THE
COMPLETE
BOOK OF
EMIGRANTS

1661-1699

*A Comprehensive Listing Compiled from English Public Records of
Those Who Took Ship to the Americas for Political, Religious,
and Economic Reasons; of Those Who Were Deported
for Vagrancy, Roguery, or Non-Conformity;
and of Those Who Were Sold to Labour
in the New Colonies*

Peter Wilson Coldham

GENEALOGICAL PUBLISHING CO., INC.

Introduction

The aim of this volume, as it was with the first in the series[1], is to bring together into one publication a comprehensive account of emigration from England to America based upon surviving sources in English public archives. To achieve this aim it has been necessary to exercise a degree of compression in the treatment of material which, while it hopefully presents the essential facts, has stripped away a wealth of circumstantial detail. This work is therefore offered merely as a comprehensive review of the raw materials available to those prepared to invest time and energy in a further exploration of the wealth of original sources.

The restoration of the English monarchy in 1660 threw into rapid reverse many of the centralising measures which had been introduced with some success by the Cromwellian administration during the preceding decade. The impact of state intervention in everyday affairs changed dramatically and, from the standpoint of the present-day researcher, the passing of the old order brought some welcome improvements in the standard of official literacy and calligraphy (though at the price of the reintroduction of shorthand Latin as a legal language) but a regrettable regression to the former system of patronage which resulted in a multiplicity of private and public administrative agencies, often with ill-defined responsibilities, many of which were to be managed with *laissez-faire* indifference and to pass into history without written records.

The Pattern of Emigration

Though the fortunes of war, political and religious conviction, and the growth of mercantilism may have brought many new figures into prominence after the Restoration, the rigid class structure had survived intact, and the lot of the peasantry and the labouring population of England was not perceptibly different from that which had induced their grandparents to seek better lives in the Americas. The early years of the restored monarchy were marked both by a conspicuous granting of new patronages[2] and a determined attempt at extirpation of undesirable elements. The principal targets were clearly those sympathetic to the disgraced Parliamentary cause and, by extension, those whose religious sympathies could place them as natural allies, chiefly the Quakers. The manner of their disposal followed a tradition as old as the colonies themselves: they were to be shipped off to labour in the plantations.

After a year of indulgence customary on the accession of a new monarch, the gaols of England were once again able to vent into the colonies not only those who had committed felony but any who were deemed to be incorrigibly idle yet also sturdy. The results within the American territories were so dire and the

i

reaction so hostile that by 1670 it became necessary to forbid the landing in Virginia of "gaol birds or others who, for notorious offences, have deserved to dye in England." Other colonies attempted to follow suit and this, combined with increasing laxity at home, led to such a crush of convicts in Newgate Prison that by 1697 special measures were introduced to compel their shipment overseas.

A similar laxity overtook the no doubt well-intentioned arrangements for monitoring the shipment of apprentices to the colonies and it is difficult to avoid censuring the system of patronage for this failure. After the petition of English merchants, planters and ships' masters (see p. 66) suggesting measures to combat abuses, one Roger Whitley was appointed by Parliament in September 1664 to a salaried office responsible for registering plantation servants in London. If such an office ever functioned, it left not a single trace in the records, and in 1682 it was found "to have served no useful purpose." The practice of "spiriting" (the kidnapping and selling of children and young adults for service in the plantations)[3], which appears to have continued unabated throughout the third quarter of the seventeenth century, reached a new height of sophistication, for now the shipping merchants began to be sued on contrived and easily obtained evidence and to be fined for conniving in this evil practice.

Finally coerced into effective action, the Privy Council in December 1682 introduced regulations (see p. 405) governing the future registration of plantation servants. Though clearly intended to extend to all such servants throughout the kingdom, the only surviving registers or lists relate to the cities of London and Bristol and the county of Middlesex, which nevertheless probably account for the great bulk of those engaged during the few years in which the regulations were enforced[4]. In 1689 Mr. Edward Thompson was granted the right for twenty-one years to register servants engaging for plantation service, but of his activities in this area no record survives.

Without doubt passenger lists were compiled throughout this period for the many ships making their annual or biannual voyages to the American colonies, but it must be assumed that these perished in the calamitous fire which destroyed the Custom House in London in 1814. Of the copies which were occasionally passed to the Exchequer there is only one battered survivor (for 1674). A partial if inadequate substitute is to be found in the run of Port Books which list the names of ships trading to the colonies and of those consigning goods by them (to determine which of the shippers were also passengers requires a comparison of names and dates given in the Port Books with those appearing in vital records).

Notes on the Records Used.

The following are brief notes on the principal records used in this compilation, but first some important qualifications must be made regarding the scope of the work:

- Only *English* sources have been used. Scotland, Wales and Ireland maintain their own records.

- With the exception of apprenticeship bindings and convict pardons, coverage has been restricted to persons connected with mainland America only.

- All dates have been rendered according to the modern calendar.

PLANTATION APPRENTICESHIP BINDINGS

1. London. Records of apprentices bound in London to plantation service begin in January 1683 with entries in the Lord Mayor's Waiting Books and end abruptly in June 1686 when there is a break in the series. These records were first abstracted by Michael Ghirelli[5] in 1968, and the revised list now included in this volume corrects several errors in the original transcription, includes the entries there omitted, and gives fuller details of the witnesses to each indenture.

By one of those curious quirks of archival history, an additional list of plantation bindings, undated but clearly appertaining to the above series, was discovered in the records of the Fishmongers' Company of London. The reason for this unlikely provenance appears to be that the Company shared their clerk with the Town Clerk of the City of London. An abridgment of the list was published in 1979[6] and the original documents have been consulted to prepare the revised list now included in this book.

2. Middlesex. A series of plantation indentures, also beginning in January 1683, but running only to September 1684, survives amongst the collections of the Greater London Record Office. Originally this series was numbered from 1 to 1,000 (suggesting a somewhat arbitrary curtailment), of which 745 survive in the Greater London Record Office, and are supplemented by a further 66 of which copies exist in the Folger Shakespeare Library in Washington. Middlesex plantation indentures were first transcribed by Cregoe Nicholson and printed in the *Genealogists' Magazine*[7] and then reprinted by the Society of Genealogists in 1965[8]. A supplementary list was later contributed by John Wareing[9]. A complete and revised listing is now included in this volume but omitting the names of witnesses except where they were clearly related to the apprentice.

3. Liverpool. The records of the City of Liverpool yield no listings of apprentices to American plantations earlier than 1697 but, between then and 1707, a rough note was made in the Town Clerk's office of some 1500 plantation indentures. If there was ever a "fair copy" it has not survived. A transcript of this source was made by Miss Elizabeth French and first published in 1910[10].

4. Dorset. In this county (and in Hampshire) apprenticeship indentures have been filed with the records of the parish in which they were registered. A short series of plantation indentures relating to Lyme Regis has been transcribed for inclusion in this volume.

PORT BOOKS

Every port in England and Wales was required to maintain its own ledgers of duty exacted upon goods shipped inwards and outwards, and yearly returns were made to the Exchequer bound up into parchment volumes. Separate returns were made for exports and imports and for coastal and overseas traffic. Within each of these separate categories as many as five overlapping books were compiled by the port officials concerned, such as Searchers, Controllers, Waiters, Customers and Surveyors. A good study of the purpose and complexities of the Port Books will be found in Marion Balderston's article "William Penn's Twenty-Three Ships."[11] The multiplicity of overlapping records to be found in this class of public record was perhaps intended to enable the Exchequer to detect fraudulence by comparing one book with another. However that may be, the Port Books provide extensive and detailed (but not comprehensive) records of the movement of shipping and of those who exported goods. That *some* of the exporters were also themselves emigrants is beyond doubt, but there exists no infallible method of distinguishing between the two. It must be remembered also that the Port Books were intended as accounting tools rather than vital archives, so the arithmetic was much more important than the personalities; hence names, both of ships and of persons, were often carelessly entered with the result that the same name may appear in three or more different guises. Moreover, the greater number of emigrants taking ship carried little more than their personal possessions which, being exempt from duty, figured not at all in the customs officers' returns.

Time and unsuitable storage have wrought disproportionate damage to this vast collection, so there are now large gaps in the series, only partly recompensed by the overlapping already mentioned. Wherever possible, therefore, at least *one* of the Port Books (usually the most extensive) for each year for which records have survived has been examined for each major port in order to abstract entries for publication. Some idea of the immensity of even this limited review may be gauged from the fact that, for the larger ports such as London or Bristol, a single book may contain over 1,000 pages of closely written entries. It will be obvious, therefore, that there remains ample scope for further research in this class of record should additional detail be sought. Nevertheless, it may be claimed that the new material now brought to light has added substantially to previously published data. As an example, many new names can now be added to the lists of passengers in William Penn's "first fleet" of 1681/2.

To keep the abstracts from this class of record within reasonable bounds the names of the most frequent London and Bristol shippers have sometimes been excluded after 1680.

CRIMINAL TRANSPORTATION ORDERS

Orders for the pardon and transportation to America and the West Indies of condemned felons were regularly issued (in Latin) to the judiciary of London, Middlesex and the seven Assize Circuits of England. Abstracts of the Patent Rolls in which these pardons were recorded were begun in 1976 and consolidated into a single alphabetical sequence in 1988[12]. The opportunity has now been taken of making a comprehensive review of the original sources to confirm or revise the content of some 300 separate orders issued between 1661 and 1699 spread over more than 100 parchment rolls. This has resulted in the location of a number of pardons previously unnoticed and a substantial number of corrections and additions. There are, nevertheless, a few unexplained gaps in the Patent Roll series, some of which have been made good by reference to comparable records in other collections.

Though each pardon included a clause specifying which of the named felons was to "depart from the kingdom," their intended destination was normally indicated in such a way as to allow room for discretion. The relevant clause would thus name the intended plantation but also give alternatives such as "parts of America already inhabited" (and occasionally even Africa), and it was left to each individual justiciary to contract with a merchant or ship's captain for the final disposition of the convicts in their charge. The abstracts included in this volume name only the destination of first choice.

Peter Wilson Coldham
Purley, Surrey, England

Whitsun 1990
AMDG

Notes

1. *The Complete Book of Emigrants 1607-1660*, ed. Peter Wilson Coldham (Baltimore: Genealogical Publishing Co., 1987).

2. For example, the grant in November 1664 to Sir James Modyford for five years of all reprieved prisoners in the gaols of England to be transported to Jamaica.

3. See Vol. I, p. *x*, and *Virginia Magazine of History and Biography* 83, pp. 280-287 (1975).

4. The archives of a few English counties (Dorset and Hampshire are known examples) contain indentures for 1683-1686 amongst their parish collections, but there is at present no published aid to identify them.

5. *A List of Emigrants from England to America 1682-1692* (1968, reprinted by Genealogical Publishing Co., 1989).

6. See the article by M. J. Chandler in the *Journal of the Barbados Museum*, 1979, pp. 28-43.

7. Vol.12, 1-16; Vol.13, 1-8.

8. *Some Early Emigrants to America*, 1965.

9. *Genealogists' Magazine*, Vol. 18, No.5.

10. See *Emigrants to America from Liverpool (New England Historical and Genealogical Register,* 1910, pp. 158 ff.)

11. Included in *Passengers and Ships Prior to 1684*, ed. Walter Lee Sheppard, Jr. (Baltimore: Genealogical Publishing Co., 1970).

12. *English Convicts in Colonial America*, Vol. II (New Orleans: Polyanthos, 1976) and *The Complete Book of Emigrants in Bondage 1614-1775*, ed. Peter Wilson Coldham (Baltimore: Genealogical Publishing Co., 1988).

References

The following is a comprehensive list of printed and manuscript sources used in the preparation of this volume:

APC =   *Acts of the Privy Council, Colonial Series, Vols. I & II*, ed. W.L. Grant, James Munro & Almeric W. Fitzroy. H.M.S.O., 1908-1910.

AW =   *American Wills and Administrations in the Prerogative Court of Canterbury 1610-1857*, ed. Peter Wilson Coldham. Baltimore: Genealogical Publishing Co., 1989.

BR =   *Bristol Registers of Servants sent to Foreign Plantations 1654-1686*, ed. Peter Wilson Coldham. Baltimore: Genealogical Publishing Co., 1988.

Bridewell = Minutes of the Court of Governors of the Bridewell, King Edward's School, Witley, Surrey, England.

CH =   *Child Apprentices in America from Christ's Hospital, London, 1617-1788*, ed. Peter Wilson Coldham. Baltimore: Genealogical Publishing Co., 1990.

CSPC =   *Calendar of State Papers, Colonial Series: America and West Indies 1661-1699*, ed. W. Noel Sainsbury and Hon. J.W. Fortescue. H.M.S.O., 1880-1908.

DRO =   Dorset Record Office, County Hall, Dorchester DT1 1XJ.

EA =   *English Adventurers and Emigrants 1661-1733*, ed. Peter Wilson Coldham. Baltimore: Genealogical Publishing Co., 1985.

EB =   *The Complete Book of Emigrants in Bondage 1614-1775*, ed. Peter Wilson Coldham. Baltimore: Genealogical Publishing Co., 1988.

GLRO =   Greater London Record Office, 40 Northampton Road, London EC1 0AB.

LaRO =   Lancashire Record Office, Bow Lane, Preston PR1 8ND.

LMCD =   *Lord Mayor's Court of London Depositions*. Washington: National Genealogical Society, 1980.

LMWB =   Lord Mayor of London's Waiting Books, Corporation of London Record Office, P.O. Box 270, Guildhall, London EC2P 2EJ.

LTB =   Liverpool Town Books, City of Liverpool Record Office, William Brown Street, Liverpool L3 8EW.

NGSQ =   *National Genealogical Society Quarterly*.

PRO =   Public Record Office, Chancery Lane, London WC2A 1LR. Such citations are followed by the reference number of the document(s).

SP Dom =   *Calendar of State Papers, Domestic Series 1661-1699*, ed. Mary Anne Everett Green, F.H. Blackburne Daniell, William John Hardy and Edward Bateson. H.M.S.O. 1860-1933.

VM =   *Virginia Magazine of History and Biography*.

1661

Undated. Petition of John Gifford, Archibald Henderson, Edward Chapman, James Bate, Henry Wilson, Robert Seymor, Edward Godfree, Theophilus Salter, John Dand, George Baxter, John Baker, Archibald Crowder and John Baxe of New England that they be delivered from oppression. (CSPC).

Undated. Petition of Lionell Copley, Thomas Foley, Thomas Pury, Nicholas Bond, John Pocock, William Heydock, John Beex, William Greenhill, George Sherpuls and William Beck, adventurers in the New England ironworks of which the managers, John Gifford and William Avery, have been imprisoned. They pray for relief. (CSPC).

Undated. Proposals by John Giffard for the development of the mines in New England based on his 20 years' residence there. (CSPC).

Undated. Petition of Archibald Henderson seeking satisfaction for the injuries caused him in New England. He arrived in Boston from Barbados in 1652, was thrown into prison and lost his ship. (CSPC).

Undated. Petition of Gyles Sylvester, merchant, for himself and other inhabitants of Shelter Island near New Haven in New England for relief from the Government of New Haven who have laid violent hands on them. He prays for restoration of their lands and goods. (CSPC).

Undated. Deposition of John Crown that he was in Boston shortly after the King's restoration when the regicides [William] Goffe and [Edward] Whalley landed there. They were embraced by Governor Endecott and were visited by John Norton, the teacher of the Independent Church. (CSPC).

1 January. The following apprenticed in Bristol: Robert Thomas, yeoman, to Christopher Alford, surgeon, 4 years Nevis; Edward Price of Churcham, Glos, yeoman, to William Limbry, mariner, 7 years Nevis; Thomas Bearnes, yeoman, to Christopher Alford, 4 years Nevis; John Gough, shoemaker, to same, 4 years Nevis; William Cole, weaver, to James Jesop, mariner, 4 years Nevis; Thomas Mills, weaver, to John Challoner, merchant, 4 years Nevis; George Ricketts, yeoman, to Roger Welsteed, mariner, 6 years Barbados; Mary Weare, spinster, to Edward Child, merchant, 4 years Nevis. (BR).

5 January. The following apprenticed in Bristol: Richard Pegley, yeoman, to James Watkin, pinmaker, 3 years Nevis. (BR).

7 January. The following apprenticed in Bristol: Thomas Williams, tailor, to Richard Thomas, mariner, 4 years Barbados; Edward Morris, clothier, to John Harris, mariner, 4 years Barbados; John West, tailor, to Joseph Day, mariner, 4 years Barbados; Elizabeth Bevan, spinster, to James Jessop Sr., 4 years Barbados. (BR).

8 January. The following apprenticed in Bristol: Morris Thomas, yeoman, to Thomas Player, merchant, 7 years Barbados; Marthah Bowden, spinster, to Christopher Harper, merchant, 3 years Barbados. (BR).

13 January. The following apprenticed in Bristol: Robert Price of Almeley, [Heref], to Thomas Watkins, surgeon, 4 years Barbados; John Blisse, yeoman, to Henry Bankes, mariner, 4 years Barbados; Mathew Vining, shoemaker, to same, 4 years Barbados; John Merriatt, cooper, to George Stocke, cooper, 4 years Barbados. (BR).

20 January. The following apprenticed in Bristol: Lewis Evans, shoemaker, to Thomas Workman, shoemaker, 4 years Barbados; Hugh Powell, yeoman, to Elizabeth Joyner, 4 years Barbados. (BR).

23 January. The following apprenticed in Bristol: John Freeman, yeoman, to Samson Dow, mariner, 4 years Barbados; James Niblett, yeoman, to Richard Lucock, yeoman, *[Entry incomplete]*; John Merriweather, yeoman, to Edmund Williams, 4 years Barbados; George Gibbs, yeoman, to George Ingleson, mariner, 3 years Nevis. (BR).

26 January. The following apprenticed in Bristol: Richard Cate, yeoman, to George Ingleson, mariner, 7 years Nevis; John James, yeoman, to same, 7 years Nevis; John Morgan, yeoman, to same, 7 years Nevis; Thomas Jones, yeoman, to same, 7 years Nevis; Walter Rosser, yeoman, to same, 7 years Nevis. (BR).

27 January. The following apprenticed in Bristol: Thomas Grigson to Christopher Harper, merchant, 4 years Nevis; Henry Morgan to James Smith, mariner, 4 years Nevis: Thomas Owen to Richard Morgan, mariner, 4 years Nevis. (BR).

28 January. The following apprenticed in Bristol: William Maurice, yeoman, to Samson Dow, carpenter, 4 years Nevis; Amy Harte, singlewoman, to John Pearson, mariner, 7 years Nevis; William Griffith to Henry Bankes, mariner, 7 years Nevis. (BR).

29 January. Deposition by Richard Pye of Poole, Dorset, sailor aged 31, re the voyage of the *Edward & Anne*, Mr. Richard Bailey, from Southampton to New England in 1660. (EA).

29 January & 5 February. Petition of John Clark seeking protection and freedom of worship for the inhabitants of Rhode Island, describing how the plantation was settled from England and granted a charter in 1644. (CSPC).

31 January. The following apprenticed in Bristol: John Mattravis to Christopher Olliver, 7 years Nevis; Alice Evans, spinster, to Francis Dorington, 5 years Barbados; Richard Lloyd, glover, to George Walker, mariner, 3 years Barbados; Elinor Jones, spinster, to Anne wife of Richard Munday, mariner, 3 years Barbados; Richard Pickerell, yeoman, to Abraham Child, ropemaker,

4 years Barbados; Griffith Inon, yeoman, to Joseph Day, mariner, 5 years Barbados. (BR).

January. Probate of will of Felix Forby of Norwich, hosier, whose son and daughter were in Virginia. (AW).

1 February. The following apprenticed in Bristol: Walter George, yeoman, to John Waters, mariner, 4 years Barbados; Thomas Mitchell of Taunton, [Som], to Walter Clarke, mariner, 5 years Barbados; John Dolling to Francis Bayly, 3 years Barbados; Richard Jones of Huntly, Glos, yeoman, to William Harris of Bristol, mariner, 4 years Barbados. (BR).

4 February. The following apprenticed in Bristol: Elizabeth Lawrence of Ludlow, [Salop], singlewoman, to Elinor wife of John Grove, merchant, 4 years Barbados; George Barnard, smith, to John Holman, baker, 4 years Barbados; James Collins, cook, to Robert Glasse, mariner, 4 years Barbados; William Rooks to Elizabeth Jayne, 4 years St. Christopher; Joane Ford of Bristol, spinster, to William Skeetch, mariner, 4 years St. Christopher; Evan Thomas, husbandman, to same, 4 years St. Christopher; Richard Evans of Caerleon, Mon, to Edward Thomas, mariner, 4 years St. Christopher; Walter Newman of Caerleon, Mon, to same, 4 years St. Christopher; John Essington of London to George Ashby, mariner, 4 years St. Christopher; Humphry Jones of Wrexham, barber, to Alexander Keisin, cooper, 4 years St. Christopher; Richard Hale, blacksmith, to John Jenning, planter, 4 years St. Christopher; Thomas Swan of Leicester, worsted comber, to same, 4 years St. Christopher. (BR).

11 February. Letter from Governor John Endecott of New England, praying the King's protection and making reference to the banishment of Quakers. (CSPC).

11 February. The following apprenticed in Bristol: John Gardner, feltmaker, to Thomas Rich, mariner, 3 years Nevis; Samuell Thatcher of Winterford, Worcs, yeoman, to Richard Rigglestone, mariner, 5 years Nevis; Francis Thatcher of Winterford to same, 7 years Nevis; Job Taylor to John Roch, 4 years Nevis; John Williams to same, 5 years Nevis; Gabriell Wibberd to Richard Lock, 5 years Nevis; Raphaell Herring, butcher, to William Limbrey, mariner, 4 years Nevis; Thomas Bradbury of Blithfield, Staffs, tailor, to Abraham Wild, ropemaker, 3 years Nevis; Christofer Wood of Blackburn, Lancs, to William Limbrey, mariner, 4 years Nevis. (BR).

13 February. The following apprenticed in Bristol: William Ferrett, glazier, to William Limbrey, mariner, 4 years Nevis; Richard Martin, blacksmith, to same, 3 years Nevis; Rowland Jones of Shrewsbury, [Salop], yeoman, to William Skeetch, mariner, 4 years Nevis; Maudlin Wilkin, spinster, to same, 6 years Barbados; Margaret Bedford of Leominster, [Heref], to William Harris, mariner, 4 years Nevis; John Crocker of Marsh, Dorset, yeoman, to Anne wife of Samuell Cole, mariner, 4 years Nevis; Elizabeth Evans of

Redwick, Mon, to Henry Banks, mariner, 4 years Nevis; Amy Phillips, spinster, to Christopher ?Hoover, mariner, 4 years; John Elison of Seagrave, Leics, to Abraham Jermin, 4 years Nevis; Daniell White to Samson Dow, 4 years Barbados; Jenkin Davis to same, 4 years Barbados; James Belshire to Elizabeth Jane, 4 years St. Christopher; John Hunt to Robert Haskins, 4 years Nevis; Robert May to same, 4 years Nevis; John Cordin to same, 4 years Nevis; George Nicholas, shoemaker, to Samuell Jones, mariner, 4 years Nevis. (BR).

15 February. The King writes to Governor Endecott promising protection. (CSPC).

18 February. The following apprenticed in Bristol: Elinor Martin, spinster, to Elizabeth Jane, 4 years St. Christopher; Margeret Richards to William Harrie, 4 years Nevis. (BR).

19 February & 14 March. Letters from Edward Godfrey, former Governor of Maine, to the King seeking relief. He has spent 30 years abroad as an original planter, has lost a vast estate, his only son has been ruined and his nearest relations killed by the Indians. Captain John Leveret, agent for Massachusetts, has taken violent action against him. (CSPC).

20 February. The following apprenticed in Bristol: George Phillips to William Barter, 3 years Barbados. (BR).

21 February. The following apprenticed in Bristol: Margeret Prickett to Henry Smith, 4 years Nevis or Barbados; Thomas Hall of Cirencester, [Glos], shoemaker, to Edward Gibbs, mariner, 3 years Barbados; Henry Hughes, yeoman, to Robert Haskins, 4 years Nevis; Andrew Geaston to Phillip Jennings, 4 years Nevis; John Cooke of Frome, [Som], to Joseph Day, 7 years Barbados; Elizabeth Ayres to Richard Lock, 4 years Barbados. (BR).

20 February. Deposition by John Oldbury of London, merchant aged 24, that Joshua Conant of Salem, New England, merchant, became indebted to John Cross of London, merchant, by bond of 5 November 1658, to be paid before or on the return to London of the *Dolphin*, Captain John Sealy. (LMCD).

25 February. The following apprenticed in Bristol: Thomas Browne to Alexander Patience, 4 years Barbados; John Bush to Thomas Jones, mariner, 11 years Barbados; Edward Thomas to Blanch Freeman, 4 years Barbados. (BR).

28 February. The following apprenticed in Bristol: Thomas Dyer, tailor, to Richard Yeamans, 3 years Barbados; Thomas Bowles to John Vincent, 5 years Barbados; Thomas Waddam of Mayfield, [Staffs], to John Jenning, 9 years Barbados; Nicholas Jones, tailor, to William Addams, ropemaker, 3 years Barbados. (BR).

28 February. Deposition by Stephen Jaye, aged 56, and Alexander Courtney, aged 46, mariners of Ratcliffe, Middlesex, that they were witnesses to a deed signed by Thomas Cowling of Teneriffe, merchant, assigning a house in Boston, New England, to Henry Shrimpton of Boston, merchant. (LMCD).

1 March. The following apprenticed in Bristol: Walter Williams to Richard Lock, 4 years Barbados. (BR).

8 March. The following apprenticed in Bristol: John Barsday to Richard Hambleton, mariner, 4 years Barbados. (BR).

9 March. The following apprenticed in Bristol: Richard Harris of Dursley, [Glos], to William Stafford, 4 years Barbados; Robert Pascall to Mathewe Steevens, ironmonger, 4 years Barbados; Thomas Hill to Richard Lock, 3 years Nevis; Thomas Reece to Henry Bankes, 5 years Nevis. (BR).

11 March. Captain Thomas Breedon reports on the state of affairs in New England which he left in 1660. (CSPC).

14 March. The following apprenticed in Bristol: William Stukly to Edward Gibbs, mariner, 3 years Barbados; John Court, yeoman, to Vincent Thorne, merchant, 5 years Nevis. (BR).

18 March. The following apprenticed in Bristol: Ann Gray to Christopher Alford, 6 years Nevis; John Baskett to Thomas Symons, merchant, 6 years Nevis; Mathew Burford to Walter Clarke, 4 years Barbados. (BR)

20 March. The following apprenticed in Bristol: John Phelpes to John Moone, 3 years Nevis; Margeret Wall to Edward Fielding, 6 years Barbados; James Brice to same, 6 years Barbados; George Mitchell to Richard Harris, 5 years Nevis; Samuell Goad to John Venson, 4 years Barbados or Nevis; Benjamin Rosser to Alexander Kason, 7 years Nevis; Morgan Davis to same, 7 years [Nevis]. (BR).

25 March. The following apprenticed in Bristol: Edward Wallington to Richard Pullin, 3 years Nevis; William Watts to William Cole, 4 years Nevis; Ann Weaver to Thomas Dolling, 5 years Nevis; Julian Hood to John Morrice, 4 years Nevis; David Howell to William Yeamans, 4 years Barbados; John Brice, yeoman, to Thomas Dolling, 4 years Nevis; John Sly, yeoman, to same, 4 years [Nevis]; Mary Lewis to Richard Pullin, 4 years Barbados; Daniell Farell to Richard Butcher, 3 years Barbados; Elinor Cox to Thomas Freeman, 7 years Barbados or Nevis; Francis Yates of Chepstow, [Mon], to William Hall, 4 years Barbados; Robert Day to Anthony Legg, 4 years Nevis; John Thomas to Jasper Crosse, 4 years Nevis; Samuell Watkins to Thomas Bower, merchant, 4 years Barbados. (BR).

2 April. Petition of Ferdinando Gorges, son and heir of John Gorges, who was the son and heir of Sir Ferdinando Gorges who was instrumental in discovering and settling New England and in 15 Charles I was granted the Province of Maine. He prays assistance against the Government of Massachusetts who have encroached upon Maine. (CSPC).

5

4 April. The following apprenticed in Bristol: Walter Newman, tiler, to William Limbry, 4 years Nevis; Dennis Brenan to Henry Bankes, 4 years Nevis. (BR).

5 April. The following apprenticed in Bristol: Martha Applan to Hester Ashly, 4 years Nevis. (BR).

8 April. The following apprenticed in Bristol: John Williams of Watchet, [Som], to Christopher Harper, 4 years Nevis; Titus Morrice to William Stringer, 3 years Barbados; Henry Winnoll to John Allyes, 3 years Nevis; William Smith to Joane Watkins, 4 years Nevis. (BR).

9 April. The following apprenticed in Bristol: William Mascall to Edward Launder, 5 years Nevis or Barbados. (BR).

10 April. The following apprenticed in Bristol: Mathew Moulton to Sarah Dixon, 3 years Nevis; Margerie Wilson to John Nethway, 4 years Barbados; William Tilly to John Roach, 4 years Nevis. (BR).

19 April. The following apprenticed in Bristol: William Tregle of Taunton, [Som], to William Hall, shoemaker, 4 years Barbados. (BR).

23 April. The following apprenticed in Bristol: Richard Price, shoemaker, to William Hall, 3 years Barbados. (BR)

24 April. The following apprenticed in Bristol: Daniel Lewis to John Nethway, merchant, 4 years Barbados; William Roe to Jeremiah Ploughman, 4 years Barbados; William Day to same, 4 years Barbados. (BR).

26 April. The following apprenticed in Bristol: John Reynolds to John Nethway, merchant, 6 years Barbados; George Johnson to Francis Short, 4 years Barbados. (BR).

29 April. The following apprenticed in Bristol: Francis Smith to Henry Willoughby, 4 years Nevis. (BR).

April. Probate of will of Joanna Griffyn of Virginia. (AW).

3 May. The following apprenticed in Bristol: John Ford to John Nethway, 4 years Nevis; Robert Leg to Frances Watkin, 4 years Nevis. (BR).

6 May. The following apprenticed in Bristol: John Turner to John Nethway, 4 years Nevis; George Bordridge to James Nethway, 4 years Nevis; Richard Niblett to William Smith, 4 years Virginia; David Loyd to John Alyes, 4 years Nevis; John Lewis to same, 3 years Nevis. (BR).

7 May. The following apprenticed in Bristol: Henry Combes to Robert Dapwell, 4 years Nevis; Charles Powell to James Watkin, 4 years Nevis; Sutton Queny to John Haskins, 4 years Virginia. (BR).

8 May. The following apprenticed in Bristol: William Rowland to Thomas Willis, 7 years Virginia. (BR).

9 May. The following apprenticed in Bristol: Thomas Ware to John Alyes, 4 years Nevis; Francis Smith to John House, 4 years Nevis. (BR).

10 May. The following apprenticed in Bristol: Thomas Cadle to John Farding, 4 years Nevis; John Cudd to John Alyes, 4 years Nevis; Stephen Bishop to same, 3 years Nevis; Woolfry Nollard to same, 3 years Nevis; John Roberts to Hugh Parry, 4 years Nevis; Rowland Jones to same, 4 years Nevis; Thomas [blank] to John [blank], Virginia. (BR).

14 May. The following apprenticed in Bristol: Roger Williams to Edward Watkins, 4 years Nevis; Mary Cauthar to Francis Short, 4 years Nevis. (BR).

15 May. The following apprenticed in Bristol: Owen Morgan to John White, 4 years Nevis; John Adney to John Haskins, 9 years Virginia; William Harlocke to Francis Short, 7 years Nevis. (BR).

16 May. The following apprenticed in Bristol: Reece Lewis to John Kingford, 4 years Nevis; Samuell Robins to John Hodges, 4 years Nevis; Ann Farding to Edmund Williams, 4 years Nevis. (BR).

17 May. The following apprenticed in Bristol: Dorothy Bowell to John Alyes, 4 years Nevis; William Aufert to Edward Fielding, 4 years Nevis. (BR)

17 May. Report to the King about the sufferings of Quakers in New England. N.N. Upthall of Boston was banished from his family; Samuel Shattock of Salem was imprisoned and banished. Signed by Thomas Coveny, Th. Moore, Giles Sylvester and Ellis Hookes. Accompanied by a letter from Samuel Shattock, Nicholas Phelps and Josiah Shatwick saying that they were banished for two years and seeking their return to Boston. (CSPC).

20 May. The following apprenticed in Bristol: John Edwards to John Kingford, 4 years Nevis; James Hawkes to David Warren, 4 years Nevis; Edward Lawles to same, 4 years Nevis; George Hoply to same, 4 years Nevis; John Skoot to John Morgan, 5 years Nevis; Elizabeth Thomas to Francis Short, 4 years Nevis; Susan Hopkins to John Nethway, 3 years Nevis. (BR).

22 May. The following apprenticed in Bristol: William Davis to Henry More, 4 years Barbados. (BR).

23 May. The following apprenticed in Bristol: Richard Allin to John Hodges, 3 years Nevis; John Clarke to Paul Williams, 6 years Nevis; George Hopley to Christopher ?Helford, 4 years Nevis; Noah Lewis to John Morgan, 4 years Nevis; John George to Morgan Jones, 4 years Nevis. (BR).

24 May. The following apprenticed in Bristol: Francis Hale to Thomas Morrice, 6 years Nevis; William Whiteing to John Nethway, 4 years Nevis; Edward Pitts to Paul Williams, 4 years Nevis; Lewis David to Charles ?Baker, 4 years Nevis; John Davie to William Hall, 3 years Nevis; Ann Price to Benjamin Blindman, 4 years Virginia; John James to John Bodenham, 6 years Barbados;

Richard Vaughan to Richard Roberts, 4 years Barbados; William Bate to John Hodge, 4 years Virginia. (BR).

28 May. The following apprenticed in Bristol: Robert Harris, yeoman, to John White, 4 years Barbados; John James to Robert Dapwell, 4 years Barbados; Anne Bell to Benjamin Blindman, 4 years Virginia. (BR)

30 May. The following apprenticed in Bristol: John Davis, yeoman, to John Kingford, mariner, 5 years Barbados; William Castle to William Zanky, 3 years Virginia; John Jenkins to Osmond Crabb, 4 years Virginia. (BR).

May. Administration of Henry Trew of Limehouse, Middlesex, who died in Virginia. (AW).

1 June. The following apprenticed in Bristol: Charles Gwyn to Edward Watkins, 4 years Barbados; Jane Morgan to John Allyes, 4 years Barbados; Suzan Morgan to same, 4 years Barbados; Thomas Wheeler to George Wilkinson, 4 years Barbados; James Olliver to William Stringer, 4 years Virginia; Elizabeth Francis to Anne Shorte, 4 years Nevis; William Fluellin to Morgan Williams, 4 years Nevis; Phillip Flower to William Zankey, mariner, 7 years Virginia; Richard Phillips to Thomas Pearson, 4 years Virginia; Joane Sheare, spinster, to Isaac Holwey, 4 years Virginia; Herbert Price to William Hall, mariner, 4 years Virginia. (BR).

6 June. The following apprenticed in Bristol: William Parker, weaver, to Walter Tocknell, merchant, 4 years Virginia; James Thomas, upholsterer, to Jasper Grimsby, mariner, 4 years Barbados; Thomas Jones of St. Mellon, [Glam], to John Haskins, mariner, 3 years Virginia; Richard Jones to same, 4 years Virginia; Edward Gally, broadweaver, to William Hale, merchant, 4 years Barbados; Roger Reede, worsted comber, to William Wakely, mariner, 4 years Virginia. (BR).

8 June. The following apprenticed in Bristol: William Gold, yeoman, to William Wakely, mariner, 4 years Virginia; Edward Richards to John Watkins, 4 years Virginia; William Jones to same, 4 years Virginia; William Price of Llangorse, Brecknock, to William Zanky, mariner, 4 years Virginia; Phillip Charles, yeoman, to Evan Jones, mariner, 4 years Virginia; Phillip Roberts, yeoman, to same, 3 years Nevis; Lazarus Jenkins to Charles Roberts, 4 years Virginia. (BR).

11 June. The following apprenticed in Bristol: Margery Chapman to John Hodge, 4 years Virginia; John Hooper, yeoman, to David Warren, mariner, 4 years Virginia; Dermod Dennovand to Robert Vickris, 3 years Virginia; John Pranch, yeoman, to James Gill, 4 years Nevis; Thomas Reede to William Hardwitch, 4 years Virginia; Joseph Read, yeoman, to same, 4 years Virginia; David Stratford to William Preed, 6 years Nevis; Anthony Sneede to Thomas Winstone, mariner, 3 years Nevis; Walter Edwards, yeoman, to Phillip Cox, mariner, 3 years Nevis; Evan Jones, yeoman, to Nicholas Morgan, merchant, 6 years Nevis; Richard Morgan to John Alyes, 4 years Nevis. (BR).

13 June. The following apprenticed in Bristol: Samuell Ascue to William Zankey, 7 years Virginia; David Jones to John Haskins, 4 years Virginia; Jenkin Thomas, yeoman, to John House, shoemaker, 4 years Nevis; Edward Lowden, yeoman, to John Roch, gent, 4 years Nevis; William Halditch, yeoman, to James James, mariner, 4 years Virginia; Howell Williams to George Hale, 4 years Virginia. (BR).

16 June. The following apprenticed in Bristol: Peter Powell to Henry Moore, 4 years Virginia; John Davis to same, 4 years Virginia; Abraham Humphry to same, 4 years Virginia; John Mathewes to same, 4 years Virginia; Reece Williams to Richard Burford, 5 years Virginia; John James to James James, 4 years Virginia; Mary Thomas, spinster, to John Osgood, mariner, 7 years Virginia; Bridget Williams to same, 7 years Virginia; Margeret Powell to same, 7 years Virginia; Edmund Hone, carpenter, to Bartholomew Penrose, mariner, 3 years Nevis; John Blisse, yeoman, to Richard Greene, mariner, 5 years Virginia; John Williams, yeoman, to John James, mariner, 4 years Virginia; John Sparkes, yeoman, to John Roch, gent, 4 years Nevis. (BR).

20 June. The following apprenticed in Bristol: John Wheeler, yeoman, to Bartholomew Penrose, mariner, 4 years Nevis; Anne Morse, spinster, to Edward Stradling, 4 years Virginia; Thomas Smith, yeoman, to John Harris, cooper, 4 years Virginia; Edward Davis, yeoman, to Walter Sherland, mariner, 4 years Virginia; William Wills, yeoman, to James Dandy, mariner, 4 years Virginia; George Hancock to Roger Gainard, 4 years Virginia. (BR).

22 June. The following apprenticed in Bristol: Prudence Edwards, spinster, to William Hardy, mariner, 4 years Virginia; Morgan Jenkins, yeoman, to John Kingford, mariner, 4 years Virginia; Richard Harris, yeoman, to John Hodge, mariner, 4 years Virginia; Mary Vizard, spinster, to John Marc——, mariner, 4 years Virginia; John Peters, yeoman, to John Reede, mariner, 4 years Virginia. (BR).

24 June. The following apprenticed in Bristol: Thomas More to Thomas Pearson, 3 years Virginia; John Poole, yeoman, to John Kingford, mariner, 4 years Virginia; Thomas Carrier, cordwainer, to Henry Moore, merchant, 4 years Virginia; William Taylor to Walter Seagar, 4 years Virginia; John Taylor, yeoman, to John Reede, mariner, 4 years Virginia; Jane Smith, spinster, to Benjamin Blindman, mariner, 4 years Virginia; Benjamin Johnstone to John Haskins, mariner, 4 years Virginia; Thomas Dukes, yeoman, to same, 4 years Virginia; Margaret Vaughan, spinster, to Hannah Hill, 4 years Virginia. (BR).

June. Administration of Richard Morgan of Islington, Middlesex, whose only child, Jude Morgan, was in Virginia. (AW).

2 July. The following apprenticed in Bristol: Edward Burristone, feltmaker, to John Haskins, mariner, 4 years Virginia; Thomas Ince, clothier, to same, 4 years Virginia; Elizabeth Holdship, spinster, to same, 4 years Virginia; Elinor Staunton, spinster, to same, 4 years Virginia; Anne Phillipps, spinster, to same,

4 years Virginia; Margery Austin, spinster, to David Warren, mariner, 4 years Virginia; Ellin Collins, spinster, to same, 4 years Virginia; Honnor Collins, spinster, to same, 4 years Virginia; Mary Collins, spinster, to same, 4 years Virginia. (BR).

4 July. Shipper by the *Marie*, Mr. David Cooper, bound from London for Virginia: Olandia de Jorden. (PRO: E190/48/4).

5 July. The following apprenticed in Bristol: Thomas Middleton to Edward Gorden, 3 years Virginia; Edward Hawkins to James Tandy, 4 years Virginia; George Hutton to John Hawkins, 4 years Virginia; Mary Cause to Joseph Steevens,4 years Virginia; Grace Hedges, widow, to David Warren, mariner, 4 years Virginia; Francis Austin, yeoman, to Edith Holloway, 5 years Virginia; Symon Watkins to James Thorpe, 4 years Nevis. (BR).

8 July. The following apprenticed in Bristol: Edward Morgan to William Fletcher, 4 years Nevis; Anne Lewis to same, 4 years Nevis; William Halling to William Jelfe, 4 years Nevis; John Taylor to John Kingford, 4 years Nevis; Samuell Morgan to Thomas Workman, 4 years Nevis; Richard Hall to same, 4 years Nevis; John Cole to Robert Steevens, 4 years Nevis. (BR).

9 July. The following apprenticed in Bristol: William Bates to John Dench, 3 years Nevis; Walter Tucker to Thomas Smarte, 3 years Nevis; Sarah Richardson to Elizabeth Shute, 4 years Nevis; Elizabeth Morgan to Richard Fielding, 4 years Nevis; Elizabeth Stead to Mathew Berrow, 4 years Nevis; Mary Philpott to James Thorpe, 4 years Nevis; Mary Attwell to Charles Bevan, 4 years Nevis. (BR).

11 July. Shipper by the *Waterhouse* bound from London for Virginia: Daniel Benon. (PRO: E190/47/2).

11 July. Probate of will of Roger Byrom, citizen and bowyer of London, who died in Barbados, and whose brother, John Byrom, went to Virginia and Barbados. (LMCD).

12 July. The following apprenticed in Bristol: John Evans to Thomas Viner, 4 years Nevis; Robert Primin to Richard Whippy, 4 years Nevis; William White to Thomas Whittey, 4 years Nevis; Hopkin Howell to William Rodney, 4 years Virginia; Thomas Whaite to Samuell Tucker, 4 years Virginia; Mary Jones to David Warren, 4 years Virginia; John Wills to James Elverd, 6 years Virginia. (BR).

13 July. The following apprenticed in Bristol: John Sherry to Thomas Whitye, 4 years Virginia; Robert Challacome to Marthah Braine, 4 years Virginia; Anne Clarke to same, 4 years Virginia; Elizabeth Abraham to same, 4 years Virginia; Eve Gold to James Shute, 4 years Virginia; Luke Gerry to Richard Whippy, 4 years Virginia; Robert Morgan to same, 4 years Virginia; Charity Hayter to Elizabeth Whippy, 4 years Virginia; Anne England to same, 4 years Virginia; Henry Reynolds to Thomas Wallis, 4 years Virginia; Edmund Davis to John

Haskins, 4 years Virginia; John Purnell to Edmund Driver, 3 years Virginia; William Morgan to same, 3 years Virginia. (BR).

16 July. Shipper by the *Honor* bound from London for Virginia: Thomas Tomlins. (PRO: E190/47/2).

16 July. The following apprenticed in Bristol: William Bennett of Stottesdon, Salop, to Richard Fielding, merchant, 5 years Virginia; Thomas Cartar to John Reede, 4 years Nevis; Mary Allin to David Warren, 4 years Nevis; Henry Norman to Christopher Alford, 4 years Nevis; Nicholas Cantar to Richard Fielding, 4 years Nevis; Mary Thomas to Christopher Birkhead, 4 years Nevis; George Tucker to Giles Bubb, 4 years Nevis; Nicholas Hillary to same, 4 years Nevis; Margaret Dowling to James Shute, 4 years Nevis; Joane Rowland to William Tayler, 4 years Nevis; Thomas Freeman to Thomas Ofield, 4 years Nevis. (BR).

18 July. Deposition by James Jenkins Sr., citizen and merchant tailor of London, aged 60, and his servant James Jenkins Jr., aged 28, that Samuel Mathews Esq., now Governor of Virginia, drew Bills of Exchange which have not been repaid. Mr. Peter Jennings of Virginia, merchant, is appointed attorney to recover. (LMCD).

19 July. The following apprenticed in Bristol: Venetia Boswick to Giles Bubb, 4 years Nevis; Elinor Cary to David Warren, 4 years Nevis; Thomas Daw to John Roch, 4 years Nevis; Alice Allin to William B———-, 4 years Nevis; Anne Clarke to same, 4 years Nevis; William Rawlins to same, 4 years Nevis; David Jones to William Sing, 4 years Nevis. (BR).

22 July. The following apprenticed in Bristol: Daniell Long to John Hodge, 4 years Virginia; Martin Young to same, 4 years Virginia; Richard Holland to John Haskins, 4 years Virginia; John Bayly to James Tandy, 5 years Virginia; Alice Griffen to same, 4 years Virginia; Francis Gleaves to Thomas Powell, 4 years Virginia; Anne Jones to same, 4 years Virginia; Hannah Combe to same, 4 years Virginia; John Combe to same, 4 years Virginia; Nicholas Cary to Jasper Grosse, 7 years Virginia; Walter Howell to David Warren, 4 years Virginia; Thomas Merry to Daniell Tayler, 4 ycars Virginia; Henry Waters to John Reed, 4 years Nevis; John Tainton to Richard Winton, 4 years Virginia; Jane Richly to Richard Evans, 4 years Virginia; William Roberts to William Reede, 7 years Virginia; Thomas Vaughan to John Tench, 4 years Virginia; Sarah Baxter to same, 7 years Virginia; Joseph Roberts to same, 6 years Virginia; Evan Davis to Charles Abevan, 4 years Virginia; George Dunne to same, 4 years Virginia; John Morgan to John Gurgenny, 4 years Virginia; Nicholas Fenott to Francis Jones, 4 years Virginia; Alice Griffin to John Davis, 4 years Virginia; Sarah Davis to Thomas Viner, 3 years Virginia; Joseph Thorne to William Cade, 6 years Virginia; John Salter to same, 5 years Virginia; Thomas Gittins to Henry Smith, 4 years Virginia; Richard Jones to Thomas Bayly, 5 years Virginia. (BR).

24 July. The following apprenticed in Bristol: Isaac Edwards to George Tayler, 4 years Virginia; Margery Woods to same, 4 years Virginia; Joane Bakehouse to William Warren, 4 years Virginia; Richard Lewis to David Warren, 4 years Virginia; John Doxy to Thomas Hatfield, 4 years Virginia; Mary Hughes to William Quarrell, 5 years Virginia. (BR).

26 July. The following apprenticed in Bristol: Anne Thomas to Timothy Cupit, 4 years Virginia; Nicholas Greene to John Fry, 4 years Virginia; Anne Lovett to same, 4 years Virginia; Jane Willis to same, 4 years Virginia; Mary Haines to Edward Kelly, 4 years Virginia; Emanuell Poole to Joseph Hardwitch, 4 years Virginia; William Smith to same, 7 years Virginia; Thomas Crosse to same, 7 years Virginia; George Munding to same, 4 years Virginia; Onisopherus Bennet to same, 4 years Virginia; Robert Clarke to same, 4 years Virginia; William David to Joseph Stephens, 3 years Virginia; Mordecai Elbury to Benjamin Blindman, 4 years Virginia; Elizabeth Bayly to Osmond Crabb, 4 years Virginia; John Steevens to Phillip Lewis, 6 years Virginia; Marthah Morgan to Elizabeth Whippy, 7 years Virginia; Stephen Cole to Thomas Pope, 7 years Virginia; Marke Bowen to James Thorpe, 4 years Nevis; Elizabeth Jones to same, 4 years Nevis; Elinor Watts to Marthah Braine, 4 years Virginia; Isabell Jones to same, 4 years Virginia; Elizabeth May to Richard Browning, 4 years Virginia; Thomas Hogin to Giles Bubb, 4 years Virginia; Margeret Thomas to John Buck, 4 years Virginia; Henry Warner to Bartholomew Smith, 4 years Virginia. (BR).

27 July. Deposition by Edward Wallis of St. Giles Cripplegate, London, aged 42, and his wife, Alice Wallis, aged 36, that William Byrom, citizen and leatherseller of London, deceased, lived in the parish of St. Mary Somerset, London, but died in Derbyshire. By his first wife he had William Byrom, citizen and leatherseller of London, by trade a brewer; Roger Byrom who went to Barbados and died there; and a daughter, Margaret, now Margaret Blount. By his second wife, Dorothy, he had Dorothy, John, Elizabeth, George, Henry, and Mary Byrom, and the deponent, Alice Wallis. The heirs of William Byrom deceased are now dead except the son William Byrom, (executor to his brother Roger Byrom), John Byrom who went long since to Virginia and is now in Barbados, and the said George Byrom who is now in Derbyshire. Mr. Samuel Osborne of Barbados has been appointed as attorney. (LMCD).

29 July. Shipper by the *Wheatsheaf* bound from London for Virginia: Henry Gross. (PRO: E190/47/2).

29 July. The following apprenticed in Bristol: Thomas Lampin to Thomas Garner (or Gainer), 4 years Virginia; Darby Daniell to William Canton, 4 years Virginia; William Mann to John Watts, 4 years Virginia; Henry Bradley to John Kingford, 4 years Virginia; John Trotnell to same, 4 years Virginia; Joseph Edmunds to Henry Hosier, 4 years Virginia; William Merret to James Tandy, 3 years Virginia; Richard Jones to Thomas Hardwitch, 5 years Virginia; Grace Adams to same, 4 years Virginia; John Butler to Richard Fielding, 4 years

Virginia; Thomas Doxy to Thomas Braine, 4 years Virginia; Mary Mandler to same, 4 years Virginia; Ursulah Doxy to same, 4 years Virginia. (BR).

30 July. Shipper by the *Friendship* bound from London for Virginia: Edward Adenbrook. (PRO: E190/47/2).

30 July-3 August. Shippers by the *Relief* bound from London for Virginia: Charles Johnson, John Tully. (PRO: E190/47/2).

31 July. The following apprenticed in Bristol: Sarah Pargeter to Richard Haskins, 6 years Virginia; Thomas Reynolds to Richard Burriat, 4 years Virginia; John Thorne to same, 4 years Virginia; Edward Reeves to John Salter, 4 years Virginia; Miles Jones to same, 4 years Virginia; Jane Merewether to Thomas Godman, 4 years Virginia; Mathew Elliott to William Zankey, 4 years Virginia; George Oakley to William Mills, 4 years Virginia; William Butler to Osmond Crabbe, 4 years Virginia. (BR).

July. Probate of will of Richard Davies of Virginia. (AW).

July. Probate of will of Mary Glover of St. Olave, Silver Street, London, widow, whose daughter, Bennett Glover, was in Virginia. (AW).

July. Probate of will of Phillip Mallory of Virginia, who died in Whitechapel, Middlesex. (AW).

1 August. Shipper by the *Golden Sheaf* bound from London for Virginia: Jane Godfry. (PRO: E190/47/2).

1 August. The following apprenticed in Bristol: Thomas Atkins to William Jinkins, 5 years Virginia; Anne Frankes to James Tandy, 6 years Virginia; Walter Chivers to Richard Homead, 4 years Virginia; Thomas Window to John Kingford, mariner, 4 years Virginia; Mary Philpott to James Thorpe, 4 years Nevis; Thomas Acton, yeoman, to Joseph Reede, 4 years Nevis; Henry Williams to Thomas Pitt, 4 years Nevis; Anthony Lancaster to William White, 4 years Nevis; Joane Stephens to John Tench, 6 years Nevis; Elizabeth Puller to same, 4 years Virginia; William Lewis to Nicholas Tovey, 5 years Nevis; Isaac Whittoes to John Woory, 4 years Nevis; John Mackworth to same, 4 years Nevis; John Harry to John Pritchard, 3 years Nevis; Julian Wootlane to same, 3 years Nevis; Eliza Butler to same, 3 years Nevis; Roger Harvey to Samuell Hucker, 3 years Nevis; Joane Smurden to same, 3 years Nevis; John Reynolds to Phillip Millard, 4 years Nevis; Cicely Poole to John Haskins, 4 years Virginia; Hester Poole to same, 4 years Virginia; Joane Hulett to Gilbert White, 4 years Virginia; Elinor Whaite to Robert Whaite, 4 years Virginia; Mary Redmond to same, 4 years Virginia; Sarah Waite to same, 4 years Virginia; John Card to same, 4 years Virginia; Arthur Flavell to Richard Powell, 4 years Virginia; Mary Whitson to John Carrell, 4 years Virginia; Blanch Jones to Christopher Reede, 4 years Virginia; Abraham Somers to Edward Hopkin, 4 years Virginia; David Salisbury to Phillip Roberts, 4 years Virginia. (BR).

6 August. The following apprenticed in Bristol: William Brickett to Henry Backrell, 4 years Virginia; Anne Whitwood to Gifford Browne, 4 years Virginia; John Lewes to Thomas Welling, 4 years Virginia; George Thomas to John Haskins, 4 years Virginia; George Betty to Nicholas Tovey, 3 years Virginia; Mary Fisher to Anthony Cupit, 3 years Virginia; Thomas Darby to John Wornell, 4 years Virginia; George Allen, yeoman, to John Needes, 4 years Virginia; Robert Sampson to Thomas Brant, 3 years Virginia; Anne Pilgram to John Luffe, 4 years Virginia; Sarah Cooke, spinster, to same, 4 years Virginia; Anthony Smith, cordwainer, to Edward Hall, surgeon, 4 years Virginia; John Powell of Esum *(sic)* to Mathias Holbrooke, 6 years Virginia; Robert Cooke of Gloucester to same, 6 years Virginia; Lawrence Whithouse to same, 6 years Virginia; Valentine Monsly to same, 6 years Virginia; Robert Salisbury to Phillip Rabby, 6 years Virginia; Joane Mockeridge to Roger Beames, 6 years Virginia. (BR).

6 August. William Stowne of Stepney, Middlesex, mariner, to answer a charge of transporting George Creech and Thomas Riddle to Virginia without authority. (VM 83/3).

10 August. The following apprenticed in Bristol: Edward Smith to William Swimmer, 4 years Virginia; David Thomas to same, 5 years Virginia; Charles Perkes to John Matts, 4 years Virginia; John Greene to same, 4 years Virginia; James By to Elizabeth Gething, 5 years Virginia; William Grindon to Hugh Cantor, 6 years Virginia; Alice Hunt to Henry Smith, 4 years Virginia; Samuell Barnard to Richard Fielding, 5 years Virginia; Olliver Spiller to John Pester, 4 years Virginia; William Griffin to same, 4 years Virginia; John Webb to John Lane, 5 years Virginia; Sarah Shepherd to Robert Lux, 4 years Virginia; Nicholas Davis to Edith Sams, 4 years Virginia; John Lymell to [blank], 4 years Virginia; Robert Roe to [blank], 4 years Virginia; Thomas St. John to [blank], 4 years Virginia; Leonard Lester to John Gurgenny; William Good to Elizabeth Whittington, 5 years [Virginia]; James Kellock to same, 7 years Virginia; James Garnesay to Abraham Roome, 4 years [Virginia]; Thomas Hall to Stephen Watts, 4 years Virginia; John James to same, 4 years Virginia; Rice Williams to same, 4 years Virginia; John Bowen to same, 4 years Virginia; Meredith Price to same, 4 years Virginia; Thomas Williams to same, 4 years Virginia; William Inon to same, 7 years Virginia; John Bayly to same, 7 years Virginia; Anne Bishop, spinster, to John Roades, 4 years Virginia; John Rosewell to John Scotto, 8 years Virginia; John Emmett to same, 4 years Virginia; Joane Spender to same, 4 years Virginia; Joyce Bowen to John Hale, 4 years Virginia; Anne Cordin to John Cox, 4 years Virginia; Elizabeth Compton to John Seward, 4 years Virginia; Mary Barnell to same, 4 years Virginia; George Painton to George Hall, 4 years Virginia; Jasper Lane to Robert Turner, 4 years Barbados; Samuell Amyes to Thomas Ofield, 4 years Virginia; Joane Smeades, spinster, to Daniell Jordan, 4 years Virginia; Edward Lloyster, yeoman, to same, 4 years Virginia; Gilbert Jones, yeoman, to same, 4 years Virginia; Phillip Griffen to Richard Hilman, 4 years Virginia; Elizabeth

Francis to John Gill, 7 years Virginia; Hannah Young to Ansell Wanklin, 4 years Virginia; Anne Watkins to Christopher Watts, 4 years Virginia; Adam Bradshaw to Robert Stephens, 4 years Virginia; Margeret Watkins to James Thorpe, 4 years Nevis; Thomas Underhill to John Dand, 4 years Virginia. (BR)

13 August. Shipper by the *Desire* bound from London for New England: Thomas Adams. (PRO: E190/47/2).

19 August-24 September. Shippers by the *Providence* bound from London for Virginia: James Drew, Henry Richards, Lucy Knightly, Patience Ward. (PRO: E190/47/2).

20 August. Shipper by the *Golden Fortune* bound from London for Virginia: John Nutchall. (PRO: E190/47/2).

21 August. Shipper by the *Brothers Adventure* bound from London for Virginia: Humphrey? Plover. (PRO: E190/47/4).

23 August. The following apprenticed in Bristol: Richard Poole, yeoman, to John Vasser, 3 years Virginia; Thomas Morgan to James Wathen, 4 years Virginia; John Williams to same, 4 years Virginia; William Cole to William Hardwick, 5 years Virginia; John Butler to John Little, 4 years Virginia. (BR).

24 August. Newgate prisoners reprieved to be transported to Jamaica by Thomas Middleton, Alexander Howe, Jeremy Bonnell and Gerrard Barnard, merchants. London: Edward Beckford; James Harris; Samuel Wethersley; Richard Syms; Sarah Wilsheire, widow; Susanna Gilham, spinster; Benjamin Childerton; Hugh Browne; Helen Thorpe, widow; William Peacock; Margaret Martin, spinster; Elizabeth Smith, spinster; Thomas Baldwin; Edward Gutch; William Elder; William Hodgson alias Hudson; Nathaniell Hubbert; Susanna James, spinster; Susanna Almond, spinster; Elizabeth Smith, wife of John Smith; John Riggs; Judith Thomas; Robert Newman; Gabriel Reynolds; Robert Wood alias Batchelor; John Harris alias Robinson; John Digby. Middlesex: Thomas Edwards of Shoreditch; Arthur Girton of Hackney; William Fuller of Bromley; John Johnson of Paddington; John Hobbs of Paddington; Bartholomew Shoare of Stepney; William Reeves of St. Giles in the Fields; John Phippy of Stepney; Thomas Bullock of St. Andrew Holborn; Thomas Cooke of St. Andrew Holborn; Francis Cole of Bedfont; Anne Mason of St. Paul Covent Garden; Alice Stewkely alias Crowley alias Cowley alias Rattenbury of Stepney; Thomas Allen of Heston; William Gunn of Stepney; Elizabeth Greene of Laleham; George Green of St. Andrew Holborn; Elizabeth Freeman of St. Sepulchre; Henry Jackson of Hammersmith; Morgan Evans of St. Paul Covent Garden; Henry Pretty of St. Botolph Aldgate; Thomas Nash of Bromley; Thomas Parr of St. Botolph Aldgate; William Keightley of St. Clement Danes; Thomas Austin of St. Clement Danes; Roger Stanbury of St. Botolph Aldgate; Elizabeth Gosgrave, spinster, alias wife of James Gosgrave of St. Botolph Aldgate; John Bowden of St. Andrew Holborn; Thomas Gadd of Hackney; George Meake of Hackney; John Holland of

Hampstead; Thomas Watson of Hampstead; George Wooler of Hampstead; George Jacob of St. Botolph Aldgate; John Hepper of St. Clement Danes; Richard Hickman of Islington; Thomas Balding of Enfield; John Thomas of Enfield; James Smith of St. Clement Danes; Elizabeth Atkins of St. Martin in the Fields; Mary Smith of St. Martin in the Fields; Elizabeth Lemon of Stepney; Richard Capper of St. Giles in the Fields; William Hawkins of Stepney; John Leach of St. Sepulchre; Humphrey Beare of St. Sepulchre. (PRO: C66/2986/1).

26 August. Shipper by the *William & Edward* bound from London for Virginia: John Bland. (PRO: E190/47/4).

27 August. The following apprenticed in Bristol: William King to William Rodney, 4 years Virginia; William Keene to William Luffe, 7 years Virginia; Winifred Field to George Hale, 4 years Virginia; William Williams to Robert Skinner, 4 years Virginia; Henry Williams to same, 4 years Virginia; John Thornbury to same, 7 years Virginia; Richard Bachelor to William Donning, 4 years Virginia; Elinor Bradnock to Katherine Bisse, 4 years Virginia; Daniell Gardner to Thomas Pearson, 6 years Virginia; Francis Gallow to William Swimmer, 4 years Virginia; Thomas Jones to James Cole, 4 years Nevis; John Higgs to John Channel, 5 years Virginia; Elinor Smith to same, 4 years Virginia; Edward Ilea to Jeremy Howell, 3 years Virginia; David Williams to John Morgan, 4 years Virginia; William Lewes to John Reede, 4 years Virginia; Joane Jackson to same, 4 years Nevis; Thomas Phillips to same, 4 years Nevis; Simon Traunter to John Crumpe, 6 years Virginia; Joane Angell to Symon Hurle, 5 years Virginia; William Powell to Richard Finch, 8 years Virginia; Margeret Butler to same, 4 years Virginia; Richard Gettings to Elizabeth Gething, 4 years Nevis; William Browne to Henry Morgan, 4 years Nevis; Barbary Culme to Godbury Dowden, widow, 4 years Barbados; Henry Herne to Godfry Widlake, 6 years Barbados. (BR).

29 August. Shipper by the *Friendship* of Poole, Mr. John Pike, bound from Poole for Virginia: William Pike & Co. (PRO: E190/879/1).

August. Administration of William Tayloe of Virginia. (AW).

6 September. The following apprenticed in Bristol: Robert Hedges to James Cole, 4 years Nevis; Arthur Evitt, yeoman, to Charles Kelly, 4 years Nevis; John Lyning to Joseph Hardwick, 8 years Nevis; Nathaniell Linley to John Wintle, 5 years Virginia; Thomas Broadrish to John Reede, 3 years Virginia; William Church to John Pearson, 5 years Virginia; Anne Reynolds to Martha Braine, 5 years Virginia; Thomas Reynolds to same, 9 years Virginia; Henry Francklin to same, 6 years Virginia. (BR).

9 September. The King orders the Governors of the New England colonies to send to England for trial all those Quakers who have been condemned and imprisoned. (CSPC).

9 September. The following apprenticed in Bristol: Robert Fulloway to Mathew Canne, 7 years Virginia; John Edmunds to J—— Bragg, 4 years Virginia; Samson Redwick to Thomas Mills, 4 years Virginia; William Gay to John Luffe, 5 years Virginia; Ann Kite to John Alflatt, 4 years Virginia; Walter Price to Morgan Williams, 4 years Virginia; Thomas Dowing to Stephen Watts, 4 years Virginia; Edward Price to Thomas Hethcott, 3 years Virginia; James Williams to Thomas Williams, 4 years Virginia. (BR).

10 September. The following apprenticed in Bristol: Robert Pearce to Morgan William, 4 years Barbados; Ansell Bayly to John Driver, 5 years Virginia; John Thomas to Richard Tomkins, 3 years Barbados; Thomas Oxford to John Smith, 5 years Virginia; Thomas Exon to John Reede, 3 years Virginia; Isaac Skinner to William Davis, 4 years Virginia; William Edwards to Evans Price, 4 years Barbados. (BR).

16 September. The following apprenticed in Bristol: Anne Reede to Anthony Eale, 4 years Virginia; John Thomas to Morgan Williams, 8 years Barbados; Margeret Bitchell to John Reede, 4 years Barbados; Edmond Williams to same, 4 years Virginia; William Coates to John Kerie, 4 years Barbados; John Shepherd to same, 4 years Barbados; Thomas Jones to John Groves, 4 years Barbados; Welthian Taylor to George Lane, 4 years Barbados; John Davis to John Harris, 4 years Barbados; Joane Clements to Francis Jones, 7 years Barbados; Thomas Ruse to Mathew Cann, 9 years [Barbados]; Phillip Burrow to Charles Ambrose, 5 years [Barbados]; Andrew Powell to William Tatten, 4 years [Barbados]; Robert Young to John Groves, 5 years [Barbados]; Margeret Perry to Roger Adams, 4 years [Barbados]; James Hooper to Walter Tocknell, 8 years [Barbados]; David Reece to Morgan Williams, 4 years Barbados; John Knight to John Tucke, 5 years Virginia; Mary Winseley to John Morgan, 4 years Virginia; Elizabeth Barnet to John Harris, 4 years Virginia; Elizabeth Williams to Elizabeth Penrose, 4 years Nevis; Mary Stone to John Harris, 4 years Nevis. (BR).

18 September. Shippers by the *Thomas & Anne* bound from London for Virginia: William Callow, William Nevitt. (PRO: E190/47/4).

25 September. The following apprenticed in Bristol: William Ruddur to John Reede, 4 years Virginia; Jonas Harris to John Luffe, 4 years Virginia; William Yeamans to John A——eaver, 4 years Virginia; Arthur Bowen to same, 4 years Virginia; Arthur Severne to John Gowing, 4 years Virginia; Anne Cooke to Francis Jones, 4 years Virginia. (BR).

30 September. The following apprenticed in Bristol: Anne Poore to John Tucke, 5 years Virginia; Mary Morse to same, 5 years Virginia; Sarah Ayleworth to same, 6 years Virginia; James Pidden to Thomas Pearson, 4 years Virginia; Robert Rusher to John Alyes, 7 years Nevis; William Wittrell to Edmund Williams, 4 years Virginia; James Harry to Richard Lucock, 7 years Virginia; Richard Vidler to John Graol, merchant, 4 years Virginia; Anne Greenhouse to John Harris, 4 years Virginia; Katherine Everley to same, 4 years Virginia;

Thomas West to Charles Andrewes, 4 years Virginia; Samuell Rooke to same, 5 years Virginia; Walter Morton to Malachy Thrustone, 4 years Virginia; Jane Harris to Thomas Packer, 6 years Virginia; John Dimick to Charles Andrewes, 4 years Virginia; David Jones to same, 4 years Virginia; John Colesell to Roger King, 4 years Virginia; William Smith to John Alflett, 3 years Virginia. (BR)

30 September-10 October. Shippers by the *John & Katherine* bound from London for Virginia: Arthur Betsworth, John Yates, John Jauncy. (PRO: E190/47/4).

September. Administration of John Cheesman of Virginia. (AW).

September. Administration of Joane Michell alias Townsend of Virginia. (AW).

5 October. Shipper by the *Royal Oak* bound from London for Virginia: Edmond Custie. (PRO: E190/47/4).

5 October. The following apprenticed in Bristol: Richard Shipley to Thomas Pearson, 3 years Virginia; William Dyer to same, 3 years Virginia; Herbert Roe to John Alflett, 3 years Virginia; Henry Jones to John Austin, 4 years Virginia; Thomas Witherington to William Square, 3 years Nevis; Robert Ward to same, 3 years Nevis; Robert Redmond to Charles Andrewes, 7 years Virginia. (BR).

12 October. The following apprenticed in Bristol: Thomas Williams to Richard Sullock, 4 years Virginia; George Southerne to Robert Yate, 5 years Barbados; Thomas Wooles to Thomas Pearson, 4 years Virginia; Francis Wrenne to same, 6 years Virginia; Thomas Barnes to same, 7 years Antigua; Dorothy Harchott to same, 6 years Antigua; James Williams to William Square, 4 years Nevis; Thomas Lewis to Richard Ward, 5 years Nevis; John Morgan to John Fairclue, 6 years Virginia. (BR).

21 October. The following apprenticed in Bristol: Daniell Shorte to Thomas Easton, 4 years Barbados; John Watkins to Elias Luke, 4 years Barbados; Joane Watkins to same, 4 years Barbados; Henry Porch to same, 4 years Barbados; William Osbourne to Joseph Day, 4 years Barbados; Robert Redditt to same, 4 years Barbados; Evan Pritchard to Robert Seward, 4 years Barbados; Richard Waring, yeoman, 4 years Barbados; Samuell Clarke to John Alyes, merchant, 4 years Barbados. (BR).

25 October. Shipper by the *King Solomon* bound from London for Virginia: Thomas Fowke. (PRO: E190/47/4).

25 October. The following apprenticed in Bristol: Thomas Williams to Margeret Webb, 4 years Virginia; Thomas Haskins to Henry Gough, 4 years Virginia; Ambrose Yorke to William Thomas, 7 years Nevis; William Rumsy to same, 7 years Nevis; Lewis Thomas to same, 7 years Nevis; Roger James to same, 4 years Nevis; Walter Williams to same, 4 years Nevis; David James to same, 4 years Nevis; John Kinton to Thomas Rippin, 4 years Nevis; Richard Ives to Richard Smith, 4 years Nevis. (BR).

October. Probate of will of Thomas Burnell, citizen and clothworker of London, whose nephew, John Morley, was in New England. (AW).

October. Probate of will of Jerman Major of St. Faith the Virgin, London, whose cousin, Ann Jones, was in New England. (AW).

4 November. The following apprenticed in Bristol: Phillys Jones to John Jones, 4 years Nevis; Robert Kitta to same, 7 years Barbados; Robert Thomas to William Reede, 4 years Barbados; Thomas Battin to Jacob Tompson, 4 years Barbados; John Lloyd to John Morris, 3 years Barbados. (BR).

8 November. Shipper by the *William & Mary* bound from London for Virginia: Charles Smith. (PRO: E190/47/4).

11 November. The following apprenticed in Bristol: Isaac Gregory to Thomas Workeman, 3 years Barbados; John Twiford to John Gurgenny, 4 years Barbados; Edward Thomas to John Jones, 4 years [Barbados]; William Preston to John Pearson, 4 years [Barbados]; David Williams to Christopher Olliver, 4 years [Barbados]. (BR).

11 November-24 February. Depositions re the voyage of the *White Dove*, Mr. Thomas Stanton, from London to Barbados, but intending for Virginia, in 1658/9 with passengers including Stephen Pett, Robert Hendray, David Griffith and Richard Merriman. (EA)

13 November. Shipper by the *Elizabeth & Mary* bound from London for Virginia: William Thompson. (PRO: E190/47/4).

18 November. The following apprenticed in Bristol: Jane Wood to John Austin, 4 years [Barbados]; Roger Painter to Richard Yates, 5 years [Barbados]. (BR).

20 November. The following apprenticed in Bristol: John Powell to William Liston, 5 years [Barbados]. (BR).

25 November. The following apprenticed in Bristol: Thomas Hull to John Jones, 7 years Barbados; Thomas Moyle to Christopher Oliver, 4 years Barbados; Henry Kirle to same, 4 years Nevis; Edward Gill to Thomas Watkins, 4 years Barbados; Charles Watts, weaver, to Thomas Barret, 4 years Barbados; John Banwell to John Alyes, 4 years Nevis; John Rooke to Arthur Stearte, 4 years Nevis; William Wilkins to Thomas Sparke, 4 years Nevis; Henry Clutterbooke to John Alflatt, 7 years Nevis; Wartus Dangerfield to Edward Fox, 4 years Barbados. (BR).

30 November. The following apprenticed in Bristol: Edward Minard to Francis Borne, 4 years Nevis; Humfry Williams to same, 4 years Nevis. (BR).

November. Administration with will of Edward Shrimpton, of Bethnal Green, Middlesex, merchant, whose children were in Boston, New England. (AW).

November. John Woodward petitions the King to be given the house and office of Assay Master of the Mint which were held by his father Thomas Woodward until he was dismissed in 1649 when he went to Virginia vowing not to return until the King was restored. (CSPC).

1 December. The following apprenticed in Bristol: John Williams to Margaret Earle, 5 years Nevis; Thomas Litman to Edward Launder, 4 years Nevis; Thomas Jones to Thomas Ady, 4 years Nevis; Edward Isles to Richard Reede, 4 years Nevis; Richard Lawrence to James West, 3 years Nevis; Hugh Holwood to Richard James, 5 years Nevis; Thomas Yates, yeoman, to Randal Judson, 4 years Virginia; John Berry to Teague Daniell, 3 years Nevis; Arthur Poole to Robert Bodinham, 4 years Virginia; Roch Hughes to Anne Morgan, 4 years Virginia; Henry Nicholas to same, 4 years Virginia; Francis Hughes to same, 4 years Virginia; John Broadrip to Thomas Seare, 4 years Nevis; Joseph Young to Francis Borne, 7 years Nevis; Lewes Williams to Evan Rice, 4 years Nevis; Thomas Williams to William Reede, 4 years Nevis; John Trotman to John Breach, 4 years Nevis; John Cockle to William Watkins, 3 years Nevis; Robert Boobier to John Samm, 4 years Nevis; Arthur Morgan to Thomas Ayleward, 4 years Nevis; William Powell to John Jones, 3 years Nevis; Judith Powell to same, 4 years Nevis; Andrew Griffin to Thomas Luckins, 4 years Nevis; Peter Langley to Randall Judson, 7 years Virginia. (BR).

30 December. The following apprenticed in Bristol: John Jobbins to Thomas Pearson, 4 years Virginia; Richard Ball to Thomas Ayleward, 6 years Virginia; Anthony Baby to Christopher Olliver, merchant, 4 years Nevis; Peter Wethers to William Janie, 4 years Nevis. (BR).

December. Probate of will of Thomas Brinley of Datchet, Buckinghamshire, whose daughter, Grissell, was wife of Nathaniel Silvester of New England. (AW).

1662

2 January. The following apprenticed in Bristol: Lodwick Tiverton to Thomas Sparkes, 4 years Barbados; Thomas Stockman to Richard ?Tullidge, 4 years Barbados; Morgan Williams to Thomas Seare, 5 years Barbados; William Williams to Richard Hambleton, 5 years Barbados; Margery Glace to Thomas Pearson, 4 years Barbados. (BR).

3 January. The following apprenticed in Bristol: John Gough to Christopher Oliver, 4 years Barbados; Francis Harris to the same, 4 years Barbados; Samuell Adams to Thomas Bradford, 6 years Barbados; Phillip Davis to the same, 4 years Barbados; Robert Nicholls to Morrice ——, 4 years Barbados; Grace Nicholls to the same, 4 years Barbados; Richard Phelps to Francis Borne, 3 years Nevis; Richard Parker to Thomas Ayleward, 3 years Nevis; Mary Nelme to Thomas Giles, 4 years Virginia; John Gunne to John Austin, 3 years Nevis; Michaell Saffin to Thomas Dunning, 4 years Nevis. (BR).

4 January. Shipper by the *Walsingham* of Bristol bound from Bristol for Virginia: Edward Gibbs. (PRO: E190/1240/6).

8 January. The following apprenticed in Bristol: John Beind to Francis Parsons, 4 years Nevis; John Abraham to Edward Langley, 4 years Nevis; Joseph Huish to Edward Launder, 6 years Nevis; John Bevan to Giles Merrick, 6 years Nevis; Anne Cording to Robert Dimock, 4 years Barbados; Jonathan Tyre to Evan Rice, 4 years Barbados; Sarah Stride to Thomas Sadler, 6 years Barbados. (BR).

10 January. The following apprenticed in Bristol: Richard Fox to John Oldbury, 5 years Barbados; Robert Bradford to Edward Wasbrow, 4 years Barbados. (BR).

11 January. The following apprenticed in Bristol: Roger Williams to Robert Heskins, 4 years Nevis; Phillip Lewis to Francis Borne, 4 years Nevis; Bartholomew Thomas to Randall Judson, 3 years Virginia; William Eleate to the same, 8 years Virginia; Mary Collins to Joseph Rivers, 4 years Nevis; Francis Yeamans to the same, 6 years Nevis. (BR).

13 January. The following apprenticed in Bristol: Phillip Jones to Alexander Jacob, 3 years Nevis; John Silly to William Reede, 4 years Barbados; Humfry Harris to George Morrice, 3 years Nevis; Edward Perrin to Thomas Pearson, 4 years Virginia; William Owen to John White, 4 years Barbados; Joseph Lawrence to John Vinson, 5 years Nevis. (BR).

15 January. The following apprenticed in Bristol: Humphry Williams to Phillip Harris, 7 years Nevis; Anthony Browne to William Limbry, 4 years Nevis; John Simkis to the same, 4 years Nevis; Cutbert Veale to James ——lly, 4 years

Nevis; Richard Stone to Edward Tocknell, 4 years Nevis; Richard Chynne to Robert Haskins, 3 years Nevis. (BR).

23 January. The following apprenticed in Bristol: Timothy Isles to Thomas Donning, 7 years New England; Humfry Barber to the same, 4 years New England; Thomas Gibbon to Joseph Day, 4 years Nevis; Mary Richards to Thomas Rice, 4 years Nevis; Edward Timewell to William Mathew, 3 years Nevis; Richard Beaton to Richard Hambleton, 3 years Nevis; Sarah Holder to William Limbry, 4 years Nevis. (BR).

25 January. The following apprenticed in Bristol: Anne Higgs to Edward Tocknell, 4 years Nevis; Thomas Moncks to Margery Fearclue, 4 years Nevis; Elinor Rogers to —— Sparkes, 4 years Nevis; Thomas Davis to William Limbry, 5 years Nevis; Roger Davis to the same, 5 years Nevis; Mary Butler to Robert Watkins, 4 years Nevis; William Fry to Thomas Donning, 7 years Nevis; John Robins to Robert Heskins, 4 years Nevis. (BR).

27 January. The following apprenticed in Bristol: Mary Channdler to Phillip Bonnet, 4 years Nevis; John Crime to Thomas Norman, 4 years Nevis; Christofer Jones to Richard Lucock, 4 years St. Christopher; John Thomas to the same, 6 years Nevis; John Nicholls to Daniel Jackson, 4 years Barbados; John Wilkins to Phillip Watkins, 4 years Nevis; Lewis Penry to Robert ?Hilzy, 4 years Nevis; Hester Plummer to Robert Haskins, 4 years Nevis. (BR)

January. Probate of will of Francis Newton of London, grocer, (bound for New England). (AW).

3 February. The following apprenticed in Bristol: Thomas Leonard to Thomas Simons, 4 years Barbados. (BR).

4 February. The following apprenticed in Bristol: Thomas Dicks to John Waters, 5 years Barbados; Margery Floyd to the same, 6 years Barbados; John Pearce to Henry Bankes, 4 years Barbados; John Trigg to the same,5 years Barbados; Robert London to Robert Merry, 4 years Nevis; William Gunne to George Watkins, 4 years Nevis; Jenkin Jones to Henry Richards, 4 years Nevis. (BR).

6 February. The following apprenticed in Bristol: James Morgan to William Skeetch, 4 years Nevis; Henry Crosby to Bartholomew Thomas, 3 years Nevis. (BR).

8 February. The following apprenticed in Bristol: Anne Warner to George Lane, 4 years New England; Fortune Roberts to John Masters, 4 years Nevis; Richard Phelps to Bartholomew Thomas, 4 years Nevis; Thomas Williams to William Hall, 4 years Nevis; Richard Harding to Thomas Donning, 4 years Nevis. (BR).

10 February. The following apprenticed in Bristol: William Watts to Phillip Harris, 4 years Nevis; Roger Edwards to Samuel Nicholls, 4 years New England; James Filla to Richard Newman, 4 years Barbados; John Harvy to Thomas Durban, 4 years Barbados; Nicholas Wrentmore to Edward Tocknell, 4 years Barbados. (BR).

14 February. The following apprenticed in Bristol: John Gough to Thomas Donning, 4 years New England; Thomas James to John Masters, 5 years Nevis; James Evilly to Jasper Crosse, 5 years Nevis. (BR).

15 February. The following apprenticed in Bristol: John Watkins to Robert Culme, 4 years Barbados; Thomas Williams to Stephen Keetch, 4 years Nevis. (BR).

17 February. The following apprenticed in Bristol: Anne Worley to Judith Daniell, 6 years Nevis; Robert Widowes to Edmund Williams, 4 years Nevis; Robert Powell to Thomas Ayson, 9 years Nevis; Tobyas Hele to Edward Watkins, 3 years Nevis; Thomas Clarke to John Turner, 8 years New England; Mary Rogers to William Clements, 10 years Barbados; Elizabeth Curtis to Stephen Humfry, 4 years Nevis. (BR).

19 February. The following apprenticed in Bristol: John Cobby to William Limbry, 4 years Nevis; Richard Williams to the same, 4 years Nevis; Anne Williams to the same, 4 years Nevis; James Jones to George Watkins, 6 years Nevis. (BR).

20 February. The following apprenticed in Bristol: Richard Burridge to Peter Peiterson, 4 years Nevis; Howell Meredith to Phillip Harris, 4 years Nevis; Thomas Thorne to Samuell Nicholls, 6 years New England; Evan Jinkins to the same, 6 years New England; Thomas Brookes to the same, 4 years New England; George Bagwell to the same, 6 years New England; Joane Gatlock to Thomas Jones, 4 years New England; Elizabeth Binner to the same, 5 years New England; John Gatly to the same, 7 years New England; George Haggat to John Swinerton, 4 years Nevis; Samuel Scripture to the same, 4 years Nevis; Joane Hill to Henry Bankes, 4 years Nevis; Thomas Jones to Henry Gough, 4 years Nevis. (BR).

24 February. The following apprenticed in Bristol: Thomas Harris to Francis Morgan, 4 years Jamaica; William Morrice to Henry Bankes, 4 years Jamaica; William Moore to the same, 4 years Jamaica; William Rogers to Thomas Donning, 4 years New England; Roger Greene to John Legg, 5 years New England; Rose Alston to Thomas Dennis, 4 years New England; Elizabeth Meredith to the same, 4 years New England. (BR).

25 February. The following apprenticed in Bristol: Richard Wilton to Edward Watkins, 4 years Virginia; William Merriman to Thomas Jones, 4 years Barbados; Thomas Williams to the same, 4 years Nevis; Simon Brimsly to Richard Pugsley, 4 years New England; Samuel Sneath to Thomas Edwards, 4 years Nevis; Roger Bevan to Phillip Harris, 4 years Nevis; Florence Mayne to Isaac Tayler, 4 years Nevis; Thomas Lewis to Henry Bankes, 4 years Nevis. (BR).

26 February-6 March. Shippers by the *Mary Fortune* of Bristol bound from Bristol for New England: John Speed for William Dunning, John Swinerton, George Lane, John Collins, John Younge. (PRO: E190/1240/6).

February. Probate of will of Henry Martin of Wapping, Middlesex, mariner, who had lands in New England. (AW).

2 March. The following apprenticed in Bristol: Richard Tuftin to Henry Bankes, 4 years Nevis; Elizabeth Williams to Thomas Northerne, 5 years Nevis; Jane Robins to William Phips, 4 years St. Christopher; John Morgan to Richard Martin, 7 years Nevis; Fabyan Price to Richard Hambleton, 5 years Nevis; Isaac Bowin to Thomas Dolling, 4 years Nevis. (BR).

5 March. The following apprenticed in Bristol: William Duke to Robert Perry, 3 years Nevis; Phillip Watkins to Giles Merrick, 7 years Nevis; Lawrence Sall to Samuell Nicholls, 4 years New England; Daniell Towne to William Hiscox, 4 years New England; William Jacob to Henry Bankes, 4 years Nevis. (BR).

7 March. The following apprenticed in Bristol: George Ashman to Stephen Humfry, 3 years Barbados; William Milsome to Thomas Sweete, 4 years Nevis; Elizabeth Jones to James Wathen, 6 years Nevis; Jane Harris to the same, 6 years Nevis; Michaell Farrington to the same, 5 years Leewards. (BR).

10 March. The following apprenticed in Bristol: Elizabeth Hammon to William Phips, 4 years Nevis; William Hix to Thomas Dolling, 5 years Nevis; Anthony Geching, 4 years Nevis; Jones Steevens to William Cole, 4 years Nevis; Thomas Williams to Henry Bankes, 6 years Nevis; William Bullock to James Wathen, 5 years Nevis; Elizabeth Jenings to the same, 4 years Nevis; Sarah Defell to the same, 5 years Nevis; Elizabeth Merchant to Thomas Covey, 7 years Nevis; Humfry Bullery to the same, 4 years Nevis; Thomas Thomas to Richard Martin, 7 years Nevis; William Philpot to John Weaver, 4 years Nevis; Thomas Berton to Richard Lucock, 4 years Nevis; John White to Henry Richard, 6 years Nevis; Anne Smith to Francis Morgan, 4 years Nevis. (BR).

17 March. The following apprenticed in Bristol: John Richards to James Wathen, 4 years Nevis; James Goodinough to Michael Deyes, 4 years Nevis; Thomas Durbin to Thomas Covey, 4 years Nevis; Edward Hix to Thomas Simons, 4 years Nevis; William Mibber to John Bevis, 4 years Nevis; Jenkin Jones to Richard Hambleton, 4 years Nevis; Jane Jones to Edward Tocknell, 4 years Nevis; William Prosser to Christopher Alford, 4 years Nevis. (BR).

18 March. The following apprenticed in Bristol: Anthony Parsons to James Wathen, 4 years Nevis; Milbrow Dicks to the same, 5 years Nevis; William Poole to the same, 5 years Nevis; Richard Evans to the same, 8 years Nevis; Edward Davis to the same, 7 years Nevis; Thomas Seconds to Robert Tilbry, 4 years Jamaica; George Collins to John Weaver, 4 years Nevis. (BR).

20 March. The following apprenticed in Bristol: Llewellin Thomas to Thomas Dolling, 5 years Nevis; Thomas Wright to the same, 4 years Nevis; John Smith to Thomas Simons, 7 years Nevis; William Arnoll to the same, 4 years Nevis; Joseph Raise to the same, 4 years Nevis; Robert Leydon to George Watkins, 4 years Nevis; Thomas Williams to Henry Bankes, 7 years Nevis; William Morgan to William Cole, 4 years Nevis; John Pritchard to the same, 4 years

Nevis; Thomas Jenkins to the same, 5 years Nevis; Adan Snow to Thomas Sadler, 3 years Barbados; William Bush to Robert Penry, 3 years Barbados; James Edmunds to the same, 3 years Barbados; Richard Hole to John Morrice, 4 years Nevis. (BR).

25 March. The following apprenticed in Bristol: Paull Prichill to Henry Bankes, 4 years Nevis; Elinor Phillips to the same, 4 years Nevis; Edward Harding to the same, 4 years Nevis; Margeret Baker to the same, 4 years Nevis; Johanne Perkes to the same, 4 years Nevis; Katherine Bevan to the same, 4 years Nevis; Edmund Thomas to the same, 4 years Nevis; Gainer Evans to Thomas Jones, 5 years Nevis; Edward Rowland to the same, 6 years Jamaica; Thomas Roger to Phillip Harris, 5 years Jamaica; John Hetherley to Elizabeth Dow, 4 years Nevis. (BR).

27 March. The following apprenticed in Bristol: Thomas Smith to John Masters, 4 years Nevis; Anne Martin to John Weaver, 4 years Nevis; Joane Jones to the same, 4 years Nevis; Elizabeth Jones to Francis Morgan, 4 years Nevis; Ralph Crow to Henry Bankes, 4 years Nevis; Robert Baker to the same, 4 years Nevis; Jenkin Jones to Thomas Dolling, 5 years Nevis. (BR).

1 April. The following apprenticed in Bristol: John Pennock to George Watkins, 5 years Nevis; Rice Thomas to Francis Morgan, 4 years Nevis; John Harden to William Lewis, 4 years Nevis; John Tippet to Robert Perry, 4 years Nevis; Elizabeth Harris to the same, 7 years Nevis. (BR).

4 April. Deposition by John Hunt, aged 20, servant of John Harvey of London, scrivener, that William Manning of Cambridge, New England, became indebted to Thomas Sandys, citizen and cutler of London, and Edmund Middleton, citizen and haberdasher of London, by deed of 21 April 1660. Samuel Bach of London, merchant, has been appointed as attorney to recover. (LMCD).

4 April. The following apprenticed in Bristol: William Dodson to Phillip Harris, 4 years Jamaica; Joane Cooke to John Grimes, 4 years Jamaica; Daniel Wood to Joseph Rivers, 6 years Jamaica; Isaac Thomas to Henry Bankes, 4 years Nevis; Humfrey Webb to the same, 4 years Nevis; John Huntur to James Watson, 4 years Nevis; John Shiviar to the same, 4 years Nevis; Robert Jerman to John Masters, 4 years Nevis; Elizabeth Elger to the same, 4 years Nevis; Thomas Stone to Thomas Michell, 4 years Nevis. (BR).

12 April. The following apprenticed in Bristol: John Gething to Thomas Taylor, 7 years Barbados; John Ball to Samuell Norrice, 5 years Barbados. (BR).

14 April. The following apprenticed in Bristol: Zachary Wheton to Robert Glasse, 4 years Barbados; Robert Bennet to John Weaver, 4 years Barbados. (BR).

15 April. The following apprenticed in Bristol: Penelope Baker to Richard Barry, 7 years Nevis; Henry Williams to Richard Winding, 5 years Barbados; Thomas

Stephens to the same, 5 years Barbados; Daniell Somers to Thomas Ofield, 4 years Nevis; Katherine Thomas to William Clarke, 4 years Barbados; Robert Hall to John Haskins, 11 years Virginia; Thomas Williams to the same, 5 years Virginia; Isaac Amorite to the same, 4 years Virginia; John Day to the same, 4 years Virginia. (BR).

21 April. The following apprenticed in Bristol: Rebecca Thomas to William Clarke, 5 years Barbados or Leewards by *Charles*; James Guy to Thomas Pincus, 4 years Barbados or Virginia by *Providence*. (BR).

24 April. The following apprenticed in Bristol: John Saunders to Thomas Pincus, 4 years Barbados or Virginia by *Providence*; John Lewis to John Weaver, 4 years Nevis or Jamaica by *William & Thomas*; Henry Powell to Robert Glasse, 4 years Barbados by *Charles*. (BR).

25 April. The following apprenticed in Bristol: Onizephorus Cornish to John Haskins, 4 years Virginia by *Providence*. (BR).

26 April. The following apprenticed in Bristol: James Jones to Daniel Punnet, 4 years Barbados by *Charles*. (BR).

28 April. The following apprenticed in Bristol: Sarah Reede to Robert Tilky, 4 years Barbados by *Charles*; Morgan Cannings to the same, 4 years Barbados by *Charles*; Mary Norris to the same, 4 years Barbados by *Charles*; Evan Bennet to John Haskins, 11 years Virginia by *Providence*; John Chandler to Robert Eilsey, 4 years Barbados by *Charles*. (BR).

29 April. The following apprenticed in Bristol: John Micail to William Donning, 4 years Virginia by *Charles*; Margaret Farly to Henry Smith, 7 years Virginia by *Charles*. (BR).

30 April. The following apprenticed in Bristol: John Ash to Edward Shadling, 4 years Virginia by *Charles*; John Williams to Thomas Elbridge, 8 years New England by *Huntsman*. (BR).

2 May. The following apprenticed in Bristol: Humfry Robins to Walter Clarke, 5 years Barbados by *Charles*; John Eastmead to John Haskins, mariner, 4 years Virginia by *Providence*; John Taylor to the same, 4 years Virginia; John Taylor to the same, 11 years Virginia; Elizabeth Taylor to the same, 11 years Virginia by *Providence*; George Harris to the same, 6 years Virginia by *Providence*; William Harris to Daniell Punnit, 7 years Barbados by *Charles*; John Lambert to Richard Winding, 7 years Barbados by *Charles*; Richard Brasie to the same, 5 years Barbados by *Charles*; John Power to Robert Tilsey, 4 years Jamaica by *Charles*; Evan Davis to the same, 4 years Jamaica by *Charles*; John Davis to the same, 3 years Jamaica by *Charles*; Lewis Jones to Blanch Freeman, 4 years Virginia by *Charles*; Prudence Yeo to the same, 4 years Virginia by *Providence*; Hugh Williams to Robert Glasse, 4 years Barbados by *Charles*; John Williams to William Hardwick, 4 years Virginia by *Providence*. (BR).

4 May. Shipper by the *Huntsman* of Bristol, Mr. John Davis, bound from Bristol for New England: Robert Yate. (PRO: E190/1240/6).

7 May. The following apprenticed in Bristol: John Jones to William Parker, 4 years Barbados by *Charles*; William Wilkison to Anselm Smarte, 4 years Virginia by *Charles*; Mary Gale to the same, 4 years Virginia; Cornelius Thomas to John Haskins, 5 years Virginia by *Charles*; Marke Randell to Thomas Archer, 4 years New England by *Huntsman*; John Thomas to James Wathin, 6 years Virginia by *Providence*; Hannah Backwell to Richard Wilding, 5 years Barbados by *Charles*. (BR).

8 May. The following apprenticed in Bristol: Samuell Simms to William Hardwick, 4 years Virginia; Elinor Pussell to William Hammonds, 4 years Barbados by *Charles*; George Nicholas to the same, 4 years Barbados; John Watkins to Ralph Williams, 4 years Barbados; Thomas Huntly to James Wathen, 4 years Virginia; William Fletcher to the same, 8 years Virginia; Elinor Barry to the same, 5 years Virginia; John Nicholas to William Freeman, 4 years Virginia; Henry Wolfe to John Davis, 4 years New England by *Huntsman*. (BR).

14 May. The following apprenticed in Bristol: Elizabeth Garrett to Blanch Freeman, 4 years Virginia; Thomas Steevens to the same, 4 years Virginia; Stephen Thomas to John Howse, 4 years Virginia; Richard Lye to John Haskins, 5 years Virginia. (BR).

20 May. The following apprenticed in Bristol: Samuell Glenne to William Hardy, 4 years Virginia; John Leere to the same, 4 years Virginia; Anne Williams to John Haskins, 4 years Virginia; Hugh Richards to the same, 4 years Virginia; Elizabeth Lydoll to Margeret Burford, 4 years Virginia; Edward Evans to Edward Brookes, 4 years Virginia; John Simons to John Farclue, 5 years Virginia; Richard Gettings to Osman Crabb, 4 years Virginia; Richard Duncombe to the same, 4 years Virginia; John Davy to the same, 4 years Virginia. (BR).

24 May. The following apprenticed in Bristol: William Edwards to Edward Crumpe, 4 years Virginia; Joyce How to John Haskins, 4 years Virginia; Mathew Richards to the same, 4 years Virginia; Elizabeth Richards to the same, 4 years Virginia; Anne Deane to the same, 4 years Virginia; John Tomalin to the same, 4 years Virginia; Charles James to Richard Burriatt, 4 years Virginia; Adam Weaver to John Bodenham, 4 years Virginia; Thomas Blinnar to the same, 4 years Virginia; Alice Woodward to the same, 4 years Virginia; Thomas Rostell to the same, 4 years Virginia; John Evans to Walter Craddock, 9 years Virginia; Mathew Hopkins to Joseph Pyrton, 5 years Virginia; Mary Lewis to Henry Smith, 5 years Virginia; Anne Wix to the same, 5 years Virginia; Mary Jones to the same, 5 years Virginia; Lewis Warren to David Warren, 4 years Virginia. (BR).

30 May. The following apprenticed in Bristol: Robert Michell to Anselme Smarte, 7 years Virginia; John Webb to Edward Stradling, 4 years Virginia; James Reynolds to Richard Dempster, 6 years Virginia. (BR).

31 May. The following apprenticed in Bristol: Geoffry Sommerford to John Tench, 4 years Virginia; Scalam Maglockly to Edward Stradling, 4 years Virginia; Samuell Churchell, shipwright, to Thomas Ninis, 4 years Virginia; Edward Jones to David Warren, 5 years Virginia; Thomas Erbury to Abraham Roome, 5 years Virginia by *Rainbow*; Thomas Robins to the same, 4 years Virginia. (BR).

May. Probate of will of Francis Carpender formerly of the City of London but late of Hereford, whose cousin, Simon Carpender, was in Virginia. (AW).

May. Administration with will of Benjamin Kaine of Glasgow, Scotland, whose father was in Boston, New England. (AW).

2 June. The following apprenticed in Bristol: Arthur Robins to Henry Smith, 3 years Virginia; Elizabeth Carter to the same, 4 years Virginia; Thomas Abram to Thomas Moody, 4 years Virginia; Hugh Gardiner to John Haskins, 6 years Virginia; William Bevan to William Hardy, 4 years Virginia; Joan Sandy to Robert Glasse, 4 years Virginia; Mary Sandy to the same, 4 years Virginia; William Sandy to the same, 4 years Virginia; Anne Bayly to Joseph Steevens, 4 years Virginia. (BR).

5 June. The following apprenticed in Bristol: John Catton to Andrew Ball, 4 years Virginia; John Tilman to the same, 4 years Virginia; John Simons to John Bodenham, 7 years Virginia; Margery Corton to Henry Daniel, 4 years Virginia; John Davies to John House, 4 years Virginia; Reece Jones to Thomas Gayner, 4 years Virginia; John Wenlock to the same, 5 years Virginia; Sarah Braban to the same, 5 years Virginia; Mary Jones to Blanch Freeman, 6 years Virginia; William Morse to John Raxwall, 6 years Virginia; David Mather to Richard Burriett, 4 years Virginia; Phillip Jones to William Hardy, 4 years Virginia; Daniel Hill to the same, 5 years Virginia; Richard Vaughan to the same, 4 years Virginia; Rosser Thomas to the same, 4 years Virginia; Hugh John to Ambrose Peiterson, 4 years Virginia; Katherine Rice to Thomas Ninis, 4 years Virginia; Richard Jones to James Tandy, 4 years Virginia; David Davids to the same, 4 years Virginia; Richard Onions to the same, 4 years Virginia; John Goldsworthy to William Hardick, 4 years Virginia; John Bovy to the same, 4 years Virginia; Mary Bath to the same, 6 years Virginia; Richard Gold to the same, 6 years Virginia; Ambrose Thomas to the same, 6 years Virginia; William Merrifield to the same, 4 years Virginia; Joane Simms to William Freeman, 5 years Virginia; Thomas Holcombe to John Rowse, 4 years Barbados; Thomas Charles to John Haskins, 4 years Virginia; Rosse Hamm to John Beare, 4 years Virginia; Francis Bridle to Abraham Roome, 4 years Virginia; Phillip Durdoe to the same, 4 years Virginia. (BR).

13 June. The following apprenticed in Bristol: John Wall to Thomas Sadler, 4 years Virginia; John Privett to Abraham Roome, 5 years Virginia; William Privett to the same, 4 years Virginia; Edward Cony to John Dowle, 4 years Virginia; William Nethway to Richard Burford, 6 years Virginia; Edward Massey to Samuell Cotner, 6 years Virginia. (BR).

16 June. The following apprenticed in Bristol: Anne Gwynne to Ralph Williams, 6 years Virginia; Francis Yates to the same, 4 years Virginia; Alexander Bevan to the same, 4 years Virginia; William Rathwell to the same, 6 years Virginia; Rice Powell to Edward Stradling, 4 years Virginia; Edward Moody to Abraham Roome, 4 years Virginia; Margeret Clarke to Martha Braine, 4 years Virginia; Temperance Benum to the same, 5 years Virginia; William Archer to William Freeman, 4 years Virginia; Thomas Edwards to William Taylor, 4 years Virginia. (BR).

21 June. The following apprenticed in Bristol: Thomas Lock to William Hardwick, 4 years Virginia; John Thomas to Morgan Williams, 4 years Virginia; Stephen Austin to William Merrick, 4 years Barbados; Anne Frowan to Phillip Smith, 4 years Virginia; John Estop to the same, 4 years Virginia; William Harris to Christopher Berkhead, 3 years Virginia; Johan Olins to Richard Burriatt, 4 years Virginia; John Cluse to the same, 4 years Virginia; John Kent to Thomas Gainer, 4 years Virginia; Robert Penn to the same, 4 years Virginia; Joseph Mayor to the same, 4 years Virginia; Elizabeth Cullinghorne to the same, 5 years Virginia. (BR).

26 June. The following apprenticed in Bristol: Amy Watts to Daniell Samm, 3 years Virginia; Isaac Hellier to Mary Steevens, 4 years Virginia; Elizabeth Hobson to Thomas Gould, 4 years Virginia by *Providence*; Nathaniel Hancock to William Hudson, 4 years Virginia by *Concord*; Richard Andrewes to David Warren, 4 years Virginia by *Concord*; Thomas Andrewes to the same, 4 years Virginia by *Concord*; Thomas Spilman to Hannah Hall, 4 years Virginia; Mary Spilman to the same, 4 years Virginia. (BR).

30 June. Shipper by the *Seahorse* of Topsham, Mr. Robert Chipp, bound from Exeter for New England: Richard Waad. (PRO: E190/953/6).

30 June. The following apprenticed in Bristol: John Elbridge to William Hudson, 4 years Virginia; John Barber to Gifford Browne, 4 years Virginia; Richard Lewis to John Tucker, 4 years Virginia; Richard Wix to George Start, 4 years Virginia. (BR).

1 July. The following apprenticed in Bristol: Thomas White to Patrick Browne, 4 years Virginia; Margeret Bevan to Ralph Williams, 4 years Virginia; Jonas Phillips to the same, 4 years Virginia; Elinor James to the same, 4 years Virginia; Thomas Saunders to the same, 4 years Virginia; William Saunders to the same, 4 years Virginia. (BR).

1 July-19 August. Shippers by the *Supply* of New England bound from Bristol for New England: John Shipway, John Hawkins. (PRO: E190/1240/6).

2 July. The following apprenticed in Bristol: John Davis to Thomas Norvell, 5 years Barbados; George Vaughan to Richard Haskins, 4 years Virginia; William Tidsum to Nicholas Tovey, 4 years Virginia; Jane Ingleton to John Tench, 4 years Virginia; John Williams to the same, 4 years Virginia. (BR).

7 July. The following apprenticed in Bristol: Richard Hick to Richard Woodward, 6 years Virginia; John Decent to John Bodenham, 4 years Virginia by *Agreement*; John Watkins to the same, 4 years Virginia; John Arthur to the same, 4 years Virginia; John Dalcott to the same, 4 years Virginia; John Jones to David Warren, 4 years Virginia; Elizabeth Williams to Joseph Tucker, 4 years Virginia; Isaac Wright to Thomas Gainer, 4 years Virginia; Anthony Goddart to the same, 4 years Virginia; Owen Davis to Richard Wood, 4 years Virginia. (BR).

9 July. Shippers by the *Providence* of Bristol bound from Bristol for Virginia: John Gale, William Dunning, Christopher Stevens. (PRO: E190/1240/6).

9 July. The following apprenticed in Bristol: John Vincent to William Butler, 4 years Virginia; Mary Blackman to the same, 4 years Virginia; William Cymber to the same, 4 years Virginia; Alice Sair to the same, 4 years Virginia; Timothy Bennet to the same, 4 years Virginia; Thomas Day to the same, 4 years Virginia; Edward Harris to Fortune Twitt, 4 years Virginia; Mary Guntur to the same, 4 years Virginia; William Henning to Thomas Nuckle, 4 years Virginia; Walter Hodges to the same, 4 years Virginia; Margeret Davis to John Tench, 4 years Virginia; Alice Milton to the same, 4 years Virginia; Samuell Dale to William Wheatly, 4 years Virginia; Robert Dale to the same, 4 years Virginia; Rachell Higgs to Edward Clarke, 5 years Virginia. (BR).

14 July. The following apprenticed in Bristol: Jane Newton to William Tayler, 4 years Virginia; David Hambleton to Benjamin Blindman, 4 years Virginia; John Thomas to the same, 4 years Virginia; Elizabeth Davis to the same, 4 years Virginia; Margeret Winter to the same, 4 years Virginia; Frances Watling to the same, 4 years Virginia; John Paradice to Thomas Knuckle, 4 years Virginia; John Ricketts to William Cave, 4 years Virginia. (BR).

15 July. The following apprenticed in Bristol: Mary Dowle to Elizabeth Roades, 4 years Virginia; Joane Roberts to the same, 4 years Virginia; Giles Parsons to John Stone, 4 years Virginia; Nicholas Heath to Arthur Grannt, 4 years Virginia; Robert Cawley to Thomas Elbridge, 5 years New England; Ralph Jenkins to Nicholas Tovey, 5 years Virginia. (BR).

16 July. The following apprenticed in Bristol: John Newman to George Hill, 3 years Virginia; Thomas Simons to the same, 3 years Virginia; Elizabeth Johnson to Anne Lugg, 4 years Virginia; Elizabeth Cooke to Aaron William, 4 years Virginia; Margaret Phillyps to the same, 4 years Virginia; David Abevan to Richard Woodward, 4 years Virginia; Alice Jones to the same, 4 years Virginia. (BR).

16 July-17 October. Shippers by the *Delight* of Bristol bound from Bristol for Virginia: Nicholas Warren, Edward Thruston, Thomas Gagecomb, Robert Skinner, Richard Allen, John Knight, Edward Crumpe, John Harris, William Bird, Thomas Tovy. (PRO: E190/1240/6).

17 July. The following apprenticed in Bristol: William Bungy to Richard Stacy, 7 years Virginia; John Berton to John Peiterson, 4 years Virginia; Adrian Martin to John Lury, 7 years Barbados; Robert Hicks to James Bisse, 4 years Barbados; Mathew Gibbs to the same, 4 years Barbados. (BR).

19 July. The following apprenticed in Bristol: John Baker to Thomas Whitop, 6 years Barbados; Simon Hooper to John Lury, 3 years Barbados; Henry Harris to Simon Steevens, 4 years Virginia; Mary West to James Bisse, 4 years Virginia. (BR).

22 July. The following apprenticed in Bristol: Francis West to John Howse, 4 years Virginia; Richard Jones to Fortune Twitt, 4 years Virginia; John Baker to Richard West, 4 years Virginia; Thomas Baker to the same, 4 years Virginia; Morrice Harris to the same, 4 years Virginia; Edward Carter to the same, 4 years Virginia. (BR).

23 July. The following apprenticed in Bristol: William Davis to David Warren, 5 years Virginia; Henry Harris to Daniel Samm, 4 years Virginia; James Dedicott to Osmond Crabb, 4 years Virginia; John Bareford to John Tench, 4 years Virginia; Joane Bareford to the same, 4 years Virginia; Thomas Hayward to Benjamin Blindman, 4 years Virginia; Alice Child to the same, 4 years Virginia; William Millard to John Clement, 4 years Virginia; John Grainger to Edward Tomlinson, 4 years Virginia; John Carpenter to John Watts, 4 years Virginia; Marthah Hulbert to the same, 4 years Virginia; Nicholas Brooke to Richard Pope, 4 years Virginia. (BR).

25 July. The following apprenticed in Bristol: Rowland Morgan to Christopher Berkhead, 10 years Virginia; John Williams to the same, 5 years Virginia; Francis Thomas to John Stone, 4 years Virginia; Joyce Davy to John Thorne, 4 years Virginia; William Stile to John Berrow, 3 years Barbados; Thomas Browne to John Kingford, 4 years Barbados. (BR).

27 July. The following apprenticed in Bristol: Maudlin Jones to Henry Walker, 5 years Virginia; Hugh Crumpton to Thomas Gainer, 4 years Virginia; Humfry Clerke to the same, 4 years Virginia; Anne Woodner to William Fox, 4 years Virginia; John Richards to the same, 4 years Virginia; Margery Bryan to William Bush, 4 years Virginia. (BR).

28 July. The following apprenticed in Bristol: Evan Williams to William Tayler, 4 years Virginia; George Williams to the same, 4 years Virginia; Robert Clarke to John Watkins, 7 years Virginia; Elizabeth Pinfold to Joseph Tucker, 4 years Virginia; Jane Dowting to Jennet Roome, 4 years Virginia; Elizabeth Scripture to Fortune Twitt, 6 years Virginia; Anne Greene to the same, 4 years Virginia; Robert Aston to Alexander Williams, 4 years Virginia; Peter Nicholas to Walter

Genings, 4 years Virginia; James Pugsly to Christopher Perkins, 4 years Virginia; Thomas Watkins to the same, 4 years Virginia; Ann Anderson to Christopher Birkhead, 4 years Virginia; Henry Anderson to the same, 4 years Virginia; Charles Cales to [blank] Thrustone, 4 years Virginia; John Charles to John Ofield, 4 years Virginia. (BR).

July. Ursula Hawkins of Walsall, Stafforshire reprieved to be transported to America. (EB).

July. Administration of William Goodman of the ship *Honor's Desire*, who died in Virginia, bachelor. (AW).

1 August. The following apprenticed in Bristol: William Richards to John Howell, 4 years Virginia; Mathew Day to Richard Story, 4 years Virginia. (BR).

2 August. The following apprenticed in Bristol: Cisely Morgan to Joseph Tucker, 4 years Virginia; Mary Smith to William Smith, 4 years Virginia; William Jones to Thomas Nuckle, 4 years Virginia. (BR).

4 August. The following apprenticed in Bristol: James Palmer to Gerard —yton, 4 years Virginia; John Whitecraft to Christopher Burkhead, 4 years Virginia; David Thomas to John Hacker, 4 years Virginia; Thomas Jones to P—— Freeman, 4 years Virginia; Martin Sale to John Tohy, 4 years Virginia; John Evans to Robert Portmann, 4 years Virginia. (BR).

4-29 August. Shippers by the *Concord* of Bristol, Mr. Nicholas Lux, bound from Bristol for Virginia: Gabriell Deane, Samuell Clarke, Stephen Watts, Humphrey Bearecroft, Thomas Atwood, Richard Ditty, John Worgan. (PRO: E190/1240/6).

5 August. The following apprenticed in Bristol: Thomas Randell to Edward Lugg, 4 years Virginia; Blanch Williams to William Hill, 6 years Virginia; Enotch Boulton to John Shipway, 4 years Virginia; John Newman to Elizabeth Matts, 4 years Virginia; Ann Jones to the same, 4 years Virginia. (BR).

6 August. The following apprenticed in Bristol: Henry Sheapard to Joseph Huntt, 4 years Virginia; George Dawkins to Henry James, 4 years Virginia; Thomas Barden to the same, 4 years Virginia; Hugh Rosser to Joseph Wicks, 4 years Virginia; Thomas Lewis to the same, 4 years Virginia; Nathaniell Bero to the same, 4 years Maryland; Christopher Wheeler to William Ward, 4 years Virginia; Robert Wood to Humphry —ter, 4 years Maryland; Richard Lister to William Bull, 4 years Virginia; Thomas Philpot to Gifford Browne, 4 years Virginia; Mary Rose to Abraham Roome, 4 years Virginia; Rachell Brune to the same, 4 years Virginia; William Linton to Peter Peters, 4 years Virginia; Thomas Glenton to John Shipway, 4 years New England; Henry Waters alias Watkins to Richard Seward, 4 years Virginia; William Johnson to William Smith, 4 years Virginia; John Higs to Henry Smith, 4 years Virginia; Howell Jones to Richard Woodward, 4 years Virginia. (BR).

8 August. The following apprenticed in Bristol: Ann Horwood to Jasper Cross, 4 years Virginia; Richard Bowen to John Hayford, 4 years Virginia; Thomas Heath to the same, 4 years Virginia; Robert Webber to William Quarrell, 4 years Virginia; Richard [blank] to Malachy Thruston, 4 years Virginia; William Edwards to David Warren, 4 years Virginia; Thomas Jones to the same, 4 years Virginia; Margery Spencer to Edward Crumpe, 4 years Virginia; Mary Chard to Thomas Wills, 4 years Virginia; Richard Vaughans to Margaret Matts, 4 years Virginia; Tobyas Marler to Thomas Norvell, 4 years Barbados; John Chard to the same, 4 years Barbados. (BR).

10 August. The following apprenticed in Bristol: Francis Jenings to Richard Shipway, 3 years New England; William Burreston to Thomas Mills, 4 years Virginia; James Hamlin to Edward Morris, 6 years Virginia; Ann Ward to Christopher Oliver, 4 years Virginia; Elizabeth Ward to the same, 4 years Virginia; John Cox to David Warren, 4 years Virginia; John Powell to John Clarke, 8 years Virginia; Richard Jones to the same, 7 years Virginia; Susanna Wilmott to John Olflatt, 7 years Virginia; Margeret Agnis to Jane Kingford, 4 years Virginia. (BR).

11 August. Robert Phage to answer a charge of transporting Edmond Gregory, an apprentice, to Virginia without the consent of his parents or master. (VM 83/3).

13 August. The following apprenticed in Bristol: Katherine Jones to William Hill, 4 years Virginia; William Thomas to Thomas Elbridge, 6 years New England; John Fox to John Forset, 3 years Virginia; Ann Peccard to Joseph Wicks, 5 years Maryland; Walter Pye to the same, 4 years Maryland; Richard Walter to James Pugsley, 4 years Virginia; John Bennett to the same, 4 years Virginia; Edward Ludlow to Henry Smith, 4 years Virginia; Elionor Parish to William Flower, 5 years Virginia; Nathaniell Dibble to William Wakely, 5 years Virginia; Grace Dole to Abraham Roome, 4 years Virginia; Simon Rench to John Tench, 4 years Virginia; Ann Guist to Thomas Freeman, 4 years Virginia; Susanna Williams to Bridgett Howell, 4 years Virginia; Reece Price to Richard Mareth, 4 years Nevis; Henry Jones to John Harke, 4 years Virginia. (BR).

13-21 August. Shippers by the *Recovery* of Bristol, Mr. Arthur Grant, bound from Bristol for Virginia: Edward Fielding, Joseph Hunt, Robert Hanridge. (PRO: E190/1240/6).

14-23 August. Shippers by the *Unity* of Topsham, Mr. Thomas Russell, bound from Exeter for Virginia: Isaac Mawditt; Endymion Walker; John Rowse; Abram Gibbs; Edward Ward. (PRO: E190/953/6).

15-23 August. Shippers by the *Samuell* of Topsham, Mr. Samuell Stoakes, bound from Exeter for Virginia: John Manington, Isaac Mawditt. (PRO: E190/953/6).

15-30 August. Shippers by the *Agreement* of Bristol bound from Bristol for Virginia: William Bullock for Thomas Bisse, Thomas Day, Francis Fisher, Joseph Wicks, William Yeomans. (PRO: E190/1240/6).

18 August. The following apprenticed in Bristol: John Tegy to Roger King, 4 years Virginia; William Jones to David Warren, 4 years Virginia; Silvanus Johnson to Edward Gibbs, 4 years Virginia; John Reece to John Reed, 4 years Virginia; Ann Price to John Record, 4 years Virginia; Thomas Roberts to Thomas Peaxton, 4 years [Virginia]. (BR).

18 August. Home counties prisoners reprieved to be transported to Barbados. Surrey: Robert Joy of St. Saviour, Southwark; Rowland Rayner of Buckland; William Lovelock of St. George, Southwark; James Singleton and Margaret Wright, spinster, of St. Olave, Southwark; Richard Plenty of Battersea; Thomas Edwards of Camberwell; John Smyth of Ewell; William Baker of Clapham; Peter Clarke of Newington; Robert Middleton of Newington; John Levett of Newington. Sussex: Thomas Penn of Felpham; John Pope of Angmering. Hertfordshire: Daniel Haydon of Hemel Hempstead; Henry Payne of Cheshunt; Thomas Nutting of Bishops Hatfield or St. Albans. Kent: William Pooley of St. Margaret, Rochester; John Cheesman of Linstead; Thomas Studman of Otterden; John Taylor of Aylesford; John Young of Farningham; Edward Colgate of Speldhurst; Anthony Langfitt of East Greenwich. Essex: Henry Johnson of Theydon Garnon; Jane Langford of Roxwell, spinster. (PRO: C66/3011/14).

18-29 August. Shippers by the *Rainbow* of Bristol bound from Bristol for Virginia: Gabriel Deane, Edward Olliver, William Crabb. (PRO: E190/1240/6).

19 August. The following apprenticed in Bristol: Benjamin Bowry to William Rodny, 4 years Virginia; William Gouldsmith to the same, 4 years Virginia; Elizabeth Racher to William Hill, 4 years Virginia. (BR).

19 August. Shipper by the *Friendship* of Bristol bound from Bristol for Virginia: Henry Smith. (PRO: E190/1240/6).

20 August. The following apprenticed in Bristol: John Wotts to Mathias Holbrooke, 6 years Virginia; Robert Wheler to the same, 6 years Virginia; Francis Abel to the same, 4 years Virginia; Samuell Audry to the same, 4 years Virginia; Phillip Sanders to the same, 4 years Virginia; George Bayton to the same, 6 years Virginia; John Harper to the same, 6 years Virginia; John Bridgman to the same, 6 years Virginia; Thomas Bridgman to the same, 6 years Virginia; Henry Farmer to the same, 6 years Virginia; Ann Morgan to the same, 4 years Virginia; Sarah George to the same, 6 years Virginia; David Smith to Zachary Tovey, 4 years Virginia; Mary Genings to James Bisse, 4 years Virginia; Thomas Lewis to Christopher Birkhead, 4 years Virginia; Thomas Morgan to Abraham Roomes, 4 years Virginia. (BR).

21 August. The following apprenticed in Bristol: Roger Phillips to William Flower, 4 years Virginia; Charles Watts to George Stearte, 4 years Virginia. (BR).

21-29 August. Shippers by the *James* of Bristol bound from Bristol for Virginia: Emanuell Averie, Williams Rogers, Edward Enbery, Charles Benan. (PRO: E190/1240/6).

22 August. The following apprenticed in Bristol: William Francis to John Tucke, 4 years Virginia; Thomas Owen to Thomas Sanders, 4 years Virginia; John Harrison to Gerrard Samson, 4 years Virginia; William Harding to David Warren, 4 years Virginia; Henry Porch to Gerrard Errington, 4 years Virginia. (BR).

23 August. The following apprenticed in Bristol: Abigell Heale to John Harris, 4 years Virginia; Richard Prise to Thomas Butler, 4 years Virginia; George Long to George Gill, 7 years Virginia; Thomas Baker to Henry Blackwell, 9 years Barbados; William Nevell to John Pearson, 4 years Barbados; Jane Nevel to the same, 4 years Barbados; Henry Butterell to the same, 4 years Barbados. (BR).

24 August. The following apprenticed in Bristol: Roger Howson to Henry Walter, 4 years Virginia; William Grene to John Alflatt, 4 years Virginia; Margeret Cowley to Edward Lugg, 4 years Virginia; Mary Poynting to George ——, 4 years Virginia; Edward Berry to Robert ——, 4 years Virginia; Ambrose Mackelow to Thomas Furlong, 4 years Virginia; Thomas Winyod to William Reay, 4 years Virginia. (BR).

25 August-12 September. Shippers by the *Black Eagle* of Yarmouth, Mr. Francis Sanders, bound from Yarmouth for Virginia: Henry Nolbrough, Richard Bellchamber, William Mead, Edward Palmer, Richard Ballard. (PRO: E190/493/5).

28 August. The following apprenticed in Bristol: John France to David Warren, 4 years Virginia; Robert Hulbright to Richard ——, 4 years Virginia; David Evan to John Brickey, 4 years Virginia; Richard Morgan to John Shuter, 4 years Virginia; Henry Smith to Thomas Winston, 4 years Virginia; Richard Pearce to Thomas Game, 4 years Virginia. (BR).

28 August. Shippers by the *Seaflower* of Bristol bound from Bristol for Virginia: Richard Smith, Robert Glass. (PRO: E190/1240/6).

30 August. The following apprenticed in Bristol: William Gwilliam to John Deffield, 4 years Virginia; Henry Williams to Edward Burrell, 4 years Virginia; Anthony Williams to Sarah Matts, 4 years Virginia; Thomas German to Joseph ?Waller, 4 years Maryland; Mary Foster to William Smith, 4 years Virginia; John Hale to Edward E—ony, 4 years Virginia; Ambrose Knight to William Prick, 5 years Virginia; William Reston to William Eles, 4 years Virginia; George Beroe to William Ellis, 7 years Virginia; William Hill to Francis Duglas, 4 years Virginia; Humphrey Wood to Thomas Gray, 4 years Virginia; Morgan Morgan to Joell Perry, 4 years Virginia. (BR).

30 August-3 September. Shippers by the *Goodwill* of Bristol, Mr. William Reepe, bound from Bristol for Virginia: Walter Stephens, Walter Tocknell. (PRO: E190/1240/6).

30 August-17 September. Shippers by the *Alexander* of Bristol bound from Bristol for Virginia: Gabriell Deane, Mathew Stephens, William Tocknell, John Gale, Richard Crabb, George Brent. (PRO: E190/1240/6).

August. Probate of will of Gregory Coffin of Stepney, Middlesex, (bound for New England). (AW).

3 September. Deposition by John Harvey of St. Swithin's, London, aged 30, that John Petter of Horsley Down, Surrey, by deed of 12 March 1662, assigned a plantation on York River, Virginia, to Richard Roffey of Horsley Down, distiller. Attached are copies of: Deed of 16 June 1660 for purchase by Humphrey Davis of Porapotank, New Kent County, Virginia, surgeon, former partner in Virginia of John Petter, gent, of a plantation which Petter purchased from Robert Jones; bill of exchange dated Virginia, 1660, drawn by John Petter on Mr. Daniel Woodgate of the Two Wainmen, Cheapside, London. Note that John Petter has appointed Richard Roffey as his attorney to recover debts from Humphrey Davis of Virginia and William Roberts of Virginia, planter. (LMCD).

3 September. The following apprenticed in Bristol: William Kinocke to William Flower, 6 years Virginia; Thomas Gregory to William Po—y, 4 years Virginia; John Monckes to William Cams, 4 years Virginia; Frances Hill to William Rodney, 4 years Virginia; William Buxton to Robert Elemond, 4 years Virginia; Hanna Hawkins to Edward ——thial, 4 years Virginia; Jane Charles to the same, 4 years Virginia. (BR).

5 September. The following apprenticed in Bristol: Thomas Harding to Robert Cutt, 4 years Virginia; George Haward to the same, 4 years Virginia; Richard Fisher to William Quarrell, 4 years Virginia. (BR).

6 September. The following apprenticed in Bristol: Owen Howell to John W——sell, 4 years Virginia; John Allen to Annes Roome, 4 years Virginia; Edward Thomas to Edward Berkle, 8 years Virginia; John Toopoot to John Harris, 4 years Virginia; Thomas Loyde to Richard Hudson, 4 years Virginia. (BR).

6-13 September. Shippers by the *Jacob* of Bristol bound from Bristol for Virginia: Robert Ward, Thomas Yeat. (PRO: E190/1240/6).

8 September. The following apprenticed in Bristol: William Berrow to James Bolcher, 4 years Virginia; Anthonie Harris to George Stearte, 4 years Virginia; Richard Martin to William Perton, 4 years Virginia. (BR).

8-24 September. Shippers by the *Bachelor* of Bristol bound from Bristol for Virginia: Richard Ditty, John Reade, Phillip Harris. (PRO: E190/1240/6).

9 September. The following apprenticed in Bristol: William Thomas to John Reece, 6 years Virginia. (BR).

10-13 September. Shippers by the *Phoenix* of Bristol bound from Bristol for Virginia: John Willoughby, David Warren. (PRO: E190/1240/6).

11 September. The following apprenticed in Bristol: Thomas Munday to Walter Sherland, 4 years Virginia; William Deffield to John Deffield, 4 years Virginia; Elizabeth Hay to Jane Kingford, 4 years Virginia; Sarah Digbie to the same, 4 years Virginia; Anne Bankes to the same, 5 years Virginia; John Wingate to Thomas Orfield, 4 years Virginia; Roger Lewis to Alice Wickam, 4 years Virginia; John Franceh to Abraham Wine, 3 years Virginia; Thomas Rickens to the same, 3 years Virginia; Joane West to David Warren, 4 years Virginia. (BR).

15 September. Shipper by the *Robert* of Bristol bound from Bristol for Virginia: Robert Yeamans. (PRO: E190/1240/6).

16 September. The following apprenticed in Bristol: Bridgett Lea to Gwenham Tovey, 4 years Virginia; Margarett Lucy to John Collins, 4 years Virginia; Francis Cable to Thomas Gagecombe, 3 years Virginia; Henry Flagg to William Rees, 4 years Virginia; George Williams to William Farwell, 4 years Virginia; Anne Davis to Elizabeth Tucker, 4 years Virginia; Mary Phillips to Anne Webb, 4 years Virginia; Josiah Willis to Richard Yareth, Barbados; Mary Evans to William Harrard, 4 years Virginia; Andrew Davis to John Harris, 4 years Virginia. (BR).

19 September. The following apprenticed in Bristol: John Lea to Thomas Winston, 4 years Virginia; Katherine Langford to Richard Allen, 5 years Virginia; Margery Clarke to the same, 6 years Virginia; Henry Baker to the same, 6 years Virginia; Edward Robinson to the same, 5 years Virginia; John Williams to Arnold Collins, 4 years Virginia; John Quelch to John Harris, 7 years Virginia; John Kenner to the same, 4 years Virginia; David Persons to Cowrell Nicholas, 5 years Virginia; George Beeders to William Rodney, 9 years Virginia. (BR).

24 September. Alexander Sheriffe, apprentice of Mr. Siviby, for running away to be sent to his father in Barbados. (Bridewell).

24 September. The following apprenticed in Bristol: William Stephens to Thomas Nean, 4 years Barbados; John English to John Roach, 4 years Virginia; Joyce Thomas to the same, 4 years Virginia; William Reyney to Robert Baker, 7 years Virginia; David Rogers to John Lane, 6 years Virginia. (BR).

26 September. The following apprenticed in Bristol: Thomas Day to Edward Crump, 4 years Virginia; Simon Bouker to William Creed, 4 years Virginia; Francis Robinson to Francis Tayler, 4 years Virginia; John Jones to Christopher Alford, 4 years Nevis. (BR).

30 September. The following apprenticed in Bristol: James Bernard to James Wathen, 4 years Virginia; Elizabeth Waller to John Tovey, 4 years Virginia. (BR).

3-24 October. Shippers by the *Elizabeth* of Bristol, Mr. Thomas Tovey, bound from Bristol for Virginia: John Seward, Nicholas Tovey, Henry Daniell, James Powell, John Coxe, Thomas Speed. (PRO: E190/1240/6).

5 October. The following apprenticed in Bristol: John Potteridge to Thomas Wotts, 4 years Virginia; Ann Kenton to Thomas Gray, 4 years Virginia. (BR).

5 October. Newgate prisoners reprieved to serve 10 years in the plantations. London: Henry Page; Katherine Ward, spinster, alias wife of Thomas Bullocke; Barbara Dawson, spinster; Elizabeth Williams; Joseph Thomlinson; Alice Williams, spinster, alias wife of Morgan Williams; Edward Houghton; Katherine Pettit, spinster, alias wife of William Pettit, goldsmith; Robert Adams; Peter Cussens; Charles Worrall; Bridget Allen, spinster; William Israell; William Gardiner. Middlesex: George Greene of St. Andrew Holborn; John Hepper of St. Clement Danes; Mark Dawson of Clerkenwell; John Harris of Islington; William Howard alias Hoord of St. Clement Danes, gent; John Johnson of Stepney; James Stanford of Stepney; Richard Hollyer of St. Giles Cripplegate; Richard Jones of St. Giles in the Fields; Thomas Nuttall of St. Martin in the Fields; Mary Bolton, spinster, alias wife of Robert Bolton, of St. Katherine by the Tower; Mary Hare of Fulham; Rebecca Davies of St. Giles Cripplegate; Elizabeth Williams of St. Andrew Holborn, spinster; Richard Smith alias Nuttall of St. Clement Danes; John Thomas of Stepney. (PRO: C66/3011/5).

8 October. The following apprenticed in Bristol: Joseph Cooke to Richard Baker, 4 years Nevis; Henry Thomas to George Lane, 4 years Virginia; Peter Nesson to Richard Pinkny, 4 years Virginia. (BR).

9 October. The following apprenticed in Bristol: Edward Phillips to Thomas N———, 4 years Barbados; James Wills to Abraham Barnes, 4 years Virginia; William Woodward to John Seward, 4 years Virginia; Edward Bradford to William Dale, 4 years Virginia; Anthony Franken to Mary Grant, 3 years Virginia; Morgan Owen to John Harris, 4 years Virginia. (BR).

10 October. The following apprenticed in Bristol: Roger Cordwint to William Pinner, 5 years Virginia; Robert Phibbal to Anthony Pearce, 4 years Virginia; John Drinkwater to John Roch, 4 years Virginia; John Williams to George Steart, 4 years Virginia. (BR).

11 October. The following apprenticed in Bristol: Thomas Cogwell to John Jones, 4 years Virginia; Elizabeth Hakens to Edward Barret, 4 years Virginia; William Cookny to Nicholas Tovey, 4 years Virginia; Samuell Clarke to the same, 4 years Virginia; Thomas Jones to Joane Cruden, 4 years Virginia; Mary Harris to John Bush, 4 years Virginia; Thomas Hitchings to James Shale, 4 years Virginia; Robert Harding to John Grinfield, 4 years Virginia. (BR).

13 October. The following apprenticed in Bristol: William Underwood to Jeremiah Howell, 4 years Virginia; William Jones to Mathew King, 4 years Virginia; Thomas Atkins to John Lane, 4 years Virginia; Stephen Prough to Richard Waker, 3 years Virginia; Ann Williams to James Lyne, 4 years Virginia. (BR).

16 October. The following apprenticed in Bristol: Samuell Woodward to Joseph White, 7 years Virginia; John Jones to John Seward, 4 years Virginia. (BR).

17 October. Depositions (ending on this date) in the Chancery case of Nicholas Bond and John Pocock v. John Giffard re the management of an ironworks in New England. The deponents include: William Heathfield of St. Mary Aldermary, London, aged 24, who was in New England in 1658; John Fuller of Lynn, New England, husbandman aged 38; Samuel Mavericke of Boston, New England, aged 58; John Purdey, collier aged 30, formerly of Lynn, New England; James Neighbor of Boston, New England, carpenter aged 43; John Blaney of Meldreth, Cambridgeshire, gent aged 33, who went to New England in 1651. (NGSQ 69/1).

17 October. The following apprenticed in Bristol: William Hopkins to William Creed, 4 years Virginia; Henry Smith to Thomas Winston, 4 years Virginia. (BR).

18 October. The following apprenticed in Bristol: John Meredeth to John Smart, 4 years Virginia; Andrew Vaughan to John Dale, 4 years Virginia. (BR).

20 October. The following apprenticed in Bristol: Barnabe Wells to John Buck, 4 years Virginia; Thomas Saul to John Williams, 4 years Virginia; Isaac Southern to John Daile, 6 years Barbados. (BR).

21 October. The following apprenticed in Bristol: Francis Proser to John Williams, 4 years Virginia; William Gould to George Smith, 4 years Virginia; Dennis Carter to the same, 4 years Virginia; William Morgan to William Merrick, 7 years Virginia; Robert Williams to Thomas Nevese, 4 years Barbados. (BR).

21 October. Probate of will of Thomas Walker of St. Michael Bassishaw, citizen and salter of London, whose son, Thomas Walker, was in Boston, New England. (NGSQ 76/3).

23 October. The following apprenticed in Bristol: William Hunnaball to John Card, 4 years Nevis; Flouranc Carter to George Smith, 4 years Virginia; John Flyd to Richard Walker, 4 years Virginia; Richard Setherard to Thomas Grant, 4 years Virginia; John Kempton to the same, 4 years Virginia; Ann Ruther to Jeremiah Howell, 7 years Virginia. (BR).

23 October. Chancery suit of Richard Hutchinson of London, ironmonger and William Mullins, gent, v. Thomas Bedingfield Esq. relating to the purchase by the plaintiffs of land in England to finance the propagation of the gospel in New England. (NGSQ 66/3).

24 October-16 November. Shippers by the *Stephen* of Bristol, Mr. John Scott, bound from Bristol for Virginia: Richard Pope, John Saffin, Jenkin Bragg, Stephen Watts, Richard Younge, William Collins. (PRO: E1290/1240/6).

28 October. The following apprenticed in Bristol: Nicholas Brewer to George Deplane, 4 years Virginia; Joseph Hambidg to Mary Grant, 4 years Virginia; David Davis to Peter Gale, 4 years Virginia. (BR).

29 October. The following apprenticed in Bristol: Richard Symons to Henry Walker, 4 years Virginia; William Gunter to Edward Waters, 7 years Barbados; William James to the same, 8 years Barbados; William Lishon to the same, 9 years Barbados. (BR).

30 October. The following apprenticed in Bristol: Elizabeth Davis to Katherine Tayler, 4 years Virginia. (BR).

October. Probate of will of Andrew Cade of East Betchworth, Surrey, whose cousin, Henry Cade, was in Virginia. (AW).

1 November. The following apprenticed in Bristol: Richard Felton to Francis Jones, 4 years Virginia; Alice Felton to the same, 4 years Virginia; James Williams to John Lane, 4 years Virginia; Mary Palmer to Alice Seburne, 4 years Virginia; Ann Davis to Edward Fielding, 4 years Virginia. (BR).

2 November. The following apprenticed in Bristol: Mary Shuter to Edward Fielding, 4 years Virginia. (BR).

4 November. The following apprenticed in Bristol: Alice Farmer to Mary Dight, 5 years Virginia; William Stephens to Thomas Liston, 5 years Virginia; Elizabeth Farle to William G——, 4 years Virginia; Henry Evere to James Shute, 4 years Virginia; Alice Jones to John Scott, 4 years Virginia; Mary Phillips to the same, 4 years Virginia; Edward Bartly to Abraham Sto——, 4 years Virginia. (BR).

7 November. The following apprenticed in Bristol: John Spencer to Christopher Alford, 4 years Virginia; Thomas Spencer to the same, 4 years Virginia. (BR).

10 November. The following apprenticed in Bristol: James Morgan to John Godsell, 4 years Virginia; Mary Banton to Joane Bucke, 4 years Virginia; Elizabeth Smith to the same, 4 years Virginia; Richard Williams to John Scot, 4 years Virginia. (BR).

12 November. The following apprenticed in Bristol: William Betayh to William Jones, 4 years Nevis; William Browne to John Lane, 4 years Virginia. (BR).

14 November. The following apprenticed in Bristol: William Milton to Mallachy Thrustone, 4 years Virginia. (BR).

15 November. The following apprenticed in Bristol: William Hosy to John Nutt, 4 years Barbados; John Fleming to William Freeman, 4 years Virginia. (BR).

17 November. The following apprenticed in Bristol: William More to William Parry, 4 years Virginia. (BR).

18 November. The following apprenticed in Bristol: George Greenway to William Collins, 4 years Virginia; Anne Hicks to William Creed, 4 years Virginia. (BR).

19 November. Chancery suit of Robert Hubbersty of London, gent, v. William Bell Esq. and others to recover property belonging to his mother, Margaret Hubbersty alias Holland, including a plantation in Maryland which she acquired from Sir William Andrewes. (NGSQ 66/3).

19 November. The following apprenticed in Bristol: John James to Charles Watts, 4 years Virginia; Charles Hodges to John Lane, 5 years Virginia; John Haulbord to Josias Hollyday, 4 years Virginia. (BR).

22 November. The following apprenticed in Bristol: Elizabeth Porch to George Griffin, 4 years Virginia. (BR).

22-24 November. Shippers by the *Pearl* of Bristol bound from Bristol for Virginia: William Yeamans, Edward Fielding. (PRO: E190/1240/6).

24 November. The following apprenticed in Bristol: Clemant Applegate to Edward Fielding, 4 years Virginia. (BR).

26 November. The following apprenticed in Bristol: Ann Price to Thomas Jones, 4 years Virginia; Richard Poole to John Union, 4 years Virginia; Elizabeth Daniell to Henry Banks, 4 years Nevis. (BR).

27 November. The following apprenticed in Bristol: Francis Haynes to Francis Duvall, 6 years Barbados; Evan Jones to George Watkins, 4 years Nevis. (BR).

28 November. The following apprenticed in Bristol: John Williams to George Watkins, 4 years Barbados; John Owen to Edward Barrat, 4 years Barbados; Thomas Biford to John Tayler, 5 years Barbados; William Biford to the same, 5 years Barbados; Walter James to Henry Banks, 4 years Nevis. (BR).

November. Probate of will of Thomas Reade of Wickford, Essex, who had lands in New England. (AW).

2 December. The following apprenticed in Bristol: John Serle to Thomas Jefferis, 4 years Barbados; Jeffery Smale to the same, 4 years Barbados. (BR).

3 December. John Lamprey, for vagrancy, to go to Virginia to work. (Bridewell).

3 December. The following apprenticed in Bristol: James Williams to John Tayler, 4 years Barbados; Evan Edwardes to George Watkins, 4 years Barbados; John King to John Herd, 4 years Nevis. (BR).

5 December. The following apprenticed in Bristol: Joan Halloway to George Ashby, 4 years Nevis. (BR).

6 December. The following apprenticed in Bristol: Thomas Smith to William Freeman, 6 years Barbados. (BR).

8 December. The following apprenticed in Bristol: John Roberts to Jinkyn Thomas, 4 years St. Christopher. (BR).

10 December. The following apprenticed in Bristol: Mary Lee to Michaell Walton, 4 years Barbados. (BR).

15 December. The following apprenticed in Bristol: Henry Seddon to John Water, 4 years Barbados; Lodwick Gwilliam to the same, 4 years Barbados; William Karkeese to George Withering, 4 years Barbados; Flurance Simmons to the same, 4 years Barbados; Edmund Pritchard to John Roch, 4 years Barbados; Edward Duvall to William Liston, 4 years Barbados; John Williams to Richard Crabb, 4 years Nevis. (BR).

17 December. The following apprenticed in Bristol: Roger Strang to Jane Engleton, 4 years Nevis; Ann Jones to George Ashby, 4 years Nevis; Charles Williams to Symon Wills, 4 years Antigua. (BR).

19 December. The following apprenticed in Bristol: William Tayler to Sampson Dowe, 4 years Nevis. (BR).

20 December. The following apprenticed in Bristol: Walter Hopkins to Thomas Simons, 4 years Nevis; John Haywood to William Stafford, 3 years Barbados; John Stone to John Waters, 4 years Barbados; Ellioner Munksly to Richard Hambleton, 4 years Nevis; Sarah Teage to the same, 4 years Nevis; Elizabeth Stand to the same, 4 years Nevis; Elizabeth Owing to the same, 4 years Nevis. (BR).

23 December. The following apprenticed in Bristol: Richard Yow to Ann Tayler, 4 years Barbados; George Williams to George James, 5 years Barbados; William Lewis to the same, 4 years Barbados; Elizabeth Waters to the same, 4 years Barbados; Phillip Luen to the same, 7 years Barbados; Thomas Trowcock to Edward Tocknell, Nevis; Edward Addis to Henry Banks, 4 years Nevis; Lewis Watkins to Francis Burne, 4 years Nevis. (BR).

29 December. The following apprenticed in Bristol: Raffe Thomas to Francis Morgan, 4 years Nevis; Peter Fontenew to George Watkins, 4 years Nevis; John West to Thomas Ellice, 4 years Nevis; William Flyd to Henry Banks, 4 years Nevis.

December. Probate of will of William Pynchon of Wraysbury, Buckinghamshire, whose daughter, Margaret Davis, and sons, John Pynchon and Eliazar Holioke, were in New England. (AW).

1663

6 January. The following apprenticed in Bristol: Thomas Garner to William Liston, 4 years Nevis; Thomas Rees to Henry Banks, 4 years Nevis; Robert Banks to John Card, 4 years Nevis; George Parker to same, 4 years Nevis; William Herne to Stephen Humphrys, 4 years Barbados. (BR).

9 January. The following apprenticed in Bristol: Edward James to George Watkins, 3 years Nevis. (BR).

10 January. The following apprenticed in Bristol: Reynold Galton to Thomas Simons, 4 years Nevis. (BR).

12 January. The following apprenticed in Bristol: Marke Snow to Francis Borne, 4 years Nevis; Roger Hunt to John Charles, 4 years Nevis; William Lluellin to Margaret Jinkin, 4 years Barbados; Mary Williams to same, 4 years Barbados; Katherine Christopher to same, 4 years Barbados; Margaret Peters to Robert Banks, 4 years Nevis. (BR).

13 January. The following apprenticed in Bristol: John Johnson to George Ashby, 4 years Nevis; Thomas Gabriell to Robert ?Hillse, 4 years Nevis; Thomas Standly to Francis Borne, 4 years Nevis; Mary Coulson to Rowland Savage, 4 years Barbados; William Carpenter to Robert Iliffe, 3 years Nevis. (BR).

15 January. The following apprenticed in Bristol: John Pritchat to Henry Banks, 5 years Nevis; John Sheapard to George Watkins, 9 years Nevis; Thomas Webb to Richard Hambleton, 4 years Nevis. Mary Webb to same, 4 years Nevis; Thomas Mathews to same, 7 years Nevis; Thomas James to Francis Borne, 5 years Nevis.(BR).

16 January. The following apprenticed in Bristol: Thomas Flyd to Giles Merrick, 4 years Nevis. (BR).

17 January. The following apprenticed in Bristol: David James to Robert Dapwell, 3 years Nevis. (BR).

19 January. The following apprenticed in Bristol: Mary Tayler to Henry Banks, 5 years Nevis; Mary Griffis to same, 5 years Nevis; John Friend to Samuell Nichols, 4 years New England; William Atkinson to William Phips, 4 years Nevis. (BR).

20 January. The following apprenticed in Bristol: Thomas Rollins to Margaret Farclew, 9 years Nevis; Roger Grizell to same, 5 years Nevis; Mary Tayler to same, 5 years Nevis; Nathaniell Perks to Richard Cicell, 9 years Nevis; Henry Woods to Francis Borne, 4 years Nevis; Mary Atwell to Thomas Powell, 4 years Nevis. (BR).

21 January. The following apprenticed in Bristol: John Sherwood to Samuell Nicholas, 4 years New England. (BR).

23 January. The following apprenticed in Bristol: Elizabeth Creed to Richard Hambleton, 4 years Nevis; Robert Law to Nicholas Smale, 4 years Nevis. (BR).

24 January. The following apprenticed in Bristol: William Blathern to John Jones, 4 years Nevis; Joane Parret to same, 4 years Nevis; Alice Hancok to Richard Hambleton, 4 years Nevis. (BR).

28 January. The following apprenticed in Bristol: Rebecca James to George Ashby, 7 years Nevis; Hugh Masters to Morgan Lewis, 4 years Barbados; Robert Crowe to John White, 4 years Barbados; Susan Phillips to Thomas Simons, 5 years Nevis; David Beaven to Thomas Tayler, 7 years Nevis; Mathew Biffard to Richard Hambleton, 4 years Nevis; Ambrosse Tayler to English Smith, 4 years Nevis. (BR).

27 January. The following apprenticed in Bristol: Abraham Royall to Alexander Cassen, 4 years Nevis; John Everet to William Hayman, 5 years New England. (BR).

28 January. The following apprenticed in Bristol: Thomas Adams to Samuell Nicholas, 4 years New England; Thomas Sturmy to same, 4 years New England; Charles Sturmy to same, 4 years New England; George Norton to Francis Borne, 4 years Nevis. (BR).

29 January. The following apprenticed in Bristol: Simple Morris to Adam Brewer, 4 years Nevis; Elizabeth Craell to same, 4 years Nevis; John Jones to Alexander Cassen, 4 years Nevis; John Warren to Nicholas Smale, 4 years Nevis. (BR).

30 January. Robert Yateman to Christopher Alford, 4 years Nevis; William Ramson to same, 5 years Nevis. (BR).

31 January. The following apprenticed in Bristol: John Bricker to Henry Backwell, 6 years Barbados. (BR).

4 February. The following apprenticed in Bristol: John Bennet to Phillip Mathews, 4 years New England; John Sheapard to Robert Haskins, 4 years Nevis; John Briant to Joshuah Hobs, 3 years Barbados; William Jones to William Lewis, 4 years New England; Francis Olliver to Edward Thomas, 4 years New England; Margaret Page to William Browne, 5 years Nevis; Ann Page to same, 5 years Nevis. (BR).

6 February. The following apprenticed in Bristol: John Freeman to Nicholas Smale, 4 years New England; Silvanus Davis to William Hayman, 8 years New England; Francis Lightfoot to William Limbre, 9 years Nevis; John Garman to same, 7 years Nevis; Margaret Morgan to Jane Edwards, 4 years Barbados. (BR).

9 February. The following apprenticed in Bristol: William Gausset to Samuell Nicholas, 6 years New England. (BR).

10 February. The following apprenticed in Bristol: William Carraway to Edward Tocknell, 4 years Nevis. (BR).

11 February. The following apprenticed in Bristol: John Carbeath to Solomon Wills, 3 years Nevis; Thomas Williams to John Harris, 4 years Nevis. (BR).

12 February. Sarah Hopwood to Mathew Stephens, 4 years Nevis; Francis Richards to William Freeman, 7 years Nevis; Thomas Jones to Phillip Bennet, 5 years Nevis; John Barbar to William Browne, 4 years Nevis; John Hawker to Thomas Sparks, 4 years Leewards; Ann Reece to Samuell Nicholas, 4 years New England; David Powell to Edward Fielding, 4 years Nevis. (BR).

13 February. The following apprenticed in Bristol: Richard Tarbert to Richard Lock, 5 years Nevis; Edward Leech to Edward Thomas, 4 years New England; Richard But to same, 4 years New England. (BR).

14 February. The following apprenticed in Bristol: Thomas Tayler to Phillip Dennet, 5 years Antigua; Mary Huffe to Mathew Lambert, 4 years New England. (BR).

17 February. The following apprenticed in Bristol: Marrian Nichols to Robert Haskins, 7 years Nevis; Allice Dymock to Samuell Nicholas, 4 years New England; John Quarrell to Thomas Wathern, 4 years Nevis.

19 February. The following apprenticed in Bristol: Thomas Bathum to Mathew Stephens, 4 years Nevis. (BR).

20 February. The following apprenticed in Bristol: Joane Williams to Phillip Bennet, 4 years Antigua; Hugh Vaughan to Mary Casen, 4 years Nevis; Henry Young to John Jones, 5 years Barbados. (BR).

21 February. The following apprenticed in Bristol: William Brook to Phillip Bennet, 4 years Antigua. (BR).

23 February. The following apprenticed in Bristol: Tobias Gregory to Phillip Bennet, 3 years Antigua; Hugh Russy to Thomas Greene, 3 years Montserrat; Dennis Horren to same, 3 years Montserrat. (BR).

26 February. The following apprenticed in Bristol: William Nevis to William Watkins, 6 years Nevis. (BR).

27 February. The following apprenticed in Bristol: Anne Bates to Edward ?Hork, 3 years New England. (BR).

28 February. The following apprenticed in Bristol: Andrew Stepmon to William Hughes, 4 years Nevis; James Baddam to Phillip Lee, 4 years Nevis; Thomas Baddam to same, 4 years Nevis; James Bayly to Edward Tocknell, 4 years Nevis; John Fetgard to Garrerd Bewly, 3 years Nevis; Ellioner Waite to Margaret Bennet, 4 years Antigua. (BR).

February. Administration of Jasper Grant of Stepney, Middlesex, who died in Virginia. (AW).

2 March. The following prisoners reprieved for transportation to Barbados: Giles Taunton of Thornbury, Gloucester, blacksmith; Richard Wakefield of Tarrington, Herefordshire; Edward Williams of Oswestry, Shropshire. (PRO: C66/3049/21).

5 March. The following apprenticed in Bristol: Allexander Vowles to John Nicholas, 6 years New England; Morgan Jones to John Osgood, 4 years Nevis. (BR).

6 March. The following apprenticed in Bristol: Jeremiah Clothier to John Vining, 8 years New England; Richard Cary to Thomas Harris, 4 years New England; Daniell Chresseham to same, 4 years New England. (BR).

7 March. The following apprenticed in Bristol: Jane Grizell to Elizabeth Browne, 5 years Nevis; John Wilmott to Richard Grant, 4 years Barbados. (BR).

9 March. The following apprenticed in Bristol: John Warie to Phillip Mathews, 4 years New England; John Bowen to John Nicholas, 4 years New England; John Rudrick to Margaret Long, 6 years Nevis; Elizabeth Constable to John Chayny, 5 years Nevis; John Greene to David Morrice, 4 years Nevis. (BR).

11 March. The following apprenticed in Bristol: Thomas Jefferis to Abraham Davis, 4 years Nevis; Henry Evans to David Morrice, 3 years Nevis. (BR).

12 March. The following apprenticed in Bristol: John Oburne to John Card, 4 years Nevis; John Weeks to same, 4 years Nevis; John Browne to same, 7 years Nevis; John Hascall to same, 5 years Nevis; Elizabeth Dibbins to same, 4 years Nevis; William Baker to same, 4 years Nevis; Nicholas Windell to same, 4 years Nevis; Margery Stone to Hester Ashby, 4 years Nevis; Edward Lowe to William Lane, 4 years Nevis. (BR).

17 March. The following apprenticed in Bristol: Thomas Backster to Samuell Nicholas, 5 years New England; Edward Laming to Richard Powell, 3 years Barbados; Merrian Davis to John Jones, 4 years Barbados. (BR).

18 March. The following apprenticed in Bristol: Katherine Juks to William Limbre, 4 years Nevis; George Tirwhitt to John Roach, 4 years Nevis; William Pew to John Harris, 4 years Nevis; William Andrews to Henry Heathcott, 5 years Nevis; Thomas Chilcott to same, 5 years Nevis. (BR).

19 March. The following apprenticed in Bristol: Michaell Crosly to William Limbre, 4 years Nevis. (BR).

20 March. The following apprenticed in Bristol: John Sampson to William Limbre, 4 years Nevis; John Challoner to Richard Lock, 4 years Nevis. (BR).

23 March. The following apprenticed in Bristol: Katherine Clark to Simon Browne, 4 years Nevis. (BR).

24 March. The following apprenticed in Bristol: Nicholas Frost to Thomas Orchard, 4 years New England. (BR).

26 March. The following apprenticed in Bristol: Elizabeth Hoxton to Robert Haskins, 4 years Nevis. (BR).

27 March. The following apprenticed in Bristol: Edward Parsons to William Limbre, 4 years Nevis. (BR).

28 March. The following apprenticed in Bristol: Walter Higgins to Robert Haskins, 4 years Nevis; Edward Buttry to same, 7 years Nevis; David Powell to Richard Powell, 4 years Barbados. (BR).

March. Administration with will of Humphrey Leigh who died overseas (bound for Virginia), bachelor. (AW).

March. Administration with will of Robert Clarke of Rotherhithe, Surrey, and of New England, who died abroad. (AW).

1 April. The following apprenticed in Bristol: Henry Webster to Henry Cole, 4 years New England; Anthony Hulls to Thomas Tayler, 4 years Barbados. (BR).

2 April. The following apprenticed in Bristol: Edward Norton to Charles Answeare, 4 years New England. (BR).

4 April. The following apprenticed in Bristol: William Love to Richard Barnet, 4 years Barbados. (BR).

11 April. The following apprenticed in Bristol: Thomas Morris to John Jones, 4 years Barbados; George Crocker to John Day, 4 years Barbados; Sarah Leveredge to George Bowcher, 4 years Barbados. (BR).

16 April. The following apprenticed in Bristol: Patrick Taylor to Robert Yeamans, 4 years Barbados. (BR).

22 April. The following apprenticed in Bristol: John Carey to Richard Rich, 4 years Barbados. (BR).

25 April. The following apprenticed in Bristol: John King to George Bowcher, 4 years Barbados. (BR).

27 April. Home Circuit prisoners reprieved for transportation to Barbados. Sussex: Joan Starr, spinster; Thomas Peters alias Weller; Robert Packenden; John Isted; Dorothy Wood, spinster. Unidentified: Oliver Pike, William Baker, Thomas Densley, Richard Etherington, Thomas Turner, Thomas Allen, William Browne, Anne Browne, spinster, James Boles, Benjamin Wood, William Wingar. (PRO: C66/3049/16).

28 April. The following apprenticed in Bristol: Edward Wallington to Jane Kingford, 4 years Barbados; Margaret Smith to same, 4 years Barbados. (BR).

30 April. The following apprenticed in Bristol: William Haskins to George Bowcher, 7 years Barbados. (BR).

April. Administration of John Booteflower of Stepney, Middlesex, who died in Virginia. (AW).

April. Administration of Nicholas Johnson of Shadwell, Middlesex, who died in Virginia. (AW).

4 May. The following apprenticed in Bristol: Mary Jefferis to Thomas Seares, 4 years Nevis; John Mills to Richard Burne, 4 years Barbados. (BR).

7 May. The following apprenticed in Bristol: John Murrey to Thomas Seares, 4 years Nevis; Thomas Roweing to Stephen Tayler, 4 years Nevis. (BR).

18 May. The following apprenticed in Bristol: William Hodges to Richard Devoe, 4 years Virginia. (BR).

22 May. The following apprenticed in Bristol: John Adlam to Thomas Sears, 4 years Nevis. (BR).

25 May. The following apprenticed in Bristol: Howell Thomas to Thomas Lukins, 4 years Nevis. (BR).

May. Probate of will of Francis Fawconer of Kingsclere, Hampshire, whose brother, Edward Fawconer, was in Virginia. (AW).

May. Administration of Richard Morton of Virginia, bachelor. (AW).

May. Probate of will of Thomas Hall of St. Katherine by the Tower, London, whose brother, John Hall, was in New England. (AW).

May. Administration of John Blake of Minehead, Somerset, who died in Virginia. (AW).

1 June. The following apprenticed in Bristol: Daniell Puddeford to Edward Morris, 4 years Virginia; Jeremiah Taylor to Robert Yeamans, 4 years Barbados. (BR).

2 June. The following apprenticed in Bristol: David Edwards to Morgan Lewis, 4 years Barbados. (BR).

3 June. The following apprenticed in Bristol: William Jenkins to Thomas Snell, 4 years Virginia; Thomas Edge to Phillip Roberts, 4 years Nevis. (BR).

6 June. The following apprenticed in Bristol: Henry Martin to Richard Burnet, 4 years Barbados. (BR).

8 June. The following apprenticed in Bristol: Humphry Curtis to Edward Morris, 4 years Virginia. (BR).

10 June. The following apprenticed in Bristol: Nicholas Evans to Walter William, 5 years Nevis; Angell Stephens to Anne Jones, 4 years Barbados. (BR).

11 June. The following apprenticed in Bristol: Joane Redman to George Bowcher, 4 years Barbados. (BR).

12 June. The following apprenticed in Bristol: Robert Farmer to John Riv——, 4 years Nevis; Dorothy Field to Thomas Williams, 4 years Nevis. (BR).

15 June. The following apprenticed in Bristol: Thomas Peale to Thomas Taylor, 4 years Nevis; Phillip Band to William Flower, 4 years Virginia; Robert Pruther to Lewis Jones, 3 years Nevis; Richard Davis to Christopher Taylor, 6 years Nevis. (BR).

16 June. The following apprenticed in Bristol: Samuell Harkwood to William Sheapard, 4 years Barbados. (BR).

17 June. The following apprenticed in Bristol: Elizabeth Davis to Richard Bennet, 4 years Nevis. (BR).

18 June. The following apprenticed in Bristol: Simon Tiner to Stephen Watts, 4 years Nevis; Phillip Johnson to William Hall, 4 years Nevis; Joane Lane to same, 4 years Nevis. (BR).

20 June. The following apprenticed in Bristol: William Fordick to William Keech, 4 years Nevis; Thomas Taylor to Peter Porter, 7 years Virginia. (BR).

22 June. The following apprenticed in Bristol: Robert Davis to Godfry Whitlock, 4 years Barbados; Richard Williams to Robert Hodge, 4 years Virginia. (BR).

23 June. The following apprenticed in Bristol: John Thomas to Richard Day, 4 years Virginia; David Morgan to Thomas Bodman, 4 years Virginia; William Jinke to William Wakely, 4 years Virginia. (BR).

24 June. The following apprenticed in Bristol: Arthur Williams to Elizabeth Munday, 4 years Barbados. (BR).

25 June. Shipper by the *Patience* of Boston, Mr. Bartholomew Cade, bound from Southampton for New England: Joseph Sweete. (PRO: E190/826/5).

June. Probate of will of Thomas Reade who died overseas (bound for Virginia). (AW).

June. Deposition by Devereux Browne of Virginia, gent aged 33, that he lived for several years with John Bateman, formerly of London and then of Maryland, haberdasher, deceased, and with Mary his wife and executrix. John Bateman brought into Maryland goods belonging to Henry Scarborough. (LMCD).

1 July. The following apprenticed in Bristol: William Harbert to Thomas Gathering, 4 years Virginia. (BR).

2 July. The following apprenticed in Bristol: Rebeckah Hughes to Elizabeth Dore, 4 years Virginia; Samuel Nowell to Walter Williams, 4 years Virginia. (BR).

3 July. The following apprenticed in Bristol: William Cole to Benjamin Blindman, 4 years Virginia; Robert Lucas to Humphrey Chiners, 5 years Virginia; William Pearson to same, 5 years Virginia; Andrew Waters to James Bridges, 4 years Virginia. (BR).

4 July. The following apprenticed in Bristol: Mary Wilkins to Sarah Jinkins, 4 years Maryland; Anne Burgesse to William Flower, 4 years Virginia; Williams Sams to Richard Bennet, 4 years Nevis. (BR).

6 July. The following apprenticed in Bristol: Anne Drew to Richard Bennet, 4 years Virginia; John Merreweather to John Rines, 4 years Nevis. (BR).

8 July. The following apprenticed in Bristol: Walter Williams to Jeremiah Hall, 4 years Virginia. (BR).

9 July. The following apprenticed in Bristol: William Briant to William More, 4 years Virginia. (BR).

10 July. The following apprenticed in Bristol: William Merreman to Joseph Hunt, 4 years Virginia; James Wood to William Fletcher, 4 years Virginia; Jane Clubb to Richard Fielding, 4 years Virginia; Elizabeth Denton to same, 4 years Virginia. (BR).

13 July. The following apprenticed in Bristol: Nathaniell Fuller to Sarah Jinkins, 11 years Virginia; Samuell Fuller to same, 13 years Virginia. (BR).

14 July. The following apprenticed in Bristol: John Price to Richard Daw, 4 years Virginia; William Paniwell to same, 4 years Virginia; Richard Davis to Thomas Whitetopp, 5 years Barbados; Katherine How to Charles Brande, 4 years Virginia; Joseph Tilly to Edward Morris, 4 years Virginia. (BR).

15 July. Newgate prisoners reprieved for transportation to Barbados. London: William Emmes; Mary Scott, spinster; Margaret Browne, spinster, alias wife of John Browne; Elizabeth Peirce, spinster; Anne Pattin, spinster, alias wife of John Pattin; Jone Wright; Edward King; Grissell Hudson, spinster, alias wife of John Hudson; James Tyler; Thomas Drew; Anne Platt, spinster, alias wife of James Osborne; Jane White alias Osborne, spinster, alias wife of John White; Richard Miller. Middlesex: Gilbert alias Owen Clarke of Littleton; Thomas Carver of Littleton; William Claver of St. Pancras; Alice Binney; Mary Wheatley of St. Clement Danes; Thomas Peake of St. Martin in the Fields; Richard Warner of South Mimms; Bridget, wife of John Jarrow of Stepney; Job Ryde of Sunbury; Johanna Farr, spinster, alias wife of William Rowe of Whitechapel; Robert Slaughter of Islington; Elizabeth Budd of Isleworth, spinster; Mary Williams of Stepney, spinster; Richard Page of Finchley; John Demetrius of Whitechapel; Samuel Taunton of St. Giles in the Fields; William Jewett of Hanwell, clocksmith; Hugh Godfrey of St. Giles Cripplegate; John Humphreys of Isleworth; Thomas Tredway of Stepney; Richard Turner alias Gardner of St. Clement Danes; Lewis Jones of St. Andrew Holborn; Thomas Nickson of St. Martin in the Fields. (PRO: C66/3048/15).

16 July. The following apprenticed in Bristol: Robert Howell to Roger Tayler, 4 years Virginia; Giles Collins to same, 4 years Virginia; Thomas Lord to same, 7 years Virginia. (BR).

17 July. The following apprenticed in Bristol: John Williams to Jesper Crosse, 5 years Virginia; Mary Cooke to William Smith, 4 years Nevis. (BR).

17 July. Oxford Circuit prisoners reprieved for transportation to Barbados: William Billingsley of Beckbury, Shropshire; Thomas Hooper, yeoman, and James Jones, miller, of Bradley, Kentchurch, Herefordshire. (PRO: C66/3048/16).

18 July. The following apprenticed in Bristol: George Makepeace to Joseph Clarke, 4 years Virginia; Joane Barksteed to William Morris, 4 years Virginia. (BR).

18 July-10 August. Shippers by the *Leviathan* of Scarborough, Mr. William Nestfield, bound from Lyme Regis for Virginia: Walter Tucker & Co., Robert Burridge. (PRO: E190/879/10).

20 July. The following apprenticed in Bristol: William Roberts to Abraham Jerning, 5 years Virginia. (BR).

21 July. Norfolk Circuit prisoners reprieved for transportation to America: Emma Greene, spinster; Robert Disney; Francis Baker; John Chilver; John Wade; Christopher Dawson; John Laughty. (PRO: C66/3048/10).

21 July. The following apprenticed in Bristol: James Winniard to Edward Lugg, 4 years Virginia. (BR).

22 July. The following apprenticed in Bristol: William Osborne to Anthony Salwey, 4 years Virginia; Sarah Perks to same, 4 years Virginia; John Luckman to same, 4 years Virginia; Nicholas Terret to same, 4 years Virginia. (BR).

23 July. The following apprenticed in Bristol: Abraham Rawley to William Flower, 5 years Virginia; Henry Thomas to Thomas Willis, 4 years Virginia. (BR).

25 July. The following apprenticed in Bristol: John Wips to Richard Phelps, 4 years Virginia; Richard Stevens to James Shute, 4 years Virginia. (BR).

27 July. The following apprenticed in Bristol: Simon Herring to Martin Morgan, 4 years Virginia; William Grimes to John Haskins, 4 years Virginia. (BR).

28 July. The following apprenticed in Bristol: Frances Gunbry to Richard Day, 4 years Virginia; Richard Berry to Jesper Crosse, 4 years Virginia. (BR).

29 July. The following apprenticed in Bristol: Margaret Bayly to Christopher Birkehead, 6 years Virginia; George Nicholas to Richard Salmon, 4 years Virginia; Samuell Hull to William Bruerton, 8 years Virginia; Katherine Foster to William Flower, 4 years Virginia; Elizabeth Hill to same, 4 years Virginia. (BR).

31 July. The following apprenticed in Bristol: Leonard Southerne to William Flower, 4 years Virginia; William Henbitch to Richard Day, 5 years Virginia. (BR).

July. Probate of will of Edward Goldstone of Limehouse, Stepney, Middlesex, mariner, who had goods in Virginia. (AW).

July. Probate of will of John Hatton of Virginia. (AW).

July. Administration with will of Thomas Browne of Plymouth, Devon, who had goods in New England. (AW).

July. Depositions in London to establish entitlement to the estate of Arthur Blackmore of Holy Cross, Winchester, Hampshire, deceased. Deponents say that Arthur Blackmore, son of the said Arthur Blackmore, married Susan Burnett in Holland in 1643 or 1644 and they had a child, Susan, baptised in the parish of St. Benet Fink in London. Susan Blackmore married Humphrey Robinson of London, merchant, whom she outlived, and then married William Corker of Virginia, surgeon, in 1649 by whom she had Susan and Judith Corker in Virginia. Deponents include: Joane, wife of James Besouth of Middleton, York County, Virginia; John Hubert of James River, Virginia, planter aged 25; Robert Holes of York River, planter; Mary Burnett of Virginia. (NGSQ 67/3).

1 August. The following apprenticed in Bristol: Hopkin Lewis to Edward Stragling, 4 years Virginia; Thomas Lloyd to John Roach, 4 years Virginia; William Pinnell to John Howell, 4 years Virginia. (BR).

3 August. The following apprenticed in Bristol: Mary Ellet to John Alflat, 5 years Virginia. (BR).

3 August. Shipper by the *George* of Southampton, Mr. Anthony Prior, bound from Southampton for Virginia: William Israel & Co. (PRO: E190/826/5).

4 August. The following apprenticed in Bristol: Walter Watkins to Mathew Barrow, 4 years Virginia; Christopher Johnson to Christopher Birkehead, 4 years Virginia. (BR).

5 August. The following apprenticed in Bristol: Thomas Bryan to John White, 4 years Virginia; Phillip Mason to William Hill, 4 years Virginia; Gabriell Parret to Richard Fielding, 3 years Virginia. (BR).

6 August. Shipper by the *Fyall Merchant* of Bideford, Mr. Edward Tapley, bound from Barnstaple for Virginia: Abraham Hennan. (PRO: E190/953/9).

6 August. The following apprenticed in Bristol: Thomas Wilson to Richard Fox, 6 years Virginia; John Jones to Christopher Berkhead, 4 years Virginia; Robert Sheapard to Jesper Crosse, 8 years Virginia; Margaret Williams to William Wakely, 4 years Virginia; Abraham Glasier to Thomas Hill, 4 years Virginia; Thomas Simons to Thomas Newman, 4 years Virginia; Anne Watkins to Sarah Jinkins, 6 years Virginia. (BR).

8 August. The following apprenticed in Bristol: John Franklin to William Luff, 4 years Virginia. (BR).

10 August. The following apprenticed in Bristol: Anne Brooks to William Jelfe, 5 years Virginia; Robert Liant to same, 4 years Virginia; James Makall to Jane Kingford, 4 years Virginia; Anne Wyett to Robert Burkett, 4 years Virginia. (BR).

11 August. The following apprenticed in Bristol: Thomas Floyd to Richard Luckett, 4 years Nevis; Thomas Trottman to Elias Trottman, 5 years Maryland; Joseph Williams to same, 5 years Maryland; Tobias Fowler to same, 7 years Maryland; John Richards to William Hazard, 4 years Virginia; Samuell Hammon to same, 4 years Virginia; Thomas Plann to same, 4 years Virginia. (BR).

12 August. The following apprenticed in Bristol: Joseph Salter to Samuell Wharton, 4 years Virginia; David Davis to William West, 5 years Virginia. (BR).

13 August. The following apprenticed in Bristol: John Cooke to George Taplady, 4 years Virginia. (BR).

13-15 August. Shippers by the *Hoper*(?) of Yarmouth, Mr. Richard So—ing, bound from Yarmouth for Virginia: Samuell Tucker, Richard Huntington. (PRO: E190/493/14).

17 August. The following apprenticed in Bristol: Ambrose Palmer to Joseph Hunt, 7 years Virginia; Mary Bicks to Blanch Freeman, 4 years Virginia; Elizabeth Miles to same, 4 years Virginia. (BR).

18 August. The following apprenticed in Bristol: Peter Edson to Richard West, 4 years Virginia. (BR).

19 August. The following apprenticed in Bristol: Richard Rogers to Richard Fielding, 4 years Virginia; William Waters to Elizabeth Jones, 5 years Virginia. (BR).

19 August. Shipper by the *Adventure* of Bideford, Mr. Samuel Whitson, bound from Barnstaple for Virginia: John Liskam & Co. (PRO: E190/953/9).

20 August. The following apprenticed in Bristol: John Skinell to Robert Hauxworth, 4 years Virginia; George Russell to same, 7 years Virginia; John Jolley to Richard Vickris, 4 years Virginia. (BR).

21 August. The following apprenticed in Bristol: Edward James to William Williams, 4 years Virginia; William Knight to John Howell, 4 years Virginia; Mary Burk to William Flower, 4 years Virginia. (BR).

22 August. The following apprenticed in Bristol: John Thomas to John Hopkins, 4 years Virginia; Robert Perreman to James Bisse, 4 years Virginia. (BR).

24 August. The following apprenticed in Bristol: William Wheeler to Richard Fielding, 4 years Virginia; Michaell Deloge to Charles Taplady, 4 years Virginia; Giles Jenings to William Flower, 6 years Virginia. (BR).

25 August. The following apprenticed in Bristol: George Avis to John Haskins, 4 years Virginia. (BR).

26 August. The following apprenticed in Bristol: James Pricklove to Abraham Roome, 4 years Virginia. (BR).

26 August. Deposition by Richard Scarlett, citizen and cooper of London, aged 49, and William Eaton of Wapping, Middlesex, mariner, that in 1654 James Phillips bound himself to the deponent Scarlett to learn the cooper's trade and completed his term with John Scotcher of Seaverne, Virginia, planter. The deponent Eaton witnessed his indenture of apprenticeship when he was in Virginia. (LMCD).

28 August. The following apprenticed in Bristol: Jane Williams to John Browne, 4 years Virginia. (BR).

28 August-9 October. Shippers by the *Diamond* of Bideford, Mr. John King, bound from Barnstaple for New England: Henry Horwood, John Lugge, Benjamin Batten. (PRO: E190/953/9).

29 August. The following apprenticed in Bristol: William Maddocks to John Read, 4 years Virginia; Edward Edwards to William Colson, 4 years Virginia. (BR).

29 August. Home counties prisoners reprieved for transportation to Barbados. Essex: John Cooke, Thomas Hawkins, Stephen Warner. Kent: Elizabeth Stretton, George Jones, Elizabeth Burges, Anne Pont, Tristram Trayner, Anthony Homan. Hertfordshire: John Dandy, John Knight alias Dimmock, Edward Bickerster. Surrey: Richard Cater, Michael Browne, Garrat Drew, Edward Boyston, John Salloway. Unspecified: John Rubbery, Stephen Starr, Edward Rushton, Samuell Asson. (PRO: C66/3048/12).

31 August. The following apprenticed in Bristol: William Steed to John Haskins, 4 years Virginia; Mary Smith to Gowen Lancaster, 4 years Virginia. (BR).

31 August-1 September. Shippers by the *Unity* of Topsham, Mr. Thomas Russell, bound from Exeter for Virginia: Endymion Walker, John Mayne, Jasper Mawditt, Isaac Mawditt. (PRO: E190/953/8).

August. Depositions in London relating to the accounts of Valentine Peyton in Virginia. (NGSQ 66/3).

1 September. The following apprenticed in Bristol: Sarah Hedges to James Shute, 4 years Virginia. (BR).

1 September. Shipper by the *Providence* of London, Mr. William Hall, bound from Southampton for Virginia: Richard Worsley. (PRO: E190/826/5).

2 September. The following apprenticed in Bristol: John Evans to Edith Smith, 12 years Virginia, Margaret Langdon to same, 3 years Virginia; Elizabeth Brannidge to same, 4 years Virginia. (BR).

3 September. The following apprenticed in Bristol: Walter Morgan to John Teage, 4 years Virginia; Lewis Cod to Joseph Tucker, 4 years Virginia. (BR).

7 September. The following apprenticed in Bristol: Thomas Jones to John Hopkins, 4 years Virginia. (BR).

8 September. The following apprenticed in Bristol: John Ellis to Mary N———, 4 years Virginia; Robert Lindsay to William Brewerton, 4 years Virginia; Thomas May to John Hopkins, 6 years Virginia. (BR).

11 September. The following apprenticed in Bristol: Peter Oakly to Abraham Roome, 4 years Virginia; Thompson Carter to John Hopkins, 4 years Virginia. (BR).

12 September. The following apprenticed in Bristol: William Rise to Giles Merrick, 4 years Virginia; Francis Hitchold to Thomas Whittey, 8 years Barbados; Peter Long to Mathew Braine, 4 years Virginia. (BR).

14 September. The following apprenticed in Bristol: William Sandiford to Abraham Roome, 4 years Virginia; Peter Cooper to John Hopkins, 4 years Virginia. (BR).

17 September. The following apprenticed in Bristol: John Vizard to Robert Noble, 4 years Virginia; John Sheapard to Richard Alley, 4 years Virginia. (BR).

18 September. The following apprenticed in Bristol: Elias Edwards to John Boxwell, 3 years Virginia. (BR).

20 September. William Preston of Shadwell, Middlesex, ship caulker, to answer the complaint of Richard Wood of Rosemary Lane, Middlesex, joiner, that he enticed away his apprentice, Isaac Bosse, and put him on board the *Golden Fortune* intending to ship him to Virginia without permission. (VM 83/3).

21 September. The following apprenticed in Bristol: Edward Harris to Blanch Freeman, 4 years Virginia. (BR).

24 September. The following apprenticed in Bristol: Filotheus Bowen to Henry Freeman, 4 years Virginia; Roger Bowen to same, 9 years Virginia. (BR).

25 September. The following apprenticed in Bristol: William Dudlett to John Wall, 4 years Virginia. (BR).

2 October. The following apprenticed in Bristol: William Berry to John Duke, 4 years Virginia; John Cooke to Daniell Baker, 4 years Virginia. (BR).

6 October. The following apprenticed in Bristol: John Price to Elizabeth Wright, 5 years Virginia. (BR).

7 October. The following apprenticed in Bristol: William Williams to James Baskerville, 4 years Virginia. (BR).

14 October. The following apprenticed in Bristol: Anne Brumadge to Jane Sayers, 6 years Virginia; John Kendall to John Harris, 4 years Virginia. (BR).

15 October. The following apprenticed in Bristol: John Jones to Matthew Stevens, 4 years Virginia. (BR).

16 October. Oxford Circuit prisoners reprieved for transportation to Barbados. Berkshire: Edward Capon Sr. & Edward Capon Jr. of Pettick, Childrey; Richard Dye of Bradfield, cordwainer. Oxfordshire: George Jackson alias Cook alias Coates of Eynsham; John Best of Fulbrook; Elizabeth, wife of William Crompton of Henley-on-Thames; Thomas Barker of St. Michael's, Oxford, carpenter; William Rowland of Piddington. Gloucestershire: William Gainsford of Dymock; Erasmus Harris of Great Barrington, cooper. Herefordshire: Mary Powell of Derrender, spinster; John Hodgetts and Margaret Hodgetts, spinster, of Woverd, Sollers Hope. Shropshire: James Davies and Edward Davies of Richard Castle; William Terratt of Drayton; John Blount of Mindtown, gent. Worcestershire: John Griffith of Norton; John Dugard of Pedmore; Staffordshire: John Higgins of Chapel Chorlton; Thomas Clempson of Milwich. Wiltshire: Thomas Wallis of Marlborough, gent. (PRO: C66/3048/8).

20 October. The following apprenticed in Bristol: John Alward to Thomas Langley, 4 years Virginia. (BR).

22 October. The following apprenticed in Bristol: Thomas Morgan to David Warren, 4 years Virginia. (BR).

24 October. The following apprenticed in Bristol: Joseph Rich to Thomas Walter, 4 years Virginia. (BR).

26 October. The following apprenticed in Bristol: Richard Roch to Roger Adams, 4 years Virginia; Thomas Jones to Giles Merrick, 4 years Virginia; Thomas Burton to John Beare, 3 years St. Christopher; Elizabeth Morgan to Charles Darby, 3 years Barbados. (BR).

27 October. The following apprenticed in Bristol: Thomas Elliot to Jinkin Bragg, 4 years Virginia. (BR).

29 October. The following apprenticed in Bristol: Thomas Starte to Roger Adams, 5 years Virginia; Jasper Gransome to Thomas Hanson, 6 years Virginia. (BR).

30 October. The following apprenticed in Bristol: Mathew Harrison to William Hill, 4 years Virginia. (BR).

October. Administration with will of Stephen Fox of the ship *Fortune*, who died near New England. (AW).

6 November. The following apprenticed in Bristol: John Cooke to John Lury, 6 years Barbados; William Miles to David Warren, 4 years Barbados; Jonathan Tayler to Edward Hassell, 4 years Barbados. (BR).

11 November. The following apprenticed in Bristol: Thomas Roberts to James Harris, 4 years Virginia. (BR).

13 November. The following apprenticed in Bristol: Lodowick Williams to Mathew Powell, 4 years St. Christopher; Thomas James to same, 5 years St. Christopher; Thomas George to same, 4 years St. Christopher; Nicholas Clement to same, 4 years St. Christopher; Thomas Williams to same, 6 years St. Christopher; Jane Thomas to same, 4 years St. Christopher; John Pynon to same, 7 years St. Christopher. (BR).

17 November. The following apprenticed in Bristol: William Sparkes to Henry Russell, 4 years Barbados. (BR).

19 November. The following apprenticed in Bristol: Ursula Hall to Mathew Powell, 5 years St. Christopher; John Fisher to John Gill, 4 years Barbados; Marthah Trayden to Richard Woodward, 4 years Virginia; Frith Lyddall to same, 4 years Virginia; Thomas Barrow to John Hunt, 4 years Virginia; Giles Underwood to John Hopkins, 4 years Virginia; Mary Jones to same, 4 years Virginia; James Jones to same, 4 years Virginia; Hester Bennet to Thomas Atwood, 5 years Virginia; Jinkin Bowen to Thomas Evans, 4 years St. Christopher. (BR).

20 November. The following apprenticed in Bristol: Katherine Williams to Mathew Powell, 5 years St. Christopher. (BR).

23 November. The following apprenticed in Bristol: George Poppin to John Smith, 6 years Barbados. (BR).

25 November. The following apprenticed in Bristol: John Powell to William Hill, 4 years Nevis; William Rosser to Stephen Tayler, 4 years Nevis; Edward Wilmot to William Freeman, 8 years Nevis. (BR).

November. Probate of will of William Grey of London, who died in Hackney, Middlesex, and whose brother, John Grey, was in New England. (AW).

3 December. The following apprenticed in Bristol: Elizabeth Holmes to William Hill, 5 years Nevis; George Fryzar to William Rodney, 4 years Barbados; Mary Jones to same, 4 years Barbados; Samuell [blank] to Robert Hilman, 4 years Barbados. (BR).

16 December. The following apprenticed in Bristol: Thomas Cox to William Davis, 3 years Barbados. (BR).

17 December. The following apprenticed in Bristol: Christopher Kirke to Robert Hilman, 3 years Barbados; Mary Vaughan to William Hill, 4 years Barbados. (BR).

19 December. The following apprenticed in Bristol: Richard Cole to William Davis, 7 years Barbados; Josias Emmett to John Bigglestone, 7 years Barbados; Evan Thomas to Robert Pratt, 4 years Barbados. (BR).

20 December. Deposition by Stephen Proctor, citizen and weaver of London, aged 45, that on 18 August 1663 Jonathan Nowell, then of London, merchant, became indebted to him for goods shipped to Virginia. He has received only part payment in tobacco from Spencer Pigott. (LMCD).

30 December. The following apprenticed in Bristol: Katherine Jones to Alice Hewman, 3 years Barbados; John Thomas to same, 4 years Barbados; Thomas Pritchard to same, 6 years Barbados; Joane Evans to same, 6 years [Barbados]; Cicely Pritchard to same, 6 years Barbados; Mary Lewes to same, 7 years Barbados; Jennet Lewes to same, 4 years Barbados; Anne Lewis to same, 7 years Barbados; Elizabeth Shereman to Robert Pratt, 4 years Barbados.

1664

4 January. The following apprenticed in Bristol: Robert Smith to Thomas Kippin, 4 years Barbados; Jane Tanner to same, 4 years Barbados. (BR).

5 January. Norfolk Circuit prisoners reprieved to be transported to Barbados. Bedfordshire: Edward Goode of Tempsford. Buckinghamshire: William Burden of Newport Pagnell. Dorset: John Martin of Bamber(?), husbandman. Norfolk: John Holden alias Alden of Foulsham; Thomas Bell of Cawston; George Copeman of North Creake; John Pitts of Rockland Tofts; Richard Wilson of North Creake; Christopher Dawson of Guist. Suffolk: Thomas Watson of Stowlangtoft; Thomas Mayor of Elmswell; Francis Langham of Great Saxham. (PRO: C66/3066/8).

7 January. The following apprenticed in Bristol: John Cox of Amesbury, [Wilts] to William Jones, 4 years Nevis; Owen Richards to Warren Lewis, 4 years Barbados; James Webb to John Robins, 4 years Barbados; William Knight, yeoman, to Thomas Kippen, 4 years Barbados; William Griffeth to William Davis, 5 years Barbados; Maudlin Davis to Morgan Stacy, 4 years Barbados; Henery Williams to Robert Dimock, 8 years Nevis; Thomas Say to Mathew Buck, 4 years New England; Ann Wattkins to Stephen Tayler, 4 years Nevis; John Higgs to same, 4 years Nevis. (BR).

13 January. Northern Circuit prisoners reprieved to be transported to Barbados: William Robson, William Nelson, Richard Pybus, Anne Harrison, Edward Savage. (PRO: C66/3066/6).

16 January. Newgate prisoners reprieved to be transported to the plantations. London: George Wood; Elizabeth Martin; Thomas Tustey; Nathaniell Harris; Francis Watson; Elizabeth Swayne, spinster; Elizabeth Bayley; William Harris; John Archer; Frances Trallacke, spinster; Margaret Wood, spinster; Elizabeth Bromhill, spinster; Susanna Ketch, spinster; Margaret Ketch, spinster, alias wife of John Ketch; William Taylor. Middlesex: Anne Walton of St. Botolph Aldgate; Francis Benbow of Whitechapel; Thomas Roberts of St. Martin in the Fields; Samuell Gilmore of Islington; John Austin of St. Clement Danes; John Symons of St. Martin in the Fields; Richard Coney of St. Martin in the Fields; John Weekes of Hornsey; Grace Brechley of Stepney; John Westwood of Marylebone; John Pound of Kingsbury. (PRO: C66/3066/5).

21 January. Newgate prisoners reprieved to be transported to Barbados. London: Richard Ridewood; John Poole; Stephen Hobson; John Johnson; Richard Trevis; George Langford; William Starkie; Abraham Drew; Henry Howard; William Stoakes; Thomas Smith alias Wingfield; Nathaniel Harris; Thomas Langshall. Middlesex: Maurice Jones; John Harvey alias Harris; Henry

Bayley; Robert Chapman; Samuel Eeles; John Smith; Margaret Parry, spinster. (PRO: C66/3049/14 & SP44/14/1).

26 January. The following apprenticed in Bristol: Thomas Phillips to John Biggles, 7 years Nevis; Anthoney Holley to John Webb, 3 years Barbados; Blanch Price to Patrick Loyd, 4 years Barbados. (BR).

29 January. The following apprenticed in Bristol: John Collins to John Collins, 4 years Barbados; William Martin to Stephen Tayler, 6 years Barbados. (BR).

1 February. The following apprenticed in Bristol: Katherin Symonds to Hector Smith, 5 years Barbados; Lewis Loyd to Robert Gerring, 4 years Nevis; Francis Hughes to Margaret Smith, 5 years Nevis. (BR).

1 February. Shipper by the *Swan*, Mr. Andrew Ashford, bound from London for New England: Samuell Sedgwick. (PRO: E190/50/1).

4 February. Shipper by the *Dolphin*, Mr. Abraham Hyett, bound from London for New England: said Abraham Hyett. (PRO: E190/50/1).

8 February. The following apprenticed in Bristol: John Francklin to Morgan Stacy, 4 years Barbados; Ann Gould to John Abbott, 4 years Nevis; Martha Waltar to same, 4 years Barbados; Edward Turford to Samuell Court, 3 years Barbados; Cadogan Jones to William Thomas, 4 years Antigua; Phillip Thomas to same, 6 years Antigua; Thomas Jones to same, 7 years Antigua; Christopher Andrewes to same, 7 years Antigua; Waltar Thomas to same, 7 years Antigua; Peter Williams to same, 4 years Antigua; Roger Apply to same, 4 years Antigua; Mary Jones to same, 9 years Antigua; James Vithnell to Edward Everatt, 7 years Nevis; John Provender to Isaac Easton, 4 years New England; John Wattkins to Symon Court, 4 years Barbados; Rowland Davice to Robert Pratt, 4 years Barbados; Michaell Symkins to Thomas Elbridge, 4 years New England; Elianor Lacy to John Morgan, 4 years New England; John Moreton to same, 5 years New England; Nathaniell Corneborough to same, 4 years New England. (BR).

9 February. Shipper by the *Dove*, Mr. Robert Walters, bound from London for New England: William Warren. (PRO: E190/50/1).

10 February. Newgate prisoners reprieved to be transported to Barbados. London: Rose Gwinne aged 40; John Seamour aged 30; John Sparkes aged 26; Daniel Poole aged 19; Jane Jones aged 40, spinster, alias wife of Richard Jones; Alice Turrell alias Parrett, spinster; Anne Peters aged 28, spinster; Ann Pettis alias Petworth alias Read alias Cade, aged 26, spinster; Rebecca Hackleton alias House aged 21, spinster, alias wife of John House; Anne Purse, spinster, alias wife of John Biggerton; Frances Beetle, aged 29, spinster; Richard Hensman; Alice Bayly aged 63, spinster, alias wife of Henry Bayly; Abigail Barrington aged 20, spinster, alias wife of John Barrington; Mary White alias Raven aged 42, widow; Giles Smithier, gardener aged 21; Francis Hall; Philip Watkins aged 21; Richard Glascocke aged 26; Edward Auckland aged 33; John Ward aged 30; George Drye; John Yate; Jacob Tomlinson; Nicholas Ridgeway. Middlesex: Elizabeth Hawkins of Hornsey, spinster aged 21; John Stockwell of Teddington aged 25; James Hatton of St. Pancras aged 30; John Cavee of Uxbridge; Richard Salter of Stepney aged 28; William Cooper of the same aged 30; Richard Guy of the same; Katherine Bentley, spinster, alias wife of Cornelius Bentley of the same; Henry Marshall aged 32 of the same, for burglary in Kent; John Payne of St. Clement Danes aged 12; Edward Ridgway of the same aged 13; Dorothy Hunt of Kensington, widow aged 21; Mary Hall of St. Botolph Aldgate. spinster aged 30; Thomas Burthwick of Edmonton aged 36; Mary Wellington aged 34, spinster, alias wife of John Wellington of Whitechapel; James Coachman of the same; Susan Wren of Clerkenwell, spinster; Thomas Procter of the same aged 23; Katherine Wright aged 19, spinster, alias wife of Jonas Wright of St. Andrew Holborn; Honor Collins of the same aged 18; Edward Davies of St. Mary Savoy aged 15; John Bayley of the same; Elizabeth Byron aged 40 of the same, widow; John Wallis of Harrow on the Hill; Anne Howard aged 20 of St. Andrew Holborn or Clerkenwell, spinster; Humphrey Underwood of Kensington; Nicholas Cambridge aged 21; Dorothy Bowdon aged 28; Ann Poore aged 40. (PRO: C66/3071/3 & SP29/92/65).

19 February. Shippers by the *Three Friends*, Mr. Walter Frank, bound from London for New England: John Harwood, William Throgmorton. (PRO: E190/50/1).

20 February. The following apprenticed in Bristol: Mary Caules to Phillip Bennet, 4 years Antigua; Oliver Richards to John Boren, 7 years New England. (BR).

22 February. The following apprenticed in Bristol: Thomas Saunders to John Stoakes, 7 years Antigua; Jane Williams to Francis French, 7 years Nevis; Elizabeth Kedger to Thomas Harris, 4 years Barbados. (BR).

26 February. The following apprenticed in Bristol: William Plowman to John Guning, 4 years Barbados. (BR).

27 February. Shippers by the *Elizabeth*, Mr. Nicholas Jaspers, bound from London for New England: John Leath, William Barrett, John Clements. (PRO: E190/50/1).

27 February-28 April. Shippers by the *Society*, Mr. John Pearse, bound from London for New England: Thomas Robinson, John Chilcott, Noah Floyd, Samuell Wilson, Daniell Whitfield, Nicholas Barnes, Thomas Bell, Lucy Knight, Sir William Peak, John Langdon, Thomas Bodley, John Fullerton, Richard Saltingstall, John Harwood, John Joram, John Pincheon, John Blinkhorn, Daniell Bridge, John Barrett, Henry Ashurst, George Gay, James Porter, John Graves, Edward Duffield, Thomas Bredon, Richard Wilks, Benjamin Hewling, Moses Brown, Edward Merryweather, Thomas Glover, John Marshall, John Kempster, Isaac Gray, Thomas Norman, Job Clement,

John Selbie, Henry Stanley, James Littleton, Thomas Carew. (PRO: E190/50/1, 50/2).

29 February. The following apprenticed in Bristol: James Lewis to William Howell, 4 years Barbados; William Hill to James Wathan, 4 years Nevis; Thomas Lewis to Morgan Williams, 4 years Barbados; Mathew Phelps to John West, 3 years Nevis. (BR).

19 February & 21 May. Norfolk Circuit prisoners reprieved to be transported to Barbados and America. Bedfordshire: Anthony Willis alias Gillars of Brammingham; Henry Benson of Leighton Buzzard; Robert Richardson of Eaton; Thomas Eaton alias Medberry alias Madberry of Eaton. Buckinghamshire: John Wright of Marsh Gibbon; Robert Cheese of Quainton; Francis Baker of Bow Brickhill; Elizabeth Urlin of Iver; Thomas Beford of Buckingham; William Cooke of Ivinghoe. Huntingdonshire: John Newman of Great Gidding; William Amber of Grafham. Norfolk: Thomas Webster of Thetford; Edward Stimpson alias Stevenson of Swaffham; Henry Boote of Belaugh; Thomas Loffen of Bexwell; John Newton of Hillington; George Smith of Bircham; Robert Clarke of Caston; William Copping of Tharston; Robert Constable of Swaffham. Suffolk: Thomas Major of Elmswell; Ann, wife of William Franck of Great Barton, Bury St. Edmunds; Anne Bickers of Bury St. Edmunds; William Pulford of Thornham; Robert Seely of Freckenham; Alice, wife of John Clarke of John of Bury St. Edmunds, yeoman; Robert Yallopp of Bungay; William Offerton of Bungay; Mary Hawkins; Christopher Hawley of Exning; William Boorn alias Boone of Mutford; Francis Langham of Great Saxham. (PRO: C66/3071/13 & 15).

4 March. The following apprenticed in Bristol: Thomas Vine to Robert Culme, 7 years Barbados; Robert Miles to same, 7 years Barbados; Thomas Harris to same, 7 years Barbados. (BR).

5 March. The following apprenticed in Bristol: William Morgan to Joane Charles, 4 years Barbados; Marke Giles to Thomas Ward, 4 years New England; Morris Chamblis to Thomas Elbridge, 4 years New England; Hugh Barnes to same, 4 years New England; Elizabeth Hewes to John West, 4 years Nevis or Antigua. (BR).

10 March. The following apprenticed in Bristol: Edmund Davis to Peter Osborne, 4 years Nevis. (BR).

12 March. The following apprenticed in Bristol: John Pitman to Jonathan Pitman, 7 years New England. (BR).

17 March-4 April. Shippers by the *Sisters*, Mr. Martin Skinner, bound from London for New England: Samuell Hinchman; Sir William Peak; John Gibbs; Obadiah Allen. (PRO: E190/50/1).

21 March-19 April. Shippers by the *Supply*, Mr. John Fairweather, bound from London for New England: Edward Floyd, Thomas Rawlinson, Edmund White,

William Bulkley, John Cooke, William Barrett, John Harwood, Richard Love, Sir William Peake, Thomas Norman, John Mascall, John Smith, Nathaniel Whitfield. (PRO: E190/50/1, 50/2).

March. Probate of will of Daniel Lluellin of Chelmsford, Essex, who had lands in Virginia. (AW).

March. Probate of will of Arthur Blackmore of St. Gregory, London, whose daughter, Susan, wife of William Corker, was in Virginia. (AW).

5 April. The following apprenticed in Bristol: Richard Knight to Bartholomew Clemmens, 4 years Barbados. (BR).

6 April. The following apprenticed in Bristol: Zacharia Clouter to John Weaver, 4 years Barbados; Griffen Morris to Phillip Lewis, 3 years Barbados; John Williams to same, 3 years Barbados; Joseph Olford to same, 4 years Barbados; Thomas Trosser to Edward Tocknell, 4 years Barbados. (BR).

8 April. The following apprenticed in Bristol: Francis Bead to Bartholomew Clemens, 4 years Nevis or Caribbees. (BR).

12 April. The following apprenticed in Bristol: John Phillips to Thomas Ellis, 4 years Barbados or Nevis. (BR).

13 April. The following apprenticed in Bristol: Margaret Brian to Elizabeth Webb, 4 years Barbados. (BR).

15 April. The following apprenticed in Bristol: Edward Jenkins to John Webb, 7 years Barbados or Nevis; Joshua Lamby to same, 6 years Barbados or Nevis; Elizabeth Thomas to Bartholomew Clemens, 5 years Nevis or Leewards. (BR).

15 April. Richard Tilley of Exeter, Devon, reprieved to be transported to Jamaica. (SP Dom).

20 April. The following apprenticed in Bristol: Owen Williams to Mathew Stephens, 4 years Nevis; Charles Jenkins to Samuell Derrough, 8 years Barbados. (BR).

21-22 April. Shippers by the *William*, Mr. Edward Harrison, bound from London for New England: Thomas Christer; John Arthur; Tobias Garbrand. (PRO: E190/50/1, 50/2).

22 April. The following apprenticed in Bristol: William Burgis to Jacob Bennet, 4 years Barbados; James Guy to James Lond, 4 years Barbados; Thomas Riggby to Robert Haskins, 4 years Nevis; Joseph Crothwine to Roger James, 4 years Nevis; Thomas Andrewes to Edward Tottnell, 4 years Barbados; Ralph Winn to same, 4 years Nevis. (BR).

30 April. Shipper by the *William & Nicholas*, Mr. Thomas Morley, bound from London for New England: Timothy Rose. (PRO: E190/50/1).

April. Probate of will of Samuel Robinson of Boston, New England, who died overseas. (AW).

1 May. Newgate prisoners reprieved to be transported to Barbados. London: Benjamin Knowles; Robert Scriven; Solomon Watts; Elizabeth Jackson, widow; Jane Whylde, spinster, alias wife of John Whylde; Thomas Wharton; William Long alias Longman; Peter Crutchfield; Richard Evans; John Greenhill; William Stedman. Middlesex: John Bird of St. Giles Cripplegate; Mary Elmes of Whitechapel, spinster; Mary Rowe of the same, spinster; James Johnson of Stepney; Daniel Brisley of the same; George Viger of St. Botolph Aldgate; William Harrison alias Procter of St. Clement Danes; William Cooke of Shoreditch; Christian Gilborne, spinster, alias wife of John Gilborne of Clerkenwell; Mary Hull of the same, spinster; William Peate of St. Martin in the Fields; Edward Jolliffe of Cranbourne, Hampshire; Thomas Wallis of Chippenham, Wiltshire. (PRO: C66/2071/2).

3 May. The following apprenticed in Bristol: Hugh Flyd to Robert Haskins, 4 years Nevis. (BR).

4 May. The following apprenticed in Bristol: William Williams to William Caines, 5 years Barbados. (BR).

4 May. Home counties prisoners reprieved to be transported to Barbados. Essex: Elizabeth Payne, Joseph Kemp, John Rosse, John Worthington, John Reynolds, John Browne, Thomas Willesmore, Richard Yorke, Richard Nasey. Hertfordshire: James Chambers. Surrey: Francis Baldwyn, James Wynne, Richard Albrooke, William Farlow alias White, John Hamming. Sussex: Margaret Pont. Unspecified: John Fuller, Charles Crust, John Bolton, William Eames, Henry Jarvys, Thomas Russell, Thomas Colvill. (PRO: C66/3071/10).

6 May. The following apprenticed in Bristol: Welthian James to John Wright, 4 years Nevis. (BR).

9 May. The following apprenticed in Bristol: Arthur Bowels to John Webb, 7 years Barbados; Anne Lane to Bartholomew Clemens, 5 years Barbados or Caribbees. (BR).

10 May. The following apprenticed in Bristol: John Erdeswicke to Edward Tocknell, 4 years Nevis. (BR).

10 May-30 June. Shippers by the *Defence*, Mr. John Webber, bound from London for New England: Benjamin Hewling, John Newell, Humphrey Hodges, Thomas Parris, James Fassett, John Fullerton, Sir William Peake, Robert Davies, Robert Knight, John Winder, Henry Culpepper, John Culpepper. (PRO: E190/50/1, 50/2).

11 May. The following apprenticed in Bristol: Jane Morgan to Robert Haskins, 4 years Nevis; James Parker to Mathew Stephens, 6 years Nevis; Mary Eves to Thomas Poape, 5 years Virginia; George Thomas to Edward Tocknell, 6 years Nevis; Thomas Radclift to Samuell Radclift, 4 years Barbados. (BR).

16 May. The following apprenticed in Bristol: William Finnis to Thomas Jones, 4 years Barbados; Henry Baily to Phillip Bis, 4 years Barbados; Thomas Prosly to Richard Poulter, 4 years Barbados; Edward Clift to same, 4 years Barbados. (BR).

18 May. The following apprenticed in Bristol: Elizabeth Chune to Richard Poulter, 4 years Barbados; Edward Williams to Richard V——, 4 years Virginia. (BR).

28 May. Shipper by the *Constant Mary*, Mr. Andrew Powlin, bound from London for New England: Obadiah Allen. (PRO: E190/50/2).

May. Probate of will of John Bly who died in Virginia. (AW)

1 June. The following apprenticed in Bristol: John Yeate to Jacob Bennet, 4 years Barbados; Thomas Harper to Thomas Jones, 4 years Barbados. (BR).

10 June. The following apprenticed in Bristol: Joane Stevens to Robert Dymock, 4 years Barbados. (BR).

16 June. The following apprenticed in Bristol: Thomas Browne to Phillip Bis, 5 years Barbados. (BR).

18 June. The following apprenticed in Bristol: Elizabeth Browne to Henry Paines, 3 years Barbados. (BR).

18-25 June. Shippers by the *Black Cock*, Mr. Henry (or Thomas) Haggerston, bound from London for New England: John Shorter, Thomas Robinson, John Taylor, Robert Brooke. (PRO: E190/50/1, 50/2).

18-30 June. Shippers by the *Daniel*, Mr. Samuel Randall, bound from London for Virginia: Richard Love, Henry Barrett, Rowland Astone, Arthur Hunt, William Mead. (PRO: E190/50/2).

22 June. The following apprenticed in Bristol: William Jones to John Farclew, 4 years Virginia. (BR).

25 June. The following apprenticed in Bristol: John Russell to Phillip Millard, 4 years Virginia. (BR).

27 June. The following apprenticed in Bristol: William Powell to Thomas Powell, 5 years Virginia. (BR).

29 June. The following apprenticed in Bristol: Thomas Weston to Robert Lawford, 4 years Virginia. (BR).

June. Probate of will of Ralph Storey of Wapping, Middlesex, who died in Virginia. (AW).

June. Probate of will of John Baker of St. Bride's, London, whose sister, Jane Gilbert, was in New England. (AW).

6 July. The following apprenticed in Bristol: William James to Richard Fielding, 4 years Virginia. (BR).

8 July. Oxford Circuit prisoners reprieved to be transported to Barbados. Berkshire: Elizabeth Williams of Hungerford; John Clifford of Inkpen; Jane Greenway of West Gynge; John Buckmaster of Kintbury. Gloucestershire: William Holliday of Bisley; Mary, wife of John Weaver of Kings Stanley; Richard Smart alias Aviland of Brimpsfield; Walter Greene of Quenington. Oxfordshire: Elizabeth Sharpe of North Newnton. Shropshire: Walter Davies of Shrewsbury. Staffordshire: Thomas Stringfellow of Hoar Cross; John Williams of Whittington; William Wilkinson of Hoar Cross; John Warburton of Stone; Barbara Gardner of Wednesbury. Worcestershire: Thomas Belcher of Bromsgrove; William Oakes of Bromsgrove. (PRO: C66/3066/23).

8 July. The following apprenticed in Bristol: Jonathan Baker to William Flettyer, 4 years Virginia. (BR).

9 July. The following apprenticed in Bristol: Francis Browne to David Fry, 4 years Virginia; Julian Leigh to Thomas Bonner, 4 years Virginia. (BR).

11 July. The following apprenticed in Bristol: Welthian Watkins to Thomas Owen, 4 years Virginia; Elinor Phillips to Owen Williams, 4 years Virginia. (BR).

12 July. Petition of merchants, planters and masters of ships to the King. There is a wicked custom to seduce or spirit away young persons to go as servants to the plantations and they pray that an appointment may be made under the Great Seal so that the names, ages, quality, place of birth and last residence of those desiring to go to the plantations may be registered. It is also proposed that an office be established for the transportation from the nearest port of all vagrants, rogues and idle persons, felons, vagabonds, gipsies and loose persons, and those resorting to unlicensed brothels; if they are under the age of 20 to be transported for four years and if over 20 for seven years. For want of such an office no account can be given of many persons of quality who were transported after the late rebellion. (CSPC).

13 July. Western Circuit prisoners reprieved to be transported to Barbados. Cornwall: Adam Hill of St. Cleer, tailor; Walter Mutchmore of Linkenhorne, tinner. Somerset: John Burge of Durleigh, husbandman; John Phillips Jr. of Milverton, husbandman; Thomas Gregory of Mells, husbandman; William Gullocke of Ileton, husbandman; Robert Gullocke of Ileton, husbandman; Robert Bennett of Horton; William Andrewes of Burnham, husbandman. Wiltshire: Philip Ranger of Warminster; Thomas Jones Jr. of Warminster. (PRO: C66/3066/21).

13 July. The following apprenticed in Bristol: Margaret Price to Thomas Poape, 4 years Virginia. (BR).

15 July. The following apprenticed in Bristol: Anne Clarke to Robert Lawford, 4 years Virginia; John Pillson to John Newman, 4 years Virginia; Grace Wayte to Bartholomew Chandler, 4 years Virginia; Christian Davis to same, 4 years Virginia. (BR).

18 July. The following apprenticed in Bristol: John Clymer to Roger Browne, 4 years Virginia. (BR).

19 July. The following apprenticed in Bristol: Mathew Lewis to John Boddenham, 5 years Virginia; Evan Lewis to John Hopkins, 5 years Virginia. (BR).

20 July. The following apprenticed in Bristol: Henry Baker to John Tucke, 6 years Virginia; Joane Baker to same, 6 years Virginia; Jane Cary to same, 7 years Virginia; Joane Cary to same, 7 years Virginia; Phillip Sanders to same, 7 years Virginia; John Sanders to same, 7 years Virginia; Margaret White to same, 7 years Virginia; Joane Sanders to same, 7 years Virginia; Evan Roberts to Henry Hosier, 4 years Virginia. (BR).

23 July. The following apprenticed in Bristol: Richard Allen to John Bodenham, 4 years Virginia. (BR).

24 July. The following apprenticed in Bristol: James Phillips to Thomas Gotherin, 4 years Virginia. (BR).

25 July. The following apprenticed in Bristol: Robert Evans to William Jelfe, 4 years Virginia; William Davis to Mathew Williams, 4 years Virginia. (BR).

25 July-31 August. Shippers by the *Isaac & Deborah*, Mr. John Tulley, bound from London for Virginia: Arthur Bayly, Christopher Johnson, Edward Swinson, John Lockey, John Currer, Thomas Toulson, Henry Collier, William Marritt, Cuthbert Witham. (PRO: E190/50/1, 50/20).

26 July. The following apprenticed in Bristol: Gerrard Warren to William Harford, 4 years Virginia. (BR).

27 July. The following apprenticed in Bristol: Robert Jones to David Clements, 4 years Virginia; Edward Bastine to Thomas Howell, 4 years Virginia. (BR).

28 July-2 September. Shippers by the *Duke of York*, Mr. Thomas James, bound from London for New England: John Jeffries, Ralph Triplett, Daniell Benyon, Richard Bray, John Harlewood, Gawin Corbett. (PRO: E190/50/1, 50/2).

29 July. The following apprenticed in Bristol: Anne Jenkins to William Frances, 5 years Barbados; William Kingsbury to John Williams, 4 years Virginia. (BR).

24 August. Justices of Westminster report that Peter Beane, Richard Winter, Thomas Hill, Joan Taylor and Susanna Menick, sturdy and incorrigible rogues found guilty at Quarter Sessions and imprisoned for four months, are ready to be transported. (APC).

24 August. Home counties prisoners reprieved to be transported to Barbados. Essex: Jane Talbott. Kent: Margaret Fowle, William Stenning, Edward Wise, Thomas Cliffe, William Bankes, Richard Crow, William Harrison, Edward Mathewes, John Iden, William Plummer. Surrey: William Conley, Richard Pettingale or Paddinghall, Jonathan Read, Thomas Stone, Thomas Tyler. Unspecified: Elizabeth Norman, John Summers, John Leigh, William Cowley, James Elliott. (PRO: C66/3066/17).

1 August. The following apprenticed in Bristol: Humphry Walker to Robert Lawford, 4 years Virginia; Paull Carter to William Ward, 4 years Virginia; Robert Blither to Thomas Jenins, 4 years Nevis; Nicholas Raggat to William Barnes, 4 years Nevis; Teague Lee to same, 7 years Nevis. (BR).

2 August. The following apprenticed in Bristol: Thomas Morgan to Thomas Cupit, 4 years Virginia. (BR).

3 August. The following apprenticed in Bristol: Lewis Stephens to William Millard, 4 years Virginia; Charity Jones to William Moore, 4 years Virginia. (BR).

3-11 August. Shippers by the *Mary*, Mr. Robert Pitts, bound from London for Virginia: William Martyn, John Greene, Thomas Browne, Thomas Webb, William Webb, John Boyd. (PRO: E190/50/1, 50/2).

4 August. The following apprenticed in Bristol: William Hossam to Richard Fielding, 4 years Virginia; Richard Curtis to Timothy Stamp, 5 years Virginia; Richard Wildgoose to same, 5 years Virginia; John Tayler to Abigal Lewis, 5 years Virginia; Katherine Semyer to Ezekiell Shepard, 4 years Virginia. (BR).

4 August. Newgate prisoners reprieved to be transported to Barbados. London: Grissell Hudson, spinster, alias wife of John Hudson; Jane Jones, spinster, alias wife of Richard Jones, aged 40; Ann Purse, spinster, alias wife of John Biggerton; Mary White alias Raven, widow aged 42; Ann Smith, spinster, alias wife of Michael Harris; Alice Saunders, spinster, alias wife of John Saunders; Elizabeth Serjeant, spinster; Mary Woodford, spinster; Matthew Burridge; Isaac Oliver; Gerrard Wayte alias White; Edward Taylor; Thomas Crumpe; James Keech; Martha Hackliut, spinster, alias wife of John Hackliut; Ursula Bunney, spinster; Elizabeth Harris, spinster; Mary Oliver, spinster, alias wife of Richard Oliver; John Savage; Jonas Pett. Middlesex: Elizabeth Wood of St. Giles Cripplegate; William Turner of Stepney; John Davis of Harrow; Fidelia Phillips of St. Giles in the Fields; Mary Marann of Stepney; John Purse of St. Giles Cripplegate; Thomas Woodward of St. Clement Danes; Henry Church of St. Andrew Holborn; Henry Ewen of Shoreditch; William Drinkwater of Shoreditch; John Smith of Shoreditch; Thomas Plowright of Shoreditch; William Purcell of St. Clement Danes; Roger Money of St. Clement Danes; Edward Godfrey of St. Andrew Holborn; Henry Thomas of St. Andrew Holborn; Bridget Harding alias Greene of St. Peter ad Vincula. (PRO: C66/3066/12).

5 August. The following apprenticed in Bristol: Mathew Hopwood to John Tuck, 5 years Virginia; Samuell Jones to same, 5 years Virginia; John Darby to David Fry, 5 years Virginia; John Johnson to William Dale, 4 years Virginia; Mathew Whitfield to same, 4 years Virginia. (BR).

7 August. The following apprenticed in Bristol: John Lovell to Jonathan Hurle, 4 years Virginia. (BR).

8 August. The following apprenticed in Bristol: John Evans to Richard Fielding, 4 years Virginia; Thomas Shall to John Igorne, 4 years Virginia; John Cox to Jenkin Bragg, 6 years Virginia. (BR).

9 August. The following apprenticed in Bristol: William James to Jenkin Bragg, 6 years Virginia. (BR).

10 August. The following apprenticed in Bristol: Edward Sapp to Thomas Millner, 4 years Virginia; Henry Price to Richard Fielding, 4 years Virginia. (BR).

11 August. The following apprenticed in Bristol: Elioner Davis to David Warren, 4 years Virginia. (BR).

12 August. The following apprenticed in Bristol: Ruth Barrat to David Warren, 4 years Virginia. (BR).

13 August. The following apprenticed in Bristol: Mary Walker to Humphrey Bonome, 4 years Virginia. (BR).

16 August. The following apprenticed in Bristol: John Addams to Anthony Cupit, 7 years Virginia; John Clarke to same, 7 years Virginia; William Roberts to John Bodenham, 4 years Virginia; Jane Bowen to Abraham Roome, 4 years Virginia; Thomas Priest to Christopher Atchly, 4 years Virginia; William Wattkins to same, 4 years Virginia; William Burdack to John Woory, 4 years Virginia. (BR).

16 August. Shipper by the *King Solomon*, Mr. Eric Croscombe, bound from London for Virginia: John Curier. (PRO: E190/50/2).

16 August-3 September. Shippers by the *Honour*, Mr. Robert Clems, bound from London for Virginia: Mary Stoner, Richard Booth, Richard Younge, Henry Burnell, Henry Andrewes, William Gould, Thomas Tomlins, John Port. (PRO: E190/50/1, 50/2).

17 August. Shipper by the *Virgin Queen*, Mr. Henry Crookes, bound from London for Virginia: John Jeffries. (PRO: E190/50/2).

17-25 August. Shippers by the *Golden Wheatsheaf*, Mr. James Conway, bound from London for Maryland and Virginia: Henry Grosse, George Cornish, James Godfrey, Thomas Martin. (PRO: E190/50/1, 50/2).

18 August. The following apprenticed in Bristol: Richard Beate to John Hisley, 5 years Virginia; Thomas Lewellen to Joseph Singer, 4 years Virginia. (BR).

19 August-1 September. Shippers by the *Brothers Adventure*, Mr. Juniper Plovier, bound from London for Virginia: Thomas Cockaine, Nicholas Jackson, Robert Glegg, Robert Wright. (PRO: E190/50/1, 50/2).

19 August-2 September. Shippers by the *Baltimore*, Mr. John Dunch, bound from London for Maryland: John Fullerton, Thomas Wills, John Long, John Gibbons. (PRO: E190/50/1, 50/2).

20-25 August. Shippers by the *Prince*, Mr. John Harrison, bound from London for Virginia: Thomas Ball, James Littlepaige. (PRO: E190/50/2).

20-29 August. Shippers by the *Golden Lion*, Mr. Thomas Harwood, bound from London for Virginia: Ralph Whisler, Anthony Stanford, John Tanner, Ralph Harwood. (PRO: E190/50/1, 50/2).

22 August. The following apprenticed in Bristol: Jane Dallen to Richard Fielding, 4 years Virginia. (BR).

23 August. The following apprenticed in Bristol: Edward Harding to John Beare, 4 years Virginia. (BR).

23 August-3 September. Shippers by the *Charles*, Mr. Samuell Cooper, bound from London for Virginia: Thomas Pearl, Thomas Lashington, James Jenkins, John Jeffries. (PRO: E190/50/1, 50/2).

25 August. The following apprenticed in Bristol: Grace Banner to Hugh Everett, 4 years Virginia; Mary Banner to same, 4 years Virginia. (BR).

25 August-8 September. Shippers by the *Richard & Francis* (elsewhere *Noah & Francis*), Mr. Robert Caning, bound from London for Virginia: Noah Floyd, John Currer, Thomas Grantam. (PRO: E190/50/1, 50/2).

25 August-26 September. Shippers by the *Tryall*, Mr. Samuell Scarlett, bound from London for New England: Benjamin Hewling, John Mansell, John Fullerton, Thomas Robinson, Thomas Stephson, William Thomas. (PRO: E190/50/1, 50/2).

26 August. The following apprenticed in Bristol: John Williams to Giles Merrick, 5 years Virginia; John Carter to Richard Collins, 5 years Virginia. (BR).

26 August. Shipper by the *Thomas*, Mr. Christopher Eveling, bound from London for Virginia: Benjamin Davis. (PRO: E190/50/2).

29 August. The following apprenticed in Bristol: John Whitten to Darby Conner, 4 years Virginia; James Phillips to Robert Noble, 4 years Virginia. (BR).

31 August. Shipper by the *Golden Fortune*, Mr. John Pearce, bound from London for Virginia: Abraham Lapworth. (PRO: E190/50/2).

August. Administration with will of Timothy Alsop of St. Mary Somerset, London, whose sister was in New England. (AW).

1 September. The following apprenticed in Bristol: Richard Avery to Richard Collins, 4 years Virginia; John Parsons to same, 4 years Virginia. (BR).

2 September. The following apprenticed in Bristol: Gilbert Lewis to Francis Webb, 4 years Virginia; Edward Hollister to same, 7 years Virginia; John Berrow to same, 4 years Virginia. (BR).

5 September. The following apprenticed in Bristol: Richard Taylor to Richard Collins, 4 years Virginia; Joane Tawer to John Vasser, 4 years Virginia; Mary Lambert to John Hopkins, 3 years Virginia. (BR).

5 September. Shippers by the *Elizabeth* of Weymouth, Mr. David Barker, bound from Weymouth for Virginia: Christopher Collier, John Tayler. (PRO: E190/879/12, 879/13).

5-12 September. Shippers by the *Henry & Francis* of Bideford, Mr. Richard Williams, bound from Barnstaple for Virginia: William Bellew, Abraham Heaman. (PRO: E190/954/2, 954/4).

9 September. The following apprenticed in Bristol: Edmund Tony to Thomas Walter, 6 years Virginia; Peter Tony to same, 7 years Virginia. (BR).

9 September. Petition by Francis Warner, Richard Russell and Richard Smith for the release of their ship *Blessing* which they sent on a voyage in 1662 to Guinea, Virginia and New England, but which was seized on her return to London. (APC).

10 September. The following apprenticed in Bristol: Elizabeth Powell to Thomas Mendam, 4 years Virginia. (BR).

10 September. Shipper by the *Edward*, Mr. Henry Avis, bound from London for Virginia: Edward Blake. (PRO: E190/50/1).

13 September. The following apprenticed in Bristol: Margaret Jones to Annis Lugg, 4 years Virginia. (BR).

15 September. London prisoner reprieved to be transported to Barbados: Alice Saunders. (PRO: C66/3066/13).

16 September. The following apprenticed in Bristol: Ambrose Lloyd to William Light, 4 years Virginia. (BR).

16 September. On a petition by Lord Baltimore who shipped servants aboard the *Reserve*, Mr. John Tully, bound for Maryland, the Governor of Plymouth, Devon, is reprimanded for allowing ashore those who claimed to have been spirited and ordered to send them back on board. (APC).

17 September-3 October. Shippers by the *John & Martha*, Mr. John Goff, bound from London for Virginia: William Bird; Thomas Grendon. (PRO: E190/50/1).

21 September. The following apprenticed in Bristol: John Willkins to Richard Arren, 4 years Virginia. (BR).

24 September. The following apprenticed in Bristol: John Roberts to Lewis Roberts, 4 years Virginia. (BR).

26 September. The following apprenticed in Bristol: William Perryman to Thomas Brereton, 9 years Nevis; Mary Phillips to Richard Collins, 4 years Virginia; John Jusale to William Light, 5 years Virginia; Margaret Haines to Elizabeth Riser, 4 years Virginia. (BR).

26-27 September. Shippers by the *Seaflower* of Bridlington, Mr. Samuell Tucker, bound from Lyme Regis for Virginia: Robert Beard; Thomas Haxby; Walter Tucker & Co.; John Waad. (PRO: E190/879/11).

28 September. Shipper at Weymouth by the *Prosperous Margaret* of Portsmouth bound from Southampton for Virginia: Robert Napper. (PRO: E190/879/13).

September. Probate of will of Elizabeth Hailes of Shadwell, Stepney, Middlesex, whose cousin, William Foster, was in New England. (AW).

September. Administration of John Ludlow of Virginia, bachelor. (AW).

1 October. The following apprenticed in Bristol: Jonathan Phillips to Thomas Jennings, 6 years Nevis. (BR).

5 October. The following apprenticed in Bristol: William Harford to Thomas Allen, 4 years Virginia. (BR).

7 October. The following apprenticed in Bristol: Nathaniell Mathews to Thomas Stark (or Stack), 4 years Nevis. (BR).

10 October. The following apprenticed in Bristol: William Smarte to Joseph Perks, 4 years Virginia; John Hawkins to same, 6 years Virginia; Thomas Hemens to same, 7 years Virginia; Elizabeth Merrick to same, 8 years Virginia. (BR).

11 October. The following apprenticed in Bristol: Elizabeth Protheroe to John Hopkins, 4 years Virginia. (BR).

12 October. The following apprenticed in Bristol: John Phillips to John Hopkins, 4 years Virginia. (BR).

13 October. The following apprenticed in Bristol: John Foard to Robert Stephens, 13 years Virginia; John Harle to Anne Butcher, 7 years Virginia. (BR).

19 October. The following apprenticed in Bristol: John Gurlen to Elizabeth Berrow, 5 years Nevis or Leewards. (BR).

22 October. Deposition by Henry Goldham of London, goldsmith aged 26 that by deed of 6 June 1657 Francis Norton of Charles Town, New England, merchant, became indebted to Thomas Pettit, citizen and cutler of London. Pettit assigned the bond to Samuel Gardner, citizen and fishmonger of London, who has appointed Peter Ledget of Charles Town, merchant, as attorney.

Thomas Pettit, aged 33, deposes that on 30 March 1659 he received part payment from John Farthing. Samuel Gardner, aged 32, deposes that he has received no payment. (LMCD).

24 October. The following apprenticed in Bristol: Symon Warland to Thomas Bartlett, 4 years Nevis; William Holliman to same, 4 years Nevis. (BR).

25 October-8 November. Shippers by the *Accomack*, Mr. Thomas Smith, bound from London for Virginia: Henry Bonner, Edward Buckridge. (PRO: E190/50/1).

31 October. Prisoners in Isle of Ely, Cambridgeshire, reprieved to be transported to Barbados: Nathaniel Denston, George Harpum, Edward Chapman, Thomas Whitecake. (PRO: C66/3066/10).

October. Probate of will of Throckmorton Trotman of St. Giles Cripplegate, London, whose cousin was in Virginia. (AW).

October. Elizabeth, wife of Edward Ford, sentenced at Middlesex Sessions to be transported to Barbados. (EB).

3 November. The following apprenticed in Bristol: Joane Burt to John Hopkins, 4 years Virginia; Lidiah Silvester to Mary Scott, 4 years Virginia; Bartholomew Romayne to Jane Banks, 4 years Nevis. (BR).

7 November. The following apprenticed in Bristol: Mary Latt to Cicely Mottis, 5 years Barbados; John Ames to John Hopkins, 4 years Virginia. (BR).

8 November. The following apprenticed in Bristol: Elioner Pearce to John Wiseman, 4 years Barbados. (BR).

9 November. The following apprenticed in Bristol: James Smith to Hugh Everett, 4 years Virginia; John Moore to John Bennt, 4 years Virginia. (BR).

12 November. The following apprenticed in Bristol: John Downe to Phillip Smith, 4 years Virginia. (BR).

15 November. The following apprenticed in Bristol: Prudence Westbury to Jasper Crosse, 4 years Virginia. (BR).

16 November. The following apprenticed in Bristol: Elizabeth Lewis to John Hopkins, 4 years Virginia; Saye Thomas to same, 4 years Virginia; Jacob Cheltnam to Jasper Crosse, 4 years Virginia. (BR).

18 November. The following apprenticed in Bristol: Richard Williams to Edward Tattnell, 5 years Virginia; Robert Chew to John Hopkins, 3 years Virginia. (BR).

23 November. The following apprenticed in Bristol: Sarah Dowlas to Jasper Crosse, 4 years Virginia; James Stampe to Hugh Everett, 3 years Virginia; Joane Pitts to same, 3 years Virginia. (BR).

24 November. The following apprenticed in Bristol: Elizabeth Cullock to Robert Pratt, 4 years Barbados. (BR).

29 November. Shipper by the *America*, Mr. William Canaham, bound from London for Carolina: Peter Cartrett. (PRO: E190/50/1).

29 November. Licence granted for five years to Sir James Modyford, Governor of Jamaica, to take all the felons convicted at the Old Bailey and on the circuits who are reprieved for transportation. (PRO: SP44/14/46).

3 December. The following apprenticed in Bristol: George Borse to Jane Wattkins, 7 years Nevis; William Evans to Stephen Taylor, 4 years Nevis. (BR).

7 December. The Sheriff of Hertfordshire is ordered to apprehend and transport Nicholas Lucas, Henry Feste, Henry Marshall, Francis Pryor, John Blendall, Jeremiah Hearne and Samuel Treherne who were convicted at the Hertfordshire Assizes, put aboard the *Anne* of London, Mr. Thomas May, to be transported, but put ashore at the Downs. Mr. May is to be arrested. (APC).

9 December. The following apprenticed in Bristol: William Reece to James Sterry, 5 years Nevis. (BR).

12 December. The following apprenticed in Bristol: David Davis to Elizabeth Webb, 4 years Barbados; William Harvey to Stephen Tayler, 6 years Nevis. (BR).

16 December. The following apprenticed in Bristol: Samuell Kellsar to Sarah Kippen, 7 years Barbados. (BR).

19 December. The following apprenticed in Bristol: John Roe to Richard Bigglestone, 4 years Nevis or Caribbees. (BR).

20 December. The following apprenticed in Bristol: Rothero Price to John Paine, 4 years Barbados; Joseph Paine to Thomas Godman, 3 years Nevis; Morgan Williams to Moses Haskins, 7 years Nevis; Thomas Speede to William Liston, 4 years Barbados. (BR).

29 December. The following apprenticed in Bristol: Phillip Dowle to Edward Hopkins, 3 years Nevis; Thomas Morgan to Charles Jones, 7 years Nevis; William Brooke to John Allen, 3 years Nevis; Thomas Williams to same, 4 years Nevis. (BR).

31 December. The following apprenticed in Bristol: David Gaines to James Sterry, 4 years Nevis. (BR).

1665

2 January. Shipper by the *Success*, Mr. Richard Covill, bound from London for Virginia: Edward Bourne. (PRO: E190/50/4).

7 January. Certificate by members of the ship's company of the *Mary Fortune* of Bristol that they put on shore three Quakers on 6 December last when they were brought to the ship to be transported because they dared not carry away innocent persons. (CSPC).

13 January. The Governors of Virginia and Maryland are instructed that ships returning to England are to go in convoy because of the shortage of seamen and the risk of capture by the Dutch. (APC).

15 January. The following apprenticed in Bristol: Edward Pounty to Thomas Jefferis, 4 years Barbados. (BR).

20 January. Robert Dutch of St. Katherine by the Tower, London, yeoman, found guilty of attempting to transport Ralph Bradshaw to Virginia by the *Elizabeth & Mary* and to sell him there. (VM 83/3).

23 January. The following apprenticed in Bristol: Edmund Thomas to Mary Pearson, 7 years Barbados. (BR).

29 January. The following prisoners held at Westminster are to be transported: Robert Bowley, William Grey, Moses Biggon, John Otter, William Downing, Ellen Downing his wife, Thomas Bradford, Margaret Bradford his wife, William Naylor, Abraham Barron, John Osborne, John Norton and James Partridge. (APC).

31 January. The following apprenticed in Bristol: John Parker to James Light, 4 years Barbados. (BR).

January. Probate of will of Richard Lee of Stratford Langton, Essex, who died in Virginia. (AW).

January. Petition of Thomas Pittman, Thomas Grigge, Mark Jarvis, John Lovicke & Co., owners of the *Recovery* which has been lying at Gravesend for five weeks waiting to sail for Virginia. She carries nearly 40 passengers, "persons utterly useless to this Kingdom and of an idle course of life" who will seek any opportunity of escaping. They pray that the embargo may be lifted. (CSPC).

January. John Francis Triponet of St. Sepulchre, goldsmith; Margaret Welsby of St. Sepulchre, widow; and Ann Hayley of St. Sepulchre, widow, sentenced at Middlesex Sessions to be transported to Jamaica for attendance at unlawful religious assembly. (EB).

1 February. The following apprenticed in Bristol: John Jones to Richard Gibson, 3 years Nevis. (BR).

6 February. The following apprenticed in Bristol: William Pullen to John Thomas, 6 years Barbados. (BR).

9 February. The following apprenticed in Bristol: Susanna Sawfutt to Robert Dapwell, 4 years Nevis; Susanna Jones to same, 4 years Nevis. (BR).

15 February. The following apprenticed in Bristol: Robert Arter to John Robs, 4 years Nevis. (BR).

16 February. The following apprenticed in Bristol: Mathew Wall to Osmond Crabb, 4 years Nevis; William Harbett to same, 4 years Nevis. (BR).

20 February. The following apprenticed in Bristol: Thomas Turner to John Robs, 3 years Nevis. (BR).

23 February. The following apprenticed in Bristol: Peter Launte to Robert Dapwell, 4 years Nevis. (BR).

23 February. Oxford Circuit prisoners reprieved to be transported to Barbados. Berkshire: Elizabeth Idens of Lambourn Woodlands, spinster; John Carter of Radley. Buckinghamshire: Thomas Phillips of Charleton. Gloucestershire: Paul Niccols of Bickleton; John Jones of Cheltenham. Oxfordshire: John Cumber of Milton, joiner. Staffordshire: Edward Bott of Wolverhampton; Isaac Creswell of the same; Edward Holmes of Huntingdon; John Sugar of Newcastle under Lyme. Worcestershire: John Harrington of Hallow. John Stephens. (PRO: C66/3073/24).

23 February. Western Circuit prisoners reprieved to be transported to Barbados. Cornwall: Sidrach Sacke of St. Stephen Branwell, husbandman. Devon: Henry Jenkins of Morchard Bishops, husbandman; William Heyne of Thorncombe. Hampshire: Nathaniel Wateridge of Hursley; William North of Hursley; William Humber of Bullington. Somerset: John Cole of Whatley; George Chippett alias Sansome of Henstridge, husbandman; John Browne of Plucknett, husbandman. Wiltshire: Edward Dewe of Warminster, husbandman; Edward Dowsewell of Purton; Humphrey Jarvis of Hacklestone. (PRO: C66/3073/25).

25 February. The following apprenticed in Bristol: Thomas Dave to William C——, 5 years Nevis. (BR).

February. Middlesex prisoners reprieved to be transported to Jamaica: John Westwood; John Pound; Anne Walton; John Austin; Thomas Roberts; Samuel Gilmore; Francis Benbow; Richard Coney; John Weekes; John Symons; Grace Beechley, for housebreaking. (EB).

2-23 March. Shippers by the *Lady*, Mr. John Pears, bound from London for New England: John Tayler, Noah Floyd, Richard Michell, Samuell Wilson, Nicholas Roberts, James Porter, Daniell Bridge, William Smith, John

76

Harwood, Richard Boyleston, Henry Ashurst, Robert Barton, Edmond White, John Fuller, William Barrett, John Bodesey, John Cornish. (PRO: E190/50/4).

7 March. Warrant to the Lord Chief Justice for the speedy disposal of those Quakers who have been condemned to be transported, calling to mind their more than ordinary insolence and the fact that there are now several ships in the Thames bound for the plantations. (SP Dom).

8 March. The following ships are appointed to carry condemned Quakers to the plantations:

Jamaica Merchant, Mr. William Gainsford, to take three Quakers to Jamaica;

John & Thomas, Mr. John Ceely, to take six Quakers to Barbados;

Amity of London, Mr. Francis Appleby, to take seven Quakers to Nevis. (APC).

15 March. Sixty Quakers now in Newgate Prison are to go to Jamaica by the *Black Eagle* of London, Mr. William Fudge, and fifty to Barbados by the *Sarah* of London, Mr. John Limbrey. (APC).

22 March. London prisoners reprieved to be transported to Jamaica: Susan Andrewes; Thomas Carryer; John Ward; Dorothy Betteris; Robert Motley; Roger Pinson; Elizabeth Long, spinster, alias wife of William; Alice Hull, spinster, alias wife of George; Rachel Barlow; John Bullocke; Anthony Gregory; Susan Stone alias Butler; Dorothy Tommey. (PRO: C66/3074/10).

1 April. Petition of John Porter Jr. of Salem, New England. For sixteen months he has been imprisoned in Boston for rebellion against his parents, having been made to stand for an hour by the gallows with a rope around his neck, then given 30 lashes and fined. (CSPC).

11 April. Deposition by John Arnold Esq. of London, aged 23, that in June 1662 he was often with Mr. John Norton, Minister of Boston, New England, brother of Thomas Norton of London, merchant, sole executor of the will of Thomas Brownest of Putney, Surrey, deceased, and father of John Norton, infant, who is the nephew of Rev. Norton. John Norton told the deponent that his brother, William Norton of New England, had assigned to him a legacy made to him by Thomas Brownest. Before he returned to New England, Rev. Norton had told his cousin, John Norton, that, if they should not meet again, he should benefit from the legacy. (LMCD).

28 April. Paul Hobson, a prisoner in the Tower of London, is permitted to embark for Carolina on condition that he does not return. (APC).

April. Probate of will of Samuel Style of Portugal, whose sister, Elizabeth Style, was in New England. (AW).

2 May. Newgate prisoners reprieved to be transported to Barbados: Stephen Collins, Nicholas Collins, Teague Connell, John Allen, Abraham Randall, Joseph Nelson, John Parker, Edward Elcocke, Edward Harris, Richard Esden,

William Blackburne, John Brooke, John Tapsfield, Edward Beamhouse, Frances Hulman, spinster, George Hopkin, Peter Scrivener, William Williams, Matthew Evans, Thomas Whitfield. (PRO: C66/3073/20).

4 May. The following apprenticed in Bristol: Richard Anderson to Robert Dymock, 5 years Barbados. (BR).

5 May. The following apprenticed in Bristol: David Price to Reece Jones, 5 years Nevis. (BR).

8 May. The following apprenticed in Bristol: Evan Rowland to Richard Gibson, 4 years Nevis. (BR).

9 May. The following apprenticed in Bristol: Mary Russell to Thomas Sparks, 4 years Nevis; William Tompkins to Robert Hilsly, 5 years Nevis; Henry Leafe to George Warren, 4 years Nevis; John Edwards to [Francis] Borne, 4 years Nevis. (BR).

22 May. The following apprenticed in Bristol: Richard Douty to Joane Wattkins, 5 years Nevis. (BR).

23 May. The following apprenticed in Bristol: William Sommers to Sarah Harding, 5 years Nevis; John Roach to John Nicholls, 1 year New England; Thomas Jones to William Attkins, 4 years Barbados. (BR).

25 May-2 June. Shippers by the ——alias *David Robin* bound from London for Virginia: —— Carpenter, Patrick Ward, Thomas Copley, James Littleton, Phillip Heron, John Cooke, William Strode, Jonathan Ash. (PRO: E190/50/4).

30 May. The following apprenticed in Bristol: Joane Woollams to Robert Dymock, 6 years Barbados. (BR).

May. Probate of will of John Cheeseman of Bermondsey, Surrey, who had lands in Virginia. (AW).

May. Probate of will of John Clarke of Great Yarmouth, Norfolk, mariner, master of the ship *Unity*, who died in Virginia. (AW).

May. Probate of will of Ralph Hooker of Barbados who died overseas and whose cousin, Richard Bennett, was in New England. (AW).

1 June. Deposition by John Ive of London, merchant aged 30, that in October 1664 he was factor in London for Nehemiah Bourne of Rotterdam and received goods to his account from Francis Willoughby of Charles Town, New England, by the *Society* of London, Mr. John Pevice. (LMCD).

3 June. The following apprenticed in Bristol: Humphry Clifford to Mary Mathews, 4 years Nevis. (BR).

14 June. The following apprenticed in Bristol: William Davis to Robert Haskins, 4 years Nevis. (BR).

22 June. The following apprenticed in Bristol: John Inion to Edward Pearce, 4 years Virginia. (BR).

26 June. The following apprenticed in Bristol: Walter Ciclett to John Weaver, 5 years Virginia; William Waters to same, 3 years Virginia. (BR).

June. Administration of John Taylor of Whitechapel, Middlesex, who died in Virginia. (AW).

June. Probate of will of Mary Godwyn of Lyme Regis, Dorset, widow, whose brother, William Hill, was in New England.

June. Ann Mayd reprieved at Middlesex Assizes to be transported to Barbados. (EB).

22 June. Western Circuit prisoners reprieved to be transported to Barbados. Devon: James Jones of Burrington, husbandman; Wilmot Ragman of Kings Nympton, spinster; Nicholas Toope of Rattery, cordwainer. Wiltshire: Emanuel Gilham of Hyndon, victualler. (PRO: C66/3074/100).

24 June. Newgate prisoners reprieved to be transported to Barbados. London: Grissell Hudson, spinster; Elizabeth Martin, spinster; Jane Wharton alias Jones, spinster; Martha Browne, spinster; John Huntresse; Thomas Whiteing; Anne Ward, spinster; Alice Hucklebone, spinster, alias wife of Ralph London; Anne Watts, spinster; Margaret Ramsden, spinster; John Copeland, scissor maker; Thomas Ward; Mary Tremayne, spinster; John Scriven; Gideon Mills; Richard Little; Richard Jones. Middlesex: James Newton of Stepney; Edward Potter of Stepney; Rebecca Clarke of Whitechapel; Oliver Cotton of St. Andrew Holborn, joiner; Humphrey Knight of Clerkenwell; John Hooke of Stepney; Florence Biscoe of St. Giles in the Fields; Thomas Scott of St. Giles Cripplegate; Henry Cole of Stepney; Thomas Owen of St. Martin in the Fields. (PRO: C66/3074/99).

5 July. The following Quakers condemned at the Hertfordshire Sessions to be transported to the plantations other than Virginia or New England by the *Nicholas* of London, Captain Gates: Nicholas Lucas, Francis Pryer, Henry Feast, Henry Marshall, Jeremiah Herne, Robert Crooke, Robert Fairman, Richard Thomas, John Brestbone, Henry Stent, Lewis Lawndey, Thomas Messe, William Burr, Robert Hart, Henry Sweeting, William Larkin, Mary Whittenbury, Samuel Wollestone, Thomas Crawley, Edward Parkin, John Witham, William Adams, John Thurrowgood, Jeremiah Deane, John Picket, William Fairman. Also to be transported by the same ship: John Blindall, Samuell Treherne, Thomas Burr and Michael Day. (APC, EB).

5 July. Shipper by the *Black Cock*, Mr. Robert Lock, bound from London for New England: Sir William Warren. (PRO: E190/50/4).

7 July. Shipper by the *Dolphin*, Mr. William Foster, bound from London for New England: said William Foster. (PRO: E190/50/4).

12 July. The following apprenticed in Bristol: John Coales to Richard Ward, 4 years Virginia. (BR).

13 July. On the death of John Woodward, the office of Master of the Royal Mint has become vacant and is to be held by John Brattle in the absence of Thomas Woodward, father of the said John, who is at a plantation in York River, Virginia, if he is still alive. (CSPC).

July. Petition of the inhabitants of Portsmouth and Strawberry Bank for protection against the Government of Massachusetts signed by: Francis Champernowne, Abraham Corbet, John Pickering, Anthony Bracket, Francis Drake, James Johnson, John Shirborne, Nathaniel Drake, Edward Clark, Samuel Fernauld, Francis Ran, John Partridge, William Cotten, Richard Sloper, George Wallis, Mark Hunking, John Johnson, John Berry, John Frost, Joseph Atkinson, John Jones, Henry Savage, Francis Jones, William Hearle, Thomas Avery, George Walton, Samuel Roby, Edward West, George Gray, Thomas Fallingsby, John Tanner and George Drake. (CSPC).

July. Probate of will of George Elliot who died overseas, mariner, (bound for Virginia in the ship *Accomack*). (AW).

3 August. The following apprenticed in Bristol: Walter Harris to John Goulder, 4 years Virginia. (BR).

7 August. The following apprenticed in Bristol: John Creede to William Morgan, 3 years Virginia; Richard Tracy to same, 4 years Virginia; Henry Lewis to same, 3 years Virginia; Anne Bassett to same, 3 years Virginia; Henry Rogers to William Bullock, 5 years Virginia. (BR).

9 August. The following apprenticed in Bristol: Robert Brookbanke to Joseph Tucker, 4 years Virginia; John Signett to Christopher Berrow, 4 years Virginia; Richard Fryer to same, 4 years Virginia; Sarah Smith to same, 4 years Virginia; Elias Lee to John Hopkins, 7 years Virginia; William Russell to Anthony Noakes, 4 years Virginia. (BR).

10 August. The following apprenticed in Bristol: Elizabeth Harris to John Crabb, 5 years Virginia. (BR).

12 August. Home Circuit prisoners reprieved to be transported to Jamaica. Hertfordshire: Robert Carman, Richard Hawkesley. Kent: Valentine Jagoe or Jacob, John Partington. Surrey: William Wright, John Smithier, Thomas Keach, John Church. Unidentified: Richard Armitage, John East, Francis Mountague, Francis Lilley. (EB & PRO: C66/3074/95).

12 August. The following apprenticed in Bristol: Walter Crow to John Walter, 5 years Virginia. (BR).

14 August. The following apprenticed in Bristol: Thomas Mudd to Anthony Noaks, 3 years Virginia; John Hotter to Henry Rich, 4 years Virginia; Gartrude Madler to Walter Gorway, 4 years Virginia; James Edwards to William

Morgan, 4 years Virginia; Richard Pew to John Golder, 4 years Virginia; Robert Holderly to John Weaver, 4 years Virginia. (BR).

15 August. The following apprenticed in Bristol: Mary Johnson to Anthony Berrow, 4 years Virginia. (BR).

17 August. The following apprenticed in Bristol: John Jenkins to Abraham Lewes, 4 years Virginia; Ursula Palmer to Christopher Berrow, 4 years Virginia. (BR).

18 August. The following apprenticed in Bristol: Elizabeth Streete to James Streete, 4 years Virginia; William Richards to William Morgan, 6 years Virginia. (BR).

19 August. The following apprenticed in Bristol: Richard Hatchnutt to Sarah Symond, 4 years Virginia. (BR).

21 August. Shipper by the *Elizabeth* of Weymouth, Mr. Thomas Barker, bound from Lyme Regis for Virginia: Walter Tucker & Co. (PRO: E190/880/2).

21 August. The following apprenticed in Bristol: Richard Sadler to Francis Morgan, 4 years Virginia. (BR).

22 August. The following apprenticed in Bristol: Nicholas Martin to Lot Richards, 4 years Virginia; Christopher Slattford to same, 4 years Virginia; Margaret Lewis to Joane Sheppard, 4 years Virginia; Thomas Pinson to Richard Middlecutt, 4 years Virginia. (BR).

23 August. The following apprenticed in Bristol: John Hobson to Alexander Williams, 4 years Virginia. (BR).

24 August. The following apprenticed in Bristol: Mary Thomas to William Downing, 4 years Virginia; Margaret Turner to William Morgan, 4 years Virginia; Joane Jenings to Jenkins Bragg, 4 years Virginia; Phillip Clay to Henry Rich, 4 years Virginia. (BR).

26 August. The following apprenticed in Bristol: Thomas Osburne to William Poore, 4 years Virginia; Edward Dangerfield to Robert Bryan, 5 years Maryland; Morgan Thomas to William Morgan, 3 years Virginia. (BR).

28 August. The following apprenticed in Bristol: Thomas Williams to Sarah Simons, 3 years Virginia; Phillip Thomas to Joane Sheppard, 3 years Virginia; James Monck to Edward Poore, 4 years Virginia. (BR).

29 August. Shipper by the *Exchange* of Bideford, Mr. William Titherly, bound from Barnstaple for New England: John Manning. (PRO: E190/954/6).

29 August. The following apprenticed in Bristol: John Jones to Joane Sheppard, 7 years Virginia; Elizabeth Baily to John Hopkins, 3 years Virginia; Richard Smith to John Scott, 4 years Virginia. (BR).

30 August. Shippers by the *Providence* of Lyme, Mr. Robert Fowler, bound from Lyme Regis for Virginia: Walter Tucker & Co., John Lisle, John Taylor. (PRO: E190/954/6).

30 August. The following apprenticed in Bristol: Henry Lane to Henry Williams, 7 years Virginia; Rebecka Robins to William Rogers, 4 years Virginia; William Willis to Richard Godwin, 4 years Virginia; Thomas Edwards to Thomas Tucke, 4 years Virginia; Phillip Payton to Thomas White, 4 years Virginia; Richard Smith to same, 7 years Virginia; Mary Tayler to same, 4 years Virginia; Anne Smith to same, 4 years Virginia; Phillip Browne to James Braithwaite, 4 years Virginia; Anne Ernell to John Weaver, 4 years Virginia; Richard Jenkins to William Morgan, 4 years Virginia; Joseph Williams to Richard Fielding, 4 years Virginia. (BR).

August. Probate of will of Martin Simpson of Hackney, Middlesex, whose niece, Hester Simpson, was in New England. (AW).

1 September. The following apprenticed in Bristol: Rowland Willson to Richard Granger, 4 years Virginia. (BR).

2 September. The following apprenticed in Bristol: Margaret Morris to Sarah Williams, 6 years Virginia; Samuell Elliott to Edward Wallis, 4 years Virginia. (BR).

4 September. Shipper by the *Phillip* of Bideford, Mr. Edmond Pickard, bound from Barnstaple for Virginia: Nicholas Sweete. (PRO: E190/954/6).

4 September. The following apprenticed in Bristol: Job Upton to William Bowyer, 4 years Virginia; Timothy Rogers to James Weaver, 4 years Virginia; Avis Row to same, 4 years Virginia. (BR).

5 September. Western Circuit prisoners reprieved to be transported to Barbados. Devon: Robert Halle of Ottery St. Mary, tanner; William Mountstephen of Payhembury, husbandman; Henry Popham alias Rowsall of Morchard Bishop, husbandman. Somerset: Lewis Evans of Higham, husbandman; Samuel Cousins of North Petherton, husbandman; Alexander Phillis of Stogumber, husbandman; Thomas Howe of Bagborough, husbandman; John Cole of Taunton, husbandman. Wiltshire: Thomas Waterland of New Sarum, husbandman; John Alford of Tisbury; William Dicke of Hankerton. (PRO: C66/3074/94).

7 September. Will of Arthur Pyne, citizen and cordwainer of London, who daughter, Hannah Johnson, was in Accamack, Virginia. (NGSQ 76/3).

7 September. The following apprenticed in Bristol: Lewis Davis to George Moody, 4 years Virginia; Jane Powell to same, 4 years Virginia; John Thomas to Mary Banister, 4 years Virginia; John Hiley to Thomas White, 7 years Virginia; William Fowle to same, 4 years Virginia; Benjamin Morratt to same, 4 years Virginia; Leonard Wray to John Crabb, 4 years Virginia; Rebecka Wray to same, 4 years Virginia; Elizabeth Beard to William Derrick, 4 years Virginia. (BR).

8 September. The following apprenticed in Bristol: Thomas Buttler to Thomas Sears, 4 years Virginia; John Grafton to William Sanders, 4 years Virginia; John Price to David Tucker, 4 years Virginia; John Viner to Abraham Lewis, 4 years Virginia; Elizabeth Evans to George Tyce, 4 years Virginia; Richard Walling to John Colburne, 4 years Virginia. (BR).

9 September. The following apprenticed in Bristol: Anne Crasway to George Tyce, 7 years Virginia; Richard Godfrey to Jasper Crasse, 4 years Virginia; Nicholas Houlder to John Webb, 4 years Virginia. (BR).

11 September. The following apprenticed in Bristol: Elizabeth Jones to David Tucker, 4 years Virginia; Mary Kempe to George Tyce, 4 years Virginia. (BR).

12 September. The following apprenticed in Bristol: Aron Powell to John Strattford, 5 years Virginia; Edward Bowen to George Tyce, 3 years Virginia; Henry Knapp to John Reede, 4 years Virginia; Mary Lane to Anne Salter, 5 years Virginia. (BR).

13 September. The following apprenticed in Bristol: Robert Curtis to Thomas Tucky, 4 years Virginia. (BR).

15 September. George Lewis to Edward Eybury, 4 years Virginia; John Alford to Robert Franck, 4 years Virginia. (BR).

16 September. The following apprenticed in Bristol: Charity Love to Thomas Hyatt, 4 years Virginia; Thomas Dale to Christopher Birkhead, 3 years Virginia; John Lyne to John Smith, 4 years Virginia. (BR).

18 September. The following apprenticed in Bristol: John Gill to Thomas Ellis, 3 years Virginia; Joane Young to Mary Wasbrow, 4 years Virginia. (BR).

19 September. The following apprenticed in Bristol: Sarah Griffen to Sarah Simons, 4 years Virginia; Peter Morgan to Jasper Crasse, 4 years Virginia; Morgan Thomas to same, 4 years Virginia; Thomas Wadly to Mary Banister, 7 years Virginia; John Player to Henry Rich, 7 years Virginia; William Lansdowne to Phillip Bisse, 9 years Virginia. (BR).

20 September. The following apprenticed in Bristol: John Lumpe to Richard Haskins, 4 years Virginia; Richard Davis to same, 4 years Virginia; Thomas Williams to Robert Dancer, 6 years Virginia. (BR).

22 September. The following apprenticed in Bristol: Elizabeth Hale to Margaret Winstone, 4 years Virginia; Sarah Horrad to Jacob Coote, 4 years Virginia; John Bullgam to Mary Banister, 4 years Virginia; Benjamin Bramsgrove to Richard Granger, 4 years Virginia; Anne Pearce to Francis Ludlow, 4 years Virginia; Susanna Hull to William Morgan, 6 years Virginia; David Jones to Robert Tyte, 3 years Virginia. (BR).

25 September. The following apprenticed in Bristol: Thomas Wales to William Jelfe, 4 years Virginia; William Jocklin to Thomas Ellis, 3 years Virginia; John Close to Arnold Collins, 4 years Virginia; Giles Wilkins to same, 3 years Virginia; John Richards to John Hopkins, 4 years Virginia; Thomas Roach to William Christy, 5 years Virginia; William Winbury to Thomas Millner, 4 years Virginia; Mathew Shellam to same, 4 years Virginia. (BR).

26 September. The following apprenticed in Bristol: Samuell Gardner to John Driver, 4 years Virginia; Christopher Cary to Thomas Sears, 3 years Virginia. (BR).

27 September. The following apprenticed in Bristol: Gabriell Trusty to Thomas Pope, 7 years Virginia; Robert Stone to same, 4 years Virginia; John Tether to same, 4 years Virginia; Edward Garnesy to same, 4 years Virginia; William Greene to Frances Morgan, 10 years Virginia; Phillip Williams to Thomas Milliner, 9 years Virginia; John Larcume to Richard Channell, 4 years Virginia. (BR).

28 September. The following apprenticed in Bristol: Sarah Marsfield to Mary Banister, 4 years Virginia; Nathaniell Tovey to Margaret Winstone, 2 years Virginia; Abraham Pullen to same, 4 years Virginia; Anne Stock to Sarah Matts, 4 years Virginia. (BR).

29 September. The following apprenticed in Bristol: Robert Love to David Tucker, 4 years Virginia; Richard Travis to John Wathen, 4 years Virginia. (BR).

30 September. The following apprenticed in Bristol: Margaret Davis to William Millden, 4 years Virginia; Samuell Baker to same, 4 years Virginia; James Coles to Roger Tayler, 4 years Virginia; Elizabeth Wood to Sarah Matts, 4 years Virginia; James Edwards to Stephen Watts, 4 years Virginia; Elizabeth Young to John Young, 4 years Virginia; Sarah Parker to Frances Tippett, 4 years Virginia; John Mayo to William Bonner, 5 years Virginia; Roger Miles to Anthony Alderson, 4 years Virginia; Thomas Buttler to George Brent, 6 years Virginia; William Marshall to same, 7 years Virginia; John Ward to same, 6 years Virginia; Robert Marshall to same, 3 years Virginia; Edward Collins to same, 7 years Virginia; John Frances to same, 7 years Virginia; Lettice Powell to Henry Daniell, 4 years Virginia. (BR).

September. The Mayor and merchants of Bristol petition for a convoy to be sent to Virginia to bring back 24 ships, a greater number than was intended, in order to protect them against the Dutch. (CSPC).

September. Probate of will of John Snooke of St. Clement Danes, Middlesex, who had lands in Virginia. (AW).

2 October. The following apprenticed in Bristol: Sibbell Higg to John Hallatt, 4 years Virginia; Margery Dee to Thomas Perks, 4 years Virginia; Elizabeth Linard to Richard Reede, 4 years Virginia; Anne Steevens to Elizabeth Hoare,

4 years Virginia; John Chares to John Pickering, 4 years Virginia; Margery Wathen to William Millden, 4 years Virginia. (BR).

3 October. The following apprenticed in Bristol: John Steevens to Richard Middlecutt, 7 years Virginia; Richard Steevens to same, 7 years Virginia; Elizabeth Emblin to same, 4 years Virginia; Mary Tayler to Susan Tompson, 4 years Virginia; Susanna Bick to John Hopkins, 4 years Virginia; Joane Tower to same, 4 years Virginia; John Gamerell to Jenkin Bragg, 4 years Virginia; William Nock to Henry Smith, 4 years Virginia; Richard Chambers to same, 4 years Virginia; William Webb to same, 4 years Virginia; George White to Edward Webb, 4 years Virginia; Elizabeth Tayler to Jacob Tompson, 4 years Virginia; William Raberson to Thomas Winston, 4 years Virginia. (BR).

6 October. Shipper by the *Samuell* of Bideford, Mr. Henry Pardon, bound from Barnstaple for Virginia: Abraham Heaman. (PRO: E190/954/6).

6 October. The following apprenticed in Bristol: Nicholas Edwards to Arthur Tanner, 4 years Barbados; William Cunnaut to same, 4 years Barbados; Robert Toms to same, 4 years Barbados; Elizabeth Nock to Henry Smith, 4 years Virginia; Thomas Arrowsmith to Gilbert Rosser, 3 years Virginia. (BR).

7 October. The following apprenticed in Bristol: Thomas Jones to Francis Burne, 4 years Nevis; Walter Preece to John Gibbs, 4 years Virginia; John Davis to William Harcume, 4 years Virginia; Mary Welch to Sarah Sanders, 4 years Virginia; William Skidmore to Fabian Hill, 4 years Virginia; William Woodcock to same, 6 years Virginia. (BR).

9 October. The following apprenticed in Bristol: John Bennett to John Scott, 4 years Virginia; Phillip Pardoe to same, 4 years Virginia; Thomas Edwards to Thomas Prewett, 4 years Virginia; Alice Norrington to Thomas Sniderbey, 4 years Virginia. (BR).

10 October. The following apprenticed in Bristol: John Licky to Thomas Way, 4 years Barbados; Margaret Griffen to Thomas Worlock, 4 years Barbados. (BR).

11 October. The following apprenticed in Bristol: David Hayce to Richard Plummer, 3 years Barbados; Robert Jones to John Ambros, 3 years Virginia; William Summerhill to Richard Ward, 4 years Virginia; John Nicholls to same, 4 years Virginia. (BR).

12 October. The following apprenticed in Bristol: William West to William Nicholls, 7 years Virginia; Richard Renn to William Coulton, 4 years Virginia; Joseph Gutheridge to Thomas Ellis, 4 years Nevis. (BR).

13 October. The following apprenticed in Bristol: Robert Arthur to Richard Cale, 4 years Virginia. (BR).

14 October. The following apprenticed in Bristol: Anne Godwin to Richard Ring, 3 years Virginia; Thomas Handey to John Owen, 4 years Virginia. (BR).

16 October. The following apprenticed in Bristol: David Jones to John Marsh, 3 years Virginia. (BR).

17 October. The following apprenticed in Bristol: Jonah Newman to Edward Alchurch, 4 years Virginia; Rowland Vaughan to Thomas Gayner, 6 years Virginia; Edith Window to John Smith, 4 years Virginia; John Pearce to Thomas Ma——, 4 years Virginia; Katherine Gwillam to Henry Rich, 4 years Virginia; Rowland Vaughan to Thomas Weaver, 4 years Virginia; John Bullock to William Christopher, 4 years Virginia. (BR).

18 October. The following apprenticed in Bristol: Francis Rennalls to Edward Fielding, 4 years Virginia; Robert Kew to Stephen Watts, 4 years Virginia; Richard Parker to Phillip Hoare, 7 years Virginia; Francis Underhill to Edward Alchurch, 4 years Virginia; Constant Underhill to same, 5 years Virginia. (BR).

19 October. The following apprenticed in Bristol: John Ashbey to John Pine, 3 years Barbados. (BR).

20 October. The following apprenticed in Bristol: Anne Hitchens to Thomas Pope, 4 years Virginia; John Bick to Edmund Borton, Maryland. (BR).

21 October. The following apprenticed in Bristol: Walter Gorway to John Luery, 4 years Virginia; Griffen Morgan to William Christopher, 4 years Virginia; John Hill to Richard Biddlestone, 4 years Virginia; Thomas Horton to Stephen Watts, 4 years Virginia. (BR).

23 October. The following apprenticed in Bristol: John Attkins to William Barwick, 4 years Virginia; Samuell England to William Christopher, 3 years Virginia. (BR).

24 October. The following apprenticed in Bristol: Richard Baker to Walter Hide, 4 years Virginia. (BR).

27 October. Shipper by the *Golden Fortune*, Mr. John Pears, bound from London for Virginia: John Long. (PRO: E190/50/4).

28 October. The following apprenticed in Bristol: Francis Creswick to Edward Lander, 4 years Nevis; Elizabeth Millsum to Richard Burriat, 4 years Virginia; John Thomas to Richard Pope, 4 years Virginia; Mary Mare to Richard Haskins, 4 years Virginia; Mary Robins to same, 4 years Virginia; Walter Griffen to William Harding, 4 years Virginia; Joane Babbett to same, 4 years Virginia. (BR).

30 October. The following apprenticed in Bristol: Robert Hooper to Henry Hosier, 4 years Virginia; Margaret Hooper to same, 4 years Virginia; Pearce Scrivill to James Thomas, 4 years Virginia. (BR).

October. Administration with will of Elizabeth Vansoldt of St. Botolph Bishopsgate, London, widow, whose son, Abraham Vansoldt, was in Virginia. (AW).

October. Probate of will of Peter Efford of Newington, Surrey, who had lands in Virginia. (AW).

October. Probate of will of John Cooper of Weston Hall, Warwickshire, whose brother, Timothy Cooper, was in New England. (AW).

2 November. Probate of will of James Loughman, citizen and saddler of London, whose youngest son, Daniel Loughman, was in Maryland. (NGSQ 76/3).

2 November. The following apprenticed in Bristol: William Belcher to John Crock, 4 years Virginia; Daniell Bishop to John Bassett, 4 years Virginia.(BR).

3 November. The following apprenticed in Bristol: Honnor Rugg to Sarah Matts, 4 years Virginia; George Hill to Arnold Collins, 4 years Virginia. (BR).

4 November. The following apprenticed in Bristol: Margery Davis to Roger Tayler, 3 years Virginia; George Courtney to Henry Jones, 4 years Virginia. (BR).

6 November. The following apprenticed in Bristol: Rcccc Morgan to John Smith, 4 years Virginia; Ratchell Morgan to same, 4 years Virginia; William Jefferis to Francis Bourne, 4 years Virginia. (BR).

7 November. The following apprenticed in Bristol: John Fisher to Thomas Pope, 4 years Virginia; John Billat to William Christopher, 4 years Virginia; Thomas Billat to same, 4 years Virginia; Thomas Beard to John Eckles, 7 years Virginia. (BR).

9 November. The following apprenticed in Bristol: Martha Addams to Sarah Matts, 4 years Virginia. (BR).

10 November. The following apprenticed in Bristol: Thomas Wilkins to Robert Lancaster, 4 years Virginia. (BR).

12-19 November. Shippers by the *Leviathan* of Scarborough, Mr. William Nesfield, bound from Lyme Regis for Virginia: Walter Tucker & Co., Thomas Weaver.

13 November. The following apprenticed in Bristol: William Ward to John Thomas, 6 years Barbados; Sibbell Arnold to Margery Tandey, 5 years Virginia. (BR).

15 November. The following apprenticed in Bristol: Moses Pearce to Tobias Pindar, 4 years St. Christopher; Tobias Greene to same, 4 years St. Christopher; William Elmes to same, 4 years St. Christopher; Thomas Browne to same, 4 years St. Christopher; Thomas Huntly to same, 4 years St. Christopher; Thomas Pinnall to same, 7 years St. Christopher; John Tanner to same, 4 years St. Christopher; John Sly to John Howell, 4 years Barbados. (BR).

17 November. The following apprenticed in Bristol: Cornelius Asson to Rebecka Thomas, 6 years Barbados . (BR).

20 November. The following apprenticed in Bristol: Richard Barly to William Sheppard, 5 years Virginia. (BR).

21 November. The following apprenticed in Bristol: Mary Badmington to John Hodge, 5 years Barbados; Daniell Venton to William Sheppard, 4 years Virginia; Thomas Venton to same, 4 years Virginia; Mary Pindar to Tobias Pindar, 4 years St. Christopher; Elizabeth Shewell to same, 4 years St. Christopher; Susanna Chandler to same, 6 years St. Christopher. (BR).

22 November. The following apprenticed in Bristol: Richard Thorne to Thomas Hillman, 4 years Barbados. (BR).

23 November. The following apprenticed in Bristol: Nicholas Branch to Thomas Beare, 4 years Jamaica. (BR).

27 November. The following apprenticed in Bristol: Thomas Horsecrofte to Thomas Kippen, 3 years Barbados; Jarome Vyerman to John Cecill, 4 years Virginia; Peter Mager to same, 4 years Virginia. (BR).

28 November. Shipper by the *Providence* of Barnstaple, Mr. Nicholas Taylor, bound from Barnstaple for Virginia: Nicholas Sweete. (PRO: E190/954/6).

28 November. The following apprenticed in Bristol: John Mallet to Jane Lond, 4 years Barbados; Mary Wilson to Elizabeth Dowlas, 5 years Barbados. (BR).

November. Probate of will of Richard Young of St. Margaret Steyning, London, who had lands in Virginia. (AW).

November. Probate of will of William Guy of St. Mildred, Broad Street, London, whose cousin, John Gate, was in Virginia. (AW).

November. Probate of will of Margaret Kembe of St. Saviour, Southwark, Surrey, widow, whose son, Thomas Kembe, was in Virginia. (AW).

7 December. The following apprenticed in Bristol: Thomas Bradburne to John Sayres, 4 years Virginia; John Whusden to Richard Purchise, 4 years Nevis. (BR).

8 December. The following apprenticed in Bristol: John Woolley to Richard Bowry, 4 years Nevis. (BR).

9 December. The following apprenticed in Bristol: William Evans to Edward Kelly, 5 years Nevis. (BR).

13 December. The following apprenticed in Bristol: Phillip Davis to William Freeman, 4 years Barbados. (BR).

14 December. The following apprenticed in Bristol: William Norgate to Richard Hamelton, 4 years Barbados; John Angell to William Steevens, 4 years Nevis. (BR).

23 December. Shipper by the *Humphrey & Elizabeth*, Mr. Robert Mead, bound from London for Virginia: James Ja———. (PRO: E190/50/4).

23 December. The following apprenticed in Bristol: William Sallmon to William Yeamans, 4 years Nevis. (BR).

29 December. The following apprenticed in Bristol: George Harris to George Hale, 4 years Nevis. (BR).

29 December. Shipper from London by the *Black Cow*, Mr. Edward Popley, bound from Plymouth for Virginia: John Rouse. (PRO: E190/1037/17).

1665. Petition for the transportation to Maryland of Mary Wood and Captain Provise, prisoners who have been pardoned. (CSPC).

1666

13 January. The following apprenticed in Bristol: Edward Clutterbuck to William Steevens, 4 years Barbados. (BR).

22 January. The following apprenticed in Bristol: William Grindall to Anthony Swymer, 4 years Barbados; William Baison to same, 4 years Barbados. (BR).

25 January. The following apprenticed in Bristol: John Cecill to Edward Tocknell, 4 years Barbados. (BR).

27 January-13 February. Shippers by the *Susan* bound from London for Virginia: Augustine Munford, Anthony Travill. (PRO: E190/50/5).

29 January. The following apprenticed in Bristol: John Peepe to Anthony Swymer, 4 years Barbados; Francis Jelford to Edmund Ditty, 7 years Barbados; Bridget Bowen to same, 4 years Barbados. (BR).

31 January. The following apprenticed in Bristol: William Gay to Anthony Swymer, 4 years Barbados; Mary Clothier to William Moore, 5 years Barbados. (BR).

January. Probate of will of Simon Smith of Stepney, Middlesex, whose granddaughter, Judith, wife of Richard Tozer, was in New England. (AW).

1 February. Deposition by John Gore, citizen and merchant tailor of London, aged 25, that Thomas Godlington, citizen and salter of London, became indebted to Richard Sherhood of Thames Street, St. Mary at Hill, citizen and merchant tailor of London. Mr. Hugh Nevitt and Mr. George Seaton of Virginia, merchants, have been appointed attorneys to recover the debt. (LMCD).

2 February. The following apprenticed in Bristol: Thomas Chillcutt to Joseph Day, 4 years Barbados; Henery Harvey to Anthony Swymer, 7 years Barbados. (BR).

3 February. The following apprenticed in Bristol: George Whiteing to Robert Moore, 4 years Barbados; John Cainton to same, 4 years Barbados. (BR).

14 February. The following apprenticed in Bristol: William Buck to Anthony Swymer, 4 years Barbados. (BR).

16-23 February. Shippers by the *Society* bound from London for New England: John Cooke, Noah Floyd, William Barrett. (PRO: E190/50/5).

23 February. The following apprenticed in Bristol: Timothy Paradice to Edward Tocknell, 3 years Barbados. (BR).

February. Probate of will of Henry Smith of Watford, Hertfordshire, whose brother, William Smith, was in Virginia. (AW).

February. Elizabeth Baily reprieved at Middlesex Assizes to be transported to Jamaica.

2 March. The following apprenticed in Bristol: William Phelps to Anthony Swymer, 5 years Barbados. (BR).

8 March. The following apprenticed in Bristol: Thomas Brucy to Roger Wade, 4 years Barbados; Welthian Dave to Edward Tocknell, 5 years Barbados. (BR).

12 March. The following apprenticed in Bristol: Edward Jones to Alexander Morgan, 6 years Barbados. (BR).

14 March. The following apprenticed in Bristol: Richard Banfield to John Walter, 4 years Barbados. (BR).

16 March. The following apprenticed in Bristol: Daniel Peacock to Nicholas Burrss, 4 years Barbados; Stephen Cornelius to Edward Tocknell, 5 years Barbados. (BR).

20 March. The following apprenticed in Bristol: John Slade to John Farewell, 4 years Barbados. (BR).

23 March. The following apprenticed in Bristol: Edward Jones to Edward Tocknell, 7 years Barbados; Hugh Mills to William West, 4 years Barbados; John Woory to John Jonston, 4 years Barbados. (BR).

24 March-21 April. Shippers by the *York Merchant* of Plymouth, Mr. Josiah Pickes, bound from Plymouth for Virginia: George Streeley, Phillip Edwards, Daniel Groce. (PRO: E190/1037/17).

31 March. The following apprenticed in Bristol: John Sheppard to Anthony Swymer, 4 years Barbados; Thomas Bull to Anthony Warden, 4 years Barbados. (BR).

March. Probate of will of Humphrey Higginson of Ratcliffe, Stepney, Middlesex, whose brother, Christopher Higginson, was in Virginia. (AW).

March. Probate of will of Luke Fawne of St. Augustine, London, whose niece, Elizabeth Clement, daughter of his brother, John Fawne, was in New England. (AW).

March. Probate of will of Thomas Reade of Colchester, Essex, carpenter, whose son, Thomas Reade, and son-in-law, Daniel Bacon, were in New England. (AW).

7 April. The following apprenticed in Bristol: William Freke to Edward Tocknell, 5 years Barbados. (BR).

9 April. The following apprenticed in Bristol: John Lamble to John Roberts, 4 years Barbados. (BR).

11 April. The following apprenticed in Bristol: John Bennett to James Backer, 4 years Barbados. (BR).

13-23 April. Shippers by the *Lady* bound from London for New England: Jeremiah Mount, John Shorter, James Littleton. (PRO: E190/50/5).

17 April. The following apprenticed in Bristol: Thomas Evans to Thomas Dixon, 4 years Barbados. (BR).

21 April. The following apprenticed in Bristol: Mary Hellier to Hugh Jones, 4 years Barbados. (BR).

22 April. The following apprenticed in Bristol: Thomas Lawford to Jonathan Prior, 4 years Barbados. (BR).

24 April-4 May. Shippers by the *Trial* bound from London for New England: John Harbin, Thomas Bodley, Richard Saltingstall, John Dayman. (PRO: E190/50/5).

April. Probate of will of Arthur Cobb of London bound for Syranum in America. (AW).

5 May. Deposition by Samuell Mitchell, aged 20, servant of Edmond Page of London, mercer, that Dr. Henry Taylor of Boston, New England, surgeon, became indebted by bond of 6 February 1664 to Page, Charles Mitchell and John Farrington of London, mercers. (LMCD).

17 May. The following apprenticed in Bristol: Margaret Pride to James Shute, 4 years Barbados. (BR).

21 May. Shipper by the *Orange Tree* of Topsham, Mr. Thomas Avery, bound from Exeter for Virginia: George Tuthill. (PRO: E190/954/17).

25 May. The following apprenticed in Bristol: Joane Williams to Richard Morgan, 5 years Barbados; Margaret Caffin to same, 7 years Barbados; Richard Brooke to Edward Tocknell, 4 years Barbados. (BR).

28 May. The following apprenticed in Bristol: Katherine Pow to John Williams, 4 years Barbados; Joane Hopkins to William Andrews, 4 years Barbados. (BR).

30 May. Thomas May, master of the *Anne*, to be taken into the Fleet Prison for setting ashore condemned Quakers. (APC).

31 May. Shipper by the *William & Mary* bound from London for New York: William M. (*sic*). (PRO: E190/50/5).

May. Probate of will of John Bolles of Clerkenwell, Middlesex, whose brother, Joseph Bolles, was in New England. (AW).

May. Elinor Robarts reprieved at Middlesex Assizes to be transported to Barbados. (EB).

6 June. Bristol prisoners reprieved to be transported to Barbados: Robert Arthur; Richard Edney; Joan Paine; John Sturgion alias Austin alias Stevens. (PRO: C66/3086/16).

7 June. The following apprenticed in Bristol: Francis Swan to Richard Morgan, 5 years Barbados; Henery Bodenar to James Shute, 4 years Barbados; James Lane to same, 4 years Barbados. (BR).

8 June. The following apprenticed in Bristol: Thomas Grangeby to William Jayne, 4 years Barbados. (BR).

8 June. Petition of Thomas May. His ship, the *Anne*, waited in the Downs for a month for a fair wind and was obliged to return to London to replenish her provisions. This was the cause of the Quakers having got away. (APC).

9 June. The following apprenticed in Bristol: Rebecka Lewis to James Shute, 4 years Barbados. (BR).

15 June. Western Circuit prisoners reprieved to be transported to Barbados. Devon: William Ewens alias Evans of Broadhempston, weaver; John Gill of Cheriton Fitzpaine, husbandman; Robert Vivian of Lamerton, carpenter; Mark Evans of Newton St. Cyres, husbandman. Hampshire: Joseph Piper of Andover, weaver; Henry Prater alias William Symes of Andover or Broughton, carpenter. Somerset: William Chivers of Batchford, weaver; William Gist of Bath, clothworker; John Perrey of Wellington, husbandman; Benjamin Palmer of Seavington St. Michael; Thomas Davies of Bath, worsted comber. Wiltshire: Robert Williams of Swindon, husbandman; Zachary Newman of Melksham, fuller; Humphrey Jarvis alias Garvis of Hacklestone, victualler; William Pinchin of Chalfield Magna, mason; Stephen Hunt of Tollard Royal. Dorset: John Dackham of North Wootton, groom. (PRO: C66/3086/17).

27 June. The following apprenticed in Bristol: Thomas Jones to Richard Martin, 7 years New England. (BR).

June. Yorkshire prisoners reprieved to be transported to Barbados: Ambrose Sheppard, James Nuttier, Thomas Smith, John Bamfield, John Johnson, Robert Pearson, John Harrison. (PRO: C66/3086/2).

5-24 July. Shippers by the *Duke of York* bound from London for New England: Timothy Poole, William Peake, Daniell Sedgwicke, Francis Parsons. (PRO: E190/50/5).

7 July. The following apprenticed in Bristol: William Jones to Thomas Lukins, 4 years Barbados; William Pallmer to same, 4 years Barbados. (BR).

11 July. On the petition of the sailors of the *Anne*, it is ordered that the ship be sold to pay their wages. (APC).

18 July. Shipper by the *Hannah & Catherine* of New England, Mr. John Phillips, bound from Weymouth for New England: said John Phillips. (PRO: E190/880/7).

30 July. Oxford Circuit prisoners reprieved to be transported to Barbados. Berkshire: Emma Phillips of Lambourne Woodland. Herefordshire: Thomas

Jones of Hereford. Oxfordshire: Andrew Sheldon of Charlbury. (PRO: C66/3086/3).

July. Administration with will of Rose Brumpsted of St. Martin in the Fields, Middlesex, spinster, whose kinsman, Thomas Breedon, was in New England. (AW).

2 August. The following apprenticed in Bristol: Thomas Low to Richard Morgan, 4 years Barbados. (BR).

7 August. The following apprenticed in Bristol: Jane Cooper to Margery Attkins, 4 years Barbados; George Cooper to Ralph Cooper, 5 years Barbados. (BR).

11 August. The following apprenticed in Bristol: David Davis to James Shute, 4 years Virginia. (BR).

18 August. The following apprenticed in Bristol: John George to John Winburne, 4 years Virginia; Francis Williams to same, 6 years Virginia. (BR).

22 August. The following apprenticed in Bristol: Humphry Thomas to Richard Plummer, 5 years Nevis. (BR).

28 August. The following apprenticed in Bristol: William Littlepage to Thomas Walter, 4 years Virginia; Henery Sparks to Edward Tocknell, 5 years New England. (BR).

31 August. The following apprenticed in Bristol: Henery Swayne to Edward Tocknell, 4 years New England. (BR).

1 September. The following apprenticed in Bristol: Christopher Watts to John Hopkins, 4 years Virginia. (BR).

3 September. Shippers by the *Nicholas* of Dartmouth, Mr. Samuell Widger, bound from Dartmouth for New England: Nicholas Isaac, Thomas Brooking. (PRO: E190/954/10).

3 September. The following apprenticed in Bristol: George Lewis to James Shute, 4 years Virginia; William Charleton to John Hopkins, 4 years Virginia. (BR).

7 September. The following apprenticed in Bristol: Reece Floyd to John Hopkins, 4 years Virginia. (BR).

8 September. The following apprenticed in Bristol: William Bale to William Hedges, 6 years Virginia. (BR).

10 September. The following apprenticed in Bristol: James Lewis to James Shute, 4 years Virginia; Mary Manning to John Hopkins, 4 years Virginia. (BR).

12 September. The following apprenticed in Bristol: William Taylor to John Morgan, 5 years Virginia. (BR).

14 September. The following apprenticed in Bristol: John Goldney to John Hopkins, 4 years Virginia; Joseph Goldney to same, 4 years Virginia; Mathew Gubden to Henry Paull Jr., 4 years Barbados or Caribbees. (BR).

17 September. The following apprenticed in Bristol: James Ellis to Humphry Lester, 4 years Virginia. (BR).

18 September-4 October. Shippers by the *Industry* of Plymouth, Mr. John Forster, bound from Plymouth for Virginia: John Thomas, Samuell Brett, Thomas Reddinge, Abraham Seavell. (E190/954/10).

19 September. The following apprenticed in Bristol: Katherine Gilbert to Daniell Sam, 4 years Virginia; John Stone to Humphry Lester, 4 years Virginia. (BR).

20 September-10 October. Shippers by the *Laurel Tree* of Dartmouth, Mr. Robert Atkins, bound from Dartmouth and Plymouth for Virginia: Ambrose Mudd & Co., Richard Sparke, Henry Corbin. (PRO: E190/954/10).

21 September. The following apprenticed in Bristol: Sarah Hunt to Thomas Gibbs, 4 years Virginia. (BR).

22 September. Shipper by the *Providence* of Dartmouth, Mr. Anthony Streate, bound from Dartmouth for Virginia: Benjamin Rooke & Co. (PRO: E190/954/10).

22 September. The following apprenticed in Bristol: Richard Cuzens to John Hodge, 4 years Virginia; Christopher Wedge to Francis Taylor, 4 years Virginia. (BR).

22-28 September. Shippers by the *Handmaid* of Dartmouth, Mr. Christopher Sellman, bound from Dartmouth for Virginia: Walter Jago & Co., Edward Seaman. (PRO: E190/954/10).

24 September. Shipper by the *Duke* of London, Mr. Robert Martyn, bound from Plymouth for New England: Henry Hatsell. (PRO: E190/1037/17).

24 September. The following apprenticed in Bristol: William Crew to John Ward, 6 years Virginia; Alice Chock to same, 4 years Virginia. (BR).

25 September-9 October. Shippers by the *Sarah* of Plymouth, Mr. Sampson Clarke, bound from Plymouth for Virginia: Endymion Walker, Richard Perry, Phillip Edwards, Joseph Pearce, Christopher Addams. (PRO: E190/1037/17).

26 September. The following apprenticed in Bristol: Thomas Wille to Humphry Lester, 4 years Virginia; William Wille to same, 4 years Virginia; John Spiller to Daniell Luffman, 4 years Maryland. (BR).

26 September. Shipper by the *Plymouth Merchant* of Plymouth, Mr. John Hack, bound from Plymouth for Virginia: George Lapthorne. (PRO: E190/1037/17).

27 September. The following apprenticed in Bristol: John Millard to Thomas Gayner, 4 years Virginia. (BR).

September. Probate of will of Thomas Tomlins of St. Bartholomew the Great, London, who had lands in Virginia. (AW).

September-October. Depositions in Plymouth, Devon, to establish the authenticity of the will of John Clarke, master of the *Unity*, who died in Virginia in 1665. John Clarke and William Browne were partners in the Virginia tobacco trade. (NGSQ 66/3).

1-5 October. Shippers by the *Thomas & William* of Poole, Mr. John Heminge, bound from Poole for Weymouth and transhipment to Virginia: John Kinge, George Ollive, George Nickles. (PRO: E190/880/6).

1 October-1 December. Shippers by the *Willing Mind* of Bideford, Mr. Stephen Dennis, bound from Barnstaple for Virginia: John Darracott, Abraham Heiman. (PRO: E190/954/9).

2 October. The following apprenticed in Bristol: Jacob Gilby to William Watkins, 4 years Virginia; Thomas Ward to Edward Noble, 4 years Virginia; Sarah Nethey to James Ellis, 4 years Virginia. (BR).

2 October. Shipper by the *Jacob* of Weymouth, foreign built and made free, Mr. Daniell Wallis, bound from Weymouth for Virginia: Daniell Wallis & Co. (PRO: E190/880/7).

2 October. Shipper by the *Weymouth Merchant* of Weymouth, Mr. George Piercie, bound from Weymouth for Virginia: John Cole & Co. (PRO: E190/880/7).

3-17 October. Shippers by the *Vinetree* of Lyme, Mr. Samuell Tucker, bound from Lyme Regis for Virginia: Walter Tucker & Co., John Mesurer. (PRO: E190/436/7).

4 October. Shipper by the *Elizabeth* of Weymouth, Mr. Thomas Barker, bound from Lyme Regis for Virginia: Walter Tucker & Co. (PRO: E190/436/7).

5 October. The following apprenticed in Bristol: William Taylor to Henry Wood, 2 years Virginia. (BR).

5-17 October. Shippers by the *Virginia Merchant* of Plymouth, Mr. John Moorsland, bound from Plymouth for Virginia: Benjamin Salt, John Cooke. (PRO: E190/1037/17).

6 October. The following apprenticed in Bristol: William Gandy to Daniel L——an, 4 years Virginia; John Rawlins to same, 4 years Maryland; Anthony Rawlins to same, 4 years Maryland; Richard Rawlins to same, 4 years Maryland; Alice Smith to John Walter, 4 years Barbados. (BR).

11 October. The following apprenticed in Bristol: Elizabeth Rusele to Edward Noble, 4 years Virginia; Anne Churchman to John Farclue, 4 years Virginia; William Bishop to William Pursell, 4 years Virginia; Daniell Dory to Robert Bound, 4 years Barbados. (BR).

12 October. The following apprenticed in Bristol: John Parker to Richard Haskins, 4 years Virginia. (BR).

13 October. The following apprenticed in Bristol: Thomas Baker to Richard Haskins, 4 years Virginia; Richard Wood to John Bodenham, 4 years Virginia; Margaret Williams to Peter Perks, 4 years Barbados; Thomas Wattkins to Nicholas Tovey, 4 years Virginia; Anne Buttler to William Sheppard, 5 years Virginia; John Barber to Charles Toplady, 5 years Virginia; Richard Arnsley to same, 4 years Virginia; Edward Thorneton to same, 4 years Virginia. (BR).

15 October. The following apprenticed in Bristol: Benjamin Caple to John Badman, 4 years Virginia; John Holwey to Benjamin Legg, 4 years Virginia; Samuell Good to John Scott, 4 years Virginia. (BR).

16 October. The following apprenticed in Bristol: William Bishop to John Lugg, 4 years Virginia; Jonathan Granger to same, 4 years Virginia; George Granger to same, 4 years Virginia; John Anthony to Daniell Gwilliam, 4 years Virginia. (BR).

17 October. The following apprenticed in Bristol: Lewis Williams to Edward Jones, 4 years Virginia; Elioner Lloyd to Joseph Chapman, 4 years Virginia; Charles Phillips to same, 4 years Virginia; Thomas Glamen to Henry Bancks, 5 years Barbados; Ambrose Lamfere to Roger Richards, 4 years Virginia. (BR).

18 October. The following apprenticed in Bristol: Mary Perren to William Bonner, 4 years Virginia; Thomas John to Joseph Chapman, 4 years Virginia. (BR).

19 October. The following apprenticed in Bristol: Phillip Wornall to John Reed, 5 years Virginia; Henery Woodland to same, 5 years Virginia; John King to same, 5 years Virginia; John Minor to Robert Noble, 5 years Virginia; Joane King to same, 7 years Virginia; Jane Walker to Thomas Boyken, 4 years Virginia; Thomas Barnes to Michaell Little, 4 years Barbados; John Haynes to same, 4 years Barbados; John Ball to same, 4 years Barbados. (BR).

20 October. Shipper by the *Elizabeth* of Weymouth, Mr. Thomas Barker, bound from Plymouth for Virginia: John Horsham. (PRO: E190/1037/17).

22 October. The following apprenticed in Bristol: Rendall Brown to James Shute, 4 years Virginia; Thomas Darby to same, 4 years Virginia; Henery Williams to John French, 4 years Virginia; Welthian Jones to Edward Thomas, 4 years Virginia; Edward Boylen to Jasper Jenkins, 5 years Virginia; Giles Hicks to Edward Millsom, 4 years Virginia; William Betty to Joseph Chapman, 10 years Virginia. (BR).

22 October. Shippers by the *Katherine* of Weymouth, foreign built and made free, Mr. William Burrod, bound from Weymouth for Virginia: Stephen Abbott for William Stanley. (PRO: E190.880/7).

22-23 October. Shippers by the *John & Francis* of Southampton, Mr. John Wall, bound from Weymouth for Virginia: John Richbell, Thomas Hide, Walter Thornhill. (PRO: E190/880/7).

23 October. The following apprenticed in Bristol: James Middleton to Thomas West, 4 years Barbados. (BR).

24 October. Chancery suit of Thomas Dowde and Margaret his wife, only surviving sister of John Whitty of London, mariner, deceased, v. Sarah, relict of John Whitty, and John Currer of London, merchant. John Whitty had plantations in Carolina, Virginia and New Jersey which he is alleged to have devised by a will to his wife. (NGSQ 69/2).

24 October. The following apprenticed in Bristol: William Davey to William Sheppard, 4 years Virginia; Jacob Board to Richard Brent, 7 years Virginia; Thomas Hill to William Harding, 7 years Virginia. (BR).

25 October. The following apprenticed in Bristol: Anne Manning to Nicholas Wyatt, 7 years Virginia; Samuell Dryer to same, 7 years Virginia; Charles Rawlins to same, 4 years Virginia; William Petticourte to same, 4 years Virginia; Justinian Brankenwell to same, 5 years Virginia; Elizabeth New to John Crock, 4 years Virginia. (BR).

25 October-6 November. Shipper by the *Francis* of Topsham, Mr. William Wilcox, bound from Exeter for Virginia: William Ware. (PRO: E190/954/7).

26 October. The following apprenticed in Bristol: John Frances to Nicholas Wyatt, 7 years Virginia; John Burte to Daniell North, 4 years Barbados; John Griffen to Phillip Hilliard, 4 years Virginia; William Carter to John Pope, 4 years Virginia; Phillis Chapple to Francis Ludlow, 4 years Virginia; Anne Foard to same, 4 years Virginia; Alice Arnold to Jasper Crasse, 5 years Virginia. (BR).

26 October. Shipper by the *Dartmouth Merchant* of Dartmouth, Mr. Thomas Grigg, bound from Dartmouth for Virginia: George Tuthill & Co. (PRO: E190/954/10).

26 October-31 December. Shippers by the *John & Martha*, Mr. John Goffe, bound from London for Virginia: John Peake, Thomas Blayton. (PRO: E190/50/5, 52/1).

27 October. The following apprenticed in Bristol: John Spracklen to John Bollen, 4 years Virginia; William Floyd to same, 4 years Virginia; John Greene to same, 4 years Virginia; Nicholas Newman to same, 4 years Virginia; William Ball to Robert Benson, 4 years Barbados; Giles Foard to same, 4 years Barbados. (BR).

29 October. The following apprenticed in Bristol: John Hicks to John Hodges, 5 years Virginia; John Collins to Jasper Crasse, 4 years Virginia. (BR).

30 October. The following apprenticed in Bristol: John Vizard to Thomas Martin, 7 years Virginia; Martha Vizard to same, 5 years Virginia. (BR).

31 October. The following apprenticed in Bristol: Samuell Abbotts to Sarah Matts, 4 years Virginia; Samuell Pearce to William Dale, 4 years Virginia;

Jonas Rouse to John Bollen, 4 years Virginia; William Copper to Stephen Watts, 4 years Virginia; Robert Thomas to Thomas Hottoste, 4 years Virginia; Thomas Paine to John Ithell, 4 years Virginia; Joseph Sillcocks to William Andrews, 4 years Virginia. (BR).

October. Administration of Robert Sharpe of Rappahannock River, Virginia, who died in Stepney, Middlesex. (AW).

October. Probate of will of Rev. Alsopp Josias, of Combe Nevell, Kingston, Surrey, whose sister, Elizabeth Rosseter, was in New England. (AW).

1 November. The following apprenticed in Bristol: Andrew Feltam to Valentine Knight, 4 years Virginia; Griffin Morris to same, 4 years Virginia. (BR).

2 November. The following apprenticed in Bristol: Thomas Arrendon to Sarah Matts, 4 years Virginia; Hopkin Williams to same, 4 years Virginia; John Williams to Thomas Jinkins, 4 years Virginia; Gyles Sydall to Daniell Sam, 4 years Virginia; Mary Burrow to John Porter, 4 years Virginia. (BR).

2 November-16 December. Shippers by the *William* of London, Mr. John Richardson, bound from Plymouth for Virginia: William Browne, Benjamin Salt, Thomas Durant, George Streeley, Samuell Brett. (PRO: E190/1037/17).

3 November. The following apprenticed in Bristol: Nicholas Sessum to Thomas Jarvis, 4 years Virginia; Thomas Waller to same, 7 years Virginia; Henery Reynolds to same, 4 years Virginia; Elizabeth Hicks to Edward Lappage, 5 years Virginia; William Ballome to Robert Taylor, 4 years Virginia; Gregory Perne to Joseph Hatton, 4 years Virginia; Thomas Jones to Jacob Elton, 4 years Virginia. (BR).

6 November. The following apprenticed in Bristol: Arthur Marsh to Thomas Gayner, 5 years Virginia; John Burrus to Edward Lappage, 5 years Virginia; John Davis to Walter Stephens, 4 years Virginia; William Whistons to Mathew Shepherd, 4 years Virginia; John Tomsey to John Waters, 4 years Barbados; Athanatius Giles to John Heattford, 4 years Virginia; John Moore to William Buttler, 4 years Virginia; John Williams to same, 4 years Virginia; Elizabeth Conway to Michaell Grand, 4 years Virginia; Mary Millsom to Laurence Raymond, 4 years Virginia; Elizabeth Bushell to same, 4 years Virginia. (BR).

7-27 November. Shippers by the *Fellowship* of Barnstaple, Mr. John Lovering, bound from Barnstaple for Virginia: Edward Fleming & Co., Joseph Reade. (PRO: E190/954/9).

8 November. The following apprenticed in Bristol: Anne Woodward to Robert Morgan, 4 years Virginia; Elizabeth Tucker to John Eyres, 7 years Virginia; Richard Tucker to same, 7 years Virginia; William Tompkins to same, 7 years Virginia; Thomas Roberts to same, 7 years Virginia; Stephen Porter to same, 7 years Virginia; William Martin to Stephen Procter, 4 years Virginia; John Tratt to same, 4 years Virginia; John Brooks to same, 4 years Virginia; Arthur

Starte to same, 4 years Virginia; Thomas Leage to same, 4 years Virginia; Pasco Bellico to Michaell Pope, 4 years Virginia. (BR).

10 November. Chester Circuit prisoners reprieved to be transported to Barbados: Gabriel Lewis, Thomas David, Jenkin Evan, Eustace Standred. (PRO: C66/3086/14).

12 November. The following apprenticed in Bristol: Martin Kelly to Stephen Procter, 4 years Virginia; Christopher Iles to same, 4 years Virginia; John Phillips to same, 4 years Virginia; John Habberfield to same, 4 years Virginia; Richard Harte to William Coleburne, 5 years Virginia; Anne Jaker to Thomas Yorman, 4 years Virginia; John Witherly to Marke Chappell, 4 years Virginia; Samuell Price to Henry Crane, 4 years Virginia; John Davis to William Wattkins, 4 years Virginia. (BR).

12-16 November. Shippers by the *Amity* of Bideford, Mr. George Powell, bound from Barnstaple for Virginia: John Liskam, William Bellow, Hartwell Buck. (PRO: E190/954/9).

13 November. The following apprenticed in Bristol: Richard Gardner to John Winburne, 4 years Virginia; Edward Gardner to same, 4 years Virginia; Thomasin Saull to Henry Gibbs, 4 years Virginia; Anne Mince to Edward Jones, 4 years Virginia. (BR).

14 November. The following apprenticed in Bristol: James Dave to Sarah Matts, 5 years Virginia; John Hargesse to George Greene, 7 years Virginia; Bodman Phillips to same, 4 years Virginia; John Collins to John Reed, 5 years Virginia; John Read to same, 5 years Virginia; Anne Legee to William Hottoste, 4 years Virginia. (BR).

15 November. The following apprenticed in Bristol: Elizabeth Mathen to William Yeamans, 4 years Virginia; James Jones to Jenkin Bragg, 4 years Virginia; James Millford to Henry Crane, 4 years Virginia. (BR).

16 November. The following apprenticed in Bristol: Robert Evans to Katherine Davis, 4 years Virginia; Ellis Jones to same, 4 years Virginia. (BR).

16 November. Shipper by the *Nightingale* of Bideford, Mr. Christopher Browning, bound from Barnstaple for Virginia: George Middleton. (PRO: E190/954/9).

16 November-14 December. Shippers by the *Bideford Merchant* of Bideford, Mr. Thomas Hamott, bound from Barnstaple for Virginia: John Darracott, John Hooper, Abraham Dennis. (PRO: E190/954/9).

17 November. The following apprenticed in Bristol: William Baker to John Bollen, 4 years Virginia; John Avery to same, 4 years Virginia; Rebecka Lovelace to same, 4 years Virginia; Grace Darby to same, 7 years Virginia; Henry Aspray to Edward Lappage, 4 years Virginia; John Wetner to same, 4 years Virginia; John Winston to same, 4 years Virginia; John Stone to same,

4 years Virginia; Elizabeth Granger to Thomas Hallett, 4 years Virginia; Elizabeth Clubb to Owen Williams, 4 years Virginia; Jane Horrard to same, 4 years Virginia; Mary Bishop to William Coleburne, 5 years Virginia; Thomasin Harte to same, 5 years Virginia. (BR).

18 November. Shipper by the *King David* of London, Mr. John Plover, bound from Dartmouth for Virginia: John Edwards. (PRO: E190/954/10).

19 November. The following apprenticed in Bristol: Ambrose Carter to William Sanders, 5 years Virginia. (BR).

20 November. The following apprenticed in Bristol: Percies Sutten to William Sanders, 5 years Virginia. (BR).

21 November. The following apprenticed in Bristol: Joane Williams to Samuell Tovey, 5 years Virginia; Andrew Attkins to Richard Jones, 6 years Virginia; John Evans to John Falkner, 6 years Virginia; Elizabeth Evans to same, 4 years Virginia; Thomas Rowland to Mary Grannte, 6 years Virginia; Robert Willis to John Orchard, 4 years Virginia; Thomas Chatle to John Bromfield, 3 years Virginia; Jonathan Smadly to same, 4 years Virginia; Richard Jelkes to same, 7 years Virginia; Richard Bennett to same, 7 years Virginia; Margaret Roberts to same, 4 years Virginia; William Morgan to John Reed, 5 years Virginia; William Daniell to James Braithwayte, 4 years Virginia; John Strugen to same, 4 years Virginia; Mary Turner to same, 4 years Virginia; Richard Rodburne to William Coleburne, 12 years Virginia; Abigall Sellwood to John French, 4 years Virginia; Elizabeth Manly to John Holbrock, 4 years Virginia; Mary Fles to same, 4 years Virginia. (BR).

22 November. The following apprenticed in Bristol: John Wilcocks to William Coleburne, 4 years Virginia; Robert Boyce to William Bane, 8 years Virginia; Phillip Everard to Thomas Mitchell, 4 years Virginia; John Arnell to Henry Lambert, 4 years Virginia; Anthony Arnell to same, 4 years Virginia; Mary Arnell to same, 4 years Virginia; Elizabeth Jacquis to same, 4 years Virginia; Alice West to same, 4 years Virginia; Joane West to same, 4 years Virginia; Joane Sloper to same, 4 years Virginia; Anne Holwey to same, 4 years Virginia. (BR).

22 November. Shipper by the *Richard & Francis*, Mr. Robert Conaway, bound from London for Virginia: John Butts. (PRO: E190/50/5).

23 November. The following apprenticed in Bristol: Henry Perry to Mathew Lambert, 3 years Virginia; William Harbett to same, 3 years Virginia; William Williams to John Bulte, 4 years Virginia. (BR).

24 November. The following apprenticed in Bristol: Robert Cocks to Marke Chappell, 4 years Virginia; George Hort to Christopher Preston, 5 years Virginia; Elizabeth Lee to James Shute, 4 years Virginia. (BR).

24 November. Shipper by the *Seraphim* of Barnstaple, Mr. Henry Wilkey, bound from Barnstaple for Virginia: John Fleming. (PRO: E190/954/9).

26 November. The following apprenticed in Bristol: Richard Sheard to Andrew Exon, 4 years Virginia; Jane Merewether to John Foyle, 4 years Virginia; Gabriell Granwell to Robert Dike, 4 years Virginia; Cornelius Lyons to Thomas Duddlestone, 4 years Virginia; Maudlin Fluellen to Richard Jones, 4 years Virginia; Nicholas Lucas to Samuell Tovey, 4 years Virginia; Richard Gay to same, 4 years Virginia. (BR).

27 November. The following apprenticed in Bristol: Joyce Warren to George Greene, 4 years Virginia. (BR).

28 November. The following apprenticed in Bristol: Lidiah Roberts to Samuell Deyes, 4 years Virginia; William Bacon to Thomas Warren, 4 years Virginia. (BR).

29 November. The following apprenticed in Bristol: Grace Stone to James Shute, 4 years Virginia; Richard Long to Richard Paull, 4 years Virginia. (BR).

November. Probate of will of William Coltman of Virginia [but shown as of Wapping, Middlesex, in Caveat Book]. (AW).

November. Probate of will of John Achley of London, merchant, who died in Virginia, bachelor. (AW).

1 December. The following apprenticed in Bristol: John Richards to Stephen Procter, 4 years Virginia; Elizabeth Cullimore to same, 4 years Virginia; Mary Jones to same, 4 years Virginia; William Diddall to Elizabeth Hyatt, 5 years Virginia; Thomas Adams to Thomas Hyatt, 4 years Virginia. (BR).

3 December. The following apprenticed in Bristol: James Hayward to John Gonning, 8 years Barbados; Nathaniell Burtonwood to Thomas Pope, 4 years Virginia; Sarah Warner to same, 5 years Virginia; Nicholas Sheppard to Daniell Luffman, 3 years Virginia; Thomasin Rosewell to same, 4 years Virginia. (BR).

4 December. The following apprenticed in Bristol: John Serjeant to Henry Norris, 4 years Barbados; Thomas Fowler to same, 7 years Barbados; John Mills to Richard Davis, 7 years Virginia; Francis Kellowhill to William Buttler, 4 years Virginia; Thomas Roberts to same, 5 years Virginia; Judith Jackson to same, 4 years Virginia; Elizabeth Jackson to same, 4 years Virginia. (BR).

5 December. The petition of Gawen Corbin & Co. that they may load materials on their Virginia ship the *Berkeley*, Mr. John Watson, in order to build a church in Virginia, is granted. (APC).

6 December. The following apprenticed in Bristol: Elizabeth Stables to William Luffman, 6 years Virginia. (BR).

7 December. Pass granted on the petition of Matthew Page of Virginia, planter, for the *Pelican* to sail to Virginia. (APC).

7 December. The following apprenticed in Bristol: John Massy to Elizabeth Hyatt, 3 years Virginia; Elizabeth Gellisoe to same, 4 years Virginia; Sarah Stiff to John Richardson, 4 years Barbados. (BR).

8 December. The following apprenticed in Bristol: Thomas Bennett to Ralph Noble, 4 years Virginia; Jane Hyatt to Robert Dunning, 5 years Virginia; Thomas Jones to James Shute, 4 years Virginia. (BR).

10 December. The following apprenticed in Bristol: William Gough to William Harle, 4 years Barbados; Richard Barnes to George Hill, 4 years Virginia; Joseph Lawrance to John Braine, 4 years Barbados. (BR).

11 December. The following apprenticed in Bristol: Christopher Williams to John Williams, 4 years Nevis. (BR).

12 December. The following apprenticed in Bristol: Anne Davis to Stephen Procter, 4 years Virginia; Charles Bennett to James Huling, 4 years Virginia; Anthony Rennals to same, 4 years Virginia; William Baldwin to same, 4 years Virginia; William Phelps to Marke Chappell, 4 years Virginia. (BR).

14-18 December. Shippers by the *Samuell* of Plymouth, Mr. Samuell Finch, bound from Plymouth for Virginia: Abraham Jennens; Benjamin Salt; Richard Perry; Thomas Durant. (PRO: E190/1037/17).

15 December. The following apprenticed in Bristol: Joseph Rowland to James Steevens, 4 years Barbados; Mary Elmes to Elizabeth Wattkins, 4 years Virginia. (BR).

17 December. The following apprenticed in Bristol: Elizabeth Corvill to Lawrance Raymond, 4 years Virginia; Martha Horship to same, 4 years Virginia. (BR).

18 December. The following apprenticed in Bristol: Thomas Attwick to Edward Fielding, 3 years Virginia. (BR).

21 December. The following apprenticed in Bristol: Howell Morgan to Anthony Brereton, 4 years Virginia. (BR).

24 December. The following apprenticed in Bristol: Thomas Burte to Joane Hillman, 4 years Virginia; Morgan Jones to John Batchelor, 4 years Virginia. (BR).

December. Administration of George Holcroft of Virginia, bachelor. (AW).

Undated. Ralph Symonds formerly of St. Botolph Aldgate, London, but late of Virginia, surgeon. Caveats by the creditors, William Lake and Thomas Elton. (AW).

1667

2 January. The following apprenticed in Bristol: John Thomas to John Shapley, 4 years Virginia. (BR).

3 January. The following apprenticed in Bristol: Christopher Henton to Edward Herren, 4 years Virginia; Mary Twiste to Henry Sampson, 7 years Virginia. (BR).

17 January. The following apprenticed in Bristol: Walter Lewis to John Basset, 4 years Virginia. (BR).

25 January. The following apprenticed in Bristol: James Stowell to Joseph Stratten, 4 years Virginia. (BR).

28 January. The following apprenticed in Bristol: David Williams to William Morgan, 4 years Virginia. (BR).

January. Probate of will of Richard Lee of St. Michael Bassishaw, London, who had goods in Virginia. (AW).

January. Probate of will of Francis Kestin of St. Olave, Southwark, Surrey, whose brother, Thomas Kestin, was in Virginia.

5 February. The following apprenticed in Bristol: Mary Marvin to Francis Ludlow, 4 years Virginia. (BR).

8 February. The following apprenticed in Bristol: Peter Edson to William Hamonds, 4 years Virginia. (BR).

12 February. The following apprenticed in Bristol: Lewis Harry to William Morgan, 4 years Virginia; Edward Price to same, 4 years Virginia. (BR).

15 February. The following apprenticed in Bristol: Edward Jones to David Tucker, 4 years Virginia. (BR).

20 February. The following apprenticed in Bristol: Elizabeth Morgan to William Morgan, 5 years Virginia. (BR).

25 February. Pass granted for the *Elizabeth*, Mr. Anthony Langston, to sail for Carolina to fetch masts. (APC).

26 February. The following apprenticed in Bristol: Jonathan Bateman to Katherine Tayler, 4 years Virginia. (BR).

27 February. The following apprenticed in Bristol: Jennet Jefferis to John ?Baring, 6 years Virginia. (BR).

February. Probate of will of James Drumont of Virginia, bachelor. (AW).

1 March. Warrant for the following London and Middlesex prisoners in Newgate to be embarked by John Pate for Virginia: William Payne, Edward Evans, John Ward, Thomas Harwood, Robert Allen, William Allen, Jonas Sonier alias Somner, Dorothy Bywater, Nicholas Danse, John English, George Windrewe, William Alexander, Matthew Cotten, William Kellam, Isaac Oliver, John Coughtland, John Smith, Mathew Jones, John Sowell, John Rivers and Nathaniel Hulbert. (PRO: SP44/29/192).

5 March. The following apprenticed in Bristol: Victoria Davis to William Morgan, 4 years Virginia; Katherine Davis to same, 6 years Virginia; Grace Hooke to John Bure, 4 years Virginia; Elizabeth Hooke to same, 4 years Virginia. (BR).

6 March. The following apprenticed in Bristol: James Weaver to Anthony ——er, 4 years Barbados; Richard Stephens to William Morgan, 4 years Virginia. (BR).

12 March. The following apprenticed in Bristol: Phillip Davis to John Tucker, 4 years Virginia; Arthur Lewis to William Hamonds, 5 years Virginia. (BR).

12 March. Depositions re the voyage of the *Susanna*, Mr. William Rock, from Portsmouth to Virginia in 1666. (EA).

18 March. The following apprenticed in Bristol: Lyeon Davis to George Mullens, 5 years Barbados; James Ricketts to Vincent Thorne, 4 years Barbados. (BR).

21 March. The following apprenticed in Bristol: Ryer George to George Stokes, 4 years Barbados. (BR).

28 March. The following apprenticed in Bristol: Elizabeth Hoyle to Vincent Thorne, 4 years Barbados. (BR).

30 March. The following apprenticed in Bristol: John David to Vincent Thorne, 6 years Barbados. (BR).

March. Probate of will of Thomas Mathew of Holborn, Middlesex, whose daughter, Mary, was in Maryland. (AW).

1 April. The following apprenticed in Bristol: Thomas Roberts to William Hooper, 3 years Barbados; Elioner Jones to Robert Warren, 4 years Barbados; Mary Davis to same, 4 years Barbados. (BR).

3 April. The following apprenticed in Bristol: Francis Hide to Robert Warren, 4 years Barbados. (BR).

4 April. Chancery suit of John Dolman, executor of John Achley of London, merchant, v. William Martin, master of the *Hope* which took goods and servants to York River, Virginia, in 1666. (NGSQ 66/3).

4 April. The following apprenticed in Bristol: Thomas Morgan to Nicholas Williams, 4 years Barbados. (BR).

5 April. The following apprenticed in Bristol: Jane Grining to Foulke Adams, 4 years Barbados. (BR).

10 April. The following apprenticed in Bristol: Evan Jones to Richard Warren, 4 years Barbados. (BR).

12 April. The following apprenticed in Bristol: David Jones to Anthony Swymer, 4 years Barbados; Mary Hicks to Evan Roberts, 4 years Barbados. (BR).

12 April. Pass for the *Phillip* of London, Mr. Henry Creyk, to sail for New York. (APC).

13 April. The following apprenticed in Bristol: Evan Lewis to Edward Noble, 6 years Barbados; Thomas Palmer to James Knight, 4 years Barbados. (BR).

15 April. The following apprenticed in Bristol: Elizabeth Collins to John Cooke, 4 years Barbados. (BR).

16 April. The following apprenticed in Bristol: John Willis to Anthony Swymer, 4 years Barbados; Michaell Williams to same, 4 years Barbados; John Willis to Thomas Lukins, 4 years Barbados; Evan Davis to Richard Warren, 4 years Barbados; William Edwins to Mathew Steevens, 4 years Barbados. (BR).

16 April. Deposition by John Whitty of the Tower of London, mariner aged 25, that he lived with Captain John Whitty and managed his affairs for eleven years. Edmond Lister alias Francis Jackson, formerly of Thornton in Craven, Yorkshire, gent, and late resident in Maryland, was indebted to Captain John Whitty, whose administratrix is Sarah Whitty. (LMCD).

17 April. The following apprenticed in Bristol: Alice Hodgkinson to Richard Warren, 4 years Barbados. (BR).

20 April. The following apprenticed in Bristol: Thomas Smith to James Knight, 4 years Barbados. (BR).

23 April. The following apprenticed in Bristol: Elizabeth Goodwen to Foulke Adams, 4 years Barbados. (BR).

24 April. The following apprenticed in Bristol: William Jones to Thomas Phelps, 4 years Barbados. (BR).

27 April. The following apprenticed in Bristol: Robert Durnell to Foulke Adams, 4 years Barbados; Elioner Lewis to Richard Tuckey, 4 years Barbados. (BR).

30 April. The following apprenticed in Bristol: William Waters to Margery Jones, 4 years Barbados; Walter Jones to James Knight, 4 years Barbados. (BR).

April(?) Petition by James Ward for the transportation to the plantations of his wife who was convicted at Oxford Quarter Sessions for stealing. (CSPC).

April. Administration of John Sharpe of New England. (AW)

9 May. The following apprenticed in Bristol: Thomas Evans to John Cooke, 4 years Barbados. (BR).

10 May. The following apprenticed in Bristol: Richard Morgan to Thomas Lukins, 4 years Barbados; Thomas Jones to same, 4 years Barbados; Anne James to Richard Warren, 5 years Barbados. (BR).

10 May. Deposition by John Orpe, citizen and scrivener of London, aged 60, that William Lowring of Huntington, Long Island, New England, clerk, and Caleb Lowring of the same, yeoman, became indebted to John Fish, citizen and fletcher of London, by deed of 26 February 1662. (LMCD).

11 May. The following apprenticed in Bristol: Reece Lloyd to Thomas Lukins, 4 years Barbados; Thomas Davis to same, 4 years Barbados; Morgan Williams to William Rodney, 4 years Barbados; John Wattkins to same, 4 years Barbados. (BR).

15 May. The following apprenticed in Bristol: Henry Bartlett to John Franck, 9 years New England. (BR).

21 May. The following apprenticed in Bristol: David Nicholls to William Rodney, 4 years Barbados; Joane Blathen to Lodowick Steevens, 4 years Barbados. (BR).

23 May. The following apprenticed in Bristol: John Reeves to Thomas Attkins, 6 years Barbados. (BR).

25 May. The following apprenticed in Bristol: John Morelly to William Rodney, 6 years Barbados. (BR).

May. Probate of will of Samuel Angier of Dordrecht, Holland, whose brother, Edmund Angier, was in New England. (AW).

May. Probate of will of William Allright of Arborfield, Berkshire, whose daughter, Margaret Avery, was in New England.

1 June. The following apprenticed in Bristol: David James to William Rodney, 4 years Barbados. (BR).

3 June. The following apprenticed in Bristol: William Hampton to William Rodney, 6 years Barbados; Elizabeth Bence to Lawrance Raymond, 4 years Barbados. (BR).

6 June. The following apprenticed in Bristol: John Hunt to Thomas Lawrance, 4 years Barbados. (BR).

7 June. The following apprenticed in Bristol: Hugh Jones to William Williams, 4 years Virginia; Elizabeth Jenkins to Richard Morgan, 4 years Barbados. (BR).

15 June. The following apprenticed in Bristol: Richard Davis to Richard Bigglestone, 4 years Barbados. (BR).

15 June. The following prisoners in Newgate to be transported with their own consent: Charles Lawrence, Edward Langley, Thomas Heritage, John Peirce, John Wright, Hugh Wogan, Robert Shipley. (PRO: SP29/205/92).

17 June. The following apprenticed in Bristol: Edward Thomas to William Rodney, 4 years Barbados. (BR).

19 June. The following apprenticed in Bristol: John Wright to David Hissing, 4 years Barbados. (BR).

June. Probate of will of Samuel Crosse of St. Saviour, Southwark, Surrey, who had assets in Boston, New England. (AW).

5 July. The following apprenticed in Bristol: John Francisco to Jasper Guerne, 4 years Barbados; Pedro Pedraldus to Guasper Guerrin, 4 years Barbados; Griffeth Bowen to William Bowen, 4 years Barbados; John Prichard to William Rodney, 4 years Barbados. (BR).

15 July. The following apprenticed in Bristol: Joane Attwood to Robert Fane, 4 years Barbados. (BR).

24 July. The following apprenticed in Bristol: Joseph Scull to Michaell Lane, 7 years Barbados. (BR).

25 July. The following apprenticed in Bristol: William Gilbert to William Swymer, 7 years Barbados. (BR).

27 July. The following apprenticed in Bristol: Arthur Parker to John Jenkins, 4 years Barbados. (BR).

30 July. The following apprenticed in Bristol: John Bird to William Hayman, 4 years Barbados. (BR).

July. Administration with will of Sir Robert Carr of Carr Island, New England, but who died in Bristol. (AW).

July. Probate of will of Sir Robert Peake of Richmond, Surrey, whose cousin, George Lyddall, was in Virginia. (AW).

2 August. The following apprenticed in Bristol: Elinor Folliott to Leonard Hancock, 4 years Barbados. (BR).

6 August. Western Circuit prisoners reprieved to be transported to Barbados. Cornwall: John Cornish of St. Ives. Devon: David Thomas of Westleigh; Anne Gibbs of Chulmleigh, spinster; Edward Lisle alias Lile of Buckland Brewer; Michael Basse of Crediton, husbandman; Thomasine Hawcombe alias Holcombe of Tiverton, spinster; Gilbert Austyne of Christow, husbandman; Anthony Paddon of East Ogwell, mason; Amos Parke alias Parkin of Westleigh, mariner; Edward Cornish of Peters Morlynge, husbandman; John Ediver alias Brooke of Barnstaple, husbandman; William Chudley of Buckland Brewer; Robert Leach of Crediton, weaver. Dorset: Thomas Pope of Candlemarsh, husbandman; John Foote of Maiden Newton, blacksmith;

John Chanings of Symondsbury, husbandman; Stephen Hallett alias Richard Dykes of Tarrant Hinton, husbandman. Somerset: Francis Greeneslade of Stogumber, carpenter; John Fricker of Frome Selwood, husbandman; William Nurcombe of Luxborough, butcher; Thomas Greene of Stogumber, husbandman; Richard Gwyre of Aishill, husbandman; Philip Cole of Kilton, worsted comber. Wiltshire: Walter Lambe of Fisherton Anger; William Hatton of Fisherton Anger; Robert Lawrence of Bromham, butcher; John Davis of Fisherton Anger; William Ball of Carle Stoke, husbandman; John Dole of Carle Stoke, husbandman. (PRO: C66/3091/5).

6 August. The following apprenticed in Bristol: William Game to Lodowick Steevens, 4 years Barbados. (BR).

12 August. The following apprenticed in Bristol: Thomas Middlemore to John Deane, 4 years Barbados; George Haward to Clement Harmant, 4 years Barbados. (BR).

16 August. The following apprenticed in Bristol: Elinor Thomas to William Swymer, 4 years Barbados; Cicillia Branch to same, 4 years Barbados. (BR).

23 August. The following apprenticed in Bristol: William Still to Gasper Guerin, 4 years Barbados; Thomas Facha to same, 4 years Barbados; George Homittslett to same, 4 years Barbados. (BR).

24 August. The following apprenticed in Bristol: John Essington to Edward Tocknell, 4 years Barbados. (BR).

28 August. The following apprenticed in Bristol: Andrew Hughs to Edward Tocknell, 4 years Barbados; Penelope Yates to John Streaton, 4 years Barbados. (BR).

29 August. The following apprenticed in Bristol: Richard Joanes to Robert Davis, 4 years Barbados. (BR).

30 August. The following apprenticed in Bristol: Hugh Eades to Mathew Steevens, 5 years Barbados; Anne Sanford to Gasper Guerrin, 4 years Barbados; Elizabeth Darby to same, 4 years Barbados. (BR).

August. Administration of Richard Collins of Bristol, who died in Virginia, bachelor. (AW).

August. Administration of Joseph Martin who died in the King's service at sea or in Virginia, bachelor. (AW).

August. Administration with will Abraham Oker of the ship *Lord Salisbury* who died at sea on the ship *Bendish* bound for Virginia. (AW).

August. Administration with will of Margaret Lane of London, widow, whose sister, Martha, wife of William Eaton, was in New England. (AW).

2 September. The following apprenticed in Bristol: Addam Perry to Gasper Guerrin, 6 years Barbados; Thomas Travell to William Keetch, 4 years Barbados; John Harding to John Gwilliam, 4 years Virginia. (BR).

5 September. The following apprenticed in Bristol: John Ward to G—— D——, 4 years Barbados. (BR).

5 September. Deposition by John Jacob, born at Ipswich, New England, but now merchant of Wapping Middlesex, aged 23, re the voyage of the *John & Sarah*, Mr. John Payne, from New England to Surinam and London in 1664. (EA).

6 September. The following apprenticed in Bristol: Mary Smith to Jacob Tomson, 4 years Virginia. (BR).

9 September. The following apprenticed in Bristol: Reece Morgan to John Bowry, 4 years Virginia; John Evans to same, 4 years Virginia. (BR).

15 September. The following apprenticed in Bristol: Thomas Washington to Peter Dyer, 4 years Barbados. (BR).

17 September. The following apprenticed in Bristol: John Steephens to William Keetch, 4 years Barbados; Margery Ames to Christopher Sadbury, 4 years Virginia. (BR).

18 September. The following apprenticed in Bristol: Elizabeth Went to William Davis, 4 years Barbados; Joseph Hemings to Richard Gottley, 5 years Virginia; John Standfell to Christopher Tricks, 4 years Barbados. (BR).

19 September. The following apprenticed in Bristol: John Morgan to John Redgwin, 4 years Virginia; Blanch Jones to John Hunt, 4 years Virginia; Elizabeth Grove to John Stoakes, 4 years Virginia. (BR).

20 September. The following apprenticed in Bristol: John Flory to Lodowick Steephens, 4 years Barbados; Mary Sheapheard to John Blisse, 7 years Virginia; Mary Atkins to same, 4 years Virginia. (BR).

23 September. The following apprenticed in Bristol: John Price to Lawrence Raymond, 4 years Barbados; Thomas Richardson to Darby Conens, 4 years Virginia. (BR).

24 September. The following apprenticed in Bristol: John Lotte to Samuell Hatton, 4 years Virginia; Humphrey Goodwin to Thomas Duddlestone, 4 years Virginia. (BR).

25 September. The following apprenticed in Bristol: Richard Rawlins to William Keech, 5 years Barbados; John Popkin to same, 4 years Barbados. (BR).

26 September. The following apprenticed in Bristol: Joane Minson to Benjamin Johnson, 5 years Virginia; Joane Lawen to same, 4 years Virginia; Nathaniell Scriven to Thomas Dunning, 4 years Nevis; Elizabeth Dyer to Martha ?Moggs, 4 years Barbados. (BR).

30 September. The following apprenticed in Bristol: John Tayler to John Pyne, 4 years Virginia. (BR).

September. Probate of will of Ralph Vizer formerly of Dublin, Ireland, but late of Bristol, whose son, Henry Vizer, was in Virginia. (AW).

September. Administration of Mathias Prosser of St. Giles Cripplegate, London, who died in Virginia. (AW).

September. Administration of Arthur Ruthra of Virginia. (AW).

September. John Byne, aged 15, apprenticed from Christ's Hospital to Mr. John Newton, merchant, to be sent to Barbados. (CH).

1 October. The following apprenticed in Bristol: Thomas Aylworth to Edward Watkins, 4 years Barbados; Jane Mathews to same, 4 years Barbados; Mary Joanes to same, 4 years Barbados. (BR).

2 October. The following apprenticed in Bristol: William Whitstone to William Keech, 4 years Barbados. (BR).

3 October. The following apprenticed in Bristol: Anne Davis to Francis Harris, 4 years Virginia; Edward Dagg to John Smith, 4 years Nevis; Arthur Norwood to Peter Stoakes, 4 years Virginia; William Davis to same, 6 years Virginia. (BR).

5 October. The following apprenticed in Bristol: Hugh Jones to Nathaniell Cadle, 7 years Virginia; Lewis Williams to Miles Carrett, 4 years Virginia; Thomas Parker to Robert Lancaster, 4 years Barbados. (BR).

4-31 October. Shippers by the *Virginia Merchant* of Bideford, Mr. Joseph Chope, bound from Barnstaple for Virginia: Abraham Heiman, Richard Williams. (PRO: E190/1009/2).

8 October. The following apprenticed in Bristol: William Bunn to Thomas Dunning, 4 years Nevis; John Henbury to Thomas Wright, 4 years Virginia; Elioner Clarke to Thomas Willis, 4 years Virginia; Nathaniell Tucker to George Markes, 4 years Virginia. (BR).

9 October. The following apprenticed in Bristol: John Hort to Thomas Willis, 4 years Virginia; John Davis to John White, 8 years Virginia; George Monke to Thomas Dunning, 4 years Nevis; William Oadams to Thomas Hyatt, 4 years Virginia; James Hughs to George Marks, 4 years Virginia. (BR).

10 October. The following apprenticed in Bristol: Precilla Draper to Richard Pawle, 4 years Virginia. (BR).

11 October. The following apprenticed in Bristol: Elizabeth Morgan to Francis Lawrence, 4 years Virginia; Anne Perrine to John Smith, 4 years Barbados. (BR).

11 October. Shipper by the *Dolphin* of Bideford, Mr. Robert Berry, bound from Barnstaple for Virginia: John Liskum. (PRO: E190/1009/2).

12 October. The following apprenticed in Bristol: John Redman to Hanniball Garlick, 5 years Barbados; Nicholas Browne to George Marks, 4 years Virginia; Elizabeth Ewins to Christopher Sadbury, 4 years Virginia; Edward Wootton to Thomas Warrin, 4 years Virginia; Thomas Martine to Anthony Cadle, 4 years Virginia; John Spinner to John Kedgiom, 4 years Virginia. (BR).

14 October. The following apprenticed in Bristol: Joseph Hedges to Thomas Willis, 4 years Virginia; Joseph Harding to John Rodway, 4 years Virginia; Thomas Jones to same, 4 years Virginia; Jenkine Jones to same, 4 years Virginia. (BR).

15 October. The following apprenticed in Bristol: John Reeve to William Busher, 5 years Virginia; Davis Dawks to George Marks, 4 years Virginia. (BR).

16 October. The following apprenticed in Bristol: Mary Pearce to Robert Morgan, 4 years Virginia; Richard Higgens to Marke Chappell, 4 years Virginia; Mary Tyle to John Lugg, 4 years Virginia; Katherine Bastable to same, 4 years Virginia. (BR).

17 October. The following apprenticed in Bristol: James Mayden to James Warren, 4 years Virginia; Charles Corens, spinster (*sic*), to Gabriell Bridges, 4 years Virginia. (BR).

18 October. The following apprenticed in Bristol: Howell Williams to John Barnes, 4 years Virginia; Jane Leveale to Thomas Speede, 5 years Barbados; Peter Humphrys to Mathew Homer, 4 years Virginia; Thomas Hamms to Edward Poore, 4 years Virginia; James Jones to John Tucker, 4 years Virginia; Anne Pounsibe to Mathew King, 4 years Virginia. (BR).

19 October. The following apprenticed in Bristol: Francis Davis to Robert Spenser, 4 years Virginia; John Ames to Nathaniell Robbins, 4 years Nevis; Anne Thomas to John Hardwick, 4 years Virginia; John Powell to George Markes, 4 years Virginia; Thomas Boyle to John Stoakes, 4 years Virginia. (BR).

21 October. The following apprenticed in Bristol: William Russell to John Stoakes, 4 years Virginia; John Smith to John Rumming, 5 years Virginia; William Sparke to John Orchard, 4 years Virginia; Andrew Mare to Thomas Willis, 4 years Virginia; George Browne to Edmund Woodruffe, 4 years Virginia; John Dibble to David Fry, 4 years Virginia. (BR).

22 October. The following apprenticed in Bristol: Robert Smith to John Willson, 4 years Barbados; Alice Crumpe to Margaret Huling, 4 years Virginia. (BR).

23 October. The following apprenticed in Bristol: Harbert Williams to Robert Spenser, 4 years Virginia; Morrice Williams to John Boyce, 5 years Virginia; Precilla Draper to John Hardige, 4 years Virginia; Thomas Ley to George

Tushingham, 5 years Virginia; Thomas Waterman to same, 5 years Virginia; Timothy Howse to John Isaacks, 5 years Nevis; Nicholas Pye to George Markes, 3 years Virginia. (BR).

24 October. Deposition by William Bower of London, scrivener aged 39, and Richard Owen of London, merchant aged 52, that Henry Sewall of Maryland became indebted by bond of 23 July 1664 to Thomas Tomlins, citizen and grocer of London, now deceased. His executors, Gilbert Metcalfe of London, merchant, and Francis Camfield, citizen and grocer of London, on 14 October 1667, signed a letter of attorney to James Husbands of London, merchant, Richard Preston of Patuxent, Maryland, merchant, and John Wilson of Stepney, Middlesex, surgeon. (LMCD).

24 October. Deposition by John Meredith, aged 23, servant and apprentice of James Johnsey, citizen and grocer of London, dwelling in Beech Lane, that he was formerly the apprentice of Andrew Middleton, citizen and grocer of London, now resident in Virginia. Four or five years ago Middleton sold goods to Sara, wife of John Godfrey of Virginia, planter, who is now married to William Porten of Virginia. He makes this deposition on behalf of Elizabeth, wife of Andrew Middleton. (LMCD).

25 October. Newgate prisoners reprieved to be transported to Barbados. London: George Anderton; Charles Lawrence; Robert Francklyn; William Payne; Edward Evans; John Ward; Thomas Haywood; William Allen; Robert Allen; Jonas Stonier alias Sommer; Penelope Dilling, spinster; Deborah Man; John Peirce alias Price; Hugh Oghen; John Wright alias Greene; Elizabeth Scott, spinster; Elizabeth Bond, spinster; Thomas Hosey; Alice Turner, spinster; Margaret Wexham, spinster, alias wife of Nicholas Wexham; Jane Jarvis, spinster, alias wife of Edward Jarvis; Jane Smith, spinster. Middlesex: Otwell Miller of Clerkenwell, yeoman; Isaac Oliver of St. Katherine by the Tower; Matthew Cotton of Islington; John Cooton (*sic*) of the same; John Turner of the same; William Kilam of Stratford by Bow; William Alexander of St. Martin in the Fields; Mary Haward of the same; Grace Hawkins, wife of John Hawkins of the same; Sarah Kirton of St. Margaret Westminster, spinster; Anne Belcherre of St. Giles Cripplegate, spinster; Anne Davies; Mary Waldron, spinster, alias wife of George Waldron of Clerkenwell; Elizabeth Milner alias Millier of St. Giles in the Fields, spinster; Adam Parrett of St. Andrew Holborn; John Gardiner of the same; Edward Garraway of Paddington; Robert Howard of Shoreditch; Thomas Austen of St. Paul Covent Garden; Margaret Grayer of St. Clement Danes, spinster. (PRO: C66/3088/4).

25 October. The following apprenticed in Bristol: John Moises to Richard Pall, 4 years Virginia; William Wottner to Robert Spenser, 5 years Virginia; Jane Jones to same, 4 years Virginia; Mary Cornish to Roger Dickason, 4 years Barbados; Paull Slade to George Markes, 3 years Virginia; William Mappett to Thomas Bowkin, 4 years Virginia; Phillip Cox to James Hewlingson, 4 years Virginia. (BR).

25 October. Shipper by the *Black Swan* of Barnstaple, Mr. Johnson Morkum, bound from Barnstaple for Virginia: Sara Dennis. (PRO: E190/1009/2).

28 October. The following apprenticed in Bristol: Julias Thruston to Edmund Woodruffe, 4 years Virginia; George Arriall to George Arriall, 4 years Virginia. (BR).

29 October. The following apprenticed in Bristol: John Pope to John Willett, 4 years Virginia; John Curtis to same, 4 years Virginia; Richard Curtis to same, 4 years Virginia; Roger Churchill to same, 4 years Virginia; John Monke to John Webb, 4 years Virginia; Humphry Curtis to James Elver, 4 years Virginia; Joane Ayly to George Tushingham, 11 years Virginia; Edith Symmes to same, 4 years Virginia; Edith Symmes Jr. to same, 11 years Virginia; Howell Davis to John Yeamans Jr., 5 years Nevis; Susanna Dutton to George Brent, 5 years Virginia; Robert Merrick to John Snow, 5 years Virginia. (BR).

30 October. The following apprenticed in Bristol: Robert Francis to John Willett, 4 years Virginia; John Fisher to same, 4 years Virginia; James Dunning to same, 4 years Virginia; Thomas Cradduck to John Seaward, 4 years Virginia; John Balding to Samuell Lewis, 7 years Virginia; Jane Bagwell to John Coleman, 5 years Virginia; Joane Toms to same, 5 years Virginia; Arthur Ayler to George Tushingham, 11 years Virginia; Edward Ayler to same, 7 years Virginia. (BR).

30 October. Shipper by the *Primrose* of Newcastle bound from Newcastle for Maryland: David Poole. (PRO: E190/194/1).

31 October. The following apprenticed in Bristol: James Joanesson to Joseph Adlam, 4 years Virginia. (BR).

October. Probate of will of William Corderoy of Virginia, bachelor. (AW).

October. Probate of will of Anne Cheyney of St. Katherine Creechurch, London, whose cousin, Anne Roe, was in Virginia. (AW).

October. Limited administration of Edward Locky of Virginia, planter, who died in St. Katherine Creechurch, London. (AW).

1 November. The following apprenticed in Bristol: Hosea Cobb to William Morrice, 5 years Virginia; John Golledge to Richard Crabb, 5 years Virginia; Edward Jeffris to Thomas Harris, 4 years Virginia. (BR).

2 November. The following apprenticed in Bristol: Anne Morrice to John Rodny, 4 years Virginia; Joseph Godward to same, 4 years Virginia; William Towers to Thomas Warren, 4 years Virginia. (BR).

6 November. The following apprenticed in Bristol: Thomas Hunt to Henry Izoe, 4 years Virginia; John Hunt to same, 4 years Virginia; Sunnell Byron to same, 4 years Virginia; John Meads to same, 4 years Virginia; Elioner Smith to same, 4 years Virginia; John Davis to John Stratton, 4 years Virginia; Thomas

Garnish to Edward Lassells, 5 years Virginia; Richard Tompson to John Joanes, 3 years Nevis. (BR).

7 November. The following apprenticed in Bristol: John Guppie to Thomas Opey, 4 years Virginia; Samuell Stepney to Thomas Jarvis, 4 years Virginia; Henry Abery to same, 4 years Virginia; Grace Cole to same, 4 years Virginia; Mary Brint to same, 4 years Virginia; Elizabeth Bevan to Henry Rich, 4 years Nevis; Elizabeth Manford to Edward Perrin, 4 years Virginia. (BR).

8 November. The following apprenticed in Bristol: John Wattkins to John Morgan, 6 years Barbados; Mathias Lewis to Thomas Warren, 5 years Virginia; Thomas Bachellor to Edward Alichurch, 7 years Virginia; Thomas James to John Redgewin, 4 years Virginia; Thomas Eden to Henry Izoe, 4 years Virginia. (BR).

9 November. The following apprenticed in Bristol: Reece Thomas to James Edwards, 4 years Nevis; Hester Earney to William Hardich, 6 years Virginia; Thomas Wayte to John Lugg, 5 years Virginia; Elizabeth Peters to John Keege, 4 years Virginia. (BR).

11 November. The following apprenticed in Bristol: Barbara Jones to Thomas Jones, 4 years Virginia; William Hart to Thomas Peasley, 7 years Virginia; Teage Ishmead to same, 7 years Virginia. (BR).

11 November-8 February. Depositions re the voyage of the *Recovery*, Mr. William Whiteing and Mr. Roger Newham, from Virginia to New England and London in 1666, including a deposition by Thomas Hawker of Stepney, Middlesex, sailor aged 28, who was born in Halton, Lancashire, and lived in Virginia before 1665. (EA).

13 November. The following apprenticed in Bristol: Thomas Joanes to Thomas Franklin, 4 years Virginia; Penelope Pretty to William Hoottest, 5 years Virginia; Pheby Carver to Anne Lugge, 6 years Virginia. (BR).

14 November. The following apprenticed in Bristol: Jonas Bennet to Robert Spencer, 9 years Virginia; Giles Waters to John Isaacks, 4 years Nevis; Margery Hughes to same, 4 years Nevis; Thomas Bindow to William Hazard, 4 years Virginia; John Trigg Sr. to Samuell Tovey, 4 years Virginia; John Trigg Jr. to same, 4 years Virginia; Walter Graunt to same, 4 years Virginia; Thomas Preston to same, 4 years Virginia. (BR).

18 November. The following apprenticed in Bristol: Edward Goodman to William Wathen, 4 years Virginia; John Towers to Lott Richards, 4 years Virginia; Elizabeth Cox to James Edwards, 4 years Nevis; Elizabeth Greenelane to same, 4 years Nevis; Richard Towsey to Thomas Blys, 4 years Virginia; Barbara Towsey to same, 4 years Virginia. (BR).

18 November. Shipper by the *Mary* of Bristol, Mr. William Light, bound from Portsmouth for Virginia: Paull Richards. (PRO: E190/826/16).

19 November. The following apprenticed in Bristol: Moses Joanes to John Morgan, 3 years Virginia. (BR).

20 November. The following apprenticed in Bristol: William Leachman to John Joanes, 4 years Nevis; Samuell James to Richard Gottly, 4 years Virginia; William Carpenter to Andrew Exon, 4 years Virginia; John Lawson to Thomas Norman, 4 years Virginia; Edith Collins to Andrew Simonds, 4 years Virginia. (BR).

21 November. The following apprenticed in Bristol: Thomas Barnes to Henry Lambert, 4 years Virginia; Isaack Caines to same, 4 years Virginia; Nathaniell Wiggmore to same, 4 years Virginia; James Caines to same, 4 years Virginia; Joane Bayly to same, 4 years Virginia; Joane Hollyer to same, 4 years Virginia; Joane Mouly to same, 4 years Virginia; Hugh Barlow to Edward Jones alias Taberfield, 4 years Virginia. (BR).

22 November. The following apprenticed in Bristol: Walter Hughs to Thomas Joanes, 3 years Virginia; John Alloway to John Bay, 3 years Virginia; John Ricroft to Thomas Attkins, 4 years Nevis; Sarah Bollen to William Prisly, 5 years Virginia; Joane West to same, 5 years Virginia; Mary Head to same, 4 years Virginia; John Peach to John Chance, 4 years Virginia. (BR).

23 November. The following apprenticed in Bristol: John Ellis to William Scott, 7 years Virginia; Anne Yeats to John Beare, 5 years Virginia; William Hickman to John Pooe (*sic*), 7 years Virginia; Henry Follett to John Gibbs, 4 years Virginia; Welthian Thomas to Mathew Stevens, 4 years Virginia; William Boysom to Robert Streete, 5 years Virginia. (BR).

25 November. The following apprenticed in Bristol: George Davis to Richard West, 4 years Virginia; Israll Prater, spinster, to John Bay, 4 years Virginia; Hopwell Wood to George Walker, 6 years Virginia; Mary Godwin to same, 4 years Virginia. (BR).

26 November. The following apprenticed in Bristol: Thomas Knight to James Edwards, 4 years Nevis; Elizabeth Mills to same, 4 years Nevis. (BR).

27 November. The following apprenticed in Bristol: Thomas George to Robert Morgan, 4 years Virginia; Rowland Pitt to William Buttler, 4 years Virginia; Richard Millard to same, 4 years Virginia; Evan Thomas to Thomas Norman, 4 years Virginia; William Arnold to Thomas Donning, 4 years Virginia. (BR).

29 November. The following apprenticed in Bristol: Edward Williams to Henry Rich, 4 years Nevis. (BR).

30 November. The following apprenticed in Bristol: John Straten to Darby Conner, 4 years Virginia; William Essex to Henry Rich, 4 years Nevis; Leonard Guntur to William Jenkins, 4 years Barbados; John Whattly to William Wathen, 5 years Virginia; John Williams to George Jones, 4 years Barbados or Leewards; James Williams to same, 4 years Barbados or Leewards; John Hawkins to same, 4 years Barbados or Leewards; James Webb to William

Paisly, 7 years Virginia; William Palmer to Tobias Ised, 4 years Virginia; Moses Dunckly to Robert Lancaster, 7 years Virginia. (BR).

2 December. The following apprenticed in Bristol: Roger Corzer to Lawrence Raymond, 6 years Barbados; Moses Dunckley to Anne Dorington, 7 years Virginia. (BR).

3 December. The following apprenticed in Bristol: Peter Atherton to William Hottost, 4 years Virginia; John Gibbs to William Hazell, 4 years Virginia. (BR).

4 December. The following apprenticed in Bristol: John Marrin to Richard Haskins, 4 years Virginia; Josias Wilcox to John Isaacks, 4 years Nevis. (BR).

5 December. The following apprenticed in Bristol: William Belcher to John Woory, 4 years Virginia; Henry Coopy to same, 4 years Virginia. (BR).

6 December. The following apprenticed in Bristol: Thomas Hichens to Thomas Aylway, 5 years Virginia; Thomas Hill to Thomas Parker, 7 years Virginia; Thomas George to Tymothy Stamp, 4 years Virginia; Benjamin George to same, 4 years Virginia. (BR).

9 December. The following apprenticed in Bristol: Anne Borsley to Anne Dorington, 4 years Virginia. (BR).

10 December. The following apprenticed in Bristol: Anne Collier to Darby Conner, 4 years Virginia. (BR).

11 December. The following apprenticed in Bristol: James Hill to George Peale, 4 years Virginia. (BR).

12 December. The following apprenticed in Bristol: Elioner James to Ezeckiell Braithwayt, 4 years Virginia; Elizabeth Cary to Henry Rich, 4 years Nevis. (BR).

13 December. The following apprenticed in Bristol: John Shelly to John Beare, 4 years Virginia. (BR).

13 December. Shipper by the *Gift* of Ilfracombe, Mr. John Perriman, bound from Barnstaple for Virginia: Mary Liskum. (PRO: E190/1009/2).

18 December. The following apprenticed in Bristol: Richard Poole to William Howell, 4 years Virginia. (BR).

19 December. The following apprenticed in Bristol: Judith Cooper to Anthony Alderson, 4 years Barbados; Luce Jones to same, 4 years Barbados. (BR).

20 December. The following apprenticed in Bristol: Anne Perren to Anthony Alderson, 4 years Barbados. (BR).

23 December. The following apprenticed in Bristol: Richard Roach to Nicholas Burroughs, 4 years Barbados; Richard Pymm to Anthony Alderson, 4 years Barbados. (BR).

24 December. The following apprenticed in Bristol: Griffith Towgood to William Dale, 7 years Virginia; John Cuffe to William Scott, 7 years Virginia; Francis Street to Christopher Birkhead, 7 years Virginia. (BR).

29 December. The following apprenticed in Bristol: Richard Harmer to Thomas Ackson, 4 years Virginia. (BR).

30 December. Shipper by the *Samuell* of Plymouth bound from Plymouth for Virginia: Henry Webb. (PRO: E190/1038/8, 1038/12).

30-31 December. Shippers by the *Constance*, Mr. Henry Edwards, bound from London for Virginia: Phillip Forster; John Dandy. (PRO: E190/52/1).

30 December-10 January. Shippers by the *Society* of Bristol bound from Bristol for Virginia: Gerrard Smart; Robert Bagnell; Edward Perryn. (PRO: E190/1137/1).

31 December. The following apprenticed in Bristol: Joane Drew to Samuell Tipton, 5 years Barbados. (BR).

31 December-7 January. Shippers by the *Stephen* of Bristol bound from Bristol for Virginia: James Lyght, Richard Crump. (PRO: E190/1137/1).

31 December-13 January. Shippers by the *John & Martha*, Mr. John Goffe, bound from London for Virginia: Thomas Blayton, Richard Brinley, Jeremiah Mount, Benjamin Peck. (PRO: E190/52/1).

1668

1 January. The following apprenticed in Bristol: Joane Golledge to Edward Ferren, 4 years Virginia. (BR).

2 January. Shipper by the *Gabriel*, Mr. Henry Roach, bound from London for Virginia: said Henry Roach. (PRO: E190/52/1).

7 January. The following apprenticed in Bristol: Jerimy Hughs to Anthony Alderson, 4 years Barbados. (BR).

8 January. Shipper by the *Humphrey & Elizabeth* bound from London for Virginia: Edward Hollingshed. (PRO: E190/52/1).

10 January. The following apprenticed in Bristol: William Browne to Mary Scott, 4 years Virginia. (BR).

13 January-7 February. Shippers by the *Endeavour*, Mr. Samuell Legg & Mr. Edward Clements, bound from London for New England: John Harwood, Robert Woolley, Margaret Bridges, William Thomas, Edmond White. (PRO: E190/52/1).

14-27 January. Shippers by the *Duke of York*, Mr. Thomas James, bound from London for Virginia: Robert Baxter, William Gold. (PRO: E190/52/1).

16-27 January. Shippers by the *Advice*, Mr. Daniell Pensax, bound from London for Virginia: Thomas Webb, Thomas Thornton. (PRO: E190/52/1).

20 January. The following apprenticed in Bristol: Richard Hall to John Lewis, 4 years Barbados. (BR).

20 January. Samuel Dunning, John Carter, Margaret Tyson and Susan Williams, prisoners in Surrey, petition to be transported to Virginia, being young and able. (SP Dom).

21 January. The following apprenticed in Bristol: William Wayt to Samuell Tipton, 4 years Barbados. (BR).

21-29 January. Shippers by the *Marigold*, Mr. Samuell Pensax, bound from London for Virginia: John Sheppard, Thomas Smith. (PRO: E190/52/1).

22 January. Shipper by the *Little Gertrude*, Mr. John Wilkinson, bound from London for Virginia: George Pott. (PRO: E190/52/1).

23 January. The following apprenticed in Bristol: William Reynald to Thomas Morgan, 4 years Barbados; John George to same, 4 years Barbados; Elizabeth Lloyd to Henry Backwell, 4 years Barbados. (BR).

29 January. The following apprenticed in Bristol: Jennett Jones to John Bourne, 6 years Barbados; Barthollomew Clark to same, 6 years Barbados; William

Allen to Thomas Liston, 5 years Barbados; Richard Harry to Daniell Samm, 4 years Barbados; Edward Morgan to same, 4 years Barbados; Dorothy Hollway to Thomas Liston, 6 years Barbados; David Mannian to Robert Pirton, 3 years Barbados. (BR).

31 January. Shipper by the *Wheatsheaf*, Mr. James Conway, bound from London for Virginia: Thomas Wilkin. (PRO: E190/52/1).

January. Shipper by the *Sarah*(?) bound from Plymouth for New England: Peter Marke. (PRO: E190/1038/12).

January. Administration of Samuel Richards of the ship *Elizabeth*, who died in Virginia on the King's service. (AW).

January. Administration of William Eastall of Virginia, who died at sea. (AW).

January. Administration of Richard Hall of London, who died in Virginia, widower. (AW).

1 February. The following apprenticed in Bristol: Phillip Joanes to Daniell Sam, 4 years Barbados. (BR).

3 February. The following apprenticed in Bristol: Jacob Perkins to Daniell Sam, 4 years Barbados; Robert Townsend to Thomas Child, 4 years Barbados. (BR).

5-29 February. Shippers by the *Rebecca*, Mr. William Redman, bound from London for Virginia: Thomas Taylor, Conyers Beckmore, John Good, William Fisher. (PRO: E190/52/1).

(6 February). Deposition by Charles Meller, citizen and vintner of London, aged 26, that Jonathan Ping of New England, merchant, became indebted to William Allen, citizen and upholder of London, by bond of 6 February 1668. (LMCD).

6 February. The following apprenticed in Bristol: John Barly to Daniell Sam, 4 years Barbados. (BR).

7-10 February. Shippers by the *Samuell & Jonathan*, Mr. William Hawes, bound from London for New England: Richard Michelborne, Noah Floyd, Robert Woolley. (PRO: E190/52/1).

8 February. The following apprenticed in Bristol: Margaret Hitchens to Daniell Sam, 4 years Barbados. (BR).

10 February. The following apprenticed in Bristol: Henry Hoger to John Biddleston, 5 years Barbados; Daniell Thomson to Thomas Berry, 3 years Barbados; Richard Bristoe to Robert Dike, 3 years Barbados. (BR).

12 February. Newgate prisoners reprieved to be transported to Barbados. London: John Butlin; Elias Vannacre; Ursula Kirke, spinster; John Niccoll; William Willis; Thomas Massey; William Brittaine; William Jerman; Humphrey Jones; John Vernon alias Verrowne. Middlesex: Edward Gladwin of St. Giles Cripplegate; Timothy Field of St. Martin in the Fields; Thomas

Fenne of the same; John Price of St. Botolph Aldgate; Thomas Hulston of St. Paul Covent Garden; William Smith alias Ridgley of the same; James Anderson of St. Giles in the Fields. (PRO: C66/3098/11).

14-26 February. Shippers by the *Supply*, Mr. John Fairweather, bound from London for New England: Robert Woolley, Noah Floyd, Samuell Sheafe, John Mansell. (PRO: E190/52/1).

18 February. The following apprenticed in Bristol: Thomas Nutt to Joseph Hunt, 4 years Barbados; Henry Summers to James Ithell, 6 years Barbados. (BR).

18 February-11 March. Shippers by the *Exchange* of Bideford bound from Bristol for New England: George Morris, John Saunders, Richard Benson, Samuell Wilson, Walter Hyde, Michaell Clothier, Thomas Scroope for John Harwood, Henry Roe, John Teige, William Reade, Edward Fielding, Thomas Walter, John Light. (PRO: E190/1137/1).

20 February. The following apprenticed in Bristol: Evan Davis to Thomas Attkins, 5 years Barbados. (BR).

21 February. Shipper by the *Elizabeth*, Mr. Stephen Dring, bound from London for New England: William Throckmorton. (PRO: E190/52/1).

22 February. The following apprenticed in Bristol: William Phelpes to John Lewis, 4 years Barbados; Mary Elbur to Thomas Saunders, 4 years Barbados; Mathew Phillips to William Sheepherd, 4 years Barbados; John Chamberlaine to William Merrick, 7 years Barbados; Henry Pym to Joseph Hunt, 4 years Barbados. (BR).

24 February. Western Circuit prisoners reprieved to be transported to Barbados. Cornwall: Richard Wyatt of St. Endellion. Devon: John Rogers of Hennock, husbandman; Robert Yalland of South Brent, husbandman; John Burnard of Sance, miller; John Woodley of Crediton, husbandman. Dorset: John Day of Sherborne, husbandman; John Coker of Great Canford. Hampshire: Thomas Thorne of Fordingbridge, husbandman; William Tilborow Jr. of Ilesfield, husbandman; Elinor Binfield of Basingstoke, singlewoman; Richard Kelsey Sr. of Romsey, husbandman. Somerset: John Penny of East Chinnock, husbandman; Charles Style of Lovington. Wiltshire: Edward Tupe of Downton, husbandman; Francis Marsh of Marlborough, husbandman. (PRO: C66/3098/2).

26 February. Colonel Edmund Scarborough, Surveyor-General of Virginia, petitions for redress against the Governor of Nevis. In August 1666 Robert Ramsden, commander of the *Providence* alias *Virginia Merchant* took his ship to Nevis and was there murdered and his ship seized. The Governor of Nevis is ordered to make satisfaction. (APC).

26 February. The following apprenticed in Bristol: Robert Griffis to Thomas Liston, 4 years Barbados; John Lonnon to William Tytherly, 4 years New England. (BR).

26 February. Shipper by the *Little Bartlet*, Mr. John Fairweather, bound from London for New England: John Mansell. (PRO: E190/52/1).

28 February. The following apprenticed in Bristol: Thomas Bennett to Thomas Berry, 4 years Barbados; Thomas Norover to William Hayman, 6 years Barbados; Walter Row to Richard Granger, 4 years Barbados. (BR).

February. Administration of John Fox of Virginia, bachelor. (AW).

2 March. The following apprenticed in Bristol: Thomas Davy to David Fox, 8 years New England. (BR).

3 March. The following apprenticed in Bristol: Darby Brayne to Owen Dorney, 2 ½ years Barbados; George Jinkins to John Howell, 5 years Barbados. (BR).

4 March. The following apprenticed in Bristol: John Ward to Cornewell Fox, 4 years Barbados; Elioner Bott to same, 4 years Barbados. (BR).

4 March-14 April. Shippers by the *Adventure* of Boston, New England, bound from Bristol for New England: John Willoughby, Richard Martyn, John Duddleston, Samuell Gould, Jeremiah Holway, Thomas Patten, Erasmus Dole, Henry Blackmore, Robert Vickris, Richard Olliver, Michaell Clothier, Thomas Deane, Richard Middlecot, Thomas Scroope, Thomas Walter. (PRO: E190/1137/1).

4-12 March. Shippers by the *Supply* of New England bound from Bristol for New England: John Machen, Thomas Leere, George Baxter, Thomas Saunders, Robert Elliot. (PRO: E190/1137/1).

6 March. The following apprenticed in Bristol: John Bull to Thomas Bedford, 4 years New England; Mary Conaway to same, 4 years New England; John Wright to John Biddlestone, 4 years Barbados. (BR).

9 March. The following apprenticed in Bristol: Jane Evans to Thomas Child, 4 years Barbados; Reece Jenkins to same, 4 years Barbados; Thomas Fry to Thomas Bedford, 9 years New England; Peter Poyner to same, 4 years Barbados; Margarett Crompton to Cornewall Fox, 4 years Barbados. (BR).

12 March. The following apprenticed in Bristol: Dorothy Tyler to Cornewall Fox, 4 years Barbados. (BR).

16 March. The following apprenticed in Bristol: Richard Bayly to Robert Ellett, 5 years New England. (BR).

19 March. Shipper by the *Fellowship* of Lyme, Mr. John Davy, bound from Plymouth for New England: Symon Orchard. (PRO: E190/1038/12).

19-28 March. Shippers by the *Constant*, Mr. Thomas Ofield, bound from London for New England: Hezekiah Usher, John Peake. (PRO: E190/52/1).

25 March. The following apprenticed in Bristol: James Browne to John White alias Cox, 4 years Barbados. (BR).

26 March. The following apprenticed in Bristol: Francis Grigory to John Read, 3 years Barbados. (BR).

27 March-17 April. Shippers by the *Nathaniel*, Mr. Thomas Smith, bound from London for New England: John Fullerton, St. Clare Raymond, William Taylor, Joseph Smart, John Sweeting, Robert Woolley, Freegrace Kendall, Samuell Wilson, George Agray, William Wyott, John Cleverley. (PRO: E190/52/1).

28 March. The following apprenticed in Bristol: Anthony Pickett to John Read, 3 years Barbados; Thomas Wall to Thomas Sanford, 4 years Barbados. (BR).

30 March. The following apprenticed in Bristol: John Rose to Phillip Jennings, 4 years Barbados or Leewards; Thomas Perrin to John Reed, 7 years Barbados. (BR).

31 March. The following apprenticed in Bristol: Henry Hill to Thomas Easton, 4 years Barbados. (BR).

31 March-5 April. Shippers by the *Dolphin*, Mr. William Foster, bound from London for New England: John Harwood, Noah Floyd, John Peake, Timothy Drake, Thomas Norman, Henry Ashurst, Henry Taylor, John Clement, Edward Shippen. (PRO: E190/52/1).

3 April. Thomas Gookin of Kingsale, Ireland, merchant, petitions for restitution of his ship *Hopewell*, Mr. John Gilson, which in 1665 was condemned in Maryland. [*See further entry of 12 August 1670*]. (APC).

4 April. Western Circuit prisoners reprieved to be transported to Barbados. Cornwall: John Congden of Lower St. Cullumb. Devon: James Tuckfield of Exeter; Thomas Holloway of Ivybridge, blacksmith; Thomas Conings of Tiverton, husbandman; Richard England of Littleham, husbandman; John Deane of Okehampton, husbandman; Andrew Bragg of Shebbear, husbandman; John Venner of Tiverton, husbandman; Robert Malcona of Parracombe, husbandman; Henry Bryar of Culmstock, husbandman; John Sheffield of Plympton St. Mary, weaver. Dorset: Thomas Bayly of Sutton Pointz, tailor; John Symes of West Kingston, husbandman. Hampshire. Richard Talbott of Titherley, husbandman. Somerset: John Drake of Crewkerne, husbandman; Jasper Dennett of Crewkerne, husbandman. Wiltshire: John Edmonds alias White of New Sarum, husbandman. (PRO: C66/3101/18).

6 April. The following apprenticed in Bristol: James Pearce to Foulke Adams, 4 years Barbados. (BR).

6 April. Shipper by the *Samuell*, Mr. John Smith, bound from London for New England: William Thomas. (PRO: E190/52/1).

7-10 April. Shippers by the *Neptune*, Mr. Christopher Hunt, bound from London for New England: James Littleton, John Harwood, Tobias Wickes. (PRO: E190/52/1).

8 April. The following apprenticed in Bristol: John Chaplin to Josias Allen, 4 years Barbados; William Mander to Thomas Stanford, 3 years Barbados; William Garland to Richard Granger, 3 years Barbados. (BR).

11 April. Home Circuit prisoners reprieved to be transported to Barbados. Essex: John Martin of Romford; Henry Sage of Theydon Bois; Bartholomew Huske of Earls Colne. Hertfordshire: Noel Hutchin of Barley; Elizabeth Wilson alias Dickson of Royston; John Broad of Abbots Langley; Ann Jones, spinster, alias wife of Charles Jones of Abbots Langley; John Jennings of Hertingfordbury. Kent: Christopher Weekes of Staplehurst; John Love and Edward Love of Cranbrook; William Peerlesse of Brasted; John Polley of Burling; Robert Wood of Brasted; Elizabeth Snipe of Maidstone; Andrew Crew of Maidstone. Surrey: Robert Barson of Kingston on Thames; John Martayne of Newington; Rose Baker, spinster, alias wife of George Baker of St. Olave, Southwark; George Keys of Newington; George Catchman of St. George, Southwark; Benjamin Johnson of Newington; Christopher Hughes of St. Olave, Southwark; Anthony Strickland of St. George, Southwark; John Rawlins of St. George, Southwark; William Connell of Newington; George Gidney of St. Saviour, Southwark; Elizabeth Cooper of St. Olave, Southwark; Joseph Smith of Newington; John Prior of St. George, Southwark. (PRO: C66/3101/22).

21 April. Home Circuit prisoners reprieved to be transported to Barbados. Surrey: William Wright of St. George, Southwark; Elizabeth Field of Cobham; Anne Smith of Cobham. Sussex: Thomas Wormelayton and Robert Wormelayton of Rusper; Robert Gosmark of Steyning; William Chambers of Horsham; William Heverdine of Chidham. Kent: Thomas Ham of Sundridge; William Hutson of Ruckinge. Suffolk: Elizabeth Shales, spinster, alias wife of Stephen Muttit, of St. Clement's, Ipswich. Essex: Hugh Glover of Orsett. Hertfordshire: Johanna Homby, spinster, alias wife of William Homby, of Welling; Rockingham Bason of Hadham; Thomas Blackett of Royston. (PRO: C66/3101/20).

16 April. The following apprenticed in Bristol: William Jones to John Read, 4 years Barbados; John Davis to James Stevens, 4 years Barbados. (BR).

22 April. Newgate prisoners reprieved to be transported to Barbados. London: John Peckett, John Price, Henry Cooper, John Tapping, Anne Jones, spinster, Margaret Dukesell, spinster. Middlesex: William Hall of Fulham; William Reynolds of Fulham; Henry Hare of St. Giles in the Fields; John Fell of St. Martin in the Fields; Jenkin Davis of the same; Christopher Williams of the same; Charles Blunt of Shoreditch; John Till of St. Andrew Holborn; William Hewitt of Stepney. (PRO: C66/3101/19).

25 April. The following apprenticed in Bristol: Roger Kenny to John Jones, 3 years Barbados. (BR).

27 April. The following apprenticed in Bristol: George Spigurnell to Phillip Jennings, 4 years Nevis. (BR).

29 April. The following apprenticed in Bristol: Ann Steevens to Walter Walton, 4 years Barbados; William Pritchard to John Hudson, 4 years Barbados. (BR).

April. Administration of Jacob Monylockes of Ratcliffe, Stepney, Middlesex, who died in Virginia. (AW).

April 1668(?) Petition of George C[*torn*] who reports that the child John Brookes has been freed again. Several other children enticed from their parents are embarked in the *Seven Brothers* which is already at Gravesend with two other ships carrying children bound for Virginia. Though their parents are allowed to see the children, because they have no money, they will not be freed. The death penalty should be imposed on those who entice children away and the ships should be stopped. (CSPC).

6 May. Shipper by the *Exchange* of Boston, New England, bound from Bristol for New England: Michaell Clothier. (PRO: E190/1137/1).

7 May. The following apprenticed in Bristol: John Willis to John Granger, 4 years Virginia; John Bethar to Arthur Lewis, 4 years Barbados. (BR).

13 May. The following apprenticed in Bristol: John Jones to William Coleston, 4 years Barbados; Elizabeth Jones to same, 4 years Barbados. (BR).

15 May-3 June. Shippers by the *Sarah*, Mr. Samuell Scarlet, bound from London for New England: Noah Floyd, Samuell Sheafe, Richard Love, John Peake, Richard Michelborne, Thomas Hayter, Thomas Glover, George Sachwell, Robert Woolley. (PRO: E190/52/1).

19 May. The following apprenticed in Bristol: William Sherman to Thomas Moore, 4 years New England; Margarett Jelfe to Thomas Smith, 4 years Nevis. (BR).

20 May. The following apprenticed in Bristol: Richard Reece to Aldworth Elbridge, 4 years New England. (BR).

23 May. The following apprenticed in Bristol: Richard Davis to William Falkner, 4 years Barbados or Leewards; Charles Lacon to same, 4 years Barbados or Leewards; Mary Abbutt to John Smith, 4 years Barbados or Leewards. (BR).

29 May-3 June. Shippers by the *Seahorse*, Mr. Francis Pille, bound from London for New England: Samuell Terrill, Peter Vandemander. (PRO: E190/52/1).

30 May. The following apprenticed in Bristol: Daniell Nicholls to John Woory, 7 years Virginia. (BR).

May 1668(?) Petition of the inhabitants of Maine for protection against the Government of Massachusetts signed by: William Phillipps, Edward Rishworth, Henry Jocelyn, Francis Hooke, John Davis, Francis Champernowne, Raphe Allanson, Jeremiah Hubbard, Abraham Corbett, William Sheldon, Thomas Williams, John Pearce, John Budstarte(?), William

Liscom, James Grant, Barnabas Chauncy, Edward Johnson, Digery Jeoffrey, James Gibbins, John Twisden, John Pudington. (CSPC).

May. Administration of John Price of the Precinct of the Tower, London, who died in Virginia. (AW).

10 June. The following apprenticed in Bristol: Job Sims to John Williams, 5 years Nevis. (BR).

15 June. The following apprenticed in Bristol: Charles Jones to John Williams, 4 years Nevis; James Jones to same, 4 years Nevis. (BR).

16 June. The following apprenticed in Bristol: William Morgan to John Woory, 4 years Virginia. (BR).

16 June 1668-23 June 1670. Depositions taken in London and Virginia to establish the extent of the Virginia estate of Francis Newton of London, grocer, who made a will in Virginia in 1661. The deponents include: John Richards of St. Mary Undershaft, London, merchant aged 44, who was in Virginia in 1660; Robert Stanton, late Clerk of the County Court in Virginia but now of Bury St. Edmunds, Suffolk, tobacconist aged 42; John Mohun, merchant aged 26, who was the trustee of Newton's estate in Surrey County, Virginia; Lt. Col. George Jordan of Virginia, aged 53; Major William Marriott of Virginia, aged 45; George Watkins of Surrey County, Virginia, gent aged 36; Thomas Binns of Virginia, aged 48; Daniel Sturdivant of Virginia, aged 45; Thomas Hunt of Virginia, aged 43; William Watkins of Virginia, aged 48. (NGSQ 69/3).

17-30 June. Shippers by the *Society*, Mr. Christopher Clarke, bound from London for New England: Benjamin Needham, Robert Woolley, St. Clare Raymond, Henry Ashurst, Richard Michelborne, John Harwood, Thomas Bodley, Noah Floyd, John Peake, Paul Darby, Thomas Elkin, Thomas Norman, William Rider, Daniell Bridge, Valentine Austin, Anthony Stockbridge, Samuel Sheafe. (PRO: E190/52/1).

18 June. Oxford Circuit prisoners reprieved to be transported to Barbados. Gloucestershire: William Greene of Hardwicke. Monmouth: William Morris of Creek, Caerwent; William Phillips alias Williams of Redwick. (PRO: C66/3101/11).

18-19 June. Shippers by the *Society* of Plymouth, Mr. James Cutteford, bound from Plymouth for New England: Thomas Yeabsley, John Lanyon. (PRO: E190/1038/8, 1038/12).

20 June. The following apprenticed in Bristol: John Benson to William Falkner, 4 years Virginia. (BR).

20 June-6 August. Shippers by the *Charles*, Mr. Robert (or Samuell) Cooper, bound from London for Virginia: Robert Jadwin, Richard Johnson, Thomas Tilsley, Samuell Caurdrey. (PRO: E190/52/1).

22 June. Deposition by George Ayray of London, draper, that he has received letters from Jonathan Newell in Virginia (defendant to John Stanford and his wife) but has never heard that he came to England at any time. (LMCD).

25 June. Shipper by the *Unity*, Mr. Christopher Clark, bound from London for New England: Robert Holt. (PRO: E190/52/1).

26 June. The following apprenticed in Bristol: Thomas Chamberlin to John Woory, 4 years Virginia; John Willmenton to George Warren, 7 years Nevis. (BR).

27 June. The following apprenticed in Bristol: John Evans to Symon Wills, 4 years Barbados; Walter Davis to Nicholas Webber, 5 years Virginia; Lewis Coner to Thomas Noell, Virginia. (BR).

29 June. The following apprenticed in Bristol: Joane Pudding to Ann Dorrington, 7 years Maryland. (BR).

30 June-28 July. Shippers by the *Blossom* of New England bound from Bristol for New England: Richard Martyn, Thomas Northerne, Thomas Pattent, Reginall Tucker, Michaell Clothier, John Beech, John Willoughby, William Tippet, Richard Bickham for John Williams. (PRO: E190/1137/1).

June. Administration of William Browne of Plymouth, Devon, who died in Virginia, widower. (AW).

3 July. The following apprenticed in Bristol: Thomas Peirce to Christopher Trip, 4 years Barbados. (BR).

6 July. The following apprenticed in Bristol: Mary Davis to Thomas Jones, 4 years Barbados. (BR).

8 July. The following apprenticed in Bristol: John Wilson to Thomas Perkins, 3 years Virginia. (BR).

9 July. The following apprenticed in Bristol: Thomas Buttler to Walter Lougher, 4 years Barbados. (BR).

11 July. The following apprenticed in Bristol: Joseph Kettle to Arthur Graunt, 4 years Nevis. (BR).

13 July. The following apprenticed in Bristol: Hester Buck to John Cary, 4 years Virginia. (BR).

16 July. The following apprenticed in Bristol: Thomas Strowd to William Allen, 10 years New England. (BR).

19 July. The following apprenticed in Bristol: John Jennings to Walter Lougher, 4 years Barbados or Leewards; Mary Jennings to same, 5 years Barbados or Leewards. (BR).

24 July. The following apprenticed in Bristol: Thomas Gibbons to Ignatius White, 4 years Virginia; Bridgett Wheeler to Anna Wisdome, 4 years Virginia. (BR).

25 July. The following apprenticed in Bristol: Thomas Strowd to George Downeing, 5 years Virginia. (BR).

27 July. The following apprenticed in Bristol: Sarah Gough to John Bumstead, 4 years Barbados; Hugh Rowland to Robert Pard, 4 years Virginia. (BR).

28 July. The following apprenticed in Bristol: George Thorne to William Sankes, 4 years Virginia; Thomas Dabenett to same, 4 years Virginia. (BR).

29 July. Shipper by the *Prosperous* of Plymouth, Mr. John Carkett, bound from Plymouth for Virginia: George Lapthorne. (PRO: E190/1038/8, 1038/12).

30 July. The following apprenticed in Bristol: John Bingham to John Cooke, 4 years Virginia; John Price to Anne Hopkins, 4 years Virginia; Mary Wildes to same, 4 years Virginia; Jane Lewis to same, 4 years Virginia; Mary Smith to same, 4 years Virginia; James Powell to John Bumsteed, 4 years Barbados. (BR).

July. Administration of William Gill of Stepney, Middlesex, who died in Virginia, widower. (AW).

July. Administration of Gilbert Mather of Whitechapel, Middlesex, who died in Virginia. (AW).

July. Administration of Richard Garraway of New England. (AW).

1 August. Shipper by the *Friendship* of London, Mr. Henry Ibrooke, bound from Newcastle for Virginia: said Henry Ibrooke. (PRO: E190/194/6).

1-25 August. Shippers by the *Agreement* bound from Bristol for Virginia: Gabriell Deane, Emanuell Deane, Thomas Whittop, William Jenning, Hugh Thomas, Peirce Bread, James Hulin, John Parkinson, Thomas Yate, Richard Crabb. (PRO: E190/1137/1).

3 August. The following apprenticed in Bristol: Judith Bowen to John Stokes, 4 years Virginia. (BR).

4 August. The following apprenticed in Bristol: Margarett Tyler to Zachary Smith, 5 years Virginia; Katherine Bray to same, 5 years Virginia. (BR).

5 August. The following apprenticed in Bristol: Elizabeth Stone to Edward Poore, 4 years Virginia. (BR).

6 August. Newgate prisoners reprieved to be transported to Barbados. London: Elizabeth Wright, spinster; Edward Tilley; Hannah Gardner, spinster; Edward Reynolds; Thomas Reynolds; John Thorpe. Middlesex: Godfrey De Hague of St. Giles Cripplegate; John Bach of St. Clement Danes; Mary Cox of St. Katherine's, spinster; Elizabeth Williams, spinster, alias wife of Joseph

Williams of St. Giles in the Fields; Mary Ascue of St. Mary le Savoy, spinster; Anne Witherington, spinster, alias wife of John Witherington of St. Martin in the Fields; Joseph Tibballs of St. Giles in the Fields; John Read of Fulham; Robert Symonds of St. Giles Cripplegate; William Smith alias Lancastell of St. Andrew Holborn; William Sherwood of St. Martin in the Fields. (PRO: C66/3101/6).

6 August. Home Circuit prisoners reprieved to be transported to Barbados. Essex: John Morris of Southchurch; Bartholomew Hull of Bocking; Thomas Boreham of Blackmore; John Bennet of Thorndon Garnon. Hertfordshire: Samuel Bugby of Ware. Kent: James Lee of Milton by Gravesend. Surrey: Margery Rawlins of St. Olave, Southwark; William Andrewes of Selscombe; William Michell of Kingston on Thames; Johanna Blewitt, spinster, alias wife of Benjamin Johnson of St. Olave, Southwark; William Martin of Leatherhead. Sussex: William Harding of Petworth. (PRO: C66/3101/6).

6 August. The following apprenticed in Bristol: William Brockett to Sarah Tandy, 4 years Virginia. (BR).

6 August. Shipper from Plymouth of goods to be sent by the *Providence* from Falmouth to Virginia: George Strelly for Thomas Teat. (PRO: E190/1038/8).

8 August. The following apprenticed in Bristol: William Hartland to John Woory, 4 years Virginia; Richard Kirke to same, 4 years Virginia. (BR).

8-18 August. Shippers by the *Prince*, Mr. Robert Conway, bound from London for Virginia: Thomas Butts, Isaac Gray, Edmond Slocomb, Charles Spendlove. (PRO: E190/52/1).

8-22 August. Shippers by the *Flowerpot* of Plymouth, Mr. Thomas Rodden, bound from Plymouth for Virginia: John Lanyon & Co., Andrew Horsman, Francis Gillhampton. (PRO: E190/1038/8, 1038/12).

10 August. The following apprenticed in Bristol: Rebecca Hill to Martha Snow, 4 years Virginia; Thomas Tasker to William Walkely, 4 years Virginia; Robert Wise to John White, 5 years Virginia; Peter Kelly to Richard Biddlestone, 4 years Virginia; Katherine Eagle to William Pennock, 4 years Virginia; Thomas Farmer to John Seaward, 4 years Virginia. (BR).

10 August. Shipper by the *Baltimore*, Mr. John Dent, bound from London for Virginia: Henry Bankes. (PRO: E190/52/1).

10 August. Shipper by the *Crown*, Mr. Anthony Young, bound from London for Virginia: Henry Richards. (PRO: E190/52/1).

10 August. Shipper by the *Employment* bound from Bristol for New England: Richard Christmus. (PRO: E190/1137/1).

12 August-1 September. Shippers by the *Joseph* of Bristol bound from Bristol for Virginia: Arthur Harte, John Knight, William Forde, Charles Jones, William Tayler, John Duddleston, Thomas Hawkridge. (PRO: E190/1137/1).

13 August. Shippers by the *Hope* of Plymouth, Mr. Joseph Pilles, bound from Plymouth for Virginia: Daniell Barker & Co., George Lapthorne, John Horsham. (PRO: E190/1038/8, 1038/12).

13 August. Shipper by the *Mercy* of Plymouth, Mr. Edward Blagg, bound from Plymouth for Virginia: Abraham Serle & Co. (PRO: E190/1038/8).

15 August. Deposition by Thomas Smith and Edward Peares of London, mariners, and William Salusbury of London, notary public, that they were witnesses to a deed of 30 October 1665 whereby Humphrey Warren of Hattons Point, Maryland, sold his plantation to William Barrett of London, merchant. (LMCD).

17 August. Shipper by the *Jonathan and Elizabeth* of Plymouth, Mr. James Clift, bound from Plymouth for New England and Virginia: John Lake. (PRO: E190/1038/12).

18 August. The following apprenticed in Bristol: Edward Morris to William Cox, 5 years Virginia; George Pustone to same, 5 years Virginia; William Hawkes to Ralph Smith, 4 years Virginia. (BR).

18 August. Shipper by the *America* bound from London for Virginia: Micajah Perry. (PRO: E190/52/1).

18-25 August. Shippers by the *Providence* of Falmouth, Mr. William Pescod, bound from Plymouth for Virginia: Bryan Rogers, William Tyack. (PRO: E190/1038/27, 1038/28).

19 August. The following apprenticed in Bristol: Richard Greene to John Eridge, 4 years Virginia. (BR).

19-26 August. Shippers by the *Patience* of Bristol bound from Bristol for Virginia: William Yeomans, Thomas Speede, George Lackey. (PRO: E190/1137/1).

20 August. The following apprenticed in Bristol: Anne Cheade to Thomas Kelly, 4 years Virginia; John Haskins to Thomas Thurston, 4 years Maryland; George Wogan to same, 4 years Virginia; George Thomas to same, 4 years Virginia; Daniell Hafield to same, 4 years Virginia; Humphry Symonds to Christopher Bearkehead, 3 years Virginia. (BR).

20 August. Shipper by the *Sarah*, Mr. Philip Heron, bound from Sandwich for Virginia: Humphrey Biggleston. (PRO: E190/662/12).

21 August. The following apprenticed in Bristol: Richard Dubbs to John Orchard, 5 years Virginia; Griffeth Bevan to John Watts, 5 years Virginia; Martha Wiles to Martha Snow, 4 years Virginia; John Meeke to Thomas Jarvis, 6 years Virginia; Morgan Jones to Richard West, 4 years Barbados. (BR).

21 August. Shipper by the *Virginia Merchant* of Plymouth, Mr. Thomas Wescott, bound from Plymouth for Virginia: George Strelly. (PRO: E190/1038/8).

21 August. Shipper by the *Michaell*, Mr. Richard Fawcet, bound from London for Virginia: John Blackston. (PRO: E190/52/1).

24 August. The following apprenticed in Bristol: John Dalby to Richard Wroth, 4 years Virginia; John Shrubshore to Thomas Jarvis, 4 years Virginia; Jeane Chapman to Robert Lancaster, 4 years Virginia; Mary Whiteing to John Seaward, 4 years Virginia; Francis South to Thurston Harris, 7 years Virginia. (BR).

25 August. Shipper by the *Francis*, Mr. Daniell Bradley, bound from Portsmouth for Virginia: James Barton. (PRO: E190/828/16).

25 August. Shipper by the *John Bonadventure*, Mr. John Holman, bound from London for Virginia: Francis Dashwood. (PRO: E190/52/1).

25-26 August. Shippers by the *Amity* of Plymouth bound from Plymouth for Virginia: Joseph Cornish, Samuell Brett. (PRO: E190/1038/8).

25 August-1 September. Shippers by the *Peter*, Mr. John Rudd, bound from London for Virginia: James Blatt, John Butts, William White, Peter Causton. (PRO: E190/52/1).

29 August. The following apprenticed in Bristol: Richard Edwards to Alexander Tompson, 4 years Virginia; Thomas Killpeck to Sarah Durand, 4 years Virginia; Elizabeth Stoakees to same, 4 years Virginia; Elizabeth Whitehouse to same, 4 years Virginia; John Mackfarly to Charles Kelly, 4 years Virginia. (BR).

31 August. The following apprenticed in Bristol: David Lloid to William Luffe, 4 years Virginia; William Dixon to same, 4 years Virginia. (BR).

August. Probate of will of Edmund Fabian of Holborn, Middlesex, whose son, Simon Fabian, was in Virginia. (AW).

1 September. The following apprenticed in Bristol: Elizabeth Pumfry to Ann Dorrington, 4 years Virginia; Jane Harper to Richard Downeing, 5 years Virginia; Phillis Edwards to Thomas Uphowell, 4 years Virginia; Elizabeth Thomas to same, 4 years Nevis. (BR).

1-18 September. Shippers by the *Concord* of Bristol bound from Bristol for Virginia: William Swymmer, William Browne, Christopher Hillier, Bartholomew Chandler, John Seaward, Richard Woodard. (PRO: E190/1137/1).

3 September. The following apprenticed in Bristol: Henry Perrisford to John Knight, 4 years Nevis; Margarett Williams to Roger Pralse, 4 years Nevis; Mary Emannuell to same, 4 years Nevis; Katherine Williams to same, 4 years Virginia; Jeremiah Densly to John Grocer, 4 years Virginia; James Martine to Alexander Thompson, 4 years Virginia; Thomas Sheapherd to Jeremy Shulevan, 4 years Virginia; William Bennell to same, 4 years Virginia. (BR).

3 September. Shipper by the *Richard & John*, Mr. Robert Munden, bound from London for Virginia: John Bagnall. (PRO: E190/52/1).

4 September. Shippers by the *William & Mary*, Mr. Samuell Groome, bound from London for Virginia: John Peake, Edward Dudson. (PRO: E190/52/1).

5 September. The following apprenticed in Bristol: William Parry to William Cox, 4 years Virginia; Edward Russell to same, 4 years Virginia; Thomas Hillard to same, 4 years Virginia; William Jones to John Running, 4 years Virginia. (BR).

7 September. The following apprenticed in Bristol: David Phillips to George Pascall, 4 years Virginia; Mary Jones to same, 5 years Virginia; Elizabeth Jones to James Pascall, 4 years Virginia; Charles Steward to Timothy Stamp, 4 years Virginia; Thomas Horseman to Richard Mansell, 4 years Virginia. (BR).

8-12 September. Shippers by the *Happy Entrance*, Mr. Robert Clems, bound from London for Virginia: William Allen, Edward Hercy, Noah Floyd, Thomas Hussey. (PRO: E190/52/1).

9 September. The following apprenticed in Bristol: Mary Price to William Paddock, 4 years Virginia; George Pearce to James Seaward, 4 years Virginia; Richard Grindall to Thomas Thurston, 4 years Virginia; David Lewis to George Marks, 4 years Virginia; Henry Lewis to same, 4 years Virginia. (BR).

11 September. Shipper by the *Adeline* of Whitby, Mr. Mascall Picknall, bound from Whitby for Virginia: William Lothrington. (PRO: E190/194/3, 194/5).

11 September. The following apprenticed in Bristol: Miles Darby to John Norman, 4 years Virginia; Miles Lewis to same, 4 years Virginia; William Morgan to same, 4 years Virginia; John Powell to Thomas Bray, 4 years Virginia; George Harper to same, 4 years Virginia; John Jones to same, 4 years Virginia; Fabian Acton to same, 4 years Virginia; Thomas Jay to same, 4 years Virginia; Mary Jones to same, 4 years Virginia; Richard Battsly to same, 4 years Virginia; Henry Bird to same, 5 years Virginia; Thomas Nicholas to same, 7 years Virginia; George Oslan to same, 7 years Virginia; Phillip Gardner to Symon Browne, 4 years Virginia; Jeremy Rod to same, 4 years Virginia; Edward Andrews to William Morgan, 4 years Virginia. (BR).

12 September. The following apprenticed in Bristol: Davy Parry to Mathew Nicholls, 4 years Virginia; Howell Reece to Peter Rudruffe, 4 years Virginia; Henry Lewis to William Richardson, 4 years Virginia; Edward Homes to Thomas Rogers, 4 years Virginia; James Evans to George Greene, 4 years Virginia. (BR).

12-15 September. Shippers by the *Samuell* of Plymouth, Mr. Samuell Finch, bound from Plymouth for Virginia: Samuell Tucker & Co., John Horsham, John Dell, Thomas Durant, Thomas Warne. (PRO: E190/1038/8).

14 September. The following apprenticed in Bristol: Henry Brayne to Abraham Lewis, 4 years Virginia; Thomas Jones to same, 4 years Virginia; John Fishlock to Peter Byon, 4 years Virginia; Ambrose Herriott to Marke Chappell, 3 years Virginia; Wattkin Thomas to Thomas Morgan, 3 years Virginia. (BR).

15 September. Deposition by John Wigley, aged 23, servant of Thomas Barker Jr. of London, linen draper, that on 2 September 1661 Thomas Barker Sr. and Thomas Barker Jr. consigned cloth to Richard Tilghman, late of London, surgeon, now resident in Maryland. No payment has been received. (LMCD).

15 September-23 October. Shippers by the *Richard* of Bristol bound from Bristol for Virginia: Gabriell Deane, John Machen, Thomas Taylor. (PRO: E190/1137/1).

17 September. The following apprenticed in Bristol: Robert Sopper to Frances Rawles, 4 years Virginia; Nathan Jones to Ann Dorrington, 12 years Virginia. (BR).

19 September. The following apprenticed in Bristol: John Smith to Cornelius Serjeant, 4 years Virginia; John Probert to Anne Millard, 4 years Virginia. (BR).

21 September. The following apprenticed in Bristol: Jane Wattkin to William Haddock, 4 years Virginia; Thomas Gough to Andrew Booth, 4 years Virginia. (BR).

22 September. The following apprenticed in Bristol: John Kayes to James Scarbrow, 4 years Virginia; Richard Bowen to Thomas Walter, 4 years Virginia. (BR).

22 September-27 October. Shippers by the *Rainbow* of Bristol bound from Bristol for Virginia: Gabriell Deane, James Biggs, Thomas Gouldsmith, Richard Christmus, Thomas Edwards, John Haymon, Henry Mills, Thomas Smarte, William Crabb, John Speede, William Gouldsmith, Robert Daniell, Miles Hobson. (PRO: E190/1137/1).

23 September. The following apprenticed in Bristol: John Colstring to Thomas Jarvis, 4 years Virginia; James Pearce to Toby Horton, 5 years Virginia; Richard Nicholas to John Channce, 4 years Virginia. (BR).

24 September-12 October. Shippers by the *Society* of Bristol bound from Bristol for Virginia: Archibald Lynsey, Richard Pope, Richard Eyre, Thomas North, Thomas Littman, Jeremiah Savelle, John Biss, Joseph Day, Robert Bagnall. (PRO: E190/1038/8).

25 September. The following apprenticed in Bristol: Ann Baker to William Hottost, 4 years Virginia; James Winard to Ralph Williams, 4 years Virginia; John Dickfield to same, 6 years Virginia; John Machell to Jeremy Shulevan, 4 years Virginia; Evan Price to same, 4 years Virginia; John Willis to William

Wathenson, 4 years Virginia; John Street to John Charles, 4 years Virginia. (BR).

27 September-23 November. Shippers by the *Industry* of Plymouth, Mr. John Mayne, bound from Plymouth for Virginia: Peter Elbiston, Samuell Fletcher, Thomas Warren, Benjamin Salt, Samuell Brett, Abraham Appleby, Phillip Edwards. (PRO: E190/1038/8).

28 September-26 October. Shippers by the *Solomon*, Mr. Edward Peirse & Mr. Ezechiel Croscomb, bound from London for Virginia: Joseph Fendall, Henry Beale, Samuell Lutton, John Sheppard. (PRO: E190/52/1).

30 September. The following apprenticed in Bristol: Daniell Thomas to William Morgan, 4 years Virginia; Edward Yearsly to William Hottost, 4 years Virginia; John Probaut to Susan Tuck, 4 years Virginia. (BR).

September. Probate of will of John Beauchamp of St. Giles Cripplegate, London, who had lands in Virginia. (AW).

September. Administration of William Glanvell of Virginia. (AW).

September. Probate of will of Nathaniel Newdigate alias Newgate of Greenwich, Kent, whose brother-in-law, Edward Jackson, was in New England. (AW).

1 October. Shipper by the *Supply* of Whitby, Mr. Thomas Peighin, bound from Whitby for Virginia: John Tomlington. (PRO: E190/194/3, 194/5).

1 October. Shipper by the *Isabel* of Whitby, Mr. Mark Lisle, bound from Whitby for Maryland: Henry Lisle. (PRO: E190/194/3, 194/5).

2 October. The following apprenticed in Bristol: Robert Wash to Margaret Goore, 5 years Virginia; Robert White to same, 5 years Virginia; George Trulove to same, 5 years Virginia; William Croucher to same, 5 years Virginia; Richard Hubbard to same, 5 years Virginia; John Powell to same, 5 years Virginia; Ezekill Jack to Richard Wilkins, 3 years Virginia. (BR).

3 October. The following apprenticed in Bristol: John Andrews to William Richardson, 6 years Virginia; Sarah Harvard to John Rumming, 4 years Virginia. (BR).

3 October. Shipper by the *John*, Mr. James Blake, bound from London for Virginia: John Warner. (PRO: E190/52/1).

5 October. The following apprenticed in Bristol: Elizabeth Parry to Thomas Bray, 4 years Virginia; James Rodgers to same, 4 years Virginia; Charles Harrington to same, 6 years Virginia; Anne Steane to Anne Millner, 4 years Virginia. (BR).

5 October. Shipper by the *Adventure* of New England bound from Bristol for New England: William Lloyd. (PRO: E190/1137/1).

6 October. The following apprenticed in Bristol: Griffith Jones to William Christopher, 4 years Virginia; Evan Richard to William Morgan, 3 years Virginia; John Davis to Thomas Hort, 4 years Virginia; John Webster to James Clifton, 5 years Virginia; Mark Saltehouse to same, 4 years Virginia; William Fletcher to same, 4 years Virginia; James Scofield to same, 4 years Virginia; Samuell Hill to same, 4 years Virginia; George Whaley to same, 5 years Virginia; William Evan to John Rumming, 4 years Virginia. (BR).

6-12 October. Shippers by the *Mary*, Mr. Robert Pitts, bound from London for Virginia: Michael Wilkins, Benjamin Whetcomb. (PRO: E190/52/1).

8 October. The following apprenticed in Bristol: Mary Bason to Fortune Twitt, 3 years Virginia; Margaret Cheadle to same, 4 years Virginia; William Cheadle to same, 4 years Virginia. (BR).

8 October. Shipper by the *Joseph & Benjamin*, Mr. Mathew Paine, bound from London for Virginia: Joseph Richardson. (PRO: E190/52/1).

9 October. The following apprenticed in Bristol: Thomas Scott to Josias Cox, 4 years Virginia; Richard Evans to Jonas M—sly, 4 years Virginia. (BR).

10 October. The following apprenticed in Bristol: John Ayres to Austin Freath, 4 years Virginia; Alice Stevens to Ann Lugg, 4 years Virginia; James Cleyton to Henry Liston, 4 years Virginia; Joane Wall to Ann Millner, 4 years Virginia; Edward Allen to William Hottost, 4 years Virginia; Enock Ellor to James Clifton, 4 years Virginia. (BR).

13 October. The following apprenticed in Bristol: Winifred Mosse to Rainstorp Bard, 4 years Virginia; Thomas Davy to Thomas Boykin, 5 years Virginia. (BR).

13 October. Shipper by the *Brothers Adventure*, Capt. Plover, bound from London for Virginia: John Bentley. (PRO: E190/52/1).

13 October. Shipper by the *Paradise*, Mr. John Day, bound from London for Virginia: Joseph Sparrow. (PRO: E190/52/1).

14 October. The following apprenticed in Bristol: Lewis Williams to Peter Rothero, 4 years Virginia; Thomas Collins to George Hall, 6 years Virginia. (BR).

15 October. The following apprenticed in Bristol: Thomas Phillips to Thomas Fisher, 4 years Nevis; Abraham Dawson to Phillip Thomas, 7 years Virginia; Anthony Underwood to Thomas Meivy, 4 years Nevis; William Carter to Leonard Hancock, 4 years Virginia; Walter Lane to same, 4 years Barbados; Jeremy Parry to John Hellier, 4 years Virginia. (BR).

15 October-2 November. Shippers by the *Diligence* of Bristol bound from Bristol for Virginia: John Knight, Nicholas Burrus. (PRO: E190/1137/1).

16 October. The following apprenticed in Bristol: John Willson to James Chiston, 4 years Virginia; Richard Shippy to same, 4 years Virginia; Christopher Tomlin to same, 4 years Virginia; William Bane to same, 4 years Virginia. (BR).

17 October. The following apprenticed in Bristol: John Hughs to Alice Thomas, 4 years Virginia; Evan Thomas to same, 3 years Virginia. (BR).

17 October-2 November. Shippers by the *St. Luce* of Falmouth, Mr. Thomas Pomeroy, bound from Truro for Virginia: William Smith, Bryant Thompson. (PRO: E190/1038/17, 1038/27).

19 October. Deposition by Thomas Bently, citizen and ironmonger of London, aged 24, that on 22 September 1663 John Hill, citizen and ironmonger of London, now deceased, (to whom the deponent was formerly servant) sold goods to Jonathan Newell, merchant, then bound for Virginia. Elizabeth Hill is the relict and administratrix of John Hill. (LMCD).

19 October. The following apprenticed in Bristol: Charles Cox to Jonathan Jones, 4 years Virginia; Mary Coleman to Abraham Olliver, 4 years Virginia; Stephen Shank to Robert Thomas, 3 years Barbados. (BR).

19 October. Shipper by the —— & *Anne*, Mr. Zachary Taylor, bound from London for Virginia: —— Camfield. (PRO: E190/52/1).

19 October-16 November. Shippers by the *Olive Branch* of Bridlington, Mr. Robert Haxby, bound from Plymouth for Virginia: Richard Perry, Walter Tucker, Henry Davis, Robert Martin, Richard Brickman, Anthony Power. (PRO: E190/1038/8).

21 October. The following apprenticed in Bristol: Benjamin Thomas to George Macks, 4 years Virginia; William Jones to George Pearce, 4 years Virginia; Thomas Roberts to same, 5 years Virginia; John Hobson to Robert Lawford, 4 years Virginia; Margarett Mettham to Ann Lugg, 4 years Virginia. (BR).

22 October. The following apprenticed in Bristol: Henry Allen to John Braine, 4 years Virginia; Daniell Gallant to Thomas Harris, 4 years Virginia; Margarett Paine to William Cox, 4 years Virginia. (BR).

24 October. Shippers by the *George* of London, Mr. John Whitty, bound from London for Virginia: Charles Clark, Edward Middleton. (PRO: E190/52/1).

25 October. Shipper by the *Richard & Mary* bound from Bristol for Virginia: Nicholas Cowlinge. (PRO: E190/1137/1).

26 October. The following apprenticed in Bristol: William Greene to Samuell Tipton, 7 years Barbados; John Morgan to Arthur Grannt, 5 years Virginia. (BR).

26 October. Shipper by the *Richard & James* bound from Bristol for Virginia: Edward Morgan. (PRO: E190/1137/1).

27 October. The following apprenticed in Bristol: Moses Dale to Olliver Machen, 7 years Virginia; William Wood to same, 4 years Virginia; Reynold Fuloflove to John Hodge, 4 years Virginia; Richard Sutton to George Tyte, 4 years Virginia; Walter Sutton to same, 4 years Virginia; Robert Tayler to same, 5 years Virginia; Thomas Curtis to same, 5 years Virginia; Elizabeth Griffis to Ann Greenfield, 4 years Virginia; John Cunney to Susanna Tuck, 4 years Virginia; Hugh Jones to same, 4 years Virginia; John Wilks to same, 7 years Virginia; Henry Knight to Edward Yeomans, 4 years Virginia. (BR).

28 October. The following apprenticed in Bristol: Morgan Wattkins to John Tucker, 4 years Virginia; William Kettle to Henry Field, 4 years Virginia; John Tayler to Morgan Jones, 4 years Virginia; George Parker to same, 4 years Virginia; Morgan Pranch to same, 4 years Virginia; Sarah Tippett to Alice Thomas, 4 years Virginia; James Lewis to William Innis, 4 years Virginia. (BR).

31 October. The following apprenticed in Bristol: Thomas Davis to Walter Bond, 4 years Virginia; James Jones to Ralph Williams, 4 years Virginia; Charles Barnes to John Batchelor, 7 years Virginia; Joseph Smith to William Hasell, 4 years Virginia; David Williams to Peter Atherwood, 4 years Virginia. (BR).

October. Administration of Richard Pearle of Virginia, bachelor. (AW).

October. Administration of John Browne of St. Michael Bassishaw, London, who died in Virginia. (AW).

2 November. The following apprenticed in Bristol: John Marrile to Arthur Allin, 4 years Virginia. (BR).

2-12 November. Shippers by the *Loyal Berkeley*, Mr. William Goodson, bound from London for Virginia: Richard Love, John Peake. (PRO: E190/52/1).

3 November. The following apprenticed in Bristol: John Daine to Peter Harrison, 4 years Virginia; Thomas Holland to same, 4 years Virginia; Jeremy Densly to Thomas Attkins, 4 years Virginia. (BR).

3-14 November. Shippers by the *George* of Plymouth, Mr. John Popplestone, bound from Plymouth for Virginia: John Horsham, George Lapthorne, Benjamin Salt, John Rouse, William Martin. (PRO: E190/1038/8).

4 November. The following apprenticed in Bristol: George Wattkin to John Norman, 4 years Virginia; Phillip Thomas to same, 4 years Virginia; John Thomas to same, 7 years Virginia; Richard Winter to Thomas Pope, 4 years Virginia; John Tayler to Edward Norman, 4 years Virginia; Thomas Williams to William Foxall, 4 years Virginia; David Williams to same, 4 years Virginia; William Jinkin to same, 4 years Virginia; Richard John to same, 4 years Virginia; Isaack Newton to John Roberts, 4 years Barbados; John Organ to Nathaniell Pall, 4 years Virginia; Jarvis Riseton to Alice Thomas, 3 years Virginia; Richard West to Francis Jones, 5 years Virginia. (BR).

4 November. Shipper by the *Maryland Merchant* bound from Bristol for Virginia: Edward Martindale. (PRO: E190/1137/1).

6 November. The following apprenticed in Bristol: Richard Fletcher to John Hunt, 4 years Virginia; Elizabeth Hopkins to John Crafford, 5 years Virginia. (BR).

7-21 November. Shippers by the *Francis & Mary* of Bristol bound from Bristol for Virginia: Richard Getley, Stephen Watts, George Markes, John Boswell. (PRO: E190/1137/1).

9-17 November. Shippers by the *Providence* of Bristol bound from Bristol for Virginia: William Dunning, James Wathen. (PRO: E190/1137/1).

10 November. The following apprenticed in Bristol: Thomas Harrison to William Walter, 4 years Virginia; John Husband to Francis Stannton, 7 years Virginia; Jinkin Price to William Hazard, 4 years Virginia; Anthony Hathur to William Saunders, 4 years Virginia; Warren Hathur to same, 7 years Virginia; Joseph Curd to Susan Smith, 7 years Virginia; Mary Morgan to John Inion, 4 years Virginia; William Bourne to Thomas Thurston, 6 years Virginia; Christopher Miles to Thomas Gibbs, 4 years Barbados; Henry Jinkins to Rosser Janie, 4 years Virginia. (BR).

10 November. Petition of David Fairvacks of London, merchant. Edmond Scarborough of Virginia, merchant, borrowed money from him which he promised to repay after his arrival in Virginia: he has now been there for many years and has built up a large estate which he has settled on his children but the petitioner has not been repaid. (APC).

12 November. The following apprenticed in Bristol: David Williams to Samuell Clovell, 4 years Virginia; Robert Blaketon to Samuell Hathway, 4 years Barbados; James Sloe to same, 4 years Virginia. (BR).

12 November. Newgate prisoners reprieved to be transported to Barbados [*but may have gone to Virginia - see petition of Emanuel Jones of May 1673*]. London: Henry Griffin; Richard Crispe; John Lively; William Field; Henry Inman; Elizabeth Burton, widow; Margaret Griffiths, spinster; Jane Rogers, widow; Mary Edwards alias Symmes, widow. Middlesex: Francis Oakley of Bromley; Elizabeth Betts of St. Giles in the Fields, spinster, [*order made in May 1669 for custody of her bastard child delivered in Newgate*]; Mary Standley of St. Giles Cripplegate, spinster; Susan Partridge of St. Paul Covent Garden, spinster; Martha Goodman, wife of Edward Goodman of St. Andrew Holborn; Margaret Tattle of St. Giles in the Fields; Mary Jones of St. Paul Covent Garden, spinster; Rose Whitehead of St. Martin in the Fields, spinster; John Cooke of Ruislip; Thomas Draper of St. Giles in the Fields; Isaac Johnson of Stepney; John Eades of Northwood; Emanuel Jones of St. Martin in the Fields; Richard Morgan of St. Giles Cripplegate; James Welling of St. Giles in the Fields; David Sirvin of St. Giles in the Fields. (EB & PRO: C66/3102/3).

13 November. The following apprenticed in Bristol: Nathaniell Lewis to Thomas Pope, 4 years Virginia; Thomas Hill to John Soller, 4 years Virginia. (BR).

16 November. The following apprenticed in Bristol: Thomas Appleyard to James Powell, 4 years Virginia; Olliver Davis to William Foxall, 4 years Virginia. (BR).

17 November. Shipper by the *William & Ellen*, Mr. Edward Watts, bound from London for Virginia: John Hill. (PRO: E190/52/1).

18 November. Shipper by the *Trial* of Bristol bound from Bristol for Virginia: William Yeomans. (PRO: E190/1137/1).

19 November. The following apprenticed in Bristol: John Hooper to Edward Robinson, 3 years Barbados; James Coder to William Kent, 3 years Virginia; Richard Butterfield to William Christopher, 5 years Virginia; Thomas Brothest to Dudly Quinton, 5 years Virginia. (BR).

20 November. The following apprenticed in Bristol: John Richards to John Batchellor, 4 years Virginia; George Jones to same, 5 years Virginia. (BR).

21 November. The following apprenticed in Bristol: Richard Quinton to William Yeomans, 5 years Virginia; Edward Jones to John Dench, 4 years Virginia; Anthony Workeman to George Marks, 4 years Virginia; Richard Parry to John Batchellor, 4 years Virginia; Richard Brooke to John Smith, 4 years Virginia. (BR).

21 November-2 December. Shippers by the *Susan*, Mr. William Goodlad, bound from London for Virginia: John Nutt, William Williams. (PRO: E190/52/1).

23 November-2 December. Shippers by the *John* of Whackett, Mr. Edward Stephens, bound from Bridgwater for Virginia: Henry Atkins for Edward Standish, Henry Woollcott. (PRO: E190/1090/6).

25 November. The following apprenticed in Bristol: John Dembry to Thomas Harris, 4 years Virginia; Archball Millard to same, 4 years Virginia; Richard Mathews to Nathaniell Cary, 4 years Virginia; Lawrence White to same, 4 years Virginia; Richard Maykins to John Smith, 4 years Virginia; Jane Williams to Margaret Huling, 5 years Virginia; William Sympson to William Langhorne, 4 years Virginia; Edith Sturgis to Alice Thomas, 4 years Virginia. (BR).

27 November. The following apprenticed in Bristol: Ambrose Chappell to William Cox, 9 years Virginia; Richard Owen to same, 4 years Virginia; Rebecca Gibbs to Martin Wakely, 4 years Virginia; William Pearce to Thomas Gibbs, 4 years Virginia. (BR).

November. Probate of will of Samuel Thompson of St. Gregory, London, whose nephew, Thomas Thompson, was to go to his mother in New England. (AW).

November. Probate of will of John Edwards of London, who died in Virginia. (AW).

November. Administration of Robert Jordan formerly of Portland Island but late of St. Giles Cripplegate London, who died in Virginia. (AW).

3 December. The following apprenticed in Bristol: Edward Emmont to John Norman, 4 years Virginia; Robert Saunders to Thomas Bridges, 6 years Virginia; Sarah Paine to Tobias Horton, 4 years Virginia; Elizabeth Peeke to Nathaniell Cary, 8 years Virginia; Susanna Edmonds to same, 8 years Virginia. (BR).

5 December. The following apprenticed in Bristol: John Cottle to Thomas Frith, 5 years Barbados; Margaret Nott to Edward Poore, 4 years Barbados; John Jones to John Smith, 4 years Virginia; James Morse to John Bryan, 5 years Nevis. (BR).

8-23 December. Shippers by the *Virginia Merchant* of Bristol bound from Bristol for Virginia: Phillip Biss for Thomas Biss, William Ellis, Jonathan Edwards, William Langhorne, William Dighton, John Speede. (PRO: E190/1137/1).

10 December. The following apprenticed in Bristol: Margaret Carter to John Rumming, 4 years Virginia; William Dellahay to same, 4 years Virginia. (BR).

14 December. Deposition by William Wilson of Southwark, Surrey, gent aged 50, and John Cox, citizen and merchant tailor of London, aged 30, that Ezechiel Fogg, citizen and skinner of London, and John Gifford of Boston, New England, merchant, became bound on 11 September 1667 to Robert Morris, citizen and skinner of London, for goods shipped to New England. (LMCD).

15 December. The following apprenticed in Bristol: Joseph Ward to Thomas Lugg, 4 years Nevis; Margarett Lewis to Edward Allchurch, 5 years Virginia; Anne Burch to same, 5 years Virginia; Humphrey Mire to same, 5 years Virginia; Elizabeth Buttler to Henry Daniell, 5 years Virginia. (BR).

17 December. The following apprenticed in Bristol: Lishom Howell to Hugh Lewis, 4 years Virginia; Mary Woods to George Morrice, 4 years Virginia. (BR).

18 December. The following apprenticed in Bristol: Thomas Richards to John Stoakes, 4 years Virginia. (BR).

19 December. The following apprenticed in Bristol: Thomas Stone to John Freeman, 4 years Virginia; Thomas Belcher to Warner Lucas, 4 years Virginia; Gabriel Tayler to John White, 4 years Virginia; William Gay to John Jones, 4 years Virginia; Ann Pitter to Thomas Allen, 4 years Virginia; John Kelly to George Morrice, 7 years Virginia; Francis Powle to Thomas Tayler, 4 years Nevis. (BR).

23 December. Shipper by the *Stephen* of Bristol bound from Bristol for Virginia: John Machen. (PRO: E190/1137/1).

29 December. The following apprenticed in Bristol: John Bannam to Thomas Allen, 8 years Virginia. (BR).

30 December. The following apprenticed in Bristol: John Roach to Margery Symonds, 4 years Virginia; Christian Pew to Thomas Reeves, 4 years Nevis. (BR).

31 December. The following apprenticed in Bristol: George Lewis to William Hughes, 3 years Nevis. (BR).

1668. Chancery suit of Francis Vassall v. Thomas Williamson re the wills and estates of Samuel and Henry Vassall of Virginia, with listing of other suits involving the Vassall family. (NGSQ 72/3).

1668(?) Petition of Dorothea, widow of Daniel Gotherson, formerly Dorothea Scott. As heir to Scott's Hall in Kent she brought a good estate to her husband but he mortgaged his property which, since his death, has been taken for debt. The petitioner has been left in poverty with six children. Her husband's debts were incurred by the purchase of houses on Long Island for her son, John Scott, who is not yet aged 17 and has been forced to labour for his bread. (CSPC).

1669

7 January. The following apprenticed in Bristol: Andrew Rogers to John Smith, 4 years Nevis; Thomas Langford to William Andrewes, 4 years Virginia; Mary Evans to Richard Bonner, 4 years Virginia. (BR).

9 January. The following apprenticed in Bristol: Edward Booth to William Andrewes, 4 years Virginia; William Horton to Edward P——ly, 4 years Nevis; George Hall to Edward Wattkins, 4 years Nevis. (BR).

12 January. The following apprenticed in Bristol: Philip David to Aron Williams, 3 years Nevis; Richard Chedbun to Jeremia Harris, 4 years Virginia; Rebecca Webb to same, 4 years Virginia; Joane Davis to same, 4 years Virginia; Griffeth Phillips to William Cum——, 4 years Virginia.

14 January. The following apprenticed in Bristol: Richard Davis to Susan Scottow, 4 years Barbados. (BR).

16 January. The following apprenticed in Bristol: John Charles to Edward Evans, 4 years Nevis; Richard Bennett to same, 4 years Nevis. (BR).

19-26 January. Deposition by Nicholas Grainger of Dover, Kent, mariner, that when he was in New England he lodged with David Hitchbourne who was still dwelling there when he left. Mary, wife of William Oswell, mariner, deposes that she was often at the house of Hitchbourne and his wife Katherine before she came with the said Katherine in the same ship to England. Katherine Hitchbourne had contrived to obtain a letter from London intimating that she had inherited a house at Stratford or Bow in England and must come with her daughter to obtain possession. David Hitchbourne is now being sued by Jeremiah Norton. (LMCD).

20 January. The following apprenticed in Bristol: Thomas Kellway to John Randall, 4 years Nevis; Robert Upward to same, 4 years Nevis; Edith Kettle to same, 4 years Nevis; Thomas Williams to William Croker, 6 years Nevis. (BR).

21 January-19 February. On the petition of John Ludlowe who was convicted of felony, he is allowed to be discharged on condition that he transports himself to the plantations. (CSPC).

22 January. The following apprenticed in Bristol: John Sharp to John Cary, 4 years Virginia; Henry Willoughby to same, 4 years Virginia; Joseph Vinson to same, 4 years Virginia; John Farclue to Charles Holt, 6 years Virginia. (BR).

24 January. Deposition by Elizabeth Sperrey, aged 32, formerly wife of Robert Parrott, citizen and grocer of London, deceased, but now wife of Henry Sperrey of St. Botolph Bishopsgate, London, that in November 1655 John

Hull, citizen and grocer of London, bought strong waters from James Wythe, citizen and innholder of London, which he took to Virginia. (LMCD).

26 January. The following apprenticed in Bristol: Griffeth Daniell to William Lyte, 4 years Virginia; Henry Comes to Christopher Smith, 3 years New England; George Daw to Thomas Pope, 4 years Virginia; Marke Snow to Thomas Lister, 4 years Barbados. (BR).

29 January. The following apprenticed in Bristol: James Wood to Thomas Winstone, 4 years Nevis. (BR).

29 January. Warrant for the discharge of Margaret Griffith who was convicted at the Old Bailey on condition that she goes to her brother in Virginia. (CSPC).

January. Probate of will of William Hardich of Nominy, Westmoreland County, Virginia, who died in Bristol. (AW).

1 February. The following apprenticed in Bristol: Mary Rogers to Edward Gerard (or Everard), 6 years Nevis; Thomas James to Edward Skinner, 3 years Barbados; Thomas Currier to Richard Sandford, 4 years Virginia. (BR).

3 February. The following apprenticed in Bristol: Thomas Jones to George Lane, 4 years Nevis. (BR).

9 February. The following apprenticed in Bristol: John Mallett to Jeffery Price, 4 years Virginia; Thomas Filkins to John Tyate, 7 years Virginia. (BR).

10 February. The following apprenticed in Bristol: Mathew Roberts to Richard Haskins, 4 years Virginia; Walter Drawey to same, 4 years Virginia. (BR).

11 February. The following apprenticed in Bristol: Jerman Beaton to Richard Haskins, 4 years Virginia. (BR).

17 February. The following apprenticed in Bristol: Peter Buttler to Richard Bonner, 4 years Virginia; Thomas Buttler to same, 4 years Virginia. (BR).

19 February. The following apprenticed in Bristol: Thomas Frome to Edward Tocknell, 4 years Barbados; John Paviott to Edward Wattkins, 4 years New England. (BR).

23 February. The following apprenticed in Bristol: Thomas Williams to William Tovey, 4 years Barbados; Robert Brayne to John Pitman, 8 years New England; Thomas Phillips to George Jones, 5 years Barbados; Susanna Parsons to Christopher Smith, 4 years Nevis; Susanna Parsons to same, 4 years Virginia; Samuell Pew to John Saunder, 4 years Nevis; Henry Wells to William Downeing, 4 years Nevis. (BR).

23 February. Western Circuit prisoners reprieved to be transported to Barbados. Devon: John Pearse of Sowton, feltmaker; Henry Snowe of Sampford Courtenay; John Gale of South Tawton, husbandman. Somerset: William Zyne of Nettlecombe; Cornelius Conway of St. Decomans; William Markes of

North Petherton, husbandman; Francis Williams of Wellington. (PRO: C66/3107/48).

February. Administration with will of John Thurmur of Calvert County, Maryland. (AW).

3 March. Warrant for Margaret Griffith to be discharged from Newgate in order to transport herself to Virginia. [*see pardon of 16 April*]. (SP Dom).

8 March. The following apprenticed in Bristol: John Humphry to George Jones, 4 years Barbados; Moses Hughs to Edward Coock, 7 years Virginia; Alexander Romsy to Margaret Winston, 4 years Nevis. (BR).

9 March. The following apprenticed in Bristol: Hugh Sheaperd to Michaell Pope, 4 years Nevis; Joane Davis to James Shute, 4 years Nevis. (BR).

11 March. Deposition by John Floyd, aged 72, citizen and tailor of London, that when he was in New England some 18 years ago he sold goods to John Coale of Boston in return for a bill for Barbados sugar to be consigned to John Freeman of London, merchant. The deponent has never received payment and his papers were lost in the Great Fire of London. (LMCD).

13 March. The following apprenticed in Bristol: Edward Morrice to Nathaniell Morrice alias Robins, 4 years Nevis; Walter Howell to William Steevens, 4 years Nevis. (BR).

19 March. The following apprenticed in Bristol: John Somers to Edward Wattkins, 4 years Nevis; William Roberts to Thomas Moore, 4 years Virginia. (BR).

25 March. The following apprenticed in Bristol: Phillip Lewis to William Stevens, 8 years Nevis; Robert Lattimore to James Downeing, 4 years Nevis *(entered twice)*. (BR).

5 April. The following apprenticed in Bristol: John Symonds to Robert Ayre, 4 years Nevis; John Thomas to William Stevens, 4 years Nevis; William Davis to William Sutherly, 5 years New England; Joane Pearcy to Samuell Winston, 4 years Virginia. (BR).

16 April. The following apprenticed in Bristol: Tarloughe Brian to Elizabeth Wattkins, 4 years Barbados. (BR).

16 April. Newgate and Home Circuit prisoners reprieved to be transported to Barbados. London: John Ludlow (a first offender aged 20 who served as a soldier in Portugal); Elizabeth Cavey, spinster; Elizabeth Carle, spinster; Penelope Johnson, spinster; Edward Thomas; Thomas Lambert; Robert Rowland; Margaret Griffith, spinster. Middlesex: Elizabeth Moate alias Baldwin of Clerkenwell, widow; Peter Jones of St. Margaret Westminster; John Trowell of St. Martin in the Fields; Richard Durnell of the same; Thomas Lambert of St. Andrew Holborn; Cornelia Banister of the same, spinster; Robert Armory of the same; Martha Goodman, wife of Edward Goodman of the same; Ruth Harrowgutt of St. Katherine's, spinster; John Cooper of St. Clement Danes; Margaret Nevison of the same, spinster; William Browne of Norton Folgate; Anne Horton, wife of William Horton of Whitechapel; John Warnum of the same; John Neale of the same; John Smith of St. Giles in the Fields; Susan Harrison, wife of Robert Harrison of the same, goldsmith; Mary Rice of Hackney; John Gibbons of St. Sepulchre; William Avery of Stepney; John Ashenhurst of Hillingdon, gent; Robert and Roger Bates of Trehiddy, Cornwall. Essex: George Glascocke of Curringham; Robert Barwell of Sandon; George Castleton of Ingatestone; John Browne of Ingrave. Surrey. Richard Terry of Bermondsey; William Clyncke of St. Mary Magdalene, Southwark; William Dickenson of St. Olave, Southwark; George Dorrell of St. Saviour, Southwark; Elizabeth Reading of St. George, Southwark; John Musgrove of Newington. Sussex: Walter Good of Salcombe. (PRO: C66/3107/47).

22 April. The following apprenticed in Bristol: Jehadah Jones to John Russell, 4 years Nevis; Susan Prest to Elizabeth Wattkins, 4 years Nevis. (BR).

24 April. The following apprenticed in Bristol: Thomas Hughes to Daniell Sam, 3 years New England. (BR).

April. Probate of will of George Morgan who died at sea or in Virginia, bachelor. (AW).

5 May. Passes for the *Hope* and the *James* to carry at least 400 Scottish traders and planters to New York. (APC).

6 May. The following apprenticed in Bristol: John Fryer to Thomas Oldfield, 3 years New England. (BR).

13 May. The following apprenticed in Bristol: John Trowbridge to Richard Martine, 6 years New England. (BR).

15 May. Deposition by William Nevett of London, merchant aged 50, that on 18 September 1668 he shipped goods for his own use on the *Loyal Berkeley* alias the *Elizabeth* of London, Mr. James Cubitt, bound for York River, Virginia. George Lee of London, merchant aged 48, deposes that he also shipped goods to Virginia for his own use. (LMCD).

21 May. The following apprenticed in Bristol: Thomas Lloid to Robert Bound, 4 years Virginia; John Wood to Thomas Oldfield, 4 years New England. (BR).

28 May. The following apprenticed in Bristol: William Hayes to Thomas Harris, 4 years Barbados; Edward Tucker to John Sunderland, 4 years New England. (BR).

May. Probate of Robert Crane of Hadleigh, Suffolk, whose aunt, —— Rogers, was in New England. (AW).

4 June. The following apprenticed in Bristol: Andrew Bevans to Thomas Stacey, 4 years Virginia; Dorothy Vaughan to John Freeman, 4 years Barbados. (BR).

7 June. The following apprenticed in Bristol: John Peckman to Thomas Oldfield, 4 years Virginia; Frances Betts to John Reed, 4 years Barbados; Robert Jones to William Wigginton, 4 years Virginia. (BR).

8 June. The following apprenticed in Bristol: John Leaff to George Downeing, 4 years Virginia. (BR).

11 June. The following apprenticed in Bristol: John Hood to John Planke, 4 years Virginia; John Edwards to John Stokes, 4 years Virginia. (BR).

11 June. Warrant to the Recorder of London for transportation to the plantations of Roger Bates and Robert Bates, found guilty of "wandering up and down the country as vagabonds with other lewd persons calling themselves Egyptians and pretending to sell fortunes." (SP Dom).

13 June. The following apprenticed in Bristol: John Colhoone to Thomas Oldfield, 4 years New England; Joseph Allen to Petoe Dyer, 4 years Virginia; John Dickeson to John Sunderland, 4 years New England. (BR).

15 June. The following apprenticed in Bristol: Ann Parr to Peter Dyer, 4 years Virginia; William Price to John Marshall, 4 years Virginia; John Smith to Thomas Harris, 6 years Barbados; James Alexander to John Stokes, 4 years Virginia; William Jones to John Wattkins, 6 years Barbados. (BR).

22 June. The following apprenticed in Bristol: William Barnard to John Williams, 3 years Virginia; William Seymor to same, 3 years Virginia; Arthur Spenser to same, 3 years Virginia; Thomas Webb to Timothy Prowt, 7 years Virginia; Francis Hobson to James Watson, 4 years Nevis. (BR).

22 June. Western Circuit prisoners reprieved to be transported to Barbados. Cornwall: William Knight of St. Teath, husbandman. Devon: William Hill of Silverton, husbandman; Andrew Branscombe of Cullompton, husbandman; George Chibbett of Cullompton, fuller; Robert Miller alias Browne of Broadhembury, butcher; Lawrence Mountstephen of Payhembury; John Giles of Walkhampton, tinner. Dorset: Robert Sherringe of Forston. Hampshire: John Flower of Chilcombe, husbandman; Thomas Bason of Swanswick, Titchfield, husbandman. Wiltshire: John Dixe of Ramesbury, husbandman; William Noyes of Swallowcliffe. (PRO: C66/3107/45).

25 June. The following apprenticed in Bristol: George Frapwell to Richard Biddlestone, 4 years Virginia; Thomas Harris to William Wakely, 4 years Virginia; John Merriwether to Richard Powell, 4 years Virginia. (BR).

29 June. The following apprenticed in Bristol: James Dicks to John Plank, 5 years Virginia; Richard Browne to Mary Tovey, 3 years Barbados; Mary Barnutt to John K——win, 4 years Virginia; Francis Hancock to John Garway, 4 years Virginia. (BR).

June. Administration of William Shortricke of York Old Fields, Virginia. (AW).

June. Administration of Richard Atkins of Maryland, bachelor. (AW).

1 July. The following apprenticed in Bristol: Thomas Young to John Garway, 5 years Virginia; Henry Hughs to James Shute, 4 years Virginia; Daniell Rowland to John Hurt, 4 years Virginia. (BR).

2 July. The following apprenticed in Bristol: Howell Davis to John Jones, 4 years Virginia; John James to Robert James, 4 years Virginia. (BR).

7 July. The following apprenticed in Bristol: William Morgan to Thomas Robins, 4 years Nevis; Richard Davy to Thomas Morrice, 4 years Nevis. (BR).

8 July. The following apprenticed in Bristol: Susanna Barber to Charles Kelly, 4 years Virginia; Charles Grindley to Robert Williams, 5 years Virginia; Rowland Davis to Fabian Hill, 4 years Virginia. (BR).

16 July. The following apprenticed in Bristol: Edward Way to Thomas Fisher, 4 years Virginia; Eliza Stone to Margaret Wall, 4 years Virginia. (BR).

17 July. The following apprenticed in Bristol: Adam Acton to Richard Morgan, 4 years Virginia. (BR).

19 July. The following apprenticed in Bristol: Mary Short to Thomas Kelly, 4 years Virginia; William Marratt to William Jayne, 4 years Virginia. (BR).

20 July. The following apprenticed in Bristol: Thomas Davis to Thomas Gurny, 4 years Virginia; Phillip Morrice to same, 4 years Virginia; John Williams to Thomas Berry, 4 years Virginia; Peter Williams to William Levander, 4 years Nevis; James Pritchard to William Wigginton, 4 years Virginia; David Jones to same, 4 years Virginia; Humphry Clayton to Andrew Griffis, 4 years Nevis; Margarett Hitchins to William Reece, 4 years Virginia; Ann Mallpus to John Smith, 4 years Nevis; John Brand to Peter Dyer, 4 years Virginia; John Lidden to William Wafery, 4 years Virginia; Rebeckah Radford to John Kedgian, 4 years Virginia; William Mathews to William George, 3 years Virginia; Thomas Willis to Joseph Day, 4 years Virginia. (BR).

23 July. The following apprenticed in Bristol: William Jinkins to Thomas Carny, 4 years Virginia; John Lloid to William Cannings, 4 years Virginia. (BR).

26 July. The following apprenticed in Bristol: James Brimble to Thomas Francklyn, 4 years Virginia; Mary Mathews to William Saunders, 4 years Virginia; John Moore to Richard Rider, 4 years Virginia; Olliver Morgan to Richard Saunders, 4 years Virginia; John Evans to Edward Adams, 4 years Virginia; Christopher Roberts to same, 4 years Virginia; John Allen to James Wallis, 4 years Nevis; Sarah Crow to Walter Richardson, 4 years Virginia. (BR).

27 July. The following apprenticed in Bristol: Joseph Sheappard to Jonas Mockley, 4 years Virginia. (BR).

28 July. The following apprenticed in Bristol: John Lewis to Robert Williams, 4 years Virginia; William Jeapson to same, 4 years Virginia; Phillip Pie to Joan

K——, 4 years Virginia; Joseph Apharry to Ralph Smith, 4 years Virginia; Elizabeth Mathews to same, 4 years Virginia. (BR).

30 July. The following apprenticed in Bristol: Dorothy Fox to Benjamin Coltman, 4 years Virginia; Thomas Lewis to Robert Evans, 4 years Virginia. (BR).

31 July. The following apprenticed in Bristol: Ann Clark to Guy Hartford, 4 years Virginia; William Powell to Charles Kelly, 4 years Virginia; Ann Newman to Margery Snow, 3 years Virginia; Margarett Burford to Thomas Lux, 4 years Virginia; William Bagg to Thomas Chamberlaine, 4 years Virginia; Mary Fletcher to same, 4 years Virginia; Honour Hall to Andrew Griffis, 4 years Nevis. (BR).

2 August. Deposition by Richard Mills of St. Andrew, Holborn, London, gent aged 47, and his wife Alice Mills, aged 53, that Robert Bullock of London, merchant, is the son and heir of William Bullock, formerly of Barking Essex, but since of Virginia, gent deceased, and that William Bullock was the son and heir of Hugh Bullock of London, deceased, who went to Virginia. (LMCD).

4 August. The following apprenticed in Bristol: Jane Tamar to Richard Joyce, 4 years Nevis; Joane Smith to John Adams, 4 years Nevis; William Man to George Wattkins, 4 years Nevis; Charles Pritchard to Richard Madox, 5 years Virginia; Mary Wright to George Wattkins, 4 years Nevis. (BR).

6 August. The following apprenticed in Bristol: John Browne to Francis Collier, 4 years Virginia; John Dowling to same, 4 years Virginia; Bartholomew Morsell to same, 4 years Virginia; Anthony Dollery to same, 4 years Virginia; Mary Bourton to same, 4 years Virginia; Mary Pickford to same, 4 years Virginia; Grace Good to same, 4 years Virginia; Jane Bayly to Richard Pope, 4 years Virginia; Dorothy Davis to William Field, 4 years Nevis; Ann Pickerin to Joice El——, 4 years Virginia. (BR).

10 August. Letter from John West [agent for the Lords Proprietors of Carolina] written aboard the *Carolina* at anchor in the Downs and enclosing a list of passengers aboard the ship: Captain [Florence] O'Sullivan and seven servants; Stephen Bull and six servants; Edward Hollis and Joseph Dalton with nine servants; Thomas and Paul Smith with seven servants; —— Hambleton and ten servants; John Rivers and four servants; Nicholas Cartwright and five servants; Morris Mathews and four servants; William Bowman and two servants; Dr. William Scrivener and one servant; William Owens and three servants; Thomas Midleton and Elizabeth his wife with two servants; Samuel West and two servants; Joseph Bailey and one servant. Passengers without servants are: Thomas Rideall, William Haughton, William Hennis, Thomas Humfreys, Elizabeth Humfreys, Marie Clerke, Sampson and Nathaniel Darkenwell, Sarah and Elizabeth Erpe, Marie Erpe, Martha Powell and Thomas Motteshed. (CSPC).

10 August. The following apprenticed in Bristol: Alice Bayly to Abraham Birken——, 4 years Virginia. (BR).

12 August. The following apprenticed in Bristol: Mary Haines to George Downeing, 5 years Virginia. (BR).

13 August. The following apprenticed in Bristol: Mary Howell to George Markes, 5 years Virginia; William Johnston to Robert Blase, 4 years Virginia. (BR).

14 August. The following apprenticed in Bristol: John Avery to John S——, 5 years Virginia; Gartry Avery to same, 4 years Virginia; Sarah Chamberlaine to James Willson, 4 years Virginia. (BR).

17 August. Letter from Henry Brayne, master of the *Carolina*, to Lord Ashley. His ship with the *Port Royal*, Mr. John Russell, and the *Albemarle*, Mr. Edward Baxter, will sail to Ireland to take on a great number of passengers to be transported to Port Royal. (CSPC)

17 August. The following apprenticed in Bristol: Elioner Richman to John Gill, 4 years Virginia; William Morgan to John Rogers, 4 years Virginia. (BR).

20 August. The following apprenticed in Bristol: Reece Jones to Abraham Alye, 4 years Virginia; Reynold Davis to Thomas T——, 4 years Virginia; Elizabeth Blessly to Thomas Gray, 4 years Virginia. (BR).

23 August. The following apprenticed in Bristol: Ann Jones to Richard Mathewes, 4 years Virginia; Mary Percivall to same, 4 years Virginia; Jane Reece to Jane Sayers, 4 years Virginia; Frances Tuften to Richard Gibbs, 4 years Virginia; Margaret Roberts to Thomas Gray, 5 years Barbados. (BR).

24 August. The following apprenticed in Bristol: Grace Davis to Thomas Gray, 4 years Barbados; Mary Holbrooke to William Jenkins, 4 years Virginia; Margaret Holbrooke to same, 4 years Virginia; Sybell Peters to Elizabeth Downeing, 4 years Virginia; Mary Budding to Richard Eastmond, 5 years Virginia; Susanna Budden to same, 3 years Virginia. (BR).

26 August. Edmund Squibb Esq. of St. Martin in the Fields, Middlesex, appoints Sir Henry Chicheley of London his attorney to recover debts assessed in judgment from Edmond Lister Esq., late of Thorney, Yorkshire, now resident in Virginia. (LMCD).

27 August. The following apprenticed in Bristol: Katherine Mann to George Markes, 5 years Virginia; Dorcus Willmot to Thomas Gray, 4 years Virginia or Barbados; Joane Joyce to same, 4 years Virginia. (BR).

28 August. Petition of John Jefferies and Thomas Colclough that they employed Giles Gale as their factor in Virginia and have paid a salary to him or his wife, but Gale has retained the petitioners' goods and has acquired a plantation. The Governor of Virginia is instructed to order Gale to come to account. (APC).

28 August. The following apprenticed in Bristol: John Jacob to William Daniell, 4 years Virginia. (BR).

30 August. The following apprenticed in Bristol: Ann Richardson to Thomas Pomfrett, 4 years Virginia; Margery Rawley to Margaret Ailward, 4 years Virginia; Barbara Hill to same, 4 years Virginia; Richard Briant to John Farnfield, 4 years Virginia. (BR).

31 August. Letter from Robert Southwell in Kinsale, Ireland, to Lord Ashley. He has tried on behalf of the Lords Proprietors of Carolina to procure servants for Port Royal but has been unable because the people are terrified at the way servants are treated in the Caribbean islands where they are sold as slaves. The writer himself has rescued many who were snatched up to be conveyed to the West Indies. (CSPC).

August. Probate of will of Moses Chaplen of St. Mary's Guildford, Surrey, whose cousin, Ester Pierce the elder, was in New England. (AW).

?August 1669. Petition by Thomas Orrell, prisoner in Newgate, that he may transport himself to a plantation being unable to undergo the labour of those sold as slaves. He was an accomplice of Mary Powell who, when she was executed, confessed that she had accused the petitioner falsely. [*See pardon of 23 September*]. (SP Dom).

2 September. The following apprenticed in Bristol: Dorothy Clarke to Guy Shattford, 4 years Virginia; Richard Williams to James Pope, 4 years Virginia; Thomas Strashing to John Orchard, 5 years Virginia; Arthur Hay to Arthur Acton, 4 years Virginia; Elizabeth Jame to Ann Brooke, 4 years Barbados. (BR).

6 September. The following apprenticed in Bristol: Joan Clarke to Thomas Francklyn, 4 years Virginia; John Samm to Thomas Carny, 4 years Virginia; Samuell Sunderland to William Morgan, 4 years Virginia; John King to same, 4 years Virginia; Evan Thomas to Jasper Creede, 6 years Virginia. (BR).

6 September. Deposition by George Gorham, citizen and merchant tailor of London, aged 25, and William Turner, citizen and woolpacker of London, aged 40, that Henry Beale Sr., citizen and merchant tailor of London, on 17 September 1668 delivered goods to John Hodgson, then of St. Mary Axe, London, but since of Accomack River, Virginia. (LMCD).

8 September. The following apprenticed in Bristol: Jane Tuick to Nathaniell Lane, 4 years Virginia; Winifred James to Abraham Aley, 4 years Virginia; Thomas Jenkins to John Jones, 4 years Virginia. (BR).

9-13 September. Shippers by the *Constance* of Weymouth, Mr. Henry Holman, bound from Weymouth for Virginia: Symon Orchard, James Budd, Samuell Cooke, Thomas Budd. (PRO: E190/880/8).

10 September. The following apprenticed in Bristol: Richard Lewis to Thomas Morgan, 5 years Virginia; Richard Jones to same, 5 years Virginia; Edward William to same, 6 years Virginia; Daniell Lewis to same, 6 years Virginia; Edward Hart to Elizabeth Day, 5 years Virginia; Thomas Hart to same, 5 years Virginia; George Mackalla to John Orchard, 5 years Virginia; George Morgan to same, 3 years Virginia; Auffris Gueff to Richard Mathews, 4 years Nevis; George Garmant to William Wattkins, 6 years Virginia. (BR).

13 September. Shipper by the *Elizabeth* of Weymouth, Mr. John Cox, bound from Weymouth for Virginia: John West. (PRO: E190/880/8).

15 September. The following apprenticed in Bristol: John Feare to Elizabeth Wattkins, 6 years Virginia; Robert Peacock to John ——ke, 4 years Virginia. (BR).

16 September. The following apprenticed in Bristol: George Hambleton to John Poole, 4 years Virginia; John Rosser to William Foxall, 4 years Virginia; James Maccadie to William Martin, 4 years Nevis; John Allery to William Rumming, 7 years Virginia; Morgan Hammond to Mathew Gay, 4 years Virginia; John Harris to same, 4 years Virginia; John Brookes to same, 4 years Virginia; Christopher Hore to John Wood, 4 years Virginia. (BR).

21 September-1 October. Depositions in London re the voyage of the *Edward* of London, Mr. Thomas Southin, from London to the Potomack River in Virginia in 1669 with passengers consigned to Mr. Corbin at Rappahannock. (EA).

23 September. Newgate and Home Circuit prisoners reprieved to be transported to Barbados. London: George Benton; John Thompson; Thomas Hendry alias Remington; Edward Mace alias Mitchell; Henry Floyd; Margery Lane, spinster, alias wife of John Lane; William Israell; William Ward; Elizabeth Wyld, spinster, alias wife of Richard Wyld; Elizabeth Scruce alias Lillington alias Garnett, spinster. Middlesex: William Petty alias Pett of St. Martin in the Fields; William Onyons of the same; John Carpenter of the same; Samuel Odwin of the same; William Fergison of the same; John Almery of the same; Thomas Orrell of St. Margaret Westminster; Thomas Acas alias Acus of the same, yeoman; Thomas Studham of Enfield; John Conner of St. Botolph Aldgate; Edward Hodge of Harrow; Henry Pritchett of Shoreditch; Tobias Wright of Islington; Anne Phillips of St. Giles in the Fields, spinster; Hendrick Jessin of the same; Robert Hacke of the same; Margaret Heathfield of Tottenham; Hannah Neale of St. Dunstan in the West, spinster; Robert Langden alias Langdall of the same; Mary Foster of the same; Grace Berry alias Hilliard of St. Clement Danes, widow; Thomas Hodges of St. Andrew Holborn; Matthew Yarrett of St. Sepulchre; Robert Haynes of St. Pancras; William Northcott of Hampton. Essex: Elizabeth Barker of Newport; John Pinner of Lambourne; Charles Parvey of Orsett; Thomas May of South Weald. Hertfordshire: George Hill of Chipping Barnet. Kent: William Ausley of Chiselhurst; James Cookham of Shoreham. Surrey: John Slate Jr. of St. Olave

Southwark; John Thaire of Frimley; Thomas Gasson of Limpsfield. Sussex: John Twyner of Wadhurst. (PRO: C66/3107/41).

27 September. The following apprenticed in Bristol: James Silvester to Paull Williams, 4 years Virginia; Harman Jonson to Nicholas Burras, 4 years Virginia. (BR).

30 September. The following apprenticed in Bristol: Robert Hallwell to Richard Lane, 4 years Virginia; Grace Gray to Nathaniel Cary, 4 years Virginia; Jane Gardner to same, 4 years Virginia. (BR).

2 October. The following apprenticed in Bristol: Richard Turner to William Scott, 5 years Virginia; Ann Yate to John Fry, 4 years Virginia; Robert Loid to Thomas Fisher, 4 years Virginia; Edward Barne to same, 4 years Virginia. (BR).

7 October. The following apprenticed in Bristol: Rachell Williams to John Crawford, 4 years Virginia; William Hughs to John Rowland, 4 years Virginia. (BR).

8 October. The following apprenticed in Bristol: Onor Macarty to Nathaniell Jefferys, 4 years Virginia; Florence Driscoll to same, 4 years Virginia; David James to Ralphe Smethwick, 4 years Virginia. (BR).

10 October. The following apprenticed in Bristol: Edward Felton to William Haggett, 4 years Virginia; Samuell Munday to Samuel Westaby, 4 years Virginia; Michaell Grayer to Henry Williams, 4 years Virginia. (BR).

11 October. The following apprenticed in Bristol: George Lockyeare to William Brian, 4 years Virginia; Joane Harris to Edward Everard, 4 years Virginia. (BR).

13 October. The following apprenticed in Bristol: William Johnson to Thomas Be——, 4 years Virginia; William Rise to John Weaver, 4 years Virginia. (BR).

15 October. The following apprenticed in Bristol: John Hogg to John ?Augate, 3 years Nevis. (BR).

18 October. The following apprenticed in Bristol: Joseph Fick to Roger Dixon, 4 years Virginia; Elizabeth Fick to same, 4 years Virginia. (BR).

20 October. The following apprenticed in Bristol: Samuell Minard to Thomas Jefferys, 4 years Virginia; George Hollard to Mathew Nottley, 4 years Virginia; John Nowell to same, 4 years Virginia; Thomas Hodge to same, 4 years Virginia; William Dicker to same, 4 years Virginia; Thomas Collins to same, 4 years Virginia; Jenkine Thomas to William Dunning, 4 years Nevis or Antigua. (BR).

24 October. John Farvacks of London, merchant, administrator of Daniel Farvacks of London, merchant, deceased, appoints Thomas Ludwell Esq. of Virginia as his attorney. (LMCD).

25 October. The following apprenticed in Bristol: Mary Dyer to Thomas Lugg, 4 years Nevis; Jane Robison to Thomas Symonds, 5 years Nevis; John Caley to John Lugg, 4 years Montserrat; John Winston to John Knight, 4 years Nevis; Evan Rice to Francis Stannton, 4 years Barbados. (BR).

29 October. The following apprenticed in Bristol: John Bryan to Francis Sparkes, 4 years Barbados; John Dorreman to Huddy Harris, 5 years Barbados; Joseph Shorney to same, 3 years Barbados; Edward Dyer to John Bullock, 4 years Barbados or Leewards; William Jay to Samuell Bevan, 4 years Barbados. (BR).

October. Administration of John Hunt of Virginia. (AW).

October. Administration of Daniel Farvacks of St. Giles Cripplegate, London, widower, who had assets in Virginia. (AW).

3 November. The following apprenticed in Bristol: John Potter to John Breach, 4 years Barbados; John Williams to William Dunning, 4 years Barbados; James Powell to Thomas Patten, 4 years Virginia. (BR).

6 November. The following apprenticed in Bristol: Richard Gribble to William Hine, 4 years Barbados; William Clarke to Henry Russell, 4 years Barbados; John Madden to same, 4 years Barbados; John Lewis to Edward Thomas, 4 years Barbados. (BR).

8 November. The following apprenticed in Bristol: Elizabeth Andersen to Thomas Fisher, 4 years Barbados; Mary Lane to same, 4 years Virginia; Thomas Parker to John England, 4 years Virginia; William Tyler to William Dunning, 4 years Virginia. (BR).

11 November. Deposition by John Wing of London, scrivener aged 29, and his servant John Starkey, aged 22, that Richard Roberts of Porobentanke, New Kent County, planter, became indebted by bond of 19 October 1667 to Stephen Porter, citizen and turner of London, and Overington Jeale, citizen and grocer of London. Deposition by John Eden of Wapping, Middlesex, mariner aged 36, and Henry Gleed of Shadwell, Middlesex, surgeon aged 36, that Richard Roberts of Porobentanke, New Kent County, Virginia, planter, became indebted by bond of 9 September 1668 to Porter and Jeale. (LMCD).

12 November. The following apprenticed in Bristol: Thomas Williams to Thomas Williams, 4 years Barbados; Morgan Williams to Robert Jones, 5 years Virginia. (BR).

13 November. The following apprenticed in Bristol: John Irish to David Churchwood, 4 years Barbados; Phillip Edmund to Thomas Simonds, 4 years Barbados. (BR).

15 November. The following apprenticed in Bristol: Mary Evan to Richard Brewer, 4 years Virginia; Sidrach Hardich to William Liston, 4 years

Barbados; Adam Clarke to Walter Hide, 4 years Barbados; Archiman Dodds to same, 4 years Jamaica. (BR).

17 November. The following apprenticed in Bristol: William Kingscutt to Richard Arrowsmith, 4 years Barbados; Richard Whately to Thomas Phillips, 4 years Barbados; Ann Mason to Thomas Symons, 4 years Nevis; John Penry to same, 4 years Nevis; Jane Williams to Thomas Gray, 4 years Barbados. (BR).

18 November. The following apprenticed in Bristol: William Pouley to Leonard Hancock, 4 years Barbados. (BR).

20 November. The following apprenticed in Bristol: Thomas Foster to Thomas Liston, 4 years Barbados; George Jones to Thomas Lewis, 4 years Barbados; Cicely Feare to William Field, 3 years Nevis; Roger Browne to Thomas Tomlinson, 4 years Nevis; John Jones to William Swymer, 4 years Jamaica; Richard Jones to same, 4 years Jamaica; Edward Jones to same, 8 years Jamaica. (BR).

24 November. The following apprenticed in Bristol: William Neale to William Field, 8 years Nevis; Phillip Webb to same, 8 years Virginia; John Vaughan to same, 4 years Virginia; Elizabeth Fisher to same, 4 years Nevis; Martha Peiterson to Ann Smith, 4 years Virginia; Richard Carter to Joseph Sweeper, 6 years Nevis. (BR).

26 November. The following apprenticed in Bristol: William Mulgrove to Edward Thomas, 4 years Nevis; William Browne to Thomas Lewis, 4 years Nevis; John Morgan to same, 4 years Nevis; Ephraim Browne to David Churchwood, 7 years Barbados; Humphrey Cockshut to John Oldbury, 7 years Barbados; Edmund Waymse to William Swymer, 4 years Jamaica; Jane Olton to Joseph Sweeper, 4 years Nevis. (BR).

3 December. The following apprenticed in Bristol: William Dyer to George Salter, 4 years Nevis; Elizabeth Price to William Swymer, 8 years Jamaica. (BR).

4 December. The following apprenticed in Bristol: David Jones to John Smith, 4 years Virginia; Elizabeth Pye to Jenkine Bragg, 3 years Barbados. (BR).

7 December. The following apprenticed in Bristol: Elizabeth Williams to Alice Field, 4 years Nevis; Reece Jones to same, 7 years Nevis; William Perrin to William Swymer, 5 years Jamaica; John Lewis to Thomas Tomlinson, 4 years Barbados; David Binoni to Thomas Lawrence, 4 years Barbados; Edith Watkins to Thomas Lugg, 4 years Nevis. (BR).

10 December. The following apprenticed in Bristol: John Williams to Henry Mudge, 4 years Nevis; John Women to same, 4 years Nevis; Joane Blunt to Osmond Crabb, 4 years Nevis. (BR).

17 December. The following apprenticed in Bristol: Thomas Rogers to William Swymer, 5 years Jamaica; John Quner to Alexander Kellwin, 4 years Nevis; Thomas Slade to John Anglesey, 3 years Nevis *(entered twice)*. (BR).

21 December. The following apprenticed in Bristol: Edward Fuse to John Sheppard, 4 years Nevis; Katherine Williams to William Millard, 4 years Nevis; George Greene to John Anglesey, 3 years Nevis. (BR).

30 December. The following apprenticed in Bristol: David Williams to Thomas Simmons, 4 years Nevis; George Johnson to same, 4 years Nevis; John Combs to John Anglesey, 4 years Nevis. (BR).

December. Administration of Daniel Bradley of Gosport, Hampshire, who died in Virginia. (AW).

December. Administration of Thomas Harrison of Rotherhithe, Surrey, who died in New England, bachelor. (AW).

1670

4 January. The following apprenticed in Bristol: William Harris to Leonard Hancock, 5 years Barbados; Thomas Tucker to Phillip Willing, 4 years Nevis; Elizabeth Randall to Thomas Speed, 4 years Nevis. (BR).

11 January. The following apprenticed in Bristol: John Williams to Leonard Hancock, 4 years Nevis. (BR).

12 January. The following apprenticed in Bristol: James Hulland to Edward Pane, 4 years Barbados; Thomas Sheappard to John Sheappard, 4 years Nevis; John Davis to Thomas Crabb, 4 years Nevis; Evan Jones to George Wattkins, 4 years Barbados or Nevis. (BR).

13 January. William Haverland imprisoned and fined for attempting to forcibly transport Thomas Stone to Virginia. (VM 83/3).

17 January. The following apprenticed in Bristol: Thomas Williams to John Stokes, 4 years Barbados; John Tripplett to John Smith, 4 years Nevis; John Symkins to Edmund Ditty, 4 years Barbados or Nevis; William Willmett to John Blannch, 4 years Barbados; Daniell Munday to Elizabeth Oldbury, 4 years Barbados; Francis Harris to John Lewin, 4 years Barbados or Nevis; Mary Steevens to Thomas Speede, 4 years Barbados or Nevis; Perrin Tayler to William Steevens, 4 years Nevis. (BR).

26 January. Petition of Ferdinando Gorges, grandson and heir of Sir Ferdinando Gorges, for the restoration to him of the Province of Maine, seized by the Governors of Boston. (APC).

31 January. The following apprenticed in Bristol: Faulke Edwards to Edmund Ditty, 4 years Barbados; William Downton to Margery Symmons, 4 years Nevis. (BR).

January. Probate of will of John Handford of Ludlow, Shropshire, whose kinsman, Tobias Handford, was in Virginia. (AW).

7 February. Warrant to allow Henry Wright, a pickpocket in Newgate who works as a tailor and has four small children, to transport himself to the plantations. (SP Dom).

8 February. The following apprenticed in Bristol: Stephen Howard to Roger Bentley, 4 years Montserrat; John Williams to same, 7 years Montserrat; John Jones to Margery Symmons, 3 years Montserrat; John Deane to John Trigg, 4 years Barbados; James Rawlins to John Hind, 4 years Barbados; Thomas Hall to Thomas Pymm, 7 years Nevis. (BR).

14 February. Warrant for Edward Maddox, prisoner in Newgate, to be set at liberty provided he gives security for his good behaviour and transports himself abroad. (SP Dom).

18 February. The following apprenticed in Bristol: George Williams to Thomas Symmons, 3 years Nevis; Elizabeth James to William Wattkins, 4 years Barbados; Mary Nash to same, 4 years Barbados. (BR).

20 February. Deposition by Daniel Bird of London, mariner aged 33, that he served as quartermaster of the *Marigold*, Mr. Samuel Pensax, which in 1669 loaded tobacco from Devereux Browne in Virginia damaged by a storm at sea before being delivered in London. (LMCD).

23 February. The following apprenticed in Bristol: William Millard to Roger Bently, 4 years Montserrat; Elias Eales to Richard Pope Jr., 5 years Nevis; Thomas Moody to Edward Coock, 3 years Nevis; Thomas Freame to Grace Smith, 4 years New England; Giles Wattkins to Thomas Symmons, 3 years Nevis; Robert Symms to same, 4 years Nevis. (BR).

28 February. The following apprenticed in Bristol: Thomas Windall to Thomas Symmons, 7 years Montserrat. (BR).

February. The following apprenticed in Bristol: Jacob Stone, taken at night in Farringdon Within and sent to labour, to be clothed by Mr. Piers who is to have him for New England provided he pays for the clothes. (Bridewell).

4 March. The following apprenticed in Bristol: Henry Richard to Edward Coockson, 3 years Montserrat; Hugh Jones to Mary Norman, 4 years New England. (BR).

5 March. Depositions by Christopher Clarke of Boston, New England, master of the *Society* of Boston, aged 52, and John Gidney Jr. of Salem, New England, master of the *John's Adventure* of Salem, aged 30, being now with their ships in the port of London, that John Sawin of Watertown, New England, by deed of 16 January 1657, conveyed to Henry Stephens of Boxford, Suffolk, his right in a house, garden and apprentices in Boxford. The deed was acknowledged before Governor Richard Bellingham in Boston on 9 September 1667. The depositions are made at the request of Henry Stephens and of Samuel Groome of Stepney, Middlesex, master of the *William & Mary* of London. (LMCD).

7 March. The following apprenticed in Bristol: Abraham Jones to Anthony Berrow, 4 years Barbados. (BR).

10 March. Deposition by Abraham Mosse, aged 22, servant of Thomas Dalton of London, scrivener, that William Daines, then of London but late of Lower Norfolk, Virginia, planter, became bound on 5 October 1668 to James Moore of St. Mary Magdalene, Bermondsey, Surrey, gent, for the delivery of tobacco. The said James Moore has now been appointed attorney to Mr. Henry Geange of London, doctor of physick, and Mr. Samuel Terrick of London, mercer. (LMCD).

10 March. The following apprenticed in Bristol: William Jones to William Wa———, 4 years Barbados. (BR).

13 March. The following apprenticed in Bristol: William Andrews to John Williams, 5 years Nevis. (BR).

15 March. The following apprenticed in Bristol: John Dodd to Thomas Symmons, 5 years Nevis; Sarah Thomas to Thomas Savadge, 4 years New England. (BR).

19 March. The following apprenticed in Bristol: Ann Bayly to Edward Coockson, 7 years Nevis. (BR).

22 March. Letter from the King to the Governor of Virginia. Richard Mompesson, son of John Mompesson of Tidworth, Wiltshire, was inveigled on board the *Elizabeth*, Mr. Richard Hobbs, in 1667 and taken to Virginia where he was delivered with John Crew and Mary Cousens to William Drummond near James Town as the consignee of John Currer in London. Richard Mompesson, who had assumed the name of Richard Davis, is to be delivered to Colonel Willis for disposal. (CSPC).

23 March. The following apprenticed in Bristol: William Cosens to John Somer, 4 years Barbados. (BR).

25 March. The following apprenticed in Bristol: Thomas Holborne to Christopher Holder, 4 years New England; William Jones to Leonard Kirton, 5 years New England. (BR).

28 March. The following apprenticed in Bristol: Mary Thorne to Roger Williams, 3 years Barbados. (BR).

30 March. The following apprenticed in Bristol: Robert Jinkins to Roger Addams, 5 years Nevis. (BR).

March. Administration with will of John Ottway of Hersom [*sic*] Surrey, who died overseas bound for New England. (AW).

March. Probate of will of Lewis Phillips of Huntingdon, whose cousin, John Throckmorton, was in Virginia. (AW).

7 April. The following apprenticed in Bristol: William Spickett to Edward Coockson, 5 years Nevis; John Long to John Williams, 3 years Nevis; William Lane to William Hayman, 4 years Barbados. (BR).

11 April. The following apprenticed in Bristol: John Smart to Edward Coockson, 3 years Nevis (*entered twice*); Thomas Davis to James Rugg, 4 years Nevis. (BR).

18 April. The following apprenticed in Bristol: William Lewis to Thomas Symonds, 7 years Montserrat; Peter Fisher to William Dunning, 4 years Nevis; John Davis to same, 5 years Nevis; William James to Christopher Davis, 4 years Nevis; Samuell Souther to John Wright, 4 years Nevis; William Everell to Thomas Dunning, 7 years Nevis or Montserrat; William Smith to James Knight, 4 years Nevis (*entered twice*). (BR).

29 April. The following apprenticed in Bristol: Samson Burch to Thomas Symmonds, 7 years Montserrat; Roger Winslow to John Williams, 7 years Virginia. (BR).

April. Probate of will of Mark Glocester alias Warkman of St. Mary Magdalen, London, whose brother Robert was in Virginia. (AW).

April. Administration of William Chambers of Virginia, bachelor. (AW).

April. Probate of will of Richard Hutchinson of Hertford, citizen and ironmonger of London, who had lands in New England. (AW).

4 May. The following apprenticed in Bristol: Katherine Williams to Martha West, 4 years Nevis; Rowland Lentall to Thomas Stevens, 4 years Nevis; Christopher Carr to same, 4 years Nevis. (BR).

5 May. The following apprenticed in Bristol: Samuell Beale to Christopher Holder, 9 years New England; John Williams to John Griffen, 4 years New England. (BR).

11 May. The following apprenticed in Bristol: Joseph Colston to John Griffen, 4 years New England; Samuell Hopkins to James Knight, 4 years Nevis; Roger Price to William Sterne, 4 years Barbados; Joan James to Edward More, 4 years Nevis; John Heale to John Millett, 4 years Virginia; Samuell Davis to Robert Welsteed, 7 years Nevis. (BR).

20 May. Deposition by William Harris, aged 23, servant of Elizabeth Ludford of London, widow, beavermaker, that William Thomas of Marshfield, New Plymouth, New England, became indebted by bond of 8 August 1664 to Elizabeth Ludford. Mr. John Hull of Boston, New England, merchant, has been appointed as attorney. (LMCD).

28 May. The following apprenticed in Bristol: George Heunnan to Henry Daniell, 4 years Virginia; Richard William Roberts to Mathew Craddock, 5 years Virginia. (BR).

May. Probate of will of Samuel Filmer formerly of Virginia and late of East Sutton, Kent, who died in Westminster, Middlesex, and whose cousin, Frances, wife of Samuel Stephens, was in Virginia. (AW).

May. Probate of will of Raphael Throckmorton of St. Gregory, London, whose brother-in-law, William Wallthall, was in Virginia. (AW).

May. Administration of John Holcombe of Virginia, bachelor. (AW).

May. Probate of will of Thomas Clarke of York, Virginia. (AW).

4 June. Deposition of William Leeke, citizen and goldsmith of London, aged 30, that John Checkley of St. Saviour, Southwark, Surrey, cooper, became indebted to Samuel Crosse, citizen and embroiderer of London, now deceased, by bond of 28 March 1657. Crosse's relict and executrix, Mary, is now married to Thomas Bullock of Shipdam, Norfolk, gent. Peter Lidget of Boston, New England, merchant, has been appointed attorney to recover debts from Checkley. (LMCD).

6 June. The following apprenticed in Bristol: Jonathan Madgwick to Henry Daniell, 4 years Virginia; Joseph Franckum to William Limbry, 7 years Virginia. (BR).

6 June. Warrant to the Recorder of London for the release on bail of Francis Stone in order that he may transport himself at his own charge. (SP Dom).

7 June. The following apprenticed in Bristol: Maurice Williams to Vallentine Knight, 4 years Barbados; William Edward to John Stokes, 5 years New England. (BR).

13 June. The following apprenticed in Bristol: Adam Wallis to David —ker, 4 years Virginia; Nathaniel Parker to Robert Penny, 5 years Barbados; John Jacob to same, 5 years Barbados. (BR).

14 June. The following apprenticed in Bristol: Joane Kent to Thomas Bodman, 4 years Barbados. (BR).

20 June. The following apprenticed in Bristol: Francis William to Thomas Gay, 4 years Virginia. (BR).

22 June. The following apprenticed in Bristol: Thomas Jones to Thomas Bodman, 4 years Barbados. (BR).

25 June. The following apprenticed in Bristol: Samuell Jones to Percivall Read, 4 years Virginia; Joane Morgan to same, 5 years Virginia; John Brookes to William Martin, 4 years Virginia; Elizabeth Griffen to William Limbry, 4 years Nevis. (BR).

27 June. Letter from Joseph West to Lord Ashley reporting on the settlements begun at Albemarle Point [above Edisto River, Colleton County] in Carolina, with servants brought from Port Royal. (SCPC).

30 June. The following apprenticed in Bristol: Edith Frankes to Mathew Craddock, 4 years Barbados; Thomas Homes to Thomas Cole, 4 years Barbados. (BR).

June. Administration of Robert Walton alias Wanton of Virginia. (AW).

June. Probate of will of Daniel Flower of London scissormaker, who had lands in Virginia. (AW).

June. Middlesex prisoners reprieved to be transported to Barbados: Elizabeth Jones, Peter Sampson, Matthew Slader, Jonathan Skudamor, Alexander Gourdian, William Tibble, Anne Niccolls alias Jenkins, Joyce Hunt, Robert Wallis, Anne Browne, Alexander Benny, Thomas Humfryes, Alison Bell alias

Webster, Thomas Edwards, Richard Corbett, Edward Coleman, Mary Chaplin, William Phillips, Anne Barnes, Thomas Higgerson, Samuel Hilton. (EB).

2 July. The following apprenticed in Bristol: John Bacon to Jonas Moxly, 4 years Virginia. (BR).

4 July. The following apprenticed in Bristol: John Townsend to Thomas Wade, 5 years Virginia. (BR).

5 July. The following apprenticed in Bristol: Sarafee James to Alice Field, 4 years Nevis. (BR).

6 July. The Governor of Virginia is ordered to ensure satisfaction to John Fairvacks, son of Daniel Fairvacks deceased, in his complaint against Edmond Scarborough. [*See entry of 6 September 1671*] (APC).

6 July. The following apprenticed in Bristol: Thomas James to Alice Field, 4 years Nevis; Thomas Mountford to Joell Penn, 4 years Virginia. (BR).

8 July. The following apprenticed in Bristol: Richard Bush to William Roberts, 4 years Virginia; Bartholomew Penn to Jonas Moxly, 4 years Virginia; Richard Kerswell to David Price, 4 years Nevis; Robert Thare to David Price, 4 years Nevis; John Morgan to Richard Day, 6 years Virginia. (BR).

14 July. Deposition by Samuel Fernihaugh of London, merchant aged 27, that on 1 February 1668 John Macken of Virginia, planter, signed a receipt for goods which he was to take to Virginia on behalf of Robert Bugnall, citizen and salter of London, and William Patton of London, scrivener. Richard Bugnall, aged 42, and William Patton, also depose. (LMCD).

15 July. The following apprenticed in Bristol: Mary Doore to James Basely, 4 years Nevis; Jenkin Williams to James Longman, 4 years Virginia. (BR).

21 July. The following apprenticed in Bristol: Sara Street to John Woolem, 4 years Virginia; Emanuell Evans to Thomas Hawkridge, 5 years Virginia; Richard Day to Christopher Roberts, 5 years Nevis. (BR).

23 July. The following apprenticed in Bristol: John Bowler to Thomas Burleton, 8 years Nevis; Deborah Bowler to same, 4 years Nevis; Elizabeth Jones to same, 4 years Nevis; Margarett Jones to same, 4 years Virginia (*sic*); Thomas Higgs to same, 4 years Nevis; Mary Davis to same, 4 years Nevis; William Lingham to same, 4 years Nevis; Richard Maylerd to same, 4 years Nevis; Timothy Clare to same, 6 years Nevis; Frances Belcher, to same 6 years Nevis. (BR).

25 July. The following apprenticed in Bristol: Margarett Clarke to Mathew Craddock, 4 years Virginia; Edward Clarke to same, 4 years Virginia; John Rennolls to same, 4 years Virginia; Mathew Walter to John Mandle, 4 years Virginia; William Rudman to Lewis Brian, 7 years Maryland. (BR).

26 July. The following apprenticed in Bristol: Thomas Lewellin to William Swymer, 5 years Nevis; Richard Howard to Jenkin Reece, 6 years Nevis; William Jenkins to same, 5 years Nevis; Thomas Davis to William Pumfrit, 4 years Virginia. (BR).

27 July. The following apprenticed in Bristol: Margarett Griffin to Richard Franke, 4 years Virginia; Joice Griffeth to same, 4 years Virginia. (BR).

28 July. The following apprenticed in Bristol: Judith Davis to John Muspratt, 4 years Nevis; Stephen Hartly to Lott Richards, 4 years Virginia; John Tripp to Aaron Browne, 4 years Virginia. (BR).

30 July. The following apprenticed in Bristol: William Jones to John Sawyer, 4 years Barbados; John Flowers to Richard Franck, 4 years Virginia; William Williams to John Randle, 4 years Virginia. (BR).

July. Leicester prisoner reprieved to be transported to America: John Bealey of South Croxton. (EB)

July. Administration of Thomas Perry of Virginia. (AW).

July. Probate of will of George Manfield of Virginia, who died overseas, bachelor. (AW).

1 August. The following apprenticed in Bristol: Walter Williams to William Carnes. 4 years Barbados; Rebecca Hellier to Margaret C—dall, 7 years Nevis; Mary Vinson to same, 4 years Virginia; Joane Chechy to Lewis Brian, 4 years Maryland. (BR).

1 August Shipper by the *John* of Absum (*sic*), Mr. John Basse, bound from Newcastle for Maryland: James Thery. (PRO: E190/194/7).

2 August. The following apprenticed in Bristol: Anthony Ewen to Thomas Hawkeridge, 3 years Virginia; John Ansin to Robert Lux, 7 years Virginia; Mary Williams to Mathew Craddock, 4 years Virginia; John Walby to Thomas Norman, 4 years Virginia by *Katherine*, Mr. Robert Dapwell; William Hort to Thomas Pope, 9 years Virginia; William Beard to Edward Fielding, 4 years Virginia. (BR).

2 August. The petition of Robert Bullock referred to the Governor of Virginia. In 1626 Captain Hugh Bullock planted an estate of 5000 acres in Virginia which, on his death 16 years ago, he bequeathed to his infant grandson Robert Bullock but other planters have entered the property. (CSPC).

5 August. The following apprenticed in Bristol: Thomas Morgan to Joseph Timber, 4 years Maryland; John Arden to Jonas Hollyday, 4 years Virginia; John Thomas to William Willett, 4 years Virginia. (BR).

9 August. The following apprenticed in Bristol: Prudence Punny to Francis Holland, 4 years Virginia; John Thomas to William Willett, 4 years Virginia; Isabell Clarke to Richard Hibbert, 4 years Virginia. (BR).

10 August. Richard Ellis, citizen and merchant tailor of London and executor of Daniell Flower, citizen and merchant tailor of London, deceased, appoints John Wright of London, gent, as his attorney to recover debts in Virginia and to sell an estate of 1080 acres on the west side of the Chickahominy River. (LMCD).

12 August. The following apprenticed in Bristol: Phillip Teverton to Henry Andrews, 5 years Maryland by *Society*; John Freeman to John Wooton, 5 years Virginia by *Submission*; George Martyn to Joseph Towgood, 4 years Virginia by *Submission*; Timothy Channter to same, 4 years Virginia by *Truelove*. (BR).

12 August. The seizure of the *Hopewell* from Mr. Gookin is declared legal and his appeal is dismissed. (APC).

15 August. The following apprenticed in Bristol: Elioner Kerby to Abraham Roome, 4 years Virginia; Ann Kerby to same, 4 years Virginia; Richard Mason to Marke Chappell, 4 years Virginia. (BR).

15-17 August. Shippers by the *Neptune* of Whitby, Mr. Daniell Jackson, bound from Hull for Virginia: Alexander Fowling, Francis Harrison, Edmond Wolfe. (PRO: E190/320/10).

17 August. The following apprenticed in Bristol: William Durbin to Alice Field, 4 years Nevis by *Nevis Adventure*. (BR).

18 August. The following apprenticed in Bristol: Margarett Reece to Mathew Hallett, 4 years Virginia; Phillip Tyler to William Saunders, 4 years Virginia; Richard Foskew to Thomas Oldfield, 5 years New England by *Content*; Mary Nilston to Winslow Christofer, 5 years Virginia. (BR).

23 August. The following apprenticed in Bristol: Thomas Lloyd to Zachery Smith, 4 years Virginia; Robert Johnson to same, 4 years Virginia; Nevill Draint to Richard Ward, 4 years Virginia (*entered twice*); Walter Welsh to John Cooke, 4 years Virginia. (BR).

24 August. The following apprenticed in Bristol: Robert Wattkins to Leyson Portry, 4 years Virginia; Edward Curtis to Thomas Pope, 4 years Virginia; John Hawkes to Thomas Bedford, 6 years Virginia by *Samuel & Mary*. (BR).

25 August. The following apprenticed in Bristol: Edward Phillip to John Hellier, 4 years Virginia; Robert Hort to John Woolton, 4 years Virginia; Christopher Parsons to John Read, 4 years Virginia; John Fisher to Henry Aley, 8 years Virginia by *Katherine*; William Phillips to Daniell Gwilliam, 4 years Virginia; Robert Lewis to same, 4 years Virginia. (BR).

26 August. The following apprenticed in Bristol: Reece Evan to Thomas Morgan, 3 years Nevis; George Dodderidge to John Hawkins, 4 years Virginia; William Winter to Mathew King, 4 years Maryland.; John Floyd to William Morgan, 4 years Virginia; George Soley to William Jones, 3 years Virginia; Alice Soley to same, 3 years Virginia; John Faddery to Timothy Slumpe, 5 years Virginia;

Richard Jones to William Jelfe, 4 years Virginia; John Drewett to William Hill, 4 years Virginia. (BR).

26 August. Deposition by John Meekes of Wapping, Middlesex, mariner aged 20, that he served aboard the *Joseph & Benjamin*, Mr. Edward Haslewood, as a seaman and his father, John Meekes, as surgeon. Dr. John Moorecroft, who resided in Maryland, purchased medicines from John Meekes Sr. when the ship was there between January and April 1670. (LMCD).

29 August. The following apprenticed in Bristol: William Payne to Jacob Thomas, 4 years Virginia. (BR).

29 August. Shipper by the *Joane* of Lyme, Mr. John Aldford, to be shipped from Lyme for Plymouth to go by the *George* for Virginia: Samuell Pike. (PRO: E190/880/10).

30 August. The following apprenticed in Bristol: Ann Morgan to Robert Williams, 4 years Virginia; Jane Bottle to Richard Ward, 4 years Virginia; John Mathyson to Thomas Bedford, 3 years *(destination not stated)*; Andrew Lloyd to Thomas Cary, 4 years Virginia by *Katherine*; Barnaby Samborne to Mawdley Samborne Esq., 4 years Barbados. (BR).

August. Administration with will of Richard Preston of Patuxent, Maryland. (AW).

August. Probate of will of Samuel Crane of Great Coggeshall, Essex, whose cousin, John Rogers, was in New England. (AW).

August. Middlesex prisoners reprieved to be transported to Barbados: Miles Zouch, Patrick McKee, William Sperrey, Francis Stone, Robert Knight, William Davies, Richard Williams, Robert Shipley, Thomas Morris, Martha Chapman, Thomas Ward, Elizabeth Herbert, Richard Morgan, Rebecca Snelling, William Cooke, Mary Kirton, John Lewes, Jane Pecke, William Piggott, John Davies (still in prison in June 1671). (EB)

2 September. The following apprenticed in Bristol: John Burges to Edward Noble, 4 years Virginia by *Unicorn*, Mr. Thomas Cooper. (BR).

5 September. The following apprenticed in Bristol: Jane Stevenson to William Bennett, 4 years Virginia by *William & Ann*, Mr. John Orchard; Jane Spurry to William Allen, 4 years Virginia by *Society*, Mr. William Sankey; Katherine Jones to same, 4 years Virginia by *Society*; John Dodderidge to same, 4 years Virginia by *Society*; John Adely to same, 4 years Virginia by *Society*; John Fidoe to Thomas Bedford, 4 years Virginia by *Samuel & Mary*, Mr. James Warren; Robert Fidoe to same, 4 years Virginia by *Samuel & Mary*; Joell Perry to Thomas Hall, 4 years Virginia by *Society*. (BR).

7-19 September. Shippers by the *Fellowship* of Lyme, Mr. John Bull, bound from Lyme for Virginia: Walter Tucker, William Smith. (PRO: E190/880/10).

8 September. The following apprenticed in Bristol: Richard Ricketts to Percivall Reed, 4 years Virginia; Mante Bisgood to John Hawkins, 4 years Virginia by *Katherine*, Mr. Robert Trapwell; John Clarke to William Bennett, 4 years Virginia by *William & Ann*; Mary Howell to Robert Nicholas, 4 years Virginia; Israell Batt to Richard M——, 7 years Virginia by *Submission*, Mr. Robert Nicholls; John Turner to Lambert George, 4 years Virginia by *Katherine*; John Craze to Giles Tayler, 4 years Virginia by *Samuel & Mary*; Benjamin Stringer to John Adams, 4 years Virginia by *Richard [&] James*; Edward Gilson to Nathaniell Hallett, 4 years Virginia by *William & Ann*. (BR).

10 September. The following apprenticed in Bristol: Mary Benson to John Godwyn, 4 years Nevis by *Nevis Adventure*; Elizabeth Oakeford to William Jones, 5 years Barbados by *Richard*, Mr. Arthur Grannt; Katherine Oakeford to same, 5 years Barbados by *Richard*; James Wright to Robert Court, 4 years Virginia by *Joseph*; John Wathen to Hugh Thomas, 3 years Maryland by *Francis & Mary*; Thomas Jones to same, 3 years Virginia by *Francis & Mary*; John Roberts to Lambert George, 4 years Virginia by *Katherine*; Roger Williams to Edward Harbert, 4 years Nevis by *Nevis Adventure*; Walter Griffis to Zachery Smith, 7 years Virginia by *Society*. (BR).

12 September. The following apprenticed in Bristol: John Bateman to John Blanke, 4 years Virginia by *Joseph*, Mr. William Jones. (BR).

12 September. Shipper by the *Nightingale* of York, Mr. John Hobson, bound from Hull for Virginia: Gawen Hodgen. (PRO: E190/320/10).

13 September. The following apprenticed in Bristol: Richard Hally to William Gorst, 4 years Virginia by *Unicorn*; Thomas Wootten to same, 4 years Virginia by *Unicorn*; John Wootten to same, 4 years Virginia by *Unicorn*; Robert Sparkes to Peter Sparkes, 4 years Maryland by *Society*, Mr. Burkett; Thomas Lewis to Robert Tanner, 4 years Virginia by *Truelove*, Mr. William Sheppard. (BR).

14 September. The following apprenticed in Bristol: Thomas Clement to William Rodney, 4 years Barbados by *Richard*; John Batchellor to John Norman, 4 years Virginia by *Francis & Mary*, Mr. John England; John Bowen to same, 4 years Virginia by *Francis & Mary*; John Owen to same, 4 years Virginia by *Francis & Mary*; Robert Champion to William Moore, 7 years Virginia by *Agreement*; John Clarke to James Wallis, 4 years Nevis. (BR).

17 September. The following apprenticed in Bristol: Richard Martin to Roger Whittfield, 4 years Virginia by *William & Ann*. (BR).

19 September. The following apprenticed in Bristol: John Browneing to Richard Dunn, 4 years Barbados by *Richard*; Ann Browneing to same, 4 years Barbados by *Richard*; William Benham to Osmond Crabb, 4 years Nevis; George Williams to William Dale, 4 years Virginia by *Agreement*; Robert Aler to John Bodenham, 4 years Virginia. (BR).

20 September. Shipper by the *Providence* of Lyme, Mr. Job Walton, bound from Lyme for Virginia: William Smith. (PRO: E190/880/10).

20 September. The following apprenticed in Bristol: Abraham Richards to Robert Tanner, 4 years Virginia by *Truelove*; Richard Lightwood to Richard Grove, 5 years Maryland by *Richard & James*; Mary Tanner to same, 4 years [Maryland] by *Richard & James*; Benjamin Thorneton to Zachery Smith, 4 years Virginia by *Society*. (BR).

22 September. The following apprenticed in Bristol: John Snow to John Barnes, 4 years Virginia by *Samuel & Mary*; William Jenkins to Richard Gibbs, 4 years Maryland by *Richard & James*; Edward Jelson to John White, 3 years Virginia by *William & Ann*. (BR).

23 September. The following apprenticed in Bristol: Anthony Norton to Richard Gibbs, 3 years Virginia. (BR).

24 September. The following apprenticed in Bristol: Thomas Harris to Winlock Christason, 7 years Maryland; Elizabeth Shipboy to same, 4 years Maryland; Grace Upton to Lewis Brian, 4 years Maryland by *Richard & James*, Mr. William Nicholas; Elizabeth Horwood to George Tyte, 4 years Virginia by *Agreement*. (BR).

26 September. The following apprenticed in Bristol: Benjamin Littlehales to Bosewell Newton, 6 years Barbados by *John*, Mr. Stokes; Thomas Gild to William Ford, 4 years Virginia by *Richard & James*; Edward Serman to Marke Darte, 4 years Virginia by *Truelove*. (BR).

27 September. The following apprenticed in Bristol: Thomas Harris to Walter Hide, 4 years Virginia by *William & Ann*; Nicholas Jones to Edward Hassell, 4 years Virginia by *Unicorn*; Zachery Cadle to Francis Holland, 4 years Virginia by *Society*; Richard Andrew to Boswell Newton, 4 years [Barbados] by *John*. (BR).

28 September-2 October. Shipper by the *Supply* of Hull, Mr. William Idle, bound from Hull for Virginia: Richard Metcalfe. (PRO: E190/320/10).

September. London prisoners reprieved to be transported to Barbados: Ambrose Bartlett, Elizabeth Page, Henry Vaughan. (EB).

September. Administration of Adam Gittings of Virginia, bachelor. (AW).

1 October. The following apprenticed in Bristol: Samuell Deareing to Percival Read, 4 years [Virginia] by *Unicorn*. (BR).

3 October. The following apprenticed in Bristol: Thomas Nicholas to Zachery Smith, 4 years Virginia by *Society*. (BR).

4 October. Shipper by the *Hope* of Lyme, Mr. William Singleton, bound from Lyme for Virginia: Samuell Tucker. (PRO: E190/880/10).

5 October. The following apprenticed in Bristol: Robert Skelton to Abraham Everett, 4 years Virginia by *Truelove*; Christopher Jones to Robert Jones, 4 years Montserrat by *Jacob*, Mr. Charles Plumer. (BR).

6 October. The following apprenticed in Bristol: John Edwards to Bryant Tandey, 4 years Virginia; John Spencer to Francis Stannton, 4 years Virginia; Mary Benson to same, 4 years Virginia; Lewis Griffeth to same, 4 years Virginia; Griffey Lloyd to same, 4 years Virginia; William Nicholas to George Tyte, 7 years Virginia by *Agreement*. (BR).

8 October. Deposition by George Ayray, citizen and merchant tailor of London, aged 50, that he began a suit against Elizabeth Lockey, relict of John Lockey, and her former husband, Anthony Hanford, in pursuance of a letter of attorney issued to him on 14 June 1667 by Jonathan Newell of York County, Virginia, merchant. On 29 September 1663 the deponent sold cloth to Newell who was then bound from London to Virginia. (LMCD).

10 October. The following apprenticed in Bristol: Edmund Punford to Thomas Harris, 4 years Virginia by *Unicorn*. (BR).

11 October. The following apprenticed in Bristol: Christian Jones to Ann Coock, 4 years Barbados by *Armes of Bristol*. (BR).

12 October. The following apprenticed in Bristol: John Rawlins to George Coyte, 4 years Virginia by *Agreement*; Charles Williams to Edward Stradling, 4 years Virginia by *Unicorn*; Thomas Powell to Joseph Berrow, 4 years Virginia by *Agreement*; John Stallard to same, 4 years Virginia by *Agreement*. (BR).

15 October. The following apprenticed in Bristol: James Sartaine to George Tyte, 4 years Virginia; Elizabeth Curtis to Jerome Jeffries, 4 years Maryland by *Unicorn*; Robert Smith to same, 4 years Maryland by *Unicorn*. (BR).

19 October. The following apprenticed in Bristol: James Browne to Osmond Crabb, 4 years Nevis by *Gabriel*, Mr. John Marsh; Thomas Harry to Robert Jones, 4 years Montserrat. (BR).

20 October. The following apprenticed in Bristol: William Harris to William Wakely, 4 years Virginia by *Unicorn*; Christopher Rowneing to David Williams, 4 years Maryland by *Unicorn*. (BR).

21 October. Warrant for Isaac Watson, Thomas Woodfield and William Parker, prisoners in Oxford, to be transported to Virginia or elsewhere. (SP Dom).

21 October. Because of the danger and disrepute brought to Virginia by the frequent sending there of felons, no more are to be sent to that colony but may continue to be sent to other plantations. (APC).

24 October. The following apprenticed in Bristol: William George to Ann Lugg, 4 years Virginia by *Unicorn*; Thomas Olliver to Francis Stannton, 4 years Virginia by *Agreement*; Thomas Spencer to same, 4 years Virginia by *Agreement*; Jane Godson to John James, 4 years Barbados by *Seaflower*. (BR).

27 October. The following apprenticed in Bristol: Edward Ledden to William Luffe, 4 years Virginia; Launcelott Webb to Percival Reade, 4 years Virginia by *Unicorn*; Elizabeth Kingson to Katherine Revell, 5 years Virginia by *Unicorn*; Judith Reeve to Thomas Bayly, 4 years Barbados by *Seaflower*, Mr. Dempster. (BR).

28 October. The following apprenticed in Bristol: Henry Windard to Thomas Bayly, 4 years Barbados by *Seaflower*; Grace Long to William Luffe, 4 years Virginia by *Unicorn*; Patience Moore to Edward Hassell, 4 years Virginia by *Unicorn*; Thomas Rendall to George Tyte, 7 years Virginia by *Unicorn*. (BR).

29 October. The following apprenticed in Bristol: Samuell Holliday to Percival Read, 6 years Virginia by *Unicorn*; Morgan Thomas to Henry Carpenter, 4 years Jamaica by *Jacob*. (BR).

October. Administration of Thomas Birt of Hershey, Gloucestershire, who died in Boston, New England, bachelor. (AW).

October. Probate of will of Nicholas Carew of St. Martin in the Fields, Middlesex, who had lands in Maryland. (AW).

October. Probate of will of Robert Rose of Rochester, Kent, whose brothers, Christopher Rose and Henry West, were in Virginia. (AW).

2 November. The following apprenticed in Bristol: Isaac Jones to Robert Jones, 11 years Montserrat by his father's consent. (BR).

3 November. The following apprenticed in Bristol: Thomas Nicholls to William Wattkins, 5 years Barbados. (BR).

7 November. The following apprenticed in Bristol: William Lewis to George Norris, 5 years Virginia by *Unicorn*; Robert Sharpe to John King, 4 years Virginia by *Agreement*, Mr. Thomas Whittop; David Penery to Robert Jones, 4 years Montserrat by *Jacob*; Jane Chegley to Phillip Ha——, 4 years Barbados. (BR).

12 November. The following apprenticed in Bristol: Henry Phillips to Thomas Cole, 4 years Nevis by *Jacob*. (BR).

14 November. The following apprenticed in Bristol: Richard Smith to Robert Jones, 3 years Montserrat by *Jacob*; John Willis to Joseph Day, 4 years Barbados; Andrew Phillips to Edward Erbury, 4 years Virginia. (BR).

16 November. The following apprenticed in Bristol: Lewis Jones to John Becon, 7 years Nevis by *Gabriel*. (BR).

18 November. The following apprenticed in Bristol: John Welch to William Hayman, 4 years Jamaica. (BR).

19 November. The following apprenticed in Bristol: Charles Slaughter to Thomas Hyett, 7 years Virginia by *Agreement*; John Bayly to William Dugglas, 4 years Nevis by *Gabriel*. (BR).

19 November. Shipper by the *Francis* of London, Mr. John Warner, bound from Portsmouth for Virginia: said John Warner. (PRO: E190/827/1).

23 November. The following apprenticed in Bristol: Mary Jefferys to Guy Shallford, 4 years Virginia by *Agreement*; Samuell Jones to Thomas King, 7 years Virginia; Robert Gilling to Jarvis Pearson, 7 years Nevis by *Love's Increase*. (BR).

26 November. The following apprenticed in Bristol: Margarett Seaward to Alice Field, 4 years Nevis by *Jacob*; Dorothy Katherine to same, 3 years Nevis by *Love's Increase*; Thomas Webb to William Cadle, 4 years Barbados; William Battle to Giles Case, 4 years Nevis. (BR).

30 November. The following apprenticed in Bristol: Phillip Davy to William Swymer, 4 years Jamaica by *Elizabeth* of Gloucester, Mr. Richard Phelpes; Edward Liddiard to same, 5 years Jamaica by *Elizabeth* of Gloucester. (BR).

November. Administration of Thomas Peer of St. Mary Magdalene, Bermondsey, Surrey, who died in Smith's Creek, St. Mary's County, Virginia. (AW).

2 December. The following apprenticed in Bristol: Hugh Pew to William Swymer, 5 years Nevis by *Elizabeth* of Gloucester; George Quarrells to same, 5 years Jamaica by *Elizabeth* of Gloucester. (BR).

7 December. The following apprenticed in Bristol: Henry Triptoe to William Swymer, 5 years Jamaica by *Elizabeth*. (BR).

12 December. The following apprenticed in Bristol: Thomas Mitchell to William Swymer, 4 years Jamaica; Margarett Hutchins to same, 5 years Jamaica by *Elizabeth* of Gloucester; Edward Robert to Edward Good, 4 years Barbados by *Golden Lion*. (BR).

14 December. The following apprenticed in Bristol: David Collins to Robert Jones, 4 years Montserrat by *Jacob*; David Price to William Wattkins, 4 years Barbados by *Reformation*, Mr. Thomas Smith. (BR).

16 December. The following apprenticed in Bristol: Thomas Newman to Richard Jones, 4 years Jamaica by *Elizabeth* of Gloucester; Peter Legg to William Southell, 7 years Barbados by *Reformation*. (BR).

19 December. The following apprenticed in Bristol: James Daulton to John Deane, 7 years Nevis by *Gabriel*. (BR).

24 December. The following apprenticed in Bristol: Richard Trew to ——— Hellier, 7 years Jamaica by *Elizabeth*; Howell Winny to John House, 4 years Montserrat by *Gabriel*; John Ives to William Swymer, 4 years Nevis or Jamaica by *Elizabeth*. (BR).

29 December. The following apprenticed in Bristol: Robert Richardson to Reginald Gurken, 5 years Barbados by *Bristol Arms*; William Blewett to

Thomas Southell, 4 years Barbados by *Reformation*; Roger Floyd to John Beaton, 4 years Nevis by *Gabriel*; Abraham Williams to John Barrett, 6 years Barbados by *Robert*, Mr. Edmund Ditty. (BR).

31 December. The following apprenticed in Bristol: Peter Fuller to John Needes, 5 years Nevis by *Love's Increase*. (BR).

December. Middlesex prisoner reprieved to be transported to Barbados: Richard Rogers (still in prison in June 1671). (EB).

1671

2 January. The following apprenticed in Bristol: Richard Martin to Thomas Smith, 5 years Barbados by *Reformation*; Andrew Baker to John Jennings, 4 years Barbados by *Robert*. (BR).

5 January. The following apprenticed in Bristol: Joane Wike to Edward Wood, 4 years Barbados by *Robert*. (BR).

6 January. Shippers by the *Tryal*, Mr. Benjamin Clarke, bound from London for New England: Thomas Delarmer, John Dowsey, William Horsey, Thomas Vele. (PRO: E190/53/3).

9 January. The following apprenticed in Bristol: John Lucas to William Swymer, 4 years Jamaica; John Ebden to Thomas Smith, 4 years Barbados by *Reformation*, said Thomas Smith Mr. (BR).

12 January. The following apprenticed in Bristol: Edward Hooper to Benjamin Howell, 9 years [Nevis or Montserrat] by *Gabriel*. (BR).

13 January. The following apprenticed in Bristol: Walter Howell to John Ridley, 4 years Nevis; William Hide to John Woory, 7 years Barbados; William Knight to Thomas Smith, 4 years Barbados. (BR).

14 January. The following apprenticed in Bristol: Richard Smith to Thomas Winstone, 4 years Barbados by *Reformation*; Henry Leafe to William Hooper, 3 years Barbados by *Robert*. (BR).

18 January. The following apprenticed in Bristol: Charles Iles to James Saunders, 4 years Barbados by *Hope*, said James Saunders Mr; Daniell Curry to William Liston, 4 years Barbados by *Golden Lion*, Mr. Nathaniell ——; Thomasin Curry to same, 4 years Barbados by *Golden Lion*. (BR).

19 January. The following apprenticed in Bristol: Ann Smith to William Hooper, 6 years Barbados by *Robert*. (BR).

19 January. America, a negro and disorderly person who ran away from his master Mr. Bolton, to work until his master transports him. (Bridewell).

20 January. The following apprenticed in Bristol: Tuberville [blank] to Thomas Templeman, 4 years [Nevis] by *Gabriel*; Hector Lewis to Richard Phelpes, 4 years Jamaica by *Elizabeth* of Gloucester; Morgan Reece to John Foord, 5 years Nevis by *Love's Increase*, Mr. John Needes. (BR).

25 January. The following apprenticed in Bristol: John Low to Edward Dyer, 4 years Barbados by *Robert*; William Thomas to John Beacon, 4 years Nevis by *Gabriel*, Mr. John Mash. (BR).

26 January. The following apprenticed in Bristol: Jane Peale to John Beacon, 4 years Nevis by *Gabriel*. (BR).

28 January. The following apprenticed in Bristol: Robert Chivers to Thomas Winstone, 4 years Barbados by *Reformation*; Thomas Munbedd to Abell Hayman, 6 years Jamaica. (BR).

30 January. The following apprenticed in Bristol: Crispian Downeing to Phillip J———, 4 years Barbados or Leewards by *Gabriel*; John Skinner to same, 4 years Barbados or Leewards by *Gabriel*; Simon Wall to William Swymer, 4 years Jamaica; Zacharia Hancock to William Hooper, 4 years Barbados by *Robert*. (BR).

1 February. The following apprenticed in Bristol: John Parry to John Knight, 6 years Nevis. (BR).

3 February. The following apprenticed in Bristol: William Jones to William England, 4 years Nevis by *Love's Increase*. (BR).

6 February. The following apprenticed in Bristol to go to Nevis by the *Love's Increase*: Walter Tacy to Walter Garroway, 4 years; Reece Williams to James Belcher, 4 years; David Knowles to same, 4 years; Elizabeth Hawkins to Alice Field, 6 years; Francis Bourne to William Collett, 4 years. (BR).

10 February. The following apprenticed in Bristol: Richard Jackson to William England, 4 years Nevis by *Love's Increase*. (BR).

11 February. The following apprenticed in Bristol to go by the *Love's Increase*: John Davis to James Belcher, 4 years Antigua; John Bacon to Richard Gibson, 4 years Nevis. (BR).

18 February. Shipper by the *Good Hope* of Southampton, Mr. John Fletcher, bound from Southampton for New England: Roger Richbell. (PRO: E190/827/2).

23 February. The following apprenticed in Bristol: Thomas Davis to Morgan Tayler, 4 years Nevis by *Blackamore*, said Morgan Tayler Mr; Jeremy Clarke to John Arden, 6 years New England by *French ship [Friendship]* of Boston; George Harris to Oliver Stratton, 4 years New England by *Robert & Hester*. (BR).

24 February. Western Circuit prisoners reprieved to be transported to Barbados. Dorset: Francis Bowcher of Lyme Regis, husbandman. Hampshire: Susan Wylde of Romsey. Somerset: Mary Jenkins alias Godwyn of Wells, spinster; John Moore of North Petherton, husbandman; Thomas Tapp of Stoke St. Gregory; Edward Harvey of St. Mary Magdalen, Taunton. Wiltshire: William Clarke of New Sarum, tailor; Robert Ragborne of Burbage, husbandman. (PRO: C66/3128/41).

24 February. Oxford Circuit prisoners reprieved to be transported to Barbados. Gloucestershire: Edward Kinge of Loughborough. Herefordshire: John

Williams of Madley. Shropshire: John Turner of Halesowen. (PRO: C66/3128/42).

February. Probate of will of William Pennoyer of London, whose kinsman, Robert Pennoyer, was in New England. (AW).

February. Probate of will of John Maplet of Bath, Somerset, whose sister, Mary Gorton, was in New England. (AW).

February. Probate of will of Matthew Haviland of Shoreditch, Middlesex, clerk, whose sister, Jane, was wife of William Torry of New England. (AW).

1 March. The following apprenticed in Bristol to go by the *Jeremy*, Mr. Thomas Mason: Thomas Mash to Thomas Mason, 4 years; David Teague to John Smith, 5 years Nevis; James Blower to Richard Gibson, 4 years; Elizabeth Cox to same, 4 years; Hannah Biker to same, 4 years; David Seard to Jenkin Rice, 5 years; David Phillips to same, 5 years; Miles Pinil to same, 5 years. (BR).

4 March. Report of John Russell, former master of the *Port Royal*, to Peter Colleton. He sailed his ship from England to Kinsale and from there to Barbados and Nevis after which they ran into bad weather and were forced to beat about for six weeks. Such was their plight that many were forced to drink their own urine. The ship was cast away on the Bahamas on 12 January 1670 where many died. (CSPC).

4 March. Deposition by Abraham Jepson of Stepney, Middlesex, ironmonger aged 30, and Thomas Painter of London, vintner, that Henry Taylor of Boston, New England, merchant, by bond of 13 April 1668, became indebted to Noah Floyd of London, draper. Eusebius Sheppard of London, merchant aged 31, deposes that Taylor also became indebted to William Meade and Ralph Ingram, citizens and merchant tailors of London, by bond of 11 April 1668; Thomas Norman Jr. of Boston, merchant, became bound to the same on 20 April 1669; and Ephraim Turner of New England, merchant, became bound to the same on 21 March 1665. (LMCD).

4 March. The following apprenticed in Bristol: Thomas James to John Mason, 4 years Nevis. (BR).

6 March. The following apprenticed in Bristol: Anthony Sloper to John Alden, 6 years New England by *French ship [Friendship]* of Boston. (BR).

7 March. William Ward of Fosdyke, Lincolnshire, reprieved to be transported to America. (PRO: C66/3128/39).

7 March. The following apprenticed in Bristol: John Harris to Jon. Dale, 4 years New England; Michael Morgan to John Smith, 4 years Nevis. (BR).

15 March. The following apprenticed in Bristol: Thomas Corsey to John Mason, 4 years Nevis by *Jeremy*; Robert James to John Smith, 4 years Nevis by *Unity*. (BR).

16 March. Deposition by John Powell, citizen and merchant tailor of London, aged 50, that the invoice dated December 1651 now produced was sent to him in a letter from Joshua Hewes of New England, merchant. (LMCD).

18 March. The following apprenticed in Bristol: Nicholas Wattkin to Vincent Thorne, 3 years Antigua by *Jeremy*. (BR).

20 March. The following apprenticed in Bristol to go by the *Jeremy* to Nevis: John Paine to Richard Gibson, 4 years; John Burle to Stephen Watts, 4 years; Mary Davis to Francis Buttler, 4 years. (BR).

28 March. The following apprenticed in Bristol: James Ash to William Thomas, 4 years Antigua by *Jeremy*; Robert Churchell to John Coock, 4 years New England by *Society*; Lewis Thomas to Christopher Davis, 7 years Nevis by *Jeremy*; Jenkin Rice to William Jenkin, 3 years Nevis by *Jeremy*; George Bartley to John Collett, 5 years Nevis by *Jeremy*. (BR).

29 March. The following apprenticed in Bristol: Anne May to William Thomas, 4 years Antigua or Caribbees by *Neptune*. (BR).

30 March. The following apprenticed in Bristol: Mathew Shepherd to Phillip Seward, 4 years Barbados by *Neptune*. (BR).

6 April. The following apprenticed in Bristol: John Short to William Thomas, 7 years Antigua or Caribbees. (BR).

7 April. The following apprenticed in Bristol: Robert Millard to Ann Rumming, 4 years New England. (BR).

8 April. The following apprenticed in Bristol: John Hort to James Braithwaite, 4 years Barbados by *Neptune*. (BR).

11 April. The following apprenticed in Bristol: Joane Martin to Grisby Christofs, 5 years New England. (BR).

18 April. The following apprenticed in Bristol: Thomas Minny to Thomas Martin, 4 years New England by *Newfoundland Merchant*. (BR).

19 April. The following apprenticed in Bristol: Isaac Wiley to John West, 7 years Barbados by *Laurel*; James Williams to same, 5 years [Barbados]; Daniell Jones to same, 6 years Nevis; Robert Richard to Stephen Seward, 5 years Barbados; John Evance to same, 4 years Barbados by *Neptune*. (BR).

21 April. Deposition by John Browne of London, gent aged 24, that John Langley Esq. of London, his wife Elizabeth, sister and administratrix of James Wych of London, merchant, deceased, and John Clarke, son and executor of Robert Clarke of Redriffe, Middlesex, and Boston, New England, mariner, deceased, by deed of 14 April 1671 appointed John Richards of Boston, New England, merchant, as their attorney. (LMCD).

26 April. The following apprenticed in Bristol: Timothy Burton to John Farrin, 4 years Barbados by *Neptune*. (BR).

1 May. Thomas Ward of Shadwell, Middlesex, waterman, to answer the charge of forcibly putting John Deane and Clement Tallis on board ship with the intention of sending them beyond the seas. (VM 83/3).

2 May. The following apprenticed in Bristol: John Hopkins to John Smith, 4 years Nevis by *Laurel*, Mr. John West. (BR).

3 May. The following apprenticed in Bristol: George Shayles to Robert Baker, 4 years Jamaica by *Hopeful Katherine*. (BR).

5 May. The following apprenticed in Bristol: Thomas Davy to Robert Watts, 4 years Jamaica by *Hopeful Katherine*, Mr. William Martin; John Price to Thomas Pixton, 4 years Jamaica or Barbados; Edmund Howell to John West, 4 years Nevis by *Laurel*. (BR).

13 May. The following apprenticed in Bristol: Nathaniell Benson to John West, 5 years Nevis or Jamaica by *Laurel*. (BR).

16 May. The following apprenticed in Bristol: Thomas Davis to John Smith, 4 years Nevis, Jamaica or New England by *Laurel*. (BR).

17 May. The following apprenticed in Bristol: William Badger to John West, 4 years Nevis by *Laurel*. (BR).

18 May. The following apprenticed in Bristol to go to Jamaica by the *Laurel*: William Harding to John Price, 4 years; Walter Berry to same, 4 years. (BR).

31 May. The following apprenticed in Bristol: Henery Masy to Thomas Boykin, 4 years Virginia. (BR).

May. Probate of will of Thomas Stegge of Virginia. (AW).

May. Probate of will of Samuel Mew of St. Mildred Poultry, London, whose brother, Ellis Mew, and sister, Sarah Cowper, were in New England. (AW).

1 June. Shippers by the *Spencer* ketch of Bristol, Mr. Michael Furlong, bound from Cowes for Virginia: Benjamin Newland, George Newland. (PRO: E190/827/2).

3 June. The following apprenticed in Bristol: William Davis to Thomas Norman, 4 years Virginia by *Katherine*. (BR).

7 June. William Thewe fined and put into the pillory for unlawfully transporting Guildford Slingsby to Virginia. (VM 83/3).

8 June. The following apprenticed in Bristol: Thomas Watkins to John Price, 4 years Jamaica by *Lion*, Mr. Samuel Cole; Edward Davis to William Merrick, 4 years Barbados by *Planter*, Mr. Bartholomew Jeffard. (BR).

8 June. Newgate prisoners reprieved to be transported to Barbados. London: Ann Poyner, widow; Martha Fox, spinster; Elizabeth Sparrow, spinster; Rebecca Harbert, spinster, alias wife of George Kirby; Peter Higlin; Elizabeth Bowden, spinster; John Minns; Richard Flower; William Swetman; William

Whitehand; Ann Wallin, spinster; Edward King; Alice Foster, spinster; Honor O'Neal alias Bowen, spinster; Margaret Hillman, spinster; Edward Gough; Nathaniel Davis; Robert Fowkes; Elias Belt; Hannah Whitford, spinster. Middlesex: Richard Rogers of St. Giles in the Fields; George Barber of the same; Mary Cuckeele, wife of James Cuckeele alias Mary Gater, spinster, of Hackney; Simon Williams of St. Mary Savoy; Robert Williams of Hillingdon; Mark Smith of Kensington; Thomas Ridley of Stepney; Richard Wells of the same; Elianor Graves, spinster, alias wife of Thomas Graves of Whitechapel; Thomas Evelin of the same; George Derrill of the same; William Wright of the same; Margaret Thomas of St. Giles Cripplegate, spinster; Thomas Powell of Hackney; John Davis of St. Clement Danes; Thomas Dancer Jr. of St. Paul Covent Garden; Thomas Hearne of Isleworth; John Crouchley of Shoreditch; John Wickers of the same; John Cooke of Hackney; Frances Jobson of St. Andrew Holborn, spinster, alias wife of Edward Jobson of Islington, alias Frances Barnes alias Frances Candler alias Frances Lusted, spinster; Richard Peirce of St. Andrew Holborn. (PRO: C66/3128/21).

9 June. The following apprenticed in Bristol: Phillip Tiler to William Merrick, 4 years Barbados by *Planter*. (BR).

9 June. Home Circuit prisoners reprieved to be transported to Barbados. Essex: John Brookes of Braintree; William Hollingsworth of Harlow. Hertfordshire: John Lincolne of Apstead [?Aspenden]; William Powell of St. Andrew, Hertford. Kent: Robert Thomas of Swanscombe; George Hall of the same; John Haslewood of the same; Robert Clarke of Erith; Nicholas Holman of Sandwich; Thomas King of Lamberhurst. Surrey: Thomas Newey of Kingston on Thames; George Deane of Lambeth; John Gyles of Newington; John Wells of the same; William Porter of St. Saviour, Southwark; Mary Fisher, spinster, alias wife of John Fisher of the same; Elizabeth Flower, spinster, alias wife of John Flower of the same; Alice Howard, spinster, alias wife of John Howard of Wandsworth; Richard Bowdey of Egham; John Britt of Redriffe; David Hewson of St. Andrew Holborn (Middlesex). Sussex: William Kidder of Bletchington; Thomas Brigman of Warbleton, husbandman. (PRO: C66/3128/17).

10 June. The following apprenticed in Bristol: Theophilus Hackett to John Price, 6 years Jamaica by *Lion*; Thomas Deare to Anthony Murry, 7 years Virginia by *Patience*, Mr. William Trego; Ellis Jones to John Hobbs, 4 years Barbados by *Planter*. (BR).

19 June. The following apprenticed in Bristol: Anne Shay to Jone Jeffard, 4 years Barbados by *Planter*. (BR).

21 June. The following apprenticed in Bristol: Jane Caple to William Sankey, 4 years Virginia by *Society*. (BR).

23 June. The following apprenticed in Bristol: Francis Reese to Peter Perkes, 4 years Virginia by *Society*. (BR).

24 June. The following apprenticed in Bristol: Elizabeth Iles to John Hodges, 4 years Virginia by *Patience*. (BR).

27 June. The following apprenticed in Bristol: Edward Whittman to Francis Little, 5 years Virginia by *Society*. (BR).

28 June-2 July. Shipper by the *William & Thomas* of Poole, Mr. Thomas Yonge, bound from Poole for Virginia: William Orchard. (PRO: E190/880/13).

30 June. The following apprenticed in Bristol: George Hughs to William Sankey, 5 years Virginia by *Society*. (BR).

5 July. The following apprenticed in Bristol: Mary Jones to John Mason, 4 years Virginia by *Trial*; Jane Gray to Martha Cradduck, 4 years Virginia by *Trial*; Edward Andrewes to Peter Perkes, 5 years Virginia by *Society*. (BR).

6 July. Western Circuit prisoners reprieved to be transported to Barbados. Cornwall: Thomas Gibbs of Stangate. Hampshire: Robert Stevens of Stratfield, husbandman; John Sedgwick of Farley, husbandman. Somerset: Thomas Dycr of Martock, husbandman; Roger Murrey of Dunster; Thomas Clarke of Watchet, husbandman; John Keate of Stoke St. Gregory, husbandman. Wiltshire: John Bolton of Preshute, blacksmith. (PRO: C66/3128/13).

7 July. The following apprenticed in Bristol: Isaac Gingell to Thomas Boykin, 4 years Virginia by *Society*; Hugh Cartwright to Abraham Roome, 4 years Virginia by *Katherine*; Charles Feakley to Lewis Bowin, 7 years Virginia by *Katherine*; Margaret Richard to Lambert George, 4 years Virginia by *Katherine*. (BR).

10 July. The following apprenticed in Bristol: Thomas Murphe to John Addams, 4 years Virginia by *Richard & James*; Anne Stradling to same, 4 years Virginia by *Richard & James*; Anne Baker to Zachariah Smith, 4 years Virginia by *Society*; Mary Sharrett to same, 4 years Virginia by *Society*; William Cole to William Cannings, 4 years Virginia by *Society*; Susan Peters to same, 4 years Virginia by *Society*; Richard Scarrutt to Thomas Opey, 4 years Nevis by *Thomas & Mary*. (BR).

11 July. The following apprenticed in Bristol: William Davis to John Mason, 4 years Virginia by *Trial*. (BR).

12 July. The following apprenticed in Bristol: Peter Hellier to Abraham Roome, 4 years Virginia by *Katherine*; William Townsend to Robert Lancaster, 4 years Virginia by *Trial*. (BR).

13 July. The following apprenticed in Bristol: Hugh Rice to Thomas Lewellin, 4 years Jamaica; Shadrick George to Lambert George, 4 years Virginia by *Katherine*. (BR).

14 July. The following apprenticed in Bristol: Thomas Moggs to John Mockesby, 8 years Virginia by *Trial*. (BR).

15 July. Northern Circuit prisoners reprieved to be transported to Barbados. Cumberland: Richard Scott of Threlkeld. Yorkshire: Jonathan Wood of York; Peter Belman of Disforth; William Ward of Thorne; William Nelson of Hompton; Jane Hardy, spinster; Robert Ramsden of Marton on Moor; John Best of Yarm; Thomas Smurfitt of York. (PRO: C66/3128/10).

15 July. The following apprenticed in Bristol: David Lloyd to Thomas Eddy, 3 years Nevis by *Thomas & Mary*; Hugh Lloyd to same, 3 years Nevis by *Thomas & Mary*; David Richard to Mathew Cradduck, 4 years Virginia by *Trial*. (BR).

17 July. The following apprenticed in Bristol: Martha Peterson to James Boone, 4 years Virginia by *Trial*. (BR).

19 July. The following apprenticed in Bristol: Richard Weaver to Robert Courte, 4 years Virginia by *Restoration*; John Chambers to same, 4 years Virginia by *Restoration*; Mary Medems to Richard Selman, 4 years Jamaica by *Lion*. (BR).

20 July. The following apprenticed in Bristol: Daniell Dune to John Rice, 3 years Jamaica by *Lion*. (BR).

21 July. The following apprenticed in Bristol: Mathias Dring to Thomas Boykin, 3 years Virginia by *Society*; James Harris to Christopher Birkhead, 4 years Virginia by *Society*. (BR).

22 July. The following apprenticed in Bristol: Thomas Browne to James Pope, 4 years Virginia by *Society*; Richard Evans to John Mason, 4 years Virginia by *Trial*; Abraham Joslin to John Lugg, 5 years Virginia by *Restoration*; Robert Pumphret to Lambert George, 3 years Virginia by *Katherine*. (BR).

26 July. The following apprenticed in Bristol: Thomas Marshall to John Hankins, 10 years Virginia by *Katherine*; John Ingrum to John Gill, 4 years Virginia; Bryan Doubty to Thomas Carney, 4 years Virginia by *Trial*. (BR).

27 July. The following apprenticed in Bristol: John White to Thomas Carney, 4 years Virginia by *Trial*; John Bennett to William Clarke, 8 years Virginia by *Katherine*. (BR).

28 July. On the petition of Thomas Bandinell, master of the *Nicholas* of Jersey which was arrested in Virginia as an illegal trader, his penalty bond is cancelled. (APC).

28 July. The following apprenticed in Bristol: Thomas Ellmore to Peter Perkes, 5 years Virginia by *Society*. (BR).

29 July. The following apprenticed in Bristol: Walter Benford to Lambert George, 3 years Virginia by *Katherine*; Thomas Turton to William Ashton, 4 years Nevis or Virginia by *William*. (BR).

31 July. The following apprenticed in Bristol: John Andrews to Peter Perkes, 7 years Virginia by *Society*; John Norrish to James Boone, 4 years Virginia by *Trial*. (BR).

July. Administration of Lancelott Hallett of River Sarifax, Maryland, bachelor. (AW).

July. Administration of Francis Ludlow of Horningham, Wiltshire, who died in Virginia. (AW).

1 August. The following apprenticed in Bristol: Morgan Thomas to Robert Lancaster, 5 years Virginia by *Trial*. (BR).

2 August. The following apprenticed in Bristol: William Williams to Maxfield Walter, 4 years Virginia by *Stephen*. (BR).

4 August. The following apprenticed in Bristol: Rebecca Knight to William Yorke, 4 years Virginia by *Hercules*; James Pendergras to Robert Pennington, 4 years Virginia by *Trial*; Richard Luse to William Bull, 4 years Virginia by *Trial*; William Whittfield to William Smith, 4 years Virginia by *Trial*. (BR).

5 August. Norfolk Circuit prisoners reprieved to be transported to Barbados. Bedfordshire: Richard Jay alias Jennings of Stagsden; Robert Langdell of Stagsden. Buckinghamshire: John Lee of Aylesbury; Samuel Wilson of Chalfont St. Peter. Cambridgeshire: Henry Watson of Barrington; William Martyn of Burrough Green. Huntingdonshire: Aaron Fountayne of Water Newton. Norfolk: Robert Lakey of Bexwell; Ralph Barrett of Topcroft; Silvester Kay of Paston; William Elwood of Dereham; William Jary of Taverham; John Bloome of East Dereham; William Hudson of Wymondham; Samuel Browne of Wymondham; Henry Brady of Necton. Suffolk: Roger Tillson of Bury St. Edmunds. (PRO: C66/3128/9).

5 August. The following apprenticed in Bristol: Sara Williams to John Mason, 4 years Virginia by *Trial*. (BR).

7 August. The following apprenticed in Bristol: Abraham Ames to William Bull, 4 years Virginia; Roger Reece to William Sanders, 4 years Virginia; Thomas Sheard to Jonas Moxley, 4 years Virginia by *Trial*; Thomas Wright to Lambert George, 6 years Virginia. (BR).

8 August. The following apprenticed in Bristol: John Clarke to Lambert George, 7 years Virginia by *Katherine*; Joane Bleathen to same, 4 years Virginia; Anne Attkins to same, 4 years Virginia; Thomas House to same, 7 years Virginia; Thomas King to Mathew Cradduck, 4 years Virginia; Richard Whitturd to Ezekiell Jones, 4 years Nevis. (BR).

9 August. The following apprenticed in Bristol: Thomas Lewis to James Moxley, 9 years Virginia by *Trial*. (BR).

10 August. The following apprenticed in Bristol: Joseph Powell to James Ryfield, 4 years Virginia; George Harbert to Abraham Field, 4 years Virginia; John Hayden to Mathew Cradock, 7 years Virginia by *Trial*; Anne Davis to Thomas Boykin, 4 years Virginia; Reece Price to Zachary Smith, 4 years Virginia. (BR).

11 August. The following apprenticed in Bristol: Thomas Newman to Thomas Carny, 4 years Virginia. (BR).

11-19 August. Shippers by the *Providence* of Lyme, Mr. Job Walton, bound for New England: Walter Tucker, Richard Hall, John Gaich. (PRO: E190/880/14).

14 August. The following apprenticed in Bristol: John Hand to Barnard Browne, 4 years Virginia. (BR).

15 August. The following apprenticed in Bristol: Thomas Harris to John Greene, 11 years Virginia. (BR).

18 August. The following apprenticed in Bristol: Jonathan St. Alban to Edward Dyer, 7 years Barbados. (BR).

19 August. The following apprenticed in Bristol: Hester Garberry to Thomas Hungerford, 4 years Virginia by *Stephen*. (BR).

20 August. Deposition by Susan Gibbs of St. Giles parish, London, widow aged 70, that her brother, Robert England of St. Clement Danes, Middlesex, butcher, deceased, has an only surviving child, Jane, wife of John Gurgany, doctor of divinity. The said Jane Gurgany is the same person named in the will of the deponent's nephew, Robert England of Virginia, deceased, as Jane Michael. Rebecca Bateman of Shoreditch, Middlesex, widow aged 71, deposes similarly as cousin to both father and son. (LMCD).

21 August. The following apprenticed in Bristol: Leonard Coate to William Scott, 5 years Virginia. (BR).

22 August. The following apprenticed in Bristol: James Morgan to Lambert George, 9 years Virginia. (BR).

23 August. The following apprenticed in Bristol: John Prance to John Bourne, 4 years Virginia by *Phoenix*. (BR).

24 August. The following apprenticed in Bristol: Susannah Davis to Thomas Daniell, 4 years Maryland. (BR).

26 August. The following apprenticed in Bristol: Thomas Gollidge to John Scott, 4 years Virginia by *Stephen*; Elizabeth Gollidge to same, 4 years Virginia by *Stephen*. (BR).

28 August. The following apprenticed in Bristol: Daniell Edwards to William Walter, 4 years Virginia. (BR).

30 August. The following apprenticed in Bristol: Robert Thomas to William Morgan, 3 years Virginia; Goodlove Bright to William Hardith, 4 years Virginia by *Francis & Mary*; William Brooke to Thomas Hodges, 4 years Barbados; Daniell Howell to Lambert George, 6 years Virginia by *Katherine*; Walter Lewis to John Norman, 4 years Virginia by *Francis & Mary*; William Bowen to same, 4 years Virginia by *Francis & Mary*; John Richards to same,

4 years Virginia by *Francis & Mary*; Thomas Wates to John Lewis, 4 years Virginia by *Phoenix*. (BR).

31 August. Shipper by the *Hope* of Lyme, Mr. William Singleton, bound for Virginia: Walter Tucker. (PRO: E190/880/14).

2 September. The following apprenticed in Bristol: Edward Provin to Thomas Daniell, 4 years Virginia by *Richard & James*; Mary Boyd to William Hardith, 4 years Virginia by *Francis & Mary*; Thomas Pitchard to Bennett Hoskins, 3 years Virginia by *Francis & Mary*; Hugh Evans to same, 4 years Virginia by *Francis & Mary*. (BR).

4 September. The following apprenticed in Bristol to go by the *Francis & Mary* to Virginia: James Garolls to Bennett Hoskins, 4 years; Thomas James to same, 7 years; Thomas Hooke to same, 7 years. (BR).

6 September. Oxford Circuit prisoners reprieved to be transported to America. Herefordshire: Thomas Jones of Munsley. Shropshire: John Harris of Tonge; Robert Welsh of Tonge; Richard Evans of Pontesbury; Richard Taylor of Tonge; Thomas Morgan of Longtown; Richard Powell of Ness; John Broadwater of Tonge. Staffordshire: Gabriel Witherell of Penkridge. Worcestershire: Robert Bray of Claines; Elianor Evans of Bromsgrove. (PRO: C66/3128/1).

6 September. Cheshire prisoners reprieved to be transported to Barbados: John Key of Nantwich; John Alcocke of Willaston. (PRO: C66/3128/2).

6 September. The following apprenticed in Bristol: John Wines to Christopher Hassell, 7 years Virginia. (BR).

7 September. The following apprenticed in Bristol: Francis Baker to Jacob Tomson, 4 years Virginia by *Samuel & Mary*; Richard Dummutt to Thomas Goodwin, 7 years Nevis by *Nevis Adventurer*. (BR).

8 September. The following apprenticed in Bristol: Lewis Howell to John Rogers, 4 years Virginia. (BR).

9 September. The following apprenticed in Bristol: Mary Hull to John Hodges, 4 years Barbados; John Gouldby to Henry Galloway, 4 years Virginia. (BR).

11 September. The following apprenticed in Bristol: Thomas Webb to John Bodman, 4 years Virginia; William Wills to William Hardith, 4 years Virginia by *Francis & Mary*. (BR).

13 September. The following apprenticed in Bristol: Sarah Jennyns to John Rogers, 4 years Virginia; Jane Jones to Michaell Hockley, 4 years Virginia by *Richard & James*. (BR).

14 September. Deposition by Edward Bacon, citizen and ironmonger of London, aged 27, that Richard Glover, citizen and ironmonger of London, shipped goods by the *Baltimore*, Mr. John Dunch, to Samuel Withers in Maryland, merchant or planter. (LMCD).

14 September. The following apprenticed in Bristol: Mary Browne to Caleb Cockrell, 4 years Virginia; William Jones to Edward Field, 4 years Barbados by *Lion*. (BR).

14 September. Shipper by the *Hope* of Lyme, Mr. William Singleton, bound from Cowes for Virginia: Benjamin Newland. (PRO: E190/827/2).

15 September. The following apprenticed in Bristol: Katharine Harris to David Price, 4 years Virginia by *Samuel & Mary*; Margaret Whitehead to Thomas Goodwin, 4 years Nevis by *Nevis Adventurer*. (BR).

16 September. Deposition by John Hutt, citizen and girdler of London, aged 31, that his brother Daniell Hutt, now in Virginia, became indebted on 19 November 1668 to Christopher Bannister, citizen and haberdasher of London, for stockings sent to Virginia. Edward Calthorp Jr. of Southwark, Surrey, grocer aged 25, deposes similarly. A letter of 5 June 1669 from Daniell Hutt to Bannister is produced in court. (LMCD).

16 September. The following apprenticed in Bristol: Edward Phillips to William Raines, 5 years Nevis by *Richard*. (BR).

18 September. The following apprenticed in Bristol: Robert Dennis to John Rogers, 4 years Virginia by *Richard & James*. (BR).

18-20 September. Shippers by the *John & Mary* of Southampton, Mr. John Milberry, bound from Southampton for Virginia: Christopher Smith, Thomas Hill, John Taylor, Peter Wale, John Loving. (PRO: E190/827/2).

19 September. The following apprenticed in Bristol: Anne Lercock to John Pitts, 4 years Virginia by *Pearl*; John Johns to John Reede, 4 years Virginia. (BR).

20 September. The following apprenticed in Bristol: Edward Avery to John Porter, 4 years Virginia by *Richard & James*. (BR).

22 September. Deposition by Thomas Hudson, aged 24, servant of John Cudworth Esq. of London, that Henry Taylor of Boston, New England, merchant, became indebted to Cudworth and to William Temple of London, citizen and cutler, now deceased, by bond of 11 April 1668 for goods shipped by the *Boston Merchant*, Captain John Peirce. (LMCD).

22 September. The following apprenticed in Bristol to go to Virginia by the *William & Anne*: Henery Tatlock to Thomas Riding, 4 years; Henry Brombill to same, 4 years; Thomas Bridge to same, 4 years. (BR).

23 September. The following apprenticed in Bristol: Faithfull Gording to Lawrence Hodges, 7 years Nevis by *Nevis Adventurer*. (BR).

25 September. The following apprenticed in Bristol: Edward Phillips to John Bodenham, 4 years Virginia by *Maryland Merchant*. (BR).

27 September. The following apprenticed in Bristol: Thomas Attwood to Phillip Millard, 4 years Virginia by *Pearl*. (BR).

28 September. The following apprenticed in Bristol: William Goose to Thomas Pope, 5 years Virginia by *Francis & Mary*. (BR).

30 September. The following apprenticed in Bristol: Judith Martin to Michaell Hockley, 4 years Virginia by *Richard & James*. (BR).

September. Deposition in London by John Bowles Jr. of Friday Street, London, merchant aged 26, re the voyage of the *Success*, Mr. James Bolton, from London to Guinea and Virginia in 1669 with a cargo of black slaves. (NGSQ 67/4).

2 October. The following apprenticed in Bristol: Barbary More to Samuell Warebridge, 4 years Virginia by *Agreement*. (BR).

4 October. The following apprenticed in Bristol: Sarah Fowler to Mary Andrews, 7 years Maryland; William Hathaway to John Becon, 4 years Barbados by *Richard*. (BR).

7 October. The following apprenticed in Bristol: Mary Weakley to Francis Stanton, 5 years Barbados by *John*; Mary Jones to same, 4 years Barbados by *John*; Lewis William to Stephen Watts, 4 years Virginia; Zacharias Thomas to same, 4 years Virginia. (BR).

7-11 October. Shippers by the *Mary* of Southampton, Mr. Thomas Martin, bound from Southampton for Virginia: George Prince, Alexander Hill, William Wells, Charles Maw, John Loving. (PRO: E190/827/2).

10 October. The following apprenticed in Bristol: Rowland Minton to Peter Wraxell, 4 years Virginia by *Maryland Merchant*. (BR).

10-12 October. Shippers by the *Elizabeth* of Weymouth, Mr. John Cox, bound from Weymouth for Virginia: Symon Orchard, Phillip Stansbie, James Guthry. (PRO: E190/880/12).

12 October. The following apprenticed in Bristol: Thomas Whiting to Fortune Twite, 4 years Maryland by *Francis & Mary*. (BR).

14 October. The following apprenticed in Bristol: Henery Mores to William Willett, 5 years Virginia; John Brumig to same, 5 years Virginia. (BR).

16 October. The following apprenticed in Bristol: William Sage to Richard Dempster, 4 years Barbados by *Seaflower*; Giles Rendall to Thomas Pope, 4 years Maryland. (BR).

17 October. The following apprenticed in Bristol: Thomas Hughs to Abraham Wild, 4 years Virginia by *Unicorn*. (BR).

19 October. The following apprenticed in Bristol: John Obonny to John England, 5 years Virginia by *Baltimore*; Walter Garratt to Bartholomew Peares, 4 years

Barbados; William John Jenkins to Edward Berkins, 5 years Virginia by *Unicorn*; Reece Thomas to same, 5 years Virginia by *Unicorn*; William Williams to same, 5 years Virginia by *Unicorn*; Henery Butler to Stephen Watts, 4 years Virginia by *Baltimore*. (BR).

23 October. The following apprenticed in Bristol to go to Virginia by the *Samuel & Mary*: Grace Jones to James Harris, 4 years; Mary Lambert to same, 5 years. (BR).

26 October. The following apprenticed in Bristol: Thomas Eltt to John Jenkins, 4 years Virginia by *Samuel & Mary*. (BR).

30 October. The following apprenticed in Bristol: Thomas Williams to John Steward, 4 years Virginia by *Samuel & Mary*. (BR).

October. Probate of will of Constant Silvester of Brampton, Huntingdonshire, who had lands in New England. (AW).

October. Probate of will of Jeremy Robins of St. Martin in the Fields, Middlesex, whose daughter, Rebecca Robins, was in Virginia. (AW).

1 November. The following apprenticed in Bristol: Moses Kingman to John Sayers, 4 years Barbados by *Richard*; Sarah Owen to William Welch, 4 years Virginia. (BR).

6 November. The following apprenticed in Bristol: Elizabeth Williams to John Howard, 4 years Virginia. (BR).

8 November. The following apprenticed in Bristol: George Butler to William Morgan, 4 years Virginia by *Agreement*; John Matthews to same, 4 years Virginia by *Agreement*; Christopher Baldwin to John West, 4 years Virginia by *Richard*; Matthew Pope to John Harvey, 5 years Virginia by *Unicorn*; Jennett Phillips to Alice Field, 4 years Nevis by *Gabriel*. (BR).

10 November. The following apprenticed in Bristol: David Bowen to William England, 4 years Barbados or Nevis by *Richard*. (BR).

11 November. The following apprenticed in Bristol: Benjamine Tovey to William Bently, 5 years Barbados by *Richard*; Richard Lamforth to Percivall Reede, 4 years Virginia by *Agreement*. (BR).

14 November. The following apprenticed in Bristol: Anne Fuller to Jane Welsh, 4 years Virginia; Aron Elsden to Edmund Young, 4 years Virginia; Elizabeth Williams to Guy Shallford, 4 years Virginia by *Agreement*. (BR).

16 November. The following apprenticed in Bristol: Richard Cole to William Bentley, 4 years Barbados by *Richard*. (BR).

17 November. The following apprenticed in Bristol: Peter Edwards to John Whitfield, 4 years Virginia by *Barbados Merchant*. (BR).

18 November. The following apprenticed in Bristol: William Thomas to John Beacon, 4 years Barbados. (BR).

21 November. The following apprenticed in Bristol: Edward Wallis to John Deane, 4 years Nevis by *Gabriel*. (BR).

23 November. The following apprenticed in Bristol: Joseph Hunt to Robert Jones, 4 years Nevis. (BR).

24 November. The following apprenticed in Bristol: Richard Samuell to William Cadle, 4 years Virginia by *Barbados Merchant*. (BR).

29 November. The following apprenticed in Bristol to go to Virginia by the *Agreement*: Charles Lewis to Guy Shalford, 4 years; Joseph David to Anthony Pearce, 6 years. (BR).

November. Administration of John Webster of Maryland, bachelor. (AW).

November. Administration of Thomas Bradford of Batcombe, Somerset, who died in Virginia, bachelor. (AW).

November. Administration of William Waite of Stepney, Middlesex, who died in Virginia. (AW).

1 December. The following apprenticed in Bristol: James Moody to Percivall Reed, 4 years Virginia. (BR).

2 December. The following apprenticed in Bristol: Thomas Lepper to William Harcam, 4 years Virginia by *Agreement*; Robert Jarvis to John Ford, 4 years Nevis by *Gabriel*. (BR).

4 December. The following apprenticed in Bristol: William Brewerton to Percivall Reed, 4 years Virginia by *Agreement*; Samuell Willett to William Willett, 4 years Virginia by *Barbados Merchant*. (BR).

6 December. The following apprenticed in Bristol: Mary Acres to John Jinkenson, 4 years Virginia by *Agreement*. (BR).

9 December. The following apprenticed in Bristol: Jone Good to Henry Sanders, 4 years Nevis by *Gabriel*; Mary Dennum to same, 4 years Nevis by *Gabriel*; Phillip Oliver to William Hooper, 4 years Nevis by *Nevis Merchant*. (BR).

11 December. The following apprenticed in Bristol: John Browne to Richard Davis, 4 years Nevis by *Nevis Merchant*; Roger Monke to Henry Sanders, 5 years Nevis by *Gabriel*. (BR).

12 December. Depositions by Dame Elizabeth Culpepper of Grays Inn Lane, London, aged 55, relict of Sir Cheny Culpepper, and Ralph Freeke Esq, aged 75, of the Middle Temple, London, that John Clark of London, merchant, went to Virginia some years ago and was killed by a falling tree on Middle Plantation at York River. He owned plantations and stock in Virginia at the time of his death. He was reputed to be the son of Sir John Clark of Wrotham, Kent, and the younger and only brother of Sir William Clark. The sole heir of the said John Clark of Virginia is therefore his nephew, John Clark Esq. of Wrotham, son of the said Sir William Clark. (LMCD).

12 December. The following apprenticed in Bristol: James Bridduck to Thomas Hilley, 4 years Nevis. (BR).

15 December. The following apprenticed in Bristol: John Anderson to Thomas Cole, 4 years Nevis by *Gabriel*. (BR).

23 December. The following apprenticed in Bristol: Christopher Blunt to Stephen Watts, 4 years Nevis. (BR).

30 December. The following apprenticed in Bristol: John West to James Russell, 4 years Nevis; George Hopkins to John Jones, 4 years Nevis by *Nevis Merchant*. (BR).

December. Administration with will of Hugh Stanley of Maryland. (AW).

December. Middlesex prisoners reprieved to be transported to Barbados: John Jones, Alice Benford, Richard Benjon alias Benioge, William Thompson, Mary Lyon alias Darton alias Carleton, Roger Medley, Richard Whitehart, Thomas Sykes, George Moles, Henry Cockdale, Jane Pellingham, Calvin Read. (EB).

1672

10-20 January. Shippers by the *Jeanney*, Mr. John Jully, bound from London for Virginia: Nicholas Roberts, Richard Long. (PRO: E190/54/1).

10 January-2 March. Shippers by the *Sea Flower*, Mr. Thomas Smith, bound from London for New England: John Addams, Henry Ashurst, Thomas Bodley, R—— Boswell, Jeremiah Chamberlaine, George Chamberlayne, John Child, Paul Darby, Thomas Deane, James Eyton, Noah Floyd, Francis French, Philip French, Thomas Glover, Peet Hagger, John Harwood, Leonard Hoare, Edward Hull, John Lewin, Edward Merriweather, Thomas Norman, John Pack, Sir William Peake, Thomas Ruck, Charles Seddon, John Sweeting, Alexander Waldren, Edmond White. (PRO: E190/53/6, 54/1).

12 January. The following apprenticed in Bristol: Robert Player to Robert Yeat, 4 years Nevis. (BR).

12 January. Shippers by the *William & Ralph*, Captain William Jeffery, bound from London for Carolina: John Stubbin, John Kingdome, John Ward. (PRO:E190/54/1).

15 January. The following apprenticed in Bristol: Joane Burgey to John Mason, 4 years Nevis by *Jeremy*; Thomas Sam to same, 4 years Nevis by *Jeremy*. (BR).

18 January. The following apprenticed in Bristol: Richard Hill to Thomas Taylor, 4 years Nevis by *Nevis Merchant*. (BR).

20 January. The following apprenticed in Bristol: Richard Wells to Thomas Symons, 5 years Montserrat by *Nevis Merchant*. (BR).

25 January. The following apprenticed in Bristol: George Thomas to Thomas Symons, 5 years Montserrat by *Nevis Merchant*. (BR).

26 January-4 March. Shippers by the *Supply*, Mr. John Fairweather, bound from London for New England: Henry Ashurst, Ralph Box, James Eaton, Noah Floyd, Edward Gallipaine, John Harwood, John Hooker, Stephen Humphreys, John Jackson, William Jacob, Mathew Jumper, John Lowen, Christopher Marshall, John Marshall, Samuell Medly, John Needham, Francis Parsons, John Peake, Spencer Piggott, Richard Plummer, George Rich, Samuell Sheafe, John Sweeting, James Swift, George Whitehead, Robert Woolley; (PRO: E190/53/6, 54/1).

27 January. The following apprenticed in Bristol: Morgan Thomas to Jane Weling, 4 years Jamaica; Laurence Frier to Thomas Symons, 4 years Montserrat by *Nevis Merchant*. (BR).

29 January. The following apprenticed in Bristol: Francis Pester to Thomas Jones, 4 years Barbados or Leewards. (BR).

31 January. The following apprenticed in Bristol: James Lewis to Thomas Tayler, 4 years Nevis; Mary Goulding to William Hooper, 4 years Nevis; William Jones to same, 4 years Nevis. (BR).

1 February. The following apprenticed in Bristol: Charles Rosser to Thomas Symons, 4 years Montserrat by *Nevis Merchant*; Elizabeth Barber to William Hooper, 4 years Nevis. (BR).

2 February. The following apprenticed in Bristol: Francis Norcomb to William Hooper, 4 years Nevis or Barbados; Anthony Bayly to Henry Jones, 9 years Nevis. (BR).

5 February. The following apprenticed in Bristol: Anne Glover to Walter Harris, 4 years Nevis. (BR).

6 February. The following apprenticed in Bristol: William Boudley Sr. to Thomas Symons, 5 years Montserrat; William Boudley Jr. to same, 10 years Montserrat; John Boudley to same, 10 years Montserrat. (BR).

8 February-2 March. Shippers by the *Endeavour*, Mr. John Fairweather, bound from London for New England: Edward Merriweather, John Bell, Richard Palleday, Christopher Banister, Richard Shipton, John Needham, Samuell Sheafe, Robert Woolley, Mathew Jumper. (PRO: E190/54/1).

14 February. The following apprenticed in Bristol: Elizabeth Jones to Margaret Tovey, 4 years Nevis by *Nevis Merchant*. (BR).

14 February. Western Circuit prisoners reprieved to be transported to Barbados. Cornwall: William Trestrayle of Kenwyn, fuller; Joan Jasper of Calstock, spinster; Katherine Wyat alias Helligan of St. Minver, spinster; Philip Dympsey of St. Stephen next Launceston, husbandman. Dorset: Thomas Bayly of Puddletrenthide, husbandman; Henry Daniell of Milborne St. Andrew, husbandman. Somerset: William Loader of Holwell, husbandman. (PRO: C66/3137/25).

17 February. The following apprenticed in Bristol: Thomas Barnes to William Jones, 7 years Nevis by *Nevis Merchant*. (BR).

21 February. The following apprenticed in Bristol: John Merrill to Phillip Seward, 4 years Barbados by *Exchange*. (BR).

23 February. The following apprenticed in Bristol: John Gwilliam to Phillip Jones, 4 years Nevis by *Nevis Merchant*. (BR).

23-27 February. Shippers by the *Bilbao Merchant*, Mr. William Neame, bound from London for New England: James Eyton, William Hanes, Michael Godfrey, Samuel Shuter. (PRO: E190/54/1).

24 February. The following apprenticed in Bristol: Maudlin Shaw to Edward Watkins, 4 years Barbados. (BR).

26 February. The following apprenticed in Bristol: Hanna Bayly to Edward Watkins, 4 years Barbados. (BR).

29 February. The following apprenticed in Bristol: Giles Jones to Thomas Symonds, 4 years Montserrat. (BR).

29 February-14 March. Shippers by the *John & Elizabeth*, Mr. Jonas Clarke, bound from London for New England: William Alleat, Henry Ashurst, Thomas Bodly, Abraham Briggs, Thomas Cockett, James Eaton, Thomas Firmin, Samuel Flownes, Noah Floyd, William Goffe, Richard Golty, John Harwood, George Heathcote, Edward Hill, Samuel Hucker, Daniel Ingoll, John Jackson, Abraham Jesson, Thomas Knight, John Knoles, John Lewin, Samuel Medley, Humphrey Nicholson, John Parker, Francis Parr, John Parsons, John Peake, Benjamin Peake, John Peake, Spencer Piggott, Anthony Ringwood, John Rosse, Thomas Ruck, Charles Seddon, William Shirley, Stephen Strutt, John Sweeting, Samuel Symonds, John Taylor, Richard Turner, Hezekiah Usher, Henry Wilkes, William Willis, Robert Woolley. (PRO: E190/53/6, 54/1).

February. Probate of will of John White, vicar of Cheriton, Wiltshire, whose nephews were in Virginia. (AW).

February. Middlesex prisoners reprieved to be transported to Barbados: Laurence Beedle, Charles Wells alias Dudley, Richard Tucker, Edward Page, Francis Nantford, Robert Pope, Thomas Lynsey, Mary Ingold, Benjamin Goodman, Joan White, Elizabeth Joddrell, John Gilder alias Gilbert. (EB).

1 March. Deposition by Edward Todd of Blackwall, Middlesex, corker (caulker) aged 53, and John Parker of London, wine cooper aged 42, that, shortly before his death five years ago, Captain John Sealey of Ratcliffe, Middlesex, promised William Tappin of Blackwall, vintner, and his wife Johanna (Sealey's daughter), warehouses and land in Piscataqua, New England, as a marriage settlement. Johanna Tappin, administratrix to her father, has nominated John Popton of New England, mariner, as her attorney. (LMCD).

5-22 March. Shippers by the *Nightingale*, Mr. Robert Bristow, bound from London for New England: Henry Ashurst, Noah Floyd, John Goulding, Edward Hull, Christopher Marshall, Thomas Norman, Robert Ox, John Parsons, Thomas Rowlington, Joseph Scott, Samuell Sheafe, John Sweeting, Hezechiah Usher, Edward White. (PRO: E190/53/6, 54/1).

8 March. Shipper by the *Margaret*, Mr. Henry Fairweather, bound from London for New England: John Banckes. (PRO: E190/54/1).

1 April. The following apprenticed in Bristol: John White to Joseph Hunt, 4 years Jamaica; David Spurle to same, 5 years Jamaica. (BR).

2 April. The following apprenticed in Bristol: George Jefferis to Joseph Hunt, 5 years Jamaica. (BR).

20 April-9 May. Shippers by the *William & John*, Mr. William Slew, bound from London for New England: Henry Ashurst, Valentine Austin, Thomas Ball, Edward Clapton, George Cole, John Cooke, John Coombes, Paul Darby, Thomas Deane, James Eyton, Thomas Firmine, Noah Floyd, Peter Gray, Edmond Hazelwood, Thomas Hollis, John Jackson, Thomas Knight, August Lynder, Edward Merrie, Humphrey Nicholson, Thomas Norman, John Parker, John Parsons, John Peake, Spencer Piggott, John Plumstead, Edward Randall, George Satchwell, William Shirley, John Shorter, Samuell Swinock, Thomas Taunton, Richard Tylden, Hezechiah Usher, John Wickins, Robert Woolley. (PRO: E190/53/6, 54/1).

22 April. Deposition by William Barkstead of St. Martin in the Fields, Middlesex, tailor aged 57, that he was a witness at the wedding of John Ball, citizen and merchant tailor of London, deceased, to his wife Joane, now dwelling near St. Paul's Wharf, London, and that her daughter, Anne Ball, was administratrix of James Ball of Waterton, New England, deceased. John and Joane Ball had a daughter Anne, now aged five and a half years. (LMCD).

25 April. Deposition by Robert Connoway, master of the *Barnaby*, aged 40, and Thomas Warren, master of the *Daniell*, aged 27, that on 31 January 1672 they saw Christopher Rigault of (Gloucester County), Virginia, planter, alive and well on board the *Barnaby*. (LMCD).

April. Administration of James Ball of Waterton near Boston in parts overseas, bachelor. (AW).

April. Administration of John Day of Rotherhithe, Surrey, who died overseas, having goods in Virginia. (AW).

April. Probate of will of William Whittingham formerly of Boston, New England, but who died in St. Mary le Savoy, Middlesex. (AW).

17 May & 17 September. Newgate prisoners reprieved to be transported to Barbados. London: Grace Long, spinster, alias wife of Thomas Long; Allan Nicholls; Robert Castleton; Christopher Townsend; William Hanson; Thomas Matchett; William Harris, butcher; William Holloway; Richard Woodmanson; Elizabeth Linlowe, spinster; Joane Palmer, spinster, alias wife of James Palmer; John Bennett; Henry Hutchings; Augustine Stanford; Robert Harvey; Samuel Reignold; Andrew Hurst; Fitzallan Crompton, scissor maker; Anne Cornwall, spinster; Henry Howard; Richard Piggott; Christopher Randall; Anne Seamour, spinster; Elizabeth Longman, spinster, alias wife of William Longman; Robert Pope. Middlesex: Edward Goddard of St. Giles in the Fields; Alice Foster of the same, spinster; Francis Nantford of the same; Allen Niccolls alias Nicholas of Heston; Joan White of Clerkenwell, spinster; Mary Ingold of St. Giles Cripplegate, spinster; Thomas Lindsey of St. Mary Savoy; Charles Wells alias Dudley of the same; Benjamin Goodman of St.

Katherine's; Richard Toocker of Perivale; Edward Page of Whitechapel; William Lennox of the same; Lawrence Beadle of Stepney; Elizabeth Jeddrell, wife of John, of the same; John Catton of the same; John Lyon of St. Martin in the Fields; John Gilder alias Gilbert of the same; James Cunningham of the same; Jane Sturgis, wife of Abraham Sturgis, of the same; Elizabeth Beare of the same, spinster; Anne Toomes of the same, spinster; Charles Browne of the same; Elizabeth Bowdley of St. Andrew Holborn, spinster; Margaret Emry of the same, spinster; Abraham Sturgis of St. Margaret Westminster; Anne Gibson of Staines, spinster. (PRO: C66/3137/2 & 17).

25 May. The following apprenticed in Bristol: John Jones to Thomas Hardick, 4 years Barbados. (BR).

May. London prisoner reprieved for Barbados: John Gardiner. (EB).

May. Probate of will of Thomas Bell the elder, of All Hallows Barking, London, whose nephew, Thomas Makins, was in New England. (AW).

May. Administration of Edward Arnold of Virginia, widower. (AW).

May. Administration of Daniel Walker of Woodbridge, Suffolk, who died in Virginia. (AW).

May. Probate of will of Roger Price of Virginia. (AW).

10 June. The following apprenticed in Bristol: Hugh Parry to John Teate, 4 years Virginia; Robert Hughs to same, 4 years Virginia. (BR).

11 June. The following apprenticed in Bristol: John Hibbs to Joane Bennett, 4 years Virginia by *Society*. (BR).

11 June-18 September. Shippers by the Dutch-built *Isabella* of Bristol, bound from Bristol for Virginia: Thomas Scroop, Richard Solloway, James Dennett, Richard Benson, John Staines, Edward Thurstone, Samuell Loye, Thomas Deane, Thomas Duddleston, Thomas Silvester, Abraham Wild, William Forde, Edward Perrin. (PRO: E190/1138/1).

14 June. The following apprenticed in Bristol: Matthias Williams to William Worrell, 4 years Virginia. (BR).

27 June. The following apprenticed in Bristol: Thomas Harris to Roger Evans, 12 years Virginia by *Trial*; Elizabeth Tayler to Edward Ithell, 4 years Virginia. (BR).

29 June. The following apprenticed in Bristol: William Evans to William Wattkins, 4 years Virginia. (BR).

1 July. The following apprenticed in Bristol: Peter Major to Roger Evans, 4 years Virginia by *Trial*; John Lovering to same, 4 years Virginia; John Foord to William Foord, 7 years Virginia by *Joseph*; Phillip Cox to same, 4 years Virginia by *Joseph*. (BR).

2 July. The following apprenticed in Bristol: William Bullock to Samuell Lloyd, 5 years Virginia; John Lewis to Joshua Davis, 4 years Virginia by *Society*; Martha Price to Christopher Birkhead, 4 years Virginia; Margaret Miskell to same, 4 years Virginia; Sarah Price to same, 7 years Virginia; John Russell to Thomas Opey, 4 years Virginia. (BR).

3 July. Western Circuit prisoners reprieved to be transported to Barbados. Cornwall: Joan Frances of Quethiock. Devon: Robert Warde of Abbots Bickington; Edward Osmond of Crediton, blacksmith; Thomas Lawrence of Luppitt; Thomas Godden of Luppitt; Thomas Morrish of Tavistock. Dorset: Giles Smith of Beaminster. Hampshire: John Over of Fordingbridge; Richard Luffe of Basing. Somerset: John Pritchard of Kill; Thomas Gullocke of Newton St. Loe; Leonard Coate of North Petherton, tailor; William Culverhowse of Heanton. (PRO: C66/3137/12).

4 July. The following apprenticed in Bristol: John Ditcher to Thomas Opey, 4 years Virginia; Thomas Olliver to Susan Ifell, 4 years Virginia. (BR).

6 July. The following apprenticed in Bristol: John Pope to William Foord, 4 years Virginia. (BR).

8 July. The following apprenticed in Bristol: William Lewis to William Swimer, 4 years Jamaica or Caribbees. (BR).

9 July. The following apprenticed in Bristol: John Bruton to Susannah Ifell, 5 years Virginia; John Pye to Thomas Bifield, 4 years Virginia. (BR).

9-20 July. Shippers by the *Black Cock*, Mr. Edward Gosling, bound from London for New England: Benjamin Peake, John Peake , George Roach, John Shorter, John Ewer. (PRO: E190/53/6, 54/1).

12 July-16 August. Shippers by the *Blessing*, Mr. William Greenough, bound from London for New England: Thomas Augier, Thomas Ball, George Banister, John Bawden, Thomas Bowerman, John Bullet, George Coale, Paul Darby, John Eltworth, Noah Floyd, Henry Foach, Jeremiah Foreman, Henry Fosh, William Greene, John Harwood, John Hatley, Edward Hitchcock, Samuel Hitchins, Ezechiel Hutchinson, Abraham Jesson, William Jesson, Nathaniel Jumper, Matthew Jumper, Noah Lloyd, Philip Manning, George Mayo, Samuel Medley, Henry Mountford, Robert Mullins, Henry Munt, Henry Muntford, Thomas Norman, John Parker, John Parsons, Benjamin Peake, Samuel Peake, John Peake, Spencer Piggott, Richard Plummer, George Roach, Nicholas Roberts, William Sherley, John Slater, Henry Speake, John Sweeting, Samuell Swinock, Elizabeth Twisden, Hezekiah Usher, John Wall, Samuel Warburton, Thomas Weatly, John Wittle, Robert Woolley. (PRO: E190/53/6, 54/1).

14 July. The following apprenticed in Bristol: John Bridgeman to Walter Habberfield, 4 years Virginia. (BR).

16 July. The following apprenticed in Bristol: Anthony Gerrard to Roger Evans, 5 years Virginia; William Horwood to same, 4 years Virginia; Charles Barneshaw to Moses Jones, 5 years Virginia by *Trial*. (BR).

18 July. The following apprenticed in Bristol: George Pearce to Sarah Smith, 7 years Virginia by *Trial*; William Penderton to Moses Jones, 4 years Virginia; Joshua Nason to same, 4 years Virginia. (BR).

19 July. Shipper by the *King Solomon*, Mr. Ezekiel Crosman, bound from London for New England: John Shorter. (PRO: E190/54/1).

22 July. The following apprenticed in Bristol: John Phillips to William Thomas, 5 years Virginia; William Evans to same, 5 years Virginia; John Reede alias Flooke to William Thomas, 4 years Virginia by *Sarah & Elizabeth*; Robert Poore to Thomas Opey, 5 years Virginia; Grace Silcockes to John Clifford, 4 years Virginia by *Trial*; Elioner Luffe to same, 4 years Virginia. (BR).

28 July. Isle of Ely, Cambridgeshire, prisoners reprieved to be transported to Barbados: John Clarke, John Cooper. (PRO: C66/3137/6).

24 July. The following apprenticed in Bristol: Morgan Jones to Peter Perken, 5 years Virginia. (BR).

26 July. The following apprenticed in Bristol: James Symons to Blanch Jackson, 4 years Jamaica; Edward Lone to Richard Taylor, 5 years Virginia; William Mishew to Thomas Newton, 5 years Maryland; William Plovey to same, 5 years Maryland; William Hall to same, 5 years Maryland; Thomas Ward to same, 7 years Maryland; George Horne to same, 9 years Maryland. (BR).

26 July-12 August. Shippers by the *Edward & Jane*, Mr. John [or Henry] Browne, bound from London for New England: John Lane, Edward Lemmon, John Cooper, Thomas Alcock, Edward Paggen, John Mauery, John Parker, John Welden, George Richards, Richard Floyd, George Baker, William Paggen, Thomas Lane. (PRO: E190/53/6, 54/1).

29 July. The following apprenticed in Bristol: Walter Kerswell to Thomas Opey, 4 years Virginia. (BR).

29 July-28 August. Shippers by the *America*, Mr. Roger Paxton, bound from London for Virginia: Daniel Allen, John Child, Robert Cole, Christopher Deynote, William Dyer, Christopher Dynet, Edward Edmons, Phessent Estwick, Noah Floyd, George Foresight, John Freeman, Samuel French, George Gosfright, Benjamin Hewling, Ezekiel Hutchinson, Abraham Jesson, Edward Man, George Mayo, Edward Merriwether, Charles Milson, Thomas Norman, Benjamin Peake, Robert Stevenson, Hezechiah Usher, Robert Woolley. (PRO: E190/53/6, 54/1).

30 July-2 August. Shippers by the *Happy Return* of Plymouth, Mr. George Orchard, bound from Plymouth for New England: John Dell, Thomas Teale. (PRO: E190/1039/5).

31 July. The following apprenticed in Bristol: George King to Mathew Davis, 4 years Virginia by *Richard & James*; Thomas Tyler to Joseph Hiscox, 5 years Virginia. (BR).

July. Probate of will of John Edmonds formerly of Collingbourne Abbots, Wiltshire, but who died in Virginia, bachelor. (AW).

July. Probate of will of Herbert Thorndike, Prebend of Westminster, Middlesex, whose nieces, Alice and Martha Thorndike, were in New England. (AW).

July. Probate of will of John Smith, citizen and cook of London, who made a bequest to Allen Whore in Virginia. (AW).

July. Probate of will of Robert Fanning of [All Hallows], Barking, London, whose kinsman, John Fanning, was in Virginia. (AW).

July. Probate of will of Zachary Irish of Windsor, Berkshire, whose brother, Edward Newman, was in Virginia. (AW).

1 August. The following apprenticed in Bristol: John Walner to Matthew Nicholas, 4 years Barbados. (BR).

1 August. Shipper by the *Resolution* of Bristol, bound from Bristol for Virginia: Anthony Gay. (PRO: E190/1138/1).

1-16 August. Shippers by the Dutch-built *Society* of Bristol, Mr. Christopher Berkhead, bound from Bristol for Virginia: Mathias Worgan, Richard Benson. (PRO: E190/1138/1).

2 August. The following apprenticed in Bristol: Stephen Marshall to Moyses Jones, 4 years Virginia by *Trial*; John Marshall to same, 4 years Virginia by *Trial*. (BR).

5 August. The following apprenticed in Bristol: William Smith to John Cooke, 5 years Virginia; John Veltum to Hester Grannger, 4 years Virginia. (BR).

5-7 August. Shippers by the Dutch-built *Joseph* of Bristol, Mr. William Jones, bound from Bristol for Virginia: William Ford, Robert Yeate. (PRO: E190/1138/1).

5-7 August. Shippers by the *Virginia Merchant* of Plymouth, Mr. William Millett, bound from Plymouth for Virginia: John Cooke, Samuell Brett, Thomas Westcott, James Chedd. (PRO: E190/1039/5).

6 August. The following apprenticed in Bristol: John Perry to Mary Bodman, 4 years Virginia by *Joseph*; Abraham Matthews to William Foord, 4 years Virginia. (BR).

7 August. Shipper by the *Swallow*, Mr. Joseph Hardy, bound from London for New England: Hezekiah Usher. (PRO: E190/54/1).

8 August. Cheshire prisoner reprieved for America: Thomas Smith alias Alexander of Trafford Bridge, husbandman. (PRO: C66/3137/5).

9 August. The following apprenticed in Bristol: William Mills to Moses Jones, 7 years Virginia by *Trial*. (BR).

10 August. The following apprenticed in Bristol: Mary Haines to Mary Bevan, 4 years Virginia by *Society*; Thomas Wells to Moses Jones, 4 years Virginia. (BR).

10-19 August. Shippers by the *Blossom*, Mr. Richard Martin, bound from London for New England: Samuel Sheafe, Noah Floyd, George Cole, Robert Woolley, George Satchwell, Mathew Jumper. (PRO: E190/53/6, 54/1).

12 August. The following apprenticed in Bristol: James Temple to William Temple, 5 years Virginia by *Katherine*, Mr. Robert Dapwell; James Wilkins to same, 7 years Virginia by *Katherine*; Thomas Wilkins to same, 5 years Virginia by *Katherine*; Elizabeth Gowing to same, 6 years Virginia by *Katherine*; Agnis Temple to same, 4 years Virginia by *Katherine*; Mary Loder to same, 6 years Virginia by *Katherine*. (BR).

13 August. The following apprenticed in Bristol: Matthew Warren to Roger Skinner, 4 years Virginia; William Tiley to John Gill, 4 years Virginia by *Concord*; Robert Phipps to Matthew King, 4 years Virginia by *Samuel & Mary*. (BR).

13-20 August. Shippers by the *Hopewell*, Mr. George Hilson, bound from London for Virginia: James Holland, William Howson, Thomas Bowdell, Jonas Hopkins. (PRO: E190/53/6, 54/1).

14-19 August. Shippers by the *Rebecca & Elizabeth* of Boston, Mr. Abraham Gourding, bound from Poole for New England: Henry Orchard, Tymothy Lindall. (PRO: E190/881/8, 881/9).

15 August. Depositions in London re the voyage of the *Advice*, Mr. George Finion, from London to Virginia in 1671 with 20 servants consigned to Mr. John Tomly. (EA).

16 August. The following apprenticed in Bristol: William Sheppard to Matthew King, 4 years Virginia by *Samuel & Mary*. (BR).

16 August. Shippers by the English-built *Patience* of Bristol, Mr. William Tregose, bound from Bristol for Virginia: John Speede, George Hanes. (PRO: E190/1138/1).

16 August. Shippers by the *Amity* of Plymouth bound for Virginia: George Searle, John Stone. (PRO: E190/1039/5).

16-19 August. Shippers by the *Concord* of Bristol, bound for Virginia: John Jones, Giles Meyrick. (PRO: E190/1138/1).

17 August. Shipper by the *Plymouth Employment*, Mr. [Joseph?] Fuge, bound from Plymouth for Virginia: Thomas Yardley. (PRO: E190/1039/5).

17-23 August. Shippers by the *Nightingale* of York, Mr. John Hobson, bound from Hull for Virginia: Edward Nightingale, Christopher Fawthropp, Michaell Taylor, John Leavens. (PRO: E190/321/4).

17 August-19 September. Shippers by the Dutch-built *Katherine* of Bristol, Mr. Robert Dapwell, bound from Bristol for Virginia: John Thomas, John Speed, James Millard, Edward Beere, James Biggs, Robert Yate, Edward Morgan, Edward Martindale, Peter Smith, John Luffe, William Crabb, John Richardson, Henry Daniell, Roger Nevill, John Lloyd, Samuell Tipton, Samuell Wharton, John Knight, Lott Richards. (PRO: E190/1138/1).

19 August. The following apprenticed in Bristol: Richard Mannington to John Borne, 4 years Virginia. (BR).

20 August. The following apprenticed in Bristol: William Talley to Blanch Jackson, 6 years Virginia by *Trial*. (BR).

20 August. Shipper by the *Experiment*, Mr. Thomas Ward, bound from London for Newcastle and Virginia: Chedley Bradshaw. (PRO: E190/54/1).

21 August. The following apprenticed in Bristol: William Roberts to Joseph Hiscox, 5 years Virginia by *Society*; James Younge to Timothy Paine, 5 years Virginia by *Society*; Richard Wilcox to Daniell Luffeman, 4 years Virginia by *Trial*; John Williams to Roger Davis, 4 years Virginia by *Stephen*; William Price to same, 4 years Virginia; Ann Lewis to Thomas Sinderley, 4 years Virginia; Able Norrice to Peter Perkes, 4 years Virginia by *Society*; Mary George to John Wright, 4 years Nevis by *Adventure*; Margarett Margan to same, 4 years Nevis; Thomas Jenkins to John Orchard, 4 years Virginia. (BR).

22 August-9 September. Shippers by the Dutch-built *Tryal* of Bristol, Mr. William Smyth, bound from Bristol for Virginia: Charles Harford, Edward Martindale, Thomas Speede, Richard Beauchamp, Anthony Gay. (PRO: E190/1138/1).

23 August. Shipper by the *Seaflower* of Poole, Mr. John Harding, bound from Poole for Maryland: George Lewen. (PRO: E190/881/8).

23 August-3 September. Shippers by the *Elizabeth & Margaret*, Mr. Nathaniel Cary, bound from London for Virginia: Robert Woolley, Abraham Jesson, Samuel Medley. (PRO: E190/53/6, 54/1).

26 August-9 September. Shippers by the English-built *Hope* of Bristol, Mr. Robert Pennington, bound from Bristol for Virginia: Richard Oliver, Samuell Wharton. (PRO: E190/1138/1).

26 August-19 September. Shippers by the Dutch-built *Stephen* of Bristol, Mr. William Scott, bound from Bristol for Virginia: James Pope, Stephen Watts, Richard Crump, John Sanders, David Parry. (PRO: E190/1138/1).

27 August. The following apprenticed in Bristol: Howell Jones to William Bull, 4 years Virginia; John Suger to William Scott, 4 years Virginia by *Stephen*;

Richard Porcher to same, 4 years Virginia by *Stephen*; John Lewis to Maxfield Walter, 4 years Virginia by *Thomas & Mary*; Jane Badge to John Mason, 4 years Virginia by *Trial*; Thomas Evans to William Pinfield, 3 years Virginia by *William & Ann*. (BR).

27 August-29 September. Shippers by the English-built *Thomas & Mary* of Bristol, Mr. Thomas Opie, bound from Bristol for Virginia: Gabriell Deane, Samuell Brett, Lyson Porter, William Morgan. (PRO: E190/1138/1).

28 August. Deposition by Edward Adamson, citizen and cutler of London, aged 30, partner of John Bell, citizen and grocer of London, and their servant Charles Hacker, aged 20, that William Maultby, formerly of Bautry, Yorkshire, but now of New England, merchant, is indebted to Adamson for goods delivered to him at Gainsborough Market. Edward Shippen of Boston, New England, has been appointed attorney. (LMCD).

29 August. The following apprenticed in Bristol: Elizabeth Probbin to Thomas Daniell, 4 years Virginia by *Society*. (BR).

29-30 August. Deposition by Francis Bennett of Poole, Dorset, merchant aged 25, that when he was in Maryland in May 1671 Phillip Shapleigh asked him to take a letter to his brother near Dartmouth, Devon, by the *William* of Dover, but the deponent never received the letter. He never knew any other person named Shapleigh in Virginia or Maryland. Randall Revell of Maryland, planter aged 61, deposes that Phillip Shapleigh had lived in Maryland for six or seven years. (LMCD).

29 August-3 September. Shippers by the *New Martin*, Mr. Roger Paxton, bound from London for New England: William Charles, Samuel Brant, Edward Edmonds. (PRO: E190/54/1).

30 August. The following apprenticed in Bristol: Bartholomew Wolfe to Richard Taylor, 4 years Virginia. (BR).

August. Probate of will of Anthony Salwey of Ann Arundell County, Maryland. (AW).

August. Administration of Benjamin Good of Virginia, bachelor. (AW).

1 September. The following apprenticed in Bristol: Richard Andrews to Marke Chappell, 4 years Virginia; Rachaell Robins to William Woodward, 5 years Virginia by *Samuel & Mary*; David Griffin to Roger Wellsted, 6 years Nevis. (BR).

6 September. Deposition by Richard Legatt of London, merchant aged 30, Thomas Malyn of London, haberdasher aged 38, and his servant, Richard Parratt, aged 21, that Thomas Williamson, when he was last in England, left an inventory dated Virginia 13 June 1668. In September 1671 letters were sent to Williamson by the *Isaac & Benjamin*, Mr. John Plover. (LMCD).

6 September. Shippers by the *[Thomas &] Edward*, Mr. John Martin, bound from London for York River, Virginia: Thomas Carew, John Butts, Henry Forman, George Richards, Thomas Pate. (PRO: E190/53/6, 54/1).

6 September. Shipper by the English-built *Endeavour* of Bristol, Mr. John Baker, bound from Bristol for Virginia: Mathew Worgan. (PRO: E190/1138/1).

6 & 15 September. The case of Fairvacks v. Scarborough is to be tried in the Chancery Court. (APC).

6 September-17 October. Shipper by the *Maryland Merchant* of Northam, Mr. John Horden, bound from Bideford for Maryland: Thomas Thurstone. (PRO: E190/955/6).

7 September. The following apprenticed in Bristol: Thomas Baker to Richard Taylor, 5 years Virginia. (BR).

8-18 September. Shipper by the *Hope* of Lyme, Mr. William Singleton, bound from Lyme for Virginia: Walter Tucker. (PRO: E190/881/2).

10 September. Shipper by the *Defence*, Mr. John Panton, bound from London for Virginia: Isaiah Bennet. (PRO: E190/54/1).

11 September. The following apprenticed in Bristol: John Baker to Richard Taylor, 5 years Virginia. (BR).

11 September. Shipper by the *John* of Plymouth, Mr. George Bayley, bound from Plymouth for Virginia: John Highams. (PRO: E190/1039/5).

11 September. Shipper by the *William* of Plymouth, Mr. William Alden, bound from Plymouth for Virginia: William Marten. (PRO: E190/1039/5).

13 September. The following apprenticed in Bristol: George Howell to William Scott, 4 years Virginia by *Stephen*; William Smith to John Sanders, 4 years Virginia by *Stephen*. (BR).

13-26 September. Shippers by the *William & Jane* alias *Richard & Jane*, Mr. Thomas Arnold, bound from London for Virginia: Henry Meese, Charles Corcellis, William Fantin, William Sherley, William Allen. (PRO: E190/53/6, 54/1).

13 September-14 October. Shippers by the *Diligence*, Mr. John Banton, bound from London for Virginia: Alexander Martin, Thomas Gee, Edward Leamon. (PRO: E190/53/6).

14 September. The following apprenticed in Bristol: John Heath to Abraham Roome, 4 years Virginia; John Tucker to Christopher Hassell, 4 years Virginia; John Cluck to same, 6 years Virginia; William Hankes to Richard Taylor, 4 years Virginia; Deborah Watts to John Carell, 4 years Virginia. (BR).

14-23 September. Shippers by the *Mary*, Mr. Abraham Wise, bound from London for Virginia: Thomas Marshall, Robert Spring. (PRO: E190/53/6, 54/1).

14 September-4 December. Shippers by the *George*, Mr. Peter Bennett, bound from London for New York and New Jersey: John Person, Joseph Canham, John Harbin, Christopher Dynot, Thomas Thorpe, John Beale, George Cole, John Barton, Samuel Swynock, Nathaniel Herne. (PRO: E190/53/6, 54/1).

16-20 September. Shippers by the *James*, Mr. Nicholas Guttridge [Goodrich], bound from London for Virginia: Francis Plumstead, John Dew, James Braines, William Crouch. (PRO: E190/53/6, 54/1).

16-23 September. Shippers by the *James & Elizabeth* of Weymouth, Mr. Thomas Barker, bound from Weymouth for Virginia: Richard Tucker, Symon Orchard, William Jare for William Twist. (PRO: E190/881/4).

17 September. The following apprenticed in Bristol: William Foord to Thomas Liston, 5 years Barbados. (BR).

17 September. Deposition by Paul Smith, citizen and fishmonger of London, aged 33, That Thomas Badcocke of Virginia owed money to James Woollball, citizen and fishmonger of London, on a bond of 21 August 1677. (LMCD).

17-19 September. In the case of George Lee of London, merchant, v. Sarah Bowler, relict and administratrix of John Bowler, deceased, whose son, John Bowler, Lee's apprentice, was sent to Virginia to manage a plantation. (NGSQ 65/3). Deposition by Martin Dallison of London, gent aged 25, and John Seares, citizen and grocer of London, aged 24, that goods and servants were taken to Virginia by Robert Whitehaire, factor for George Lee of London, merchant, and to be sold in Virginia by John Bowler, then apprentice to Lee. The deponent Dallison, then assistant to Lee in Virginia, saw Bowler receive goods and slaves from the ships *Charles and Dundee* and the *St. Andrew*. John Bowler arrived in London in May 1671 but had refused to come to account with Lee. George Lee, aged 51, deposes that Bowler defrauded him in Virginia. In January 1671 Richard Clarke arrived in Virginia to replace Bowler who, in order to deceive his creditors, set off again for Virginia. (LMCD).

18 September. The following apprenticed in Bristol: James Thomas to William Nicholas, 4 years Virginia. (BR).

18-19 September. Shippers by the *Industry* of Plymouth, Mr. Edward Blagg, bound from Plymouth for Virginia: Arthur Cotton, James Strong. (PRO: E190/1039/5).

19 September. Shippers by the *Blessing* of Southampton, Mr. William Baker, bound from Southampton for Virginia: Robert Richbell, Andrew Hunt. (PRO: E190/827/5).

21 September. The following apprenticed in Bristol: Joseph Rogers to Richard Sanders, 4 years Virginia by *Elizabeth & Sarah*; John Buxton to Matthew King, 4 years Virginia; Benjamin Blacklock to same, 4 years Virginia; William Reede to Percivall Reede, 4 years Virginia. (BR).

23 September. Shipper by the *Elizabeth* of Weymouth, Mr. John Cox, bound from Weymouth for Virginia: John Cox & Co. (PRO: E190/881/4).

23 September. The following apprenticed in Bristol: Charles Jones to Henry Andrews, 5 years Maryland. (BR).

23 September-3 October. Shippers by the *Dolphin*, Mr. Joseph Pyle, bound from London for Virginia: Arthur Bayly, Joseph Blest, Henry Meese, Gawen Corbin. (PRO: E190/54/1).

26 September. The following apprenticed in Bristol: Robert Phillips to Nathaniell Day, 4 years Virginia; John Knight to Percivall Reede, 4 years Virginia; William Penn to William Sanders, 7 years Virginia; Henery Davis to Joseph Hide, 4 years Virginia. (BR).

27 September-19 October. Shippers by the Dutch-built *William & Ann* of Bristol, Mr. John Orchard, bound from Bristol for Virginia: John Walter, John Luffe. (PRO: E190/1138/1).

27 September-28 November. Shippers by the *Baltimore*, Mr. John Dunch, bound from London for Maryland and Virginia: Benjamin Blunt, Richard Booty, William Browne, Mark Carleton, Thomas Collingwood, John Collingwood, Thomas Glover, James Godfrey, Thomas Hedge, John Hodges, Robert Lang, Edward Leaman, Joseph Lister, Job Nut, Robert Ray, Nicholas Roberts, Robert Whitehorne, Samuel Young. (PRO: E190/54/1)

28 September. The following apprenticed in Bristol: William Wheler to James Paine, 4 years Virginia. (BR).

30 September. The following apprenticed in Bristol: Thomas Mitchell to Roger Evans, 3 years Virginia; Thomas Skudamore to William Lancaster, 4 years Virginia; Susannah Wray to Susannah Ifield, 4 years Virginia. (BR).

September. Shipper by the *Providence* of Lyme, Mr. Job Walter, bound from Lyme for Virginia: Walter Tucker. (PRO: E190/881/1).

September. Probate of will of William Hickman of St. Swithin, London, whose kinsman, Joseph Hickman, was in Virginia. (AW).

September. Probate of will of Richard Sturman of Nomini, Westmoreland, Virginia. (AW).

1 October. Deposition by Samuel Auckland of Bexley, Kent, yeoman aged 50, that his son, Samuel Auckland, now living with Mr. Peter Knight in Virginia, was born in January 1649 and baptised on 28 January 1649 according to an entry in the Bexley parish register. (LMCD).

1 October. The following apprenticed in Bristol: James Johnson to Aldworth Elbridge, 4 years Jamaica. (BR).

1 October-26 November. Shippers by the *John*, Mr. James Treffrey [Terfrey], bound from London for Virginia: Richard Boss, John Price, Edward Benson, Matthew Wilkinson, Nathaniel Wilkinson, William Sayer, William Scarce. (PRO:E190/53/6, 54/1).

3 October. The following apprenticed in Bristol: John Hartily to George Cowley, 4 years Maryland by *Richard & James*; William Holland to same, 4 years Maryland; Thomas Camme to same, 4 years Maryland; Edward Smith to same, 4 years Maryland; Stephen Pegg to same, 4 years Maryland; Thomas Roe to same, 4 years Maryland; John Dammes to same, 4 years Maryland; Grace Turner to same, 4 years Maryland; Richard Attkison to same, 7 years Maryland. (BR).

3 October-9 November. Shippers by the *Trades Increase* of Basildon, Mr. Henry Davis, bound from Southampton for Virginia: Charles Maw, Thomas Cornelius. (PRO: E190/827/5).

4 October. The following apprenticed in Bristol: Jane Windsor to Nicholas Hart, 4 years Virginia; Thomas Griffith to Roger Nevell, 4 years Virginia; Abraham Morgan to same, 4 years Virginia. (BR).

4-19 October. Shippers by the Dutch-built *Robert* of Bristol, Mr. Morgan Taylor, bound from Bristol for Virginia: Henry Deighton, Robert Yeamans, Michael Pope. (PRO: E190/1138/1).

5 October. The following apprenticed in Bristol: Thomas Petley to Thomas Reede, 4 years Virginia by *Endeavour*; Symon Purdue to William Bayly, 4 years Virginia; Thomas Crumpton to William Nicholas, 4 years Virginia; Elizabeth Davis to William Scott, 4 years Virginia; George Davis to John Cotten, 4 years Virginia; Thomas Cooke to William Suddaby, 4 years Virginia. (BR).

5-7 October. Shippers by the *Batchelor*, Mr. Nicholas Churchwood, bound from London for Maryland: Richard Chandler, Michael Clipsham. (PRO:E190/54/1).

6 October. Shipper by the *William & John* of Lyme, Mr. William Osborne, bound from Lyme for Virginia: Walter Tucker. (PRO: E190/881/2).

7 October. Shipper by the *King Solomon*, Mr. Ezekiel Crosman, bound from London for Virginia: James Coniers. (PRO: E190/54/1).

8 October. The following apprenticed in Bristol: Nicholas Holloway to Edward Newberry, 4 years Virginia; Thomas Norvill to Thomas Hardwicke, 4 years Virginia. (BR).

8 October. Shippers by the *Willing Mind*, Mr. William Ginge, bound from London for Virginia: Deverax Browne, Henry Browne. (PRO: E190/53/6, 54/1).

9 October. The following apprenticed in Bristol: John Crumpe to Thomas Carvey, 7 years Virginia. (BR).

10-24 October. Shippers by the Dutch-built *Maryland Merchant* of Bristol, Mr. John Holbrooke, bound from Bristol for Virginia: Joseph Fisher, Joseph Fincher, Edward Dale, John Potter, John Duddlestone. (PRO: E190/1138/1).

10 October-2 December. Shippers by the English-built *Samuell & Mary* of Bristol, Mr. James Harris, bound from Bristol for Virginia: Henry Dobbins, William Hayman, Laurance Avory, John Sand, Jonas Holliday, Phillip Stanton, James Tregoe, John Hawkins, Richard Streamer, John Grant, Gabriell Deane, Thomas Edwards, William Davis. (PRO: E190/1138/1).

12 October-8 December. Shippers by the *Daniel*, Mr. Thomas Warren, bound from London for Virginia: Isaac Merritt, Thomas Glover, Samuel Young, Richard Booth, Robert Ray, Robert Whitehorne, Benjamin Blunt, Nicholas Roberts, John Hutton, John Hind, John Parker, Mark Carleton, Matthew Carlton, Edward Lemon, George Richards, Bernard Mitchell, John Jefferys, James Court, John Hagget. (PRO: E190/53/6, 54/1).

14 October. The following apprenticed in Bristol: Ann Salisbury to John Adams, 4 years Virginia. (BR).

15 October. The following apprenticed in Bristol: Dorothy Bayly to Richard Brittaine, 4 years Virginia. (BR).

16 October. The following apprenticed in Bristol: Josias Hussey to Thomas Hellerd, 4 years Virginia. (BR).

17 October-8 November. Shippers by the *Thomas & Mary*, Mr. John Body, bound from London for Virginia: Robert Burdett, John Harres, Nathaniel Stiles. (PRO: E190/53/6,54/1).

18 October. The following apprenticed in Bristol: Anne Ince to William Hazard, 5 years Virginia. (BR).

19-24 October. Shippers by the Dutch-built *Richard & James* of Bristol, Mr. William Nicholas, bound from Bristol for Virginia: Mathew Rogers, Richard Pope, George Cowley. (PRO: E190/1138/1).

21 October. The following apprenticed in Bristol: Anne Rider to Samuell Sandford, 4 years Virginia; Daniell Haines to same, 4 years Virginia. (BR).

21 October. Shippers by the Dutch-built *Sarah & Elizabeth* of Bristol, Mr. William Harris, bound from Bristol for Virginia: Jeremy Holway, John Luffe, Edward Martindale. (PRO: E190/1138/1).

21 October-2 December. Shippers by the Dutch-built *Agreement* of Bristol, Mr. Richard Speed, bound from Bristol for Virginia: Thomas Speed, John Speed, George Tyte, Edmond Light, William Davis, Thomas Burges. (PRO: E190/1138/1).

22 October. The following apprenticed in Bristol: Griffith Griffiths to Thomas Castle, 4 years Virginia. (BR).

22 October. Shipper by the *Crown Mallago*, Captain Dunch, bound from London for Virginia: said Captain Dunch. (PRO: E190/54/1).

22 October-6 December. Shippers by the *Prince*, Mr. Robert Conway, bound from London for Virginia: Thomas Stepkin, William Edmonds, Ralph Horwood, James More, Robert Forth, Gawen Corbin, Richard Booth, John Osborne, Charles Stephens, Thomas Cowell. (PRO: E190/53/6, 54/1).

23 October. The following apprenticed in Bristol: John Stronge to Thomas Fisher, 4 years Virginia. (BR).

24 October. The following apprenticed in Bristol: James Chalcrofte to Henry Rich, 4 years Virginia; Richard Cobner to Robert Noble, 4 years Virginia. (BR).

25 October. The following apprenticed in Bristol: William Lodum to Daniell Hardick, 4 years Virginia; John Baldwin to Thomas Harris, 4 years Virginia. (BR).

26 October. The following apprenticed in Bristol: David Stradling to William Nichols, 4 years Virginia; Florence Stradling to same, 4 years Virginia; Joane Crocker to John Light, 5 years Virginia; Thomas Wrentmore to same, 5 years Virginia; John Membry to same, 5 years Virginia; Benjamine Vickrey to same, 10 years Virginia; John Gefford to same, 10 years Virginia; Morgan Davis to Mary Slack, 4 years Virginia; John Powell to same, 4 years Virginia; Alice Games to John Rosser, 4 years Virginia; Joseph Almond to Richard Gottley, 6 years Virginia. (BR).

28 October. The following apprenticed in Bristol: Mary Jones to Edward Hassell, 4 years Virginia; Martha Short to William Weaver, 4 ycars Barbados; William Hickes to John Adams, 4 years Virginia; George Webber to Tobias Dunne, 5 years Barbados; Thomas New to Christopher Haswell, 5 years Virginia. (BR).

29 October. The following apprenticed in Bristol: Alice Onion to John Willett, 4 years Virginia; Zachariah Deane to William Luffe, 7 years Virginia. (BR).

29 October-27 November. Shippers by the *Unicorn* of Bristol bound from Virginia: Emanuell Avory, Thomas Fisher, John Machen, John Duddlestone, William Cannings. (PRO: E190/1138/1).

30 October. The following apprenticed in Bristol: John Phillips to John Breach, 7 years Barbados; Richard Lane to John Willett, 3 years [Virginia]. (BR).

31 October. The following apprenticed in Bristol: Matthew Hoppells to John Rogers, 4 years Virginia; William Christopher to John Adams, 4 years Virginia; Francis David to William Wiggington, 4 years Virginia. (BR).

31 October. Shipper by the *Charles*, Mr. John Perry, bound from London for New England: John Freeman. (PRO: E190/54/1).

October. Probate of will of John Cole of Weymouth and Melcombe Regis, Dorset, merchant, who had lands in New England. (AW).

2 November. The following apprenticed in Bristol: Dorothy England to Thomas Sweete, 4 years Nevis; John Paine to William Wiggington, 4 years Virginia; Roger Groves to John Willett, 4 years Virginia; John Jones to John Wootters, 4 years Virginia; John Sansbury to same, 4 years Virginia; Thomas Harding to same, 4 years Virginia; Henery Ayles to same, 7 years Virginia. (BR).

2 November-2 December. Shippers by the *Richard & Martin [Martha]*, Mr. James Conaway, bound from London for Virginia: John Elowes, Thomas Hedge, Anthony Ringwood, Leonard Towne, Edward Pate, Samuel Mewington, Michael Standcliffe, Edward Mackins, Ignatius Harmer. (PRO: E190/54/1).

4 November. The following apprenticed in Bristol: Richard Williams to Edward Newberry, 4 years Virginia; Alice Williams to Robert Noble, 4 years Virginia. (BR).

4 November. Shipper by the *Virginia Merchant* of Bideford, Mr. Joseph Chope, bound from Bideford for Virginia: Abraham Heiman. (PRO: E190/955/6).

6 November. The following apprenticed in Bristol: Elizabeth Penduck to John Wootters, 6 years Virginia. (BR).

6 November. Shipper by the *Fortune*, Mr. John Noore, bound from London for Virginia: John Kemble. (PRO: E190/54/1).

6-26 November. Shippers by the *Isaac & Benjamin*, Mr. John Plomer, bound from London for Virginia: Nicholas Jackson, Benjamin Shute, John Mundford, Humphrey Lenens, Joseph Sabim, Joseph Sparrow. (PRO: E190/54/1).

6 November-4 December. Shippers by the *Duke of York*, Mr. John Purvis, bound from London for Virginia: Samuel Shipton, John Raymond, John Alder, John Jeffs, William Thompson, Samuel Sharshunt, Symon Masters, David Cary, Henry Cornish, Obadiah Livesey, James Baily. (PRO: E190/54/1).

6 November-9 December. Shippers by the Dutch-built *Phoenix* of Bristol, Mr. Henry Roche, bound from Bristol for Virginia: Edward Fielding, George White, William Morgan, John Challenor. (PRO: E190/1138/1).

7-20 November. Shippers by the *Rebecca*, Mr. Christopher Embling [Endling], bound from London for Virginia: Francis Camfield, Robert Terrell, John Browne, Edward Leamon. (PRO: E190/54/1).

7 November-14 December. Shippers by the *William & Mary*, Mr. Thomas Smith, bound from London for Virginia: Thomas Elliot, Thomas Linne, Henry Salter, Anthony Standford, Richard Love, Henry Meese, Marke Mortimer, Robert Roe, Thomas Eyle, Marmaduke Moosely, Richard Lane. (PRO:E190/54/1, 53/6).

8-14 November. Shippers by the *Salisbury*, Mr. Richard Cowell, bound from London for Virginia: Randolph Renell, John Powell. (PRO: E190/54/1).

9 November. The following apprenticed in Bristol: Thomas Lock to William Sanders, 4 years Virginia. (BR).

9-28 November. Shippers by the *John & Martha*, Mr. Thomas Gearie?, bound from London for Virginia: John Drew, Robert Forth, Arthur Baily. (PRO:E190/53/6, 54/1).

12 November. The following apprenticed in Bristol: Sarah Fowler to John Light, 5 years Virginia; Thomas Harris to John Woolvin, 4 years Virginia; Thomas Bessant to John Clarke, 4 years Virginia; John Guyett to same, 4 years Virginia. (BR).

12 November. Shipper by the *Elizabeth & Thomas*, Mr. Thomas Smith, bound from London for Virginia: Richard Lane. (PRO: E190/54/1).

12 November-2 December. Shippers by the *Hopewell*, Mr. John Rudds, bound from London for Virginia: John Sadler, Henry Richards, James Janney, David Kilway, Nicholas Roberts. (PRO: E190/54/1).

12 November-3 December. Shippers by the *Peace*, Mr. Michael Pack, bound from London for Virginia: Arthur Baily, John Parker, Humphrey Lewin, John Corey, Edmond Clark. (PRO: E190/54/1).

13 November. The following apprenticed in Bristol: Robert Briant to William Wiggington, 4 years Virginia; Joseph Jenkins to Thomas Horhurse, 4 years Nevis; Reece Thomas to James Jones, 4 years Virginia. (BR).

13 November. Shipper by the *James*, Mr. James Foskett, bound from London for Virginia: Richard Moore. (PRO: E190/54/1).

13-29 November. Shippers by the *Post Horse*, Mr. John More, bound from London for Virginia: John Smith, Samuel Richson, Humphrey Lewen. (PRO: E190/54/1).

13 November-11 December. Shippers by the *Batchelor* of Hull, Mr. William Idle, bound from Hull for Virginia: John Peckett, Thomas Carter, Thomas Clarke. (PRO: E190/321/4).

14 November. The following apprenticed in Bristol: John Davis to James Harris, 4 years Virginia; John Wely to William Wells, 4 years Virginia. (BR).

14 November-4 December. Shippers by the *Elias*, Mr. Benjamin Cooper, bound from London for Virginia and Maryland: John Stone, Strang Mud, Gawen Corbin, William Johnson, Richard Lone, Thomas Crundall, Ralph Harwood, Noah Floyd. (PRO: E190/54/1).

15 November. The following apprenticed in Bristol: Thomas Richards to John Willett, 4 years Virginia; Thomas Cuffe to same, 4 years Virginia. (BR).

16 November. The following apprenticed in Bristol: Richard Rake to John Adams, 7 years Virginia; Phillip Lawrance to Peter Archer, 4 years Virginia; Anne Jones to same, 4 years Virginia. (BR).

16-23 November. Shippers by the *Griffin*, Mr. Robert Griffin, bound from London for Virginia: John Harris, Richard Lone. (PRO: E190/54/1).

18 November-4 December. Shippers by the *Friendship*, Mr. William Wheatly, bound from London for Virginia: John Collingwood, John Raymond, Jacob Forman, Joseph Sparrow, Henry Sprigg. (PRO: E190/54/1).

20 November-4 December. Shippers by the *Pearl* of Bristol bound for Virginia: Thomas Biss, Thomas Speede, Reginald Tucke, Richard Codrington, John Knight, John Grant, John Reade, James Millard, John Jackson, William Bullocke, William Willett, Edward Fielding, Richard Locke. (PRO: E190/1138/1).

21 November. The following apprenticed in Bristol: Richard Denham to William Wiggington, 3 years Virginia. (BR).

21 November-10 December. Shippers by the *Madras*, Mr. Roger Newham, bound from London for Virginia: Thomas Russell, John Hood, Thomas Hill, Thomas Curle. (PRO: E190/54/1).

22 November. The following apprenticed in Bristol: John Owen to George Tyte, 4 years Virginia. (BR).

25 November. The following apprenticed in Bristol: Anne Peddement to John Creede, 4 years Virginia; Dennis Clarke to George Cary, 4 years Virginia; Robert Hughs to John Reade, 4 years Virginia. (BR).

26 November. The following apprenticed in Bristol: Anne Foord to Peter Archer, 4 years Virginia. (BR).

26 November-14 December. Shippers by the *Pelican*, Mr. John Bowman [Mr. Matthew Paine], bound from London for Virginia: Matthew Wilkinson, Thomas Morden, Symon Masters, Matthew Stocks, William Nut. (PRO: E190/54/1).

27 November. The following apprenticed in Bristol: John Thornehull to Thomas Hancock, 4 years Virginia. (BR).

28 November. The following apprenticed in Bristol: William Widows to William Bayly, 4 years Virginia; William Border to William Fley, 4 years Virginia. (BR).

28 November. Shipper by the *Dragon*, Mr. John Webb, bound from London for Virginia: John Flagen. (PRO: E190/54/1).

29 November. The following apprenticed in Bristol: William Lester to James Harris, 4 years Virginia; Edward Rann to Thomas Harris, 4 years Virginia; William Lightley to Charles Harris, 4 years Virginia; Giles Rockett to John Sayer, 4 years Virginia. (BR).

29 November-11 December. Shippers by the *Symon & Francis*, Mr. Daniel Pensax, bound from London for Virginia:, John Cust, John Clarke, Symon Clarke. (PRO: E190/54/1).

30 November. The following apprenticed in Bristol: Joane Hill to John Tippett, 4 years Virginia. (BR).

30 November. John Keynes of Marlborough, Wiltshire, gent, attests that William Burges, Thomas Taylor, Nathaniel Heathwicke and George Puddington have been appointed as attorneys to secure possession of land in Ann Arundel County, Maryland, assigned to Benjamin Lawrence of Marlborough, chandler. (LMCD).

November. Probate of will of Joseph Burges of Marlborough, Wiltshire, but late of Maryland, who died in the City of London, merchant. (AW).

November. Administration of John Somers of Virginia, bachelor. (AW).

1 December. Shipper by the *Exchange* of Bideford, Mr. George Tytherly, bound from Bideford for Virginia: William Tytherly. (PRO: E190/955/6).

2 December. The following apprenticed in Bristol: Mary Grigg to John Creed, 4 years Virginia; John Whafer to George Tyte, 4 years Virginia; Phillip Streete to John Willett, 4 years Virginia. (BR).

2 December. Shippers by the *Mary*, Mr. Thomas Smith, bound from London for Virginia: William Stonestreete. (PRO: E190/54/1).

2 December. Shipper by the *Hope* of Plymouth, Mr. John Griffith, bound from Plymouth for Virginia: Abraham Searle. (PRO: E190/1039/5).

2-6 December. Shippers by the *Canary Bird*, Mr. John Lucam, bound from London for Virginia:, John Jeffrey, Joseph Greene, John Freeman. (PRO: E190/54/1).

4 December. Shipper by the *Mary & Elizabeth*, Mr. Samuel Pensax, bound from London for Virginia: Isaac Merrit. (PRO: E190/54/1).

5 December. The following apprenticed in Bristol: Robert Mens to James Harris, 5 years Virginia; John Bushell to Henry Roach, 5 years Virginia. (BR).

6 December. Deposition by Elizabeth Denny of Limehouse, Stepney, Middlesex, widow aged 71, and Ann Kibe of the same, widow aged 66, that Randall Harle and his wife Mary had two sons Randall and Henry. Randall Harle Sr. more than 20 years ago went as master of the *London* to Virginia where he purchased lands before returning to London. In order that his estate in Virginia should be cared for he sent his son Randall there but he died a bachelor and the father died in 1661 or 1662 in Limehouse leaving only his said son Henry Harle who was killed at sea in 1666 during the Dutch wars. Henry Harle had a son, Henry Harle Jr., who is heir to both his father and grandfather. Nathaniell Sherman and his wife Elizabeth Sherman are guardians of the said Henry Harle Jr., a minor. Daniel Pensax, master of the *Simon & Frances* of London, now bound to Virginia, has been appointed attorney to recover Randall Harle's plantation in Nandue Creek, Accomack County, occupied by Captain John West. (LMCD).

6 December. Shipper by the *Maryland Merchant* of Newcastle, Mr. Roger Rey, bound from Plymouth for Virginia: Michaell Taylor. (PRO: E190/1039/5).

9 December. The following apprenticed in Bristol: Roger Cooke to George Warren, 4 years Virginia. (BR).

12 December. The following apprenticed in Bristol: Elizabeth Villers to Robert Turpin, 4 years Virginia. (BR).

13 December. The following apprenticed in Bristol: Robert Trevent to Thomas Fysher, 4 years Virginia. (BR).

16 December. The following apprenticed in Bristol: John Cooper to John Flyfoote, 4 years Virginia; George Tomson to Thomas Bedford, 4 years Virginia. (BR).

18 December. Shipper by the *Reformation* of Bristol bound for Virginia: Edward Baugh. (PRO: E190/1138/1).

19 December. The following apprenticed in Bristol: Mary Evans to William Luffe, 4 years Virginia; Cicely Evans to same, 4 years Virginia. (BR).

23 December. John Tailoe and others declare that Robert Walton alias Wauton became indebted to them for cloth but, having had himself imprisoned in the King's Bench, escaped with the goods to Virginia where he bought a large plantation. In 1669 Walton died, leaving his plantation to his wife Elizabeth and appointing Thomas Mathew as his executor. The petitioner Tailoe, having taken out letters of administration to Walton's estate, was unable to secure it because it was ruled that Walton's debts were incurred before his arrival in Virginia. (APC).

24 December. The following apprenticed in Bristol: William Hodge to John Swayne, 4 years Nevis. (BR).

27 December. The following apprenticed in Bristol: Henry Whitehead to William Hooper, 4 years Nevis. (BR).

December. Probate of will of Thomas Middleton of London, who had lands in New England. (AW).

December. Probate of will of Thomas Juxon of Mortlake, Surrey, whose cousin, William Juxon, was in Virginia. (AW).

1673

1 January. Deposition by Ezechiel Fogg, aged 34, citizen and skinner of London, but late of Bristol, that David Anderson of Charles Town, New England, mariner, owed money to John Williams of Bristol arising out of the voyage of the *Elizabeth & Mary* of New England, Mr. David Anderson, from Bristol to New England and Virginia in 1669. (LMCD).

2 January. Petition of John Tailoe and others referred to the Governor of Virginia. They are creditors of Robert Walton who, to avoid payment, went to Virginia and purchased an estate there. (CSPC).

3 January. The following apprenticed in Bristol: Evan Barrett to William Cottle, 9 years Barbados; Anthony Quarrell to Stephen Luffe, 6 years Virginia; John Weaver to William Wells, 4 years Barbados. (BR).

6 January. The following apprenticed in Bristol: David Edwards to William Morgan, 3 years Virginia; Michaell Rous to James Keire, 4 years Barbados. (BR).

8 January. The following apprenticed in Bristol: George Foorde to George Tyte, 4 years Virginia; Richard Hopkins to William Cannings, 12 years Virginia. (BR).

11 January. The following apprenticed in Bristol: Elizabeth Jones to William Hardidge, 3 years Virginia; Katherine Jones to same, 3 years Virginia; Richard Chiner to George Thomas, 4 years Virginia. (BR).

13 January. The following apprenticed in Bristol: William Felton to John Stephens, 4 years Barbados; Prudence Davis to Edward Field, 4 years Virginia; John Auter to same, 4 years Virginia. (BR).

14 January. The following apprenticed in Bristol: Mary Probert to Walter Cecill, 4 years Nevis. (BR).

24 January. The following apprenticed in Bristol: Austin Jenkins to Richard Dempster, 4 years Virginia; Richard Pope to John Neades, 4 years Nevis. (BR).

January. Administration of Thomas Benbowe of the ship *St. Andrew* granted to Joanna, wife of the principal creditor, Roger Frost, in Virginia. (AW).

January. Administration with will of John Woodbury of New England, who died on the ship *Crown* at sea. (AW).

January. Administration of George Allen of Queen's Ferry, Scotland, who died at sea near Virginia, bachelor. (AW).

1 February. Northern Circuit prisoners reprieved to be transported to Barbados. Cumberland: John Munkhouse of Brackenthwaite. Durham: Susan Roseden of Gateshead, spinster. Northumberland: William Clarke of Newtown;

Eleanor Dainton of Newcastle upon Tyne; Cuthbert Hobson of Crookhouse. Westmorland: Miles Atkinson of Asby. Yorkshire: Robert Snawden of York; Abraham Parker of York; Richard Lancaster of Selby; Jonathan Wood of York; Edward Ingram of York. (PRO: C66/3148/18).

6 February & 26 October. Newgate prisoners reprieved to be transported to Barbados. London: Thomas Man alias Mather; Dorothy Moore, spinster; Thomas Denman; Mary Shingfield, spinster, alias wife of Michael Shingfield; Elizabeth Butler, spinster, alias wife of William Longman; Richard Ewdall alias Evedall; John Jackson alias Coxe; Ann Lowe, spinster, alias wife of Thomas Lowe, mariner; Ann Sutton, spinster, alias wife of William Sutton; Judith Trott alias wife of Robert Trott; Grissell Hudson, spinster, alias wife of William Hudson; Elizabeth Soe alias Jackson, spinster; Richard Evins; John Jackman, carpenter; John Briggs alias Boys; Mary Jolopp, spinster; Ann Smith alias Twist, spinster; James Mathews; Robert Devenish; Charles Smith; Francis Shepherd; Mary Elsmore, spinster, alias wife of Robert Elsmore; Elizabeth Croft, spinster; John White alias Wayte; Martha Parker, spinster; Helen Farmer, widow; Martha Houghton, spinster; Joseph Syvett; Evan Davies, Jane Watts, spinster; Elizabeth Burch, spinster. Middlesex: Mary Bromley, spinster, alias wife of Francis Griffith of St. Margaret Westminster; Thomas Phillips of the same; Elinor Rigby of St. Martin in the Fields, spinster; Bridget Ward of the same; Thomas Towers of the same; William Kirton of the same; Amy Guy of the same for manslaughter; John Draper of the same; John Hawksworth alias Green of St. Paul Covent Garden; Thomas Sadler of the same; Thomas Harris of Staines; Thomas Harris of Hayes; Jasper Smith of Islington; William Brewett of Stepney; Jeremy Sowell of the same; William Ridgway of Marylebone; Jane Bride, wife of Thomas Bride of the same; George Gee of Enfield; John Burton of St. Giles in the Fields; William Ireland of the same; Margaret Watson of the same, spinster; Elizabeth Prince of Whitechapel; John Slaughter of the same; Grace Tucker, wife of Richard Tucker of the same; Richard Cowley of St. Clement Danes; Clement Toulson of the same for manslaughter; Joan Stanley, wife of Thomas Stanley of St. Mary Savoy; Thomas Bingham of St. Giles Cripplegate; Susan Fostiker of the same; Sarah Onesby of St. Sepulchre, spinster; Thomas Leech of Friern Barnet. (PRO: C66/3145/2, 3148/17).

10 February. The following apprenticed in Bristol: George Loshley to Richard Dempster, 4 years Barbados; Elizabeth Norman to same, 4 years Barbados. (BR).

15 February. Western Circuit prisoners reprieved to be transported to Barbados. Cornwall: George Kent of Lanteglos. Devon: Margaret Hoskins of Exeter, spinster; Matthew Piddesley of Shobrooke; Joan Bampfield of Sandford, singlewoman; Peter Crosse of Scitvole, Exeter, woolcomber. Somerset: James Morgan of Brislington, husbandman; Charles Bayley of Wells, husbandman; Samuel Peryn of Axbridge, husbandman; John Wiseman of Burton, blacksmith; Henry West of Beckington, husbandman; Edward Baker of Chard, husbandman. (PRO: C66/3148/20).

15 February. Oxford Circuit prisoners reprieved to be transported to America. Gloucestershire: John Hayward of Frogg Mill; Richard Cooke of Upton St. Leonard. Herefordshire: Richard Fisher of Linton; James Powle of Dilwyn. Monmouthshire: David William of Abergavenny; John George of Abergavenny; William Price of Newport. Staffordshire: Robert Orme of Burton on Trent; Robert Dodd of Adbaston. Worcestershire: John Knight of Dudley. (PRO: C66/3148/19).

February. Administration of John Powell of New England, who died at sea on the frigate *Moncke*, bachelor. (AW).

March. Administration of William Hind of Virginia, widower. (AW).

March. Administration of John Pate of Virginia, bachelor. (AW).

March. Probate of will of Susan Bell of All Hallows Barking, London, widow, who made a bequest to Anne, wife of John Elliott, of New England. (AW).

April. Probate of will of Robert Parker of Bosham, Sussex, who had lands in Virginia. (AW).

April. Probate of will of Bartholomew Wall of Blakenham on the Waters, Suffolk, whose daughter, Anna Jacob, was in New England. (AW).

9 May. Shipper by the *Court of Kent*, Mr. John Should, bound from London for New England: George Scott. (PRO: E190/59/1).

9 May-8 July. Shippers by the *Blessing*, Mr. William Greenough, bound from London for New England: John Freeman, Thomas Bodly, Benjamin Peake, Christopher Dynott, George Knight, Ralph Box, Christopher Banister, John Parker, Sampson Sheafe, Thomas Pall, Spencer Piggott, Robert Hackshaw, John Ive, John Knapp, Henry Redman, John Brice, Edward Shippen, John Goodman, Robert Woolley, William Antleby, Nicholas Roberts, Christopher Gore, Joseph Freeman, John Harwood, Joseph Muscot, John Wise, Noah Floyd, James Edwards, Thomas Bluck, Oswald Cornish, Ezechiel Hutchinson, Abraham Jesson, John Jackson, Daniel Allen, James Eyton, Maximilian Gore, John Child, John Wickins, Richard Nowell, Richard Hodgkins. (PRO: E190/59/1).

10 May. Shippers by the *Roger & Mary*, Mr. John Laming, bound from London for New England: Thomas Knight, John Lavin. (PRO: E190/59/1).

?May. Petition of Emanuel Jones, a prisoner in Newgate, who was apprehended seven years ago for stealing a coat and was sent to Virginia where he stayed five years. He pleads a pardon for having returned. [*See Newgate pardon for 12 November 1668*]. (SP Dom).

6 June-13 August. Shippers by the *Sea Flower*, Mr. Thomas Smith, bound from London for New England: Thomas Norman, David Waterhouse, Edward Shippen, John Kiffety, Josias Dewye, Nicholas Roberts, Ezechiel Hutchinson, Richard Turner, John Price, John Child, Henry Ashurst, Francis Parsons, Nathaniel Hubbard, Robert Woolley, William Hatwill, Thomas Sontley, John Jackson, Gawen Corbin, Edward Merriwether, Abraham Jackson, William Shirley, Abraham Briggs, Edward Mountfort, Thomas Hollis, Samuel Medley, Elizabeth Hutchinson, Thomas Bodley, Stephen Burton, Nicholas Webb, Thomas Glover, Edward Hull, Gerrard Roberts, Nicholas Floyd, Isaac Chetwood, Isaac Grey, John Harwood, John Kempster. (PRO: E190/59/1).

28 June. Pass for the *Blessing*, Mr. William Greenway, to go to New England to fish. (APC).

June. Administration of Philip Bolton of St. Leonard Eastcheap, London, who died in Virginia. (AW).

1 July. Oxford Circuit prisoners reprieved to be transported to America. Gloucestershire: Margaret Francis of St. Philip, Gloucester, spinster. Herefordshire: David Huggins of Almeley, glover. Shropshire: Elizabeth Doughty of Thongland, spinster; Mary Williams of Whitchurch, spinster; William Spencer of Neen Savage. Staffordshire: John Joydrell of Stafford; Henry Lush of Stafford. Worcestershire: William Rea of Worcester; Roland Jackson of Bromsgrove. (PRO: C66/3148/5).

1 July. Midland Circuit prisoners reprieved to be transported to America. Leicestershire: Richard Johnson Jr. of Bagworth; Richard Loseby of Barkby Thorpe. Lincolnshire: Edward Peacocke of Elkington; Nicholas Walton of Long Sutton; Richard Thompson of Leverton; Alan Elwand of Slowby; George Hassen of North Kelsey; James Gould of Methringham; Edward Friskney of Partney. Northamptonshire: William Wells of Brixworth. Nottinghamshire: David Jefford of Mansfield. Warwickshire: Valentine Hallifield of Fenny Compton; James Band of Ausley; Samuel Highhorne of Knighton; Richard Floyd of Ausley; Thomas Morris of Ausley; Abraham Beaumont alias Harridge of Dalton, (Yorkshire). (PRO: C66/3148/4).

1-22 July. Shippers by the *Katherine*, Mr. Thomas Frizell, bound from London for New England: Edward Hull, Charles Sweeting, James Swift, John Langham, Thomas Ruck, Edward Shippen, John Bawdon, Thomas Bodley, Abraham Jesson, Christopher Gore, Christopher Taylor, Robert Woolley, Richard Tue, Samuel Medley, Edward Edmonds, Nicholas Floyd, Thomas Knight. (PRO: E190/59/1).

9-24 July. Shippers by the *Blossom*, Mr. Richard Martin, bound from London for New England: George Cole, Thomas Bates, Thomas Powell. (PRO: E190/59/1).

30 July. The following apprenticed in Bristol: Thomas Jones to John Seward, 8 years Nevis. (BR).

July. Probate of will of William Parker of Stepney, Middlesex, who had goods in Maryland. (AW).

2 August. Deposition by Dorothy Spencer, aged 62, wife of John Spencer, citizen and merchant tailor of London, deposes that she is the sister of Thomas Whitgreave of Moseley, Staffordshire, gent, and his wife Frances, formerly wife of Dr. Jeremy Harrison deceased, and afterwards of Captain Giles Brent, as she understands from letters from Virginia directed to her husband. Thomas Whitgreave is the only brother of the deponent and of Frances, lately also deceased. John Spencer, citizen and merchant tailor of London, aged 64, deposes that Captain Giles Brent has informed him by letter from Virginia that he had married Frances Harrison. (LMCD).

6 August. The following apprenticed in Bristol: John Jones to Thomas Boykin, 4 years [Virginia]. (BR).

9 August. The following apprenticed in Bristol: George Dobbins to Anthony Barrow, 5 years Nevis. (BR).

12-22 August. Shippers by the *Society*, Mr. Benjamin Moore, bound from London for New England: Christopher Marshall, John Harwood, Nehemiah Bourne, Edward Mann, Samuel Medley. (PRO: E190/59/1).

22 August-13 September. Shippers by the *Katherine*, Mr. John Andrews, bound from London for New England: Maximilian Gore, William Stonestreet, John Jurin, Samuel Wickins, Thomas Cluter, Charles Corsellis, Henry Mountfort, Christopher Gere, James Littleton, Robert Goodman, Robert Chaplin, Thomas Knights, John Child, Abraham Jesson, Thomas Norman, William Shirley, John Eaton, John Richardson. (PRO: E190/59/1).

28 August. The following apprenticed in Bristol: John Boore to Andrew Limbry, 4 years Barbados; Cornelius Larden to John Bodenham, 4 years Virginia; John Tayler to Phillip Browne, 4 years Nevis. (BR).

August. Administration of George Foxwell of Virginia, bachelor. (AW).

2 September. The following apprenticed in Bristol: Joseph Muspott to John Gill, 4 years Virginia. (BR).

4 September. Shipper by the *Neptune* of Whitby, Mr. Daniell Jackson, bound from Whitby for Maryland: William Linskell & Co. (PRO: E190/195/3).

5 September. Deposition by William Pate, citizen and ironmonger of London, that he has revoked a letter of attorney appointing James Whetcombe of New England, merchant, and now appoints Thomas Clouter of London, mariner, bound for New England by the *Katherine* of London. (LMCD).

22 September. The following apprenticed in Bristol: Alice Read to James Wathen, 4 years Barbados; Mary Williams to Richard Britton, 4 years Virginia. (BR).

25 September. The following apprenticed in Bristol: Elizabeth Jones to William Hagget, 4 years Nevis; Gartred Cottle to William Ford, 5 years Virginia. (BR).

3 October. Deposition by Henry Had of Redrith, Surrey, mariner aged 26, that William Ginger, now deceased, was master of the *Willing Mind* which in October 1672 went from London to Virginia. During the voyage William Stiffe now deceased bought the freedom of Elizabeth Mitchell, a maidservant in Virginia. Stephen Marsh of Redriffe, mariner aged 28, deposes that Stiffe took a boy on the voyage who was to be left in Virginia. (LMCD).

3 October-21 November. Shippers by the *Golden Lyon*, Mr. Leonard Webber, bound from London for Virginia: Richard Banks, Richard Booth, Thomas Hanson, John Munford, Isaac Merritt, Thomas Jordan. (PRO: E190/59/1).

4 October. The following apprenticed in Bristol: Charles Harris to Jonah Quarrell, 4 years Barbados; William Low to William Jelfe, 4 years Maryland; Elizabeth Barnelines to Joseph Fookes, 4 years Barbados; Hannah Brideley to same, 4 years Barbados. (BR).

6 October. Shipper by the *James*, Mr. Nicholas Goodridge, bound from London for Virginia: Arthur Bailey. (PRO: E190/59/1).

7 October. Shipper by the *Thomas* of Hull, Mr. Edward Harrison, bound from Newcastle for Maryland: said Edward Harrison. (PRO: E190/195/7).

9 October. The following apprenticed in Bristol: Joane Page to Christopher Hasell, 4 years Virginia; John Parker to John Synschall, 4 years Virginia. (BR).

12 October. Certificate that Robert Beverley of Peankedanke, Virginia, has been appointed attorney for Anne Day of Redrith, Surrey, relict and administratrix of John Day of Redrith, who died overseas. (LMCD).

13 October. The following apprenticed in Bristol: Katherine Reynolds alias Reves to Leonard Phelps, 4 years Barbados. (BR).

13-31 October. Shippers by the *George*, Mr. Thomas Grantham, bound from London for Virginia: George Baker, John Kent, Robert Forth, Matthew Meriton, Nicholas Funnell, Edward Leamon. (PRO: E190/59/1).

14 October. The following apprenticed in Bristol: Gregory Reyland to Thomas Speede, 4 years Virginia by *Thomas*. (BR).

20 October-11 November. Shippers by the *Martha*, Mr. Abraham Wheelock, bound from London for Virginia: Edward Thompson, Perient Trott. (PRO: E190/59/1).

20 October-17 November. Shippers by the *Samuel & Jonathan*, Mr. John Hilson, bound from London for Virginia: Humphrey Nicholson, William Hawes. (PRO: E190/59/1).

21 October. The following apprenticed in Bristol: Maurice Benfield to Jonas Hollyday, 4 years Virginia. (BR).

25 October. The following apprenticed in Bristol: Thomasin Webb to John Needes, 4 years Nevis; Sarah Northerne to same, 4 years Nevis. (BR).

27 October. The following apprenticed in Bristol: Thomas Window to John Bodenham, 4 years Nevis; Daniel Price to Thomas Bedford, 4 years Virginia. (BR).

28 October. The following apprenticed in Bristol: Mary Sheppley to Francis Cockhill, 4 years Virginia. (BR).

31 October. The following apprenticed in Bristol: Richard Lewis to Thomas Bedford, 4 years Virginia; William Hopkins to Thomas Willett, 4 years Virginia; William Pridley to John Jeffries, 4 years Maryland. (BR).

31 October-7 November. Shippers by the *Willing Mind*, Mr. George Ginge, bound from London for Virginia: John Clarke, Richard Banks, Isaac Merritt. (PRO: E190/59/1).

October. Administration of Rawleigh Hance of Shadwell, Middlesex, who died in Virginia, bachelor. (AW).

October. Probate of will of Samuel Jones of Gloucester, New England, and of the ship *Warspight* in the King's service, who died in St. Thomas, Southwark, Surrey. (AW).

October. Probate of will of John Phipps of London, whose son, Henry Phipps, was in Maryland. (AW).

October. Administration of William Stiffe of Upton, Essex, who died on the ship *Rainbow*, bachelor, a trader to Virginia. (AW).

3 November. The following apprenticed in Bristol: Edward Smith to Christopher Birkhead, 4 years Virginia. (BR).

3 November-22 December. Shippers by the *Charles*, Mr. Benoni Eaton, bound from London for Virginia: Henry Foreman, Henry Meese, John Olive, Jeremiah Foreman, Isaac Merritt, Thomas Mathews. (PRO: E190/59/1).

4 November. The following apprenticed in Bristol: Thomas Hagget to Thomas Willet, 7 years Virginia; Thomas Reece to Christopher Birkhead, 4 years Virginia. (BR).

9 November. The following apprenticed in Bristol: Henry Gupway to John Woolvin, 4 years Virginia; Jane Pritchard to Francis Cockhill, 4 years Virginia; Robert Foorte to Percivall Reade, 4 years Virginia. (BR).

10 November. The following apprenticed in Bristol: Francis Thomas to Daniell Sommers, 4 years Virginia. (BR).

12 November. The following apprenticed in Bristol: Robert Evans to William Thomas, 4 years Virginia; Dorothy Kezle to Edward Morgan, 4 years Virginia. (BR).

15-21 November. Shippers by the *Francis*, Mr. John Warner, bound from London for Virginia: Joseph Saunders, Richard Deane, Edward Beacon. (PRO: E190/59/1).

17 November. Deposition by Thomas Walsh of London, haberdasher aged 28, and William Walsh of Whitchurch, Shropshire, gent aged 31, that by deed of 2 October 1673 John Nevett, son of Richard Nevett of Whitchurch, turner, assigned to Jane, Susanna and Anne Nevett, daughters of William Nevett of London, merchant, all the legacies bequeathed to him by the will of his uncle, Hugh Nevett of Virginia, merchant, deceased. Deposition by John Nevett, aged 23, son of William Nevett, citizen and haberdasher of London, that on 18 April 1672 Laurence Smith consigned tobacco from York River, Virginia, to Nicholas Harrison by the *Industry*, Mr. Phineas Hide, and the deponent was sent by his father to Hugh Nevett in Virginia with goods. (LMCD).

18 November. The following apprenticed in Bristol: John Wade to Edward Jackson, 4 years Virginia; John Minthen to Edward Gibbes, 6 years Virginia; Thomas Shine to same, 6 years Virginia; Timothy Shine to same, 4 years Virginia; Henry Strickland to same, 5 years Virginia; William Nauty to same, 6 years Virginia; Edward Wise to same, 4 years Virginia. (BR).

19 November. The following apprenticed in Bristol: Elizabeth Carr to Thomas Pope, 4 years Virginia; Thomas Hopkins to John Mason, 4 years Virginia; John Scripture to same, 4 years Virginia; Richard Wigg to same, 5 years Virginia; Thomas Tayler to same, 7 years Virginia. (BR).

22 November. The following apprenticed in Bristol: Mary Nash to Thomas Hooker, 4 years Virginia; Elioner Smart to Benjamin Lawrence, 4 years Virginia; John Nicholl to Samuell Richardson, 4 years Virginia; John Lullet to same, 5 years Virginia. (BR).

22-27 November. Shippers by the *Industry*, Mr. Fineas Hide, bound from London for Virginia: Richard Deane, John Travis, Mabel Harvey. (PRO: E190/59/1).

24 November. The following apprenticed in Bristol: Anne Masters to Edward Skinner, 4 years Virginia; Anne Hewell to Edward Morris, 4 years Virginia; Thomas Williams to Samuell Drayton, 4 years Virginia; James Lecke to Elizabeth Marden, 4 years Virginia. (BR).

25 November. Agnes Summers of Ilminster, Somerset, widow, appoints Hubert Farrell of Virginia, merchant, as her attorney. (*See administration of John Somers, November 1672*). (LMCD).

25 November. The following apprenticed in Bristol: John Mills to Zackariah Smith, 4 years Maryland; Hopkin Williams to Edward Jackson, 4 years Virginia; Thomas Barrow to Thomas Bush, 4 years Virginia. (BR).

25 November. Shipper by the *City Stoade*, Mr. John Vanflexten, bound from London for Virginia: said John Vanflexten. (PRO: E190/59/1).

November. Administration of Bartholomew Thomas of Virginia. (AW).

November. Administration of John Bracegirdle of London, who died in Virginia, bachelor. (AW).

November. Administration of George Southen of Virginia. (AW).

November. Administration of Richard Evans of Virginia. (AW).

1 December. The following apprenticed in Bristol: William Thomas to Edward Birkin, 4 years Virginia; Anne Waters to John Cecill Jr. & John Dymer, 5 years Maryland. (BR).

2 December. Western Circuit prisoners reprieved to be transported to Barbados. Cornwall: Henry Lewis of Launceston. Devon: George Hore of Buckland Brewer, husbandman; Robert Chalice of Broadhembury, husbandman. Somerset. William Smyth of North Petherton, husbandman. (PRO: C66/3145/6).

6 December. The following apprenticed in Bristol: David Vaughan to Thomas Pope, 4 years Virginia. (BR).

10 December. The following apprenticed in Bristol: John Wills to John Mason, 4 years Virginia; Thomas Merrifield to same, 4 years Virginia. (BR).

11 December. Shipper by the *St. Peter* of Hamburg, Mr. Vincent Johnson, bound from Portsmouth for Virginia: Stephen Van Ettsen. (PRO: E190/828/3).

11 December. The following apprenticed in Bristol: John Orchard to Richard Britten, 6 years Virginia; Anne Thomas to John Snow, 4 years Jamaica. (BR).

12 December. The following apprenticed in Bristol: John Lowrin to Jane Sayers, 4 years Virginia; John Griffeth to Jedidiah Pickford, 4 years Virginia; Lettice Foord to Thomas Hooker, 4 years Maryland. (BR).

20 December. The following apprenticed in Bristol: Mary Huskins to Nicholas Olliver, 4 years Virginia. (BR).

22 December. The following apprenticed in Bristol: Mary Hobson to Margerie Snow, 4 years Jamaica; Evan Jones to Mathew Stookes, 4 years Virginia. (BR).

29 December. The following apprenticed in Bristol: John Jones to Mary Oliver, 6 years Virginia. (BR).

December. Thomas Price, aged 11, apprenticed from Christ's Hospital to Robert Smith, commander of the *Mary* bound for Barbados. (CH).

December. Administration of Christopher Watkins of St. Botolph Aldersgate, London, whose kinsman, George Watkins, was in Virginia. (AW).

1674

2 January. The following apprenticed in Bristol: Anne Markes to Benjamin Lawrence, 5 years Virginia; Avis Howman to Mathew Stoakes, 4 years Virginia; John Lullet to Margery Snow, 4 years Virginia. (BR).

5 January. The following apprenticed in Bristol: Henry Howard to John Woolvin, 4 years Virginia; Theophilus Wattkins to John Creed, 4 years Virginia; John Sheppard to same, 4 years Virginia; John Williams to Robert Alexander, 5 years Virginia. (BR).

15 January. Deposition by Clement Kettle of London, innholder aged 40, that Reynold Henly of Chickahominy, Virginia, planter, became indebted on 20 November 1672 to Mathew Wilkinson, citizen and skinner of London, for goods shipped on the *John*, Mr. Josias Pickes, to be paid for in tobacco. (LMCD).

15 January. The following apprenticed in Bristol: Thomas Manson to Mary Tayler, 5 years Virginia. (BR).

15 January. Western Circuit prisoners reprieved to be transported to Barbados. Hampshire: Thomas Hussey of St. Bartholomew, Winchester; Eleazer Elcombe of Hambledon. Somerset: James Bishopp of Trent; Henry Slocombe of Huish Champflower; Amos Randoll of Martock, carpenter; James Dupe of Norwood; Edward Stevens of Cothelstone, blacksmith; Thomas Cooke of Wells; Robin Holloway of North Perrot; Thomas Rudman of Mells. Wiltshire: William Hutchins of Cherhill. (PRO: C66/3166/1).

19 January. The following apprenticed in Bristol: John Plummer to Edward Birkin, 4 years Virginia. (BR).

26 January. The following apprenticed in Bristol: John Bridges to Nicholas Oliver, 4 years Virginia; John Mottershitt to Thomas Pope, 10 years Virginia; William Penkston to same, 4 years Virginia; John Bate to William Hardidge, 4 years Virginia. (BR).

26 January. Bill presented to Parliament to prevent the transportation of prisoners beyond the seas with the exception of those pardoned on condition of transportation. (SP Dom).

27 January. The following apprenticed in Bristol: Stephen Bentler to Edward Birkin, 6 years Virginia; Phillip Mattson to William Ford, 6 years Virginia. (BR).

28 January. The following apprenticed in Bristol: Thomas Safford to William Buttler, 4 years Virginia. (BR).

29 January. The following apprenticed in Bristol: Andrew Brady to John Brown, 4 years Virginia. (BR).

31 January. The following apprenticed in Bristol: John Searle to John Jones, 4 years Virginia; Cicely Hall to Anne Salter, 4 years Virginia. (BR).

January. Probate of will of Mary Neeve of Virginia, spinster. (AW).

2 February. The following apprenticed in Bristol: Samuell Britten to Richard Britten, 4 years Virginia. (BR).

4 February. The following apprenticed in Bristol: Richard Hood to Richard Britten, 4 years Virginia. (BR).

12 February. The following apprenticed in Bristol: Dorothy Swettman to Phillip Whellin, 4 years Virginia; Anne Hardidge to John Seyre, 4 years Virginia; Richard Drake to John Covill Esq., 4 years Virginia. (BR).

13 February. The following apprenticed in Bristol: Cicely Peasely to Elizabeth Webb, 4 years Virginia; John Thomas to Christopher Cooper, 5 years Virginia; Thomas Oliver alias Williams to Thomas Hobson, 4 years Virginia; James Blunt to same, 4 years Virginia. (BR).

16 February. The following apprenticed in Bristol: Thomas Dax to Christopher Cooper, 4 years Virginia; William Pilchert to Abraham Willett, 5 years Virginia; Henry Benfield to William Kaine, 10 years Virginia. (BR).

19 February. The following apprenticed in Bristol: William Morgan to Christopher Cooper, 4 years Virginia; John Mortimore to Aaron Prance, 4 years Virginia; Richard Burgis to Robert Parsmon, 4 years Virginia; John Gwilliam to same, 4 years Virginia. (BR).

20 February. The following apprenticed in Bristol: James Alwood to John Ar——, 4 years Virginia. (BR).

23 February. The following apprenticed in Bristol: Mary Williams to Simon Burton, 4 years Virginia; Susanna Grandier to Edward Skinner, 4 years Virginia. (BR).

24 February. The following apprenticed in Bristol: Mary Fowler to Edward Yeamans, 4 years Virginia; Robert Williams to William Willett, 4 years Virginia. (BR).

26 February. Deposition in London re the voyage of the *Little Bartlett*, Mr. Nicholas Prinn, from London to Virginia in 1672, her capture by the Dutch and return to London. (EA).

27 February. The following apprenticed in Bristol: John Hacker to Thomas Harris, 4 years Virginia; Robert Ellis to William Merrick, 4 years Barbados; Mary Evans to Thomas Pope, 4 years Virginia; Thomas Lloyde to same, 7 years Virginia; Richard Hopkins to John Peasley Jr., 4 years Virginia; William Mundey to George Willis, 4 years Virginia. (BR).

28 February. The following apprenticed in Bristol: Thomas Chick to Edward Yeamans, 4 years Virginia; Katherine Macy to Thomas Pope, 4 years Virginia. (BR).

February. Administration of John Bird of St. Sepulchre, London, who died in Virginia. (AW).

February. Administration of John Martin of New England, who died at sea on the ship *Jersey*, bachelor. (AW).

2 March. The following apprenticed in Bristol: Nicholas Huskstone to John Jenkins, 4 years Virginia; George Lloyd to John Wattkins, 4 years Virginia; Anthony Guest to Anthony Bayly, 4 years Stanton Drew (*sic*); Samuell Ellis to William Morgan, 4 years Nevis. (BR).

5 March. The following apprenticed in Bristol: Ursula Hammell to Henry Wise, 4 years Virginia; Sarah Edwards to Benjamin Powell, 4 years Virginia. (BR).

9 March. The following apprenticed in Bristol: William Greatehead to Matthew King, 4 years Virginia; Robert Andrewes to Thomas Pope, 5 years Virginia. (BR).

11 March. The following apprenticed in Bristol: Robert Burnoll to Simon Hinds, 4 years Virginia; Thomas Andrewes to James Harris, 4 years Virginia; John Hill to John Harris, 4 years Maryland. (BR).

13 March. Home Circuit prisoners reprieved to be transported to Barbados or Jamaica: Mary Catlin, spinster, alias wife of Nathaniel of Ovington; William Hollingsworth of Harlow; Grace Hull of Barking; Joseph Smith of Woodford; Ann Miller of Sandon. Kent: Bartholomew Allen of Milton by Sittingbourne; John Saunders of Plumpstead or Brasted; Edward Allen of Milton by Sittingbourne; William Saunders of Plumpstead or Brasted; Edward Milstead of Bethersden; Peter Plisson of Milton next Gravesend; William Mallyon of Maidstone. Surrey: John Bullen of Walton on Thames; Robert Walker alias Weedon of Bermondsey; Katherine Randoll, spinster, alias wife of Edward of West Molesey; Francis Corbett of St. Saviour, Southwark; Anne Coster of St. George, Southwark, spinster; Thomas Browne of St. Olave, Southwark; Elianor Lye of West Molesey, spinster, alias wife of Richard; George Gowers of Newington; Sarah Norgate of St. Saviour, Southwark, spinster; Elizabeth Owen of St. Olave, Southwark. (PRO: C66/3167/2).

13 March. The following apprenticed in Bristol: Thomas Percivall to Matthew King, 4 years Virginia; Joane Wood to Christopher Trix, 4 years Nevis; Anne Thomas to Daniell Fowler, 7 years Virginia; Charles Baker to same, 7 years Virginia. (BR).

14 March. The following apprenticed in Bristol: Thomas Wakefield to Matthew King, 4 years Virginia; Henry Evans to James Harris, 4 years Virginia; William Lucas to William Minor, 4 years Nevis; Thomas Haswell to same, 4 years Nevis. (BR).

20 March. The following apprenticed in Bristol: Richard Parkar to Christopher Trix, 4 years Nevis. (BR).

21 March. The following apprenticed in Bristol: Richard Downton to Edward Morris, 6 years Nevis; John Sharrow to William Morgan, 4 years Nevis; William Jones to same, 4 years Nevis; John Jones to same, 4 years Nevis; William Poole to John Jones, 4 years Nevis. (BR).

30 March. The following apprenticed in Bristol: Baldwine Thomas to Thomas Simmons, 4 years Nevis; Peter Tithing to William Rodney, 4 years Nevis; William Eyres to John Hand, 4 years Nevis. (BR).

March. Probate of will of Richard Tew of Newport, Rhode Island. (AW).

March. Probate of will of Elizabeth Foster of Crutched Friars, London, relict of Henry Foster of Virginia. (AW).

3 April. The following apprenticed in Bristol: Charles Digby to Thomas Simmons, 5 years Montserrat. (BR).

6 April. The following apprenticed in Bristol: William Bick to Sir James Russell, 4 years Nevis; William Jones to same, 4 years Nevis; William Hughes to same, 4 years Nevis. (BR).

8 April. The following apprenticed in Bristol: Richard Eastbury to Anthony Warner, 4 years Barbados. (BR).

22 April. Petition of William Idle, master of the *Batchelor* of Hull that his ship was seized at New York in July 1673 and taken to Calais. On 24 March 1674 he and eight of his men re-took the ship and sailed her to Plymouth. He askes for her discharge. (APC).

22 April. The following apprenticed in Bristol: Thomas Dale to John Cecill, 4 years Barbados. (BR).

23 April. The following apprenticed in Bristol: Annah Coleman to Thomas White, 4 years Barbados; John Shipsea to John Cecill Esq., 4 years Barbados. (BR).

27 April. The following apprenticed in Bristol: John Aylesworth to George Warren, 4 years New England. (BR).

29 April. The following apprenticed in Bristol: Richard Stophill to Joseph Fincher, 7 years Nevis; Thomas Millson to John Cecill, 4 years Barbados; Sylvester Washing to same, 4 years Barbados; John Williams to same, 4 years Barbados. (BR).

1 May. The following apprenticed in Bristol: Thomas Jones to Matthew Stephens, 4 years New England; Matthew Tayler to same, 4 years New England; Jeremiah Bridges to Zachariah Tovey, 4 years Nevis. (BR).

6-14 May. Depositions in London re the capture of the *Bachelor*, Mr. William Idle, by the Dutch in New York from where she was taken to Cadiz and there freed by her master and sailed to Plymouth. Deponents include Robert Vauquellin alias de la Prairie, aged 50, Surveyor of Lands in New Jersey but raised in Caen, Normandy; William Pardon of Elizabeth Town, New Jersey, planter aged 57; and Henry Coustreer, merchant of London aged 50, formerly resident in New York. (EA).

7 May. The following apprenticed in Bristol: Morgan Jones to Sir James Russell, 4 years Nevis; Joane Jarvis to John Cary, 4 years New England. (BR).

11 May. The following apprenticed in Bristol: Arthur Challoner to William Roberts, 5 years New England; Lenox Beverlin to same, 7 years New England. (BR).

12 May. The following apprenticed in Bristol: William Drew to Thomas Teague, 4 years Barbados; William Davis to Zachariah Tovey, 4 years Nevis; Thomas Bick to Sir James Russell, 5 years Nevis; Thomas Turner to same, 5 years Nevis; John Hunt to same, 5 years Nevis; Benjamin Rolfe to same, 5 years Nevis; Jeremiah Longden to same, 5 years Nevis; William Bowen to same, 5 years Nevis; Thomas Rigges to same, 5 years Nevis; Elizabeth Turner to same, 5 years Nevis. (BR).

13 May. The following apprenticed in Bristol: John Roberts to Pugh Tucker, 4 years New England; John Baugh to Thomas Whittopp, 4 years Barbados. (BR).

14 May. The following apprenticed in Bristol: Christian Pendelin to Thomas Hardwick, 4 years Barbados. (BR).

15 May. The following apprenticed in Bristol: John Long to William Wigginton, 4 years Nevis; William Plomer to Thomas Hardwick, 4 years Nevis; Thomas Smith to Lewis Mayor, 4 years Nevis; Lidia Carter to Thomas Walter, 4 years Virginia; Elizabeth White to Richard Earle, 4 years Barbados. (BR).

18 May. The following apprenticed in Bristol: John Oldburge to John Cecill, 4 years Barbados. (BR).

22 May. The following apprenticed in Bristol: Edward Chichester to William Wigginton, 5 years Nevis; Walter Jackson to Thomas Cooper, 4 years Nevis. (BR).

23 May. The following apprenticed in Bristol: Thomas Griffen to Thomas Hardwick, 4 years Barbados or Nevis. (BR).

25 May. The following apprenticed in Bristol: Henry Webb to James Phipps, 4 years Virginia; Lucy Byes to Thomas Speede, 4 years Nevis; Thomas Baker to Pugh Tucker, 4 years New England; Humphry Wall to same, 4 years New England; John Sclanders to William White, 4 years New England; Martha

Round to same, 4 years New England; Elizabeth Morgan to Richard Earle, 4 years Barbados. (BR).

29 May. The following apprenticed in Bristol: Elizabeth Polden to Thomas Hardwick, 4 years Barbados. (BR).

30 May. The following apprenticed in Bristol: John Harrington to Cadwallader Palmer, 4 years Nevis. (BR).

29 June. The following apprenticed in Bristol: Mary Veere to Thomas Muspratt, 5 years Nevis. (BR).

30 June. The following apprenticed in Bristol: John Geare to Josias Rootes, 5 years New England; John Dodge to same, 5 years New England. (BR).

June. Administration of Robert Whitehaire of Willesden, Middlesex, who died in Virginia. (AW).

June. Probate of will of Peter Moulson of St. Bartholomew the Less, London, whose brother, Foulke Moulson, was in Virginia. (AW).

3 July. Chancery proceedings in the case of Judith Garrett v. Mary Yates, relict and executrix of Michael Yates of Limehouse, Middlesex, mariner, deceased, who declares that George and Joan Garrett of London had a son and heir, John Garrett, now living in Virginia. (NGSQ 61/4).

3 July. The following apprenticed in Bristol: Daniell Langly to Henry Daniell, 5 years Virginia. (BR).

4-6 July. Depositions in London re the voyage of the *Thomas & Mary*, Mr. William How, from James River, Virginia, in 1672, her capture by the Spanish and the setting adrift of some of her crew and a woman passenger. The master and others of the crew were thrown into prison in Havana and again in Cadiz. The deponents include Richard Ashall of St. Gregory's, London, merchant aged 25, who was born in Virginia. (EA).

6 July. The following apprenticed in Bristol: Henry Thomas to Robert Nicholas, 4 years Barbados or Virginia; Giles Brace to same, 4 years Barbados or Virginia; Richard Turk to same, 4 years Barbados or Virginia; William Hawkins to same, 4 years Barbados or Virginia. (BR).

14 July. The following apprenticed in Bristol: William Ashbey to William Saunders, 4 years Virginia. (BR).

17 July. The following apprenticed in Bristol: Joseph Hill to Edward Thrustone, 9 years Barbados; Jacob Wall to Edward Herbert, 7 years Nevis; David Jenkins to William Saunders, 4 years Maryland. (BR).

18 July. Newgate prisoners reprieved to be transported to Barbados. London: Grissell Hudson, spinster, alias wife of William Hudson; Priscilla Devenish, spinster, alias wife of Robert Devenish; Mary Davis, spinster; John Mackrell; Jane Wapshott, spinster; Nicholas Cloyse, yeoman; Mary Ireland, spinster;

Elizabeth Williams, spinster; Thomas Browne; William Groves; Robert Larrett; Thomas Vardell; Richard Terry; Michael Bird; Mary Parker, widow; William Browne; Henry Busby; Mary Fisher, spinster, alias wife of Thomas Fisher, yeoman; Robert Williams; Katherine Keeling, widow; Thomas Hutchens. Middlesex: Edward Goddard of St. Giles in the Fields; Elizabeth Harris alias Harrison of the same; Jasper Smith of Islington; Mary Rugmar of Hampstead, spinster; William Kingham of Shoreditch; Anne Baker, wife of John Baker of St. Margaret Westminster; Sarah Baily of the same, spinster; Lucy Wolfrey of St. Martin in the Fields, spinster; Robert Motley of the same; George Merchant of the same; William Birch of the same; Roger Pullison of the same; Robert Johnson of the same; Thomas Walters of Stepney; Richard Greene of the same; David Martin of the same; Walter Field of the same; John Yarpe of the same; Elizabeth Williams of St. Andrew Holborn, spinster; Elizabeth Ball of the same; William Mitchell of the same; Frances Ellett of Whitechapel; John Jones of St. Paul Covent Garden; John Harbridge of St. Mary Savoy; Mary Nevill of Clerkenwell; John Jordaine of Enfield; Walter Field of St. Giles Cripplegate; John Yarpe of the same; John Williams of Hampstead. (PRO: C66/3167/1).

20 July. The following apprenticed in Bristol: John Williams to Thomas Cardney, 4 years Virginia. (BR).

21 July. Shipper by the *Flower* ketch of Boston, Mr. Joseph Penwill, bound from Newcastle for Boston, New England: said Joseph Penwill. (PRO: E190/195/13).

22 July. The following apprenticed in Bristol: Ellis Northerne to Thomas Ellis, merchant, 4 years Nevis; John Reade to same, 9 years Nevis. (BR).

23 July. Midland Circuit prisoners reprieved to be transported to America. Derbyshire: William Ellis of Derby. Leicestershire: William Ball of Leicester. Northamptonshire: John Smith of Luffeswick; John Robinson of Twywell; William Palmer of Kilsby. Warwickshire: John Hall of Birmingham; James Howse of Farnborough; John Bingham of Folshill, Coventry. Unspecified: Robert Smith. (PRO: C66/3167/3).

27 July. The following apprenticed in Bristol: Mary Slade to Anne Fletcher, 4 years Barbados. (BR).

28 July. The following apprenticed in Bristol: Elizabeth Farley to Elizabeth Saunders, 5 years Virginia; John Rigges to Edward Jackson, 4 years Virginia. (BR).

30 July. Shipper by the *Prosperous* of Newcastle, Mr. Francis Partis, bound from Newcastle for Virginia: said Francis Partis. (PRO: E190/195/13).

31 July. The following apprenticed in Bristol: John Combes to William Styles, 4 years Virginia; Joane Ford to William Millard, 4 years Virginia; Rebecca

Cuffe to Thomas Pope, 4 years Virginia; Walter Parrey to Elizabeth Sanderson, 4 years Virginia; William Gadd to Mary Beacon, 8 years Virginia. (BR).

July. Administration of George Gunnell of Shoreditch, Middlesex, who died in Virginia. (AW).

July. Administration with will of Thomas Bache of Over Pen, Staffordshire, whose nephew, Peter Buck, was in Virginia. (AW).

July. Mary Pritchard apprehended says she was married in Virginia and her husband is at sea: to be set to work. (Bridewell).

3 August. The following apprenticed in Bristol: Rendall David to William Saunderson, 4 years Virginia; John Wood to Thomas Harris, 4 years Virginia; James Williams to Thomas Tovey, 7 years Nevis. (BR).

10 August. The following apprenticed in Bristol: James Publin to Edward Everard, 4 years Virginia; Henry Parry to Thomas Bowen, 5 years Virginia. (BR).

12-14 August. Shippers by the *Concord* of Newcastle, Mr. Edward Robinson, bound from Newcastle for Maryland: Ambrose Barnes, Michaell Taylor. (PRO: E190/195/13).

17 August. The following apprenticed in Bristol: Sarah Smith to Thomas Tandy, 9 years Virginia. (BR).

18 August. Shipper by the *Endeavour* of Hull, Mr. John Newton, bound from Newcastle for Maryland: Robert Farrar. (PRO: E190/195/13).

20 August. The following apprenticed in Bristol: Anne Husdey to William Tovey, 5 years Virginia. (BR).

21 August. The following apprenticed in Bristol: Anne Chelcutt to Mary Long, 5 years Nevis. (BR).

22 August. The following apprenticed in Bristol: Maudlin Jones to Jonah Moxley, 5 years Virginia. (BR).

26 August. The following apprenticed in Bristol: Griffeth Jones to Jonah Moxley, 4 years Virginia; William Lowrey to William Jelfe, 4 years Virginia; William Jenkins to Edward Thomas, 4 years Virginia. (BR).

27 August. The following apprenticed in Bristol: Jane Ketty to Robert Edwards, 5 years Virginia. (BR).

28 August. The following apprenticed in Bristol: Edward Jenkins to John Cecill, 4 years Virginia; William Reece to same, 4 years Virginia; George Walter to Thomas Tovey, 4 years Virginia; Thomas Pritchard to same, 4 years Virginia; Reice Evan to William Worgan, 4 years Virginia. (BR).

29 August. The following apprenticed in Bristol: John Morgan to Thomas Tandy, 5 years Virginia; William Robinson to William Lovell, 5 years Virginia. (BR).

August. Administration with will of George Harris of Westover, Charles County, Virginia. (AW).

2 September. The following apprenticed in Bristol: John Allen to William Faulkner, 4 years Virginia. (BR).

4 September. The following apprenticed in Bristol: Welthian Williams to Richard Thomas, 4 years Maryland; Sarah Rennolls to John Gough, 4 years Virginia. (BR).

5 September. The following apprenticed in Bristol: John Sherry to John Smith, 3 years Virginia; George Matthewes to Thomas Casewell, 5 years Virginia. (BR).

9 September. The following apprenticed in Bristol: Richard Thompson to John Walter, 4 years Barbados; Anne Gardener to Thomas Tovey, 4 years Nevis; Evan Jones to Robert Williams, 5 years Maryland; Luke Yerden to Henry Hellier, 5 years Barbados. (BR).

11 September. The following apprenticed in Bristol: Sarah Bifield to Henry Hellier, 5 years Barbados; Charles Harris to John Cluff, 8 years Virginia. (BR).

11 September. The Commissioners of Customs report on the petition of Henry Meese. The *King David* cleared the port of London for Virginia on 3 February 1674 but has not yet returned. The King's indulgence for the ship is requested. (APC).

12 September. The following apprenticed in Bristol: Cicely Williams to John Pickering, 4 years Maryland. (BR).

14 September. The following apprenticed in Bristol: Mary Randell to Patrick Spence, 4 years Virginia; Katherine Reade to same, 4 years Virginia; William Reade to same. 5 years Virginia; John Gale to same, 4 years Virginia. (BR).

15 September. The following apprenticed in Bristol: William Ricketts to John Nutt, 4 years Virginia; John Hilton to same, 4 years Virginia; Matthew Perry to Leonard Phelps, 4 years Virginia. (BR).

16 September. The following apprenticed in Bristol: Francis Roode to Hillary Stringer, 4 years Virginia; Richard Price to John Jordan, 6 years Virginia; Margaret Phillips to Thomas Tandy, 4 years Virginia; Hannah Ware to James Wallis, 4 years Virginia. (BR).

18 September. The following apprenticed in Bristol: Elizabeth Clarke to Thomas Tandy, 4 years Virginia; Edward Evans to John King, 4 years Virginia; Mary Browne to Edward Morris, 4 years Virginia. (BR).

19 September. The following apprenticed in Bristol: Maudlin Lewis to Thomas Davis, 4 years Barbados; Rowland Williams to William Prichard, 4 years Virginia; Matthew Willes to Alexander Maggs, 5 years Barbados; Margaret Sallett to Thomas Willett, 9 years Virginia; Anne Muttlebury to same, 9 years Virginia. (BR).

22 September. The following apprenticed in Bristol: John Price to John Hollett, 5 years Virginia. (BR).

23 September. The following apprenticed in Bristol: Elizabeth Prudrow to William Sankyn, 4 years Virginia. (BR).

25 September. The following apprenticed in Bristol: Nicholas Jones to Thomas Alford, 4 years Virginia; Joseph Browne to Phillip Hanger, 4 years Virginia; Simon Smith to same, 4 years Virginia. (BR).

26 September. The following apprenticed in Bristol: Martha Upton to John Jones, 4 years Virginia; Elizabeth Collins to Joseph Fookes, 4 years Virginia. (BR).

28 September. The following apprenticed in Bristol: William Ithill to Thomas Hounslow, 8 years Virginia; William Wassard to Simon Stephens, 4 years Nevis; John Hughes to Martin Wakely, 4 years Virginia; John Hollis to Joseph Fookes, 4 years Virginia; Richard Baron to Edward Wasborough, 4 years Virginia; Roger Bishop to Nathan Smith, 5 years Virginia; David Evans to William Worgan, 4 years Virginia; Reece Jones to same, 4 years Virginia. (BR).

September. Administration of George Garrett of St. Botolph Bishopsgate, London, and of the ship *Mermaid*, whose son, John Garrett, was in Virginia. (AW).

September. Administration of Peter Rowland of Shadwell, Middlesex, who died in Virginia. (AW).

?September. Petition of John Fussell for relief. The loyalty of his father to the King ruined the petitioner who was obliged to send his two sons as common servants to Virginia. (SP Dom).

2 October. The following apprenticed in Bristol: Mary Gay to William Worgan, 4 years Virginia; Edward Washer to Matthew Jordan, 4 years Virginia; Richard Wattkins to Andrew Morgan, 4 years Nevis. (BR).

3 October. The following apprenticed in Bristol: Henry Perry to Roger Welstead, 6 years Nevis; George Morgan to Nicholas Smith, 4 years Virginia. (BR).

5 October. The following apprenticed in Bristol: Robert Fletcher to Thomas Sylvester, 4 years Virginia; William Court to Edward Gibbes, 4 years Virginia; John Court to same, 4 years Virginia; Henry Grazier to same, 4 years Virginia; Joseph Strickland to same, 4 years Virginia; Richard Hogchitch to Walter Broadhurst, 5 years Virginia; Richard Jarvis to same, 5 years Virginia; James Hogchitch to same, 5 years Virginia; Richard Priestly to same, 5 years Virginia; Arthur Scriven to Nathan Smith, 4 years Virginia; Thomas Bayly to same, 5 years Virginia; James Griffen to John Griffen, 4 years Virginia; Robert Phillips to Thomas Chamberlaine, 4 years Virginia; William Sydenham to same, 7 years Virginia; Israell Watham to same, 4 years Virginia. (BR).

7 October. The following apprenticed in Bristol: John Light to Brian Tandy, 4 years Virginia; Margaret Trippick to same, 4 years Virginia; Elizabeth Blackwell to William Carey, 4 years Nevis; Giles Barrett to Thomas Pope, 4 years Virginia. (BR).

8 October. Richard Batt of St. Katherine by the Tower, London, haberdasher, found guilty of unlawfully conveying James Simmons, apprentice of Thomas Ball, to the *George* intending to convey him to Virginia and sell him. (VM 83/3).

8 October. The following apprenticed in Bristol: Bartholomew Avenell to John Phillipps, 4 years Nevis; Richard Avenell to same, 4 years Nevis; Anne Roberts to Jonas Holwy, 4 years Virginia; Grace Jones to William Foord, 5 years Virginia; Walter Evans to Isaac Davis, 4 years Virginia; Thomas Knight to Samuell Clarke, 4 years Nevis; Henry Reece to Symon Stephens, 4 years Nevis. (BR).

12 October. The following apprenticed in Bristol: Samuell Ostler to William Jelfe, 4 years Virginia; George Young to Sylvester Davis, 4 years Virginia. (BR).

14 October. The following apprenticed in Bristol: Robert Davis to Henry Baker, 4 years Virginia; John Jacob to same, 4 years Virginia. (BR).

16 October. The following apprenticed in Bristol: Edward Mills to John Seward, 4 years Virginia; William Hill to William Watters, 4 years Virginia; Thomas Bowden to Simon Stephens, 8 years Virginia; Margarett Farmer to Samuell Pilsworth, 4 years Virginia. (BR).

17 October. The following apprenticed in Bristol: Richard Gill to Phillip Hanger, 4 years Virginia; William Carter to Robert Arnoll, 4 years Barbados; William Meeke to John Sanders, 6 years Virginia. (BR).

17 October-4 November. Shippers by the *Loving Friendship* of Newcastle, Mr. Thomas Greene, bound from Newcastle for Maryland: Ralph Grey, Mark Milbank, George Wallis. (PRO: E190/195/13).

19 October. The following apprenticed in Bristol: Thomas Willson to Robert Arnoll, 4 years Virginia; Richard Williams to John Brooke, 4 years Barbados; John Vincent to William Morgan, 4 years Nevis; Robert Carver to William Bush, 4 years Nevis. (BR).

20 October. The following apprenticed in Bristol: Theodorus Lewis to Thomas Pope, 4 years Virginia; John Beare to John Genn, 4 years Virginia. (BR).

24 October. The following apprenticed in Bristol: John Wallway to George Mason, 4 years Virginia; John Williams to Robert Williams, 4 years Maryland; John Merrick to Thomas Starkes, 4 years Virginia; William Wilkins to William Morgan, 4 years Virginia; Joane Watts to same, 4 years Virginia; Samuell Warner to Nathaniell Smith, 1½ years Virginia; Susannah Abbott to Robert

Williams, 4 years Virginia; William Norcutt to Patrick Spence, 4 years Virginia. (BR).

26 October. The following apprenticed in Bristol: Henry Rogers to Thomas Pope, 4 years Virginia; Henry Williams to John Lysons, 4 years Virginia. (BR).

27 October. The following apprenticed in Bristol: Elizabeth Arnold to Arthur Duck, 4 years Virginia. (BR).

28 October. The following apprenticed in Bristol: Moses Jones to John Sanders, 4 years Virginia; Nicholas Stafford to Edward Morris, 4 years Nevis. (BR).

29 October. The following apprenticed in Bristol: Edward Short to William Backworth, 5 years Virginia; Richard Thomkins to William Andrews, 4 years Virginia; Howell Francis to Nicholas Tyler, 4 years Virginia; William Wilkes to Thomas Pope, 7 years Virginia. (BR).

30 October. The following apprenticed in Bristol: Mabell Uxley to Ann Ring, 4 years Virginia; Thomas Boules to Martin Wakely, 7 years Virginia. (BR).

31 October. The following apprenticed in Bristol: Joseph Gouldsney to Thomas Pope, 4 years Virginia. (BR).

October. Administration of Joshua Meriton of Virginia. (AW).

October. Administration of James Wheeler of Maryland, bachelor. (AW).

October. Administration with will of Philip Gibbs of Bristol, bound for Virginia. (AW).

2 November. The following apprenticed in Bristol: Anne Johnson to James Newland, 5 years Virginia; Elizabeth Williams to John Saunders, 4 years Virginia. (BR).

3 November. The following apprenticed in Bristol: Rowland Williams to Christopher Berry, 4 years Virginia. (BR).

4 November. The following apprenticed in Bristol: Mary Bull to William Olliffe, 3 years Virginia; George Turley to John Henry, 4 years Virginia; William Ferryman to John Baynam, 4 years Barbados; William Howard to Henry Baker, 4 years Virginia. (BR).

6 November. The following apprenticed in Bristol: Wattkin Andrewes to Robert Fouler, 4 years Barbados. (BR).

9 November. The following apprenticed in Bristol: Richard Andrewes to Richard Sweete, 5 years Barbados; George Jones to John Bodenham, 4 years Nevis; Jane Reece to same, 4 years Nevis; John Lung to same, 6 years Nevis; James Richards to Ellis Poole, 3 years Barbados; Thomas Wickham to same, 3 years Barbados; John Lambert to John Abbott, 4 years Nevis; Owen Jones to Richard Earle, 4 years Barbados. (BR).

10 November. The following apprenticed in Bristol: Elizabeth Bolton to John Abbott, 4 years Nevis. (BR).

11 November. The following apprenticed in Bristol: Thomas Hughes to John Bodenham, 8 years Nevis; Morgan Williams to same, 8 years Nevis. (BR).

(11 November). Mary Bateman of London, spinster, daughter and heir of John Bateman of London and of Patuxent River, Maryland, haberdasher, deceased, and of his wife Mary, afterwards widow of Henry Scarborough of North Walsham, Norfolk, gent, exhibits a deed of 18 November 1674 whereby Resurrection Manor in Maryland was conveyed to Richard Perry of Patuxent River. (LMCD).

13 November. The following apprenticed in Bristol: Thomas Nilie to John Ansell, 5 years Nevis. (BR).

14 November. The following apprenticed in Bristol: Edward Jones to John Bodenham, 4 years Nevis. (BR).

16 November. Shipper by the *Adventure* of Whitby, Mr. Robert Raine, bound from Whitby for Maryland: John Peckett. (PRO: E190/195/12).

16 November. The following apprenticed in Bristol: Edmund Rogers to John Bodenham, 4 years [Nevis]; Edward Lewis to Edward Morris, 8 years Nevis. (BR).

17 November. The following apprenticed in Bristol: Richard Sandell to William Neale, 4 years Barbados; James Kendall to John Bodenham, 5 years Barbados or Nevis; William Morgan to Thomas Bodenham, 4 years Nevis. (BR).

18 November. The following apprenticed in Bristol: Anthony Coles to John Bodenham, 4 years Nevis. (BR).

19 November. The following apprenticed in Bristol: John Clarke to John Hand, 4 years Nevis; John Jones to Richard Earle, 4 years Barbados; John Roswell to William Cooke, 4 years Barbados. (BR).

23 November. The following apprenticed in Bristol: Robert Browne to James Lewis, 4 years Barbados; William Stuckey to same, 4 years Barbados. (BR).

24 November. The following apprenticed in Bristol: Joane Jones to William Cary, 4 years Barbados; Elizabeth Gardener to same, 4 years Barbados; William Avent to John Ansell, 4 years Nevis. (BR).

25 November. The following apprenticed in Bristol: Thomas Bull to William Crocker, 4 years Nevis. (BR).

25 November 1674-11 March 1675. Shippers by the *Industry*, Mr. Phineas Hide, bound from London for Virginia: John Travis, George Layfield, Benjamin Beake, Charles Stepkins, Lucie Knightley, William Mead, Thomas Parker. (PRO: E190/62/5).

26 November. The following apprenticed in Bristol: Richard Jones to John Hand, 4 years Nevis; Matthew Bland to Samuell Clarke, 4 years Nevis; Saunder Judicott to John Adams, 4 years Nevis. (BR).

28 November. The following apprenticed in Bristol: Joseph Horton to John Hare, 4 years Nevis; George Sterte to Richard Earle, 4 years Barbados. (BR).

30 November. The following apprenticed in Bristol: James Sprake to Samuell Clarke, 4 years Nevis. (BR).

November. Administration of Simon Cole of Boston, New England, who died at sea, bachelor. (AW).

November. Probate of will of Henry Henderson of York River, Virginia, who died in Clerkenwell, Middlesex. (AW).

1 December. The following apprenticed in Bristol: William Lawrence to John Hand, 4 years Nevis; Edward Ansell to John Ansell, 4 years Nevis; William Chedsey to same, 4 years Nevis; Edward Thomas to Griffin Lawrence, 4 years Nevis. (BR).

5 December. The following apprenticed in Bristol: Nathan Bayly to William Hedges, 5 years Nevis. (BR).

9 December. The following apprenticed in Bristol: Henry Reekes to John Knight, 4 years Nevis; Thomas Ellison to same, 4 years Nevis; Richard Browne to John Bodenham, 4 years Nevis; Richard Richardson to same, 4 years Nevis. (BR).

10 December. The following apprenticed in Bristol: Thomas Fitzgerald to John Knight, 4 years Nevis. (BR).

11 December. The following apprenticed in Bristol: Thomas Preece to Thomas Bartlett, 4 years Nevis; Thomas Haines to same, 4 years Nevis; Jeremiah Rose to same, 4 years Nevis; John Richardson to John Adams, 6 years Nevis; Peter Gill to George Morris, 4 years Nevis; Alexander Killman to John Ansell, 4 years Nevis. (BR).

12 December. The following apprenticed in Bristol: Edward Puberly to Edward Cooke, 3 years Nevis; George Jenkins to Thomas Wright, 4 years Nevis; John Parry to John Gill, 7 years Nevis. (BR).

17 December. The following apprenticed in Bristol: Joane Edwards to Nathaniell Jefferys, 4 years Nevis; Thomas Woodley to William Cary, 4 years Barbados. (BR).

18 December. The following apprenticed in Bristol: Howell Thomas to Michaell Perry, 4 years Nevis; William Edwards to Charles Hopkins, 6 years Nevis. (BR).

19 December. The following apprenticed in Bristol: Jane Parry to Nathaniell Jeffereys, 4 years Nevis; Anne Hunt to same, 4 years Nevis; Lewis Sherive to

John Gill, 4 years Nevis; Peter Sherive to same, 4 years Nevis; Nicholas Aust to John Rosewell, 4 years Nevis; Llewellin Morgan to Andrew Vivers, 4 years [Nevis]. (BR).

22 December. The following apprenticed in Bristol: George Morris to Benjamin Viner, 4 years Nevis; Thomas Gengill to Michaell Hunt, 6 years Nevis. (BR).

23 December. The following apprenticed in Bristol: John Pester to John Poore, 5 years Barbados. (BR).

24 December. The following apprenticed in Bristol: Reece Morgan to John Knight, 4 years Nevis. (BR).

29 December. The following apprenticed in Bristol: Sarah Trevord to Mary Slaughter, 4 years Nevis; William Gramford to George Buse, 4 years Nevis. (BR).

29 December 1674-10 February 1675. Shippers by the *Francis*, Mr. John Warner, bound from London for Virginia: Robert Bray, John Ewing, John Kent, Phillip Forster, Benjamin Peake, Charles Stepkin, John Ludwell, Samuell James, William Mead, Samuell Young. (PRO: E190/62/5, 62/1).

30 December. The following apprenticed in Bristol: Richard Fisher to Phillip Cooke, 4 years Montserrat; Sarah Cullymore to Samuell Baker, 7 years Nevis; John Froud to William Hedges, 4 years Nevis; John Woods to same, 4 years Nevis. (BR).

30 December. Shippers by the *St. Nicholas*, Mr. John Johnson, bound from London for Maryland: William Johnson, William Tigh. (PRO: E190/62/5).

31 December. The following apprenticed in Bristol: Evan Davis to John Foord, 4 years Nevis; William Greenall to John Gill, 4 years Nevis; Anthony Vavely to William Morris, 4 years Nevis. (BR).

December. Probate of will of Edmund White of St. Giles Cripplegate, London, whose son-in-law, Humphrey Davie, was in Boston, New England. (AW).

1675

1 January. The following apprenticed in Bristol: John Ballard to Phillip Cooke, 4 years Montserrat; Thomas Casum to Charles Hopkins, 4 years Montserrat. (BR).

2-16 January. Shippers by the *North Boare*, Mr. Bury Anderson, bound from London for Virginia: William Mead, Peter Hanson. (PRO: E190/62/5).

4 January. Shipper by the *Catherine* of Poole, Mr. John Skues, bound from Poole for Maryland: George Carew. (PRO: E190/882/5).

7 January. The following apprenticed in Bristol: Edward Minord to Thomas Cole, 4 years Nevis. (BR).

8 January. The following apprenticed in Bristol: Edward Lewis to William Morris, 3 years Nevis; Penelope Grubb to Christopher Andrewes, 4 years Nevis; Elizabeth Forley to same, 5 years Nevis. (BR).

9 January-26 March. Shippers by the *Rebecca*, Mr. Thomas Larimore, bound from London for Virginia: William Prescott, Thomas Gold, Thomas Page, Thomas Athowe, Samuell Shute, Thomas Dunster. (PRO: E190/62/5, 62/1).

11 January. The following apprenticed in Bristol: Robert Royer to Christopher Andrewes, 4 years Nevis or Antigua; Charles Roe to George Buse, 4 years Nevis. (BR).

14 January. The following apprenticed in Bristol: Susannah Clarke to Edward Yeamans, 4 years Nevis; Katherine Jones to same, 4 years Nevis. (BR).

15 January. The following apprenticed in Bristol: Thomas Woodward to Richard Wastfield, 4 years Nevis. (BR).

16 January. The following apprenticed in Bristol: Edmond Day to Thomas Mills, 4 years Nevis or Antigua. (BR).

18 January. The following apprenticed in Bristol: Samuel Hurlestone to John Gill, 4 years Nevis; John Anderton to same, 4 years Nevis. (BR).

19 January. Shipper by the *Fortune*, Mr. Olla Michalls, bound from London for Virginia: William Paggen. (PRO: E190/62/5).

21 January. The following apprenticed in Bristol: Ann Buggin to Marke Chappell, 4 years Nevis; Roger Collins to same, 4 years Nevis. (BR).

21 January. Deposition by George Copping of London, scrivener aged 37, that John Blany of Lynn, New England, gent, became indebted to Ralph King of Watford, Hertfordshire, deceased, by bond of 8 April 1659. Sarah Neale, aged 65, sole executrix of her husband Andrew Neale, draper, deceased, who was

234

executor of the said Ralph King, deposes that the bond was not satisfied. Jacob Jeffson of New England is appointed attorney. (LMCD).

22 January. The following apprenticed in Bristol: Gabriell Allen to Edward Yeamans, 5 years Nevis; John Haines to Christopher Andrewes, 4 years Nevis. (BR).

22 January. Western Circuit prisoners reprieved to be transported to Barbados. Hampshire: Nicholas Knight of Penton; Edward Sutton of Basingstoke. Somerset: James Buxton of St. Cuthbert, Wells; John Sutton of Wedmore; John Sperring of St. Cuthbert, Wells, tailor; John Blatchley of Wedmore. Wiltshire: Robert Combes of Hilperton; Robert Shargold of Shrewton. Unspecified: Thomas Leeke of London, silversmith; Robert Hutchings of Belfast, Ireland. (PRO: C66/3178/15).

23 January. The following apprenticed in Bristol: William Reed to George Bewes, 4 years Antigua; George Burford to Anthony Hedges, 4 years Montserrat. (BR).

25 January. The following apprenticed in Bristol: Leversedge Huxley to Humphry Nason, 4 years Nevis; Edward Wolfe to Marke Chappell, 7 years Nevis. (BR).

27 January. The following apprenticed in Bristol: William Thomas to Thomas Mills, 4 years Nevis. (BR).

28 January. The following apprenticed in Bristol: Thomas Stillard to John Luxford, 4 years Nevis; Jacob Johnsons to same, 7 years Nevis; John Parmiter to Richard Gottley, 3 years Nevis; James Herring to same, 4 years Nevis; Jane Martin to Henry Baker, 5 years Nevis. (BR).

29-31 January. Shippers by the *King David*, Mr. Adrian Francen, bound from London for Virginia: Thomas Barker, William Depester. (PRO: E190/62/5).

January. Administration of Thomas Mason of Virginia, bachelor. (AW).

January. Probate of will of John Allen of Holborn, Middlesex, who died in Maryland. (AW).

January. Probate of will of Henry Knight of Maryland. (AW).

3 February. The following apprenticed in Bristol: Anne Powell to Nathaniell Cary, 4 years Nevis. (BR).

4 February. The following apprenticed in Bristol: John Hullett to Stephen Hubbard, 4 years Nevis. (BR).

5 February. The following apprenticed in Bristol: John West to Christopher Andrewes, 4 years Nevis; Thomas Martin to William Morgan, 4 years Nevis. (BR).

6 February. Petition of Francis Foxcroft, master of the *Carolus Secundus*, John Harlow, master of the *Charitas*, and Joroen Jeroenson, master of the *Liefde*, that as Dutch subjects they have brought over their ships and families desiring to sail to Virginia. Passports granted. (APC).

6 February. The following apprenticed in Bristol: Thomas Wells to Richard Gottly, 4 years Nevis; Thomas Rossome to Stephen Hubbard, 4 years Nevis. (BR).

10 February. The following apprenticed in Bristol: William Fisher to Thomas Hobson, 4 years New England. (BR).

11 February. The following apprenticed in Bristol: Jane Taylor to Stephen Hubbart, 4 years Nevis. (BR).

12 February. The following apprenticed in Bristol: Katherine Purvice to John England, 4 years Nevis. (BR).

15 February. Newgate prisoners reprieved to be transported to Barbados. London: William Sadler; Jonathan Bates; Mary Floyd; John Corbett; William Cox; William Hopkins; Elizabeth Snead, spinster; Margaret Dealtry, spinster; Peter Dalton; Elizabeth Green, spinster; Edward Staniell; Thomas Collins; Thomas Desborough; Joan Bickerton, spinster, alias wife of John; Thomas Jones; Henry Robinson; Richard Bowen; Seth Holdsworth; Robert Kerby; Hugh Shinningfield; Simon Halifax; Daniel Clarke. Middlesex: Elizabeth Howell of St. Martin in the Fields, spinster; Samuel Carrell alias Kaurhell of the same; George Babbidge of the same; Katherine Ogle, spinster, alias wife of Thomas Ogle of the same; Thomas Sadler of the same; John Whitwell of St. Paul Covent Garden; Elizabeth Wright of St. Clement Danes, spinster; Susan Taylor of the same, widow; Elizabeth Lloyd of the same; Joan Childersley, wife of Thomas Childersley of the same; Thomas Christofer of St. Giles in the Fields; Elizabeth Vaughan of the same, widow; Margaret Ransum, spinster, alias wife of Robert Inman of the same; Edith Collett of St. Margaret Westminster, widow; William Ashley of Paddington; Edward Rivis of Paddington; Matthew Coppinger of St. Giles Cripplegate; John Harrison of Isleworth; William Olden of the same; Thomas Collins of Cranford; William Read of Clerkenwell; John Serjeant of Stepney; Richard Green of the same; John Spencer of Finchley; Charles Wilmer of St. Botolph Aldgate; John Taylor of St. Andrew Holborn; Daniel Hocknell of Enfield; John Simonds of the same; William Hartnes of the same; John North of St. Mary Savoy or St. Clement Danes; Margaret Wadlow of St. Botolph Aldersgate, spinster; Mary West of Tottenham; John Seely of Norwood; John White alias Williams alias Matchett of Harmondsworth. (PRO: C66/3173/3).

16 February. The following apprenticed in Bristol: Rice Griffen to Thomas Hollard, 4 years New England. (BR).

18 February. The following apprenticed in Bristol: Robert Legg to John Shewell, 4 years Barbados; Nathaniell Boyer to same, 4 years Barbados. (BR).

19 February. Shipper by the *Dove* of Plymouth bound from Plymouth for New England: John Trenicke. (PRO: E190/1041/1).

20 February-2 March. Shippers by the *Golden Falcon*, Mr. Edward Peirce, bound from London for Virginia: John Percy, Robert Beverley, Francis Plumsted, Samuell Ongley, Thomas Cowell, Samuell Young, John Swan, Robert Terrell, William Sare, Samuell Welden. (PRO: E190/62/5).

20 February-16 March. Shippers by the *Adventure*, Mr. John Balston, bound from London for New England: Hezechiah Usher, Isaac Barton. (PRO: E190/62/1).

22-25 February. Shippers by the *James*, Mr. John Warner, bound from London for Virginia: John Willford, Edward Howell. (PRO: E190/62/1).

22-25 February. Shipper by the *Hope*, Mr. William Singleton, bound from London for Virginia: Mark Mortimer. (PRO: E190/62/5).

23 February. Shipper by the *Fortune*, Mr. Edward Batt, bound from London for Virginia: Thomas Parker. (PRO: E190/62/5).

23-26 February. Shippers by the *Unicorn*, Mr. Samuel Pensax, bound from London for Virginia: Hugh Mortimer, Richard Lone. (PRO: E190/62/5).

23 February-9 March. Shippers by the *Humphrey & Elizabeth*, Mr. Robert Medford, bound from London for Virginia: John Kent, William Allen, Noah Floyd, William Dolby, John Haggett, Phillip Forster, Thomas Rawlinson, William Juxon, Thomas Lane, Henry Meese, George Richards, Robert Warner, Thomas Parker, William Paggen, Arthur Bayley, Peter Jones, John Jefferys, Joseph Hill. (PRO: E190/62/5).

24 February. The following apprenticed in Bristol: Francis Baker to Thomas Hardwick, 4 years Nevis; Deborah Jefferies to same, 4 years Nevis. (BR).

25 February. Pass granted to Samuel Pensax, master of the *Unicorn* of London, to sail from London for Virginia with 26 men. (APC).

25 February. The following apprenticed in Bristol: William Robins to Thomas Hollard, 4 years New England. (BR).

25 February-15 April. Shippers by the *Society*, Mr. Edward Clements, bound from London for New England: Abraham Jesson, Edward Floyd, John Matthews, John West, Giles Shute, Richard Shipton, John Chudworth, George Roach, Thomas Firman, Francis Parsons, William Parker, Edward Hull, Edward Man, Thomas Elkin, John Child, Henry Ashurst, David Sidney, Noah Floyd, Thomas Shaw, Thomas Jeffery, Thomas Ball, John Parker, William Dye, Ralph Gibbon, William Window, James Sotheby, Nathaniel Greene, John Jackson, John Margetts, Maximilian Gore, Arthur Sedgwick, Peter Gray, Edward Mumford, Samuell Butler, William Sotheby, Gerrard Roberts, Alexander Hosea, William Sherley, James Leman, Thomas Lane, Christopher Marshall, Edward Merriweather, John Harwood, Samuell Sheafe, Thomas

Sherley, Charles Sweeting, Robert Woolley, Thomas Ruck, William Hattrell, Spencer Pigott, Nathaniel Byfield, Christopher Gore, William Antleby, Samuell Tatum, William Crowch, Edward Sidney, John Combe, William Smith, Anthony Ringwood, William Hulls, John Boake, Edward Shaston, Thomas Lone, Henry Salter, Thomas Jorden, William Williams, William Webb, James Hayes, William Mead, Thomas Sontley, George Scott, James Eyton, Richard Lloyd, John Hickson [or Frickson], William Dingley. (PRO: E190/62/5).

26 February. The following apprenticed in Bristol: Richard Stone to John Moore, 5 years New England. (BR).

February. Shippers by the *Queen of Sweden*, Mr. Henry Verburgh, bound from London for Virginia: Nathaniell Paine, William Depester. (PRO: E190/62/5).

February. Administration of Robert Cubitt of Virginia, bachelor. (AW).

February. Probate of will of Benjamin Fenn of New England, who died in Milford, Connecticut. (AW).

1-9 March. Shippers by the *Submission*, Mr. Robert Bristow, bound from London for New England: Daniel Allen, Matthew Roper, Thomas Doxey. (PRO: E190/62/1).

2-17 March. Shippers by the *Relief*, Mr. John Tully, from London bound for Maryland: William Barrett, John Parsons, George Banister, William Mead, Nicholas Lowe. (PRO: E190/62/5).

4 March. The following apprenticed in Bristol: Charles Powell to Thomas Lewellin, 4 years Nevis; John Stout to same, 4 years Nevis; Llewis Price to John Templeman, 4 years Barbados. (BR).

5-9 March. Shippers by the *Joanna*, Mr. John Holmes, from London for Virginia: Richard Drinkwater, William Goulston. (PRO: E190/62/5).

5-24 March. Shippers by the *Owners Delight*, Mr. Thomas Phelps, bound from London for Maryland: John Broome, Robert Taverner, Robert White, Thomas Bowne, William Withers. (PRO: E190/62/5).

11 March. The following apprenticed in Bristol: Joane Harris to John Shewell, 4 years Barbados; Mellisant Try to same, 4 years Barbados; Elizabeth Phillips to same, 4 years Barbados; Emanuell Stringer to John Nicholas, 4 years Barbados. (BR).

11 March. Shippers by the *Gift*, Mr. Peter Bosse, bound from London for Virginia: Thomas Roberts, Edward Man, Gerrard Robertson, William Meade. (PRO: E190/62/5).

13 March. Shipper by the *Little Bartlett*, Mr. George Purvis, bound from London for Virginia: Benjamin Bradley. (PRO: E190/62/5).

1675

15 March. The following apprenticed in Bristol: Richard Phelps to John Nicholas, 4 years Barbados; Margaret Mills to John Templeman, 6 years Barbados; Martin Yeamanson to William Briscoe, 4 years Barbados. (BR).

16 March. Shippers by the *Canary Bird*, Mr. John Lucombe, bound from London to Virginia: John Brames, John Haggett, Edmond Harman, William Mead. (PRO: E190/62/5).

17-18 March. Shippers by the *Grane*, Mr. Richard Angell, bound from London for Maryland: James Brames, William Mead. (PRO: E190/62/5).

17-22 March. Shippers by the *Friendship*, Mr. John Hull, bound from London for New England: Ezechiell Hutchinson, Thomas Roberts, John Dyne, Edward Bromfield. (PRO: E190/62/1).

17-26 March. Shippers by the *Duke of York*, Mr. John Purvis, bound from London for Virginia: William Atwood, Thomas Pouley, John Jefferys, Henry Mees, Symon Master, Francis Camfield, William Garfoote, Robert Beverley, Samuell Botley, Thomas Hasted, John Kent, Richard Hancock, Gawen Corbin, Henry Cornish, James Lordell, Isaac Houblon, James Hayes, Samuell Putt, William Meade, Peter Jones. (PRO: E190/62/5).

17-27 March. Shippers by the *William & Mary*, Mr. Thomas Smith, bound from London for Virginia: William Storke, William Bides, Maurice Moseley, Samuell Read, Nicholas Roberts, Richard Lone, Thomas Spencer, William Wavell, Thomas Parker. (PRO: E190/62/5).

19-20 March. Shippers by the *Hopewell*, Mr. John Rudds, bound from London for Virginia: Thomas Grindon, Thomas Sands, Richard Ballard, John Jennings, Thomas Parker, Richard Walton. (PRO: E190/62/5).

20-26 March. Shippers by the *Griffin*, Mr. Robert Griffin, bound from London for Virginia: Richard Yardley, Richard Lone, Thomas Jervase, Thomas Parker, Wilbert Daniell, Benjamin Hobson, John Morrice, Benjamin Thorowgood, Samuell Shute. (PRO: E190/62/5).

20-26 March. Shippers by the *Good Hope*, Mr. George Heathcott, bound from London for New York: Joseph Strutt, Humphrey Willis, John Eburne, John Harwood, Benjamin Hewling. (PRO: E190/62/1).

21-27 March. Shippers by the *Rebecca*, Mr. Eveling, bound from London to Virginia: Francis Cranfield, John Hawes, Thomas Hammersley, Mary Righton, Thomas Parker. (PRO: E190/62/5).

23-26 March. Shippers by the *Happy Return* of Plymouth bound from Plymouth for New England: David Teage, Thomas Creese. (PRO: E190/1041/1).

26-31 March. Shippers by the *Providence*, Mr. John Waite, bound from London for Virginia: Edward Blake, Nicholas Lock, Benjamin Hobson, Edward Rowland, Samuell Young, Edward Carter, John Jennings. (PRO: E190/62/5).

239

26 March-6 April. Shippers by the *Joseph & Benjamin*, Mr. Gregory Marlow, bound from London for Virginia: George Cornish, James Godfrey. (PRO: E190/62/5).

27-28 March. Shippers by the *Constance*, Mr. Samuell Edwards, bound from London for Virginia: Edward Lemon, Thomas Lloyd. (PRO: E190/62/5).

27-31 March. Shippers by the *Symon & Francis*, Mr. Daniell Pensax, bound from London for Virginia: John Blenton, Samuell Scott, Isaac Merritt, John Preston. (PRO: E190/62/5).

27 March-3 April. Shippers by the *Pelican*, Mr. John Bowman, bound from London for Virginia: William Hattrill, Thomas Toulson, Thomas Parker, Thomas Wetheridge, William Welsh, Joseph Rooksby. (PRO: E190/62/5).

28 March-2 April. Shippers by the *Phoenix*, Mr. Richard Pidgeon, bound from London for Virginia: James Jancey, Thomas Grindon, Thomas Parker. (PRO: E190/62/5).

29 March. The following apprenticed in Bristol: Thomas Edwards to Edward Herbert, 4 years Montserrat. (BR).

30 March. Shippers by the *Truelove*, Mr. Robert Symonds, bound from London for Virginia: John Cooper, Thomas Parker, Michaell Clipsham. (PRO: E190/62/5).

30 March. Shipper by the *Priscilla* of Plymouth bound from Plymouth for New England: Sir John Frederick. (PRO: E190/1041/1).

30 March. The following apprenticed in Bristol: David Griffeth to Bartholomew Jefford, 4 years Antigua, Montserrat or Nevis; Reece Gwinne to same, 4 years Antigua, Montserrat or Nevis. (BR).

31 March. Shipper by the *Liberty*, Mr. Thomas Beale, bound from London for Virginia: Richard Bankes. (PRO: E190/62/5).

March. John Dunfield to work until he can find a master willing to carry him beyond the sea. (Bridewell).

March. Administration of Jonathan Newell of Virginia. (AW).

March. Administration of Stephen Dring of Deptford, Kent, who died in Virginia. (AW).

1 April. Shippers by the *May Flower*, Mr. William Richardson, bound from London for Maryland: Ralph Ingram, William Mead. (PRO: E190/62/5).

1 April. Shippers by the *Four Anns*, Mr. Thomas Scott, bound from London for New England: John Harwood, David Sidney. (PRO: E190/62/5).

2-18 April. Shippers by the *Swan*, Mr. Stephen Dring, bound from London for Virginia: Mathew Page, Cuthbert Potter, Sir Thomas Chicheley. (PRO: E190/62/5).

7-9 April. Shippers by the *Riga Merchant*, Mr. Joseph Ball, bound from London for Virginia: Richard Glover, John Shorter, William Mead. (PRO: E190/62/5).

8 April-4 May. Shippers by the *Sampson*, Mr. Richard Spragg, bound from London for New England: William Parker, Francis Parsons, Henry Hobbs, John Potter, Arthur Sedgwick, James Rosewell, Stephen Humphries. (PRO: E190/62/1).

9 April. Shipper by the *Adventure*, Mr. James Dowell, bound from London for New England: John Hunlock. (PRO: E190/62/1).

11-14 April. Shippers by the *Constant Friendship*, Mr. William Wheatley, bound from London for Virginia: Joseph Sparrow, George Sturman, Edward Lloyd, Luke Read, Thomas Parker. (PRO: E190/62/5).

13-24 April. Shippers by the *Prince*, Mr. Robert Conway, bound from London for Virginia: Matthew Carleton, Edward Blake, Edward Leaman, Nicholas Harrison, Sir Thomas Chicheley, Lawrence Chappell, James Rayley, Thomas Parker, John Jennings, William Dingley, Nowell Bassano, William Mead, John Bowerman. (PRO: E190/62/5).

17 April. The following apprenticed in Bristol: Gabriell Joice to John Shewell, 6 years Nevis. (BR).

18-20 April. Shippers by the *Mary*, Mr. William Knott, bound from London for Virginia: Thomas Warren, Henry Foreman, Thomas Parker. (PRO: E190/62/5).

21 April. The following apprenticed in Bristol: Joseph Gooding to Paull Mohun, 4 years Nevis. (BR).

24 April. The following apprenticed in Bristol: John Stoute to Richard Reece, 4 years Nevis. (BR).

24 April-7 May. Shippers by the *Olive Branch*, Mr. Clement Ingram, bound from London for New England: George Cole, John Rice, Thomas Gardner, Thomas Gerrard, John Child, Joseph Hayes, Richard Hutchinson. (PRO: E190/62/5).

26-29 April. Shippers by the *Adventure*, Mr. John Woolley, bound from London to New England: William Limbrey, Paul Allestry. (PRO: E190/62/1).

28 April. The following apprenticed in Bristol: Esekiell Langley to Thomas Harris, 4 years Nevis. (BR).

28 April-2 December. Depositions in London re the voyage of the *Golden Phoenix*, Mr. Richard Pidgeon, from London to Virginia in 1674 and her return to London in 1675. Deponents include John Conyers of Virginia, planter aged 23, who was born at St. Sepulchre's, London. (EA).

29 April-9 May. Shippers by the *Wheatsheaf*, Mr. James Strong, bound from London for Virginia: Edward Lloyd, Barnaby Dunch, Lawrence Fullone, William Mead, Samuell Young. (PRO: E190/62/5).

30 April. The following apprenticed in Bristol: William Cotton to William Shuter, 4 years Jamaica. (BR).

30 April. Shipper by the *Diamond*, Mr. Richard Griffith, bound from London for New York: John Jennings. (PRO: E190/62/5).

2 May. Shipper by the *Mary*, Mr. James Pulman, bound from London for New England: Jonathan Haddock. (PRO: E190/62/5).

3 May. The following apprenticed in Bristol: William Jones to Moses Jones, 4 years Nevis. (BR).

4 May. Deposition by John Powell of London, loriner aged 20, that John Hunlocke of New England, merchant, became indebted to Walter Moncke of London, draper, by bond of 29 March 1675. (LMCD).

4 May. The following apprenticed in Bristol: William Harris to William Martin, 4 years Jamaica. (BR).

4-16 May. Shippers by the *Ruby*, Mr. Julius Anderson, bound from London for New England: Edward Edmonds, Christopher Gore, Richard Goodlad, William Kirwood, Phillip Manning, John Blewett. (PRO: E190/62/5).

7 May. The following apprenticed in Bristol: Howell Thomas to Joseph Lewis, 4 years Nevis; Daniell Lawson to Andrew Vivers, 4 years Nevis; Alexander Morgan to George Maggs, 4 years Barbados; Elizabeth Harrison to Arthur Grant, 4 years Jamaica; Mary Hawkins to William Shotter, 4 years Jamaica. (BR).

8 May. The following apprenticed in Bristol: Charles Prattin to John Creed, 5 years Nevis. (BR).

8 May-5 June. Shippers by the *Society*, Mr. Benjamin Moore, bound from London for New England: Jane Bodley, George Pochin, Christopher Taylor, Robert Wynn, Edward Hubbold, Thomas Stonley, Edward Jones, Thomas Firman, Robert Hooker, Benjamin Moore, Christopher Marshall, Phillip Poole, Thomas Jenner, Warwick Evans, Henry Rose, Henry Loades, Thomas Tookey, Valentine Adams, Thomas Woodford, Edmond Jones, John Harwood, John Freeman, Thomas Hill, Samuell Shute, Richard Shipton. (PRO: E190/62/5).

11 May-3 June. Shippers by the *Zebulon*, Mr. William Greenough, bound from London for New England: Thomas Glover, Benjamin Hewling, Edward Man, Edward Montforth, John Barwood, Benjamin Peake, Joseph Hubbard, Thomas Foweracre, John Lewin, Peter Bent, James Rawling. (PRO: E190/62/1).

12-24 May. Shippers by the *Edistow Dogger*, Mr. John Cummings, bound from London for Carolina: Earl of Shaftesbury, Richard Chandler, Lords Proprietors of Carolina, William West, Edward Thornburgh. (PRO: E190/62/5).

13 May. The following apprenticed in Bristol: Thomas Jones to Edward Cooke, 4 years Nevis. (BR).

14 May. The following apprenticed in Bristol: William Powell to Henry Baker, 4 years New England; William Morris to same, 4 years New England; John Robert to same, 4 years New England; Thomas Waynehouse to Samuell Tipton, 4 years New England; Evan Davis to same, 4 years New England; Andrew Lugg to same, 4 years New England. (BR).

15 May. The following apprenticed in Bristol: Anthony Wood to William Martin, 4 years Virginia; Joan Buddin to same, 4 years Jamaica; William Cosser to Maxfield Walter, 4 years Jamaica. (BR).

15 May-6 June. Shippers by the *Friendship*, Mr. Zachariah Long, bound from London for New England: Paul Allestrey, Robert Buckle, Edward Hull, John Wing, Thomas Elkin, Thomas Ball, William Wood, Bartholomew Parr, John Ballot, Noah Lloyd, Joseph Scott, Abraham Jesson, John Winer, Robert Hooker, Robert Woolley, William Baxter, Thomas Saltonstall, John Slater, Hezechiah Usher, Samuell Shcafe, Richard Roberts, Daniell All——, James Littleton, Phillip Whistler, Nicholas Roberts, Christopher Taylor. (PRO: E190/62/5).

16-20 May. Shippers by the *Bonadventure*, Mr. John Holman, bound from London for New England: Nehemiah Bourne, John Peake. (PRO: E190/62/5).

17 May. The following apprenticed in Bristol: John Woodman to William Martin, 4 years Jamaica. (BR).

18 May. Shipper by the *Two Friends*, Mr. John Bawton, bound from London for New England: James Littleton. (PRO: E190/62/1).

28 May. The following apprenticed in Bristol: John Window to Aaron Cook, 4 years Barbados; Thomas Cooke to same, 4 years Barbados; William Pen to John Vance, 4 years New England. (BR).

31 May. The following apprenticed in Bristol: Howell Thomas to Samuell Clarke, 5 years Virginia. (BR).

31 May-9 June. Shippers by the *Dove*, Mr. Robert Cannon, bound from London for New England: John Imay, John Wargon, Henry Tew, Francis Jaggard. (PRO: E190/62/1).

May. Probate of will of Phillip Chesley of York County, Virginia. (AW).

May. Depositions in London re the appointment of Richard Longman as factor in Virginia for Benjamin Cowell of London, merchant, deceased. (NGSQ 64/2).

1-12 June. Shippers by the *Hope*, Mr. John Thompson, bound from London for New England: Thomas Ewer, Mathew Page, John Harwood, Samuell Stenton, Thomas Elkin. (PRO: E190/62/5).

2 June. Shipper by the *Castle* frigate, Capt. Griffith, bound from London for New York: Anthony Brookhold. (PRO: E190/62/5).

2-25 June. Shippers by the *Jane* & ——, Mr. Elias Parkin, bound from London for New England: Joseph Rooksby, Elias Parkman, Thomas Ruck, John Legg, Christopher Taylor, Andrew Robinson, Richard Cowthorne, Thomas Elkin, Edmond Haslewood, Robert Cockram, Edward Edmonds, William Antleby, James Eyton. (PRO: E190/62/5).

2 June-15 July. Shippers by the *Hopewell* of Plymouth bound from Plymouth for New York: Thomas Turner, George Lapthorne, John Horsham, John Warren, John Hingston. (PRO: E190/1041/1).

4 June. The following apprenticed in Bristol: Richard Lambert to Hercules Hodges, 4 years Barbados; William Thomas to same, 4 years Barbados; Charles Waters to same, 4 years Barbados. (BR).

5 June. The following apprenticed in Bristol: Richard Thous to Thomas Bowen, 4 years Virginia. (BR).

8-25 June. Shippers by the *Exchange*, Mr. John Cushing, bound from London for New England: Hezekiah Usher, Thomas Bryan, Thomas Cornish, Stephen Burton. (PRO: E190/62/1).

9 June. The following apprenticed in Bristol: William Salmun to Thomas Carry, 4 years Virginia; John Folkes to Thomas Bowen, 4 years Virginia; Kingsmill Maynard to same, 5 years Virginia; William Moore to same, 4 years Virginia; George Roberts to Rowland Williams, 4 years Virginia; Howell Jones to same, 4 years Virginia. (BR).

9-12 June. Shippers by the *Robert & Anthony*, Mr. William Day, bound from London for New York: Daniell Allen, John Lewin. (PRO: E190/62/1).

10 June. The following apprenticed in Bristol: John Jones to Thomas Bowen, 4 years Virginia; Margaret May to Thomas Norman, 4 years Virginia. (BR).

11 June. Petition of William Harris of New England, one of the first to buy land in Narragansett Bay, for the restoration of lands called the Proprieties of the Men of Patuxet seized by John Harrad of Warwick, Rhode Island, and others. (APC & CSPC).

12 June. The following apprenticed in Bristol: William Winter to Hercules Hodges, 4 years Virginia; Thomas Warmer to same, 4 years Virginia; John Mathias to same, 4 years Virginia; George Wadham to same, 4 years Virginia; John Bartlett to same, 4 years Virginia; John Nickolls to same, 4 years Jamaica. (BR).

12-25 June. Shippers by the *Elizabeth & Mary*, Mr. Joseph Dell, bound from London for New England: Joseph Harvey, Christopher Marshall, Thomas Revis, William Donfellow. (PRO: E190/62/1).

14 June. The following apprenticed in Bristol: Thomas Lees to Samuell Clarke, 4 years Virginia. (BR).

16 June. The following apprenticed in Bristol: John Higgins to Thomas Speed, 4 years York River. (BR).

17 June. The following apprenticed in Bristol: John Hughes to Thomas Bowen, 5 years Virginia. (BR).

19 June. The following apprenticed in Bristol: Barbara Andrews to Maxfield Walter, 4 years Virginia. (BR).

21 June. The following apprenticed in Bristol: Thomas Higgins to William Godwin, 4 years Virginia; Ellioner Langford to Maxfield Walter, 4 years Virginia; Henry Williams to Arthur Grant, 5 years Virginia. (BR).

23 June. Petition of Francis Morison, Thomas Ludwell and Robert Smith, agents for Virginia, that the King may incorporate the plantation of Virginia and the territory of Accomack. (APC).

23 June. The following apprenticed in Bristol: Charles Lewis to Robert Finch, 4 years Virginia. (BR).

23 June. Home Circuit prisoners reprieved to be transported to Barbados or Jamaica. Essex: William Gillett of Abbots Roothing; William Parish of St. Osyth; Richard Evans of Layton; (all three still in prison in July 1677). Kent: Francis Jones of East Peckham. Surrey: Margaret Eager of Christchurch; John Heyward of Tooting; William Barnes of St. George, Southwark; John Floyd of Christchurch; Katherine Aspinall of St. George, Southwark. Sussex: John Perring of East Grinstead. (PRO: C66/3173/23).

24 June. The following apprenticed in Bristol: John Trapni to John Mardin, 4 years Virginia; William Conner to David Parry, 5 years Virginia; John Price to William Holliday, 4 years Virginia; Anne Jones to Arthur Grant, 5 years Virginia; Ruth West to same, 4 years Virginia; Ellioner Cullis to same, 4 years Virginia; Blanch Jones to Thomas Tayler, 4 years Maryland; Joane Jones to same, 4 years Virginia; William Winthrip to Charles Harris, 4 years Virginia. (BR).

26 June. Northern Circuit prisoners reprieved to be transported to Barbados. Cumberland: John Ellott of Tronghead. Yorkshire: Thomas Shaw of Ottley; John Law; John Fetherstone of York City; Nathaniel Haythorn alias Smythhurst of Leathley; Samuel Shaw of Brampton Brearley. (PRO: C66/3173/22).

25 June. Shipper by the *Mary*, Mr. John Dolman, bound from London for Virginia: Thomas Webb. (PRO: E190/62/1).

29 June. The following apprenticed in Bristol: James Edwards to William Holliday, 4 years Virginia; Giles Olpin to same, 4 years Virginia; John Holliday to same, 4 years Virginia; James Bendall to same, 4 years Virginia; John Bath to Daniell Gwilliam, 4 years Virginia; Daniell Auston to same, 4 years Virginia; Nicholas Haskins to same, 4 years Virginia. (BR).

30 June. The following apprenticed in Bristol: Mary Harford to John Curtis, 4 years Virginia. (BR).

June. Administration of Simon Dawkins of Petsworth, Hampshire, who died in Long Island in New England, bachelor. (AW).

June. Probate of will of Nicholas Tovey of Maryland. (AW).

June. Administration of Mathew Pinder of Virginia, bachelor. (AW).

June. Administration with will of Henry Grey of St. Botolph Aldgate, London, who died in Virginia. (AW).

June. John Mercer, an idle, pilfering person, says he was born in Newcastle and lately came from Virginia, but none came against him. (Bridewell).

1 July. Norfolk Circuit prisoners reprieved to be transported to Barbados (counties not stated): William Morris, Henry Jessop, Andrew Dickins, George Orchard. (PRO: C66/3174/16).

1 July. Oxford Circuit prisoners reprieved to be transported to America. Berkshire: Fortunatus Pearce alias Noone of Newbury. Gloucestershire: Nicholas Johnson of Broad Campden; Thomas Wilse of Tuffley; Henry Newman of Marshfield; Anthony Gastrell of Haresfield; Thomas Crosse of Sevenhampton; Richard Sexton of Winchcombe. Herefordshire: Philip Grosvenor of Middleton on Hill; Thomas Jones of Hampton Bishop; Jane Pewteres of Tarrington; Thomas Watkins of Michaelchurch Escley; Thomas Davys; William Howell of Pedwardine. Monmouthshire: Thomas Water of Lower Kemeys; William Pritchard alias Cadogan of Caldicote; William Giles of Bedwelty. Oxfordshire: Thomas French of Sarsden; Edward Wenlock of Cottesloe; William Okey alias Sessions of Kingham. Shropshire: William Davies of Oswestry; John Sayce of Ludlow; George Fewterell of Greet; Henry Bowdler of Bridgnorth. Staffordshire: Ralph Wovenden of Newcastle under Lyme; William Mason of Cannock. Worcestershire: Richard Davis of Bromyard; Elizabeth Taylor of Pedmore. Radnor: Anne Price of New Radnor. (PRO: C66/3174/17).

2 July. The following apprenticed in Bristol: Thomas Marshall to Arthur Grant, 5 years Virginia; Blewett Beamont to Robert James, 4 years Virginia; Jane Case to same, 4 years Virginia; Rebecca Jee to same, 4 years Virginia; Watkin Llewis to Alexander Thomas, 4 years Maryland. (BR).

5 July. The following apprenticed in Bristol: Daniell Peirce to William Holliday, 4 years Virginia; James Benning to Phillip Seward, 4 years Virginia; James Richards to Arthur Grant, 4 years Virginia; Thomas Richards to same, 4 years Virginia; David Roberts to same, 5 years Virginia. (BR).

7 July. The following apprenticed in Bristol: James Hardy to Thomas Fisher, 7 years Maryland; Mary James to Aaron Prance, 4 years Virginia. (BR).

7-18 July. Shippers by the *Prosperous*, Mr. Francis Partis, bound from London for Maryland: William Barrett, William Mead. (PRO: E190/62/5).

9 July. The following apprenticed in Bristol: Thomas Mathews to John Holliday, 4 years Virginia. (BR).

11-30 July. Shippers by the *Sea Flower*, Mr. Thomas Smith, bound from London for New England: Henry Loads, George Beach, Robert Hooker, Spencer Pigott, James Blackman, William Sherley, Ezechiell Twisleton, Thomas Bentley, John Child, William Crowch, Charles Dixon, Arthur Stone, Edward Merryweather, Thomas Ruck, John Price, Andrew Phillips, Daniell Allen, John Hubbard, Edward Hull, Francis Parsons, Thomas Elkin, Samuell Shelbury, John Jackson, John Peake, James Eyton, Edward Smith, Thomas Norman, Thomas Hollis, Matthew Whatton, Robert Sedgwick, Thomas Glover, Maximilian Gore, John Harwood, Henry Ashurst, George Cole, John Bartlett, Joseph Beake, Nicholas Roberts, John Rust, George Sturman, Joseph Hayes, Richard Lloyd, Isaac Vinck, John Cresner, Thomas Papillon, John Cooke, George Hockenhull. (PRO: E190/62/5).

12 July. The following apprenticed in Bristol: Walter White to William Mills, 8 years Virginia; Elizabeth Solomon to Thomas Tayler, 4 years Virginia; Mathew Gaudrum to William Morgan, 4 years Virginia. (BR).

13 July. The following apprenticed in Bristol: William Woodly to William Hampsteed, 5 years Virginia; Thomas Goodwin to same, 5 years Virginia; Robert Smith to same, 5 years Virginia; John Heale to same, 6 years Virginia. (BR).

13-23 July. Shippers by the *Barnaby*, Mr. Ryder, bound from London for Virginia: John Kent, James Bayly, Ralph Harwood, Andrew Robinson, James Donalson, Edward Porteus, Samuell Weldon, Thomas Lane, Richard Booth, John Jefferys, John Mumford, William Meade, John Stone, Thomas Parker. (PRO: E190/62/5).

14 July-3 August. Shippers by the *Blessing*, Mr. James Elson, bound from London for New England: Ralph Box, Spencer Pigott, Thomas Bentley, Nicholas Roberts, James Bosiar, William Antleby, Ezechiell Hutchinson, Noah Lloyd, Thomas Elkin, Thomas Bodley, James Eyton, Thomas Firmin, Thomas Norman, John Child, Thomas Glover, Isaac Winck. (PRO: E190/62/5).

16-24 July. Shippers by the *Sarah*, Mr. Richard Rich, bound from London for New England: Isaac Chetwood, Maximilian Gore, Anthony Ringwood, Richard Lloyd. (PRO: E190/62/5).

17 July. The following apprenticed in Bristol: Abraham Butcher to William Sheppard, 4 years Virginia. (BR).

17 July. Shippers by the *Pelican* of Plymouth bound from Plymouth for Virginia: John Merring, Richard Harper. (PRO: E190/1041/1).

18 July-20 August. Shippers by the *Diamond*, Mr. Richard Griffiths, bound from London for New York: Robert Woolley, Maj. Edmond Andrews, Thomas Griffith, John Odell, Thomas Worledge, John Knapp, John Jennings. (PRO: E190/62/5).

19 July. Shipper by the *Flower* ketch of Boston, Mr. Joseph Penwell, bound from Newcastle for Boston, New England: Robert Gibb. (PRO: E190/196/2).

20 July. The following apprenticed in Bristol: Robert Brock to Robert James, 4 years Virginia; Samuell Wheeler to William Holliday, 4 years Virginia. (BR).

21 July. The following apprenticed in Bristol: Evans Thomas to Christopher Pitt, 4 years Virginia; Mary Martin to Charles Haynes, 4 years Virginia. (BR).

22 July. The following apprenticed in Bristol: John Strude to Barnabas Robertson, 4 years Virginia; George Nest to Maxfield Walter, 4 years Virginia; Mary Nest to same, 4 years Virginia; William Hardin to Francis Rawles, 4 years Virginia; Mark Kelly to John Snow, 4 years Virginia; George Childs to Thomas Robins, 4 years Virginia; Katharine Clarke to John Fifoote, 4 years Virginia. (BR).

26 July. The following apprenticed in Bristol: Walter Lewis to John Mason, 4 years Virginia; John Percell to Thomas Cary, 7 years Virginia; Jane Willson to Caleb Cockerell, 4 years Virginia by *Nevis Merchant*. (BR).

28 July-20 August. Shippers by the *Swallow*, Mr. Joseph Hardy, bound from London for New England: Christopher Gore, William Antleby, Thomas Bodley, Robert Hooker, Spencer Pigott, Hezechiah Usher, Robert Woolley, Daniell Lathum, Thomas Crundall, William Lovell, Charles Rives. (PRO: E190/62/5).

29 July. Newgate prisoners reprieved to be transported to Barbados. London: John Goldin; William Mooreton alias Martin; Alice Powell, spinster, alias wife of John Masters, yeoman; Anne Harris, widow, alias Anne Freeman, spinster; Mary Morris, spinster; Charles Lewis; Daniel Austen; Thomas Symonds; John Ashmore; Margaret Biggs, widow, alias wife of Thomas Grove, yeoman; Lydia Hallifax, spinster; Elizabeth Chamberlaine, spinster; William Bonner; Ambrose Ford; Yard Yarde; Sarah Barlow, spinster; Elizabeth Greene, spinster, alias wife of John Greene; Joshua Slater; William Motley. Middlesex: Elizabeth Howell of St. Martin in the Fields, spinster; Jane Kates, wife of John Kates, alias Jane Symonds of the same, spinster; William Hunt of the same; George Poore of the same; Andrew Death of the same; Richard Stephens of New Brentford; Richard Shorte of Heston; John Rouse of Ealing; James Davies of Fulham; John Stubbins alias Stebbins of Willesden or Acton; Matthew Turner of St. Sepulchre; Samuel Page of St. Andrew Holborn; William Longman of the same; Michael Jones of the same; William Robinson of the same; John Tyley of Stepney; John Oulson of the same; Charles Chambers of the same; Benjamin Hutchinson of the same; Augustine Punt of the same; Michael Burroughs of the same; Susan Tutt, wife of Alexander Tutt of St. Clement Danes; Anne Windwright of Whitechapel, spinster; Alexander Douglas of Hampstead; Humphrey Beckett of the same; Benjamin Tompkins of St. Botolph Aldersgate; Richard Fountaine of St. Giles in the Fields; James Wilson of St. Dunstan in the West; Thomas Treane alias Tearne of Shoreditch; Joane Hughes, spinster, alias wife of John Piper of Marylebone. (PRO: C66/3170/38).

29 July. Deed of bond signed by Eliazar Hathorne of Salem, New England, merchant, to Robert Woolley, citizen and clothworker of London. (LMCD).

29 July. The following apprenticed in Bristol: Roger Evans to John Mason, 4 years Virginia. (BR).

30 July. The following apprenticed in Bristol: Mary Wall to John Mason, 4 years Virginia; Michaell Conway to Phillip England, 7 years Virginia; Jane Price to Andrew Limbry, 4 years Virginia or Barbados; Thomas Lewis to Richard Jones, 4 years Virginia; Morgan Phillips to Lewis Heath, 4 years Virginia; Evan Thomas to same, 4 years Virginia. (BR).

30 July-18 August. Shippers by the *Rappahannock Merchant*, Mr. John Plover, bound from London for Virginia: John Clark, John Bellamy, Thomas Malin, Gawen Corbin, Henry Meese. (PRO: E190/62/5).

31 July-5 August. Shippers by the *Robert & James*, Mr. John Mosse, bound from London for Virginia: Robert Woolley, Joseph Sparrow, John Freeman, Richard Emes, John Preston. (PRO: E190/62/5).

July. Administration of Thomas Lucas the younger of Virginia, bachelor. (AW).

July. Administration of Thomas Joyner of Stepney, Middlesex, who died in Virginia. (AW).

July. Administration of John Connell of Youghall, Ireland, who died in Virginia, bachelor. (AW).

July. Probate of will of Ambrose Fielding of Virginia. (AW).

3 August. The following apprenticed in Bristol: Elizabeth Trindall to Abraham Evans, 4 years [Virginia]; Richard Band to Barnabas Robertson, 4 years Virginia; Richard Winn to Briant Tandy, 4 years Virginia; James Hurne to Richard Phillips, 4 years Virginia; John Smith to Richard Robins, 4 years Virginia; Elizabeth Woodly to Zacharias Smith, 4 years Virginia; William Woodly to same, 4 years Virginia; John Lafwell to Robert Turpin, 4 years Virginia. (BR).

4-17 August. Shippers by the *Daniell*, Mr. Thomas Warren, bound from London for Virginia: John Parker, Edward Leamon, John Rowe, Samuell Powell, John

Forth, John Jennings, Ralph Harwood, Nowell Bassano, Thomas Parker, Thomas Abney. (PRO: E190/62/5).

6 August. Shippers by the *Young Prince*, Mr. Robert Morrice, bound from London for Virginia: Thomas Dands, John Jennings. (PRO: E190/62/5).

6 August. Shippers by the *Crown Mallaga*, Mr. Walter Dunch, bound from London for Virginia: Francis Finch, Thomas Elwys, William Phillips, John Puttiford, John Stone, William Mead. (PRO: E190/62/5).

6 August. Shipper by the *Griffin* of London, Mr. Robert Griffin, bound from Portsmouth for New Jersey: Roger Hucking. (PRO: E190/828/9).

6-18 August. Shippers by the *Castle* frigate, Capt. Burton, bound from London for New York: Andrew Hunt, James Saught, John Lewin, Phillip Cartwright, James South, Charles Rives, John Hobbs, William Sturt, Thomas Boone, Samuel Swinnock, John Peake, William Dyer, Robert Woolley. (PRO: E190/62/5).

6-20 August. Shippers by the *Hope*, Mr. William Browne, bound from London for New England: Thomas Powell, James Burkin, William Sherley, William Dingley, Samuel Shute. (PRO: E190/62/5).

7 August. The following apprenticed in Bristol: James Upadine to Thomas Daniell, 4 years Virginia; John Jones to Edward Stradly, 4 years Virginia; James Jobbins to same, 4 years Virginia; Elizabeth Trindall to Christopher Berry, 4 years Virginia; Thomas Gilbert to Thomas Austin, 4 years Barbados. (BR).

10-11 August. Shippers by the *Tryall*, Mr. Ezechiel Croscomb, bound from London for Virginia: Samuell Shepheard, Thomas Parker. (PRO: E190/62/5).

11 August. The following apprenticed in Bristol: Edward Jenkin to Mathew Cradock, 4 years Virginia; Maria West to Edward Jackson, 4 years Virginia; Mary West to same, 5 years Virginia; Sarah West to same, 5 years Virginia; Elizabeth Mantell to same, 7 years Virginia; John Blanch to Walter Thomas, 4 years Virginia. (BR).

13 August. The following apprenticed in Bristol: Elizabeth Bush to Joseph Fookes, 4 years Barbados. (BR).

13-28 August. Shippers by the *Augustine*, Mr. Zachary Taylor, bound from London for Virginia: Thomas Bentley, Henry Foreman, Richard Booth, John Parker, George Layfield, Phillip Foster, Nicholas Roberts, Joshua Stony, Gabriell Marden, William Hawes, Samuell Young, William Paggen, John Jennings, William Dingley, Richard Glover, Gawen Corbin, William Meade. (PRO: E190/62/5).

14 August. The following apprenticed in Bristol: Abraham Foord to Michaell Pole, 4 years Virginia. (BR).

15-27 August. Shippers by the *Virginia Factor*, Mr. James Conway, bound from London for Virginia: Michael Stancliff, Thomas Banford, Edward Lloyd, Thomas Lane, Timothy Harmer, Ralph Sedgwick, William Meade, Thomas Parker. (PRO: E190/62/5).

16 August. The following apprenticed in Bristol: Carnan Hutton to Thomas Caidny, 4 years Virginia; Humphry Jones to John Belcher, 6 years Virginia; Joseph Merryweather to Maxfield Walter, 4 years Virginia; Mary Miller to Abraham Evans, 4 years Virginia. (BR).

17 August. The following apprenticed in Bristol: Richard Rugg to James Boond, 4 years Virginia; John Rugg to same, 7 years Virginia; Michaell Godwin to Richard Sutton, 7 years Virginia; James Cousins to same, 7 years Virginia; Richard Sutton to Thomas Whitehead, 5 years Barbados. (BR).

17-21 August. Shippers by the *Joseph & Benjamin*, Mr. Matthew Paine, bound from London for Virginia: Benjamin Whitchcott, Giles Bullock, James Brames, John Haggett, Francis Paine, Strangeways Mudd, John Jennings, William Mead. (PRO: E190/62/5).

18 August. The following apprenticed in Bristol: James Bridgeford to John Lancaster, 4 years Virginia; Daniell Cooksey to Daniell Jordan, 9 years Virginia; George Eke to same, 5 years Virginia; Joan Eke to same, 4 years Virginia; Edward Richards to same, 5 years Virginia; Michaell Harpfield to Mary Morris, 9 years Virginia; Edward Jones to Francis Rawles, 4 years Virginia. (BR).

19 August. Deposition by John Wayne, citizen and merchant tailor of London, aged 65, that he knew Sir Thomas Temple of Boston, New England, for 40 years before his death and witnessed a bond which he signed to the use of Sir Thomas Longville of Woolverton, Buckinghamshire, on 29 June 1655. Thomas Russell of New England has been appointed as attorney. (LMCD).

20 August. The following apprenticed in Bristol: Thomas Newsham to Thomas Peasely, 4 years Virginia; Leonard Newsham to Robert Lancaster, 4 years Virginia; Elizabeth Jones to John Maston, 4 years Virginia; Susanna Stone to Thomas Willet, 4 years Virginia; Henry Warnfoord to William Yorke, 4 years Virginia. (BR).

20 August. Shipper by the *John*, Mr. John Poulson, bound from London for Virginia: Richard Reeve. (PRO: E190/62/5).

21 August-2 September. Shippers by the *Susanna* of Plymouth bound from Plymouth for Virginia: Arthur Cotton, Isaac Harwood, John Prowse, Edward Blagg, Thomas Powell, John Monyon, Samuell Brett, Richard Cowes. (PRO: E190/1041/1).

24 August. The following apprenticed in Bristol: Paule Williams to Zachariah Smith, 4 years Virginia; Bridgett Lowe to Richard Speed, 4 years Nevis. (BR).

25-29 August. Shippers by the *John & Anne*, Mr. Joseph Guillam, bound from London for New England: John Loggin, Richard Sweeting, Henry Beresford, Christopher Taylor, William Longstaffe, Henry Bernford, William Ragdale, Hezechiah Usher, Robert Woolley, Edmond Edmonds, John Shorter, Roger Arkinstall, Benjamin Hewling, Charles Mitchell. (PRO: E190/62/5).

25 August-3 September. Shippers by the *Anne*, Mr. Benjamin Cooper, bound from London for Virginia: Henry Mees, Thomas Williamson, Strangeways Mudd, Thomas Parker. (PRO: E190/62/5).

25 August-4 September. Shippers by the *Marygold* of Plymouth bound from Plymouth for Virginia: Edward Jeffery, Thomas Ford, Richard Opie, Samuell Brett, Abraham Beele, Derringe Blackborne, John Stone. (PRO: E190/1041/1).

25 August-8 September. Shippers by the *Adventure*, Mr. John Moore, bound from London for Virginia: John Welden, William Rayton, Bernard Mitchell, William Meade. (PRO: E190/62/5).

26 August. The following apprenticed in Bristol: John Berryman to Thomas Speed, 4 years Virginia; John Leake to John Williams, 4 years Virginia; Edward Morgan to Thomas Lock, 4 years Virginia. (BR).

27 August. The following apprenticed in Bristol: John Roberts to Thomas Preston, 4 years Virginia; Margaret Gregory to same, 4 years Virginia; John Rogers to John Nutt, 4 years Virginia. (BR).

28 August. The following apprenticed in Bristol: Benjamin Bevis to George Packer, 4 years Maryland. (BR).

30 August. The following apprenticed in Bristol: William Brittin to Richard Willcock, 4 years Virginia; William Easton to William Bennet, 4 years Virginia; Thomas Richards to same, 4 years Virginia; Thomas Cooke to Henry Spooner, 5 years Virginia; John Knowling to Robert Welsh, 4 years Virginia; Moses Horton to Edward Jackson, 6 years Virginia; Thomas Turner to John Snow, 4 years Virginia; Mary Liniore to John Mason, 4 years Virginia; Elizabeth Gaine to same, 4 years Virginia. (BR).

31 August. The following apprenticed in Bristol: Richard Glover to Thomas Speed, 4 years Virginia; Sarah Nash to Abraham Burkhead, 5 years Virginia. (BR).

31 August-1 September. Shippers by the *Zebulon*, Mr. Joseph Pile, bound from London for Virginia: John Kent, Edward Lemon, Samuell Shute, Gawen Corbin. (PRO: E190/62/5).

31 August-14 September. Shippers by the *Honor & Dorothy*, Mr. John Moore, bound from London for Virginia: William Thomas, Thomas Bassett, Isaac Merritt, Edward Carter, Nicholas Roberts, Thomas Grindon, William Juxon, William Antleby, Thomas Baker. (PRO: E190/62/5).

31 August-30 October. Shippers by the *Elizabeth & Mary*, Mr. Roger Newham, bound from London for Virginia: Jonathan Brewen, Ralph Goldsmith, Henry Phillips, John Rutland, Elizabeth Hutchinson, Samuell Groome, John Kent, Sir Boyle Maynard. (PRO: E190/62/5).

August. Probate of will of Isaac Brookesbancke of the ship *Anne* who died at sea bound for Maryland. (AW).

August. Administration of George Story of Stepney, Middlesex, who died in Virginia. (AW).

August. Administration of Richard Sanckley of Virginia, bachelor. (AW).

August. Administration of Thomas Neale of Maryland. (AW).

1-17 September. Shippers by the *Virginia Merchant* bound from Plymouth for Virginia: Thomas Yeabsley, Thomas Westcott, John Hodge, Joseph Bridger, Thomas Phillips. (PRO: E190/1041/1).

2 September. Deposition by Samuel Gillart of Rye, Sussex, aged 26, that Charles Sarys of Blessland, New Kent County, Virginia, planter, became indebted by bond of 2 July 1670 to George Ongley Jr. of Maidstone, Kent, mercer. (LMCD).

2 September. The following apprenticed in Bristol: John Browne to James Boond, 4 years Virginia; Henry Harris to Richard Sollway, 4 years Virginia; Andrew Wright to Henry Baker, 4 years Virginia; Jane Payne to George Perry, 4 years Virginia; Charles Young to same, 4 years Virginia. (BR).

3 September. The following apprenticed in Bristol: William Phillips to Thomas Daniell, 4 years Virginia; John Staty to John Mason, 4 years Virginia; Elizabeth Rawbone to Lewis Heath, 5 years Virginia; Elizabeth Bartlam to Christopher Burkhead, 4 years Virginia; Richard Wells to John Gill, 4 years Nevis. (BR).
3 September-12 October. Shippers by the *Crown* of Plymouth bound from Plymouth for Virginia: John Pearne, George Jackson, Thomas Brooking, Andrew Horsman, Samuell Brett. (PRO: E190/1041/1).

4 September. The following apprenticed in Bristol: Daniell Tayler to Thomas Walter, 4 years Virginia. (BR).

4-8 September. Shippers by the *Recovery*, Mr. John Wood, bound from London for Virginia: Thomas Taylor, William Lock, Robert Forth, Richard Booth, Robert Woolley, John Smith, Thomas Elliott, Richard Bankes, Isaac Merritt, William Meade, William Duke, Richard Glover, Thomas Bassett. (PRO: E190/62/5).

5 September. Shipper by the *Advance*, Mr. John Baddily, bound from London for Virginia: Isaac Merritt. (PRO: E190/62/5).

6 September. The following apprenticed in Bristol: Richard Newman to Zachariah Smith, 4 years Virginia; Thomas Heath to Thomas Jefferis, 4 years Virginia; Daniell Galland to William Swimer, 4 years Jamaica. (BR).

7 September. Deposition by Giles Steele of London, scrivener aged 32, that John Edmondson of Talbot County, Maryland, merchant, became bound by deed of 14 August 1672 to John Edwards of North Shields, Northumberland, gent. The deed provided that Edmondson should procure 200 acres called Edwards Desire or Edwards Choice in Marsh Creek, Choptank River, Maryland, for Edwards. (LMCD).

7 September. The following apprenticed in Bristol: William Luton to Jacob Wheeler, 6 years Virginia; Robert Brocklesby to John Lowden, 4 years Virginia; William Braine to same, 4 years Virginia; Deborah Cozens to Nicholas Cradling, 5 years Virginia; Mary Holder to same, 5 years Virginia; Onner Blake to Thomas Bishop, 5 years Virginia; Thomas Bissell to William Scott, 4 years Virginia. (BR).

8-11 September. Shippers by the *Swan*, Mr. William Foster, bound from London for New England: Samuell Hinks, Spencer Pigott, Edward Merryweather, Edward Haslewood, Robert Parker, Robert Woolley, Thomas Lucas, Thomas Burkin, Abraham Bond, William Pate. (PRO: E190/62/5).

9 September. John Rudd of Whitechapel, Middlesex, yeoman, found guilty of forcibly transporting John Hewlett, apprentice of William Burbridge, tailor, to Virginia and selling him there for profit. (VM 83/3).

9 September. The following apprenticed in Bristol: William Moody to Bryan Tandy, 4 years Virginia; John White to William Bull, 4 years Virginia. (BR).

11 September. The following apprenticed in Bristol: William Thomas to Thomas Hodge (or Dodge), 7 years Virginia; Thomas Maddox to Thomas Phillips, 3 years Virginia. (BR).

13 September. The following apprenticed in Bristol: Richard Carter to John Stephens, 4 years Virginia; Mary Gwillim to John Mason, 4 years Virginia; Hester Handy to James Wall, 5 years Virginia; Samuell Franklyn to same, 5 years Virginia. (BR).

14 September. The following apprenticed in Bristol: Thomas West to Thomas Cades, 4 years Virginia; Sarah Dawson to Lawrence Herder, 4 years Virginia; Elizabeth Lowe to same, 7 years Virginia; John Farmer to John Jones, 3 years Barbados; Dorothy Jones to Edmond Davies, 4 years Virginia; Peter Steward to Phillip Eggleston, 4 years Virginia. (BR).

14 September-13 October. Shippers by the *Abraham & Sarah* of Plymouth bound from Plymouth for Virginia: Edward Dyer, Digory Tonking, Thomas Brooking, John Monyon. (PRO: E190/1041/1).

15 September. The following apprenticed in Bristol: Mary Burges to Giles Sandford, 4 years Virginia. (BR).

15-22 September. Shippers by the *Hopewell*, Mr. Michael Yoakley, bound from London for Virginia: John Mills, John Singleton, John Smith, Edward Rownd, Isaac Hine. (PRO: E190/62/5).

16 September. The following apprenticed in Bristol: James Shute to Francis Cockhill, 4 years Virginia; Mary Thomas to Thomas Wade, 4 years Virginia; Elizabeth Thomas to same, 4 years Virginia; John Thomas to Thomas Hobson, 4 years Virginia; Thomas Williams to Edward Skinner, 4 years Virginia; William End to Thomas Hawkins, 10 years Virginia; Griffin Evans to John Mason, 4 years Virginia. (BR).

17 September. The following apprenticed in Bristol: Ursula Thomas to Thomas Nelson, 4 years Virginia. (BR).

18 September. The following apprenticed in Bristol: Phillip Watts to Thomas Nelson, 5 years Virginia; William Powell to John Tucker, 5 years Virginia. (BR).

20 September. The following apprenticed in Bristol: James Wall to William Barrow, 5 years Virginia; John Stutchberry to Phillip Hanger, 4 years Virginia; John Tucker to John Millsom, 7 years Virginia; Stephen Peterson to John Addams, 4 years Virginia; William Baker to John Woolvin, 7 years Virginia; William Thomas to Francis Harris, 4 years Virginia; John Harris to same, 4 years Virginia; William Popley to William Clement, 4 years Virginia. (BR).

21 September. Deposition by Nicholas Laney, citizen and merchant tailor of London, aged 50, and John Beart of St. Bride's, London, feltmaker aged 40, that Arthur Boldero, citizen and stationer of London, is the brother and heir of John Boldero, citizen and haberdasher of London, deceased, and that both were sons of John Boldero, haberdasher of London, deceased, and his wife, Mary Brent deceased, who was the sister and heir of Edmond Brent of Westmoreland County, Virginia, gent, deceased. The son, John Boldero, as heir to Edmond Brent, enjoyed an estate in Fleet Street, London, which he sold to the son, Arthur Boldero. (LMCD).

21-23 September. Shippers by the *William* of Plymouth bound from Plymouth for Virginia: William Martin, Thomas Hunte. (PRO: E190/1041/1).

23 September. Deposition by John Lodge of London, merchant aged 30, John Bynnes of London, gent aged 34, and William Scorey of London, notary public aged 30, that Christopher Watkins, citizen and haberdasher of London, who lived at White Hart Court, Long Lane, London, was a Yorkshire man and was born at Carlton where his father was minister. He married Jane Walker at St. Vedast, Foster Lane, London, on 28 June 1663. When he died, Watkins left two sons and a daughter as well as a brother, sister and other relations in Yorkshire. He had often spoken of George Watkins in Virginia who had left him a considerable legacy in his will. Jane Watkins is the relict and administratrix of Christopher Watkins. (LMCD).

25 September. The following apprenticed in Bristol: Susan Dempston to John Filer, 4 years Virginia; Anne Kenner to same, 4 years Virginia. (BR).

27 September. Deposition by Thomas Heath of London, scrivener aged 46, that Samuel Slany, citizen and grocer of London, on 21 January 1664 assigned to George Hudson, citizen and haberdasher of London, lands and goods which William Hodgskins of Rappahannock, Virginia, had assigned to Slany by deed of 10 March 1663. (LMCD).

27 September. The following apprenticed in Bristol: Thomas Mountslow to John Harris, 5 years Virginia; Samuell Painter to Brian Tandy, 5 years Virginia; John Allen to same, 5 years Virginia. (BR).

28 September. Deposition by Thomas Somerley of Shadwell, Middlesex, notary public aged 50, and his servant, Theophilus Haydock, aged 20, that Anthony Trevillian of Whitechapel, Middlesex, and Samuel Trevillian of Virginia, planter, undertook on 4 December 1672 to ship goods from York River, Virginia, to John Plator of Shadwell, cheesemonger. (LMCD).

28 September. The following apprenticed in Bristol: Joseph Moxham to Isaac Sheere, 4 years New England; Joseph Fry to John Arnee, 4 years Maryland. (BR).

28 September-3 November. Shippers by the *James & Thomas* of Plymouth, Mr. George Bayly, bound from Plymouth for Virginia: John Horsham, Thomas Ford, James Chedd, James Ingledon, Roger Gooding, John Francis. (PRO: E190/1041/1).

29 September. The following apprenticed in Bristol: James Bayliffe to John Harris, 4 years Maryland. (BR).

30 September. The following apprenticed in Bristol: David Jones to Robert Wynn, 5 years Maryland or Virginia; Thomas Palmer to Richard Roberts, 4 years Virginia; Henry Fish to Ellis Pearle, 4 years Barbados. (BR).

1 October. The following apprenticed in Bristol: John Burroughs to Henry Packer, 4 years Virginia; Blanch Pritchett to Thomas Cary, 4 years Virginia. (BR).

2 October. The following apprenticed in Bristol: Thomas Perry to Thomas Spinke, 4 years Virginia; Edward Slade to same, 4 years Virginia; Thomas Hidde to same, 4 years Virginia; Edward Hidde to same, 4 years Virginia. (BR).

4 October. The following apprenticed in Bristol: Joshua Lee to Martin Weekly, 4 years Virginia; Thomas Jones to John Wilcockes, 4 years Virginia; Mary Fishpell to Christopher Perry, 5 years Virginia; John Hoskins to William Sankey, 4 years Virginia. (BR).

6 October. The following apprenticed in Bristol: Bridgett Morgan to Robert Wynn, 5 years Virginia; William Davis to William Springett, 4 years Virginia; Robert Leather to Thomas Hobson, 4 years Virginia; Thomas Clarke to same, 4 years Virginia; Thomas Larrimuir to William Sankey, 4 years Virginia; Edward Ellis to John Whitfield, 4 years Virginia. (BR).

9 October. The following apprenticed in Bristol: Mary Eastmett to William Bruett, 4 years Virginia by *Lilly* of Bristol, Mr. John Filer; Jonathan Smith to Thomas Clandy, 7 years Virginia by *Alithea*, Mr. Edward Watkins; William Hipsly to Benjamin Sealy, 4 years Virginia by *Stephen*, Mr. William Scott; Edward Jones to Sarah Smith, 7 years Virginia by *Alithea*; David Bevan of Swansea, Wales, to Henry Baker, 4 years Virginia by *Stephen*. (BR).

12 October. Shipper by the *John & Mary* of Plymouth bound from Plymouth for Virginia: Abraham Searle. (PRO: E190/1041/1).

12 October-3 November. Shippers by the *Mary* of Plymouth bound from Plymouth for Virginia: John Addis, Abraham Searle. (PRO: E190/1041/1).

13 October. The following apprenticed in Bristol: Arthur Davis of Laugharne, Glam, to William Morgan, 4 years Virginia by *Stephen;* Morgan Lysons to William Jefferis, 4 years Virginia by *Providence*, said William Jefferis Mr; Alexander Richards to Robert Wynn, 4 years Virginia by *William & Anne*, Mr. Phillip (*elsewhere William*) Hanger. (BR).

16 October. The following apprenticed in Bristol: Henry Piper to Thomas Whitwood, Barbados by *Lion*, Mr. Nathaniell Saunders. (BR).

18 October. The following apprenticed in Bristol: Rebecca Langton to John Filer, 4 years Virginia by *Lilly* of London, Mr. John Moore: John Price to Alexander Thompson, 4 years Virginia by *Star*, Mr. Christopher Burcott (*elsewhere Burchen*); Thomas Napper to Robert Hayne, 4 years Virginia by *Exchange*, Mr. Richard Speed; Anne Ireland to Robert Wynn, 4 years Virginia by *William & Anne*. (BR).

19 October. The following apprenticed in Bristol to go to Virginia by the *Alithea*: William Spuraway to Thomas Fisher, 5 years; Charles Low to William Tovy, 4 years. (BR).

20 October. The following apprenticed in Bristol: Robert Tayler to Phillip Haskins, 9 years Virginia by *Love's Increase*, Mr. John Needs; John Bowles to same, 5 years Virginia by *Love's Increase*; Michaell Webb to same, 4 years Virginia by *Love's Increase*; Joseph Thomas to same, 7 years Virginia by *Love's Increase*; John Smith to Thomas Symons, 4 years Montserrat by *Prosperous Catch*, Mr. Samuell Pomfret. (BR).

21 October. The following apprenticed in Bristol: Lawrence Pratt to William Bennet, 4 years Virginia by *Constant Martha*, Mr. William Heaver; Michaell Whitewood to Thomas Symons, 5 years Montserrat by *Prosperous Catch*. (BR).

22 October. The following apprenticed in Bristol: Griffin Evans to Robert Wynn, 4 years Virginia by *William & Anne*. (BR).

23 October. The following apprenticed in Bristol: Joseph Poynt to Henry Lewis, 5 years Virginia by *William & Anne*; John Wynn to William Druett, 4 years Virginia by *Lilly*. (BR).

25 October. The following apprenticed in Bristol to go to Virginia by the *William & Anne*: William Marrow to George Hackett, 4 years; Richard Prece to Henry Lewis, 4 years. (BR).

26 October. The following apprenticed in Bristol: Thomas Boulton to Ralph Poole, 4 years Virginia by *Dogger* of Yarmouth, Mr. Thomas Crofford; Christopher Veale to same, 4 years Virginia by *Dogger* of Yarmouth; William Abbis to William Morris, 4 years Nevis, Antigua or Virginia by *Exchange* of Bristol; John Downe to John Nutt, 6 years Virginia by *Stephen*; Simon Rice to William Bennet, 4 years Virginia by *Alithea*; Joan Fry to Thomas Prewet, 4 years Virginia by *Star*; Thomas Marlique to Richard Wellsteed, 4 years Virginia by *Love's Increase* of Bristol. (BR).

28 October. The following apprenticed in Bristol: Robert Price to Richard Wellsteed, 4 years Virginia by *Love's Increase*. (BR).

October. Thomas Vicars, aged 14, sent from Christ's Hospital to his grandfather, William French, living in New Rents, Southwark, to be sent to his father Mr. Thomas Vicars, now a Minister living in Petson Parish, Gloucester Co., Virginia. (CH).

1 November. The following apprenticed in Bristol to go by the *Love's Increase*: John Woodheard to Hugh Thomas, 4 years Maryland; Mary Evans to Richard Wellsteed, 5 years Virginia. (BR).

2 November. The following apprenticed in Bristol: William Beedle to Stephen Watts, 4 years Virginia by *John* of Bristol. (BR).

3 November. The following apprenticed in Bristol: Andrew Lake to John Newland, 4 years Virginia by *John* of Bristol. (BR).

7 November. Probate of will of Ann Dafforne of St. Leonard, Shoreditch, Middlesex, widow, whose son John Dafforne was in New England. (NGSQ 76/3).

8 November. The following apprenticed in Bristol: Mary Sprake to William Jelfe, 5 years Virginia by *Constant Martha*, Mr. William Hanman. (BR).

9 November. The following apprenticed in Bristol: James Peale to Stephen Watts, 4 years Virginia by *John* of Bristol, Mr. Peter Wraxall Jr; William Stand to Edward Brock, 4 years Jamaica by *Neptune* of Bristol. (BR).

13 November. The following apprenticed in Bristol: George Beaker to James Ithell, 5 years Virginia by *John* of Bristol; William Powell to Sarah Smith, 4 years Virginia by *Star*, Mr. Christopher Burkhead. (BR).

15 November. The following apprenticed in Bristol: William Richardson to Edmond Driver, 11 years Virginia by *John* of Bristol; James Parry to Samuell Scott, 4 years Virginia by *Love's Increase*; William Glue to same, 4 years Virginia by *Love's Increase*; John Alderton to William Bayly, 4 years Virginia by *Constant Martha*; William Johns to Mathew Bowen, 7 years Virginia by *Star*; Richard John Morsly to same, 7 years Virginia by *Star*; John Jenkin Davy to same, 7 years Virginia by *Star*. (BR).

18 November. The following apprenticed in Bristol: Sylvester Saunders to John Needs, 4 years Virginia; Thomas James to William Jelf, 6 years Virginia by *Constant Martha*. (BR).

24 November. The following apprenticed in Bristol: Richard Lloyd to Isaac Webb, 4 years Virginia by *Constant Martha*; Thomas Perry to John Sawyer, 4 years Virginia by *Reformation*, Mr. William Harris; Richard Stone to William Clement, 4 years Virginia by *Reformation*; Anne Tayler to William Jelf, 5 years Virginia by *Constant Martha*; Mary Davis to same, 5 years Virginia by *Constant Martha*; Lewis Davis to same, 5 years Virginia by *Constant Martha*; John Smith to John Hyatt, 9 years Virginia ; Daniell Bugle to same, 5 years Virginia. (BR).

27 November. The following apprenticed in Bristol to go to Virginia by the *Star*: More Morgan to Francis Pitts, 4 years; Henry Jenkins to same, 4 years. (BR).

29 November. The following apprenticed in Bristol: Thomas Hughes to Francis Pitts, 4 years Virginia by *Star*; Joseph Hunt to William Hanman, 4 years Virginia by *Constant Martha*, said William Hanman Mr. (BR).

November. Probate of will of Hannah Walker of St. Giles Cripplegate London, widow, whose son, Thomas Walker, was in New England. (AW).

1 December. The following apprenticed in Bristol to go to Virginia by the *Constant Martha*: Ellioner Frank to Thomas Fisher, 5 years; James Frank to same, 10 years. (BR).

4 December. The following apprenticed in Bristol: Jonas Lewis to Edward Driver, 4 years Virginia; Joseph Crumpe to Thomas Woolaston, 4 years Maryland by *Star*; William Jones to Thomas Fisher, 4 years Virginia. (BR).

6 December. The following apprenticed in Bristol to go to Virginia by the *Constant Martha*: Valentine Stephenson to William Jelf, 4 years; Mabella Tent to same, 4 years; Francis Weekfull to Isaac Webb, 4 years. (BR).

10 December. The following apprenticed in Bristol: Arthur Whiteby to Thomas Fisher, 4 years Maryland by *Constant Martha*. (BR).

11 December. Shippers by the *Adventure* of Plymouth bound from Plymouth for Virginia: William Martin, Joseph Fuge. (PRO: E190/1041/1).

11 December. The following apprenticed in Bristol: Guilliam Thomas to Edward Jackson, 4 years Virginia by *Reformation*; Thomas Hanman to Robert Williams, 5 years Virginia by *Star*. (BR).

13 December. The following apprenticed in Bristol: Robert Wayte to Thomas Fisher, 4 years Virginia by *Constant Martha*. (BR).

15 December. The following apprenticed in Bristol: William Stretch to Robert Edwards, 4 years Virginia by *Constant Martha*. (BR).

17 December. On the petition of James Therry of London, merchant, a pass is granted for the *Sampson* of London to sail from Plymouth for Virginia. (APC).

20 December. The following apprenticed in Bristol: William Lambert to William Clement, 5 years Virginia by *Reformation*. (BR).

23 December. Deposition by Joseph Whitehead of Cliffords Inn, London, gent aged 24, that on 9 July 1671 Arthur Price of York River, Virginia, became indebted to Mathew Wilkinson, citizen and ironmonger of London, for goods shipped by the *Richard & Jane* of London. (LMCD).

30 December. The following apprenticed in Bristol: Samuell Churchhouse to William Jelf, 4 years Virginia by *Constant Martha*. (BR).

1676

3 January. Deposition by John Custis of Virginia, merchant, Colonel of Horse in the Northampton and Accomack Militia, Virginia, aged 47, that in 1662 he was deputed by Thomas Martin and Ambrose Hampson to sue Devereux Browne in Virginia for goods held by one Anscombe to whom Browne was indebted. The deponent found the case too weak to sustain. In 1664 or 1665 John Martin, brother of Thomas Martin, went to Virginia to sue Browne but he let the case lapse. (LMCD).

5 January. The following apprenticed in Bristol: Walter Dodimet to Thomas Lugg, 5 years Barbados by *Katherine*, Mr. Robert Dapwell; Elizabeth Osborne to Anselm White, 4 years Barbados. (BR).

8 January. The following apprenticed in Bristol: John Fryer to John Gottly, 7 years Virginia. (BR).

10 January. The following apprenticed in Bristol: John Williams to John Broadwinter, 4 years Barbados. (BR).

11 January. The following apprenticed in Bristol: John Tally to Thomas Lugg, 4 years Barbados by *Katherine*; Grace Phellps to John Kent, 4 years Barbados by *Nathaniel* of London, said John Kent Mr. (BR).

12 January. The following apprenticed in Bristol: Henry Belshire to John Harris, 4 years Barbados by *Gabriel*, Mr. Thomas Simons. (BR).

14 January. The following apprenticed in Bristol: Elizabeth Osborne to John Harris, 4 years Barbados by *Gabriel*. (BR).

15 January. Shipper by the *Hannah*, Mr. Henry Creeke, bound from London for Virginia: Richard Booth. (PRO: E190/67/3).

21 January. The following apprenticed in Bristol: Reece Williams to John Friend, 4 years Virginia by *Baltimore*. (BR).

22 January. The following apprenticed in Bristol: Joseph Hall of Coventry, [Warw], weaver, to Richard Bridges, 4 years Barbados; John Wakecombe of Stockland [?Stockton], Wilts, to James Bush, 4 years Barbados by *Katherine*; John Haggason to John Bowen, 4 years Barbados. (BR).

26 January. The following apprenticed in Bristol: William Tiley to John England, 4 years Virginia; Charles Mines to Daniell Greening, 4 years Virginia by *Baltimore*, Mr. James Porter; John Gardner to same, 4 years Virginia by *Baltimore*. (BR).

28 January. The following apprenticed in Bristol: Thomas Deane of Swallowfield [?Swallowcliffe], Wilts, blacksmith, to James Porter, 4 years Virginia by *Baltimore*. (BR).

29 January. The following apprenticed in Bristol: Robert Shuring to Thomas Lugg, 4 years Barbados by *Katherine* of Bristol; John Price to Mr. Thomas Symmons, 4 years Caribbees by *Gabriel*; Robert Browne to same, 4 years Caribbees by *Gabriel*. (BR).

January. Administration of William Booth of Wapping, Stepney, Middlesex, who died in Virginia, bachelor. (AW).

1 February. The following apprenticed in Bristol to go to Virginia by the *Baltimore*: Robert Webb of Marbury [Marlborough], Wilts, to John Nutt, 4 years; Reece Williams of Trevethin, Mon, to John Harris, soapboiler, 4 years; Theophilus Watkins of Amsley [?Aymestrey], Heref, to James Porter, 4 years; John Jones of Lannwerth [?Llanwern], Mon, to John Harris, 4 years. (BR).

4 February. The following apprenticed in Bristol: John Evans to Moses Jones, 4 years Virginia by *Rochelle Merchant*, Mr. Joseph Lewis. (BR).

5 February. Elizabeth Collier, wife of James Collier of Shadwell, Middlesex, yeoman, found guilty of forcibly transporting Sarah Price, spinster, by the *Rebecca* to Virginia. (VM 83/3).

5 February. The following apprenticed in Bristol: Thomas Harris to John Harris, 4 years Virginia by *Baltimore*. (BR).

9 February. The following apprenticed in Bristol: John Russell of Gillsif (*sic*), Montgomery, yeoman, to Thomas Lugg, 4 years Barbados by *Katherine*; Frances Knowles of Caernarvon, spinster, to Peter Palmer, 4 years Barbados by *Nathaniel* of London. (BR).

12 February-4 March. Shippers by the *Good Hope*, Mr. George Northcott, bound from London for New York: John Hawes, William Antleby, Phillip French, Edward Mann, John Atterbury, Thomas Hart, Robert Woolley, William Depeyster, Benjamin Hewling. (PRO: E190/67/3).

15 February. The following apprenticed in Bristol: Thomas Marder of Taunton, Som, woolcomber, to John Friend, 4 years Virginia by *Baltimore*; Richard Reeves to Moses Jones, 4 years Virginia by *Rochelle Merchant*; Richard Griffin to same, 4 years Virginia by *Rochelle Merchant*; Evan Jones of Carmarthen to Mark Piggs, 4 years Virginia by *Baltimore*. (BR).

18 February. Home Circuit prisoners reprieved to be transported to Barbados or Jamaica. Essex: Richard Halls of Wanstead; William Mott of Lambourne. Hertfordshire: Judith Ancell of Ayot, spinster, for infanticide. Kent: Henry Keable of Halling; Silvan Johnson of Woolwich; William Powell of Bobbing; Anthony Chesson of High Halden; William Hills of Stockbury. Surrey: John Bentley of Walton on Thames; Sarah Ancher, spinster, alias wife of John Ancher of St. Saviour, Southwark; Elizabeth Tucker of St. Olave, Southwark; Margaret Scott, spinster, alias wife of William of St. Olave, Southwark (still in prison in July 1677). Sussex: John Bartholomew of Cuckfield. (PRO: C66/3187/24).

1676

19 February. The following apprenticed in Bristol: Herbert Morgan of Panteg, Mon, to Thomas Williams, 7 years Virginia by *John*, Mr. Edward Lewis; Thomas Ree of Aust, Glos, to Joseph Tucker, 5 years Barbados by *Katherine*; Jane Hodges to John Howell, 4 years Virginia by *Rochelle Merchant*; Michaell Smith of Bristol to Frances Morgan, 4 years Jamaica by *America Merchant*. (BR).

19 February-7 March. Shippers by the *John's Adventure*, Mr. John Whalley, bound from London for New York: Hezekiah Usher, William Depeyster, Robert Woolley. (PRO: E190/67/3).

21 February. Deposition by Thomas Sondes, late servant of Edward Allen of London, scrivener, that Samuel Wilson, citizen and merchant tailor of London, became indebted to John Jackson, citizen and merchant tailor of London, by bond of 3 May 1670. James Franck, aged 20, apprentice to John Jackson, deposes that Wilson also became indebted to Jackson by a bond of 3 June 1674. William Pinhorne of New York has been appointed attorney. (LMCD).

22 February-9 March. Shippers by the *Zebulon*, Mr. William Greenoway, bound from London for New England: William Gore, John Child, Hezekiah Usher. (PRO: E190/67/3).

23 February-6 March. Shipper by the *Increase* of Boston bound from Plymouth for Boston, New England: John Horsham. (PRO: E190/1041/14).

February. Probate of will of William Lloyd of Redcliffe, Bristol, who had lands in Rhode Island. (AW).

February. Administration of Robert Taverner of Maryland, bachelor. (AW).

February. Probate of will of Henry Anderson of Bantam, East Indies, whose father John Anderson was in New England. (AW).

2 March. Shipper by the *Mary & Sarah*, Mr. John Foy, bound from London for New England: Thomas Smith. (PRO: E190/67/3).

6 March. Deposition by Samuel Roberts of London, leatherseller aged 21 that John Hooper signed a receipt for goods sent on 18 March 1676 by Mr. Hastings Clarke to William Phillips of Boston, New England, merchant, by the *Zebulon*, Mr. William Greenough. (LMCD).

9-10 March. Shippers by the *Fortune*, Mr. John [or James] Hoddy, bound from London for New York: Robert Woolley, David Conyard. (PRO: E190/67/3).

13 March. Shipper by the *Welcome*, Mr. John Smith, bound from London for New England: Hezekiah Usher. (PRO: E190/67/3).

14 March-5 April. Shippers by the *Blessing*, Mr. David Anderson, bound from London for New England: Robert Woolley, Hezekiah Usher, Noah Lloyd, John Spicer, Abraham Jesson, William Nicholls, Benjamin Hewling, Joseph Scott. (PRO: E190/67/3).

17 March. The following apprenticed in Bristol: Mary Manning to Nathaniel Stephens, 4 years Barbados. (BR).

20 March. Shipper by the *Blossom* of Bideford, Mr. John Quance, bound from Bideford for New England: William Titherly. (PRO: E190/956/7).

25 March. The following apprenticed in Bristol: Thomas Phillips to Thomas Sparks, 5 years Jamaica; Elinor Jones of Aresmon (*sic*), Pembroke, spinster, to Thomas Masters, 4 years Jamaica by *America Merchant*; Richard Constant to same, 4 years Jamaica by *America Merchant*; Thomas Allen to Thomas Lock, 6 years Jamaica by *Primrose*, Mr. Robert Haskins. (BR).

3 April. The following apprenticed in Bristol: Maurice Phillips to Thomas Cock, 4 years Jamaica. (BR).

5 April. The following apprenticed in Bristol: Robert Pollman to Robert Smith, 7 years [not stated]. (BR).

6 April. The following apprenticed in Bristol to go by the *Primrose*: John Williams to Nathaniell Stephens, 4 years Barbados; David Nicholas to same, 4 years Barbados; Simon Griffin to same, 4 years Barbados; Daniell Close of Shudwater [?Shurdington], Glos, aged 15, to William Swymer, 6 years Jamaica. (BR).

7 April. The following apprenticed in Bristol to go by the *America Merchant* to Jamaica: Ann Tuston of Withington, Glos, to Thomas Masters, 4 years; Isaack Lane of Petworth, Sussex, to Joseph Fisher, 4 years. (BR).

22 April. Petition of John and Sarah Bland of Virginia. John Bland bought large plantations in Virginia and settled his two brothers there but one died and the other left only a widow so he sent his son, Giles Bland, to manage his property. A quarrel arose between Giles Bland and Thomas Ludwell which was adjudicated in favour of the latter. (CSPC).

24 April. The following apprenticed in Bristol: Thomas Bradshaw of Winsell [?Winsley], Wilts, to Griffith Jones, 4 years Barbados by *Success*, Mr. William Head. (BR).

24 April & 25 May. Deposition by John Balston of Boston, New England, mariner aged 28, on behalf of John Kempster, plaintiff against William Mead, that he was master of the *Adventure* of Boston and in June 1675 took on board barrels of oil which were delivered to Henry Phillips and Ansted Williams in London. (LMCD).

26 April-23 May. Shippers by the *Sea Flower*, Mr. John Harris, bound from London for New England: Ambrose Harrison, Christopher Marshall, John Kynaston, Phillip French. (PRO: E190/67/3).

27 April. The following apprenticed in Bristol: Samuell Tayler to Oliver Stratton, 5 years Barbados by *Success*. (BR).

April. Administration of Christiana Rodling of Virginia. (AW).

2 May. Shipper by the *Providence*, Mr. Samuel Andrews, bound from London for New England: Henry Ashurst. (PRO: E190/67/3).

8 May. John Kent, Lancelot Shank, labourer, and Richard Rawlins, architect, of King Street, Middlesex, indicted for forcibly putting John Cressop on board ship to be transported to Virginia. (VM 83/3).

10-12 May. Shippers by the *Adventure*, Mr. John Balston, bound from London for New England: Ralph Preston, William Mead. (PRO: E190/67/3).

19 May. The following apprenticed in Bristol: Nicholas Greene to John Perkins, 4 years Newfoundland. (BR).

30 May. Depositions by James Elson of Boston, New England, and Benjamin Ayloffe of London, merchant, that the *Endeavour* of Boston, Mr. Samuel Smith, is bound to the Baltic with a cargo of salt and does not carry prohibited goods. (LMCD).

May. Probate of will of Robert Roane of Chaldon, Surrey, whose son, Charles Roane, was in Virginia. (AW).

May. Probate of will of Henry Baskerville, citizen and fishmonger of London, whose brother, John Baskerville, was in Virginia. (AW).

May. Probate of will of Maurice Thompson of Haversham, Buckinghamshire, who had lands in Virginia. (AW).

May. London prisoners reprieved to be transported to Barbados: Frances Watson, Frances Russell alias Wright, Robert Smyth, Richard Davis, John Atkins, Mary Mills alias Stephens, Mary Jenkins, Benjamin Poole, William Mooreton alias Martin, Elizabeth Garland, John Holmes, John Parsons, Mary Davis, Elizabeth wife of John Minns, John Scalthropp, Griffith Robarts, William Wilmott, Joseph Rowley, Elizabeth Hewitt, Charles Horton, Mary Lee, Robert Appletree, John Prince alias Bates, George Starling, Miles Smyth. (EB).

1 June. Shipper by the *Rebecca* of Plymouth bound from Plymouth for Virginia: George Counter. (PRO: E190/1041/14).

1 June. The following apprenticed in Bristol: Richard Strange to Phillip Seward, 4 years Nevis. (BR).

6 June. The following apprenticed in Bristol: Hugh Tayler to Phillip Seward, 4 years Nevis. (BR).

12 June. Shipper by the *Hopewell*, Mr. Christopher Morse, bound from London for New England: William West. (PRO: E190/67/3).

22 June. The following apprenticed in Bristol: David Williams to William Morgan, 4 years Nevis. (BR).

28 June. The following apprenticed in Bristol to go to Barbados or Virginia by the *Blackmore*: John Harburt to William Bayly, 4 years; Charles Davis to same, 4 years; George Edwards to same, 4 years. (BR).

June. Probate of will of Edward Peck, sergeant at law of the Inner Temple, London, whose son, Edward [Peck], was in New England. (AW).

3 July. Shipper by the *Adventure*, Mr. James Gilbert, bound from London for Virginia: Arthur Bayly. (PRO: E190/67/3).

10 July. The following apprenticed in Bristol: Henry Jones to Robert Passmor, 4 years Virginia by *Phoenix*, Mr. Anthony Alston; William Jones to Arthur Grant, 4 years Virginia by *Nevis Merchant*, said Arthur Grant Mr. (BR).

12 July. The following apprenticed in Bristol: Frances Strattford to John Compton, mariner, 5 years Virginia by *Alexander*, Mr. William Jones; James Ash to William Smith, 4 years Virginia by *Bristol Merchant*, said William Smith Mr. (BR).

18 July. Shipper by the *Elizabeth & Katherine*, Mr. Peter Payne, bound from London for Virginia: William Pagan. (PRO: E190/67/3).

18 July. Shipper by the *Richard & Elizabeth*, Mr. Nicholas Pryn, bound from London for Virginia: William Paggen. (PRO: E190/67/3).

18-20 July. Shippers by the *Bohemia*, Mr. William Fowles, bound from London for Virginia: William Kissen, Robert Williams. (PRO: E190/67/3).

19 July. The following apprenticed in Bristol to go to Virginia by the *Nevis Merchant*: Alice Edwards to Arthur Grant, 5 years; Elizabeth Offer, widow, to same, 5 years; Ellinor Fell, spinster, to same, 5 years. (BR).

20 July. The following apprenticed in Bristol: Mary James to Joseph Clarke, 4 years Virginia by *Alexander*. (BR).

21 July. The following apprenticed in Bristol to go to Virginia by the *Nevis Merchant*: Humphry Scott to Maxfield Walter, 4 years; Richard Floyd to same, 4 years; Robert Evans to same, 4 years; Richard Jones to same, 4 years; John Dowty to same, 4 years. (BR).

21 July. Shipper by the *Young Prince*, Mr. Robert Morris, bound from London for Virginia: Thomas Sandes. (PRO: E190/67/3).

22 July. The following apprenticed in Bristol: Henry Baily to Samuell Clarke, 4 years Virginia by *Alexander*. (BR).

24 July. The following apprenticed in Bristol: John Salter to John Bicknell of Bristol, tailor, 4 years Virginia by *Alexander*. (BR).

28 July. The following apprenticed in Bristol: Edward Rawlins to William Wigginton, 5 years Virginia by *Richard & James*, Mr. Thomas Opey. (BR).

29 July. Shipper by the *Heron*, Mr. John Ely, bound from London for Virginia: Richard Bankes. (PRO: E190/67/3).

29 July. The following apprenticed in Bristol: Edward Weston to John Stephens, 5 years Virginia by *Nevis Merchant*. (BR).

31 July. The following apprenticed in Bristol: Benjamin Addington to Thomas Opy, 4 years Virginia by *Richard & James*. (BR).

July. Administration of John Brand of the ship *Prince*, who died in Virginia, bachelor. (AW).

July. Probate of will of Thomas Isham of the Middle Temple, London, whose cousin, Henry Isham, was in Virginia. (AW).

July. Administration of Harman Derickson of Virginia, bachelor. (AW).

July. Limited administration with will of Richard Fassaker of Stafford County, Virginia, who died on the ship *Rappahannock Merchant* at sea. (AW).

July. Administration of William Connington of Baltimore County, Maryland, bachelor. (AW).

July. Administration with will of David Anthony of Virginia, bachelor. (AW).

3 August. Shipper by the *Hopewell*, Mr. Michael Yoakley, bound from London for Maryland: William Rousby. (PRO: E190/67/3).

4 August. The following apprenticed in Bristol: William Blackgrove to John Snow, 4 years Virginia by *Batchelor*, said John Snow Mr. (BR).

5 August. The following apprenticed in Bristol: Richard Farmer to Caleb Cotterell, mariner, 4 years Virginia by *Richard & James*. (BR).

5-9 August. Shippers by the *Crown Mallaga*, Mr. Thomas Applethwait, bound from London for Virginia: Edward Leman, William Dorpe, Thomas Parker, —— Collingwood. (PRO: E190/67/3).

7 August. The following apprenticed in Bristol: John Fransum to Robert Welch, 4 years Virginia by *Stephen*, Mr. John Read. (BR).

7-14 August. Shippers by the *Mary*, Mr. John Consett, bound from London for Virginia: Samuel Wickins, Micajah Perry, —— Luddington, John Rutland. (PRO: E190/67/3).

8 August. The following apprenticed in Bristol: Hester Marchfield to Abraham Olliver, mariner, 4 years Virginia by *Phoenix*; Thomas Baker to Thomas Daniell, mariner, 4 years Virginia by *Richard & James*; Roger Squire to Robert Begham, tobacco cutter, 4 years Virginia by *Stephen*. (BR).

10 August. The following apprenticed in Bristol: Edward Lawrence to William Price, mariner, 4 years Virginia by *Unicorn*, Mr. Thomas Cooper; Samuell Gerrard to Arthur Grant, 4 years Virginia by *Nevis Merchant*. (BR).

10 August-4 September. Shippers by the *Increase*, Mr. John Holland, bound from London for New England: John Harwood, Edward West, Noah Floyd, Jeremiah Johnson, George Baron, Samuel Wickins, Miles Foster, Robert Woolley, Robert Day. (PRO: E190/67/3).

14 August. The following apprenticed in Bristol: John Bevill to Caleb Cockerell, 4 years Virginia by *Richard & James*; William Packer to Zacharias Smith, 5 years Virginia by *Maryland Merchant*, Mr. William Trego; John Phillips to same, 5 years Virginia by *Maryland Merchant*; Richard Sidenham to Thomas Gamon, 4 years Barbados by *Blackmore*, said Thomas Gamon Mr; Mary Horseman to Abraham Olliver, mariner, 4 years Virginia by *Phoenix*; Richard Knight to Abraham Evans, mariner, 5 years Virginia by *Bristol Merchant*; Richard Glosty to Nathaniell Peddar, 7 years Virginia by *Batchelor*; John Bradshaw to John Charles, 9 years Nevis by *Endeavour*, Mr. Simon Emery; Jane Woods to John King, 4 years Virginia by *Phoenix*. (BR).

15 August. Chester Circuit prisoners reprieved to be transported to Barbados. Cheshire: William Roberts of Bloverdstone, husbandman. Flintshire: Robert Porter and John Arthur of Flint. Denbighshire: John Morgan and Edward ap Evan of Wrexham; William Thomas and Robert Thomas of Ruthin; Hugh Thomas of Brefford; Griffin Jones of Llangollen; John Roberts of the same; Owen Hughes of the same; Thomas Abell of Denbigh, husbandman. (PRO: C66/3186/11).

15 August. The following apprenticed in Bristol: George Mathews to Robert Lancaster, 4 years Virginia by *Bristol Merchant*. (BR).

15 August. Shipper by the *Susanna* bound from Plymouth for Virginia: Andrew Phillips. (PRO: E190/1041/14).

16 August. The following apprenticed in Bristol: William Harris to John Marden, 4 years Virginia by *Phoenix*; Thomas Compton to Richard Hooper, mariner, 4 years Virginia by *Unicorn*, Mr. Thomas Cooper. (BR).

16-29 August. Shippers by the *Virginia Factor*, Mr. James Conway, bound from London for Virginia: Edward Cooke, Micajah Perry, Edward Round, James Godfrey, Richard Carter. (PRO: E190/67/3).

17-26 August. Shippers by the *Friends Increase*, Mr. John Martin, bound from London for Virginia: John Jennings, Micajah Perry, William Sherley, John Webb, Isaac Merritt. (PRO: E190/67/3).

17 August-4 September. Shippers by the *Providence*, Mr. Andrew Boone, bound from London for New York: [Phillip] French, Elisha Holliock, Thomas Boyston, Benjamin Davis, Samuell Himby, —— Kingsland, Samuel Wickins, Jeremiah Forman, Benjamin Hewling, Edward Woodgate. (PRO: E190/67/3).

18 August. The following apprenticed in Bristol: Samuell Gayner to Thomas Speed, 5 years Virginia [by *Agreement*]; Thomas Ward to same, 5 years Virginia [by *Agreement*]; Susanna Brayne to John Wathen, 4 years Maryland by *Susanna*, Mr. William Neades; Hanna Ford to Lewis Heath, mariner, 4 years Virginia by *Bristol Merchant*; Edward Wallis to same, 4 years Virginia by *Bristol Merchant*; John Thomas to Maxfield Walter, 4 years Virginia by *Nevis Merchant*. (BR).

18-25 August. Shippers by the *William* of Plymouth bound from Plymouth for Virginia: William Martin, John Luke. (PRO: E190/1041/14).

18-29 August. Shippers by the *Virginia Merchant* bound from Plymouth for Virginia: William Martin, Richard Vinson, John Merring, Nicholas Jory, Robert Hodge, Nicholas Curle. (PRO: E190/1041/14).

19 August. The following apprenticed in Bristol: Lewis Francis to Richard Hawkins, 4 years Virginia by *Richard & James*; James Russe to Ralph Smith, 4 years Virginia by *John*, Mr. Peter Wraxall; Joseph Farworth to Robert Lancaster, 4 years Virginia. (BR).

21 August. The following apprenticed in Bristol: John Taylor to Henry Hieron, soap boiler, 4 years Virginia by *George*, Mr. John Isaac; Henry Kent to Peter Smith, mariner, 4 years Virginia by *Unicorn*; Nicholas Westcott to Thomas Yates, mariner, 4 years Virginia by *Agreement*; James Prince to Phillip Neason, 4 years Virginia by *Agreement*; Mary Coles to Charles Haynes, 4 years Virginia by *Susanna*; Joseph Edmund to Caleb Cockerill, 4 years Virginia by *Richard & James*. (BR).

23 August. The following apprenticed in Bristol: Elizabeth Chamberlin to John Fearne, 4 years Virginia by *Batchelor*; James Penn to Ralph Smith, 4 years Virginia by *[St.] John*; Robert Bicham to Richard Lloyd, shipwright, 5 years Virginia by *Susanna*; Brydgett Shippman to Zachariah Smith, mariner, 5 years Virginia by *Maryland Merchant*. (BR).

26 August. The following apprenticed in Bristol: William Seye to Jasper Jenkins, 4 years Maryland by *Susanna*; Richard Powell to same, 4 years Maryland by *Susanna*; Thomas Price to same, 4 years Maryland by *Susanna*; Mary Jenkins to same, 4 years Maryland by *Susanna*; Jane Boole to same, 4 years Maryland by *Susanna*; Edward Boole to same, 4 years Maryland by *Susanna*; John Jones to Simon Gethin, 7 years Virginia by *Nevis Merchant*; William Harrwarr to William Upington, 4 years Virginia by *Susanna*; Edward Phillips to William S—ley, 4 years Virginia by *William & John*; Robert White to John Fearne, 4 years Virginia by *Batchelor*; Sarah Bay to Lawrence Herder, mariner, 4 years Virginia by *William & Ann*; Rebecca Stephens to Lewis Heath, 4 years Virginia by *Bristol Merchant*. (BR).

26 August-4 September. Shippers by the *Joseph & Benjamin*, Mr. Matthew Payne, bound from London for Virginia: John Coldham, John Ebsworth, John Steventon. (PRO: E190/67/3).

28 August-2 September. Shippers by the *James & Thomas* of Plymouth bound from Plymouth for Virginia: John Stone, Thomas Powell, Abraham Edgcombe, Ezechiell Marsh, James Trewells. (PRO: E190/1041/14).

28 August-18 September. Shippers by the *Love*, Mr. Oswell Wheatly, bound from London for Maryland: George Parker, Richard Banks, James Holland. (PRO: E190/67/3).

29 August. The following apprenticed in Bristol: Anthony Blanchard to Thomas Horsington, planter, 4 years Virginia by *Unicorn*; Jenkin Thomas to Mathew Cradock, 4 years Virginia by *Unicorn*; Alice James to Charles Haynes, 4 years Potuxan River by *Susan*. (BR).

29 August-6 September. Shippers by the *Marygold* of Weymouth, Mr. John Cox, bound from Weymouth for Virginia: Richard Byles, Symon Orchard. (PRO: E190/882/8).

29 August-11 September. Shippers by the *Concord*, Mr. Thomas Grantham, bound from London for Virginia: [Thomas] Baker, Thomas Jaques, Richard Glover, Robert Johnson, George Baker, Richard Hutchinson. (PRO: E190/67/3).

30 August. Shipper by the *Concord* of Newcastle, Mr. Edward Robinson, bound from Newcastle for Virginia: Christopher Gresham. (PRO: E190/196/6).

30 August. The following apprenticed in Bristol: Christopher Norton to Richard Wilcox, mariner, 4 years Virginia by *Unicorn*; Walter Wheath to Caleb Cockerill, mariner, 7 years Virginia by *Richard & James*; Thomas Jenkin to Thomas Edwards, planter, 4 years Virginia by *Unicorn*. (BR).

30-31 August. Shippers by the *Relief*, Mr. George Purvis, bound from London for Virginia: Maximilian Petty?, Edward Lemon, John Reade. (PRO: E190/67/3).

31 August. Deed of release by Eleanor Young, relict and administratrix of Paul Young of Stepney, Middlesex, cutler, deceased, of her claim on her husband's estate to Thomas Notley of Maryland, merchant. (LMCD).

31 August. The following apprenticed in Bristol: Charles Greene to Edward Watts, 5 years Virginia by *Bristol Merchant*. (BR).

31 August-6 September. Shippers by the *Baltimore*, Mr. John Dunch, bound from London for Virginia and Maryland: George Cornish, Thomas Elwes, Thomas Harwood. (PRO: E190/67/3).

August. Administration of Thomas Boys of Patochnick River, Virginia, widower. (AW).

August. Probate of will of Richard Bennett of Nansemond River, Virginia. (AW).

August. Administration of John Jenney of St. Mary at Hill London, who died in Virginia, bachelor. (AW).

4 September. The following apprenticed in Bristol: Thomas Goodwin to Richard Hooper, 4 years Virginia by *Unicorn*; William Sely to Peter Archer, 4 years Maryland [by *Agreement*]; Margery Lewis to same, 5 years Maryland [by *Agreement*]; Herbert Power to Thomas Speed, 7 years Virginia by *Agreement*. (BR).

4 September. Shipper by the *Friendship*, Mr. John Holland, bound from London for New England: Edward Ellis. (PRO: E190/67/3).

4-11 September. Shippers by the *Duke of York*, Mr. John Purvis, bound from London for Virginia: James Johnson, Thomas Fern, William West. (PRO: E190/67/3).

5 September. The following apprenticed in Bristol: Richard Bayneham to William Clarke, 4 years Virginia by *Susanna*; Henry Freke to William Alford, 4 years Virginia by *Maryland Merchant*, Mr. William Trego; Phillip Dennis to Caleb Cockerill, 5 years Virginia by *Richard & James*; Edith Collins to Nathaniell Day, 4 years Virginia by *Agreement*; Mary Price to Abraham Oliver, 4 years Virginia by *Maryland Merchant*. (BR).

5-6 September. Shippers by the *America* of Plymouth bound from Plymouth for Virginia: Samuell Brett, Edward Jeffery. (PRO: E190/1041/14).

6 September. Deposition by William Odeon of Stepney, Middlesex, mariner aged 25, and Giles Nash of St. Botolph Aldersgate, London, surgeon aged 27, that on 22 April 1676 Richard Taylor of South Branch, Elizabeth River, Lower Norfolk County, Virginia, appointed William Taylor of London, merchant, as his attorney. (LMCD).

6 September. Deposition by Robert Barton of London, notary public aged 28, that William Dorrington of Potuxon River, Calvert County, Maryland, signed a deed on 15 August 1666 in the house of Barnaby Dunch of Leadenhall Street, London, whereby he became indebted to Walter Dunch of London, mariner, in order to provide a marriage portion for his wife, Mary Johnson alias Dunch, late wife of Walter Dunch and daughter of Anne Johnson, now Mary Dorrington. The marriage was performed in Potuxon in January 1664. (LMCD).

6 September. Shippers by the *Fortune*, Mr. Bartholomew Clements, bound from London for Virginia: Thomas Parker, William? Evans, James Hayes(?). (PRO: E190/67/3).

6 September. Shippers by the *Bideford Merchant*, Mr. William Mosey, bound from Bideford for Maryland: Henry Cadd, John Davie. (PRO: E190/956/7).

6 September. Shipper by the *Beginning* of Bideford, Mr. John Courtis, bound from Bideford for Maryland: Thomas Power. (PRO: E190/956/7).

7 September. Shippers by the *Noah's Ark*, Mr. Noah Band, bound from London for Maryland: Giles Bullock. (PRO: E190/67/3).

7 September. Shipper by the *Fortune* of Bideford, Mr. Ethelred Darracott, bound from Bideford for Maryland: Andrew Hopkins. (PRO: E190/956/7).

8 September. Thomas Gore of St. Katherine by the Tower, London, found guilty of forcibly putting Edward Meade aboard the *Charles* to be conveyed to Virginia and sold there. (VM 83/3).

8-13 September. Shippers by the *Augustine*, Mr. Zachary Taylor, bound from London for Virginia: Francis Tysen, Richard Booth, [Hugh] Hartshorne, Francis Camfield. (PRO: E190/67/3).

11-27 September. Shippers by the *Francis*, Mr. John Warner, bound from London for Virginia: John Ewing, Edward Leman, Benjamin Peake. (PRO: E190/67/3).

13 September. Thomas Luckett of London, scrivener aged 35, deposes that William Dunkerton, then of London, merchant, but late of Baltimore County, Maryland, signed a deed of 22 September 1675 whereby he mortgaged to Robert Hawkins, now of London, ropemaker, but then of Maryland, three plantations: 700 acres called Colleton on Chesapeake Bay, 150 acres called Triangle on Chesapeake Bay, and 600 acres called Two Necks on Old River. The deeds of sale were acknowledged in Baltimore County and entered into the Register Book. (LMCD).

13 September. The following apprenticed in Bristol: Roger Davis to Abraham Oliver, 4 years Virginia by *Maryland Merchant*. (BR).

13-22 September. Shippers by the *Hopewell*, Mr. John Rudd, bound from London for Virginia: Thomas Grindon, Thomas Dearsley. (PRO: E190/67/3).

16 September. Deposition by Robert Greenwood, aged 17, clerk to John Fisher of Grays Inn, London, gent, that George Halfhide alias Harris of Ware, Gloucester County, Virginia, merchant, signed a bond of 27 August 1676 to Elizabeth Edwards of Long Alley, St. Leonard Shoreditch, Middlesex, spinster, by which a 250 acre plantation in Ware occupied by Halfhide alias Harris and by George Sanders was assigned in trust to Richard Basnett of Ware, tailor. (LMCD).

16 September. Shipper by the *Constant Katherine*, Mr. Benjamin Masters, bound from London for Virginia: George Gay. (PRO: E190/67/3).

16 September. The following apprenticed in Bristol: Richard Howell to William Swymmer, 4 years Jamaica. (BR).

18-22 September. Shippers by the *Barnaby*, Mr. Matthew Ryder, bound from London for Virginia: Ralph Harwood, George Richards. (PRO: E190/67/3).

19 September. The following apprenticed in Bristol: Daniell Hurly to William Worrell, 4 years Virginia by *Maryland Merchant*; Robert Seward to Richard Tovey, 4 years Nevis. (BR).

20 September. The following apprenticed in Bristol: Mary White to Abraham Oliver, 4 years Virginia by *Maryland Merchant*; George Millard to Richard Tovey, 7 years Nevis by *Sarah*, Mr. William Sheppard. (BR).

22 September. The following apprenticed in Bristol: Thomas Crippin to Thomas Cock, 4 years Virginia by *William & Ann*, Mr. Philip Hanger; Richard Tomlinson and Helen his wife to Thomas Walter, 4 years Virginia by *Maryland Merchant*. (BR).

22 September. Shipper by the *Anne*, Mr. Benjamin Cooper, bound from London for Virginia: John Cooper. (PRO: E190/67/3).

22-30 September. Shippers by the *Charles*, Mr. Walter Dunch, bound from London for Maryland: James Godfrey, Peter Devell. (PRO: E190/67/3).

22 September-11 December. Shippers by the *Prince*, Mr. Robert Conway, bound from London for Virginia: Hugh Hartshorne, Edward Leman, John Lewin. (PRO: E190/67/3).

23 September. The following apprenticed in Bristol to go by the *Maryland Merchant*: Hester Price to Arthur Young, 4 years Virginia; David Evans to same, 4 years Virginia; John Davis to same, 4 years Virginia; John Price to same, 4 years Virginia; Thomas Bevan to Benjamin Lawrence, 4 years Maryland; Richard Winson to same, 5 years Maryland; Mary Ano to same, 5 years Maryland; Elizabeth Wedmore to William Norman, 4 years Virginia. (BR).

25 September. The following apprenticed in Bristol: Elizabeth Austin to John Whittfield, 4 years Virginia by *William & Ann*; James Sutton to Isaac Sheares, 5 years Virginia by *Francis & Mary*, Mr. William Nicholas. (BR).

27 September. Shipper by the *Thomas & Edward*, Mr. John Browne, bound from London for Virginia: William Antleby. (PRO: E190/67/3).

28 September. The following apprenticed in Bristol: John Smith to Henry Earle, 7 years Virginia by *William & Ann*. (BR).

30 September. The following apprenticed in Bristol to go to Virginia by the *William & Ann*: Martha Steven to John Whittfield, 4 years; Nathaniell Mason to Phillip Hanger, 4 years. (BR).

30 September-2 October. Shippers by the *Exeter Merchant*, Mr. Derby Hickey, bound from Exeter for Virginia: Richard Bounsford, Joseph Mauditt, Jasper Radcliffe, Thomas Brooking. (PRO: E190/956/14).

September. Administration of Ralph Couch of Stepney, Middlesex, who died in Virginia. (AW).

2 October. The following apprenticed in Bristol to go to Virginia by the *Francis & Mary*: Hannah Pate to Richard Milsham, 4 years; John Thompson to Isaac Sheares, 6 years. (BR).

4 October. The following apprenticed in Bristol: Mordecay Jones to Richard Milsum, 4 years Virginia by *Francis & Mary*. (BR).

7 October. The following apprenticed in Bristol: Thomas Price to Matthew Court, 4 years Virginia. (BR).

10 October. The following apprenticed in Bristol: Joseph Parry to Henry Baker, 4 years Virginia; Jane Harvy to William Mussaven, 4 years Virginia. (BR).

12 October. The following apprenticed in Bristol: Benjamin Gildar to John Baker, 4 years Virginia by *George*, Mr. Samuel Isaac; Dorothy Adams to William Harcum, 4 years Virginia by *Francis & Mary*; Mary Gardner to John Mason, 4 years Virginia by *George*. (BR).

13 October. The following apprenticed in Bristol: Rachell Shelton to John Whittfield, 4 years Virginia by *William & Ann*. (BR).

16 October. The following apprenticed in Bristol: John Downing to Thomas Tandy, 5 years Virginia by *William & Ann*; Jane Powter to William Walls, 4 years Virginia by *Francis & Mary*. (BR).

17 October. The following apprenticed in Bristol: Nicholas Savory to Richard Tovey, 4 years Nevis; John Wattkins to William Walls, 4 years Virginia by *Francis & Mary*. (BR).

23 October. Shipper by the *John's Adventure*, Mr. Edward Winslow, bound from London for New England: Morris Moseley. (PRO: E190/67/3).

24 October. The following apprenticed in Bristol to go to Virginia by the *Francis & Mary*: Elinor Foord to Charles Meredith, 4 years; Elizabeth Constant to Thomas Stevens, 4 years. (BR).

26 October. Deposition by Richard Stonehill of London, notary public aged 28, that John Gifford of New England, merchant, became bound to John Wright Esq. of Wrightsbridge, Essex, by deed of 4 June 1673. (LMCD).

27 October. The following apprenticed in Bristol: George Hanks to Thomas Stevens, 4 years Virginia by *Francis & Mary*. (BR).

30 October. The following apprenticed in Bristol: Thomas Rake to Osmond Crabb, 5 years Virginia; John Collins to John Whittfield, 7 years Virginia by *William & Ann*. (BR).

October. Administration of Phebe Smith of Virginia, spinster. (AW).

October. Probate of will of Daniel Wyld of Brewerton, York County, Virginia. (AW).

1 November. The following apprenticed in Bristol to go to Virginia by the *Francis & Mary*: Reece Jenkins to Lewis Markham, 4 years; Stephen Morgan to same, 4 years; Thomas Jenkins to same, 4 years; William Morgan to same, 4 years; Ann Davis to same, 4 years. (BR).

4 November. The following apprenticed in Bristol: John How to Thomas Cock, 4 years Virginia by *William & Ann*. (BR).

7 November. The following apprenticed in Bristol: Jeremiah Perry to William Bull, 4 years Virginia by *William & Ann*; Hannah Foord to John Mason, 4 years Virginia by *George* ; Richard Sherman to William Andrewes, 4 years Virginia by *Francis & Mary*; Elizabeth Sampson to Thomas Nelson, 5 years Virginia by *George*. (BR).

9-16 November. Shippers by the *Constant [Jacob]*, Mr. Jacob Hay, bound from London for Virginia: John Jennings, Bernard Mitchell. (PRO: E190/67/3).

10-29 November. Shippers by the *Anne*, Mr. Benjamin Cooke, bound from London for Virginia: Henry Maynard, William Dolby, Thomas Crundall, Godfrey Webster. (PRO: E190/67/3).

13 November. The following apprenticed in Bristol: John Warrell to Thomas Tandy, Virginia by *William & Ann*. (BR).

14 November. The following apprenticed in Bristol: Daniell Underwood to John Woolven, 4 years Virginia by *Francis & Mary*; (BR).

15 November. The following apprenticed in Bristol: Richard Tarbutt to Richard —Isham, 4 years Virginia by *Francis & Mary*; Joseph Roberts to Lewis Markham, 4 years Virginia by *Francis & Mary*; Diana Nokes to Thomas Compton, 4 years Antigua by *Mary*, Mr. Thomas Berry. (BR).

17 November. The following apprenticed in Bristol to go to Virginia by the *George*: John Reeves to Samuell Isaac, 5 years; Robert Davis to same, 5 years. (BR).

23 November. The following apprenticed in Bristol: Elionor Evans to Thomas Parsons, 4 years Antigua by *Mary*; Rowland Gwin to Richard Tovey, 5 years Nevis by *Planter*, Mr. Robert Hawkins; David Philipps to John Marden, 5 years Virginia by *Francis & Mary*. (BR).

24 November. The following apprenticed in Bristol: Isaac Bishopp to Thomas Nelson, 4 years Virginia by *George*; Thomas Richards to same, 5 years Virginia by *George*; Ann Crow to Lawrence Hatter, 4 years Virginia by *Francis & Mary*; Daniell Simon to Isaac Sheares, 5 years Virginia by *Francis & Mary*; Elizabeth Cooper to Richard White, 4 years Virginia by *Sarah & Elizabeth*, said Richard White Mr. (BR).

25 November. Edward Nelthorpe of London has appointed Benjamin Rozier of Maryland, merchant, as his attorney. (LMCD).

29 November. The following apprenticed in Bristol: Joane Leeke to Richard White, 4 years Virginia by *Sarah & Elizabeth*; Elizabeth Edmonds to John Mason, 4 years Virginia by *George*, said John Mason Mr. (BR).

30 November. The following apprenticed in Bristol: David Rosser to Lewis Markham, 4 years Virginia by *Francis & Mary*. (BR).

November. Administration of Edward Yardley of Virginia bachelor. (AW).

November. Probate of will of Margaret Stone of St. Peter le Poor, London, widow, whose husband, William Stone, was in Virginia. (AW).

2 December. The following apprenticed in Bristol: Robert Berkly to Robert Williams, 4 years Virginia by *Francis & Mary*; Henry Powter to John Mason, 7 years Virginia by *George*; Lewis Williams to John Obridge, 7 years Maryland by *Alithea*, Mr. Edward Watkins; Hugh Addison to Thomas Tandy, 4 years Virginia by *Francis & Mary*; Thomas Whittchelly to Joseph Adlam, 4 years Virginia by *Francis & Mary*. (BR).

4 December. Deposition by John Flowerdewe, aged 29, citizen and grocer of London, that Sir Henry Chicheley of Rappahannock, Virginia, and his wife Dame Agatha, assigned their plantations in Virginia to John Jefferies Esq. and Thomas Coleclough of London by deed of 26 August 1669. Depositions to similar effect made by John Keylway of St. Giles in the Fields, London, spinster (*sic*) aged 34, and John Burgess of London, gent aged 30. (LMCD).

13 December. The following apprenticed in Bristol: Margarett Harris to John Willett, 4 years Virginia by *William & Ann*; Michaell Davis to Richard Bubb, 4 years Barbados by *Batchelor*. (BR).

15 December. The following apprenticed in Bristol: Phillipp Evans to William Swymmer, 4 years Jamaica by *America Merchant*. (BR).

18 December. The following apprenticed in Bristol: Richard Widdus to Richard Gottley, 4 years Virginia by *George*; John Radford to John Willett, 4 years Virginia by *William & Ann*. (BR).

19 December. The following apprenticed in Bristol: Reece Davis to John Woolvyn, 4 years Virginia by *George*. (BR).

21 December. The following apprenticed in Bristol: William Davis to Thomas Nelson, 4 years Virginia by *Charles*. (BR).

23 December. The following apprenticed in Bristol: John Adis to Christopher Guys, 4 years Nevis by *Love's Increase*. (BR).

29 December. Shipper by the *Sicillia*, Mr. John Body, bound from London for Virginia: Richard Banks. (PRO: E190/72/1).

29 December-8 January. Shipper by the *Relief*, Mr. George Purvis, bound from London for Virginia: William Rousby. (PRO: E190/80/1).

December. Probate of will of William White of St. Bride, London, whose brother, John White, was in Virginia. (AW).

1677

3-14 January. Shippers by the *Francis*, Mr. Richard Covill, bound from London for Virginia: Thomas Parker, Joseph Stephens. (PRO: E190/80/1).

10 January. The following apprenticed in Bristol: Cornelius Giles to William Swymmer, 4 years Jamaica by *America Merchant*. (BR).

11 January-10 March. Shippers by the *Adventure*, Mr. Arthur Fanner, bound from London for New England: Henry Phillips, Phillip French, Samuell Stone, Richard Lucas, Richard Holt, Thomas Walker, Samuel Whislem, Walter Mico, William Crowch, William White, Richard Merin, Edward Hull, William Stonestreet, George Shallcross, Thomas Lane, William Meade, Edward Mann, Alexander Hosea, Thomas Wilkins, Joseph Hayes, Henry Greenwood. (PRO: E190/72/1).

16 January. The following apprenticed in Bristol: Benjamin Thomas to George Mason, 4 years Barbados by *Golden Lion*, Mr. Nathaniell Saunders; Robert Vibian to William Swymmer, 4 years Jamaica by *America Merchant*; Robert Window to Robert Kirke, 4 years Jamaica by *America Merchant*; Alice Dickes to William Colton, 4 years Jamaica by *America Merchant*. (BR).

18 January. The following apprenticed in Bristol to go to Jamaica by the *America Merchant*: Elizabeth Collins to Joseph Bryan, 4 years; John Curtis to same, 4 years. (BR).

19 January. The following apprenticed in Bristol to go to Jamaica by the *America Merchant*: Abraham Nicholas to William Swymmer, 4 years; John Newman to William Martyn, 4 years. (BR).

22 January. The following apprenticed in Bristol: Welthian Savage to Michaell Colton, 4 years Jamaica by *America Merchant*. (BR).

24 January. The following apprenticed in Bristol: John Brebery to John Snow, 4 years Barbados by *Batchelor*, said John Snow Mr; Robert Nickins to Roger Williams, 4 years Barbados by *Golden Lion*. (BR).

26 January. The following apprenticed in Bristol: Charles Buttler to William German, 4 years Barbados by *Batchelor*. (BR).

28 January-12 February. Shippers by the *Fortune*, Mr. Bartholomew Clement, bound from London for Virginia: Peter Walraven, John Cary. (PRO: E190/80/1).

January. Probate of will of Robert Tavernor of London, who died in Virginia, merchant. (AW).

1 February. The following apprenticed in Bristol: Samuel Curtis to Abraham King, 6 years Newfoundland by *Mary & Joane*, Mr. William Ashton. (BR).

277

2 February. The following apprenticed in Bristol to go to Nevis by the *Exchange*, Mr. Richard Speed: John Bushell to Elias Loud, 5 years; Ansell Williams to John Eason, 4 years. (BR).

5 February. The following apprenticed in Bristol: Stephen Goun to John Fern, 4 years Barbados by *Batchelor*. (BR).

6-28 February. Shippers by the *Two Sisters*, Mr. Samuell Johnson, bound from London for New England: Edward Hull, Humphrey Warren, Thomas Stone, Robert Carnell, William Crouch, Richard Studing, William Thomas, Charles Phillips, Thomas Lane, John Lake, Thomas Hartley, William Stonestreet, Peter Gray, James Parke, Robert Thorner, John Tipton, Richard Creswell, John Sharp, William Barron, John Lasher, Robert Lucas, Spencer Piggott, Thomas Hill, Marmaduke Roundall, Samuell Wickins, John Ive, Joseph Cox, William Mead, John Ind, William Chambers, John Cresner. (PRO: E190/80/1)

7 February. The following apprenticed in Bristol: Daniell Millard to Charles Richards, 6 years Barbados by *Society*, Mr. Edmund Ditty; Rose Brindall to John Snow, 4 years Barbados by *Batchelor*; Katharine Howell to same, 4 years Barbados by *Batchelor*. (BR).

8 February. The following apprenticed in Bristol: Robert Sprewell to Richard Speed, 4 years Nevis by *Exchange*; Walter Denham to same, 4 years Nevis by *Exchange*; John Hewins to Thomas Buttler, 4 years Nevis by *Exchange*; William Baylis to John Neades, 4 years Barbados by *Love's Increase*, said John Neades Mr. (BR).

8 February-8 March. Shippers by the *Elizabeth*, Mr. John Wild, bound from London for New England: Edmond White, Francis Fox, William Barron, John Cresner, William Gore, Richard Stopforth. (PRO: E190/80/1).

9 February. The following apprenticed in Bristol: Lawrence Foweracre to David Price, 4 years Barbados by *Golden Lion*. (BR).

10 February. The following apprenticed in Bristol: Philipp Saunder to Abraham King, 9 years Newfoundland by *Jacob*, Mr. Thomas Edwards. (BR).

12 February. The following apprenticed in Bristol: Owen Hugh to John Neson, 4 years [Nevis] by *Exchange*; Richard Cullin to John Curtis, 4 years Barbados by *Batchelor*. (BR).

12-15 February. Shippers by the *Concord*, Mr. William Tennant, bound from London for Virginia: Lawrence Kilby, William Belfore, Richard Glover, Sary Bradbent. (PRO: E190/80/1).

14-27 February. Shippers by the *Albemarle*, Mr. Peter Welcom, bound from London for New England: William Shirley, Thomas Tryon, Thomas Roach, Thomas Rock, Richard Banks, Edward Merriweather, Ralph Box, Thomas Hollis, James Bush, William Jordan, Robert Buckley, Phillip French, Abraham Jesson, James Hayes, Thomas Fermin, Henry Phillips, Daniell Allen, Allen

Hackshawe, Samuell Wickins, Thomas Lane, Robert Stone, Edward Hull, William Roulston, Gabriell Wheatley, James Bush, William Prout, Joshua Dinsdall, John Reynolds, John Blackhall, John Read, James Eyton, Alexander Hosea, Francis Fox, Richard Lloyd, Benjamin Gerrard, John Cresner. (PRO: E190/80/1).

15 February. The following apprenticed in Bristol: Thomas Newcome to Richard Speed, 4 years Nevis by *Exchange*. (BR).

16 February-30 April. Shippers by the *Blessing*, Mr. David Anderson & Mr. John Phillips, bound from London for New England: William Crowch, Edward Hull, Thomas Gatton, Abraham Jesson, Thomas Hill, Robert Oxe, Samuel Watkins, John Palmer, Benjamin Mumford, John Wase, William Middleton, John Baldwin, John Ebwin, Robert Woolley, David Potter, John Knapp, Samuell Eaton, Timothy Waldo, John Crowe, Phillip French, Giles Long, George Roach, Francis Parsons, Valentine Adams, Daniell Ingle, William Ambler, John Sabin, Spencer Piggott, William Shirley, Arthur Cooke, William White, Francis Fox, George Leggatt, James Child, John Reynolds, Christopher Marshall, Clement Stockwell, Thomas Major, Thomas Smith, Thomas Hill, Thomas Ruck, Thomas Humphreys, Thomas Powell, Joseph Freeman, John Loggin, Blaze Clarke, William Hubert, Richard Burden, Thomas Glover, Ezekiell Hutchinson, James Goldham, William Whiting, Walter Mico, Elizabeth Harwood. (PRO: E190/72/1, 80/1).

20 February. The following apprenticed in Bristol: Henry Williams to Dennis Lond, 7 years Nevis or Antigua by *Exchange*; William Whiteacre to William Bradly, 4 years Barbados by *Gabriel*; Giles English to same, 4 years Barbados by *Gabriel*; William English to same, 4 years Barbados by *Gabriel*; Thomas Lawrence to Richard Treherne, 7 years Jamaica by *Isabella*, Mr. Dennis Tayler. (BR).

24 February. The following apprenticed in Bristol: Robert Cripps to Abraham King, 5 years Newfoundland by *Jacob*; George Capp to John Snow, 4 years Barbados by *Batchelor*. (BR).

26 February. The following apprenticed in Bristol: Elioner Peirce to John Snow, 4 years Barbados by *Batchelor*. (BR).

26 February-23 March. Shippers by the *Diligence*, Mr. Thomas Palmer, bound from London for New England: James Burkin, Henry Warren, Nicholas Harrison, William Potter, John Hunkes, Robert Scudamore, Henry Mumford, Thomas Tryon, Francis Fox, Thomas Buck. (PRO: E190/72/1).

27 February. The following apprenticed in Bristol: Rebeccah Browne to Roger Bagg, 5 years Barbados by *Batchelor*. (BR).

February. Administration of James Nedham of Virginia, bachelor. (AW).

1 March. The following apprenticed in Bristol: Edmund Farre to John Comber, 4 years Nevis by *Gabriel*; Sarah Pope to George Marks, 5 years Barbados by *Dolphin*. (BR).

3 March. Newgate prisoners reprieved to be transported to Barbados. London: John Woolfe; Sarah Comford, spinster, alias wife of Edward Comford; Elizabeth Whitehead, spinster; Mary Tool alias White alias Taffe alias Fowler; Sara Trangmore, spinster; William Cole; Mary Hawley,spinster, alias wife of Richard Hawley; James Parker; Walter Bailey; John Flower; Thomas Powell; John Wilson alias Cox; William Sowdell; James Lloyd; Jane Harris; Nicholas Cockerell; Martin Shinfield; Thomas Harper; William Tabor; Dorothy Moore, spinster; James Mathews. Middlesex: Rose Goodman alias Wheeler of Whitechapel or St. Giles Cripplegate, spinster; Elizabeth Smith of St. Margaret Westminster, widow; Elizabeth Evans of the same, spinster; Richard Wootten of the same; Francis Dewitt alias Rolls of the same; Uriel, wife of Thomas Wittens, alias Uriel Hodges, spinster, of the same; Mary Phillips of St. Giles Cripplegate, spinster; William Neale of the same for manslaughter; Elizabeth Whitehorne of Shadwell, spinster; Elizabeth Bishop of the same, spinster; Ruth Webber of the same, spinster; Sarah Bowen, wife of John Bowen, alias Sarah Smith, spinster, of St. Botolph Aldgate; Charles Constantine of Stepney; Jane Price of Islington, spinster; James Newton of Whitechapel; John Salley of Enfield; James Tivey of Chelsea or St. Margaret Westminster; William Motley of Acton; Gilbert Jackson of Willesden. (PRO: C66/3188/6).

3-26 March. Shippers by the *John & Thomas*, Mr. Thomas Jenner, bound from London for New England: Stoph Maberly, James Gouldham, John Wase, Spencer Pigott, Robert Wynn, John Arnold, John Richardson, James Sotheby, John Oulton, Matthew Hatton, William Antleby, William Crowch, Abraham Jesson, Gabriel Whitely, Edward Shipping, Edmond Buckridge, Robert Woolley, Henry Syms, John Child, John South, Thomas Cooper, Thomas Giles, John Crow, William Stonestreet, Hugh Davis, John Reynolds, Joseph Taylor, Edward Fenton, William Buckler, John Richard, Abraham Jessell, John Nathan, Thomas Clark, Thomas Bowtell. (PRO: E190/72/1).

4-30 March. Shippers by the *Benjamin*, Mr. Arthur Tanner, bound from London for New England: Spencer Piggott, Joseph Bowles, John Tipton, Thomas Matthews, John Upton, William Crouch, Robert Hook, William White, Thomas Lane, Henry Phillips, Timothy Waldo, Edmond Hale, John Rignold, Christopher Taylor, Edward Hulls, Jonathan Leigh, John Harden, Richard Martin, Gabriell Whitely, Daniell Allen, John Reynolds, Benjamin Rantin, Peter Gray, Henry Blaymor, Caleb Mayes, George Aires, Richard Martin, John Harwood, William Withers, Samuell Shute, Luke Foster, William Mead. (PRO: E190/80/1).

5 March. The following apprenticed in Bristol: Robert Anderson to William Swymmer, 4 years Jamaica. (BR).

8 March. The following apprenticed in Bristol to go to Jamaica by the *Isabella*: Hannah Legg to John Towne, 4 years Jamaica not to be employed in fields but as household servant; William Harris to Christopher Andrews, 5 years. (BR).

10 March. The following apprenticed in Bristol: Thomas Whittle to Daniell Legg, 5 years New England by *Speedwell*. (BR).

11 March-9 April. Shippers by the *Recovery*, Mr. Edward Clements, bound from London for Virginia: John Harwood, Edward Hulls, Thomas Griffith, Robert Wynn, David Conguard, Abraham Jesson, Joseph Butts, Sir John Peake. (PRO: E190/80/1).

12 March. Deposition by Edward Asherst of Wapping, Middlesex, surgeon aged 24, and William Hall, aged 22, servant of Henry Lewes of London, scrivener, that they were witnesses to the will made out by George Alcock of St. Katherine Creechurch, London, gent, on 27 February 1677. The will was proved by Benjamin Walker, citizen and pewterer of London, and Peter Thatcher of New England, clerk. (LMCD).

16 March-3 April. Shippers by the *Kent*, Mr. Gregory Marlow, bound from London for New Jersey: Adam Skinner, Robert Wade, Robert Powell, Richard Guy, Jonathan Woodhouse, Thomas Nossiter, William Strumpton, Abraham Manie, William Dolby, Thomas Olive, Thomas Batting, Morgan Drewitt, William Moore, Daniel Wills, Jasper Robins, William Perkin, William Buckler, Francis Plumstead, George Sturman, John Habbuck, Henry Salter. (PRO: E190/72/1).

18 March. Shipper by the *New York* Pink, Mr. William Merritt, bound from London for New York: Benjamin Hewling. (PRO: E190/80/1).

21 March. The following apprenticed in Bristol: Charles Lane to Henry Baker, 4 years New England by *Daniel*, Mr. Daniell Legg. (BR).

23 March-7 April. Shippers by the *Edistow Dogger*, Mr. John Comings, bound from London for Carolina: Peter Hudson, William Rutter, William Buckler, George Barr. (PRO: E190/72/1).

26 March. The following apprenticed in Bristol to go to Jamaica by the *Isabella*: John Webb to Richard Thorne, 5 years; Margarett Howell to same, 5 years. (BR).

28 March. The following apprenticed in Bristol to go to Jamaica by the *Primrose*, Mr. Robert Haskins: Edward Knight to William Swymmer, 4 years; John Parke to same, 4 years. (BR).

29 March. The following apprenticed in Bristol: James Pew to Christopher Andrews, 4 years Jamaica by *Isabella*. (BR).

March. Probate of will of Anne Grave of St. Botolph Aldgate, London, widow, whose kinsman, George Grave, was in Hartford, Connecticut, and kinsman, John Grave, in New Haven, New England. (AW).

March. Probate of will of George Alcock of St. Katherine Creechurch, London, who had lands in New England. (AW).

March-May. Declarations of loyalty, petitions and grievances presented following the rebellion of Nathaniel Bacon in Virginia:

James City County: William Browne; Matthew Collins; Nicholas Bush; Thomas Bobby; John Dean; Thomas Glover; Andrew Goedean; Henry Gord; William Hoare; Henry Jenkins, tanner; John Johnson; James Barrow; Edward Lloyd, mulatto; John Williams.

Rappahannock County: Warwick Cammock; Alexander Doniphann; Henry Torndey; Ellen Awley; Thomas Gouldman; Cadwallader Jones of Sittingbourne parish; John Bowsie of the same.

Stafford County: Richard Gibson; Samuel Maynard.

Surrey County. Thomas Busby; George Procter; W. Wyatt on behalf of William and Elizabeth Rookings, orphans of William Rookins.

Isle of Wight County: Richard Jorden Sr.; Richard Penney; John Marshall; Edward Miller; John Davis; Thomas Fulgham; John Bridger; John George; James Powell; Edward Wickins; John Jennings.

Henrico County: William Glam; John Pleasants; Solomon Knibbe; William Hatcher; John Lewis.

Gloucester County: Philip Lightfoot.

New Kent County: Robert Lowder; John Cocker; Robert Porter; Stephen Tarleton.

York County: Nicholas Toope, tanner.

Unspecified: Four orphans of Anthony Arnold; Elizabeth, James, Thomas and William Dudley; Thomas Lushington; Thomas Palmer; William Rowland; William Whore. (CSPC).

2 April-22 July. Shippers by the *William & John*, Mr. Samuel Legg, bound from London for New England: Henry Phillips, James Goldham, John Richards, Abraham Jesson, Thomas Smith, Robert Scott, Phillip French, Thomas Norman, George Balch, Phillip Manning, Edward Ellis, Thomas Glover, Nicholas Butler, Matthew Denis, Henry Finch, William Crouch, Richard Davis, Robert Woolley, Nicholas Richardson, Edward Randall, Thomas Lacy, Joseph Hiller, Gabriel Whitely, Richard Swething, Edward Merryweather, Ralph Fox, George Shalcrosse, Samuel Alford, Spencer Piggott, Jeremiah Johnson, Edward Carter, Henry Hovernor, Thomas Elkin, John Marshall, Thomas Griffith, William Jordan, Edward Hulls, William Meade, Thomas Carleton, Giles Scruton, Henry Sandys, Thomas Jenner, George Roch, Valentine Adams, John Cooke, Richard Smith, Henry Smith, Thomas French, Ralph Frewin, Champion Ashby, William Nicholls, Stephen Cooke, William

Hodges, John Drake, Richard Gawthorne, Ralph Ingram, Nicholas Brattle, Charles Phelps, Thomas Hogg, Joshua Drydall, Robert Lavis, Thomas Dudson, Robert Cockram, William Skinner, Adam Leveridge, James Cleghorne, John Whaley, Joseph Parker, John Richardson, William Buckler, Peter Hudson, Nicholas Chaplin, Ebenezer Shrimpton, Edward Ball, Richard Buckley, George Gay, Richard Lloyd. (PRO: E190/72/1, 80/1).

4 April. The following apprenticed in Bristol: Richard Cuffe to Christopher Andrews, 4 years Jamaica by *Isabella*; Bartholomew Gornly to William Swymmer, 4 years Jamaica by *Primrose*; Darby Hanning to same, 4 years Jamaica by *Primrose*. (BR).

5 April-5 May. Shippers by the *Mary & Sarah*, Mr. John Foy, bound from London for New England: Ralph Box, Spencer Piggott, James Eyton, John Garrett, Samuel Wilkins, Christopher Taylor, John Mayleigh, Humphrey Roger, John South, Jonah Leigh, John Ive, Robert Woolley, Thomas Buckham, John Crow, John Freeman, Reginald Tucker, Bartholomew Layton, Thomas Sontley, Gabriel Whitley, Abraham Jesson, John Ward, Edward Mumford, Joseph Pinchen, Thomas Glover, Thomas Norman, Edward Hull, Joseph Parton, William Paine, John Harwood, John Greene, Henry Smith, John Child, Francis Hunter. (PRO: E190/72/1).

8 April. The following apprenticed in Bristol: Thomas Archer to Thomas Lock, 4 years Jamaica by *Primrose*. (BR).

9 April. The following apprenticed in Bristol: Samuell Berry to William Swymmer, 4 years Jamaica by *Primrose*. (BR).

9 April-5 June. Shippers by the *Blossom*, Mr. Richard Martin, bound from London for New York: William Depeyster, Edward Gravenor, Edward Merriweather, Benjamin Tanton, Richard Holt, James Rawlins, Humphrey Nicholson, Gerrard Vanheythusen, William Leveridge, Peter Bearsly, Thomas Elkin, John Freeman, Sir Edmond Andrews, Thomas Moore, John Lewin, William Wilson, Benjamin Hewling, Edward Griffith, William Smith, John Bradenham, William Crouch, Anthony Stoner, John Jackson, Thomas Marden, Thomas Hart, Thomas Bating, Thomas Selwood, Augustine Lynn, Edmond Buckeridge, John Pagett, George Gay, Robert Woolley, Robert Kerrington, Widow Simpson, William Williams, Samuell Palmer, Samuell Scott, Luke Foster, Nathaniell Denew. (PRO: E190/80/1).

11 April-26 May. Shippers by the *Greyhound*, Mr. John Wasey, bound from London for New York: David Conyard, Humphrey Nicholson, Abraham Jesson, Ralph Marshall, William Antleby, John Smith, Thomas Bateing, Edward Bradwill, Benjamin Hewling, Edward Griffith, John Freeman, Jonathan Woodhouse, Edward Man, William Bare, John Kensey, Josiah Dewy, Nathaniel Wade, William Buckler, Thomas Hare, Benjamin Blagg, Samuel & John Swinnock, James Jackson, Joseph Taylor. (PRO: E190/72/1).

12-20 April. Shippers by the *Jacob*, Mr. Elisha Bennett, bound from London for New England: ――― Bentley, James Burkin, Eliab Roberts, Thomas Lane. (PRO: E190/72/1).

13 April-23 May. Shippers by the *Providence*, Mr. Samuell Andrews, bound from London for New England: Thomas Norman, Robert Bolter, John Impey, Thomas Lane, William White, John Sampson, John Reynolds, Ralph Box, William Bendree, Thomas Morden, Samuell Dashwood, Thomas Sontley, Robert Woolley, Roger Pitkins, William May, Henry Ashurst, Edmond Hall, Edmond White, Thomas Hoggs, John Powell, John Cutlove, William Gore. (PRO: E190/80/1).

25 April. The following apprenticed in Bristol: Francis Beard to John Holbrooke, 4 years Newfoundland by *Hopewell*, said John Holbrooke Mr. (BR).

27 April. Deposition by William Antleby, citizen and grocer of London, aged 51, that Abraham Bartholomew, then of Boston, New England, became indebted by bond to Robert Hooker, citizen and merchant tailor of London, and Daniel Adkins, ropemaker. A witness to the bond was Silas Shrimpton, now beyond the seas. (LMCD).

28 April-15 May. Shippers by the *Bohemia Merchant*, Mr. William Fowles, bound from London for Virginia: William Riffin, Clement Lunn. (PRO: E190/72/1).

30 April. The following apprenticed in Bristol: Robert Gillum to John Orchard, 4 years Jamaica by *Primrose*. (BR).

April. Administration of Samuel Wilson of Ledbury, Herefordshire, who died in Virginia. (AW).

1 May. The following apprenticed in Bristol: Richard Davis to Thomas Pearce, 4 years Newfoundland by *Hopewell*; William Hopkins to John Baker, 4 years Jamaica by *Mary*, said John Baker Mr. (BR).

3-14 May. Shippers by the *Black Cock*, Mr. Michael Pack, bound from London for New England: James Hayes, Henry Kyte, John Freeman, Sir William Warren, Joseph Bowles, Ralph Ingram, Thomas Wilkins, Edward Merriweather, Thomas Griffith, Sir John Shorter, Robert Orchard, John Ive, Francis Peacock. (PRO: E190/80/1).

4-13 May. Shippers by the *King Solomon*, Mr. Gabriell Morgan, bound from London for New England: Gregory Page, William Warren. (PRO: E190/80/1).

8 May-23 July. Shippers by the *Robert*, Mr. Nathaniel Hayman alias Hammond, bound from London for New England: Francis Fox, Joseph Stapley, Edward Hulls, Samuell Eaton, James Parke, George Heathcott, Phillip French, William Hodges, Samuell Alford, William Mead, Richard Merriweather, William Crouch. (PRO: E190/72/1, 80/1).

284

17 May. The following apprenticed in Bristol: Evan Phillipps to John Holbrooke, 4 years Newfoundland by *Hopewell*. (BR).

28 May. Thomas Chamberlaine, aged 16, apprenticed from Christ's Hospital to James Kendall, commander of the *Clara* bound for Jamaica. (CH).

31 May. The following apprenticed in Bristol: Thomas Price to William Neads, 6 years Virginia by *Susanna*, said William Neads Mr. (BR).

May. Administration of Laurence Washington of Luton, Bedfordshire, who died in Virginia. (AW).

May. Administration of Henry Taylor of St. Margaret Westminster, Middlesex, who died in Virginia. (AW).

May. Probate of will of Benony Eaton of Bermondsey, Surrey, who had lands in Virginia. (AW).

May. Administration of John Watson of Shadwell, Middlesex, who died in Virginia, widower. (AW).

May. Probate of will of Elizabeth Howe of St. Giles Cripplegate, London, widow, whose son-in-law, Edward Hill, was in Virginia. (AW).

6 June. The following apprenticed in Bristol: David Dennis to William Smith, 4 years Virginia by *Bristol Merchant*, said William Smith Mr; Thomas Hillman to William Neads, 4 years Virginia by *Susanna*. (BR).

7 June-4 September. Shippers by the *Mehitabel*, Mr. William Browne, bound from London for New England: Daniell Atkins, Edmond White, William Shirley, Edward Merriweather, Thomas Powell, John Pitman, Thomas Glover, Samuell Alford, Joseph Harvey, Elie Roberts, Thomas Southley, George Barron, Peter Hudson, James Eyton, John Freeman. (PRO: E190/72/1, 80/1).

9 June. The following apprenticed in Bristol: William Southern to William Neads, 4 years Virginia by *Susanna*. (BR).

11 June. The following apprenticed in Bristol to go to Virginia by the *Susanna*: Thomas Gilbert to William Neads, 6 years; James Gilbert to same, 7 years. (BR).

12 June. The following apprenticed in Bristol: Nathaniel Williams to William Mills, 4 years Virginia by *Sapphire*, Mr. William Jones. (BR).

13 June. Shippers by the *Mary*, Mr. Edward Bayly, bound from London for New York: William Depister, John Richardson. (PRO: E190/72/1).

14-27 June. Shippers by the *Unity*, Mr. Bartholomew Ketcher, bound from London for Virginia: Robert Woolley, Richard Yardley, Nathaniel Wilkinson, Benjamin Mitchell, Thomas Skevington. (PRO: E190/72/1).

18 June. The following apprenticed in Bristol: Morgan Howell to William Neads, 4 years Virginia by *Susanna*. (BR).

23 June. Shipper by the *Owners Adventure*, Mr. Roger Laming, bound from London for New York: John Smith. (PRO: E190/72/1).

25 June-26 July. Shippers by the *Increase*, Mr. John Holland, bound from London for New England: Thomas Elkin, William Wright, Nicholas Bratell, Richard Woodcock, William Crowch, Jehosaphat Smith, John Hubbard, John Sturt, James Park, William White, Henry Bray, Henry Syms, John Hartwood, William Sherley, Thomas Lane, Ann Pain, Thomas Simonds. (PRO: E190/72/1).

27 June. The following apprenticed in Bristol: Ann Bone to Richard Budds, 4 years Virginia by *Susanna*. (BR).

27 June-2 August. Shippers by the *Sarah*, Mr. Thomas Tuck, bound from London for New England: Samuel Watkins, Abraham Jesson, Agnes Linn, William Bendry, Robert Woolsey, Peter Hudson, Alexander Hosea, Thomas Southley, Samuel Wickins, John Reynolds, Francis Fox, Bethell Goodwyn. (PRO: E190/72/1).

30 June-17 October. Shippers by the *Willing Mind*, Mr. John Lucomb & Mr. Roger Newton, bound from London for New Jersey (& Virginia): William Clark, Francis Forest, Edward Leaman, William Snowden, James Hewitt, John Salter, Henry Salter, John Jones, Henry Mees, Gilbert Metcalfe, Micajah Perry, Miles Berife, Richard Onslow. (PRO: E190/72/1, 80/1).

June. Probate of will of Leonard Southcot of the ship *Loyal Rebecca*, who died in Virginia. (AW).

June. Administration of James Edmonds of Boston, New England, bachelor. (AW). 1677B.

2 July. The following apprenticed in Bristol: Elias Edins to Thomas Gamon, 5 years Virginia by *Blackmore*, said Thomas Gamon Mr. (BR).

2-9 July. Shippers by the *Elizabeth*, Mr. Jeremiah Jackson, bound from London for New England: Francis Fox, Robert Wynn, Thomas Elkin. (PRO: E190/72/1).

4 July. The following apprenticed in Bristol: Francis Ward to William Neads, 4 years Virginia by *Susanna*. (BR).

4 July-6 August. Shippers by the *Constant Mary*, Mr. Edward Roades, bound from London for Virginia: Mathias Walraven, Thomas Sands, Edward Lemon, John Mahew, John Jaggard, Thomas Mason, Edward Harper, Barnaby Dunch, William Evans, Edward Bristow, Robert Bristow, Michaell Perry, Micajah Perry, James Croxton, Gawen Corbin, John Jennings, Andrew Bolt, William Mead. (PRO: E190/72/1, 80/1).

5 July. Deposition by Henry Faucon of London, scrivener, aged 39, that David Anderson of Charles Town, New England, owed money to William Middleton and Andrew Hebb of Wapping, Middlesex, rope merchants. on a bond of 19 March 1676. (LMCD).

5 July. The following apprenticed in Bristol: Daniell Holmes to John Compton, 4 years Virginia by *Sapphire*; Thomas Harly to Jasper Jenkins, 4 years Virginia by *Susanna*; John Hicks to same, 4 years Virginia by *Susanna*; Edward Ellis to same, 4 years Virginia by *Susanna*. (BR).

6 July. The following apprenticed in Bristol: Thomas Hill to Thomas Wintle, 4 years Virginia by *Blackmore*. (BR).

7 July. The following apprenticed in Bristol: Abigall Mayfield to William Neads, 4 years Virginia by *Susanna*; Jerves Williams to Mathew Cradock, 4 years Virginia by *Bristol Merchant*. (BR).

9 July. Shipper by the *Coronation*, Mr. William Barker, bound from London for New England: Robert Knightly. (PRO: E190/72/1).

10 July. Deposition by Jacob Strange, citizen and merchant tailor of London, aged 55, and Robert Wynne, citizen and haberdasher of London, aged 42, that Robert Spring of London, merchant, and Thomas Webb of London, clothworker, became indebted to the said Jacob Strange and to John Strange, citizen and merchant tailor of London, by bond of 3 June 1675 relating to the voyage of the *Mary* of London, Captain John Doleman, to York River, Virginia. (LMCD).

10 July. The following apprenticed in Bristol: Katharine Williams to Richard Budds, 7 years Virginia by *Susanna*; Jeremy Warner to Richard Wilson, 4 years Virginia by *Susanna*; Thomas Seabrett to Anthony Male, 4 years Virginia by *Sapphire*; Mary Wyatt to same, 4 years Maryland by *Sapphire*; Joseph Holt to William Neads, 4 years Virginia by *Susanna*; Alice Bird to Eliener Jenkins, 5 years Maryland by *Susanna*. (BR).

10-12 July. Shippers by the *Society*, Mr. William Gard, bound from London for New England: Robert Cravell, William Crouch, William Shirley, George Shagrose, Thomas Downes, Joseph Bowles, John Ive, John Ward, Daniell Atkins, Alexander Hosea, Rebecca Love, Clement Manistry, Elizabeth Stevens, Samuell Eaton, Edward Mann, Edward Hulls, Francis Hiller, William Dingly, Samuell Taylor, Thomas Parker, William Mead. (PRO: E190/80/1).

13-19 July. Shippers by the *Mary & Ann*, Mr. Thomas Rose, bound from London for New England: Robert Cockram, Joseph Bowles, William Crouch, John Ive, Richard Horton. (PRO: E190/80/1).

13-20 July. Shippers by the *John & Thomas*, Mr. John Laming, bound from London for Virginia: Mathias Walraven, Richard Foot. (PRO: E190/72/1).

16 July. Home Circuit prisoners reprieved to be transported to Barbados or Jamaica. Essex: Elizabeth Smith of Dagenham; Richard Craven of Chelmsford; Emma Phillips of Epping. Hertfordshire: Edward Denny of

Hadham; John Swingley of Hemel Hempstead (still in prison in July 1679). Kent: Anne Thurston of Lewisham, spinster; Richard Durrant of Dartford; Joseph Baker of Norborne (still in prison in July 1678). Surrey: John Hussey of Kingston on Thames; John Richardson of Christchurch; Susan Rond of Lambeth; Margaret Newey, spinster, alias wife of John of Lambeth; Elizabeth Wainewright of St. George, Southwark; Thomas Stringer of Camberwell; Martha Austen of St. Saviour, Southwark; Thomas Cowley of Putney; Elizabeth Tucker of St. Olave, Southwark; John Bentley of Walton on Thames; Mary Smalman of St. Saviour, Southwark; John White of Bagshot; John Scott alias Trott of Lambeth; Thomas Townesend of Bagshot. Sussex: Ralph Tulley of Portslade. (PRO: C66/3200/17).

16 July. Midland Circuit prisoners reprieved to be transported to America. Lincolnshire: Nathaniel Livesly of Charleton; Charles Browne of Morton. Northamptonshire: Thomas Witty of Buxworth, (Derbys). Edward Barton of Tamworth, (Staffordshire). Edmund Banbury of Thorney, Isle of Ely, (Cambridgeshire). Warwickshire: John Halford of Halford; John Palmer of Olcester; James Winckles of Rugby (still in prison in July 1679). (PRO: C66/3200/25).

16 July. Deposition by James Cary of London, merchant aged 45, and his servant, Daniel Sheriffe, aged 22, that they consigned goods to Mr. James Waddinge of Virginia by the *Planters' Adventure*, Mr. Ellis Ellis. In October 1673 Mr. Robert Workman sent tobacco from Virginia by the *Price* of London, Mr. Robert Connaway, and in August 1674 by the *George* of London, Mr. Thomas Grantham. (LMCD).

17 July. Memorial by the Bishop of London concerning abuses in the plantations. The want of public burial places in Virginia gives rise to the profane custom of burying the dead in private gardens, orchards and other places. (CSPC).

18 July-26 October. Shippers by the *John*, Mr. Thomas Groves, bound from London for Virginia: Thomas Mudd, George Gosfright, William Nicholls, James Comber, Robert Calderwood. (PRO: E190/72/1, 80/1).

20 July. The following apprenticed in Bristol to go by the *Susanna*: Thomas James to Henry Powell, 6 years Maryland; Jeremy Harris to same, 4 years Maryland; John Foord to Robert Lancaster, 7 years Virginia; George Radford to same, 7 years Virginia. (BR).

20 July-17 August. Shippers by the *Crown Mallago*, Mr. Thomas Applewaite, bound from London for Virginia: John Abington, Mathias Walraven, William Garfoot, George Cornish, Barnaby Dunch, William Drope, James Bayly, Silvester Durham, Thomas Truman, Samuell Roper, William Maddox. (PRO: E190/72/1, 80/1).

21 July. Oxford Circuit prisoners reprieved to be transported to America. Gloucestershire: Richard Roberts of Dowdeswell; Eleanor Baker alias Jane, spinster, alias wife of Fortunate of Woolaston; David Harris of Woolaston;

Humphrey Jarvis of Thornbury. Herefordshire: Thomas Gingell of Ledbury; William Harry of Abbey Dore. Shropshire: William Symcocks of Condover; Anne, wife of David Williams of Bridgenorth; William Deame of Church Stretton. Staffordshire: John Ingleby of Cannock; Christopher Dugmore of Sheriff Hales; Elizabeth Cassy of Walsall. Worcestershire: William Dowley of Inkberrow; Joseph Cowell of Eckington. (PRO: C66/3200/24).

21 July. Northern Circuit prisoners reprieved to be transported to Barbados. Derbyshire: Michael Deane of Hath. Yorkshire: George Wilson of York Castle; Peter Barber of Hodden; Simon Noble. (PRO: C66/3200/23).

21 July-2 August. Shippers by the *Samuel & Jonathan*, Mr. George Hillson, bound from London for Virginia: Richard Yallop, Edward Davis, Edward Leman. (PRO: E190/72/1).

21 July-6 August. Shippers by the *Planters Adventure*, Mr. Robert Ransom, bound from London for Virginia: Charles Stepkins, John Jefferys, Benjamin Hobson, George Richards, Elizabeth Shirley, Thomas Arnold, Thomas Parker, Henry Mees, John Cooper, George Richards, Peter Pett, Henry Hammond, William Garfoot, Peter Hudson, Arthur North, Richard Glover, Isaac Merritt, John Jennings, Nowell Bassano, Thomas Hemmings. (PRO: E190/72/1, 80/1).

21 July-11 August. Shippers by the *Friends Increase*, Mr. John Martin, bound from London for Virginia: Henry Foreman, Mathew Paige, Daniel Park, Daniel Clark, Thomas Worledge, Francis Lee, William Haig, James Donalson, Hugh Hartshorn, Edward Leman, Robert Bristow, Isaac Merritt. (PRO: E190/72/1).

25 July. Chester Circuit prisoners reprieved to be transported to Barbados. Cheshire: Robert Yardsley of Gloverstone; Charles Weston of Gloverstone. (PRO: C66/3200/22).

23 July. The following apprenticed in Bristol to go to Virginia by the *Susanna*: William Bunchcombe to William Neads, 4 years; George Martyn to Edward Beckin, 4 years. (BR).

24-30 July. Shippers by the *Employment*, Mr. John Wally, bound from London for New England: Abraham Jesson, Robert Woolley. (PRO: E190/80/1).

24 July-24 September. Shippers by the *Love*, Mr. Oswald Wheatly, bound from London for Virginia: Abraham Jesson, William Burgis, John Collingwood, George Cornish, William Matthews, Thomas Ogden, Richard Moore, Nicholas Greenberry, William Skrimshere, James Holland. (PRO: E190/72/1, 80/1).

25 July. The following apprenticed in Bristol: John Reece to Matthew Craddock, 4 years Virginia by *Bristol Merchant*. (BR).

26 July-8 August. Shippers by the *Young Prince*, Mr. Robert Morris, bound from London for Virginia: Thomas Sands, Mathias Walraven, Nicholas Bland. (PRO: E190/72/1).

27 July. The following apprenticed in Bristol: Mary Searle to James Brayne, 4 years Virginia by *Bristol Merchant*; assigned to Robert Page 24 August. (BR).

27 July-1 August. Shippers by the *Providence*, Mr. Jacob Green, bound from London for New England: Phillip French, James Parker, William Hodges, James Taylor, Francis Hiller, Daniell Atkins, John Askew. (PRO: E190/80/1).

27 July-26 August. Shippers by the *Mary*, Mr. John Conset, bound from London for Virginia: Henry Foreman, Richard Buller, John Osbourne, Joseph Smart, Nicholas Ree, Edward Smith, Robert Winston, John Cary, Samuel Wilkins, Edward Blake, John Habbuck, Joseph Gray, Thomas Parker, Thomas Wickmans. (PRO: E190/72/1, 80/1).

27 July-12 September. Shippers by the *Humphrey & Elizabeth*, Mr. Robert Medford, bound from London for Virginia: Francis Wheeler, John Chumley, William White, John Cary, Thomas Bennett, Josiah Dowce, Thomas Grindon, George Richards, George Baker, Robert Mitford, John Richardson, Robert Walker, Henry Mees, Edward Lemon, Arthur Bayly, Richard Buller, John Showell, Samuell Proby, Thomas Rawlinson, Nathaniell Wilkinson, Dormer Shepherd, James Fowles. (PRO: E190/72/1, 80/1).

27 July-31 August. Shippers by the *Success*, Mr. Stephen Nicholls, bound from London for New Jersey: George Prono, William Sureing, John Essington, Mathew Roper, John Sabin, Henry Stacy, William Crouch, Edward Mann, Hugh Hartshorne, Samuell Jacobs, James Goldham, Marmaduke Roundall, John Hawes, John Denn, John Richardson. (PRO: E190/80/1).

28 July. Western Circuit prisoners reprieved to be transported to Barbados. Devon. William Benham of Crediton; James Worth of West Teignmouth; Richard Darracott of Great Torrington; Thomas Weekes of Barnstaple. Hampshire: Robert Dowty of Andover, woolcomber; Richard Austin of Basingstoke; Edward Saunders of Romsey; James Cooper of Winchester. Somerset: James Salman of Stratton; John Barfield alias Warfield alias Wastfield of Balconsbury. (PRO: C66/3200/21).

28 July. Joseph Terry, aged 15, apprenticed from Christ's Hospital to Matthew Yates, commander of the *Recovery* bound for Jamaica. (CH).

30 July. The following apprenticed in Bristol: Daniell Banks to John George, 6 years Virginia by *Bristol Merchant*; Thomas Hinson to John Adams, 8 years Virginia by *New England Merchant*. (BR).

30 July-21 August. Shippers by the *Fraternity*, Mr. Deliverance Parkman, bound from London for New England: Henry Grigg, John Kynaston, Peter Pett, William Nicolls, Robert Viney, Michael Bradley. (PRO: E190/72/1).

July. Administration of Stephen Willoughby of Virginia. (AW).

July. Administration of Thomas Richards of Alverstoke, Hampshire, who died in Virginia. (AW).

July. Administration of Sir William Berkeley, Governor of Virginia, who died in Twickenham, Middlesex. (AW).

July. Administration of Daniel Taylor of St. Martin Ludgate, London, who died in Maryland. (AW).

July. Administration of Thomas Lane of London, who died in Virginia, bachelor. (AW).

1-5 August. Shippers by the *Richard & Michaell*, Mr. Nathaniell Hayman, bound from London for New England: Richard Merriweather, Abraham Jesson, Nicholas Bratch, William Shirley, James Wanklin, Philip French, John Foster, Peter Gray. (PRO: E190/80/1).

2-20 August. Shippers by the *William & Henry*, Mr. Jeremy Cushing, bound from London for New England: John Smith, Edward Merryweather, Richard Sweeting, John Blackhall, William White, William Antleby, Spencer Piggott, Robert Woodhouse, William Crouch, Robert Gutteridge, William Parren, John Freeman, William Sherley, John Jackson, Bethell Goodwin, William Crouch, Thomas Roberts, Charles Phelps. (PRO: E190/72/1).

2-28 August. Shippers by the *Thomas & Susan*, Mr. David Edwards, bound from London for New England: Thomas Smith, John Lewin, Edward Hull, Thomas Firmin, Jeremy Johnson, Joseph Cox, Edward Merryweather, James Eyton, John Gee, John Jeffreys, Benjamin Ayloffe. (PRO: E190/72/1).

3 August. Shipper by the *Endeavour*, Mr. Robert Dawson, bound from London for Virginia: Charles Stepkins. (PRO: E190/72/1).

3-18 August. Shippers by the *Samuel & Jonathan*, Mr. George Hilson, bound from London for Maryland: John Singleton, John Collingwood, William Sherley, Dormer Sheppard, Nicholas More, William Skrimshire, Edward East, Isaac Bennett, James Bayly, Edward Boulston, Richard Banks. (PRO: E190/72/1).

3-28 August. Shippers by the *New York*, Mr. Nicholas Vanbrake, bound from London for New York: Abraham Jesson, John Sherly, Robert Woolley, Edward Staverton, Thomas Firmin, Benjamin Hewling, Phillip French, Alexander Hosea, Benjamin Dejean, Vallentine Adams, Edward Mann, William Darvall, Thomas Ball, Gerrard Vanheythusen, Thomas Eccleston, Samuell Shute, Peter Kesterman, Elias Beak. (PRO: E190/80/1).

3 August-16 September. Shippers by the *Bohemia [Merchant]*, Mr. William Fowles, bound from London for Virginia: Henry Lucas, William Kiffin, John Skinner, Joseph Hayes, Thomas Parker. (PRO: E190/80/1).

4 August. The following apprenticed in Bristol: Sarah Rawleigh to Philipp Neason, 4 years Virginia; Ann Peck to Thomas Hall, 5 years Virginia by *Bristol Merchant*. (BR).

6 August. The following apprenticed in Bristol: Jenkin Rogers to Matthew Craddock, 4 years Virginia by *Bristol Merchant*; Robert Meredith to Thomas Gamon, 4 years Virginia by *Blackmore*; Sarah Muskett to —— Jarvis, 4 years Virginia by *Bristol Merchant*. (BR).

7 August. Shipper by the *Hopewell*, Mr. John Baker, bound from London for New England: John Ive. (PRO: E190/80/1).

8 August. Abraham Dumbleton, aged 15, apprenticed from Christ's Hospital to James Kendall, commander of the *Clara* bound for Jamaica. (CH).

9 August. James Applin, aged 15, apprenticed from Christ's Hospital to Robert Morris, commander of the *Young Prince* bound for Virginia. (CH).

9 August. The following apprenticed in Bristol: John Hughs to Anthony Broad, 4 years Maryland by *Maryland Merchant*; Elizabeth Soloman to Richard Whitt—e, 4 years Virginia by *Nevis Merchant*. (BR).

9 August. Shipper by the *Thomas & Mary*, Mr. William Adams, bound from London for Maryland: Adrian Vanchisperroot. (PRO: E190/72/1).

10 August-26 October. Shippers by the *Recovery*, Mr. Thomas Hasted, bound from London for Virginia: Arthur Bayly, Henry Dandy, John Jones, William Hayes, Joseph Taylor, Edmond Harper, Gawin Corbin, Henry Burdett, Richard Foster, Isaac Bennett, John Marshall, Samuel Scott, Phillip Whistler, William Trevithian, William Smith, John Sturt. (PRO: E190/72/1, 80/1).

12 August-19 September. Shippers by the *Kent*, Mr. Henry Treganow, bound from London for Virginia: Richard Buller, John Richardson, Francis Hiller, Robert Maddox, Seth Sothell, John Taylor, William Gosnell, Henry Holford, John Jennings. (PRO: E190/80/1).

13 August-14 September. Shippers by the *Elizabeth & Sarah (Katherine)*, Mr. Peter Pagan, bound from London for Virginia: Richard Booth, Henry Foreman, Charles Singleton, John Tasker, John Collingwood, Gawen Corbin. (PRO: E190/72/1, 80/1).

13 August-22 September. Shippers by the *Baltimore*, Mr. John Dunch, bound from London for Maryland: George Cornish, Mathias Walraven, John Enbree, Joseph Smart, James Parker, George Gosfright. (PRO: E190/72/1).

13 August-3 October. Shippers by the *Concord*, Mr. Thomas Grantham, bound from London for Virginia: Gawin Corbin, Anthony Ringwood, Edward Harper, James Carey, John Kent, Thomas Jaegell, Micajah Perry, Letia Newell, William Howard, William Paggen, Samuel Wakins, Thomas Fyfe, John Kent, Henry Foreman, Stephen Math(ews), Hugh Hartshorn, Richard Burdon, Robert Terrell, Robert Crisp, Richard Glover, Samuel Young, Francis

Levin, Richard Booth, Thomas Jacques, Ann Waters, Thomas Palmer, Anthony Phillips, Israell Morgan, Robert Farrer, John Pike, Charles Stepkins, Robert Bristow, Robert Woolley, Richard Banks, William Mead, Christopher Harris, Andrew Bolt, Paul Palmer, John Jennings. (PRO: E190/72/1, 80/1).

14 August. The following apprenticed in Bristol to go to Virginia by the *Nevis Merchant*: Nicholas Windover to Abraham Oliver, 4 years; Anthony Drew to same, 4 years. (BR).

15 August. The following apprenticed in Bristol: John Allen to Arthur Bible, 4 years Jamaica by *Lamb*. (BR).

15-21 August. Shippers by the *Good Hope*, Mr. George Heathcott, bound from London for New York: Ralph Ingram, William Mead, John Richards, Thomas Crundall. (PRO: E190/80/1).

15 August-25 September. Shippers by the *Providence*, Mr. Andrew Boone, bound from London for New York: Moses Rusdon, William Antleby, Anthony Poole, Edward Merryweather, Andrew Willett, Abraham Jesson, John Richardson, William Mead, Daniel Ingoll, Benjamin Hewling, William Crowch, Robert Wynn, Christopher Dynot, James Walklin, Henry Smith, Edward Man, Humphrey Nicholson, Thomas Leeds, James Hayes, John Harwood, Jeremiah Horman, Thomas Batting, Edward Thornburgh, Alexander Hosea, William Smith, Samuel Groome, John Essington. (PRO: E190/72/1).

16 August. Shipper by the *Concord* of Newcastle, Mr. Edward Robinson, bound from Newcastle for Maryland: Michaell Taylor. (PRO: E190/197/2).

17 August-5 September. Shippers by the *Mary*, Mr. John Constant, bound from London for Virginia: Charles Dyos, Nathaniel Broxup, Francis Wheeler, Michaell Perry, John Beale, Thomas Parker, George Richards, Thomas Wickins, Humphrey Levins, Edward Smith, Luke Cropley, Robert Maddox, Samuell Sheppard, Andrew Bolt. (PRO: E190/80/1).

20 August. The following apprenticed in Bristol: John Giles to Thomas Opie, 4 years Virginia by *Richard & James*. (BR).

20 August-14 September. Shippers by the *Edward & Ann*, Mr. Nathaniel Green, bound from London for New York: Samuell Taylor, Robert Farrer, Mach. Barry, John Jackson, Sir John Peake, Phillip French, Edward Hull, Ezekiel Hutchinson, John Ive, Elizabeth Matkins, Thomas Lane, John Freeman, Abraham Jesson, William Chambers, John Savage, Andrew Kendrick. (PRO: E190/80/1).

21 August-12 September. Shippers by the *Blessing*, Mr. James Elson, bound from London for New England: Jeremy Johnson, Phillip French, John Johnson, John Heale, Spencer Piggott, Robert Woolley, Francis Fox, Edward Mann, William White, Clement Fanster, Thomas Lane, Francis Hiller, Joseph Bowles, John Spendler, Edward Hull, George Wood, Bartholomew Parr,

Abraham Jesson, Richard Gawthorne, Charles Phelps, John Bawdon, Champion Ashby, Luke Foster, James Eyton, William Barron, Richard Langford, William Crouch, Edmond Harrison, Samuell Clarke, Andrew Kendrick, William Mead. (PRO: E190/80/1).

23 August-1 September. Shippers by the *Adventure*, Mr. John Balston, bound from London for New England: John Ellis, Robert Woolley, William White, Thomas Elkin, Edward Hull, Richard Sweething, Samuel Wickins, Elnath Chacey, Abraham Jesson, Gabriel Whitley, Richard Baker, Charles Phelps, William Crowch, John Reynolds, Thomas Lane, John Wase, Thomas Cable, Edward Allan, Thomas Moore. (PRO: E190/72/1).

23 August-5 September. Shippers by the *Joseph & Benjamin*, Mr. Edmond Paine, bound from London for Maryland and Virginia: John Taylor, Robert Horn, Joseph Pook, Thomas Lyme, Hugh Hartshorn, Henry Meese, William Shakerly, Thomas Bard, Strangwater Mudd, John Ebsworth, John Flavell, William Pate. (PRO: E190/72/1).

23 August-2 October. Shippers by the *Zebulon*, Mr. Nicholas Gutteridge, bound from London for Virginia: Henry Lucas, William West, Hugh Hartshorn, William Lock, George Blackwell, Joseph Bishop, Thomas Ellis, Arthur Bayly, Gilbert Metcalfe, Edward Leman, James Parke, Thomas Ellis, Andrew Bolt. (PRO: E190/72/1, 80/1).

24 August. The following apprenticed in Bristol: Mary Morgan to John Adams, 4 years Virginia by *New England Merchant*; Edward Creed to Thomas Pope, 5 years Virginia by *John*; Susannah Norcutt to Alexander Willcox, 4 years Virginia by *New England Merchant*. (BR).

24 August. Deposition by Thomas Grantham of Tower Street, London, mariner aged 35, that he was in Virginia in March 1677 in the *Concord* and was at the house of Governor William Berkeley when tobacco belonging to Alexander Walker was seized. (LMCD).

24 August-7 October. Shippers by the *Beaver*, Mr. Jacob Morrice, bound from London for New York: John Vanwatchtendunke, Edward Mann, Ralph Ingram, John Bradenham, Samuell Groome, Benjamin Dejeane, James Hayes, William Buckler, Robert Dale, Mathew Chitty, Thomas Hart, Samuell Burdon, Thomas Tennant, George Gay, Isaac Marriott, Joseph Dickinson, Abraham Jesson, James & Joseph Hayes, Gerrard Vanheythusen, John Osgood, Hend. Contre. (PRO: E190/80/1).

25 August. The following apprenticed in Bristol: Elienor Price to Arthur Barrett, 4 years Maryland by *Maryland Merchant*; Alice Trow to same, 4 years Maryland by *Maryland Merchant*; Edward Williams to John Sprackland, 4 years Virginia by *Unicorn*. (BR).

27 August. The following apprenticed in Bristol: Margarett Smith to John Frogley, 4 years Virginia by *John*; Thomas Baily to Bartholomew Holland, 5 years Virginia by *Unicorn*; Thomas Jeanes to Thomas Goldby, 4 years Virginia by *Susanna*. (BR).

28 August-24 September. Shippers by the *Duke of York*, Mr. John Purvis, bound from London for Virginia: Robert Suckling, John Naylor, Thomas Mallins, Jane Hoyle, John Kent, Henry Dandy, Henry Meese, Samuel Hersent, Anthony Ringwood, John Jeffreys, Isaac Merritt, John Savage, William Smith, Robert Briscowe, Arthur Bayly, Phillip Foster, Gawen Corbin, John Chandler, Samuell Shute. (PRO: E190/72/1, 80/1).

29 August. The following apprenticed in Bristol: George Stanly to Richard Sutton, 4 years Virginia by *Maryland Merchant*; William Jones to Robert Price, 4 years Virginia. (BR).

31 August. The following apprenticed in Bristol: Mary Major to Bartholomew Holland, 4 years Virginia by *Unicorn*; William Lawrence to Abraham Oliver, 6 years Virginia by *Nevis Merchant*. (BR).

31 August-7 September. Shippers by the *Assistance*, Mr. James Strange, bound from London for Virginia: Richard Lloyd, Thomas Norman, Thomas Moore, John Phillips, Henry Coursly, William Grover. (PRO: E190/80/1).

31 August-27 September. Shippers by the *Elizabeth & Mary*, Mr. Roger Newham, bound from London for Virginia: Richard Buller, James Cumber, Mary Smith, Edward Day, Thomas Parker, Hugh Hartshorne, William Hodges, James Braine, George Gaye, James Fowlis, John Whiting, Edmond Roberts, John Man, Abraham Jesson, John Sadler. (PRO: E190/72/1, 80/1).

3 September. The following apprenticed in Bristol: Nathaniell Davis to Thomas Peares, 4 years Virginia by *Maryland Merchant*. (BR).

4 September. Newgate prisoners reprieved to be transported to Barbados. London: Jane Vosse alias Stephens, spinster; Jane Sadler, spinster; Thomas Halstaff; Joseph Melton; John Bradley. Middlesex:. Elizabeth Hewitt of St. Giles in the Fields, spinster; Eleanor Jones of the same, spinster; Humphrey Stephenson of Enfield; Richard Chaplin alias Chapman of the same; John Page of St. Margaret Westminster; Alice Chilton of St. Mary Savoy, spinster; Elizabeth Gibson of the same, spinster; Matthew Elsley of Fulham; Richard Devonrex of Finchley. (PRO: C66/3200/15).

4 September. The following apprenticed in Bristol: Thomas Carline to John Drake, 4 years Virginia by *Stephen*, Mr. John Read; John Tackley to Anthony Broad, 8 years Virginia by *Maryland Merchant*; William Tackley to same, 10 years Virginia by *Maryland Merchant*; John Williams to William Morgan, 4 years Virginia; Elizabeth Pope to John Harris, 4 years Virginia by *Lamb*, Mr. Arthur Bible; Benjamin Ricketts to same, 4 years Virginia by *Lamb*; Joyce Holder to same, 4 years Virginia by *Lamb*. (BR).

4 September-24 October. Shippers by the *Carolina*, Mr. Zachary Gillam, bound from London for Carolina: Thomas Sands, John Abell, George Dinant, John Jennings. ((PRO: E190/72/1, 80/1).

5 September-15 November. Shippers by the *Virginia Factor*, Mr. James Conway & Mr. Robert Joules, bound from London for Virginia: Spencer Piggott, Thomas Elwes, Edward Leman, Micajah Perry, Mathias Walraven, Edward Crisp, John Richardson, Edward Floyd, James Godfrey, Richard Lloyd, James Grunwin, Thomas Parker. (PRO: E190/72/1, 80/1).

7 September-10 October. Shippers by the *Augustine*, Mr. Zachary Taylor, bound from London for Virginia: John Thornbush, Samuel Hoyle, John Sabin, James White, Mark Jarratt, Robert Carnall, Mathew Carlton, John Jeffreys, Francis Lee, Richard Langford, Hugh Hartshorn, Samuel Young, Arthur North, Henry Meese, George Richards, Phillip Foster, George Walkely, Henry Foreman, Francis Camfield, Thomas Jones, Benjamin Smart, James Wagstaff, Edward Lemon, Robert Briscoe, Gilbert Salisbury, Thomas Parker, Samuell Onely. (PRO: E190/72/1, 80/1).

8 September. Shipper by the *Speedwell*, Mr. Thomas Lawrence, bound from London for Virginia: John Phelps. (PRO: E190/72/1).

8 September-14 October. Shippers by the *Herne*, Mr. John Ely & Mr. John Buckey, bound from London for Maryland & Virginia: Richard Beckford, John Haggett, Mathias Walraven, Roger Lillington, Samuel Herne, Andrew Bolt, Michaell Shemcliff, John Handford, Thomas Ball. (PRO: E190/72/1, 80/1).

9 September. The following apprenticed in Bristol: Henry Gosmoore to Richard Franklin, 5 years Virginia by *Expectation*; Ann Nagis to William Oldys, 5 years Virginia by *Comfort*, Mr. William Stevens; William Jones to Arthur Grant, Virginia by *Nevis Merchant*, said Arthur Grant Mr. (BR).

10 September. The following apprenticed in Bristol: Mary Hancock to John Harris, 4 years Jamaica by *Lamb*. (BR).

11 September. The following apprenticed in Bristol: James Briant to Thomas Russell, 4 years Virginia by *Unicorn*; William Bassett to Richard Francklin, 7 years Virginia by *Expectation*. (BR).

12 September. Edward Flood, aged 16, apprenticed from Christ's Hospital to Joseph Wilde, commander of the *Prince* bound for Jamaica. (CH).

12 September-15 October. Shippers by the *Richard & Elizabeth*, Mr. Nicholas Pryn, bound from London for Virginia: Micajah Perry, William Paggen, Mathew Page, Samuel Frith, Richard Booth, Samuell Sanford, John Jennings, Edward Whitwell. (PRO: E190/72/1, 80/1).

12 September-12 November. Shippers by the *Constant Jacob*, Mr. Jacob Haye, bound from London for Virginia: John Phelps, Adam Skinner, Richard

Chambers, William King, Reginald Tucker, Israell Morgan, Richard Rennington, Randall Raper, Edward Carter. (PRO: E190/72/1).

13 September. The following apprenticed in Bristol: James Clubb to Maurice Orchard, 7 years Virginia by *John*; Richard Symonds to George Berry, 4 years Virginia by *Expectation*. (BR).

13 September-8 November. Shippers by the *Thomas & Edward*, Mr. John Brown, bound from London for Virginia and Maryland: John Reynold, John Collingwood, Thomas King, Nathaniel Mathews, Joseph Taylor, Joseph Sparrow, Henry Foreman. (PRO: E190/72/1, 80/1).

14 September. Shipper by the *Hope*, Mr. Andrew Boone, bound from London for New York: William Botton. (PRO: E190/72/1).

14 September. The following apprenticed in Bristol: Ann Okey to John Sheppard, 4 years Virginia by *Stephen*; Henry Williams to same, 5 years Virginia by *Stephen*. (BR).

15-22 September. Shippers by the *Adventure*, Mr. John Nore, bound from London for Maryland: William Crowch, John Kemble, John Habuck, John Richards, Thomas Hare, John Robotham. (PRO: E190/72/1).

16-17 September. Shippers by the *Dolphin*, Mr. Thomas Cowell, bound from London for New England: John Freeman, Abraham Jesson. (PRO: E190/80/1).

17 September. The following apprenticed in Bristol: Ephraim Axford to George Squire, 4 years Virginia by *Bristol Merchant*; Barbara Collins to Richard Welstead, 4 years Virginia by *Abraham & Isaac*, Mr. John Jones; William Wadly to Isaac Knight, 6 years Virginia; Charles Jones to same, 6 years Virginia; Robert Watts to same, 6 years Virginia; Richard Hawkins to Margaret Phelps, 5 years Virginia by *Alathea*; Hesekiah Blank to Isaac Haynes, 5 years Virginia by *Comfort*. (BR).

17 September. Shipper by the *Planters Adventure*, Mr. James Conway, bound from London for Maryland: William Nutt. (PRO: E190/72/1).

18 September-14 October. Shippers by the *Hopewell*, Mr. John Rudds & Mr. Michael Yoakley, bound from London for Virginia: Lawrence Crabb, Thomas Grindon, Henry Hartwell, Edward Leman, Edward Alder, Charles Dyos, John Freeman, Thomas Hartley, Thomas Parker, William King, Samuell Sale, Thomas Jordan, Nowell Bassano, Samuell Sheppard, Thomas Grindon, William Wilson, John Sabin, John Osgood. (PRO: E190/72/1, 80/1).

19 September. The following apprenticed in Bristol: Hannah Silley to Matthew Craddock, 4 years Virginia by *Bristol Merchant*; John Harding to William Bennet, 5 years Virginia by *Francis & Mary*; John Storks to William Chambers, 6 years Virginia by *Maryland Merchant*; William Legg to Richard Milsum, 4 years Virginia by *Francis & Mary*; Frances Folkner to Joseph Hiscox, 4 years Virginia by *Francis & Mary*; Elizabeth Griffiths to John

Marden, 4 years Virginia by *Francis & Mary*; Thomas Lockyer to Theophilus Turford, 4 years Virginia by *Comfort*; Samuell Jones to Charles Stevens, 4 years Virginia by *Sarah & Elizabeth*, Mr. William White; Nathaniel Daye to Hugh Lewis, 4 years Virginia by *Bristol Merchant*; Griffith Griffiths to same, 4 years Virginia by *Bristol Merchant*. (BR).

24 September-23 October. Shippers by the *Friends Increase*, Mr. Jonathan Hilson, bound from London for Virginia: John Osborne, Micajah Perry, Joseph Sparrow, Christopher Tomlinson, Hugh Rowcliff, William Mead. (PRO: E190/80/1).

25 September. The following apprenticed in Bristol: Richard Reed to Barnett Browne, 4 years Virginia by *Bristol Merchant*. (BR).

25 September-26 November. Shippers by the *Merchants Consent*, Mr. Francis Partis, bound from London for Virginia: Jane Moore, William Haig, Henry Foreman, Thomas Stark, Richard Foote, Robert Woolsey, William Barrett, John Stephenson, Benjamin Whitchcott, Henry Wildman, Richard Langford. (PRO: E190/72/1, 80/1).

26 September. Shipper by the *Coaster*, Mr. Thomas Gurdis, bound from London for Virginia: Alexander Mars. (PRO: E190/72/1).

26 September. Shipper by the *Heron*, Mr. John Ellis, bound from London for Virginia: Roger Lillington. (PRO: E190/72/1).

26-27 September. Deposition by John Savile of St. Leonard, Shoreditch, Middlesex, weaver aged 72, and Roger Hunt of St. Ethelburga without Bishopsgate, London, citizen and merchant tailor of London, aged 61, that Mathew Crewes, citizen and leatherseller of London, had two sons: Francis Crewes of (?), Middlesex, citizen and grocer of London, by trade a silkman, deceased; and Colonel James Crewes of Virginia, now also deceased. Deposition by Arthur Miles of London, scrivener aged 53, and Giles Sussex of London, citizen and gardener of London, aged 52, that Sarah Whittingham, whom they have known since her infancy, is the only surviving daughter of Edward Crewes of London, merchant, deceased, and administratrix of Col. James Crewes of Virginia, deceased. A certificate of the ages of Edward, Francis and James Crewes, taken from the register of St. Pancras, Soper Lane, London, is produced. (LMCD).

27 September. The following apprenticed in Bristol: John Haskins to Thomas Stibbins, 4 years Virginia by *Sarah & Elizabeth*. (BR).

September. Joseph Wells, aged 15, apprenticed from Christ's Hospital to John Munford, citizen and grocer of London, to serve in Virginia. (CH).

September. Administration of John Robotham of the ship *Dartmouth*, who died in Virginia, bachelor. (AW).

September. Administration of James Crewes of Virginia, widower. (AW).

September. Administration of Esau Halsey of Suffolk, New England, bachelor. (AW).

September. Probate of will of John Prise of Shadwell, Middlesex, who died overseas (bound for Virginia). (AW).

1 October. The following apprenticed in Bristol: John Stone to George Tyte, 4 years Virginia by *Maryland Merchant*; Christopher Earle to Robert Court, 4 years Virginia by *Maryland Merchant*; Jonathan Budge to John Townson, 4 years Virginia by *George*, Mr. Samuel Isaac; Josias Budge to same, 4 years Virginia by *George*; Thomas Gough to same, 4 years Virginia by *George*; Isaac Hopkins to same, 4 years Virginia by *George*; Thomas Collins to same, 4 years Virginia by *George*; Mary Thomas to Robert Williams, 4 years Virginia by *Francis & Mary*. (BR).

1-28 October. Shippers by the *Charles*, Mr. Walter Dunch, bound from London for Virginia and Maryland: Mathias Walraven, Barnaby Dunch, Edward Floyd, Thomas Poyntz, Lord Baltimore, Daniel Norris, John Osgood, Henry Constable, Thomas Elwys. (PRO: E190/72/1, 80/1).

1-31 October. Shippers by the *Cecilia* (*Caselius*), Mr. John Body, bound from London for Virginia: Henry Lucas, William Dodson, Richard Burk, John Singleton, John Collingwood, William Skrimshire, Arthur Storer, George Cornish, John Daniell, William Mead, Richard Banks. (PRO: E190/72/1, 80/1).

1 October-9 November. Shippers by the *Barnaby*, Mr. Mathew Ryder, bound from London for Virginia: Barnaby Dunch, Charles Stepkins, Thomas Parker, John Jennings, Anthony Dansy, Joseph Taylor, William Mumford, Samuel Powell, Andrew Bolt, Walter Bettell, Jacob Lumpkins, John Gore, Isaac Merritt, Ralph Harwood, William Evans, Mathias Walraven, Walter Monke, Daniel Dunch, William Haig, Thomas Lee, Richard Banks. (PRO: E190/72/1, 80/1).

2-10 October. Shippers by the *Young Prince*, Mr. Robert Morrice, bound from London for Virginia: John Freeman, Michaell Bland, Thomas Sands, John Jennings. (PRO: E190/80/1).

3 October. Shipper by the *Owners Goodwill*, Mr. Samuel Cuttance, bound from London for Virginia: Abigall Lee. (PRO: E190/72/1).

3 October. Shipper by the *Coronet*, Mr. John Bibby, bound from London for New England: John Eyles. (PRO: E190/72/1).

3 October-6 November. Shippers by the *Henry & Ann*, Mr. Thomas Arnold, bound from London for Virginia: Ralph Goldsmith, Edward Man, Clement Plumsted, Edward Lemon, Mathew Hardman, Joseph Ashton, Robert Carter,

William Devall, William Lane, William Sherley, John Taylor, Thomas With. (PRO: E190/72/1).

4 October. Passengers embarked (from London) for Virginia by the *Concord*, Mr. Thomas Grantham: Thomas Johnson from Scotland, aged 40; John Prigg from Suffolk, aged 20; Samuell Harris from Worcestershire, aged 23; [*and possibly in continuation of the same list*] Harry [——]; George Wilson from Worcestershire, aged 16; Henry(?) Hall from London, aged 26; Nicholas Miller from [?], aged 21; William Hopkins from Bedford, aged 24; Hannah Chaceley from London, aged 19; Hester Phillips from [?], aged 19; Richard Magott from London, aged 21; Nathaniell Holland from Northamptonshire, aged 15; Robert Raynard from Virginia, aged 18. (NSGQ 64/2).

Passengers embarked by [*name illegible*] for Maryland: Richard Bennett from Leicestershire, aged 15; Joseph Gostwick, aged 24; Elizabeth Bassett from Yorkshire, aged 18; Elizabeth Roo— from Yorkshire, aged 18; Sarah Cook from Suffolk, aged 23; Anne Kent from Oxford, aged 21; Anne Turner from Virginia, aged 30; Samuell Godfrey from London, aged 20; Anne Colnetman aged 16; Charles Turner from Virginia, aged 5; Moses White; Mr. Clarke. (NGSQ 64/2).

5 October. Shippers by the *Hope*, Mr. Robert Parsons (Pearson), bound from London for Virginia: John Freeman, Robert Lawson. (PRO: E190/72/1).

6 October. The following apprenticed in Bristol: William Cox to Edmund Moore, 4 years Nevis by ——, Mr. Jeffries; Henry Wall to Marke Sloper, 4 years Virginia by *Bristol Merchant*; Joane Twist to George Knight, 5 years Virginia; Bridgett Griffith to Matthew Walter, 4 years Virginia by *Maryland Merchant*. (BR).

8 October. Passengers embarked by the ship *John*, Commander Mathew Norwood, from London to Barbados: George Toker from Bermuda, aged 25; Mary Middlelow from Hertford, aged 37; Mr. Troott; Francis Joanes. (NGSQ 64/2).

8 October. The following apprenticed in Bristol: Henry Symons to Robert Pomry, 4 years Virginia by *Maryland Merchant*; Robert Kellway to Thomas Masters, 4 years Jamaica by *America Merchant*. (BR).

9-11 October. Shippers by the *Honor & Dorothy*, Mr. John Moore, bound from London for Virginia: Anthony Reynolds, Thomas Sanders. (PRO: E190/72/1).

10 October. Shipper by the *Hannah*, Mr. Anthony Gester, bound from London for Virginia: Luke Burse. (PRO: E190/80/1).

12 October-13 December. Shippers by the *Stephen & Edward*, Mr. Sebastian Gingey, bound from London for Virginia: Edward Harper, Richard Banks, Walter Kilner, Thomas Walker, Micajah Perry, Mathew Scarbrow, James Bayly. (PRO: E190/72/1, 80/1).

14 October-6 December. Shippers by the *Ann*, Mr. Benjamin Cooper, bound from London for Virginia: John Harrington, Stephen Barecroft, Thomas Crundall, William Holgate, Thomas Place, John Crispe, Henry Mees, Francis Lee, Ralph Edwards, John Steventon, John Jefferies, Peter Causton. (PRO: E190/72/1, 80/1).

15 October. The following apprenticed in Bristol: Christopher Legg to William Symmes, 4 years Jamaica by *America Merchant*; Richard Attwood to John Hare, 4 years Virginia by *Francis & Mary*; Richard Pritchatt to Thomas Shepherd, 4 years Virginia by *Sarah & Elizabeth*. (BR).

17 October-19 November. Shippers by the *Baltimore*, Mr. George Purvis, bound from London for Virginia: Edward Mitton, James Godfrey, Thomas Tibbe, John Adams, John Bartlett. (PRO: E190/80/1).

17 October-5 December. Shippers by the *Speedwell*, Mr. John Lorimer, bound from London for Virginia: John Hamon, Micajah Perry, Richard Butler, Stephen Montague, Nathaniel Whitchurch, William Shakerly, James Wagstaffe, Arthur Bayly, George Richards, Thomas Sherington, Thomas Salter, Thomas Parker. (PRO: E190/72/1, 80/1).

18 October. The following apprenticed in Bristol: Thomas Greenfield to Thomas Lawrence, 4 years Virginia by *Maryland Merchant*; Andrew Bomer to Richard White, 4 years Virginia by *Sarah & Elizabeth*. (BR).

19 October. Shipper by the *Dolphin*, Mr. Samuel Jones, bound from London for Virginia: Thomas Ball. (PRO: E190/72/1).

19 October. Shipper by the *Good Hope*, Mr. Abraham Wheelock, bound from London for Virginia: Henry Lucas. (PRO: E190/72/1).

19 October. Petition of Sarah Drummond, relict and administratrix of William Drummond of Virginia who, after the rebellion there, was stripped and taken before Governor Sir William Berkeley and sentenced by martial law to death. Her husband had not borne arms nor was he charged with any offence. Though even the arch rebel Nathaniel Bacon was not stripped of his estate, her husband's small plantation was taken and the petitioner, with her five small children, was forced to flee and to wander in deserts and woods. She prays a pardon for her husband and reinstatement of his property. *See also entry for 2 November*. (APC).

19 October. Petition of Richard Booth, Samuel Story, Samuel Claphamson and William Clapham of London, merchants. In July 1676 they loaded goods on the *Richard & Elizabeth* of London, Mr. Nicholas Prynn, which were consigned to their agent in Virginia, William Hunt. The goods were seized by the Governor on suspicion that Hunt was concerned in the rebellion. (APC).

19-27 October. Shippers by the *Rappahannock Merchant*, Mr. Robert Gowland, bound from London for Virginia: Adam Skinner, Thomas Hanwell, Gawen Corbin, James Wagstaffe. (PRO: E190/72/1).

20 October. The following apprenticed in Bristol: Richard Somersett to Francis Morgan, 4 years Jamaica by *America Merchant*; William Burgis to John Mason, 4 years Virginia by *George*; Francis Thomas to Edward Lane, 4 years Virginia by *George*. (BR).

23 October. Shipper by the *Rebecca*, Mr. Thomas Larimer, bound from London for Virginia: John Good. (PRO: E190/72/1).

27-30 October. Shippers by the *James*, Mr. Solomon Blackledge, bound from London for Carolina: Joseph Finch, Christopher Rose, William Crowch. (PRO: E190/72/1).

31 October-23 December. Shippers by the *Globe*, Mr. Samuel Groome, bound from London for Virginia and Maryland: John Sabin, Barnaby Dunch, John Taylor, James Brames, Josia Bacon, John Flanell, George Gosfright, William Skrimshire, Ralph Ingram, Samuell Sheppard, William Mead. (PRO: E190/72/1, 80/1).

October. Probate of will of Henry Derrick of St. Stephen, Bristol, who died in Virginia. (AW).

October. Administration of William Drumond of Virginia. (AW).

October. James Becknall, aged 14, to be sent from Christ's Hospital to Col. Newton in Barbados to serve him. (CH).

2 November. The following apprenticed in Bristol: Humfry Mills to William Walls, 4 years Maryland by *Francis & Mary*; Edward Millard to same, 4 years Virginia by *Francis & Mary*; William Johnson to same, 4 years Virginia by *Francis & Mary*; William Morris to Thomas Yate, 4 years Virginia by *Agreement*; Francis Meeke to Richard Page, 4 years Virginia by *Francis & Mary*. (BR).

2 November. Further petition of Sarah Drummond for restitution of goods seized from the *Francis* in Virginia. (APC).

3 November. Deposition by Thomas Hinsley of London, tobacco cutter aged 52, that Francis Butlin of Ware parish, Gloucester County, Virginia, became indebted to Francis Camfield of St. Bartholomew the Great, London, by bond of 19 June 1675. (LMCD).

3 November. The following apprenticed in Bristol: William Games to Samuell Carpenter, 4 years Virginia by *George*; William Window to William Walls, 4 years Maryland by *Francis & Mary*; Phyllis Goulding to George Cary, 4 years Virginia by *Francis & Mary*. (BR).

6 November. Petition of Richard Carver, son and heir of William Carver of Lower Norfolk County, Virginia, who was executed in the late rebellion, for restitution of his father's estate. (CSPC).

6 November. The following apprenticed in Bristol to go to Virginia by the *Agreement*: Edward Watts to William Bradley, 4 years; William Harris to Thomas Yate, 4 years. (BR).

8 November. The following apprenticed in Bristol: William Shaw to John Webb, 4 years Virginia by *Agreement*. (BR).

8 November-20 December. Shippers by the *St. Ann*, Mr. Anthony Fenn, bound from London for Virginia: Robert Green, Henry Lucas, Edward Smith, Thomas Parker, William Mead. (PRO: E190/80/1).

12 November. The following apprenticed in Bristol to go to Virginia by the *George*: Henry Isdill to John Mason, 4 years; David Jones to same, 4 years. (BR).

14 November. The following apprenticed in Bristol: Edward Eckly to John Woolvin, 4 years Virginia. (BR).

15 November. The following apprenticed in Bristol: John Richards to Robert Gibbs, 4 years Virginia by *Reformation*; James Brookes to same, 6 years Virginia by *Reformation*; Thomas Tucker to Richard Luffe, 4 years Barbados by *Olive Tree*, Mr. Thomas North; Richard Leech to Ellis Ashby, 5 years Barbados by *Humility*. (BR).

16-24 November. Shippers by the *Francis*, Mr. John Warner, bound from London for Virginia: Henry Lucas, Samuel Curle. (PRO: E190/72/1).

16 November-10 December. Shippers by the *Hannah*, Mr. Henry Creake, bound from London for Virginia: Henry Hore, George Billers, James Hind, John Baden, Joseph Smith, John Osbourne. (PRO: E190/72/1).

20 November-24 December. Shippers by the *[Golden] Fortune*, Mr. William Jeffreys, bound from London for Virginia: Robert Porten, John Raymond, William Jefferies, Michaell Clipsham, John Littleboys, William & Walter Hands, William Sare, Robert Bristow. (PRO: E190/72/1, 80/1).

21 November. Petition of Henry West, a native of Virginia, planter. He requests a pardon for his brother, William West, who accepted a commission from Nathaniel Bacon to go against the Indians but then resigned the commission and surrendered to Sir William Berkeley. Nevertheless he was sentenced to death but, after a long imprisonment, was required to give a bond to transport himself to England to the ruin of himself, his wife and their several small children. [*See entry of 22 February 1678*] (APC & CSPC).

23 November. The following apprenticed in Bristol to go to Virginia by the *Agreement*: William Mason to John Webb, 4 years; Mary Powell to Thomas Willis, 4 years. (BR).

November. Probate of will of Robert Huggins of Carolina, bachelor. (AW).

November. Probate of will of Robert Terrell of London, merchant, who had goods in Virginia. (AW).

November. Deposition by Thomas Wells of London, merchant aged 25, that he consigned goods by the *Golden Lyon*, Mr. Leonard Webber, to Mr. Roger Thorpe or John Blackfan of Potomack River, Virginia, for which he has not received payment. (LMCD).

1 December. The following apprenticed in Bristol: James Curnock to Jonas Moxley, 4 years Jamaica by *Primrose*, Mr. Thomas Lock. (BR).

4 December. The following apprenticed in Bristol: John Baker to William Bagg, 4 years Barbados by *Batchelor*, Mr. Roger Bagly. (BR).

4-19 December. Shippers by the *Leghorn Merchant*, Mr. Thomas Smith, bound from London for Virginia: Samuel Hoyle, Edward Eaton, John Matthews, Ralph Eddows. (PRO: E190/72/1).

5 December. Deposition in London by Thomas Bacon Esq. of Woodbridge, Suffolk, aged 57, that Nathaniel Bacon, lately deceased, who went to Virginia was his son. (NGSQ 61/4).

6 December. Shipper by the *Dover*, Mr. John Harris, bound from London for Virginia: John Taylor. (PRO: E190/72/1).

7 December. Admiralty estimates for the freightage of merchant ships taken into war service by Sir William Berkeley in Virginia include the following: The *Young Prince*, Mr. Robert Morrice; the *Rebecca*, Mr. Thomas Larimore; the *Adam and Eve*, Mr. Thomas Gardiner; and the *Richard & Elizabeth*, Mr. Nicholas Prynn. (APC).

7 December-23 January. Shippers by the *Angel Gabriel*, Mr. John Reade, bound from Bristol for Virginia: Richard Fitt——, William Swymer, John Sandford, Abraham Saunders, Peter Heale, John Bubb, Samuell Pilsworth, Richard Crumpe, William Willett. (PRO: E190/1139/3).

10-19 December. Shippers by the *Constant*, Mr. Thomas Smith, bound from London for Virginia: John Bell, John Sabin, Edward Leman, Thomas Parker, Thomas Malin. (PRO: E190/80/1).

11 December. The following apprenticed in Bristol: Sarah Perrin to Thomas Pattfield, 4 years Virginia by *Agreement*; Howell Price to William Lock, 4 years Jamaica by *Primrose*; Stephen Jones to Richard Tuck, Barbados by *Angel Gabriel*, Mr. Perkins. (BR).

12 December. Petition of Thomas Gardiner, late master of the *Adam & Eve*. He seized the rebel Nathaniel Bacon and 40 other armed men embarked on a sloop in James River, Virginia, and delivered them to the Governor at James Town but was committed to prison on the charge of having caused the loss of the sloop. (APC).

12-20 December. Shippers by the *York Merchant*, Mr. Christopher Eveling, bound from London for Virginia: Francis Camfield, Joseph Taylor. (PRO: E190/80/1).

15 December. Shipper by the *Charles*, Mr. George Brown, bound from London for Virginia: Joshua Lasher. (PRO: E190/72/1).

19 December. Shipper by the *Margaret*, Mr. George Crone, bound from London for New England: Christopher Hambleton. (PRO: E190/80/1).

22 December. Petition of Otto Thorpe of York County, Virginia, newly arrived in the plantation by the *Planters Adventure*, for restoration of his goods plundered by the rebels and by Sir William Berkeley. (APC)

22 December. Petition of William Mumford of London, merchant, on behalf of Alexander Walker of Virginia, planter, whose tobacco crop was seized by Sir William Berkeley. (APC).

22 December. Petition of Sands Knowles of Gloucester County, Virginia, for restoration of his estate plundered by Robert Beverley. (APC & CSPC).

22 December. Petition of Elizabeth, widow of William Dudley Sr. of Middlesex County, Virginia, for recompense in respect of tobacco seized by Sir William Berkeley. (APC).

24 December. The following apprenticed in Bristol: David Clarke to Joseph Lawrence, 4 years Nevis by *Exchange*, Mr. Richard Speed. (BR).

24 December. Shipper by the *Charles & Mary*, Mr. Thomas Bowman, bound from London for Virginia: Roger Baker. (PRO: E190/72/1).

December. Probate of will of Tobias Handford, formerly of Ware, Gloucester County, Virginia, who died in the parish of St. George Botolph Lane, London. (AW).

December. Administration of John Warner of Stepney, Middlesex, mariner, who had goods in Virginia. (AW).

1677. Passengers by unknown ship (from London) to Virginia: George [———], aged 17; Elizabeth Hatt; Martha Curtis; Robert Lockhard, aged 26; Elizabeth Gorring, aged 21; Hannah East, aged 17; Mary Neight, aged 20; Henry Charrol, aged 27. (NGSQ 64/2).

1677. Passengers by unknown ship (from London) to America(?): Elizabeth (?) Short, aged 20; Ann Harbett from Durham, aged 20; John Whitehouse from Leicester, aged 20; Eleoner Fox from Shropshire, aged 22; Elizabeth Parsons from Warwick, aged 20; Francis Mas—— from Kent, aged 2?; Susan Wells from Bristol, aged 22; Josiah ———; Jane Nasir(?) from London; Jane Wood from Essex (?); Jone Shelton from Buckinghamshire, aged 21; Mary ——— from Ireland, aged 15; William Foster from Ha——, aged 18; Elce Hill from Virginia, aged 12; Francis Hill from Berkshire, aged 17(?). (NGSQ 64/1).

1678

3 January. The following apprenticed in Bristol: Joane Curtis to David Phelps, 4 years Wickacomico, Virginia, by *Angel Gabriel*, Mr. John Roach. (BR).

4 January. The following apprenticed in Bristol: Hugh Jones to Thomas Pope, 4 years Virginia by *Angel Gabriel*; Ann Madocks to William Dicksey, 4 years Barbados by *Society*. (BR).

5 January. Deposition by Peter Peele of London, gent aged 27, that Thomas Roberts of London, merchant, by deed of 31 December 1677, assigned to Job Boulton of London, goldsmith, a debt owed by Miles Forster of Boston, New England. (LMCD).

7 January. The following apprenticed in Bristol: John Jeffry to John Johnson, 5 years Virginia by *Angel Gabriel*; Simon Hughes to William Curtis, 4 years Virginia by *Angel Gabriel*; Jane Wilkins to Isaiah Gribble, 4 years Barbados by *Batchelor*; John Foord to George Knight & Elizabeth his wife, 6 years Virginia. (BR).

15 January. Deposition by Robert Stangroome of Ratcliffe, Middlesex, scrivener aged 49, that Frances Warner, relict and administratrix of John Warner of Ratcliffe, Middlesex, mariner, deceased, has appointed as her attornies Richard Covell of Ratcliffe, mariner, and John Porter of the Eastern Branch of Elizabeth River, Virginia. (LMCD).

18 January. The following apprenticed in Bristol: Thomas Humphreys to Joseph Lawrence, 4 years Nevis by *Exchange*; William Banfield to same, 4 years Nevis by *Exchange*; Mary Webb to same, 4 years Nevis by *Exchange*; Arthur Springnesh to Samuell Pillsworth, 4 years Virginia by *Angel Gabriel*; Benjamin Charme to same, 6 years Virginia by *Angel Gabriel*; Richard Worgan to John Walter, 4 years Barbados by *William & Ann*; John Durban to John Collins, 5 years Barbados; William Mitchell to Thomas Cock, 4 years Barbados by *William & Ann*; Thomas Hitchman to Richard Davy, 4 years Virginia by *Charity*, said Richard Davy of Lyme Mr; Thomas Davis to Thomas Pym, 4 years Antigua by *Fellowship*, said Thomas Pym Mr; John Kirtland to Thomas Tovey, 4 years Virginia by *Gabriel*; James Hallings to —— Owen, 5 years Barbados by *Arthur & Mary*, Mr. Michael Perry; —— Cannum to same, 5 years Barbados by *Arthur & Mary*; Mathew Payne to Thomas Pope, 4 years Nevis by *Gabriel*; Thomas Sheppard to same, 4 years Nevis by *Gabriel*; John Morris to same, 4 years Nevis by *Gabriel*; Mary Syms to same, 4 years Nevis by *Gabriel*. (BR).

18 January. Gawen Corbin to pay Thomas Gardner from money which he holds on behalf of the Assembly of Virginia following the annulment of a bond given by Gardner to Nathaniell Bacon Jr. (APC).

January. Probate of will of Robert Thurston of St. Sepulchre, London, bound for Virginia. (AW).

January. Administration of David Anderson of Boston, New England, who died at sea. (AW).

22 February. On the petition of Henry West of Isle of Wight County, Virginia, his brother William West is granted a pardon, is to have his estate restored and is to be permitted to return to his wife and children. (APC).

24 February. Petition to the Council of Plantations from merchants, planters and masters of ships trading to the plantations in America. In 1664, on their petition, an officer was appointed to register the names, descriptions and covenants of those going voluntarily to the colonies. It is now necessary to set down rules for the future so that the plantations may be supplied. Signed by William Wood, Robert Forthe, William Howston, William Allen, Thomas Mathew, Philip Foster, Henry Meese, John Harris, Thomas Griffith, Thomas Sandes and A. Stanford. (PRO: CO 389/2).

24 February. A further petition representing that certain evil-minded persons enlist voluntarily for the plantations but, when they come to be cleared at Gravesend, they pretend they have been carried away without their consent, to the loss of the signatories. To control such abuses, a person in or near the City of London should be appointed to register the names, ages, quality, place of birth and last residence of those taking ship. Signed by James Goodwin, Robert Chemix, Jeremy Fisher, Richard Glover, Anthony Fenn, Martin Gardener, James Conaway, John Gardner, Richard Longman, William Tuxon, Robert Conaway, John Mohun, Richard Owen, John Thornebush, John Smyth, William Weede, John Port, Thomas Jordan, John Jeffery, John Dunch, Thomas Webbe, Robert Gill, John Midleton, William Goodlas, James Jenkins, John Benborne, Marke Warkeman, John Harris, Ihr. Sutter, Samuell Cooper, Thomas Mathews, Thomas Jones, Thomas Colclough, John Rokey, Thomas Griffith, A. Stanford and William Barrat.

The petitions are referred to the Solicitor-General who reports as follows:

On 18 July 1664 it came to notice that the mischief of spiriting was prevalent and that there was scarce any voyage to the plantations but some were carried there against their will. It was recommended that a Register of Passengers be established to provide a remedy. Though the King might erect such an office, it could only be effective on the passing of an Act of Parliament so that a fee could be paid in recompense. On 7 September 1664 it was agreed that Roger Whitley Esq. should become the master of the proposed office to be called "The office of taking and registering the consents, agreements and covenants of such persons, male or female, as shall voluntarily go or be sent as servants to the plantations in America." The register was to be kept in a parchment or strong paper book and a common seal used by masters of ships to be employed solely for the purposes of registration. This grant was not to apply to factors, apprentices or menial servants of any merchant, planter and the like going to the plantations.

Enclosed with the report are the following affidavits:

Robert Smart, aged 2-, tall, sanguine complexion, blind in one eye, long brown hair, grey coat, from Dartford, Kent, says that he was to go to Virginia on the account of George Potts in the *Jamaica Factor*, Mr. Constable. 1 August 1670.

Mary, wife of Marke Collens, barber surgeon, living at the *Lyon and Sampson* in St. Katherine's Lane near Tower Hill, says that she spoke with Mr. Haverland, generally called a spirit, who was taking a young man, a servant to Sir Thomas Bateman. She threatened to get a warrant from the Lord Chief Justice against Haverland but he said he did not care a turd for the Lord Chief Justice and would wipe his arse with the warrant. When she met Haverland again, he drew his sword and swore he would make her fly to the devil. 9 January 1671.

Thomas Stone of Battlebridge, Southwark, says that Haverland, whom he met last November, touched him on the shoulder and called him "country man." When Haverland discovered he was from Wiltshire, he pretended he was from the same part, plied him with drink and delivered him to Captain Wheeler of the *Martha.* 10 January 1671.

William Haverland of St. Katherine's parish, Middlesex, says that John Steward has spirited 500 persons a year to Barbados, Virginia, Jamaica and elsewhere overseas for twelve years . He ususally gave 25 shillings to anyone who brought him a person to be transported and received 40 shillings a head from the interested merchant. William Thiew of Marlings Rents in East Smithfield, shoemaker, used to spirit persons in the same manner for twelve years or more and in one year spirited 840 persons away. John Hartley, a fat man lodging at St. Katherine's who was a soldier, has been a spirit for three months. Robert Bayley, an old spirit who lives sometimes in St. Katherine's and sometimes in St. Giles, had no other livelihood but spiriting. Richard Ingram, a cobbler lodging in St. Katherine's Court, is sometimes a bailiff but has also been a spirit for three years. Thomas Harris, a shoemaker at Ratcliffe Cross, has spirited persons for the last year. The following have also been spirits for up to four years: Richard Batt of Mill Bridge, St. Katherine's, haberdasher; Stephen Micher of Southwark, seaman; William Jones of East Smithfield; Richard Perry, of St. Katherine's, ostler; Thomas Griggs, labourer; Robert Taylor, waterman at Pickle Herring Stairs, Southwark; Mt. Davies in Bear Lane, London, victualler; William Stubbs, brewer's servant of St. Katherine's; Marke Collens, a soldier in Captain Howard's Company; John Rammage, victualler at the Iron Gate in the Tower. Thomas Ridley, who had agreed with Captain Wheelock to serve him for four years in Virginia, was carried by Wheelock to Edward Rickett's house on Ratcliffe Highway where he was robbed. 30 January 1671.

Griffith Jones says that last Christmas Marke Collens tried to get him to become a clerk in Barbados, promised him books and took him to an alehouse in Billingsgate from where he was carried by boat aboard the *Exchange* and sold for 50 shillings. It cost the deponent three pounds to get off the ship. 1 February 1671.

Joshua Pretty of St. Leonard, Shoreditch, weaver, says that at Christmas he was plied with drink by John Hartley, Robert Taylor and Marke Collens who offered him ten pounds and tobacco if he would go to Jamaica. When he refused he was beaten so badly that he was unable to work for two weeks. Marke Collens then went by the name of Captain Stanford. 6 February 1671.

Martha, wife of William Tanner, says that at Christmas John Steward, Joane Steward his wife, and George Hardisty confessed that they had spirited away the deponent's husband on the *Nathaniel* to Barbados and had kept him in drink for three days in order to get him aboard. William Kirke, Steward's partner, shared in the 50 shillings they received from Thomas Bodley, a merchant living in Houndsditch, who was in partnership with another merchant, Robert Merriot. The deponent had received two letters from her husband while he was on board the ship saying that he wished to get off. 17 February 1671.

The report concludes by stating that an Act to prevent the stealing and transportation of children and other persons was passed on 18 March 1671, and that such actions were punishable by death. (CO 389/2). [N.B. In 1682 the Privy Council concluded that Whitley's office was failing to achieve its purpose and ordered that plantation servants must register before a Mayor, Justice of the Peace or magistrate].

14 February. Depositions in London re the voyage of the *Alexander*, Mr. William Harris, from to Virginia in 1677 and her return in 1678. (EA).

27 February-5 March. Shippers by the *Unity* of Topsham, Mr. William Condey, bound from Exeter for New England: John Mayne, John Lane, Matthias Jenkins, John Pope, Robert Hutchings. (PRO: E190/957/3).

February. Probate of will of Marmaduke Goode of Upton, Berkshire, clerk, whose brother, John Goode, was in Virginia. (AW).

February. Administration of Edward Rawlins of New York, bachelor. (AW).

February. Probate of will of Anne Jones of St. Clement Danes, Middlesex, whose son, Thomas Daniell, was in Virginia. (AW).

February. Probate of will of Mary Hoskins of Richmond, Surrey, widow, whose brother, John Githins, was in Maryland. (AW).

February. Probate of will of Nathaniel Eeles of Harpenden, Hertfordshire, whose son, John Eeles, was in Virginia. (AW).

February. Probate of will of John Anderson of New England. (AW).

1 March. Essex prisoners reprieved to be transported to Barbados or Jamaica: Daniel Albon of Broxted; John Dixon of Arksden; William Starnell of Hornchurch. (PRO: C66/3204/14).

1 March. The following apprenticed in Bristol: Thomas White to —— ——, 5 years Barbados by *Mary*, Mr. Richard Brittain; Ann Payne to Andrew Dolbery, 4 years Barbados by *Two Brothers*, said Andrew Dolbery Mr. (BR).

9 March. Northern Circuit prisoners reprieved to be transported to Barbados. Cheshire: Thomas Woodcocke of Church Hulme; Mary Leighe of Glovers Stone. (PRO: C66/3204/5).

13 March. Deposition by Andrew Willett of London, merchant aged 35, that his uncle, Jacob Willett, late citizen and haberdasher of London, on 10 May 1672 appointed Nicholas Giffard, citizen and painter stainer of London as his attorney. In 1675 he sent an order from New England revising the appointment. (LMCD).

20 March. Deposition by Richard Walton, aged 21, servant of Thomas Ball, citizen and leatherseller of London, that Bernard Trott of Boston, New England, merchant, became indebted to his master by bond of 25 June 1674. (LMCD).

29 March-30 April. Shippers by the *Desire* of Bristol bound from Bristol for New England: John Richardson, Erasmus Dole, Thomas Scroope, William Middlecott, Richard Smith, Thomas Tayer, Thomas Saunders. (PRO: E190/1139/3).

March. Administration with will of Thomas Todd the elder, of Baltimore, Maryland. (AW).

March. Probate of will of Henry Roach of Abbots Leigh, [Somerset], mariner, who had lands in Virginia. (AW).

March. Margaret Rogers of Ipswich, New England, widow. Administration to the principal creditor, William Hubbard. (AW).

March. Administration of Thomas Sharpe of Virginia. (AW).

20 April. Deposition by Samuel Brown of London, merchant aged 27, and John Powell of London, merchant aged 30, that William Greenough of New England, mariner, and John Hoper of London, merchant, became indebted to the deponent Powell by bond of 9 February 1676. (LMCD).

26 April. Deposition by Thomas Allen, aged 25, and John Bulkley, aged 20, linen drapers of London, that Abraham Bartholomew of Salem, New England, became indebted to Francis Warner Esq. by bond of 19 July 1674. (LMCD).

28 April. Shipper by the *Success* of Topsham, Mr. Thomas Rost, bound from Exeter for New England: John Cholwill. (PRO: E190/957/3).

1678

2 May. Newgate prisoners reprieved to be transported to Barbados. London: Walter Bailey; Jane Harris, spinster; Nicholas Cockerell; Susan Banser alias Gibson alias Greene, spinster. Middlesex: Hepsibah Cobb, wife of James Cobb of St. Clement Danes; Elizabeth Watts, wife of Thomas Watts of St. Margaret Westminster; Sarah Good of the same; Thomas Callespine of the same; Elizabeth Evans of the same, spinster; Susan Hinsell of Whitechapel; Roger Minsher of Clerkenwell; Joane Smith of Stepney, spinster; Anne Steward alias Wanarton of St. Martin in the Fields; Alice Chilton of St. Mary Savoy, spinster. (PRO: C66/3204/7).

30 May. Petition of Sir John Peake and John Harward, owners of the *Recovery*, Mr. Edmond Clements, for a pass for the ship to sail from London for New York. (APC).

31 May. Mr. Edward Randolph is to be confirmed in his appointment as Collector of Customs at Boston, New England. (APC).

May. Administration of William Lloyd of Westminster, Middlesex, who died in Virginia, bachelor. (AW).

May. Administration of Edward Phelps of Virginia, bachelor. (AW).

May. Probate of will of James Turpin of Virginia, widower. (AW).

19 June. Petition of Thomas Gould, John Jeffreys, Alexander Culpepper, George Richards, Edward Carter, Henry Meese, Thomas Lane, James Tubb, Micajah Perry and Thomas Sands for payment of bills of exchange issued by the Treasury of Virginia. (APC).

23 June. Shipper by the *Endeavour* of Piscataway, Mr. Lawrence Catt, bound from Dartmouth for New England: John Haynes. (PRO: E190/957/11).

25 June. Shipper by the *Hopewell* of Piscataway, Mr. Thomas Miller, bound from Dartmouth for New England: John Cutt. (PRO: E190/957/11).

28 June. Deposition in London re the voyage of the *Constant Martha*, Mr. William Hanman, from to Maryland in 1676 with goods consigned to Cadwallader Palmer. (EA).

? June. The following apprenticed in Bristol: Samuel Ferris to William Smith, 4 years Virginia by *Bristol Merchant*, said William Smith Mr. (BR)..

June. Administration of Edmund Wharton of New England, bachelor. (AW).

June. Administration of William Cuthbertson of the ship *Elizabeth and Catherine*, who died in Virginia, bachelor. (AW).

June. Probate of will of Joseph Hayes of Ware, Gloucester County, Virginia. (AW).

June. Administration of John Beton of Ratcliffe, Stepney, Middlesex, who died in Virginia. (AW).

June. Administration of Josias Alleine of New England, bachelor. (AW).

1 July. Oxford Circuit prisoners reprieved to be transported to America. Berkshire: Richard Plumridge of White Waltham; Anne Bartlemer of Kintbury. Gloucestershire: Edward Cutler of Tewkesbury; Alice Williams alias Steele of Westbury. Herefordshire: William Hill of Hereford; James Owens of Wigmore. Monmouthshire: Richard Hopson of Abergavenny; Thomas Powell alias David Higgins of Llanellen; John Forster of St. Maughans. Oxfordshire: John Bradshawe of Oxford. Shropshire: Hugh David of Shrewsbury; William Coston of Winstanstow; John Charles of Pockington; Thomas Gilbert of Shrewsbury; Howell Probert of Bromfield. Staffordshire: Thomas Naden of Wallspring; Richard Naden of Donhead; Nicholas Jones of Wolverhampton. Worcestershire: James Gilbert of All Saints, Worcester; Dorothy Yarrington of Hanley Child; Thomas Chaundler of Hampton Lovett; John Heminge of Worcester. (PRO: C66/3204/9).

2 July. Certificate that Jonathan Allein (of London) is the lawful brother and next-of-kin of Josias Allein of New England, bachelor deceased, whose administration has been granted in the Prerogative Court of Canterbury. (LMCD).

2 July-2 August. Shippers by the *Return* bound from Bristol for New England: Thomas Edwards, John Richardson, William Middlecott, Thomas Saunders, Richard Spragg. (PRO: E190/1139/3).

2 July-12 August. Shippers by the *Relief* bound from Bristol for New England: William Marshall, Robert Hayne, Phillip Cook, Walter Stephens, John Richardson, Thomas Tayer. (PRO: E190/1139/3).

3 July. Petition of Richard Smith for himself and for John Winthrop, Josiah Winslow, William Harris, John Vyall and other proprietors of Narriganset, New England, for the Government of Rhode Island to restore the territory to the Government of Connecticut. (APC).

3 July. Home Circuit prisoners reprieved to be transported to Barbados or Jamaica. Essex: Matthew Porter alias Pourcher of Stamford Rivers or High Ongar; William Browne of Ongar; John Pledger of All Saints, Colchester, (the last two still in prison in July 1679). Hertfordshire: Oliver Turpin of Barnet (still in prison in July 1679). Kent: Thomas Gassoone of Charing. Surrey: Edward Ayres of Newington. (PRO: C66/3204/10).

9 July. Shipper by the *Susan* of Boston, Mr. John Frost, bound from Newcastle for Boston, New England: Martin Bodkin. (PRO: E190/197/12, 198/6).

10 July. Western Circuit prisoners reprieved to be transported to Barbados. Cornwall: William Poynter of St. Clements; John Merrell of Truro. Devon: William Stone alias Richards of Sandford; William Clarke of Tamerton Foliot. Dorset: Thomas Snooke of Stalbridge. Hampshire: Dorothy Kyte of Penton Grafton; John Lawrence of Portsmouth; Samuel Worledge of Portsmouth;

Henry Tovey of Portsmouth, ropemaker. Somerset: James Foweracre of Taunton St. James. (PRO: C66/3206/20).

10 July. Midland Circuit prisoners reprieved to be transported to America. Derbyshire: Edward Sikes of Asher; Robert Houghton of Chesterfield. Leicestershire: Richard Wiggins of Ragdale; Thomas Glover of Loughborough; Bartholomew Dawson of Loughborough; William Davis of Loughborough; Elias Blackston of Anstey; Thomas Smith of Sneston; Robert Read of Thurnby; Mordecai Radford of Ashby de la Zouch. Lincolnshire: Edward Mease of Lincoln; Simon Tingle of Gainsborough; William Beels of Wigtoft; Philip Melton of Faldingworth; John Burnett of Biskerthorpe; Christopher Meynell of Long Leadman; William Fairfax of Lincoln; Zacharias Groome of Whapload; Nicholas Lemmon of Long Leadenham; Edward Pacey of Helpingham; John Chester of Grantham. Northamptonshire: James Perkins of Whilton; Edward Perkins of Whilton; Edward Robinson of Pilton; Thomas Burges of Walton; Thomas Wainwright of Kings Cliffe; William Smith of Dodford; William Shipman of Northampton; Thomas Stroud of Northampton; Thomas Collins of Northampton, shoemaker; Henry Spencer of Watford. Nottinghamshire: Robert Pearson of Great Markham; Robert Ratcliffe of West Retford; John Espin of Nottingham; William Greisby of Wellor; James Tayler of Newark on Trent; William Healowe of Nottingham; George Espin of Nottingham; Stephen Slack of Retford; Thomas Cooper of Ruddington. Rutland: Robert Remmington of Uppingham; Richard Randall of Oakham; Francis Fry of Empingham. Warwickshire: Randolph Langham of Monks Kirby; James Rowley of Warwick; John Newey of Killingworth; Daniel Veares of Warwick; Edward Corbett of Warwick; Thomas Whitmore of Coton; William Charley of Coventry; John Court alias Smith of Killingworth; William Canning of Stratford on Avon; Robert Wells of Killingworth; William Whitenit of Birmingham. Unspecified: Thomas Stanley. (PRO: C66/3204/13).

11 July. Deposition by Jonas Armstrong, citizen and waterman of London, of St. Olave, Southwark, Surrey, aged 36, that, before he went to Virginia, Thomas Webb of London, merchant, now deceased, had declared that he and Robert Spring owed money to George Peake of London, merchant, now deceased. Richard Peake of Southwark, gent, is administrator of George Peake. (LMCD).

12 July. The following apprenticed in Bristol: Moses Found to Philipp Cole, 9 years New England by *Return* of Boston. (BR).

16 July. The following apprenticed in Bristol: Katharine Griffin to Robert Turpin, 4 years Virginia by *Unicorn*. (BR).

17 July. Petition of Randall Holden and John Green for the town of Warwick to be restored to the Government of Connecticut. (APC).

18 July. Deposition by John Jones of Charles Town, New England, mariner aged 34, that on 7 November 1677 he received into his ship the *Swallow* of Charles

Town, goods and horses to be delivered to Captain Joseph Crisp of St. Christopher's, merchant. (LMCD).

18 July. The following apprenticed in Bristol: Richard Laud to Bernard Browne, 4 years Virginia by *Bristol Factor*, Mr. Roger Drewe; Sarah Clarke to William White, 4 years Virginia by *Bristol Factor*; Ann Tidcombe to Philipp Cooke, 5 years New England by *Return* of Boston; Mary Ball to same, 4 years New England by *Return* of Boston; Ann Wharton to same, 4 years New England by *Return* of Boston. (BR).

18 July-22 August. Shippers by the *Martha & Sarah* bound from Bristol for Virginia: Alexander Thompson, Nicholas Pope. (PRO: E190/1139/3).

20 July-2 August. Shippers by the *Bristol Factor* bound from Bristol for Virginia: Stephen Watts, Richard Hughes, Richard Marsh, James Still. (PRO: E190/1139/3).

26 July. The following apprenticed in Bristol: William Bastin to George Squire, 4 years Virginia by *Bristol Factor*. (BR).

26 July. Deposition by James Glavin of Grays Inn Lane, London, victualler aged 60, that his brother, Thomas Glavin of Lymington, Hampshire, deceased, was the father of Bartholomew Glavin of Maryland, surgeon, deceased, and of Thomas Glavin of Lymington, gent, the oldest brother now living of the said Bartholomew. (LMCD).

27 July. Deposition by John Dent of Christchurch, Surrey, gent aged 60, John Lee of the same, waterman aged 40, and Mary Pitts, aged 27, wife of Francis Pitts of the same, waterman, that a negro named Black Tom who now calls himself Tom Hackleton, was a slave belonging to Mrs. Hackleton of Christchurch, now deceased, while he was in England and she let him out at her pleasure. He was never christened because Mrs. Hackleton feared that, once he was, he would sue for his freedom. She sent him to her brother Thomas Kemp of Maryland, planter. (LMCD).

27 July. The following apprenticed in Bristol: Elizabeth Poticary to George Squire, 4 years Virginia by *Bristol Factor*. (BR).

30 July. Shipper by the *John & Francis*, Mr. John Wall, bound from Weymouth for Virginia: said John Wall. (PRO: E190/882/10).

30 July. The following apprenticed in Bristol: Ann Matthewes to George Wilson, 4 years Virginia by *Bristol Factor*; Christopher Meade to William Neads, 4 years Virginia by *Martha & Sarah*, said William Neads Mr. (BR).

July. Probate of will of Jehosaphat Smith of London, who died in Boston, New England. (AW).

July. Administration of Theophilus Potts of Virginia, bachelor. (AW).

July. Administration of Peter Greene of the ship *Charles*, who died in Virginia. (AW).

July. Administration of Peter Sibbet of Haddington, Scotland, who died in Virginia, bachelor. (AW).

July. Administration of Francis Young of Stepney, Middlesex who died in Virginia. (AW).

1 August. The following apprenticed in Bristol: Andrew Dyer to George Wilson, 4 years Virginia by *Martha & Sarah*; Thomas Lewes to Barnabas Robertson, 8 years Virginia by *Bristol Factor*; Miles Williams to Lydia Harcum, Virginia by *Martha & Sarah*; John Thomas to William Mills, 8 years Virginia. (BR).

4 August. The following apprenticed in Bristol: David Jones to Phillip Neason, 4 years Virginia by *Nevis Merchant*. (BR).

5 August. Shipper by the *Francis* of Southampton, Mr. John Wall, bound from Southampton for Virginia: Robert Richbell. (PRO: E190/829/9).

6 August. The following apprenticed in Bristol: Mary Dorman to George Wilson, 5 years Virginia by *Bristol Factor*. (BR).

7 August. The following apprenticed in Bristol: Hanna Elvins to Phillip Ireson, 4 years Virginia by *Nevis Merchant*; Joshua Jackson to Philipp Turdin, 4 years Virginia; Katharine Jones to Philipp Cooke, 4 years New England by *Return*, Mr. Thomas Edwards; Priscilla Wattkins to same, 4 years New England by *Return*. (BR).

8 August. Deposition by John Taylor, rector of Westmill, Hertfordshire, aged 63, that John Sykes, vicar of Yardley, Hertfordshire, officiated at the marriage of John Stanley, then of Gutter Lane, London, who went to Virginia in 1666 and is since deceased, and Elizabeth, daughter of Richard Taylor, vicar of Westmill. (LMCD).

12 August. The following apprenticed in Bristol: Philipp May to Barnard Browne, 4 years Virginia by *Bristol Factor*; Thomas Jerkins to Robert Worgan, 4 years Virginia by *Victory*, Mr. William [*elsewhere* John] Jones; Humfry Axall to Francis Haynes, 5 years New England by *Return* of Boston. (BR).

14 August. Shipper by the *Endeavour* of Ramsgate, Mr. Henry Curling, bound from Lyme for Virginia: John Burridge. (PRO: E190/882/11).

14 August. The following apprenticed in Bristol: Elizabeth Pittman to William Harwood, 4 years Virginia by *Bristol Merchant*; William Lucus to William Neads, 4 years Virginia by *Mary & Joan*; Elizabeth Harding to Richard Follington, 4 years Virginia by *Bristol Factor*; Mary Dorney to Charles Tilden, 4 years Virginia by *Victory*. (BR).

19 August. Shippers by the *Armes of Southampton*, Mr. Anthony Pryar, bound from Southampton for Virginia: Thomas Cornelius, William Puckle. (PRO: E190/829/9).

21 August. Shipper by the *Providence* of Lyme, Mr. Solomon Andrew, bound from Lyme for Virginia: said Solomon Andrew. (PRO: E190/882/11).

21 August. The following apprenticed in Bristol: Jonathan Hurd to John Spragdon & Robert Turpin, 4 years Virginia by *Unicorn*; Elizabeth Howell to Philemon Bird, 4 years Virginia by *Victory*. (BR).

22 August. The following apprenticed in Bristol: Joane Morris to Arthur Grant, 4 years Virginia by *Nevis Merchant*, said Arthur Grant Mr; Richard Martyn to John Brinsey, 4 years Virginia by *Bristol Merchant*; Katharine Griffin to Browne Biddleston, 4 years Virginia by *Victory*. (BR).

24 August-8 September. Shippers by the *Prosperous* of Lymington, Mr. John Brading, bound from Southampton for Virginia: John Tayler, William Jolliffe, Nathaniell Provo. (PRO: E190/829/9).

25 August. Petition of George Baron of London, merchant, sole owner of the *Elizabeth* of London, Mr. William Prout. The ship is now in Boston, New England, and he seeks a pass for her return to London. (APC).

26 August. The following apprenticed in Bristol: James Williams to Robert Worgan, 4 years Virginia by *Victory*. (BR).

28 August. Deposition by Tobias Russell of East Smithfield, Aldgate, London, tobacconist aged 51, and John Stripling of Wapping, Middlesex, mariner, that James Barret of London and Virginia, merchant, became indebted to Jonathan Leigh of London by bond of 20 November 1672. (LMCD).

28 August. The following apprenticed in Bristol: Robert Lindsay to Foulke Adams, 4 years Virginia by *Concord*. (BR).

30 August. The following apprenticed in Bristol: Mary Dollman to Samuell Carder, 4 years Virginia by *Blackmore*. (BR).

30 August-16 October. Shippers by the *Victory* bound from Bristol for Virginia: George Webb, John Bubb, Edward Dyer, Stephen Watts, John Hawkins, Michaell Hunt, James Phelps, William Coulson, Thomas Speed, Cadwallader Jones, Benjamin Adlam, John Woodward, Edward Fielding, James Freeman, John Richardson, Samuell Parker. (PRO: E190/1139/3).

31 August-4 September. Shippers by the *Concord* bound from Bristol for Virginia: William Swymer, James Biggs, Joseph Clark, Nicholas Lux, Thomas Scuse, John Bubb, John Sandford, Edward Fielding, Michael Pope, Henry Daniell. (PRO: E190/1139/3).

31 August-28 September. Shippers by the *Unicorn* bound from Bristol for Virginia: Richard Finch, Roger Nevill, David Parry, James Millard, Richard

Harris, Richard Bickham, John Belcheir, William Scott, Joseph Bridger. (PRO: E190/1139/3).

August. Administration of Richard Mavell of Hanley Castle, Worcestershire, who died in Virginia, bachelor. (AW).

August. Administration with will of Robert Wynne of Jordans, Charles City, Virginia. (AW).

2 September. Depositions taken in London to establish the authenticity of the will of George Moone of Fremington, Devon, master of the *Dublin Merchant*, who died in Virginia in 1677. A search was made both in Virginia and in Bideford, Devon, for John Helliar, who witnessed Moone's will, but he could not be found and was presumed dead. (NGSQ 69/3).

2 September. The following apprenticed in Bristol: Jennet Edwards to Zachariah Smith, 4 years Virginia by *Expectation*; Mary Haverd to Philipp Neason, 4 years Virginia by *Nevis Merchant*; Michaell Dare to Kadwallader Jones, 4 years Virginia by *Bristol Merchant*; Henry Brice to same, 4 years Virginia by *Bristol Merchant*; John Hughes to same, 4 years Virginia by *Bristol Merchant*; John Anderson to George Stevens, 4 years Virginia by *Sarah & Elizabeth*, Mr. Richard White; Francis Sutton to Lot Richards, 4 years Virginia by *Victory*. (BR).

4 September. Shippers by the *Nevis Merchant* bound from Bristol for Virginia: John Bubb, John Duddlestone. (PRO: E190/1139/3).

4-13 September. Shipper by the *Marygold* of Weymouth, Mr. John Cox, bound from Weymouth for Virginia: James Gould. (PRO: E190/882/10).

5 September. Deposition of Joseph Randall, aged 27, servant of John Dowley, citizen and fishmonger of London, that he has seen the account between his master and Mr. George Bagnall, deceased, relating to goods consigned to Mr. John Winder of New York. (LMCD).

5 September. The following apprenticed in Bristol: William Jones to Robert Parker, 4 years Virginia by *Victory*. (BR).

6 September. Shipper by the *Hopewell* of New England, Mr. John Baker, bound from Lyme for New England: John Aning. (PRO: E190/882/11).

6 September. Shipper by the *Charity* of Lyme, Mr. Richard Davy, bound from Lyme for Virginia: John Burridge. (PRO: E190/882/11).

6 September. The following apprenticed in Bristol: Thomas Blake to Samuell Carder, 6 years Virginia by *Blackmore*. (BR).

6-25 September. Shippers by the *Blackamore* bound from Bristol for Virginia: Edward Martindale, William Smith, Thomas Speed. (PRO: E190/1139/3).

7 September. The following apprenticed in Bristol: George Browne to John Stevens, 4 years Virginia by *Sarah & Elizabeth*; Richard Shepherd to Henry

Hieron, 5 years Virginia by *Victory*; Sarah Killuck to same, 5 years Virginia by *Victory*; Ann Otridge to same, 5 years Virginia by *Victory*. (BR).

9 September. The following apprenticed in Bristol: Dorothy Haverd to Charles Andrews, 4 years Virginia by *Reformation*; Robert Smith to Henry Hieron, 4 years Virginia by *Victory*; John Collins to John Stevens, 4 years Virginia by *Bristol Merchant*; Welthian Jones to Thomas Stevens, 4 years Virginia by *George*. (BR).

11 September. The following apprenticed in Bristol: John Chapman to William Ennott, 4 years Virginia by *Richard*, Mr. Philipp Patch. (BR).

12 September. The following apprenticed in Bristol: Thomas Turner to George Wilson, 4 years Virginia by *Bristol Merchant*; William Edwards to same, 4 years Virginia by *Bristol Merchant*; Elizabeth Abbott to John Thedam, 4 years Virginia by *Victory*; John Carroll to John Stevens, 4 years Virginia by *Sarah & Elizabeth*; John Poole to John Staynes, 4 years Virginia by *Sarah & Elizabeth*. (BR).

17 September. The following apprenticed in Bristol: Edward Clement to Margaret Phelps, 4 years Virginia by *Victory*. (BR).

18 September. The following apprenticed in Bristol: Charles Glover to Zachary Smith, 4 years Virginia by *Maryland Merchant*, Mr. George Tyte. (BR).

18-27 September. Shippers by the *Richard* of Bristol bound from Bristol for Virginia: Richard Pope, James Pope, Robert Bayley, John Porter, Samuell Wharton. (PRO: E190/1139/3).

20 September. The following apprenticed in Bristol: John Bowers to Mary Tildin, 4 years Virginia by *Victory*; John Spencer to Mark Sloper, 4 years Virginia by *Bristol Merchant*; Elizabeth Bache to Thomas Gamon, 5 years Virginia by *Blackmore*, said Thomas Gamon Mr; Elizabeth Daybrinke to same, 5 years Virginia by *Blackmore*. (BR).

21 September. Deposition by Benjamin Mosse of London, scrivener, that on 18 September 1678 John Hussey of Shottesbrook, Berkshire, cordwainer, and Mary his wife, formerly Mary Harden, daughter of Mary Harden and an heir of John Singleton of Maryland, deceased, signed a letter of attorney to Henry Coursey of Chester River, Talbot County, Maryland, merchant. (LMCD).

24 September-9 October. Shippers by the *Sarah [or Hannah] & Elizabeth* bound from Bristol for Virginia: John Orchard, John Stayne, Charles Harford, Michaell Pope, Richard Hughes, Edward Fielding, Charles Allen. (PRO: E190/1139/3).

25 September. Deposition by James Scrape of London, haberdasher aged 30, that on 5 July 1677 Arthur Price, then in London but now in Virginia, became bound to the deponent's father, Robert Scrape of London, merchant, to pay

Mathew Wilkinson of London, merchant, for goods which were shipped to him. (LMCD).

26 September. The following apprenticed in Bristol: Grace Tammas to William Mills, 4 years Virginia by *Mary & Joan*, Mr. William Nego; John Coward to Joseph Clarke, 6 years Virginia by *Blackmore*; John Singer alias Smith to same, 6 years Virginia by *Blackmore*. (BR).

27 September. Shipper by the *Seaflower* of Poole bound from Poole for Maryland: Alexander Maynard. (PRO: E190/882/13).

27 September. On the petition of Ralph Williamson who has undertaken to transport 50 felons from Scotland to the plantations, an order is to be sent to allow their landing in Virginia. (APC).

27 September. The following apprenticed in Bristol: John Rogers to Philipp Eggleston, 4 years Virginia by *Expectation*, Mr. William Davis. (BR).

27 September. Shipper by the *Bonadventure* of Topsham, Mr. Michaell Hooker, bound from Exeter for Virginia: John Pym. (PRO: E190/957/3).

27 September-12 October. Shippers by the *Exeter Merchant*, Mr. Derby Hickey, bound from Exeter for Virginia: John Pym, Robert Dabynett, James Cheed, Thomas Ford, James Fulwood, William Buckley, Henry Tanner, Endymion Walker, James Clutterbuck. (PRO: E190/957/3).

28 September. Shipper by the *Comfort* bound from Bristol for Virginia: Samuell Wharton. (PRO: E190/1139/3).

30 September. The following apprenticed in Bristol: Alice Wattkins to Robert Williams, 4 years Virginia; William Morgan to Robert Miller, 4 years Virginia by *Sarah & Elizabeth*. (BR).

September. Administration of William Munford of Virginia, who died in London, bachelor. (AW).

September. Administration of Nathaniel Knight of James Town, Virginia. (AW).

September. Administration of James Senior of Kingston-upon-Hull, Yorkshire, who died in Virginia, bachelor. (AW).

September. Administration of Bartholomew Walker of the ship *Robert and William*, who died on the King's service in Virginia, bachelor. (AW).

1 October. Deposition by Nathaniel Mason, citizen and cooper of London, aged 38, that Thomas Barbour of York River, Virginia, became indebted to John Rawlins of Wapping, Middlesex, mariner, by bond of 20 October 1673. (LMCD).

2 October. The following apprenticed in Bristol: Priscilla Kingman to Zachary Smith, 4 years Virginia by *Maryland Merchant*; John Butcher to John Thedam,

4 years Virginia by *Victory*; Joseph Merchant to William Jones, 4 years Virginia by *Victory*. (BR).

2 October. Shipper by the *William* of Weymouth, Mr. Jacob Chubb, bound from Weymouth for Virginia: said Jacob Chubb. (PRO: E190/882/10).

7 October. The following apprenticed in Bristol: Mary Powell to Philemon Bird, 4 years Virginia by *Victory*; Christopher Harrell to Anthony Thieron, 8 years Virginia by *Victory*; Henry Harrell to same, 10 years Virginia by *Victory*; George Semine to Thomas Tandy, 7 years Virginia by *Alithea*; George Wattkis to same, 7 years Virginia by *Alithea*; Margaret Jones to Richard White, 4 years Virginia by *Sarah & Elizabeth*; Francis Cotton to same, 4 years Virginia by *Sarah & Elizabeth*. (BR).

9 October. The following apprenticed in Bristol: William Stidman to Thomas Robins, 4 years Virginia by *Expectation*; Arthur Williams to John Walter, 3 years New York by *Katharine*, Mr. Robert Dapwell; Edward Williams to same, 3 years New York [by *Katharine*]; Samuell Minor to same, 5 years New York; John Lokyer to John Hort, 7 years Virginia by *John*, Mr. Peter Wraxall. (BR).

9-19 October. Shippers by the *Expectation* bound from Bristol for Virginia: Marmaduke Bowdler, Abraham Edwards, Phillip Jordan, Mathew Worgan, Abraham Wild, Thomas Huntley. (PRO: E190/1139/3).

11 October. The following apprenticed in Bristol: Rebecca Walter to Zachary Smith, 4 years Virginia by *Maryland Merchant*; Edward Badman to William Mills, 8 years Virginia by *Mary & Joan*; Martha Barnett to same, 8 years Virginia by *Mary & Joan*. (BR).

12 October. The following apprenticed in Bristol: David Llewellin to Robert Worgan, 4 years Virginia by *Victory*; Jane Shakefoote to John Abbott, 4 years Nevis by *New England Merchant*; Roger Meredith to John Marden, 4 years Virginia by *Francis & Mary*. (BR).

12-23 October. Shippers by the *Stephen* bound from Bristol for Virginia: Walter Stephens, Martha Deane, Henry Daniell, Symon Harle, Robert Smith, Michaell Pope, Stephen Watts, John Sandford, David Phillips, William Yeamans, John Read. (PRO: E190/1139/3).

15 October. The following apprenticed in Bristol: Thomas Ware to Thomas Yate, 3 years Virginia by *Agreement*, Mr. William Stratton; Patience Walker to Edith Guest, 4 years Virginia by *Richard*; Constant Cotton to John Cromwell, 4 years Virginia by *Richard*; Thomas Tanner to same, 8 years Virginia by *Richard*; William Watts to same, 7 years Virginia by *Richard*; John David to Roger Ferrier, 6 years Virginia by *Victory*. (BR).

16 October. Shipper by the *Elizabeth* of Poole, Mr. William Pike, bound from Poole for Maryland: said William Pike. (PRO: E190/882/13).

16-23 October. Shippers by the *Reformation* bound from Bristol for Virginia: Edward Fielding, Michaell Pope, John Bubb, Charles Andrewes, Thomas Turner. (PRO: E190/1139/3).

16-26 October. Shippers by the *John* bound from Bristol for Virginia: John England, Jonathan Packer, John Bubb, Stephen Watts, Thomas Edwards, John Dymer. (PRO: E190/1139/3).

17 October. The following apprenticed in Bristol: James Eton to Richard Ferrier, 5 years Virginia by *Victory*; William Edwards to Thomas Griffin, 4 years Virginia by *George*; Sarah Bennett to same, 4 years Virginia by *George*; Timothy Haines to John Frogly, 4 years Virginia by *John*. (BR).

19 October-15 November. Shippers by the *George* bound from Bristol for Virginia: Richard Farrier, Samuell Carpender, John Wasbrow, Jenkin Morgan, Richard Benson, Edward Martindale, Richard Olliver, Richard Gibbons. (PRO: E190/1139/3).

23 October. Certificate that Priscilla Holland of London, spinster, daughter and administratrix of her father James Holland, citizen and grocer of London, deceased, has appointed Simon Wilmer, her father's late factor, as attorney in Maryland, or, on his decease, Nathaniel Heathcott of Maryland, merchant. (LMCD).

24 October-2 November. Shippers by the *Agreement* bound from Bristol for Virginia: William Stratton, Thomas Yate, Henry Daniell, John Wasbrow. (PRO: E190/1139/3).

26 October. The following apprenticed in Bristol: Richard Daggett to Abraham Wilde, 4 years Maryland by *Agreement*. (BR).

29 October. The following apprenticed in Bristol: Mary Couzens to John Stratton, 5 years Virginia or Maryland by *Agreement*. (BR).

31 October-2 November. Shippers by the *Alathea* bound from Bristol for Virginia: Richard Benson, William Jones. (PRO: E190/1139/3).

October. Probate of will of Margaret Chalfont of St. Sepulchre, London, widow, whose sister, Susanna Harris, was in New England. (AW).

October. Probate of will of John Baker of Stepney, Middlesex, who died in New England. (AW).

October. Administration of James Hay of Cloughton near Scarborough, Yorkshire, who died in Virginia. (AW).

October. Probate of will of Mary More of Kennington, Surrey, whose son, Samuel Hardy, was in New England. (AW).

2 November. The following apprenticed in Bristol: John Rice to Thomas Pope, 5 years Virginia by *Richard & James*, Mr. Thomas Opie; Thomas Freeman to Thomas Willis, 4 years Virginia by *Agreement*. (BR).

4 November. The following apprenticed in Bristol: John Jones to John Marden, 5 years Virginia by *Francis & Mary*, Mr. William Nicklas; William Penbrooke to Abraham Wylde, 4 years Maryland by *Agreement*; George Beard to Richard Bennett, 4 years Nevis by *Antego Merchant*, Mr. John Mason; John Roberts to Thomas Daniell, 5 years Virginia by *Maryland Merchant*; Richard Williams to Robert Parker, 4 years Virginia by *George*; George Hartupp to same, 4 years Virginia by *George*; Thomas Kirby to William Hazard, 4 years Barbados by *Exchange*, Mr. Francis Laurence; George Curryer to John Williams, 5 years Virginia by *Maryland Merchant*. (BR).

6-15 November. Shippers by the *Richard & James* bound from Bristol for Virginia: Thomas Pope, William Morgan, Henry Daniell, Thomas Harris, John Friend. (PRO: E190/1139/3).

9 November. The following apprenticed in Bristol: John Johnson to William Sauchy, 4 years Virginia by *Maryland Merchant*; Margaret Dugden to Richard Milsom, 4 years Virginia by *George*. (BR).

12 November. The following apprenticed in Bristol: Anthony Poole to Richard Milsom, 4 years Virginia by *George*. (BR).

14 November. The following apprenticed in Bristol to go by the *Maryland Merchant*: Thomas Sweete to George Tyte, 4 years Virginia; John Turner to Anthony Broad, 4 years Maryland; Thomas Barker to same, 4 years Maryland; Thomas Fowler to same, 4 years Maryland. (BR).

16 November. The following apprenticed in Bristol: William Williams to John Marden, 5 years Virginia by *Francis & Mary*; Ann Deverell to Zachariah Smith, 4 years Virginia by *Maryland Merchant*. (BR).

23 November. The following apprenticed in Bristol: Mary Young to Robert Mason, 4 years Virginia by *Rainbow*; Thomas Griffith to Thomas Stevens, 4 years Virginia by *George*; John Burnett to Richard Carpenter, 7 years Virginia by *William & Joseph*; George Wilkenson to Richard Milsom, 4 years Virginia by *George*; Thomas Powell to Brian Tandy, 4 years Virginia by *Maryland Merchant*; John Rodd to William Sauty, 4 years Virginia by *Maryland Merchant*. (BR).

25 November. The following apprenticed in Bristol: Mary Swetman to Thomas Wauklin, 5 years Virginia by *George*. (BR).

26 November. The following apprenticed in Bristol: Robert Masters to William M *(sic)*, 4 years Virginia by *Rainbow*. (BR).

26 November-9 December. Shippers by the *Francis & Mary* bound from Bristol for Virginia: John Richardson, William Nicholas, Thomas Speed, Stephen Watts, Robert Day, Edward Thurston, James Thomas. (PRO: E190/1139/3).

26 November-6 December. Shippers by the *Maryland Merchant* bound from Bristol for Virginia: John Richardson, John Rogers, William Crabb, Richard Crump, Peter Younge, John Friend. (PRO: E190/1139/3).

27 November. Certificate that John Jefferies Esq. of London and Thomas Coleclough of London, merchant, have revoked the appointment of Francis Morrison Esq. as their attorney and have appointed Thomas Ludwell Esq., John Page and John Bournham, planters, as their attornies in Virginia. (LMCD).

27 November-10 December. Shippers by the *Vine* of Liverpool, Mr. William Preeson, bound from Liverpool for Maryland: David Poole, Edward Greene, John Pemberton, John Adison, John Lawson. (PRO: E190/1341/3).

29 November. The following apprenticed in Bristol: John Pavier to Matthew Stephens, 4 years Virginia. (BR).

November. Administration of Edward Blagrave of St. Margaret, Westminster, Middlesex, who died in Virginia, bachelor. (AW).

November. Probate of will of Bezaliel Angier of Dedham, Essex, whose brother, Edmund Angier, was in New England. (AW).

1 December. John Morris of Stepney, Middlesex, yeoman, found guilty of having transported Thomas Russells on board the *Cambridge* to Virginia. (VM 83/3).

2 December. The following apprenticed in Bristol: John Yarranton to William French, 4 years Virginia; William Reece to John Waters, 4 years Virginia by *Rainbow*. (BR).

2-10 December. Shippers by the *Beginning* bound from Bristol for Virginia: Samuell Tipton, Edward Morgan, George Hosier, Edward Martindell, John Sandford, Abraham Edwards, John Willett. (PRO: E190/1139/3).

6 December. The following apprenticed in Bristol: Jacob Roch to Christopher Pitt, 4 years Nevis; Nathan While to same, 4 years Nevis; Francis Rafe to George Tyte, 5 years Virginia by *Maryland Merchant*; Joane Nickolls to Abraham Wild, 4 years Maryland; Mary Attwood to Richard Swymmer, 4 years Barbados by *Fellowship*; Matthew Buttler to William Andrews, 5 years Virginia by *Francis & Mary*; John Parsons to Isaac Haynes, 4 years Virginia by *Rainbow*. (BR).

10-24 December. Shippers by the *Rainbow* bound from Bristol for Virginia: Edward Martindell, Erasmus Dole. (PRO: E190/1139/3).

12 December. Shipper by the *William & Ann* bound from Bristol for Virginia: John Walter. (PRO: E190/1139/3).

13 December. The following apprenticed in Bristol: Thomas Elcock to Stephen Tuck, 4 years Virginia by *Society*; Richard Cox to William T——, 4 years Virginia by *Rainbow*. (BR).

16 December. Shipper by the *New York* of New York, Mr. Nicholas Verbreake, bound from Southampton for New York: William Darvall. (PRO: E190/829/9).

16 December. The following apprenticed in Bristol: William Cheilds to Christopher Pitts, 4 years Nevis by *Abraham & Isaac*; Sarah Foord to Samuel James, 4 years Barbados by *Society*; assigned to son Samuel James in Barbados; Ann Williams to William Worgan, 4 years Nevis by *Dolphin*. (BR).

20 December. Petition of Randall Holden. Forty years ago he and others in Rhode Island were seized by the Government of Massachusetts. He was imprisoned in Boston and made to work before being banished. He seeks the repeal of the order of banishment which was dated 1644. (APC & CSPC).

23 December. The following apprenticed in Bristol: Daniel Christon to John Millis, 4 years Nevis by *Abraham & Isaac*; James Warnum to Richard Jones, 4 years Virginia by *Rainbow*; William Batchelor to William Hooper, 4 years Nevis by *[Golden] Hart*. (BR).

24 December. The following apprenticed in Bristol: Ruth Andrews to William Worgan, 4 years Nevis by *Dolphin*. (BR).

27 December. Jane Gurgany of London, widow, produces a deed by which 250 acres in Melbury Island parish, Warwick County, Virginia, known as Quarraluh(?) and formerly belonging to her brother Robert Pyland, have been sold to James Hire of James River, Virginia. (LMCD).

30 December. Shipper by the *York Merchant*, Mr. [Christopher] Eveling, bound from London for Virginia: George Richardson. (PRO: E190/84/1).

30 December-2 January. Shippers by the *Thomas*, Mr. Henry Fenn, bound from London for Virginia: Edward Carter, Benjamin Hobson, John Jennings. (PRO: E190/84/1).

31 December. Shipper by the *Constant*, Mr. Thomas Smith, bound from London for Virginia: Thomas Pointz. (PRO: E190/84/1).

December. Administration of Abel Beauchamp of Worcester, who died in Virginia, bachelor. (AW).

1679

2 January. The following apprenticed in Bristol: Thomas Pinchen to John Dunn, 4 years Barbados by *Industry*; Ann Dempsy to William Rayne, 4 years Virginia by *Rainbow*. (BR).

3-7 January. Shippers by the *John*, Mr. Daniel Pensax, bound from London for Virginia: Richard Banks, John Thomas. (PRO: E190/84/1).

3 January-28 May. Shippers by the *Providence*, Mr. Andrew Boone, bound from London for New York: Abraham Jesson, Thomas Bowman, John Freeman, John Warren, John Richardson, David Conyard, Richard Ellis, John Asken, John Moore, James Eyton, Francis Fox, Thomas Ball, John Sabin, Thomas Parker, John Middleton, Edward Fenwick, Robert Woolley, John Harwood, William Antleby, Thomas Firmin, Gerrard Vanheythusen, Phillip French, Andrew Willett, Daniell Ingoll, Anthony Stoner, Vallent Adams, James Nicholson, Robert Holt, Humphrey Nicholson, James Wanklin, Jonathan Leigh, George Grove, Edmond Buckeridge, John Delavall, Jacob Leveller, Alexander Hosea, Rainsford Waterhouse, Jacob Leyster, Benjamin Hewling, John Corsley, Samuell Frost, Samuell Shute, Francis Lodwick, William Mead, William Scowen. (PRO: E190/84/1).

4 January. By the *Old Head*, Mr. Robert Barker, from Barbados to the Leeward Islands: Matthew Williams; Jane Crillick, servant of John Follitt. (PRO: CO1/44/47).

6 January. The following apprenticed in Bristol: Elizabeth Broadbeard to Thomas Peares, 4 years Virginia; Francis Dew to Joseph Hopton, 5 years Virginia by *Rainbow*. (BR).

7-14 January. By the *Joseph & Ann*, Mr. Samuell Evans, from Barbados to Carolina: Elizabeth Paty; William Slaughter, servant of John Jennings; Elinor Carter; Jeremiah Chaplin; Richard Serjeant. (PRO: CO1/44/47).

7 January-12 March. Shippers by the *Blessing*, Mr. Thomas Berry, bound from London for New England: Francis Fox, John Sindry, William Scruten, Benjamin Smith, Jeremy Johnson, Edward Challenham, Edward Hull, Abraham Jesson, William White, James Taylor, Thomas Taylor, Thomas Clarke, John Cooke, William Day, Thomas Ratherington, Samuell Wickins, Robert Patten, Walter Mico, Edmond Hales, Timothy Waldo, William Baron, John Knap, Spencer Piggott, Ralph Box, Mathew Hatton, John Wright, Gabriel Whitley, George Roch, James Taylor, John Smith, Robert Patten, John Blackhall, Gabriell Patten, Thomas Humphrey, Samuell Stone, Thomas Lane, John Reynolds, Johnathan Leigh, Robert Woolley, Vallent Adams, John Archer, Thomas Trimm, William Stonestreet, William Crouch, Henry Bartholomew, Timothy Waldo, Andrew Kendrick, Edward Tarleton, Thomas

Elson, Peter Hudson, Josias Dewy, Robert Paston, Richard Gawthorne, John Ellis, John Loggin, Isaac Waldin, John Riches, William Gow, Henry Russell, William Gore, Henry Forman, John Catlond, Thomas Wilkin, Sir William Warren, Nathaniel Colston. (PRO: E190/84/1).

13 January. Newgate prisoners reprieved to be transported to Barbados. London: Jane Vosse alias Stephens, spinster; Jane Sadler, spinster; Elizabeth Carleton, spinster; James Powell; William Rowlandson; Sarah Demerick alias Davis, spinster; Elizabeth Staines, spinster; Dorothy Clarke alias Atkinson, spinster; Elizabeth Allen, spinster, alias wife of Edward Allen; Susan Banser alias Greene, spinster; Jane Middleton, spinster. Middlesex: Elizabeth Courtney alias Holcroft of St. Martin in the Fields, spinster; John Spittle of the same; Alice Morgan of St. Giles in the Fields, spinster; Mary Kiteley, spinster, alias wife of Edward Woodden, of Whitechapel; Beatrice Breeden of Shoreditch, spinster; Thomas Gregory of Chiswick; Anne alias Mary Wynn, wife of Thomas Wynn of Paddington; Thomas Quinton alias Humpston alias Humpton of St. Andrew Holborn; John Leake of Whitechapel; Edward Preston of Hanwell; Mary Penryn, wife of Benjamin Penryn, alias Mary White alias Fowler alias Taffe of Isleworth; Robert Peters of Islington. (PRO: C66/3205/31).

13 January. The following apprenticed in Bristol: William Cheesman to Christopher Pitt, 4 years Nevis; Tristram Davis to John Burroughs, 7 years Jamaica by *Royal Oak*; Thomas Johnson to Nicholas Smith, 4 years Virginia by *Rainbow*. (BR).

13 January-12 March. Shippers by the *Herne*, Mr. Thomas Barrett, bound from London for New England: Anthony Turney, William Bridges, William Dingly, William Gore, Richard Lloyd, James Eyton, William Mead, John Cutlove, Nathaniel Lee, John Eborne, John Ongly, Phillip French, Thomas Ruck, James Blackman, Thomas Malyn, Joseph Smart, William Shirley, Samuel Wickins, Abraham Jesson, Samuel Alford, John Freeman, Joseph Hearne, Francis Kemp, Henry Russell, Henry Forman, Thomas Wilkin, Sir William Warren, Nathaniel Colston. (PRO: E190/84/1).

21 January. The following apprenticed in Bristol: William Jones to Christopher Pitt, 4 years Barbados or Nevis. (BR).

21 January-28 February. Shippers by the *Elizabeth*, Mr. Thomas Saxton, bound from London for New England: Ann Carter, John Knap, John Reynolds, Charles Phelps, William White, Thomas Simonds, John Crow, Edward Whitehall, Thomas Clark, John Lake, Charles Oughtred, Joseph Bowles, John Freeman, Spencer Piggott, Thomas Baymer, Jeremy Johnson, Josias Hulls, William Crouch, Ralph Box, Thomas Tryon, William Harrison, Henry Meese, Thomas Caddon, John Merriton, James Hayes, John Blackhall, John Loggin, Cham Ashby, Thomas Lane, John Richards, Edward Bass, William Buckler, Joseph Hayes, Richard Dawkins, Thomas Hill, James Eyton, Thomas Farrington, Edward Bass, Samuell Gerrard, John Sturt. (PRO: E190/84/1).

24 January. The following apprenticed in Bristol: John Ayleworth to Christopher Pitt, 4 years Nevis. (BR).

25 January. The following apprenticed in Bristol: Samuel Ockford to Christopher Pitt, 4 years Barbados or Nevis. (BR).

27 January. The following apprenticed in Bristol: Robert Pomry to William Worgan, 7 years Nevis by *Dolphin*, Mr. James Turner; Ann Prewett to same, 6 years Nevis by *Dolphin*; Hester Wells to same, 4 years Nevis by *Dolphin*; Joane Evans to same, 4 years Nevis by *Dolphin*; Ann Priddie to same, 4 years Nevis by *Dolphin*; John Prosser to John Porter, 4 years Barbados by *Gabriel*, Mr. James Limbry; William Tomkins to William Hopper, 4 years Nevis by *Golden Hart*, said William Hopper Mr. (BR).

28 January-13 February. By the *James*, Mr. William Sweetland, from Barbados to New York: Jarvis Marshall; Andrew Bowdler; Abraham Hayem; Phillip Smith; Samuell Symons. (PRO: CO1/44/47).

31 January. The following apprenticed in Bristol to go to Virginia by the *Dolphin*: Amos Spraggott to James Turner, 5 years; Robert Bennett to same, 5 years. (BR).

31 January. By the *Friendship*, Mr. Joseph Hardy, from Barbados to New England: John Cragg. (PRO: CO1/44/47).

31 January-14 February. Shippers by the *Elizabeth*, Mr. Thomas Saxton, bound from London for New England: William Baron, William Mead, Thomas Cuddon. (PRO: E190/84/1).

January. Probate of will of Rebecca Saintbury alias Sainbry of St. Olave, Southwark, Surrey, who had kin in Virginia.

January. Administration of Thomas Boreman of Virginia, bachelor. (AW).

January. Administration of Alexander Lloyd of Bristol, who died in Virginia. (AW).

January. Probate of will of Thomas Ludwell of Bruton, Somerset, who died in Virginia. (AW).

4 February. The following apprenticed in Bristol: John Powell to Humfry Mason, 4 years Nevis by *Arthur & Mary*. (BR).

6 February. By the *Diligence*, Mr. Jeremiah Jackson, from Barbados to New England: Andrew Fanning. (PRO: CO1/44/47).

6-7 February. Shipper by the *Endeavour*, Mr. Henry Edgett, bound from London for Virginia: Richard Worsam. (PRO: E190/84/1).

7 February. Petition of Mr. John Crown on behalf of his father, William Crown, to be granted the lands of Mounthope, New England, to compensate for his father's losses following the surrender to the French of Nova Scotia. (APC).

12 February. The following apprenticed in Bristol: Hester Harrison to Henry Masters, 4 years Barbados by *William & Ann*, Mr. Thomas ——ger. (BR).

13 February. By the *Two Brothers*, Mr. Rice Jefferies, from Barbados to Jamaica. James Forbush; John and Mary Stockley; Samuell Sherwood. (PRO: CO1/44/47).

14 February. The following apprenticed in Bristol: Abigal Whittwood to Humfry Mason, 4 years Nevis. (BR).

14-18 February. By the *Resolution*, Mr. John Ingleby, from Barbados to Nevis and Montserrat: Margaret Dang; John Blake. (PRO: CO1/44/47).

15 February. The following apprenticed in Bristol: Joseph Rowne to Joseph Ball, 4 years Barbados by *[St.] Peter*, Mr. Thomas Hillman. (BR).

17 February. By the *Adventure*, Mr. Christopher Berrow, from Barbados to Antigua: Rachaell Brown, Nicholas Lynch and Alice his wife. (PRO: CO1/44/47).

19 February. Northern Circuit prisoners reprieved to be transported to Barbados. Cheshire: John Banne of Glovers Stone; John Yardsley of Glovers Stone. Northumberland: John Howd of Newcastle upon Tyne. (PRO: C66/3210/6).

19-25 February. Shippers by the *Anthony & Jasper*, Mr. Thomas Canham, bound from London for Virginia: James Bigger, John Jeffries, John Baesh, Richard Foot. (PRO: E190/84/1).

21 February. By the *Endeavour*, Mr. Abraham Newman, from Barbados to Virginia: John Denton. By the *Fellowship*, Mr. Thomas Pimm, from Barbados to Antigua: Richard Travis. (PRO: CO1/44/47).

22 February. The following apprenticed in Bristol to go to Nevis by the *Dolphin*: Richard Bowden to William Worgan, 4 years; Daniel Rogers to Thomas Bowen, 6 years. (BR).

22 February. By the *Bachelor's Delight*, Mr. Robert Greenway, from Barbados to New York: Norton Claypoole. (PRO: CO1/44/47).

22 February-7 March. Shippers by the *Three Brothers*, Mr. Peter Boss, bound from London for New Jersey: John Essington, John Richardson, Edward Hind, Edward Man. (PRO: E190/84/1).

25 February. The following apprenticed in Bristol: Judith Bond to Joseph Bull, 6 years Barbados by *St. Peter*. (BR).

25 February. By the *Plantation*, Mr. Aser Sharpe, from Barbados to Carolina: Hester Smith. (PRO: CO1/44/47).

25 February-3 April. Shippers by the *Richard*, Mr. Thomas Jowles, bound from London for New England: Abraham Jesson, Andrew Kendrick, Richard Scudamore, John Daniell, Thomas Taylor, Samuell Austin, Edward Lardner,

Edward Hulls, George Walker, Nicholas Bratch, Isaac Waldron, John Blacknell, Jeremy Johnson, Richard Parrett, John Blackhall, William Gore, George Whitehead, Jeremy Whitchcott, Thomas Lane, Thomas Brailsford, Richard Worledge, Humphrey Fenn, Edward Tarleton, Nicholas Brattle, John Crow, Richard Glover, John Archer, Samuell Blewitt, John Lake, William Antleby, William Shirly, Thomas Mayor, George Roach, Edmond White, John Clark, John Knap, John Freeman, Charles Somers, Henry Bartholomew, William Houghton, Jacob Preston, Samuell Clarke, William Johnson, Benjamin Cox, Richard Lloyd, William Chambers. (PRO: E190/84/1).

28 February-18 March. Shippers by the *Increase*, Mr. John Holland, bound from London for New England: Edmond Marchant, Thomas Ackworth, Henry Dandy, Thomas Lane, Thomas Elye, John Hull, John Askew, Richard Joyce, Spencer Piggott, Nicholas Warner, Alice Waltham, Thomas Deane, William Ashurst, Alexander Hosea, John Eyston, Benjamin Ayloff, Giles Long, John Loggin, Robert Welly, Samuell Round. (PRO: E190/84/1).

February. Administration of James Pennington of St. Bartholomew by the Exchange, London, who died in Maryland. (AW).

February. Probate of will of Robert Lucas of Hitchin, Hertfordshire, who had lands in New England. (AW).

February. Probate of will of Ezekiel David of Charles Town, South Carolina. (AW).

1 March. By the *William & John*, Mr. John Sanders, from Barbados to New England: Jacob Tinico. (PRO: CO1/44/47).

3 March. By the *Vineyard*, Mr. Henry Perrin, from Barbados to Virginia: Symon Ryder, servant of George Moor. By the *Beginning*, Mr. Thomas Bossinger, from Barbados to Virginia: William Piper. (PRO: CO1/44/47).

5 March. The following apprenticed in Bristol: John Jones to William Hooper, 7 years Nevis by *[Golden] Hart*. (BR).

5 March. Western Circuit prisoners reprieved to be transported to Barbados. Cornwall: John Marratt alias May of Verran. Dorset: Christopher Rasker of Fordington. Hampshire: John Stubberfield of Portsmouth, feltmaker. Somerset: Margaret Churchman of Bath. (PRO: C66/3210/2).

5 March. By the *Expedition*, Mr. John Harding, from Barbados to Virginia: Job Perwidge. (PRO: CO1/44/47).

5-10 March. By the *Seaventure*, Mr. George Battersby, from Barbados to Antigua: James Bilford; Richard Cary. (PRO: CO1/44/47).

6 March. The following apprenticed in Bristol: John Willis to William Hooper, 4 years Nevis. (BR).

6 March. By the *Blessing*, Mr. John Thwing, from Barbados to New York: Thomas Cooper. (PRO: CO1/44/47).

7-11 March. By the *Society*, Mr. William Guard, from Barbados to Boston: Henry Armitage; Symon Jarmin; John Nevill; Andrew Dolberry; Ambrose Collyer; Anthony Weltden; Michaell Stokes; W. Stacy; William Morris. (PRO: CO1/44/47).

8 March. Deposition by Cornelius De Gelder of London, merchant aged 57, that in September and October 1676 he was engaged by Wilbors Daniells and Abraham Christian to discharge the debts of Giles and Peter Meunix of Middleborough; as security they assigned to him the plantations and debts owed to them by Mr. John Blake of Barbados and goods and plantations in Virginia in the possession of Mr. Barnaby Kerne. (LMCD).

8 March. The following apprenticed in Bristol: Lawrence Tanner to Thomas Harris, 7 years Newfoundland by *Olive Branch*; William Allen to Thomas Edwards, 5 years Newfoundland by *Olive Branch*; Thomas Boone to same, 7 years Newfoundland by *Olive Branch*; Encoh Billings to William Hooper, 4 years Barbados by *[Golden] Hart*; William Britten to Thomas Burroughs, 7 years New England by *Supply*. (BR).

10 March. By the *James*, Mr. Paul Crean, from Barbados to Antigua: Anthony Viner. By the *Diligence*, Mr. Abraham Newman, from Barbados to Virginia: John Wills. (PRO: CO1/44/47).

12 March. By the *Susanna*, Mr. Hugh Babell, from Barbados to Carolina: William Pile; Edward Smith. (PRO: CO1/44/47).

12-14 March. By the *Ann & Mary*, Mr. John Johnson, from Barbados to Antigua: Alexander Robinson; Oliver Enderby; William Jackson; Timothy Melony. (PRO: CO1/44/47).

12-22 March. By the *William & Susan*, Mr. Ralph Parker, from Barbados to New England: James Barton; Joseph Banks; Ann Lock; William Ross; Isaac Herrick; Adam Hamilton; Samuell Colwell; John Querk, servant of Thomas Allen. (PRO: CO1/44/47).

12-27 March. Shippers by the *Sapphire* bound from Bristol for New England: Robert Yate, Robert Hayne, Thomas Earle, William Morgan, John Cann, Thomas Scroope. (PRO: E190/1140/3).

15 March-7 April. Shippers by the *Supply* bound from Bristol for New England: William Jones, Erasmus Dole, Richard King, Thomas Scroope, John Richardson, Thomas Tayer, Thomas Sanders, Dennis Moone, Henry Baker. (PRO: E190/1140/3).

18-20 March. By the *Beginning*, Mr. William Play, from Barbados to New York: William Elson; Mary Whittee; Robert & Mary Wright; Isaac Morris; Joane Maddox; Benjamin Sanders. (PRO: CO1/44/47).

18 March-17 April. Shippers by the *Recovery*, Mr. James (Thomas) Brown, bound from London for New York: Richard Booth, Richard Isard, William Depester, Humphrey Nicholls, John Harwood, Benjamin Hewling, Joseph Butts, John Paggott, Gerrard Vanheythusen, Benjamin Gerrard, William Williams, Samuell Shute, Edward Griffith, Peter Hudson. (PRO: E190/84/1).

20-30 March. Shippers by the *Black Cock*, Mr. Michael Pack, bound from London for New England: John Shorter, Jone Onely, Thomas Wilkins, John Shelton, Sir William Warren, Henry Forman, Joseph Hayes. (PRO: E190/84/1).

22 March. Norfolk Circuit prisoners reprieved to be transported to Barbados. Bedfordshire: Joseph Warner of Leighton Buzzard; John Bland of Maulden; Richard Knight of Cardington. Buckinghamshire: John Knight of Wavendon; Richard Huffe of Stony Stratford; Eleanor Huffe wife of Richard *(qv)* of Stony Stratford; William French of Pitchcott. Huntingdonshire: John Cotton alias Jarvis of Stanground. Norfolk: John Barker of Stow Bardolph; Edward Smith alias Morley of Munford. Suffolk: Thomas White of Great Horningheath. (PRO: C66/3210/3).

22-24 March. By the *Mary*, Mr. John Gardner, from Barbados to Boston: Benjamin Gerish; John Higley. (PRO: CO1/44/47).

26 March. Shipper by the *Society* bound from Bristol for New England: Henry Gibbs. (PRO: E190/1140/3).

26 March. Thomas Baxter, late of New Plymouth, New England, who lost part of his right hand by accident while defending the town against the Indians, to be recommended for an allowance following his petition. (APC).

26 March-8 May. Shippers by the *William & Henry*, Mr. Jeremy Cushing, bound from London for New England: William Shirly, Joshua Sheppard, Richard Woolridge, George Shalcross, Daniell Atkins, John Blackhall, John Crowe, Richard Ellis, Thomas Cooper, Joseph Calvin, William Antleby, Henry Hovenor, William Crouch, Thomas Carleton, Richard Banks, John Sayer, John Lake, Spencer Piggott, John Jackson, John Daniell, Joseph Potter, Abraham Jesson, Nicholas Brattle, Robert Woolley, John Freeman, Alexander Hosea, Joseph Cam, William Sheely, Peter Butler, John Sturt, Stephen Cole, John Wase, Matthew Gibbon, George Day, Richard Lloyd, Thomas Hill, William Dingly, Epaphras Shrimpton, Thomas Parker. (PRO: E190/84/1).

27 March. By the *Mary & Sarah*, Mr. George Conway, from Barbados to Carolina: Barnard Humphry; Richard Wright. (PRO: CO1/44/47).

28 March-4 April. Shippers by the *Abraham & Francis*, Mr. Henry Turpin, bound from London for New England: Henry Foreman, Richard Boone. (PRO: E190/84/1).

28 March-15 April. Shippers by the *Adventure*, Mr. John Balstone, bound from London for New England: Joseph Harvey, John Haggett, Thomas Lane, John

Reynolds, Robert Carnall, Joseph Bowles, James Wanklyn, John Freeman, Edward Mann, John Haynes, John Hill, Thomas Norman, John Balam, William Crouch, Joseph King, Richard Dawkins, Richard Merriweather, John Sturt, William Mead, Ralph Ingram. (PRO: E190/84/1).

29 March-1 April. By the *Swallow*, Mr. Joseph Hardy, from Barbados to Rhode Island: Mordecai Campanell; Thomas Pead; Miles Haviland; Richard Sailes. (PRO: CO1/44/47).

29 March-15 April. Shippers by the *Elizabeth* of Boston, Mr. Thomas Shaxten, bound from Plymouth for Boston, New England: Richard Cowes, William Shepheard. (PRO: E190/1043/17).

29 March-28 April. By the *Mary*, Mr. Nicholas Lockwood, from Barbados to Carolina: Mary Cooper; Thomas Maul; Thomas Drayton Jr.; Henry Gittes; Robert Daniell; Robert Grigg; Alice Grigg; Mary Godfrey; Ann Albert; Stephen Fox; Phillis Fox; Dennis Canting; Sarah Jipson. (PRO: CO1/44/47).

31 March. By the *John & Thomas*, Mr. Thomas Jenour, from Barbados to Providence: John Sewer. (PRO: CO1/44/47).

31 March. The following apprenticed in Bristol: Richard Browne to Thomas Moore, 4 years New England by *Sapphire*. (BR).

31 March-15 April. By the *Robert*, Mr. Nathan Hayman, from Barbados to Boston: Lawrence Row; Amos Whitefoot; Henry Sandiford; Henry Webster. (PRO: CO1/44/47).

31 March-17 April. By the *Blessing*, Mr. Francis Watlington, from Barbados to Providence: Joseph Fransum; Nicholas Barnes; William Major. (PRO: CO1/44/47).

1 April. By the *Blessing*, Mr. Samuel Rickard, from Barbados to Boston: William Crossing; Francis Dickinson. (PRO: CO1/44/47).

1-28 April. By the *Unity*, Mr. James Rainy, from Barbados to Virginia: William Smith; Lewis Evans; Ralph Sedgwick; George Adamson; Margaret Anderson. (PRO: CO1/44/47).

2-4 April. By the *Rutter*, Mr. Edward Duffield, from Barbados to Jamaica: John Bagnall; George Ridley. (PRO: CO1/44/47).

4 April. The following apprenticed in Bristol: Lettice Jones to Peter Liscombe, 5 years Barbados by *Bristol Factor*; Thomas Saunders to Joseph Bowry, 4 years New England by *Sapphire*, said Joseph Bowry Mr; John Wrentmore to same, 4 years New England [by *Sapphire*]; Nathaniel Thornes to Dennis Moore Jr., 4 years New England by *Supply*. (BR).

5-7 April. By the *May Flower*, Mr. Edward Hubbert, from Barbados to Providence and Bermuda: John Plummer; Samuell Peniston; Thomas Bickle. (PRO: CO1/44/47).

7 April. By the *Adventure*, Mr. Daniell Ridley, from Barbados to Carolina: William Dukes. 7 Apr. (PRO: CO1/44/47).

8 April. Deposition by Richard Walton of London, gent aged 25, (former servant of Thomas Ball, citizen and leatherseller of London, deceased) and Benjamin Williams, citizen and leatherseller of London, aged 37, (executor to Thomas Ball), that they shipped goods by the *Providence*, Mr. Andrew Boone, and the *Endeavour*, Mr. Richardson, to William Dervall of New York, merchant. (LMCD).

9 April. By the *John's Adventure*, Mr. John Welch, from Barbados to Antigua. John Daniell. (PRO: CO1/44/47).

9-14 April. Shippers by the *Betty*, Mr. William Duncomb, bound from London for New England: John Hoole, John Loggin. (PRO: E190/84/1).

9 April-6 May. By the *Providence*, Mr. Marke Hunking, from Barbados to New England: John Jacob; John Brome. (PRO: CO1/44/47).

10 April. By the *Providence*, Mr. Francis Watlington, from Barbados to Bermuda: Sarah Howell. By the *Resolution*, Mr. Daniell Acklin, from Barbados to Providence: Daniell Wilkinson. (PRO: CO1/44/47).

11 April. By the *William & John*, Mr. John Sanders, from Barbados to New England: Abraham Burgess. (PRO: CO1/44/47).

12 April. By the *Bonetta*, Mr. Richard Ripley, from Barbados to Jamaica: Joseph Gooding. (PRO: CO1/44/47).

15 April. By the *Elizabeth*, Mr. Peter Major, from Barbados to Nevis: Almons Sfrane? (PRO: CO1/44/47).

17 April. By the *Pearl*, Mr. Richard Williams, from Barbados to Antigua: William Bushell. (PRO: CO1/44/47).

18 April. By the *Recovery*, Mr. Thomas Chinnery, from Barbados to New York: Mary Holliday; Nathaniell Stephens; Richard Roth.

19-28 April. By the *Friends Adventure*, Mr. John Long, from Barbados to Antigua: Daniell Mahony; Nathaniell Johnson. (PRO: CO1/44/47).

24 April-15 May. Shippers by the *Benjamin* bound from Bristol for New England: John Richardson, Thomas Saunders, Erasmus Dole, Edmond White, John Perowne, Francis Ballard, Samuell Price. (PRO: E190/1140/3).

25-29 April. By the *Nathaniel*, Mr. William Clarke, from Barbados for Boston: Richard Mitchell and his servant, Mary Fitznicholls; John Mitchell; Richard Townsend and his servant, Jane Davies; John Turner; Richard Snacknell; Edward Webster; John Wilkins; George Elliston; William Atherton. (PRO: CO1/44/47).

26 April. By the *Brother's Adventure*, Mr. John Selleck, from Barbados to New York: Margaret Smith, servant of Thomas Doxey. By the *Francis*, Mr. Peter Jefferys, from Barbados to the Leeward Islands: Symon Williams. (PRO: CO1/44/47).

29 April. By the *Francis*, Mr. Peter Jefferys, from Barbados to Antigua: Ann Armstrong. (PRO: CO1/44/47).

30 April-28 July. Shippers by the *Crown Mallago*, Mr. Samuel Phillips, bound from London for Virginia: John Jennings, William Garfoot, Hugh Hartshorne, Nathaniel Ashcombe, Nicholason Nicholls, Barnaby Dunch. (PRO: E190/84/1).

April. Edward Richards, aged 15, apprenticed from Christ's Hospital to David Lockwood, commander of the *Dragon* bound for Jamaica. (CH).

April. Savell Wright, aged 16, apprenticed from Christ's Hospital to Capt. John ——, commander of the *Hope* bound for Barbados. (CH).

1 May. The following apprenticed in Bristol: Peter Coffy to John Snow, 4 years Nevis by *Jamaica Merchant*, Mr. John Cary. (BR).

2 May. The following apprenticed in Bristol: Christopher Talbot to Richard Follint, 4 years New England by *Benjamin* of Boston; Thomas Pritchard to same, 4 years New England; William Price to same, 4 years New England. (BR).

2-13 May. By the *Prosperous*, Mr. David Fogg, from Barbados to Virginia: Katherine Arthur; Luke Rainy; Samuell Davies; John Pinke; Mathew Whitfield; Dennis Burne; Ann Box; Francis Southworth. (PRO: CO1/44/47).

2 May-2 June. Shippers by the *Jacob & Mary*, Mr. Richard Moore, bound from London for New Jersey: Samuell Field, John Sabin, Richard Pickman, Mathew Roper, John Wrenn. (PRO: E190/84/1).

3-8 May. By the *Bachelor*, Mr. Peter Swaine, from Barbados to the Leeward Islands: Richard Holsey; William Wheeler. (PRO: CO1/44/47).

5 May. The following apprenticed in Bristol: Evan Rodrah to John Snow, 5 years Nevis by *Jamaica Merchant*. (BR).

6 May. By the *John & Thomas*, Mr. Thomas Jenour, from Barbados to Providence: Thomas Feaghery. (PRO: CO1/44/47).

8 May. By the *May Flower*, Mr. Robert Kitchin, from Barbados to Boston: John Blackleech. (PRO: CO1/44/47).

8-23 May. Shippers by the *Edistowe*, Mr. John Comings, bound from London for Carolina: John Ashby, Edward Thornburgh, John Freeman, Earl of Shaftesbury, Valentine Adams, Joseph Puddefatt, Benjamin Thorowgood. (PRO: E190/84/1).

8 May-4 June. Shippers by the *Mehitable*, Mr. William Browne, bound from London for New England: Robert Hinde, Thomas Soutley, William White, Robert Clarke, Phillip French, Thomas Lane, Jeremy Clutterbuck, Henry Damarin, Henry Ashurst, Thomas Cuddon, Robert Hudson, Thomas Levenworth, Thomas Ball, William Antleby, Richard Glover, William Crouch, John Doggett, Abraham Jesson, William Shirly, William Kenniston, Edward Proby, James Yound, Nicholas Caplin, William Mead. (PRO: E190/84/1).

10-20 May. By the *Resolution*, Mr. John Ingleby, from Barbados to Antigua: Benjamin Wickham; Pearce Stanton. (PRO: CO1/44/47).

13 May. The following apprenticed in Bristol: William Waple to William Bye, 4 years Newfoundland by *William*. (BR).

14-24 May. By the *Supply*, Mr. John Mellowes, from Barbados to Boston: Isaac Smith; Vines Ellicott; John Duboyes. (PRO: CO1/44/47).

19-29 May. By the *William & John*, Mr. Samuel Legg, from Barbados to Boston: Edward Rainsford; Edward Russell; Robert Richbell; Samuell Sparkes; Rich(ard) Salter; Sylam Mason; Richard Mosely. (PRO: CO1/44/47).

20-31 May. By the *Nicholas & Rebecca*, Mr. Nicholas Blake, from Barbados to New York: John Helmes; Sylvester Stephens. (PRO: CO1/44/47).

21 May. By the *Elizabeth*, Mr. John Fletcher, from Barbados to Boston: Thomas Bond. (PRO: CO1/44/47).

21 May. The following apprenticed in Bristol: William Tomkins to John Snow, 4 years Nevis by *Jamaica Merchant*. (BR).

22-28 May. By the *Prudence & Mary*, Mr. Jacob Green, from Barbados to Boston: James Fontleroy; William Jordan; George Thomas; John Sherlan; John Kyte; Phillip Watkins; Nicholas Morrell; Eliazer Allin. (PRO: CO1/44/47).

22 May-17 June. By the *Joseph (and Mary)*, Mr. Abraham Knott, from Barbados to New York: John Johnson; Samuell French; John Davies of Christ Church; Daniell Hooper; John Platt. (PRO: CO1/44/47).

23 May. Petition of Benedict Arnold to the King. His grandfather, William Arnold of Patuxet, Rhode Island, by his will made the petitioner his heir but Stephen Arnold, the youngest son of William Arnold, detains the will and deeds. (CSPC).

26 May. By the *Francis & Susan*, Mr. Philip Knell, from Barbados for Boston: Angus Abraham; William Whiteing. (PRO: CO1/44/47).

28 May. On the petition of Rene Petit [the King's agent at Rouen] and Jacob Guerard of Normandy, gents, two ships are to be provided to transport to Carolina 80 foreign protestant families skilled in the manufacture of silk, oils and wines. [*See further entry of 24 October 1679*]. (APC & CSPC).

28 May. By the *William & John*, Mr. Samuel Legg, from Barbados to Boston: Edward Cornish, servant of John Harris. (PRO: CO1/44/47).

30 May-6 August. Shippers by the *Samuel & Thomas*, Mr. Peter Butler, bound from London for New England: William Crouch, Thomas Soutley, Samuell Wick, John Archer, Richard Merriweather, Spencer Piggott, Samuell Wiggin, Ralph Frewin, Elkanah Bois, Francis Marriott, Thomas Ball, John Titchbourne, Edward Tarleton, Ralph Burfoot, Benjamin Tainton, Thomas Ruck, John Goldham, Abraham Jesson, Thomas Allen, John Harwood, Joshua Dimsdall, Edward Hull, Gabriell Whitley, John Ellis, Edward Edmonds, Benjamin Bullivant, Jeremy Johnson, Phillip French, John Freeman, Peter Pett, Allen Ackworth, Francis Walker, William Gore, Samuell Shute, Walter Mico, Matthew Eben, John Ive, Robert Patten. (PRO: E190/84/1).

31 May. By the *True Friendship*, Mr. Charles Callahane, from Barbados to Nevis: Thomas Cloven (*see also entry for 2 October*). (PRO: CO1/44/47).

May. Probate of will of Mary Whitehead of Binfield, Berkshire, whose son, Richard Whitehead, was in Virginia. (AW).

May. Administration of Herbert Jeffreys, Governor of Virginia, who died in Virginia. (AW).

May. Administration of Richard Longman of Virginia, bachelor. (AW).

May. Administration of George Hilson master of the ship *Friends Increase*, who died in Virginia. (AW).

May. Probate of will of Joseph Stocker of Wiveliscombe, Somerset, whose son, Ephraim Stocker, went to Virginia. (AW).

4 June. The following apprenticed in Bristol to go to Barbados by the *Robert & Hester*: Robert Harrison to William Stoakes, 4 years; Gilbert Cooke to same, 4 years; John Crookshanke to same, 4 years. (BR).

5 June. Shippers by the *Susannah* of New York, Mr. David Johner, bound from Southampton for New York: Richard Loving, Nicholas Byard, Ramard Parker, Thomas Lodgwick. (PRO: E190/830/6).

5 June. The following apprenticed in Bristol: Edward Poole to Edward Perrin, 6 years Virginia. (BR).

6 June. Deposition by James Rawlins, citizen and merchant tailor of London, that on 22 March 1675 he sold goods to John Winder of New York for which payment has not been received. (LMCD).

11 June. By the *John & Sarah*, Mr. Peter Carew, from Barbados to New York: Lidia Fell. (PRO: CO1/44/47).

13 June. Shipper by the *Blessing* of Boston, Mr. Samuell Pelton, bound from Plymouth for New England: George Orchard. (PRO: E190/1043/17).

13 June. By the *Hopewell*, Mr. Nicholas Morrell, from Barbados to Boston: William Hook. (PRO: CO1/44/47).

14-17 June. By the *John's Adventure*, Mr. Edward Winslow, from Barbados to Jamaica: Thomas Allison; Elizabeth How; Owen Jenkins. (PRO: CO1/44/47).

14-30 June. Shippers by the *Elizabeth & Hannah* of Boston, Mr. Lot Gordin, bound from Dartmouth for New England: Nicholas Manning, Thomas Tewsey, John Atkins, John Hayne. (PRO: E190/957/18).

18 June. By the *Thomas & Susan*, Mr. David Edwards, from Barbados to Boston: Emanuell Wolfe; James Wood. (PRO: CO1/44/47).

21 June-8 July. Shippers by the *Hopewell*, Mr. Francis Richardson, bound from London for New York: James Hayes, Robert Holt, Thomas Ball, Walter Newberry, Thomas Moore, John Richardson, Robert Smith, John Bradenham, George Woodward, John Pagett, Jeremy Forman, Thomas Hart, Peter Short, William Adams, Nicholas Tyack, William Mead, Luke Foster, John Osgood. (PRO: E190/84/1).

22 June-1 July. By the *Providence*, Mr. Timothy Prout, from Barbados to Boston: Thomas Bread; Nicholas Ingleby; John Hunt; Eliazer Phillips; John Richbell. (PRO: CO1/44/47).

June. Administration of Nathaniel Stevens of St. Merrin, Cornwall, who died on the ship *Margaret* in Virginia. (AW).

June. Administration of David Thompson of Stepney, Middlesex, who died on the ship *Willing Mind* in Virginia. (AW). 1679B

2-21 July. By the *Neptune*, Mr. John Knott, from Barbados to Carolina: John Collins; Edward Evans; Peter Davies. (PRO: CO1/44/47).

7 July. Deposition by Josiah Jones of London, notary public aged 25, that Captain John Quigley of Maryland is indebted by bond to John Bawdon of London, merchant. (LMCD).

7 July. The following apprenticed in Bristol: William Robinson to Arthur Grannt, 4 years Virginia or West Indies by *Nevis Merchant*, said Arthur Grannt Mr. (BR).

8-28 July. Shippers by the *Love*, Mr. Oswald Wheatley, bound from London for Virginia: Richard More, Nicholas Lowe, John Collingwood, John Lloyd, William Meade. (PRO: E190/84/1).

10 July. The Government of New Hampshire is to be established and to exercise jurisdiction over the towns of Portsmouth, Hampton, Dover and Exeter. (APC).

10-16 July. Shippers by the *Constant Mary*, Mr. Edward Rhodes, bound from London for Virginia: Henry Meese, Edward Leman, Thomas Leman, Gawen

Corbin, Thomas Wickham, Thomas Sands, John Jennings, John Rose. (PRO: E190/84/1).

11 July. The following apprenticed in Bristol: Francis Foord to William Swymmer, 4 years Jamaica by *Primrose*, Mr. Thomas Cock; Robert Vyne to Arthur Grannt, 4 years Nevis by *Nevis Merchant*. (BR).

12 July. The following apprenticed in Bristol: Richard Nicholas to John Lord, 4 years Jamaica by *Primrose*. (BR).

15-20 July. By the *Elizabeth*, Mr. John Bonner, from Barbados to Boston: Robert Mansell; Abigall Newton. (PRO: CO1/44/47).

15-22 July. By the *Rebecca*, Mr. Thomas Williams, from Barbados to Virginia: Thomas Rule; James Richard; Chester Pearshouse; Thomas Scott; Thomas Stannage; Nathaniell Verin; John Needler; John McEnree; William Wilson; Edmond Welch, servant of John Hopcroft; Samuell Frith. (PRO: CO1/44/47).

16 July. Northern Circuit prisoners reprieved to be transported to Barbados: Northumberland: John Lawder of ?Yatem, Scotland. Yorkshire: John Nevinson of Wortley; John Todd of Etton; Thomas Cousins of York Castle. (PRO: C66/3214/7).

16 July. The following apprenticed in Bristol: John Beale to William Richards, 5 years Nevis or Jamaica by *Amity*, Mr. William Falkner. (BR).

16-31 July. Shippers by the *Planters Adventure*, Mr. Robert Ransom, bound from London for Virginia: Richard Glover, Jeremy Handford, George Richards, William Garfoot, Thomas Jefferys, William Smith, Thomas Packer. (PRO: E190/84/1).

17 July. The following apprenticed in Bristol: Thomas Edwards to William Falkner, 4 years [Nevis or Jamaica]. (BR).

17 July. By the *Society*, Mr. William Guard, from Barbados to Boston: Nathaniell Thayer. By the *Brother's Adventure*, Mr. Robert Darkin, from Barbados to New York: Thomas Rudge. (PRO: CO1/44/47).

18 July. By the *Prosperous*, Mr. David Fogg, from Barbados to Virginia: Thomas Yates, servant of Francis Southworth. (PRO: CO1/44/47).

19 July. Home Circuit prisoners reprieved to be transported to Barbados or Jamaica. Essex: Mary Tarnell of Navestock; Maurice Price of West Horndon; Mary Frost of Woodham. Hertfordshire: Hambleton Swinstead of Ware. Kent: Emblyn Redge of Bexley; Walter Stritch of Sutton at Hone; Charles Kelly of Charlton; Oliver Hawley of Charlton. Surrey: Anne Brockhouse of Bermondsey; Ralph Parker of Battersea; Mary Moreman, spinster, alias wife of William of St. Saviour, Southwark; Sarah Osmore wife of Richard of St. Olave, Southwark; Peter Howell of Kingston on Thames; George Bowdry of St. Saviour, Southwark; Alice Wright wife of Peter of St. Thomas Apostle,

Southwark. Sussex: Edward Batchelor of Horsham; William Tutfold alias Taylor of Petworth. (PRO: C66/3214/13).

19 July. Western Circuit prisoners reprieved to be transported to Barbados. Devon: Richard Luckis of Salcombe; Elizabeth Steere of Plymouth; Elizabeth Mathewes of Heavitree; Abednego Heard of Cadeleigh; Thomas Salter of Clayhiddon; Henry Tose of Holcombe. Somerset: Anne Thomas of Pinchead; Charles Lane of Curry Rivel; Henry Hobbs of Cutcombe; Richard Daniel of Taunton, husbandman; John Lane of Cleese. Wiltshire: George Wornell of Burbridge. (PRO: C66/3214/10).

19 July. Oxford Circuit prisoners reprieved to be transported to America. Gloucestershire: Thomas Hopson of St. Mary, Gloucester; John Shattersley of Clifton. Herefordshire: David Higgins alias Thomas Powell of Byford. Oxfordshire: Nicholas Merryman of Thame. Shropshire: William Pitt of Albrighton; William Jones of Bishops Castle. Staffordshire: Jane Foster alias wife of Thomas Turner of Burton on Trent; Joane Parks of Rowley Regis. Worcestershire: John Gill of St. Peter, Worcester. (PRO: C66/3214/17).

19 July. Midland Circuit prisoners reprieved to be transported to America. Lincolnshire: Edward Newton of Hale; Thomas Crow of Spalding; Alexander Rogers of Spalding; Thomas Morris of Spalding. Northamptonshire: John Briggs of Northampton; David Pecke of Towcester; Thomas Golding of Northampton. Nottinghamshire: Francis Browne of Lenton. (PRO: C66/3214/16).

21 July. Deposition by Roger Williams of Providence, Rhode Island, the first beginner of the mother town of Providence, aged nearly 80, that Roger Smith Sr. deceased for conscience sake left a good estate in Gloucestershire [England] and adventured with his relations to become a leading man in Taunton, Plymouth Colony. But differences arose there and he removed to Narragansett where he erected the first English house. On his death his estate was inherited by Captain Richard Smith. (CSPC).

22 July. By the *Endeavour*, Mr. Lawrence Cutt, from Barbados to New England: Robert Gray. (PRO: CO1/44/47).

23 July. The following apprenticed in Bristol: Philipp Grubb to William Swymmer, 8 years Jamaica; John Griffith to Philipp Biss, 4 years Barbados by *Antego Merchant*, Mr. John Mason. (BR).

25 July. The following apprenticed in Bristol: Robert Burrell to Arthur Grannt, 5 years Nevis or Virginia by *Nevis Merchant*. (BR).

26 July. The following apprenticed in Bristol to go to Virginia by the *Bristol Factor*, Mr. Roger Drew: Archibald Johnson to George Squire, 4 years; Robert Johnson to same, 4 years. (BR).

26 July-5 August. Shippers by the *Diamond*, Mr. Phillip Edwards, bound from London for Virginia: John Tongue, William Robins, Charles Stepkins, John Grice, Edward Leman, Micajah Perry, William Tyghe. (PRO: E190/84/1).

26 July-12 August. Shippers by the *Maryland Merchant* of York, Mr. Robert Raine, bound from Hull for Virginia: Thomas Hutchinson, Thomas Stacy, Joseph Wright, Richard Metcalfe, Edward Nightingale. (PRO: E190/323/1).

29 July. The following apprenticed in Bristol: Morgan Jenkin to Evan Lewis, 4 years Nevis by *Nevis Merchant*. (BR).

29 July. By the *Dove*, Mr. John Grafton, from Barbados to Antigua: Miles Poor; Maren Dran, servant of Jacob Leroux. (PRO: CO1/44/47).

30 July. The following apprenticed in Bristol: Arthur Bowen to Robert Hawkins, 7 years Montserrat by *Montserrat Merchant*, Mr. Richard ——. (BR).

30 July-5 August. Shippers by the *Mary*, Mr. John Consett, bound from London for Virginia: Richard Dull, John Jackson, John Richardson, William West, Micajah Perry, William Lock, John Bale, Hugh Hartshorne, James Dryden, Andrew Bolt, Thomas Parker, William Mead. (PRO: E190/84/1).

30 July-11 August. Shippers by the *Assistance*, Mr. James Strong, bound from London for Virginia: William Rathborne, Roger Lillington, Peter Sayre, Thomas Parker, Thomas Allen. (PRO: E190/84/1).

31 July. By the *John & Mary*, Mr. John Parreck, from Barbados to Boston: Giles Hall. (PRO: CO1/44/47).

July. Probate of will of John Kellond of Paignsford, Devon, whose son, Thomas Kellond, was in Boston, New England. (AW).

July. Lancashire prisoners reprieved to be transported to Barbados: John Turner alias Colly of Manchester, husbandman; George Harwood of Livesay. (EB).

1 August. The following apprenticed in Bristol: William Dedbridge to Arthur Grannt, 4 years Virginia by *Nevis Merchant*; John Sheppard to Edward Birkin, 5 years Virginia by *Bristol Factor*; John Griffith to John Hodge, 4 years Jamaica by *Richard & Ann*, said John Hodge Mr. (BR).

1 August & 6 October. Deposition by John Wintle of London, aged 20, servant of Richard Hawthorne, citizen and skinner of London, that Nathaniel Elkin of Boston, New England, merchant became indebted by bond of 29 August 1677 to Hawthorne. Deposition by Timothy Bond, aged 16, servant of Gerard Usher of London, scrivener, that James Lloyd of Boston, New England, became indebted to Hawthorne by bond of 14 March 1678. (LMCD).

1 August. By the *Return*, Mr. Thomas Harvey, from Barbados to New England: John Wheeler. (PRO: CO1/44/47).

1-4 August. By the *Young William*, Mr. Thomas Cornish, from Barbados to Virginia: Martin Bodkin; Nicholas Bodkin; James Rice; John Rice; Martin

Neagle; Henry Keith; William Dundas; Katherine Davies; John Emery, servant of Lt. Col. Hallett; Richard Cawfield. (PRO: CO1/44/47).

1 August-3 October. Shippers by the *Sarah*, Mr. Thomas Tuck, bound from London for New England: Thomas Cuddon, Vallentine Adams, Thomas Maylin, John Bawden, Phillip French, Abraham Jesson, Thomas Lane, Spencer Piggott, Samuell Wickins, William Cray, Edward Lardner, William Crouch, William Gore, James Goldham, Edmund White, John Blackhall, Charles Phelps, Edward Hall, Thomas Inds, John Inds, James Eyton, John Reynolds, Nicholas Brattle, Richard Sweeting, Oliver Westland, William Stougham, Michael Stanclift, Thomas Wetterne, Nathaniell Letten, Francis Miller, William Dingley, Ralph Ingram, Jonathan Belt, William Meade. (PRO: E190/84/1).

2 August. By the *Elizabeth*, Mr. Silvanus Paine, from Barbados to Jamaica: Katherine Cottingham; Tremmit Dawson. (PRO: CO1/44/47).

4 August. The following apprenticed in Bristol: George White to Thomas Opie, 4 years Virginia by *Richard & James*, said Thomas Opie Mr; Walter Williams to Arthur Grannt, 5 years Virginia or Nevis by *Nevis Merchant*; Rowland Pytherch to Bartholomew Tayler, 4 years Virginia by *Richard & James*; William Nicholls to Thomas Stevens, 4 years Virginia by *Bristol Factor*. (BR).

6 August-6 September. Shippers by the *Henry*, Mr. Thomas Arnold, bound from London for Virginia: Gilbert Metcalfe, Thomas Washington, Benjamin Cowell, Thomas Parker, James Cary, Henry Mees, Henry Hammond. (PRO: E190/84/1).

7 August. The following apprenticed in Bristol: William Jones to Thomas Stevens, 4 years Virginia by *Bristol Factor*; Thomas Cornish to same, 6 years Virginia by *Bristol Factor*; William Gouldin to same, 6 years Virginia by *Bristol Factor*; Richard Williams to same, 7 years Virginia by *Bristol Factor*; Charles Clift to John Gouldby, 4 years Virginia by *Samuel & Mary*, Mr. William Deane; James Rice to George Squire, 7 years Virginia by *Bristol Factor*; Roger Jones to Arthur Grannt, 4 years Virginia or Nevis by *Nevis Merchant*; Philipp Waters to Francis Rogers, 4 years Barbados by *Antego Merchant*; Sarah Moody to Thomas Foster, 5 years Virginia by *Bristol Factor*. (BR).

9-14 August. By the *Plantation*, Mr. Aser Sharpe, from Barbados to Carolina. John Collins; Richard Quintyne and his servant, James Mahone; Elizabeth Jones; George Gordon. (PRO: CO1/44/47).

13 August. The following apprenticed in Bristol: Francis Thomas to Evan Lewis, 4 years Virginia by *Nevis Merchant*. (BR).

13 August. By the *Hopewell*, Mr. Thomas Curle, from Barbados to Virginia: James Jackson. (PRO: CO1/44/47).

13-19 August. By the *Neptune*, Mr. John Knott, from Barbados to Virginia: Gilbert Godfrey, Elinor Butler and Mary Poor, servants of William Bulkley; Robert Pickford; Thomas Callay; John Gorton, servant of John Browne; Patrick McDaniell; Arthur Middleton; Henry Sealy and his servant, Thurlow Smith; John Turdall. (PRO: CO1/44/47).

14 August. The following apprenticed in Bristol: Latimer Willmott to John Adams, 7 years Virginia by *Bristol Factor*; Robert Camell to Richard Whittacre, 5 years Virginia by *Nevis Merchant*. (BR).

14 August-18 September. Shippers by the *Samuell & Mary* bound from Bristol for Virginia: William Jackson, Thomas Harris. (PRO: E190/1140/3).

15 August. The following apprenticed in Bristol: William Philipps to John Adams, 6 years Virginia by *Bristol Factor*; Sarah Obryan to Arthur Grannt, 4 years Nevis or Virginia by *Nevis Merchant*. (BR).

15 August. By the *Friendship*, Mr. William Murphy, from Barbados to New England: John Bedingham. By the *Postillion*, Mr. John Praul, from Barbados to New England: Robert Rich. (PRO: CO1/44/47).

15-20 August. Shippers by the *Joseph & Benjamin*, Mr. Edward Payne, bound from London for Virginia: William Stonestreet, Henry Mees, John Pryor, Ishmael Batton. (PRO: E190/84/1).

18 August. The following apprenticed in Bristol to go to Virginia by the *Bristol Factor*: Robert Baber to Thomas Foster, 4 years; Thomas Crispe to same, 4 years. (BR).

19 August. By the *True Friendship*, Mr. Charles Callahane, from Barbados to Nevis: Jeremiah Wolfenden. (PRO: CO1/44/47).

19 August. The following apprenticed in Bristol: Richard Jones to Edward Berkin, 4 years Virginia by *Bristol Factor*; Ann Bobett to William White, 4 years Virginia by *Bristol Factor*; Henry Morgan to Arthur Grannt, 4 years Virginia or Nevis by *Nevis Merchant*. (BR).

20 August-17 September. Shippers by the *Hannah*, Mr. Anthony Gester, bound from London for Virginia: Luke Nurse, Gawin Corbin, William Hayes, Anthony Palmer, Daniell Jackson, John Shelton, Robert Hall, John Daniell. (PRO: E190/84/1).

22 August. The following apprenticed in Bristol: Joane Ricketts to John Adams, 4 years Virginia by *Bristol Factor*. (BR).

23 August. Shipper by the *Beginning* of Bideford, Mr. John Atkins, bound from Bideford for Maryland: John Davie. (PRO: E190/957/16).

23 August. Shipper by the *Mayflower* of Bideford, Mr. John Ilsco, bound from Bideford for Maryland: William Titherly. (PRO: E190/957/16).

25 August. By the *John & James*, Mr. Giles Hamlin, from Barbados to New England: Francis Cox. (PRO: CO1/44/47).

25 August. Newgate prisoners reprieved to be transported to Barbados. London: John Holland; Mary Stephens alias Robinson alias Hipkins, spinster; Dorothy Thomas, spinster; Arthur Boswell; Abraham Chissers; Elizabeth Drury, spinster; George Seigniour; Sarah Layton, spinster; Richard Hill; John Quarles; Elizabeth Plummer, spinster; Elizabeth Hanson; Ruth Webber, spinster; Thomas Fairchild; Mary Needum, spinster; Thomas Lambert. Middlesex: Mary Barker of St. Martin in the Fields; Andrew Spire of the same; Robert Lant of the same; Elizabeth Johnson of the same, widow; Abigail Darke of St. Andrew Holborn; Prudence Hill of the same; Thomas Smith of Acton; Henry Weller of the same; Elizabeth Martin of Stepney; John Thatchwell alias Tanner of St. Giles Cripplegate; Edward Grady of Whitechapel; Elias Hutchins of St. Margaret Westminster or St. Mary Savoy; Edward Swaine alias Coleman of St. Margaret Westminster; Joseph Wright of Hillingdon; Anne Slye of Clerkenwell, spinster, for infanticide; Mary Cattle of St. Paul Covent Garden, spinster, for infanticide. (PRO: C66/3214/25).

26 August. The following apprenticed in Bristol to go to Virginia by the *Bristol Factor*: Bridgett Whitethorne to George Squire, 4 years; John Nicholas to Zachary Smith, 4 years; William Matthews to Barnard Browne, 4 years; Joane Gooding to John Adams, 4 years. (BR).

26 August-11 September. Shippers by the *Increase*, Mr. John Holland, bound from London for New England: John Hubbard, George Roshe, Thomas Lane, Giles Long, William White, Thomas Deane, James Hayes, Edward Mann, John Crow, Edmund Hale, William Crouch, Thomas Cuddon. (PRO: E190/84/1).

27 August. The following apprenticed in Bristol: Samuell Warren to [blank], 4 years Virginia; John Rudman to Lyson Portry, 4 years Virginia by *Bristol Factor*; Edward Rudman to same, 4 years Virginia by *Bristol Factor*; Edward West to Roger Drew, 4 years Virginia by *Bristol Factor*; Elizabeth Dyer to William Norman, 4 years Virginia by *Maryland Merchant*, Mr. George Tyte. (BR).

27 August-27 September. Shippers by the *Humphrey & Elizabeth*, Mr. Robert Medford, bound from London for Virginia: John Sadler, Arthur Bayley, John Good, John Blavor, John Jefferies, John Shewell, John Rawlinson, William Tyghe. (PRO: E190/84/1).

28 August. The following apprenticed in Bristol: Walter Lewis to Arthur Grante, 4 years Virginia by *Nevis Merchant*; John Brothurst to John Cromwell, 7 years Virginia. (BR).

28 August. Shipper by the *Virginia Merchant* of Bideford, Mr. John Heiman, bound from Bideford for Maryland: said John Heiman. (PRO: E190/957/16).

28 August-18 September. Shippers by the *Concord*, Mr. Thomas Grantham, bound from London for Virginia: Arthur Bayley, John Kent, William Pinchback, Vincent Goddard, Richard Booth, Robert Farrer, Edward Pate, William Dolby, John Taylor, Gilbert Upton, Thomas Hill, Thomas Frampton, Nowell Bassano, John Brett, Richard Clements. (PRO: E190/84/1).

28 August-28 September. Shippers by the *Recovery*, Mr. Thomas Hasted, bound from London for Virginia: Cuthbert Best, Edward Harper. (PRO: E190/84/1).

29 August. The following apprenticed in Bristol to go to Virginia by the *Bristol Factor*: Richard Watkins to Bernard Browne, 4 years; Thomas Hall to Henry Hunt, 4 years. (BR).

29 August-24 September. Shippers by the *Augustine*, Mr. Zachary Taylor, bound from London for Virginia: Gawen Corbin, John Brett, Francis Camfield, Samuell Young, Edward Tiplady, Robert Bristow, Phillip Foster, Arthur Nort(h), Hugh Hartshorne, Richard Nicolson, George Richards, John Wagstaff, Richard Ash, Samuell Hoyle, Thomas Parker, Edward Leman, John Grice, Hes(ter) Pitchard, John Putford, Gilbert Salisbury, John Wood, Thomas Dalton, John Roberts. (PRO: E190/84/1).

30 August. The following apprenticed in Bristol: Francis Jenkins to Edmund Reddish, 7 years Jamaica. (BR).

30 August-18 December. Shippers by the *Agreement* bound from Bristol for Virginia: Thomas Pearce, Richard Yate, William Smith, Thomas Phelps, John England. (PRO: E190/1140/3).

August. Probate of will of Sir Nathaniel Herne, alderman of London, whose niece, —— Whitlock, was in Virginia. (AW).

August. Administration of Edward Laight of Virginia, bachelor. (AW).

August. Deliverance Cotterell, aged 14, apprenticed from Christ's Hospital to John Consett, commander of the *Mary* bound for Virginia. (CH).

1 September. The following apprenticed in Bristol: Alexander Wise to William Davies, 9 years Virginia by *Samuel & Mary*, said William Davies Mr; Robert Davis to Robert Worgan, 4 years Virginia by *Samuel & Mary*; Godfrey Clarke to Thomas Mountjoy, 4 years Virginia by *Bristol Factor*. (BR).

1 September. Ann Servant, wife of Ralph Servant of Stepney, Middlesex, yeoman, found guilty of forcibly transporting Alice Flax to Virginia by the *Elizabeth & Katherine*. (VM 83/3).

1 September. By the *Barbados Merchant*, Mr. Edward Griffin, from Barbados to the Leeward Islands: Thomas Westbury. (PRO: CO1/44/47).

1-2 September. By the *John & Francis*, Mr. John Howard, from Barbados to Antigua: James Cole; Dennis Griffin; Elizabeth Wickham. (PRO: CO1/44/47).

1-8 September. By the *Trent*, Mr. George Mountjoy (Munjoy), from Barbados to Boston: Joseph Pollard; Mary Pendleton. (PRO: CO1/44/47).

1-25 September. Shippers by the *Duke of York*, Mr. John Purvis, bound from London for Virginia: John Rawlins, John Paine, Henry Meese, Arthur Bailey, Phillip Foster, John Purnis, John Jefferys, Gawen Corbin, Francis Lee, Edward Leman, James Parker, Andrew Bolt, Edward Tomlins, Isaac Merritt, John Jennings. (PRO: E190/84/1).

4 September. The following apprenticed in Bristol: Thomas Tanner to John Cromwell, 8 years Virginia by *Richard & James*; John Hall to Roger Adams, 4 years Jamaica by [*Richard & Ann*], Mr. John Hodge. (BR).

4 September. By the *Joseph*, Mr. Stephen Clay, from Barbados to New York: Richard James, servant of Col. Samuel Newton; William Robotham. By the *Pearl*, Mr. Edward Peirson, from Barbados to the Leeward Islands: John Nevill; Robert Pickford. (PRO: CO1/44/47).

5-8 September. Shippers by the *Bombay*, Mr. John Wood, bound from London for Virginia: James Hayes, John Crowe, John Eburne, Robert Holt, John Hubbard, Thomas Papelion, Edward West, James Goldham, George Benson. (PRO: E190/84/1).

6 September-1 October 1689. Shippers by the *Barnaby*, Mr. Matthew Ryder, bound from London for Virginia: Richard Glover, Silvester Deane, Edward Leman, Andrew Bolt, Thomas Parker, Barnaby Dunch, Thomas Fife, John Morgan, Samuell Powell, Isaac Puller, James Bayley, Isaac Merritt, Ralph Ingram. (PRO: E190/84/1).

9 September. Attestation of Thomas Arnold of Redrith, Surrey, mariner aged 34, that he was master of the *Henry & Ann* during her last voyage from Virginia to London and delivered tobacco which is claimed by Richard Wilson and his wife Sarah, relict and administratrix of Samuel Partridge, deceased, as creditors of Robert Beverley. (LMCD).

9-24 September. Shippers by the *Hopewell*, Mr. John Rudds, bound from London for Virginia: Michael Purefoy, Thomas Grindon, John Potts, William King, Thomas Parker, George Richards, Edward Carter, Thomas Askew. (PRO: E190/84/1).

10 September. Deposition by Jeremy Stancliffe, servant of John Crawley, citizen and haberdasher of London, that by deed of 2 August 1678 John Pinchon of Boston, New England, merchant, became indebted to Crawley and to Michael and Samuel Stancliffe of London. (LMCD).

10 September. The following apprenticed in Bristol: Thomas James to David Nicholls, 4 years Virginia by *Richard & James*; John Robins to Thomas Foster, 4 years Virginia by *[Bristol] Factor*. (BR).

10-30 September. Shippers by the *Elizabeth*, Mr. Thomas Saxon, bound from London for New England: Edward Lardner, Edward Hull, John Blackall, Spencer Piggott, James Eyton, Thomas Humphreys, John Crowe, Abraham Jesson, John Richardson, William Crouch, Joseph Cox, John Loggin, Sir Patrick Ward, John Eburne, Francis Fox. (PRO: E190/84/1).

11 September. The following apprenticed in Bristol: Owen James to Thomas Bishopp, 4 years Montserrat by *Patience*, Mr. William Andrews; Jabez Greening to William Davis, 4 years Maryland by *Expectation*, said William Davis Mr; Margaret Harris to John Adams, 4 years Virginia by *[Bristol] Factor*; Elizabeth Jones to Thomas Foster, 4 years Virginia by *Bristol Factor*. (BR).

12 September. By the *Portsmouth*, Mr. Joseph Briar, from Barbados to Rhode Island: William Ellinsworth. (PRO: CO1/44/47).

12-17 September. Shippers by the *Baltimore*, Mr. George Purvis, bound from London for Virginia: John Handford, William Hull, Thurston Whitwell, Henry Eatherton. (PRO: E190/84/1).

12-25 September. Shippers by the *Richard & Elizabeth*, Mr. Nicholas Prynn, bound from London for Virginia: John Mann, Richard Booth, Henry Robins. (PRO: E190/84/1).

12-27 September. Shippers by the *Willing Mind*, Mr. John Lucombe, bound from London for Virginia: Henry Meese, Richard Worgan, Thomas Joulson, William Hancock, William Meade, Thomas Harke, Andrew Bolls, John Hanford. (PRO: E190/84/1).

13 September. The following apprenticed in Bristol: Reece Price to Thomas Foster, 7 years Virginia; John Price to same, 7 years Virginia; William Price to same, 7 years Virginia; James Groves to same, 7 years Virginia; John Clark to same, 7 years Virginia. (BR).

13-23 September. Shippers by the *Prince*, Mr. Robert Conway, bound from London for Virginia: Edward Round, John Cooper, Robert Bristow, Thomas Parker, William Nutt, John Jaggard, Edward Bale, John King, John Jefferys, Edward Leman, William Taylor, Samuell Harris. (PRO: E190/84/1).

13-30 September. Shippers by the *Owners Adventure* of London, Mr. Thomas Lurting, bound from Liverpool for Virginia: Thomas Clayton, Mathew Talbott, John Pemberton, Edward Booker. (PRO: E190/1341/24).

13 September-7 October. By the *True Friendship*, Mr. Charles Callahane, from Barbados to Nevis, Antigua and Jamaica: Nathaniell Johnson; Richard Lynch; Henry Elliott; Thomas Greenslatt; Patrick Madden; John Mountaine; William Jennings; James Belfour; John Butcher; Richard Banister; Alexander Hancock; Thomas Wickham; Thomas Clovan; Evan Charles; Thomas Swinny. (PRO: CO1/44/47).

15 September. The following apprenticed in Bristol: John Wedmore to Bernard Browne, 8 years Virginia by *[Bristol] Factor*. (BR).

15-18 September. By the *Hope*, Mr. John Price, from Barbados to New England: Edward Pilson; John Harker; Daniell Nasy. (PRO: CO1/44/47).

15-27 September. Shippers by the *Zebulon*, Mr. Nicholas Goodridge, bound from London for Virginia: John Bayly, Henry Dandy, Thomas Ellis, Josiah Keeling. (PRO: E190/84/1).

16-20 September. By the *Blessing*, Mr. Francis Watlington, from Barbados to Bermuda: Francis Browne; George Sone. (PRO: CO1/44/47).

18 September. Deposition by James Godfrey, citizen and ironmonger of London, aged 43, and Rowland Platt of London, merchant aged 38, that the son and heir of Richard Jennings, citizen and grocer of London, deceased, is Alexander Jennings of London, merchant. In 1674 Richard Jennings empowered the deponent Godfrey, then bound for Maryland, to sell his estate there which he had acquired on 6 December 1665. (LMCD).

18 September. The following apprenticed in Bristol: Dorothy Hibberd to John Adams, 4 years Virginia by *Bristol Factor*; Roger Popkin to Thomas Lane, 4 years Maryland by *Friendship*, Mr. Thomas Whittopp. (BR).

19 September. The following apprenticed in Bristol: James Rice to Thomas Gibbons, 4 years Virginia by *Bristol Factor*; John Stanton to Henry Oakey, 4 years Nevis by *Nevis Merchant*, Mr. Arthur Grant. (BR).

19 September-2 October. By the *Lisbon Merchant*, Mr. Roger Whitfield, from Barbados to New York: George Blunt; Jane Jenkins. (PRO: CO1/44/47).

20 September. The following apprenticed in Bristol: Susanna Farrow to Richard Welsteed, 4 years Virginia by *Bristol Factor*. (BR).

20-27 September. Shippers by the *Merchants Consent*, Mr. Francis Partis, bound from London for Virginia: Nicholas Hayward, John Steventon, William Barrett, Peter Causton. (PRO: E190/84/1).

22 September. Deposition by Thomas Luke of St. Mary Savoy, Strand, Middlesex, merchant aged 35, and his servant, Ambrose Buckley, aged 33, that in August 1675 they delivered goods to John Minor, then in London as Colonel Spencer's servant, which he was to dispose of in Virginia. No payment has been received. (LMCD).

22 September-3 October. Shippers by the *Richard*, Mr. Thomas Jowles, bound from London for New England: John Reynolds, Nicholas Brattle, James Lane, Edward West, Edward Tarleton, Eros Norwick, Jeremy Johnson, Abraham Jesson, William Shirley, Walter Mico, John Clarke, Peter Buckley, Richard Gawthorne, Richard Shipton, James Swift, Abraham Tillard, Nicholas Chaplin, Richard Russell, Richard Parrett, Edward Hall, John Blackall, John Silvester, Edward Ellis, Benjamin Scrivener, William Crouch, Epaphras

Shrimpton, William Sloughton, Ezekiel Hutchinson, George Walker, John Loggin, James Eyton, Richard Franklin, John Norman, Andrew Kendrick, Richard Lloyd, George Benson, Stephen Cole, Jacob Preston, Edmond Hall. (PRO: E190/84/1).

23 September. The following apprenticed in Bristol: Richard Edwards to Thomas Gibbons, 4 years Virginia by *Bristol Factor*; Ann Catter to David Jones, 5 years Virginia by *Victory*, Mr. William Jones; Ann Wheeler to Roger Drew, 4 years Virginia by *Bristol Factor*. (BR).

23-26 September. Shippers by the *John*, Mr. Thomas Groves, bound from London for Virginia: Richard Buller, Robert Chamberlain, James Fowles, Edward Blake. (PRO: E190/84/1).

23 September-16 October. Shippers by the *Bristol Factor* bound from Bristol for Virginia: William Smith, Stephen Watts, Bartholomew Bach. (PRO: E190/1140/3).

24-27 September. Shippers by the *Sarratt Merchant*, Mr. Nathaniell Reynolds, bound from London for Virginia: Edward Leman, Joseph Carpenter, Edward Carter, Francis Strutt. (PRO: E190/84/1).

24 September-23 December. Shippers by the *Thomas & Edward*, Mr. John Browne, bound from London for Virginia: John Collingwood, Thomas Taylor, William Collett, Jane Moore, Sarah Broadbent. (PRO: E190/84/1).

25 September. The following apprenticed in Bristol to go to Virginia by the *Bristol Factor*: Joane Iles to Roger Drew, 4 years; George Hort to Richard Franklyn, 4 years. (BR).

26 September. Shipper by the *Providence* of Lyme, Mr. Solomon Andrew, bound from Lyme for Virginia: said Solomon Andrew. (PRO: E190/883/4).

26 September-2 October. By the *Rutter*, Mr. Edward Duffield, from Barbados to Jamaica: Richard Searfle, servant of James Coates; Ann O'Neal; Henry Gother; Richard Gorton; William Muskett; Michaell Jennings; Elizabeth Brandby, servant of David Watkins. (PRO: CO1/44/47).

27 September. Deposition by Joseph Clapton Jr., son and servant of Joseph Clapton of London, merchant, that the bill now shown him is for goods delivered to Giles Godward, carpenter, formerly dwelling within Bishopsgate, London, but now resident in New England. (LMCD).

27 September. By the *Supply*, Mr. John Ady, from Barbados to Virginia: Wilbert Daniell. (PRO: CO1/44/47).

29 September. The following apprenticed in Bristol: Simon Evans to Robert King, 4 years Virginia by *Friendship*. (BR).

September. Administration with will of Daniel Parke of London, who died in Virginia. (AW).

September. Probate of will of Joseph Austin of Shadwell, Middlesex, and late of New England. (AW).

September. Henry Cordwell, aged 15, apprenticed from Christ's Hospital to Nathan Reynolds, commander of the *Sarratt Merchant* bound for Virginia. (CH).

1-3 October. By the *Barbados Merchant*, Mr. James Cock, from Barbados to Virginia: Christopher Barton; Francis Fear; Martha Short; John Sandford. (PRO: CO1/44/47).

4 October. The following apprenticed in Bristol to go to Barbados by the *Unicorn*: Thomas Sherman to Peter Fay, 4 years; Sarah Baker to same, 4 years; Elizabeth Treasure to same, 4 years. (BR).

4 October. By the *Virgin*, Mr. Thomas Allumby, for the Leeward Islands and Virginia: James McIloly; Thomas Bishop. (PRO: CO1/44/47).

4 October. Shipper by the *Elizabeth* of Weymouth, Mr. John Bull, bound from Weymouth for Virginia: John Burridge. (PRO: E190/883/2).

6 October. The following apprenticed in Bristol to go to Virginia by the *Bristol Factor*: Edward Hathway to George Squire, 4 years; Cornelius Serjeant to Thomas Gibbons, 4 years. (BR).

6-7 October. Shippers by the *Prince*, Mr. Robert Morrice, bound from London for Virginia: Barnaby Dunch, Thomas Sands, William Bough, Jacob Bell, William Mead. (PRO: E190/84/1).

7 October. The following apprenticed in Bristol: Elizabeth Herbert to David Nicholls, 4 years Virginia by *Richard & James*. (BR).

7-8 October. By the *Africa*, Mr. Anthony Bugess, from Barbados to Antigua: John Hilk; Oliver Willoughby. (PRO: CO1/44/47).

8 October. The following apprenticed in Bristol: Bridgett Griffiths to Richard Pearce, 4 years Virginia by *Maryland Merchant*. (BR).

9 October. The following apprenticed in Bristol: Benjamin Buggin to Thomas Tiler, 4 years Virginia by *Richard & James*. (BR).

9-23 October. Shippers by the *Richard & James* bound from Bristol for Virginia: Peter Waddinge, Francis Watkins, Marmaduke Williams, Edward Sleeman, George Mason, Henry Gibbs. (PRO: E190/1140/3).

9 October-4 November. By the *Endeavour*, Mr. Thomas Shaw, from Barbados to Carolina: Mary Benson; Julian Battison; Thomas Yarwood; Christopher Portman; Magnus Popple. (PRO: CO1/44/47).

10 October. The following apprenticed in Bristol: Walter Sayn to Bartholomew Taylor, 6 years Virginia by *Richard & James*; Morgan Jones to Thomas Jones,

4 years Barbados by *John*, Mr. Peter Wraxall; Thomas Foot to Edward Swettnam, 5 years Virginia by *Richard & James*. (BR).

13 October. Deposition by Jonathan Davies, citizen and dyer of London, aged 38, that he was present when Edmond Browne of London, merchant, married Martha Davies at St. Mary's, Newington, Surrey, on 27 June 1677. Browne was taken by the Turks while on a voyage to Virginia and is since deceased. (LMCD).

13 October. The following apprenticed in Bristol: William Welworth to Bartholomew ——, 4 years Virginia by *Richard & James*; Marke Clyent to Walter Phelps, 5 years Maryland. (BR).

14 October. The following apprenticed in Bristol: John Browne to Zacharia Smith, 4 years Nevis by *Abraham & Isaac*, Mr. John Jones. (BR).

15 October. Shipper by the *John's Love* of Hull, Mr. Lionell Ripley, bound from Hull for Virginia: John Burnsall. (PRO: E190/323/1).

15-25 October. Shippers by the *Golden Lyon*, Mr. Jeremy Rich, bound from London for Maryland: William & Walter Jarvis. (PRO: E190/84/1).

16 October. The following apprenticed in Bristol: Thomas Browning to George Paine, 5 years Virginia by *[Bristol] Factor*; George Hopton to Francis Wattkins, 6 years Maryland by *Richard & James*; Mary Jones to same, 5 years Maryland by *Richard & James*; Thomas Rice to John Stevens, 4 years Virginia by *Bristol Merchant*, said John Stevens Mr. (BR).

16 October-20 November. Shippers by the *James*, Mr. Anthony Young, bound from London for Virginia: James Brace, Walter Atwood. (PRO: E190/84/1).

18 October. The following apprenticed in Bristol: Francis Williams to Thomas Pope, 5 years Virginia by *Victory*; Samuel Gottly alias Dowle to William Jones, 4 years Virginia or Barbados by *Victory*; Mary Hewett to John Chiney, 4 years Virginia by *Richard & James*. (BR).

20 October. By the *John & Sarah*, Mr. James Shoare, from Barbados to New York: Walter Butler. (PRO: CO1/44/47).

20 October-10 November. Shippers by the *Virginia Factor*, Mr. Robert Joules, bound from London for Maryland: Barnaby Dunch, Richard Carter, Samuell Lane, Henry Rowland, Micajah Perry, Thomas Elwys, John Edwards. (PRO: E190/84/1).

21 October. The following apprenticed in Bristol: Thomas Lockheart to Thomas Howel, 4 years Virginia; Elisha Davis to Robert Parker, 4 years Virginia by *[Bristol] Factor*. (BR).

23 October. The following apprenticed in Bristol: Jane Williams to David Charles, 4 years Virginia by *Bristol Merchant*. (BR).

23 October-7 November. Shippers by the *James* of Plymouth, Mr. Edward Blagg, bound from Plymouth for Virginia: William Martyn, Abraham Beele. (PRO: E190/1043/17).

24 October. Rene Petit and Jacob Guerard report that many of the families seeking to settle in Carolina have now arrived in London and could be transported by the *Richmond* shortly sailing for Barbados. A list of passengers is to be submitted. (APC).

24 October. The following apprenticed in Bristol: Mary Evans to William Smith, 7 years Virginia by *Bristol Merchant*; Philipp Hilsey to John Howell, 4 years Virginia by *Richard & James*. (BR).

27 October. The following apprenticed in Bristol: Simon Smelt to Abraham Cook, 6 years Virginia by *Unicorn*, Mr. Thomas Cooper; Evan Thomas to Thomas Greene, 4 years Maryland by *Planter*, Mr. Matthew Nicholas; Francis Warren to same, 5 years Maryland by *Planter*; Peter Morgan to same, 6 years Maryland by *Planter*; Mary Lilly to same, 4 years Maryland by *Planter*; Margaret Cole, 4 years Maryland by *Planter*; William Smith to same, 5 years Maryland by *Planter*; James Lilly, 6 years Maryland by *Planter*; William Bradley to same, 4 years Maryland by *Planter*. (BR).

27 October-8 November. Shippers by the *James & Thomas* of Plymouth, Mr. George Bayley, bound from Plymouth for Virginia: Thomas Warne, Marke Batt, John Peale, Francis Spurrell, Nathaniell Young, Joseph Fugge. (PRO: E190/1043/17).

27 October-28 November. Shippers by the *Sarah & Elizabeth* bound from Bristol for Virginia: Charles Harford, George Hawes, Thomas Turner, William Morgan, Michaell White. (PRO: E190/1140/3).

28 October. The following apprenticed in Bristol: Thomas Reynolds to John Marden, 4 years Virginia by *Richard & James*. (BR).

29 October. By the *Dove*, Mr. Anthony Jenour, from Barbados to Nevis. John Parker, Barnaby Hale, Thomas How and John Smith, servants of Col. Christopher Codrington; Morgan John; Jacob Senior; Hugh Farrell. By the *Hopewell*, Mr. John Ayres, from Barbados to Antigua: Joseph Holt. (PRO: CO1/44/47).

30 October. Petition of Jane Beaumont. Her husband, William Beaumont, plasterer, about two months ago left her with five small children and she heard nothing from him until three days ago when she received a letter from him written aboard the *Charles*, Mr. Walter Dunch, then in the Downs bound for Maryland. He says he was inveigled on board the ship by a carpenter and sold to the boatswain as a slave. The Admiralty is ordered to stop the ship and put Beaumont on shore. (APC).

30 October. The following apprenticed in Bristol: Thomas Coleman to Thomas Tandy, 4 years Virginia by *Alithea*, Mr. Edward Wattkins. (BR).

31 October. Deposition by John Owen, citizen and merchant of London, that Stephen Burton of Boston, New England, became indebted by bond to Thomas Malyn, citizen and haberdasher of London, resident at the White Horse without Aldgate. (LMCD).

31 October. The following apprenticed in Bristol: John Notly to John Jones, 4 years Nevis by *Bonadventure*, Mr. William Wraxall. (BR).

October. Probate of will of John White alias Wampers of Boston, New England, who died while travelling in Stepney, Middlesex. (AW).

1 November. By the *Three Brothers*, Mr. Peter Boss, from Barbados to New York: Joseph Whitehead. (PRO: CO1/44/47).

3 November. The following apprenticed in Bristol: Joane Bishopp to John Harris, 4 years Virginia; Thomas Arnold to Bryan Tandy, 4 years Virginia by *Planter*. (BR).

3-7 November. By the *Adventure*, Mr. Edward Duffield, from Barbados to Jamaica: Katherine Reddin, servant of Martin Hayes; Luke Hunt; Moses Henriques Cotinho; Henry Siddy; Thomas Babbington, servant of Thomas Gladdin. 7 Nov. (PRO: CO1/44/47).

4-14 November. Shippers by the *David* of Plymouth, Mr. William Ginny, bound from Plymouth for Virginia: Rees Evans, David Teage. (PRO: E190/1043/17).

6-8 November. By the *Hopewell*, Mr. William Murphy, from Barbados to Antigua: William Tremills; Abel Oldridge; Arthur Williams; William Courtney; George Salter; William Jones; Hector Jones; Alexander Urquhart. (PRO: CO1/44/47).

7 November. The following apprenticed in Bristol: Joseph Higgins to Thomas Speed, 4 years Virginia by *Maryland Merchant*; David Jones to George Cary, 5 years Virginia by *Francis & Mary*. (BR).

7 November. Shipper by the *Richard* of London, Mr. Thomas Jouls, bound from Plymouth for New England: Sir John Frederick. (PRO: E190/1043/17).

8 November. The following apprenticed in Bristol: Thomas Tacy to Samuel Cole, 4 years Virginia by *Hannah & Elizabeth*, said Samuel Cole Mr; Humphrey Williams, 4 years Virginia by *Hannah & Elizabeth*. (BR).

8-12 November. Shippers by the *Adventure* of Hull, Mr. John Longdon, bound from Hull for Virginia: Charles Bollard, John Baker, Anthony Wells, Robert Scott, Edward Stampe. (PRO: E190/323/1).

11 November. The following apprenticed in Bristol to go to Virginia by the *Francis & Mary*: Luke Lockly to Peter Bache, 5 years; William Smith to same, 6 years; Richard Cardell to same, 10 years. (BR).

11-27 November. Shippers by the *Unicorn* bound from Bristol for Virginia: Joseph Clark, Richard Finch, Patience Read, William Mynor, Robert Smith,

James Millard, William Swymer, Henry Daniell, John Mechen, Thomas Cooper, John Duddlestone, Jonas Holliday, Henry Harris, John Richardson, Michaell Pope. (PRO: E190/1140/3).

11 November-5 December. Shippers by the *Victory* bound from Bristol for Virginia: Thomas Phillips, John Haskins, Marmaduke Bowdler, John Woodward, Perowne Biddlestone, Thomas Pope, Richard Gotley, John Harris, William Crabb. (PRO: E190/1140/3).

12 November. The following apprenticed in Bristol: John Philipps to Edward Stoakes, 4 years Nevis by *New England Merchant*, Mr. Nathaniel Plom; William Rogers to Richard Carpenter, 5 years Jamaica by *Mary*, Mr. William Whetstone. (BR).

13-14 November. Shippers by the *David* of Plymouth, Mr. William Ginny, bound from Plymouth for Virginia: Rees Evans, David Teage. (PRO: E190/1043/17).

14 November. The following apprenticed in Bristol: John Davy to Thomas Clement, 4 years Virginia by *George*, Mr. Samuel ———. (BR).

14-28 November. Shippers by the *Planter* bound from Bristol for Virginia: Symon Pickmore, George Tyte, John Hudson, Thomas Scroope, Nicholas Gwilter(?). (PRO: E190/1140/3).

15 November. The following apprenticed in Bristol: Richard Grabom to Simon Stephens, 4 years Virginia by *Sarah & Elizabeth*, Mr. Richard White. (BR).

15-29 November. By the *Resolution*, Mr. Thomas Gilbert, from Barbados to Antigua: Stephen Dewer; Nicholas Kew; Morgan Lynch, servant of John Codrington; Owen Parris. (PRO: CO1/44/47).

19 November. The following apprenticed in Bristol: John Jenkins to John Harris, 4 years Virginia by *Sarah & Elizabeth*. (BR).

19-25 November. Shippers by the *Golden Fortune*, Mr. William Jefferies, bound from London for Virginia: John Handford, Isaac Merritt, George Ludlor, Edward Lane. (PRO: E190/84/1).

20 November. The following apprenticed in Bristol: Thomas Swarford to William Threlfa, 4 years Barbados by *Abraham & Mary*, Mr. Jeffris. (BR).

20-24 November. By the *Mary & Sarah*, Mr. George Conway, from Barbados to Providence: Martin Bently; Robert Osburne, servant of Richard Lilburne; John Ogle; Richard Lilburne. (PRO: CO1/44/47).

21-25 November. By the *Phoenix*, Mr. Robert Flexny, from Barbados to Antigua and the Leeward Islands: Thomas Bread; Arthur Bread; Nathaniell Mannerick; Gideon Rowland; Abraham Abudient. (PRO: CO1/44/47).

24 November. The following apprenticed in Bristol to go to Maryland by the *Sarah & Elizabeth*: Joseph Hosier to Samuel Alford, 4 years; Daniel

Morgaison to same, 4 years; Michael Martyn to same, 4 years; Ann Carswell to same, 4 years. (BR).

25-29 November. By the *Katherine*, Mr. Andrew Gall, from Barbados to Antigua: Sarah Are; Katherine Alsop; Robert Spittle; William Corbett; Andrew Hannah, servant of William Stickland; Roger Farrell. (PRO: CO1/44/47).

27 November-5 December. Shippers by the *Francis & Mary* bound from Bristol for Virginia: Michaell Pope, Thomas Speed, Edward Fielding, Richard Gotley, Samuell Tipton. (PRO: E190/1140/3).

27 November-6 December. Shippers by the *Dorothy*, Mr. John More, bound from London for Virginia: Richard Buller, Micajah Perry, John Culpepper. (PRO: E190/84/1).

28 November-6 December. Shippers by the *Fortune*, Mr. William Fowles, bound from London for Virginia: Thomas Crundall, Thomas Parker, Stephen Bearcroft. (PRO: E190/84/1).

November. Administration of Thomas Norwood of Virginia, widower. (AW).

November. Probate of will of Hopkin Price formerly of Stepney, Middlesex, but late of Rappahannock River, Middlesex County, Virginia. (AW).

November. Administration of William Smith of St. John the Baptist, Bristol, who died in Virginia. (AW).

November. Administration of Foulk Moulton of Westover, Virginia. (AW).

2 December. Deposition by Robert Bayly of Barking, Essex, surgeon aged 23, and Joseph Alsford of Limehouse, Middlesex, mariner aged 36, that they served in the *Leonard & James* of London, Mr. John Wilson, on a voyage from London to Virginia. On 23 November 1678 Thomas Jackson, aged 20, boarded the ship at Deptford as a passenger to Virginia and on 28 November all 74 passengers were examined and registered at Gravesend. No person named William Odams was registered but, after a week at sea, it was reported that Thomas Jackson's real name was William Odams and he was delivered with others to Elizabeth Hull in Virginia to whom he belonged. (LMCD).

3 December. Shipper by the *Sampson* of London, Mr. William Saunders, bound from Southampton for Virginia: Benjamin Newland for James Thiery. (PRO: E190/830/6).

4 December-9 February. Shippers by the *Bristol Merchant* bound from Bristol for Virginia: Abraham Sanders, Charles Harford, George Burgess, John Jones, Mathew Lambe, Stephen Watts, Thomas Gamon, James Wall, Thomas Gibbons, John Baber, John Dymer. (PRO: E190/1140/3, 1141/1).

6 December. By the *Unity*, Mr. Lawrence Sluce, from Barbados to Jamaica: Nathaniell Warner. (PRO: CO1/44/47).

6-13 December. Shippers by the *Alathea* bound from Bristol for Maryland: John England, Robert Dowding, James Wall, Edward Watkins. (PRO: E190/1140/3).

6-18 December. Shippers by the *Rose & Crown*, Mr. Bartholomew Clements, bound from London for Virginia: Micajah Perry, William Lane, John Allen, William Shakerly, George Richards, Dorman Norman, Thomas Salter. (PRO: E190/84/1).

8 December. Shippers by the *Nathaniell* bound from Bristol for Virginia: Thomas Moore, Charles Allen. (PRO: E190/1140/3).

8 December-2 January. Shippers by the *Expectation* bound from Bristol for New England: Robert Yate, Thomas Earle, Robert Alexander, Edward Jones, Thomas Lodge. (PRO: E190/1140/3, 1141/1).

10 December. Shippers by the *St. George*, Mr. Richard Sheppard, bound from London for Virginia: John Bawden, Samuell Shute. (PRO: E190/84/1).

11 December. Shipper by the *Oxford* frigate, Captain Mason, bound from London for Virginia: Lord Culpepper. (PRO: E190/84/1).

15-22 December. By the *Laurel*, Mr. Robert Oxe, from Barbados to Nevis and the Leeward Islands: John Sidney; John Downing. (PRO: CO1/44/47).

15-29 December. Shipper by the *Abraham & Sarah*, Mr. Godfrey Stephens, bound from Plymouth for Virginia: Samuell Rooke. (PRO: E190/1043/17, 1044/21).

17 December. Middlesex prisoners reprieved to be transported to Barbados: Richard Hughes of Friern Barnet; Francis French of St. Giles in the Fields; Richard Wheeler of Tottenham; Alice Kipp of Stepney, spinster; Elizabeth Jacey of the same, spinster; Thomas Beacham of New Brentford; Maurice Hunt of Stanmore; John Meaten of St. Clement Danes; Hannah Andrews of St. Botolph Aldgate, spinster; John Weale of Bedfont; Mary Kiteley, spinster, alias wife of Edward Woodden of Whitechapel; Joan Blackwell of London, spinster. (PRO: C66/3208/4).

20-22 December. Shippers by the *Globe*, Mr. Samuell Groom, bound from London for Maryland: Richard Eley, John Hubbock, Thomas Bassett. (PRO: E190/84/1).

22 December. Shipper by the *Rainbow* bound from Bristol for Virginia: Erasmus Dole. (PRO: E190/1140/3).

22 December. Shipper by the *Elizabeth* of Poole, Mr. William Pike, bound from Poole for Maryland: Jane Gould. (PRO: E190/883/2).

23-31 December. By the *Recovery*, Mr. James Brown, from Barbados to Jamaica: Robert Marriott; John Sindry; Robert Barnewell; Mary Sharpe; Telles Lopez. (PRO: CO1/44/47).

24 December-30 December. By the *True Friendship*, Mr. Charles Callahane, from Barbados to Antigua: Roger Holeman; Jeffery Burke. (PRO: CO1/44/47).

December. Administration of Patrick Moone of Shadwell, Middlesex, who died in Virginia. (AW).

December. Probate of will of Samuel Hitchins of All Hallows Barking, London, whose nephews, Daniel and Joseph Hitchins, were in New England. (AW).

December. Probate of will of David Griffin of St. Michael Bassishaw, London, whose brother, Samuel Griffin, was in Virginia. (AW).

1680

2-19 January. Shippers by the *Maryland Merchant*, Mr. John Fyle—, bound from Liverpool for Maryland: Samuell Jeferson. (PRO: E190/1343/17).

3 January-20 February. Shippers by the *Herne*, Mr. Thomas Barrett, bound from London for New England: Joseph Herne, Robert Blackborne, Thomas Cuddon, John Benson, Thomas Lee, Owen Buck, John Doggett, Edward West, Benjamin Marshall, Robert Cornall, John Crow, Thomas Underwood, Thomas Potter, Thomas Lediard, Peter Hudson, William Bridges, Timothy Waldo, William Ladd, Joseph Butts, Hugh Strode, William East, Joseph Caum, George Roach, Humphrey Edwin, Thomas Cuddon. (PRO: E190/91/1).

7-10 January. Shippers by the *Delight*, Mr. Joseph Eaton, bound from London for Virginia: Thomas Dassey, John Burgis, Henry Portman, Thomas Cooke, Thomas Hunt. (PRO: E190/91/1).

20 January. Shipper by the *Anne & Elizabeth* of Liverpool, Mr. Hugh Renald, bound from Liverpool for Maryland: Anthony Wood. (PRO: E190/1343/17).

20-24 January. Shippers by the *Crowned Lyon* of Bristol bound from Bristol for Virginia: Richard Wastfield, Nicholas Pembourne. (PRO: E190/1141/1).

21-27 January. Shippers by the *Alexander* of Bristol bound from Bristol for Virginia: Samuell Clarke, James Thomas, Edward Thurston, Alexander Tompson, John Moone. (PRO: E190/1141/1).

27 January-11 March & 24 September-8 October. Shippers by the *Dolphin*, Mr. John Foye, bound from London for New England: Joseph Hyde, John Gould, Symon Wynn, Thomas Tryon, Thomas Hartley, John Philpott, Samuell Blewett, Robert Hudson, Thomas Humphrey, John Sundry, Philip Bartlett, John Ellers, Benjamin Swaine, Jonathan Leigh, Thomas Hogg, Peter Hudson, Robert Hind, William Roby, William Disher, John James, Francis Burroughs, Dillington Tankard, William Tatnall, Thomas Tervin, Thomas Mayer, John Crowe, Richard Franklin, Josias Dowry, John Sindry, Richard Shipton, Thomas Gatton, Jacob Jesson, Thomas Southby, John Hyde. (PRO: E190/91/1).

28 January. Petition of John Ward. By bond of 17 July 1674 John Winder of New York, now deceased, became indebted to him. He obtained judgment against Winder's relict and executrix, who afterwards married John Palmer, but the judgment was reversed on appeal. (APC).

4-13 February. Shippers by the *Diligence* of Bristol bound from Bristol for Virginia: James Phelps, John Seward & Co., William Morgan, Francis Ballard, Richard Dempster. (PRO: E190/1141/1).

4-20 February. Shippers by the *Hopewell*, Mr. Francis Richardson, bound from London for New York: Richard Holt, Joseph Hay, John Richardson, John Delavale, Ralph Hatley, Peter Kesterman, Peter Rich, William Cockram, Benjamin Defrane, Thomas Eccleston, Thomas Crundall. (PRO: E190/91/1).

7 February-15 March. Shippers by the *Bombay*, Mr. Joseph Bartholomew & Mr. John Wood, bound from London for New England: Benjamin Wilkes, Joseph Saudon, Grace Levingworth, Edward Middleton, Thomas Gould, John Ebourne, Edmond White, Robert Hackshaw, Thomas Hogg, Nathaniel Geuether (*sic*), Edward Hurlock, John Brett, Bedin Higham. (PRO: E190/91/1).

9 February. Shipper by the *Sarah & Elizabeth* of Bristol bound from Bristol for Virginia: Edmond Willis. (PRO: E190/1141/1).

10 February. Shipper by the *Unicorn* of Bristol bound from Bristol for Virginia: John Bubb. (PRO: E190/1141/1).

10 February. The following apprenticed in Bristol to go to Virginia by the *Chatham*, Mr. William Cole: David Pritchard to Samuel Carpendar, 4 years; Thomas Jones to same, 4 years. (BR).

12 February. The following apprenticed in Bristol to go to Antigua by the *St. Peter*, Mr. Thomas Hillman: Mary Whittwood to Thomas Hillman, 4 years; James Wells to Bartholomew & Richard Avenell, 3 years. (BR).

13 February. John Sturmey, aged 13, apprenticed from Christ's Hospital to John Jewell, commander of the *Batchelor* bound for Barbados. (CH).

18 February-16 March & 26 October-24 November. Shippers by the *Elizabeth*, Mr. John Wild, bound from London for New England: Burkett Wade, Moses Browne, Samuell Danvers, Peter Ducane, Peter Vandeputt, Bedin Higham, Richard Druen, Henry Merry, Henry Wood, Edward Fenton, William Withers, Henry Wade, Luke Nurse. (PRO: E190/91/1).

21 February. Deposition by Henry Edon, aged 22, apprentice of Abraham Jesson, citizen and tyler/bricklayer of London, that Thomas Sexton of Boston, New England, mariner, became indebted by bond of 26 September 1679 to Jesson. (LMCD).

23 February. The following apprenticed in Bristol to go to Nevis by the *Constant Martha*, Mr. John Triggs: Thomas Walker to James Cicell, 4 years; Charles Prescutt to same, 4 years; John Coxell to same, 4 years; John Mountstephens to same, 5 years; John Gwilliam to same, 4 years. (BR).

26 February-2 March. Shippers by the *John* of Boston bound from Bristol for New England: John Cary, Thomas Saunders, Thomas Lodge, John Richardson, Erasmus Doale, Thomas Dudlestone, John Purnell. (PRO: E190/1141/1).

27 February. The following apprenticed in Bristol: William Probert to Thomas Watts, 4 years Nevis by *Constant Martha*. (BR).

28 February-27 March. Shippers by the *Success* of Topsham, Mr. Stephen Withall, bound from Exeter for New England: Edward Hickman, Robert Hutchings, John Pym, Sarah Holditch, William Farwell, John Cholwell, John Ellwill, Christopher Broadridge, Humphrey Luscombe. (PRO: E190/958/8).

February. Richard Hodgskins, aged 14, apprenticed from Christ's Hospital to Peter Blake, commander of the *Elizabeth* bound for Jamaica. (CH).

February. Probate of will of Sir George Carteret, Vice-Chamberlain of the Royal Household, who had lands in New Jersey. (AW).

February. Administration of James Cox of Bristol, who died in Maryland, bachelor. (AW).

February. Middlesex prisoners reprieved to be transported to Barbados: William Blake; Dorothy Thomas; John Sutton; Ellen Holland; Mary North; Mary Dashashire alias Duck; Anne Green; William Harvey; Edward Richardson; Thomas Castilion; James Rawlings; Daniel Lathbury; Elizabeth Richardson; Sarah Mason. (EB).

2 March. Home Circuit prisoners reprieved to be transported to Barbados or Jamaica. Hertfordshire: Ann Taster of Watford; Thomas Cowper of Reed. Kent: Sarah Crofts of Beckenham; Thomas Blackman of Westerham; Hugh Cope of Westerham; Elizabeth Bateman of Westerham; William Wyles of Ash cum Ridley. Surrey: Jane Bassett wife of Basil, alias Hill alias Graves, of St. Saviour, Southwark; George Moore of Cheam; Elizabeth Smith, spinster, alias wife of John of St. Olave, Southwark. (PRO: C66/3216/32).

2 March. Oxford Circuit prisoners reprieved to be transported to America. Berkshire: Thomas Birch of Wokingham; John Quelsh of Bray; William Tarrs of Shinfield. Gloucestershire: John Stone of Oldland; Samuel Steele of Westbury; Stephen Seare of Flaxley; Katherine Smith of Westbury; John Hudson of Sodbury; William Tucker of Oldland. Herefordshire: Robert Smith of Ross; Mary Jones of ?Glascall; John Tyther of Sarnesfield. Oxfordshire: Robert Salloway of Oakerton, butcher; Francis Spratt of Wootton; John Holliocke of Adderbury; William Tanner of Ducklington; John Dickson of Wootton. Shropshire: William Coward of Whitchurch. Worcestershire: William Seymore of Alvechurch; William Phipps; Henry Wilkins of Evesham; Thomas Wood of Worcester. (PRO: C66/3217/6).

3 March. The following apprenticed in Bristol to go to Barbados by the *Constant Martha*: John Taylor to John Cicell, 4 years; Robert Fox to same, 4 years; Maurice Dawson to same, 4 years. (BR).

4-24 March. Shippers by the *Providence*, Mr. Andrew Boone, bound from London for New England: William Wright, Francis Lodwick, Henry Cotterell,

John Boyce, Anthony Storer, John Reyse, Thomas Scowen. (PRO: E190/91/1).

7-30 March. Shippers by the *Delight*, Mr. William Reyden, bound from London for New Jersey: Walter Humphreys, William Wrighton, Samuell Scott, John Reene, Thomas Rawlinson. (PRO: E190/91/1).

12 March. Norfolk Circuit prisoners reprieved to be transported to America. Bedfordshire: Thomas Morgan of Hockluffe. Norfolk: Symon Rands of West Harling; John Holland of Methwold; William Middleton of Necton; Henry Williams of Welney. Suffolk: Symon Bladwell of Barton; Thomas Rice of Gislingham. (PRO: C66/3216/33).

20-29 March. Shippers by the *Vine*, Mr. Edward Norwood, bound from London for New England: John Loggin, John Norton. (PRO: E190/91/1).

25 March. Deposition by Andrew Harbin, citizen and leatherseller of London, aged 28, that Abraham Bartholomew of Boston, New England, merchant, became indebted to Thomas Taylor, citizen and leatherseller of London, by bond of 5 July 1674. (LMCD).

22-26 March. Shippers by the *Martha & Sarah* of Bristol bound from Bristol for Virginia: Edward Thurston, Martha Higgins. (PRO: E190/1141/1).

29 March-17 April. Shippers by the *Welcome*, Mr. Edward Clements, bound from London for New York: Amos Ford, Francis Lodwick, Ralph Frewin, Henry Cotton, Francis Plumsteed, Corne Vanbostler. (PRO: E190/91/1).

27 March. The following apprenticed in Bristol: Thomas Escott to Roger Adams, 4 years Virginia. (BR).

29 March. The following apprenticed in Bristol: John David to William Falkner, 4 years Jamaica by *William & Mary*, said William Falkner Mr. (BR).

March. Administration of John Ferne of the ship *Catherine*, who died in Virginia, bachelor. (AW).

March. Somerset prisoner reprieved to be transported to Barbados: Robert Selfe of Rodden. (EB).

1 April. The following apprenticed in Bristol: Timothy Burne to Robert Hawkins, 4 years Jamaica; John Carouthers to John Harris, 4 years Virginia by *Bristol Merchant*, Mr. John Stephens. (BR).

5-22 April. Shippers by the *Black Cock*, Mr. Michaell Pack, bound from London for New England: John Shelton, John Phelps. (PRO: E190/91/1).

6 April. The following apprenticed in Bristol: John Gallaston to John Whitfield, 4 years Jamaica by *William & Mary*; John Morgan to William Williams, 4 years Barbados by *Bristol Merchant*; Walter James to same, 4 years Barbados by *Bristol Merchant*; John Severs to Edward Lane, 5 years Nevis by *Sarah*, Mr. John Snow. (BR).

19 April. The following apprenticed in Bristol: Thomas Peirson to James Bond, 4 years Virginia by *Bristol Merchant*, Mr. John Stevens. (BR).

20 April-10 May. Shippers by the *Supply* ketch bound from Bristol for New England: Samuell Price, Henry Harris, Ichebod Chacey, Henry Baker, Robert Hame(?), Thomas Saunders. (PRO: E190/1141/1).

April. Administration of William Stent of Portsmouth, Hampshire, who died on the ship *Planters Adventure* in Virginia, bachelor. (AW).

3 May. The following apprenticed in Bristol: George Chappell of Baddleton *(sic)* to Joseph Ball, 4 years by *Supply*, Mr. David Saker; William Barton to John Whitfield, 10 years Jamaica by *William & Mary*; William Inon of Haverfordwest, [Pembroke], to John Snow, 4 years Nevis by *Sarah* of Bristol. (BR).

7 May. The following apprenticed in Bristol: Jonathan Gibbons to Abraham Adams, 5 years Jamaica by *William & Mary*. (BR).

7-25 May. Shippers by the *Carolina*, Mr. John Comings, bound from London for Carolina: Earl of Shaftesbury, Joseph Puddefatt, Sir Peter Colleton, Sir Peter Filts, John Ashby, Christopher Smith, Peter Neale. (PRO: E190/91/1).

19 May-14 June. Shippers by the *Paradise*, Mr. William Eveling, bound from London for New Jersey: Edward Round, John Butcher, Francis Jaggard. (PRO: E190/91/1).

26 May. The following apprenticed in Bristol: Simon Swimer of Alvington [?Albrighton], Salop, to John Snow, 4 years Nevis by *Sarah*, said John Snow Mr. (BR).

28 May. Shipper by the *Fidelity* of New England, Mr. John Jackson, bound from Bideford for Piscataway: said John Jackson. (PRO: E190/958/5).

May. Administration of Johnson Morcombe of Bideford, Devon, who died in Virginia. (AW).

May. Administration of Isaac Key of St. Saviour, Southwark, Surrey, who died in Virginia. [*Act not completed*]. (AW).

8-21 June. Shippers by the *Hopewell* of Boston, Mr. Thomas Towley, bound from Exeter for Boston, New England: Nathaniell Pearse, Robert Tristram, Hugh Able, Robert Hutchings, Benjamin Brinley, John Cooke, Thomas Carter. (PRO: E190/958/8).

12 June. The following apprenticed in Bristol: John Griffiths of Carmarthen to William Morgan, 4 years Barbados by *Comfort*. (BR).

17 June-6 July. Shippers by the *Content*, Mr. William Johnson, bound from London for New Jersey: Richard Worgan, Isaac Warner, Henry Cotre, Thomas Hogg, David Conyard, Thomas Potter. (PRO: E190/91/1).

18 June. The following apprenticed in Bristol: Richard Britten of Audley, [?Staffs], to William Hooper, 7 years Nevis by *Sarah*. (BR).

21 June-28 July. Shippers by the *Assistance*, Mr. James Stronge, bound from London for Virginia: Marina Goodhand, John Collingwood, Thomas Hollis, Pres (*sic*) Fenton, Thomas Hogg, Roger Lillington, Margaret Prewe, Margaret Green, John Bowley, John Blake. (PRO: E190/91/1).

22-25 June. Shippers by the *James*, Mr. Joseph Oliver, bound from London for New England: James Farmer, Richard Walton, Richard Young. (PRO: E190/91/1).

23-25 June. Shipper by the *Unity* of London bound from Plymouth for New England: James Boarken, George Orchard. (PRO: E190/1044/21).

25 June. Shipper by the *Exchange* of Newcastle, Mr. John Wettwang, bound from Newcastle for New England: said John Wettwang. (PRO: E190/199/4).

26 June. The following apprenticed in Bristol: Thomas Jones of Llantrishen, Glam, to Maryland by *Samuel*, Mr. Warnes. (BR).

30 June. Deposition by John Whitlock of Mansfield, Nottinghamshire, clerk aged 55, and Johanna Harris, aged 62, wife of Henry Harris of Finchley, Middlesex, gardener, that Anthony Whitlock of Lambeth, Surrey, husbandman, is the only child now living of John Whitlock, formerly of Lambeth, silk weaver, deceased, who was a brother of Thomas Whitlock of Rappahannock River, Virginia, planter. (LMCD).

June. Probate of will of Henry Isham of Henrico County, Virginia. (AW).

June. Probate of will of John Bland of St. Olave Hart Street, London, whose wife, Sarah Bland, was in Virginia. (AW).

June. Administration of Thomas Sexton of Boston, New England, who died in Deal, Kent. (AW).

June. Probate of will of Elizabeth Kent of Sonning, Berkshire, widow, whose brother, Carey Latham, was in New England. (AW).

June. Administration with will of John Mayow of Bath, Somerset, who died in St. Paul Covent Garden, Middlesex, doctor of laws, whose daughter, Mary Slater, was in New York. (AW).

June. Probate of will of Richard Smith of the ship *Duke of York*, who died in Virginia or at sea, bachelor. (AW).

1 July-31 August. Shippers by the *Henry & Ann*, Mr. Thomas Arnold, bound from London for Virginia: Isaac Butler, Samuell Pownall, John Brett. (PRO: E190/91/1).

2 July. The following apprenticed in Bristol: Thomas Smart of Glamorganshire to Abraham Wilde, 4 years Barbados by *Samuel*; Walter Thomas to same, 7 years Barbados by *Samuel*. (BR).

3 July. The following apprenticed in Bristol: Hugh Reece to Abraham Wilde, 4 years Maryland. (BR).

9 July. The following apprenticed in Bristol: James Fry to Abraham Wilde, 4 years Maryland by *Samuel*. (BR).

12 July. The following apprenticed in Bristol to go to Virginia by the *Richard & James*, Mr. John Opie: William Jones to Bridget Parker, 6 years; John William Griffits to William Morgan, 4 years. (BR).

13 July. The following apprenticed in Bristol: William Webb to Abraham Wilde, 5 years Maryland by *Samuel*. (BR).

13-17 July. Shippers by the *Love*, Mr. Oswald Wheatly, bound from London for Virginia: Richard Nicholson, John Welch, William Withers. (PRO: E190/91/1).

13-23 July. Shipper by the *Unicorn*, Mr. Norrington, bound from London for Virginia: Peter Gill. (PRO: E190/91/1).

13 July-17 August. Shippers by the *Mary*, Edward Roads, bound from London for Virginia: James Biggs, Stephen Montague, Thomas Peachey, Anthony Reynolds, William Tyghe. (PRO: E190/91/1).

14 July. The following apprenticed in Bristol to go to Virginia by the *Richard & James*: David Bynam to William Morgan, 4 years; John Price to same, 4 years. (BR).

14 July-31 August. Shippers by the *Adventure*, Mr. Robert Ransom, bound from London for Virginia: George Richards, Stephen Mountague. (PRO: E190/91/1).

15 July. The following apprenticed in Bristol: Thomas Pondle to William Morgan, 4 years Virginia by *Richard & James*. (BR).

19 July. The following apprenticed in Bristol: George Morgan to Abraham Wilde, 6 years Maryland by *Samuel*. (BR).

19-21 July. Shippers by the *Crown Mallago*, Mr. John Francis, bound from London for Virginia: Barnaby Dunch, William Mead. (PRO: E190/91/1).

20 July-13 August. Shippers by the *Endeavour*, Mr. Benjamin Gillam, bound from London for New England: Joshua Pordage, Josiah Newy, Robert Patten, Granad Chester, John Sherbrooke, Christopher Hamilton, James Seely. (PRO: E190/91/1).

20 July-17 August. Shippers by the *Richard* of Bristol bound from Bristol for Virginia: Richard Pope, Peter Waddinge. (PRO: E190/1141/1).

20 July-20 September. Shippers by the *Return* of Boston bound from Bristol for New England: John Bennett, Thomas Dudlestone, Samuell Price, William Minor, John Hollister, John Richardson, Joseph Bullock, Michaell Pope, Richard Buckham, John England, Thomas Tayer. (PRO: E190/1141/1).

22 July. The following apprenticed in Bristol: Andrew Wauklyn to George Cary, 4 years Virginia by *Samuel*, Mr. William Sanby. (BR).

24 July-4 August. Shippers by the *Prosperous* of Hull, Mr. William Marr, bound from Hull for Virginia: Edward Nightingale, Richard Metcalfe, George Conner. (PRO: E190/323/12).

27 July. The following apprenticed in Bristol: Joseph Westeson, a Dane, to David Jones, 4 years Virginia by *Richard & James*; Jonathan Wyn to Henry Hidron, 4 years Virginia. (BR).

27 July-28 August. Shippers by the *Richard*, Mr. Thomas Jowles, bound from London for New England: John Orme, Michael Standcliff, Benjamin Tayton, John Saxton, Joshua Pordage, William Yate, James Pack, Richard Parrott, John Fisher, Richard Boswell, Thomas Bands, Edward Lardner, James Tryton. (PRO: E190/91/1).

28-31 July. Shippers by the *Samuell & Mary* of Bristol bound from Bristol for Virginia: William Swymer, Nicholas Lux. (PRO: E190/1141/1).

28 July-19 August. Shippers by the *Comfort* of Bristol bound from Bristol for Virginia: John Dudlestone, Thomas Dudlestone, Richard Pope, Francis Fisher, Edward Field. (PRO: E190/1141/1).

30-31 July. Shippers by the *Adventure*, Mr. Ralph Cooper, bound from London for Virginia: John Forth, John Wall. (PRO: E190/91/1).

July. Administration of Thomas Whitlock of Virginia, bachelor. (AW).

July. Probate of will of Margaret Cheeseman of Bermondsey, Surrey, widow, whose kinsmen, Lemuel Mason, Elizabeth Theleball and John Matthews, were in Virginia. (AW).

July. Administration of Gilbert Cage of the ship *Hopewell*, who died in Virginia. (AW).

July. Isaac Ward, aged 11, apprenticed from Christ's Hospital to Robert Conaway, commander of the *Prince* bound for Virginia. (CH).

2 August. The following apprenticed in Bristol: James Stankliffe to Philip Neson, 4 years Nevis by *Nevis Merchant*. (BR).

2-27 August. Shippers by the English-built *Phoenix* of Bridlington bound from Bristol for New England: Michaell Hunt, John Willoughby, Thomas Speede. (PRO: E190/1141/1).

3 August. The following apprenticed in Bristol to go to Maryland by the *Samuel*, Mr. Thomas Warnes: Thomas Hayford to John Parker, 4 years; Philip Morgan to Abraham Wilde, 4 years. (BR).

3-5 August. Shipper by the *Margaret*, Mr. Edward Watkins, bound from London for Virginia: John Bawden. (PRO: E190/91/1).

3-10 August. Shippers by the *Dispatch*, Mr. Josiah Willis, bound from London for Virginia: Francis Bill, William Cox. (PRO: E190/91/1).

4 August. Shipper by the *David* of Weymouth, Mr. Robert Barker, bound from Weymouth for Virginia: Mathew Pitt. (PRO: E190/883/13).

4 August. The following apprenticed in Bristol: John Hagly to William Sanky, 4 years Virginia by *Samuel*; George Millard of Wotton Underedge, [Glos], glover, to Edward Fielding, 5 years Jamaica by *Lamb*; John Harding to William Sanky, 6 years Virginia by *Samuel*. (BR).

4 August. Petition of Captain Henry Wilkinson that he may be granted use of the fireship *Spanish Merchant* lying at Deptford to transport himself, his servants, and 150 passengers to Carolina. (APC).

4 August-3 September. Shippers by the *Benjamin*, Mr. Edward Paine, bound from London for Virginia: Edward Round, Thomas Godsell, John Bryton, Edward Pye, Ann Hoyle, Nicholas Hayward, Strangeway Mudd, John Pryor, John Houblon. (PRO: E190/91/1).

7 August. Shipper by the *Merchants Delight* of Bideford, Mr. Robert King, bound from Bideford for Virginia: Hartwell Buck. (PRO: E190/958/5).

7-26 August. Shippers by the *Samuell* of Yarmouth bound from Bristol for Maryland: Joseph Saunders, Peter Waddinge, William Morgan, Thomas Pope. (PRO: E190/1141/1).

7-27 August. Shippers by the *Mary*, Mr. John Consett, bound from London for Virginia: Joseph Dyes, Richard Buller, Thomas Walsh, Edward Blake, Hugh White, Frederick Gronen. (PRO: E190/91/1).

10 August. The following apprenticed in Bristol to go by the *Comfort*, Mr. William Andrews: Richard Williams to George Tyte, 4 years Virginia; William Popejoy to Thomas Lawrence, 7 years Maryland. (BR).

10 August. Shippers by the *Hopewell*, Mr. Michael Yoakly, bound from London for Virginia: John Blackall, John Osgood. (PRO: E190/91/1).

11-19 August. Shippers by the *Thomas & Nicholas* of Bideford, Mr. Thomas Courtis, bound from Bideford for Maryland: Henry Brayley, Hartwell Buck. (PRO: E190/958/5).

11-23 August. Shippers by the *Elizabeth*, Mr. Peter Paggen, bound from London for Virginia: John West, John Brett. (PRO: E190/91/1).

12 August. Shipper by the *Elizabeth* of Weymouth, Mr. John Cox, bound from Weymouth for Virginia: James Gould. (PRO: E190/883/13).

14 August. Deposition by John Crouch of Westminster, Middlesex, gent aged 60, that William Freeman of King Street, Westminster, gent, is the oldest surviving son of Thomas Freeman, formerly of Wallingford Castle, Berkshire, gent, deceased, and brother of Col. Bridges Freeman and Bennett Freeman of Virginia, deceased. William Freeman also had a sister, Elizabeth Freeman, who went to her brother Bridges in Virginia. Deposition by David Bennett of St. Martin in the Fields, Middlesex, gent aged 51, that his father, David Bennett, was a brother of Thomas Freeman's wife. (LMCD).

16 August. The following apprenticed in Bristol: Thomas Gillman to John Ring, 4 years Virginia by *Nevis Merchant*, Mr. Arthur Grant. (BR).

16-21 August. Shippers by the *Richard & Elizabeth*, Mr. Nicholas Prynn, bound from London for Virginia: Richard Booth, John Mann, John Strange. (PRO: E190/91/1).

17-31 August. Shippers by the *Susan*, Mr. Hugh Davis, bound from London for New York: Mark Mortimer, Thomas Hart, John Banden, Henry Cott, Thomas Forshaw, Henry Maynard, Thomas Phipps. (PRO: E190/91/1).

17 August-4 September. Shippers by the *Charles*, Mr. Samuel Phillips, bound from London for Virginia: William Dodson, Thomas Ellers, Edward Rounde, John Worthington, Richard Burke, John Abbington. (PRO: E190/91/1).

19 August. The following apprenticed in Bristol to go to Virginia by the *Comfort*: Henry Foote to Abraham Wilde with his father's consent, 7 years; George Holmes to Christopher Haswell, 4 years; Ann Smith to William Dymor, 4 years. (BR).

19 August-7 September. Shippers by the *Constant*, Mr. Thomas Smith, bound from London for Virginia: Thomas Parker, Jacob David, John Fleete. (PRO: E190/91/1).

20 August. The following apprenticed in Bristol: Alicia Wattkins to John C——dy, 4 years Maryland by *Richard & James*; Joseph Brookes to Abraham Wilde, 5 years Maryland by *Samuel*; Peter Barchis of Chester to Peter Liss——, 4 years Nevis by *Bristol Factor*, Mr. Roger Drew. (BR).

21 August. The following apprenticed in Bristol to go to Nevis by the *Nevis Merchant*: Mary Puttley to Arthur Grant, 4 years; Joel Burnhole to William Herd, 4 years. (BR).

21 August-17 September. Shippers by the *Recovery*, Mr. Thomas Hasted, bound from London for Virginia: Daniell Jackson, John Redman, Luke Nurse. (PRO: E190/91/1).

25 August. Shipper by the *William* of Bristol bound from Bristol for Virginia: Arthur Hart. (PRO: E190/1141/1).

25 August-2 September. Shippers by the *John* of Bristol bound from Bristol for Virginia: Thomas Pope, Edward Dyer, James Holloway. (PRO: E190/1141/1).

26 August-8 September. Shippers by the *Concord* of Bristol bound from Bristol for Virginia: Thomas Skuse, William Swymer, Robert Day, Roger Nevill, Joseph Clark, Symon Hurle. (PRO: E190/1141/1).

29 August. The following apprenticed in Bristol: Alexander Mocollock to John Fowles, 4 years Barbados by *Arthur & Mary*. (BR).

30 August. Shipper by the *Concord* of Newcastle, Mr. Edward Robinson, bound from Newcastle for Virginia: Michaell Taylor. (PRO: E190/198/13).

30 August. Deposition by George Shallcross of London, salter aged 33, that on 5 March 1676 he shipped goods on board the *Zebulon* of Boston, New England, Mr. William Greenough. (LMCD).

30 August-1 September. Shipper by the *Submission* of Liverpool, Mr. James Settle, bound from Liverpool for Maryland: Thomas Clayton. (PRO: E190/1343/17).

30 August-4 September. Shippers by the *Thomas & Edward*, Mr. John Browne, bound from London for Virginia: John Wagstaff, Peregrine Browne, John Collingwood. (PRO: E190/91/1).

August. Frances Guy of St. Botolph Bishopsgate, London, widow, whose brother, William Clutterbuck, was in New England. Probate to John Heyth, M.D. (AW).

August. Administration of William Thrasher of the ship *Success*, who died at sea, widower. (AW).

August. Administration of Samuel Nevett of London, who died in Virginia, bachelor. (AW).

1 September. The following apprenticed in Bristol: Robert Lawrence to Robert Lancaster, 7 years Virginia by *Bristol Factor*. (BR).

2-20 September. Shippers by the *Diligence* of Bristol bound from Bristol for Virginia: James Holloway, Richard Dempster, James Wall, Samuell Combs. (PRO: E190/1141/1).

7 September. Deposition by James Hulbert of London, draper aged 24, that he was servant to William Welles of London, draper, who in August 1678 shipped goods to Samuel Haugh of Boston, New England. (LMCD).

8-9 September. Shippers by the *Mary* of Bristol bound from Bristol for Virginia: Thomas Pope, James Holloway. (PRO: E190/1141/1).

8 September-2 October. Shippers by the *Duke of York*, Mr. John Purvis, bound from London for Virginia: Thomas Poyntz, William Churchill, Robert Tay. (PRO: E190/91/1).

9 September-13 October. Shippers by the *Samuel & Thomas*, Mr. Thomas Jenner, bound from London for New England: William Palmer, Thomas Jenner, John Crow, Isaac Tellers, John Rayner, William Disher. (PRO: E190/91/1).

10 September. The following apprenticed in Bristol: William Lewis to John Shidder, 3 years Barbados by *Speedwell*, Mr. Hugh Rainstubb; Richard Roberts of Salop to Robert Williams, 4 years Virginia by *Richard & James*. (BR).

10-13 September. Shippers by the *Friendship*, Mr. William Hindmore, bound from London for Virginia: Anthony Mason, Thomas Wych. (PRO: E190/91/1).

13-18 September. Shippers by the *Expedition* of Bideford, Mr. John Atkins, bound from Bideford for Maryland: Thomas Lawrence, John Davie. (PRO: E190/958/5).

13 September-14 October. Shippers by the *Richard & James* bound from Bristol for Virginia: Marmaduke Bowdler, George Hawes, Henry Gibbs, Peter Waddinge, Robert Bayly, Robert Smith, Francis Watkins, James Pope, Edward Perrin, Thomas Day, William Saulsbury. (PRO: E190/1141/1).

14 September-2 October. Shippers by the *Prince*, Mr. Robert Conway, bound from London for Virginia: William Clapton, Thomas Hemming. (PRO: E190/91/1).

16 September. The following apprenticed in Bristol: John Thomas to ———— ———, 4 years Maryland by *Richard & James*; George Barnaby to Arthur Grant, 4 years Nevis or Montserrat by *Nevis Merchant*. (BR).

16 September-1 October. Shippers by the *Barnaby*, Mr. Matthew Ryder, bound from London for Virginia: Thomas Starke, Thomas Fife, Silvester Deane. (PRO: E190/91/1).

20-23 September. Shippers by the *Augustine*, Mr. Zachary Taylor, bound from London for Virginia: Richard Nicholson, Ann Hoyle, Francis Crampfield, Samuell Pettiford, Arthur North, John Viner, Nowell Bassano. (PRO: E190/91/1).

22 September. Shipper by the *Truelove* of Bideford, Mr. James Hunkins, bound from Bideford for Maryland: Abraham Heiman. (PRO: E190/958/5).

22 September-4 October. Shippers by the *Hopewell*, Mr. John Rudds, bound from London for Virginia: James Steward, Henry Robins, Sarah Drymond, Thomas Askew. (PRO: E190/91/1).

23 September. Shipper by the *Robert* of Poole, Mr. Robert Bennett, bound from Poole for Virginia: William Orchard. (PRO: E190/883/11).

24 September. The following apprenticed in Bristol: Edward Davis to Thomas Cary, 4 years Virginia by *[Bristol] Factor*; Ann Douding to Marmaduke

Williams, 4 years Maryland by *Richard & James*; Thomas Williams to same, 4 years Maryland by *Richard & James*. (BR).

24 September-4 October. Shippers by the *John*, Mr. Daniell Bradley, bound from London for Virginia: Lawrence Fines, John Forth, William Woolfe, Thomas Nisbett, Thomas Wych. (PRO: E190/91/1).

25 September. The following apprenticed in Bristol: Mary Urlin to Robert Lancaster, 4 years Virginia by *Bristol Factor*; Mary Attwood to Thomas Attwood, 4 years Virginia by *Richard & James*. (BR).

26 September. Shipper by the *Unity* pink of Lyme, Mr. Robert Cox, bound from Lyme for Virginia: John Burridge. (PRO: E190/883/14).

28 September-25 October. Shippers by the *Crowned Lyon* of Bristol bound from Bristol for Virginia: Charles Plomer, William Clark, Richard Wastfield, Alexander Doleman, William Carpenter, John Knight, Samuell Tipton, William Swymer. (PRO: E190/1141/1).

30 September-6 October. Shippers by the *Hanna*, Mr. Peter Poyson, bound from London for Virginia: Ellis Best, Hugh Rowcliff, Thomas Rodbart, John Tubley, Thomas Frampton, Thomas Boughey. (PRO: E190/91/1).

September. Administration of William Anderson of Shadwell, Middlesex, who died in Virginia, bachelor. (AW).

1 October. The following apprenticed in Bristol: William Griffin to Edward Berkin, 4 years Virginia by *[Bristol] Factor*. (BR).

1-4 October. Shippers by the *Speedwell*, Mr. Thomas Larimore, bound from London for Virginia: Henry Lucas, William Anderson, Thomas Salter. (PRO: E190/91/1).

1-11 October. Shippers by the *Increase*, Mr. John Lynes, bound from London for Virginia: Thomas Cooke, Thomas Alcock. (PRO: E190/91/1).

1-19 October. Shippers by the *Merchants Content*, Mr. Charles Partis, bound from London for Maryland: Thomas Elwys, Samuell Gibbs, William Tyghe. (PRO: E190/91/1).

4 October. The following apprenticed in Bristol: Andrew Wild to Samuel Clarke, 4 years Nevis by *Content*; Thomas Hamond to Roger Drew, 4 years Virginia by *[Bristol] Factor*. (BR).

6 October. The following apprenticed in Bristol: John Fisher to Edward Birkin, 4 years Virginia by *[Bristol] Factor*. (BR).

7 October. The following apprenticed in Bristol: Tobias Fowler to William James, 4 years Virginia by *Bristol Factor*. (BR).

8-19 October. Shippers by the *Lyon*, Mr. Jeremy Rich, bound from London for Maryland: Benjamin Roser, Matthew Paine. (PRO: E190/91/1).

8-22 October. Shippers by the *John*, Mr. Daniel Pensax, bound from London for Maryland: Thomas Cooke, George Cornish. (PRO: E190/91/1).

9 October. Deposition by John Foye of Boston, New England, mariner aged 40, that Samuel Shrimpton signed a general release to Thomas Nosman on 12 July 1680. (LMCD).

11 October. The following apprenticed in Bristol: Richard Parker to Robert Lancaster, 4 years Virginia by *Bristol Factor*. (BR).

12 October. Shipper by the *Supply*, Mr. Thomas Canham, bound from London for Virginia: Henry Lucas. (PRO: E190/91/1).

13 October. Shipper by the *Seraphim* of Barnstaple, Mr. Walter Gist, bound from Bideford for Maryland: said Walter Gist. (PRO: E190/958/5).

13-14 October. Shippers by the *Virginia Factor*, Mr. Robert Joles, bound from London for Maryland: Francis Maulden, Thomas Elwayes. (PRO: E190/91/1).

13-19 October. Shippers by the *Exeter Merchant*, Mr. Thomas Friend, bound from Exeter for Virginia: Richard Connant, John Pym, Robert Dabinet, Samuell Axe. (PRO: E190/958/8).

15 October. The following apprenticed in Bristol: Mary Clarke to Peter Liscombe, 4 years Virginia by *[Bristol] Factor*. (BR).

15 October-3 November. Shippers by the *Vine* of Liverpool, Mr. William Preeson, bound from Liverpool for Maryland: Robert Crossman, William Browne. (PRO: E190/1343/17).

15 October-6 November. Shippers by the *Delight*, Mr. Thomas Greeneway, bound from London for New York: Benjamin Dejeane, John Middleton, John Dawden, Thomas Hogg. (PRO: E190/91/1).

16 October. Shipper by the *Baltimore*, Mr. George Purvis, bound from London for Virginia: Edward Leman. (PRO: E190/91/1).

19-23 October. Shippers by the *Elizabeth* of Exeter, Mr. Nicholas Sainthill, bound from Exeter for Virginia: Thomas Brooking, Malachy Keale, James Fulwood, Joseph Maudit. (PRO: E190/958/8).

19-26 October. Shippers by the *Rose & Crown*, Mr. Bartholomew Clements, bound from London for Virginia: William Shakerly, Richard Ballard, Nathaniel Grantham. (PRO: E190/91/1).

20 October. The following apprenticed in Bristol to go to Virginia by the *Bristol Factor*: Anthony Drew to Robert Lancaster, 4 years; Reece Lloyd to Edward Birkin, 4 years; Lewis Lloyd to same, 4 years. (BR).

21-27 October. Shippers by the *Bristol Factor* bound from Bristol for Virginia: Stephen Watts, Richard Franklin, John Jones, Bartholomew Robinson, William Smith. (PRO: E190/1141/1).

22 October. Shipper by the *Hart* of Bideford, Mr. Henry Perrin, bound from Bideford for Virginia: John Ford. (PRO: E190/958/5).

22 October. The following apprenticed in Bristol: William Attkins to William Carpendar, 4 years Virginia by *Richard & James*. (BR).

25 October. The following apprenticed in Bristol: Edward Hulbert to William Carpendar, 4 years Virginia by *Richard & James*. (BR).

25-26 October. Shippers by the *Globe*, Mr. Samuel Groome, bound from London for Virginia: Jeremy Tedder, James Braine. (PRO: E190/91/1).

26 October. The following apprenticed in Bristol: Thomas Merchant to Robert Parker, 6 years Virginia by *[Bristol] Factor*. (BR).

October. Administration of George Joy of Boston, New England. (AW).

October. Administration with will of Hugh Nevett of Virginia, bachelor. (AW).

3-11 November. Shippers by the *John & Benjamin*, Mr. Mathew Trim, bound from London for Virginia: Edward Harper, John Mathew. (PRO: E190/91/1).

5 November. The following apprenticed in Bristol: Roger Griffith to John Harris, 4 years Maryland by *Maryland Merchant*, Mr. George Tyte. (BR).

6 November. Shippers by the *Sarah & Elizabeth* bound from Bristol for Virginia: Richard Hart, Daniell Inon, Henry Phelps. (PRO: E190/1141/1).

10 November. The following apprenticed in Bristol to go to Virginia by the *Maryland Merchant*: John Davis to Thomas Speed, 4 years; Richard Millard to Zacharias Smith, 7 years; William Millard to same, 9 years; George Sanders to Bryan Tandy, 4 years; Ann Sanders to same, 4 years. (BR).

10-20 November. Shippers by the *James* of Plymouth bound from Plymouth for Virginia: Arthur Cotten, William Martyn, John Light. (PRO: E190/1044/21).

13-20 November. Shippers by the *Maryland Merchant* bound from Bristol for Virginia: Thomas Speed, George Tite, John Hudson, Francis Rogers, John Woodward. (PRO: E190/1141/1).

15-18 November. Shippers by the *James & Thomas* of Plymouth bound for Virginia: Thomas Warne, John Rogers, Marke Batt. (PRO: E190/1044/21).

15-20 November. Shippers by the *Francis & Mary* bound from Bristol for Virginia: Thomas Pope, Samuell Clarke, Edward Dyer, Michaell Pope. (PRO: E190/1141/1).

15 November-6 December. Shippers by the *John*, Mr. Thomas Groves, bound from London for Virginia: Thomas Bird, Richard Buller, John Morris. (PRO: E190/91/1).

17 November. The following apprenticed in Bristol: John Argos to John Hudson, 7 years Virginia by *Maryland Merchant*. (BR).

18 November. Shipper by the *Concord*, Mr. Thomas Hurlock, bound from London for Virginia: John Handford. (PRO: E190/91/1).

19 November. The following apprenticed in Bristol to go to Virginia by the *Maryland Merchant*: Ann Browne to Zacharia Smith, 4 years; Ann Martyn to same, 4 years. (BR).

24-25 November. Shippers by the *Alathea* bound from Bristol for Virginia: Richard Benson, Edward Watkins. (PRO: E190/1141/1).

24-27 November. Shippers by the *Victory* of Bristol bound from Bristol for Virginia: Edward Perrin, John Haskins, Samuell Packer, Thomas Burges, Peter Younge. (PRO: E190/1141/1).

24-27 November. Shippers by the *Alexander* bound from Bristol for Virginia: Alexander Tompson, Samuell Clarke, Edward Thurston, James Thomas. (PRO: E190/1141/1).

November. Administration with will of Thomas Stolyon of Warbleton, Sussex, who had goods in New England. (AW).

November. Probate of will of George Moone of Fremington, Devon, who died in Virginia, mariner. (AW).

1 December. Shipper by the *Maryland Merchant* of Hull, Mr. Robert Raine, bound from Hull for Virginia: Edward Nightingale. (PRO: E190/323/12).

3 December. The following apprenticed in Bristol: George Sherland to William Scott, 4 years Virginia by *Resolution*, said William Scott Mr. (BR).

5 December. The following apprenticed in Bristol: William Tayler son of William Tayler of Landsend, Wilts, to Joseph Mocker, 5 years Virginia by *Unicorn*, Mr. Thomas Cooper. (BR).

7 December. Home Circuit prisoners reprieved to be transported to Barbados or Jamaica. Essex: Daniel Alban of Epping. Kent: Richard Spratt of Kennington; John Hinde of Rainham. Surrey: Thomas Goodyer of St. Olave, Southwark. Susex: William Gandy of Chissington. (PRO: C66/3218/16).

7 December. The following apprenticed in Bristol: Robert Sample to Christopher Jones, 5 years Virginia by *Stephen*; Edward Evins to William Scott, 4 years Virginia by *Resolution*; Nathaniel Jones to same, 4 years Virginia by *Resolution*. (BR).

7-18 December. Shippers by the *Resolution* bound from Bristol for Virginia: William Smith, Edward Martindale, Peter Waddinge, James Biggs, Samuell Davis, Walter Stephens, Michaell White, Michael Pope, Thomas Scroope. (PRO: E190/1141/1).

11 December. The following apprenticed in Bristol: Mary Price to William Jackson, 4 years Maryland by *Society*, Mr. Philip Jordan; Thomas Ragland to same, 9 years Maryland by *Society*; Samuel Workeman to same, 9 years Maryland by *Society*; John Peirce to Thomas Roch, 4 years Jamaica by *[Royal] Oak*. (BR).

11-17 December. Shippers by the *[Constant] Friendship*, Mr. William Fowles, bound from London for Virginia: Stephen Mountague, Micajah Perry. (PRO: E190/91/1).

13-15 December. Shippers by the *Unicorn* bound from Bristol for Virginia: Rachel Finck, Joseph Clark, James Millard, William Ollive. (PRO: E190/1141/1).

13 December. Shippers by the *Stephen* of Bristol bound from Bristol for Virginia: Richard Crump, William Carpender. (PRO: E190/1141/1).

23 December. Shipper by the *Anne & Elizabeth* of Liverpool, Mr. Hugh Renald, bound from Liverpool for Maryland: John Hodgson. (PRO: E190/1343/17).

December. Probate of will of John Curtis of Boston, New England, who died on H.M. ship *English Tyger*, bachelor. (AW).

1680. John Howman, aged 13, apprenticed from Christ's Hospital to Richard Cobb, commander of the *Resolution* bound for Barbados. (CH).

1680. Charles Sherbourne, aged 15, apprenticed from Christ's Hospital to Samuel Jones, commander of the *Joanna* bound for Jamaica. (CH).

1681

1-17 January. Shippers by the *Friends Adventure* of London, Mr. James Tattnam, bound from Southampton for New York: Richard Loving for William Darvall, Cornelius Darvall and Peter Jacobson. (PRO: E190/831/6).

1-20 January. Shippers by the *George*, Mr. Richard Shepherd, bound from London for Maryland: Barnaby Dunch, John Bawdon. (PRO: E190/99/1).

1-27 January. Shippers by the *Daniel*, Mr. Thomas Browne, bound from London for Virginia: John Forth, Thomas Sandes, Joshua Hassell. (PRO: E190/99/1).

3 January. Shipper by the *Elizabeth* of Poole, Mr. William Pike, bound from Poole for Maryland: James Gould. (PRO: E190/884/6).

7 January. The following apprenticed in Bristol: Phillip Lambert to Thomas Rosser, 4 years Virginia by *Society*. (BR).

11-12 January. Shippers by the *Society* of Bristol bound from Bristol for Virginia: Phillip Jorden, George Hawes. (PRO: E190/1142/3).

12 January. The following apprenticed in Bristol: William Prigg of Westerleigh, Glos, yeoman, to John Knight, merchant, and Anne his wife, 7 years Nevis. (BR).

22 January. Shipper by the *Ark* of Brighton, Mr. James Fendall, bound from Weymouth for Virginia: David Arbuthnot. (PRO: E190/884/2).

26 January. Shipper by the *Hope*, Capt. Sampson, bound from London for New England: John Loggins. (PRO: E190/99/1).

26 January-28 February. Shippers by the English-built *Gabriel* of Bristol, Mr. James Limbry, bound from Bristol for New England: Thomas Cole, James Porter, Thomas Lodge. (PRO: E190/1142/3).

28 January-1 March. Shippers by the *Freeman* of Liverpool, Mr. Edward Tarlton, bound from Liverpool for Maryland: James Jones, Marke Condea. (PRO: E190/1343/2).

3 February-14 March. Shippers by the *Edward & Ann*, Mr. John Wally, bound from London for New England: Samuel Grant, William Talbot, John Lake, Robert Hind, William Gore, John Ward, Thomas Carleton, John Wase, Joseph Pordage, George Moncke, David Waterhouse, Richard Joyce, Robert Rowland, John Sindry, William Pate, Lawrence French, Nehemiah Bourne, John Van Brookhoven, Thomas Elkin, Joseph Cam, Robert Carnoll, John Daniell, Daniel Foxcroft, Ralph Ingram, James Goldham, John Anderton, Edward Harrington. (PRO: E190/99/1).

9-12 February. Shipper by the *Hopewell*, Mr. George Heathcott, bound from London for New York: Edward Barker. (PRO: E190/99/1).

16 February. Shipper by the *William & Elizabeth* of Poole, Mr. William Phippard, bound from Poole for Newfoundland and Virginia: said William Phippard. (PRO: E190/884/6).

17 February. Midland Circuit prisoners reprieved to be transported to America. Lincolnshire: Joseph Ward alias Manners of Hagnaby; Thomas Jackson of Glentham. Northamptonshire: Matthew Cooper of Northampton. Warwickshire: John Gardner of Birmingham; Humphrey Bucknall of Birmingham; John Ryley of Birmingham. London: Thomas Arres. Worcestershire: Richard Friend of Easum. (PRO: C66/3222/20).

19 February. Norfolk Circuit prisoners reprieved to be transported to America. Bedfordshire: Peter Clarke of Edworth; Henry Clifton alias Clipps of Thornecutt, Morhill. Norfolk: Edward Murgett of Baconsthorpe; Adam Lucocke of Blickling; Francis Browne of Walsoken. Suffolk: John Brand of Bildeston. (PRO: C66/3219/7).

19 February. Oxford Circuit prisoners reprieved to be transported to America. Gloucestershire: Edward Devett alias Dewitt of Stroud; John Inon of Almondsbury & Westbury on Trym; Peter Barron of Thornbury. Herefordshire: William Sergeant of Peterstow; Thomas Merick of Woolhope; John Clarke of Ledbury. Oxfordshire: Robert Waite of Long Hanborough. Shropshire: Richard Hamonds of Hopesay. Staffordshire: Thomas Cooper of Leek; Dorcas Dugmore of West Bromwich; John Ireland alias Chambers. Worcestershire: John Perkes of Stourbridge; Elizabeth Botfield of St. John, Worcester. (PRO: C66/3219/11).

25 February-7 April. Shippers by the *Endeavour*, Mr. Francis Richardson, bound from London for New York: Benjamin De Jeane, James Hayes, Francis Lodwick, Edward Baxter, George Rosh, John Essington, William Markes, John Wright, Thomas Forshew, Thomas Crundall. (PRO: E190/99/1).

February. Samuell Burgis, aged 15, apprenticed from Christ's Hospital to Christopher Ravens, commander of the *Loyal Goring* bound for Barbados. (CH).

5 March. Newgate prisoners reprieved to be transported to Barbados. London: Susan Smith, widow; Elizabeth Sparkes alias Zouch, spinster; Thomas Bates; Elizabeth Wilkinson, spinster; Simon Lee; Thomas Bolton alias Demarry; Katherine Nevill, spinster; Mary Smith; Isabel Marsh, spinster. Middlesex: Elizabeth Hicks, wife of John Hicks of St. Martin in the Fields; Blanch Thomas of the same, spinster; Edward Conway alias Connoway of Islington; Mary Johnson of St. Paul Covent Garden, spinster; Priscilla Wynne alias Fielder of the same, spinster; Isabel Gawden, wife of John Gawden of St. Andrew Holborn; Dorothy Mathews, wife of James Mathews of the same; John Wright of Bow; Elizabeth Hull of St. Giles in the Fields; Katherine Johnson alias

Dodson of the same, spinster; Anne Ditcher, wife of John Ditcher of the same; Francis Small of Enfield; Anne Carter, wife of John Carter, alias Anne Harman, spinster, of Whitechapel; Philip Demerry of Hornsey; Martha Cooke of St. Mary Savoy, spinster; John Watkins and Edward Whitwick of Clerkenwell for manslaughter; Thomas Grandwell alias Bigge; Elizabeth Staines alias Allen of St. Botolph Aldgate, spinster; Elizabeth Husk of the same, spinster; John Ayris of St. Pancras; John Bayley of Stepney; Thomas Mare of the same; William Abbott of the same. (PRO: C66/3222/17).

5 March-8 April. Shippers by the *Elizabeth*, Mr. John Wild, bound from London for New England: Jacob Jesson, James Hayes, Thomas Maylin, John Hill, Robert Gower. (PRO: E190/99/1).

7 March. Shipper by the *Adventure* of Mostyn, Mr. John Thomas, bound from Liverpool for Virginia: David Poole. (PRO: E190/1343/2).

11 March-7 May. Shippers by the *St. Christopher*, Mr. William Chambers, bound from London for Carolina: Henry Wilson, George Warburton, Sir Peter Colleton, Richard Urry. (PRO: E190/99/1).

19 March-9 April. Shippers by the *Sarah* of Bristol bound from Bristol for New England: William French, John Richardson, William Middlecott, Thomas Gouldny, Thomas Saunders. (PRO: E190/1142/3).

21-26 March. Shippers by the *Dove* of Bristol bound from Bristol for New England: Robert Yate, Thomas Earle, Giles Tapley. (PRO: E190/1142/3).

23 March-6 May. Shippers by the *Elizabeth & Francis*, Mr. John Brookes, bound from London for New England: John Crow, Christopher Hamilton, Edmond White & Thomas Hunt, Robert Holt, Jonathan Leigh, George Roche, John Bawdon. (PRO: E190/99/1).

26 March. Deposition by Thomas Comberford, citizen and draper of London, by trade a plate maker of Stepney, Middlesex, lately come from New York and shortly to return there, aged 30. At the request of Lidia Poole, relict and executrix of Anthony Poole, deceased, citizen and skinner of London and assignee of Robert Barlow of New York, he declares that James Carteret of London became indebted to Barlow by bond of 2 December 1680 signed in New York. (LMCD).

29 March-6 May. Shippers by the *Blossom*, Mr. Richard Martin, bound from London for New York: William Depester, Ralph Manwaring, Richard Martin, John Huggett, Edward Lardner. (PRO: E190/99/1).

29 March-3 June. Shippers by the *Herne*, Mr. Thomas Barrett, bound from London for New England: Phillip French, Timothy Waldoe, Dillington Tankard, Joshua Shephard, Joseph Bowles, Ezekiel Hutchinson, George Satchwell, John Hubbard, Benjamin Skinner, Thomas Lee, Thomas Papillon, Thomas Underwood, Robert Bolter, John Reynolds, Thomas Tryon, William

Stonestreet, Francis Walker, Richard Gawthorne, Francis Good, John Lewin, John Onley, Sir William Warren. (PRO: E190/99/1).

March. John West, aged 16, apprenticed from Christ's Hospital to James Manby, commander of the *Arabella* bound for Barbados. (CH).

9-29 April. Shippers by the *Success* of Topsham, Mr. Thomas Rost, bound from Exeter for New England: John Cooke, Richard Freake, John Cholwell. (PRO: E190/959/8).

15 April. Petition of Thomas Darvall, merchant, against judgment in favour of Richard Hall given at the New York Assize Court in October 1680. (APC).

18 April-3 May. Shippers by the *Sarah* of Boston bound from Bristol for New England: William French, William Jackson, Thomas Tayer, Michaell Pope, Henry Gibbs, Richard Smith, Erasmus Dole, Francis Middlecott. (PRO: E190/1142/3).

29 April. Deposition by John White, aged 17, clerk to John Smith of London, scrivener, that John King of London, master of the *Two Brothers*, now deceased in New England, assigned his ship, then called the *Deliverance*, to John Temple, William Temple and John Sealy. They then assigned the ship to Emanuel Winsor. Emanuel Winsor of London, merchant aged 49, deposes that he is the owner of the *Two Brothers*. Enclosed is a letter of 29 November 1680 from John King in New York to Emanuel Winsor at the Golden Anchor, Little Wood Street, London, reporting on a voyage from St. George's to New York. (LMCD).

29 April. Deposition by Henry Edon of London, ironmonger aged 24, that William Darvall of New York became indebted to Abraham Jesson of the High Street, Aldgate, London, ironmonger, now deceased, by bond of 27 August 1679. Jesson's relict and executrix is Elizabeth Jesson of London. (LMCD).

April. William Driver of Virginia, bachelor. Administration to the father, Edward Driver. (AW).

8 May-13 June. Shippers by the *Susanna* of Boston, Mr. Thomas Carter, bound from Exeter for Boston, New England: Christopher Brodridge. (PRO: E190/959/8).

18 May. Edward Williams, citizen and vintner of London, and his wife Elizabeth, relict and executrix of Benjamin Scrivener of St. Botolph Aldgate, London, deceased, appoint Thomas Barrett, master of the *Heron*, now bound for New England, as their attorney. (LMCD).

May. Administration of Leonard Corneforth of Stepney, Middlesex, who died in Virginia. (AW).

8 June. Shipper by the *Olive Branch* bound from Bristol for New England: George Hart. (PRO: E190/1142/3).

13 June. Shipper by the *Abigall*, Mr. Wood, bound from London for Carolina: Henry Headly. (PRO: E190/99/1).

16 June. Shipper by the *Crowned Lyon* of Bristol, Mr. Nicholas Seaborne, bound from Bristol for Barbados and Virginia: said Nicholas Seaborne. (PRO: E190/1142/3).

20 June-19 July. Shippers by the *Welcome*, Mr. Edward Clements, bound from London for New York: Amos Ford, John Bawdon, Edward Hull, Benjamin Williams. (PRO: E190/99/1).

21 June. Shipper by the *Francis*, Mr. Peter Bennett, bound from London for New England: Thomas Todd. (PRO: E190/99/1).

21 June. Shipper by the *Beginning* of Bideford, Mr. Thomas Phillips, bound from Bideford for Virginia: Joseph Comer. (PRO: E190/959/4).

25-30 June. Shipper by the *Endeavour* of Piscataway, Mr. John Hunkins, bound from Dartmouth for New England: John Hayne. (PRO: E190/959/10).

June. Probate of will of Thomas Crooke the younger of London (bound for Virginia), who died abroad. (AW).

June. Administration of Anne Evans of St. Bartholomew, London, who died in Virginia or at sea, spinster. (AW).

4 July. Western Circuit prisoners reprieved to be transported to Barbados. Cornwall: William Williams of Ruan Minor. Devon: George Bridford; John Bond of Halberton; William Coles of Crediton. Dorset: Ezechiel Wills of Broadwindsor; Richard Bayly alias Densloe of Netherbury; Richard Spittle of Wellridge; John Luckis of Frampton; Jane Bugden of Tarrant Kingston. Hampshire: Cyprian Southake of Faccombe, scrivener; Jeremy Coates of Kingscleere. Somerset: Elizabeth Osborne alias Potter; Ann Symonds of Northleigh. Wiltshire: Giles Blanford of Devizes; William Ely of All Commons. (PRO: C66/3223/4).

4 July. Northern Circuit prisoners reprieved to be transported to Barbados. Cumberland: Robert Davis alias Devis of Brampton. Lancashire: James Grundy of Lancaster; Israel Arrundel of the same. Northumberland: Robert Fram of Newcastle upon Tyne; Richard Hutton of Newcastle upon Tyne. Yorkshire: Margaret Johnson alias Simpson of York. (PRO: C66/3223/5).

7 July. Deposition by John Reed of Deal, Kent, mariner aged 46, John Gant of Romangate, Kent, mariner aged 36, and John Savage of Waterford, Ireland, mariner aged 22, that they served on the *Heron* of London, which went to Boston, New England, and to Barbados. (LMCD).

4 July. Shipper by the *Bonadventure*, Mr. William Wilkinson, bound from London for Carolina: Richard Adams. (PRO: E190/99/1).

5-11 July. Shipper by the *Hopewell*, Mr. Michael Yoakly, bound from London for Maryland: John Abbington. (PRO: E190/99/1).

5-12 July. Shippers by the *Adventure*, Mr. Ralph Cooper, bound from London for Virginia & Maryland: Christopher Eveling, John Collingwood, William Rathborne, Elizabeth Dunch. (PRO: E190/99/1).

9 July. Oxford Circuit prisoners reprieved to be transported to America. Berkshire: Hugh Billemore of Ufton. Oxfordshire: Thomas Hart of Standlake. Staffordshire: George Bennett of Harborne, blacksmith. Elizabeth wife of Edward Stockin of Bury St. Edmunds, Suffolk. Worcestershire: John Fownes of Cradley. (PRO: C66/3223/1).

9 July. Shipper by the *Crown Mallaga*, Mr. John Francis, bound from London for Maryland: Thomas Bellgrave. (PRO: E190/99/1).

9 July-11 August. Shippers by the *Elizabeth & Mary*, Mr. Elisha Bennett, bound from London for New England: Jacob Jesson, Henry Ecton(?), Zachary Morris, John Ryder, William Shirley, Vallentine Adams, Edward Ellis, Thomas Hunt, Samuel Penn, Thomas Higgins. (PRO: E190/99/1).

11 July. Richard Hart apprenticed from Christ's Hospital to Joseph Graves, commander of the *Bohemia Merchant* bound for Barbados. (CH).

11 July-5 August. Shippers by the *Henry & Ann*, Mr. Thomas Arnold, bound from London for Virginia & New Jersey: William Biddle, Gilbert Metcalf, Francis Collins, James Caron, Thomas Hogg. (PRO: E190/99/1).

18 July. Shipper by the *Dolphin*, Mr. Christopher Morgan, bound from London for Virginia: John Osburne. (PRO: E190/99/1).

18 July. Shipper by the *John & Thomas*, Mr. Michael Wilkins, bound from London for Virginia: William Garfoot. (PRO: E190/99/1).

23 July. Shipper by the *Merchants Delight* of Bideford, Mr. William Bratton, bound from Bideford for Virginia: Henry Ginnings. (PRO: E190/959/4).

27 July. Shipper by the *Cambridge*, Mr. John Lomax, bound from London for Virginia: Richard Booth. (PRO: E190/99/1).

28 July. Shipper by the *Richard & Elizabeth*, Mr. Edward Burford, bound from London for Virginia: Richard Booth. (PRO: E190/99/1).

28 July-3 August. Shippers by the *Elizabeth & Katherine*, Mr. Timothy Keyser, bound from London for Virginia & Maryland: Richard Booth, John Foster. (PRO: E190/99/1).

July. Administration of Arthur Carleton of Maryland, widower. (AW).

July. Administration with will of William Toms of Topsham, Devon, who died in Virginia, bachelor. (AW).

July. Administration of Jane Vaughan alias Jones of Kent County, Maryland. (AW).

July. Essex prisoner reprieved to be transported to Barbados or Jamaica: John Cooke of Dulleland. (EB)

2 August. John Alday apprenticed from Christ's Hospital to John Mumford, citizen and grocer of London, to serve in Virginia. (CH).

2 August. Shipper by the *Patience*, Mr. Eman Hudson, bound from London for Virginia: John Clagett. (PRO: E190/99/1).

2-22 August. Shippers by the *Constant Mary*, Mr. Edward Rhodes, bound from London for Virginia: John Taylor, Edward Round, Thomas Potter, James Bigger, James Archer. (PRO: E190/99/1).

2 August-6 September. Shippers by the *Prosperous* of Hull, Mr. William Marr, bound from Hull for Virginia: John Yates, John Cockerell, Charles Naylor, Richard Metcalfe, Richard Wilson, Anthony Wells, Joshua Ibbetson, William Skinner, Philip Wilkinson, William Prescott. (PRO: E190/324/5).

4 August. Shipper by the *Love*, Mr. Oswald Wheatley, bound from London for Maryland: John Collingwood. (PRO: E190/99/1).

6 August. Shipper by the *Mary*, Mr. Benjamin Hall, bound from London for Virginia: Richard Buller. (PRO: E190/99/1).

8 August. Shipper by the *Stephen & Edward*, Mr. Sebastian Gingey, bound from London for Maryland: Thomas Starke. (PRO: E190/99/1).

9-20 August. Shippers by the *Comfort* of Bristol bound from Bristol for Virginia: John Standbank, Joseph Saunders, John Porter. (PRO: E190/1142/3).

10 August. Shipper by the *William & Thomas*, Mr. Francis Partis, bound from London for Virginia: William Drope. (PRO: E190/99/1).

11 August. Deposition by Robert Godson, citizen and silkthrower of London, aged 58, that William Parker of Calvert County, Maryland, became indebted for tobacco on 5 December 1674 to his father-in-law, Edward Lloyd, then of Stepney but now of Whitechapel, Middlesex, gent. By deeds of the same date William Parker also undertook to deliver cattle that his mother, Grace Lloyd, had inherited by her husband's will and to supply tobacco to William Parker's sister, Elizabeth Parker. Edward Lloyd, aged 70, deposes that he is owed the balance of the estate of his son-in-law William Parker, deceased. (LMCD).

11 August. Shipper by the *Thomas & Edward*, Capt. [John] Browne, bound from London for New England: Joseph How. (PRO: E190/99/1).

11 August-19 September. Shippers by the *John* of Bristol bound from Bristol for New England: Erasmus Dole, Thomas Dudlestone, Michaell Pope, William French, James Pope, Edward Dowding, Henry Harris, Thomas Waldinge. (PRO: E190/1142/3).

15-26 August. Shipper by the *Content*, Mr. William Johnson, bound from London for Maryland: Thomas Elwes. (PRO: E190/99/1).

17 August-10 October. Shippers by the *Richard*, Mr. Thomas Joles, bound from London for New England: Francis Marrett, Thomas Cooper, John Wood, William Harrison, Edward Tarlton, Edward Lardner, David Waterhouse, Francis Emberton, William Gore, Benjamin Harwood, Robert Rowlands, Samuel Porter, Joseph Alford. (PRO: E190/99/1).

19-25 August. Shippers by the *John*, Mr. Daniel Bradly, bound from London for Virginia: Henry Harman, Francis Wheeler, Thomas Wych. (PRO: E190/99/1).

19-27 August. Shippers by the *Joseph & Benjamin*, Mr. Edmond Paine, bound from London for Virginia: John Watson, Gerrard Sly. (PRO: E190/99/1).

19-30 August. Shipper by the *Recovery*, Mr. Thomas Hasted, bound from London for Virginia: James Wagstaff. (PRO: E190/99/1).

25 August-5 September. Shippers by the *Culpepper*, Mr. John Conset, bound from London for Virginia: Thomas Parker, Elizabeth Dunch, Edward Carter, Arthur North, Joseph Pile. (PRO: E190/99/1).

26 August-12 September. Shippers by the *Samuell*, Mr. John Clifford, bound from London for Carolina: William Cox, James Ball, John Symms, Samuell Lamott. (PRO: E190/99/1).

30 August-17 September. Shippers by the *Unicorn*, Mr. William Norrington, bound from London for Virginia: Henry Meese, Thomas Starke, Samuel Richards, Thomas Bassett, Daniel Ackhurst, Stephen Bearcroft. (PRO: E190/99/1).

31 August. Shipper by the *Hart* of Bideford, Mr. Henry Perrin, bound from Bideford for Virginia: John Ford. (PRO: E190/959/4).

31 August-1 September. Shippers by the *Hannah*, Mr. Anthony Gester, bound from London for Virginia: John Child, Anthony Palmer. (PRO: E190/99/1).

31 August-5 September. Shippers by the *Baltimore*, Mr. George Purvis, bound from London for Virginia: Arthur Bailey, Robert Akers. (PRO: E190/99/1).

31 August-19 September. Shippers by the *Hopewell*, Mr. John Rudds, bound from London for Virginia: Michael Purefoy, John Mann. (PRO: E190/99/1).

August. Administration of Andrew Dickeson of St. Mary Magdalene, Bermondsey, Surrey, who died in Virginia, bachelor. (AW).

2 September. Shipper by the *Windmill* of Plymouth bound from Plymouth for Virginia: John Rogers. (PRO: E190/1045/21).

2-7 September. Shipper by the *Shield* of Stockton, Mr. Daniel Toaes, bound from Hull for Virginia: George Horner. (PRO: E190/324/5).

7 September. Shipper by the *Abigall & Mary*, Mr. John Dicks, bound from London for Virginia: John Tongue. (PRO: E190/99/1).

7 September-20 October. Shippers by the *Samuel & Thomas*, Mr. Thomas Jenner, bound from London for New England: John Anderton, Thomas Todd, Thomas Powell, Richard Edmondson, Joseph Ashton, Richard Goodall, William Ashurst, William Baker, Christopher Keen, James Ivers, Francis Terens. (PRO: E190/99/1).

10 September-14 October. Shippers by the *Elizabeth* of Topsham, Mr. Nicholas Sainthill, bound from Exeter for Virginia: Joshua Davies, Robert Dabynett, Endymion Walker, Thomas Whithaire, Joseph Maudit, James Brownsford. (PRO: E190/959/8).

10 September-21 October. Shippers by the *Humphrey & Elizabeth*, Mr. John Martin, bound from London for Virginia: Phillip Manning, Thomas Cheesman, Vincent Goddard, William Dingley. (PRO: E190/99/1).

14-15 September. Shippers by the *John* of Bristol, Mr. Henry Totterdell, bound from Bristol for Virginia: Thomas Puxton, Richard Franklin. (PRO: E190/1142/3).

14-28 September. Shippers by the *Unity*, Mr. John Bull, bound from Lyme for Virginia: John Burridge, Robert Fowler, Thomas Way, Thomas Carswell, James Tucker. (PRO: E190/884/3, 884/7).

14 September-10 October. Shippers by the *Duke of York*, Mr. John Purvis, bound from London for Virginia: Francis Lee, Henry Hovenor, Peter Hales, Luke Nourse. (PRO: E190/99/1).

15 September. Shipper by the *Endeavour* of Stockton, Mr. Daniell Toaes, bound from Newcastle for Virginia: Michaell Taylor. (PRO: E190/199/1).

15-22 September. Shipper by the *Lamb* of Liverpool, Mr. John Tench, bound from Liverpool for Maryland: Thomas Johnson. (PRO: E190/1343/2).

16-20 September. Shippers by the *Diamond*, Mr. John Baddason, bound from London for Virginia: Stephen Monteage, Robert Bristow. (PRO: E190/99/1).

17 September. Deposition by George Weekes Sr. of London, aged 63, that he was bred and served his apprenticeship in Romsey, Hampshire, where he knew Hugh Dowding who went 40 years ago to Virginia, returned to Romsey 18 years ago and died there 14 years ago. He had a younger brother, Richard Dowding, and both were the sons of Richard Dowding of Romsey, husbandman, and the said Richard Dowding Jr., master of the *Royal Oak* of London, is the only brother of Hugh now alive. (LMCD).

19 September. Shipper by the *Robert* of Poole, Mr. Robert Bennett, bound from Poole for Virginia: William Orchard. (PRO: E190/884/6).

20 September. Shipper by the *Prince*, Mr. Robert Conway, bound from London for Virginia: Richard Glover. (PRO: E190/99/1).

21 September. Diana Middleton of St. Martin in the Fields, Middlesex, widow, found guilty of abducting Mary Hartley, spinster, and Margaret Towers, and putting them on board a ship to be conveyed to Virginia and sold there. (VM 83/3).

22 September. Shippers by the *David* of Plymouth bound from Plymouth for Virginia: George Orchard, John Taylor, Nicholas Tripe, Joseph Brooking. (PRO: E190/1045/21).

22 September-13 October. Shippers by the *Augustine*, Mr. Zachary Taylor, bound from London for Virginia: Thomas Cheesman, John Puttiford, Richard Nicholson, Samuel Young, Thomas Jaques. (PRO: E190/99/1).

23 September. Shipper by the *Royal Oak*, Mr. Richard Dowding, bound from London to Virginia: said Richard Dowding. (PRO: E190/99/1).

23 September-20 October. Shippers by the *Dolphin*, Mr. John Foy, bound from London for New England: Francis Burroughs, Thomas Maylin, Joseph Hide, Ralph Box, Mathew Page, William Disher, James Browne, Robert Hudson, John Lake, John Crow, Christopher Booth, Jonathan Lee. (PRO: E190/99/1).

26 September. Deposition by Edward Fanshaw, citizen and upholder of London, aged 25, that on 18 October 1680 he packed a box containing law books on behalf of William Jameson of Wye River, Talbot County, Maryland, gent, to be delivered to Richard Royston then bound for Maryland. (LMCD).

26 September-1 October. Shippers by the *Assistance*, Mr. James Strong, bound from London for Maryland: Robert Ellis, Henry Kent, Edward Fanshaw, James Conway. (PRO: E190/99/1).

26 September-17 October. Shippers by the *Charles*, Mr. Samuel Phillips, bound from London for Maryland: John Ladd, John Welsh, Thomas Turner, Henry Constable, George Webb, William Osbaldston, Nicholas Low. (PRO: E190/99/1).

26 September-24 October. Shippers by the *John & Sarah*, Mr. Henry Smith, bound from London for Pennsylvania: Walter Marten, Phillip Ford, William Smith, John Moore, George Cole, James Hayes. (PRO: E190/99/1).

27 September-6 October. Shippers by the *Barnaby*, Mr. Matthew Rider, bound from London for Virginia: James Waters, Thomas Thackham, John Handford, Silvester Deane. (PRO: E190/99/1).

28 September. Shippers by the *Bristol Merchant* of Bristol bound from Bristol for Pennsylvania: Thomas Coborne, Nathaniell Allem. (PRO: E190/1142/3).

September. Administration of John Moody of Virginia. (AW).

September. Administration of Tristian Harrendon of New England, bachelor. (AW).

September. Administration of Benedict Pritts of the ship *Merchant's Delight*, who died in Virginia, bachelor. (AW).

1-4 October. Shippers by the *Endeavour*, Mr. Peter Welcome, bound from London for New England: Edmond White, Francis Hiller. (PRO: E190/99/1).

1-17 October. Shippers by the *Bristol Factor* bound from Bristol for Virginia: William Tims, Stephen Watts, John Beazer, Nathaniell Allen. (PRO: E190/1142/3).

3 October. Shipper by the *Paradise*, Mr. William Eveling, bound from London for Virginia: William Morley. (PRO: E190/99/1).

4-10 October. Shippers by the *Concord* of Bristol bound from Bristol for Virginia: William Daines, William Swymer, Lott Richards, William Hayman, John Sandford, James Millard, Henry Daniell. (PRO: E190/1142/3).

4-19 October. Shippers by the *John*, Mr. Daniel Pensax, bound from London for Maryland: George Cornish, Samuel Richards. (PRO: E190/99/1).

5 October. Licence granted to Nicholas Love, merchant, to export firearms to Maryland to defend the English there against the natives. (APC).

5 October. Shipper by the *Friends Increase*, Mr. John Lines, bound from London for Maryland: said John Lines. (PRO: E190/99/1).

6-26 October. Shippers by the *Gerrard*, Mr. John Harris, bound from London for Virginia & Maryland: Hugh Hammersley, John Pryor, John Ebsworth. (PRO: E190/99/1).

6 October-2 January. Shippers by the *Richard & James* bound from Bristol for Virginia: George Masson, John Knight, James Pope, Peter Waddinge. (PRO: E190/1142/3, 1144/1).

10 October. Shipper by the *Flanell*, Mr. Christopher Flanell, bound from London for New England: Joseph Bowles. (PRO: E190/99/1).

10-21 October. Shippers by the *Genoa Merchant*, Mr. John Wynn, bound from London for Virginia: John Smith, William Dingley, Charles Dyos, Thomas Falkner, James Warburton, Mathew Robinson. (PRO: E190/99/1).

14-20 October. Shippers by the *Maryland Merchant* of Hull, Mr. Robert Paine, bound from Hull for Virginia: Edward Nightingale, Richard Metcalfe, George Greenfield. (PRO: E190/324/5).

15 October-7 November. Shipper by the *Vine* of Liverpool, Mr. William Preeson, bound from Liverpool for Virginia: Hugh Stedman. (PRO: E190/1343/2).

19 October. Shipper by the *Willing Mind*, Mr. John Lucombe, bound from London for Virginia: James Curey. (PRO: E190/99/1).

20 October. Shipper by the *Globe*, Mr. Bartholomew Watts, bound from London for Virginia: Samuel Groome. (PRO: E190/99/1).

20 October. Shipper by the *Planters Adventure*, Mr. Robert Ranson, bound from London for Virginia: George Richards. (PRO: E190/99/1).

20-31 October. Shippers by the *Virginia Factor*, Mr. Robert Joles, bound from London for Virginia & Maryland: James Park, Thomas Elwes. (PRO: E190/99/1).

21 October. Deposition by William Pott, draper aged 26, servant of John Rawlinson of London, that on 5 September 1679 Stephen Burton, merchant, took goods to New England to dispose of, and that further goods were sent to him by the *Endeavour*, Mr. Benjamin Gillam, on 27 July 1680. John Rawlinson, aged 30, deposes that the goods have not been paid for and that William White, merchant, now bound for New England, has been appointed attorney. (LMCD).

24 October. Shipper by the *Speedwell*, Mr. Thomas Larimore, bound from London for Virginia: Micajah Perry. (PRO: E190/99/1).

2 November. Shipper by the *Experiment*, Mr. James Condon, bound from London for Virginia: John Marshall. (PRO: E190/99/1).

2 November-19 December. Shippers by the *Victory* of Bristol bound from Bristol for Virginia: Thomas Colston, Samuell Tipton, Richard Marsh, Edward Perrin, Edward Fielding, William Jones, William Challenor. (PRO: E190/1142/3).

7 November. Shipper by the *Jonas* of Weymouth, Mr. Edward Tucker, bound from Weymouth for Virginia: David Arbuthnot. (PRO: E190/884/2).

8-22 November. Shippers by the *Concord*, Mr. William Jeffreys, bound from London for Virginia: Edward Round, Thomas Nelson, Sarah Matthews, John Palmer, William Grantham. (PRO: E190/99/1).

8-28 November. Shippers by the *Rose & Crown*, Mr. John Boddy, bound from London for Virginia: John Bawdon, Edward Bleek, William Bates. (PRO: E190/99/1).

10-20 November. Shippers by the *Alathea* of Bristol bound from Bristol for Virginia: James Pope, Richard Benson, Ann Romsy, Richard Benson. (PRO: E190/1142/3).

10 November-17 January. Shippers by the *Francis & Mary* bound from Bristol for Virginia: John Grant, William Nicholas, Thomas Hartly, James Hardwick, Thomas Colston. (PRO: E190/1142/3, 1144/1).

11 November. Shipper by the *Frederick* of Plymouth bound from Plymouth for Baltimore: John Toule. (PRO: E190/1045/21).

17 November. Shipper by the *John*, Mr. Thomas Groves, bound from London for Virginia: Micajah Perry. (PRO: E190/99/1).

17 November. Shipper by the *Alexander* of Bristol bound from Bristol for Virginia: Ambrose Marshall. (PRO: E190/1142/3).

19 November. Shippers by the *Exeter Merchant* [? for Virginia]: Mr. Jasper Radcliffe, Thomas Whithair. (PRO: E190/959/8).

22 November-8 December. Shippers by the *Unicorn* of Liverpool, Mr. William Gant, bound from Liverpool for Virginia: Robert Fechom, Thomas Clayton. (PRO: E190/1343/2).

23 November. Shipper by the *David* of Weymouth, Mr. Robert Barker, bound from Weymouth for Virginia: William Horsey. (PRO: E190/884/2).

24 November-7 December. Shippers by the *Bilboa Merchant*, Mr. James Pulman, bound from London for Carolina: Sir Peter Colleton, James Ball, Thomas Wych, John Ashby, Robert Bellamy, William Pulman. (PRO: E190/99/1).

24 November-8 December. Shippers by the *Bristol Merchant* bound from Bristol for Virginia: Edward Martindale, John Baber, Samuell Rogers, Jacob Beale, Edmond Driver, Thomas Griffen. (PRO: E190/1142/3).

November. Administration of Martha Jones alias Ironmonger, wife of John Jones of Virginia. (AW).

November. Administration of Corderoy Ironmonger of Virginia, bachelor. (AW).

5 December. Shipper by the *Elizabeth*, Mr. Timothy Pike, bound from Poole for Maryland: James Gould. (PRO: E190/884/6).

6 December. Shipper by the *Advantage*, Mr. Edward Barrow, bound from London for Virginia: Christopher Dodsworth. (PRO: E190/99/1).

7 December. Newgate prisoners reprieved to be transported to Barbados. London: Elizabeth Owen, spinster; Susan Heard, widow; Mary Snell, spinster; Sarah Chapman alias Good, spinster; Elizabeth Rycroft, spinster; Francis Russell; Elizabeth Clements, spinster; Helen Browne, spinster; Elizabeth Wolfe, spinster, alias wife of John Wolfe; Anne Smith, spinster; Mary Rowley, spinster; Anne Smith alias Greene, spinster; Mary Lane, spinster; Lancelot Dodson; John Parke. Middlesex: Anne Carter alias Harman, spinster, alias wife of John Carter of Whitechapel; Thomas Hewitt of St. Martin in the Fields; Roger Swiney of the same; Thomas Jepson of Islington; John King of Shoreditch; John Wall of St. Mary Savoy; Henry King of Marylebone; Mary Marshall of Chiswick, spinster; Elizabeth Warner of Shadwell, spinster; Anne Price of St. Margaret Westminster, spinster, for infanticide; Susan Powell of St. Dunstan in the West, spinster, for infanticide. (PRO: C66/3225/7).

7-14 December. Shippers by the *Constant*, Mr. Thomas Smith, bound from London for Virginia & Maryland: George Richards, Henry Bellamy, John Kirk. (PRO: E190/99/1).

1681

8-20 December. Shippers by the *Maryland Merchant* of Bristol bound from Bristol for Virginia: George Tyte, John Hudson, Richard Crump. (PRO: E190/1142/3).

17 December-9 January. Shippers by the *Golden Fortune*, Mr. Robert Arbuckle, bound from London for Virginia: Samuell Scott, Micajah Perry, John Raymond, William Sare. (PRO: E190/99/1, 106/1, 132/1).

19-23 December. Shippers by the *Stephen* of Bristol bound from Bristol for Virginia: George Masson, Richard Crump, James Pollonay. (PRO: E190/1142/3).

December. Probate of will of Edmund Goddard of Virginia, bachelor. (AW).

1682

20 January. Western Circuit prisoners reprieved to be transported to Barbados. Bristol: Robert Evered, mariner. Devon: Edward Newberry of Brixham, husbandman. Somerset: John Surfitt of West Buckland, husbandman. Wiltshire: Thomas Rogers of Fisherton Anger, cutler. (PRO: C66/3224/12).

24 January-17 February. Shippers by the *Society*, Mr. Peter Clarke, bound from London for New England: William Shirley, John Wood, Jacob Jesson, John Reynolds, John Sindry, Joseph Came, Anthony Stockbridge, William Ladds, Samuel Kirk, Robert Bolter, John Harwood, John Crow, James Hayes. (PRO: E190/106/1, 132/1).

24 January-15 April. Shippers by the *Edward & Ann*, Mr. Nathaniel Green, bound from London for New England: Jacob Jesson, Samuel Grant, Thomas Carleton, Delington Tankard, Thomas Firmin, Robert Hodson, Thomas Goddard, John Norton, Thomas Weeks, Samuel Wilkins, Joseph Bowles, Joseph Cox, George Roach. (PRO: E190/106/1, 132/1).

27 January. Shipper by the *Rebecca* of Weymouth, Mr. Henry Feaver, bound from Weymouth for New England: Stephen Pitts. (PRO: E190/884/9).

1 February-7 March. Shippers by the *Hester & Hannah*, Mr. William East, bound from London to Pennsylvania: William Guest, Phillip Ford, William Toesen, Charles Coldham, Samuel Shepherd. (PRO: E190/132/1).

3-8 February. Shippers by the *Hopewell*, Mr. George Heathcott, bound from London for New England: Robert Hackshaw, Charles Lodwick, Thomas Bolton, Thomas Crundall. (PRO: E190/106/1, 132/1).

4-6 February. Shippers by the *John & Mary*, Mr. John Cosway, bound from London for New York: James Hayes, Thomas Bolton, Sir Humphrey Nicholson, Henry Wheatley, John Freeman, William Mead, Edward Barker. (PRO: E190/106/1, 132/1).

14-25 February. Shippers by the *William* of Bristol bound from Bristol for New England: George Hart, Henry Baker, John Bowry, Richard Gibbons. (PRO: E190/1144/1).

16 February-4 April. Shippers by the *Windsor Bridge*, Mr. David Kelly, bound from London for New York: David Conyard, Edward Barker, Anthony Tomkins, Thomas Wenham, Henry Collier, Richard Pulford, Benjamin Hewling. (PRO: E190/106/1, 132/1).

17 February-5 April. Shippers by the *Herne*, Mr. Thomas Barrett, bound from London for New England: Thomas Deane, Thomas Holmes, Thomas Cudd, Joseph Gray, John Drake, Henry South, Lydia Dutton, John Daniel, John Page,

Richard Morrice, John Cook, John Wise, Robert Hodson, Martha Hunlick, John Cutch. (PRO: E190/106/1, 132/1).

18 February. Shipper by the *Industry* of Guernsey, Mr. Aaron Anly, bound from Dartmouth for New England: John Forty. (PRO: E190/961/2).

21 February-15 April. Shippers by the *Amity*, Mr. Richard Dymond, bound from London for Pennsylvania: Thomas Ogden, Griffith Jones, John Taylor, John Gibbon, William Fleetwood, James Boydon, Francis Collins, Thomas Holmes, Thomas Bowman, Henry Stacey, Philip Ford, Abraham Chitty, Joseph Richards, Thomas Sear, John Richardson, John Blunston, William Evans, John Smith. (PRO: E190/106/1, 132/1).

23 February-4 April. Shippers by the *Black Cock*, Mr. Michael Pack, bound from London for New England: Samuel Wilkins, Sir William Warren, Henry Lewis. (PRO: E190/106/1, 132/1).

27 February. Shipper by the *Olive Branch* of Bristol bound from Bristol for New England: George Hart. (PRO: E190/1144/1).

February. Probate of will of William Tatton of St. Mary Aldermary London, who made a bequest to John Machen in Virginia. (AW).

2 March. Midland Circuit prisoners reprieved to be transported to America. Leicestershire: Elianor Day of Burbage. Lincolnshire: Simon Smith of Wigtoft. Nottinghamshire: Mary Strutt wife of Samuel of Worksop; Alice Hill of Kattford; Jane Robinson of Hucknell Torkend. (PRO: C66/3228/10).

2 March. Shipper by the *Jonathan* of Exeter, Mr. William Richards, bound from Exeter for Virginia: George Tuthill. (PRO: E190/960/7).

2-24 March. Shippers by the *Hopewell* of Boston bound from Exeter for New England: Richard Freake, Christopher Coke, Thomas Tawley. (PRO: E190/960/7).

4 March. Home Circuit prisoners reprieved to be transported to Barbados or Jamaica. Essex: Roger Bowden of Waltham Abbey; John Corder of Waltham Abbey; John Walbancke of Waltham Cross; and the following still in prison in February 1683: Thomas Withers of Stratford Langthorne; John Lee of Stratford Langthorne; Daniel Alban of South Weald; William Browne of Blackmore; Mary Dawkins of Castle Hedingham; Samuel Sharpe of Rainham; John Smith of Stratford Langthorne. Hertfordshire: Richard Waddington of All Saints, Hertford. Kent: John Collins of North Cray; Richard Leggatt of Gleham; Isaac Brissenden of Kennington; Thomas Mills of Wateringbury; John Penny of Farningham; John Brooker of Edenbridge. Surrey: John Stephens alias Billing of St. Saviour, Southwark; George Pinfold of Farnham; Francis Stocker of Croydon; and the following still in prison in March 1683: William Tooth of St. Olave, Southwark; Benjamin Wilkinson of St. Saviour, Southwark; William Bishopp of St. George, Southwark; Ann James of Bermondsey; Jane Steward of Bermondsey. (PRO: C66/3228/2).

4 March. Oxford Circuit prisoners reprieved to be transported to America. Gloucestershire: Mary Emley of Hawkesbury. Staffordshire: Humphrey Richards of Armitage; Joshua Harris of Wolverhampton; Philip Morris of Wolverhampton. Worcestershire: Sarah Jones of Worcester; John Smith of Cradley; John Jones of Powick; John Lord of Ombersley. (PRO: C66/3230/11).

6-9 March. Shippers by the *Industry*, Mr. Peter Peake, bound from London for Carolina: Foulk Jones, Christopher Short, Christopher Dodsworth. (PRO: E190/132/1).

9 March-3 June. Shippers by the *Thomas & Susan*, Mr. David Edwards, bound from London for New England: Godfrey Webster, Thomas Dean, Walter Mico, Edward West, John & Thomas Lane, Richard Chivet, Benjamin Dejeane, Anthony Tomkins, Moses Browne, John Crow, Richard Atkinson. (PRO: E190/106/1, 132/1).

10-15 March. Shippers by the *Barnard* of Bristol bound from Bristol for New England: Abraham Saunders, Valentine Trim. (PRO: E190/1144/1).

13 March. Shipper by the *Merchants Delight*, Mr. Joseph Eaton, bound from London for Virginia: John Jeffries. (PRO: E190/132/1).

14-20 March. Shippers by the *John Bonadventure*, Mr. Andrew Cratey, bound from London for New England: Thomas Thackham, Daniel Royse, Joseph Cox. (PRO: E190/132/1).

16-22 March. Shippers by the *Pine Tree* of Topsham, Mr. William Showers, bound from Exeter for Boston, New England: Joseph Tuckfield, Robert Hutchings, Christopher Coke, Sarah Holditch, John Pym. (PRO: E190/960/7).

20-27 March. Shippers by the *Success* of Topsham, Mr. Thomas Rost, bound from Exeter for New England: William Sandford, Christopher Coke, Roger Wood, Sarah Holditch, John Chollwell, William Farnell, Edward Seaward. (PRO: E190/960/7).

28 March. Chester Circuit prisoners reprieved to be transported to Barbados. Chester: Christopher Moore of Dodcott; William Wilkinson of Aston by Budworth. Montgomery: John ap Edwards of Hussington, yeoman; Griffin Richard of Llangen. (PRO: C66/3229/2).

30 March-8 April. Shippers by the *Elizabeth*, Mr. John Wild, bound from London for New England: George Barron, William Baron, James Hayes, Thomas Sontley, Joshua Forster, Edward Ellis, Samuel Wilkins. (PRO: E190/106/1, 132/1).

March. Edward Sheldon, aged 16, apprenticed from Christ's Hospital to Andrew Cratey Jr., commander of the *Bonadventure* bound for New England. (CH).

1 April-16 May. Shippers by the *Providence*, Mr. Andrew [or Gresham] Boon, bound from London for New York: John Johnson, Thomas Crundall, Phillip French, John Harwood, Jeremy Tedder. (PRO: E190/106/1, 132/1).

7 April. Deposition by Daniel Jefferies of London, merchant aged 23, that in May 1677 he arrived in Boston, New England, to regulate the account between his master, Philip French of London, merchant, and Samuel Sheafe in Boston. He lived with Sheafe until December 1680. (LMCD).

10-27 April. Shipper by the *Virgin* of Jersey, Mr. John Browne, bound from Dartmouth for New England: Edward Marret. (PRO: E190/960/6).

12 April-3 May. Shippers by the *Society* of Bristol bound from Bristol for Pennsylvania: Thomas Pascall, Charles Plomley, Walter Reave, Phillip Jorden, Francis Fisher, John Reade, Joseph English, Kenball Britten, John Somers, Giles Knight, Nathaniell Rickards, Thomas Bradford, James Croaft, Mathew Lambert, Thomas Freme, James Freman. (PRO: E190/1144/1).

12 April-22 May. Shippers by the *Samuell*, Mr. John Adey, bound from London for Pennsylvania: John Sheene, John Bannes, Robert Young, John Marten, Robert Carter, John Burges, Thomas Hutton, Francis Plumsted. (PRO: E190/132/1).

13 April. Shippers by the *Exeter Merchant* bound from Exeter [?for Virginia]: Robert Hutchings, Tristram Bartlett. (PRO: E190/960/7).

13-24 April. Shippers by the *Comfort* of Bristol bound from Bristol for Virginia: Thomas Turner, John Lysons. (PRO: E190/1144/1).

19 April. The petition of Robert Orchard complaining against the Government of Boston to be referred to the Governor of Boston. (APC).

20 April-4 May. Shippers by the *Joseph* of Bristol bound from Bristol for New England: Jonathan Stone, Olliver Stratton, Abraham Elton, Archibald Erskin, Joseph Bullock, Thomas Lodge, James Holloway, Joseph Hoyforde, Roger Williams. (PRO: E190/1144/1).

20 April-23 May. Shippers by the *Teneriffe Merchant*, Mr. Elias Clifford, bound from London for Carolina: Edward Barker, James Banner, William Sadler, George Cox, Sir Peter Colleton, William Smith, John Rose, Joseph Himons, Thomas Hogg, Erasmus Fetter, Samuel Lamot. (PRO: E190/106/1, 132/1).

21 April. Shipper by the *Lyon* of Liverpool, Mr. John Crompton, bound from Liverpool for Pennsylvania: said John Crompton. (PRO: E190/1345/11).

April. Administration of William Fellowes of St. Martin Vintry, London, who died in Virginia. (AW).

April. Administration of George Purkis of New England, who died in Algiers. (AW).

April. Administration of William Jacob of Deptford, Kent, who died in Virginia, bachelor. (AW).

April. Probate of will of Henry Meese of St. Katherine Creechurch, London, who had lands in Virginia. (AW).

8 May-1 June. Shipper by the *Merchants Adventure*, Mr. John Babb, bound from London to Carolina: Henry Foreman. (PRO: E190/132/1).

10 May-13 July. Shippers by the *Elizabeth & Mary*, Mr. Elisha Bennett, bound from London for New England: Edward Davis, Frd. Eyles, George Barron, Henry Collier, John Gardner, John Smith, Francis Furrows, Thomas Wight, John Halford. (PRO: E190/106/1, 132/1).

11-30 May. Shippers by the *Seafare* of Bideford, Mr. John Titherly, bound from Bideford for New England: Joyce Lamb, Bartholomew Shipton. (PRO: E190/960/3, 960/14).

12-19 May. Shippers by the *Samuel*, Mr. John Ady, bound from London for Pennsylvania: John Martens, Thomas Hooton, John Babb. (PRO: E190/106/1).

12 May-13 June. Shippers by the *Adventure*, Mr. John Coleman, bound from London for Carolina: John Phelps, Peter Underwood, Walter Ryan, Christopher Dodsworth, Nathaniel Thornburgh, Walter Byon. (PRO: E190/106/1, 132/1).

15 May. Shipper by the *William & Elizabeth* of Poole, Mr. William Phippard, bound from Poole for Virginia: said William Phippard. (PRO: E190/884/8).

15-30 May. Shippers by the *Friendship* of Liverpool, Mr. Robert Croston, bound from Liverpool for Pennsylvania: John Simcocke, William Tayler, Randle Vernon, John Sharples, James Kenerey. (PRO: E190/1345/11).

19 May. Shipper by the *Mary* of Fowey, Mr. William Lugger, bound from Fowey for Pennsylvania: Joseph Growden. (PRO: E190/1046/10).

23 May-3 June. Shippers by the *Freeman* of Liverpool, Mr. George Southern, bound from Liverpool for Pennsylvania: Samuell Ellis, Bartholomew Coppacle, Joseph Powell, John Neeld, Thomas Brasey. (PRO: E190/1345/11).

26 May-29 July. Shippers by the *Rainbow* of Bristol bound from Bristol for New England: William French, Edmond White, Francis Fowles, Walter Stephens, Thomas Cock, Henry Gibbs, Henry Baker. (PRO: E190/1144/1).

31 May. Probate of will of Thomas Teere, citizen and blacksmith of London, whose son Thomas Teere was in New England. (NGSQ 76/3).

31 May-4 July. Shippers by the *Friends Adventure* of Liverpool, Mr. Thomas Wallis, bound from Liverpool for Pennsylvania: William Yardley, John Clewes, John Brooke, George Powell, Shadrach Whaley, George Pownell,

Charles Richeson(?), Samuell Buckley, Edward Tomlinson, Charles Pickering, John Hynch. (PRO: E190/1345/11).

May. Administration of Bernard Sykes of London, who died in Virginia. (AW).

May. Administration of Richard Bancks of Carolina. (AW).

9-10 June. Shippers by the *Golden Hind*, Mr. Edward Read, bound from London for Pennsylvania & New Jersey: Francis Colman, John Hinde, Thomas Mathews. (PRO: E190/132/1).

12-22 June. Shippers by the *Robert*, Mr. Richard Burt, bound from London for New York: Joseph Bowles, John Boswell, John Cary, Edward Mann. (PRO: E190/106/1, 132/1).

17 June. Report on the petition of Thomas Sands of London, merchant, for permission to ship tobacco from Virginia free of impost. (APC).

20 June. Shipper by the *Mary* pink of Bristol bound from Bristol for Virginia: Edmond Fcaveryeare. (PRO: E190/1144/1).

23 June. The following convicted at Quarter Sessions in Devon as wandering rogues and dangerous to the inferior sort of people to be banished to the plantations: Richard Stanley, Thomas Stanley, Peter Stanley and Matthew Eyres. (APC). [*See further entry of 29 November*].

26 June-14 July. Shippers by the *Lamb* of Liverpool, Mr. John Tench, bound from Liverpool for Pennsylvania: Cuthberd Heyhurste, William Hall, James Dilworth, Richard Coulborn, Robert Eaton, Charles Lee, Thomas Wigleworth, Nicholas Walme, John Dodsworth, Thomas Clayton. (PRO: E190/1345/11).

27 June-12 August. Shippers by the *Fly*, Mr. William Adams, bound from London for Carolina: Walter Ryan, Nathaniel Hudson, Owen Davis, John Fann, John Ashby, Sir Peter Colleton, Ann Smith, James Ball. (PRO: E190/106/1, 132/1).

28 June. Shipper by the *Hopewell* of Bideford, Mr. Peter Prust, bound from Bideford for Virginia: Peter Luxon. (PRO: E190/960/3, 960/14).

28 June-22 July. Shippers by the *Mary* of Salem bound from Bristol for New England: Edmond Feaveryeare, William Pugsly, Thomas Adams. (PRO: E190/1144/1).

June. Probate of will of Ralph Kinsey of St. Botolph Aldersgate, London, who had lands in Pennsylvania. (AW).

1-27 July. Shippers by the *Isabel & Mary*, Mr. Thomas Hudson, bound from London for Pennsylvania: Phillip Alford, William Clark, John Harwood, Isaac Marten, John Day, John Mason, Thomas Merritt. (PRO: E190/106/1, 132/1).

7-27 July. Shippers by the *Hopewell*, Mr. Michael Yoakly, bound from London for America [*destinations shown as Pennsylvania, Carolina & Virginia*]:

Daniel Wherley, John Archdell, John Dorman, John Richardson, Nicholas Finkley, Samuel Groome. (PRO: E190/106/1, 132/1).

7 July-21 August. Shippers by the *Welcome*, Mr. Robert Greenway, bound from London for Pennsylvania: Phillip Ford, Daniell Wherley, Robert Smith, John West, Denis Rochford, John Wilmer. (PRO: E190/106/1, 132/1).

11-19 July. Shippers by the *Richard & Michael*, Mr. Samuel Hayman, bound from London for New England: Daniel Causton, James Wass, William Wright. (PRO: E190/132/1).

12 July. Northern Circuit prisoners reprieved to be transported to Barbados. Cumberland: William Wigham alias Thomas Greene of High Crosby. Northumberland: Robert Wilson alias Morley of Newcastle upon Tyne; Stephen Taylor of Newcastle upon Tyne; Thomas Hall of Corsenside. Yorkshire: John Smathwit alias Johnson alias Jackson of Pennistone. Archibald Johnson alias Johnston of Mussleborough, Scotland. (PRO: C66/3228/15).

14 July. Norfolk Circuit prisoners reprieved to be transported to America. Bedfordshire: John Collett of Luton. Huntingdonshire: Thomas Mawson of St. Neot's. Norfolk: Walter Towler of Shipdam; Thomas Stilling of Heverland (still in prison in July 1683). Suffolk: Henry Vintner of Assington. (PRO: C66/3228/14).

14 July. Chester Circuit prisoner reprieved to be transported to Barbados: John Thomas John of Machynlieth, Montgomery. (PRO: C66/3229/3).

17 July. Midland Circuit prisoners reprieved to be transported to America. Derbyshire: Peter Waterfall of Derby; John Waterfall of Derby. Northamptonshire: Thomas Letherland of Northampton; John Pitts of Northampton; Samuel Shaw of Northampton. Nottinghamshire: Henry Ward of Nottingham. Warwickshire: Joseph Veares of Birmingham; Mary Steeres of Birmingham; Humphrey Dormant of Warwick; John White of Coventry; Robert Fenton of Birmingham. (PRO: C66/3228/1).

17 July. Oxford Circuit prisoners reprieved to be transported to America. Gloucestershire: Benjamin Williams of Henbury. Herefordshire: John James of Garway; James Edwards of Hereford. Shropshire: Evans Jones of Ryton. Staffordshire: Ursula Hawkins of Walsall, spinster. Worcestershire: Richard Downe of Lindridge, carpenter; William Hyde of Claines; Ruth Barnes of Offenham. (PRO: C66/3229/1).

18 July. Shipper by the *Providence* of Scarborough, Mr. Robert Hooper, bound from Scarborough for Pennsylvania: Phillip Ford. (PRO: E190/325/10).

19 July. Shipper by the *Providence*, Mr. Robert Harper, bound from London for Pennsylvania: said Robert Harper. (PRO: E190/132/1).

21-27 July. Shippers by the *John*, Mr. Peter [or Phillip] English, bound from London for New England: Joseph Cox, William Barron. (PRO: E190/106/1, 132/1).

22 July. Shipper by the *Recovery*, Mr. Thomas Hasted, bound from London for Virginia: Edward Leman. (PRO: E190/132/1).

22-31 July. Shippers by the *Dolphin*, Mr. Anthony Horth & Benjamin Hall, bound from London for Virginia: Giles Bullock, Micajah Perry, Samuel Blewitt, Arthur North, James Harris. (PRO: E190/106/1, 132/1).

24 July-3 August. Shippers by the *Crown Mallago*, Mr. John Francis, bound from London for Maryland: Thomas Shaw, John Abbington, William Drope. (PRO: E190/106/1, 132/1).

26 July. Shipper by the *Own Adventure*, Mr. Thomas Lurting, bound from London for Virginia: William Garfoot. (PRO: E190/106/1).

26 July-26 August. Shippers by the *Bristol Factor*, Mr. Roger Drew, bound from Bristol for Pennsylvania: Tobias Leech, William Browne, John Blunston, Humphry Ellis, Evan Oliver, Robert Lancaster, John Jones, Phillip James, Charles Jones, John Child. (PRO: E190/1144/1).

27 July. Shipper by the *Abraham & Francis*, Mr. Peter Paggen, bound from London for Virginia: William Paggen. (PRO: E190/106/1, 132/1).

27 July. Shipper by the *Richard*, Mr. Edward Burford, bound from London for Virginia: William Paggen. (PRO: E190/106/1, 132/1).

27 July. Shipper by the *Elizabeth & Katherine*, Mr. Timothy Keyser, bound from London for Virginia: William Paggen. (PRO: E190/106/1, 132/1).

28 July-8 August. Shippers by the *Thomas & Edward*, Mr. John Brown, bound from London for Virginia: John Glover, Thomas Wych, Samuel Phillips, Henry Forman. (PRO: E190/106/1, 132/1).

July. Administration of John Haswell of Stepney, Middlesex, who died in Virginia. (AW).

July. Administration of Nathaniel Heathcote of Anne Arundell County, Maryland. (AW).

July. Probate of will of John Johnson of the ship *Concordat*, who died in Virginia, bachelor. (AW).

July. Administration of Jeremiah Rich of Stepney, Middlesex, who died in Virginia. (AW).

July. Probate of will of Richard Cutt of Portsmouth in Piscataqua in parts overseas. (AW).

1 August. Shipper by the *Stephen*, Mr. Sebastian Ginge, bound from London for Virginia: Edward Leman. (PRO: E190/106/1).

1-9 August. Shippers by the *William & Thomas*, Mr. Francis Partis, bound from London for Virginia: John Wagstaff, Henry Darnell, Richard Carter, Thomas Starke, William Hickock, John Phelps, Thomas Wych, Nicholas Lowe. (PRO: E190/106/1, 132/1).

2 August. Shipper by the *John & Mary* of Bideford, Mr. Thomas Courtis, bound from Bideford for Maryland: John Barnes. (PRO: E190/960/3, 960/14).

2-3 August. Shippers by the *Adventure*, Mr. Ralph Cooper, bound from London for Maryland & Virginia: John Taylor, George Cornish, Peter Leedes, Agnis Gibbons. (PRO: E190/106/1, 132/1).

3 August 1682. Report on the petition of Captain William Dyer who in May 1681 was accused by Samuel Winder in New York of treason for levying customs in New York. (APC).

3-31 August. Shippers by the *Richard*, Mr. Thomas Jowles, bound from London for New England: Joseph Bowles, Jac. Jesson, Peter Gray, John Westbrook, Edward Tarlton, Nathaniel Troughton, Peter Hudson, Henry Blannyer. (PRO: E190/106/1, 132/1).

4 August. Shipper by the *Thomas*, Mr. Nicholas Funnell, bound from London for Virginia: Arthur Bailey. (PRO: E190/106/1, 132/1).

4-14 August. Shippers by the *Samuell & Mary* of Bristol bound from Bristol for Virginia: Thomas Scuse, William Jackson, Richard Townsend, Richard Finch, James Millard. (PRO: E190/1144/1).

5-9 August. Shipper by the *Henrietta* of Bideford, Mr. John Atkins, bound from Bideford for Maryland: John Davie. (PRO: E190/960/3, 960/14).

5-11 August. Shippers by the *Potomack Merchant*, Mr. Charles Partis, bound from London for Virginia & Maryland: John Wagstaff, Richard Piggs, Anthony Stretton. (PRO: E190/106/1, 132/1).

5-14 August. Shippers by the *Agreement* of Bristol bound from Bristol for Carolina: Abraham Wilde, Benjamin Blake, Thomas Bradly, John Gwyn, William Fisher, William Lewis, Thomas Thurston. (PRO: E190/1144/1).

8 August. Shipper by the *Samuell* of London, Mr. Thomas Bowman, bound from Southampton for Virginia: said Thomas Bowman. (PRO: E190/832/9).

10-17 August. Shippers by the *Friendship* of Bristol bound from Bristol for Virginia and Maryland: Joseph Saunders, John Porter, Thomas Whittop, Joseph Britten, John Sandford, John Chaird. (PRO: E190/1144/1).

10-28 August. Shippers by the *Boston Merchant*, Mr. John Wally, bound from London for New England: Richard Merryweather, John Wood, Charles Duke, Thomas Humphreys, Thomas Tuckwell, Jonathan Toft, John Ballet, Francis Hiller, Edward Ellis, Thomas Cuddon, Robert Hodson, John Guntee. (PRO: E190/106/1, 132/1).

11-28 August. Shippers by the *Content*, Mr. William Johnson, bound from London for Maryland & Virginia: John Smith, John Cresner, John Wilson, William Osbaldston, Thomas Elwayes, John Shelton, Thomas Goddard. (PRO: E190/106/1, 132/1).

11 August-23 September. Shippers by the *Globe*, Mr. Samuel Groome, bound from London for New York: John Gardner, Samuel Wheeler, Ralph Hatley, Thomas Crundall, John Newton. (PRO: E190/106/1, 132/1).

12 August. Shipper by the *Beginning* of Bideford, Mr. John Limbry, bound from Bideford for Virginia: Richard Cockhill. (PRO: E190/960/3, 960/14).

12-18 August. Shippers by the *Reformation* of Bristol bound from Bristol for Virginia: Edward Fielding, Thomas Hardy. (PRO: E190/1144/1).

16-31 August. Shippers by the *Submission* of Liverpool, Mr. James Settle, bound from Liverpool for Pennsylvania: Phineas Pemberton, Raph Pemberton, James Harrison, Thomas Winn, Randle Blackshaw, Arthur Wood. (PRO: E190/1345/11).

18 August-4 September. Shippers by the *Constant Mary*, Mr. Edward Rhodes, bound from London for Virginia: James Bigger, Edmond Littlepage, Samuel Dean, Roger Burroughs, John Sole, Richard Laundy, Francis Lee. (PRO: E190/106/1, 132/1).

19-23 August. Shippers by the *Charles*, Mr. Anthony May, bound from London for Virginia: John Hand, James Harris. (PRO: E190/106/1, 132/1).

19-30 August. Shippers by the *John* of Bristol bound from Bristol for Virginia: Henry Totterdell, Richard Gotly, Francis Ballard, George Tyte. (PRO: E190/1144/1).

21 August-28 September. Shippers by the *Sarah* bound from Bristol for New England: Edmond Feaveryeare, Thomas Tyler, Daniell Kill, James Wilkins, Thomas Adams, Thomas Burroughs, Richard Kinge, Thomas Walden. (PRO: E190/1144/1).

22 August. Shipper by the *Richard* of Weymouth, Mr. Richard White, bound from Weymouth for Virginia: said Richard White. (PRO: E190/884/9).

22-29 August. Shippers by the *Unicorn* for Virginia and Pennsylvania: John Grant, John Kinoy, William Cloude, Anthony Elton, James Hill, Michaell White, Nicholas Cuny. (PRO: E190/1144/1).

23 August-8 September. Shippers by the *Jefferys*, Mr. Thomas Arnold, bound from London for Virginia & Pennsylvania: Mathew Walraven, Society of Quakers, Society of Traders to Pennsylvania, William Shirley, John Cary, Robert Bristow, Nicholas Moore, John Fordham, Robert Smith, James Claypoole, John Shelton, Stephen Montage, Peter Daile, William Woodbee. (PRO: E190/106/1, 132/1).

26-29 August. Shippers by the *Dolphin*, Mr. John Sherbone, bound from London for New England: Henry Merry, John Reynolds, William Whiteing, Samuel Allen. (PRO: E190/106/1, 132/1).

26 August-14 September. Shippers by the *Assistance*, Mr. James Strong, bound from London for Maryland & Virginia: John Welsh, Roger Lillington, John Moore, Edward Round. (PRO: E190/106/1, 132/1).

28 August. Deposition by John Hanford of London, merchant aged 61, that John Rogers of Virginia, planter, has appointed Captain Thomas Arnold as his attorney. (LMCD).

29 August-5 October. Shippers by the *Charles*, Mr. Arthur Tanner, bound from London for New England: John Peacock, Thomas Crisp, John Lyons. (PRO: E190/132/1).

29 August-4 September. Shippers by the *Hound*, Mr. Phineas Hide, bound from London for Virginia: Andrew Bolt, George Cornish, Thomas Hide. (PRO: E190/106/1, 132/1).

30 August. Shipper by the *Richard & Mary*, Mr. John Parrick, bound from London for New England: Josiah Dewye. (PRO: E190/132/1).

31 August-8 September. Shippers by the *Hannah*, Mr. Anthony Gester, bound from London for Virginia: Edward Burrish, John Brett, Robert Carnoll, Benjamin Layton. (PRO: E190/106/1, 132/1).

31 August-18 September. Shippers by the *John*, Mr. Daniel Bradley, bound from London for Virginia: Henry Moor, Richard Buller. (PRO: E190/106/1, 132/1).

August. Limited administration of William White of James City, Virginia. (AW).

1-20 September. Shippers by the *Baltimore*, Mr. James Conway, bound from London for Virginia: James Round, William Garfoot, Henry Constable, Benjamin Taffey, Thomas Petter. (PRO: E190/106/1, 132/1).

4-19 September. Shippers by the *White Fox*, Mr. George Purvis, bound from London for Virginia: John Steel, Edmond Pagett, Arthur Forbess, Joseph Woodall. (PRO: E190/106/1, 132/1).

5 September. Deposition by Katherine Crutchell, aged 72, wife of John Crutchell of Norton Folgate, London, glover, and Elinor Clifford of the same, widow aged 60, that William Stone, tailor, and his wife Margaret of Norton Folgate lived together for two years and had a daughter, Sarah, now aged 12, before William went to Virginia in about 1670. Sarah Stone now lives with Joseph Godwin, citizen and skinner of London, and his wife Sarah, sister of the said Margaret Stone of St. Peter le Poor, London, widow, deceased. Godwin is sole executor of Margaret Stone and has appointed Mr. Samuel Griffin of New York, merchant, as his attorney. (LMCD).

5-26 September. Shippers by the *Hopewell*, Mr. John Rudds, bound from London for Virginia: John Constantine, Charles Dyos, William Winch, Jonathan Tetlow. (PRO: E190/106/1, 132/1).

7 September. London prisoners reprieved to be transported to Barbados: Hester Wainewright, Thomas Stockdale, William West, John Belcher, John Platts, Samuel Neve, Christopher Smyth, John Merriden, Dorothy Bishopp, Anne Smyth alias Greene, Mary Harris, John Welling, Anne Bland, Peter Merveillean, Lidia Garrington alias Garlington alias Arlington, Elizabeth Scott, Elizabeth Wolfe. (PRO: C66/3225/7).

7 September. Shipper by the *Windmill* of Plymouth bound from Plymouth for Virginia: John Rogers. (PRO: E190/1046/4).

7-13 September. Shipper by the *Merchants Delight* of Bideford, Mr. William Brutton, bound from Bideford for Maryland: Samuell Dennerd. (PRO: E190/960/3).

7-26 September. Shippers by the *Mary*, Mr. John Harris, bound from London for Virginia: Anne Lascoe, William Dodson, John Bowman, John Wilder, Samuel Richards, John Prior. (PRO: E190/106/1, 132/1).

8 September. Shipper by the *Joane* of Exeter, Mr. John Seaward, bound from Exeter for Virginia: Isaac Gibbs. (PRO: E190/960/7).

9 September. Shipper by the *Ann* of New England, Mr. Elia Nicholls, bound from Dartmouth for New England: said Elia Nicholls. (PRO: E190/960/6).

9-28 September. Shippers by the *Concord* of Bristol bound from Bristol for Virginia: William Swymer, John Codner, James Millard, John Peirson, William Searle, Symon Hurle, Mathew Fackman, William Scott, Robert Shaw. (PRO: E190/1144/1).

9 September-14 October. Shippers by the *Augustine*, Mr. Zachary Taylor, bound from London for Virginia: Elizabeth Gibbon, John Putteford, Arthur North, William Goddard, Henry Loads, George Richards, Thomas Wynn. (PRO: E190/106/1, 132/1).

11 September. Shipper by the *Exchange* of Bideford, Mr. William Titherly, bound from Bideford for Maryland: Mark Chappell. (PRO: E190/960/14).

11 September. Shipper by the *Dolphin* of New England, Mr. John Sherborne, bound from Dartmouth for New England: John Hayne. (PRO: E190/960/6).

11-30 September. Shippers by the *Greyhound*, Mr. Joseph Wasey, bound from London for New Jersey: Thomas Goddard, William Dingley. (PRO: E190/132/1).

11 September-9 October. Shippers by the *Dolphin*, Mr. John Foy, bound from London for New England: Ezekiel Hutchins, John Marshall, Noah Lawrence,

John Lake, Richard Chiswell, Erasmus Warwick, Robert Avey, Edward Cheltman, William Pinder. (PRO: E190/106/1, 132/1).

12 September. Shipper by the *Zebulon*, Mr. Nicholas Goodridge, bound from London for Virginia: Henry Dandy. (PRO: E190/132/1).

13 September. Shipper by the *John* of Exeter, Mr. John Lyle, bound from Exeter for Virginia: Robert Lyle. (PRO: E190/960/7).

14 September-16 October. Shippers by the *Samuel & Thomas*, Mr. Thomas Jenner, bound from London for New England: Samuel Wickins, William Ashurst, Benjamin Gerrard, John Anderson, John & Thomas Lane, John English, Theophilus Charte, Robert Hyne, Richard Parrat, Joseph Martin. (PRO: E190/106/1, 132/1).

15 September. Shipper by the *Elizabeth* of Weymouth, Mr. John Cox, bound from Weymouth for Virginia: James Gould. (PRO: E190/884/9).

18-25 September. Shippers by the *Constant Friendship*, Mr. William Fowles, bound from London for Virginia: Thomas Wych, Richard Cliffe, Ralph Hatley, Thomas James. (PRO: E190/106/1, 132/1).

19 September. Shipper by the *Globe*, Mr. Bartholomew Watts, bound from London for New Jersey: William Crouch. (PRO: E190/132/1).

20 September. Memorandum by the Lords of Trade and Plantations. No person pardoned on condition of transportation should be sent to the plantations except on security of one hundred pounds each to ensure that they remained in a plantation for at least four years. On this condition 300 malefactors will be delivered to anyone who undertakes to transport them to St. Christopher's. (CSPC).

20 September. Newgate prisoners reprieved to be transported to Barbados. London: Mary Snell, spinster; Samuel Neeve; Hester Wainwright, spinster; Francis Russell; Anne Smith alias Greene, spinster; Elizabeth Woolfe, spinster, alias wife of John Woolfe; Mary Harris, spinster; Elizabeth Scott, spinster; John Platts; Peter Merveillean; John Belcher; William West; John Welling; Anne Bland, spinster; John Merriday; Thomas Stockdale; Christopher Smith. Middlesex: Dorothy Bishopp of St. Andrew Holborn, spinster; Lydia Garrington alias Garlington alias Arlington of St. Clement Danes, spinster; Elizabeth White of St. Martin in the Fields, spinster; Joyce Coe of the same; Anne Parkinson alias Goodell, spinster, alias wife of John Parkinson of the same; Anne Ditcher alias Stubbs, spinster, alias wife of John Ditcher of St. Giles in the Fields; John Spittle of Clerkenwell; Thomas Mountague of Shoreditch; Mary Williams alias Sharp alias Harris, spinster, alias wife of John Williams of Stepney; Anne Caster alias Harman, spinster, alias wife of John Caster of Whitechapel; Richard Trebarfoote alias Woolley of St. Clement Danes; Peter Hodge of Ealing; Robert Rogers of the same. (PRO: C66/3229/4).

20-22 September. Shipper by the *Shield* of Stockton, Mr. Daniell Toes, bound from Newcastle for Virginia: Joseph Eyon. (PRO: E190/199/9).

20 September-22 October. Shippers by the *Mary*, Mr. Richard Tibbot, bound from London to Virginia: Micajah Perry, John Dove. (PRO: E190/106/1, 132/1).

20 September-11 November. Shippers by the *Sarah*, Mr. George Kennedy, bound from London for Carolina: Richard Hobson, John Ashby, Sir Peter Colleton. (PRO: E190/132/1).

22 September. Shipper by the *Adventure* of Barnstaple, Mr. Philip Greenslade, bound from Barnstaple for Maryland: Andrew Hopkins. (PRO: E190/960/10).

22 September-22 October. Shippers by the *Culpepper*, Mr. Christopher Morgan, bound from London for Virginia: Micajah Perry, Mary Lucas. (PRO: E190/106/1, 132/1).

25 September. Shipper by the *Seraphim* of Barnstaple, Mr. John Darracott, bound from Barnstaple for Maryland: John Fleming. (PRO: E190/960/10).

26 September. Shipper by the *Resolution*, Mr. William Scott, bound from London for Virginia: John Osgood. (PRO: E190/106/1, 132/1).

26 September. Shipper by the *Concord* of Newcastle, Mr. Edward Robinson, bound from Newcastle for Maryland: Michaell Taylor. (PRO: E190/199/9).

26 September. Bennet Smith, aged 14, apprenticed from Christ's Hospital to Captain Benjamin King, commander of the *Biscay Merchant* bound for Barbados. (CH).

27 September. Deposition by Henry Damarine of Stepney, Middlesex, ropemaker aged 60, that he consigned goods to Joseph Parsons of Boston, New England, by the *Zebulon*. (LMCD).

28-30 September. Shippers by the *James & Thomas* bound from Plymouth for Virginia: Thomas Warne, John Rogers, Marke Batt, John Pryn. (PRO: E190/1046/4).

29 September. Shipper by the *Friendship*, Mr. John Burton, bound from Lyme for Virginia: John Burridge. (PRO: E190/884/11).

September. John Peckover alias Pettifer, aged 15, apprenticed from Christ's Hospital to Joseph Bartholomew, commander of the *Providence* bound for Jamaica. (CH).

September. Administration of John Neale alias Oneale of Stepney, Middlesex, who died in Virginia. (AW).

September. Administration of George Mawer of the Durham Bishopric, who died in Virginia. (AW).

2-16 October. Shippers by the *Duke of York*, Mr. John Purvis, bound from London for Virginia: Robert Bristow, Francis Lee, Thomas Starke, Robert Fairman, John Fryer. (PRO: E190/106/1, 132/1).

3 October. Shipper by the *Seaflower* of Poole, Mr. William Cock, bound from Poole for Maryland: said William Cock. (PRO: E190/884/8).

3 October. Shippers by the *Robert* of Poole, Mr. Robert Bennett, bound from Poole for Virginia: William Orchard, George Lewen. (PRO: E190/884/8).

3-4 October. Shippers by the *Charles* of Plymouth bound from Plymouth for Virginia: Andrew Horsham, Joseph Cornish, William Holster, George Lapthorne. (PRO: E190/1046/4).

3-30 October. Shippers by the *Exeter Merchant* bound from Exeter for Virginia: Jasper Radcliffe, Joseph Mauditt, Robert Fairmouth, Joseph Sanders. (PRO: E190/960/7).

4 October. Shipper by the *Daniell & Elizabeth* of Plymouth bound from Plymouth for Virginia: William Martyn. (PRO: E190/1046/4).

6-21 October. Shippers by the *Humphrey & Elizabeth*, Mr. John Martin, bound from London for Virginia: Henry Freeman, Giles Bullock. (PRO: E190/132/1).

9-11 October. Shippers by the *Vine* of Liverpool, Mr. William Preeson, bound from Liverpool for Virginia: William Kendell, Thomas Johnson, Walter Skrimshire. (PRO: E190/1345/11).

9 October-9 November. Shippers by the *Barnaby*, Mr. Matthew Ryder, bound from London for Virginia: Giles Blayfield, William Paggen, William Hiccocks, James Harris, William Drope, Anthony Worme, George Richards, Thomas Thackham, John Littleboys. (PRO: E190/106/1, 132/1).

10-20 October. Shippers by the *Industry* of Bristol bound from Bristol for Virginia: Roger Williams, Richard Gotly, John Vinor. (PRO: E190/1144/1).

10 October-15 November. Shippers by the *Paradise*, Mr. William Eveling, bound from London for Virginia: John Cary, Richard Goodall, Isaac King. (PRO: E190/106/1, 132/1).

13-23 October. Shippers by the *Francis & Mary* of Bristol bound from Bristol for Virginia: Peter Waddinge, Abraham Lewis, John Fivefoote, Jenkin Morgan, William Roberts, William Dymer. (PRO: E190/1144/1).

16 October-4 November. Shippers by the *Unicorn*, Mr. William Norrington, bound from London for Virginia & Maryland: Thomas Starke, Samuel Richards, Gerrard Slye, John Loton, Samuel Coulsen, Richard Dowding, John Letton. (PRO: E190/106/1, 132/1).

19-23 October. Shippers by the *Diligence* of Liverpool, Mr. William Trenew, bound from Liverpool for Virginia: James Prescott, Alexander Dawe, William Pippard. (PRO: E190/1345/11).

20 October. Shipper by the *Blackamore* bound from Bristol for Virginia: Mathias Worgan. (PRO: E190/1144/1).

20 October. Deposition by Edmund Bannister, citizen and cordwainer of London, aged 52, that by his bond of 11 October 1680, Benjamin Rozer of Maryland, merchant, became indebted to Matthew Payne of Wapping, Middlesex, mariner. (LMCD).

20-30 October. Shippers by the *Elizabeth*, Mr. John Martin, bound from London for Virginia: Robert Brion, Giles Bullock, Samuel Scott. (PRO: E190/106/1).

23 October. Shippers by the *Maryland Merchant* bound from Bristol for Virginia: John Burt, William Pope. (PRO: E190/1144/1).

23-31 October. Shippers by the *Alexander* of Bristol bound from Bristol for Virginia: Alexander Tompson, Thomas Williams, Edward Thurston, James Thomas, Samuell Packer, William Fry. (PRO: E190/1144/1).

24 October-8 November. Shippers by the *Bristol Merchant* bound from Bristol for Pennsylvania and Virginia: Walter Kinge, John Barnes, Stephen Watts, Richard Phillips, Jane Collett, Francis Chadsey, William Cloude, John Hardculst, James Ranson, John Jones, John Harris, Thomas Day, John Trotter, John Moone, William Beakes, Robert Donn. (PRO: E190/1143/1, 1144/1).

25 October-22 December. Shippers by the *Thomas & Anne*, Mr. Thomas Singleton, bound from London for New York: Daniell Wherly, Ezechiell Woolley, Ralph Halsey, John Blackall, Richard Crockford, William Mead. (PRO: E190/106/1, 132/1).

October. Probate of will of William Wade of Westham, Sussex, (bound to Pennsylvania), bachelor. (AW).

October. Administration of Mary Hooker of Virginia, spinster. (AW).

October. Probate of will of Roger Rayner of Burnham Abbey, Buckinghamshire, whose kinsman, John Rayner, was in New England. (AW).

October. Probate of will of Henry Smith of Wraysbury, Buckinghamshire, whose daughter, Mary Lord, was in New England. (AW).

3 November. Petition by merchants with estates in Virginia representing that several persons have been prosecuted or threatened with prosecution for sending servants to the colonies even though they were entered in the office created for the purpose as going voluntarily. Some merchants have been heavily fined. The result is that no one dares send servants to the colonies. The generality of volunteers for transportation are the scum of the world brought to volunteer by their own prodigality. If they do not go to the gallows they will probably go to Tyburn. The petitioners pray that they may be protected by regulation. [*See further entry of 13 December*]. (CSPC).

4-9 November. Shippers by the *Alathea* of Bristol bound from Bristol for Virginia: Henry Jeffris, Richard Benson, Francis Hawkins, Edward Perrin, Francis Fisher, George White, Edward Kemp, Edward Watkins. (PRO: E190/1144/1).

8 November, Shipper by the *Grace* of Plymouth bound from Plymouth for Virginia: John Addis. (PRO: E190/1046/4).

14-23 November. Shippers by the *America* of Liverpool, Mr. Thomas Goller, bound from Liverpool for Maryland: James Jones, Thomas Clayton. (PRO: E190/1345/11).

15 November. The following apprenticed in London: Thomas Wisdome to Robert Marshall, 4 years Barbados, to be given 4 cwt. of sugar at the end of his term. (LMWB13/106).

27 November. Declaration made in London by Elizabeth Adkins, aunt and next-of-kin of Thomas Rubell of Virginia, bachelor, deceased, that his estate includes money received from the estate of his uncle, John Webb, deceased, now in the hands of Rubell's mother, Sarah Russell. (NGSQ 74/1).

28 November-16 December. Shippers by the *Genoa Merchant*, Mr. John Wynn, bound from London for Virginia: Charles Dyos, John Mann, William Shackerley, Francis Wheeler, Joseph Pile, William Paggen, James Harris, Edward Ellis, Arthur North, Micajah Perry, Francis Quarterman, Robert Bristow. (PRO: E190/106/1, 132/1).

29 November. Contract made with Walter Kelland, merchant, for the transportation to Barbados of those convicted in Devon. (APC).

November. Administration of Hanse alias John Cornelison of Virginia, bachelor. (AW).

November. Administration of Erasmus Joy of Plymouth, Devon, who died in Virginia. (AW).

November. Administration of William Chapell of Stepney, Middlesex, who died in Virginia. (AW).

November. Probate of will of Edward Carter of Edmonton, Middlesex, who had lands in Virginia. (AW).

4-22 December. Shippers by the *Anne & Elizabeth* of Liverpool bound from Liverpool for Maryland: Mathew Brytell, Edward Booker, John Shaw, David Poole, William Yonge, Henry Withington, John Crowder, Allen Noble. (PRO: E190/1345/11).

7 December. Shippers by the *Margaret* of New York, Mr. Richard Jefferies, bound from Southampton for New England: Frederick Sh—ipson, Peter Teller. (PRO: E190/832/9).

10 December. Mathew Trim of St. Katherine by the Tower and Sarah Falconer of the same found guilty of forcibly transporting Elizabeth Partridge, spinster, to Virginia by the *Indee* and selling her there. (VM 83/3).

13 December. On the representation made to the King that people called "Spirits" seduce many of his subjects to go on shipboard where they are seized and carried by force to the plantations in America, and that many idle persons who have enlisted voluntarily to go to the plantations but have afterwards pretended that they were taken against their will and have caused the transportation merchants to be prosecuted, it is ordered that the following methods be used in future:

1. Indentures are to be executed in the presence of a magistrate and filed separately;

2. A Clerk of the Peace is to keep a fair book into which the names of those indentured are to be entered alphabetically;

3. Every person aged more than 21 is to be bound in the presence of a Justice of the Peace or a Mayor;

4. Persons under the age of 21 are to be bound in the presence of the Lord Mayor of London or a justice or alderman of London and are to have their parents' consent;

5. Persons under the age of 14 are to be bound with their parents present and with their consent and are not to be taken on shipboard before the expiry of fourteen days.

The patent granted to Roger Whitley [on 7 September 1664] for registering the covenants of plantation servants is to be withdrawn as being of no use. Note that this order was renewed on 26 March 1686. (APC & CSPC).

30 December-13 January. Shippers by the *Thomas & Ann*, Mr. Thomas Singleton, bound from London for New York: Thomas Crundall, Henry Toone, John Essington, John Loverod, Edward Barker, Martin Wolley. (PRO: E190/115/1).

1683

4 January. The following apprenticed in London: Elizabeth Humes, William Davis, Mathew Hall and Thomas Wakely to Andrew Hardy of Virginia, planter, 4 and 5 years Virginia. (LMWB13/ 136).

4 January. Shipper by the *Genoa Merchant*, Mr. John Wynn, bound from London for Virginia: Thomas Hogg. (PRO: E190/115/1).

8 January. Shipper by the *Thomas & Anne* of London, Mr. Thomas Singleton, bound from London for New York and Pennsylvania: Simon Bow. (PRO: E190/125/1).

9 January. Petition of John Bawdon and William Bolton of London, merchants, that they may not be proceeded against after their conviction for illegally transporting subjects to Barbados and Maryland. (SP Dom).

10 January. Petition of Jaques Guibal and other French gentlemen for free passage and provisions to be provided to transport 15 men to Virginia. Signed by [Abraham] Guiball, J[acob] Baillergeau, I[saac] Veyrel, D[aniel] Bernard, [Theophile] Morin, P[aul] de Rosemond and [Henry] Delaplace. (CSPC).

13-29 January. Shippers by the *Merchants Delight*, Mr. Joseph Eaton, bound from London for Virginia & Maryland: John Gore, Ralph Harwood, Anthony Stretton, Thomas Potter, Edward Cartwright, George Grabham. (PRO: E190/115/1).

15-21 January. The following apprenticed in Middlesex to William Haveland of St. Katherine by the Tower, merchant, to go to Barbados: John Tyler, bricklayer, 4 years; Henry Blake, smith aged 21, 4 years; Richard Harris 4 years. (GLRO: MR/E/593).

19 January. The following apprenticed in London: Anne Wall, daughter of Richard W. of Hereford, dyer, to John Whittamore, mariner, 5 years (no destination shown); Edward Calignon, Jean Louis Patrone, Augustine Soux and Samuel Gueshard to James Bullay of Maryland, planter. (LMWB13/140,141).

22 January. The following apprenticed in Middlesex: Elizabeth Fletcher, aged 15, whose father and mother are dead, to Edward Patteson of Whitechapel, 7 years Pennsylvania, with the consent of her uncle John Jackson and the churchwarden of Aldgate. (GLRO: MR/E/593).

23 January. The following apprenticed in Middlesex: Christopher Graygoose to John Wallis of Shadwell, mariner, 4 years Jamaica. (GLRO: MR/E/593).

25 January-3 February. The following apprenticed in Middlesex to be sent by the *John & Elizabeth*, Mr. Jonas Leach, to Barbados for four years: Charles

Webb, aged 23, to Jonas Leach of London, mariner; Thomas Smith of Ireland, aged 22, to William Haveland; Thomas Holland of Yorkshire, tailor aged 23, to the same; Joel Jones of Shropshire, tailor aged 23, to the same; William Symmons of Suffolk, aged 23, to the same; Mary Sandyford of Yorkshire, spinster aged 20, to the same; Peter Hainsley, aged 21, to the same; Samuel Hill, aged 23, to the same. (GLRO: MR/E/593).

26 January. The following apprenticed in London: Robert Gilford to George Pye, mariner, 4 years (destination not stated); William Jackson to serve John Fleming of Jamaica 4 years. (LMWB13/144).

27 January. The following apprenticed in Middlesex: Lambeth Despur, aged 22, to William Smyth, 4 years Jamaica; Micah Seyre, aged 21, to Francis Branson, 4 years Barbados. (GLRO: MR/E/593).

29 January. Warrant for 42 French Protestants to take passage to Jamaica in one of the King's ships. (CSPC).

29 January-28 March. Shippers by the English-built *William* of Bristol, Mr. John Bowry, bound from Bristol for New England: Arthur Hart, Samuell Price, John Wasborow, Richard Gibbons, John Batchelor. (PRO: E190/1146/1).

January. Administration of Matthew Helcott of H.M. ship *Robust*, who died in New York. (AW).

January. Probate of will of Robert Nelson of Carolina, bachelor. (AW).

1 February. Shipper by the *Industry* of Poole, Mr. John Pelly, bound from Poole for Barbados and Virginia: Roger Biggs. (PRO: E190/885/5).

1 February-5 March. Shippers by the *Society*, Mr. Peter Clark, bound from London for New England: John Crow, John James, Richard Merriweather, William Prince, Samuell Ball, Joshua Pordage, Alexander Mearell, Richard Chare, Robert Carroll, John Bateman, Peter Hudson, Isaac Ash, Banks Kenten. (PRO: E190/115/1).

1 February-10 March. The following apprenticed in Middlesex to go by the *Hopewell*, Mr. Joseph Ball, to Barbados for four years. To Joseph Ball of Redrith, Surrey, mariner: Joseph Marsh of Oxford, aged 27; John Morerie of Lincolnshire, labourer aged 30; Robert Reynolds of Hawston [?Harston], Cambridgeshire, aged 26; Lewis Sergiant of Wales, labourer aged 22; Charles Scrue of London, tapster aged 21; John Cooke of Grays, Essex, "friendless," aged 18; Trustram Hollmore from near Exeter, Devon, gardener aged 21; John Prince of Munslow, Shropshire, tailor aged 23; Thomas Barratt from Worcestershire, labourer aged 21; Richard Crocker of Farnum, Hampshire, [?Farnham, Surrey], aged 18; Henry Davis from the Bridewell, aged 18; Thomas Norton of Worcestershire, tailor aged 26; Richard Snell of London, labourer aged 27; Charles Gaint of Cambridge, labourer aged 21; Marmaduke Ayles of London, tailor aged 22; John Rogers from the Bridewell, aged 18; John Benerley from the Bridewell, aged 18; John Peachie of Warmington,

Northamptonshire, aged 22; John Bradford of Downe, Kent, aged 21; John Clifford from the Bridewell, aged 23; Samuell Price of Shropshire, labourer aged 22; Thomas Webster of Yorkshire, weaver aged 21; Robert Bettally of West Chester, Lancashire, coachman aged 22; Thomas Bramly of Repton, Derbyshire, labourer aged 29; Jacob Ruffs of Watford, Hertfordshire, coachman aged 22; Thomas Walters of Naizborough [?Knaresborough], Yorkshire, cordwainer aged 24; Thomas Barratt of Essex, butcher aged 25; Charles Fluellen of Bristol, labourer aged 23; John Worster of Middlesex, throwster aged 22; Jacob Symmons of Oxford, coachman aged 28; Edmond Bullock of Kent, coachman aged 29; James Habbergam from the Bridewell, aged 22; John Laymard of France, aged 30; Abell Steene of Kent, labourer aged 20; Thomas Barlow of Shropshire, ostler aged 21; Richard Jackson from the Bridewell, aged 31; George King of Bristol, comb maker; John Hawkins of Wiltshire, clothworker aged 26; John Fairbank of Yorkshire, yeoman aged 31; John Goodland of Kent, aged 25; John Croft of Lancashire, labourer aged 21; Thomas Harrison of London, ostler and groom aged 21; Nathaniell Powell of Lancashire, wool comber aged 22; Godfrey Beard of Derbyshire, tailor aged 22; Nicholas Leatherington of Yorkshire, aged 21; John Tubb of Wantage, Berkshire, aged 25; Aaron Lake of St. Ives, Huntingdonshire, aged 21; James Hooper of Ireland, blacksmith aged 26; John Edwards of Devon, aged 23; Robert Borrodon of Lincolnshire, coachman aged 21; Walter Cobham of Berkshire, husbandman aged 29, (date uncertain). To William Haveland, merchant: Gilbert Gordone from Scotland, gent aged 30; Martin Finch of Ruskington, Lincolnshire, labourer aged 28; William Mayhoe, aged 23. (GLRO: MR/E/593).

7 February. The following apprenticed in London: Robert Ashenden, son of Robert A., to Crafurn Fetter, 7 years Carolina, with the consent of his father; Edward Hayward, son of John H., to William Cherrey, 7 years Barbados, with the consent of his father. (LMWB13/151).

9 February-8 March. Shippers by the *Pine Tree* of Exeter, Mr. William Shower, bound from Exeter for New England: Walter Morgan, John Pym, Mathew Pyne. (PRO: E190/961/5).

9 February-3 April. Shippers by the *Adventure*, Mr. William Condey, bound from London for New England: Nicholas Brattle, George Walker, Ephraim Harmer, Ezechiel Hutchinson, Henry Allen, Thomas Humphreys, Richard Humphreys, Francis Gerrard, Nathaniel Higginson, William Kemp, Sampson Sheath, Peter Hudson, John Gilchrist, John Wase, Edward Ellis. (PRO: E190/115/1).

12 February. The following apprenticed in Middlesex: Charles Webb, aged 22, to Samuel Nash of London, merchant, 4 years Jamaica. (GLRO: MR/E/593).

14 February. The following apprenticed in London: William Parker to serve John Fleming of Jamaica, merchant. (LMWB13/155).

14 February. Appeal of Robert Wright and Francis Pew of New York against judgments awarded against them in New York in favour of Robert Cornwall. (APC).

14 February-9 March. Shippers by the *Success* of Exeter, Mr. Thomas Ross, bound from Exeter for New England: Nathaniell Gist, Edward Seaward, John Cholwell, Robert Tristram. (PRO: E190/961/5).

20 February. Home Circuit prisoners reprieved to be transported to Barbados or Jamaica. Hertfordshire: William Dison of Hitchin; Hanna wife of Edward Stephens of Broxbourne; Edward Watson of Hitchin; John Hoasden of Curricott. Kent: John Stannum of Preston; Margaret wife of William Gennett of Gillingham. Surrey: Elizabeth Finney alias Quennell of Lambeth; Henry Slaughter of Rotherhithe; Joyce Feakes of Lambeth; Samuel Johnson of St. George, Southwark; Elizabeth Booth of Bermondsey; Walter Knightley of St. Saviour, Southwark; Walter Gilman alias Fowler of Thursby. Sussex: Thomas Blakeman of Hurst; George Goffe of Aldingbourne. (PRO: C66/3235/36).

20 February. Midland Circuit prisoners reprieved to be transported to America. Leicestershire: Robert Burges. Lincolnshire: John Wetherill; Richard Moncke. Nottinghamshire: Elizabeth Erby. Warwickshire: Richard Eden; Richard Flavell; Edward Cooke of Birmingham; Henry Garrett (still in prison in August 1685). (PRO: C66/3235/38).

20 February. The following apprenticed in London: Thomas Brathwaite, son of Simon B. of Ripon, Yorkshire, butcher, deceased, and William Smith of Longstock, Hampshire, vintner, to John Gibbs of Norfolk, gent, 5 years Carolina. (LMWB13/161).

21 February. The following apprenticed in Middlesex: William Wilsheire, aged 40, and Richard Browne, aged 33, to Francis Richardson, 4 years New York or New Jersey. (GLRO: MR/E/593).

26 February. The following apprenticed in London: John Payne of Norfolk to John Gibbs, gent, 5 years Carolina. (LMWB13/162).

26 February -20 March. Shippers by the *Endeavour*, Mr. Francis Richardson, bound from London for New York: James Conguard, Humphrey Merry, Thomas Byfield, John Dunlop, George Barr, Robert Stepney, James Brains, Samuel Barker, Thomas Heaton. (PRO: E190/115/1).

28 February-4 April. Shippers by the *Expedition*, Mr. John Hasted, bound from London for Carolina: Richard Goodall, John Monk, Francis Southworth, William Cox, Thomas Wych, William Batch, John Rose. (PRO: E190/115/1).

February. Petitions for pardons for those implicated in Edward Gove's rebellion by: Hannah Gove on behalf of her husband Edward Gove; Robert and Sarah Wadleigh of Exeter, New Hampshire, on behalf of their three sons; Elizabeth Gillman and Elizabeth Lad on behalf of Nathaniel Lad; William Healy, servant of Edward Gove; Thomas Rawlins. (CSPC).

February. Administration with will of Lavall De Thomas of New York City. (AW).

1 March. The following apprenticed in Middlesex: John Wetton to Robert Lessels of Stepney, mariner, 4 years Jamaica. (GLRO: MR/E/593).

2 March. The following apprenticed in Middlesex: Richard Hepart, ostler, to serve Thomas Ward of Jamaica, planter, for 4 years. (GLRO: MR/E/593).

2 March. The following apprenticed in London: Mathew Pryor of Norfolk, labourer, Martha Cradock, widow, midwife, and John Barber of Kent to John Gibbs, gent, 4 & 5 years Carolina. (LMWB13/166).

2 March-27 April. Shippers by the *Thomas & Susan*, Mr. David Edwards, bound from London for New England: William Crouch, Thomas Cuddon, John James, John Lake, John Lyons, Thomas Dodson, Roger Kilcup, Henry Sandys, Benjamin Bullivant, Joshua White, Francis Hiller, George Barber, Robert Hyne. (PRO: E190/115/1).

2-4 March. Shippers by the *Samuell*, Mr. John Atkins, bound from London for New England: Samuell Allen, Anthony Burrow. (PRO: E190/115/1).

3 March. The following apprenticed in Middlesex: Anthony Hambleton to Michael Purefoy of Limehouse, mariner, 7 years Virginia. (GLRO: MR/E/593).

4 March. Deposition by Robert Gilpin of Cornhill, London, linen draper aged 50, and Richard Baldwin of Cornhill, linen draper aged 54, that they knew William Darvall of New York, merchant, who in August 1678 was indebted to Samuel Shute and Benjamin Shute, then of Cornhill, linen drapers. Mr. John Robinson of New York, merchant, is appointed attorney. (LMCD).

6 March. Newgate prisoners reprieved to be transported to Barbados. London: Thomas Potts; John Cotton; Mary Gilbert, widow; Ann Dukes alias Lambe, widow; Edward Dickens; Ann Slowe, spinster, alias wife of Thomas Abraham; Gertrude Dirick, spinster; William Whitehead; James Martin; Joshua Bowes; Daniel Fry; Robert Norman; Edward Arthur; Henry Harris; Thomas Rumsey alias Hale, gent; Timothy Bolton. Middlesex: Anne Gambeling of Stepney, widow; Charles Evans of St. Margaret Westminster; John Prince of the same; Mary Gurney of St. Martin in the Fields; Anne Adams, wife of John Adams of the same; Martha Harvey of the same; Nathaniel Dowty of the same; Thomas Newman of the same; Elizabeth Neale of the same, spinster, for infanticide; Sarah Bowen alias Browne of Stepney; Thomas Faulkner of St. Clement Danes; Arthur Pembrooke of the same; William Fitton of the same; Edward Horner of St. Katherine's; John Macklyn of Whitechapel; John Marsh of St. Pancras; John Smith of St. Andrew Holborn; Samuel Sadler of Stoke Newington; William Dawtrey of Clerkenwell; Peter Williams of Chiswick; Anne Archer of St. Giles in the Fields, spinster. (PRO: C66/3235/30).

6-20 March. Shippers by the *Elizabeth*, Mr. John Wild, bound from London for New England: George Baron, William Darby, Thomas Maylin, Thomas Potter, Hugh Strode, John Degrave. (PRO: E190/115/1).

7 March. The following apprenticed in London: Sarah Braywood to Henry Sutton, 4 years Carolina, with the consent of her father. (LMWB13/169).

7 March. The following apprenticed in Middlesex: Thomas Sharp, aged 26, to John White of Ratcliffe, 4 years Barbados. (GLRO: MR/E/593).

8 March. Shipper by the *Mary Jane* of Jersey, Mr. Laurance Remmon, bound from Southampton for New England: Peter Seale & Co. (PRO: E190/832/13).

9 March. Shipper by the *Seaflower* of Jersey, Mr. Jerman Aubin, bound from Southampton for New England: William Button & Co. (PRO: E190/832/13).

9 March. Shippers by the *Martha* of Jersey, Mr. John Le Cras, bound from Southampton for New England: Phillip Le Coustuer & Co., Edward Le Brunn. (PRO: E190/832/13).

10-26 March. Shippers by the *Zant* of Bristol bound from Bristol for New England: Robert Nicholas, Thomas Tayer, Roger Williams. (PRO: E190/1146/1).

13 March. The following apprenticed in London: Samuell Binns to Francis Richardson, 4 years New York. (LMWB13/174).

13 March. The following apprenticed in Middlesex: Jone Diggerey, aged 22, to Francis Black, 4 years Barbados. (GLRO: MR/E/593).

16-17 March. Shippers by the *John Bonadventure*, Mr. Andrew Cratey, bound from London for New England: Edward Ellis, Joseph Bowles. (PRO: E190/115/1).

17 March. Shippers by the *John*, Mr. Christopher Keeble, bound from London for New England: Rayner Grove, Thomas Bands. (PRO: E190/115/1).

20 March. Shipper by the English-built *William & Ann* of Bristol, Mr. Phillip Jeffris, bound from Bristol for New England: Thomas Mosely. (PRO: E190/1146/1).

23 March. Petition of George Walton of New Hampshire. In 1681 Robert Mason confirmed to him certain lands on Great Island but a Massachusetts jury has now found in favour of Jeremy Walford and John Amazeen on the basis of a town grant of 1658. (CSPC).

24-27 March. Shippers by the *Hambro* frigate, Mr. Gregory Sugar, bound from London for Carolina: Lawrence Chicking, Benjamin Bradly. (PRO: E190/115/1).

26 March. Shipper by the *Wren*, Mr. William Deering, bound from London for New York: Benjamin Hewling. (PRO: E190/115/1).

28 March. Shipper by the *Bristol Ketch* bound from Bristol for New England: William Evans. (PRO: E190/1146/1).

29 March-2 April. Shippers by the *Endeavour* of Guernsey, Mr. Aaron Anly, bound from Dartmouth for New England: John Forty, John Hayne. (PRO: E190/962/1).

29 March-28 April. Shippers by the New England built ketch *Adventure*, Mr. Pyam Blowers, bound from Bristol for New England: Edward Willy, Thomas Dudlestone, Abraham Elton. (PRO: E190/1146/1).

31 March. Deposition by Josiah Jones of London, notary public aged 28, that he has obtained from the parish of Wheathampstead, Hertfordshire, a certificate establishing that Richard, John, William and Edward Smith were baptised as the sons of Richard Smith and his wife Grace. The third son, William Smith, now of Aldenham, Hertfordshire, yeoman, was born after John Smith of the Grove, Carolina, planter, now deceased. Richard Smith of Carolina, planter, deposes that he has known the family for several years and went to Carolina in 1675 with the son, John Smith, now deceased; the son, Richard Smith, is vicar of Aldenham. William Ewer of Aldenham, shoemaker aged 24, deposes that he witnessed a letter appointing John Arsdel Esq. of Carolina as attorney. (LMCD).

March. Probate of will of Nathaniel Burrough of Limehouse, Stepney, Middlesex, whose son, George Burrough, was in New England. (AW).

March. Administration of William Crosse of Blandford, Dorset, who died in Maryland, widower. (AW).

2 March. Oxford Circuit prisoners reprieved to be transported to America. Herefordshire: Thomas Lloyd of Ross. Monmouthshire: Mary John of Newport, spinster. Staffordshire: Paul Jarvis of Bushbury, carpenter; Thomas Horton of Bradley. Worcestershire: John Sheldon of Dudley, nailer; Joseph Edwards of Evesham; Edward Wheeler of Evesham. (PRO: C66/3235/31).

7 April-18 May. Shippers by the *Mary & Elizabeth*, bound from London for New York: Francis Hiller, Jeremiah Johnson, Moses Browne, Joshua Shepherd, Joshua Pordage, John Loder. (PRO: E190/115/1).

11-19 April. The following apprenticed in Middlesex to go by the *Barbados Merchant*, Mr. Christopher Prissick, to serve 4 years. To William Haveland: Humphrey Palmer of Somerset, aged 21; Samuel Bennett of Derbyshire, aged 21; Peirce Jones of Shropshire, aged 22. To Christopher Prissick: John Rowles of Worcestershire, aged 21. (GLRO: MR/E/593).

12 April. Shipper by the *Olive Branch* of Bristol bound from Bristol for New England: Richard Mittins. (PRO: E190/1146/1).

13 April-7 May. Shippers by the *Vine*, Mr. William Thompson, for New York and Pennsylvania: Robert Fairman, Anthony Tomkins, Samuel Baker, John Sanders. (PRO: E190/115/1).

17 April-19 June. Shippers by the *Blossom*, Mr. Richard Martin, bound for New York: John Wilkes, George Wells, Daniel Ingoll, Robert Holt, Godfrey Webster, John Royse, John Rawlinson, —— Rogerson, Thomas Cockrell, Gabriel Odingsells, Jeremiah Tothill. (PRO: E190/115/1).

18 April. The following apprenticed in Middlesex: Alice Leniell, spinster aged 21, to William Thompson, mariner, 4 years Pennsylvania. (GLRO: MR/E/593).

19 April. The following apprenticed in Middlesex: John Bayly of Warwickshire, aged 16, to Daniel Huickson, 4 years Barbados; (GLRO: MR/E/593).

19-24 April. Shippers by the *Liver* or *Leopard* of Liverpool, Mr. James Kilner, bound from Liverpool for Pennsylvania: Joseph Massey, Phillip Engd [?England], Amos Stretell. (PRO: E190/1345/13).

20 April. Shipper by the *Friendship* of Bristol bound from Bristol for Virginia: Joseph Saunders. (PRO: E190/1146/1).

24 April-18 May. Shippers by the *Elizabeth & Mary*, Mr. John Bowman, bound from London for New York: James Boyer, William Prince, John Essington, Gershon Boone. (PRO: E190/115/1).

26 April. The following apprenticed in Middlesex: Barenthia England, aged 21, to Thomas Cannington, 4 years Jamaica; John Marsh, aged 24 and more, to William Emberly of Limehouse, Middlesex, mariner, 4 years Barbados. (GLRO: MR/E/593).

30 April. Shipper by the *Judith* of Exeter, Mr. William Younge, bound from Plymouth for New England: Walter Maryon. (PRO: E190/1047/13).

30 April. Shipper by the *Expedition* of London, Mr. John Hasted, bound from Plymouth for Carolina: John Harris. (PRO: E190/1047/13).

April. Administration of William Chambers of Stepney, Middlesex, who died in Carolina. (AW).

April. Administration of Arthur Showell of Carolina. Marked "vacat" and the next entry shows a grant of the administration of Arthur Showell of Rotherhithe, Surrey. (AW).

April. Administration of John Smith of Carolina. (AW).

April. Administration of Samuel Osborne of St. Olave, Southwark, Surrey, who died in Carolina. (AW).

2 May. The following apprenticed in Middlesex: John Floyd of Wapping, Middlesex, aged 38, to Richard Batts, 4 years Jamaica by the *Golden Fleece*, Mr. Joseph Banister. (GLRO: MR/E/593).

3-31 May. Shippers by the *America*, Mr. Joseph Wasey, bound from London for Pennsylvania: Edward West, Edward Hastwell, Benjamin Whitehead, John Hall, Richard Carter, Richard Whitfield, Daniel Whearley, Daniel Duchais. (PRO: E190/115/1, 125/3).

9 May. Shippers by the *Expectation* bound from Bristol for New England: John Batchelor, Thomas Porter. (PRO: E190/1146/1).

9-24 May. The following apprenticed in Middlesex to go by the *Elizabeth & Mary*, Mr. John Bowman, to Maryland to serve William Haveland for 4 years: John Watson of Yorkshire, tanner aged 28; James Stretton of Scotland, aged 32; John Ramsay of Westminster, framework knitter aged 29; John Martin of Middlesex, joiner aged 27; Charles Parry of Glamorganshire, sawyer aged 29; Richard Gent of Chippenham, Wiltshire, broadweaver aged 28. Thomas Annis of London, joiner aged 23, to John Bowman of London, mariner, 4 years Virginia by the same ship. (GLRO: MR/E/593).

14-19 May. The following apprenticed in Middlesex to go by the *Nicholas*, Mr. John Eaton, to serve Eaton for 4 years in Barbados: Edmond Smyth, bricklayer aged 38; Thomas Willson of Cumberland, aged 22; Thomas Pulling of Thornbury, Gloucestershire; Humphrey Golding of Huntingdonshire, tailor aged 22; John Fray of Yorkshire, husbandman aged 26; Henry Hye of Lancashire, aged 22; John Williams of Gloucestershire, husbandman aged 23. John Johnson of Coventry, Warwickshire, to William Haveland, 4 years Barbados by the same ship. (GLRO: MR/E/593).

16 May. The following apprenticed in London: Arthur Dove, son of Humfrey D. of London, gent, to Thomas Wyche of London, apothecary, 4 years Carolina; Elizabeth Lawes to Gerrard Slye and Israel Morgan, 6 years Maryland; Thomas Carter, son of William C., citizen and cook of London, deceased, to Emmanuel Hutson, mariner, 7 years Barbados. (LMWB13/206,207).

18-25 May. The following apprenticed in Middlesex to John Williams to serve him in Maryland: Thomas Battey, aged 21, 5 years; Mary Hillyard Jr., aged 18, 4 years; Mary Hillyard Sr., aged 35, 4 years. (GLRO: MR/E/593).

19-26 May. The following apprenticed in Middlesex to go by the *Concord*, Mr. Thomas Hurlock, to Virginia: William Turner of Somerset, aged 19, to serve John Oakey of Virginia, planter, for 9 years; Thomas Claymore, aged 18, to Thomas Hurlock, 5 years. (GLRO: MR/E/593).

22 May. Apprentices from Christ's Hospital: Charles Laughorne, aged 17, to William Jefferys, commander of the *Concord* bound for Virginia; Richard Crockett, aged 16, to Thomas Hazelwood, commander of the *Katherine* bound for Virginia; Nathaniel Long, aged 15, to Bartholomew Clement, commander of the *Rose & Crown* bound for Virginia. (CH).

23 May. Deposition by John Brett Jr., aged 50, and William Wagstaff Jr., aged 37, both citizens and merchant tailors of London, and by Thomas Browne, citizen and haberdasher of London, aged 50, that Joshua Atwater of New England, deceased, was indebted to Brett for goods sent in 1671 by the *Society*, Mr. Edward Clements, and in June 1674 by the *House of Friendship*, Mr. Zachary Long. (LMCD).

23 May-26 June. Shippers by the *Comfort* of Bristol bound from Bristol for Pennsylvania: George Morris, Alexander Beardsly, Robert Burrows, Elizabeth Smith, Francis Yarnall, Thomas Howell, John Houlston, Francis Fisher, Thomas Groome, Richard Owen, John Wayte, John Grant, Millisent Hopkins, Thomas Peerson, Enock Flower, Walter Stephens, Ralph Smith, William Browne, John Gibbons, Edward Beazar, Ann Smith, John Luff, William Lovell, Edward Hackett. (PRO: E190/1146/1).

25 May. The following apprenticed in Middlesex: Charles Oldridge, aged 35, to Richard Batt, 4 years Virginia. (GLRO: MR/E/593).

?May. Note by Lord Baltimore. My father used to allow 50 acres of land for every servant imported for which the transporter was required to swear that he never had rights to land in Maryland. Recently such rights have mostly been bought from merchants and [ship] commanders by Collectors or Surveyors of the province who then disposed of them at excessive rates to the poorer inhabitants. The conditions have now been altered and in place of a right for the transportation of a servant one hundredweight of tobacco will be accepted for every 50 acres. (CSPC).

May. Administration of Richard Sanford of Virginia, bachelor. (AW).

4 June. The following apprenticed in Middlesex: John Edwards of Somerset to Richard Charlett, merchant, 5 years Maryland. (GLRO: MR/E/593).

4-6 June. The following apprenticed in Middlesex to serve Richard Moss for 4 years in Maryland: John Whittle of Craden, aged 21; John Boswell of Cranford, [Northamptonshire], aged 21; Barbara Coliour of Chatham, Kent, aged 22. (GLRO: MR/E/593).

4-25 June. Shippers by the *Speedwell* of Boston, Mr. Thomas Tawley, bound from Exeter for Boston, New England: Nathaniel Peirce, Edward Seaward. (PRO: E190/961/5).

4 June-4 July. The following apprenticed in Middlesex to go by the *Samuell*, Mr. Thomas Bowman, to Maryland or Virginia: John Taylor of Newcastle upon Tyne, Northumberland, aged 22, to William Haveland, 4 years Maryland; Jonathan Fuller of Somerset, tailor aged 23, to the same, 4 years Virginia; James Wallwood of Northumberland, house carpenter aged 21, to the same, 4 years Maryland; Edward Allison of Bedfordshire, aged 31, to Richard Batt of

London, merchant, 4 years Virginia; George Groombright of London, labourer, to the same, 4 years Virginia; James Slose, aged 24, to Thomas Bowman, 4 years Maryland. (GLRO: MR/E/593).

5 June. The following apprenticed in London: John Wilkinson to James Manby, 4 years Barbados. (LMWB13/214).

6 June. Benjamin Watson, aged 15, apprenticed from Christ's Hospital to Peter Paggen, commander of the *Booth* bound for Virginia. (CH).

8 June. The following apprenticed in Middlesex: John Crane of St. Andrews Major, [Glamorgan], aged 21, to William Hunton, 4 years Maryland. (GLRO: MR/E/593).

9-22 June. The following apprenticed in Middlesex to Richard Batt to serve him for 4 years in Virginia: James Millner of Harwich, [Essex], aged 21; William Rawlins of Huntingdon, aged 25; John Steward, aged 20; William Steward (Steuard), aged 19. (GLRO: MR/E/593).

13 June-9 July. Shippers by the *Hopewell*, Mr. Michael Yoakley, bound from London for Virginia and Maryland: John Bunting, Ann Jones. (PRO: E190/115/1).

13 June-19 July. Shippers by the *Katherine*, Mr. Thomas Haslewood, bound from London for Carolina: Jeremiah Clark, Peter Barr, Mary Randall, John Ashby, Josias Dewye, Sir Matthew Johnson. (PRO: E190/115/1).

14-30 June. Shippers by the *Samuell*, Mr. Thomas Bowman, bound from London for Virginia: Samuel Groome, John Tayler. (PRO: E190/115/1).

15 June-11 July. Shippers by the *Endeavour* of Liverpool, Mr. George Thorpe, bound from Liverpool for Pennsylvania: Francis Russell, Richard Hough, William Pemberton, John Clowes, Henry Madocke, Thomas Jenny, Henry Thorpe, James Fletchar, Francis Stanfeld. (PRO: E190/1345/13).

21 June-4 August. Shippers by the *Richard*, Mr. Thomas Joles, bound from London for New England: Thomas Weekes, Andrew Dolberry, John Letton, Timothy Waldoe, Samuell Stringer, Thomas Nicholls, Samuell Blewitt, Thomas Goldsmith, William Disher, William Gore, Robert Carnoll, Francis Merritt, Paul Collins, Thomas Holmes, John Ingersole, Edward Tarleton, Joseph Sivett, Daniell Atkins, James Dark, Charles Duke, Gervas Lock, John Lugger. (PRO: E190/115/1).

22 June. The following apprenticed in Middlesex: Thomas Newman of Kent, aged 18, to Ralph Milborn, 4 years Maryland. (GLRO: MR/E/593).

22-25 June. Shippers by the *Lyon* of Liverpool, Mr. John Crompton, bound from Liverpool for Pennsylvania: Henry Lucas, John Nixon, Francis Tucker. (PRO: E190/1345/13).

25 June. Shippers by the *Mary* of Southampton, Mr. Anthony Pryar, bound from Southampton for Pennsylvania: Robert Leigh, John Swifte & Co. (PRO: E190/832/13).

25 June. The following apprenticed in Middlesex: Elizabeth Free of London, aged 21, to Robert Bucker of Limehouse, merchant, 4 years Maryland. (GLRO: MR/E/593).

26 June-16 August. Shippers by the *Concord*, Mr. William Jeffreys, bound from London for Pennsylvania: John Gardner, John Viner, William Hard, Phillip Crook, Daniell Styles, John Allen, Edward Blake, Hugh Lamb, John Harwood. (PRO: E190/115/1, 125/3).

27 June-20 July. Shippers by the *Dolphin*, Mr. Benjamin Hall, bound from London for Virginia: Benjamin Stephens, Giles Bullock, Arthur North, John Warman. (PRO: E190/115/1).

28 June. The following apprenticed in Middlesex: Richard Chesher, aged 24, to Nathaniel Smith, merchant, 4 years Virginia; Richard Kitchin (Kichin), aged 18, to Richard Cooper, master of the *Adventure*, 4 years Maryland. (GLRO: MR/E/593).

June. Administration of James Brighouse of Virginia, bachelor. (AW).

June. Administration of Samuel Blaydes of Virginia, bachelor. (AW).

June. Administration of John Simpson of Stepney, Middlesex, who died in Virginia. (AW).

June. Administration of John Boddy of Stepney, Middlesex, who died in Maryland. (AW).

2 July. The following apprenticed in London: Francis England bound to [*entry not completed*] with the consent of his father. (LMWB13/228).

3 July. The following apprenticed in Middlesex: Ann Hutchinson (Huchison), aged 22, to William Orton, 4 years Virginia; Gregory Dakeyn, aged 35, to William Jefferies of Ratcliffe, Middlesex, mariner, 4 years Pennsylvania; John Gamon, aged 21, to Ralph Bourn, 4 years Maryland. (GLRO: MR/E/593).

4 July. Shipper by the *William & Ann* bound from Bristol for Virginia: Abell Deane. (PRO: E190/1146/1).

4 July. The following apprenticed in Middlesex: Joyce Bibbsell of Hatfield, [Hertfordshire], aged 21, to Charles Bartholomew, 4 years Virginia; Elizabeth Lovelock, aged 21, to Michael Staples, 5 years Maryland. (GLRO: MR/E/593).

4 July. The following apprenticed in London: Edward Hargrave to George Bickerton, 4 years (no destination stated), witnessed on behalf of the father by Mr. Phillips near Holborn Hill, brazier. (LMWB13/229).

4 July. Chester Circuit prisoners reprieved to be transported to Barbados. Cheshire: Henry Lithgoe of Etchells; Ralph Johnson of High Legh; John Biccarstaff of Macclesfield; John Jones of Huntington (*sic*). Denbighshire: Thomas Lloyd of Wrexham. Flint: Lewis Williams of Fackington. Montgomery: John Mackenchin of Llanaveren; Thomas Vaughan of Castlewright. (PRO: C66/2329/30).

6 July-7 August. Shippers by the *Bristol Factor*, Mr. Roger Drew, bound from Bristol for Pennsylvania: John Bevan, Samuell Packer for Charles Jones, Stephen Watts, Philip James, Edward Harford, Joseph Baugh, Anthony Sturgis, William Smith, Nicholas Downing, Walter Humphrys, John Holland, Walter Stephens. (PRO: E190/1146/1).

6 July-17 August. Shippers by the *Unicorn* of Bristol bound from Bristol for Pennsylvania: Samuell Packer for William Penn, Thomas Skinker, Michaell White, Thomas Banks, John Ithell, Alexander Dolman. (PRO: E190/1146/1).

7-19 July. Shippers by the *Sea Flower*, Mr. Michael Cobie, bound from London for New York: Benjamin Williams, John Gardner. (PRO: E190/115/1).

9-24 July. Shippers by the *Thomas & Edward*, Mr. John Brawne, bound from London for Virginia: Henry Forman, Thomas Ellis, Thomas Bell. (PRO: E190/115/1).

10 July. Norfolk Circuit prisoners reprieved to be transported to America. Bedfordshire: John Jenkins of Aspley Guise. Buckinghamshire: John Stratton of Aylesbury. Huntingdonshire: George Grason of Huntingdon; John Lawson of Huntingdon. Norfolk: Edward Hipkin of Spixworth; William Prior of Towlesham. Suffolk: Richard Potter of Hunnington. (PRO: C66/3239/26).

10 July. Western Circuit prisoners reprieved to be transported to Barbados. Devon: Charity Arundell of Buckfontleigh; Robert Elstone of Crediton. Dorset: John James of Margaret Marsh; Elizabeth Harvey of Chinnock. Hampshire: Thomas Willis of Tangley. Somerset: Henry Stone of Hockworthy; Richard Sully of Milverton. Wiltshire: John Millard of Bradford. (PRO: C66/3239/27).

12 July. Midland Circuit prisoners reprieved to be transported to America: Ralph Hancock; Caleb Johnson. Lincolnshire: William Dickons; Thomas Wawby; Anne Bernard; John Mason. Northamptonshire: Nicholas Woodcocke Sr. Nottinghamshire: Robert Browne; John Richardson; Margaret Smith. Rutland: Robert Grime of Rutland; Samuel Lawrence. Warwickshire: John Eldersheire; John Newey. (PRO: C66/3239/24).

12 July. Northern Circuit prisoners reprieved to be transported to Barbados. Cheshire: Henry Lithgoe of Etchells; John Biccarstaffe of Macclesfield; John Jones of Huntingdon; Ralph Johnson of Hunley, butcher. Cumberland: Gawin Parrott of Brampton, yeoman; Mabel Blathwaite alias Yawdell of Warchott; George Thompson of Botcherby, yeoman. Flint: Lewis Williams of Facknait.

Lancashire: Joshua Broadhead of Manchester; Susan Ayanson of Egton cum Newland, spinster; Henry Hartley of Lostock, miller; Hugh Browne of Chorley, hatmaker; Thomas Garnett of Galeston; Richard Widdowson of Bootle cum Lineaker; Henry Greene of West Haughton, fustian weaver; William Wood of Castle. Northumberland: Jeanette Graham of Stanwix; Robert Browne of Allington. Westmorland: Robert Smart of Knadeby; Thomas Todhunter of Orton. Yorkshire: Robert Taylor Jr. of Leeds; Edward Brothericke of Leeds; John Kirby of Blacktoft. (PRO: C66/3239/25).

13 July. Shipper by the *Elizabeth & Ann*, Mr. William Orten, bound from London for Virginia: Francis Wheeler. (PRO: E190/115/1).

16 July-3 August. Shippers by the *Potomack Merchant*, Mr. Charles Partis, bound from London for Virginia: John Phelps, William Peel, Thomas Elwes, Caleb Heathcot, William Osbaldeston, William Hiccocks, James Dryden. (PRO: E190/115/1).

16 July-16 August. Shippers by the *Concord*, Mr. Thomas Hurlock, bound from London for Virginia: James Wagstaffe, John Harwood. (PRO: E190/115/1).

18 July. The following apprenticed in Middlesex: Ursilla Pepper, aged 17, to Richard Bills of Bermondsey, Surrey, mariner, 4 years Jamaica. (GLRO: MR/E/593).

18-19 July. Shippers by the *Owners Adventure*, Mr. Thomas Lurthy, bound from London for Virginia: John Smith, Nathaniel Bland. (PRO: E190/115/1).

19 July-23 August. Shippers by the *Morning Star* of Chester, Mr. Thomas Hayes, bound from Chester for Pennsylvania: Hugh Roberts, John Roberts, William Jones, David Davies, Robert Davies, George Edge, Edward Jones, Richard Thomas, John Edwards, Katherine Roberts, Kadwallader Morgan, Thomas Lloyde, Gayner Roberts, William Morgan, Thomas Prichard, James Prescott. (PRO: E190/1345/1).

20 July-4 August. Shippers by the *Richard & James* of Bristol, Mr. Thomas Opie, bound from Bristol for Virginia: Peter Waddinge, William Parker, Robert Adridge, Richard Benson. (PRO: E190/1146/1).

21 July-7 August. Shippers by the *Adventure*, Mr. Ralph Cooper, bound from London for Maryland: Francis Malden, Mathew Walraven, Richard Carter, Nicholas Lowe. (PRO: E190/115/1).

26 July-21 August. Shippers by the *Crown Mallaga*, Mr. John Francis, bound from London for Virginia: John Abbington, Thomas Shaw, John Langley, Sarah Garfoot. (PRO: E190/115/1).

27 July-17 August. Shippers by the *Jeffreys*, Mr. Thomas Arnold, bound from London for Pennsylvania and New Jersey: William Woodby, James Cary, William Shardlow, Percivall Toll, John Forth, John Harwood, Thomas

Crundall, Phillip Ford, George Richards, Hugh Lamb, Clement Plumsted, William Steward, William Dolbe. (PRO: E190/115/1, 125/3).

28 July. The following apprenticed in Middlesex: Elizabeth Harvey, aged 21, to serve John Edwards of Maryland, merchant, 5 years. (GLRO: MR/E/593).

30 July. Oxford Circuit prisoners reprieved to be transported to America. Gloucestershire: Margaret Tyler of Cirencester; Rotherick Williams of Cirencester; Elizabeth Gill Jr. of Stowell Inferior, spinster; Elizabeth Gill Sr. wife of Ralph Gill Sr. of Stowell Inferior; Ralph Gill Jr. of Stowell Inferior, miller. Oxfordshire: William Mason of Woodstock. Shropshire: John Teague of Moreton; John Edwards of Atcham. Staffordshire: Anthony Lunns of Baswich; John Terrell of Tettenhall; William Sheldon of Handsworth, nailer. Worcestershire: John Farley of Hanley Castle. (PRO: C66/3239/20).

30 July. The following apprenticed in Middlesex: Dorothy Goodrick, aged 20, to Charles Partis, 4 years Maryland by the *Potomack*, said Charles Partis Mr. (GLRO: MR/E/593).

30 July. Shipper by the *Abraham & Francis*, Mr. Edward Burford, bound from London for Virginia: William Paggen. (PRO: E190/115/1).

30 July. Shipper by the *Elizabeth & Katherine*, Mr. Timothy Keyser, bound from London for Virginia: William Paggen. (PRO: E190/115/1).

30 July-14 August. Shippers by the *Booth*, Mr. Peter Paggen, bound from London for Virginia: William Paggen, John Mann, Theophilus Turner. (PRO: E190/115/1).

1 August. The following apprenticed in London: Elizabeth Wood to Capt. Simon Flew, 4 years Jamaica. (LMWB13/247).

2-20 August. Shippers by the *Friendship* of Bristol bound from Bristol for Virginia: John Porter, Thomas Whittop. (PRO: E190/1146/1).

2 August-4 September. Shippers by the *Friendship* of Liverpool, Mr. William Crosman, bound from Liverpool for Pennsylvania: Henry Madocke, John Hodkinson, Richard Smithson, George Woodiard, Thomas Pemberton, John Pennington, Jonathan Scafe, Joseph Drake, John Hough, Jonathan Hayes, Gilbert Woolman, Samuell Borges, Joseph Clayton, Symon Ellis, Robert Hardman, William Stocker, Robert Crossman, John Sharples, Robert Crossman. (PRO: E190/1345/13).

3 August-6 September. The following apprenticed in Middlesex to go for four years to Maryland by the *Content*, Mr. William Johnson: Robert Boyer of Berkshire, sawyer aged 25, to William Johnson; Elizabeth Mason of London, spinster aged 21, to the same; Samuel Richardson of Banbury, Oxfordshire, pinmaker aged 21, to Richard Murphy of London, merchant; John Holmes of Yorkshire, aged 21, to the same; George Everygen of Dorset, aged 61, to the same, (7 years). (GLRO: MR/E/593).

4-25 August. Shippers by the *Endeavour*, Mr. John Quixley, bound from London for New England: Henry Hatley, Thomas Ingram, Joseph Hayes, Edward Cheltenham, Francis Fox, William Ashurst, Edmond White, Thomas Wells, Thomas Potter, Samuell Porter. (PRO: E190/115/1).

7 August. Shippers by the *Friendship*, Mr. Samuell Edwards, bound from London for Virginia: Thomas Stark, John Letton. (PRO: E190/115/1).

9 August. The following apprenticed in London: Robert Dey, formerly of Norwich but now of London, weaver, to John Burroughs of Northampton Co., Accomack, Virginia, merchant, to serve him 4 years. (LMWB13/252).

9 August. Mr. William Sanny, citizen and currier of London, appoints Mr. John Floyd near Boston, New England, as his attorney. (LMCD).

10 August. The following apprenticed in London: Edward Davenport of Waltham Cross, Essex, labourer, to Samuel Gilham of London, blacksmith, 4 years Virginia. (LMWB13/252).

11 August. Shipper by the *Hound*, Mr. Phineas Hide, bound from London for Maryland: Arthur Bailey. (PRO: E190/115/1).

13 August-1 September. Shippers by the *Agreement* of Plymouth, Mr. Isaac Blake, bound from Plymouth for Virginia: John Rogers, George Lapthorne. (PRO: E190/1047/13).

14-29 August. Shippers by the *Benedict Leonard*, Mr. Francis Partis, bound from London for Maryland: Richard Jelly, Edward Hollinshed, Corresby Cave, John Cherrey, John Gore. (PRO: E190/115/1).

14-23 August. Shippers by the *Globe*, Mr. Bartholomew Watts, bound from London for Virginia and Maryland: Samuell Greene, John Pryor, John Kirk. (PRO: E190/115/1).

15 August. Shipper by the *Welcome* of Bristol bound from Bristol for Virginia: Henry Daniell. (PRO: E190/1146/1).

15 August. Shipper by the *John* of Topsham, Mr. John Lyle, bound from Exeter for Virginia: Thomas Chrispin. (PRO: E190/961/5).

16 August. Shipper by the *William* of Bristol bound from Bristol for Virginia: John Collett. (PRO: E190/1146/1).

17 August. Shipper by the *Judith* of Plymouth, Mr. John Leane, bound from Plymouth for Virginia: Roger Mills. (PRO: E190/1047/13).

17 August. The following apprenticed in Middlesex: George Bate of Staffordshire, aged 21, to Francis Parties of London, mariner, 4 years Maryland by the *Benedict Leonard*, said Parties master. (GLRO: MR/E/593).

18 August. Shipper by the *Pearl* of Bideford, Mr. George Hanford, bound from Bideford for Virginia: John Smith. (PRO: E190/961/1).

18-23 August. Shippers by the *John* of Bristol bound from Bristol for Virginia: Henry Totterdell, Richard Gotly, Edward Briscoe. (PRO: E190/1146/1).

18 August-4 September. Shippers by the *Speedwell*, Mr. Benjamin Shapley, bound from London for New England: Gerrard Vanheythusen, Ralph Hatley. (PRO: E190/115/1).

20-25 August. Shippers by the *Stephen & Edward*, Mr. Sebastian Gurley [Ginge?], bound from London for Virginia: Robert Bristow, Thomas Starke, Hugh Aldworth, George Parke. (PRO: E190/115/1).

20-25 August. Shippers by the *John*, Mr. Daniel Bradley, bound from London for Virginia: Benjamin Bradley, Thomas Stark, Henige Robinson, Isaac Delytree. (PRO: E190/115/1).

20-29 August. Shippers by the *Assistance*, Mr. James Strong, bound from London for Virginia: Richard Wynn, John Harwood, Thomas Adams. (PRO: E190/115/1).

21-22 August. Shippers by the *Vine* of Liverpool, Mr. John Bankes, bound from Liverpool for Virginia: Thomas Johnson, Nathaniell Bacon, William Kendell, John Stranger, William Preeson. (PRO: E190/1345/13).

21 August-12 September. Shippers by the *White Fox*, Mr. George Purvis, bound from London for Virginia: Henry Lucas, Silvanus Thomas. (PRO: E190/115/1).

22 August. Shipper by the *Joseph & Ann*, Mr. Christopher Marsh, bound from London for Carolina: Abraham Carie. (PRO: E190/115/1).

22 August. Shipper by the *Henrietta* of Bideford, Mr. John Atkins, bound from Bideford for Maryland: John Davie. (PRO: E190/961/1).

22 August-5 September. Shippers by the *Resolution* of Bristol bound from Bristol for Virginia: Richard Griffeth, Giles Linscott, Jonathan Stone, Richard Finch, Michaell Shile, Henry Westover. (PRO: E190/1146/1).

23 August. Shipper by the *Industry*, Mr. Peter Peak, bound from London for Maryland: Margaret Fisher. (PRO: E190/115/1).

23-29 August. Shippers by the *Hopewell* of London bound from Bristol for Virginia: Abraham Wilde, Abraham Raven, Thomas Owen. (PRO: E190/1146/1).

24 August. Shipper by the *Dove* of Plymouth, Mr. Edward Blagg, bound from Plymouth for Virginia: John Addis & Co. (PRO: E190/1047/13).

25 August. The following apprenticed in London: Francis East to Phillip Redwood, 4 years Tobago. (LMWB13/270).

25 August. Petition of Robert Wadleigh, attorney for Jeremy Walford and John Amazeen of New England, planters, against George Walton for the award of lands in Great Island, New Hampshire. (APC).

25 August-11 September. Shippers by the *Maryland Merchant* bound from Bristol for Virginia: William Dorrington, George Tyte, Francis Hawkins, Guy Finch, Walter Uppington, Bryan Tandy, Anthony Mayle, Thomas Turner. (PRO: E190/1146/1).

25 August-10 October. Shippers by the *Recovery*, Mr. Thomas Hasted, bound from London for Carolina: Thomas Lone, John Plover, Richard Mees, William Thornburgh, James Ball, William Nottell. (PRO: E190/115/1).

27 August-12 September. Shippers by the *Content*, Mr. William Johnson, bound from London for Maryland: Thomas Elwes, James Galway, Francis Hiller. (PRO: E190/115/1).

28 August-7 September. Shippers by the *Culpepper*, Mr. Christopher Morgan, bound from London for Virginia: John Plover, James Harris, Micajah Perry. (PRO: E190/115/1).

28 August-28 September. Shippers by the *Zebulon*, Mr. Nicholas Goodridge, bound from London for Virginia and New Jersey: Robert Thorowgood, Joseph Pile, John Ellis, Solomon Weeks, Jane Metcalfe, Henry Dandy, Gawen Lawrey, William Dockwra, Nicholas Russell. (PRO: E190/115/1).

28 August-1 October. Shippers by the *Constant Mary*, Mr. Edward Rhodes, bound from London for Virginia: John Hill, John Hanford, Francis Deane, Thomas Nelson, Thomas Jaques, Stephen York, Edward Pate, Anthony Palmer. (PRO: E190/115/1).

28 August-11 October. Shippers by the *Experiment*, Mr. James Congdon, bound from London for Virginia: John Plover, Francis Hiller, John Hubbuck, Richard Hattolph. (PRO: E190/115/1).

29 August. Shipper by the *Happy Return* of Plymouth, Mr. Robert Goodinge, bound from Plymouth for Virginia: David Teage. (PRO: E190/1047/13).

29-31 August. Shippers by the *Blackamore* bound from Bristol for Virginia: Thomas Tayer, John Williamson. (PRO: E190/1146/1).

29 August-4 September. Shippers by the *Hannah*, Mr. Anthony Gester, bound from London for Virginia: John Brett, Francis Lee. (PRO: E190/115/1).

29 August-27 September. Shippers by the *Samuell & Thomas*, Mr. Thomas Jenner, bound from London for New England: Edward White, Joshua Pordage, Benjamin Gerrard, Ralph Mannering, Charles Duke, Thomas Cockerill, Hugh Strode, Richard Fawcet, John Terry, Elizabeth Scott, John Boult, Thomas Todd, Richard Goodall. (PRO: E190/115/1).

August. Administration with will of John Avery of Dorchester County, Maryland. (AW).

1 September. Shipper by the *Elizabeth* of Exeter, Mr. Nicholas Sainthill, bound from Exeter for Virginia: Thomas Whitehair. (PRO: E190/961/5).

1-13 September. Shippers by the *Society* of Bristol, Mr. Thomas Jordan, bound from Bristol for Virginia: John Hort, John Cooper, Samuell Packer, William Diggs, William Crabb, William Alloway. (PRO: E190/1146/1).

3-18 September. Shippers by the *Samuell & Mary* of Bristol, Mr. Thomas Skeves, bound from Bristol for Pennsylvania and Virginia: William Sallaway, Thomas Jaques, Barnaby Wilcox, Andrew Barnes, Samuell Beake, Joseph Kirle, John Perce, John Hughs, John Batchelor, John Lysons, James West, William Alway, John Armstrong, John Parrott, Henry Davis, John Moone, Thomas Masters, Edward Comly, John Bristow, Joseph Blease, Joseph Browne, John Hodge, Christopher Mathews, John Wyse, Francis Bedford. (PRO: E190/1146/1).

4 September. The following apprenticed in Middlesex to serve John Galwith of Maryland, planter: Henry Sutheth, aged 15, 7 years, witnessed by James Galwith; Phillip Ryan, aged 21, 5 years, witnessed by the same. (GLRO: MR/E/593).

4-7 September. The following apprenticed in Middlesex to go by the *Mary*, Mr. John Harris, to Maryland: Hugh Owen (Owin) of London, aged 21, to Walter Hatch of London, merchant, 4 years; George Obie of London, gardener aged 24, to the same, 4 years; Lawrence Clay of London, aged 21, to Joseph Dayne of London, merchant, 5 years; Rebecca Dorson of Chatham, Kent, spinster aged 16, to William Haveland, 5 years. (GLRO: MR/E/593).

4-29 September. The following apprenticed in Middlesex to go by the *Richard & Elizabeth*, Mr. Nicholas Pryn, to serve him for four years: Richard Elkins of Dorset, aged 22, to Virginia; Roger Crosdell of London, aged 32, to Maryland; Joseph Marshall of London, aged 22, to Virginia; John Williamson of London, accountant aged 21, to Virginia; William Withers of London, husbandman aged 22, to Virginia; Thomas Sisson, aged 21, to Virginia; Mary Wrinch, aged 27, to Maryland; Martha Kimber, aged 22, to Virginia; Simon Pooke, aged 24, to Virginia. Isaac Shafield, aged 18, to Virginia. (GLRO: MR/E/593).

5 September. Deposition by Basil Lambe, citizen and girdler of London, aged 26, that Isaac Waldron of Boston, New England, physician, became indebted by bond of 22 February 1679 to Daniel Blundell, citizen and girdler of London, now deceased, for haberdashery sent by the *Blessing*, Mr. John Berry. Mary Blundell, relict and executrix of Daniel Blundell, has appointed Mr. Daniel Allin of Boston, merchant, as her attorney. (LMCD).

5 September. The following apprenticed in Middlesex: Rebecca Bignall of St. Giles in the Fields, aged 29, to Joseph Doyne, 4 years Virginia; Grace Sheppard of Whitechapel, aged 21, to Edward Brook, 4 years Jamaica. (GLRO: MR/E/593).

5-22 September. Shippers by the *Southampton Merchant*, Mr. Andrew Belcher, bound from London for New England: John Wood, John Hall, John Lyons, William White, Joseph Alford, William Grand. (PRO: E190/115/1).

6 September. The following apprenticed in Middlesex: Margaret Rogers, aged 19, to John Wilson, 4 years Maryland. (GLRO: MR/E/593).

6 September. Deposition by Thomas Hene, citizen and joiner of London, aged 37, that Benjamin Rozer of Maryland, merchant, became indebted by bond of 4 September 1680 to Stephen Kendricke of St. Martin in the Fields, Middlesex. Mr. Humphrey Warren of Maryland, merchant, has been appointed attorney. (LMCD).

6 September. Shipper by the *Eagle* of Bideford, Mr. Eusebius Easterbrook, bound from Bideford for New England: said Eusebius Easterbrook. (PRO: E190/961/1).

6-7 September. The following apprenticed in Middlesex to serve Richard Batt of London for four years in Maryland: Margaret Mastys, aged 27; Thomas Peter Fenix Lightwich, aged 24. (GLRO: MR/E/593).

6-11 September. The following apprenticed in Middlesex: George Adamson, aged 18, to John Wilson, 6 years Maryland; Thomas Nason, aged 21, to the same, 4 years Maryland. (GLRO: MR/E/593).

7 September. The following apprenticed in Middlesex: James Gooding of London, aged 21, to John Lee of London, merchant, 4 years Maryland by the *Hanna*, Mr. Guester; John Dowson of London, aged 18, to the same, 7 years Maryland by the same ship; Thomas Owens (Owines), aged 28, to James Phillips, 4 years Virginia; Elizabeth Jackson, aged 17, to Ernesto (Arnatt) Keckerbart, 4 years Virginia. (GLRO: MR/E/593).

7-12 September. Shippers by the *Concord* of Bristol bound from Bristol for Virginia: John Shewell, John Peirson, Faulke Adams, Symon Hurle. (PRO: E190/1146/1).

8 September. Deposition by Christopher Rigault of London, merchant aged 56, that he has not received payment for brandy consigned in 1674 by the *Barnaby*, Captain Matthew Ryder, to George Seaton of Virginia, gent, despite an order made in Gloucester County Court on 16 May 1683. (LMCD).

8 September. Shipper by the *Friendship* of Lyme, Mr. John Burton, bound from Lyme for Virginia: John Burridge. (PRO: E190/885/7).

8-18 September. Shippers by the *Mary*, Mr. John Harris, bound from London for Virginia and Maryland: Stephen Bearcroft, William Palmer, John Letton. (PRO: E190/115/1).

10 September. Shippers by the *Two Brothers* of London, Mr. Thomas Smith, bound from Southampton for New York: Thomas Trench, James Barton, Phillip Trench. (PRO: E190/832/13).

10 September. The following apprenticed in Middlesex: Howell Jones, aged 21, to John Woosley, 4 years Jamaica. (GLRO: MR/E/593).

10-14 September. Shippers by the *Daniell & Elizabeth* of Plymouth, Mr. William Ginnes, bound from Plymouth for Virginia: Thomas Constable, George Orchard. (PRO: E190/1047/13).

10-17 September. Shippers by the *Diligence* bound from Exeter for Virginia: Joseph Mauditt, John Vicary, Adam Gupwell, James Fulwood, Richard Coles, William Elston. (PRO: E190/961/5).

11 September. Shipper by the *Francis & Mary* of Bristol bound from Bristol for Virginia: Peter Waddinge. (PRO: E190/1146/1).

11 September. Symon Coombe of Lyme Regis, Dorset, bound to John Davie of Lyme Regis, mariner, to serve 4 years in America. (DRO B7/M9).

11 September. The following apprenticed in Middlesex: Henry Sury, aged 21, to Samuel Phillips, 4 years Maryland; Jeane Lewis, aged 22, to John Jackson, 4 years Virginia. (GLRO: MR/E/593).

11-18 September. The following apprenticed in Middlesex to James Conaway, master of the *Baltimore*, to serve him in Maryland: Samuell Northerow of Leicestershire, aged 25, 4 years; Martha Reader of Hertfordshire, spinster aged 19, 6 years; John Harwood of London, aged 22, 4 years; Thomas Knightsmith of London, aged 21, 4 years; John Start of London, aged 16, 8 years; Frances Francklin of Battersea, Surrey, aged 20, 4 years; John Smith of London, aged 21, 4 years; John Hannam of London, aged 20, 4 years. (GLRO: MR/E/593).

13 September. The following apprenticed in Middlesex: William Thomas, aged 24, to serve William Webb of Rappahannock, Virginia, 4 years as a shipwright. (GLRO: MR/E/593).

13 September. Humphry Face of Petherton, Somerset, bound to John Bull of Lyme Regis, mariner, to serve 4 years in America. (DRO B7/M9).

13 September. Shippers by the *Beginning* of Bideford, Mr. Richard Southcott, bound from Bideford for Virginia: Josias Ellett, Nicholas Docton. (PRO: E190/961/1).

13-14 September. Shippers by the *Sarah* of Exeter, Mr. Christopher Hetty, bound from Exeter for Carolina: Thomas Smith, Thomas Harris. (PRO: E190/961/5).

14 September. George Kyte of Coombe, Somerset, bound to John Burridge of Lyme Regis, Dorset, to serve 4 years in America & to go by the *Friendship*, Mr. John Davie. (DRO B7/M9).

14-17 September. Shippers by the *Baltimore*, Mr. James Conway, bound from London for Maryland: Richard Clagett, James Kelk. (PRO: E190/115/1).

15 September. The following apprenticed in Middlesex: Mary Peirson, aged 21, to Richard Lucey, 4 years Maryland; John Kinsbury of London, aged 30, to William Haveland, 4 years Jamaica and to seek his redemption after arrival. (GLRO: MR/E/593).

17 September. William French of Cullyford (*sic*), Devon, bound to John Davie of Lyme Regis, mariner, to serve 4 years in America; John Blythman of Eversley, Hampshire, bound to the same to serve 4 years in America; John Davies of Somerset bound to Samuell Alford of Taunton, Somerset, tucker, to serve 4 years in Virginia. (DRO B7/M9).

17 September. The following apprenticed in Middlesex: John Mitchell of London, aged 26, to Christopher Eveling of London, mariner, 4 years Virginia by the *William & Thomas*, said Christopher Eveling Mr.; Mary Weaver, aged 23, to John Becker, 4 years Virginia; Benjamin Cooper, son of John C. of Bermondsey, Surrey, victualler, to William Cooper of Stepney, merchant, 4 years Virginia, witnessed by his father John Cooper. (GLRO: MR/E/593).

17-18 September. Shippers by the *William & Thomas*, Mr. Christopher Eveling, bound from London for Virginia: Richard Atkinson, George Layfield. (PRO: E190/115/1).

17-22 September. Shipper by the *Submission* of Liverpool bound from Liverpool for Virginia: James Settle. (PRO: E190/1345/13).

18 September. The following apprenticed in Middlesex: John Trowell of St. Leonard, Shoreditch, Middlesex, blacksmith aged 30, to William Dockwra of London, merchant, 4 years New Jersey, and to receive 25 acres of land, etc., witnessed by Joseph Trowell. (GLRO: MR/E/593).

18 September. Shipper by the *Elizabeth* of Weymouth, Mr. John Cox, bound from Weymouth for Virginia: James Gould. (PRO: E190/885/1).

18 September-16 October. Shippers by the *Augustine*, Mr. Zachary Taylor, bound from London for Virginia: George Baker, John Viner, Matthew Jones, Stephen Sykes, John Thornburgh, John Nason, Vincent Goddard, John Shert, Richard Bent, John Sole. (PRO: E190/115/1).

19 September. The following apprenticed in Middlesex to serve Thomas Sloper of Pertuxen, Maryland, gent, for four years: Jone Young, aged 21; Martha Barton, aged 22; Mary Glover, aged 21. (GLRO: MR/E/593).

20 September. The following apprenticed in Middlesex: Mary Jenkins, aged 23, to Francis Parsons of Stepney, mariner, 4 years Virginia; John Wilson, aged

21, to William Yorke of Stepney, mariner, 4 years Virginia. (GLRO: MR/E/593).

20-24 September. The following apprenticed in Middlesex to Thomas Wyche of London, merchant, to go by the *Recovery*, Mr. Thomas Hasted: Zachariah Smale of London, sawyer aged 21, 4 years Carolina; Mary Chiswell of London, spinster aged 24, 4 years Virginia; Richard Hind of Kent, basket maker aged 24, 4 years Virginia; John Bennett of London, aged 21, 4 years Virginia. (GLRO: MR/E/593).

20 September-1 October. The following apprenticed in Middlesex to James Galwith of London, silk thrower, to serve him for five years in Maryland: Mary Freeman of London, spinster aged 22; John Malin Jr., gardener aged 18, witnessed by his father John Malin Sr. (GLRO: MR/E/593).

21 September. The following apprenticed in London: Charles Mills, son of Andrew M., deceased, to Richard Owen, 7 years Maryland, witnessed by his brother-in-law, Robert Thompson. (LMWB13/282).

21 September. The following apprenticed in Middlesex: Everilday Prichard, [spinster] aged 21, to Samuel White, 4 years Virginia; Ann Browne, aged 22, to John Thorne, 4 years Virginia. (GLRO: MR/E/593).

22 September. The following apprenticed in London: Edward Cammocke, son of William C., deceased, to serve Samuel Bourne of Maryland, gent, for 10 years, with the consent of his mother. (LMWB13/283).

22-25 September. Shippers by the *Hope* of Plymouth, Mr. John Rudds, bound from Plymouth for Virginia: Phillip Willcox, Thomas Yeabsley, John Luke, Joseph Brookinge. (PRO: E190/1047/13).

22 September-17 October. Shippers by the *Genoa Merchant*, Mr. John Wynn, bound from London for Virginia: Thomas Curtis, Jeremiah Bradfield. (PRO: E190/115/1).

24 September. Shipper by the *Unity* of Lyme, Mr. John Burton, bound from Lyme for Virginia: John Burridge. (PRO: E190/885/7).

24 September. The following apprenticed in Middlesex: Sarah Green, aged 22, to John Banks, 4 years Virginia; Abigall Taylor, aged 24, to Nathaniel Snow, 4 years Barbados; Mary Harris, aged 25, to James Congden, 4 years Virginia; Frances Goreham, aged 24, to the same, 4 years Virginia. (GLRO: MR/E/593).

26 September. The following apprenticed in Middlesex: Thomas Greene, blacksmith aged 30, to William Fles of Wapping, mariner, 4 years Jamaica. (GLRO: MR/E/593).

27 September. Shipper by the *Swallow* of Boston, Mr. John Carter, bound from Weymouth for New England: said John Carter. (PRO: E190/885/1).

27 September. The following apprenticed in Middlesex: Edward Taylor, aged 24, to Thomas Green, 4 years Jamaica. (GLRO: MR/E/593).

27 September-26 October. Shippers by the *Duke of York*, Mr. John Purvis, bound from London for Virginia: Robert Fairman, William Smith, Francis Camfield, Susanna Marriot, Edward Pate. (PRO: E190/115/1).

29 September. The following apprenticed in Middlesex: Nicholas Rowlson to Joseph Paine, 4 years Maryland. (GLRO: MR/E/593).

30 September. Shippers by the *Shield* of Stockton, Mr. Daniell Toes, bound from Hull for Virginia: Gilbert Metcalfe [*elsewhere* Heathcote], Richard Metcalfe, George Spencer. (PRO: E190/325/3).

September. Administration of John Fitzer of Maryland, bachelor. (AW).

1 October. Shipper by the *Richard & Elizabeth*, Mr. Nicholas Pryn, bound from London for Virginia: Edward Leman. (PRO: E190/115/1).

1 October. Shipper by the *Hart* of Bideford, Mr. Henry Perrin, bound from Bideford for Maryland: Richard Laud. (PRO: E190/961/1).

1-2 October. Shippers by the *Industry* of Bristol bound from Bristol for Virginia: Jonathan Stone, Timothy Davis. (PRO: E190/1146/1).

1-2 October. Shippers by the *James & Thomas* of Plymouth, Mr. Thomas Shepherd, bound from Plymouth for Virginia: Thomas Warne, Abraham Beele, John Edgcombe. (PRO: E190/1047/13).

2 October. Shipper by the *Swallow* of Liverpool, Mr. Thomas Withington, bound from Liverpool for Virginia: John Pemberton. (PRO: E190/1345/13).

2-15 October. Shippers by the *Industry* bound from Plymouth for Virginia: Samuell Brett, Joseph Braking, John Rogers. (PRO: E190/1047/13).

2 October-9 November. Shippers by the *Barnaby*, Mr. Matthew Ryder, bound from London for Virginia and Pennsylvania: Richard Goodall, Samuell Billing, John Todd, John Ingles, John Knight. (PRO: E190/115/1).

3 October. Shipper by the *Love*, Mr. Samuel Phillips, bound from London for Maryland: Thomas Elwes. (PRO: E190/115/1).

3-8 October. Shippers by the *Constant*, Mr. Thomas Smith, bound from London for Virginia: George Richards, William Stonestreet. (PRO: E190/115/1).

3-23 October. Shippers by the *Paradise*, Mr. William Eveling, bound from London for Virginia: Henry Lucas, James Carey, Richard Halley. (PRO: E190/115/1).

3-24 October. Shippers by the *Priscilla*, Mr. Joseph Moulton, bound from London for New England: Edward Mann, Benjamin Alsop, Edward Harrington, Joseph Cleare, Samuel Porter, Samuel Bail, John Dunton, Robert Patten, Gilbert Bakewell. (PRO: E190/115/1).

5-16 October. Shippers by the *Hopewell*, Mr. John Rudds, bound from London for Virginia: John Phelps, Andrew Kenrick, Bartholomew Parr, Elizabeth Preston. (PRO: E190/115/1).

5-16 October. Shippers by the *Alithea* of Bristol bound from Bristol for Virginia: Edward Perrin, Richard Benson, Samuell Chambers, George Webb. (PRO: E190/1146/1).

6 October. Shippers by the *Mary*, Mr. Richard Tibbot, bound from London for Virginia: Edward Leman, Micajah Perry. (PRO: E190/115/1).

6 October. The following apprenticed in Middlesex: James Edwards of London, aged 20, to James Randall Esq. of London, 4 years Maryland. (GLRO: MR/E/593).

8 October. Shipper by the *Windmill* of Plymouth, Mr. James Trefry, bound from Plymouth for Virginia: John Rogers. (PRO: E190/1047/13).

8-19 October. The following apprenticed in Middlesex to serve Thomas Carey, master of the *Adventure*: Robert Cooper of London, aged 16, 8 years Maryland; Rachell Ethewe of London, spinster aged 22, 4 years Maryland; John Henry of London, groom aged 23, 4 years Maryland; Richard Jones of London, aged 21, 4 years Maryland; Charles Guy of London, aged 23, 4 years Maryland; Susanna Beatson, aged 19, 5 years Virginia; Stephen Hargoose of London, groom aged 23, 4 years Maryland. (GLRO: MR/E/593).

9 October. Shipper by the *Young Prince*, Mr. Thomas Heron(?), bound from London for Virginia: Thomas Sands. (PRO: E190/115/1).

10 October. The following apprenticed in Middlesex: William Tingler?, aged 21, to William Phillips, master of the *Love*, 4 years Virginia; John Rogers, aged 31, and his wife Hester Rogers, aged 20, of London, to the same, 4 years Maryland; Barbary Field, aged 19, to serve Thomas Boile of Jamaica, surgeon, 4 years. (GLRO: MR/E/593).

10-26 October. Shippers by the *Isaac & Sarah* bound from Bristol for Virginia: Edward Martindale, John Baber, Walter Tayler, John Moore, Alexander Davy, Samuell Kitchener, John Temple, William Rother. (PRO: E190/1146/1).

11 October. Shipper by the *Penelope* of Salem, Mr. William Lord, bound from Plymouth for New England: Robert Hutchings. (PRO: E190/1047/13).

12 October. Shipper by the *Adventure*, Mr. Thomas Carey, bound from London for Virginia: Richard Booth. (PRO: E190/115/1).

15 October. Shipper by the *Alexander* of Bristol bound from Bristol for Virginia: William Wakely. (PRO: E190/1146/1).

15-20 October. Shippers by the *Unicorn*, Mr. William Norrington, bound from London for Virginia: Anthony Phillips, Thomas Petter, John Letten, Nicholas Hayward. (PRO: E190/115/1).

15-27 October. The following apprenticed in Middlesex to go by the *Unicorn*, Mr. John Norrington: Michael Askin of Middlesex, aged 22, to William Haviland, 4 years Maryland; David Lewis of Middlesex, aged 18, to John Clarke, 7 years Virginia; John East of Middlesex, aged 19, to John Norrington, 4 years Maryland. (GLRO: MR/E/593).

15 October-12 November. The following apprenticed in Middlesex to go by the *Mary*, Mr. Tippett: Jone Churchill of Middlesex, dairymaid aged 26, to William Haveland, 4 years Maryland; Lydea Coaks of Middlesex, spinster aged 18, to the same, 4 years Maryland; John Evered (?) of Middlesex, aged 16, to the same, 6 years Maryland, witnessed by his father-in-law and mother, John and Elizabeth Stephenson; Anne Shipperson of Middlesex, spinster aged 21, to the same, 4 years Maryland John Stansell of Middlesex, aged 21, to the same, 4 years Virginia; Francis Farrow of Middlesex, aged 16, to Edmund Putman of London, merchant, 8 years Maryland; William Meade of Middlesex, aged 27, to John Smith, merchant, 4 years Virginia. (GLRO: MR/E/593).

16 October. The following apprenticed in London: Isaac Steele, aged 21, of Nantwich, Cheshire, clockmaker, to serve Henry Hartwell of Virginia, merchant, 5 years. (LMWB13/300).

16 October. Shipper by the *Leopard* of Liverpool, Mr. Jeremiah Wilson, bound from Liverpool for Maryland: David Procter. (PRO: E190/1345/13).

16-23 October. The following apprenticed in Middlesex to go by the *Duke of York*, Mr. John Purvis: John Gillmore of Middlesex, aged 21, to John Clarke of London, merchant, 4 years Maryland; William Fisher of Middlesex, aged 21, to the same, 4 years Virginia; Richard Stafford of Middlesex, aged 23, to William Haveland, 4 years Virginia; Joseph Priestley of Middlesex, accountant aged 24, to the same, 4 years Virginia; Thomas Cattbury of Middlesex, aged 20, to the same, 7 years Virginia; John Horne of Middlesex, tanner aged 32, to the same, 4 years Virginia; Christopher Morton of Middlesex, aged 18, to John Purvis of London, mariner and merchant, 8 years Virginia; Robert Steele of Middlesex, tailor aged 21, to Francis Lee of London, merchant, 4 years Virginia. (GLRO: MR/E/593).

17 October-9 November. The following apprenticed in Middlesex to go to Virginia by the *Barnaby*, Mr. Matthew Ryder: William Howlett of Middlesex, aged 16, to Christopher Deane of London, merchant, 7 years Virginia; James Johnson of Middlesex, aged 22, to the same, for Virginia; James Jones of Middlesex, aged 21, to the same, 4 years Virginia; Henry Harbridge of Middlesex, aged 22, to the same, 4 years Virginia; James Elliott of Middlesex, aged 22, to the same, 4 years Virginia; John Bowles of Middlesex, aged 22, to the same, 4 years Virginia; Edmund Rice of Middlesex, aged 21, to the same, 4 years Virginia; Robert Morton of Middlesex, shipwright aged 30, to John Norrington, 4 years Virginia; Thomas Stevens to the same, 7 years Virginia; Isaac Steel, aged 23, to Mathew Ryder, 4 years Virginia. (GLRO: MR/E/593).

19 October. The following apprenticed in London: Sybilla Cartwright, spinster, to Francis White of Virginia, merchant, with the consent of her mother. (LMWB13/302).

19-23 October. Shippers by the *Virginia Factor*, Mr. William Hill, bound from London for Maryland: John Welch, Thomas Elwes. (PRO: E190/115/1).

19 October-12 November. Shippers by the *Rose & Crown*, Mr. Bartholomew Clements, bound from London for Virginia: John Lloyd, George Richards. (PRO: E190/115/1).

22 October. The following apprenticed in London: Thomas Tansly, aged 34, to Gilbert Ashley, carpenter, 4 years New Providence; John Bernard to the same, 4 years, with the consent of his father; John Jenkins to the same, 6 years, with the consent of his father; Jane Purton to the same, 4 years, with the consent of her father, John P.; Alice Jones to the same, 4 years. (LMWB13/304).

22 October. The following apprenticed in Middlesex: Theophilus Willoby, aged 19, to John Clarke, 6 years Maryland; William Moors, aged 18, to James Emmerson of Stepney, mariner, 4 years Virginia. (GLRO: MR/E/593).

24 October-2 November. Shippers by the *Exchange* of Bideford, Mr. Mark Chappell, bound from Bideford for Maryland: William Titherly, William Champlin. (PRO: E190/961/1).

26 October. The following apprenticed in Middlesex: Joseph Betts of Middlesex, aged 22, to John Smith of London, merchant, 4 years Virginia by *Virginia Factor*, Mr. John Hill. (GLRO: MR/E/593).

26 October. Shipper by the *Maryland Merchant* of Bideford, Mr. John Scweek (*sic*), bound from Bideford for Maryland: John Davie. (PRO: E190/961/1).

27 October. The following apprenticed in Middlesex: Hannah Atkins, aged 21, to Phillip Gower, 4 years Jamaica. (GLRO: MR/E/593).

October. Administration of George Ludlowe of Hedingham Sible, Essex, who died in Virginia, bachelor. (AW).

October. Administration of Richard Gibbs of St. Dunstan in the West, London, who died in New York. (AW).

2 November. The following apprenticed in London: William Cox to Philip Gower, 4 years Jamaica. (LMWB13/322).

2 November. The following apprenticed in Middlesex: Elizabeth Selnister, aged 16, whose father and mother are dead, to John Purvis, 6 years Virginia. (GLRO: MR/E/593).

3-5 November. The following apprenticed in Middlesex to go by the *Charles*, Mr. Daniel Bird: Mathew Greene of Middlesex, aged 16, to Edmund Putman, 8 years Virginia; John Smith of Middlesex, aged 30, to William Haveland, 4 years Maryland; Nicholas Easton of Middlesex, aged 21, to the same, 4 years Virginia. (GLRO: MR/E/593).

6 November. The following apprenticed in Middlesex: William Foredom, aged 22, to William Haveland, 4 years Virginia. (GLRO: MR/E/593).

6 November. Shipper by the *Charles*, Mr. Daniel Bird, bound from London for Virginia: Charles Stepkins. (PRO: E190/115/1).

7 November. The following apprenticed in Middlesex: Katherine Thompson, aged 22, to Mathew Prince, 4 years Virginia; Peter Johnson, aged 25, to Matthew Trynion of Shadwell, mariner, 4 years Virginia. (GLRO: MR/E/593).

7-16 November. Shippers by the *America* of Liverpool, Mr. Thomas Goller, bound from Liverpool for Maryland: Cornelius Madocke, Thomas Clayton, Richard Banister. (PRO: E190/1345/13).

7 November-11 December. The following apprenticed in Middlesex to go by the *William*, Mr. John Bennett, to Jamaica: Evan Evans of Middlesex, aged 30, to John Bennett of London, merchant & mariner, 4 years; William Key of Middlesex, aged 21, to the same, 6 years; Humphrey Dixon, aged 26, to the same, 4 years; Hannah Miles, aged 18, to the same, 4 years; John Hennagin, aged 23, to the same, 3 years; Thomas Kelson of Middlesex, cordwainer aged 22, to William Haveland, 4 years; William Bird of Middlesex, aged 21, to John Rose of London, merchant, 4 years. (GLRO: MR/E/593).

8-17 November. Shippers by the *Sarum Merchant* of Poole, Mr. William Dolbery, bound from Poole for Maryland: James Bennett, Thomas Cooker, Francis Harbin, William Toope, William Dowse. (PRO: E190/885/5).

8 November-21 January 1684. The following apprenticed in Middlesex to go to Barbados for four years by the *William & Robert*, Mr. Giles Bond: John Ellis of Middlesex, aged 21, to Tobias Frare of London, merchant; Joseph Wilson of Middlesex, aged 21, to the same; Robert Hill of Middlesex, aged 23, to Anthony Wallinger of London, merchant, William Whaley of Middlesex, aged 24, to the same; William Giles of Middlesex, currier aged 28, to William Haveland; Henry Underwood of Middlesex, farrier smith aged 28, to the same; Thomas Gobell of Middlesex, aged 31, to the same; John Birt of Middlesex, tobacco pipe maker aged 23, to the same; John Kym of Middlesex, smith, to the same, to seek his redemption on arrival; Samuel Johnson of Middlesex, house carpenter, aged 24, to the same; Francis Colman of Middlesex, ploughman aged 30, to the same; Joseph Midleton of Middlesex, blacksmith aged 24, to the same; John Brittland of Middlesex, tailor aged 21, to the same; Samuel Norman of Middlesex, aged 21, to the same; John Seddick of Middlesex, bricklayer aged 22, to the same; Andrew Ashley, aged 24, of Roso [?Rocester], Staffordshire, son of John A., deceased, to the same; John Owen of Middlesex, aged 22, to John Williams of London, merchant; Thomas Paine, ploughman aged 21, son of Thomas Paine of Northleach, Gloucestershire, deceased, to Sir Peter Collington of London, merchant. (GLRO: MR/E/593).

9-15 November. Shippers by the *Lamb* of Liverpool, Mr. William Glover, bound from Liverpool for Virginia: Peter Allerton, Nathaniell Marier, Thomas Sandeford. (PRO: E190/1345/13).

9-17 November Shippers by the *Reserve* of Liverpool bound from Maryland: Christopher Phanmoore, Thomas Clayton. (PRO: E190/1345/13).

10 November. The following apprenticed in London: Israell Say to Thomas Walsh, merchant, 5 years Virginia. (LMWB13/326).

10 November-6 December. The following apprenticed in Middlesex to go to Virginia by the *Judith*, Mr. Trym: Thomas Wootton of Middlesex, aged 21, to William Haveland, 4 years; Kabell Dibdon of Middlesex, aged 16, to John Williams of London, mariner, 9 years. (GLRO: MR/E/593).

13 November. Shipper by the *Hope* of Whitehaven, Mr. John Walls, bound from Liverpool for Maryland: David Poole. (PRO: E190/1345/13).

16 November-5 December. Shippers by the *Judith*, Mr. Matthew Trim, bound from London for Virginia: Joseph Webb, Edmond Clark, Edward Calthorp, John Jeffreys, Joshua Hassell. (PRO: E190/115/1).

22-24 November. Shipper by the *Speedwell* of Poole, Mr. John Skott, bound from Poole for Maryland: said John Skott. (PRO: E190/885/5).

29 November-8 December. Shippers by the *Owners Goodwill* of Hull, Mr. William Yeilder, bound from Hull for Virginia: Richard Metcalfe, George Spencer, Elizabeth Chapellow, William Idle. (PRO: E190/325/3).

1 December. The following apprenticed in Middlesex: William Davis, aged 22, to Francis Pain of Limehouse, mariner, 4 years Virginia. (GLRO: MR/E/593).

3 December. The following apprenticed in Middlesex: George Ivory, aged 18, to serve Roger Adams of Jamaica, planter, and Ann his wife, 6 years. (GLRO: MR/E/593).

5 December. Shipper by the *Thomas & Ann*, Mr. Thomas Singleton, bound from London for New York: said Thomas Singleton. (PRO: E190/115/1).

7-8 December. The following apprenticed in Middlesex to serve Robert Russell of Stepney, mariner, in Barbados: Richard Betham, 6 years; Henry Boddard, aged 22, 4 years. (GLRO: MR/E/593).

8 December. The following apprenticed in London: Isaack Steel to Christopher Prissick, 4 years Barbados. (LMWB13/340).

10 December. Shipper by the *John & Elizabeth*, Mr. Jonas Leech, bound from London for Virginia: Thomas Potter. (PRO: E190/115/1).

12 December. Newgate prisoners reprieved to be transported to Barbados. London: Thomas Potts, merchant; William Riggs; John Butler; William Knowles; Joseph Dunckley; Sarah Pearson, spinster; Frances Marshall alias Whipple alias Flower, spinster; Laurence Addington; Joseph Curtis; Peter Deverson; James Hancorne; Sidley Vandelo; Charles Roberts; Jonathan Parsons; Robert Valliony; Samuel Mathews. Middlesex: Francis Johnson of Shoreditch; Thomas Walker of St. Andrew Holborn; Thomas Cariffe of St. Martin in the Fields; Isabel Syms, wife of William Syms, alias Isabel Hayles, spinster, of the same; Elizabeth Bird, wife of George Bird of the same; Peter Anderson of St. Mary le Bow or St. Botolph Aldgate; Thomas Barratt of Hornsey; John Knott of Islington; Mary Marsh, wife of Daniel Marsh, alias Mary Bryant, spinster, of Stepney; Richard Smith of the same; Christopher Moore of St. Clement Danes; Humphrey Hoggins of the same; John Knight of Enfield; John Peybody of the same; Thomas Edmonds of the same; William Smith of Chelsea; John Greene of Whitechapel; Roger Samuell of Wrexham, Denbighshire, for manslaughter; Peter Davison of Hawarden, Flint. (PRO: C66/3236/12).

12 December. The following apprenticed in Middlesex: Joseph Johnson, aged 27, to Richard Batts, 4 years Barbados; John Parish of Essex, aged 16, to James Conaway, master of the *Baltimore*, 7 years Maryland by the said ship. (GLRO: MR/E/593).

13 December. The following apprenticed in Middlesex: John Lomax, aged 15, to serve Robert Adams of Jamaica, planter, and Ann his wife, 7 years. (GLRO: MR/E/593).

18 December-5 January. The following apprenticed in Middlesex to go for four years to Nevis by the *St. George*, Mr. Thomas Dunn: Daniel Arundell of Middlesex, aged 23, to William Wrayford of London, merchant; Thomas Smith of Middlesex, aged 23, to the same; Thomas Swann of Middlesex, aged 23, to the same; Thomas Honywell of Middlesex, aged 18, to Thomas Dunn, mariner, witnessed by his father, William Honywell; William Symmons of Middlesex, aged 21, to the same. (GLRO: MR/E/593).

19 December. The following apprenticed in London: Charles Mortlack, son of John M. of Nottingham, ironmonger, to Barbara Orgill, 4 years Jamaica, with the consent of his father. (LMWB13/346).

20 December. The following apprenticed in London: Katherine Bull, aged 24, of Shoreditch, Middlesex, spinster, to Christopher Jefferson Esq. of London, 5 years St. Christopher's; (LMWB13/347).

28 December. The following apprenticed in London: James Cotmore, son of James C. of St. Giles Cripplegate, London, victualler, to John Bawdon of London, merchant, 3 years Nevis to serve as a cooper. (LMWB13/350).

1683-1685?. Fishmongers' Company records of apprentices bound to foreign plantations [*See note in Introduction*].

Bound to Robert Bristow [Briscoe] for Virginia: William Colewell; Joseph Motley, with the consent of his mother.

Bound to Rainsford Waterhouse for Jamaica: Francis Nicholls, aged 25; Robert Rouse, aged 25; Thomas King, aged 35; Joseph Norman of Christchurch, Surrey; William Sanderson, aged 23.

Bound to Mathew Yates for Jamaica: Henry Bourne, aged 27; William Smyth, aged 39.

Bound to John Bennett for Jamaica: Ruth Gosse, aged 28; John Peters, aged 23.

Bound to Henry Bignall for Jamaica: Samuell Dawson, aged 26; James Barrow, aged 26; William Archer, aged 40; Henry Freeborne, aged 30; Samuell Fairefax, aged 25.

Bound to James Claypoole for Jamaica: Edward Tavernor, aged 32.

Bound to John Spencer for Jamaica: Isaac Steele; Edward Phillipps, aged 22.

Bound to Edward Smyth for Jamaica: William Guise, aged 23; Thomas Constable of Tedbury, aged 21; Jonathan Foster, aged 22.

Bound to John Stubbs for Jamaica: Elizabeth Bromfield of London, widow.

Bound to Francis Mingham for Jamaica: George Simpson Jr., aged 24; George Steward of Islip, Oxon.

Bound to Daniell Brewer for Jamaica: Henry Masson, aged 25.

Bound to Thomas Hunt for Jamaica: John Chelsham, aged 24.

Bound to Peter Bennett for Jamaica: Charles Boote, son of Samuel B. of St. Bride's, London; Joane Henley of St. Martin Ludgate, [London].

Bound to Henry Sutton of Rotherhithe for Barbados: Alice Radford; Grace Walton.

Bound to Samuell Wilson for Carolina: John Crane of Moore Mitchell; Markham Thomasman.

Bound to William Condy for New England: John Symms, son of Robert S. of Aldersgate Street, [London].

Bound to John Kingsford for Jamaica: Sara Mackcloth of St. James, Middlesex; Hanna Quint of St. Giles in the Fields, Middlesex.

Bound to John Hasted for Carolina: John Milford Jr., aged 22.

Bound to Hercules Smyth for Barbados: Joseph Palmer, aged 25.

Bound to Nicholas Gregson for Jamaica: Daniell Hull, aged 33.

Bound to Francis Richardson for Jamaica: Thomas Cheese, aged 22.

Bound to Thomas Richardson for Jamaica: Jane Buck, aged 23; Elizabeth Francklyn of Bishopsgate, [London], aged 20; Richard Francklyn, aged 23; Thomas Ellis, aged 21; Mary Myles, aged 22.

Bound to Alexander Pollington for Antigua: James Bayley of Elsfield, Oxon.

Bound to Robert Bennett for Barbados: John Norris, aged 38.

Bound to Samuell Baker for Pennsylvania: Paul Hamber, aged 34; Richard Barton, aged 24; Mary David, parents dead, spinster aged 18; John White, with the consent of his mother.

Bound to Mechly Williamson for Carolina: Charles Nicholls, aged 21.

Bound to William Biddle for New Jersey: Stephen Watts, aged 16, parents dead.

Bound to George Stone for Jamaica: Sarah Maggott of St. Olave, Southwark; Richard Beamont, aged 30.

Bound to Joseph Waysey for Pennsylvania: Elinor Wayman, with the consent of her father.

Bound to Christopher Prissick: Mary Swan, aged 21, for Pennsylvania; David Broid of Aldgate, [London], for Barbados.

Bound to John Monck for Carolina: Margery Fullwood, aged 17; Richard Stiffe, aged 22.

Bound to Samuell Kellett for Jamaica: Elizabeth Gatehouse, spinster.

Bound to John Williams: Elinor Hanbury, aged 22, for Virginia; William Archer, aged 30, for Virginia; John Honour of Amfield [?Ampthill], Beds, for Virginia; John Wright of Wakefield, Yorkshire, for Virginia; John Saby of Thingdon [?Thenford], Northants, for Barbados; James Sidney of St. Andrew Holborn, London, for Virginia; Thomas Morthey of Munster, Ireland, for Virginia; Dorcas Pratt of Abingdon, Berks, for Virginia; Isaac Titmash, aged 25, for Barbados; William Edson, aged 22, for Barbados; Thomas Carver, aged 25, for Barbados; Joseph Willis, aged 22, for Barbados; Robert Newell, aged 22, for Barbados; John Belling, aged 22, for Barbados.

Bound to Thomas Hurlock for Virginia: Mary Needham, aged 22; Jane Turley, aged 23.

Bound to Anne Atkey for Maryland: Elizabeth Burgan, aged 21; Elizabeth Peele of St. Ethelburga [London], aged 17.

Bound to Edward Leach for Maryland: Samuell Dendy, witnessed by his mother.

Bound to Roger Newman for Maryland: Mary Middleton.

Bound to William Wyatt for Jamaica: Joane Baker, spinster.

Bound to John Grice for Jamaica: Joane Greene of St. Clement Danes, [Middlesex], spinster.

Bound to Nathaniell Gale for New Providence: Richard Arrowsmyth.

Bound to Walter Ryan for South Carolina: Samuell Linnell, aged 32.

Bound to Samuell White for Maryland: Richard Avery of Newbury, Berkshire.

Bound to John Hance for Maryland: Martha Woodward of Huntingdon, aged 20.

Bound to James Congdon for Maryland: Thomas Gatton, aged 30.

Bound to Edward Evans for Virginia: Mabell Rosse of Westminster; Sarah Rosse of Westminster; Elizabeth Prescott, aged 21; Jane Bailey, aged 22.

Bound to Jonathan Francis for Jamaica: William Skinner, aged 23; Mary Howard, aged 29; Robert Howard, aged 30.

Bound to Robert Carlile for Jamaica: Mary Harris of Bishopsgate, [London]; George Denersh, aged 25; Elizabeth Robinson, aged 22; Elizabeth Palmer.

Bound to Francis Lee for Virginia: James Devolne, aged 21.

Bound to Charles Smarte for Barbados: Henry Warnford, aged 36.

Bound to George Harmar for Barbados: James Manton, aged 24.

Bound to George Scrongie for Barbados: William Jedds of Edinburgh, Scotland.

Bound to Francis Brooking for Barbados: Richard Parr of Tower Hill, [London].

Bound to Phillipp Goare for Jamaica: William Foard, aged 22.

Bound to Richard Batts for Barbados: William Hathaway, aged 27; Thomas Martin, aged 24; Archibald Moir, aged 26; Robert Hall, aged 23; Michaell Goodson, aged 32.

Bound to Richard Batt(s) for Virginia: John Knight, aged 22; Francis Jones, aged 22.

Bound to William Seyward for Jamaica: Mary Goffe, aged 22.

Bound to Thomas Dann: William Hillary, aged 22, for Nevis; Margaret Lodge of Sherburn, Durham, for Nevis; Elizabeth Spicer, aged 25, for Barbados.

Bound to John Bawden for Nevis: James Coytmore of Cripplegate, Middlesex, victualler.

Bound to John Wyatt, merchant, for Barbados: John Wyatt.

Bound to Anne Clarke for Pennsylvania: William Butler of Reading, [Berkshire].

Bound to John Ross for Jamaica: Henry Holston of St. Clement Danes, Middlesex.

Bound to Robert Raworth for Teneriffe: Richard Eaton, aged 33.

Bound to William Dockwra for New Jersey: Christopher Cockinskell, aged 31; Richard Hodgekins, son of John H., glover; Mary Smyth, aged 21; Sara Smyth, aged 21; Anne Penell of Balderston, Notts; Thomas Horne, aged 36; Marmaduke Barnard, aged 48; James Smyth, aged 24; John Tankyn, aged 22; John Wood, aged 27; Henry Page, aged 28; Henry Gray, aged 27; John Stevens, aged 22; Robert Ham, aged 22; Thomas Palmer, aged 38.

Bound to Francis Hiller for Jamaica: Isabell Purvis, aged 26.

Bound to John Handford for Virginia: Thomas Godbold of St. Andrews in High Suffolk (*sic*); Richard Claxton, aged 22; Mary Athy of St. George Botolph Lane, [London].

Bound to William Haveland: Thomas Potts, aged 26, for Virginia; Antipas Taylor, aged 24, for Barbados.

Bound to Samuell Roberts for Maryland: Elizabeth Bryan, aged 20; Elizabeth Grinson, aged 18.

Bound to Thomas Hollyday: George Bevis of Bishops Stortford, [Herts], for Maryland; Thomas Symonds of Stepney, Middlesex, for Maryland; Jonathan Patrick, aged 20, for Virginia; Daniell Thomas of Lambeth, [Surrey], for Maryland: Joseph Morunt of Norton Folgate, [London], for Maryland; Jonathan Ward of St. Martin Outwich, [London], for Maryland.

Bound to Francis Partis for Maryland: Robert Harris of St. Sepulchre, [London]; Elizabeth Mitchell of Wapping, [Middlesex].

Bound to Phillip Clarke for Maryland: Rebecca Maughan of St. Edmund's, Exeter, [Devon].

Bound to Henry Dryden: Henry How of St. Olave, Southwark, for Virginia; William Fyfield of St. Olave, Southwark, for Maryland; Thomas Palmer, aged 20, for Virginia.

Bound to Joshua Hollingshed for Maryland: Elizabeth Lovell of St. Swithin's, London.

Bound to Thomas Tasker for Maryland: Elizabeth Sergeant of Highgate, [Middlesex]; Elinor Gunn, aged 21; Mary Taylor of Coventry, [Warwickshire]; Anne Thomas, aged 23.

Bound to Walter Smyth for Maryland: John Johnson of St. Andrew Holborn, [London]; Ralph Collwell of Northampton; Thomas Mollinex of St. Clement Danes, [Middlesex]; John Phillips, a German.

Bound to James Gorden for Barbados: William Adamson of Scotland.

Bound to John Pym for Jamaica: Anne Mercy of Bristol, aged 18; Margaret Marcy (*sic*) of Bristol.

Bound to Francis Clark of New Jersey: Sara Beck, aged 26.

Bound to Francis French for Maryland: Samuell Miles of Aldgate, [London].

Bound to Thomas Dryden? for Maryland: John Eaton of St. Botolph Bishopsgate, [London].

Bound to Symon Flew for Jamaica: Frances Teague of St. Mary's, Dover, [Kent]; Katherine Osborne of St. James, Dover.

Bound to Margaret Stanley for Jamaica: Jane Poe, aged 21.

Bound to Benedict Leonard for Maryland: Charles Baker, aged 22.

Bound to Joseph Pyle for Maryland: Elizabeth Cheese of St. George, Southwark; Michaell Green, aged 21.

Bound to Thomas Starkey for Maryland: William Williamson of Cumberland.

Bound to Abraham Clarke for Maryland: Thomas Day, aged 23.

Bound to Nicholas Painter for Maryland: Susanna Drake, widow aged 27.

Bound to Arthur Forbass for Virginia: Andrew Grey, aged 28.

Bound to Richard Cox for Virginia: John Baxter of Lancashire.

Bound to John Browne for Virginia: Mary Monnseir, aged 21.

Bound to Benjamin Johnson: John Betson, aged 21, for Virginia; Arthur Munday, aged 20, for Virginia; Thomas May, aged 21, for Virginia; John Wall, aged 22, for Virginia; Daniell Habgood, aged 21, for Barbados; John Thompson, aged 22, for Barbados; Thomas Nonson for Barbados; Thomas Miller, aged 23, for Virginia; Humphrey Tedder, aged 23, for Virginia; John Williamson, aged 21, for Virginia; William Elton, aged 28, for Virginia; Thomas Allen of St. Martin in the Fields, [Middlesex], for Virginia; Robert Downey, aged 22, for Virginia; William Dale, aged 26, for Virginia; Robert Strides, aged 21, for Virginia; Alexander Cock, aged 24, for Virginia; Richard Jones, aged 21, for Virginia; Abraham Taylor, aged 30, for Virginia; David Higgs, aged 24, for Virginia; John Briteridge, aged 24, for Virginia; William Kendall of Wilburton, [Cambs], for Virginia; William Ryley, aged 22, for Virginia; William Blades, aged 23, for Virginia; Richard Highfield, aged 21, for Virginia; Elizabeth Gale, aged 22, for Virginia; James Black of St. Martin in the Fields, [Middlesex], for Virginia; William Rolfe, aged 21, for Virginia; Edward Smyth, aged 27, for Virginia; William Clay, aged 24, for Virginia; Robert Cooke, aged 22, for Virginia; Oliver Bancks, aged 26, for Virginia; Phebe Rumney of St. Bride's, [London], for Virginia; Ralph Gibbs, aged 22, for Virginia; Michaell Rudlidge, aged 29, for Virginia; Elizabeth Jones of Gloucester, for Virginia; William Eckley, aged 28, for Virginia; Hugh Edward of Denbigh, aged 18, for Virginia; William Page, aged 21, for Virginia; William Lloyd, aged 22, for Virginia; Robert Boyce, aged 39, for Virginia; Jane Kitchen, aged 21, for Virginia; William Jones, aged 24, for Virginia; Thomas Clark, aged 23.

Bound to Thomas Nelson for Virginia: Thomas Hall, aged 21.

Bound to Bartholomew Clements for Virginia: Henry Goldson, aged 30.

Bound to John Gore for Jamaica: Thomas Gilbert, aged 21; Thomas Jones, aged 23.

Bound to Benjamin Pym for Jamaica: Johanna Stiles, aged 21.

Bound to Peter Greene for Virginia: John Snow of Newbury, [Berkshire].

Bound to Vincent Goddard for Virginia: Timothy Fry of St. Sepulchre, [London].

Bound to John Ros(s)e: John Marshall, aged 34, for Virginia; William Randall, aged 30, for Jamaica.

Bound to Thomas Sanders for Jamaica: Francis Reed of Stepney, [Middlesex].

Bound to David Lockwood for Jamaica: Dorcas Finch of Waltham, Essex; Robert Bilton of St. Stephen Coleman Street, [London].

Bound to John Dykes: John Clarke of Lancashire, butcher, for Barbados; Thomas Rogers of Suffolk, for Barbados; Thomas Porter of Lancashire, tanner, for Barbados; Richard Gillard, aged 31, for Jamaica; Wentworth Greenhath, aged 25, for Jamaica; Peter Clarke, carpenter aged 21, for Jamaica; Edmond Barrett, aged 24, for Jamaica; Ralph Osborne, aged 21, for Jamaica; John Watts, aged 23, for Jamaica; James Roach of St. Olave, Southwark, for Barbados; William Lands of King Street, Westminster, for Barbados.

Bound to William Winter for Nevis: Thomas Snelling of Greenwich, [Kent].

Bound to John Bathurst for Jamaica: Anthony Tutt, cooper.

Bound to James Galwith for Maryland: Charles Darbishire, aged 21; Sara Marsh, aged 21; Mary Savaker, aged 18; John Hawkes, aged 19; Margaret Stimson, aged 21; Elizabeth Cooke, aged 19; Mary Beanes, aged 21; John Kidd, aged 25; Mary Carman, aged 19; Susanne Woolfe, aged 32; Judith Mullins, aged 16; Alice Smyth, aged 22; Anne Barton, aged 25.

Bound to Robert Ashurst for Virginia: Sarah Clisby of Westminster.

Bound to John Thornbury for Jamaica: Elizabeth Low, aged 23; John Sherman, aged 38.

Bound to John Pearson for Barbados: William Garway, aged 22; Daniell Mackenna, aged 28; Edward Watton, aged 21; John Lockwood, aged 26.

Bound to John Shaw: Gilbert Movett, aged 22, for Jamaica; William Rone of [King's] Lynn, Norfolk, carpenter, for Barbados.

Bound to Thomas Mountague for Jamaica: Mary Summers of Guildford, [Surrey], spinster; Robert Singleton, aged 42; William Morgan, aged 25.

Bound to Symon Rogers for Jamaica: John Wallis, aged 33.

Bound to John Richards: David Simpkin, aged 30, for Maryland; John Slade, aged 22, for Barbados; Elizabeth Worsencroft, aged 21, for Barbados; Daniell Reynolds, aged 29, for Barbados; Nicholas Bryan, aged 24, for Barbados; Rice Jones, aged 26, for Barbados; William Lane, aged 22, for Barbados; Thomas Lewys, aged 22, for Barbados; Phillip Cursham, aged 21, for Barbados; Virtue Woods, aged 25, for Barbados; George Edsor, aged 32, for Virginia; Jacob Allen, aged 22, for Maryland; John Bruerton, aged 26, for Barbados; John White, aged 21, for Barbados; William Clayton, aged 22, for Barbados; Joseph Winterborne, aged 21, for Barbados; Mary Littleton, aged 18, for Barbados; John Hare, aged 23, for Barbados; Richard Collier, aged 25, for Barbados; William Burton, aged 22, for Maryland; Richard Jones, aged 29, for Barbados; Daniell Carr, aged 25, for Maryland; William Serrell, aged 28, for Barbados; William Harrenden, aged 29, for Barbados; Henry Hamling, aged 32, for Barbados; John Coles, aged 25, for Barbados; Walter Jones, aged 28, for Barbados; Robert Hill, aged 22, for Barbados; Richard Emmery, aged 22, for Barbados; Robert Carne, aged 23, for Barbados; James Ashford, aged 26, for Barbados; John Williams, aged 35, for Barbados; James Davis, aged 23, for Barbados; William Ravill, aged 21, for Barbados; George Thomas, aged 25, for Barbados; George Cooke, aged 21, for Barbados; Thomas Rogers, aged 30, for Maryland; William Skidmore, aged 27, for Maryland; James Lloyd, aged 23, for Barbados; John Waters, aged 27, for Maryland; William Hallett, aged 23, for Maryland; Rowland Benson, aged 24, for Maryland; James Jannins, aged 22, for Maryland.

Bound to Archibald Archer for Virginia: John Ashlock, aged 26.

Bound to Richard Park for Virginia: John Vaughan, aged 23; Mary Edling, aged 21; Thomas Clare, aged 22; Thomas Shephard, aged 25; Barbara Kemp of Hertfordshire; Elizabeth Crispe of Warwickshire; Henry Tilson, aged 22; Edward Edwards, aged 24; William Cooper, aged 26; Robert Coles, aged 27; Edward Sallock, aged 23.

Bound to John Park for Virginia: Thomas Ashton, aged 22.

Bound to John Cooper for Virginia: Thomas Scales, aged 14, of St. Olave's, [Southwark]; John Smith of St. Olave, Southwark.

Bound to Thomas Stapleton for Virginia: Elizabeth Soper, aged 21.

Bound to Thomas Walsh for Virginia: Joseph Sheriffe, aged 23.

Bound to Thomas Clark for Maryland: John Mills, aged 24.

Bound to James Emmerson for Virginia: Joseph Rumball, aged 22.

Bound to Robert Lee for Maryland: Charles Jones, aged 32.

Bound to James Williams: Jonathan Newton, aged 26, for Maryland; John Mooreton, aged 24, for Barbados; Isaack De Camps, aged 21, for Barbados;

Thomas Sparks, aged 30, for Barbados; Thomas Thomas, aged 22, for Barbados; Charles Abbott, aged 23, for Barbados.

Bound to William Hill for Maryland: Daniell Yates, aged 29; Thomas Wilson, aged 21.

Bound to John Thomas for Virginia: John Thomas, aged 25.

Bound to Clement Tudway for Antigua: Thomas Middleton, aged 50; James Harris, aged 46.

Bound to John Scampion for Virginia: Francis Clements, aged 23.

Bound to William Cooke for Jamaica: John Harrison, aged 22.

Bound to William Martyn for Jamaica: Anne Taverner, aged 24.

Bound to Stephen Sikes for Virginia: John Neve of St. Mary Woolnoth, London.

Bound to William Bradley for Jamaica: William Bell of Cambridge, aged 20.

Bound to Francis Snead for Jamaica: John Orme, aged 21.

Bound to Sion Hill for Barbados: Edward Yorke of Bishopsgate, [London], aged 15; Thomas Joy, aged 23.

Bound to Seger Walter for Jamaica: John Motley, aged 30.

Bound to John Moorehead: Gilbert Maddox of Wallingford, [Oxon], blacksmith, for Jamaica; Thomas Meakins of Aldgate, [London], for Jamaica; Thomas Roberts of Sunninghill, [Berks], for Jamaica; William Church of Battersea, Surrey, for Jamaica; Timothy Reddin of Windsor, [Berks], for Barbados; Reynald Parsons, aged 30, for Barbados; Robert Riggs, aged 22, for Barbados; Robert Sheppard, aged 22, for Barbados; John Smyth, aged 21, for Barbados; William Orchard, aged 22, for Barbados; John Hopper, aged 21, for Barbados.

Bound to Robert Wilkinson for Barbados: Mary Goddard, aged 21.

Bound to Thomas Savill: William Howell of London for Barbados; George Ratcliffe, aged 26, for Barbados; Joseph Slaughter of Derbyshire, aged 20, for Barbados; Nathaniell Penner, aged 22, for Barbados; John Shaw, aged 28, for Barbados; John Kilby, aged 22, for Jamaica; Charles Knapp of Oxford, tailor, for Jamaica; Barnard Scott, aged 21, for Barbados.

Bound to Thomas Serjeant for New England: Samuell Weaver.

Bound to John Netheway for Nevis: George Watkins; William Edwin of Berkshire, carpenter; John Jenn; Thomas Wilkenson; Thomas Dunckley of Hackney, [Middlesex], gardener; George Ricketts of Stepney, [Middlesex].

Bound to James Fossett for Barbados: Anne Long, aged 22; Elizabeth Wrenn, aged 23; Elizabeth Haynes, aged 19; Edward Forster, aged 34; Jonathan Bindon, aged 22.

Bound to Thomas Patman for Barbados: Joseph Coleburne, aged 28; Thomas Simpson of Yorkshire; Henry Cooper, aged 23.

Bound to Davy Breholt for Barbados: John Capell, aged 22; Peter Charleton, aged 28.

Bound to William Brockett for Barbados: John Brockett, aged 19.

Bound to Edward Parsons for Barbados: Joane Taylor, aged 24.

Bound to Richard Gardner for Maryland: William Napper of Oxford; Francis Swailes of London.

Bound to William Thorowgood for Carolina: Daniel Honfrey Aveny; Anthony Dodsworth; Henry Collis.

Bound to Charles Lodwick for New York: William Greene.

1684

11 January. Shippers by the *Resolution* of Dartmouth, Mr. Humphrey Goodridge, bound from Dartmouth for Carolina: Thomas Smith, Aaron Atkins, James Gelbenon, William Wilkins. (PRO: E190/964/13).

18 January. John Bottle of Offculme (*sic*), Devon, husbandman, bound to Robert Fowler of Lyme Regis, mariner, to serve 4 years in Barbados. (DRO B7/M9).

21 January-25 February. The following apprenticed in Middlesex to go to Barbados by the *Barbados Merchant*, Mr. Christopher Prissick: James Gray, groom aged 21, of Haddon [?Hutton], Somerset, son of John G., deceased, to William Precept, mariner, 4 years; Richard Petty, aged 21, of Canterbury, Kent, son of John Petty, deceased, to Christopher Prissick, 5 years; Hugh Parkington, aged 22, of Rinohenty (?), Cheshire, son of George P., to the same, 4 years to serve as a ploughman; Abraham Ricky of Norwich, aged 21, son of Isaac Ricky, to the same, 4 years; Anders Mattson, a Swede aged 18, to the same, 4 years; Mathew Scott of Scotland, aged 23, to the same, 4 years; Humphrey Jones of Burnham, Essex, aged 19, son of William J., to the same, 6 years, with the consent of his father and mother; Joseph George of Litchfield, Staffordshire, aged 31, son of John G., to the same, (4) years, to be employed as a tailor; Richard Spurling, aged 17, son of Alexander S. of Kent, to the same, 5 years; Pauls Cornelius of Zeeland, Holland, aged 18, to the same, 5 years; John Clapp, aged 19, of Cherrick (*sic*), Dorset, son of William C., to the same, 5 years; Thomas Greenlees, husbandman aged 21 and more, to the same, 4 years; Abell Bartram of Middlesex, aged 24, to the same, 4 years; Robert White of Middlesex, aged 28, to the same, 4 years; Henry Flack, aged 21, of Colchester, Essex, to the same, 5 years; Elizabeth Tarbutt, aged 16, whose father and mother are dead, to the same, 4 years; Mary Rime, aged 19, whose father and mother are dead, to the same, 4 years; Charles Towell of Devon, aged 20, son of Thomas T., to the same, 6 years; John Rice of Lancashire, aged 21, son of David R., to the same, 4 years, to be employed as a distiller; Mary Burnley, aged 19, whose father and mother are dead, to the same, 4 years; William Street of Middlesex, glazier aged 24, to the same, 4 years; William Frost of Windham [?Wymondham], Norfolk, aged 18, son of Edward F., to the same, 7 years; Henry Agar of Middlesex, accountant aged 21, to the same, 4 years; John Colpis of Middlesex, ribbon weaver aged 22, to the same, 4 years. (GLRO: MR/E/593).

26 January. Deposition by Edmond Farrow of Redrith, Surrey, mariner aged 30, that he was in New England a year ago and saw William Pullridge throwing out limestones from the *Charles*, Mr. Arthur Tanner. (LMCD).

January. Administration of Dorothy Elsam of New England, spinster. (AW).

5 February. Gascoyne Hampton of Staple, Somerset, bound to Robert Fowler of Lyme Regis, Dorset, mariner, to serve 5 years in Barbados. (DRO B7/M9).

6 February. John Granfield of Broomfield, Somerset, husbandman, bound to Robert Fowler of Lyme Regis, mariner, to serve 4 years in Barbados. (DRO B7/M9).

8 February. The following apprenticed in London: John Joverell of Gloucester, glass bottle seller of full age, to Joseph Martin of London, merchant, 4 years Pennsylvania. (LMWB13/371).

18 February-4 March. The following apprenticed in Middlesex to Richard Batt of Tower Hill, gent: George Wrangham, aged 19, 5 years Barbados; Edward Powell, carpenter aged 30, 4 years Barbados. (GLRO: MR/E/593).

18 February-29 March. The following apprenticed in Middlesex to John Humphreys of East Smithfield, mariner: William Thomson, aged 12, 7 years Jamaica, with the consent of his father, Richard T.; Dorothy Hutchinson, spinster aged 21, 4 years Jamaica; Elizabeth Wilkinson, spinster aged 21, 4 years Jamaica. (GLRO: MR/E/593).

19 February. Shipper by the *Hopewell*, Mr. Singleton, bound from London for New England: Joshua Shepherd. (PRO: E190/124/1).

21 February. Home Circuit prisoners reprieved to be transported to Barbados or Jamaica. Essex: Robert Scull alias Rogers of Wakes Colne; John Harvey of Halstead; William Draper of Saffron Walden; Ann Osborne of St. James, Colchester. Kent: John Teward of Sittingbourne; Jane Johnson of Hurst; Henry Cockerill of Offham. Surrey: John Browne of Bermondsey; Mary Dendy of Chertsey; John Harris of St. Saviour, Southwark; Mary Nolder of Rotherhithe; Elizabeth Briscoe of St. Saviour, Southwark; Ann Emerton of Bermondsey; Thomas Toll of St. George, Southwark; William Brasyer of St. George, Southwark; William Hopkins of Camberwell; Elianor wife of Robert Bampsfield of St. Saviour, Southwark; Samuel Hall of Camberwell; Abraham Morton of Lambeth; Miriam Arthur alias Magdalene of St. George, Southwark. Sussex: James Freeman of Chailey; Stephen Whetten alias Whitehorne alias Whitehall of Boxgrove; James Beech of Wisborough Green. (PRO: C66/3245/13).

21 February. Norfolk Circuit prisoners reprieved to be transported to America. Buckinghamshire: Jenkin Thompson of Great Marlow. Norfolk: Thomas Carrow alias Crow of Grimston; John White of Thetford; Peter Lee of Thetford; George Thurston of Thetford. (PRO: C66/3245/12).

21 February-10 March. Shippers by the *Society*, Mr. Peter Clark, bound from London for New England: Thomas Edwards, Thomas Mordin, Charles Duke, Thomas Goodwin, Edward Rooke, Isaac Delillers. (PRO: E190/124/1).

21 February-12 March. Shippers by the *Thomas & Ann*, Mr. Thomas Singleton, bound from London for New York & New Jersey: David Corryard, William

Crouch, William Gibbs, John Hamlin, William Fortune, John Morrey, William Shewin. (PRO: E190/124/1).

25 February. Oxford Circuit prisoners reprieved to be transported to America. Berkshire: Perry White of Hampstead Marshall. Gloucestershire: Samuel Williams of Cam; John Morley of Barton Regis. Herefordshire: James Owens of Titley. Oxfordshire: Jane Tanner of Ducklington. Staffordshire: Leonard Hutton of Cannock; Thomas Naden of Aldridge; William Hugitt of Leek. (PRO: C66/3245/14).

25 February. Western Circuit prisoners reprieved to be transported to Barbados. Cornwall: John Nicholls of Egloshayle. Devon: John Gayge of Clayhidon. Devon: Elizabeth Good of Modbury; Thomas Yeavsley of Teignmouth; Nicholas Cooke of Dodbrooke, miller. Dorset: John Munfie of Marshwood; Thomas Durneford of Marnehall; George Durneford of Marnhull, blacksmith. Hampshire: John Weene of Colemore; Humphrey Walker of Portsmouth. Somerset: William Prowse of Nether Stowey; John Stacey of Chedzoy; William Pulman of Martock. Somerset: Henry Codd of Wiveliscombe. (PRO: C66/3245/11).

26 February-3 March. Shippers by the *Elizabeth*, Mr. John Wild, bound from London for New England: John Cutcher, John Knapp, Samuel Helland, Anthony Greene, Robert Hooker, Hugh Strode, John Bendon, Joseph Came. (PRO: E190/124/1).

27 February. The following apprenticed in Middlesex: John Beddoe, aged 21, to Richard Coning of Wapping, mariner, 4 years Jamaica. (GLRO: MR/E/593).

27 February-4 March. The following apprenticed in Middlesex to go by the *Crown*, Mr. Thomas Croft, to serve in Barbados for 4 years: Edward Heather of Petersfield, Hampshire, joiner and cabinet maker aged 25, to John Dix of London, merchant; James Backwell of Middlesex, cordwainer aged 25, to the same; George Troope, aged 21, to the same, to be employed as a "slicker"; John Williams of Chester, aged 24, son of Connerigg W., to William Haveland, to work as a farrier smith; Michael Drummer, aged 21, to John James of London, mariner; George Mason of Oxfordshire, gent aged 21, son of Thomas M., to John Sanders of London, merchant; Henry Wilson of Middlesex, groom aged 23, to William Goodburne of London, merchant; John King of Middlesex, accountant aged 26, to John Pearson of London, merchant; John Ast of Cawston [?Calstone Wellington], Wiltshire, aged 24, son of John A., to John Shawe of London, merchant, to work as a sawyer; George Brace of Hereford, aged 24, son of George B., to James Williams of London, merchant, to work as a wheelwright and carpenter; William Greene of Middlesex, ploughman aged 21, to John Jones of London, merchant. (GLRO: MR/E/593).

27 February-19 March. Shippers by the *Guillielmo*, Mr. William East, bound from London for Pennsylvania: John West, Pennsylvania Society, Richard Martin, Joseph Martin, John Pemble, Samuel Shepherd. (PRO: E190/124/1).

29 February. The following apprenticed in London: John Wyatt, son of Thomas W. of Stoke (Golding), Leicestershire, to John Wyatt of London, merchant, 5 years Barbados. (LMWB13/382).

29 February. The following apprenticed in Middlesex: Jacob Paice, aged 22, to William George, 4 years Barbados. (GLRO: MR/E/593).

4 March. Deposition by Richard Bussell of St. Olave, Southwark, Surrey, that he has appointed Samuel Bussell of Boston, New England, as his attorney; Deposition by Walter Alico of London, merchant aged 53, that he has seen a true account of his dealing with Isaac Waldron of Boston, New England. (LMCD).

6 March. The following apprenticed in Middlesex: Benjamin Levens of Colchester, Essex, aged 21, son of William L., to John Dix of London, merchant, 4 years Nevis and Antigua by the *George*, Mr. Bridgman. (GLRO: MR/E/593).

6 March. Shipper by the *Success* of Topsham, Mr. Thomas Ross, bound from Exeter for New England: John Chetwell. (PRO: E190/962/4).

6-8 March. Shipper by the *Diamond* of Topsham, Mr. Edward Shower, bound from Exeter for New England: Charles Mayne. (PRO: E190/962/4).

6-29 March. The following apprenticed in Middlesex to go by the *Providence*, Mr. Bartholomew, to serve 4 years in Jamaica: Giles Haddock of Middlesex, ploughman aged 21, to John Neale of London, merchant; John Browne of Middlesex, butcher aged 33, to the same; John Rawlings of Middlesex, sawyer aged 27, to John Norris of London, merchant; James Kimson of Middlesex, glazier aged 21, to John Rowe of London, merchant; Humphrey Martin of Devon, aged 27, to the same; John Smith of Middlesex, brickmaker aged 28, to John Jones of London, merchant; Samuel Gent of Warwickshire, aged 27, to Richard Batts; Zachariah Gray of Middlesex, ploughman aged 22, to Richard Waterhouse of London, merchant; David Adamson of Scotland, aged 23, to John Williams; Joseph Sparkes of Willner [?Wichnor], Staffordshire, smith aged 23, to John Stone of London, merchant. (GLRO: MR/E/593).

7-27 March. The following apprenticed in Middlesex to go by the *Francis & Dorothy*, Mr. Richard Brigham, to serve in Antigua: Henry Phelix of Middlesex, cooper aged 22, to John Earle of London, merchant, 4 years; Thomas Agersall of Middlesex, aged 20, vagrant held in the House of Correction, to the same, 6 years; Richard White of Middlesex, aged 21, vagrant held in the House of Correction, to the same, 4 years; Robert Abell of Middlesex, sawyer aged 28, to John Pearson of London, merchant, 4 years; Nicholas Browne of Middlesex, groom aged 24, to John Williams of London, merchant, 4 years; Daniel MacQuin of Scotland, aged 21, to John Rose of London, merchant, 4 years; Robert Weston of Rye, Sussex, aged 22, to Thomas Wise of London, merchant, 4 years; Thomas Frame of Middlesex, ploughman aged 30, to John Mason of London, merchant, 4 years. (GLRO: MR/E/593).

8 March. The following apprenticed in Middlesex: Richard Price of Middlesex, cooper aged 23, held in Whitechapel Prison for debt, to John Earl, 4 years Jamaica by *Joseph*, Mr. John Brakes. (GLRO: MR/E/593).

8 March. Declaration by Sir Edmond Andros of London that he has appointed Stephen Courtland of New York, merchant, and Mr. Philip Wells of Staten Island, New York, planter, as his attorneys. (LMCD).

9 March. Deposition by Robert Blagrave, aged 22, servant of George Alder of London, scrivener, that George Lockhart and English Smith of New York, merchants, became indebted to Richard Adkinson, citizen and shipwright of London, by bond of 30 June 1683. (LMCD).

10 March. The following apprenticed in London: John Moore, glass bottle maker, to Joseph Martin, agent for the Pennsylvania Society, 4 years Pennsylvania to work as a bottle maker. (LMWB13/387).

10 March-10 April. Shippers by the *Hopewell*, Mr. Samson Stoddard, bound from London for New England: Daniel Adkins, Henry Bourne, Henry Hall, Hugh Horton, Thomas Pattin, Robert Yalden, Daniel Foe, John Daniell, Nathaniel Crynes, John Hancock. (PRO: E190/124/1).

12 March. Deposition by Roger Mott, citizen and merchant tailor of London, aged 40, that on 15 September 1679 he consigned goods to Isaac Waldron of Boston, New England, merchant. (LMCD).

12 March. Shippers by the *Friends Adventure*, Mr. John Browne, bound from Exeter for New England: Edward Seaward, Robert Tristram. (PRO: E190/962/4).

12 March. Shippers by the *Recovery* of Exeter, Mr. Joseph Parsons, bound from Exeter for New England: Edward Seaward, Thomas Edmonds, Peter Edbrooke. (PRO: E190/962/4).

12 March-17 April. Shippers by the *Rebecca*, Mr. Edward Clements, bound from London for New York: John Hall, Godfrey Webster, Thomas Wheeler, Reg[inald] Heber, John Loveroo, Jacob Milburne, Nathaniel Whitfield. (PRO: E190/124/1).

14 March. Deposition by William Hawys of London, merchant aged 34, that Henry Taylor of Boston, New England, became indebted to John Jackson, citizen and merchant of London, and William Jackson, citizen and merchant tailor of London, now deceased, by bond of 30 March 1668. Thomas Crundall Jr. of Devonshire House, Bishopsgate, London, has been appointed attorney. (LMCD).

14-15 March. Shippers by the *Sarah & Elizabeth* of Exeter, Mr. Nicholas Downe, bound from Exeter for New England: Thomas Tanner, Thomas Lee. (PRO: E190/962/4).

15 March. The following apprenticed in Middlesex: Mary May, aged 21, to Samson Stodder, 4 years New England. (GLRO: MR/E/593).

19 March. The following apprenticed in Middlesex: William Phillips, aged 27, to Edmund Paine of Stepney, mariner, 4 years Pennsylvania. (GLRO: MR/E/593).

20 March-7 March 1685. Depositions in London re the voyage of the *Blessing*, Mr. David East, belonging to John Parmeter of Boston, New England, from Jamaica, her capture by the Spanish, and the imprisonment of her crew in Havana. (EA).

22-26 March. Shippers by the *Joane* of Topsham, Mr. John Seaward, bound from Exeter for New England: Isaac Gibbs, John Cholwell. (PRO: E190/962/4).

22 March-14 April. Shippers by the *Reformation*, Mr. George Beare, bound from Exeter for New England: Edward Seaward, Malachy Pyne, John Cooke. (PRO: E190/962/4).

23 March-1 April. The following apprenticed in Middlesex to go by the *George*, Mr. Jones: William Hope of Cranbrook, Kent, aged 21, son of Anthony H., to Harks Garbrane of London, merchant, 4 years Jamaica; John Solley of Ash, Kent, aged 21, son of Thomas S., to the same, 4 years Jamaica; John Rachell of Middlesex, aged 21, to James Moore of London, merchant, 4 years Jamaica; Francis Wardle of Cheshire, husbandman aged 22, to William Somes of London, merchant, 4 years Jamaica; Robert Pettenreck of Scotland, accountant aged 21, to Richard Batts, 4 years Jamaica; John Reed of Scotland, groom aged 21, to the same, 4 years Jamaica; William Whiting of Huckett [?Holcot], Northamptonshire, aged 21, son of William W., to John Wiseman of London, merchant, 4 years Jamaica, to serve as a husbandman. Richard Holt of Bromidge(?), Lancashire, groom aged 23, to the same, 4 years Jamaica. (GLRO: MR/E/593).

24 March. Shipper by the *Robert* of Guernsey, Mr. Samuell Gampaine, bound from Weymouth for Boston, New England: said Samuell Gampaine. (PRO: E190/886/3).

24 March-4 April. The following apprenticed in Middlesex to go to Barbados by the *Katherine*, Mr. Emberley, to serve for four years: Thomas Dymond of Leeds, Yorkshire, aged 21, to William Jones of London, merchant; John Seethings of Banham, Norfolk, aged 21, to the same; John Thompson of Middlesex, ploughman aged 22, to John Shawe, to serve as a ploughman. (GLRO: MR/E/593).

24 March-18 April. The following apprenticed in Middlesex to go by the *Anne & Mary*, Mr. Isaac Harvey, to serve 4 years in Antigua: Richard Reynolds of Bristol, aged 21, son of Richard R., to John Hall of London, merchant; Thomas Burton of Bistone [?Boston], Lincolnshire, aged 24, to the same, to serve as an accountant; Thomas Dyer of Pangbourne, Berkshire, aged 20, to the same;

Patrick Sarsfield of St. Giles in the Fields, barber aged 21, to the same; William Braisnett of Hethersett, Norfolk, labourer aged 21, to the same; Jonathan Miller of Northamptonshire, aged 24, to Edmund Pattman of London, merchant; Elizabeth Merring of Nottingham, spinster aged 23, to Daniell Heyward of London, mariner. (GLRO: MR/E/593).

25 March. Shipper by the *John Bonadventure*, Mr. Andrew Cratey, bound from London for New England: Edward Ellis. (PRO: E190/124/1).

26 March. Shipper by the *Black Cock*, Mr. Michael Pack, bound from London for New England: John Shorter. (PRO: E190/124/1).

26 March. The following apprenticed in London: John Combes to Daniell Duthaes of London, merchant, 7 years Pennsylvania. (LMWB13/397).

26-28 March. The following apprenticed in Middlesex to serve Thomas Richardson, citizen and surgeon of London, for four years in Jamaica: John Smith of London, shoemaker aged 28; Jane Whitfield of Alston Moor, Cumberland, spinster aged 21; Margaret Jones of Waterford, Ireland, aged 22. (GLRO: MR/E/593).

28 March. Deposition by John Stacie of London, merchant aged 24, that Jeremy Child of Boston, New England, became indebted to John Jackson, citizen and merchant of London, by bond of 30 April 1678. (LMCD).

28 March. The following apprenticed in Middlesex to serve George Lehunt, citizen and merchant of London, for four years in Jamaica: Alice Duckett of Pembridge, Herefordshire, widow aged 24; Mary Flack of Portsmouth, Hampshire, widow aged 22. (GLRO: MR/E/593).

29 March-11 April. Shippers by the *Richard* of Bristol bound from Bristol for New England: Charles Pope, Alexander Penny, Phillip Patch, George Squire, David Saunders, Henry Combs. (PRO: E190/1147/1).

March. Administration of Thomas Grimditch of New York. (AW)

March. Probate of will of Sir Edward Brett of Bexley, Kent, who died in St. Margaret, Westminster, Middlesex, and whose nephew, Henry Isham, was of Virginia. (AW).

March. Administration of Jonathan Davis of Barne Elms, Surrey, who died in Virginia. (AW).

4-9 April. The following apprenticed in Middlesex to serve Edmond Payne of Stepney, mariner, in Maryland: James Almond, aged 11, 9 years, with the consent of his father-in-law, Edward Bedford, and his uncles, John Beardmore and John Harford, his own father and mother being dead; Joseph Vaughan, aged 33, 4 years. (GLRO: MR/E/593).

4-27 April. The following apprenticed in Middlesex to go by the *Joseph & Ashton*, Mr. John Jones, to serve for four years in Carolina: Adam Gregory of

Lancashire, aged 21, to Sir Henry Johnson of London, merchant; Abell Crode of Cutlock(?), Dorset, husbandman aged 26, to the same; Daniel Gardner of Bewdley, Worcestershire, labourer aged 26, to the same; Alice Gardner of Bewdley, Worcestershire, spinster aged 24, to the same; John Law of Scotland, aged 32, to John Smith, merchant; Richard Hicks of Montgomeryshire, accountant aged 26, to the same; George Preston of Towcester, Northamptonshire, aged 21, to John Jones of London, mariner; Benjamin Phillips, aged 21, to the same. (GLRO: MR/E/593).

9 April. Richard Wilkinson, aged 17, apprenticed from Christ's Hospital to James Leech, commander of the *John & Elizabeth* bound for Barbados. (CH).

9 April-2 May. The following apprenticed in Middlesex to Edmond Payne of London, merchant, to serve four years in Pennsylvania: Abraham Amis, aged 31; Benjamin Porter, aged 21. (GLRO: MR/E/593).

10 April. Shipper by the *William* of Bristol bound from Bristol for New England: Henry Baker. (PRO: E190/1147/1).

11 April. The following apprenticed in Middlesex: William Ford, aged 27, to Rainsford Waterhouse of Wapping, merchant, 4 years Jamaica. (GLRO: MR/E/593).

14-16 April. Deposition by John Phillips, clerk aged 57, that he officiated at the wedding in the church of St. Mary Somerset, London, on 1 November 1683 of George Marrison of London, gent, and Elizabeth Bucknell, relict and executrix of Ferdinando Bucknell, citizen and girdler of London. James Cripps of Lincolns Inn, London, gent aged 20, deposes that letters from Ferdinando Bucknell to his wife dated December 1677 were written in his hand. James Needler, citizen and scrivener of London, aged 50, deposes that Samuel Bucknell of Boston, New England, became indebted to Ferdinando Bucknell by bond of 17 May 1661. (LMCD)

17 April. The following apprenticed in Middlesex: Stephen Williams, aged 31, to Edward Padley of Poplar, mariner, 4 years Antigua. (GLRO: MR/E/593).

17-29 April. Shippers by the *Joseph & Ashton*, Mr. John Jones, bound from London for Carolina: James Bull, William Cox, Robert Ayres, Matthew Walraven, Samuel Shepherd, Sir Nathaniel Johnson. (PRO: E190/124/1).

18-26 April. The following apprenticed in Middlesex to go by the *John & Elizabeth*, Mr. Jonas Leech, to serve for four years in Barbados; Thomas Savage of St. Clement Danes, Middlesex, tailor aged 24, to John May of London, merchant; John Ford of Wotton under Edge, Gloucestershire, weaver aged 21, to John Hall of London, merchant; George Bryant of Leicester, weaver aged 25, to the same: Thomas Heyward of Ore, Sussex, ploughman aged 22, to the same: Henry Wilson of Aderston [?Atherstone], Warwickshire, groom aged 21, to the same; John Hollis of Staffordshire, aged 24, to the same: Abraham Taylor of Ashton under Lyne, Lancashire, aged 20, to the same;

Martin Gardner of Edinburgh, [Scotland], husbandman aged 28, to the same; Francis Bromfield of Sussex, farrier smith aged 24, to William Haveland. (GLRO: MR/E/593).

21 April-14 June. Shippers by the *Rainbow* of Bristol bound from Bristol for New England: Giles Merricke, Thomas Carleton, Henry Harris, James Fox, Thomas Saunders. (PRO: E190/1147/1).

22 April. The following apprenticed in London: Rachel Thompson to Daniel Howard, joiner, 4 years Carolina. (LMWB13/409).

24 April. The following apprenticed in Middlesex: Ann Hill, aged 21, whose father and mother are both dead, to William Orton of Ratcliffe, mariner, 4 years Virginia, witnessed by her sister, Hosea Cole. (GLRO: MR/E/593).

25 April-6 May. The following apprenticed in Middlesex to go by the *Richard & Sarah*, Mr. Thomas Stubbs, to serve four years in Jamaica: Thomas Rowland of Montgomeryshire, aged 21, to George Smith of London, merchant, to serve as a husbandman; Henry Bisford of York, husbandman aged 28, to the same; James Swain of Cogges, Oxfordshire, aged 21, to Thomas Stubbs, mariner; James Thorp of Uppingham, Rutland, miller aged 21, to John Smith of London, merchant; Joseph Pagrowne of Blofield, Norfolk, gardener aged 21, to the same; Edward Button of Attleborough, Norfolk, baker aged 28, to the same; Robert Mercer of Lowding [?Lothian], Scotland, baker aged 28, to the same. (GLRO: MR/E/593).

26 April. The following apprenticed in Bristol: Ann Evans of Bristol to John Hort, 7 years Jamaica by *America Merchant*, Mr. Thomas Masters. (BR).

26 April-7 June. The following apprenticed in Middlesex to go by the *Friendship*, Mr. William Beeding, to serve for four years in Barbados: Richard Kilner of Westmorland, labourer aged 25, to William Haveland; Joshua Browne of Halifax, Yorkshire, clothier aged 26, to the same; Francis Pearse of Bridge Norton, Gloucestershire, husbandman aged 21, to the same; George Parsons of Shropshire, ploughman aged 21, to the same; Walter Hooper, glazier aged 23, son of Walter H. of Atherley [?Alderley], Gloucestershire, to the same; William Printice of Latton, Essex, aged 25, son of William P., to the same; John Harding, husbandman aged 30, son of John H. of Penrith, Cumberland, deceased, to the same; Francis Poole, husbandman aged 29, son of Matthew P., deceased, of Northampton, to the same; Thomas Herricke, gent aged 21, son of William H. of Woodhouse, Leicestershire, to the same; Obadiah Buck, girdler aged 27, son of James B. of Wells, Somerset, to the same, with the consent of his wife, Henrietta; Daniel Church, turner aged 23, son of James Church of [Hemel] Hempstead, Hertfordshire, to the same; John Andrew of Mawkcon(?), Hertfordshire, husbandman aged 22, son of John A., ploughman, deceased, to the same; Richard Trelford of Kirkham, Lancashire, smith aged 26, to Richard Batts; William Harrison of Masham, Yorkshire, tailor aged 30, to James Williams, merchant; Hugh Sneath of St. Martin [in the Fields], Middlesex, vintner aged 28, to John Smith; Benjamin Maple of Ipswich, Suffolk, aged 21, to the same, to serve as a husbandman; Thomas Lingwood, coachman aged 27, son of Christopher L. of High Easter, Essex, to John Jones, merchant; John Passmore, surgeon aged 22, son of John Passmore of Exeter, Devon, to the same; John Lee, locksmith aged 21, son of John L. of Cillell(?), Warwickshire, deceased, to the same; Thomas Sclater, aged 18, son of Henry S. of London, to Sir Peter Collington; William Pearson, citizen of London aged 22, to William Beeding of Wapping, mariner. (GLRO: MR/E/593).

29 April. The following apprenticed in Middlesex: Savile Jackson, aged 21, to Nathaniell Taylor of Stepney, mariner, 4 years Barbados. (GLRO: MR/E/593).

29 April-10 June. Shippers by the *Adventure*, Mr. John Balston, bound from London for New England: Thomas Hunt, John Pitt, John James, Thomas Ruck, Joseph Martin, Thomas Sontley, Robert Gower, Thomas Deane, John Child, John Colman, Joseph Paice, William Disher, Thomas Rutty, Peter Hudson. (PRO: E190/124/1).

30 April-17 May. Shippers by the *Charles*, Mr. Edmond Paine, bound from London for Pennsylvania: Thomas Warner, Daniel Whearley, Richard Goodall, William Boulton, John Shelton. (PRO: E190/124/1).

April. Probate of will of Thomas Jarvis formerly of Virginia but late of St. Olave, Old Jewry, London. (AW).

1 May. The following apprenticed in London: Robert Gibble, son of William G. of Exeter Street, Strand, Middlesex, gent, deceased, and Philip Philizot, son of Odo P. of Paris, France, wool spinner, to Rene Drignion, goldsmith, 4 years Pennsylvania. (LMWB13/416).

1 May-11 June. The following apprenticed in Middlesex to William Orton of Ratcliffe, mariner: Elizabeth Ivory, aged 23, 4 years Carolina; Richard Nibbs, aged 32, 4 years Virginia or Carolina; William Bagott, aged 26, 4 years Carolina or Virginia. (GLRO: MR/E/593).

7 May. Petition of Christopher Jeaffreson, agent for St. Christopher's. In November 1682 he asked for 300 convicts to be transported to St. Christopher's on the King's order but none have yet been delivered to him though many have been sent to other colonies. (CSPC).

8 May. The following apprenticed in Bristol: Arthur Marwood, tailor, to Anthony Swymmer, merchant, 7 years Jamaica. (BR).

10 May. The following apprenticed in Middlesex: Rebeccah Hill, aged 21, to serve John Morehead of Jamaica, merchant, 4 years. (GLRO: MR/E/593).

12 May. The following apprenticed in Middlesex: John White of Aldgate, London, aged 15, to John Turpin of Wapping, mariner, 6 years Barbados. (GLRO: MR/E/593).

12-14 May. Shippers by the *Expectation* of Bristol bound from Bristol for New England: William Curtis, Richard Gibbons, Edward Jones. (PRO: E190/1147/1).

13 May. The following apprenticed in London: William Prosser and David Tristid to Richard Whitpaine, citizen and butcher of London, 4 years Pennsylvania. (LMWB13/426).

17 May-2 July. Shippers by the *Patience*, Mr. William Smith, bound from London for Pennsylvania: William Roydon, Thomas Crundall, Thomas Cope, Edward Hasted, Isaac Testard, William Woodbee, John Brogett, Richard Witpan, John Pemble. (PRO: E190/124/1).

19 May. The following apprenticed in London: Francis Turton to serve Nicholas Moor Esq. of Philadelphia 4 years, with the consent of Mr. John Pemble. (LMWB13/429).

20 May. The following apprenticed in Middlesex: Elizabeth Harris to James Phillip of Plymouth, Devon, mariner, 4 years Virginia or Carolina. (GLRO: MR/E/593).

21 May. The following apprenticed in London: Caleb Hill to Thomas Adams, 4 years in Port Royal, Jamaica. (LMWB13/430).

23 May. The following apprenticed in Middlesex: Robert Tasker, aged 21, to William Smith of Wapping, mariner, 4 years Pennsylvania; Francis Stott, aged 28, to the same, 4 years Pennsylvania; Charles Horton, aged 13, to William Pewsey of Tower Hill, London, merchant, 9 years Jamaica, with the consent of his father, William H. (GLRO: MR/E/593).

23 May. Newgate prisoners reprieved to be transported to Barbados or Jamaica. London: Stephen Bumpstead; John Hopkins; Robert Wheatley; Christopher Ashley; James Watkins; William Flanck; Margaret Paul, spinster; John Valliony; John Bernard; Gerrard Middleton; James Harding; Joan Nicholls; John Carcy alias Carus; John Denn; John Francis; James Griffith; Joseph Curtis; Robert Valliony; John Howard; Elianor Adams, spinster, for infanticide; John Smith; William Fletcher. Middlesex: William Russell alias Nappier of St. Giles in the Fields; William Marshall of the same; Christopher Parris alias Parry of the same; Samuel Manarty of the same; John Atwood of St. Margaret Westminster; Richard Ford of St. Pancras; Roger Weekley of St. Giles in the Fields; Robert Barbadoes of St. Giles Cripplegate; Mary Desoe, spinster, alias wife of John Desoe of St. Paul Covent Garden; Alice Cranfield of St. Andrew Holborn, spinster; Richard Cudd of St. Katherine's; John Wheeler alias Stone of Hampstead; John Codd of St. Bartholomew Cripplegate (*sic*); Charles Atley of Stepney; Nathaniel Sunderland of St. Martin in the Fields. (PRO: C66/3245/16).

27 May. The following apprenticed in London: Francis Fullam, son of Jacob F. of Dublin, Ireland, tailor, deceased, to Peter Noyce of Sudbury, Middlesex, gent, 8 years New England. (LMWB13/433).

28 May. Petition of Edward Gove of New Hampshire, a prisoner in the Tower of London, to be released from his irons and to have the liberty of the Tower. (APC).

28 May-1 July. Shippers by the *Ann & Elizabeth*, Mr. William Orton, bound from London for Carolina: John Morris, Robert Hind, Jane Hall, John Ashby, William Thornburgh, Benjamin Laker, Sir Nathaniel Johnson, Robert Christopher, Samuel Ball, Henry Barnard. (PRO: E190/124/1).

29 May-2 June. The following apprenticed in Middlesex to serve James Galwith of Stepney, mariner, for four years in Maryland: Elizabeth Beman, aged 23; Hannah Webb, aged 19, with the consent of her father, William W., and her mother, witnessed by her aunt, Hannah Booker. (GLRO: MR/E/593).

30 May. The following apprenticed in London: Richard Hill, son of Nathan Hill of St. Giles Cripplegate, London, silk stock winder, deceased, to Roger Edwards of Stepney, Middlesex, mariner, 8 years Jamaica. (LMWB13/434).

30 May-30 June. The following apprenticed in Middlesex to go by the *William & Mary*, Mr. Mingian, to serve four years in Jamaica: Gregory Price, labourer aged 24, son of John Price, deceased, of Bowthered(?), Herefordshire, to Richard Batts of London, merchant; Evan Price, husbandman aged 21, son of David P. of Manafon, Montgomery, to John Browne, merchant; Richard Worrell, husbandman aged 27, son of Richard W. of Great Budworth, Cheshire, to John Browne; Gabriel Ely of Duffield, Derbyshire, ploughman aged 21, son of George E., deceased, to the same; Thomas Lodge of Clitheroe, Lancashire, ploughman aged 21, son of John Lodge, deceased, to the same; William Hippy of Derrington, Northamptonshire [?Staffordshire], labourer aged 21, to the same; John Johnson of Liverpool, Lancashire, accountant aged 29, son of John J., to the same; William Littlemore of Great Budworth, Cheshire, ploughman aged 30, son of William L., to the same; Cornelius Campion, barber aged 27, son of Michael C. of Thackford, Essex [?Thaxted, Essex or Thetford, Suffolk], to John Jones, merchant. (GLRO: MR/E/593).

May. Administration of Paul Pouls alias Poulson of Virginia, bachelor. (AW).

May. Administration of George Knight of Virginia, bachelor. (AW).

May. Administration of William Greenough of Boston, New England, who died abroad or at sea. (AW).

May. Probate of will of Nicholas Prinn of Stepney, Middlesex, who died in Virginia. (AW).

2 June. The following apprenticed in London: Sarah Mably, aged 16, daughter of Thomas M., to Robert Watkins, citizen and leatherseller of London, 4 years

Jamaica; George Ellison, son of William E. of St. Olave, Southwark, Surrey, deceased, to William Mingham, mariner, 5 years Jamaica. (LMWB13/437).

3 June. The following apprenticed in Bristol: Charles Morgan alias Williams to William Smith, 6 years Pennsylvania by *Bristol Merchant*, said William Smith Mr; Elizabeth Gibbs of Worcester to William Swymmer, 4 years Jamaica; John Thomas of Llandaff, to John Tompson, 6 years Pennsylvania by *Bristol Merchant*. (BR).

3 June. The following apprenticed in London: Elizabeth Whittle to William Smith, mariner, 4 years Pennsylvania. (LMWB13/438).

3 June. The following apprenticed in Middlesex: John Moody, aged 22, to Robert Lockton of Shadwell, mariner, 4 years Jamaica. (GLRO: MR/E/593).

3-13 June. Shippers by the *Vine* of Liverpool, Mr. William Preeson, bound from Liverpool for Pennsylvania: Griffeth Owen, William Hatton, Henry Baker, John Stedman. (PRO: E190/1346/9).

3 June-30 July. The following apprenticed in Middlesex to go by the *Booth*, Mr. Peter Pagan: John Gatchell, aged 19, son of John G. of Up Hatch, Somerset, to John Bright of London, merchant, 6 years Virginia; Nicholas Barnes, labourer aged 23, son of Henry B. of Norwich, to the same, 4 years Virginia; Elizabeth Skipp of East Smithfield, Middlesex, spinster aged 21, daughter of Francis S., deceased, to the same, 4 years Virginia; William Jarratt, aged 19, son of William J. of Hartycross(?), Cheshire, deceased, to the same, 5 years Virginia; John Bird, cordwainer aged 21, son of Edward B. of Shaftesbury, Dorset, to the same, 4 years Virginia; John Browne, aged 18, son of John B. of Tillingham, Essex, deceased, and at the desire of that parish, to the same, 5 years Virginia; William Scarr, labourer aged 26, son of Arthur S. of Aldgate High Street, Middlesex, originally from Ireland, to the same, 4 years Virginia; John Hannam, aged 21, son of John H. of Dorchester, to the same, 4 years Virginia, to serve as a labourer; John Whithead, barber aged 21, son of Thomas W. of Ubley, Somerset, to the same, 4 years Virginia; William Tompson, husbandman aged 21, son of William T. of Huttingham(?), Cambridgeshire, to the same, 4 years Virginia; William Holmes, labourer aged 21, son of William H. of St. Ives, Huntingdonshire, to the same, 4 years Virginia; John Elderkin, groom aged 25, son of John E. of St. Peter, Aldwinkle, Northamptonshire, to the same, 4 years Virginia; Thomas Howarth, weaver aged 21, son of James H. of Haslingden, Lancashire, to the same, 4 years Virginia; John Porter, aged 22, son of George P. of the Isle of Ely, Cambridgeshire, to the same, 4 years Virginia; Mary Saly, spinster aged 26, daughter of George S. of Kirton [?Kenton], Devon, to the same, 4 years Virginia; John Fitch, aged 20, son of John F. of Arrington, Cambridgeshire, deceased, to the same, 4 years Virginia; Richard Peaty, labourer aged 22, son of John P. of Canterbury, Kent, to the same, 4 years Virginia; Samuel Ratcliff, husbandman aged 24, son of William R. of Mellor, Derbyshire, to the same, 4 years Virginia; Thomas Smeethes, accountant aged 22, son of John S. of

Bewdley, Worcestershire, to the same, 4 years Virginia; John Towne, aged 18, son of John T. of Worminghall, Buckinghamshire, to the same, 7 years Virginia; Henry Snellgrove, aged 21, son of John S. of Evershot, Dorset, to the same, 4 years Virginia; Edward Osmond, tailor aged 24, son of Edward O. of Broadworth [?Broad Town], Wiltshire, to the same, 4 years Virginia; James Gresham, groom aged 21, son of James G. of Canterbury, Kent, to the same, 4 years Virginia; Bartholomew Stowell, husbandman aged 21, son of George S. of Albury, Surrey, to the same, 4 years Virginia; Thomas Johnson, labourer aged 19, son of Ralph J. of Portsmouth, Hampshire, to the same, 4 years Virginia; Luke Williams of Llandeusant, Carmarthenshire, groom aged 28, son of John Jones, to the same, 4 years Maryland; Andrew Oswald of Edinburgh, Scotland, clerk aged 22, son of James O., to the same, 4 years Virginia; Thomas Lewis of Peterchurch, Herefordshire, gardener aged 22, to the same, 4 years Virginia; John Bailey [Baly], groom aged 21, son of Lancelot B. of Todicke(?), Derbyshire, to the same, 4 years Virginia; Elizabeth Johnson, spinster aged 21, daughter of John J, of Sevenoaks, Kent, to the same, 4 years Virginia; Robert Peal, groom aged 23, son of Daniell P. of Monks Eleigh, Suffolk, to the same, 4 years Virginia; Phillip Hide of Hereford, tailor aged 21, son of Andrew H., to the same, 4 years Virginia; Nicholas Sharp of Mayfield [?Metfield or Mickfield], Suffolk, son of Nicholas S., to the same, 4 years Maryland; John Harris of Cripplegate, Middlesex, aged 22, son of John H., to the same, 4 years Virginia; Ann Dowly, aged 25, to Peter Pagan of London, merchant, 4 years Maryland. (GLRO: MR/E/593).

4 June-23 July. The following apprenticed in Middlesex to Nicholas Smith of Ratcliffe, mariner, to serve him for five years in Maryland: Elizabeth Piddock, aged 24; Dorcas Rawlett, aged 19, witnessed by her brother Charles R., her mother and father being dead; Margaret Weller, aged 22; Susan Clark, aged 20. (GLRO: MR/E/593).

5-7 June. The following apprenticed in Middlesex to Rainsford Waterhouse, merchant, to serve him in Jamaica for four years: John Horton, aged 23; Robert Littler, aged 22. (GLRO: MR/E/593).

6 June. The following apprenticed in Bristol: Thomas Eyre of East Farndon, Northants, to Giles Merrick, 4 years New England by *Rainbow*, Mr. William Henry; William Powell of Caldicote, Mon, to same, 4 years Nevis by *William & Ann*, Mr. Adam Combes. (BR).

6 June. The following apprenticed in Middlesex: Thomas Foller, aged 21, to David Carr of London, mariner, 4 years Virginia or Carolina. (GLRO: MR/E/593).

7 June. Deposition by Richard Watson, aged 27, citizen and haberdasher of London, that Stephen Burton of Boston, New England, merchant, became indebted in London by bond of 29 September 1679 to Thomas Ball, citizen and leatherseller of London, deceased, whose executor is Benjamin Williams, citizen and leatherseller of London. (LMCD).

7 June. The following apprenticed in Middlesex: Christopher Dosper of Goldas [?Gouldhurst], Kent, ploughman aged 27, son of Henry D., to John Browne, merchant, to serve in Jamaica. (GLRO: MR/E/593).

9 June. The following apprenticed in Middlesex: Susan Clark, aged 21, to Robert Hassett of London, merchant, 4 years Jamaica; William Downes, husbandman aged 27, son of John D. of Tenbury, Worcestershire, to William Haveland, 4 years Maryland. (GLRO: MR/E/593).

10-17 June. The following apprenticed in Middlesex to go by the *Brothers Adventure*, Mr. Henry Tragany, to serve in Maryland: John Lowdon of Exeter, Devon, shoemaker aged 19, to William Hutchens of London, merchant, 5 years; Andrew Breeding of Scotland, aged 20, son of Thomas B., to William Haveland, 4 years; Thomas Crampton, husbandman aged 22, son of John C. of Manchester, Lancashire, to Henry Tragany of London, merchant, 4 years . Francis Haires, aged 16, son of Edward H. of Penkridge, Staffordshire, "a miserable, wandering boy whose father and mother are dead," to the same, 7 years; William Fraser of Orkney, Scotland, accountant aged 21, son of William F., to the same, 4 years; Mark Watts, husbandman aged 21, son of George Watts of Pirbright, Surrey, to the same, 4 years; Thomas Lestrange, accountant aged 29, son of Thomas L. of Woodbridge, Suffolk, to the same, 4 years; John Perkins [Pirkins] of Tiverton, Devon, husbandman aged 28, son of William P., to the same, 4 years; Joseph Guy, cordwainer aged 29, son of William G. of Westbury, Wiltshire, to the same, 4 years; Henry Chambers, scholar aged 30, son of John C. of Holderness, Yorkshire, to the same, 4 years, to serve as an accountant; Thomas Martin, aged 16, son of Gilbert M. of Morpeth, Northumberland, deceased, and a ward of the parish of Newcastle, [Northumberland], since the death of his mother, to the same, 7 years; John Haster, labourer aged 21, son of John Haster of Edinburgh, Scotland, to the same, 4 years. (GLRO: MR/E/593).

11 June. Recommendation by the Lords of Trade and Plantations that convicts pardoned in London should be sent to St. Christopher's to the number of 300. (CSPC).

12 June. The following apprenticed in Middlesex to serve David Carr of London, mariner, for 4 years in Carolina or Virginia: William Thomson, aged 21; John Shelton, aged 18, with the consent of his father, his mother being dead; Thomas Lucas, aged 30. (GLRO: MR/E/593).

16 June. The following apprenticed in London: Elizabeth Peate, spinster, to serve James Matthew of Jamaica, vintner, 7 years. (LMWB13/448).

17 June. Deposition by Thomas Sorrell, citizen and vintner of London, aged 52, that Thomas Chinnery of Ratcliffe, Middlesex, mariner, became indebted by deed of 14 August 1678 to John Sole of Ratcliffe, citizen and tallow chandler of London. John Lloyd of Rumney Marsh, New England, has been appointed attorney to recover the debt. (LMCD).

17 June. The following apprenticed in Bristol: Henry Powell of Usk, Mon, to Philip Jefferies, 7 years Jamaica by *Amity*, Mr. Reece Jefferies; Sarah Neale of Barton, Glos, daughter of Alexander Neale, to —— ——, 7 years Jamaica by *Dragon*. (BR).

19-23 June. Shippers by the *Shield* of Stockton, Mr. Daniell Toaes, bound from Newcastle for Pennsylvania: Alexander Robinson, Nicholas Pendry. (PRO: E190/200/9).

20 June. Midland Circuit prisoners reprieved to be transported to America. Derbyshire: William Pilkington; William Wardle; Edward Browne; William How of Witton le Wear; John Green of Bithburn. Lincolnshire: Thomas Prim; John Freshney; Michael Noell; John Nettleton; Robert Taylor; Jane Blakeley. Northamptonshire: William Wormer of Peterborough; Nathaniel Good; William Smith. Unspecified: Edward Roberts. (PRO: C66/3245/17).

20 June. Home Circuit prisoners reprieved to be transported to Barbados or Jamaica. Essex: Allanson Clarke of Waltham; Charles Rumball of Stapleford Tawney. Hertfordshire: Anthony Strangwich of Ware; John Stratford of Hemel Hempstead. Kent: William Taswell of Sittingbourne; Valentine Cogswell of Deptford; Joseph Robinson of Dartford; George Wakeford of Dodington. Surrey: Margaret Floyd of Newington; Hannah Hallett of St. Saviour, Southwark; John Broman of Guildford. (PRO: C66/3245/18).

21 June-5 July. Shippers by the *Loyal Chapman*, Mr. George Clark, bound from London for Carolina: John King, Francis Hartley, John Scot. (PRO: E190/124/1).

23 June. The following apprenticed in London: Richard Hall, whose father and mother are dead, to serve John Lightfoot, planter, 9 years Virginia, with the consent of his grandmother, Elizabeth Chidley; Mary Miller, widow, to William Smith, mariner, 4 years Pennsylvania; Henry Stephens to the same, 12 years Virginia, with the consent of his mother, Rebecca, wife of Lewis Isles. (LMWB13/454).

23-30 June. The following apprenticed in Middlesex to go by the *Prince*, Mr. Jonathan Wilson, to serve for four years in Barbados: William Whiting, accountant aged 20, son of Thomas W. of St. Clement Danes, Middlesex, to William Haveland; Nathaniell Mayne, coachman aged 21, son of Nathaniell M. of Newton Bushell, Devon, to the same; John Mather, husbandman aged 22, son of John M. of Ratley [?Radcliffe], Lancashire, deceased, to the same; Simon Leeson, tailor aged 21, son of Benjamin L. of Hartpool [?Hatfield], Hertfordshire, to James Williams of London, merchant, (for 4 years in Virginia); Simon Wilson, citizen and merchant tailor of London aged 31, son of William W. of Kingham, Oxfordshire, to William Thomas of London, merchant; George Rock of Cowcross, Middlesex, labourer aged 21, son of William R., deceased, to John Johnson of London, merchant. (GLRO: MR/E/593).

24 June. The following apprenticed in Middlesex: Thomas York, aged 21, to Peter Peake of London, mariner, 4 years Maryland. (GLRO: MR/E/593).

24-30 June. Shipper by the *Elizabeth* of Weymouth, Mr. John Cox, bound from Weymouth for Virginia: James Gould. (PRO: E190/886/3).

25 June-31 July. Shippers by the *Dolphin*, Mr. John Foy, bound from London for New England: Zachary Taylor, Noah Lawrence, Thomas Humphreys, Hugh Horton, Thomas Gibbs, John Hilton, Thomas Puckle, Richard Deane, John Butler, Joshua Spurrier, William Barnes, John Wood, Charles Lidget, Richard Humphries, Samuel Hacker. (PRO: E190/124/1).

26 June. The following apprenticed in Middlesex: Katherine Gardner, aged 22, held in the Bridewell for pilfering, to George Clark of London, mariner, 4 years Carolina; Mary Dwaite, aged 21, held in the Bridewell for pilfering, to the same, 4 years Carolina; Elizabeth Bird, aged 14, held in the Bridewell for pilfering, to the same, 5 years Carolina, with the consent of her father and mother; William Harrison, aged 31, to Thomas Everard of Limehouse, mariner, 4 years Barbados. (GLRO: MR/E/593).

26 June. Shipper by the *Baltimore*, Mr. James Conway, bound from London for Virginia: Dean Cocks. (PRO: E190/124/1).

26 June-11 July. Shippers by the *Bristol Factor* bound from Bristol for New England: Archibald Erskin, Samuell Packer, Joseph Baugh, Thomas Gouldny. (PRO: E190/1147/1).

27 June. The following apprenticed in Middlesex: Sarah Phillips, aged 21, to Thomas Sweet of London, mariner, 4 years Maryland; Mary Spence, aged 21, to James Brayner of London, merchant, 4 years Virginia. (GLRO: MR/E/593).

27 June. The following apprenticed in Bristol: Francis Sansom of Broseley, Salop, baker, to Henry Loyd, 4 years Virginia or Pennsylvania. (BR).

30 June. The following apprenticed in Bristol: William Edwards of Oxford to John Napper, 6 years Barbados by *Samuel*, Mr. Henry Driver; William Courtney of Exeter, [Devon], to same, 4 years Jamaica by *Samuel*. (BR).

30 June. The following apprenticed in Middlesex to Francis French of London, merchant: Samuell Lee, aged 18, and Joseph Lee, aged 14, both held in the Bridewell, 6 & 7 years Maryland with the consent of their mother, Alice L., their father being dead. (GLRO: MR/E/593).

June. Probate of will of James Swift of St. Mary Abchurch, London, who died in Hackney, Middlesex, having goods in Boston, New England. (AW).

1 July. The following apprenticed in Middlesex: Thomas Lankford, aged 20, to Peregrine Browne of London, 6 years Maryland; William Wainright, aged 24, held in Whitechapel Prison, to John Dodsworth of London, merchant, 4 years Maryland; Thomas Bummer, aged 25, held in the Bridewell, to the same, 4 years Maryland. (GLRO: MR/E/593).

1-30 July. The following apprenticed in Middlesex to go by the *Benedict Leonard*, Mr. Francis Partis, and to serve him in Maryland: Robert Harrison of Godmanchester, Huntingdonshire, ploughman aged 28, son of John H., 4 years; John Curren of Kilkenny, Ireland, groom aged 21, son of William C., 4 years; John Wright, groom aged 23, son of William W. of Markington, Yorkshire, 4 years; Sarah Carter, spinster aged 19, daughter of John C. of Newcastle under Lyme, Staffordshire, deceased, 4 years; Joseph Johnson of London, aged 22, son of Joseph J., 4 years, to serve as a "slooper"; David Ogilvie of Banff, Scotland, scholar aged 21, son of Alexander O., 4 years; Stephen Wright of Pebrey(?), Lincolnshire, husbandman aged 22, son of Stephen W., 4 years; Michael Drummer, labourer aged 21, son of Francis D. of Brandborough [?Brant Broughton], High Holland, [Lincolnshire], 4 years; Hannah Kible of Ellastone, Staffordshire, spinster aged 21, daughter of John K., 4 years; William Harris, groom aged 23, son of William H. of Atcham, Shropshire, 4 years; William Standley, cordwainer aged 22, son of William S. of Kingston on Thames, Surrey, 4 years; Mary Busby, aged 18, 5 years, with the consent of her mother, Margaret B., her father being dead; Frances Clark, aged 15, 5 years, with the consent of her mother, Elizabeth C., her father being dead; William Cannaby, husbandman aged 20, son of John C. of Backwell, Somerset, 4 years; John Griggs, aged 16, son of Timothy G. of St. Clement's, [Ipswich], Suffolk, to 7 years; John Dunbarr, tailor aged 22, son of John D. of Glasgow, Scotland, 4 years; Hugh Price, aged 21, son of Thomas P. of Glasbury, Brecon, 4 years; Daniell Francis, slooper aged 26, son of William F. of Shantly(?), Essex, 4 years; Mary Jenkins, spinster aged 23, daughter of William J. of Wapping, Middlesex, 4 years; William Tagwell, a friendless person aged 17, son of John T. of Cleeve, Wiltshire, 7 years; Richard Swann of Dublin, Ireland, aged 16, son of Richard S., deceased, 7 years, with the consent of his brother, Joseph S., for the mother in Ireland. (GLRO: MR/E/593).

2 July. The following apprenticed in Middlesex: Richard Humphreys, aged 21, to Richard Bayly of Maryland, boatwright, 4 years; John Stanton, aged 17, to the same, 7 years; John Bullock, aged 25, to Isaac Lyon of London, mariner, 4 years Virginia. (GLRO: MR/E/593).

2 July. John Mare of Marydowne (*sic*), Devon; and Thomas Wiltsheire of North Petherton, Somerset, bound to John Bull of Lyme Regis, mariner, to serve 4 years in Virginia or Maryland. (DRO B7/M9).

3 July. Northern Circuit prisoners reprieved to be transported to Barbados. Cumberland: John Barwis of Dovenby. Durham: John Wright of Carlehouses. Northumberland: William Orocke of Ouseburn. Yorkshire: Samuel Man of Great Preston; Isabel Partridge, spinster; John Martin of Leeds. (PRO: C66/3245/15).

3 July. Western Circuit prisoners reprieved to be transported to Barbados. Bristol: Robert Deale of St. James, Bristol. Cornwall: John Howard of Hennock

(Devon); Stephen Painter of Mewan; Joseph Kneebone; John Webb of Jacobstowe; Dorothy Pope of Landrake; James Pope of Dulver. Devon: Richard Howard of Crediton. Hampshire: John Davyes of Long Sutton. Wiltshire: Thomas Harman of Calne; Isaac Jessope of Malmesbury. (PRO: C66/3245/19).

4 July. The following apprenticed in London: The following pilfering boys who "lie day and night in the markets and streets (of London) and haveing noe friends or relacions to take care or provide for them .. bound themselves .. to John Lightfoot, planter lodging at Mr. Edmond Lightfoot's without Newgate, to serve him in Virginia" for 10 or 15 years: William Gentleman, son of William G. of Charing Cross, Middlesex, porter, deceased; William Jones, son of William J. of Whitechapel, Middlesex, tailor, deceased; Thomas Hathorne, son of Thomas H. of Cross Lane, Holborn, Middlesex, joiner, deceased; Dukesell Browne, son of John B. of Hereford, carrier, deceased; Henry Harding, son of Nicholas H. of Hampshire, labourer, deceased; Richard George, son of Richard G. of Deptford, Kent, gardener, deceased; Robert Ipey, son of Robert I. of Rosemary Lane, London, deceased; William Hagar, son of Robert H. of Bishopsgate Street, London, weaver, deceased. (LMWB13/464,465).

4 July. The following apprenticed in Middlesex: James Davis, aged 22, to John Brown, merchant, 4 years Virginia; William Horrox, cooper aged 23, son of Ralph H. of Warrington, Lancashire, deceased, to James Whaley of London, merchant, 4 years Antigua by [blank], Mr. Bowman, to serve as a cooper; Elizabeth Bever, aged 21, to John Wilkey of London, mariner, 4 years Maryland; Sarah Hilton, aged 16, to Charles Parle of London, mariner, 4 years Maryland, with the consent of her mother, Elizabeth Hill, her father being dead. (GLRO: MR/E/593).

4 July-9 August. The following apprenticed in Middlesex to go by the *Abraham & Francis*, Mr. Edward Burford, to serve him in Maryland: William Bruin(?) of Bulwick, Northamptonshire, gardener aged 28, son of William B., 4 years; Robert Clapshoe of Newbury, Berkshire, wool comber aged 22, son of Robert C., 4 years; Benjamin Rose, aged 16, son of John R. of Selby, Yorkshire, 6 years; Elizabeth Hanworth, spinster aged 27, daughter of James H. of Godstone, Surrey, 4 years; Timothy Clarkson, groom aged 21, son of John C. of Cockcross(?), Lancashire, 4 years; Peter Snelling, aged 16, son of John S. of Piccadilly, Middlesex, 5 years, with the consent of his father and of his mother, Cornelia S.; Richard Edgar, ropemaker aged 27, son of Richard Edgar of Middlesex, 4 years; Amy Hawes, spinster aged 21, daughter of Robert H. of Tichwell, Norfolk, to Edward Burwell, 4 years; Edward Phillips, aged 21, son of Thomas P. of Orleton, Herefordshire, 4 years; George Key, shoemaker aged 21, of Bury, Lancashire, son of Richard K., 4? years; Richard Baxter, tailor aged 21, son of William B. of Pershore, Worcestershire, deceased, 4 years; Jeremiah Arnold of Coventry, Warwickshire, weaver aged 22, son of Thomas A., deceased, 4 years; Henry Wood of East Smithfield, Middlesex, labourer aged 20, son of Henry W., deceased, 4 years; George Terrold of Boston, Lincolnshire, clerk aged 23, son of Joseph T., 4 years. (GLRO: MR/E/593).

6 July. The following apprenticed in Middlesex: Lidea Pike, aged 22, to Jacob Acres and Thomas Jordain of Limehouse, mariners, 4 years Maryland. (GLRO: MR/E/593).

7 July. The following apprenticed in London: James Collins, son of John C. of Woolvercott, Oxfordshire, labourer, deceased, an idle boy taken up in the streets, to John Lightfoot, planter, 12 years Virginia. (LMWB13/467).

7 July. The following apprenticed in Middlesex: Samuell Champley, aged 25, to Peregrine Browne of London, merchant, 4 years Maryland; Richard Norcott, aged 14, to Robert Hatton of East Smithfield, mariner, 10 years Maryland, with the consent of his mother, Ann N., and his brother, Henry N., his father being dead. (GLRO: MR/E/593).

7-11 July. The following apprenticed in Middlesex to serve Luis Evans of Maryland, planter: Arabella Tempest, aged 22, 5 years; Joyce Harvey, aged 25, 4 years. (GLRO: MR/E/593).

7-26 July. Shippers by the *Adventure*, Mr. Ralph Cooper, bound from London for Virginia and Maryland: Thomas Martin, Joseph Brock, Thomas Sands. (PRO: E190/124/1).

8-27 July. Shippers by the *Samuell*, Mr. Thomas Bowman, bound from London for Virginia: Samuel Groome, John Taylor, Robert Burman, Stephen Robe. (PRO: E190/124/1).

9 July. The following apprenticed in London: Anne Meadowes, daughter of [blank] of St. Sepulchre, London, shoemaker, to John Lightfoot, planter, 5 years Virginia, with the consent of her sister Elizabeth, wife of Richard Child. (LMWB13/469).

9 July. The following apprenticed in Middlesex to serve Captain John Brown of London, mariner, for four years in Maryland: William Fidler, aged 22; Robert Wright, aged 21. (GLRO: MR/E/593).

9 July. Shipper by the *Brothers Adventure*, Mr. Henry Tregany, bound from London for Virginia: James Braines. (PRO: E190/124/1).

9-21 July. The following apprenticed in Middlesex to serve John Dix of London, mariner, for four years in Maryland: John Hall, aged 21; Sarah Troke, aged 18; Thomas Kimberly, aged 21. (GLRO: MR/E/593).

9-26 July. The following apprenticed in Middlesex to go by the *Adventure*, Mr. Ralph Cooper, to serve Edward Talbott of London, merchant, in Maryland: John Morrall of Newcastle under Lyme, Staffordshire, gardener aged 22, son of William M., 4 years; Mary Goldsmith, widow aged 30, daughter of Henry Lester of Southwark, Surrey, 4 years, to serve as housemaid, with the consent of her said father and of her mother, Sarah Lester; Seth Everill, aged 15, son of Seth E. of Shrewsbury, Shropshire, 8 years. (GLRO: MR/E/593).

10 July. The following apprenticed in London: Margaret Morgan, daughter of Richard M. of St. Giles in the Fields, Middlesex, to John Lightfoot, planter, 5 years Virginia, with the consent of her father. (LMWB13/470).

10 July-15 August. The following apprenticed in Middlesex to serve Richard Moss of London, merchant and mariner, in Maryland: John Crofts, aged 32, 4 years; William Hardin, aged 24, 4 years; Richard Coles, aged 20, 4 years; Richard Peacock, aged 32, 4 years; Thomas Wakefield, son of John & Mary W., deceased, 5 years; John Johnson, aged 15, 9 years; Jonathan Ward, aged 30, 4 years; William Freeman, aged 18, 7 years; Ursula Child, aged 25, 4 years; Joseph Boreman, aged 22, 5 years; Henry Ingram, aged 16, 4 years; John Boyter, gardener aged 24, 4 years; John Greenwood, seaman aged 21, 4 years; Sarah Searl, aged 20, 4 years; Susan Wharton, aged 21, 4 years (in Virginia); Mary Michell, aged 21, 4 years; Margaret Pilkington, aged 23, 4 years; Mabell Tynn, aged 18, 4 years; Edmond Ward, aged 23, 4 years. (GLRO: MR/E/593).

11 July. The following apprenticed in London: William Ovendell, son of William O. of St. Olave, Southwark, Surrey, and John Cash, son of Thomas C. of Jamaica, planter, to Richard Heath, 7 years Maryland. (LMWB13/470).

11 July. The following apprenticed in Middlesex: John Robinson, aged 28, to Jonas Cock of Wapping, carpenter, 4 years Maryland. (GLRO: MR/E/593).

11 July. Shipper by the *Margaret* of Boston bound from Exeter for [?Boston, New England]: Samuell Terrell. (PRO: E190/962/4).

11 July-16 August. The following apprenticed in Middlesex to go by the *Crown Malago*, Mr. Michael Staples: Robert Scofield, a poor youth aged 16, son of John S. of Hodgesdone (*sic*), Middlesex, [? Hoddesdon, Hertfordshire], to Edward Talbott, 8 years Maryland; Thomas Walker of Yorkshire, aged 17, son of George W., deceased, to the same, 7 years Maryland or Virginia; Susanna Perry of Early [?Arley], Staffordshire, spinster aged 20, daughter of James P., to the same, 4 years Maryland or Virginia; Anne Price of St. Andrew's, Worcester, dairymaid aged 22, daughter of John P., to the same, 4 years Maryland; William Stroud, aged 14, son of Robert S., to Michael Staples of Stepney, mariner, 7 years Maryland, with the consent of his father. (GLRO: MR/E/593).

14 July. The following apprenticed in London: Henry Eades, son of Henry E. of Godmanchester, Huntingdonshire, tailor, deceased, to John Lightfoot, 7 years Virginia; Rachell Greenwood to the same, 5 years Virginia; Henry Carter to Robert Burman, 6 years Maryland; Alexander Fullerton to John Haslewood of London, mariner, 4 years Virginia. (LMWB13/473,476).

14 July. The following apprenticed in Middlesex: Edward Holt, aged 22, to John Perce of Limehouse, mariner, 4 years Maryland; William Gurlin, aged 14, to

Daniel Claphamson of Whitechapel, mariner, 6 years Virginia, with the consent of his father-in-law, Thomas Stokes, and his mother, Susanna Stokes, his father being dead, and with the agreement of his master, William Pinkard. (GLRO: MR/E/593).

14-15 July. Shipper by the *Tryall* of Boston, Mr. Nathaniell Pearce, bound from Exeter for New England: Joseph Sanders. (PRO: E190/962/4).

14 July-1 August. Shippers by the *Nevis Merchant*, Mr. Timothy Clark, bound from London for New England: Jacob Jesson, Thomas Hunt & Co., Anthony Burren, Anthony Tourney (PRO: E190/124/1).

14 July-9 August. The following apprenticed in Middlesex to Michael Yoakley of London, mariner, to serve in Maryland: John Stennett, aged 46, 4 years; Abraham Ogden, son of Samuel O., 8 years, with the consent of his father. (GLRO: MR/E/593).

15 July. The following apprenticed in London: Anne Mongomery, daughter of Robert M. of Newcastle, Northumberland, waterman, to Robert Burman of London, factor, 5 years Maryland. (LMWB13/477).

15 July. The following apprenticed in Middlesex: Thomas Darnell, aged 26, to Richard Molborn of Stepney, mariner, 4 years Maryland. (GLRO: MR/E/593).

16 July. The following apprenticed in Middlesex: Elizabeth Lynes, aged 25, to Isaack Lyon of Rotherhithe, mariner, 4 years Maryland. (GLRO: MR/E/593).

16 July. The following apprenticed in Bristol: Steward Haddick of North Molton, Devon, to John Whitfield, 4 years Jamaica by *Dragon*; Godfry Waterson of Gloucester to Robert Kirke, 4 years Jamaica by *Dragon*. (BR).

16 July. The following apprenticed in London: Mary Breadcott, daughter of Richard B. of Dorchester, Oxfordshire, mariner, to John Heslewood of London, mariner, 6 years Virginia; Mary Crane, daughter of John C. of St. Martin le Grand, London, shoemaker, deceased, to the same, 6 years Virginia. (LMWB13/478).

16-18 July. Shipper by the *Hopewell*, Mr. Michael Yoakley, bound from London for Virginia and Maryland: William Yoakley. (PRO: E190/124/1).

16-19 July. Shippers by the *Potomack Merchant*, Mr. Charles Partis, bound from London for Virginia: John Jeffreys, William Peele. (PRO: E190/124/1).

17 July. The following apprenticed in London: Robert Barbadoes to be delivered to John Harwood and John Saunders to be transported to Barbados. (*See list of reprieved convicts for May 1684*). (LMWB13/480).

17 July. Shipper by the *Industry*, Mr. Peter Peak, bound from London for Virginia: Christopher Dodsworth. (PRO: E190/124/1).

17-24 July. Shippers by the *Booth*, Mr. Simon Emerly, bound from London for Virginia: Thomas Jennings, Thomas Stark. (PRO: E190/124/1).

19 July-21 August. The following apprenticed in Middlesex to serve Richard Batt of London, merchant: John Cruse, cooper aged 21, son of Thomas C. of Plympton, Devon, 4 years Barbados; Jeffery Badger, aged 29, 4 years Maryland; Richard Chapman, aged 30, 4 years Maryland; William Hanly, aged 28, 4 years Virginia; Robert Johnson, aged 30, 4 years Virginia. (GLRO: MR/E/593).

21 July. The following apprenticed in London: Thomas Hancocks, son of John H. of Worcester, bargeman, to Thomas Warren of London, merchant, 7 years Maryland. (LMWB13/488).

21 July. Shipper by the *Christopher*, Mr. Benjamin Hall, bound from London for Virginia: Giles Bullock. (PRO: E190/124/1).

21 July. The following apprenticed in Middlesex: Ambrose Wigglesworth, aged 24, to serve Thomas Morley of Barbados, planter, 4 years. (GLRO: MR/E/593).

22 July. The following apprenticed in London: Elizabeth Search, daughter of Joseph S., deceased, to John Haslewood of London, merchant, 5 years Virginia; William Brookes, son of William B. of Great Witley, Worcestershire, husbandman, to Christopher Rousby, 4 years Maryland; Richard Griffin, son of Richard G. of Whitechapel, Middlesex, seaman, deceased, to Michaell Petry and Thomas Lane of London, merchants, 10 years Virginia; William Downes, son of James D. of Basinghall Street, London, to the same, 4 years Virginia or elsewhere. (LMWB13/488,489).

22 July. Shipper by the *Thomas & Susan*, bound from London for New England: Francis Baker. (PRO: E190/124/1).

22-26 July. Shippers by the *William & Mary*, Mr. Benjamin Hall, bound from London for Virginia: Micajah Perry, John Brodnax. (PRO: E190/124/1).

22 July-29 August. Shippers by the *Blossom*, Mr. Richard Martin, bound from London for New York and New Jersey: Alvaro Dacosta, David Conguard, John Jackson, John Loveroo, Nathaniel Rookby, George Keth, Robert Bridgman, Thomas Marden, John Tutt, Henry Parker, Robert Hodskins, John Greening. (PRO: E190/124/1).

23-24 July. Shippers by the *Thomas & Edward*, Mr. John Browne, bound from London for Virginia: Edward Lightfoot, John Plover, Thomas Glover. (PRO: E190/124/1).

23-24 July. Shippers by the *John & William*, Mr. Thomas Dell, bound from London for Virginia: James Harris, Richard Cox. (PRO: E190/124/1).

24 July. The following apprenticed in London: John Wright, son of John W. of King's Bench Alley, Southwark, Surrey, tailor, deceased, to John Heslewood of London, mariner, 8 years Virginia. (LMWB13/491).

24-26 July. Shippers by the *Benedict Leonard*, Mr. Francis Partis, bound from London for Virginia and Maryland: James Wagstaffe, Nicholas Giffard, Thomas Elwes. (PRO: E190/124/1).

25 July. The following apprenticed in London: John Grant, son of John G., mariner, to John Lightfoot, gent, 10 years Virginia; Mary Read, servant of Jane Corfield, committed to the Bridewell for stealing chickens, to Richard Heath of London, merchant, 4 years Maryland; Mary Pond, aged 21, (who was committed to Bridewell Prison), daughter of Abraham P. of Margate, Kent, to the same, 4 years Maryland, provided she is willing to go; Ambrose Shipwash of Oxfordshire to serve Philip Clarke of Maryland 7 years; George Willowes and Elizabeth Brent to the same, 4 years; Christopher Lathorne, son of William L. of Southwark, Surrey, map maker, deceased, to Thomas Tench of London, merchant, 9 years Maryland; William Davis, son of William D. of Barnet, Hertfordshire, starchmaker, deceased, to the same, 7 years Maryland; John Harrison, son of Sidrick H. of Bluecoats Field, Ratcliffe, Middlesex, mariner, deceased, to the same, 9 years Maryland. (LMWB13/492-495).

26 July. The following apprenticed in Bristol: Edward Evans of Dollwrell (*sic*), Worcs, tailor, to John Orchard, 4 years Pennsylvania by *Society*, Mr. John Read; Samuel Pepper of Kings Lynn, Norf, to William Swymmer, 4 years Jamaica by *Dragon*. (BR).

26 July-4 September. The following apprenticed in Middlesex to go by the *Hound*, Mr. Phileas Hinde, to Maryland to serve for four years: William Sanders, aged 21, to Captain Phileas Hide; William Fenwick of Lincoln, aged 21, son of Robert F., to the same; John Darling, cordwainer aged 21, son of John D. of Scotland, to the same; Richard Holmes, cordwainer aged 21, son of Richard H. of Bewdley, Worcestershire, to John Moore; John Skinner of Wivelsfield, Sussex, aged 21, son of William S., to John Dix of London, merchant. (GLRO: MR/E/593).

28 July. The following apprenticed in London: William Fray, son of Thomas F. of Canterbury, Kent, deceased, and Daniel Rust, late of Norwich, to Thomas Tench, merchant, 4 years Maryland; John Tomlinson (Thomplinson), son of Mathew T. of Bramfield, Hertfordshire, butcher, to the same, 5 years Maryland; Elizabeth Lloyd, daughter of Jeremy L. of St. Sepulchre, London, chimney sweep, to serve Philip Clarke of Maryland, planter, 8 years; Margaret Williams of Tanworth, Warwickshire, spinster, to the same, 4 years Maryland; William Buxton, son of William B. of Southwark, Surrey, gardener, deceased, to John Haslewood, mariner, 9 years Virginia. (LMWB13/500,501).

28 July. The following apprenticed in Bristol: John Parker alias Padgett of Sturbridge, Worcs, to Robert Kirke, 4 years Jamaica by *Dragon*, Mr. William Dawes; Roger Price to Roger Beck, 4 years by *Bristol Merchant*. (BR).

28 July. The following apprenticed in Middlesex: William Horton, aged 18, son of William H., to Thomas Newbold of London, merchant, 5 years Maryland, with the consent of his father; Deborah Falconer, aged 19, daughter of Robert & Sarah F., to Daniel Clapham, 4 years Maryland, with the consent of her father and mother; John Igne, aged 24, to James Longman of Ratcliffe, mariner, 4 years Virginia. (GLRO: MR/E/593).

28 July. Shipper by the *Golden Lyon*, Mr. John Haslewood, bound from London for Virginia: Arthur Baily. (PRO: E190/124/1).

28-31 July. Shippers by the *John*, Mr. Daniel Bradley, bound from London for Virginia: John Constantine, Richard Buller, Edward Edmonds. (PRO: E190/124/1).

28 July-4 August. Shippers by the *Owners Adventure*, Mr. James Bowman, bound from London for Virginia: John Plover, Arthur Baily. (PRO: E190/124/1).

28 July-2 September. Shippers by the *Maryland Merchant* of Hull, Mr. Joseph Eyon, bound from Hull for Pennsylvania: Walter Fawcett, John Bambrigg, Thomas Fox, Robert Shackleton, Thomas Nisbett, John Langstaff, Cornel Empson, George Horsley. (PRO: E190/327/7).

29 July. The following apprenticed in Bristol: Robert Curry of Stoke St. Mary, Som, to John Porter, 4 years Maryland by *Society*, Mr. John Read. (BR).

29 July. The following apprenticed in London: William Smith, son of William S. of Scotland, deceased, to Richard Heath, merchant, 4 years Maryland. (LMWB13/502).

30 July. The following apprenticed in Middlesex: William Evans, aged 17, to serve Edward Burford of Virginia, planter, 5 years. (GLRO: MR/E/593).

30 July-13 September. Shippers by the *Priscilla*, Mr. Joseph Moulten, bound from London for New England: John Dunton, William White, Joshua Boult, William Puryour, Thomas Same, John Lake, Thomas Goddard, John Roper, James Rolleston. (PRO: E190/124/1).

31 July. The following apprenticed in London: Elizabeth Fann of St. Botolph Bishopsgate, London, spinster, and Patience Knight of Southwark, Surrey, spinster, to Phillip Clarke, planter, 4 years Maryland; Isaac Vigoreux of Rochelle, France, to Daniel Duthaes, 4 years Pennsylvania. (LMWB13/502,503).

31 July. The following apprenticed in Bristol: John Coombe of Abingdon, Berks, mason, to William Smith, mariner, 2 years Virginia, to be employed in his trade and to have an additional 50 acres. (BR).

July. Administration of William Stephens of Bristol, who died in Virginia. (AW).

July. Administration of John Brooks of Stepney, Middlesex, who died in Virginia. (AW).

1 August. The following apprenticed in London: William Roberts, son of William R. of St. Botolph Aldersgate, London, deceased, to William Frisby, merchant, 12 years Maryland. (LMWB13/506).

1 August. The following apprenticed in Middlesex: William Townsend, aged 18, to James Galwith, 4 years Maryland; Mary Gilbert, aged 20, to William Johnson of London, mariner, 5 years Maryland, with the consent of her father-in-law and of her mother, Ellen Davis; Dinah Wells, aged 21, to Edward Corbett of London, mariner, 5 years Virginia; George Croson, aged 21, to the same, 4 years Virginia; Dorothy Jennings, aged 21, to the same, 5 years Virginia; (GLRO: MR/E/593).

1 August. Shipper by the *Endeavour*, Mr. John Lawrence, bound from London for Virginia: John Pile. (PRO: E190/124/1).

1-7 August. The following apprenticed in Middlesex to serve Robert Hall of London, mariner, in Maryland: Thomas Holtham, aged 19, 5 years; James Bankes, aged 18, 6 years. (GLRO: MR/E/593).

1-7 August. The following apprenticed in Middlesex to go by the *Elizabeth & Katherine* [elsewhere *John & Elizabeth*], Mr. Keazar, to serve John Moore of London, merchant, for four years in Maryland: Henry Willis of Wantage, Berkshire, labourer aged 21, son of Leonard W.; Elizabeth Liptrapp, spinster aged 21, daughter of Edward L. of Tinkby [?Tugby], Leicestershire; Frances Speakman, spinster aged 16, daughter of George S. of Uxbridge, Middlesex, deceased; John Smart, tailor aged 21, son of John S. of Middleton, Warwickshire, deceased. (GLRO: MR/E/593).

1-8 August. Shippers by the *Mary*, Mr. John Gardner, bound from London for New England: Peter Hudson, Nicholas Day, John Freeman. (PRO: E190/124/1).

1-9 August. The following apprenticed in Middlesex to go by the *Hannah*, Mr. James Kendall, to serve him for four years in Jamaica: Mary Gibbs, spinster, witnessed by Thomas Gibbs, citizen and leatherseller of London; Elizabeth Jones, widow aged 26; Robert Cross, aged 17; Lawrence Howard, aged 30. (GLRO: MR/E/593).

1-22 August. Shippers by the *Globe*, Mr. Samuel Prior, bound from London for Maryland: John Thorp, Degory Marshall, William Farmer, Strangways Mudd. (PRO: E190/124/1).

2 August. The following apprenticed in London: Anne Boylston of London, spinster, to Samuell Roberts, mariner, 4 years Maryland; Nathaniel Brisco, aged 21, shoemaker, to Richard Heath, merchant, 4 years Maryland. (LMWB13/508).

2 August. The following apprenticed in Bristol: John Stevens of London to John Lord, 4 years Jamaica by *Samuel*; Ann Doggett of Bristol to Richard ——, 4 years Virginia by *Society*; Mary Chandler of Bristol to same, 4 years Virginia by *Society*; Richard Salisbury of London to Joseph ——, 4 years Maryland by *Society*; John Whitfield to William Stoakes, 4 years Barbados by *Diligence*, said William Stoakes Mr. (BR).

2 August-10 September. Shippers by the *Richard*, Mr. Thomas Joles, bound from London for New England: Erasmus Norwich, Samuell Dawes, Anthony Tanner, Anthony Burren, James Whitcomb, William Whitcomb, John Wood, Lawrence Baskervile, Stephen Cooke, Ezekiel Hutchinson, Richard Parratt, Richard Seale. (PRO: E190/124/1).

4 August. The following apprenticed in London: Sarah Boice, daughter of Rowland B. of Worcester, clothier, deceased, to Sebastian Gingee, mariner, 4 years Virginia; Richard Fennell, son of Richard F. of Epsom, Surrey, blacksmith, deceased, to Thomas Tench, merchant, 8 years Maryland. (LMWB13/509).

4 August. The following apprenticed in Middlesex: Ellinor Draper to Richard Swanwell of Newcastle, [Northumberland], mariner, 4 years Maryland; John Curtis, aged 30, to Bartholomew Watts of London, mariner, 4 years Maryland. (GLRO: MR/E/593).

4-19 August. Shippers by the *Barbados Merchant*, Mr. James Cocke, bound from Plymouth for Virginia: Thomas Hull, Phillip Willcox, Peter Baker. (PRO: E190/1048/8).

4-21 August. Shippers by the *Culpepper*, Mr. Christopher Morgan, bound from London for Virginia: John Plover, Micajah Perry. (PRO: E190/124/1).

5 August. The following apprenticed in Middlesex: John Bond, aged 23, to serve Edmond Sandeford of Barbados, planter, 4 years; Charles Siviter, aged 12, to serve Abraham Clark of Maryland, planter, 9 years, with the consent of his father and mother, Richard and Elizabeth S. (GLRO: MR/E/593).

5 August. The following apprenticed in London: George Procter, son of William P. of Wednesbury, Staffordshire, tailor, to Thomas Tench, 6 years Maryland. (LMWB13/510).

5 August. Shipper by the *Abraham & Francis*, Mr. Edward Burford, bound from London for Virginia: Anthony Phillips. (PRO: E190/124/1).

5 August. Shipper by the *Elizabeth & Katherine*, Mr. Timothy Keyser, bound from London for Virginia: William Paggen. (PRO: E190/124/1).

5-14 August. Shippers by the *Society* of Bristol bound from Bristol for Virginia: Francis Fisher, John Porter, Edward Perrin, Francis Bowry, Jane Pope, John Reade. (PRO: E190/1147/1).

5-16 August. Shippers by the *Greyhound*, Mr. Joseph Marty, bound from London for Pennsylvania: John Grey, Thomas Bawman, John Osgood, Thomas Bud, Daniel Burton, John West, Francis Hulcupp, Michael Clark. (PRO: E190/124/1).

5 August-6 September. Shippers by the *Southampton Merchant*, Mr. Andrew Belcher, bound from London for New England: John Ives, Edward Hull, John Mills, Thomas Evans, John Jurin, Jeremy Elwes. (PRO: E190/124/1).

6 August. The following apprenticed in London: Margaret Wales, daughter of Alexander W. of Brightshine (*sic*), Angus, Scotland, to Richard Fyfe, merchant, 4 years Maryland; Thomas Barnes, son of Thomas B. of Chichester, (Sussex), butcher, deceased, to Richard Moss, merchant, 4 years Maryland; Susanna Coe, daughter of Andrew C. of London, printer, deceased, to Philip Clarke, 5 years Maryland. (LMWB13/511).

6 August. The following apprenticed in Middlesex: Mary Wood, aged 21, to John Potter of Old Gravel Lane, mariner, 5 years Maryland; Richard Eastopp of Petticoat Lane, Stepney, Middlesex, aged 16, son of John E., deceased, to Thomas Rogers of London, merchant, 5 years Maryland by *Loyal Subject*, Mr. Thomas Rogers, with the consent of his grandmother, Precilla Eaton, and his uncle, Richard Eaton. (GLRO: MR/E/593).

6 August. Thomas Symes of Ycovil, Somerset, bound to John Burridge of Lyme Regis, merchant, to serve 4 years in Virginia or Maryland. (DRO B7/M9).

6-9 August. The following apprenticed in Middlesex to Thomas Tench of London, merchant, to serve him in Maryland: James Riggs, aged 22, 4 years; Mary Harris, aged 21, 5 years; Edward Taylor of London, aged 17, 6 years; Elizabeth Watts, aged 19, 4 years; Elizabeth Williams, aged 20, 4 years. (GLRO: MR/E/593).

6-18 August. Shippers by the *Friends Adventure*, Mr. Richard Angell, bound from London for Carolina: Richard Goodall, William Thorowgood, William Gibbs, Anthony Stretton, Richard Woosley. (PRO: E190/124/1).

7 August. The following apprenticed in London: Thomas Peirceson, son of Thomas P. of Kingston on Thames, Surrey, plasterer, deceased, to Thomas Tench, merchant, 4 years Maryland. (LMWB13/512).

7 August. The following apprenticed in Middlesex: Robert Williams, aged 30, to George Green of London, mariner, 4 years Virginia; Elinor Marchbank, aged 22, to Thomas Bradshaw of London, mariner, 5 years Maryland. (GLRO: MR/E/593).

7 August-2 September. The following apprenticed in Middlesex to serve John Twitt of London, mariner, in Maryland: Luke Allyn, aged 18, 7 years; Frances Banister, aged 21, 5 years; Frances Darrant, aged 18, 4 years; Mary Atwell, aged 22, 4 years; Edward Nelson, aged 23, 4 years; John Hall, aged 25, 4 years; Ann Hutton, aged 21, 4 years; Susan Hutton, aged 21, 4 years. (GLRO: MR/E/593).

8 August. Shippers by the *Torrington Merchant* of Barnstaple, Mr. Henry Nicholls, bound from Barnstaple for Maryland: John Smith, Thomas Penhorwood. (PRO: E190/962/5).

9 August. Shipper by the *Agreement* of Plymouth, Mr. Isaac Blake, bound from Plymouth for Virginia: James Blackbourne. (PRO: E190/1048/8).

9 August. The following apprenticed in London: Andrew Ervin, aged 16, son of Andrew E. of Shetland, Scotland, to Thomas Ross, 6 years Barbados. (LMWB13/513).

9 August. The following apprenticed in Bristol: George Lloyd of Wiston, Pembroke, to John Kingsford, 5 years Virginia by *Friends Adventure*, Mr. Samuel Hartnoll; Daniel Marlow of Coventry, Warw, tailor, to John Whitfield, 4 years Jamaica by *Dragon*. (BR).

9 August. The following apprenticed in Middlesex: Mary Hewitt, aged 18, whose father and mother are dead, to Richard Cook of London, mariner, 4 years Virginia. (GLRO: MR/E/593).

11 August. The following apprenticed in London: Grace Daveson, daughter of Henry D. of Plymouth, Devon, mariner, deceased, to Richard Flye of London, merchant, 5 years Maryland; Daniell Osborne, son of Thomas O. of Stowmarket, Suffolk, hatband maker, deceased, to Thomas Tench, 4 years Maryland; John Smith, son of John S., citizen and tailor of London, to Phillip Clarke, 7 years Maryland. (LMWB13/515).

11 August. The following apprenticed in Bristol: Jacob Bosley of Chipping Norton, Oxon, to John Hort, mariner, 4 years Pennsylvania by *Bristol Merchant*. (BR).

11 August. The following apprenticed in Middlesex: Elizabeth Powell, aged 21, to Thomas Cocking of London, mariner, 4 years Virginia; William Peckden, aged 21, to Robert Arche of London, merchant, 4 years Virginia; Jacob Barrownouch of Poland, aged 18, to William King of London, merchant, 4 years Maryland. (GLRO: MR/E/593).

11 August. Shippers by the *Crown Mallaga*, Mr. Michael Staples, bound from London for Maryland: Walter Dunch, Thomas Shaw. (PRO: E190/124/1).

11 August-3 September. The following apprenticed in Middlesex to go by the *Jefferies*, Mr. Thomas Arnold [*from 30 August master is shown as Thomas Strong*]: Thomas Williams of Llandaff, Glamorgan, groom aged 18, son of William W., deceased, to Thomas Arnold of London, merchant, (4) years Virginia; John Winch, pastry cook aged 25, son of Richard W. of St. Sepulchre, London, to the same, 4 years Virginia; John Wood of Ambry(?), Yorkshire, groom aged 22, son of John W., deceased, to the same, (4) years Virginia; William Jackson of Hinxton, Cambridgeshire, husbandman aged 30, son of Mathew J., deceased, to the same, 4 years Virginia; Thomas Luke, husbandman aged 30, son of William L. of Beasly [?Barnsley], Gloucestershire, deceased, to the same, 5 years Virginia; William Alligin, labourer aged 30, son of Robert A. of Copthall, Essex, to the same, 4 years Virginia; William Dyer of Martock, Somerset, labourer aged 21, son of George

D., deceased, to the same, 5 years Virginia; George Herne, groom aged 21, son of George H. of Woolaston, Gloucestershire, to the same, 4 years Virginia; Thomas Naylor, aged 31, to the same, 4 years Virginia; Thomas Brigdon, aged 16, son of William B. of Hell[ingly], Sussex, deceased, to the same, 7 years Virginia; Mary Evans, spinster aged 19, daughter of William E. of Brewood, Staffordshire, deceased, to the same, 4 years Virginia; Francis Barker, labourer aged 21, son of Ruben B. of London, to the same, 5 years Virginia; John Brooks, blacksmith aged 24, son of John B. of Woolaston, Worcestershire, deceased, to the same, 5 years Virginia; William Roger, ploughman aged 21, son of Walter R., to the same, 5 years Virginia; Henry Brisco, aged 21, son of Henry B. of Tamworth, Warwickshire, to the same, 6 years Virginia; Elizabeth Lawton, spinster aged 21, daughter of William L. of Lincoln, to the same, 5 years Virginia; John Morrall, gardener aged 22, son of William M. of Stock [?Stoke upon Trent], Staffordshire, to the same, 4 years Virginia, previously bound [on 9 July, with same signature]; James Wood, tailor aged 20, son of William W. of West Chester, [Lancashire], to the same, 4 years Virginia; William Lyle of Whickham, Durham, barber surgeon aged 22, son of Thomas L., to John Carter of London, merchant, 4 years Virginia; Edward Clayton of Berkshire, husbandman aged 32, to the same, 4 years Virginia; Thomas Grindy, farmer aged 23, son of Phillip G. of Cardiff, Glamorgan, to the same, 4 years Virginia; Edmund Hudson, aged 19, son of John H. of Northallerton, Yorkshire, to the same, 4 years Virginia; Moses Rust, husbandman aged 26, son of Finch R., of Allington, Kent, to the same, 5 years Virginia; Thomas Dunkley of Newbold, Leicestershire, aged 17, to the same, 5 years Virginia; John Armstrong of York, aged 15, to the same, 6 years Virginia; Nathaniell Palmer, groom aged 21, son of Elizahias P. of Pippall Abbey (*sic*), Northamptonshire, to the same, 5 years Virginia; Joseph Banton, aged 17, son of Charles B. of Leeds, Yorkshire, to the same, 7 years Virginia; William Carpenter of Skipton on Craven, Yorkshire, butcher aged 27, son of Patrick C., to the same, 4 years Maryland; Robert Whitby of Helsby, Cheshire, groom aged 24, son of Randall W., to the same, 4 years Maryland; Walter Wright of Whiston, Northamptonshire, groom aged 22, son of William W., to the same, 4 years Virginia. (GLRO: MR/E/593).

12 August. The following apprenticed in London: Robert Cobby, son of Robert C. of Buckingham, maltster, deceased, to Thomas Tench, 7 years Maryland; John Downes, son of Samuell D. of Lincoln, deceased, to the same, 4 years Maryland. (LMWB13/516).

12 August. The following apprenticed in Middlesex: Robert Cheesman, aged 21, to Thomas Chamberlain of London, mariner, 4 years Virginia; Abigall Manning, aged 30, to Thomas Bennett, shipwright of London, 4 years Virginia; Ralph Barrow, aged 23, to Christopher Daniell of London, mariner, 4 years Maryland. (GLRO: MR/E/593).

13 August. The following apprenticed in London: Margaret Owen, daughter of Richard O. of Coleman Street, London, packer, deceased, to Richard Fyfe, 5 years Maryland; Stephen Pilcher, son of Stephen P. of Sandwich, Kent, merchant, deceased, to the same, 5 years Maryland; Anthony Annis, son of Lazarus A., scrivener, to Thomas Tench, 4 years Maryland; Joseph Scale, son of William S. of Hemel Hempstead, Hertfordshire, labourer, to the same, 4 years Maryland; Robert Clay, son of John C. of Norwich, to the same, 4 years Maryland. (LMWB13/517).

13 August. The following apprenticed in Middlesex: Susan Arden, aged 15, daughter of John A., to serve Edmond Sandeford of Barbados, planter, 5 years, with the consent of her father. (GLRO: MR/E/593).

13 August. Shipper by the *Robert & William* of Barnstaple, Mr. William Brutten, bound from Barnstaple for Maryland: James Cock. (PRO: E190/962/5).

13-19 August. Shippers by the *Elizabeth & Mary*, Mr. Roger Newham, bound from London for Virginia: Gabriel Grunwyn, Richard Butler, Jonathan Matthews, Ralph Ingram. (PRO: E190/124/1).

14 August. The following apprenticed in Middlesex: Oliver Palmer, aged 15, to serve William Frisby of Maryland, 7 years, with the consent of his uncle, his father and mother being dead; Frances Baldwin, aged 16, to Bartholomew Oates of London, mariner, 5 years Maryland, witnessed by Ann Billion and John Ewbanck who swear that her father and mother are dead; Matthew Swanson, aged 23, to Thomas Grubb of Rotherhithe, mariner, 4 years Virginia. (GLRO: MR/E/593).

14 August. The following apprenticed in Bristol: Alice Powell of Taunton Deane, Som, spinster, to George Cary, mariner, 4 years Virginia by *Francis & Mary*; Francis Clarvo of Bristol to Ambrose Bradford, 4 years Maryland by *Society*; Walter Harris of Christchurch, Mon, to William Stoakes, 4 years Barbados by *Diligence*; Ann Fox of London to Thomas Bowditch, 5 years Barbados by *Diligence*. (BR).

14 August. The following apprenticed in London: Thomas Arnold, son of Jeremiah A. of St. Sepulchre, London, silversmith, to William Thorowgood, 5 years Carolina. (LMWB13/518).

15 August. The following apprenticed in London: John Cressill, son of Phillip C. of Colchester, Essex, weaver, deceased, to John Burgis, citizen and mariner of London, 6 years Virginia. (LMWB13/519).

15 August. The following apprenticed in Middlesex: Mary Hutchins, aged 22, to Frederick Johnson of London, mariner, 4 years Maryland; John Hill, aged 18, to William Haveland, 5 years Virginia; Jacob Francis of Holland, aged 34, to the same, 4 years Virginia. (GLRO: MR/E/593).

15 August. Edward Paine of Somerset bound to Samuell Alford of Taunton, Somerset, fuller, to serve 4 years in Maryland. (DRO B7/M9).

15 August. Shipper by the *Content* of Plymouth, Mr. Mathew Hutchins, bound from Plymouth for Virginia: Allen Furse. (PRO: E190/1048/8).

15-19 August. Shippers by the *Susanna* of Plymouth, Mr. James Bartlett, bound from Plymouth for Virginia: John Kendall, Walter Ingram, Richard Opie, Thomas Weston. (PRO: E190/1048/8).

15-27 August. Shippers by the *Reserve* of Dartmouth, Mr. Caleb Barnes, bound from Dartmouth for Virginia: William Juyce, William Laven, William Mannory Jr. (PRO: E190/964/13).

15-30 August. The following apprenticed in Middlesex to go by the *Assistance*, Mr. James Strong: Ralph Horsey of Elminster(?), Somerset, labourer aged 21, son of Phillip H., to John Moore of London, merchant, 4 years Virginia; Phillip Dycer, tailor aged 29, son of Phillip D. of Flushing, Zeeland, to the same, 4 years Virginia; Thomas Weldon of Durham, clerk aged 21, son of Thomas W., to the same, 4 years Virginia; Henry Lee, aged 18, to the same, 5 years Virginia; William Hasteed, husbandman aged 21, son of Thomas H. of Boxgrove, Sussex, to John Bright of London, merchant, 4 years Virginia; Thomas Eavens of Devon, aged 18, son of Lewis E., to the same, 4 years Virginia, to work as a husbandman; Richard Howes of Oswestry, Shropshire, husbandman aged 21, son of William H., deceased, to the same, 4 years Virginia; John Beckett of Bushbury, Staffordshire, nailer aged 24, son of Thomas B., to the same, 4 years Virginia; George King of St. Botolph Aldgate, London, aged 18, to the same, 5 years Virginia, with the consent of his mother, Grace K.; Richard Hillard, groom aged 19, son of Peter H. of Arpithe(?), Dorset, to the same, 5 years Virginia; Richard Rose, husbandman aged 31, son of Richard R. of Mancetter, Warwickshire, to the same, 4 years Virginia; John Billing, aged 18, son of John B. of Tinwell, Rutland, deceased, to the same, 6 years Maryland; Thomas Correy, tanner aged 23, son of Archibald C. of Chester, to the same, 4 years Maryland; Thomas Lolley, aged 21, son of John L., to the same, 4 years Maryland; Alice Stevens, aged 18, daughter of John S. of London, to the same, 5 years Virginia; David Williams, husbandman aged 31, son of William W. of Mould, Flint, to the same, 4 years Maryland; James Markley, aged 22, son of James M. of Ayre, France, to the same, 5 years Maryland; John Reeve, feltmaker aged 32, son of Edward R. of Watford, Northamptonshire, to the same, 4 years Maryland; Peter Davison, aged 22, son of John D. of Dundee, Scotland, to the same, 5 years Maryland; Thomas Kynner, sawyer aged 40, son of Edward K. of Worksey(?), Wiltshire, to the same, 4 years Maryland; Nicholas Cock of Exeter, Devon, aged 21, son of John C., to the same, 4 years Maryland; Benjamin Kett of Norwich, barber aged 19, son of Henry K., to the same, 5 years Maryland; John Crackwell of Burrough Green, Cambridgeshire, aged 21, son of Richard C., to the same, 4 years Maryland; Joseph Honywell, accountant aged 30, son of William H. of St. Austell, Cornwall, to the same, 4 years Maryland; John Floyd, aged 18, son of John F. of Knighton, Herefordshire, to the same, 4 years Maryland; Robert Stanmore, aged 18, son of John S. of Barbury [?Barlborough], Derbyshire, to the same, 7 years Maryland. (GLRO: MR/E/593).

16 August. The following apprenticed in Bristol: Henry Hart of Bedminster, Dorset, to John Porter, 5 years Virginia by *Society*; Silvester Stillingfleet of Pontefract, Yorks, to John Whitfield, 4 years Jamaica by *Dragon*. (BR).

16 August. The following apprenticed in Middlesex: Hannah Barton, aged 30, to Joseph Wosey of London, merchant, 4 years Barbados; William Edmonds to Peter Greene of London, 5 years Virginia. (GLRO: MR/E/593).

16 August. Shipper by the *Unity*, Mr. John Bull, bound from Lyme for Virginia: John Burridge & Co. (PRO: E190/886/2).

16 August-6 September. Shippers by the *Jeffreys*, Mr. Thomas Arnold, bound from London for Virginia: John Hanford, James Young, John Jeffreys, Amy Carpenter, Robert Stepney, Nathaniel Wyerdale. (PRO: E190/124/1).

17 August. Shipper by the *Swallow* of Boston, Mr. John Carter, bound from Weymouth for New England: Samuell Gampaine & Co. (PRO: E190/887/2).

18 August. The following apprenticed in London: Joane Pollard, spinster, Mary Tidwell, spinster, and Mary Savery, spinster, to Abraham Wilde of Bristol, merchant, 4 years Maryland; Matthew Randall to the same, 4 years Maryland; Thomas Hocroft to Christopher Robinson of London, merchant, 9 years Virginia. (LMWB13/524,525).

18-19 August. The following apprenticed in Middlesex to serve Abraham Wild of London, merchant, in Maryland: James Bower, aged 18, 6 years; Mary Bennett, aged 18, 4 years. (GLRO: MR/E/593).

19 August. The following apprenticed in Middlesex: Edward Makerness, aged 23, to Andrew Peterson of Ratcliffe, mariner, 4 years Virginia; Thomas Cary from the House of Correction, aged 15, to Christopher Daniell of London, mariner, 9 years Maryland; John Collins, aged 30, to Thomas Jennings of Poplar, mariner, 4 years Maryland. (GLRO: MR/E/593).

19 August. The following apprenticed in London: John Sewell, discharged from the Bridewell Prison, to Abraham Wilde, merchant, 7 years Maryland; Thomas Tattnell, tailor, to Philip Clarke, planter, 4 years Maryland; Thomas Tullis to serve Robert Gray of Barbados 5 years. (LMWB13/526).

19 August. The following apprenticed in Bristol: Edward Pinnick of Seend, Wilts, to Robert Crewde, 7 years Pennsylvania by *Bristol Merchant*; John Pinnick of Seend to same, 3 years Pennsylvania by *Bristol Merchant*; John Evans of Newcastle, Staffs, to James Newland, 4 years New England by *New England Merchant*, Mr. Palmer. (BR).

19 August. Shipper by the *Success* of Plymouth, Mr. John Ford, bound from Plymouth for Virginia: Marke Batt. (PRO: E190/1048/8).

19 August-24 September. Shippers by the *Thomas & Susan*, Mr. David Edwards, bound from London for New England: James Blackman, Thomas Newman, Richard Bartlett, John Degrave, John Dunton, Richard Fawcet, Benjamin Dejeane, Nathaniel Low, William Barnes, Sefton Long, John Warner. (PRO: E190/124/1).

20 August. Nicholas Hearris of Somerset bound to Samuell Alford of Taunton, Somerset, fuller, to serve 4 years in Maryland. (DRO B7/M9).

20-22 August. Shippers by the *Hope*, Mr. John Radden, bound from Plymouth for Virginia: Robert Parrott, Abraham Searle, Thomas Stutt, Joseph Fuge, John Veale, Nicholas Ginnes, Nathaniell Young, Samuell Carkett, Thomas Martyn. (PRO: E190/1048/8).

20-25 August. Shippers by the *Stephen & Edward*, Mr. Sebastian Ginsey (*sic*), bound from London for Virginia: Robert Bristow, George Ayray, Samuel Lamb. (PRO: E190/124/1).

20 August-1 September. Shippers by the *Hound*, Mr. Phineas Hyde, bound from London for Maryland: John Tayler, Henry Bray. (PRO: E190/124/1).

21 August. The following apprenticed in London: Ruth Upfield, spinster, to Christopher Robinson, merchant, 4 years Virginia; Bridget Mundy to Nicholas Painter, 5 years Maryland; Elizabeth Parker, spinster, to Emmanuel Winsor, 4 years in America; George Bradley to serve James Bowman of Barbados 3 years; Robert Citterson and John Oldfield to Abraham Wilde, 4 years Maryland; Martha Hollymon, spinster, to John Hanford of Botolph Lane, London, merchant, 5 years Virginia. (LMWB13/527-529).

21 August. Deposition by Israel Morgan of the Old Bailey, London, merchant, that he agreed on 8 August 1683 with Gerrard Slye of Maryland for the freighting of the *Concord*, Captain Thomas Hurlock, from London to Virginia. The ship was lost at sea but her passengers were saved. (LMCD).

21 August. The following apprenticed in Bristol: Mary Jones of St. Brides, Glam, to Philip Willis, shipwright, 4 years Pennsylvania or Virginia. (BR).

22-28 August. The following apprenticed in Middlesex to serve Richard Bray: Peter Geay, aged 20, 4 years Virginia but not to work in the fields; Mary Hastings, aged 23, 4 years Maryland; Frances Atkinson, aged 22, 4 years Maryland; Margaret Prou, aged 24, 4 years Virginia but not to work in the fields; Cyprian Prou, aged 21, 4 years Virginia but not to work in the fields. (GLRO: MR/E/593).

22 August-6 September. Shipper by the *Seraphim* of Barnstaple, Mr. John Darracott, bound from Barnstaple for Maryland: John Fleming. (PRO: E190/962/5).

23 August. The following apprenticed in London: John Burgis to Jonathan Matthew, 4 years Virginia. (LMWB13/531).

23 August. The following apprenticed in Middlesex to serve Thomas Berrisford of London, merchant and mariner, for four years in Virginia: John Ball, aged 23; Jane Trunkett, aged 30; John Hadley; Frances Hildridge, aged 28. (GLRO: MR/E/593).

23-25 August. Shippers by the *Isaac & Sarah*, Mr. Thomas Griffin, bound from London for Maryland: Abraham Wilde, James Harris. (PRO: E190/124/1).

23 August-6 September. Shippers by the *Resolution* of Bristol, Mr. William Scott, bound from Bristol for Virginia: Stephen Watts & Co., Richard Finch, William Sheerestone, Phillip Tyler, James Millard, Erasmus Dole, Symon Peters. (PRO: E190/1147/1).

25 August. The following apprenticed in Middlesex: Elizabeth Mercer, aged 29, to Samuell Williams of London, shipwright, 4 years Virginia; Charles Winter, aged 22, to Moses Fulborne of London, mariner, 4 years Maryland. (GLRO: MR/E/593).

25 August. The following apprenticed in Bristol: William Goldsmith of Falmouth, Corn, to John Steevens, 4 years Pennsylvania or Virginia; William Golden of London to Jonathan Stone, 7 years Virginia or Maryland by *Resolution* or *Society*; Richard Athay of Litton, Som, cordwainer, to John Hort, mariner, 4 years Pennsylvania by *Bristol Merchant*. (BR).

25 August. Shipper by the *Friends Adventure* of Bristol, Mr. Samuell Hartnell, bound from Bristol for Virginia: Mathias Worgan. (PRO: E190/1147/1).

25 August-1 September. Shippers by the *Assistance*, Mr. James Strong, bound from London for Virginia: John Pym, Thomas Ellis, Francis Maldon. (PRO: E190/124/1).

25 August-10 September. Shippers by the *Daniell* of Boston, Mr. Abraham Gorden, bound from Bristol for New England: William Jones, Walter Stephens, William Window, Henry Lloyd. (PRO: E190/1147/1).

26 August. The following apprenticed in Middlesex: Nicholas Smith, aged 19, to Maximilian Robinson of London, merchant, 6 years Virginia; Catherine Harding, aged 21, to William Ballard of London, shipwright, 4 years Virginia. (GLRO: MR/E/593).

26 August. Ralph Box Esq. of London, signs a letter appointing James Tailor of Boston, New England, as his attorney. (LMCD).

26 August. Shipper by the *Jonathan* of Exeter, Mr. George Bass, bound from Exeter for Virginia: George Tuthill. (PRO: E190/962/4).

26-30 August. Shippers by the *Bonadventure* of Exeter, Mr. William Pennell, bound from Exeter for Virginia: Barnard Goddard, Thomas Wood. (PRO: E190/962/4).

26 August-1 September. Shippers by the *Mary*, Mr. John Harris, bound from London for Virginia: John Lucombe, Mary Sweningham, Richard Chandler, Robert Hattoft, William Palmer. (PRO: E190/124/1).

26 August-18 September. Shippers by the *Margaret & Elizabeth*, Mr. Elisha Bennett, bound from London for New England: John Gardner, Thomas Hunt, Thomas Theed, Edmond White & Co. (PRO: E190/124/1).

27 August. The following apprenticed in London: Solomon Johnson and his wife Elizabeth to Hugh Gardner, 4 years Virginia; Mary Jewell, daughter of Joseph J., deceased, to the same, 4 years Virginia; Thomas Mills to Robert Shanks, mariner, 4 years Virginia. (LMWB13/535,536).

27 August. The following apprenticed in Bristol: William Hall of Liverpool, Lancs, to Robert Coleman, 5 years Virginia by *Samuel*. (BR).

27 August. The following apprenticed in Middlesex: Jacob Morris, aged 14, born in France, to serve Nicholas Pamle of Maryland, gent, for 7 years; James Hyland, aged 29, to serve Nicholas Painter of Maryland, gent, 4 years. (GLRO: MR/E/593).

27 August. Abraham Hancoke of Somerset bound to Samuell Alford of Taunton, Somerset, fuller, to serve 4 years in Maryland. (DRO B7/M9).

27 August. Shipper by the *John* of Exeter, Mr. John Lyle, bound from Exeter for Virginia: John Carpenter. (PRO: E190/962/4).

27 August-2 September. The following apprenticed in Middlesex to go by the *Recovery*, Mr. Thomas Hasteed [Hastings]: Ellioner Barnes of Middlesex, spinster aged 21, daughter of James B., to Thomas Hasteed of London, merchant, 4 years Maryland; Richard Swaisland, groom aged 22, son of Henry S. of Seal, Kent, to the same, 4 years Maryland; John Tompkin, groom aged 28, son of John T. of Dunton, Bedfordshire, to the same, 4 years Maryland; George Laurence of Nottingham, aged 31, son of William L., to the same, 4 years Maryland; Mary Stanton, spinster aged 17, daughter of Phillip S. of London, to the same, 4 years Maryland; John Powter, aged 17, son of John P. of Harrietsham, Kent, to the same, 7 years Maryland; Ann Diptale, spinster aged 21, daughter of John D. of Bristol, looking glass maker, to the same, 5 years Maryland; Sarah Lefeavre, spinster aged 16, daughter of Charles L. of Leyden, Holland, dyer, to the same, 7 years Maryland; Hugh Jones of Flintshire, aged 21, son of John J., to the same, 4 years Maryland; Thomas Matthews, aged 18, to John Moore of London, merchant, 6 years Virginia; William Bings of Radford, Nottinghamshire, tailor aged 24, son of Richard B., to the same, 4 years Maryland; John Baker of Walthamstow, Essex, husbandman aged 21, son of Bartholomew B., to the same, 4 years Virginia; Thomas Fowler, aged 17, son of William F. of Melton Mowbray, Leicestershire, to the same, 7 years Maryland or Virginia; Edward Danby of Mitton, Lancashire, groom aged 21, son of John D., to John Carter, 5 years Maryland. (GLRO: MR/E/593).

27 August-2 September. The following apprenticed in Middlesex to serve Nicholas Painter of Maryland for four years: John German, aged 21; John Naylor, aged 22. (GLRO: MR/E/593).

27 August-4 September. Shippers by the *Hannah*, Mr. Arthur Gester, bound from London for Virginia: John Plover, James Foulis, John Pelling, William Farmer. (PRO: E190/124/1).

27 August-5 September. Shippers by the *Diamond* of Exeter, Mr. William Shower, bound from Exeter for Boston, New England: William Lobb, John Meane, John Pym, Thomas Turner, John Prickman. (PRO: E190/962/4).

27 August-8 September. Shippers by the *Baltimore*, Mr. James Conway, bound from London for Virginia: Edward Round, Sarah Garfoot. (PRO: E190/124/1).

28 August. The following apprenticed in Bristol: Richard Day of Shepton Mallet, Som, broadweaver, to James Hardwick of Virginia, planter, 5 years Virginia by *Francis & Mary*; Mary Whitwood of Winscomb, Som, spinster, to same, 5 years Virginia by *Francis & Mary*, Mr. William Nicholas; Grace Hardwith of Wedmore, Som, to same, 5 years Virginia by *Francis & Mary*. (BR).

28 August. John George of Hampstead Marshall, Berkshire, bound to John Bull of Lyme Regis, mariner, to serve 4 years in Virginia or Maryland. (DRO B7/M9).

28-29 August. Shippers by the *John's Adventure*, Mr. John Francis, bound from London for Maryland: Henry Everett, Thomas Potter. (PRO: E190/124/1).

28-31 August. The following apprenticed in Middlesex to serve William Webb of Ratcliffe, shipwright, for four years in Virginia: John Robson, aged 21; Francis Coffin, aged 27. (GLRO: MR/E/593).

28 August-1 September. Shippers by the *John* of Bristol, Mr. Edward Watts, bound from Bristol for Virginia: Nicholas Downing, Thomas Pope, William Lovell. (PRO: E190/1147/1).

28 August-3 September. Shippers by the *Sarah*, Mr. Thomas Edwards, bound from Yarmouth for New England: John Tuthill, George Spillman, John Carter, John Harper. (PRO: E190/502/5).

29 August. The following apprenticed in Middlesex: Walter English, aged 13, son of Walter E., to Samuel Berry of Bow, surgeon, 7 years Virginia, with the consent of his father. (GLRO: MR/E/593).

29 August-1 September. The following apprenticed in Middlesex to serve Richard Bayly of Maryland, planter: John Stokely, aged 16, 8 years; Ann Banks, aged 22, 5 years. (GLRO: MR/E/593).

29 August-1 September. Shipper by the *Windmill*, Mr. James Trefry, bound from Plymouth for Virginia: John Roberts. (PRO: E190/1048/8).

29 August-1 September. Shippers by the *Charles* of Plymouth, Mr. Edward Blagg, bound from Plymouth for Virginia: John Rogers, Thomas Couch. (PRO: E190/1048/8).

29 August-4 September. The following apprenticed in Middlesex to serve Richard Jackson of Barbados, merchant, for three years: Sarah Parker, aged 24; Bozoun Goodrick, aged 26; Charles Church, aged 38. (GLRO: MR/E/593).

29 August-4 September. Shipper by the *Brothers Adventure* of New England, Mr. Joseph Benwell, bound from Newcastle for New England: George Morton. (PRO: E190/200/9).

29 August-13 September. Shippers by the *Richard & James* of Bristol, Mr. Thomas Opye, bound from Bristol for Virginia: Peter Waddinge, Robert Bayly, Symon Pickmore, Richard Prigg. (PRO: E190/1147/1).

30 August. The following apprenticed in Middlesex: Thomas Williams, aged 19, to serve John Worthington of Maryland, merchant, 9 years, with the consent of his father-in-law, William Marry, his own father and mother being dead. (GLRO: MR/E/593).

30 August-9 September. Shippers by the *Zebulon*, Mr. Nicholas Goodridge, bound from London for Virginia: Richard Cliffe, Thomas Mayleigh, Jane Metcalfe. (PRO: E190/124/1).

30 August-25 September. Shippers by the *Constant Mary*, Mr. Edward Rhodes, bound from London for Virginia: Thomas Sands, Robert Fairman, Henry Loades, Vincent Goddard, Abraham Molyn, Daniel Winch, Andrew Pegle. (PRO: E190/124/1).

August. Administration of James Brownsford of Virginia. (AW).

August. Administration of Richard Glover of Virginia who died at sea on the ship *Maryland*, widower. (AW).

August. Administration of John Curtis of Virginia, bachelor. (AW).

1 September. The following apprenticed in Bristol: Samuel Smith of Bristol to Thomas Opie, 4 years Virginia by *Richard & James*, said Thomas Opie Mr. (BR).

1 September. The following apprenticed in London: Arthur Mabb, aged 20, to serve Nicholas Painter of Maryland, gent, 4 years. (LMWB13/542).

1 September. The following apprenticed in Middlesex: Mary Richerson, aged 18, to Richard Batt, 4 years Maryland; Elizabeth Grey, aged 21, to John Brown of London, mariner, 4 years Virginia. (GLRO: MR/E/593).

1 September-7 October. Shippers by the *Concord*, Mr. William Jeffreys, bound from London for Virginia: George Baker, James Harris, William Bradford,

Matthew Jones, John Viner, Edward Round, Edward Witton, William Sare, Robert Warkman. (PRO: E190/124/1).

3 September. Shipper by the *Dove* bound from Dartmouth for Virginia: William Elliott. (PRO: E190/964/13).

3-4 September. The following apprenticed in Middlesex to go by the *Mary*, Mr. John Harris, to serve John Bowman of London, merchant, in Maryland for four years: Elizabeth Webb of Elston [?Elkstone], Gloucestershire, spinster aged 25, daughter of Richard W.; Arthur Hancock of Bristol husbandman aged 28, son of Roger H. (GLRO: MR/E/593).

3-10 September. Shippers by the *Unicorn* of Bristol, Mr. Thomas Cooper, bound from Bristol for Virginia: George Masson, Charles Perks, Richard Swetnam, Joseph Nash, Abraham Elton, Michaell White, Anthony Alderson. (PRO: E190/1147/1).

3 September-16 October. Shippers by the *Samuel & Thomas*, Mr. Thomas Jenner, bound from London for New England: John Ellis, Samuel Sheaf, Thomas Cartwright, Thomas Checkley, William Blackwell, Henry Smart, Robert Hyne. (PRO: E190/124/1).

4 September. The following apprenticed in London: Thomas Brooke and James Harris, glass bottle makers, to Joseph Martin, agent for the Free Society of Traders in Pennsylvania, 4 years Pennsylvania. (LMWB13/544).

4 September. The following apprenticed in Middlesex: David Williams, aged 18, to Thomas Gadsden of London, merchant, 4 years Barbados; John Hall, aged 22, to John Tanner of Limehouse, mariner, 4 years Virginia; Thomas Hearne, aged 21, to Edward Brook of London, merchant, 4 years Jamaica; Margaret Ash, aged 21, to the same, 4 years Jamaica; Mary Pelham, aged 21, to the same, 4 years Jamaica; Frederick Harris, aged 22, to John Day, merchant, 4 years Maryland. (GLRO: MR/E/593).

4 September. The following apprenticed in Bristol: Elizabeth Worne of Taunton, Som, to John Hockle, 7 years Virginia. (BR).

4 September. Shipper by the *Content*, Mr. William Johnson, bound from London for Virginia: Thomas Mayleigh. (PRO: E190/124/1).

4-11 September. Shippers by the *Daniell & Elizabeth*, Mr. William Ginnes, bound from Plymouth for Virginia: William Martyn, John Woods, John Rogers. (PRO: E190/1048/8).

4-13 September. Shippers by the *Samuell & Mary* of Bristol, Mr. James Harris and Mr. Thomas Skuse, bound from Bristol for Virginia: William Hayman, George Atwood, Symon Hurle. (PRO: E190/1147/1).

4-15 September. Shipper by the *White Fox*, Mr. George Purvis, bound from London for Virginia: Robert Silk. (PRO: E190/124/1).

5 September. The following apprenticed in Bristol: Margaret Green of Colthall Green near Waltham Abbey, Essex, spinster, to Thomas Opie, 4 years Virginia; Thomas Griffin of Halleston, Glam, to John Dunn, 4 years Jamaica; John Mors of Tidenham, Glos, to Edward Fielding, mariner, 4 years Virginia by *Richard & James*. (BR).

5 September. The following apprenticed in London: John Baxter, son of David B. of Cornisle(?), Lancashire, tallow chandler, deceased, to Richard Cox of London, merchant, 4 years Virginia. (LMWB13/545).

5 September-1 December. Shippers by the *Exeter Merchant*, Mr. James Friend, bound from Exeter for Virginia: Robert Faremouth, Robert Dabinet, Thomas Smith. (PRO: E190/962/4).

6-10 September. Shipper by the *Leaver* of Liverpool, Mr. Gilbert Livesley, bound from Liverpool for Maryland: Thomas Johnson. (PRO: E190/1346/9).

8 September. Deposition by Samuel Briggs of Stenton, Westmorland, carrier aged 33, made at the request of Mr. Edward Jenkinson of London, innholder, that Samuel Shaw, vicar of Kirby Stephen, Westmorland, and Lydia his wife, on 29 August 1684 appointed Mr. Clement Hill of St. Clement's Bay, Maryland, as their attorney to recover debts; deposition by James Olliver of Ratcliffe, Middlesex, mariner aged 28, and Adam Johnston of Ratcliffe, mariner aged 25 that they served in the *Zebulon*, Mr. Nicholas Goodridge, on a voyage from London to East Jersey near New York and to Virginia before returning to London. (LMCD).

8 September. The following apprenticed in Bristol: Richard Sledge son of Richard Sledge of Pensford, Som (*sic*), to John Longworth, 5 years Virginia; Richard Langford of Ightfield, Salop, to John Tibolt, mariner, 4 years Jamaica by *Lamb*, Mr. George Colwell; Job Cholmley of Whitchurch, Salop, to same, 5 years Jamaica by *Lamb*; Elizabeth Davis of Worcester, spinster, to George Wilkinson, 4 years Jamaica by *Lamb*; Elizabeth Thomas of Bristol, spinster, to same, 4 years Jamaica by *Lamb*; John Bond of Clipsham, Northants, to same, 4 years Jamaica by *Lamb*. (BR).

8 September. The following apprenticed in London: Thomas Fox, son of John F. of Berry Pomeroy, Devon, butcher, deceased, to John Walters, 5 years Virginia; John Mounfield, son of Thomas M. of Graffham, Sussex, maltster, deceased, to John Worthington, 4 years Maryland. (LMWB14/3).

9 September. The following apprenticed in London: John Fulstone to John Prim of London, merchant, 7 years Virginia, with the consent of his mother. (LMWB14/5).

11 September. The following apprenticed in London: Sarah Ames, daughter of Thomas A. of Leather Lane, London, labourer, to John Worthington of Maryland for 4 years, with the consent of her father. (LMWB14/6).

10-16 September. Shippers by the *Submission* of Liverpool bound from Liverpool for Maryland: James Settle, John Fisher. (PRO: E190/1346/9).

12 September. The following apprenticed in Bristol: George Chappell son of Samuel Chappell of Allingsey (*sic*), Som, husbandman deceased, to Richard Browning, 4 years Jamaica by *Abraham & Mary*. (BR).

13-27 September. Shippers by the *William & Thomas*, Mr. Christopher Eveling, bound from London for Maryland: Isaac Goddard, Robert Davis, Richard Atkinson, Charles Lord Baltimore. (PRO: E190/124/1).

15 September. Shippers by the *Diligence* of Exeter, Mr. Walter Lyle, bound from Exeter for Virginia: Thomas Barron, Tristram Bartlet. (PRO: E190/962/4).

15-27 September. Shippers by the *Concord* of Bristol, Mr. John Shewell, bound from Bristol for Virginia: Edward Colston, William Swymer, Faulke Adams, James Harris, Charles Jones. (PRO: E190/1147/1).

15 September-1 October. Shippers by the *Genoa Merchant*, Mr. John Wynn, bound from London for Virginia: John Crofts, Jacob Bridgwater, Benjamin Bradley, Thomas Mundin, Thomas Cudden, John Cooper, William Penn. (PRO: E190/124/1).

16 September. The following apprenticed in London: Thomas Reynolds to John Yanows of London, 9 years Virginia, with the consent of his mother, Ann. R.; John Eves to serve Francis Edwin of Virginia, merchant, 6 years. (LMWB14/9).

16 September. The following apprenticed in Bristol: Nathaniel Lawly of Culmington, Salop, to Francis Rawley, 4 years Virginia by *Maryland Merchant*. (BR).

17 September. The following apprenticed in Bristol: John Morris of Oswestry, Salop, tobacconist, to Richard Browning, 4 years Jamaica by *Abraham & Mary*; Edward Howell of Oswestry to same, 4 years Jamaica by *Abraham & Mary*. (BR).

18-26 September. Shippers by the *Morning Star* of Liverpool, Mr. Thomas Heyes, bound from Liverpool for Virginia: John Bradshaw, James Prescott. (PRO: E190/1346/9).

18 September-20 October. Shippers by the *Despatch*, Mr. Henry Patrick, bound from London for New York and Pennsylvania: William Dockwra, Daniel Wright, George Hutchinson, Thomas Budd, William Woodbee, Thomas Mayleigh, Richard Witpan, John Hall, John Pemble. (PRO: E190/124/1).

19 September. The following apprenticed in Bristol: Thomas Harris of Worcester to Robert Coleman, mariner, 5 years Jamaica by *Abraham & Mary*. (BR).

19 September-16 October. Shippers by the *Augustine*, Mr. Zachary Tayler, bound from London for Virginia: Clement Plumsted, Richard Nicholson,

Stephen Sykes, Jonathan Fisher, Thomas Dalton, John Simpkin, Edward Calthorp, John Loggin, John Elwick. (PRO: E190/124/1).

22 September. The following apprenticed in London: Andrew Niccoll, aged 26, to Archibald Arthur, surgeon, 4 years Virginia. (LMWB14/15).

22 September-3 October. Shippers by the *Lyon* of Liverpool, Mr. John Crompton, bound from Liverpool for Maryland: Peter Atherton, Thomas Brookbank, William Lloyde. (PRO: E190/1346/9).

23 September. The following apprenticed in Bristol: William Hurd of Shepton Mallet, [Som], to Anthony Swymmer, 4 years Jamaica. (BR).

23-24 September. Shippers by the *Recovery*, Mr. Thomas Hasted, bound from London for Virginia: Thomas Ellis, Robert Burroughs. (PRO: E190/124/1).

23-25 September. Shippers by the *James* of Bristol bound from Bristol for Virginia: John Blackwell, Henry Jeffris, Robert Price. (PRO: E190/1147/1).

23 September-7 October. Shippers by the *Constant*, Mr. Thomas Smith, bound from London for Virginia: Jeremy Elwes, John Cully, Nicholas Hayward. (PRO: E190/124/1).

23 September-25 October. Shippers by the *Maryland Merchant* of Bristol, Mr. George Tyte, bound from Bristol for Virginia: John Reddinge, Charles Jones, Jane Pope, Bryan Tandy, Richard Mellin, Richard Champneys, Walter Upington, Jacob Moggs, Nicholas Rideout. (PRO: E190/1147/1).

24 September. The following apprenticed in Bristol: John Pottinger of Sittingbourne, Kent, to Francis Lawler, 4 years Maryland by *Maryland Merchant*. (BR).

24 September. The following apprenticed in London: Charles Denton to John Barry, merchant, 5 years Barbados. (LMWB14/18).

24-30 September. Shippers by the *Francis & Mary* of Bristol, Mr. William Nicholas, bound from Bristol for Virginia: Abraham Lewis, William Roberts, James Hardwick, William West, George Cary. (PRO: E190/1147/1).

24 September-2 October. Shippers by the *Lamb* of Liverpool, Mr. William Glover, bound from Liverpool for New York: Humphrey Traford, Henry Ashton. (PRO: E190/1346/9).

25 September. The following apprenticed in London: Henry Whitby, son of Thomas Whitby of London, porter, to Richard Bull, 4 years Maryland. Later entry (LMWB14/31) of 15 October 1684 shows him as bound to William Hill. (LMWB14/18).

25 September. The following apprenticed in Bristol: Ann Thomas of Llanvihangel Rogiet, Merioneth, to Whyte Dorening, 5 years Nevis by *Nevis Merchant*. (BR).

2? **September**. The following apprenticed in Bristol: Christopher Allen of Carlton, Yorks, to John Longworth, 5 years Virginia by *Francis & Mary*. (BR).

25 **September**. Jane Price of St. Andrew, Holborn, Middlesex, fined for abducting Richard Jackson with the intention of transporting him to Virginia by the *Jeoffrey* and selling him there. (VM 83/3).

26 **September**. Mary Gwyn, wife of William Gwyn of St. Botolph Aldgate, London, and Thomas Black of the same, found guilty of abducting Alice Deakins, aged 16, daughter of Robert Deakins, and putting her on board the *Concord* to be transported and sold in Virginia. (VM 83/3).

26 **September**. The following apprenticed in London: John Gibbons, son of Henry G. of Mells, Somerset, mealman, deceased, to John Wynn, mariner, 6 years Virginia; Joshua Payton, son of John P. of London, sailor, deceased, to the same, 8 years Virginia; John Gray, son of John G. of St. Martin in the Fields, Middlesex, tailor, deceased, to Francis and Elizabeth Edwin, 14 years Virginia, with the consent of his mother; John Dyke of Cattistock, Dorset, labourer, to Robert Shanks, mariner, 4 years Jamaica. (LMWB14/19).

26-30 **September**. Shippers by the *Love*, Mr. Samuel Phillips, bound from London for Maryland: Henry Bray, Edmond Sleeth. (PRO: E190/124/1).

29 **September**. The following apprenticed in London: Mary Curd, daughter of William C. of London, deceased, and Phillis Smith, daughter of Edward S. of London, deceased, to Robert Shanks, mariner, 4 years Jamaica. (LMWB14/22).

30 **September**. The following apprenticed in London: Francis Gibbs of London, labourer, and Thomas Batterton of London, labourer, to Francis and Elizabeth Edwin, 5 & 7 years Virginia; Mary Haykins, daughter of William H. of Norwich, deceased, and Martha Richardson, daughter of William R. of York, pewterer, deceased, to Robert Shanks, 4 years Virginia. (LMWB14/22).

30 **September**. The following apprenticed in Bristol: John Kyppen of Sherborne, Dorset, button mould cutter, to John Shewell, mariner, 4 years Virginia by *Concord*, said John Shewell Mr; Elizabeth Pacie of Almondsbury, [Glos], spinster, to Henry Driver, 4 years Jamaica by *Samuel*. (BR).

30 **September**. Shipper by the *Maryland Merchant* of Liverpool, Mr. Joseph Glover, bound from Liverpool for Virginia: Samuell Jeferson. (PRO: E190/1346/9).

30 **September-6 October**. Shippers by the *Mary*, Mr. Richard Tibbotts, bound from London for Virginia: Micajah Perry, John Plover. (PRO: E190/124/1).

30 **September-11 October**. Shippers by the *Comfort* of Bristol, Mr. Abraham Hooke, bound from Bristol for Virginia: John Bubb, William Wakely, John Irish. (PRO: E190/1147/1).

September. Administration of Thomas Powys of London, who died in Boston, New England, bachelor. (AW).

1 October. The following apprenticed in London: Elizabeth Hamden of London, widow, to John Wynn, 5 years Virginia; Joshua Cross, son of Joshua C., Doctor of Laws, deceased, to Samuel Hanson, merchant, 4 years Barbados; Bridget Greenaway, daughter of William G., waterman, deceased, to Francis and Elizabeth Edwin, 7 years Virginia. (LMWB14/23).

2 October. The following apprenticed in London: Martin Franklyn, son of Richard F. of Kilburn, Middlesex, husbandman, deceased, to Peter Barton, 4 years Virginia; Joseph Scott, son of Caleb S., citizen and cooper of London, deceased, to John Hill of London, merchant, 5 years Barbados. (LMWB14/23).

2 October. The following apprenticed in Bristol: Cornelius Hunt of Castle Morton, Worcs, to Francis Thomas, mariner, 5 years Maryland by *Alithea*, Mr. Edward Watkins; John Watson of Hamilton, Scotland, to John Needs, 5 years Barbados by *Maryland Merchant*. (BR).

4 October. The following apprenticed in Bristol: Bertredge King of Emory (*sic*), Heref, to John Swymmer, 4 years Jamaica by *Providence*; Hester Way of Bristol to Josias Moxley, 4 years Jamaica by *Lamb*; Jane Jenkins of Tenby, Pembroke, to Albertus Stan——, mariner, 4 years Jamaica by *Lamb*. (BR).

4-15 October. Shippers by the *Alathea* of Bristol bound from Bristol for Virginia: William Wakely, Richard Benson, Edward Watkins, John Sayers. (PRO: E190/1147/1).

6 October. The following apprenticed in London: Richard Whaley, son of Richard W. of Great Marlow, Buckinghamshire, deceased, to David Browne, mariner, 4 years Virginia; John Clayton, son of Richard C. of Bloomsbury, Middlesex, baker, to Thomas Cason, mariner, 8 years Virginia, with the consent of his mother, Jane C.; Mary Fich, daughter of Robert F. of Goswell Street, St. Giles Cripplegate, London, weaver, deceased, to Henry Turner of London, merchant, 4 years Virginia. (LMWB14/26).

7 October. The following apprenticed in Bristol: William Wheeler of Barton Regis (*sic*), to —— Youll, cooper, inhabitant of Jamaica, 5 years Jamaica by *Lamb*. (BR).

7 October. The following apprenticed in London: John Savage and his brother, Thomas Savage, sons of Abraham Savage of Canterbury, Kent, weaver, deceased, to Thomas Taylor of London, mariner, 5 & 6 years Virginia; John Roffe, son of Humphrey R. of Cambridge, bricklayer, deceased, to Samuell Phipps of Stepney, Middlesex, surgeon, 4 years Virginia; Samuel Turner, son of Henry T. of Exminster, Devon, tanner, deceased, to Robert Shanks, 4 years Jamaica; Symon Harvey, son of Symon H. of Oxford, cordwainer, to the same, 8 years Jamaica. (LMWB14/27).

8 October. The following apprenticed in Bristol: Simon Weyford of Wells, Som, comber, to James Porter, 4 years Barbados by *Diligence*. (BR).

9 October. The following apprenticed in Bristol: William Hackock of Overseal, Leics (*sic but prob. Derbys*), to George Wilkinson, 4 years Jamaica by *Lamb*; John Phelps of Matherntivy (*sic*), Pemb, to Francis Pills, 4 years Jamaica by *Lamb*; Thomas Postons of Bowchurch (*sic*), Heref, to John Needs, 4 years Barbados by *Martha & Sarah*; Ann Sledge of Pensford, Som, spinster, to Thomas Howell, 4 years Virginia by *Alithea*; Elizabeth Moir of Pensford, spinster, to same, 4 years Virginia by *Alithea*; Ann Addis of Minehead, [Som], spinster, to Richard Thorne, 4 years Virginia by *Sarah*. (BR).

9 October. The following apprenticed in London: Mary Lockson, daughter of John L. of Long Lane, London, pipe maker, deceased, to Robert Shanks, 4 years Jamaica; Thomas Jeffrey, son of John J., ragman, to David Browne of Blackwall, Middlesex, mariner, 7 years Virginia; Elizabeth Smith, daughter of James Whittle of Chesterfield, Derbyshire, deceased, to Richard Cornwallis of Wapping, mariner, 5 years Virginia; Charles Leverland, son of Lewin L. of Oxford, deceased, to the same, 4 years Virginia; Mary James, daughter of Edward J. of Chillington, Somerset, to the same, 5 years Virginia; Sarah Passell, daughter of Jonathan P. of Tilbury, Kent (*sic*), deceased, to the same, 5 years Virginia; John Dennis, son of Thomas D. of Higham, Kent, deceased, to Robert Cox of Blackwall, Middlesex, mariner, 9 years Virginia. (LMWB14/28,29).

10-17 October. Shippers by the *Virginia Factor*, Mr. William Hill, bound from London for Virginia and Maryland: Henry Phillips, Hugh White, Henry Constable, James Galwith. (PRO: E190/124/1).

11 October. The following apprenticed in London: Elizabeth Posterne, daughter of William P. of Blackfriars, London, glover, deceased, and Margaret Hills, daughter of Thomas H. of Sawston, Cambridgeshire, deceased, to Nicholas Richardson, 4 years Jamaica. (LMWB14/29).

11-20 October. Shippers by the *Exchange*, Mr. Christopher Haycroft, bound from Exeter for Virginia: Thomas Smith, Robert Dabinet, Richard Farr. (PRO: E190/962/4).

11-27 October. Shipper by the *Industry* bound from Plymouth [? for Virginia]: Samuell Brett, Joseph Brooking, John Moulton, Samuell Allyn, Thomas Stutt, Joseph Frye, Nicholas Carkett, John Baslove. (PRO: E190/1048/8).

13 October. The following apprenticed in Bristol: John Steevens, son of William Steevens of Devizes, Wilts, gent, to Anthony Swymmer, 4 years Jamaica by *Lamb*. (BR).

14 October. The following apprenticed in London: John Olibear to Robert Shanks, 4 years Virginia; William Knewstubb to John Brookes of Wapping, Middlesex, mariner, 4 years Jamaica. (LMWB14/30).

14-20 October. Shippers by the *James & Elizabeth*, Mr. John Beer, bound from Weymouth for Pennsylvania: James Jacob & Co., David Arbuthnot. (PRO: E190/886/3, 887/2).

15 October. The following apprenticed in London: Henry Whitby, son of Thomas Whitby of London, porter, to William Hill of Ratcliffe, Middlesex, mariner; William Scarborough of Northampton, haberdasher, to Christopher Squire of Wapping, Middlesex, shipwright, 4 years Jamaica; John Bradley, son of Simon B. of Worcestershire, yeoman, to Roger Giles of London, mariner, 4 years Virginia; Joseph Bowtell to serve Richard Jackson of Barbados 4 years; Mary Clarke, spinster, daughter of John C. of London, shoemaker, to the same, 4 years Barbados. (LMWB14/31).

15 October. The following apprenticed in Bristol: John Fisher of Horsington, Som, to Nicholas Ridout of Shaftesbury, Dorset, 5 years Pennsylvania by *Maryland Merchant*; Samuel Veale of Keynsham, Som, ribbon weaver, to same, 5 years Pennsylvania by *Maryland Merchant*; Caesar Hoskins of Llantverne (*sic but poss. Llanwarne*), Heref, ribbon weaver, to same, 4 years Pennsylvania by *Maryland Merchant*; Christopher Groyn of Abbey Dore, Heref, to John Wathen, 4 years Maryland by *Comfort*; Thomas Williams of Dewchurch, [Heref], to same, 4 years Maryland by *Comfort*; James Williams of Dewchurch to same, 4 years Maryland by *Comfort*. (BR).

16 October. The following apprenticed in London: Richard Fennell, son of Richard F. of East Smithfield, London, blacksmith, to Robert Cox of Blackwall, shipwright, 7 years Virginia; John Simpkin, son of John S. of Shadwell, Middlesex, mariner, to the same, 9 years Virginia; Thomas Gardner of Northampton to the same, 4 years Virginia; Henry Sims, son of Henry S. of Somerset, to Robert Shanks, 6 years Jamaica; Henry Chapman, son of Henry C. of Hertford, weaver, and John Clarke, son of John C. of Suffolk, weaver, to serve Edward Brook of Jamaica 4 years; Christopher Phillips, son of John P. of Cornwall, husbandman, to John Richards of London, mariner, 4 years Maryland after the arrival there of the ship *Virginia Factor*; John Macguider, aged 22, to the same, 4 years Maryland; John Stanton, aged 26, to Robert Shanks, 4 years Maryland; William Read, son of William R., deceased, to Mathew Hubbard, mariner, 7 years Virginia. (LMWB14/33,35,36).

18 October. The following apprenticed in Bristol: John Blandford of Shaftesbury, Dorset, to John Wathen, 4 years Jamaica by *Lamb*. (BR).

20 October. The following apprenticed in Bristol: George Jefferies of North Petherton, Som, aged 14, to Henry Driver, mariner, 6 years Nevis by *Samuel*. (BR).

20 October. The following apprenticed in London: John Ball, son of John B., deceased, to Francis Curnock, mariner, 4 years Virginia. (LMWB14/38).

21 October. The following apprenticed in London: Thomas Martin, aged 24, to Walter Pye, merchant lodging in St. Swithin's Lane, London, 4 years Jamaica;

Isaac Powell, son of Oliver P., wool comber, deceased, and Thomas Norton, son of Thomas N., labourer, to Matthew Trimm of Lower Shadwell, Middlesex, mariner, 4 years Virginia. (LMWB14/39).

22 October. The following apprenticed in London: Robert Munday, aged 21, to William Pogson, 4 years Nevis; James Storey, aged 22, to John Richards, 4 years Maryland. (LMWB14/40).

23 October. The following apprenticed in London: Roger Morrow, aged 25, and Ann Stannicot, spinster aged 23, to John Dix, mariner, 4 years Maryland; Robert Grimes, aged 23, to Thomas Thatcher, mariner, 4 years Jamaica. (LMWB14/41).

23 October. The following apprenticed in Bristol: John Butler of Awre, Glos, to Richard Browning, 4 years Jamaica by *Abraham & Mary*. (BR).

24 October. The following apprenticed in Bristol: William Rowde of Oxfordshire to George Wilkinson, 4 years Jamaica by *Lamb*; Leonard Symes of St. Olave, Southwark, Surrey, dyer, to Anthony Swymmer, 4 years [Jamaica]; Nicholas Leaverne of Alcester, Warw, to same, 4 years [Jamaica]; Joane Kerswell of Exeter, [Devon], spinster, to same, 4 years Jamaica; Mary Brewer of Exeter, spinster, to same, 4 years Jamaica; Isaac Williams of Llandower, Pemb, to William Normand, 4 years Virginia by *Maryland Merchant*. (BR).

24 October. The following apprenticed in London: Elizabeth Cornish, spinster aged 25, to John Wiseman, 4 years Virginia; Mary Davis, daughter of Francis D., and Mary Harrison, widow aged 26, to William Flood, 4 years Jamaica. (LMWB14/42).

24-29 October. Shippers by the *Swallow* of Liverpool, Mr. Thomas Withington, bound from Liverpool for Virginia: John Pemberton, Nathaniell Bacon. (PRO: E190/1346/9).

24 October-7 November. Shippers by the *Duke of York*, Mr. John Purvis, bound from London for Virginia: Francis Camfield, Robert Camell, John Liquorish, George Richards, Francis Lee, Solomon Weekes. (PRO: E190/124/1).

25 October. The following apprenticed in London: Robert Clarke, aged 27, to Richard Abbott, planter, 3 years Nevis; James Turner, aged 23, to William Pogson, merchant, 3 years St. Christopher's. (LMWB14/43,44).

25 October. The following apprenticed in Bristol: William Bryan of Lydeard St. Lawrence, Som, to John Lord, 4 years Jamaica by *Samuel*; Richard Tayler of Court (*sic but poss. Corse*), Glos, to John Shewell, 4 years Virginia. (BR).

27 October. The following apprenticed in Bristol: Richard Westwood of Oldswinford, Worcs, nail seller, to Anthony Swymmer, 4 years Jamaica by *Providence*; William Cooke of Kingswinford, [Worcs], to same, 4 years Jamaica; Richard Dally of Wells, [Som], husbandman, to William ——, shipwright, 4 years Jamaica by *Abraham & Mary*; John Kerslake of Exeter, [Devon], cordwainer, to —— Kempe, 4 years Barbados by *Diligence*; Jeremy Hunt of Brimfield, Heref, tailor, to Anthony Swymmer, 4 years Barbados by *Lamb* and to be employed as a tailor; Francis Mingo of Gedington, Northants, to same, 4 years Jamaica by *Providence*; Thomas Webster of Hanham, [Glos], cordwainer, to same, 4 years Jamaica by *Providence*; Daniel Baldwyn of Kings County (*sic*) to James Porter, 4 years Barbados by *Olive Tree*. (BR).

27 October. The following apprenticed in London: John Burroughs of Shoreditch, Middlesex, labourer, to John Richards, mariner, 4 years Barbados; Maurice Tucker, aged 36, of Ludgvan, Cornwall, labourer aged 36, to Mathew Trim, mariner, 4 years Virginia; Robert Reeker, labourer aged 21, of Kingston, Dorset, to David Lockwood, mariner, 4 years Jamaica; Thomas Baker, son of Thomas B. of St. George, Southwark, Surrey, deceased, and Thomas Taylor, son of Thomas T., brickmaker, to William Bradley, mariner, 5 years Jamaica; William Ridgell to Robert Shanks, mariner, 4 years Jamaica. (LMWB14/45,46).

29 October. The following apprenticed in Bristol: Andrew Jones of Holywell, Flint, to James Parker, 4 years Barbados by *Olive Tree*; Francis Carter of Ilminster, Som, tanner, to same, 4 years Barbados by *Olive Tree*. (BR).

30 October. The following apprenticed in London: Ann Ong, daughter of William O., clerk, deceased, to Anthony Ensdale, mariner, 5 years Jamaica. (LMWB14/47).

31 October. The following apprenticed in London: William Wetton of London, labourer, to Robert Shanks, 4 years Jamaica; John Plumpton of London, labourer, to Thomas Green, mariner, 4 years Jamaica; Walter Williams, son of Thomas W. of Monmouth, husbandman, to Andrew Perry, mariner, 4 years Jamaica; Richard Helleway of London, labourer, to Thomas Green, mariner, 4 years Jamaica; John Martin of London, labourer, to William Cooke, ship carpenter, 4 years Jamaica. (LMWB14/47).

30 October-12 November. Shippers by the *Antelope* of Liverpool, Mr. George Hull, bound from Liverpool for Virginia: David Poole, John Stanley, Edward Booker. (PRO: E190/1346/9).

October. Probate of will of John Martin of Stepney, Middlesex, who had lands in Virginia. (AW).

3 November. The following apprenticed in Bristol: John Thomas of Week Va——, Glam, to William Neel, cooper, 2 years Jamaica by *Lamb*; Ann Crooke of Bristol to Thomas Sober, 5 years Barbados by *Diligence*. (BR).

3 November. The following apprenticed in London: Thomas Whittingham of Wrenbury, Cheshire, gardener, to David Lockwood of Wapping, Middlesex, mariner, 4 years Jamaica. (LMWB14/49).

4 November. The following apprenticed in London: Robert Allen, son of Thomas A. of Worcester, weaver, deceased, Francis Chamberlen, son of Edward C. of Dublin, Ireland, shoemaker, and Daniell Purchase alias Purchis, son of John P. of Ottery St. Mary, Devon, chandler, deceased, to David Lockwood, 4 years Jamaica; George Belgood, son of John B. of Cambridge, baker, deceased, to Issachar Dalby of London, mariner, 4 years Jamaica; John Sheen, son of John S. of Lewisham, Kent, watchmaker, deceased, to Robert Shanks, 4 years Jamaica. (LMWB14/49).

6 November. Deposition by John Milner of London, gent aged 50, that in Easter Term 1675 Matthew Travers of London, merchant, and John Essington, since deceased, sued James Pennington for debts. Travers has appointed Christopher Rousby of Potuxon River, Maryland, merchant, and Francis Billingsley of the Clifts near Potuxon, planter, as his attorneys. (LMCD).

6 November. The following apprenticed in Bristol: Elizabeth King of Stapleton, [Glos], to Robert Kirke, 4 years Jamaica by *Lamb*; Sarah Holcomb of Taunton, Som, to Anthony Swymmer, 4 years Jamaica by *Lamb*; Alexander Prichard of Sodbury, [Glos], to Charles Stoakes, 4 years Barbados; Edward Bodman of Westerleigh, [Glos], to same, 4 years Barbados; George Myttins of Bath, [Som], shoemaker, to Robert Kirke, 4 years Jamaica by *Lamb*; Joane Russell of Westbury, Som, to same, 4 years Jamaica by *Lamb*; James Pound of Munster, Ireland, to William Stoakes, 4 years Barbados. (BR).

6-19 November. Shippers by the *Assistance*, Mr. Roger Kemp, bound from London for Maryland: Gerrard Slye, Joseph Webb. (PRO: E190/124/1).

6-27 November. Shippers by the *Judith*, Mr. Matthew Trim, bound from London for Virginia: Thomas Bowser, Robert Christopher, Jeremy Bradfield, Samuel Scott. (PRO: E190/124/1).

7 November. The following apprenticed in London: William Savage, son of Francis S. of Blankney, Lincolnshire, blacksmith, deceased, Hugh Davies, son of Richard D. of Portsmouth, Hampshire, gunner, deceased, and Peter Eades, son of Peter E. of Butcher Row, Whitechapel, Middlesex, cooper, deceased, to David Lockwood, mariner, 4 years Jamaica; Dorothy Nicholls to Bartholomew Biggs of Ratcliffe, Middlesex, mariner, 4 years Barbados; Sarah Roulston to Arthur Easdell of Ratcliffe, Middlesex, mariner, 4 years Virginia; Henry Midglee, son of John M. of Bletchingley, Surrey, dyer, deceased, to John Newton of Wapping, Middlesex, mariner, 4 years Jamaica. (LMWB14/51).

7-19 November. Shipper by the *Liverpool Merchant*, Mr. William Marshall, bound from Liverpool for Maryland: Thomas Stanley. (PRO: E190/1346/9).

8 November. The following apprenticed in London: John Daine, son of John D. of Sherborne, Dorset, gardener, deceased, and Thomas Hellier, son of Robert H. of Chudleigh, Devon, lime burner, to David Lockwood, 4 years Jamaica;

Sarah Damster, daughter of William D. of Southam, Warwickshire, joiner, to Nicholas Crainsborough of London, gent, 4 years Virginia. (LMWB14/52).

8 November. Shipper by the *Elizabeth*, Mr. Jonathan Martin, bound from London for New England: John Daniell. (PRO: E190/124/1).

10 November. The following apprenticed in London: Ann Fulligar, daughter of Matthias F. alias Dominee of Upchurch, Kent, to John Triggs of London, surgeon, 4 years Virginia; Easter Harrison, widow, daughter of Elias Shie of Wapping, Middlesex, shipwright, and Katherine Sigsworth, spinster, daughter of Thomas S., victualler, to Matthew Trim, mariner, 4 years Virginia; William Rogers of Newnham, Northamptonshire, blacksmith, to John Richards of London, mariner, 4 years Barbados; John Rust, son of Thomas R. of Aylsham, Norfolk, hosier, to serve Richard Adams of Jamaica, merchant, 4 years. (LMWB14/55,56).

11 November. The following apprenticed in London: William Read, son of Michael R. of Bullwell, Nottinghamshire, deceased, to Robert Shanks, 4 years Jamaica; Joseph Davies, son of Thomas D. of Long Alley, London, weaver, to Humphrey Buncarr of Plymouth, Devon, mariner, 4 years Virginia; Edward Butler, son of John B. of Earls Colne, Essex, to Richard Bent of Ratcliffe, Middlesex, mariner, 4 years Virginia. (LMWB14/56).

12 November. The following apprenticed in London: Walter White, son of Edward W. of Cork, Ireland, to Robert Shanks, 4 years Jamaica. (LMWB14/57).

12 November. The following apprenticed in Bristol: Mary Powell of Caerleon, Merioneth, to Elizabeth Tyson, 4 years Barbados by *Diligence*. (BR).

13 November. The following apprenticed in London: Anne Goodin, daughter of Thomas G. of Shoreditch, Middlesex, gent, to Richard Anniver of Deal, Kent, mariner, 4 years Jamaica; Thomas Dunkley, son of Abraham D. of Newbold, Leicestershire, labourer, to David Lockwood, 5 years Jamaica. (LMWB14/58).

14 November. The following apprenticed in London: Robert Mortimer, son of William M. of Upavon, Wiltshire, to Thomas Green, 4 years Jamaica; Thomas Duckenfield, son of William D. of Brindle, Lancashire, husbandman, to David Lockwood, 4 years Jamaica; Sarah Thorne, daughter of George T. of St. Martin's, London, harness maker, to William Wilson of Stepney, Middlesex, mariner, 4 years Jamaica. (LMWB14/59).

14 November. Deposition by Francis Bass, citizen and vintner of London, aged 40, that Mr. Richard Hanslop of London, merchant, has appointed Mr. Hugh Aldworth of London, merchant, to recover his debts in Virginia, Maryland and New York. (LMCD).

15 November. The following apprenticed in Bristol: John Martin of London, tailor, to William King, 4 years Barbados by *Martha & Sarah*. (BR).

15 November. Shipper by the *Hope* of Liverpool, Mr. William Renald, bound from Liverpool for Maryland: Charles Scarsbrick. (PRO: E190/1346/9).

17 November. The following apprenticed in Bristol: Richard Pavy of Stoke Abbott, Dorset, to James Porter, 4 years Barbados; Richard Maunder of Portbury, Som, to William Abbot, 4 years Barbados by *Diligence*. (BR).

17 November. The following apprenticed in London: Mary Willington of London, spinster, to Seager Walter, mariner, 4 years Jamaica; John Edlington, son of Henry E. of London, weaver, deceased, to the same, 7 years Jamaica. (LMWB14/64).

18 November. The following apprenticed in London: John Gardiner, aged 25, to Richard Pateson, 4 years Jamaica; Suzanna Wicks of Stanwell, Middlesex, spinster, to Josias Dowell, 4 years Jamaica. (LMWB14/67).

18 November. The following apprenticed in Bristol: Henry Fonken, a Dutchman, to John Tovey, 4 years Barbados by *Olive Tree*. (BR).

19 November. The following apprenticed in Bristol: John Williams of Llangattock, [Mon], to William Stoakes, 4 years Barbados. (BR).

19 November. The following apprenticed in London: Samuel Collins, aged 21, to John Richards, mariner, 4 years Barbados; Mary Coggill of London, spinster, and Mary Hughes of London, spinster, to Matthew Trim, 5 years Virginia; John Lomsdale to David Lockwood, 4 years Jamaica. (LMWB14/68).

20 November. The following apprenticed in London: Edward Browne, aged 21, and Thomas Wickham, aged 28, to Robert Shanks, 4 years Jamaica; John Everard, aged 23, to Christopher Squire, 4 years Jamaica. (LMWB14/69).

20 November-6 December. Shippers by the *Charles & Jane*, Mr. Edward Poulson, bound from London for Maryland: John Jackson, William Hiccocks, Henry Lee. (PRO: E190/124/1).

21 November. The following apprenticed in London: John Kaham, aged 22, to Richard Pateson, mariner, 4 years Jamaica; Mary Hardy, aged 23, spinster, to John Triggs, surgeon, 4 years Virginia; Gabriel Buck, aged 21, to Robert Shanks, 4 years Jamaica; Thomas Ball, aged 23, discharged from Bridewell Prison, to Robert Shanks, mariner, 4 years Virginia. (LMWB14/70).

22 November. The following apprenticed in London: Miles White, aged 30, to Robert Shanks, 4 years Jamaica; John Stevenson, aged 26, to John Elliot, 4 years Jamaica. (LMWB14/72).

22-28 November. Shippers by the *Charles*, Mr. John Wiseman, bound from London for Virginia: James Harris, Henry Eden, Francis Nelson, John Pym. (PRO: E190/124/1).

24 November. The following apprenticed in London: John Watson of London, labourer aged 26, and Thomas Nell of London, labourer aged 22, to Robert Shanks, 4 years Jamaica. (LMWB14/73).

25 November. Shipper by the *America Merchant*, Mr. John Vevers, bound from London for Virginia: James [or Jane] Bell. (PRO: E190/124/1).

26 November. The following apprenticed in London: Frances Simpson of Westminster, spinster, and John Simpson of London, aged 30 and more, to John Triggs, surgeon, 4 years Virginia; James Anderson of Douglas, Clydesale, Scotland, labourer, to John Balson, mariner, 4 years Jamaica; Elizabeth Hodges of London, spinster aged 21, to John Oakley, 4 years Maryland. (LMWB14/74).

27 November. The following apprenticed in London: James Browne of London, labourer aged 21, to Robert Shanks, 4 years Jamaica; Frances Webb of Southwark, Surrey, spinster aged 25, to William Cooke, ship carpenter, 4 years Jamaica. (LMWB14/75,76).

27 November. The following apprenticed in Bristol: John Tibbott of Cheddar, Som, to James Porter, 4 years Barbados. (BR).

28 November. The following apprenticed in London: Allian Keyr of London, labourer aged 35, and his son, Caleb Keyr, aged 15, to Robert Shanks, 4 years Jamaica; Peter Smith, aged 11, son of William S. of London, bricklayer, to Henry Low, merchant, 4 years Maryland. (LMWB14/77).

29 November. The following apprenticed in London: Richard Dewhurst, aged 30, of London, labourer, to Henry Low, merchant, 4 years Maryland; George Wilson, aged 17, son of George W. of Buxton, Norfolk, husbandman, deceased, to Christopher Squire, 6 years Jamaica. (LMWB14/78).

29 November. The following apprenticed in Bristol: Isaac Williams of Usk, Mon, to James Porter, 4 years Barbados by *Olive Tree*; John Jefferies of Beaminster, Dorset, weaver. to —— Reed, 4 years Barbados by *Diligence*. (BR).

30 November. The following apprenticed in Bristol: Elizabeth Driver of Berkeley, [Glos], spinster, to Henry Huet, surgeon, 4 years Jamaica by *George*; Richard Marker of Charlton Kings, [Glos], husbandman, to James Porter, 4 years Barbados by *Olive Tree*. (BR).

November. Administration with will of John Gwin of James City, Virginia. (AW).

1 December. The following apprenticed in London: John Jones, aged 17, son of John J. of Mile End, Middlesex, deceased, to Alexander Pollington, citizen and haberdasher of London, 6 years Antigua; John Wilson, aged 22, son of John W. of Helmsley, Yorkshire, husbandman, deceased, to Robert Shanks, 4 years Jamaica; James Walker, aged 22, son of Henry W. of Halifax, Yorkshire, weaver, deceased, to the same, 4 years Jamaica; James Milburne, son of

Nicholas M. of Bishop Auckland, Durham, deceased, to Anthony Elliot of Shadwell, Middlesex, mariner, 4 years Virginia. (LMWB14/82,83).

2 December. The following apprenticed in London: James Russ, aged 22, son of John R. of Bemcroft Hill, Bremhill, Wiltshire, to Robert Shanks of Wapping, Middlesex, mariner, 4 years Jamaica. (LMWB14/85).

5 December. The following apprenticed in Bristol: John Male of Hatfield, Heref, to William Swymmer, 4 years Jamaica by *America Merchant*. (BR).

5 December. The following apprenticed in London: John Provist, aged 18, son of John P. of St. Giles in the Fields, Middlesex, painter, deceased, to James Parsons, surgeon, 4 years Jamaica, with the consent of his sister, his mother being also dead; John Coldwell, aged 28, singleman, son of William C. of Black Barnsley, Yorkshire, husbandman, deceased, to John Peirson of Wapping, Middlesex, 4 years Jamaica. (LMWB14/87).

6 December. The following apprenticed in London: Sarah Mills, spinster aged 19, daughter of Henry M. of Horsham, Sussex, sawyer, deceased, to Joseph North of Wapping, Middlesex, mariner, 4 years Jamaica, witnessed by Mary Hobson. (LMWB14/89).

6 December. The following apprenticed in Bristol: Walter Griffith of Llanharvan (*sic*), Glam, weaver, to Robert Kirke, 4 years Jamaica by *America [Merchant]*. (BR).

9 December. The following apprenticed in London: Stephen Goddard, son of Stephen G. of Shoe Lane, London, deceased, to Robert Shanks, 4 years Jamaica with the consent of his mother, Elizabeth G.; William Sleath, son of Edward S., butcher, deceased, and Thomas Vye, both of Grimston, Leicestershire, to William Martin of Bristol, mariner, 4 years Jamaica. (LMWB14/93).

10 December. The following apprenticed in Bristol: Walter Welsh of Cheltenham, Glos, to William Worgan, 4 years Barbados by *Rose*; George Trotter of London, silk thrower, to same, 4 years Barbados by *Rose*; Mary, wife of George Trotter, to same, 4 years Barbados by *Rose*. (BR).

11 December. The following apprenticed in Bristol: Thomas Orchard of Westerleigh, Glos, to James Porter, 4 years Barbados by *Olive Tree*. (BR).

15 December. The following apprenticed in London: William Proudman, son of William P. of London, bricklayer, deceased, to William Emberley, mariner, 5 years Barbados. (LMWB14/95).

16 December. The following apprenticed in London: Ellenor Clerke, aged 21, of London, spinster, to Thomas Clark, merchant, 4 years Barbados; William Strange, aged 22, to William Martin, mariner, 4 years Barbados. (LMWB14/95).

16 December. The following apprenticed in Bristol: David Stephens of Salop, broad weaver, to James Porter, 4 years Barbados by *Olive Tree*. (BR).

17 December. The following apprenticed in London: George Andrewes and Jane his wife to Samuel Pratt, surgeon, 4 years Jamaica; George Barber, aged 27, to Richard Pattison, mariner, 4 years Jamaica. (LMWB14/97).

18 December. The following apprenticed in London: Thomas Amps, aged 30, to Charles Smith, ship carpenter, 4 years Jamaica; Elizabeth, wife of Stephen Day, sawyer, to Andrew Herring, mariner, 4 years Virginia with the consent of her husband; William Jeane, aged 22, to Robert Shanks, 4 years Jamaica. (LMWB14/99).

19 December. The following apprenticed in London: Katherine Pory, spinster aged 24, to David Lockwood, mariner, 4 years Jamaica, witnessed by Mr. Pory near Barking Church, merchant. (LMWB14/101).

19 December. Shipper by the *Dublin Merchant*, Mr. John Haws, bound from London for New England: Humphrey South. (PRO: E190/124/1).

20 December. The following apprenticed in London: William Warren, singleman aged 44, to Thomas Dann, mariner, 4 years Nevis; Abraham Kent, aged 22, to William Martin, mariner, 4 years Jamaica, with the consent of his brother and sister. (LMWB14/102,103).

22 December. The following apprenticed in London: John Johnson, aged 30, of Cottenham, Cambridgeshire, carpenter, to Robert Shanks, 4 years Jamaica. (LMWB14/104).

23 December. The following apprenticed in Bristol: William Pierce of Ham, Mddx, to Robert Kirke, 4 years Jamaica by *America Merchant*. (BR).

24 December. George Chick of Beaminster, Dorset, husbandman, bound to Robert Fowler of Lyme Regis, mariner, to serve 4 years in Barbados. (DRO B7/M9).

29 December. The following apprenticed in London: Owen Oubley, aged 23, son of Edward O. of Cobham, Surrey, coachman, deceased, to Rainford Waterhouse of Wapping, Middlesex, 4 years Jamaica. (LMWB14/108).

29 December. The following apprenticed in Bristol: Peter Maxy of Newton St. Cyres, Devon, to Robert Kirke, 4 years Jamaica by *America Merchant*; Thomas West of Taunton, [Som], tucker, to Thomas Tildy, mariner, 4 years Barbados by *Olive Tree*; Edmond Quayle of Taunton to same, 4 years Barbados by *Olive Tree*. (BR).

30 December. The following apprenticed in Bristol: John Ashford of Shepton Mallet, [Som], to William Clarke, 4 years Barbados by *Olive Tree*. (BR).

31 December. The following apprenticed in London: John Clarke, son of John C. of the Minories, London, painter, to William Martin of Wapping,

Middlesex, 4 years Jamaica; Thomas Lowther, singleman, son of Thomas L. of Berwick on Tweed, Northumberland, deceased, to John Rose of London, cooper, 4 years Jamaica, witnessed by his friend, William Randall; Richard Smith, singleman, son of George S. of Cockermouth, Cumberland, deceased, to the same, 4 years Jamaica, with the consent of his friend, James Williams. (LMWB14/109-111).

December. Administration with will of Benjamin Acrod of Hackney, Middlesex, who died in Pennsylvania. (AW).

December. Petition of Joseph Eaton to the Lord Chief Justice. Complaint has been made against him for carrying a boy named Goodwin to Maryland against his will. For many years the petitioner has commanded a ship to Virginia but has never carried a passenger without his consent. (CSPC).

1685

3 January. The following apprenticed in Bristol: James Webb of Bristol, tailor, to Roger Bagg, 4 years Barbados by *Batchelor*. (BR).

3 January. The following apprenticed in London: John Bewitt, aged 17, son of Mathew B. of Cheam, Surrey, writing master, to Benjamin Goodwin of Cheam, mariner, 4 years Jamaica, with the consent of his father; John Paine, aged 23, son of Richard P. of Barnstaple, Devon, to Robert Shanks, 4 years Jamaica. (LMWB14/111,112).

5 January. The following apprenticed in London: William Adams, aged 26, from Somerset, to James Fawcett, 4 years Maryland. (LMWB14/113).

5 January. The following apprenticed in Bristol: Moses Lott of St. Georges, Som. (*sic*), to John Davis, 4 years Barbados by *Batchelor*. (BR).

6 January. Shipper by the *Elizabeth* of Dublin, Mr. John Hayes, bound from Newcastle for New England: Sir William Creagh. (PRO: E190/201/6).

6 January. The following apprenticed in Bristol: John Prosser of Ullingswick, Heref, to James Porter, 4 years Barbados by *Olive Tree*. (BR).

7 January. The following apprenticed in London: Elizabeth Davies of Bristol, spinster aged 22, and Margaret Frazer of St. Martin in the Fields, Middlesex, to Robert Barrington of London, mariner, 4 years in West Indies; William Giles, son of John G. of Mitcham, Surrey, to Benjamin Goodwin of Cheam, Surrey, mariner, 6 years Jamaica, with the consent of his mother, Mary G. (LMWB14/114).

8 January. The following apprenticed in London: John Walton, singleman, gunsmith aged 23, son of Roger W. of Cockshutt, Shropshire, to George Pye of Redriffe, Surrey, 4 years Jamaica, on the affirmation of John Smith of Rosemary Lane, London, plasterer; Robert Clitheroe, aged 24, of Litleplun (?Litherland), Lancashire, to John Nugent of Wapping, Middlesex, mariner, 4 years Jamaica, witnessed by John Childe of Petticoat Lane, London, bricklayer; Richard Ellgood of Market Dereham, Norfolk, labourer, to John Dykes of Shadwell, Middlesex, mariner, 4 years Jamaica. (LMWB14/115).

10 January. The following apprenticed in London: Nicholas Mundy, son of Robert M. of Steeple Langford, Wiltshire, to John Richards, 4 years Jamaica; John Morton alias Norton, son of Richard M. or N. of Old Bedlam, London, to James Williams, 4 years Jamaica. (LMWB14/117).

12 January. The following apprenticed in Bristol: Francis Ra—— of Wisbeach, Cambs, to George Walwyn, 4 years ?Antigua; Tobey Gray of Dusselton (*sic*), Som, to William Canes, 4 years Jamaica. (BR).

501

13 January. The following apprenticed in Bristol: George Wilcocks of Chewton Mendip, Som, to John Napper, 4 years Jamaica by *George*. (BR).

13 January-7 February. Shippers by the *Penelope* [elsewhere the *Antelope*], Mr. William Lord, bound from London for New England: Daniel King, Hugh Horton, Thomas Powell, Thomas Weekes, Jeremy Johnson, Samuel Dawes, Samuel Ball, Thomas Bell, Nathaniell Lew, William Baron, Alexander Hosea. (PRO: E190/129/1).

14 January. The following apprenticed in Bristol: William Bazen, son of James Bazen of Bedminster, Som, clothier, to Nicholas Lott, merchant, 6 years Jamaica. (BR).

15 January. The following apprenticed in Bristol: Nicholas Huling of Shrewsbury, [Salop], collier, to Robert Kirke, 4 years Jamaica by *America Merchant*; Jacobus Iles of Shepton Mallet, Som, to Matthew Jones, 4 years Barbados by *Olive Tree*; Robertus Hordley of Hampshire to John Pragg, 4 years Barbados by *Batchelor*. (BR).

15 January. The following apprenticed in London: Thomas Fenn, carpenter aged 22, to John Richards, 4 years Nevis.(LMWB 14/123).

16 January. Shipper by the *Adventure*, Mr. Andrew Cratey, bound from London for New England: William Stafford. (PRO: E190/129/1).

20 January. The following apprenticed in London: Hester Turner, daughter of Thomas T. of Plymouth, Devon, sailor, deceased, to James Parsons, 4 years Jamaica, witnessed by Susan Turner of Duke Street, Covent Garden, Middlesex; Sarah Wood of London, singlewoman, to the same, 4 years Jamaica, witnessed by George Atkin of New Street, Shoe Lane, London; John Rice, aged 18, of Crayford, Kent, to John Gibbs, 5 years Barbados, witnessed by Anne Grime of St. Clement's Lane, Lombard Street, London, widow, whose husband was Gibbs' master; William Trebitt, singleman aged 22, of Crayford, Kent, to the same, 5 years Barbados; James Welch, aged 28, of Crayford, Kent, to the same, 3 years Barbados. (LMWB14/129).

21 January. The following apprenticed in Bristol: Richard Morris of Swansea, Glam, to Robert Kirke, 4 years Jamaica; John Harcourt of Bontmore, Ireland, to Thomas Kirke, 4 years Jamaica by *America Merchant*. (BR).

22 January. The following apprenticed in Bristol: William Philipp of Llangavelly, Glam, to Giles Hall, 4 years Barbados by *Batchelor*. (BR).

23 January. The following apprenticed in Bristol: Abel Whiteman of Bristol to Mathew Nicholas, 7 years Jamaica by *George*; Charles Jefferis of Upton upon Severn, Worcs, to Thomas Kirke, 4 years Jamaica by *America Merchant*. (BR).

23 January. The following apprenticed in London: Jonathan Dickins, singleman of Stepney, Middlesex, bricklayer, to John Netheway, merchant, 4 years Nevis as a bricklayer, witnessed by Jonathan Bonns of Phoenix Street, Spitalfields,

Middlesex; Lucq Le Jeun alias Young, native of Jersey, to the same, 4 years Nevis; James Wills, singleman aged 23, citizen and grocer of London, to Philip Beckett, planter, 4 years Jamaica, with the consent of his mother of Plaistow, Essex, his father being dead witnessed by Abraham Rescons. (LMWB14/133).

23 January-28 February. Shippers by the *Amity*, Mr. Richard Dymond, bound from London for Pennsylvania: Edward Parsons, James Blackman, John Gray, Joshua Bramley, Francis Richardson, Jacob Hall, William Phillips, Walter Benthall, Peter Boss, Edward Hastwell, Thomas Cooper, Ralph Hatley. (PRO: E190/129/1).

30 January-18 March. Depositions in London re the *Adventure*, Mr. John Balstone of New England, the *Amity*, Mr. Gersham Browne, and the *Elizabeth*, Mr. William Condy of Boston, New England, all witnesses to the activities of a French privateer, the *Trompeuse*, in New England. Consignments to London merchants were made by the following New England merchants: James Taylor, Joseph and Humphrey Parsons of Boston, Nathaniel Byfield, John Eyre, Daniel Allin, Isaac Walker, William Brinley, William Robie, John Floyd, Frances Foxcroft, Richard Banks, Edward Shippen, William Lewis, Francis Burroughs and Benjamin Walker. (EA).

31 January. The following apprenticed in Bristol: Richard Morgan of Penmarke, Glam, to Samuel Gibbons, 4 years Barbados by *Olive Tree*. (BR).

January. Probate of will of Joseph Thorowgood of London, who died in Carolina, bachelor. (AW).

January. Probate of will of Richard Richmond of St. Leonard Foster Lane, London, whose sister, Margaret Richmond, was in Virginia. (AW).

January. Administration of Christopher Rousby of Maryland, widower. (AW).

January. Administration with will of William Gibson of St. Edmund the King, London, who had goods in New Jersey and Pennsylvania. (AW).

2 February. The following apprenticed in Bristol: Thomas Marchant of Westmorland to John Napper, 4 years Jamaica by *America Merchant*. (BR).

3 February. Chancery proceedings re a settlement drawn up on 12 May 1670 relating to the intended marriage of Samuel Shrimpton of London and Elizabeth Roberts, daughter of Nicholas Roberts, citizen and ironmonger of London, who died in August 1676. Shortly after their marriage, Samuel and Elizabeth Shrimpton departed for New York. (NGSQ 63/3).

3 February. The following apprenticed in Bristol: Henry Evans of Newton Nottidge, Glam, to Martin Weakley, 6 years Jamaica by *America Merchant*. (BR).

3-25 February. Shipper by the *Thomas & Ann*, Mr. Andrew Elton, bound from London for New York: William Sanders. (PRO: E190/129/1).

4 February. The following apprenticed in Bristol: Nathaniel Cory of Hullavington, Wilts, tailor, to Andrew Lack, 4 years Jamaica by *America [Merchant]*. (BR).

5 February. The following apprenticed in Bristol: John Davis of Bath, Som, to Henry Taylor, 4 years Jamaica by *America Merchant*; Joseph Lokier of Broad Masson, Som (*sic, ?Broad Marston, Glos, intended*) to John Napper, 4 years Jamaica by *America Merchant*; John Pooler of Yeovil, Som, to same, 7 years Jamaica by *America Merchant*; William Margery of Netherbury, Dorset, to same, 4 years Jamaica by *America Merchant*; Robert Morgan of Tenby, Pembroke, to Thomas Masters, 4 years Jamaica by *America Merchant*. (BR).

6 February. The following apprenticed in Bristol: Charles, son of Charles Edgell of West Harptree, Som, tanner deceased, to John Hort, 9 years Jamaica by *[America] Merchant*; Joseph Brookes of Gloucester to Thomas Masters, 4 years Jamaica by *America Merchant*; Mary Davis of Minehead, Som, spinster, to Thomas Kirke, 4 years Jamaica by *America Merchant*; Samuel Jones of Monmouth to Thomas Foster, 9 years Virginia by *Mary*, Mr. William ——stone; John Sturgis of Shepton Mallet, Som, to Henry David, 4 years Jamaica by *America Merchant*; Trustrum Chilkin of Spaxell [?Spaxton intended], Som, to Thomas Kirke, 4 years Jamaica by *America Merchant*. (BR).

8 February. The following apprenticed in Bristol: Mathew Phillips of Llanethly, Glam, to Thomas Masters, 4 years Jamaica by *America Merchant*. (BR).

11 February. The following apprenticed in Bristol: Rebecca Sperin of Bristol to Thomas Masters, 7 years Jamaica by *America Merchant*. (BR).

16 February. The following apprenticed in Bristol: John Jenkins of Llanlyntwood (*sic*) to Thomas Foster, 5 years Virginia by *Mary*; John Gibbons of Loxley, Oxon (*sic, Warw perhaps intended*), to Anthony Swymmer, 5 years Jamaica by *Mary*. (BR).

16 February. The following apprenticed in London: William Newarke, aged 19, son of John N. of Fenchurch Street, London, to John Salmon, merchant, to serve in Jamaica. (LMWB14/157).

17-25 February. Shippers by the *John & Charles*, Mr. Timothy Armitage, bound from London for New England: Christopher Booth, Jonathan Luck, Arthur Tanner. (PRO: E190/129/1).

19 February. Shipper by the *Rebecca*, Mr. Edward Clements, bound from London for New York: Henry Plomer. (PRO: E190/129/1).

20 February. Shipper by the *Mehitabell*, Mr. John Thwing, bound from London for New England: Joseph Whetham. (PRO: E190/129/1).

20 February. Shipper by the *Antego*, Mr. Gershon Boon, bound from London for New York: said Gershon Boon. (PRO: E190/129/1).

20 February. The following apprenticed in London: Jane Pepper of London, widow with no children, to William Bartrum, mariner, 4 years Antigua, witnessed by Ellin Angsdell of Holborn, London; Elizabeth Marshall of London , spinster aged 16 and more, to the same, 6 years Antigua, witnessed by Elizabeth Fletcher and Elizabeth Biggs at the house of John Fletcher in Cole Yard, St. Giles in the Fields, Middlesex. (LMWB14/161).

20 February. The following apprenticed in Bristol: Richard Hedon of Landbathurne (*sic*), Cardigan, to John Codnall, 4 years New England by *Laurel*; William Evans of Bristol, pipe maker, to Robert Kirke, 4 years Jamaica by *Mary*; Mary Vick of Berkeley, (Glos), spinster, to William Whetston, 9 years Barbados by *Mary*. (BR).

21 February. The following apprenticed in Bristol: John Cripps of St. Dunstan in West, (London), stationer, to John Broom, 4 years Nevis by *[America] Merchant*. (BR).

22-26 February. Shippers by the *Society*, Mr. Peter Clarke, bound from London for New England: William Barnes, Thomas Mardin, Thomas Edwards, Joseph Thompson, Edward Ellis, John Crow, Charles Duke, Joseph Waldow, Thomas Moulton, Edward Hunlock, Thomas Goodwin, Ralph Ingrave, John Brett. (PRO: E190/126/5).

23 February. The following apprenticed in Bristol: Thomas Davis of Commis (*sic*), Pembroke, to John Codner, 4 years New England by *Laurel*. (BR).

25 February. Report on the circumstances of the murder of Christopher Rousby, Collector of Customs in Maryland, by Colonel George Talbott. (APC).

25 February. The following apprenticed in Bristol: Thomas Bleakeman of Landinium, Montgomery, to Thomas Foster, 5 years Virginia by *Mary*; Timothy Yeamans of Stuckersell (*sic*), Som, to Caleb Winter, 7 years Jamaica by *Mary*; Josias Jeffrys of Bridgenorth, Salop, to Robert Kirke, 4 years Jamaica by *Mary*. (BR).

25 February-14 March. Shippers by the *Lawrell* of Bristol, Mr. John Codner, bound from Bristol for New England: Sir Thomas Earle, Henry Lloyd, Francis Ballard. (PRO: E190/1147/2).

27 February. The following apprenticed in Bristol: Katherine Powell of Laysters, Heref, to Thomas Kirke, 4 years Jamaica by *Dragon*. (BR).

27 February. The following apprenticed in London: Thomas Franklin, son of Abraham F. of Dunnings Alley, Billingsgate Street, London, weaver, to Thomas Nicchols of St. Giles in the Fields, Middlesex, gent, 4 years Jamaica, with the consent of his father and mother. (LMWB14/165).

28 February. The following apprenticed in London: Peter Allett, aged 30, son of Thomas A. of Over, Cheshire, weaver, deceased, to John West of Bermondsey, Surrey, ship carpenter,4 years Jamaica; Simon Dodd, aged 31, son of Thomas D. of Newcastle, Staffordshire, shoemaker, deceased, to the same, 4 years Jamaica; Thomas Barnard, aged 20, son of Phillip B. of Aberford, Yorkshire, pipe maker, deceased, to the same, 4 years Jamaica; Elizabeth Bryan, aged 20, daughter of Benjamin B. of Salisbury, Wiltshire, deceased, to the same, 4 years Jamaica. (LMWB14/166).

February. Probate of will of Edward Bettris of Oxford, surgeon, who had lands in Pennsylvania. (AW).

2 March. The following apprenticed in London: Thomas Broadwater, son of Robert B. of St. Mary, Newington, Surrey, to Thomas Hunt, 4 years Jamaica; Martha Martin, daughter of William M. of St. Mary Magdalene, Bermondsey, Surrey, cordwainer, to the same, 4 years Jamaica. Elizabeth Bigg, daughter of John B. of St. Giles, Middlesex, coachman, deceased, and Elizabeth Fletcher, aged 22, daughter of John Fletcher of Drury Lane, St. Giles, Middlesex, porter, to Nathaniel Jones of Deptford, Kent, mariner, 4 years Jamaica; Thomas Challenor, son of Arthur C. of Lysborne(?), Yorkshire, gent, to Phillip Gower of St. Christopher's, London, merchant, 4 years Jamaica; Abraham Lightfoot, son of Thomas L. of Exeter, Devon, worsted comber, to the same, 4 years Jamaica; John Martin of Dumfries, Scotland, singleman, to Hugh Horton of Milk Street, London, 4 years Jamaica, witnessed by William Thompson at the Angel and Crown, Cheapside, London, haberdasher. (LMWB14/167).

2 March. The following apprenticed in Bristol: Thomas Murry of Felton (*sic*), Som, to Thomas Kirke, 4 years Jamaica by *Dragon*; Thomas Ball of Cold Ashton, Glos, to same, 4 years Jamaica by *Dragon*; William Ball of Cold Ashton to same, 4 years Jamaica by *Dragon*; Thomas Jervis of Dyrham, Glos, to same, 4 years Jamaica by *Dragon*. (BR).

4 March. The following apprenticed in London: Peter Wells of Little Waltham, Essex, to Micajah Perry, 4 years Virginia, with the consent of his brothers, John W. of St. George's, Southwark, and James W. of St. Katherine Creechurch, London; William Dowling, son of Thomas D. of Spitalfields, Stepney, Middlesex, silk thrower, to Percival Milner, Captain of the *Rose* of London, 9 years Jamaica, with the consent of his father. (LMWB14/169).

4 March. The following apprenticed in Bristol: Jenkin Lloyd of Stradmerrick, Cardigan, to Thomas Kirke, 4 years Jamaica by *Dragon*. (BR).

5 March. The following apprenticed in Bristol: Daniell Guest of Dudley, Worcs, to William Hooper, 6 years Nevis by *[Golden] Hart*. (BR).

6 March. The following apprenticed in London: Edward Seabin, son of John S. of Wardington, Oxfordshire, yeoman, to Philip Gower, 4 years Jamaica; Joseph Whittell of Reading, Berkshire, shearman, to the same, 4 years Jamaica. (LMWB14/170).

7 March. The following apprenticed in London: Thomas Elsey, millwright, son of Thomas E. of Dalby Thould (?Great Dalby), Leicestershire, husbandman, to John Dikes, 4 years Jamaica. (LMWB14/171).

7 March. Newgate prisoners reprieved to be transported to Barbados or Jamaica. London: Elizabeth Ratcliffe, spinster; Christian Bromfield alias Jorden alias Christian, spinster; Robert Todd; Mary Vosse, spinster; John Pett; John Fuller; Sarah Carter alias Eden; Barbara Williams, spinster; John Thurowgood; John Morgan; Dorcas Morgan, spinster; John Harrupp; William Fincham; Mary Ryves, spinster; John Walker; Edward Perkins; John Holmes; Thomas Smith; Elizabeth Townsend alias Wolfe, spinster. Middlesex: Richard Enos of St. Katherine's; William Thomas of the same; John Walbanck of St. Martin in the Fields; Jane Arnaux of the same; Joseph Key of the same; Silvanus Morris of the same; Katherine Cotterell alias Irish alias Jones of the same, spinster; George Clarke of the same for clipping coins; Henry Curley of Stepney; Henry Lift of the same; Ralph Harrison of the same; Thomas Stephenson of the same; William Williams of the same; William Clarke of the same; William Temple of St. Andrew Holborn; William Butler of the same; Thomas Viccars of St. Giles Cripplegate; Roger Adams of the same; John Hayes of the same; John Clutton of the same; William Pearce of Hornsey; Jane Bourne of St. Clement Danes, spinster; Matthew Harwar of Enfield; Philemon Adams of Clerkenwell; Francis Abraham of St. Giles in the Fields; Richard Scarlett of Whitechapel; Charles Buckler of Friern Barnet; John Holtam alias Holtham of Islington; (PRO: C66/3275/2).

9 March. The following apprenticed in London: Sarah Palmer, spinster aged 23, to John Dikes, mariner, 4 years Jamaica. (LMWB14/177).

9 March. The following apprenticed in Bristol: Arthur Rice of Haverfordwest, Pembroke, to William Swymmer, 4 years Jamaica by *Dragon*; Samuel Plumley of Clapton, Som, to same, 5 years Jamaica by *Dragon*. (BR).

9-26 March. Shippers by the *Black Cock*, Mr. Michael Isaacs(?), bound from London for New England; John Shorter, Michael Pack. (PRO: E190/126/5).

10 March. The following apprenticed in London: Richard Rawlings, aged 23, to William Emberry, mariner, 4 years Barbados; John Stacy, aged 26, to Roger Edwards, mariner, 4 years Jamaica; James Stewart, aged 21, and Elizabeth Foster, aged 21, to John Shaw, carpenter, 4 years Jamaica. (LMWB14/178,179).

10 March. Shipper by the *Mary* of Bristol bound for Barbados and Virginia: Jacob Beale. (PRO: E190/1147/2).

11 March. Order for the release of Christopher Sibthorpe from the Wood Street Counter, London, on condition that he transports himself and his family to Pennsylvania. (APC).

11 March. The following apprenticed in London: Abell Fisher, aged 22, blacksmith, to John Shaw, carpenter, 4 years Jamaica, witnessed by John Peirson at the Crooked Billet, Petticoat Lane, London. (LMWB14/181).

11 March. The following apprenticed in Bristol: William Bliss of Pensford, Som, weaver, to Anthony Swymmer, 4 years Jamaica by *Mary*. (BR).

12 March. The following apprenticed in London: Abraham Potto, aged 21, to John Williams, mariner, 4 years Virginia, witnessed by his father Jacob P. of Pearl Street, Spitalfields, Middlesex; Andrew Wilson, aged 21, to the same, 4 years Virginia; Daniel Lambert, aged 31, to the same, 4 years Virginia; Samuel Robinson, aged 21, to the same, 4 years Virginia; Edward Browne, aged 21, to Thomas Hunt, mariner, 4 years Jamaica, witnessed by Lawrence Simcot at the Vineyard, Horsley Down, Surrey, ship carpenter. (LMWB14/181,182).

13 March. The following apprenticed in London: Phillis Rakes, spinster aged 21, to Robert Porten, mariner, 4 years Antigua; James Bradshaw, aged 24, and Thomas Carmell, aged 28, to John Williams, mariner, 4 years Barbados. (LMWB14/183).

13 March. The following apprenticed in Bristol: William Webb of Chepstow, Mon, cooper, to Robert Kirke, 4 years Jamaica by *Mary*; Robert Stephens of Bridport, Dorset, to Richard Downe, 3 years Newfoundland by *Supply*. (BR).

13 March. Shipper by the *Friends Adventure* of Exeter, Mr. John Browne, bound from Exeter for New England: Edward Seaward. (PRO: E190/963/1).

14 March. The following apprenticed in Bristol: Henry Chapman of Sutton, Dorset, to Shadrach Burt, 4 years Newfoundland by *Jeremy*; Charles Shirrey of Yetminster, Dorset, to Thomas ———, 3 years Newfoundland by *Jeremy*; Edward Browne of Chippenham, Wilts, to Daniel Jones, 4 years Newfoundland by *Jeremy*. (BR).

16 March. The following apprenticed in London: Samuel Evans, aged 21 and more, singleman, son of Ellis E. of Southwark, Surrey, labourer, deceased, to John Williams, 4 years Virginia, with the consent of his father-in-law, Paul Milbourne of Kent Street, Southwark, basketmaker. (LMWB14/189).

16 March. The following apprenticed in Bristol: John Woods of Gurtontubborod, Ireland, barber surgeon, to Anthony Swymmer, 4 years Jamaica by *Mary*; John Queele of Chepton Sled (*sic*), Wilts, to same, 4 years Jamaica by *Mary*. (BR).

17 March. The following apprenticed in London: James Bland, aged 22, of Penrith, Cumberland, glazier and plumber, and Ralph Grant, aged 22, of Rochester, Kent, blacksmith, to William Dockwra of London, merchant, 4 years East New Jersey; Richard Allinson, son of Richard A. of Oxford, to David Greenhill, 4 years Jamaica; Thomas Chetwin, aged 24, of London, labourer and singleman, to John West, shipwright, 4 years Jamaica; Gerrard Everlings, aged 20, formerly of The Hague in Holland, shoemaker, to Thomas Hunt, mariner, 4 years Jamaica. (LMWB14/189).

17 March. Shipper by the *Diamond* of Exeter, Mr. Edward Shower, bound from Exeter for Boston, New England: John Cholwell. (PRO: E190/963/1).

17 March. Shipper by the *Success* of Exeter, Mr. Thomas Ross, bound from Exeter for Boston, New England: John Cholwell. (PRO: E190/963/1).

18 March. The following apprenticed in London: John Woolnough, aged 15, son of Thomas W. of Gloucester, clerk, deceased, to Thomas Black, 5 years Barbados, witnessed by his mother's brother, Samuel Dobson, of Wood Street, London, silver wire drawer, both his father and mother being dead; William Hooper, labourer aged 21, son of William Hooper of Taunton, Somerset, labourer, deceased, and his mother being also dead, to John Langley, 5 years Barbados. (LMWB14/190,191).

19 March. The following apprenticed in London: Mary Williamson, daughter of William W. of Deptford, Kent, mariner, deceased, to Edward Coomes, 4 years Jamaica; William Chamberlaine, aged 14, son of William C. of Stroudwater, Gloucestershire, deceased, to Emanuel Windsor of London, merchant, 7 years New York. (LMWB14/191,192).

19 March. The following apprenticed in Bristol: Anne Jayne of Bristol, spinster, to Anthony Swymmer, 4 years Jamaica by *Dragon*. (BR).

20 March. The following apprenticed in Bristol: Judith Lemon of Blagdon, Som, to Robert Kirke, 4 years Jamaica by *Dragon*; John Andrews of Llantwit, Glam, to Robert Kirke, 4 years Jamaica by *Dragon*. (BR).

20 March. The following apprenticed in London: William Mills of London, singleman, labourer aged 26, to James Williams, mariner, 4 years Barbados; Thomas Watts of London, singleman, mariner aged 29, to Thomas Hunt, mariner, 4 years Jamaica, witnessed by William Hodges of Rotherhithe, Surrey, waterman. (LMWB14/192).

21 March 1684. The following apprenticed in London: Thomas Lewis of London, singleman aged 30, sawyer, to John Williams, 4 years Barbados, witnessed by John Rogers of Shoe Lane, London, cooper. (LMWB14/193).

23 March. The following apprenticed in Bristol: Henry Stone of Wells, Som, to Edward Manshipp, 4 years Barbados by *Mary*, Mr. William Cowes; John Stanly of Pidworth [Petworth perhaps intended], Sussex, to same, 4 years Barbados by *Mary*; Edward Isles of Leeds, Yorks, to Robert Kirke, 4 years Jamaica by *Samuel & Mary*. (BR).

25 March. The following apprenticed in London: Christian Atkins, spinster, daughter of Michaell A. of Newcastle, (?Northumberland), brewer, deceased, to Phillip Gower, 4 years Jamaica, witnessed by Sarah Hopper; Elizabeth Towsey, aged 15, daughter of George T. of St. Anne's Lane, Westminster, Middlesex, carpenter, to the same, 4 years Jamaica. Rebecka Ashley, aged 20, spinster, daughter of Jeremiah A. of Benfleet, Essex, tailor, deceased, to Thomas Blake of Redrith, Surrey, mariner, 4 years Barbados; Jubily Harrison, aged 22, daughter of William H. of Shrewsbury, Shropshire, stationer, deceased, to Emanuell Winsor of London, merchant, 4 years New York. (LMWB14/195,196).

26 March. The following apprenticed in London: William Hall, aged 12, son of Alexander H. of Great Baddow, Essex, carpenter, deceased, to Phillip Gower, 9 years Jamaica, with the consent of his mother, Maudlen H. (LMWB14/196).

26 March. The following apprenticed in Bristol: David Williams of Llandenny, Mon, to William Swymmer, 4 years Jamaica by *Samuel & Mary*; John Evans of Winterbourne, Glos, to same, 5 years Jamaica. (BR).

26 March-2 April. Shippers by the *Recovery* of Exeter, Mr. Joseph Parsons, bound from Exeter for Boston, New England: Edward Seaward, Thomas Edmonds, Joseph Sanders. (PRO: E190/963/1).

27 March. The following apprenticed in London: Thomas Russell, singleman aged 23, of Wanstead, Essex, husbandman, to Rowland Buckley Esq., 4 years Barbados; John Twycrosse of Wanstead, Essex, singleman aged 23, to the same to serve as his head groom for 4 years in Barbados, both witnessed by William White, late coachman to Sir Josiah Childe; Richard Thomas, aged 17, son of Richard T. of Bristol, to Joseph Bartholomew of Wapping, Middlesex, mariner, 4 years Jamaica, with the consent of his uncle, James T.; Mary Orrill, aged 19, daughter of Richard O. of Hatton Garden, London, smith, to the same, 4 years Jamaica, with the consent of her father; Elizabeth Morris, daughter of John M. of Ewell, Surrey, bricklayer, deceased, to Phillip Gower, 4 years Jamaica, with the consent of her aunt, Anne Strange. (LMWB14/198,199).

30 March. The following apprenticed in London: John Freeze to John Williams of Lambeth, Surrey, mariner, 4 years Barbados. (LMWB14/203).

31 March. The following apprenticed in London: Waller Williams, son of John W., citizen and merchant of London, deceased, to Thomas Hilton of Port Royal, Jamaica, apothecary, for 7 years, with the consent of his mother, Dorothy W. of Drury Lane, Middlesex; Thomas Morgin, son of William M. of Bishopsgate Street, London, blacksmith, to James Foster of London, mariner, 4 years Montserrat; Mary Shield, aged 23, daughter of John S. of Cotton (*sic*), Yorkshire, to the same, 4 years Montserrat; Elizabeth Ayres, daughter of Edward A. of Launceston, Cornwall, cloth drawer, to Joseph Bartholomew, 4 years Jamaica, with the consent of her aunt, Elizabeth Volereen, wife of Anglebert V. of the Old Artillery Ground, Spitalfields, Middlesex, joiner. (LMWB14/205).

31 March. The following apprenticed in Bristol: George Ridon of Burnham, Som, to Thomas Chester, 4 years Virginia by *Mary*; Francis Toby of Wenvoe, Glam, to same, 4 years Virginia by *Mary*; John Hastings of Huntspill, Som, to Robert Kirke, 4 years Jamaica by *Dragon*; Katherine Bassett of Padsford (*sic*), Glos, to same, 4 years Jamaica by *Dragon*; James Mackdonnell of Cork, Ireland, to Thomas Kirke, 4 years Jamaica by *Dragon*. (BR).

1 April. The following apprenticed in London: Mary Bullock, aged 22, daughter of John B. of Benson, Oxfordshire, carpenter, to Phillip Gore of London, merchant, 4 years Jamaica; Richard Mountford of Kinlett, Shropshire, wheelwright, to Rowland Buckley, 4 years Barbados. (LMWB14/206).

1 April. The following apprenticed in Bristol: Ezekiel Jeanes of Taunton, Som, to William Swymmer, 7 years Jamaica by *Dragon*; James Cutler of Taunton to same, 7 years Jamaica by *Dragon*; Frances Sealy of Taunton to same, 7 years Jamaica by *Dragon*. (BR).

2 April. The following apprenticed in London: William Collins of Kent, carpenter, to James Williams, 4 years Jamaica; Isaiah Brinkwell, son of John B. of Petticoat Lane, Whitechapel, Middlesex, to James Foster, 7 years Montserrat; Frances Eves, daughter of John E. of Epping, Essex, to same, 4 years Montserrat, witnessed by William Morgin of Bishopsgate Street, London, blacksmith, and Ann Balchin, widow, that the relations of the last two were all dead. (LMWB14/209).

4 April. The following apprenticed in London: Elizabeth Ashley, daughter of Richard A. of White Lion Street, St. Giles in the Fields, Middlesex, deceased, Katherine Simmons, daughter of Thomas S. of Mitcham, Surrey, deceased, and Martha Yates, aged 20, daughter of John Y. of White Lion Street, St. Giles in the Fields, Middlesex, to John Pelly of Poole, Dorset, mariner, 4 years Barbados. (LMWB14/211).

6 April. The following apprenticed in London: Nevill Warren, aged 23, and Edward Ledger, aged 28, to John Dikes, mariner, 4 years Barbados; Thomas Barnes, wheelwright aged 27, to John Richardson, mariner, 4 years Pennsylvania. (LMWB14/213).

7 April. The following apprenticed in London: Allan Twiggs, aged 30, to Thomas Saywell, mariner, 4 years Barbados; James Beacham of Stratford, Essex, smith, to Rowland Bulkeley, late of Barbados but now of London, 4 years Barbados; Edward Harrison, aged 30, to John Dikes, mariner, 4 years Barbados. (LMWB14/214).

8 April. The following apprenticed in London: Robert Cotswell, son of Thomas C., baker, deceased, and Thomas Hardy, aged 22, to John Dikes, mariner, 4 & 6 years Barbados; John Baiton, aged 21, to Thomas Saywell, mariner, 5 years Barbados. (LMWB14/214).

9 April. The following apprenticed in London: Mary Pitts, daughter of William P. of Greenwich, Kent, mariner, deceased, to Phillip Gower, to serve him in Jamaica; Sara Browne, aged 21, to James Foster, mariner, 4 years Montserrat. (LMWB14/216).

10 April. The following apprenticed in London: Thomas Smith, aged 23, and Thomas Woodward, aged 26, to Philip Gower, 4 years Barbados; Joseph Shelley, aged 21, to John Moorhead, mariner, 4 years Barbados; Mary

Middleton, aged 21, to the same, 4 years Barbados. Mary Norwood, daughter of Edward N., tinker, deceased, Ellenor Smith, daughter of William S., gardener, deceased, and Elizabeth Fleet, daughter of William F, butcher, deceased, to William Lock, mariner, 4 years Montserrat; Thomas Watts, aged 23, to Robert Forbus, surgeon, 4 years Jamaica. (LMWB14/217,218).

11 April. The following apprenticed in Bristol: Edward Morley of Paxford, Glos, to Robert Kirke, 6 years Jamaica by *Dragon*. (BR).

13 April. The following apprenticed in London: Elizabeth Bray, aged 17, daughter of William B. of London, bricklayer, to Joseph Bartholomew, 4 years Jamaica with the consent of her mother. (LMWB14/219).

13 April. The following apprenticed in Bristol: George Cock of Pridden [Priddy perhaps intended], Som, to Martin Darby, 4 years Jamaica by *Dragon*; William Adsley of Chatham, Kent, to same, 4 years Jamaica by *Dragon*; John Gyles of Christchurch, Mon, to William Paines, 4 years Jamaica by *Dragon*. (BR).

14 April. The following apprenticed in Bristol: Charles Foord of Clippen (*sic*), Som, to Robert Kirke, 4 years Jamaica by *Dragon*. (BR).

14 April. The following apprenticed in London: Joseph Spinnedge of London, gent, singleman aged 24, gent, to John Viccars, mariner, 3 years St. Christopher's, witnessed by Oliver King of Brooks Wharf, (London); Mary Edwards, aged 23, of London, spinster, and Anne Pretty, aged 16, daughter of William P. of Old Windsor, Berkshire, basket maker, deceased, to Joseph Bartholomew, 4 years Jamaica, witnessed by Grace Jordan near the Maypole, St. Olave, Southwark, Surrey; Francis Cherrey, son of Francis C. of Collingtree, Northamptonshire, husbandman, deceased, to William Goring, 5 years Barbados, witnessed by Robert Manning of Execution Dock, Wapping, Middlesex, cooper, his mother being also dead. (LMWB14/219).

16 April. The following apprenticed in London: Thomas Belcher, aged 22, singleman of London, baker, to Philip Gower, 4 years Jamaica, witnessed by Elizabeth Johnson, widow, living in Houndsditch, London. (LMWB14/220).

16 April. The following apprenticed in Bristol: John Clarke of Tring, Herts, to Martin Darby, 4 years Jamaica by *Dragon*. (BR).

18 April. The following apprenticed in Bristol: William Carter of Axbridge, Som, aged 12, to William Clarke, 9 years Jamaica. (BR).

21 April. The following apprenticed in Bristol: Christopher Tayler of Falmouth, Corn, to Martin Darby, 4 years Jamaica by *Dragon*. (BR).

22 April. The following apprenticed in London: Rachaell Bray, aged 18, daughter of Charles B. of Farrington, Berkshire, freemason, deceased, and Jane Jones, daughter of John J. of Denbigh, glover, deceased, to William Lawes of Wapping, Middlesex, mariner, 4 years Jamaica. (LMWB14/221).

24 April. The following apprenticed in London: Edward Atkins, aged 25, son of Thomas A. of Wilden, Bedfordshire, shoemaker, deceased, to John Williams, 4 years Barbados, witnessed by William Chadburne of Knightsbridge, Middlesex, carter; William Hancock, aged 23, singleman, son of Walter H. of Mark, Somerset, farrier, deceased, to the same, 4 years Barbados, witnessed by his friend and countryman, John Child; Edward Holden, aged 16, son of Edward H. of the Minories, London, Customhouse officer, to George Phillips of London, merchant, 4 years Jamaica. (LMWB14/222, 223).

24 April. The following apprenticed in Bristol: Thomas Honywell of Bristol to Thomas Kirke, 4 years Jamaica by *Dragon*. (BR).

25 April. The following apprenticed in Bristol: Elizabeth Meeres of Portskewet, Mon, to Thomas Kirke, 7 years Jamaica by *Dragon*; Mary Warrington of Bristol to Robert Kirke, 4 years Jamaica by *Dragon*. (BR).

27 April. The following apprenticed in Bristol: Samuell Stirt of Langford, Som, to William Beven, 4 years Jamaica by *Joseph*. (BR).

28 April. The following apprenticed in Bristol: Winifred Harris of Trostrey, Mon, to Robert Kirke, 4 years Jamaica. (BR).

28 April. The following apprenticed in London: Charles Mollone and Denny Shaw, Irishmen, to John Moorhead, 4 years Jamaica; Charles Taylor, son of Isaac T. of Redbrooke, Gloucestershire, to the same, 4 years Jamaica; John Burnett to Barnaby Cater, 4 years Barbados; William Ingull, singleman aged 28, of Roding Abbess, Essex, husbandman, Sarah Smart to the same, 4 years Barbados; James Armstrong to the same, 4 years Barbados, witnessed by his sister, Elizabeth A. of Castle Alley, Holborn, London; Abigall Simpson, daughter of David S. of Holborn, London, tallow chandler, deceased, to Thomas Montagu, citizen and clothworker of London, 4 years Jamaica, with the consent of her mother, Sarah Gawes of St. Giles in the Fields, Middlesex; Charles Griffin, son of George G. of Shipston upon Stour, Worcestershire, turner, to George Phillips of Alley Street, Goodmans Fields, London, merchant, 4 years Jamaica. (LMWB14/227, 228).

29 April. The following apprenticed in London: Lavinia Doyley, daughter of Edward D. of Bloomsbury, Middlesex, deceased, to Phillip Gore of London, merchant, 4 years Jamaica, witnessed by William Phillips of Distaff Lane, London, skinner; Thomas Bagley, son of Ralph B., of Fleet Street, London, deceased, to the same, 4 years Jamaica, with the consent of his mother, Mary Dixon, and his father-in-law, John Dixon of Three Fox Court, Long Lane, London, shoemaker; Henry Holmes, son of Henry H. of Shoreditch, Middlesex, deceased, to the same, 4 years Jamaica, same witnesses; William Trimor and John Trimor, sons of John T. of Three Horseshoe Alley, Old Street, London, to Barnaby Cater, 6 & 8 years Barbados, with the consent of their mother, Frances T. (LMWB14/228).

29 April. Deposition by Anthony Dickins of Mortlake, Surrey, gent aged 21, that on 23 October 1684 John Godfrey Esq. of Carolina appointed Andrew Percivall Esq. of Carolina and William Revell and Richard Walters of Barbados, gents, as his attorneys. (LMCD).

30 April. The following apprenticed in Bristol: James White of Cork, Ireland, to Martin Darby, mariner, 4 years Jamaica by *Dragon*. (BR).

30 April. The following apprenticed in London: Thomas Parr, son of Thomas P. of Aldersgate Street, London, confectioner, to Barnaby Cater of London, mariner, 5 years Barbados, with the consent of his mother; Frances Swetnam, daughter of Thomas S. of St. Andrew. Holborn, London, deceased, to the same, 4 years Barbados, with the consent of her father-in-law, Thomas Davies, of Middle Row, Holborn, London, tailor; Elizabeth Reynolds, spinster, daughter of John R. of Cornwall, shoemaker, deceased, to the same, 4 years Barbados, witnessed by her mother, Elizabeth R. of Shoreditch Street, Covent Garden, Middlesex; William Selby, son of Robert S. of Peterborough, Northamptonshire, to John Moorhead, 5 years Jamaica, witnessed by Ambrose Cox of Rosemary Lane, London, victualler. (LMWB14/229).

April. Limited probate of will of Thomas Grendon of Westover, Charles City County, Virginia. (AW).

April. Administration of John Allen the elder of the Island of New Jersey. (AW).

1 May. The following apprenticed in London: John Martin, son of Phillip M. of Sourton, Devon, husbandman, deceased, to John Moorhead, 4 years Jamaica, witnessed by Joseph White of St. Margaret, Westminster, joiner; Charles Parker, lodging with Richard and Mary Wareing, son of Charles P. of Pearsell (Pelsall?) near Eckle (?), Staffordshire, mason, deceased, to the same, 4 years Jamaica, witnessed by Mary, wife of Richard Harding of Tower Ditch, Aldgate, London, victualler; William Palmer at the sign of the Anchor, the Hermitage, Middlesex, to John Williams of Lambeth, Surrey, 4 years Barbados, witnessed by Benjamin Arnall of the Hermitage; Francis Roberts, bricklayer aged 30, son of William R. of Bristol, tailor, to James Williams, 4 years Jamaica, witnessed by John Oakely living near the Catherine Wheel, St. Giles in the Fields, Middlesex, labourer. (LMWB14/229-231).

1 May. The following apprenticed in Bristol: James Jones of St. Davids, Pembroke, to William Beven, 4 years Jamaica by *Dragon*, Mr. Berkin; John Tapling of Newport, Glos, to William Swymmer, 6 years Jamaica by *Dragon*. (BR).

2 May. The following apprenticed in Bristol: Samuel Eales of Wrington, Som, to Thomas Kirke, 4 years Jamaica by *Dragon*; Thomas Jayne of Tidenham, Glos, to same, 4 years Jamaica by *Dragon*; William Fivian of Yeovil, Som, to John Napper, 7 years Jamaica by *Dragon*; Thomas Collins of Bridgewater, Som, to same, 7 years Jamaica by *Dragon*. (BR).

2 May. The following apprenticed in London: Charles Booth, aged 20, son of Charles Booth of Shifnal, Shropshire, to John Moorehead, 4 years Jamaica, witnessed by Elizabeth Hammond of Smithfield, Middlesex; John Murton, aged 22, son of John M. of Kent, deceased, to the same, 4 years Jamaica, witnessed by Thomas Pattman of St. Katherine by the Tower, London, shoemaker; Jane Sutor, aged 21, daughter of William S. of Blackfriars, London, deceased, to Barbara Hopps, 4 years Jamaica, with the consent of her mother, Jane Rosse of Westminster. (LMWB14/232).

4 May. The following apprenticed in London: Diana Bowell, spinster, daughter of Robert B. of Bath and Wells, Somerset, scrivener, deceased, to Thomas Thackster, 4 years New England, witnessed by Richard Williams of Golden Lane, weaver; Phillis Davison of London, spinster aged 22, to John Moorhead, mariner, 4 years Jamaica, witnessed by Mary Cox of Pennington Street, Ratcliffe, Middlesex; Michael Cornish, son of Michael C. of Drury Lane, Middlesex, joiner, deceased, to John Williams, mariner, 4 years Jamaica, witnessed by his master, Peter Cheltenham of Noble Street, joiner, and his guardian and father's executor, Thomas Watson. (LMWB14/236).

4 May. The following apprenticed in Bristol: Walter Summers of Preston, Som, to Thomas Kirke, 4 years Jamaica by *Dragon*; Sarah Cribb of Beer, Dorset, to Robert Kirke, 4 years Jamaica by *Dragon*; James Thomas of Halberton, Devon, to same, 4 years Jamaica by *Dragon*. (BR).

5 May. Deposition by Thomas Poore of London, gent aged 28, that Josiah Wills, merchant, and Sampson Sheafe, both of Boston, New England, became indebted by bond of 3 November 1678 to Samuel Smith of London, merchant. (LMCD).

5 May. The following apprenticed in London: Richard Clarkson, aged 26, to John Moorhead, 4 years Jamaica, witnessed by Joseph Randall of Monmouth Street, St. Giles, Middlesex, joiner; Thomas Gualter, aged 22, to the same, 4 years Jamaica, witnessed by John Rogers of Shoe Lane, London, cooper; William Dixon, aged 22, to Robert Roades, mariner, 4 years Jamaica, witnessed by John Wadley of Deptford, Kent, waterman; Frances Newton, aged 21, whose parents live in Cock Alley, Shoreditch, Middlesex, to the same, 4 years Jamaica. (LMWB14/237).

6 May. The following apprenticed in London: Mary Rice, daughter of Thomas R. of Shoreditch, Middlesex, shoemaker, deceased, to Christopher Eyre, surgeon, 4 years Jamaica, with the consent of her mother; Elizabeth Butterfield, daughter of John B. of Gravesend, Kent, waterman, deceased, to the same, 4 years Jamaica, witnessed by Margaret Bradley of Shadwell Dock, Middlesex; Elizabeth Kibblewight, spinster aged 25, to John Mapleston, mariner, 4 years Jamaica, witnessed by Thomas Price of the Minories, London, shoemaker. (LMWB14/238,240).

6 May. The following apprenticed in Bristol: Richard Crisp of Cheddar, Som, to John Heathfield, 4 years Jamaica by *Samuel & Mary*; Sarah Thomas of Salisbury, [Wilts], to same, 4 years Jamaica by *Samuel & Mary*; Edward Rawlins of Dorsington, Glos, to John Napper, 4 years Jamaica by *Dragon*; John Whoms of Frinton (*sic*), Som, to William Swymmer, 4 years Jamaica by *Dragon*. (BR).

7 May. The following apprenticed in Bristol: Richard Salter of Longley [perhaps Langley, Wilts], to William Swymmer, 4 years Jamaica by *Dragon*. (BR).

7 May. The following apprenticed in London: Mary Pithibridge, widow aged 22, to Joseph Bartholomew, 4 years Jamaica, witnessed by her mother in Nightingale Lane, (London). (LMWB14/241).

8 May. Shipper by the *Mary* of Boston, Mr. James Smith, bound from Plymouth for New England: Thomas Bound. (PRO: E190/1049/15).

8 May. The following apprenticed in London: Joseph Bedding, aged 23, to John Moorhead, mariner, 4 years Jamaica, witnessed by Ambrose Cox at the Blackamoor's Head, Nightingale Lane, London; Nicholas Appleton, son of Ralph A. of Colne, Lancashire, clothier, deceased, to the same, 4 years Jamaica, witnessed by John Okeley at the Catherine Wheel, St. Giles in the Fields, Middlesex. (LMWB14/243).

8 May. Deposition by Josiah Jones of London, notary, that Stephen Burton of Boston, New England, became indebted to John Clagett by bond of 7 October 1678. (LMCD).

8 May. The following apprenticed in Bristol:William Luntley of Haverfordwest, Glos (*sic, but Pembroke probably intended*), to Robert Kirke, 4 years Jamaica by *Dragon*; Meredith Abevan of Glamorganshire to same, 4 years Jamaica by *Dragon*; Abraham Roome of Bristol to same, 4 years Jamaica by *Dragon*. (BR).

9 May. The following apprenticed in Bristol: Daniell Lloyd of Leechfield (*sic*), Devon, to John Napper, 4 years Jamaica; Edward Spooner of Birmingham, Warw, to Robert Kirke, 6 years Jamaica by *Dragon*. (BR).

9-18 May. Shippers by the *Expectation* of Bristol bound from Bristol for New England: William Dan, John Collins, John Batchelor, Robert Alexander. (PRO: E190/1147/2).

13 May. The following apprenticed in London: William Letten, aged 17, son of William L. of London, cooper, deceased, to William Nash, 5 years Jamaica, with the consent of his mother of Blanchapple Court, London(?); Mathew Ansley, son of Mathew A. of Banbury, Oxon, linen draper, deceased, to Thomas Bannister, plasterer, 8 years New England, witnessed by Thomas Harcott, servant to the Banbury carrier. (LMWB14/249, 250).

14 May. The following apprenticed in Bristol: David Jones of Clanorthin (*sic*), Glam, to Robert Kirke, 4 years Jamaica by *Dragon*. (BR).

15 May. Deposition by Thomas Jackson of London, merchant aged 21, that John Grafton of Salem, New England, deceased, became indebted by bond of 18 December 1682 to Thomas Parker, citizen and haberdasher of London. (LMCD).

16 May & 14 December. Deposition by John Bawdon and John Gardner of London that they have appointed Moses Jones and John Loader of Boston, New England, merchants, as their attorneys. (LMCD).

17 May-28 June. Shippers by the *Patience*, Mr. William Smith, bound from London for Pennsylvania: Daniel Wherely, William Royden, Thomas Crundall, William Cox, Thomas Coope, Edward Mann, William Weaver, Edward Hastens, John Brogett, John Howard, Richard Wilson, John Pemble, John Osgood. (PRO: E190/126/5).

18 May. The following apprenticed in London: Sarah Hill, daughter of Isabell Hill of Highgate, Middlesex, widow, to serve Samuell Bradway of Jamaica, merchant, 4 years, witnessed by Mr. Deane Mounteage. (LMWB14/255).

18 May. The following apprenticed in Bristol: Mathew Bagg of Taunton, Som, to Robert Kirke, 4 years Jamaica by *James & Mary*. (BR).

19 May. The following apprenticed in Bristol: Walter Williams of Abergavenny, Mon, to William Bevan, 5 years Jamaica by *Samuel & Mary*; Mary Goodwing of Wrington, Som, to Robert Kirke, 4 years Jamaica by *Samuel & Mary*; John Cooke of Yarpole, Heref, tailor, to William Swymmer, 4 years Jamaica by *Samuel & Mary*. (BR).

19 May. The following apprenticed in London: Griffith Jones, aged 19, son of David J. of Coychurch, Glamorgan, yeoman, deceased, to William Boniface of Bermondsey, Surrey, shipwright, 4 years Jamaica, witnessed by John Burton of St. Mary Magdalene, Bermondsey, Surrey; Thomas Reames, aged 40, son of Thomas R. of Faversham, Kent, farmer, deceased, to the same, 4 years Jamaica. (LMWB14/258).

21 May. Deposition by Thomas Williams, citizen and haberdasher of London, aged 29, that John Givan of London, distiller, signed articles of agreement on 4 June 1673 with Mr. John Bawdon and Mr. John Gardner of London, merchants, for the establishment of a distilling trade in Boston, New England. (LMCD).

21 May. The following apprenticed in Bristol: John King of Langathen (*sic*), Carmarthen, to Robert Kirke, 4 years Jamaica by *Samuel & Mary*; Richard Thorne of London to same, 4 years Jamaica by *Samuel & Mary*. (BR).

22 May. The following apprenticed in London: John Whiteing, blacksmith aged 20 and more, late prisoner in the Wood Street Compter, to serve Rainsford

Waterhouse of London, merchant, for 5 years in Jamaica; Simon James, aged 40, son of Thomas J. of Chepstow, Monmouthshire, husbandman, deceased, and John Collins, aged 20, son of Robert C. of Farrington, Dorset, husbandman, deceased, to Phillip Gower, 4 years Jamaica. (LMWB14/260).

23 May. The following apprenticed in Bristol: Stephen Lewis of Longtown, Heref, to Robert Kirke, 4 years Jamaica by *Samuel & Mary*. (BR).

23 May. Anthony Payne, aged 16, apprenticed from Christ's Hospital to Thomas Aubone, commander of the *Hopewell* bound for Barbados. (CH).

25 May. The following apprenticed in Bristol: Robert English of Frampton upon Severn, Glos, to John Napper, 4 years Jamaica by *Samuel & Mary*. (BR).

26 May. The following apprenticed in London: Ann White, aged 23, daughter of John W. of Lambeth, Surrey, deceased, to serve Samuell Bradway of Jamaica, mariner, witnessed by her aunt, Margaret Biddle of Brick Lane, Whitechapel, Middlesex. (LMWB14/264).

27 May. The following apprenticed in Bristol: Margarett Pumroy of Wincanton, Som, to Thomas Skuse, 4 years Jamaica by *Samuel & Mary*; Trevilian Tayler of Trent, Som, to John Napper, 4 years Jamaica by *Samuel & Mary*. (BR).

28 May. The following apprenticed in Bristol: Samuel Millicheap of Clee St. Margaret, Salop, to Thomas Kirke, 4 years Jamaica by *Samuel & Mary*. (BR).

28 May. The following apprenticed in London: Thomas Johnson, husbandman aged 26, son of Thomas J. of Boylestone, Derbyshire, to Phillip Gower, 4 years Jamaica, witnessed by Mr. Marmaduke Procter; Cipper Ellwood to Thomas Sawell of Southwark, Surrey, mariner, 5 years Jamaica; Thomas Randall, singleman aged 20, son of Thomas R. of Cheshunt, Hertfordshire, deceased, to the same, 4 years Jamaica, witnessed by William Randall of Old Bedlam, London, shoemaker. (LMWB14/264, 270).

28 May-30 July. Shippers by the *Dolphin*, Mr. John Foye, bound from London for New England: Robert Carnoll, Zachary Taylor, John Woodcock, Noah Lawrence, Hugh Horton, William Athurst, James Blackman, Samuel Holland, Robert Key, Charles Dick, Richard Dean, John Butler, Thomas Puckle, Christopher Hamilton, Joshua Spurrier, John Langham, Isaac Ash, Thomas Byfield. (PRO: E190/126/5).

30 May. The following apprenticed in Bristol: Cornelius Collins of Sandwich, Kent, to Thomas Kirke, 4 years Jamaica by *Samuel & Mary*; Joseph Moore of Birmingham, Warw, to same, 4 years Jamaica by *Samuel & Mary*; Lewis Roberts of St. Tiswells (*sic*), Pembroke, to William Swymmer, 5 years Jamaica by *Samuel & Mary*; John Cornish of Taunton, Som, to same, 4 years Jamaica by *Samuel & Mary*; Thomas Wilshire of Chippenham, Wilts, to Robert Kirke, 4 years Jamaica by *Samuel & Mary*. (BR).

May. Probate of will of Davey Wyett of St. Gregory Stoke, Somerset, who died in Carolina, bachelor. (AW).

May. Probate of will of Benjamin Blanchflower of Fitzhead, Somerset, who died in Virginia. (AW).

1 June. The following apprenticed in London: Philip Cappur, son of Harrington C. of London, gent, to Philip Gower, 7 years Jamaica with his father's consent. (LMWB14/265).

1 June. The following apprenticed in Bristol: Griffen Morris Carmorden (*sic*) of Charmorden (*sic*), cooper, to William Beven, 4 years Jamaica by *Samuel & Mary*; Charles Elliott of Dublin, Ireland, to Robert Kirke, 4 years Jamaica by *Samuel & Mary*; Isaac Wilton of Llangibby, Mon, to John Napper, 4 years Jamaica by *Samuel & Mary*; Walter Reece of Langinney (*sic*), Glam, to Joseph Browne, 4 years Jamaica by *Samuel & Mary*. (BR).

2 June. Deposition by Henry Bray of London, glazier aged 40, that Edward Winslow of Boston, New England, became indebted by bond of 24 July 1678 to James Swift of London, merchant, deceased, whose relict and executrix is Sarah Swift. John Martin, citizen and fishmonger of London, aged 55, deposes that John Hunlocke of Boston, New England, became indebted to James Swift by bond signed at the latter's house in Abchurch Lane, London. (LMCD).

2 June. Shipper by the *Richard & Michaell* of New England, Mr. Samuell Hayman, bound from Cowes for Pennsylvania: Abraham Hill. (PRO: E190/834/4).

2 June. The following apprenticed in Bristol: Phillip Weald of East Ham, Essex, to William Swymmer, 4 years Jamaica by *Samuel & Mary*; John Deere of Milverton, Som, to Samuel Alford, 4 years Jamaica by *Samuel & Mary*; Stephen Hide of Somerset to John Napper, 4 years Jamaica by *Samuel & Mary*; Mary Williams of Bristol, spinster, to Henry Davis, 4 years Nevis by *Joseph*; Jane Downe of Little Cheverell, Wilts, to Robert Kirke, 4 years Jamaica by *Samuel & Mary*; Griffith Morgan of Llangellian, Carmarthen, to Joseph Browne, 4 years Jamaica by *Samuel & Mary*. (BR).

5 June. The following apprenticed in London: Richard Gay, aged 24, to Thomas Gay Esq., 4 years Jamaica. (LMWB14/273).

5 June. The following apprenticed in Bristol: John Blake of Bristol to William H——, 4 years Jamaica by *Samuel & Mary*. (BR).

6 June. The following apprenticed in Bristol: Edward Brears of Leicester, wool comber, to Joseph Browne, 4 years Jamaica by *Samuel & Mary*. (BR).

8 June. The following apprenticed in London: Joseph Garrett of London to Thomas Chinery, mariner, 4 years Jamaica; Rebecca Butler, aged 24, of St. Giles in the Fields, Middlesex, spinster, to Thomas Niccolls, gent, 4 years Jamaica with the consent of her mother, Margery B.; Joseph Jones, singleman aged 22, of London, miller, to William Goodman, mariner, 4 years Jamaica, witnessed by Thomas Slade of Rosemary Lane, East Smithfield, London, blacksmith, who knew him when he lived at Monmouth Bridge. (LMWB14/275).

9 June. The following apprenticed in Bristol: George Masters to John ———, 7 years Jamaica. (BR).

10 June. The following apprenticed in Bristol: Susanna Jones of Litton [Linton perhaps intended], Heref, to Robert Kirke, 4 years Jamaica. (BR).

11 June. The following apprenticed in Bristol: Thomas Burkoxe of Humber, Heref, mason & tiler, to Thomas Kirke, 4 years Jamaica; Eliener Burkoxe his wife to same, 4 years Jamaica; Humphrey Lamb, son of Eliener Burkoxe, to same, 8 years Jamaica; Thomas Browne of Whitchurch in Kemeys, Pembroke, to William Swymmer, 4 years Jamaica. (BR).

12 June. The following apprenticed in Bristol: Richard Head of Winchester, [Hants], to Robert Kirke, 4 years Jamaica by *Samuel & Mary*; Robert Milton of Windsor, Berks, to same, 4 years Jamaica by *Samuel & Mary*; Colon Risdon of Exeter, [Devon], gunsmith, to same Jamaica by *Samuel & Mary*, and to be employed as gunsmith. (BR).

12 June. The following apprenticed in London: Daniel Golding, aged 18, tailor, whose mother is dead and father is in Jamaica, to Thomas Sawell, mariner, 4 years Jamaica, witnessed by Isaac Johnson of Moorfields, London. (LMWB14/277).

12 June. Petition of John Clippingdale, master of the *John & Catherine*, for a pass for his ship to proceed to the Caribbean to load and return to England, he having inadvisedly contracted to carry 200 French people to Carolina. (APC).

13 June. The following apprenticed in Bristol: James Watkins of Madley, Heref, to John Napper, 4 years Jamaica by *Samuel & Mary*. (BR).

14-21 June. Shippers by the *Chapman*, Mr. George Clarke, bound from London for Carolina: Francis Hartley, John Ling, John Scott, Thomas Fountaine, John Fountaine, Luke Forster. (PRO: E190/126/5).

15 June. The following apprenticed in Bristol: William Payne of Bristol, silk weaver, to John Napper, 4 years Jamaica by *Samuel & Mary*; Francis Dately of Gloucester, hat maker, to same, 4 years Jamaica by *Samuel & Mary*; Richard Fall of New England to Robert Kirke, 7 years Jamaica by *Samuel & Mary*. (BR).

17 June. The following apprenticed in Bristol: David Williams of Mitchel Troy, Mon, to John Napper, 7 years Jamaica by *Samuel & Mary*; Jacob Boyce of The Lea, Heref, to same, 4 years Jamaica by *Samuel & Mary*. (BR).

19 June. The following apprenticed in Bristol: Robert Dickenson of Bristol to John Napper, 4 years Jamaica by *Samuel & Mary*; Thomas Darke of Studley,

Wilts, husbandman, to John Whiteing, 4 years Jamaica by *Samuel & Mary*. (BR).

22 June. The following apprenticed in Bristol: William Symons of Cam, Glos, broadweaver, to Thomas Kirke, 4 years Jamaica by *Samuel & Mary*; Davies John of Llandarvy, Carmarthen, & now of Cowbridge, Glam, to John Napper, 4 years Jamaica by *Samuel & Mary*. (BR).

25 June-10 July. Shippers by the *Rebecca* of Liverpool, Mr. James Skinner, bound from Liverpool for Pennsylvania: Richard Coulborne, Edmond Butler, James Ratcliffe, Richard Cureton, Jeremy Scott, Thomas Orme, William Worall, John Lytham. (PRO: E190/1346/16).

26 June. Shipper by the *Henry & Francis* of Newcastle, Mr. Richard Hutton, bound from Newcastle for Pennsylvania: said Richard Hutton. (PRO: E190/201/6).

27 June. The following apprenticed in Bristol: Thomas Harris of Gloucestershire, collier, to John Napper, 4 years Jamaica by *Samuel & Mary*; Morgan Lewis of Newent, Mon, to same, 5 years Jamaica; James Bishe of Pensford, Som, to Joseph Browne, 4 years Jamaica by *Samuel & Mary*. (BR).

30 June. The following apprenticed in London: Elizabeth Waters, spinster aged 27, to Robert Thorne, 4 years Virginia, witnessed by Mr. Cole of Ratcliffe Cross, Middlesex, waterman; Elizabeth Woodhouse, spinster, to the same, 4 years Virginia, also witnessed by Mr. Cole; William Noble of Christchurch, Southwark, Surrey, to Richard Heath of London, merchant, 4 years Maryland, with the consent of his mother in Southwark. (LMWB14/305,306).

June. Administration of Mary Knight of Virginia, spinster. (AW).

June. Probate of will of John Wise of Virginia. (AW).

June. Probate of will of John Harwood of St. Leonard, Shoreditch, Middlesex, whose brother, Thomas Harwood, daughter, Elizabeth Sedgwick, and other kin were in New England. (AW).

June. Administration with will of George Derickson of Shadwell, Middlesex, who died on the ship *Unicorne* in Virginia, bachelor. (AW).

1 July. The following apprenticed in Bristol: John Edmonds of Cornwall, Mon (*sic*), to John Napper, 4 years Jamaica; John Carter of Bristol to same, 4 years Jamaica. (BR).

2 July. The following apprenticed in Bristol: Thomas Hilman of Bristol, joiner, to John Napper, 3 years Jamaica; George Glasier of Kingston upon Thames, Surrey, butcher, to same, 4 years Jamaica; Israel Batt of Bishops Hull, Som, to same, 3 years Jamaica. (BR).

3 July. Mr. John Heathcoate to go from London to Gravesend, Kent, to take passage for Jamaica by Captain William Mingham's ship, witnessed by Mr. Barron of Coleman Street, London. (LMWB14/309).

5 July. Pass for John Butcher to go from London to New England on the *Mary* of Boston, Mr. John Gardner, witnessed by Nicholas Strange of Paternoster Row, London, tailor. (LMWB14/317).

5-24 July. Shippers by the *Benedict*, Mr. Francis Partis, bound from London for Virginia: James Wagstaff, Edward Hollings, Thomas Elwys, John Abington, William Osbaldaston. (PRO: E190/126/5).

6 July. The following apprenticed in London: William Whitehead, aged 13, son of Samuel W. of Southwark, Surrey, to Richard Heath, mariner, 8 years Maryland, witnessed by his brother, Samuel W. on behalf of the father and by Gabriel Wilkinson of the Mint, Southwark; Elizabeth Core, aged 17, of London, spinster, to the same, 4 years Maryland with the consent of her mother of Moorfields, London; Henry Windell of London, leather gilder aged 20, to John and Elizabeth Haynes, 4 years Maryland, with the consent of Silvester Bonniface of Soho Fields, Middlesex. (LMWB14/317).

6 July. Newgate prisoners reprieved to be transported to Barbados or Jamaica. London: Elizabeth Ratcliffe, spinster; Robert Todd; William Rawson; Eleanor Mitchell, spinster; John Thompson alias Silke; John Price; John Pilborow; Thomas Saltmarsh; Hugh Jones. Middlesex: Sarah Bell of St. Giles in the Fields, spinster; Julia Pell of the same; William Lippey of the same; Elizabeth Hill of St. Martin in the Fields, widow; Benjamin Crooke of the same; Lionel Fennick of the same; Thomas Parlow of the same; Edward Parlow of the same; John Price of the same; Charles Davis of the same; Nowell Greene of the same; Edward Littleton of the same; Daniel Mackrow of the same; Ralph Watson of Kensington; Richard Maiden of the same; Anne Dye of St. Clement Danes, spinster; Jane Suckloe of the same, spinster; Christopher Orchard of St. Margaret Westminster; Richard James of Willesden; Charles Middleton of St. Andrew Holborn; Mary Cary alias Davis of St. Giles Cripplegate, spinster; Mary Rapier, spinster, alias wife of Joseph Rapier of Stepney; Samuel Wheeler of the same; Thomas Browne of Whitechapel. (PRO: C66/3276/12).

7 July. The following apprenticed in Bristol: William George of Shepton Mallet, Som, cordwainer, to John Napper, 5 years Jamaica by *Samuel & Mary*; Thomas Britton of Marshfield, Glos, tailor, to same, 4 years Jamaica; William Hardwick of Locking, Som, to same, 7 years Jamaica. (BR).

7-26 July. Shippers by the *Advance*, Mr. Samuel Cooper, bound from London for Virginia: Thomas Martin, John Fowles, George Cornish, Phillip Lloyd, Thomas Sands, Ralph Ingram. (PRO: E190/126/5).

8 July. Shipper by the *Adventure*, Mr. Henry Treganey, bound from London for Virginia: James Braines. (PRO: E190/126/5).

8 July. The following convicted before Chief Justice Jefferies at the Court of Oyer and Terminer for Dorset, Somerset and Devon for waging war against the King and sentenced to be transported to the Americas [sentence enrolled on 4 February 1691]: Francis Smith, Richard Green, William Mathews [or Marthers], John Facey, William Greenway, Richard Daniell, Edward Kent, Christopher Jewell, Abraham Thomas, John Baker, Samuel Pinson, Robert Clarke, George Ebdon, Samuel Dolbeare, Benjamin Whicker, John Whicker, John Hitchcott [or Hutchcombe], Thomas Forcey, William Gyles, Joseph Gage, Robert Mullens, Roger Bryant alias Hooper, Charles Broughton, Richard Parke or Parker, John Hayne, John Conant [or Connett], Bernard Lowman, John Heathfield, Edward Venn, Richard Pyne, Thomas Pester, John Sam, Henry Symes, William Deale, William Haynes, Thomas Francklyn, William Guppy, Azarias Pinney, John Bovett, Robert Sandys, Thomas Dolling, Edward Marsh, John Easemond [or Eastmont], John Vincent, Allen England, Robert Vater, John Prew [or Peyce], Oliver Hobbs, Philip Coxe, Peter Ticken, William Clarke, Richard Hoare, Robert Foane [or Fawne], Bartholomew Barge, Daniel Barker [or Parker], Edward Wale, Peter Bagwell, Thomas England, Francis Puckett, William Combden, John Lock, John Gardner, William Lush, John Sturrick, Samuel Paul, Robert White, John Woodward, William Sellwood, John Shinler, Matthew Elliott, John James alias Jeanes, John Sprake, John Bagwell, Abraham Hunt, Christopher Cooper, Edmund [or Edward] Bovett, John Follett, Peter Bird, John Kemplin, William Edwards, James Combes, John Hooper, John Smith, Bernard Periam, Robert Shoesmith, John Phinnimore, Jacob King, John Pope, Thomas Whyttie, William Hayes, Josias [or John] Hart, Walter Blew, John Gardiner, Robert Barge, Edward Lugg, John Furber, John Lyde, Thomas Cutler, Henry Hooper, Elisha Davis, Richard Long [or Lang], Thomas Bray, Thomas Adams, William Goodland, Alexander Townsend, John Hensley, Isaac Kingston, William Row, Hugh Gill, James Glanvill, Henry Wrentmore, Thomas Cross, John Hoare, Tobias Dryer, William Bayly, Richard Masters, John Gibbs, William Spreate, William Crafte [or Crofte], John Hucker Jr., Robert Brodbeare, Joseph Lacey, Nathaniel Musgrave, Thomas Curtis, William Page, Robert Mead, Samuel Saxbee, John Fowler Sr., John Fowler Jr., Richard Perkins, Humphrey Slade, William Venting, William Tapscott, Benjamin Sparke, Bartholomew Davy, Robert Brookes, William Norman, Andrew Boyce, John Grace [or Grise], James Soper, Thomas Howell, Peter Shorland, George Lee, Humphrey Saunders, John Butfield, Samuel Totell, Edward Eves [or Edes], Thomas Debnam, Thomas Hendy, Giles Crane, Walter Phillips, Richard Drake, Matthew Pottle, George Robertson, John Metyard, Henry Hamett, James Gallop [or Golloppe], William Bull, Andrew Nabrick, George Smith, Thomas Markes, Daniel Rutter, Jeremy Poole, John Baker, Robert Pearce, Leonard Staple, Edward Kent, Charles Bennett, John Parsons, John Gibbs, John Bryer, Thomas Gould, John Harty, William Pitts, James Webb, Nicholas Collins Jr., Richard King, Emanuel Merchant, William Merchant, John Slade, Samuel Bond, John Rogers, Bernard Loveridge, Percival Nowis, William Saunders,

William Verryard, Henry Chambers, Thomas Rowsewell, John Crane, Charles Burridge, William Leigh, John Robins, Luke Porter, Thomas Priest, Cornelius Radford, Philip Cheeke, Robert Earle, John Mogridge, Henry Randall, James Maynard, John Culverwell, George Trubbs, Sylvester Lyde, Mathew Cooke, William Phelpes, Elias Lockbeare, Silvester Poole, Thomas Moore, Laurence Priest, William Gould, Henry Priest, Enoch Gould, John Bennett, James Baker, Samuel Mountstephen, Thomas Buglar, Stephen Jeffryes, John Morse, William Scurrier, John England, Jacob Powell, John Godsall, John Andrews, Samuel Sweeting, George Rowsall, Edward Bellamy, William Crosse, Jonas Browne, John Crosse, Christopher Knight, Thomas Meade, John Needs, Thomas Pitt, Robert Richards, Christopher Rowe, Matthew Craft Jr., Richard Peircy, John Miller, George Snow, Samuel Collins, John Cockram, James Cockram, Christopher Hoblyn, John Marwood, John Timothy, Thomas Austin, Moses Osborne, Walter Hacker, Randall Babington, John Knight, Job Hunt, William Woodcock, John Adams, Thomas Pomfrett, James Patten, Thomas Bambury, James Clift, Thomas Chamberlyn, Humphrey Justin, Isaac Dyer, Richard Symons, Richard Stephens, Richard Edgar, Charles Lucas, George Gray, John Bartlett, John Stoodley, Robert Paul, Robert Mitchell, John Gale, Bartholomew Randall, John Rogers, William Haynes, William Bernard, Thomas Matthews, Henry Meyer [or Mayor], John Bressett, Richard Allen, John Poole, John Burges, John Farmer, Richard Backham, Henry Gibbons, John Bason [or Busson], George Nowell, Morris Furse alias Vosse, Humphrey Trump, John Warren, George Warren, Humphrey Pope, Osmond Read, Henry Quant, William Burroughs, William Dawe, William Parker, Robert Sease, Thomas Middleton, James Hillman [or Helman], John Bray, Ambrose Winter, Laurence Hussey, Robert Seaman, Edward Lyde, John Chappell, Robert Easton, John Walter, Thomas Brock, George Mullins, Daniel Pomeroy, Jeremy Atkins, Samuel Boone, John Edwards, George Michill, William Drew, Thomas Dennis, John Avoake, William Tiverton, Joseph Vinicott, John Seymore, John Leaker, Simon Poole, John Wale, Richard Wadham, Stephen Rodway, Francis Came, Michael Powell, John Kerle, Thomas Galhampton, George Carrow [or Garrold], Abraham Pollard, John Budge, William Harvy, William Hall, William Phippen, John Chilcott, Robert Coward, John Cantlebury [or Chantlebury], William Woolridge, William Smith, John Smith, William Mead, George Keel, Edward Councell, Joseph Wickham, John Harris, Justinian Guppy, William Combe, James Baker, Thomas Gamage, William Walter, Robert Teape, Timothy Hawker, William Smith, John Smith, John Clode, Jonas Crosse, John Bragge, William Hutchins, John Mitchell, Edward Vildey, Richard Alwood, James [or Jacob] Adams, Samuel Blackmore, John Browne, James Broughton, Charles Baker, Thomas Bridgwood, John Bright, William Bush, Thomas Browne, Francis Bagwell, John Browne, John Bartlett, James Bickley, Robert Court, John Classey, John Croom, Samuel Clarke, John Clarke, John Collins, John Coleman, Henry Collins, John Cox, Nicholas Cummins, Robert Clarke, Benjamin Keeble [or Cable], Richard Chaplin, Joseph Cowes, John Colebourne, William Coles, Thomas Churchhouse, Peter

Drayton, James Dew, William Dew, Thomas Daniell, Richard Denham, Richard Dyer, Francis Dunning, John Dunning [or Denning], Philip England, Richard Easton, Richard Edgehill, James Ellford, Cornelius Elliott, John Ervin, Thomas Ferris, Edward Ford, Samuel Farmer, Arthur Ford, Walter Freston, Richard Fouracres, John Fowler [or Flower], John Foster, William Feare, Francis Gamlyn [or Gambull], Joseph Gale [or Geale], James German, Thomas Gamlin, Nehemiah Goffe, William Guppy, Edward Goodman, Peter Goodgroome, John Holmes, John Henson, Thomas Hooper, James Herring, Thomas Hutchins, Humphrey Hodge, Robert Hannan, Richard Howells, Edward Harris, Andrew Howard, John Hull, Moses Higwell, Thomas Humphryes, Francis Hales, William Higden, George Halfeyard, Josias Howard, James Harman, Thomas Hill, William Jackson, Joseph Jerman [or Jermyn], John Jones, Richard Jacob, Charles Jones, William Johnson, Samuel Knight, Philip Keeping, William Key, John Lewis, John Larkham, John Lock, John Lawrence, William Locke, John Langford, Paul Morse, Henry Quick, Samuel Farmer, Arthur Ford, Gabriel Smart, Henry Cooke, Isaac Pryor, William Eyres, James Payne, Nicholas Kelford, John Butcher, Christopher Candy, John Bennett, Thomas Archett alias Orchard, Nathaniel Dennick, Humphrey Davyes, Henry Syms, Jonathan Drew, John Jones, Robert Millard, Robert Stuckey, James Field Jr., Isaac Bolster [or Balster], John Hussey, Andrew Staley, John Reynells [or Reignolds], Arthur Everard, Robert Reeves, Robert Norton, Edmund Hurd, Thomas Hurd, Thomas Lawrence, George Hallett, Giles Whittle, John Hart, John Lawrence, James Aymes, Samuel Elworthy, John Holloway, James Hurd, John Field, John Weech, William Staunton, Thomas Salisbury, Thomas Andersey, James Heale [or Heath], Robert Beaton, Simon Chynn, John Portnell, Robert Drower, Eli Holman, James Puttman, Thomas Mills, Joshua Sully, Ambrose Vining, Peter Durden alias Durdant, Joseph Hawker, Thomas Snooke, Henry Snooke, George Harding, William Chynne, Nicholas Davidge, John Hanning, James Moore, Henry Mills, James Wake, John Atwood, William Lacey, Adam Smith, Robert Beale, John Rosseter, Allegan Leversedge, Christopher Gray, John Woodrow, Anthony Woodrow, Roger Cole, Edward Vile, Philip Lacey, William Best, Edward Wilmott, William Prowse, Christopher Masters, Thomas Redbeard, James Best, Robert Best, John Stower, Thomas Laver, John Baker, Edward Vagg, Robert Clarke, Joseph Robins, Thomas Pittard, Timothy Toleman, James Sheppard, James Elford, John Harwood, Roger Channing, Thomas Channing, Charles Pople, John Webb, George Allen, John Palmer, Robert Burridge, John Morley, Humphrey Maundry, James Moody, Thomas Mitchell, Ralph Middleton, William Merrick, Edward Mitchell, John Muttlebury, Joseph Mullins, Roger Mortimer, Nathaniel Weale, Baldwin Parker, William Priest, Andrew Palmer, Silas Phillips, John Pope, Francis Plummer, James Parker, James Peirce, John Palmer, George Russell, Christopher Richards, Henry Rooke, William Read, Alexander Robinson, Argentine Rust, Robert Smith, Robert Slye, William Sheppard, William Smith, William Sherry, John Simon, Francis Savage, William Selfe, George Searle, John Saunders,

Jonathan Sutton, James Smith, John Say, Jonas Say, Richard Spiller, Richard Selwood, Richard Symes, John Skyff, Thomas Tuckey, Richard Tapper, Richard Turner, John Tilley, Lewis Tricks, Peter Welly, Robert Wilkins, Richard Wilcox, John Williams Sr., John Williams Jr., John Worrall, Joseph Warren, Thomas Walter, William Warren, Richard West, Robert Willis, John Watts, Stephen Walsh, Richard Young, Matthew Woodland, Thomas Waggott, Edward Kemp, Hugh Banton, William Clotworthy [or Clatworthy], Thomas Carden, Edward Gilbert, William Greenland, Thomas Goodson, Richard Hooper, Henry Hunt, William Harris, Robert Jennings, Richard Lyne, William Lyneing, John Lush, Charles Mason, Richard Milward [or Miller], Thomas Norton, James Norvill [or Navell], John Stone, Henry Roper, Francis Carter, John Fathers, John Laver, Shadreck Morley, Matthew Pryor, Nicholas Gill, John Hurle, John Lease alias Gamlin, Samuel Denham, John Oram, Robert Haywood [or Heyward], John Helps, John Peircy, Richard Wilmott, Thomas Speed, Robert Drower*, Elias Holman*, John Rosseter*, Allegan Leversedge*, [*these appear to have been entered twice*] Thomas Anderson, Richard Hoare, James Smith, James Baker, John Joliffe, Robert Peirce, John Dods, Henry Pitman, Nathaniel Beaton [or Benton], Peter Cordelion, William Biggs, William Puttman, John Cooke, John Harcombe, John Collins, Nathaniel Standerwick, Richard Dyke, Abraham Gooden, John Brice [or Price], Andrew Holcombe, John Hooper, Thomas Venner, Lawrence Caswell, Thomas Body, James Price, Samuel Davison, Samuel Weaver, Robert Batt, John Gould, John Hooper, John Coake [or Cooke], John Johnson, John Wills [or Willis], Richard Nash alias Lissant, John Foot, John Reeves, John Giles [or Gill] Jr., Edward Rawbone, Thomas Nashion, Richard Wiseman, Thomas Eglin, Richard Snook, Thomas Lockyer, Moses Moore, Samuel Ruddle, John Parsons, Robert Mudford alias Munford, John Bishop, John Sprake, Thomas Viles, David Thomas, William Powell, William Prowse, Robert Sweet Jr., Edward Hody, John Wythyman Jr., Joseph Wytherell, William Sweet, Josiah Gillham, John Partridge, John Bramble, George Butcher, Edward Abbott, Matthew Goodman, Benjamin Trask, Henry Noon, John Key, Philip Smith, John Westlake, William Redbeard, John Dinnett, John Quick, Thomas Saunders, William Chilcott, Thomas Vile, Thomas Doleman [or Coleman], Robert Carter, Edward Halsey, William Brodbeare, Edward Chedzoy, John Hill, Thomas Trott, William Collier, John Parsons, John Rotherton, John Arnold. (PRO: C66/3339/1 & SP (Domestic) James II Vol.1 No.159).

9 July. The following apprenticed in London: William Hill, late grocer of London, to John Pym, merchant, 4 years Jamaica, witnessed by his brother, John H. of Fenchurch Street, London. (LMWB14/321).

9 July-1 September. Shippers by the *Hinde*, Mr. Phineas Hyde, bound from London for Virginia: George Cornish, Daniel Styles, Thomas Buck, Henry Bray. (PRO: E190/126/5).

10 July. The following apprenticed in London: Charles Williams, aged 14, son of Charles W. of St. Giles in the Fields, Middlesex, deceased, to George Couch, mariner, 4 years Barbados, with the consent of his uncle, Edward Williams, of Hampton, Middlesex. (LMWB14/321).

11 July. Thomas Trippett, aged 12, apprenticed from Christ's Hospital to Benjamin Hall, commander of the *William & Mary* bound for Virginia. (CH).

12-18 July. Shippers by the *Samuel*, Mr. Thomas Bowman, bound from London for Virginia: Samuel Groome, John Pym, Robert Bowman, James Dryden, Richard Carter. (PRO: E190/126/5).

14 July. The following apprenticed in London: John Harman and his brother, Matthias Harman, sons of William H. of Hanslope near Stony Stratford, Buckinghamshire, labourer, to John Glover of Barbados, merchant, to serve him 4 years with the consent of their father. (LMWB14/326).

14 July. The following apprenticed in Bristol: Phillipp Smith of Winterbourne, Glos, haberdasher, to Thomas Kirke, 4 years Jamaica; John Mose of Wimborne, Dorset, brick maker, to John Napper, 7 years Jamaica by *Samuel & Mary*. (BR).

15-23 July. Shippers by the *Potomack Merchant*, Mr. Charles Partis, bound from London for Virginia: John Jeffreys, Francis Lee, John Seaman, Thomas Elwes, William Peece, John Bookey, Benjamin Thorowgood. (PRO: E190/126/5).

16 July. The following apprenticed in London: Sarah Kewell, daughter of Thomas K. of Husson (?Hunston), Sussex, yeoman, deceased, to Thomas Allen of the Middle Temple, London, 5 years Virginia, witnessed by Elizabeth Hall. (LMWB14/328).

16 July. The following apprenticed in Bristol: Richard Dymery of Dursley, Glos, broadweaver, to John Napper, 4 years Jamaica. (BR).

16-18 July. Shipper by the *Hopewell*, Mr. John Yokely, bound from London for Virginia: Ralph Ingram. (PRO: E190/126/5).

16 July-6 August. Shippers by the *Antelope* of Liverpool, Mr. George Hoole, bound from Liverpool for Maryland: David Poole, William Kelley, Charles Green. (PRO: E190/1346/16).

17 July. The following apprenticed in London: Anthony Kaine, aged 13, son of Charles K. of Horsley Down, Southwark, Surrey, mariner, deceased, to Richard Stephens of Southwark, carpenter, 7 years Virginia, with the consent of his mother, Judith K. of Horsley Down. (LMWB14/329).

17 July. Shipper by the *Industry*, Mr. Peter Peake, bound from London for Virginia: Christopher Dodsworth. (PRO: E190/126/5).

17-27 July. Shippers by the *Booth*, Mr. Simon Emberley, bound from London for Virginia: Thomas Penning, William Paggen, Thomas Starke, Arthur North. (PRO: E190/126/5).

18 July. The following apprenticed in London: William Rowland, aged 18, son of John R. of Shoreditch, Middlesex, brewer, deceased, to Samuell Woodfield of Wapping, Middlesex, mariner, 5 years Virginia, with the consent of his mother, Rebeccah R. (LMWB14/330).

18 July. The following apprenticed in Bristol: James Morris of South Brent, Devon, husbandman, to Robert Kirke, 4 years Jamaica; Thomas Baggs of Chippenham, Wilts, broadweaver, to Joseph Browne, 4 years Jamaica; John Gunton of Rumerston (*sic*), Suffolk, to same, 4 years Jamaica. (BR).

18 July-4 August. Shippers by the *John*, Mr. Daniell Bradley, bound from London for Virginia: Richard Buller, John Constantine, Edmond Edmonds, Arthur North, Noell Bassano, Henry Turner. (PRO: E190/126/5).

19-23 July. Shippers by the *Edward*, Mr. John Browne, bound from London for Virginia: Edward Lightfoot, Thomas Ellis, Richard Cliffe, John Glover. (PRO: E190/126/5).

20 July. The following apprenticed in London: Jonathan Cole, a poor boy left in the parish of (St. Mary) Colechurch, to Thomas Gadsden of Limehouse, Middlesex, mariner, 7 years Barbados. (LMWB14/331).

20 July. John March, resident of London for seven weeks, to pass to New England to reside. (LMWB14/331).

20 July. The following apprenticed in Bristol: Richard Jones of Ludport [Ludford perhaps intended], Heref, farrier, to John Napper, 4 years Jamaica; William Marcher of Malpas, Chesh, to same, 4 years Jamaica; John Oxenbourd of Streaton (*sic*), Salop, tailor, to same, 4 years Jamaica; William Ellis of Chewstoke, Som, tanner, to same, 4 years Jamaica. (BR).

21 July. The following apprenticed in Bristol: George Pegg of Epping Forest, Essex, butcher, to Robert Kirke, 4 years Jamaica by *Samuel & Mary*; Walter Pitman of Ditcheat, Som, to same, 4 years Jamaica by *Samuel & Mary*; Thomas Drury of Alderchurch (*sic*), Lincs, husbandman, to John Napper, 4 years Jamaica by *Samuel & Mary*; John Dowler of Wicke near Pershore, Worcs, husbandman, to same, 4 years Jamaica by *Samuel & Mary*; Samuel Watkins of Painswick, Glos, to William Swymmer, 4 years Jamaica by *Samuel & Mary*. (BR).

21 July. The following apprenticed in London: Stephen Wells, son of John W. of Suffolk, blacksmith, to Robert Burman of London, merchant, 5 years Maryland, witnessed by his uncle, John Lucas of Ivy Lane, London; James Dennis, son of James D. of Whitechapel, Middlesex, deceased, to the same, 8 years Maryland, with the consent of his mother, Elizabeth Davis of Catherine Wheel Alley, Whitechapel, Middlesex; Joseph Peregois, Frenchman of full age, to the same, 5 years Maryland; John Royston, son of Robert R., to the same, 5 years Maryland, with the consent of his sister in Spitalfields, Middlesex; Jacob Wilbow, son of Eustace W., to the same, 5 years Maryland, witnessed by Ann Guffee of Spitalfields, Middlesex; John Guffy, son of Francis G. of the French Almshouse in Spitalfields, Middlesex, to the same, 5 years Maryland, with the consent of his father and sister; Edward Wootton, son of John W. of the Savoy in the Strand, Middlesex, bellman, to Moses Pullborne of Wapping, Middlesex, mariner, 7 years Virginia, with the consent of his father; Thomas Poyner and Mary Tate, late in the New Prison, to John Furle of Wapping, Middlesex, mariner, 4 years Maryland; Isabella Curtis, spinster of full age, and Mary Lindsey, spinster of full age, to Ernesto Keckerbecke of Whitechapel, Middlesex, mariner, 4 years Virginia; Sarah Bird, spinster of full age, to the same, 4 years Jamaica; Sarah Jones to Phillip Holland of Clerkenwell, Middlesex, mariner, 6 years Maryland, on the recommendation of her nurse, Susannah Marshall of Whitefriars, London. (LMWB14/332-334).

21-26 July. Shippers by the *Christopher*, Mr. Benjamin Hall, bound from London for Virginia: Micajah Perry, John Broadnax. (PRO: E190/126/5).

22 July. The following apprenticed in London: Elizabeth Newton to William Boulton of Wapping, Middlesex, mariner, 4 years Virginia, witnessed by Ann Forger of Wapping, Middlesex; William Pounsey, to Richard Stephens of Redriffe, Surrey, mariner, 8 years Maryland, with the consent of her mother, Alice Pounsey of Shad Town, Southwark, Surrey. (LMWB14/334).

22 July. The following apprenticed in Bristol: Charles Mullocke of Handmore, Flint, tiler, to John Napper, 5 years Jamaica; Walter Power of Kenshore [Kenchester perhaps intended], Heref, to same, 4 years Jamaica; Thomas Lawrence of Trelleck, Mon, to same, 4 years Jamaica; William Stibbins of Dundry, Som, to same, 4 years Jamaica; Thomas Oakey of Worcester, broadweaver, to same, 7 years Jamaica; Francis Lyes of Worcester to same 7 years Jamaica; William Berrey of Newton, Lancs, weaver, to Thomas Kirke, 4 years Jamaica by *Samuel & Mary*. (BR).

22 July-7 August. Shippers by the English-built *Bristol Merchant*, Mr. John Stephens, bound from Bristol for Pennsylvania and Virginia: Richard Crabb, Aron Williams, William Browne, Joseph Hort, Richard Hellier, Charles Harford, John Hassell, Peter Waller, John Bristoll, John Lovell, Richard Fuse, William Fry, Francis Hickman, John Horwood, Robert Lux, John Bristow. (PRO: E190/1147/2).

22 July-30 August. Shippers by the *Blossom*, Mr. Richard Martin, bound from London for New York: Abraham Decosta, David Conguard, Richard Martaine, Godfrey Webster, Anthony Rodregos, George Keth, Robert Bridgman, Thomas Mardin, Thomas Henchman, Michael Russell, George Heath. (PRO: E190/126/5).

23 July. Northern Circuit prisoners reprieved to be transported to Barbados. Lancashire: Adam Hibbart of Jute; William Baldwyn of Caleston; Samuel Felgate of Mitton, yeoman; James Barton of Liscoe St. Michael; Stephen Read of Mitton, yeoman; John Pilkington of Mitton, yeoman; John Richardson of Curedale; John Browne of Great Hoole; Edmond Hankinson of Great Hoole, miller; Robert Molineux of Castle. Yorkshire: Richard Holmes of Adwalton; George Elliott of Helay in Swaledale; Michael Chadwick of Huntslett. (PRO: C66/3276/6).

23 July. The following apprenticed in Bristol: Howell Reece of Bowling Grove, Carmarthen, to Robert Kirke, 5 years Jamaica by *Samuel & Mary*; John Evans of Swansea, Glam, to same, 6 years Jamaica by *Samuel & Mary*; John Jones of Milton, Oxon, clothworker, to John Napper, 4 years Jamaica; Robert Jones of Westerleigh, Glos, husbandman, to same, 4 years Jamaica; William Warner of Worcester, brick maker, to same, 4 years Jamaica. (BR).

23 July. The following apprenticed in London: Peter Matthews to Richard Phillips of London, mariner, 8 years Maryland, witnessed by Sarah Matthews of Shoe Lane, Fleet Street, London; Easter Hescock, widow aged 18, daughter of Richard Pemberton, deceased, to the same, 5 years Maryland, witnessed by her sister, Anne Pemberton of St. Anne's Lane, Aldersgate, London; John Brerey of Otley, Yorkshire, lately disbanded from military service, to Fitzwilliam Lawrence of London, merchant, 4 years Virginia; Ananias Baylee, cordwainer, to Marmaduke Larkin of Queen Street, London, packer, 4 years Maryland, witnessed by Caleb Dutch of Southwark, Surrey, cordwainer; Blanch Glover to the same, 4 years Maryland, witnessed by Hester Whittaker of the Strand, Middlesex, joiner's wife; Humphrey Penhellick to the same, 4 years Maryland, witnessed by his relation, Chichester Young of the Middle Temple, London; Joshua Seecell, goldsmith of full age, to the same, 4 years Maryland. (LMWB14/336-338).

23-27 July. Shippers by the *Lawrell* of Liverpool, Mr. Gilbert Livesley, bound from Liverpool for Maryland: Thomas Johnson, George Robotham. (PRO: E190/1346/16).

24 July. The following apprenticed in London: Katherine Hall to Robert Burman of London, merchant, 4 years Maryland, witnessed by her aunt, Sarah Hall, porter's wife; Thomas Hanley, son of Thomas H. of St. Giles in the Fields, Middlesex, to John and Elizabeth Haines, 4 years Maryland, witnessed by his mother, Dennis H.; Mary Gilbert, daughter of Mary G. of Long Lane, Smithfield, London, to the same, 5 years Maryland. (LMWB14/338).

24 July. The following apprenticed in Bristol: Richard Vickerry of Halberton, Devon, husbandman, to John Napper, 4 years Jamaica; John Gibbs of Worcester, clothworker, to same, 4 years Jamaica. (BR).

25 July. The following apprenticed in Bristol: Miles Hennis of Gloucester, glass maker, to Thomas Whittop, 4 years Maryland by *Society*; Nathaniell Barnett of Barton Regis, Glos, cordwainer, to John Napper, 4 years Jamaica. (BR).

25 July. The following apprenticed in London: Grace Browne, daughter of Richard B. of St. Andrew Holborn, London, to Robert Burman, 5 years Maryland, witnessed by her father and mother, Katherine (Browne); Margaret Harris, aged 22, daughter of John H. of Wotton under Edge, Gloucestershire, currier, to Ernesto Keckerbecke of London, surgeon, 4 years Maryland; William Neviston, son of John N. of Ireland, deceased, to serve Thomas Newbold of Virginia, merchant, 8 years, witnessed by Katherine Young of Whitecross Street, Middlesex. (LMWB14/340, 341).

27 July. The following apprenticed in London: John Cooke, son of Samuel C. of Stepney, Middlesex, weaver, to Ernesto Keckerbecke, surgeon, 5 years Virginia, with the consent of his father of Bethnal Green (*sic*); Thomas Gentleman, son of Evers G., deceased, to Richard Smith, merchant, 7 years Maryland; Robert Thwaites, son of Robert T., deceased, to the same, 7 years Maryland, witnessed by Thomas Gregory of Maiden Lane, Westminster; George Clarly, aged 52, John Jones, aged 22, and Joshua Hartley, aged 21, prisoners in New Prison, to John Seaman, merchant, 4 years Maryland; Elizabeth Hickman, daughter of William H. of London, porter, to John and Elizabeth Haynes, 7 years Maryland, with the consent of her father of Long Lane, London; Margaretta Maria Cooper, spinster aged 22, to the same, 4 years Maryland, witnessed by Mrs. White of Long Lane, London; Elizabeth Midgley, spinster aged 23, to Richard Phillips, grocer, 5 years Maryland, with the consent of her mistress in Bartholomew Lane, London. (LMWB14/343-345).

27 July. The following apprenticed in Bristol: Robert Allen of Trowbridge, Wilts, aged 15, to Peter Griffith, 5 years Jamaica by *Primrose*, Mr. Thomas Lock; Joseph Nash of Worcester, waterman, to John Napper, 4 years Jamaica by *Samuel & Mary*; Joseph Mathews of Manchester, Lancs, weaver, to same, 4 years Jamaica by *Samuel & Mary*; Christopher Harrison of Maxford (*sic*), Chesh, cordwainer, to same, 5 years Jamaica; Katharine Orwell of Christian Malford, Wilts, spinster, to John Shewell, 4 years Jamaica. (BR).

29 July. Shipper by the *Hope* of Boston, Mr. John Clutterbuck, bound from Newcastle for New England: said John Clutterbuck. (PRO: E190/201/6).

29 July. The following apprenticed in London: Robert Carver, son of Richard C. of Westminster, deceased, to John Burton, fellmonger, 9 years Virginia, witnessed by Edward Crosse of Baldwins Gardens, tailor, and John Clarke of the Hermitage, Wapping, Middlesex. (LMWB14/347).

29 July. The following apprenticed in Bristol: Edward Bower of Dursley, Glos, to Alexander Lidden, 4 years Jamaica by *Samuel & Mary*; John West of Westerleigh, Glos, to John Napper, 4 years Jamaica by *Samuel & Mary*;

Thomas Phillipps of Handmore, Flint, glover, to same, 4 years Jamaica; Thomas Cox of Peterstone, Mon, cordwainer, to same, 4 years Jamaica by *Samuel & Mary*. (BR).

30 July. The following apprenticed in London: William Starling, son of William S. of St. John's Street, Middlesex, porter, deceased, to Ernesto Keckerbecke, surgeon, 7 years Virginia, with the consent of his father; Mary Rawlins, daughter of John R. of Bethnal Green, Middlesex, deceased, to John Rafe, ship carpenter, 7 years Virginia, witnessed by Christopher Sandon of the Minories, London, looking glass maker, and her father-in-law, John Towers of Bethnal Green. (LMWB14/348).

30 July-19 September. Shippers by the *Thomas & Susan*, Mr. David Edwards, bound from London for New England: Humphrey Hutchins, James Blackman, Thomas Norman, Joseph Priday, Gerrard Taylor, John Dunton, John Wood, David Edwards, Benjamin Denine, Sefton Long, John Warner, Gilbert Bateman, Samuell Ball, Jacob Sessions, John Degrave, Thomas Weekes. (PRO: E190/126/5).

30 July-5 October. Shippers by the *Priscilla*, Mr. Joseph Mortien, bound from London for New England: Nicholas Gifford, John Dunstone, William Purryer, Daniel Adkins, Joseph Boult, Thomas Goddard, John Lake, Joseph Spurrier, William Fawcett, Jonathan Ashton, Thomas Phipps, John Roper, Thomas Wheeler, James Rolleston, Samuel Allen, Samuel Hart. (PRO: E190/126/5, 129/1).

31 July. Shipper by the *Hopewell* of Boston, Mr. Samuell Vesey, bound from Hull for New England: Ferdinando Hacker. (PRO: E190/328/1).

31 July. The following apprenticed in London: Francis Lloyd, son of Francis L. of Pershore, Worcestershire, gardener, deceased, to Ernesto Keckerbecke, 7 years Virginia, witnessed by Mary Hardy near Whitechapel church, Middlesex; James Garnet, son of John G. of St. Botolph Bishopsgate, London, deceased, to Richard Solley, mariner, 7 years Maryland, with the consent of his mother of St. John's Street near Spitalfields, Middlesex. (LMWB 14/349,350).

31 July. The following apprenticed in Bristol: John Lidard of Ruckeley (*sic*), Wilts, tailor, to John Napper, 4 years Jamaica by *Samuel & Mary*. (BR).

1 August. The following apprenticed in London: Thomas Vaughan, son of John V. of Deptford, Kent, farmer, deceased, to John Cooper, surgeon, 4 years Barbados, witnessed by Thomas Cooper of Southwark, Surrey, cabinet maker. (LMWB14/352).

1 August. The following apprenticed in Bristol: Gabriell Waters of Newport, Mon, cooper, to Joseph Saunders, 4 years Virginia by *Society*; Mary Adams of Thornbury, Glos, to Thomas Lock, 4 years Jamaica by *Primrose*; Jeffery Ellis of Potterne near Devizes, Wilts, clothier, to Thomas Philpott, 4 years

Jamaica by *Samuel & Mary*; William Carter of Conistreet (*sic*), brick maker, to John Napper, 4 years Jamaica; John Lodge of Dymoke, Glos, miller, to same, 4 years Jamaica. (BR).

1-5 August. Shipper by the *Elizabeth*, Mr. Timothy Keyser, bound from London for Virginia: William Paggen. (PRO: E190/126/5).

2-6 August. Shippers by the *John's Adventure*, Mr. John Francis, bound from London for Maryland: Henry Ewer, Thomas Potter, Hannah Smith. (PRO: E190/126/5).

2-16 August. Shippers by the *Mary*, Mr. John Gardner, bound from London for New England: Nicholas Day, Peter Hudson, John Freeman, John Ive. (PRO: E190/126/5).

3 August. The following apprenticed at the request of the French Church in London to Marmaduke Larkin to serve in Jamaica: Moyse Aubier of London, mason; John Baron of London, shoemaker; Daniel Bance, son of John B. of London, buttonmaker, deceased; Henry Reynault of London, labourer, and Elizabeth his wife, and Francois, Elizabeth and Marie, their children; Pierre Viellet of London, labourer. (LMWB14/353).

3 August. The following apprenticed in London: Jean Fleuriott of London, labourer, Louise his wife, and their sons Jean Fleuriott, aged 14, and Daniel Fleuriott, aged 15; Andre Le Doux, Frenchman lately dismissed from the Army; Jean Bauldry and Elizabeth his wife, and Jeanne Le Tort, French Protestants, to Marmaduke Larkin, 4 years Maryland; Elizabeth Bayly to the same, 4 years Maryland, her husband (?Ananias Baylee) having already been bound; Thomas Herve of London, labourer aged 19, to the same, 4 years Maryland; John Underwood, aged 15 and more, son of George U. of St. Giles in the Fields, Middlesex, victualler, deceased, to Edward Brooke, grocer, 5 years Maryland, with the consent of his mother, Anne Wetheridge of the Barber's Pole near the Almshouses by the church of St. Giles in the Fields; Jonathan Eakins, aged 14, son of Richard E. of London, deceased, to Nicholas Smith, 6 years Virginia. (LMWB14/354).

3 August. The following apprenticed in Bristol: Thomas Barlam of Handmore, Flint, to John Reade, 4 years Maryland or Virginia by *Society*; Richard Weeks alias Davis of Sherston, Wilts, to Joseph Saunders, merchant, 4 years Virginia by *Society*; William Griffith of Carmarthen, husbandman, to John Napper, 4 years Jamaica by *Samuel & Mary*. (BR).

4-8 August. Shippers by the *Adventure*, Mr. Peregrine Browne, bound from London for Virginia: Clement Plumsted, Arthur Bayly, John Plomer. (PRO: E190/126/5).

4-17 August. Shippers by the *James*, Mr. John Cox, bound from Weymouth for Virginia: James Gould, David Arbuthnot. (PRO: E190/887/5).

4 August-3 October. Shippers by the *Culpepper*, Mr. Christopher Morgan, bound from London for Virginia: Francis Wheeler, Micajah Perry. (PRO: E190/126/5).

5 August. The following apprenticed in London: Andrew Anderson, aged 21, of Selkirk, Scotland, and Ambrose Hogg, aged 20, of Urcester (?Uttoxeter), Staffordshire, labourer, soldiers discharged from the Army, to Robert Burman, merchant, 4 years Maryland. (LMWB14/355).

5 August. The following apprenticed in Bristol: William Hill of Ross, Heref, glover, to Philip Skrine, 4 years Jamaica by *Samuel & Mary*; Thomas Browne of Ross, aged 15, to same, 4 years Jamaica by *Samuel & Mary*. (BR).

5 August. Shipper by the *Windmill* of Plymouth, Mr. James Trefry, bound from Plymouth for Virginia: John Rogers. (PRO: E190/1049/15).

5-26 August. Shippers by the *Greyhound*, Mr. Joseph Macey, bound from London for Pennsylvania: Thomas Plowman, John Grey, Hugh Lamb, Thomas Budd, Joseph Carpenter, John West, William Woodbe, John Spire, Clement Plumsted, Thomas Goddard. (PRO: E190/126/5).

6 August. The following apprenticed in Bristol: Richard James, son of Thomas and Elizabeth James of High Littleton, Som, to Samuel ——, 7 years Barbados; Richard Mitchell of Lanhevett (*sic*), Corn, tailor, to Thomas Kirke, 4 years Jamaica by *Providence*; John Dew of Kidlington, Oxon, to John Napper, 4 years Jamaica by *Providence*; John Saunders of Whitchurch, Salop, tailor, to same, 5 years Jamaica; Thomas Raby of Low Layton, Surrey (*sic but Essex perhaps intended*), to same, 4 years Jamaica. (BR).

6 August. The following apprenticed in London: Richard Bridgman of Hertford to James Harding, 7 years Jamaica, with the consent of his father; William Morgan, singleman of London, shoemaker, to Marmaduke Larkin, 4 years Maryland, witnessed by Edmond Burnham of Bishopsgate Street, London. (LMWB14/357).

7 August. The following apprenticed in Bristol: William Stathorne of Bristol, waterman, to Richard Harris, 4 years Jamaica by *Samuel & Mary*; Thomas Merry of Frampton upon Severn, Glos, broadweaver, to John Shewell, 4 years Virginia by *Conqueror*; John England of Frampton upon Severn, to same, 4 years Virginia. (BR).

8 August. The following apprenticed in Bristol: Tobias Sprior of Henton near Norton St. Philip, Som, broadweaver, to Gabriell Cox, 4 years Jamaica by *Samuel & Mary*; James Cathew of St. Telom (*sic*), Corn, husbandman, to John Napper, 4 years Jamaica by *Samuel & Mary*. (BR).

10 August. The following apprenticed in Bristol: Phillipp Pope of Bristol, tobacconist, to William Swymmer, 4 years Jamaica by *Primrose*; James Goddin of Leominster, Heref, tinker, to John Napper, 4 years Jamaica; Richard Blower of Handmore, Flint, cook, to same, 4 years Jamaica. (BR).

10 August. The following apprenticed in London: Thomas Davies, apprentice of Richard Stephens of London, mariner, since 1684, son of Richard D. of Bristol, merchant, deceased, bound for 3 years (no destination shown); Mary Newman, aged 22, daughter of William N. of Sundridge, Kent, gent, deceased, to John Tanner of Stepney, Middlesex, merchant, 4 years Maryland, witnessed by Sibilla Dunn of Ludgate Hill, London, widow, on behalf of the mother; Mary Jones, spinster aged 28, daughter of Robert Jones near Ruthin, Denbighshire, mason, to the same, 4 years Virginia; Mary Pippin, aged 21, daughter of John P. of the Strand, Middlesex, trass? maker, deceased, to the same, 4 years Maryland, witnessed by her aunt, Mary Letherland; Mary Baker, spinster, daughter of Gyles B. of Yarmouth, Norfolk, tailor, deceased, to serve Henry Hawkins of Maryland, tanner, 4 years; Jane Harris, daughter of Elizabeth, now wife of Abraham Medcalfe of St. Thomas, Southwark, Surrey, and with their consent bound to the same, 10 years Maryland. (LMWB14/361, 362).

10 August. Shippers by the *Elizabeth* of Exeter, Mr. John Williams, bound from Exeter for Virginia: William Harris, Joshua Sanders. (PRO: E190/963/1).

10-20 August. Shippers by the *Globe*, Mr. Bartholomew Watts, bound from London for Virginia: John Thorpe, Degory Marshall. (PRO: E190/126/5).

11 August. The following apprenticed in Bristol: Ann Besor of Bristol, spinster, to William Holden, 4 years Virginia by *Bristol Merchant*. (BR).

11 August. The following apprenticed in London: Jane Edwards, spinster, daughter of John E. of Thame, Oxfordshire, shoemaker, deceased, and Thomas Harris, singleman aged 28, son of John H. of Bristol, distiller, deceased, to Ernesto Keckerbecke, 4 years Virginia; Solomon Burch, son of John B. of Guildford, Surrey, clerk, deceased, to serve John Payne of Maryland 13 years, with the consent of his mother, Elizabeth B.; Anne Brookes, aged 20, daughter of Richard B. of Stamford, Lincolnshire, baker, deceased, to the same, 4 years Maryland, witnessed by Katherine Freizby of Shoe Lane, London, widow; John Harbottle, son of John H. of St. Giles in the Fields, Middlesex, brewer's clerk, to Roger Newman of London, merchant, 7 years Maryland, with the consent of his father. Martha Shimpson, spinster aged 18, daughter of Richard S. of Norwich, butcher, deceased, to the same, 5 years Virginia; Mary Foster, spinster aged 19, daughter of Robert F. of Norwich, maltster, deceased, to the same, 5 years Maryland. (LMWB14/363,364).

12 August. The following apprenticed in London: Barbarah Whitefield, widow without children, aged 26, daughter of Edward Scholler of the Orkneys in Scotland, husbandman, deceased, to Ernesto Keckerbecke of Whitechapel, Middlesex, surgeon, 4 years Virginia. (LMWB14/365).

12 August-16 September. Shippers by the *Globe*, Mr. Anthony Pryor, bound from London for Maryland: Samuel Groome, John Cary, James Wagstaff, William Farmer, Strangeways Mudd, Richard Booth, John Brett, Ralph Ingram. (PRO: E190/126/5).

13 August. The following apprenticed in London: Thomas Daughton, son of Thomas D. of Nightingale Lane, East Smithfield, Middlesex, tobacco pipe maker, to Daniell Claphamson of Whitechapel, Middlesex, mariner, 8 years Maryland. (LMWB14/366).

14 August. The following apprenticed in London: John Taylor, singleman aged 22, son of Richard T. of Holcombe Regis, Devon, yeoman, to Myles Staples of Stepney, Middlesex, mariner, 4 years Maryland; Thomas Eades, singleman aged 20, and Elizabeth Eades, spinster aged 23, children of John E. of Wellesbourne Munford, Warwickshire, gent, deceased, to the same, 4 years Maryland. (LMWB14/369).

14 August. The following apprenticed in Bristol: Joan Pittman of Bristol to Richard ——, 4 years Jamaica by *Samuel & Mary*. (BR).

15 August. The following apprenticed in Bristol: Susanna Hollard of Hullock (*sic*), Som, to John Read, 4 years Virginia by *Great Society*, said John Read Mr; John Raby of Pensford, Som, felt maker, to John Hort, 4 years Virginia or Maryland by *Great Society*; Mary Evans of Cardiff, Glam, to John Read, 4 years Virginia or Maryland by *Society*; Nathan Eeff of Usk, Mon, to William Clarke, 4 years Virginia by *Society*. (BR).

15-19 August. Shippers by the *Elizabeth*, Mr. Roger Newham, bound from London for Virginia: Richard Butler, Gabriel Grunwin, John Constantine, Ralph Ingram, Jonathan Mathews, Richard Cox. (PRO: E190/126/5).

16 August-14 October. Shippers by the *Jefferies*, Mr. Thomas Arnold, bound from London for Virginia: John Handford, Amy Carpenter, Robert Stepney, Thomas Potter, Robert Bristow, Robert Wessey, John Gosling, Thomas Nutting, Edmond Littlepage. (PRO: E190/126/5, 129/1).

17 August. The following apprenticed in London: Christian Skarfe, aged 19, daughter of John S. of Hundwell near Whitby, Yorkshire, to Silvester Wooton of Wapping, Middlesex, mariner, 4 years Maryland, witnessed by her sister, Mary S., servant near Execution Dock; Elizabeth Vincent, widow aged 40, to Robert Morris of Ratcliffe, Middlesex, mariner, 4 years Barbados, witnessed by Robert Musgrove near Clements Inn Gate, London, porter. (LMWB14/370).

17-25 August. Shippers by the *Concord* of Bristol, Mr. John Shewell, bound from Bristol for Virginia: William Swymer, James Harris, George Atwood, Symon Hurle, John Pearson. (PRO: E190/1147/2).

17-28 August. Shippers by the *Society* of Bristol, Mr. John Reade, bound from Bristol for Virginia: William Clearke, Nathaniell Day, Richard Champneys, William Hellier. (PRO: E190/1147/2).

18 August. The following apprenticed in London: Richard Bennett and Edward Bennett, sons of Richard B. of Fleet Lane, St. Sepulchre, London, to serve Robert Howard of Jamaica 4 & 5 years; Elizabeth Browne to the same to serve

4 years, with the consent of her sister, Elizabeth Townsend, wife of John Townsend; William Long, son of Humphrey L. of St. Martin in the Fields, Middlesex, feltmaker, deceased, to Francis Partis of Wapping, Middlesex, mariner, 8 years Maryland, witnessed by his mother, Ann Kittson; Mary Taylor, aged 19, daughter of John T. of New Inn Yard, Shoreditch, Middlesex, to John Parrick of Shadwell, Middlesex, mariner, 5 years Maryland, witnessed by her said father and mother, Anne Taylor. (LMWB14/371, 372).

18 August. Deposition by Gabriel Briscoe of London, surgeon aged 20, that he delivered a cask of brandy to the storehouse of Richard Heath on Severn River, Maryland, on behalf of John Clares. (LMCD).

18 August. The following apprenticed in Bristol: Jenkins Llewellin of Neath, Glam, yeoman, to Jane Pope, 4 years Virginia or Maryland by *Society*. (BR).

18 August-13 September. Shippers by the *White Fox*, Mr. George Purvis, bound from London for Virginia: Francis Lee, Micajah Perry, John Jeffreys, Roger Burrough. (PRO: E190/126/5).

19 August. The following apprenticed in Bristol: Olliver Freeman of Bromsgrove, Worcs, to Joseph Saunders, 4 years Virginia or Maryland by *Society*; John Bryan of Rochester, Kent, husbandman, to William Swymmer, 4 years Virginia or Maryland by *Society*. (BR).

19-25 August. Shippers by the *Richard* of Bristol, Mr. Phillip Patch and Mr. Alexander Pinney, bound from Bristol for Virginia: Peter Waddinge, Charles Pope. (PRO: E190/1147/2).

20 August. Shippers by the *Content* of Plymouth, Mr. Mathew Hutchins, bound from Plymouth for Virginia: George Lapthorne, Amos Doidge. (PRO: E190/1049/15).

20 August. The following apprenticed in London: Henry Gray, singleman aged 20, son of William G. of Durham, to Robert Thorne of Ratcliffe, Middlesex, mariner, 4 years Virginia, witnessed by Jeffrey Barnes of Ratcliffe Cross, waterman; Katherine Daintye, daughter of William D., to Nathaniel Anderton to be assigned to John Abbington, 5 years Maryland, witnessed by her mother, Ellenor D.; Susan Pepper, daughter of John P. of Walnut Tree Alley, Southwark, Surrey, to Anthony Dent of Southwark, surgeon, 5 years Virginia, witnessed by her aunt, Adine Woodburne; Mary Woodburne, aged 17, daughter of Thomas W. of Southwark, porter, to the same, 4 years Virginia, witnessed by her mother Adine W. of Walnut Tree Alley, Southwark. (LMWB14/374).

20 August. The following apprenticed in Bristol: Elizabeth Nicholls of Bristol, spinster, to Zacharia Smith, 4 years Virginia or Maryland by *Patience*. (BR).

20-23 August. Shippers by the *Stephen*, Mr. Sebastian Ginge, bound from London for Virginia: Robert Bristow, Micajah Perry, Samuel Lamb, George Corbin, John Brett. (PRO: E190/126/5).

21 August. The following apprenticed in Bristol: Margarett Napp of Brockley, Som, to John Read, 4 years Virginia or Maryland by *Great Society*; Edith Napp of Brockley to same, 4 years Virginia or Maryland by *Society*. (BR).

21 August. The following apprenticed in London: Edward Hickman, aged 21, son of Edward H. of Newport Pagnell, Buckinghamshire, corn chandler, deceased, to serve Thomas Newbold of Maryland, merchant, 5 years, witnessed by his father-in-law, John Wilson of Little Old Bailey, London, cutler. (LMWB14/375).

21-25 August. Shippers by the *Isaac & Sarah*, Mr. Thomas Griffin, bound from London for Maryland: Abraham Wild, Thomas Parker. (PRO: E190/126/5).

22 August. The following apprenticed in London: John Goffe, son of Roger G. of St. Paul, Shadwell, Middlesex, butcher, deceased, to serve Edmond Sandiford of Barbados, merchant, 5 years, witnessed by his mother, Bennett Pickford, and father-in-law, William Pickford, near the new church at Shadwell. (LMWB14/375).

24 August. The following apprenticed in London: Benjamin Hamond, aged 26, and Moses James, singleman without father or mother, aged 21, to William Holliday, tallow chandler, 5 years Maryland, witnessed by Lucy Dushmay of Quaker Street, Spitalfields; Nicholas White, son of John W. of London, ostler, to the same, 10 years Maryland, with the consent of his father and mother. (LMWB14/378).

25 August. The following apprenticed in London: Roger Glassebrooke, singleman aged 27, lately discharged as a soldier, to John Marden, mariner, 4 years Virginia; Elizabeth Warner, spinster aged 21, to John Burford, mariner, 5 years Maryland; Elizabeth Pawling, spinster aged 21, to the same, 4 years Maryland, witnessed by Sarah Read of Meeting House Alley, Wapping, Middlesex. (LMWB14/379).

25 August. The following apprenticed in Bristol: John Roberts of Gloucester, hosier, to John Cart of Tewkesbury, Glos, 5 years Pennsylvania by *[Bristol] Factor* or *Unicorn*; Frances Rayes of Bristol, spinster, to John Blewett, mariner, 4 years Barbados by *Prosperity*, Mr. Samuel Legg. (BR).

25 August. Abell Barnard, aged 17, apprenticed from Christ's Hospital to Thomas Gardner, commander of the *Fortune* bound for Virginia. (CH).

25 August. Order by the Lord Mayor of London in respect of the complaint lodged by Arthur Partridge, waterman, that his daughter, Elizabeth Partridge, aged 17, was taken as a servant to Virginia without his consent by Matthew Trim of Wapping Wall, Middlesex, mariner. It is found that Elizabeth Partridge embarked voluntarily at Gravesend and was not of good repute. Trim is ordered to pay the cost of her return passage and to recompense the father. (LMWB 14).

26 August. Midland Circuit prisoners reprieved to be transported to America. Derbyshire: Thomas Melborne. Leicestershire: Mary Ellis, widow, John Hodgson. Lincolnshire: Elizabeth Browne alias Boswell, William Elderkin, Thomas Coxon, Nathaniel Ian. Northamptonshire: Matthew Yelverton of Peterborough, John Evans. Nottinghamshire: George Handley, Richard Plomer, Francis Shallett. Warwickshire: Christopher Johnson, Thomas Smith, John Smith, Robert Sweetman, George Taylor, William Wood. (PRO: C66/3276/1).

26 August. The following apprenticed in Bristol: William Tapley of West Chester, cooper, to Robert Kirke, 4 years Jamaica by *Lamb*; Ralph Fabyn of London to William Stoakes, 4 years Barbados by *New England Merchant*; William Raynolls of Usk, Mon, to Joseph Saunders, 4 years Virginia by *Society*. (BR).

26 August. The following apprenticed in London: Joseph Eastop, singleman, son of John E. of London, glover, deceased, to Mathew Dawson, mariner, 5 years Maryland, witnessed by Richard Eaton of Spitalfields, Middlesex. (LMWB14/381).

26-31 August. Shippers by the *John* of Exeter, Mr. John Lyle, bound from Exeter for Virginia: Thomas Chrispin, Stephen Shower, William Wootten. (PRO: E190/963/1).

26 August-2 September. Shippers by the *Mary*, Mr. John Harris, bound from London for Virginia: Mary Vanswaring, Stephen Bearcroft, Richard Chandler, James Braines, Thomas Andrews, Anthony Sedgwick. (PRO: E190/126/5).

26 August-10 September. Shippers by the *Richard*, Mr. Thomas Jowles, bound from London for New England: Erasmus [or Eros] Norwich, Samuel Dawes, Anthony Farmer, William Whitcombe, John Parsons, Peter Greene, Lawrence Baskervile, William Shirley, Thomas Jolls, William Scowen. (PRO: E190/126/5).

27 August. The following apprenticed in London: Richard Smith, aged 14, to Thomas Broomer, merchant, 8 years Virginia, with the consent of his mother Anne S. at Cripplegate; John Fort, son of Richard F. of Aldgate, Middlesex, husbandman, deceased, to Elizabeth Norris, 4 years Maryland, with the consent of his mother Jane F. near the King's Slaughterhouse, Swedeland Street, widow, and of his master Josiah Wallop of New Fleet Street, Spitalfields; Richmond Smith, son of John S. of Leather Lane, Holborn, Middlesex, cloth drawer, to the same, 4 years Maryland, with the consent of his father. (LMWB14/382).

27 August. Deposition by Robert Vesey, citizen and merchant tailor of London, aged 55, that he received no account from his brother, Richard Vesey, deceased, of sales made by him, and has appointed Joseph Ford of Warwicksqueak Bay, James River, Virginia, planter, as his attorney for goods sent by the *Constant Mary*, Mr. Edward Rhodes, in September 1683, and by the *Jeffrey*, Mr. Thomas Arnall, in September 1684. (LMCD).

27 August. Shippers by the *Exeter Merchant*, Mr. James Friend, bound from Exeter for Virginia: Thomas Smith, Robert Dabinet. (PRO: E190/963/1).

27 August-1 September. Shippers by the *Bridget*, Mr. Richard Journall, bound from London for New England: Thomas Hunt, William Pate, William Wrayford, John Seller, Thomas Tryon, Thomas Heath, John Hull, Samuel Ball, John Gyles, Thomas Elliott, James Deanes, Christopher Merriweather, John Halsey, William Hibbert, William Withers, Phillip Newman, John Fentzell, Lewin Robins, Richard Yerbury. (PRO: E190/126/5).

27 August-9 September. Shippers by the *Zebulon*, Mr. Nicholas Goodridge, bound from London for Virginia: Ann Dedman, Jane Metcalfe, Thomas Wasleigh, Henry Dandy, Thomas Ellis. (PRO: E190/126/5).

27 August-6 October. Shippers by the *Baltimore*, Mr. James Conway, bound from London for Virginia: Sarah Garfoot, Edward Round, Anthony Cornwell, John Constantine. (PRO: E190/126/5, 129/1).

28 August. The following apprenticed in London: Benjamin Stephens, aged 14, to Richard Smith, merchant, 9 years Maryland, with the consent of his mother Abigail Stephens of Clare Market, Middlesex, widow; Elizabeth Dunckley, spinster aged 22, to George Wilson, mariner, 4 years Maryland; Joseph Jennings, son of Bartholomew J. of Southwark, Surrey, deceased, to John Tanner, mariner, 8 years Maryland, with the consent of his mother Joane J. of Houndsditch, London; John Vangoodinghouse, aged 17, to Elizabeth Norris, 4 years Maryland, witnessed by his master, John Hayley, and by his nearest relation, Samuel Goodinghouse, his father and mother being dead; Richard Fowkes, aged 32, to George Phillips, merchant, 4 years Jamaica, witnessed by Rice Thomas of Catherine Wheel Alley, Whitechapel, Middlesex. (LMWB14/383, 384).

28 August-14 October. Shippers by the *Hannah*, Mr. Ambrose [or Anthony] Gester, bound from London for Virginia: James Fowles, Ang. Crow, William Farmer, John Pelling, Peter Mortimer, William Jaggard, John Plover, Grace Edwards, William Everard, John Hobbs. (PRO: E190/126/5, 129/1).

29 August. The following apprenticed in London: Martha Morrice, spinster aged 19 without father or mother, to serve her uncle, Francis Morrice of Bloomsbury, Middlesex, sawyer, in Virginia; Peter Burnley, singleman aged 21, to George Norris, mariner, 4 years Maryland, witnessed by Enoch Bemister of Canterbury, Kent. (LMWB14/384, 385).

29-31 August. Shippers by the *Barbados Merchant* of Liverpool, Mr. Cuthbert Sharples, bound from Liverpool for Virginia: Isaac Holroid, William Houghton, Henry Withington, Joseph Withington. (PRO: E190/1346/16).

29 August-2 September. Shipper by the *Vine* of Liverpool, Mr. Thomas Preeson, bound from Liverpool for Maryland: William Preeson. (PRO: E190/1346/16).

31 August. The following apprenticed in London: John Atkins, aged 12, son of Robert A. of London, periwig maker, deceased, to Henry Robinson, merchant, 10 years Maryland, with the consent of his mother Elizabeth Robinson; Elizabeth Brown, daughter of Thomas B. of London, corn chandler, deceased, to Richard Feverson, 4 years Maryland, with the consent of her mother Dorothy Lugg of St. Olave, Southwark, Surrey; Elizabeth James of Wapping, Middlesex, spinster, to Jeremiah Resler, mariner, 5 years Maryland, witnessed by Deborah Boynton of Meeting House Alley, Wapping, Middlesex. (LMWB14/386, 387).

31 August. The following apprenticed in Bristol: Mary Knowles of St. Phillipps, [Bristol], spinster, to Zachary Smith, 4 years Virginia or Maryland by *Patience*. (BR).

31 August. Shipper by the *Margaret* of Jersey, Mr. James Leicester(?), bound from Dartmouth for New England: John Browne. (PRO: E190/963/3).

August. Administration of Elizabeth Peele of Maryland, spinster. (AW).

August. Probate of will of Catherine Northcote of Hoxton, Middlesex, widow, whose kinswoman, Joane Poole, and her son, Theophilus Poole, were in Boston, New England. (AW).

August. Probate of will of Robert Lancaster of Bristol, who died at sea, surgeon, having goods in Virginia. (AW).

August. Probate of will of Richard Cary of Barbados, merchant, who had goods in New York. (AW).

1 September. The following apprenticed in London: Adam Van Rike, son of John Jacobson Van Rike of Stockholm, Sweden, deceased, to Thomas Tooley, merchant, 4 years Jamaica; Thomas Price, aged 13, son of Thomas P., labourer, to Richard Smith Jr., merchant, 9 years Maryland. (LMWB14/387).

1-7 September. Shipper by the *America* of Liverpool, Mr. Jonathan Livesley, bound from Liverpool for Maryland: Silvanus Richmond. (PRO: E190/1346/16).

2 September. Deposition by John Clarke, citizen and tallow chandler of London, aged 44, and Penelope Ingles, aged 42, wife of Jonathan Ingles, citizen and pewterer of London, that Edward Osborne of St. Paul, Covent Garden, Middlesex, pewterer, and Elizabeth his wife, sold a plantation of 800 acres in Stafford, Virginia, to Nicholas Hayward, now aged over 21. Edward Osborne as the only son of Henry Osborne of London, wine cooper, deceased, who was the only brother of Robert Osborne of Stafford County, Virginia, is therefore heir to his said uncle, Robert Osborne. Elizabeth, wife of Edward Osborne, agrees to assigning the lease of 27 August 1685 to Nicholas Hayward and she and her husband have appointed as their attorneys Captain George Brent, Samuel Hayward and Sigismund Massey. (LMCD).

2 September. Shippers by the *Martha & Mary* of Fowey, Mr. John Rodden, bound from Plymouth for Virginia: John Phillips, John Veale. (PRO: E190/1049/15).

2-7 September. Shippers by the *Morning Star* of Liverpool, Mr. Thomas Heyes, bound from Liverpool for Virginia: James Doe, James Prescott. (PRO: E190/1346/16).

3 September. The following apprenticed in Bristol: Thomas Thurston, son of Thomas Thurston of Twineing (*sic*), Wilts, to Joshua Cart of Tewkesbury, saddler, 10 years Pennsylvania by *[Bristol] Factor*; Owen Morgan of Cardiganshire to Abraham Moore, 4 years Virginia or Maryland. (BR).

3 September. The following apprenticed in London: Robert Tomlin, son of John T. of Southwark, Surrey, hatter, deceased, to John Baxter, mariner, 7 years Maryland, with the consent of his mother Elizabeth Oakes; John Clark, son of John C. of Bocking, Essex, woolcomber, deceased, to George Elkin, 7 years Jamaica, witnessed by the overseers of the poor in Bocking; Margaret Hilton of London, spinster aged 28, to Thomas Ridder, tailor, 4 years Maryland, witnessed on behalf of her brother by Katherine, wife of said Thomas Ridder. (LMWB14/389).

3 September. Shipper by the *James* of Bristol, Mr. William Dymer, bound from Bristol for Virginia: James Dymer. (PRO: E190/1147/2).

3 September. Shipper by the *Mary* of Dartmouth, Mr. Elliott, bound from Dartmouth for Virginia: Henry Lane. (PRO: E190/963/3).

3 September. Shipper by the *Jonathan* of Exeter, Mr. George Bass, bound from Exeter for Virginia: George Tuthill. (PRO: E190/963/1).

3 September. Shippers by the *Agreement* of Plymouth, Mr. Isaac Blake, bound from Plymouth for Virginia: James Blackborne, Peter Row. (PRO: E190/1049/15).

3-18 September. Shippers by the *Reserve* of Liverpool, Mr. George Hardman, bound from Liverpool for Virginia: Christopher Moore, James Vanbobart, Nathaniell Bacon. (PRO: E190/1346/16).

3 September-18 October. Shippers by the *Samuel & Thomas*, Mr. Thomas Jenner, bound from London for New England: John Lyons, Thomas Sadd, Anthony [or Arthur] Burren, Richard Fawcett, Edward Lamb, William Blackwell, Thomas Cartwright, John Pym, Josiah Dewey, Andrew Kendrick, Elizabeth Norman, Bennett Swaine, Richard Sprigg, Francis Comins, Joseph

Alford, Andrew Belcher, Thomas Lane, John Adams, Joseph Hardy, Samuel Holden, John Mason. (PRO: E190/126/5, 129/1).

4 September. The following apprenticed in London: Margaret McGregor (MackGrigger) of Wapping, Middlesex, spinster, to John Pye, mariner, 4 years Virginia, witnessed by Margaret Toulloch of the Hermitage, Wapping, Middlesex; Henry Cook, aged 19, son of John C. of St. Giles in the Fields, Middlesex, butcher, deceased, to Solomon Niccolls, mariner, 4 years Maryland, witnessed by his sister Elizabeth C. of Cow Cross. (LMWB14/389,390).

4 September. The following apprenticed in Bristol: Robert Thomas of Virginia to George Colwell, 4 years Jamaica by *Lamb*; Katherine Pert of Sandwich, Kent, singlewoman, to Thomas Coyner, 4 years Virginia by *Patience*; Francis Creech of Devizes, Wilts, to Philip Cooke, 4 years Virginia by *James*. (BR).

4 September-12 January. Shippers by the *Augustine*, Mr. Zachary Taylor, bound from London for Virginia: John Hartford, Clement Plumsted, Samuel Young, James Wagstaff, William Wilks, Edward Calthorp, Daniell Sheriffe, Stephen Laming, Jacob Camfield, Abraham Ewer, Samuell Hart, William Hiccocks. (PRO: E190/126/5, 129/1, 139/1).

4 September-24 October. Shippers by the *Content*, Mr. William Hill, bound from London for Virginia: Thomas Mayleigh, Richard Cliff, James Galwith, James Thomson, Richard Seale. (PRO: E190/126/5, 129/1).

4 September-7 November. Shippers by the *Recovery*, Mr. Thomas Hasted, bound from London for Virginia: Thomas Ellis, Roger Burroughs, Thomas Weekes, James Sheret. (PRO: E190/126/5, 129/1).

5 September. The following apprenticed in London: Laurence Russell, French boy aged 14, to John Boullay, 7 years Maryland, witnessed by his cousin, Abraham Michaell, Frenchman of Dorset Street, Spitalfields, Middlesex; Peter Ellett, son of Thomas E. of London, deceased, to Mary Rosewell, widow, 3 years Jamaica. (LMWB14/391).

5-10 September. Shippers by the *Liverpool Merchant*, Mr. Joseph Marchall, bound from Liverpool for Maryland: Thomas Clayton, John Crowther. (PRO: E190/1346/16).

5-23 September. Shippers by the *Alexander* of Bristol, Mr. Francis Fisher, bound from Bristol for Virginia: Robert Curtis, Thomas Lowe, Michaell Wharton, James Thomas, William Shephard, James Wallis, Richard Ditty. (PRO: E190/1147/2).

7 September. Shipper by the *Submission* of Liverpool bound from Liverpool for Virginia: James Settle. (PRO: E190/1346/16).

7 September. The following apprenticed in London: John Schoale, singleman aged 25, son of Ralph S. of Wakefield, Yorkshire, to George Elwes of Milk Street, London, 4 years Maryland. (LMWB14/392).

8 September. The following apprenticed in London: Thomas Ayres, aged 11, son of Thomas A. of Drury Lane, Middlesex, soldier, to serve John Bare of Jamaica, merchant, 10 years, with the consent of his mother Elizabeth A.; George Fawne, aged 10, son of George F. of Guernsey, woolcomber, to the same, 12 years Jamaica, his father and mother being unable to support him. (LMWB14/393).

8 September. The following apprenticed in Bristol: Randolph Garland of Rolstone (*sic*), Chesh, to Abraham Hooke, 4 years Maryland or Virginia by *Comfort*; Margaret Evans of Thornbury, Glos, to John Bruton, 4 years Virginia by *Comfort*. (BR).

8 September. Shipper by the *David* of Plymouth, Mr. Joseph Cornish, bound from Plymouth for Virginia: David Teage, William Chafe. (PRO: E190/1049/15).

9 September. The following apprenticed in Bristol: Elizabeth Williams of Crickhowell, Brecknock, spinster, to Abraham Hooke, 4 years Maryland by *Comfort*. (BR).

9 September. The following apprenticed in London: Isaack Holton, aged 16, son of Richard H. of London, linen draper, deceased, to his father-in-law, Robert White, 5 years Barbados, with the consent of his mother Mary White. (LMWB14/393).

9-16 September. Shippers by the *Comfort* of Bristol, Mr. Abraham Hooke, bound from Bristol for Virginia: Michaell Pope, John Wraxell, Charles Harford, Elizabeth Bruton, Ralph Smith, Richard Prigg, Anthony Alderson, Joshua Carte. (PRO: E190/1147/2).

9-23 September. Shippers by the *Genoa Merchant*, Mr. John Wynn, bound from London for Virginia: William Fenton, John Crofts, Jacob Bridgwater, Thomas Cudden, John Cooper, Micajah Perry, William Penn. (PRO: E190/126/5).

10 September. The following apprenticed in London: Henry Perry, son of Henry P. of Hackney, Middlesex, butcher, deceased, to John Dangerfield of Hackney, Middlesex, 5 years Virginia, with the consent of his mother Susanna P. (LMWB14/393).

10-14 September. Shippers by the *Friendship* of Bristol bound from Bristol for Virginia: Thomas Whittop, Jacob Beale, Phillip Berrow, John Kinge. (PRO: E190/1147/2).

11 September. Shipper by the *Seaflower* of Poole, Mr. Robert Bennett, bound from Poole for Virginia: George Lewen. (PRO: E190/887/3).

11-22 September. Shippers by the *Dolphin* of Poole, Mr. John Christian, bound from Poole for Maryland: Henry Lawes, Robert Bennett. (PRO: E190/887/3).

12 September. Shipper by the *Lyon* of Plymouth, Mr. James Blight, bound from Plymouth for Virginia: Phillip Pentire. (PRO: E190/1049/15).

12-25 September. Shippers by the *Daniell & Elizabeth* of Plymouth, Mr. William Ginnes, bound from Plymouth for Virginia: George Orchard, John Woods, Peter Newchurch. (PRO: E190/1049/15).

13-25 September. Shippers by the *William & Thomas*, Mr. Christopher Eveling, bound from London for Maryland: Richard Atkinson, Isaac Goddard, Robert Davis, William Thompson, John Thompson, Charles Lord Baltimore, Richard Channey. (PRO: E190/126/5).

14 September. The following apprenticed in London: Mary Maddin, daughter of James M. of St. Giles in the Fields, Middlesex, to John Rudds of Ipswich, Suffolk, mariner, 4 years Virginia, witnessed by Elizabeth Hopton of St. Giles; Robert Mapletoft, son of Peter M. of Stamford, Lincolnshire, grocer, to John Meares of Stamford, 4 years Barbados, witnessed by his uncle John Hill of Doctors Commons, proctor; James Drunckcourt, son of Anthony D. of Quaker Street, Spitalfields, Middlesex, reed maker, to Samuel Roberts of Limehouse, Middlesex, mariner, 7 years Maryland, witnessed by his said father and his mother, Susanna D.; John Crosse, son of Leonard C. of Newgate Street, London, to Margaret Chelderey of Newgate Street to be assigned to serve Michael Tauny of Maryland 9 years, with the consent of his mother Jane C.; Jonathan Whitehead, son of Ninian W. of Southwark, Surrey, barber, to William Serocold of Poplar, Middlesex, gent, 6 years Virginia, witnessed by his mother-in-law, Jane [blank]. (LMWB14/400).

14 September. The following apprenticed in Bristol: Sarah Knapp, daughter of William Knapp, rector of Brockley, Som, to Philip Cooke, mariner, 5 years Virginia by *Comfort*. (BR).

15 September. The following apprenticed in London: Abraham Deshawns, son of James D. of Germany, to Augustin Boullay of Petticoat Lane, London, 7 years Maryland, witnessed by William Aller of Bishopsgate Street, London, weaver. (LMWB14/401).

15-26 September. Shippers by the *Mary*, Mr. Edward Roads, bound from London for Virginia: Robert Fairman, Vincent Goddard, Abraham Molque, Daniel Winch, Andrew Neagles. (PRO: E190/126/5).

16 September. The following apprenticed in London: Hester Speed, widow, whose husband was killed in Monmouth's rebellion, to Robert Lurting, of Stepney, Middlesex, mariner, 5 years Virginia, witnessed by Mary Johnson of St. Olave, Southwark, lacemaker; Sarah Hackley, spinster, sister of Thomas H. of Clement's Lane, London, barber, to Thomas Jackson of London, merchant, 4 years Virginia; Deborah Smith, spinster, daughter of Edward S. of Cambridge, deceased, to William Flood of Wapping, Middlesex, mariner, 4 years Jamaica, witnessed by her uncle, Henry Moss of the Royal Exchange, London, victualler; Jane Williams of Newgate Street, London, to John Clarke of Warwick Lane, London, 4 years Virginia, witnessed by her mother, Lyddy W.; Isaac Guille, his wife Anna and his children Magdalene, John, Peter, Stephen and Joseph G., to serve Augustine Boullay of Virginia, merchant. (LMWB14/402-404).

16 September. The following apprenticed in Bristol: David Miles of Llantrissant, Glam, to Lewis Markham, 4 years Virginia by *John*; Dorothy Price of Carmarthen Town to same, 4 years Virginia by *John*; Elizabeth Norton of Cardiff, Glam, to same, 6 years Virginia by *John*; Katherine Thomas of Llandedgouth (*sic*) to same, 4 years Virginia by *John*; Reece Edwards of Llanquidd (*sic*) to same, 4 years Virginia by *John*; Morgan Llewis of Fagan (*sic*) to same, 6 years Virginia by *John*. (BR).

16 September-10 October. Shippers by the *Unicorn* of Bristol, Mr. John Teague, bound from Bristol for Virginia and Pennsylvania: Joshua Carte, William Collett, Edmond Tucker, William Symmons, Mary Bradwell, Mary Townsend, Henry Lackye, Elizabeth Price, Thomas Hobbs, Hannah Smith, Uzzell Bussell, William Richards, Mary Whitehead, Richard Mellichap, Roger Drew, Francis Ballard, John Dudlestone, Joseph Paule, John Persons, Anthony Alderson, Thomas Martin, William Harmer, Thomas Dickenson, Abraham Elton, Mathew Andrews, Edward Lone, William Smith, Francis Smith, Phillip Deninge, John Grant, Phillip Tyler, Roger Adams, Edward Pocknell, Thomas Freeman, Phillip Cooke. (PRO: E190/1147/2).

18 September. The following apprenticed in London: Mary Hill of London, spinster, to Samuel Claphamson of Whitechapel, Middlesex, merchant, 4 years Virginia, witnessed by Lawrence Davenport near the Three Inkhorns in Houndsditch, London, joiner; Sarah Garnett, spinster aged 20, to the same, 4 years Virginia, witnessed by Elizabeth Cramp of Houndsditch, London. (LMWB14/405).

18 September. The following apprenticed in Bristol: Sarah Winsloe of Bristol, widow, late servant at Bull Tavern, to Philip Cooke, 4 years Virginia by *John*; Mary Bryan, daughter of Andrew Bryan of Blagdon, Som, yeoman deceased, to same, 4 years Virginia. (BR).

18-24 September. Shippers by the *Charles* of Plymouth, Mr. Edward Blagg, bound from Plymouth for Virginia: Charles Evans, Thomas Lanyon, William Davis, Thomas Shipard. (PRO: E190/1049/15).

19 September. The following apprenticed in Bristol: Thomas Rackes of London, cooper, to Jerome Plowman, 18 months Virginia by *Lamb*; Joseph Morgan of Llanwortis, Brecknock, to Joshua Cart, 6 years Pennsylvania by *Unicorn*, Capt. Cooper; Benjamin Morgan of Llanwortis to same, 6 years Pennsylvania by *Unicorn*; Elizabeth Phillpotts of Bristol, spinster, to same, 6 years Pennsylvania by *Unicorn*. (BR).

19 September. The following apprenticed in London: Joseph Powell and his sister, Elizabeth Powell, of Whitechapel, Middlesex, to Samuel Roberts of

Limehouse, Middlesex, mariner, 9 & 8 years Virginia, with the consent of the mother Elizabeth P., basket woman. (LMWB14/409).

20 September. Letter from the King to the Governors of Plantations. Having shown mercy to the late rebels by ordering their transportation, we instruct that those sent to Jamaica shall serve their masters for ten years without being allowed to redeem themselves. [*But see revocation of 9 January 1690*]. (CSPC).

21 September. The following apprenticed in London: Samuel Hacon, aged 12, to William Flood, mariner, 8 years Jamaica, witnessed by his sister Mary, wife of Anthony Porter; John Blaton, aged 15, to John Clarke, mariner, 5 years Virginia, witnessed by his aunt, Ellinor Wilson of Newgate, London; John Prime, aged 20, son of John P. of Ratcliffe Highway, Middlesex, to Anthony Gester, 4 years Virginia, with the consent of his said father; Alice Wild, spinster aged 20, to the same, 4 years Virginia, witnessed by Robert Young of Ratcliffe Highway. (LMWB14/406).

22 September. The following apprenticed in London: Elizabeth Green, aged 16, spinster, to John Rudds, mariner, 4 years Virginia, with the consent of her father, Peter G. of the Minories, London, weaver; Mary Clarke, spinster aged 18, to the same, 4 years Virginia, with the consent of her mother Margaret Gillam of Duke Street, St. James, coachman (*sic*). (LMWB14/410).

22 September-5 October. Shippers by the *Diligence* of Liverpool, Mr. William Trenew, bound from Liverpool for Virginia: George Robotham, Leonard Andrews, Peter Atherton, Thomas Sandiford. (PRO: E190/1346/16).

23 September. The following apprenticed in London: John Godfrey, singleman aged 23, to his cousin William Nash, merchant, 4 years Jamaica; Elizabeth Ansell, spinster aged 17, to Peter Febber, mariner, 4 years Virginia, witnessed by Prudence Ansell of Mile End, Stepney, Middlesex, widow; Richard Connor, singleman aged 21, to John Paine, merchant, 4 years Maryland. (LMWB14/413, 414)

23-24 September. Shippers by the *Swallow* of Liverpool bound from Liverpool for Virginia: William Jones, Thomas Withington, Daniell Forster. (PRO: E190/1346/16).

23 September-4 October. Shippers by the *Dispatch*, Mr. Henry Patrick, bound from London for Pennsylvania: D—— Wright, George Hutchinson, William Rackstro, William Woodbe, Christopher Williams, Thomas Mayleigh, Digery Marshall, John Guy, Francis Chamberlin, Thomas Budd, Richard Witpan, John Pemble, Mathew Chitty, Simon Lewis. (PRO: E190/126/5).

24 September. Shipper by the *Susanna* of Plymouth, Mr. James Bartlett, bound from Plymouth for Virginia: John Kenall. (PRO: E190/1049/15).

24 September-6 October. Shippers by the *Diligence* of Exeter, Mr. Walter Lyle, bound from Exeter for Virginia: Charles Cunningham, Barnard Goddard,

William Elston, John Pike, Tristram Bartlett, Endymion Walker, Samuel Axe, Mary Peal. (PRO: E190/963/1).

25 September. The following apprenticed in London: Patrick Udall, aged 20, to Daniell Hill, mariner, 5 years Maryland, witnessed by Mr. Knightly of Hackney, Middlesex. (LMWB14/417).

25 September. Rebels convicted after Monmouth's rebellion to be transported from Dorchester Gaol by James Kendall to Barbados.

John Minifie; Joseph Hallett; William Bennett; John Markes; Robert Shale; Roger French; Nicholas Warren; William Foode; John Truren.

And the following transported from Weymouth by the *Happy Return* of Poole, Capt. Roger Wadham, to Barbados and sold there in January 1686: Edward Luther; John Downe; Benjamin Crow; Thomas Bennett; John Fisher; John Manning; Robert Lambert; William Madford; Richard Keech; George Plumley; Thomas Allen; John (Thomas) Reason; John Speering; Mathew Porter; Robert Spurway; John Edwards; John Hardiman; Bernard Bryant; John White (Witte); James Pomeroy; Thomas Hoare; Peter Row; Elias Stephens; John Bridle; Thomas Parsons; Nicholas Palmer; Thomas Williams; Mathew Hutchins; Nicholas Smith; Emanuel Collins; Roger Hobbs; John Guy; Nathaniel Webber; Edward Morton; James Salter; John Loveridge; Ambrose Ashford; William Wills; John Prior; William Tucker; William Browne; Samuel Lawrence; John Hutchins; William Clarke; John Browne; Robert Burridge; Henry Tucker; Thomas Burridge; Robert Burridge; John Allambridge; Thomas Cornelius; Humphrey Moulton; Edward Willmott; William Williams; Thomas Marshall; Richard Paul; Joseph Paul; Hugh Willmott; John Johnson; Richard Allen; John Pitts; Stephen Gamage; Andrew Rapson; William Cozens; Thomas Townsend; Jasper Diamond; Thomas Gregory; John Allen; Robert Hellier; Thomas Allen; Thomas Best; Thomas Hellier; John Long; John Mitchell; John Madders; Thomas Hallett; John Alston; George Macey; John Penny; Charles Strong; William Saunders; James Spence; John Wilson; Edward Adams; John Adams; Arthur Lush; John Hutchins; Thomas Bovett; James Fowler; John White; Francis Langbridge. (PRO: SP31/1/159).

26 September. The following apprenticed in London: William Rayner, aged 17, to John Clarke, mariner, 4 years Virginia, witnessed by his brother-in-law, Charles Povey in the Strand, Middlesex; Elizabeth Brett, aged 12, to John Drapentier, engraver, 8 years Virginia, with the consent of her mother Elizabeth B. of Whitefriars, London; John Binion, aged 14, to the same, engraver, 7 years Virginia, with the consent of his mother Elizabeth B. of Whitefriars, London. (LMWB14/418,419).

26 September. Rebels convicted after Monmouth's rebellion and to be transported by Jerome Nepho to Barbados.

From Dorchester Gaol: Abraham Thomas; John Baker; George Ebdon; Benjamin Whicker; John Whicker; Roger Bryant; Bernard Lowman; Azarias Pinney (taken away to Bristol to be transported); Peter Tickin; Walter Osborne; Peter Bagwell. And the following embarked on the *Betty* of London, Mr. James May, at Weymouth to be transported to Barbados: John Moggeridge; Thomas Quick; Nicholas Salter; Francis Smith; Richard Green; William Madder (died on shore in Barbados); John Facey; William Greenway (died on passage); Richard Daniel; Peter Kent; Christopher Jewell; Samuel Pinson; Robert Clarke; Samuel Dolbeare; John Hitchcock; Thomas Forcey; William Gyles; Joseph Gage (Gaich); Robert Mullens; Charles Broughton; John Kemplin; Richard Parker; John Hayne; John Connett; John Heathfield; Edward Venn (died on passage); Richard Pine; Thomas Pestor; John Sam; Henry Sims; William Deale; William Hayne; Thomas Franklyn; William Guppy (died on passage); John Bovett; Robert Sandy; Thomas Dolling; Edward Marsh; John Eastmond; John Vincent; Allen England; Robert Vawter (died on passage); John Prew; Oliver Hobbs; Philip Cox (died on passage); William Clarke; Richard Hoare; Robert Fowne; Daniel Parker.

From Exeter Gaol: John Scamplyn; Walter Teape. And the following embarked on the *Betty* of London, Mr. James May, at Weymouth to be transported to Barbados: Abraham Hunt; Christopher Cooper; Edmond Bovett; John Follett; Peter Bird (died on passage).

From Wells: John Joliffe; Nathaniel Beaton; John Cooke; Richard Dyke; John Denham; John Mead; John Brice; Thomas Chyn; Robert Batt; John Hooper; John Goald; John Johnson. And the following embarked on the *Betty* of London, Mr. James May, at Weymouth to be transported to Barbados: Robert Pearce; John Dodds; Henry Pitman; Peter Cordelion; William Biggs; William Pitman; John Harcombe; John Collins; Nathaniel Standerwick; Abraham Gooden; Andrew Holcombe; Thomas Venner (died on passage); Lawrence Caswell; Samuel Weaver; John Cooke; John Willis (died on passage); Richard Nash alias Lyllant; John Foot; John Reeves; John Gill Jr. Also a servant woman, Susannah Toleman.

All the above, with the exception of those who died, were landed in Barbados in January 1686 and allocated to masters there. (PRO: SP31/1/159).

26 September-1 October. Shippers by the *Rainbow* of Bristol, Mr. John Holbrooke, bound from Bristol for Virginia: William Crabb, John Reade. (PRO: E190/1147/2).

26 September-24 October. Shippers by the *Love*, Mr. Samuell Phillips, bound from London for Maryland: Henry Braye, Edward Sleeth, George Cornish, John Payne. (PRO: E190/126/5).

27 September-7 January. Shippers by the *Concord*, Mr. William Jeffries, bound from London for Virginia: George Baker, William Bradford, Nowell Bassano,

William Evans, Mathew Malraven (*sic*), James Harris, Thomas Nelson, William Maslin. (PRO: E190/126/5, 139/1).

28 September. The following apprenticed in London: Hannah Smith, spinster, to John Paine, mariner, 4 years Maryland, with the consent of her cousin Mary Harridge of Rotherhithe, Surrey; William Sismore, son of Michael S. of London, deceased, to Francis and Elizabeth Weeks, 9 years Virginia. (LMWB14/420).

29 September. The following apprenticed in London: Samuel Gold, son of John G. of London, cabinet maker, deceased, to George Doughty, mariner, 5 years Virginia, with the consent of his mother; Mary Gun of London, spinster aged 18, to James and Margaret Skinner, 4 years Jamaica, with the consent of her brother John G. and Mr. Lockett of Tuttle Street, Westminster, pipe maker; Elizabeth Farwell, spinster, to the same, 4 years Jamaica; Mary Button of London, spinster aged 20, to Thomas Niccolls, 4 years Jamaica, with the consent of her brother-in-law Henry Conyers of St. Martin's Lane, London. (LMWB14/420).

30 September. The following apprenticed in London: Samuel Hodges, aged 12, son of John H., deceased, to John Drapentier, 8 years Virginia, with the consent of his mother; Philadelphia Weston to go to Virginia as servant of Lady Berkeley. (LMWB14/420).

30 September. The following apprenticed in Bristol: Thomas Powell of Raglan, Mon, husbandman, to Philip Cooke, 4 years Virginia by *John*. (BR).

30 September-8 October. Shippers by the *Lyon* of Liverpool, Mr. John Crompton, bound from Liverpool for Virginia: Edmond Croston, Robert Seacome, Ellen Jones. (PRO: E190/1346/16).

30 September-18 December. Shippers by the *Mary*, Mr. Richard Tibbott, bound from London for Virginia: Micajah Perry, Thomas Starke, Henry Turner, Richard Cox, Thomas Salter, John Done. (PRO: E190/126/5, 129/1).

1 October. The following apprenticed in London: John Norris of London, porter aged 26, to John Cutcher, 4 years Jamaica, with the consent of his mother, Eleanor N. (LMWB14/420).

1 October. Shipper by the *Constant*, Mr. Thomas Smith, bound from London for Virginia: Walter Hope. (PRO: E190/129/1).

1-5 October. Shippers by the *Averilla*, Mr. Abraham Wild, bound from London for Maryland: John Gresham, Micajah Perry. (PRO: E190/129/1).

1-8 October. Shippers by the *Friendship* of Liverpool, Mr. Henry Marten, bound from Liverpool for Virginia: William Moss, Robert Crosman, Cornelius Maddock, John Lawson, Silvanus Richmond, Richard Ratlife, Elner Hall, William D—house. (PRO: E190/1346/16).

1-9 October. Shippers by the *Barnaby*, Mr. Matthew Ryder, bound from London for Virginia: Vincent Goddard, John Wing, James Bray. (PRO: E190/129/1).

2 October. The following apprenticed in London: Margaret Burnell, aged 19, spinster, to William Bird, 4 years Nevis, with the consent of her mother. (LMWB14/421).

2 October. The following apprenticed in Bristol: Daniel Flower aged 18 of Marshfield, Glos, carpenter, by consent of his mother Mary Flower, to Thomas Martin of Great Bedwin, Wilts, wheelwright, 2 years Pennsylvania by *Unicorn*; Margarett Hartland of Ashlode (*sic*), Glos, spinster, to Bartholomew Holland, mariner, 4 years Virginia by *Unicorn*; Henry Pearce, son of Anthony Pearce of Calne, Wilts, clothier deceased, to Francis Smith of Devizes, 7 years Pennsylvania by *Unicorn*. (BR).

2-13 October. Shippers by the *Mary* of Stockton, Mr. Thomas Anderson, bound from Newcastle for Maryland: Daniell Toaes, Nicholas Milbourne, Rowland Place & Co. (PRO: E190/201/6).

3 October. The following apprenticed in Bristol: Benjamin Hickes of Bristol, by consent of his mother Martha Hickes, to John Collett, 5 years Barbados by *Welcome*; Hanna Minchin of Pershore, Worcs, spinster, to Robert Brent, 5 years Virginia by *Maryland Merchant*, Mr. Thomas Smith. (BR).

3-9 October. Shippers by the *Katherine*, Mr. Samuel Dodson, bound from London for Carolina: John Bays, Jacob Phelps, Zachary Breedon. (PRO: E190/129/1).

5 October. Shipper by the *Richard & Elizabeth*, Mr. Richard Williams, bound from London for Virginia: William Paggen. (PRO: E190/129/1).

5 October. Shipper by the *Arran* pink of Bristol, Mr. Edward Fenshaw, bound from Bristol for Virginia: Charles Jones. (PRO: E190/1147/2).

5 October. The following apprenticed in London: William Bould, singleman, son of Thomas B. of Ganthorpe, Yorkshire, clothier, to John Underlay of Redrith, Surrey, mariner, 4 years Nevis, witnessed by his cousin, Thomas Stapleton, servant at the King's Arms, Leadenhall Street, London; John Turner, aged 23, son of John T. of Gravesend, Kent, doctor of physick, deceased, to the same, 4 years Nevis, with the consent of his mother, Martha Cull, widow; William Davies, singleman aged 24, son of Richard D. of St. Martin in the Fields, Middlesex, mariner, deceased, to the same, 4 years Virginia, with the consent of his aunt, Jane Wybourne, spinster; Robert Bainham, son of Thomas B. of St. Clement Danes, Middlesex, tailor, deceased, to George Purvis of Ratcliffe, Middlesex, mariner, 8 years Virginia, with the consent of his mother Mary, wife of Thomas Armstrong of Grub Street, London, labourer; John Fairland, aged 28, son of John F. of Selby, Yorkshire, yeoman, deceased, to John Brooke of London, mariner, 4 years Virginia, witnessed by his cousin Henry Horner, journeyman of Fenchurch Street, London; (LMWB14/423, 424).

6 October. The following apprenticed in London: John Smith, aged 14, son of Thomas S. of St. Giles in the Fields, Middlesex, brewer's servant, deceased, to Edward Brooke of Bloomsbury, Middlesex, grocer, 7 years Maryland, with the consent of his mother Sarah S., widow; George Topper, son of Christopher T. of Bury, Sussex, yeoman, deceased, to John Taylor of London, salter, 4 years Virginia, witnessed by his brother Thomas T. (LMWB14/425).

6 October. Shipper by the *Judith* of Plymouth, Mr. John Lean, bound from Plymouth for Virginia: Roger Mills. (PRO: E190/1049/15).

6-24 October. Shippers by the *Prosperous*, Mr. Edward Conway, bound from London for Pennsylvania: John Thomas, Jacob Hall. (PRO: E190/129/1).

7-9 October. Shippers by the *Francis & Mary* of Bristol, Mr. William Nicholas, bound from Bristol for Virginia: Robert Taunton, Peter Waddinge, Thomas Burgis. (PRO: E190/1147/2).

8-13 October. Shipper by the *Hope* of Liverpool, Mr. Joseph Glover, bound from Liverpool for Virginia: David Poole. (PRO: E190/1346/16).

8-17 October. Shippers by the *Virginia Merchant*, Mr. William Hill, bound from London for Virginia: John Thorpe, Percival(?) Ellis. (PRO: E190/126/5).

8 October-11 November. Shippers by the *John* of Bristol, Mr. Edward Watts, bound from Bristol for Virginia: Michaell Pope, Thomas Hartly, William Lovell, Nicholas Downing, Richard Gotly. (PRO: E190/1147/2).

9 October. The following apprenticed in London: Armstrong Parker, son of George P. of Aslocton, Nottinghamshire, gent, to Anthony Guest of Stepney, Middlesex, 7 years Virginia, with the consent of his father. (LMWB14/427).

10 October. The following apprenticed in London: Joseph Niccolls, aged 12, son of Thomas N. of Woolwich, Kent, to serve Simon Bashford of Virginia 7 years, with the consent of his mother Jane N. (LMWB14/427).

10 October. Shippers by the *Reserve* of Newcastle, Mr. Joseph Greane, bound from Newcastle for Virginia: Michaell Taylor, Ralph Estob. (PRO: E190/201/6).

12 October. Rebels convicted after Monmouth's rebellion and designed to be shipped by John Rose, merchant, to Barbados or Jamaica: Charles Bennett; John Parsons; John Hartey; William Marchant; Thomas Rowsewell; John Crance; John Robins; Henry Randall; John Culverwell; Thomas Moore; Lawrence Preist; William Gould; John Bennett; Samuell Mountstephen; Thomas Buglar; Stephen Jeffreyes; John Morse; John England; Jacob Powell; Samuell Sweeting; William Crosse; Christopher Knight; John Needes; Samuell Collins; John Marwood; Moses Osborne; Walter Hucker; Randall Babington; John Knight; John Adams; Thomas Pomfrett; James Patten; Thomas Bambury.

And the following shipped on the *Jamaica Merchant* on 9 December 1685 for Barbados, landed and sold there in March 1686:

Luke Porter, aged 20, shoemaker; Edward Kent, aged 19; Bernard Loveridge, aged 23, soap boiler; Silvester Poole, aged 24, butcher; John Godsall, aged 27, butcher; Silvester Lyde, aged 27, butcher; William Verryard, aged 17, carpenter; Edward Bellamy, aged 27, carpenter; Job Hunt, aged 26, carrier; Jeremiah Poole, aged 30, clothier; John Rogers, aged 38, clothier; Robert Pearce, aged 25, clothier; William Saunders, aged 19, clothier; William Woodcock, aged 19, comber; John Andrews, aged 27, wool comber; Richard Pearcey, aged 20, comber; John Cockram, aged 18, comber; James Cockram, aged 21, comber; Thomas Pitts, aged 18, comber; George Rowsell, aged 30, wool comber; Charles Burrage, aged 27, comber; George Snow, aged 19, comber; Isaack Dyer, aged 25, comber; Humfrey Justin, aged 17, comber; William Pitts, aged 28, wool comber; Henry Chambers, aged 25, wool comber; Thomas Meade, aged 22, glover; Percivall Nowes, aged 23, hatter; James Webb, aged 18, husbandman; Thomas Chamberline, aged 20, shoe maker; John Bruer, aged 25, mason; John Baker, aged 27, mason; Thomas Austin, aged 27, mercer; John Miller, aged 35, plowman; Leonard Staples, aged 20, plowman; Jonas Browne, aged 20, plowman; John Cross, aged 18, plowman; John Gibbs, aged 19, plowman; Richard King, aged 18, plowman; James Maynard, aged 22, plowman; George Trubbs, aged 28, plowman; Robert Earle, aged 24, plowman; Phillip Cheeke, aged 16, plowman; William Lee, aged 20, plowman; Mathewe Cooke, aged 25, plowman; William Phelpes, aged 26, plowman; Henry Preist, aged 22, plowman; Emanuell Merchant, aged 20, plowman; Thomas Gould, aged 35, tailor; Robert Richards, aged 28, tailor; Elias Lockbeare, aged 18, tanner; John Timothy, aged 29, ribbon weaver; James Clift, aged 20, weaver; Christopher Hoblyn [or Holbin], aged 40, weaver; Richard Symons, aged 33, weaver; Daniell Rutter, aged 20, serge weaver; Thomas Preist, aged 20, serge weaver; Samuell Bond, aged 20, serge weaver; John Slade, aged 25, serge weaver; Nicholas Collins Jr., aged 20, weaver; Cornelius Radford, aged 20, weaver; John Mogridge, aged 23, weaver; Christopher Row, aged 34, weaver; William Scurrier, aged 22, weaver; John Baker, aged 35, serge weaver; Enock Gould, aged 15, weaver; Mathew Craft Jr., aged 19, weaver. (PRO: SP31/1/159).

12 October. The following apprenticed in London: Thomas Griggs, son of Thomas G. of Golden Lane, London, joiner, deceased, to Joel Kent of Limehouse, Middlesex, shipwright, 7 years Virginia, with the consent of his sister Mary G., servant of Stocklinch, Somerset, witnessed by Jane, wife of Richard Davies of Moor Lane, London, weaver. (LMWB14/430).

13 October. Deposition by Jeremy Rouse of London, scrivener aged 44, that in March 1679 Isaac Waldron of Boston, New England, became indebted to James Goldham Sr., citizen and draper of London, for goods shipped on the *Blessing* of Boston, Mr. Thomas Berry. Stephen Burton of Boston had also become indebted to Goldham by bond of 7 October 1679. James Goldham Sr. declares that he has appointed his son, James Goldham of Boston, as his attorney. (LMCD).

14 October. Shipper by the *Supply* ketch of Bristol bound from Bristol for Barbados and Virginia: Richard Olliver. (PRO: E190/1147/2).

14-19 October. Shippers by the *Alathea* of Bristol bound from Bristol for Virginia: Richard Benson, Edward Watkins. (PRO: E190/1147/2).

15-22 October. Shippers by the *Swallow*, Mr. Joseph Eldridge, bound from London for New England: Edward Hull, Charles Duke, Thomas Hopkins, Richard Beaumont, Noah Lawrence, Benjamin Alford, Ralph Ingram. (PRO: E190/129/1).

16 October. The following apprenticed in London: John Valliant to Samuel Phillips of Limehouse, Middlesex, mariner, 4 years Maryland, with the consent of his mother, Mary Devallock, living near the Elephant and Castle in Piccadilly, Middlesex, and his uncle, Renny V., of Lincolns Inn Fields; Richard Spence, aged 24, of Richmond, Surrey, to Thomas Goddard of Coleman Street, London, merchant, 4 years Jamaica. (LMWB14/432).

17 October. The following apprenticed in London: Marmaduke Smeaton, son of John S. of Thieving Lane alias Bow Street, Westminster, Middlesex, cordwainer, to Anthony Gester of Stepney, Middlesex, mariner, 5 years Virginia, with the consent of his father. (LMWB14/433).

18 October-9 November. Shippers by the *Exchange* of Exeter, Mr. Christopher Haycraft, bound from Exeter for Virginia: Thomas Smith, Robert Dabinet, John Kew, John Whiteborough, John Haycroft. (PRO: E190/963/1).

19 October-2 December. Shippers by the *Ann & Sarah* of Liverpool, Mr. Edward Tarleton, bound from Liverpool for Virginia: Isaac Holroid, John Mills, John Hill. (PRO: E190/1346/16).

20 October. The following apprenticed in London: John Austin, aged 22, and his sister, Elizabeth Austin, spinster aged 23, to Anthony Cornwell, merchant, 4 years Maryland, witnessed by [blank], waterman of Gravesend, Kent; Catherine Taylor, widow of Christopher Quick, Christopher Q., deceased, and her daughter, Mary Quick, aged 15, to Mathew Tazzard, mariner, 4 years Nevis, witnessed by Robert Sumpter of Virginia Street. (LMWB14/435).

20 October-6 November. Shippers by the *Industry* bound from Plymouth [? for Virginia]: Samuell Brett, Phillip Willcocks, John Dell, Abraham Cole, Joseph Webb. (PRO: E190/1049/15).

22 October. The following apprenticed in London: Elizabeth Judkin, spinster aged 14, to Anna Keckerbecke, 7 years Virginia, with the consent of her father William J. of Northumberland Alley, Fenchurch Street, London, shoemaker;

William Green, aged 16, to John Guyet, merchant, 7 years Maryland, witnessed by his mother-in-law Mary Phillips of Distaff Lane, London; Bridget Scofell, spinster aged 23, to Margaret Skinner, 4 years Jamaica, with the consent of her sister Elizabeth Scofell of St. James's Market; Elizabeth Selwood, spinster, to the same, 4 years Jamaica, witnessed by her cousin, Anne Ratcliffe of Pall Mall. (LMWB14/437).

23 October. The following apprenticed in London: John Bunnford, aged 13, to John Hosea, 8 years Jamaica, with the consent of his mother, Mary Powell. (LMWB14/438).

23 October. The following apprenticed in Bristol: William Beard of Defford, Worcs, to Robert Brent, 4 years Virginia by *Maryland Merchant*; Thomas Tustin of Defford to same, 4 years Virginia. (BR).

24 October. The following apprenticed in Bristol: Charles Stone of Elverton (*sic*), Glos, to John Piles, 4 years Nevis by *Rose*, Mr. William Worgan. (BR).

24 October. Rebels convicted after Monmouth's rebellion and transported from Bristol to Barbados by the frigate *John*, Mr. William Stokes.

From Somerset: William Drew of Bridgwater; John Seamer of Chilton; William Smith of Road (died at sea); William Hall of Chard; Justinian Guppy of Taunton (died at sea); George Carrow of Bridgwater; Thomas Dennis of Bridgwater; Ambrose Winter of West Buckland; Thomas Galhampton of West Zoyland (died at sea); William Daw of Taunton; Henry Gibbons of Taunton; Robert Easton of Taunton; George Michell of Bridgwater (died at sea); Daniel Pomeroy of Taunton; Edward Counsell of Allerton (died at sea); John Wall of Bridgwater; John Leake of Huntspill; Edward Vildy of Taunton; Robert Teape of Bridgwater; Joseph Wickham of Burnham (died on passage); Jeremiah Atkins of Taunton; Samuel Boone of Taunton; John Buston of Milverton; John Walters of Taunton; Robert Sears of Taunton; George Mullins of Taunton; Thomas Brocke of Taunton; Robert (George) Seaman of Taunton; Lawrence Hussey of Wellington; William Tiverton of Bridgwater; George Warren of Milverton; Robert Coward of Road; John Chappell of Petherton; William Burrows of Corfe; William Haynes of Beckington; George Keele of Chilton (died at sea); Stephen Rodway of Frome; Henry Quant of Taunton; William Mead of Bridgwater (died at sea); Thomas Gamage of Taunton; James Baker of Milverton; Humphrey Pope of Taunton; John Warren of Milverton; Joseph Vinicott of Bridgwater; Henry Mire of Bridgwater; John Harris of Huntspill; Francis Came of Huntspill (died at sea); Richard Stephens of North Curry; George Nowell of Taunton; Morris Fusse of Milverton; James Hillman of Milverton; John Stoodley of Trent; William Barnard of Huish; Bartholomew Randall of West Coker; John Rogers of Mackington (?Maperton); Robert Mitchell of Ilton; Jonas Crosse of Cucklington (died at sea); Richard Allen of Creech; Thomas Middleton of Taunton; Richard Bickham of Dosin; John Budge of Chard; Robert Paul of Ilton (died at sea);

Osmond Read of Taunton; John Burgess of Taunton; William Parker of Taunton; John Farmer of Taunton; Abraham Pollard of Chard.

From Devonshire: Timothy Hawker of Thorncombe; John Mitchell of Thorncombe; John Bagg of Thorncombe; William Smith Jr. of Upottery; Michael Powell of Neath, Glamorganshire; William Walters of Membury; Humphrey Trump of West Sandford; John Bartlett of Pitminster (Somerset); John Chilcot of Tiverton; William Harvey of Membury; William Hutchings of Upottery (died at sea); John Smith of Honiton; John Clode of Upottery; John Cantlebury of Sampford Peverell; Richard Wadham of Frome; William Woolridge of Tiverton; Simon Poole of Beaminster, Dorset (died at sea); William Coombe of Broadwindsor (Dorset); Richard Edgar of Mosterton (Dorset); William Phippin of High Church; John Gale of Coscam (?Croscombe, Somerset); Thomas Matthews of Chideock (Dorset); John Keele of Chilton (died).

The *John* arrived in Barbados in January 1686 and the rebels landed were sold to local masters. (PRO: SP31/1/159).

24 October. The following apprenticed in London: Julian Morris, spinster aged 15, to Samuel Phillips, mariner, 4 years Maryland, with the consent of her mother Mary, wife of Samuel Lennell near Stationers' Hall; Mary Hunt, spinster aged 17, to John Lloyd, mariner, 4 years Nevis, witnessed by her brother, Samuel Upshaw of Southwark, Surrey, painter; Nathaniel Hudson, singleman aged 25, to Elizabeth Wicks, 5 years Virginia, witnessed by his sister, Mary Wheeler of Holborn Bridge, widow. (LMWB14/438).

25 October-18 December. Shippers by the *Duke of York*, Mr. John Purvis, bound from London for Virginia: Robert Carnoll, John Liquorish, Francis Lee, Francis Camfield, John Weekes, Robert Fairman, John Little, Giles Sprackling, Arthur Burren, Peter Temple. (PRO: E190/126/5, 129/1).

26 October. Shipper by the *Joane* of Exeter, Mr. John Seaward, bound from Exeter for Virginia: Isaac Gibbs. (PRO: E190/963/1).

31 October. The following apprenticed in Bristol: John Canterbury of Litton, Som, but resident for some years at Chewton, Som, to Samuel Burge, 4 years Virginia by *Swallow*; Stephen Spear of Chewton, Som, to same, 5 years Virginia by *Swallow*, Mr. Thomas Witherington. (BR).

October. Memorandum of shipment of rebels John Edwards and Edward Lloyd to York River, Virginia, signed by John Baker of Hamwood, Somerset. (CSPC).

October. Probate of will of Nicholas Paynter of Anne Arundell County, Maryland. (AW).

October. Probate of will of Thomas Pope of St. Philip and James, Bristol, merchant, who had lands in Virginia. (AW).

October. Probate of will of George Read of Whitechapel, Middlesex, who died on the ship *Culpepper* in Virginia. (AW).

October. Administration with will of William Sterry of Bristol, who died in Boston, New England. (AW).

October. Probate of will of Thomas Weare of Charfield, Gloucestershire, whose brother, Peter Weare, was in York, New England. (AW).

2 November. The following apprenticed in London: Robert Stanton, aged 16, son of Lawrence S. of St. Katherine by the Tower, London, tubman, deceased, to serve Elizabeth Wicks, wife of Francis Wicks of Virginia, planter, 8 years, with the consent of his mother Elizabeth Ruth. (LMWB14/441).

3 November. Shipper by the *Grace*, Mr. John Dottinge, bound from London for Maryland: John Verner. (PRO: E190/129/1).

3 November. The following apprenticed in London: John Evans, son of John E. of Aldgate, London, porter, deceased, to George Purvis of Limehouse, Middlesex, mariner, 7 years Virginia, with the consent of his mother Helen E. (LMWB14/441).

3-7 November. Shippers by the *Abraham & Mary* of Bristol, Mr. Samuell Hartnell, bound from Bristol for Virginia: William Daines, Joseph Jeffris, Edward Fielding. (PRO: E190/1147/2).

4-7 November. Shipper by the *Swallow* of Liverpool, Mr. Thomas Withington, bound from Bristol for Virginia: Samuell Packer. (PRO: E190/1147/2).

6-12 November. Shippers by the *Assistance*, Mr. Roger Kempe, bound from London for Maryland: Joseph Webb, Gerrard Slye, Pog—— Craven. (PRO: E190/126/5).

7 November. The following apprenticed in London: John Gosse, aged 18, and Robert Gosse, aged 12, sons of Robert G. of St. Katherine by the Tower, London, waterman, deceased, to Elizabeth, wife of Francis Weeks of Virginia, 6 & 10 years Virginia, with the consent of their mother, Elizabeth G.; Thomas Rogers, son of Evan R. of Oswestry, Shropshire, labourer, deceased, to the same, 6 years Virginia. (LMWB14/443).

9 November. The following apprenticed in Bristol: William Sanders of Canterbury, Kent, to Thomas Jones of Marsh Street, mariner, 4 years Virginia or Maryland by *Maryland Merchant*; William Dennott of Bridgewater, [Som], to same, 4 years Virginia or Maryland. The two boys above came to town with the soldiers and have been wandering about and have offered themselves voluntarily. (BR).

9 November. The following apprenticed in London: Thomas Barton, singleman, to Samuel Pratt of London, surgeon, 4 years Jamaica, witnessed by his sister, Merrian Day, and her husband, Leonard Day, and Francis Thomas, solicitor; Elizabeth Browne, daughter of William B. of London, bricklayer, deceased, to Fossett Gardner of Ratcliffe, Middlesex, tailor, 5 years Virginia, witnessed by her brother-in-law, Thomas Butler of Clerkenwell Green, Middlesex, gent, who says she was discharged from Clerkenwell prison where she was held for pilfering. (LMWB14/445).

10 **November**. The following apprenticed in London: Anthony Harding, singleman, to serve James Harding of Jamaica, merchant, 4 years, witnessed by his cousin, Simon Webb of Goodmans Yard, London, cutler. (LMWB14/445).

11 **November-11 December**. Shippers by the *Maryland Merchant* of Bristol, Mr. George Tyte, bound from Bristol for Virginia: Edward Dyer, Thomas Smith, George Pyle, John Sandford, James Ifield, John Browne, William French. (PRO: E190/1147/2).

12 **November**. Shipper by the *Thomas & Francis*, Mr. Richard Summers, bound from London for Virginia: Thomas Walsh. (PRO: E190/129/1).

12 **November**. The following apprenticed in London: Robert Craine, aged 30 and formerly overseas and William Croppin, aged 26, of Brixham, Devon, to Arthur Smith of Limehouse, Middlesex, mariner, 3 years Antigua; John Baites, son of Edward B. of Amersham, Buckinghamshire, to William Wills of Lamb's Chapel, London, merchant, 5 years Virginia, with the consent of his father, witnessed by Hannah Holdshipp, blacksmith's wife of St. John's Street; James Deboard, aged 22, of Berwick upon Tweed, Northumberland, tailor, to Edward Williams of Shadwell, Middlesex, cooper, 4 years Jamaica. (LMWB14/447,449).

13 **November**. The following apprenticed in Bristol: Ann Glassingham of St. Mary Redcliffe, [Bristol], spinster, to John ——, 4 years Virginia by *Maryland Merchant*. (BR).

14 **November**. The following apprenticed in London: John Rogers to John Gandy of Whitechapel, Middlesex, mariner, 6 years Maryland, with the consent of his mother Mary P. (LMWB14/450).

16 November. The following apprenticed in Bristol: Simon Straw, a Frenchman, to Luke Mason, 7 years Barbados or Nevis by *Rose*. (BR).

17 **November**. The following apprenticed in London: Elizabeth Marryott, spinster aged 22, to John Lock of Bermondsey, Surrey, mariner, 4 years Maryland, witnessed by George Browne of St. Olave, Southwark, Surrey, waterman. (LMWB14/452).

18 **November**. The following apprenticed in London: John Hyfield, aged 17, to Thomas Cradock, mariner, 4 years Virginia, with the consent of his mother Rebecca, wife of William Noakes of Whitechapel, Middlesex, clothier; Richard Cottam of London, vintner, to Gregory Dorset, citizen and barber surgeon of London, 4 years Barbados. (LMWB14/453).

19 November. The following apprenticed in London: Suzanna Clifford, aged 17, spinster, to Alice Bare, widow, 4 years Nevis, witnessed by her mother, Suzanna C. of Holborn, Middlesex; Anne Sheppard, spinster aged 22, to the same, 4 years Nevis, witnessed by said Suzanna Clifford; Elizabeth Price, spinster, to Christopher Keen, citizen and turner of London, 2 years Jamaica, witnessed by said Christopher Keen of Threadneedle Street, London, instrument maker. (LMWB 14/453, 454).

21 November. William Wise, aged 15, apprenticed from Christ's Hospital to Arthur Smith, commander of the *Amity* bound for the West Indies. (CH).

23 November. The following apprenticed in London: Anthony Goff, aged 27, of London, vintner, to Francis Mingham, 4 years Jamaica; James Rither, aged 13, to John Pheasant, carpenter, 7 years Virginia. (LMWB14/459).

23 November. The following apprenticed in Bristol: Luke Wernall, a Frenchman, to Richard Millsome, 4 years Barbados or Nevis by *Rose*. (BR).

24 November. The following apprenticed in London: Agnes Day of London, spinster aged 16, to Alice Bare, widow, 4 years Nevis, with the consent of Elizabeth Franklyn of the Three Cranes near Joiners' Hall. (LMWB14/459).

26 November. The following apprenticed in London: John Cruickshanks to Nicholas Dove of London, tailor, 3 years Jamaica; Elizabeth Simpson of London, spinster, to the same, 4 years Jamaica; John Barnes, son of Robert B. of London, bricklayer, deceased, to Thomas Stockin, porter, 7 years Virginia. (LMWB14/460,461).

24 November-15 December. Shippers by the *Charles*, Mr. Edward Poulson, bound from London for Maryland: John Jackson, Thomas Elwes, Samuell Greene, William Hiccocks, George Eshall, Henry Loe, Samuell Glasse, Charles Sessions. (PRO: E190/126/5).

26 November. Shiper by the *Rainbow* of Bristol bound from Bristol for Virginia: William Crabb. (PRO: E190/1147/2).

26 November. The following apprenticed in Bristol: John James of Nash, Mon, to Robert Mason, 4 years Virginia by *Maryland Merchant*. (BR).

27 November. The following apprenticed in London: John Gravell, aged 16, to Francis Hanson Esq., 5 years Jamaica. (LMWB14/463).

27 November-9 December. Shippers by the *Globe*, Mr. Joseph Payne, bound from London for Virginia: Jeremy Bradfield, George Elwes, Henry Pryor. (PRO: E190/129/1).

28 November. Deposition by Matthew Travers of London, merchant aged 40, that he and John Rodway of Talbot County, Maryland, deceased, signed a receipt to Captain Webber for the cost of importing eight men and seven women servants. The deponent has assigned to Josiah Bacon of London, merchant, debts due from the heirs of John Rodway and from John Wilson of Herrington, Maryland, planter. (LMCD).

30 November. The following apprenticed in London: Richard Garth, aged 19, son of Avery G. of Haugham, Lincolnshire, gent, deceased, to William Kirkham of London, merchant, 4 years Barbados; John Hammon, aged 16, son of John H. of Chichester, Sussex, needle maker, to William Tailby of London, merchant, 4 years Jamaica, with the consent of his father. (LMWB14/465).

1 December. The following apprenticed in Bristol: William Morgan, son of Ann Morgan of Brockworth, Glos, to Thomas Dennet of the same, mariner, 4 years Virginia by *Maryland Merchant*. (BR).

2 December. The following apprenticed in Bristol: John Muspratt, son of Thomas Muspratt of Claverton, Som, and by his consent, to John Grant, 6 years Nevis by *Content*; David Jenkins of Swansea, [Glam], carpenter, to Lambrook Thomas, tailor, 4 years Maryland by *Maryland Merchant*; Richard France of Cromwell [Cromhall perhaps intended], Glos, to same, 4 years Maryland; Henry Jones of Whitson, Mon, husbandman, to Francis ———, 5 years Maryland by *Maryland Merchant*; John Purnell of Bussellton (*sic*), Glos, to Thomas Smith, 4 years Virginia by *Maryland Merchant*. (BR).

2 December. The following apprenticed in London: Thomas Baison, aged 26, son of William B. of Wick Cambee (*sic*), Northants, husbandman, deceased, to Thomas Howard, 4 years Virginia; Thomas Jones, aged 22, son of Richard J. of Monmouth, husbandman, deceased, to Thomas Austin of Limehouse, Middlesex, mariner, 4 years Antigua; Mary Granger, aged 28, daughter of Anne Dawson of Princes Street, Leicester Gardens, widow, to William Tayleby of London, merchant tailor, 4 years Jamaica; Walter Winter, aged 14, son of William W. of Wallingford, Berkshire, tallow chandler, to Gilbert Crouch of London, gent, 5 years Maryland, with the consent of his father and of his uncle, Richard Coombes, near the Temple Bar, hatmaker. (LMWB14/466, 467).

2-5 December. Shippers by the *Zebulon*, Mr. Nicholas Goodridge, bound from London for Virginia: Joseph Pile, William Wills, Richard Howard. (PRO: E190/129/1).

4 December. William Davis, aged 14, apprenticed from Christ's Hospital to Nathaniel Bacon of Virginia, merchant. (CH).

4 December. The following apprenticed in London: Mary Bowston, aged 29, widow, daughter of John Williams of Spitalfields, Middlesex, deceased, to William Levett of London, draper, 4 years Barbados; Mary Billing, aged 22, spinster, to Samuell Cox of London, merchant, 4 years Barbados; Thomas Evans, aged 18, son of Thomas E. of London, porter, deceased, to serve

Thomas Baily of North Carolina 5 years, with the consent of his mother Elizabeth E. (LMWB14/468).

5 December. The following apprenticed in London: Francis Scorfield, aged 21, son of James S. of Emley, Yorkshire, husbandman, deceased, to serve John Bayne of Maryland 4 years; Joseph Johnson, singleman aged 30, of Piddington, Oxfordshire, to the same, 4 years Maryland, witnessed by Walter Breynton of Aldermanbury, London; Robert Eddington, aged 33, son of Thomas E. of Ludgershall, Wiltshire, broadcloth weaver, deceased, to James Fidler of Ratcliffe, Middlesex, mariner, 4 years Virginia. (LMWB14/469).

7 December. The following apprenticed in London: Katherine Hands, spinster aged 25, to serve Thomas Baylee of Carolina 5 years, witnessed by Diana Roman of Golden Lane, orange woman; Matthias Childe, son of Matthias C. of London Wall, silkman, deceased, to the same, 4 years Carolina, with the consent of his mother Margaret C. of Little Wood Street, London, silkwoman. (LMWB14/473).

7 December. The following apprenticed in Bristol: Edmond Williams of St. Peter's, Bristol, to Lambert Thomas, 4 years Maryland by *Maryland Merchant*; Mary, wife of Edmond Williams, to same, 4 years Maryland by *Maryland Merchant*; Sarah Reed of Bristol to same, 4 years Maryland by *Maryland Merchant*. (BR).

8 December. The following apprenticed in London: Thomas Peirson, son of William P. of Shoe Lane, St. Bride's, London, to Edward Tomlin of Ratcliffe, Middlesex, mariner, 7 years Virginia, with the consent of his father. (LMWB14/473).

9 December. Shipper by the *William & Thomas*, Mr. Francis Harbyn, bound from London for Maryland: Roger Craven. (PRO: E190/129/1).

9 December. Shipper by the *America Merchant* of Bristol, Mr. Thomas Masters, bound from Bristol for Virginia: Sir William Hayman. (PRO: E190/1147/2).

9 December. The following apprenticed in London: Margaret Dunsmore, daughter of Richard D. of London, innholder, now in prison, to William Bennett of London, surgeon, 5 years Virginia, witnessed by Thomas Bennett of Whitecross Street, physician; Thomas Wicks to the same, 5 years Virginia, with the consent of his mother, Jane Copplee, wife of Samuel C. of St. Martin le Grand, London. (LMWB14/474, 475).

10 December. The following apprenticed in Bristol: Joanna Medley of Bridgewater, [Som], spinster, to Thomas Smith, 4 years Virginia by *Maryland Merchant*. (BR).

12-23 December. Shippers by the *Judith*, Mr. Matthew Trim, bound from London for Virginia: John Mumford, Robert Christopher, Anthony Stratton, William Woodham, Samuel Dixon. (PRO: E190/129/1).

14 December. The following apprenticed in London: Benjamin Smithson, aged 24, to Thomas Hall, merchant, 4 years Jamaica, witnessed by Joshua Smith of London Wall, clothworker; Edward Raymond, aged 20, son of Saintclear H. of Winchester Park, Southwark, Surrey, to the same, 4 years Jamaica, with the consent of his said father; Charles Clayson, aged 21, to John Munford, 4 years Virginia, witnessed by Francis Clayson and by his mother, Katherine C. of Dyers Yard, Old Bedlam, London; Katherine Chidley, aged 24, spinster, to Matthew Trim, 4 years Virginia, witnessed by her brother, Stephen Michell of Whitechapel, Middlesex, tailor; Francis Sampson, aged 20, to serve William Winter of Virginia, planter, 4 years, witnessed by William Rogers of Hammersmith, Middlesex, brandy seller. (LMWB14/478, 479).

14 December. The following apprenticed in Bristol: William Purnell, son of Thomas Purnell of Stanton Drew, Som, to John Pilt, mariner, 4 years Barbados or Caribbees by *Rose*. (BR).

15 December. The following apprenticed in London: Mathew Palmer, aged 18, to serve Thomas Lee of Virginia, planter, 4 years. (LMWB14/479).

16 December. The following apprenticed in London: Joachim Henrick, aged 24, to Jane Hayes to serve him 4 years in Jamaica as a tailor. (LMWB14/480).

17 December. The following apprenticed in London: Anne Smith, spinster aged 24, to Thomas Hale, merchant, 4 years Jamaica, witnessed by her brother Samuell S. near the Exchange, London. (LMWB14/480).

18 December. Report on the petition of Edward Plampin, administrator to John Bagnall deceased, for repayment of a debt owed to Bagnall by Edmund Scarborough deceased. (APC).

18 December. Shipper by the *Dolphin*, Mr. Robert Clark, bound from London for Virginia: Micajah Perry. (PRO: E190/129/1).

30 December. The following apprenticed in London: Rebecka Flicknoll, aged 15, daughter of Henry F. of Coleman Street, London, tailor, deceased, to Richard Cornwallis of Wapping, Middlesex, mariner, 5 years Virginia, with the consent of her mother Rebecka, wife of William Bond. (LMWB14/488).

30 December. The following apprenticed in Bristol: Richard Morris of Harrow on the Hill, Mddx, to William Gallopp, mariner, 4 years Barbados by *Fellowship*, Mr. Nathaniel King. (BR).

31 December. The following apprenticed in London: Elizabeth Wilson, daughter of John W. of Grub Street, London, joiner, to serve Francis Jervis of Virginia 5 years, with the consent of her father. (LMWB14/488).

December. Probate of will of Samuel Shute of St. Peter Cornhill, London, a trader to New York. (AW).

1686

2 January. The following apprenticed in Bristol: Richard Clarke, son of Thomas Clarke of Winterbourne, Glos, and with his consent, to John Dickenson, merchant, 4 years Barbados. (BR).

2 January. The following apprenticed in London: Anthony Jerman, aged 17, son of John J. of Hatton Garden, Middlesex, tailor, to Gabriell Bonner of London, merchant, 4 years Virginia, with the consent of his father. (LMWB14/489).

8 January. The following apprenticed in Bristol: Amy Putman of Bridgewater, Som, late servant to a baker in Redcliffe Street, [Bristol], to William Abbott, mariner, 4 years Barbados by *Fellowship*. (BR).

11 January. The following apprenticed in London: Elizabeth Jones, spinster aged 17, to Robert Eldridge, mariner, 4 years Virginia, witnessed by Mrs. Chandler of Coventry Street, Middlesex; Richard Cole, aged 21, to Thomas Ackerman, mariner, 4 years Virginia. (LMWB14/495).

14 January. The following apprenticed in London: Elizabeth Thompson, spinster aged 25, to Thomas Nicholls, surgeon, 4 years Barbados; Penelope Wheatley, spinster aged 21, to Robert Eldridge, mariner, 4 years Virginia, witnessed by Margaret Wilson of Ratcliffe Cross, Middlesex. (LMWB14/496).

14-26 January. Shippers by the *Jefferies*, Mr. Thomas Arnold, bound from London for Virginia: William Anderson, Thomas Stark, John Mumford. (PRO: E190/139/1).

19 January. The following apprenticed in Bristol: Nicholas Persons of Limington, Som, husbandman, to Thomas Smith, 4 years Virginia by *Maryland Merchant*, said Thomas Smith Mr. (BR).

20 January. The following apprenticed in London: Mary Hall, aged 15, of Southwark, Surrey, to Gabriell Bonner, 6 years Virginia, witnessed by her brother, Richard Prosgrove of Southwark, Surrey. (LMWB14/500).

22 January. The following apprenticed in London: Thomas Dicken formerly of Cannock, Staffordshire, but now of London, to Clement Tudway, 3 years Antigua. (LMWB14/501).

24 January-3 February. Shippers by the *Unicorn*, Mr. William Norrington, bound from London for Virginia: Anthony Stratton, Thomas Porter, Jonathan Woodley. (PRO: E190/139/1).

25 January. The following apprenticed in London: James Devonport, aged 10, son of Edward D. of Red Cross Street, London, printer, to William Tyleby of London, sailman, 10 years Jamaica. (LMWB14/504).

26 January-9 February. Shippers by the *Thomas & Anne*, Mr. Andrew Elton, bound from London for New York: William Sanders, David Conguard, Anthony Tomkins, Thomas Hart, Thomas Heaton, Christopher Gore. (PRO: E190/139/1).

28 January. The following apprenticed in London: George Fox, aged 35, son of James Fox of Teviotdale, Scotland, blacksmith, deceased, to William Tyleby of London, merchant tailor, 4 years Jamaica. (LMWB14/506).

January. Probate of will of John Brett of St. Andrew Undershaft London, who had lands in New England. (AW).

January. Probate of will of Richard Watson of St. Margaret, Westminster, Middlesex, whose stepson, Robert Boodle, was in Virginia. (AW).

1 February. The following apprenticed in London: Elizabeth Booth, spinster aged 23, of Hackney, Middlesex, daughter of Thomas B. of Clapton, Middlesex, deceased, to Joseph Athy, 4 years Montserrat, witnessed by William Bradshaw; Hester Paine, spinster aged 23, daughter of Harbett P. of Shoreditch, Middlesex, deceased, to the same, 4 years Montserrat, witnessed by William Bradshaw of Moorgate, London. (LMWB14/510).

3 February. Report of the examination in Barbados of Randolph Babington and Daniel Manning. Babington was born in London and kept a warehouse there. In July 1685 he went to the West Country on business where he was merely a spectator of Monmouth's Army. Nevertheless he was arrested and tried, pleaded guilty and was condemned to be sent to Barbados to serve Sir William Booth. Since he had money, he was allowed to travel as a free passenger and to serve his time as a free man. Daniel Manning was a blacksmith's apprentice neat Taunton, Somerset, and was pressed by Monmouth's Army but later joined the King's Army. After Monmouth's rout he went to London where he was questioned on suspicion of being a rebel. He met a man on Tower Hill who promised him employment if he would serve for four years in Barbados and was shipped there with 22 other men, none of whom had served with the rebels. (CSPC).

5 February. Shipper by the *Thomas*, Mr. Thomas Colbrook, bound from London for New York: John Teshmaker. (PRO: E190/139/1).

6 February. Home Circuit prisoners reprieved to be transported to Barbados or Jamaica. Essex: Ann Brookes, spinster, alias wife of Richard of Chelmsford; William Ricketts of Dagenham; John Whitfield of Waltham Cross; John Bassett of Waltham Abbey; William Sayers of Woodham Mortimer; George Smith of Hornchurch; John Lloyd alias Floyd of Waltham Cross; Richard Jackson of Little Wakering; Laurence King alias Kecke alias White of East Ham. Hertfordshire: Elizabeth Sharpe of Cheshunt; Richard Haynes of Redbourn; Edward Coopes of Bishops Stortford; Susan Howard of Tring. Kent: William Sutton of Lewisham; Richard Butler of Chart. Surrey: John Flixon of St. George, Southwark; Mary Pinck alias Mountsley of St. Saviour,

Southwark; John Jessop of Holy Trinity, Guildford; William Hill of Christchurch; John Summers of St. Saviour, Southwark. Sussex: Thomas Simpson of Wadhurst. (PRO: C66/3282/7).

9 February. The following apprenticed in London: James Jones, aged 23, and Edward Bolton, aged 21, to Phillip Quinton, merchant, 4 years Barbados; Ethell Cawdrey, aged 20, spinster, to Thomas Gadsden, 4 years Virginia. (LMWB14/517).

11 February. The following apprenticed in London: Isaac Steele of London, tailor, to Joseph Pendlebury of London, merchant, 4 years Barbados. (LMWB14/520).

11 February. The following apprenticed in Bristol: Katherine White of Exeter, [Devon], to Richard Dempster, 4 years Barbados by *Abigail*; David Williams of Kilpeck, Heref, to same, 4 years Barbados. (BR).

12 February-3 March. Shippers by the *Blessing*, Mr. Ralph Potts, bound from London for Carolina: Sir Mathew Johnson, Arthur Shallett, James Niccolls, Thomas Potts, John Caroon, John Rose. (PRO: E190/139/1).

12 February-7 April. Shippers by the *Adventure* of Exeter, Mr. John Browne, bound from Exeter for New England: Edward Seaward, Hugh Bidwell, Mary Freeke, Bartholomew Anthony. (PRO: E190/964/1).

13 February. The following apprenticed in Bristol: Grace Grove of Caerleon, Mon, to Richard Dempster, 4 years Barbados. (BR).

13 February. The following apprenticed in London: Elizabeth Parsons, daughter of Richard P. of Gloucester, spinster aged 21, to Joseph Athy, mariner, 4 years Montserrat, witnessed by William Pott of Cheapside, London, linen draper, on behalf of the father. (LMWB14/521).

13 February-2 March. Shippers by the *Elizabeth*, Mr. John Wild, bound from London for New England: James Lever, Phillip Norroway, Froud Emberley, Joseph Bowles, Francis Fox, John Whetham, Edward Ellis, Daniell Foe. (PRO: E190/139/1).

15 February. The following apprenticed in Bristol: Thomas Broadrife of Wells, Som, shoemaker, to Edward Marston, 4 years Barbados by *Abigail*. (BR).

15 February. The following apprenticed in London: Hugh Newton to Christopher Jefferson, 5 years St. Christopher's. (LMWB14/523).

19 February. The following apprenticed in London: Thomas Basier, aged 16, to Christopher Byerley, 7 years Carolina; Byworth Horsford of London, labourer, to the same, 4 years Carolina, with the consent of his mother; Ralph Browne of London, labourer, to the same, with the consent of his half-brother, Robert Chesman of the Strand, Middlesex; John Draper of London, clothmaker, son of Samuel D., to Andrew Kerr, 4 years Jamaica, with the consent of his said father of Broad Street, London. (LMWB14/525).

20 February. The following apprenticed in London: Katherine Skelton to Christopher Jefferson, 5 years St. Christopher's. (LMWB14/526).

23 February. The following apprenticed in London: Edmond Darson, aged 25, son of James D. of Shrewsbury, Shropshire, farmer, to Christopher Jefferson of Westminster, gent, 4 years St. Christopher's; William Johnson, aged 30, son of William J. of Abergavenny, Monmouthshire, deceased, to the same, 4 years St. Christopher's; Edmond Willis, singleman aged 26, son of Thomas W. of Benson, Oxfordshire, farmer, deceased, to the same, 4 years St. Christopher's; William Taylor, aged 16, son of Richard T. of St. Clement Danes, Middlesex, tailor, to James Hobbart of Stepney, Middlesex, mariner, 6 years Jamaica, with the consent of his father; Thomas Harris, an Indian aged 16, and Mary Hewett, aged 19, spinster, daughter of Thomas H. of Nottingham, tailor, deceased, both from Westminster Bridewell, to Richard Ally of Westminster, gent, 4 years West Indies. (LMWB14/529).

23 February. Oxford Circuit prisoners reprieved to be transported to Jamaica, Barbados or Bermuda. Berkshire: John Gowing of Harwell; James Smith of Sonning; William Stanney of New Windsor. Gloucestershire: Christopher Tilley of North Nibley; Elizabeth Lambert of Leckhampton; Samuel Asplyn of Ashleworth; Edward Thomas alias Roberts of Newnham. Herefordshire: Nathaniel Priest of Hereford. Monmouthshire: John Martin of Abergavenny. Oxfordshire: Elizabeth wife of Richard Symonds of Burford; Elianor wife of Richard Willier of Burford. Shropshire: Mary wife of David Thomas of Horton; Jane Jones of Ludlow. Staffordshire: Joseph Hoyle of Uttoxeter; William Lawrence alias Moulton of Huntingdon; John Dilloway of Wolverhampton; Isabel Duffield of Dudley; Walter Russell of Uttoxeter; Elizabeth Symonds of Tipton, widow. Worcestershire: John Dale of Pirton; Joseph Raughton of Worcester; William Bowater of Dudley; Thomas Raughton of Worcester; Richard Wilson of Stourbridge; Andrew Inckoe of Chaddesley. (PRO: C66/3282/14).

24 February. Newgate prisoners reprieved to be transported to Barbados or Jamaica. London: John Thompson; Thomas Draper; Cassandra Widdowes, spinster; Herbert Thompson, yeoman; Mary Fisher, spinster, alias wife of William Fisher; Edward Hawley; Robert Brookes; Richard Osborne; John Dikes; Thomas Drew, victualler. Middlesex: George Atwell of Hanwell; Samuel Alderton of Stepney; John Smith of the same; David Barton of the same; Mary Hancock of St. Giles in the Fields; Thomas Goldsborough alias Goldsberry of St. James [Westminster]; Richard Jones of the same; Leonard Beale of the same, apothecary; Matthew Morgan of St. Martin in the Fields; Mary Collard, spinster, alias wife of John Collard of the same; Anne Davis, wife of John Davis of the same; Lionel Fenwick of the same; Elizabeth Hacker alias Thacker alias Webb, spinster, alias wife of John Hacker of St. Andrew Holborn ; Thomas Glamster of the same; George Smith of the same; Thomas Gardner of St. Mary Savoy; Richard Coy of Hillingdon; Zachary Thompson of St. Botolph Aldgate; Ambrose Stapling of Islington; Sarah Worrell of St. Clement Danes; Isaac Smith of the same. (PRO: C66/3282/10).

25 February-20 March. Shippers by the *William & Anne*, Mr. William Deering, bound from London for New York: Richard Merriweather, Daniell Ingoll, William Maynerd, William Yeomans, Henry Haile, Peter Hacker. (PRO: E190/139/1).

25 February-15 April. Shippers by the *Society*, Mr. Thomas Fairweather, bound from London for New England: Jacob Jesson, Jeffrey Stoner, John Goltman, Thomas Brattle, Andrew Kendrick, Samuell Procter, Thomas Mayer, John Crow, Chowning Rudliffe, Robert Peter, Thomas Dodge, Francis Chamberlain, William Shotton, Thomas Brindly, Samuell Mercer. (PRO: E190/139/1).

27 February-1 March. Shippers by the *Gally* frigate of Liverpool, Mr. John Gally, bound from Liverpool for Virginia: David Poole. (PRO: E190/1347/1, 1348/6).

27 February-27 March. Shippers by the *Diamond* of Exeter, Mr. Edward Shower, bound from Exeter for Boston, New England: John March, John Cholwill, John Foxwell, Richard Sheares. (PRO: E190/964/1).

1 March. Shipper by the [blank], Mr. John Wing, bound from London for Virginia: Jeremy Bradfield. (PRO: E190/139/1).

1 March. The following apprenticed in London: Hannah Wood, spinster, to Abraham Barrow Lassado of London, merchant, 4 years Barbados, witnessed by Benjamin Francis; Jane Cockin and Mary Davies, daughter of Mary D. of Clare Market, Middlesex, to Thomas Colebeech of London, mariner, 4 years Virginia, witnessed by the latter's mother, Mary D. (LMWB14/533).

1 March. Deposition by John Bawdon and John Gardner of London, merchants, that they have appointed Humphrey Luscombe of Boston, New England, as their attorney. (LMCD).

1 March. Norfolk Circuit prisoners reprieved to be transported to America. Bedfordshire: John Infield of Chelson. Buckinghamshire: Charles Hambleton of Burnham. Cambridgeshire: Francis Browne of Soham; Thomas Moule of Coton. Huntingdonshire: Judith Skelton of Wood Walton. Norfolk: Richard Fuller of Great Fransham; John Howard of Saham Toney; Dina alias Diana Reeve of Downham Market; William Woods of Saham Toney; John Woodcocke of Great Yarmouth. Suffolk: John Dawson of Stanton; John Gower of Claydon. (PRO: C66/3282/5).

1 March. Western Circuit prisoners reprieved to be transported to Barbados. Devon: Nathaniel Baker of Shute; Charles Twist of Plymouth; John Thorne of Rewe; Henry Wyatt of Ottery, tanner; William Sherwell of Modbury, weaver; Richard Doe of Plymouth; James Baker of Halwell. Dorset: Susan Gerrard of Beaminster; Nicholas Burd alias Bird of Shaston. Hampshire:

George Swetman of Brockenhurst; Nicholas Chaunter of Soake near Winchester; John Durneford of Portsmouth; Hercules Hayes of Portsmouth, mariner. Somerset: Robert Kidner of Bromfield; Nicholas Bennett of Bromfield; John Wheeler alias Whidler of Winford; James Walter of Culmersdon; Mary Sealey alias Cooksley of Dunster; Samuel Clutterbuck of London. (PRO: C66/3282/6).

2 March. The following apprenticed in London: James Trinity to Jonathan Martin of London, mariner, 7 years Barbados, with the consent of the churchwardens of Holy Trinity, London. (LMWB14/534).

3 March. The following apprenticed in London: Jeffery Pollard, son of William P. of All Hallows the Less, London, porter, to Samuel Ayres, citizen and dyer of London, 4 years Barbados, witnessed by his master, John Huffam of All Hallows, London, salter, and his mother, Sarah P. of Thames Street, London, widow. (LMWB14/535).

4 March. John Davis, aged 17, apprenticed from Christ's Hospital to John Benson, commander of the *Scipio* bound for Barbados. (CH).

4 March-10 April. Shippers by the *Dolphin*, Mr. John Foy, bound from London for New England: Anthony Burren, John Ward, Charles Feltham, Edward O'Holtenhan, George Howard, John James, Benjamin Bullivant, Thomas Gibbs, Charles Morton, Rowland Tryon, Robert Carnall, Charles Sebright, John Vascey, John Balstone, John Sholton, Christopher Tooley. (PRO: E190/139/1).

5 March. The following apprenticed in London: Leonard Foster, a poor boy, to serve Edward Peirce of Antigua, shoemaker, 9 years with the consent of the churchwardens of St. Leonard, Foster Lane, London. (LMWB14/537).

6 March-24 April. Shippers by the *Loyal Society*, Mr. Peter Clark, bound from London for New England: Walter Monk, Thomas Powell, Christopher Booth, John Baker, Arthur Shallett, Thomas Hunt, John Crow, Anthony Ball, William Tirrey, Laurence French, Thomas Bless, Edward Rook, Thomas Bletsoe, John Reynolds, Josias Dewye, Thomas Dodge. (PRO: E190/139/1).

10 March. Shipper by the *John* of Jersey, Mr. John Nicholls, bound from Dartmouth for New England: said John Nicholls. (PRO: E190/964/6).

10 March. The following apprenticed in London: Edward Warrington, aged 16, son of Francis W. of Whitefriars, London, shoemaker, to John Pearce, goldsmith, 4 years Barbados, with the consent of his said father. *Entry of 8 April shows him as bound to Charles Richards to serve 5 years in Jamaica.* (LMWB14/558). (LMWB14/542).

11 March-26 April. Shippers by the *Amity*, Mr. Richard Diamond, bound from London for Pennsylvania: Joseph Richards, James Blackman, George Barr, Peter Kekwich, Richard Thacker, Richard Willard, William Cockram. (PRO: E190/139/1).

12-31 March. Shippers by the *Desire* of Plymouth, Mr. Peter Baker, bound from Plymouth for Pennsylvania: James Fox, Thomas Mathew, John Homes, John Shilston, Nicholas Pearse, James Cooke, John Light, Francis Rawle. (PRO: E190/1050/16).

15 March. The following apprenticed in London: Samuel Rowton, aged 13, to Thomas Nixon, 5 years Virginia, with the consent of his father-in-law, Henry Arthur of St. Martin in the Fields, Middlesex; James Brough, aged 13, to Alexander Rowland, 5 years Jamaica, witnessed by his mother, Sarah (Brough) of Hog Lane, London. (LMWB14/544).

16 March. The following apprenticed in London: John Betson of London, pinmaker, to Robert Forbes, 4 years Jamaica. (LMWB14/544).

16 March-21 April. Shippers by the *Thomas*, Mr. Thomas Colbeard, bound from London for New York: Gerrard Vanheythusen, Robert Lineing, William Fortune, Nicholas Fortune, Joseph Billopp, Paul Freeman, Thomas Crundall. (PRO: E190/139/1).

17 March. Shipper by the *Sarah & Elizabeth* of Exeter, Mr. Nicholas Downe, bound from Exeter for Boston, New England: Thomas Turner. (PRO: E190/964/1).

17 March-1 April. Shippers by the *Recovery* of Exeter, Mr. Joseph Parsons, bound from Exeter for Boston, New England: Edward Seaward, Thomas Edmonds, Samuell Sampson. (PRO: E190/964/1).

20 March. The following apprenticed in Bristol: Joseph Bennet of Northampton to William Whetstone, 5 years Barbados or Nevis by *Europe*, said Joseph Bennet Mr. (BR).

22 March. The following apprenticed in London: William Trewlove, aged 30, son of William T. of Prees, Shropshire, silver wire drawer, deceased, to Charles Richards of Bloomsbury, Middlesex, merchant, 4 years Jamaica; George Moore of St. Giles in the Fields, Middlesex, carpenter, to the same, 4 years Jamaica; Robert Waterfield, carpenter, and his wife, Mary Waterfield, of St. James in the Fields, Middlesex, to the same, 4 years Jamaica. (LMWB14/547).

24 March. The following apprenticed in London: John Arkinstall, singleman aged 22, son of John A. of Wem, Shropshire, bodice maker, deceased, to Charles Richards of Bloomsbury, merchant, 4 years Jamaica. (LMWB14/549).

29 March. The following apprenticed in London: Edward James, son of William J. of Rotherhithe, Surrey, carpenter, deceased, to Thomas Nicholls of Deptford, Kent, surgeon, 8 years America, witnessed by his half-brother, William Partridge of Little Moorfields, barber; Henry Lodge, aged 40, of Deptford, Kent, to Charles Richards of Bloomsbury, Middlesex, merchant, 3 years Jamaica; Dorothy Forrester of King Street, Bloomsbury, Middlesex, spinster aged 23, to the same, 4 years Jamaica. (LMWB14/552).

30 March. The following apprenticed in London: John Tomes, son of John T. of Christchurch, Southwark, Surrey, soldier, to Nathaniel Bryer of Weymouth, Dorset, 7 years Pennsylvania; Charles Raines of Long Acre, London, carpenter, with Mary his wife, and William Richards with Elizabeth his wife (sister of Charles Raines), to Charles Richards of Looe, Cornwall, mariner, 4 years Jamaica; James Davies, singleman aged 21, son of Hugh Davies of Devon, husbandman, to Phillip Hodge, 4 years Jamaica, witnessed by Michael Vallis of Southwark, Surrey. (LMWB14/553).

30 March. The following apprenticed in Bristol: Henry Goddard of Whaddon, Glos, sergeweaver, to Peter Ware, planter, 4 years New England by *Boston Merchant*; John Miles of Whaddon, sergeweaver, to William Curtis, 4 years New England by *Boston Merchant*, said William Curtis Mr; Susanna, wife of John Miles, to above, 4 years New England by *Boston Merchant*. (BR).

31 March. The following apprenticed in London: Susanna Warton of St. Sepulchre, London, widow, to Thomas Nicholls of Deptford, Kent, surgeon, 5 years Pennsylvania; Solomon Baynam, son of Richard B. of Bishopsgate, London, weaver, to Christopher Prissicke of London, mariner, 4 years Barbados, with the consent of his father and Pleasant, his mother; Mary Greenoway, spinster, daughter of Henry G. of St. Paul's Wharf, London, gent, deceased, to the same, 4 years Barbados, witnessed by her cousin Rebbecah, wife of Charles Session of Lower Shadwell, Middlesex. Samuel Field to Charles Richards, 7 years Jamaica, witnessed by his mother Dorothy F. of Bloomsbury, Middlesex. (LMWB14/554,555).

March. Administration of John Sayer of Virginia. (AW).

1 April. The following apprenticed in London: William Mackerith, aged 26, of Piccadilly, Middlesex, bricklayer, to James Finch of St. Giles in the Fields, Middlesex, 4 years Pennsylvania; Timothy Burch, aged 16, to the same, 7 years Pennsylvania, with the consent of his brother William B. of St. Giles, victualler. (LMWB14/556).

2 April. The following apprenticed in London: John Honnott and his wife, Mary H., of Alresford, Hampshire, to James Streater, 4 years Pennsylvania; Joseph Wright of Oxford, aged 24, and Henry Wheatley of Warwickshire, aged 25, to Charles Jones of Rotherhithe, Surrey, mariner, 4 years Jamaica, witnessed by Richard Raines of Shadwell, Middlesex, waterman. (LMWB14/557).

3 April. Shipper by the *Augustine*, Mr. Zachary Taylor, bound from London for Virginia: John Jefferies. (PRO: E190/139/1).

3 April. Deposition by Joseph Butts of London, merchant aged 38, that John Grafton of Salem, New England, mariner, deceased, became indebted to Thomas Ball, citizen and leatherseller of London, by bonds of 24 August 1675 and 20 December 1682 for goods delivered on board Grafton's ship *Dolphin*. Benjamin Williams, citizen and leatherseller of London, is Ball's executor. Charles Barcroft of Watford, Hertfordshire, gent aged 20, deposes that Richard Crispe of Boston, New England, merchant, also became indebted to Benjamin Williams by several bonds. David Jefferys of Boston, New England, has been appointed as Williams' attorney. (LMCD).

5 April. The following apprenticed in London: Samuel Standish, aged 24, and William Laughton, aged 24, to Charles Richards, merchant, 4 years Jamaica. (LMWB14/558).

8 April. The following apprenticed in London: Michael Kennedy, aged 20, to John Pym, merchant, 4 years Jamaica, with the consent of his mother Elizabeth Jones, widow. (LMWB14/559).

9 April. The following apprenticed in London: Elizabeth Rameage, spinster aged 18, to Thomas Nicholls, surgeon, 6 years Pennsylvania or West Jersey, witnessed by her mother, Susannah R. of the Minories, London, widow; Henry Ambrose, aged 14, to the same, 7 years Pennsylvania or West Jersey, with the consent of his mother Alice Paine; Joseph Thompson, aged 16, whose parents are both dead, to Simon Rogers, 7 years Pennsylvania, witnessed by Richard Mercer of St. John's Street, soldier; Edward Pratt, aged 15, to Nathaniel Redman, citizen and carpenter of London, 5 years Jamaica, witnessed by Anthony Smith, surgeon at Fishmongers' Hall. (LMWB14/559,560).

9-28 April. Shippers by the *Charles*, Mr. Edmond Coppin, bound from London for Carolina: John Singleton, William Fry—, Charles Stepkins, John Rayne, Benjamin Bradley. (PRO: E190/139/1).

9 April-17 June. Shipper by the *Elizabeth*, Mr. John Balston, bound from London for New England: Joseph Cox, Nathaniell Boston, Thomas Godfry, Joseph Thompson, Ezekiel Hutchinson, Edward Schopens, Ralph Cook, Robert Partridge, Thomas Lane, John Hill, John Smallwood, Richard Parrott, Thomas Major, Richard Seal, John Bigg, John Teshmaker, Henry Allin, Noah Laurance, Samuell Holden, Thomas Cabell, Jonathan Leigh, John Beighton, Thomas Ruck, Hugh Horton, Thomas Dodge, John Rawson, Charles Savage, Thomas Sutton. (PRO: E190/139/1).

10 April. The following apprenticed in London: Margaret Finch, aged 17, spinster, to James Finch, shoemaker, 7 years Pennsylvania, witnessed by William Burch, victualler, and William Mackrith, bricklayer, both of St. Giles in the Fields, on behalf of the mother. (LMWB14/561).

16 April. The following apprenticed in London: Jane Hill, aged 15, to Samuel Sleigh, 7 years Jamaica, witnessed by her mother Katherine H. of Fenchurch Alley, London. (LMWB14/560).

16 April. The following apprenticed in London: Thomas Hawkins of Abingdon, Berkshire, to John Bunce, 4 years Pennsylvania, with the consent of his father. (LMWB14/562).

16 April-8 May. Shippers by the *Shield* of Stockton, Mr. John Howell, bound from Hull for Virginia: Daniell Toaes, James Marshall, William Hudson, Christopher Watkin, John Richardson, Richard Darkin, William Gibbitus, Benjamin Knapton, Thomas Clifton, John Watkin, John Cornwall, George Robotham. (PRO: E190/329/5).

17 April. The following apprenticed in London: Samuel Keepe, aged 19, to Charles Richards, 4 years Jamaica, with the consent of his master, Thomas Cole of Bloomsbury, Middlesex, joiner. (LMWB14/562).

19 April. The following apprenticed in London: Richard Bray, singleman aged 22, and William Mechin, singleman aged 20, to Charles Richards of Bloomsbury, merchant, 4 years Jamaica, witnessed by Thomas Arnes of Trumball Street, butcher; Joseph Osborne, aged 15, son of Joseph O., to Thomas Nicholls of London, surgeon, 7 years Pennsylvania or West Jersey, witnessed by his said father and mother, Margaret O. (LMWB14/565).

20 April. The following apprenticed in London: George Blaize, singleman aged 32, to Robert Forbes of St. Botolph Aldgate, London, surgeon, 4 years Jamaica, witnessed by Thomas Simpson of Lothbury, London, tailor; Robert Pullman, aged 15, to Thomas Nicholls, 7 years Pennsylvania or West Jersey, with the consent of his mother Elizabeth P. of Wapping, Middlesex. (LMWB14/566).

21 April. The following apprenticed in London: Thomas Norris, aged 22, of Leicester, to Thomas Nicholls, surgeon, 4 years Pennsylvania or West Jersey. (LMWB14/568).

24 April. The following apprenticed in London: Charles Carricke to serve Francis Foxcroft of Boston, New England, 4 years, witnessed by John Smith of St. Lawrence Lane, London. (LMWB14/569).

24 April. The following apprenticed in Bristol: John Wilkenson of Hertford to William Smith, 4 years Jamaica by *Anna Maria*; Thomas Smallwood of Stone, Staffs, to same, 4 years Jamaica by *Anna Maria*. (BR).

27 April. The following apprenticed in London: Daniell Robinson, aged 17, to John Richards of St. Botolph Aldgate, London, mariner, 7 years Barbados, with the consent of his father-in-law, George Kewland of Petticoat Lane, London, and his mother, Deborah K.; Francis Hartwell, singleman aged 23, to Thomas Price, 4 years Jamaica, witnessed by his brother, Thomas H. of Covent Garden, Middlesex, coachman. (LMWB14/576).

29 April. The following apprenticed in London: Nicholas Randall to John Richards, mariner, 4 years Barbados, witnessed by William Attwell of Soho, Middlesex. (LMWB14/578).

30 April. Shipper by the *Robert*, Mr. Elisha Bennett, bound from London for New England: James Ivery. (PRO: E190/139/1).

1 May. Deposition by Edward Carleton of London, merchant, that he has appointed Thomas Bolton of Charles Town, Carolina, as his attorney. (LMCD).

1 May. The following apprenticed in London: Margaret Delamott, formerly of the Isle of Wight but now of London, spinster aged 26, and Anne Hayne, formerly of Norfolk but now of London, spinster aged 26, to John Robinson of Shadwell, Middlesex, mariner, 4 years Jamaica, witnessed by Phillip Atkins of Spitalfields, Middlesex, tailor; Joane Browne, aged 19, Rebeccah Robinson, aged 19, and Mary Hutton, aged 19, to John Robinson, 4 years Jamaica, witnessed by Mary Trevailer of King Street, Westminster. (LMWB14/580).

4 May. Shipper by the *Tryal*, Mr. William Fry, bound from London for New England: John Hackshaw. (PRO: E190/139/1).

6 May. The following apprenticed in London: Henry Bennet, aged 28, to John Robinson, 4 years Jamaica, witnessed by Thomas Hollowell of Coleman Street, London, tailor; John Bell, aged 18, son of Thomas Bell of Maidwell Street, Golden Lane, London, coachman, to John Robinson, 4 years Jamaica, witnessed by his said father and by his mother, Mary Bell; Richard Lawrence, aged 20, to the same, 4 years Jamaica, with the consent of his master, Martin Wilkinson of Clerkenwell, Middlesex, carpenter. (LMWB14/587).

7 May. The following apprenticed in London: James La Casteel, singleman aged 30, to James Williams, mariner, 4 years Barbados. (LMWB14/588).

11 May. The following apprenticed in London: John Rowley of Long Sutton, Lincolnshire, husbandman aged 22, to James Williams, mariner, 4 years Barbados; John Dowzin, aged 21, labourer, to the same, 4 years Barbados. (LMWB14/591).

12 May. The following apprenticed in London: Thomas Loveday of Coggeshall, Essex, gardener, to John Richards, 4 years Barbados; Robert Mawson of Gateside, Westmorland, yeoman, to the same, 4 years Barbados. (LMWB14/591).

15 May. The following apprenticed in London: Henry Mathews of Greatworth, Northamptonshire, sawyer, to John Richards, 4 years Barbados; Cornelius Smewrey, aged 24, of Berwick on Tweed, Northumberland, weaver, to the same, 4 years Barbados. (LMWB14/592).

19 May. The following apprenticed in London: Anne Pashellor, aged 18, daughter of William P. of Beech Lane, Cripplegate, London, lead refiner, to Alexander Rowland, 4 years Jamaica, with the consent of her father of the Hermitage, Middlesex, cooper, and her mother-in-law, Anne. (LMWB14/595).

22 May. The following apprenticed from Christ's Hospital: John Browne, aged 15, to Christopher Keeble, commander of the *Vealz Merchant* bound for New England; Jacob Ward, aged 16, to Leonard Browne, commander of the *Anne* bound for Angola and Jamaica. (CH).

27 May-4 June. Shippers by the *Veles Merchant*, Mr. Christopher Keeble, bound from London for New England: Thomas Banes, Sir John Shorter, John Brailsford, Francis Chamberlaine, Joseph Rideon, John Pennington. (PRO: E190/139/1).

27 May-25 June. Shippers by the *Elizabeth & Katherine*, Mr. Richard Martin, bound from London for New York: John Stacy, Shem Bracebridge, Samuell Holland, John Greenhill, Jeremy [or Joseph] Hindmarsh. (PRO: E190/139/1).

28 May. The following apprenticed in London: Mary Cooke, daughter of Thomas C., blacksmith near St. Thomas's Hospital, Southwark, Surrey, to Godfrey Cummin of London, mariner, 4 years Jamaica, with the consent of her father and of her mother, Lucy C. (LMWB14/600).

May. Probate of will of James Rand of St. Mary Colechurch, London, a creditor of William Bancks in Virginia. (AW).

1-7 June. Shipper by the *Beake*, Mr. Edward Hill, bound from London for Virginia: John Gill. (PRO: E190/139/1).

3 June. Petition of James Smailes, master of the *Bachelor's Adventure*. When bound to Carolina he was driven into Bermuda by adverse winds where a passenger, Richard Phillips, demanded that his goods be unloaded. When the petitioner refused he was thrown into gaol and his vessel seized. (CSPC).

3 June. The following apprenticed in London: John Boill, singleman aged 22, to Josias Leech, mariner, 4 years Barbados, witnessed by Richard Lawrence of St. Paul Shadwell, Middlesex, wherryman. (LMWB14/603).

5-28 June. Shipper by the *Susanna*, Mr. Thomas Meech, bound from London for New York: Samuell Burlingham. (PRO: E190/139/1).

10 June-13 July. The following apprenticed in Liverpool to Gilbert Livesley of Liverpool, mariner, to serve 4 years in Virginia or Maryland: Hugh Owen of Wrexham, Denbighshire, labourer aged 24; Elizabeth Jones of West Chester, [Lancashire], spinster aged 21; John Jones [Joanes] of Wrexham, labourer aged 21; George Walker of Astbury, Cheshire, blacksmith aged 27; Ann Cooper of Lydiate, Lancashire, spinster aged 21; William Evans of Bristol, labourer aged 24; Alice Jenkinson of Warrington, Lancashire, spinster aged 21. (LaRO: QSP 625/2).

11 June. The following apprenticed in London: Jane Thunder, aged 18, to Bartholomew Sprint, 4 years New York, with the consent of her mother of Old Jewry, London; Mary Coates, aged 18, to the same, 4 years New York, with the consent of her mother; Elizabeth Bray, aged 20, spinster, to Jeremiah Hawthorne, 5 years Barbados. (LMWB14/608,609).

12 June. Deposition of James Goldham, citizen and draper of London, that Stephen Burton of Boston, New England, by bond of 7 October 1679 became indebted to Roger Mott, citizen and merchant tailor of London. Francis Hunlocke, citizen and ironmonger of London, deposes that Edward Hunlocke of Boston, New England, merchant, became indebted to Mott by bond of 10 March 1684. Roger Mott deposes that he has not received payment from Richard Buckley of Boston for gowns. (LMCD).

12 June. The following apprenticed in Bristol: The following apprenticed in Bristol: Daniel West of Brockenborough, Wilts, to Thomas C——, 4 years Montserrat by *Patience*. (BR).

14-26 June. Shippers by the *Success* of Exeter, Mr. Thomas Rost, bound from Exeter for New England: John Cholwill, Malachy Pyne, Pasche Minnes, Henry Pafford. (PRO: E190/964/1).

15 June. The following apprenticed in London: Joseph Halliday, singleman of Sunderland, Durham, to Edward Hill of Limehouse, Middlesex, mariner, 4 years Barbados. (LMWB14/613).

16 June. The following apprenticed in London: Robert Winton, aged 24, son of Edward W. in the King's Bench Prison, to serve Edward Marshall of Barbados 4 years, with the consent of his father and witnessed by Walter Curidon of Red Lion Court, Fleet Street, London, tailor; Ahazuerus Fromanteel of the Old Bailey, London, printer aged 24, to Thomas Meach of London, mariner, 4 years New York, witnessed by Bartholomew Sprint of the Old Change, London, printer; George Anderhill of the Temple, London, printer, to the same, 4 years New York, witnessed by Bartholomew Sprint. (LMWB14/616).

17 June. The following apprenticed in London: Elizabeth Davies, spinster, daughter of William D. of Ockley, Surrey, husbandman, deceased, and Elizabeth Jackman, daughter of John J. of Ockley, husbandman, deceased, to Thomas Davies of Limehouse, Middlesex, mariner, 4 years Barbados; Sarah Gibbs, aged 18, daughter of Nicholas G. of Bishopsgate, London, silkweaver, deceased, to Thomas Meach, 4 years New York, with the consent of her mother, Amy Gibbs of Whitecross Street, Middlesex. (LMWB14/616).

17 June. Shipper by the *Swan*, Mr. Thomas Meek, bound from London for New York: Paul Sheeman. (PRO: E190/139/1).

17 June-16 July. Shippers by the *Betty*, Mr. Edward Henfield, bound from London for New England: John Ivey, Charles Duke, Samuell Smithurst, Timothy Fowler, Nicholas & James Relk, John Ballentine, George Spilman, John Ive, Humphrey Rich, Francis Fox, Samuell Spicer, Stephen Alexander. (PRO: E190/139/1).

18 June. The following apprenticed in London: Mary Haite, spinster aged 18, daughter of John H. of Bozeat, Northamptonshire, labourer, deceased, to John Haslewood of Whitechapel, Middlesex, mariner, 4 years Virginia. (LMWB14/617).

25 June-19 July. Shippers by the *Endeavour* of Exeter, Mr. Samuell Paull, bound from Exeter for Barbados and Virginia: John Barons, Robert Burrage. (PRO: E190/964/1).

28 June-15 July. Shippers by the *Susan*, Mr. Edward Tatnall, bound from London for Virginia: Richard Bullard, Thomas Jennings, Blewit Bemont. (PRO: E190/139/1).

29 June. Deposition by Henry Smith, aged 33, servant of Robert Maurice of London, merchant, that on 31 January 1682 Samuel Winder of New York bought cloth from his master for which no payment has been received. Jacob Milbourne of London, merchant, is appointed attorney. (LMCD).

30 June-5 July. Shippers by the *King David* of Stonehouse, Mr. John Colloum, bound from Plymouth for Carolina: James Barbott, John Harris, John Warren. (PRO: E190/1050/16).

June. Administration of John Dewar of St. Michael Crooked Lane, London, who died in Quitto, Virginia, bachelor. (AW).

June. Probate of will of William Spencer of Cople, Bedfordshire, whose brother, Nicholas Spencer, was in Virginia. (AW).

5 July-3 August. Shippers by the *Hopewell*, Mr. Nicholas Smith, bound from London for Maryland: Robert Hatton, George Ayray, Michaell Yoakley, James Park, Benjamin Harwood, John Ironmonger. (PRO: E190/139/1).

6 July. Oxford Circuit prisoners reprieved to be transported to America. Gloucestershire: Christopher Woodward of Wotton Under Edge; Thomas Davies of Lydney. Herefordshire: Humphrey Davies of Weobley. Shropshire: Mary Walker of Ashford Carbonell; Evan Evans of Broseley; James Turner of Shrewsbury; Robert Williams of Wellington. Staffordshire: John Crowder alias Strowder of Longdon; Thomas Rowland alias Harrison of Kingswinford, blacksmith. (PRO: C66/3287/7).

6 July-4 August. Shippers by the *Margaret & Elizabeth*, Mr. Elisha Bennett, bound from London for New England: Thomas Hunt, William Coleman, Abraham Churchill. (PRO: E190/139/1).

9 July. Deposition by Paul Allestree of London, merchant aged 58, that in May 1686 Dr. John Battyn of Barbados shipped three servants named James Lancasteel, Robert Gore and John Steward on the *Carolina*, Mr. John Harding. At the end of May he embarked another servant, John Barford, who then ran away with Gore and Steward. On 22 June Battyn shipped two further servants, Bartholomew Guttridge and Robert Haise. (LMCD).

10 July. Deposition by John Ellingworth of London, mariner aged 39, that Charles Redford of Salem, New England, merchant, is indebted by bond of 2 May 1683 to Edward Ellis of London, silkman, for goods shipped by the *Thomas & Susan*. (LMCD).

10 July. The *Elizabeth & Katherine* of London bound for New York stopped in Plymouth by order of Customs officers. (PRO: E190/1050/16).

13 July. Midland Circuit prisoners reprieved to be transported to America. Derbyshire: John Ball; Henry Potts. Leicestershire: Francis Rivington. Lincolnshire: George Baxter; Mary Pauson; John Harris; William Stewkly; William Burneham; Richard Raynsford; William Eley; Laurence Fox. Northamptonshire: William Tasker; John Leverett. Nottinghamshire: William Brearly; Hannah Taylor; Richard Browne; Robert Jackson; Margaret Swaff. Warwickshire: John Romanstoe. (PRO: C66/3288/28).

13-23 July. Shippers by the *Samuell*, Mr. Daniell Bradley, bound from London for Virginia: Thomas Stark, Micajah Perry, Arthur North. (PRO: E190/139/1).

15 July. Shipper by the *Rose*, Mr. William Tucker, bound from London for New England: Abraham Tillard. (PRO: E190/139/1).

15 July. Northern Circuit prisoners reprieved to be transported to Barbados. Northumberland: William Hopper of Newcastle upon Tyne; Isabel Urwin alias Margaret Douglas of Newcastle; James Scott alias Generall of Gostonfield Head; Thomas Hasty of Millhouse, Haltwistle, shoemaker; John Reed of Charlton. Yorkshire: Ann Benson of Swillington, widow. (PRO: C66/3288/25).

16 July. Marshalsea prisoner reprieved on condition that he transports himself overseas: Christopher Cook of Wilton, Somerset, baker. (PRO: C66/3288/21).

16-23 July. Shippers by the *Brothers Adventure*, Mr. Henry Tregany, bound from London for Virginia: Francis Wheeler, Richard Cox. (PRO: E190/139/1).

16-31 July. Shippers by the *Dove*, Mr. John Wally, bound from London for New England: Edward Hull, Joseph Alford, John Reynolds, John Richardson, William Crowch. (PRO: E190/139/1).

16 July-25 September. Shippers by the *Endeavour*, Mr. John Quixly, bound from London for Carolina: Lionell Elliott, Walter Ryan, John Garrett, Lewis Sowlard, William Thornburgh, Zachary Burras, Lewis Gervaire, James Caley, Jacob Marium, Claude Hayes, Rene Bodewin, William Cook, William Geare, Charles Michell, James Watson, Anthony Dugar, John Richardson. (PRO: E190/139/1).

17 July. Newgate prisoners reprieved to be transported to Barbados or Jamaica. London: Elizabeth Wilson alias Ryecroft, spinster; Maurice Archer; William Cole; John Hilliard; Nathaniel Johnson; Richard Alborough of Ilford (Essex). Middlesex: John Lewis of Clerkenwell; Charles Homersham of the same; Daniel Flower of Stepney; John Crofts of the same; Elizabeth Tisdell of the same; Robert Robinson of St. Paul Covent Garden; John Thacker of Shadwell; Elinor Rogers of the same, widow; John Steeres of Whitechapel; Rebecca Rose, spinster, alias wife of Pasch Rose of the same; Richard Higginson of the same; Mary Cale of St. Martin in the Fields, spinster; John Mancroft of St. James Westminster; Mary Lush, wife of Thomas Lush of St. Mary Savoy; Francis Symonds of St. Giles in the Fields; William Roach of the same; Henry Clarke of Shoreditch. (PRO: C66/3288/20).

19 July. Shipper by the *William & Mary*, Mr. Benjamin Hall, bound from London for Virginia: Micajah Perry. (PRO: E190/139/1).

19 July. Shipper by the *Freeman* of Whitehaven bound from Liverpool for Virginia: George Ribton, Isaac Holroid. (PRO: E190/1347/1, 1348/6).

19-27 July. Shippers by the *John & Sarah*, Mr. John Francis, bound from London for Virginia: Micajah Perry, Joseph Strutt. (PRO: E190/139/1).

19 July-3 August. Shippers by the *Anne & Elizabeth*, Mr. William Orton, bound from London for Virginia: Richard Sherly, Robert Christopher, Josias Dewye. (PRO: E190/139/1).

20 July. Shipper by the *Katherine*, Mr. William Tucker, bound from London for New England: said William Tucker. (PRO: E190/139/1).

22 July-9 August. Shippers by the *Antelope* of Liverpool, Mr. George Hull, bound from Liverpool for Virginia: David Poole, James Read, John Barron, William Floyd, George Hull. (PRO: E190/1347/1, 1348/6).

26-28 July. Shippers by the *Booth*, Mr. Symon Emberley, bound from London for Virginia: William Paggen, Walter Furnis, Henry Dennis. (PRO: E190/139/1).

27 July. Shipper by the *Owners Adventure*, Mr. Peregrine Browne, bound from London for Maryland: Arthur Baily. (PRO: E190/139/1).

27 July-4 August. Shippers by the *Golden Lyon*, Mr. John Haslewood, bound from London for Virginia: Arthur Baily, Francis Lee. (PRO: E190/139/1).

27 July-7 August. Shippers by the *Charles & Jane*, Mr. Edward Poulson, bound from London for Maryland: John Abbington, Anthony Lacon. (PRO: E190/139/1).

27 July-28 August. Shippers by the *Mary*, Mr. James Smith, bound from London for New England: Arthur Shallett, Anthony Burren, Thomas Lane, William Burtwell, Jonathan Leigh. (PRO: E190/139/1).

29 July-13 August. The following apprenticed to James Hornby of Liverpool, mariner, to serve 4 years in Virginia or Maryland: Phillis Ferne of Blurton, Staffordshire, spinster aged 21; Roger Browne of Llandlehide, Caernarvonshire, singleman aged 21; Ann Johnson of Kinsley, Cheshire, spinster aged 21. (LaRO: QSP 625/2).

31 July-9 August. Shippers by the *Thomas & John*, Mr. John Browne, bound from London for Virginia: Thomas Ellis, Thomas Mark, John Tayler, Thomas Harman. (PRO: E190/139/1).

July. Administration of Samuel Partridge of Rappahannock, Virginia. (AW).

July. Probate of will of Otho Thorpe of All Hallows on the Wall, London, whose cousin, John Grice, was in Virginia. (AW).

July. Probate of will of John Style of Stepney, Middlesex, whose nephew, George Burrough, clerk, was in New England. (AW).

July. Probate of will of William Hawkins of Kingston-on- Thames, Surrey, who died in New England. (AW).

July. Administration of Thomas Power of St. Margaret Lothbury, London, who died in Virginia. (AW).

3 August. Shipper by the *Brothers*, Mr. James Braine, bound from London for Virginia: said James Braine. (PRO: E190/139/1).

3-12 August. Shippers by the *Samuell*, Mr. Thomas Bowman, bound from London for Maryland: Henry Loads, Anthony Stretton, John Monell, Robert Burman, John Constable. (PRO: E190/139/1).

3-18 August. Shippers by the *Elizabeth & Katherine*, Mr. Timothy Keyser, bound from London for Maryland and Virginia: Samuell Thayer, William Paggen, Edmond Harrison. (PRO: E190/139/1).

3-27 August. Shippers by the *Elizabeth*, Mr. Peter Butler, bound from London for New England: Arthur Shallett, John Smallwood, Charles Sebright, John Masters, Mathew Page, John Maxwell. (PRO: E190/139/1).

4-12 August. Shippers by the *Adventure*, Mr. Peter Peake, bound from London for Maryland: Thomas Coman, John Hubbuck. (PRO: E190/139/1).

4-14 August. Shippers by the *John*, Mr. Daniell Pensax, bound from London for Virginia: Thomas Stark, John Ransome. (PRO: E190/139/1).

5-9 August. Shippers by the *Lawrel* of Liverpool, Mr. Gilbert Livesley, bound from Liverpool for Maryland: Thomas Johnson, Clement Sayle, Edward Booker. (PRO: E190/1347/1, 1348/6).

5-11 August. Shippers by the *Crown Mallago*, Mr. [Michael] Staples, bound from London for Maryland: Thomas Martin, John Tayler. (PRO: E190/139/1).

6 August. Anna Shute, relict and executrix of Samuel Shute, citizen and dyer of London, deceased, late partner of his father-in-law Samuel Shute who is joint executor, have revoked a letter of attorney granted to Mr. John Robinson of New York, merchant, and have appointed Christopher Gore of New York, merchant, by letter of 13 July 1686. (LMCD).

6 August-2 October. The following apprenticed in Liverpool to Edward Tarleton of Liverpool, mariner, to serve 4 years in Virginia or Maryland: Joan Norres of the Isle of Man, spinster aged 26; Alice Lacie of the Isle of Man, spinster aged 21; Theophilus Basnett of Kelsall, Cheshire, singleman aged 22; Richard Thomas of Clanriott [?Llanrhydd], Denbighshire, butcher aged 30. (LaRO: QSP 625/2).

7 August. Shipper by the [blank], Mr. John Boone, bound from London for Maryland: Thomas Harman. (PRO: E190/139/1).

9-16 August. Shippers by the *Jacob*, Mr. Charles Reeves, bound from London for Maryland: Samuell Groome, James Dryden, Edward Carlton, Dudley Carlton. (PRO: E190/139/1).

11-31 August. Shippers by the *Hopewell*, Mr. Sampson Stoddard, bound from London for New England: John Smith, Joseph Alford, Benjamin Susan, Anthony Stretton, Samuell Ball, John Blackall, Sir John Shorter, Ambrose Crawley. (PRO: E190/139/1).

11 August-20 December. Shippers by the *Dragon*, Mr. Roger Whitfield, bound from London for New York and Pennsylvania: Bartholomew Hart, John West, John Greening, Phillip Ford, Samuell Burlingham, Mathew Robinson, Jonah Smith. (PRO: E190/139/1).

12-26 August. Shippers by the *Vine* of Liverpool, Mr. Thomas Preeson, bound from Liverpool for Virginia: William Preeson, Robert Bridge, John Molineux, Jacob Hall, Josias Keyme. (PRO: E190/1347/1, 1348/6).

12 August-1 September. Shippers by the *Morning Star* of Liverpool, Mr. Thomas Heyes, bound from Liverpool for Virginia: Samuell Minchall, John Barnes, Thomas Wynne, Robert Taylor, Richard Starkie, Robert Smith, Mary Stevenson, Thomas Read, Joseph Powell, Henry Maddock, James Sykes, Randle Blackshaw, Phineas Pemberton, Bryan Peart. (PRO: E190/1347/1, 1348/6).

13-25 August. Shippers by the *Benedict Leonard*, Mr. Francis Partis, bound from London for Maryland: Jeremy Callaway, James Wagstaffe, John Seaman. (PRO: E190/139/1).

14 August. Shipper by the *Abraham & Francis*, Mr. Edward Burford, bound from London for Virginia: William Paggen. (PRO: E190/139/1).

17 August. Shipper by the *Thomas & Richard*, Mr. Thomas Wynn, bound from London for Carolina: Samuell Burdett. (PRO: E190/139/1).

17-23 August. Shippers by the *John* of Exeter, Mr. Isaac Stoneham, bound from Exeter for Virginia: Thomas Chrispin, Thomas Smith. (PRO: E190/964/1).

17 August-4 September. Shippers by the *Hopewell*, Mr. John Rudds, bound from London for Virginia: Gabriel Grunwin, John Tutt, Robert Christopher, William

Aldersey, Thomas Sellon, Katherine Gawler, Richard Cox, Edward Braine. (PRO: E190/139/1).

18 August-4 September. Shippers by the *Thomas & Susan*, Mr. Robert Lewis, bound from London for New England: Nicholas & James Relk, William Chambers, Paul Bristoe [or Bustoe], Edward Ellis, Henry Hatford, Castor Higgs. (PRO: E190/139/1).

19 August-10 September. The following apprenticed in Liverpool to John Bankes of Liverpool, mariner, to serve 4 years in Virginia or Maryland: Isabell Wilkinson of Carlisle, [Cumberland], spinster aged 22; Alice Turner of Goosnargh, Lancashire, widow aged 30. (LaRO: QSP 625/2).

20-21 August. Shippers by the *Windmill* of Plymouth, Mr. James Trefry, bound from Plymouth for Virginia: John Rogers, Robert Brockendon, Thomas Jackson. (PRO: E190/1050/16).

20 August-13 September. Shippers by the *Potomack Merchant*, Mr. Charles Partis, bound from London for Virginia: Francis Lee, Edward Carlton, Richard Buck, William Peel, Ambrose Crawley, James Dryden. (PRO: E190/139/1).

23-26 August. Shipper by the *Elizabeth*, Mr. John Williams, bound from Exeter for Virginia: William Drake. (PRO: E190/964/1).

25 August. Shippers by the *Culpepper*, Mr. Christopher Morgan, bound from London for Virginia: Francis Wheeler, John Constantine. (PRO: E190/139/1).

25 August. Shipper by the *Hopewell*, Mr. Roger Elliott, bound from Exeter for Virginia: Robert Dabinet. (PRO: E190/964/1).

25 August-16 September. Shippers by the *Swan*, Mr. William Coggan, bound from Exeter for Virginia: John Manckly, Humphrey Bawden, Symon Mayowe, Hugh Bidwell, Joseph Saunders, John Foxwell, John Coly. (PRO: E190/964/1).

26 August. Shipper by the *Averilla*, Mr. Abraham Wild, bound from London for Maryland: Arthur Baily. (PRO: E190/139/1).

26 August. Shipper by the *Submission* of Liverpool, Mr. James Hornby, bound from Liverpool for Virginia: James Settle. (PRO: E190/1347/1, 1348/6).

26-31 August. Shippers by the *Constant*, Mr. William Burnham, bound from London for Maryland: Richard Davies, Samuell Field, Nicholas Hayward. (PRO: E190/139/1).

26 August-1 September. Shippers by the *Unity* of Lyme, Mr. John Bull, bound from Lyme for Virginia: John Burridge & Co., James Tucker, John Nicholas & Co. (PRO: E190/887/1).

26 August-10 September. Shippers by the *Bristol Merchant*, Mr. Samuell Woodbury, bound from London for New England: John Wase, William

Stonehewer, John Mills, William Dockwra, Michaell Russell, Samuell Kirk, Robert Plumstead. (PRO: E190/139/1).

27 August. Shipper by the *Adventure*, Mr. Ralph Cooper, bound from London for Virginia: Daniell Hickman. (PRO: E190/139/1).

28-31 August. Shippers by the *Stephen & Edward*, Mr. Sebastian Ginge, bound from London for Virginia: Hugh Aldworth, Robert Bristow, Edward Corbett. (PRO: E190/139/1).

30 August. Shipper by the *Truelove*, Mr. Ralph Constance, bound from London for Virginia: Sir Benjamin Ayloffe. (PRO: E190/139/1).

30 August. Shipper by the *Mercy* of Plymouth, Mr. Edward Blagg, bound from Plymouth for Virginia: Abraham Searle. (PRO: E190/1050/16).

30 August-6 September. Shippers by the *Hound*, Mr. Phineas Hide, bound from London for Virginia: Robert Burman, George Cornish, Nicholas Patrick. (PRO: E190/139/1).

31 August. Shipper by the *Aaron*, Mr. Edward Hanshaw, bound from London for Virginia: John Tayler. (PRO: E190/139/1).

31 August-3 September. Shippers by the *Samuell*, Mr. John Atkins, bound from London for Carolina: Alice Boudenell, Peter Malacha, Peter Albert. (PRO: E190/139/1).

August. Administration with will of James Jesson of St. Andrew Undershaft, London, who had lands in New England. (AW).

1-13 September. The following apprenticed in Liverpool to Thomas Sandiford Jr. of Liverpool, merchant, to serve 4 years in Virginia or Maryland: Joseph Low of Ashton in Makerfield, [Lancashire], labourer aged 22; Margaret Thomas of Whitchurch, Shropshire, spinster aged 23; Thomas Jones of Northopp, Flint, milliner aged 22; Sarah Barber of Tamworth, Staffordshire, spinster aged 22. (LaRO: QSP 625/2).

1 September. Shipper by the [blank] *John?*, Mr. John Tanner, bound from London for Virginia: Thomas Welch. (PRO: E190/139/1).

1-3 September. Shippers by the *Dewie*(?), Mr. Alexander Notey(?), bound from London for Virginia: John Hoolby, Daniell Foe. (PRO: E190/139/1).

3 September. Shipper by the *William & Elizabeth*, Mr. Richard Williams, bound from London for Virginia: Charles Middleton. (PRO: E190/139/1).

4-28 September. Shippers by the *Jefferies*, Mr. Thomas Arnold, bound from London for Virginia and Pennsylvania: William Woodbee, Thomas Laurence, Samuell Newson, Edward Round, Samuell Round, Hugh Lamb, Richard Whitpan, Oliver Williams, Nicholas Dawes, Thomas Beer, Walter Benthall. (PRO: E190/139/1).

6-9 September. Shippers by the *Exeter Merchant* bound from Exeter [?for Virginia]: John Lile, Thomas Smith. (PRO: E190/964/1).

7 September. Shippers by the *America*, Mr. John Venner, bound from London for Virginia: Edward Leman, William Forster. (PRO: E190/139/1).

7 September. Shipper by the *Margaret*, Mr. John Bowman, bound from London for Virginia: Benjamin Braine. (PRO: E190/139/1).

8 September-4 October. Shippers by the *Content*, Mr. William Johnson, bound from London for Virginia and Maryland: Edward Leman, Thomas Courtney, Thomas Birdsey. (PRO: E190/139/1).

9-20 September. Shippers by the *Love*, Mr. James Till, bound from London for Maryland: George Cornish, Samuell Phillips. (PRO: E190/139/1).

9-27 September. Shippers by the *Barbados Merchant*, Mr. Samuell Legg, bound from London for New England: John Boucher, Charles Duke, Richard Stracey, Richard Bechar, John Beighton, Thomas Gibbs, William Ashurst. (PRO: E190/139/1).

10 September. Deposition by John Harrison of London, gent aged 30, that Edmund Roberts Esq. of Canterbury, Kent, agreed with Francis Jarvis of London, gent, to become partners in trade with Virginia. (LMCD).

10-17 September. Shippers by the *Lamb* of Liverpool, Mr. William Glover, bound from Liverpool for Virginia: Daniell Clark, Peter Atherton, Thomas Sandiford. (PRO: E190/1347/1, 1348/6).

11 September. Joane Broadeway of Pitminster, Somerset, spinster; and Margarett Bellrenger of North Petherton, Somerset, spinster, bound to John Bull of Lyme Regis, mariner, to serve 4 years in Virginia or Maryland. (DRO B7/M9).

14 September. Shipper by the [blank] *Mary?*, Mr. John Gardner, bound from London for New England: Joseph Tayler. (PRO: E190/139/1).

17 September. Deposition by Mr. Robert Ellis, formerly of Maryland but now of St. Martin in the Fields, Middlesex, gent, that he has appointed Mr. Thomas Courtney of St. Mary County, Maryland, as his attorney. (LMCD).

17 September-11 October. Shippers by the *Barnaby*, Mr. Mathew Rider, bound from London for Virginia: Edmond Littlepage, Richard Atkinson, Richard Marsh, Henry Loades, Thomas Mynn, Francis Tyson. (PRO: E190/139/1).

20 September. Shippers by the *Agreement* of Plymouth bound from Plymouth for Virginia: Peter Rowe, John Rogers. (PRO: E190/1050/16).

21 September-2 October. Shippers by the *Virginia Factor*, Mr. William Hill, bound from London for Maryland: Nicholas Bell, Samuell Hincks, Edward Round. (PRO: E190/139/1).

22 September. Shipper by the *Hannah & Sarah* of Boston, Mr. Isaac Carter, bound from Dartmouth for New England: said Isaac Carter. (PRO: E190/964/6).

23 September-6 October. The following apprenticed in Liverpool to Edmund Croston of Liverpool, mariner, to serve 4 years in Virginia or Maryland: William Alsea of Farnham, Hampshire, painter aged 22; Samuell Chapman of Brundsley, Derbyshire, tailor aged 21; John Richardson of Mansfield, Nottinghamshire, bricklayer aged 22; John Gerrard of Parr, Lancashire, blacksmith aged 30; John Shipabottome of Elton near Bury, Lancashire, husbandman aged 27; Samuell Sedwell of Manchester, Lancashire, weaver aged 24; Amy Pendleton of Manchester, spinster aged 26; Joseph Howard of Broadston, Derbyshire, joiner aged 36. (LaRO: QSP 625/2).

23 September-13 October. Shipper by the *America*, Mr. John Marshall, bound from Liverpool for Virginia: Nathaniell Bacon, Thomas Clayton, Richard Ratlife. (PRO: E190/1347/1, 1348/6).

24 September-22 November. Shippers by the *Katherine*, Mr. Edmond Paine, bound from London for Maryland: Ambrose Crawley, James Dryden. (PRO: E190/139/1).

25 September-6 October. Shippers by the *Two Brothers*, Mr. William Welstead, bound from London for New England: Joseph Bishop, Ralph Cook, Sir Edmond Andrews, Thomas Powell. (PRO: E190/139/1).

25 September-11 October. Shippers by the *Turkey Merchant*, Mr. Thomas Burrell, bound from London for Virginia: Richard Cox, Jeremy Trewooley. (PRO: E190/139/1).

27 September. The following apprenticed in Liverpool to Richard Radcliffe of Liverpool, merchant, to serve 4 years in Virginia or Maryland: John Naylor, aged 28, son of Thomas N. of Bowas, Staffordshire. (LaRO: QSP 625/2).

28 September. Shipper by the *Young Prince*, Mr. Robert Lurting, bound from London for Virginia: William Paggen. (PRO: E190/139/1).

28 September. Shipper by the *John & Thomas*, Mr. Miles Cook, bound from London for Virginia: James Skorrell. (PRO: E190/139/1).

30 September-1 October. Shippers by the *Daniell & Elizabeth*, Mr. William Ginnis, bound from Plymouth for Virginia: William Martyn, Thomas Warren. (PRO: E190/1050/16).

September. Administration of Nicholas Best of Stratford by Bow, Middlesex, who died in Maryland, widower. (AW).

September. Probate of will of Zaccheus Breedon (bound for Carolina or Maryland) who died at sea or abroad.(AW).

September. Administration of William Watson of Rotherhithe, Surrey, who died at sea near Carolina. (AW).

September. Administration of Josias Jones of Greenwich, Kent, who died in Virginia. (AW).

September. Administration of John Dunn of the ship *Resolution*, who died at sea, bachelor. (AW).

September. Probate of will of William Balfoure of Virginia. (AW).

1-7 October. Shippers by the *Diligence* bound from Exeter [?for Virginia]: Giles Browne, Edward March, Walter Lyle. (PRO: E190/964/1).

2 October. Shippers by the *Maryland*, Mr. John Dorman, bound from London for Virginia: John Smith, Micajah Perry. (PRO: E190/139/1).

2 October. Shipper by the *Hope*, Mr. John Clutterbuck, bound from London for New England: Daniell Atkins. (PRO: E190/139/1).

2-15 October. Shipper by the *White Fox*, Mr. George Purvis, bound from London for Virginia: John Marks. (PRO: E190/139/1).

5 October. Shipper by the *Endeavour* of Plymouth bound from Plymouth for Virginia: John Rogers. (PRO: E190/1050/16).

6 October. The following apprenticed in Liverpool to Richard Houghton of Liverpool, merchant, to serve 4 years in Virginia or Maryland: John Walker of Belfast, Ireland, merchant aged 19; Judith Wiresdell of Wolverhampton, Staffordshire, widow aged 19. (LaRO: QSP 625/2).

6-18 October. Shippers by the *Exchange* of Exeter, Mr. Christopher Haycroft, bound from Exeter for Virginia: Robert Dabinet, Thomas Smith, Hugh Bidwell. (PRO: E190/964/1).

7-12 October. Shippers by the *Reserve* of Looe, Mr. John Jory, bound from Plymouth for Virginia: John Woods, Thomas Weston. (PRO: E190/1050/16).

8-13 October. Shippers by the *Mary*, Mr. John Harris, bound from London for Virginia and Maryland: James Beaumont, Stephen Bearcroft, Richard Drafgate, Richard Booth. (PRO: E190/139/1).

9 October. John White, aged 16, apprenticed from Christ's Hospital to Thomas Warren, commander of the *Society* bound for Barbados. (CH).

9-16 October. Shippers by the *St. Thomas*, Mr. Henry Sutton, bound from London for Virginia: Edward Leman, William Conly. (PRO: E190/139/1).

11 October. Shipper by the *Elizabeth* of Jersey, Mr. Daniel Janurin, bound from Dartmouth for Virginia: said Daniel Janurin. (PRO: E190/964/6).

11 October. Shipper by the *William & Mary* of Dartmouth, Mr. William Elliott, bound from Dartmouth for Virginia: said William Elliott. (PRO: E190/964/6).

11 October. Deposition by John Jones, servant of Thomas Cuddon of London, merchant, that Thomas Jenner of Boston, New England, became indebted to Cuddon by bond of 6 October 1685. (LMCD).

15-21 October. Shippers by the *Loyalty* of Liverpool, Mr. Edward Tarleton, bound from Liverpool for Virginia: Silvester Richmond, Christopher Robinson. (PRO: E190/1348/6).

15-30 October. Shippers by the *Advantage* of Liverpool, Mr. John Fisher, bound from Liverpool for Virginia: Randle Gallaway, Jonathan Livesley, Ralph Foster, Alexander Norres. (PRO: E190/1347/1, 1348/6).

15 October-10 November. Shippers by the *Samuell & Thomas*, Mr. John Tebbott, bound from London for New England: Thomas Sontley, Walter Monck, John Coltman, Richard Bocher, John Teshmaker, John Smart, Elizabeth Procter, Henry Hale, Thomas Weynell, Francis Wyell. (PRO: E190/139/1).

19-21 October. Shippers by the *William & Thomas*, Mr. Francis Harbin, bound from London for Maryland: Hugh Ecclestone, John Richards, Ann Hart. (PRO: E190/139/1).

19-21 October. Shippers by the *Bristol Frigate* bound from Plymouth for Virginia: George Lapthorne, William Tom. (PRO: E190/1050/16).

21 October. Shipper by the *Constant Mary*, Mr. Edward Rhodes, bound from London for Virginia: said Edward Rhodes. (PRO: E190/139/1).

21 October. Shipper by the *Friendship*, Mr. Henry Martin, bound from London for Maryland: said Henry Martin. (PRO: E190/139/1).

21-22 October. Shippers by the *Diligence* from Liverpool [*destination not stated*]: Jeffrey Theckstone, Edward Rose, John Pluckington. (PRO: E190/1348/6).

23 October-15 November. Shippers by the *Augustine*, Mr. Zachary Taylor, bound from London for Virginia: Albertus Warren, Francis Wheeler, Jeremy Bradfield, Richard Atkinson, Edward Calthrop, Stephen Sykes, John Munfield, Thomas Chisman. (PRO: E190/139/1).

26 October. Shipper by the *Isaac & Sarah*, Mr. Samuell Isaac, bound from London for Virginia: George Williams. (PRO: E190/139/1).

26 October-8 November. Shippers by the *Reserve* of Liverpool, Mr. Christopher Moore, bound from Liverpool for Virginia: James Graham, John Rimers. (PRO: E190/1347/1).

27 October-27 January 1687. Depositions in London re the voyage of the *Friends' Adventure*, Mr. Richard Angell, from London to Carolina and Maryland in 1684, her condemnation in Maryland in 1685, and her sale there to Mr. Philip Lynes. (EA).

27 October-20 November. Shippers by the *Globe*, Mr. Bartholomew Watts, bound from London for Maryland: Richard Goodall, Samuell Yong, Robert Lee, Thomas Ellis, William Osbaldeston, Joseph Strutt. (PRO: E190/139/1).

30 October. Shipper by the *Elizabeth & Mary*, Mr. Dean Cock, bound from London for Virginia: William Wills. (PRO: E190/139/1).

October. Shipper by the *Dolphin* of Bideford, Mr. Daniel Heynes, bound from Bideford for Maryland: John Buck. (PRO: E190/964/9).

October. Administration of Samuel Cooke of Rotherhithe, Surrey, who died in Virginia, bachelor. (AW).

October. Administration of Mathew Payne of Pennsylvania, widower. (AW).

October. Administration of William Dickson of Virginia, bachelor. (AW).

October. Probate of will of Oliver Smith of Ratcliffe, Stepney, Middlesex, who died on the ship *Susanna* in Virginia. (AW).

2-6 November. Shipper by the *William & Elizabeth* of Belfast, Mr. Adam Gillis, bound from Liverpool for Virginia: Robert Black. (PRO: E190/1348/6).

3-29 November. Shippers by the *Concord*, Mr. William Jefferies, bound from London for Virginia: John Gore, Edmond Littlepage, Samuell Poynter, Humphrey Nelson, Samuell Deane, Francis Reeves, Samuell Austin. (PRO: E190/139/1).

4 November. Shippers by the *Lyon* from Liverpool [*destination not stated*]: Henry Willington, Ann Hesketh. (PRO: E190/1348/6).

4 November-3 December. Shippers by the *Recovery*, Mr. Thomas Hasted, bound from London for Carolina: Richard Goodall, Thomas Wych, Elias Baudinell, Peter Falconer, Edward Lloyd, John Ashby, Tryon & Perkins, Phillip Speed, Francis Noble, Francis Plumstead, James Lennier, David Dufoy, Josias Bull, William Grace. (PRO: E190/139/1).

8 November. Shippers by the *Mary*, Mr. Richard Tibbott, bound from London for Virginia: Thomas Stark, Thomas Birchill, William Fulwood. (PRO: E190/139/1).

8 November. Shipper by the *Merchants Adventure*, Mr. Richard Langley, bound from London for Virginia: Thomas Stark. (PRO: E190/139/1).

12-18 November. Shippers by the *Mary*, Mr. Edward Bicknall, bound from London for New England: John Beighton, John Jackson, Edward Whitehall. (PRO: E190/139/1).

22 November. Deposition by Paul Wicks of London, scrivener, that on 1 September 1662 Mainwaring Hammond of Rickohocke, New Kent County Virginia, mortgaged his plantations in Virginia to William Wheatley, citizen and grocer of London. (LMCD).

22-23 November. Shippers by the *Susan*, Mr. Richard Featherstone, bound from London for Virginia: Thomas Wych, William Wills, John Strechley. (PRO: E190/139/1).

23 November-1 December. Shippers by the *Judith*, Mr. Mathew Trim, bound from London for Virginia: Mathew Jones, Richard Hammon, Robert Pharo, Thomas Cuddon. (PRO: E190/139/1).

25 November. Shipper by the *Antelope*, Mr. Henry Cooke, bound from London for Virginia: James Monckles(?). (PRO: E190/139/1).

30 November. Deposition by Robert Yardley of London, draper, that Daniel Royse of Boston, New England, merchant, became indebted by bond of 13 March 1686 to James Eyton of New Fish Street, London, draper. (LMCD).

30 November. Deposition by John Marissall of London, weaver, and his wife, Elizabeth Marissall alias Parris, that they have appointed Mr. Edward Gouge of Boston, New England, merchant, as their attorney. (LMCD).

November. Probate of will of John Royse of London merchant, who died in Gravesend, Kent, (bound for New York). (AW).

1 December-5 January. Shippers by the *Robert*, Mr. Richard Burt, bound from London for New York: Walter Benthall, Robert Green, Nathan Rookby, Daniell Foe, Samuell Kirk, John Loveroo, Henry Hale, John Ongly, William Stonehewer. (PRO: E190/139/1, 147/1).

2-14 December. Shippers by the *Katherine*, Mr. Samuell Dodson, bound from London for Virginia and Maryland: James Skerrett, Anthony Burren, Thomas Potter, Samuell Yong. (PRO: E190/139/1).

17-22 December. Shipper by the *Planters Adventure*, Mr. Jeremy Tayler, bound from London for Maryland: Alexander Armstrong. (PRO: E190/139/1).

20 December. Western Circuit prisoners reprieved to be transported to Barbados. Devon: Francis Dew of Plymouth; John Evans of Cadbury; Edward Turvey of Plymouth; William Ward of Plymouth; William Jones of Broad Clyst. Wiltshire: Henry Beaman of Chippenham. (PRO: C66/3290/11).

24 December. Shipper by the *Speedwell*, Mr. Marmaduke Gamly, bound from London for Virginia: said Marmaduke Gamly. (PRO: E190/139/1).

24 December. Deposition by Elizabeth Appleyard, aged 40, wife of Thomas Appleyard of St. Paul, Shadwell, Middlesex, mariner, and daughter of John Sanders of Barbados, planter, deceased, that her father had four children by his wife Elizabeth, also deceased: Richard Sanders of Stepney, Middlesex, merchant, since deceased overseas; John Sanders of Fenny Stratford, Buckinghamshire, draper; Henry Sanders who went many years ago to Barbados and then to New England and, not having been heard of for 20 years, is now supposedly dead; and the deponent. The heir-at-law of John Sanders Sr. is the deponent's brother, John Sanders, who has appointed Mrs. Dorothy

Cecill of Barbados, widow, and Mrs. Dorothy Nixon of London, widow (now bound for Barbados), as his attorneys. (LMCD).

29 December. Shipper by the *Richard* of Bristol, Mr. Thomas Codner, bound from Bristol for Virginia: Michaell Wharton. (PRO: E190/1148/1).

29-30 December. Shippers by the *Alathea* of Bristol, Mr. Phillip Jeffris, bound from Bristol for Virginia: Richard Benson, Uzzell Bussell. (PRO: E190/1148/1).

December. Administration of Henry Thompson of Boston, New England. (AW).

December. Probate of will of Mary Langhorne alias Ingoldsby of Holborn, Middlesex, who died in Staughton, Huntingdonshire, and whose nephew, Oxenbridge, was in New England. (AW).

1687

3-15 January. Shippers by the *Unicorn*, Mr. William Norrington, bound from London for Virginia: William Billop, James Waters, Vincent Goddard, Nicholas Hayward, Thomas Elsing. (PRO: E190/147/1).

17-24 January. Shipper by the *Crown*, Mr. William Thompson, bound from London for Carolina: said William Thompson. (PRO: E190/147/1).

14 January. Shipper by the *James & Thomas* of Plymouth, Mr. Sampson Clarke, bound from Plymouth for Virginia: John Clarke. (PRO: E190/1051/13).

19 January. Shipper by the *Blessing*, Mr. John Budge(?), bound from London for Virginia: said John Budge. (PRO: E190/147/1).

21 January. Shipper by the *Susanna* of Plymouth, Mr. John Ford, bound from Plymouth for Virginia: Marke Batt. (PRO: E190/1051/13).

1 February-17 March. Shippers by the *Jerusalem* of Bristol, Mr. John Pepwell, bound from Bristol for Boston, New England: Erasmus Dole, Sir Thomas Earle, John Elsworthy, Henry Gibbs, John Trimmer, Charles White, John Newman. (PRO: E190/1148/1).

4 February-17 March. Shippers by the *Amity*, Mr. Gresham Boone, bound from London for New York: John Gardner, Elizabeth Skelton, John Longe, Thomas Lodwick, Ralph Hadley, Jasper Shephard, John Button, Peter Hudson, Christopher Willing. (PRO: E190/147/1).

7 February-15 March. Shippers by the *Endeavour*, Mr. John Richardson, bound from London for New York: John Blackwell, Benjamin Braine, Joseph Pipping, Humphrey Edwin. (PRO: E190/147/1).

8-21 February. Shippers by the *Mary & Elizabeth*, Mr. Thomas Gadsden, bound from London for Virginia and Carolina: Richard Buller, Peter Hudson, Thomas Dodd, Thomas Parker, Henry Royall. (PRO: E190/147/1).

12 February-12 March. Shippers by the *Society*, Mr. Thomas Fairweather, bound from London for New England: John Margetts, John Coltman, Thomas Plummer, James Blackman, John Crow, Noah Lawrance, Joseph Alford, Jeremy Johnson, Cockram & Hume, Joseph Hide, Lawrence French, John Pettit, Nathaniell Ware, Thomas Noake, Nathaniell Wood, Israell Wormall. (PRO: E190/147/1).

14 February-11 May. Shippers by the *Dolphin*, Mr. John Foy, bound from London for New England: John Thwing, Sarah Harris, David Hutton, Thomas Godfry, Mathew Cadwell, William Gore, Richard Beeker, Nehemiah Borne, Richard Prockter, Joseph Crayker, Daniell Ingoll, Richard Drafgate, Anthony Burren, Nicholas & James Kelk, Thomas Goldsmith, Joseph Came, Morice

Mosely, Edmond Wildbore, Sir John Shorter, Ann Penny, Castor Higgs, John Rolston, Nathaniell Marshall, Henry Hatfield, Samuell Hackaday, John Dunston, John Harvey, Richard Beacher, Joseph Webb. (PRO: E190/147/1).

17 February-2 March. Shippers by the *Timberlog*, Mr. John King, bound from London for Pennsylvania: John Pitts, William Cockram, Daniell Wherley. (PRO: E190/147/1).

19 February-10 March. Shippers by the *Susan*, Mr. John Rose, bound from London for Carolina: Elias Bowdenett, Richard Goodall, William Thornburgh, Peter Burtell, Daniell Brulon, Joseph Barker, Benjamin Bradyll. (PRO: E190/147/1).

21 February. Newgate prisoners reprieved to be transported to Barbados or Jamaica. London: Elinor Davis, spinster; Sarah Deane, spinster; Joseph Hensley; John Culverwell; John Mills; John Elered; John Dunkin. Middlesex: Elias Smith of Islington; John Jennings of the same; William Austin Hyde of St. Clement Danes; Edward Newgent of the same; Elizabeth Banfield alias Katherine Carter alias Howard alias Smith of the same, spinster; Thomas Fann of Stoke Newington; Edward Anthony of St. Andrew Holborn; Isaac Vaughan alias Ward of the same; James Deale alias Reynolds of St. Paul Covent Garden; Thomas Gibbs of St. Martin in the Fields; John Clarke of St. Anne Westminster; (PRO: C66/3291/11).

21 February. Oxford Circuit prisoners reprieved to be transported to America. Berkshire: John Goodson of New Windsor. Gloucestershire: Benjamin Smith of Burton on Hill; Charles Haynes of Bourton on the Hill. Monmouthshire: John Thomas of Llanthewy Skirrid. Staffordshire: Thomas Challoner of Leek. (PRO: C66/3291/14).

24 February. Norfolk Circuit prisoners reprieved to be transported to America. Norfolk: William Poynton of North Lopham; Edward Kemp of Crimplesham. Suffolk: Joseph Warner of Kedington; Robert Pulham of Kedington. (PRO: C66/3291/9).

February. Administration of Charles Larrence of Boston, New England. (AW).

1-15 March. Shippers by the *Expectation* of Bristol, Mr. William Jones, bound from Bristol for New England: Robert Yate, John Hine, Michaell White, Robert Alexander, George Masson, Thomas Porter, Daniell Packer. (PRO: E190/1148/1).

3 March. Deposition by Richard Vaughan of Wapping, Middlesex, mariner aged 24, that he was in Pennsylvania in August 1686 when William Dorritt had a chest belonging to him on board the *Industry*. The ship sailed without him. (LMCD).

5-17 March. Shippers by the *Boston Merchant* of Boston, Mr. William Custis, bound from Bristol for New England: John Richardson, John Price, John Wyre, Benjamin Baylye, Margaret Streamer, Richard Gibbons, Walter

Stephens, Thomas Lodge, Peter Saunders, James Moore. (PRO: E190/1148/1).

16 March-22 April. Shippers by the *James & John*, Mr. George Clark, bound from London for Carolina: Ambrose Crawley, Thomas Price, James Ball, Thomas Spence, Claude Hayes, James Frontine. (PRO: E190/147/1).

23 March-1 April. Shipper by the *Windmill* of Plymouth, Mr. Robert Brockendon, bound from Plymouth for Dublin and Virginia: George Lapthorne. (PRO: E190/1051/13).

23 March-7 April. Shippers by the *William*, Mr. John Way, bound from London for Carolina: John Greening, Arthur Shallett, Daniell Brulan. (PRO: E190/147/1).

26 March-2 April. Shippers by the *Francis & Dorothy*, Mr. Richard Bridgman, bound from London for New England: John Gardner, Edward Browne. (PRO: E190/147/1).

March. Probate of will of Thomas Mather who died at sea bound for New York. (AW).

March. Probate of will of William Strachey of St. Augustine, London, whose daughter, Arabella, wife of John Waters, was in Virginia. (AW).

March. Rutland prisoner reprieved to be transported to America: Thomas Wood. (EB).

6 April-13 June. Shippers by the *Elizabeth*, Mr. John Balston, bound from London for New England: Ezekiel Hutchinson, John Smith, Nehemiah Crossley, Herriat Master, Sir John Shorter, Christopher Fowler, Edward Lewis, William Ashurst, John Ive, Jeremy Dike, Dorman Newman, Robert Livist, Nathaniell Pretty, Timothy Waldoe, Benjamin Feneuill, Ezekiel Grosilia, Gilbert Kerk, Robert Linch, Robert Cornall, Isaac Bartrand. (PRO: E190/147/1).

7-12 April. Shippers by the *Samuell*, Mr. Peter Clongen, bound from London for Virginia: James Bastian, William Lysons. (PRO: E190/147/1).

11 April. Deposition by Daniel Harris of London, gent aged 21, and Thomas Crome of London, merchant tailor aged 33, that William White of Boston, New England, merchant, by bond of 11 May 1685 became indebted to the deponent Crome. David Robertson of Boston, New England, mariner, has been appointed as attorney. (LMCD).

20 April. Shipper by the *Timberlog* of Pennsylvania, Mr. John King, bound from Weymouth for Pennsylvania: said John King. (PRO: E190/888/3).

22 April-24 May. Shippers by the *Blessing*, Mr. Samuell Chooke, bound from London for New England: Thomas Betcliff, John Smallwood, John Scott, Ellis & Cheesley, Jonathan Leigh. (PRO: E190/147/1).

April. Probate of will of Elizabeth Harwood of Bethnal Green, Middlesex, widow, whose brother, Hezekiah Usher, was in New England. (AW).

6 May. Shipper by the *Swallow* of Liverpool bound from Bristol for Virginia: John Jones. (PRO: E190/1148/1).

10 May-10 June. Shippers by the *Brothers Adventure*, Mr. Henry Tregany, bound from London for Pennsylvania: Mathew Robinson, Joseph Harris, Richard Sherbrook, John Evans, Thomas Parrott, Joseph Shaw, Jonas Smith, Jeremy Collett. (PRO: E190/147/1).

27 May. Shipper by the *William & Daniell*, Mr. Thomas Wilkinson, bound from London for New England: Daniell Foe. (PRO: E190/147/1).

May. Probate of will of William Yeamans of St. Giles in the Fields, Middlesex, whose brother, Christopher Yeamans, was in New York. (AW).

May. Administration of Abraham Hutchinson of Virginia, bachelor. (AW).

May. Administration of Charles Comer of Stepney, Middlesex, who died in New York. (AW).

1 June. Oxford Circuit prisoners reprieved to be transported to America. Berkshire: Francis Cisson of Cookham. Gloucestershire: Richard Wilkins of Woodchester; John Keyte of Berkeley; Thomas Turner of Hempstead; Thomas Budding of Berkeley. Herefordshire: Roland Jackson of Bircher; William Lewis of Dorston. Staffordshire: William Lyon of Uttoxeter. Worcestershire: William Shakspeare of Dudley; Alice Bullowes of Stourbridge, widow; Isaac Jones of Alvechurch. (PRO: C66/3296/2).

17 June-20 August. Shippers by the *Elizabeth & Katherine*, Mr. John Wake, bound from London for New York: Ralph Lodwick, Benjamin Dejane, John Greening, John Palmer, Jacob Lucy, Herk. Busay, John Cressingham, John Fisher, James Galwith, John Spragg. (PRO: E190/147/1).

24 June. Western Circuit prisoners reprieved to be transported to Barbados. Cornwall: Jane Blewett of Madderne, singlewoman. Devon: Thomas Hooper of Payhembury. Hampshire: William Borer of Sharley, Milbrooke. Somerset: Robert Harman of Bishops Lydeard; Robert Westerne of St. Decumans. Wiltshire: Richard Cater of Whaddon. (PRO: C66/3296/1).

28 June-25 August. Shippers by the *Phoenix*, Mr. James Duncan, bound from London for New England and Pennsylvania: John Loveroo, Samuell Swynock, Nathaniell Thompson, George Hogg. (PRO: E190/147/1).

June. Administration of Thomas Morris of Shadwell, Middlesex, who died on the ship *Dunbarton* in Virginia. (AW).

June. Probate of will of John Kempster of Plaistow, Essex, whose cousin, John Wilkins, was in Boston, New England. (AW).

June. Probate of will of William West of Eton, Buckinghamshire, whose son, William West, was in Virginia. (AW).

1 July. Midland Circuit prisoners reprieved to be transported to America. Derbyshire: Richard Fogg; John Boulton; Thomas Holt; William Wilson. Leicestershire: William Middleton; Edward Rayner. Lincolnshire: Robert Keele; Robert Rhodes. Northamptonshire: Thomas Robinson of Peterborough; William Parr (2); John Wright. Nottinghamshire: John Wells. Warwickshire: Daniel Parr; Ann Sparry; Edward Davyes; Thomas Hopkins alias Heritage; Humphrey Muckley; Thomas Wildblood. (PRO: C66/3297/23).

1 July. Home Circuit prisoners reprieved to be transported to Barbados or Jamaica. Essex: Sarah Brookes, spinster of St. Peter, Colchester; George Fuller of Epping; John Grissell of Waltham Abbey. Hertfordshire: William Alderkin of Braughing; John Fisher of North Mimms; Peregrine Rolphe of Hatfield; Hugh Bryant of North Mimms; Thomas Gudden of Northchurch. Kent: John Badenham of Tunbridge; John Merchant of Tunbridge. Surrey: Blackstone Thorneton of Camberwell; Charles Browning of St. Saviour, Southwark; Thomas Hollett of Clapham; William Cotton of Epsom; Thomas Knight of St. Saviour, Southwark. (PRO: C66/3296/4).

1-2 July. Shippers by the *Desire* of Plymouth bound from Plymouth for Pennsylvania: James Cock, Thomas Jackson. (PRO: E190/1051/13).

1 July-11 August. Shippers by the *Swan*, Mr. Andrew Belcher, bound from London for New England: Francis Chamberleyne, John Stace, William Cleave, Henry Hatly, Richard Dymond, Thomas Bauds, John Daniell, Robert Orchard, Andrew Greenfinch. (PRO: E190/147/1).

2 July. Shipper by the *Blessing*, Mr. Gilbert Attwood, for London and transhipment to New England: John Harper. (PRO: E190/503/3).

5 July-11 August. Shippers by the *Friendship*, Mr. John Ware, bound from London for New England: Joseph Webb, Lady Andrews, Thomas Hunt, Anthony Burren, Benjamin Harwood, Peter Devall, Benjamin Suzan, Edmond Skinner, Peter Gardner, John Ware, John Uzzill, Peter Devaux, Jonathan Everard. (PRO: E190/147/1).

6 July. Shipper by the *Prosperous*, Mr. John Wallis, bound from London for Virginia: Benjamin Whichton. (PRO: E190/147/1).

6-19 July. Shippers by the *John*, Mr. Daniell Pensax, bound from London for Virginia: John Abington, Richard Cliffe. (PRO: E190/147/1).

9 July. Shipper by the *Hannah*, Mr. Thomas Deale, bound from London for Virginia: John Constantine. (PRO: E190/147/1).

9-16 July. Shippers by the *Hopewell*, Mr. Nicholas Smith, bound from London for Maryland: Michael Yoakley, Michael Godfry. (PRO: E190/147/1).

10 July. Western Circuit prisoners reprieved to be transported to Barbados. Devon: Robert Elston of Crediton, weaver; Charity Arundell of Buckfontleigh, singlewoman. Dorset: John James of Margaret Marsh; James Sprackland of Lyme Regis; Elizabeth Harvey of Chideock, singlewoman. Hampshire: Thomas Willis of Tangley, husbandman; Robert Wisham of Tattam, husbandman. Somerset: Henry Stone of Hockworthy. Wiltshire: John Millard of Bradford. (PRO: C66/3239/27).

12 July. Shipper by the *Susan*, Mr. Thomas Dill, bound from London for Virginia: Richard Cox. (PRO: E190/147/1).

13 July. Shipper by the *Adventure*, Mr. Thomas Lurting, bound from London for Maryland: Samuell Groome. (PRO: E190/147/1).

15 July. Shippers by the *Adventure*, Mr. Ralph Cooper, bound from London for Maryland: John Bennett, John Cooper. (PRO: E190/147/1).

16 July. Shipper by the *Virginia Merchant* of Bideford, Mr. John Atkin, bound from Bideford for Virginia: said John Atkin. (PRO: E190/965/4).

16 July. Deposition by Benjamin Bartlett of London, gent aged 37, that Thomas Pate of Poropotank, Gloucester County, Virginia, merchant, deceased, became indebted by deed of 19 October 1683 to his father, Edward Pate of London, merchant. (LMCD).

18 July. Shipper by the *Loyalty*, Mr. Edward Tarleton, bound from London for Virginia: William Bellamy. (PRO: E190/147/1).

18 July. Shipper by the [blank] *Samuell?*, Mr. Daniell Bradley, bound from London for Virginia: Thomas Stark. (PRO: E190/147/1).

18 July-9 August. Shippers by the *Adventure*, Mr. Robert Coles, bound from London for Carolina: Henry Gould, Edmond White, Jeremy Clarke, David Sanders, John Ashby, Daniell Brulove, Thomas Clagett, Zachary Burrough, George Moore, Walter Ryon. (PRO: E190/147/1).

19 July. Newgate prisoners reprieved to be transported to Barbados or Jamaica. London: John Carpenter; Daniel Crookes alias Penn; Charles Hopton; Elizabeth Fuller, spinster. Middlesex: Timothy Beaton of Hendon; Domingo Cerda of St. Dunstan in the West; Thomas Griffith of St. Giles in the Fields; Edward Crookes of St. Margaret Westminster; Thomas Jarvis of St. James Westminster; John Sherland of St. Clement Danes; William Griffith of St. Pancras; Thomas Wintour of Isleworth; Richard Hollis of St. Andrew Holborn; Francis Lowe of St. Martin in the Fields; Katherine Jones of the same, spinster. (PRO: C66/3297/16).

21 July-29 August. Shippers by the *Friendship* of Bristol bound from Bristol for Virginia: Richard Townsend, John Lord, Thomas Goulding, Jeremy Pearce, Edward Mitchell. (PRO: E190/1148/1).

26 July. Shipper by the *Bird*, Mr. Edward Audley, bound from London for Virginia: Micajah Perry. (PRO: E190/147/1).

26 July. Cheshire prisoners reprieved to be transported to America: Elizabeth Lowndes of Stapeley; John Wilson of Chester. (PRO: C66/3297/11).

27-29 July. Shipper by the *Thomas & John*, Mr. John Browne, bound from London for Virginia: Walter Bentall. (PRO: E190/147/1).

29 July. Shipper by the *Thomas & Sarah*, Mr. Richard Bill, bound from London for New England: John Eston. (PRO: E190/147/1).

29 July-1 August. Shippers by the *Adventure*, Mr. William East, bound from London for Virginia: Richard Buller, Benjamin Wiston. (PRO: E190/147/1).

29 July-11 August. Shippers by the *[Golden] Lyon*, Mr. Anthony Gester, bound from London for Virginia: Arthur Baily, Robert Boodly, Thomas Birdsey. (PRO: E190/147/1).

29 July-11 August. Shippers by the *Success*, Mr. Edward Tatnall, bound from London for Virginia: Thomas Jennings, George Echell. (PRO: E190/147/1).

July. Administration of John Broadribb of Chester River, Talbot County, Maryland. (AW).

July. Administration of Daniel Axtell of Stoke Newington, Middlesex, who died in Carolina. (AW).

July. Probate of will of James Ashton of Stafford County, Virginia. (AW).

1-12 August. Shippers by the *Samuell*, Mr. Thomas Bowman, bound from London for Virginia and Maryland: Anthony Strutton, Jonathan Murrell. (PRO: E190/147/1).

2-3 August. Shippers by the *Crown Mallago*, Mr. Michael Staples, bound from London for Maryland: Michael Yoakley, John Pettit. (PRO: E190/147/1).

3-8 August. Shippers by the *Endeavour*, Mr. Robert Harne, bound from London for Maryland: Richard Atkinson, Joseph Tomblins, Joseph Thomas. (PRO: E190/147/1).

3-8 August. Shipper by the *Jacob*, Mr. Charles Reeves, bound from London for Maryland: William Foxon. (PRO: E190/147/1).

4-10 August. Shipper by the *Margaret*, Mr. Ralph Crow, bound from London for Virginia: Micajah Perry. (PRO: E190/147/1).

4-12 August. Shippers by the *Elizabeth*, Mr. William Orton, bound from London for Virginia: Joseph Woodland, Nicholas Pasfield. (PRO: E190/147/1).

4-17 August. Shippers by the *Desire*, Mr. Alexander Notts, bound from London for Virginia: Micajah Perry, Jonathan Mathew. (PRO: E190/147/1).

4-18 August. Shippers by the *Robert*, Mr. Richard Burt, bound from London for New York: Walter Bentall, Robert Plumstead, William Prince, Thomas Ashfield, Robert Hacks, Henry Lacount. (PRO: E190/147/1).

6 August. Shipper by the *James*, Mr. Symon Emberley, bound from London for Virginia: William Paggen. (PRO: E190/147/1).

8-12 August. Shippers by the *James & Elizabeth*, Mr. John Beere, bound from Weymouth for Virginia: Richard Ireland, Thomas Bower, Hugh Hext, Benjamin Wilson. (PRO: E190/888/3).

9 August. Shipper by the *Dolphin* of Poole, Mr. John Christian, bound from Poole for Maryland: Henry Lawes. (PRO: E190/888/4).

9 August. Shipper by the *Samuell*, Mr. Daniell Bradley, bound from London for Virginia: William Paggen. (PRO: E190/147/1).

10 August. Shipper by the *Adventure*, Mr. Peregrine Browne, bound from London for Virginia: said Peregrine Browne. (PRO: E190/147/1).

10-12 August. Shippers by the *Unity*, Mr. John Bull, bound from Lyme for Virginia: John Burridge & Co., Richard Davy. (PRO: E190/888/1).

15 August. Robert Scutt of Sydling, Dorset, tailor, bound to John Bull of Lyme Regis, mariner, to serve 4 years in Virginia or Maryland. (DRO B7/M9).

20 August. Shipper by the *America* of Bideford, Mr. Thomas Phillips, bound from Bideford for Maryland: Hartwell Buck. (PRO: E190/965/4).

21-25 August. Shippers by the *Unity* of Bristol bound from Bristol for Virginia: Richard Champneys, Hugh Raynstrope. (PRO: E190/1148/1).

25-31 August. Shipper by the *Thomas & Mary* of Bristol bound from Bristol for Virginia: Thomas Atkins. (PRO: E190/1148/1).

25 August-1 September. Shippers by the *Henrietta* of Bideford, Mr. Phillip Greenslade, bound from Bideford for Virginia: John Davie, James Busuargus. (PRO: E190/965/4).

27 August-13 September. Shippers by the *Bristol Merchant* bound from Bristol for Virginia: John Stephens, Samuell Packer, John Beaton. (PRO: E190/1148/1).

26 August. Shipper by the *Merchants Delight* of Bideford, Mr. John Land, bound from Bideford for Virginia: said John Land. (PRO: E190/965/4).

26 August. Shipper by the *Truelove* of Bideford, Mr. Peter Prust, bound from Bideford for Maryland: John Smith. (PRO: E190/965/4).

28 August. Shipper by the *Chester Merchant* of Bideford, Mr. Samuell Elliott, bound from Bideford for Virginia: John Smith. (PRO: E190/965/4).

August. Deposition by Henry Minchard of London, notary aged 52, that Thomas Jenner of Boston, New England, mariner, became indebted to Thomas Powell, citizen and cutler of London, by bond of 10 October 1685. Thomas Powell, aged 58, deposes that he has not received payment. Mr. John Foster of Boston, New England, merchant, is appointed attorney. (LMCD).

3-9 September. Shippers by the *Hopewell* of Bristol bound from Bristol for Virginia: Faulke Adams, Hugh B——-ham, Peter Mitchell, Joseph Whitchurch. (PRO: E190/1148/1).

8-13 September. Shippers by the *Mary* of Bristol bound from Bristol for Virginia: William Daines, Samuell Hartnell. (PRO: E190/1148/1).

12 September. Shipper by the *Seaflower* of Barnstaple, Mr. John Darricott, bound from Barnstaple for Waterford and Maryland: John Fleming. (PRO: E190/965/4).

17 September. Shipper by the *Prosperous* of New York, Mr. John Prenstes (*sic*), bound from Plymouth for New York: Nicholas Edgcombe. (PRO: E190/1051/13).

23 September. James Vaughan, aged 15, apprenticed from Christ's Hospital to Mr. Henry Hartwell of James Town, Virginia, merchant. (CH).

September. Administration of Christopher Thompson of Virginia, widower. (AW).

September. Probate of will of Sarah Binding of Chertsey, Surrey, widow, whose daughter, Sarah, wife of Richard Buckley, was in Boston, New England. (AW).

4 October. Shipper by the *Lyon* of Plymouth, Mr. James Blight, bound from Plymouth for Virginia: said James Blight. (PRO: E190/1051/13).

5-20 October. Shippers by the *Comfort* of Bristol, Mr. William Brisco, bound from Bristol for Barbados and Virginia: Edward Jones, Richard Prigg. (PRO: E190/1148/1).

7 October. Shipper by the *Two Brothers* of Poole, Mr. William Bascombe, bound from Poole for Maryland: William Tompson & Co. (PRO: E190/888/4).

12-17 October. Shippers by the *Hopewell* of Topsham, Mr. Walter Lyle, bound from Plymouth for Virginia: Phillip Pentire. (PRO: E190/1051/13).

13-14 October. Shipper by the *Elizabeth & Samuell*, Mr. Richard Friend, bound from Weymouth for Virginia: said Richard Friend. (PRO: E190/888/3).

15 October. Shipper by the *Bristol Factor* bound from Bristol for Virginia: Francis Fisher. (PRO: E190/1148/1).

15-21 October. Shippers by the *Potomack Merchant* of Bristol bound from Bristol for Virginia: Thomas Dudlestone, Richard Crump, Edmond Mountjoy, Thomas Tayer. (PRO: E190/1148/1).

22 October. Shipper by the *Swallow* of Poole, Mr. Richard B——, bound from Poole for Virginia: George Lewen. (PRO: E190/888/4).

27 October. Shipper by the *Thomas & Elizabeth* of Poole, Mr. Thomas Hide, bound from Poole for Maryland: said Thomas Hide. (PRO: E190/888/4).

2 November. John Newsam, aged 15, apprenticed from Christ's Hospital to George Richards of St. Botolph Aldgate, merchant, to be assigned to Col. John Page of York River, Virginia. (CH).

8-25 November. Shippers by the *Unicorn* of Bristol, Mr. Thomas Cooper, bound from Bristol for Virginia: Edward Fielding, William Opye. (PRO: E190/1148/1).

10-23 November. Shippers by the *Concord* of Bristol bound from Bristol for Virginia: Charles Jones, James Millard, William Swymer, Michaell Wharton, John Peirson, George Bryan. (PRO: E190/1148/1).

24 November-31 December. Shippers by the *Daniell & Elizabeth* of Plymouth, Mr. William Ginnis, bound from Plymouth for Virginia: Peter Row, William Martyn. (PRO: E190/1051/13, 1052/21).

28 November-7 December. Shippers by the *Endeavour* of Plymouth, Mr. Robert Gooding, bound from Plymouth for Virginia: William Martyn, John Woods. (PRO: E190/1051/13).

30 November. Deposition by George Echell, citizen and merchant tailor of London, aged 30, John Faldoe of London, slopseller aged 28, and Edward Partridge of London, shipwright aged 28 that Thomas Rowe, then in Dover, Kent, bought goods from Thomas Potter of London, merchant. Nathan Stanbury of Boston, New England, merchant, has been appointed as attorney. (LMCD).

November. Administration of Elizabeth Burbridge alias Burges alias Church of St. Giles in the Fields, Middlesex, widow, granted to Charles Raven, husband of the sister, Mary Nicholas alias Raven, in New England. (AW).

November. Administration of William Clarke of the ship *Kings Fisher*, who died in Boston, New England. (AW).

November. Administration of Thomas Goddard of Talbot County, Maryland. (AW).

November. Administration of David Mordoch of New York. (AW).

19 December-10 January. Shippers by the *John* of Bristol bound from Bristol for Virginia: Thomas Speede, Anthony Saunders, George Mason, Samuell Parker. (PRO: E190/1148/1, 1149/1).

December. Probate of will of Richard Bacon of Stepney, Middlesex, (bound for Virginia). (AW).

1688

16 January. Shipper by the *Industry* of Plymouth, Mr. Phillip Harwood, bound from Plymouth for Virginia: said Phillip Harwood. (PRO: E190/1052/21).

January. Administration with will of Roger Baker of Wapping, Middlesex, who had lands in Maryland and died overseas. (AW).

1 February-7 March. Shippers by the *John & Elizabeth*, Mr. Jonas Leech, bound from London for New England: Daniell Adkins, Jeremy Johnson, John Berry, Thomas Rogers, Thomas Smith, Samuell Ball, Thomas Fairweather, John George, Abram Mitchell, John Crow, William Harrison, Henry Hatfield, Jacob Bell, James Rawlinson, Joseph Alford, Thomas Hancox, Nicholas Gregson, John Uzzell, Edmond Skinner. (PRO: E190/145/1).

3 & 25 February. Western Circuit prisoners reprieved to be transported to Barbados. Cornwall: Sarah Paschoe of Roach, singlewoman; Thomas Buttland of Tregony, wool comber. Devon: Nicholas Dennett of Sadbury, gunsmith; Ralph Keene of Creacombe or Ermington, yeoman; Emma Hart of Chulmleigh, singlewoman; Charles Cornish alias Pedrick alias Johnson of Fremington, potter. Somerset: James Priest alias Hancock of Wiveliscombe, weaver; Samuel Tolman of St. Michaelchurch, mason; Francis Brooke Jr. of Minehead; John Tilley of Glastonbury, woolcomber; John Chard alias Charter of Blackford, husbandman; Francis Hixe of Hornblotton. Wiltshire: George Langton Jr. of Bourton Shrivenham; Thomas Hayward of Bourton Shrivenham, blacksmith. (PRO: C66/3302/9 & 3303/11).

7-9 February. Shippers by the *Maryland Merchant* of Bristol bound from Bristol for Virginia: William Crabb, Walter Upington, John Hollister, Jacob Moggs, Robert Siclaton. (PRO: E190/1149/1).

8-22 February. Shippers by the *Elinor* of Bristol bound from Bristol for New England: Giles Tapley, Abraham Elton, Mathew Higgens, James Swetnam, Sir Thomas Earle. (PRO: E190/1149/1).

10-15 February. Shippers by the *Alathea* of Bristol, Mr. Rice Jefferis, bound from Bristol for Virginia: John Dowding, Richard Benson, George Novis. (PRO: E190/1149/1).

14 February-24 April. Shippers by the *Bordeaux Merchant*, Mr. Lawrence Sturman, bound from London for New York: Nicholas Cullen, William Cornelison, Jacob Harwood, Robert Fenwick, Thomas Wenham, executrix of John Loveroo, James Foulis, Thomas Coman, John Long, Paul Minivill, John Barberie. (PRO: E190/145/1).

17 February-26 March. Shippers by the *York*, Mr. George Heathcott, bound from London for New York: Francis Hunter, John Garaton. (PRO: E190/145/1).

21 February. Shipper by the *Supply* of Bristol, Mr. Thomas Templeman, bound from Bristol for New England: Thomas Edwards. (PRO: E190/1149/1).

21 February-4 April. Shippers by the *Boston Merchant* of Bristol, Mr. William Curtis, bound from Bristol for New England: Richard Gibbons, Abraham Evans, Samson Sheafe, Edward Dyer, John Wyer, John Hollister. (PRO: E190/1149/1).

22 February. Shippers by the *Alexander* of Bristol, Mr. John White, bound from Bristol for Virginia: James Thomas & Co. (PRO: E190/1149/1).

22 February. Depositions taken in London in the case of Coldham v. Cade re the descent of the Manor of Wonham in Betchworth, Surrey. Andrew Cade, who held the Manor, died testate in 1662 leaving great-nephews Henry and Peter Cade. Depositions were taken in Warwick Court House from: John Noble of Denbigh, Warwick County, Virginia, planter aged 67; Mary Stow, aged 57, wife of John Stow of Denbigh; Ann Noble, aged 64, wife of John Noble of Denbigh, planter; Mary Thurmore of Denbigh, widow aged 39; Peter Cade of Denbigh, planter aged 40; Jane Ridge of Elizabeth City County, widow aged 56, who was born in Sutton, Surrey, England, and went to Virginia in 1646; Ann Daniell, aged 43, wife of Darby Daniell of Warwick County, planter; and Robert Grove of Denbigh, planter aged 47. They testify that Walter Cade, a nephew of the testator, used to keep a confectioner's shop in London, left a son, Andrew Cade, in England before going first with his wife Grace to Old Pocoson, Virginia, and then to Denbigh, before his death in 1666. Walter and Grace Cade had two sons in Virginia: Henry Cade, who in about 1642 married Ann, daughter of Samuel Grove of Newports News, Virginia, and died testate; and Peter Cade who is still living. Henry and Ann Cade had a daughter, Ann Cade, now aged 23, who married Henry Royall in 1686. (NGSQ 69/1).

23 February-24 April. Shippers by the *George*, Mr. John Wild, bound from London for New England: Ambrose Crawley, John Hills, Thomas Weekes, Jonathan Price, Richard Parrott, Holgate & King, Thomas Fairweather, Stephen Mason, Joshua Webb, Roger Hazard, William Sheldon, Tabitha Lascoe, David Clarkson, James Blackman, Thomas Wilkin, Thomas Bands, Thomas Osborne. (PRO: E190/145/1).

25 & 28 February. Norfolk Circuit prisoners reprieved to be transported to America. Bedfordshire: Susan Fairley of Leighton Buzzard; John Bandy of Pulloxhill. Buckinghamshire: Richard Williams of Chipping Wycombe; Richard Pinckard of Bierton; Nathaniel Harteshorne of Denham. Huntingdonshire: John Slow of Stanground. Norfolk: Henry Thompson of Holverston. Suffolk: Andrew Reader of Bradfield St. George; Bartholomew

Kettle alias Green of Clinsett (*sic*); Richard Weekes alias Wicks of Beccles; Thomas Smith of Bradwell; William Gauslin of Poslingford. (PRO: C66/3302/10 & 3303/12).

25 February-10 March. Shippers by the *John Bonadventure*, Mr. Andrew Cratey, bound from London for New England: Daniell Whearly, Thomas Haden. (PRO: E190/145/1).

27 February. Shipper by the *B[arbados?] Merchant*, Mr. Edmond Copping, bound from London for Virginia: Joseph Low. (PRO: E190/145/1).

27 February-21 April. Shippers by the *Dolphin*, Mr. John Foy, bound from London for New England: James Kelk, Gabriel Berman, Thomas Kettlebrough, Richard Becher, Eliza Biggs, John Vesey, Richard Dakins, John Luck, Robert Bedford, Wigfall & Bell, Humphrey Edwin, Thomas Noakes, John Uzzell, Samuell Spicer, Thomas Riddell, William Sly. (PRO: E190/145/1).

28 February. Warrant to the Recorder of London for the pardon of James Williams convicted of seducing and carrying away the King's subjects to foreign plantations. (SP Dom).

February. Administration of Thomas Saffin of Boston, New England, who died in Stepney, Middlesex, bachelor. (AW).

February. Probate of will of John Hill of St. Olave Hart Street, London, merchant, whose brother, Valentine Hill, was in New England. (AW).

February. Probate of will of John Pargiter of St. Martin in the Fields, Middlesex, whose cousin, Sarah Lovell, was in Virginia. (AW).

3 March. Oxford Circuit prisoners reprieved to be transported to Jamaica, Barbados or Bermuda. Gloucestershire: John Thompson of Cirencester; Thomas Roberts of Chipping Camden; John Bradford of Barton, Temple Guiting; Susan Davies of Owen by Gloucester, spinster; Herefordshire: Mary Gibbons of St. John Baptist, Hereford; Francis Sawford of Cradley; Worcestershire: William Hagar of Worcester; Roger Rees of the same; Francis Rhodes of the same; Jervase Jones of Astley; Shropshire: Samuel Hughes of Horton; Richard Nucke of Wellington. (PRO: C66/3302/8).

5 March. Newgate prisoners reprieved to be transported to Barbados or Jamaica. London: Robert Andrewes; Lewis Heager; William Eley; Thomas Pafford alias Reynolds; Thomas Ward alias Wyatt; Isaac Buffield. Middlesex: Joseph Booth of Teddington; John Sutton of St. Giles in the Fields; Christian Hartley of St. Botolph Aldgate, spinster; Thomas Tracey of the same; Mary Burton of the same, widow; Elizabeth Mellard of St. Martin in the Fields; Margaret Meeke of the same, spinster; Florence Vaughan of the same; Armaine Depoure of the same; Ann Child of St. Sepulchre, spinster; George Ogleby of St. Andrew Holborn; Charles Hughes of the same; John Cooper of the same; Mary Wootten, spinster, alias wife of Edward Wootten of the same; Thomas Garrett alias Knowles of Hampstead; Thomazine alias Elizabeth Tally of Stepney; Thomas Jones of the same; George Clerke of the same; Robert Browne alias Beames alias Betty of the same; John Greene of St. Clement Danes; George Clerke of Isleworth; Elizabeth Morris alias Clansey of St. James Westminster, spinster; Anthony Dyer of Fulham; Solomon Spring of Hornsey. (PRO: C66/3301/1).

10 March. Oxford and Western Circuit prisoners reprieved to be transported to America. Berkshire: Richard Higgs of Bisham. Dorset: William Gough of Wimborne, butcher; Thomas Harris of the same, clothworker; Thomas Shutler alias Shuckler of Blandford, innholder; Christopher Pownell of the same, tailor. Monmouth: Samuel Berrington of Monmouth, gunsmith; John Sinclare of the same; James Sinclare of the same, gunsmith. Oxfordshire: Margaret Sanderson, wife of John Sanderson of Woodstock; Peter Beare of Banbury; John Carter of Shipton, miller. Staffordshire: Henry Flint of Midwich. Worcestershire: Bridget Court of Worcester, widow; Francis Pingrey of Tenbury. (PRO: C66/3304/25).

13 March. Home Circuit prisoners reprieved to be transported to Barbados or Jamaica. Essex: Edward Gallant of Heybridge; Richard Chalker of South Weald; John Greene of Inworth; John Palmer of West Tilbury; William Boxer of South Weald. Kent: Thomas Coachman of Great Chart; Susan Wilson of Hollingbourne, spinster; George Porch Jr. of Sutton at Hone; Mary Butler of Deptford. Surrey: Alice Yates of St. Saviour, Southwark. (PRO: C66/3302/6).

16 March-9 April. Shippers by the *Tryal*, Mr. Bernard Darby, bound from London for New England: Daniell Foe, Daniell Williams, David Clarkson, Richard Jenkinson, James Causton. (PRO: E190/145/1).

23 March. William Robinson, aged 14, sent from Christ's Hospital to his uncle Richard Robinson and aunt Mary Curtis to serve William Stretton, commander of the *Golden Lyon* bound for Barbados with the agreement of his mother Mary R. (CH).

28 March-11 April. Shippers by the English-built *Jerusalem* of Bristol, Mr. John Pepwell, bound from Bristol for New England: Sir Thomas Earle, Henry Gibbs, John Maine, James Hallidge, John Hardon, Tryall Underhill, Sir Richard Crumpe. (PRO: E190/1149/1).

4 April. Francis Claxton, aged 15, apprenticed from Christ's Hospital to Mr. William Wrayford, merchant in Bow Lane, to be sent to Nicholas Tippett and Mary his wife in St. Christopher's. (CH).

12 April. Shipper by the *Charles* of Plymouth, Mr. Aquila Wallis, bound from Plymouth for Virginia: George Lapthorne. (PRO: E190/1052/21).

12-26 April. Shippers by the English-built *Delaware* of Bristol, Mr. John Cane, bound from Bristol for New England: Charles Jones, John Elsworthy, Oliver Field, Michaell White. (PRO: E190/1149/1).

14 April. Deposition by Francis Comyn, citizen and fishmonger of London, aged 40, and Thomas Wells, citizen and girdler of London, aged 37, that Daniel Royce Jr. of Boston, New England, merchant, became indebted by bond of 3 April 1685 to the deponent Wells. Henry Sargent of Boston, New England, has been appointed as attorney to recover. (LMCD).

11 May. Deposition by Jeremy Rouse of London, scrivener aged 47, that Joshua Storey of Mattaponi, York River, Virginia, became indebted by bond of 21 September 1675 to John Worger, citizen and girdler of London, now deceased. (LMCD).

31 May-9 July. Shippers by the *Batchelor*, Mr. Humphrey Ayles, bound from London for New England: Edmond Leake, John Boniton, John Paige, William Whiting, Walter Benthall, John Tatem, Mark Manbert, Jacob Harwood, Charles Seabright, Samuell Standcliffe, Thomas Brinley, Richard Seale. (PRO: E190/145/1).

May. Probate of will of John Wyron of Reading, Berkshire, whose daughter, Grace, wife of William Rackstraw, was in Pennsylvania. (AW).

9-22 June. Shippers by the *Brothers Adventure*, Mr. Henry Tregany, bound from London for Pennsylvania: Thomas Lawrance, James Marshall, John West. (PRO: E190/145/1).

12 June-7 August. Shippers by the *President*, Mr. Arthur Tanner, bound from London for New England: Edward Adams, Moses Lamonche, Benjamin Suzan, Nathaniell Williams, Edward Rook, James Mell, Thomas Hollis, Peter Longueville, John Surman. (PRO: E190/145/1).

16 June-11 August. Shippers by the *Friendship*, Mr. John Ware, bound from London for New England: John Hill, Sir Benjamin Ayloffe, Sir John Shorter, Robert Rowland, Charles Fenace, John Uzzall, Edward Crisp, John Smallwood, John Bedell, John Daniell, William Maxwell, John Ryder, Joseph Alford. (PRO: E190/145/1).

21 June-4 July. Shippers by the *Friendship*, Mr. Edward Watkins, bound from London for Maryland: John Abbington, John Hill. (PRO: E190/145/1).

21 June-11 July. Shipper by the *Hopewell*, Mr. Nicholas Smith, bound from London for Maryland: Michael Yoakley. (PRO: E190/145/1).

25 June. Shipper by the *Adventure*, Mr. William Parker, bound from London for New England: Giles Bigg. (PRO: E190/145/1).

26 June. The following apprenticed from Christ's Hospital: Richard Francklin, aged 15, sent to Mrs. Margaret Farewell living in Basinghall Street to be bound to her son George Farewell, an attorney in Boston, New England; Nathaniell Crockford, aged 13, sent to his mother Rebecca Crockford to go with Mr. Thomas Brinley, merchant, to Boston, New England. (CH).

June. Probate of will of Moses Browne of St. Margaret Lothbury, London, whose sister, Sarah Noyse, was in New England. (AW).

June. Administration of Robert Tonstall of St. Olave, Southwark, Surrey, who died on the ship *Dumbarton* in Virginia, mariner. (AW).

4-17 July. Shippers by the *Friends Adventure*, Mr. William East, bound from London for Virginia: John Robinson, Samuell Hill, Joseph Bosworth, Edward Steele, Gabriel East. (PRO: E190/145/1).

6 July. Shipper by the *Adventure*, Mr. Ralph Cooper, bound from London for Virginia: said Ralph Cooper. (PRO: E190/145/1).

12 July. Shipper by the *Margaret*, Mr. Dean Cock, bound from London for Maryland: Samuell Groome. (PRO: E190/145/1).

12 July. Shipper by the *Crown Mallago*, Mr. James Till, bound from London for Maryland: John Tayler. (PRO: E190/145/1).

12-16 July. Shipper by the *Adventure*, Mr. Michael Staples, bound from London for Maryland: Robert Hatton. (PRO: E190/145/1).

13-19 July. Shippers by the *Baltimore*, Mr. Samuell Phillips, bound from London for Maryland: John Taylor, William Hiccocks. (PRO: E190/145/1).

13-20 July. Shippers by the *Henry*, Mr. Thomas Bowman, bound from London for Maryland: Edward Carleton, Mary Ashcomb. (PRO: E190/145/1).

13-18 July. Shippers by the *Endeavour*, Mr. Robert Herne, bound from London for Virginia: Thomas Martin, Joseph Pile. (PRO: E190/145/1).

14 July. Midland Circuit prisoners reprieved to be transported to America. Derbyshire: Thomas Lomas. Leicestershire: John Hartshorne. Lincolnshire: Francis Sisson; Alexander Cutforth; Robert Keywood; Francis Bond. Northamptonshire: William Stephens. Nottinghamshire: John Roe; William Langton; John Trolley. Warwickshire: John Brooks; John Evans. (PRO: C66/3305/13).

14 July. Western Circuit prisoners reprieved to be transported to Barbados. Devon: Josias Westcoate of Sidmouth; Robert Richard of Chudleigh; Richard Roberts of Kentisbeare. Dorset: Isaac Clarke of Hermitage. Hugh Bryan of London, ship carpenter; Thomas Darby of London; William Davys of Southwark (Surrey), pinmaker. Hampshire: Edward Harnaman of Portsmouth; Somerset: Grace Putt of D——, widow; Thomas Bagg of Gregory Stoke; John Sandford of Okehampton (Devon) alias Robert Greedy of Wiveliscombe, blacksmith; John Hammett of Taunton, yeoman; Thomas Kerton Jr; Peter Walling of Charlton Mackrell. Wiltshire: James Pearson of Malmesbury; Benjamin Hutchins of Devizes; Ishmael Andrews of Calne; William Williams of Malmesbury. (PRO: C66/3305/14).

17 July. Shipper by the *Dolphin* of Poole, Mr. John Christian, bound from Poole for Maryland: Moses Durrell. (PRO: E190/888/8).

18 July. Shipper by the *John*, Mr. Daniel Pensax, bound from London for Virginia: said Daniel Pensax. (PRO: E190/145/1).

18 July. Oxford Circuit prisoners reprieved to be transported to America. Herefordshire: William Watkins of Llangarren. Oxfordshire: William White of Benson. Thomas Rogers of Wimborne (Dorset), clothworker. (PRO: C66/3305/11).

19 July. Shipper by the *Susanna*, Mr. Thomas Dell, bound from London for Virginia: Richard Cox. (PRO: E190/145/1).

19 July. Shipper by the *Thomas & Francis*, Mr. John Turner, bound from London for Virginia: Phillip Grimes. (PRO: E190/145/1).

19 July. Shipper by the *James & Elizabeth*, Mr. John Beer, bound from Weymouth for Virginia: said John Beer. (PRO: E190/888/9).

19 July. Home Circuit prisoners reprieved to be transported to Barbados or Jamaica. Essex (all still in prison in February 1690): Thomas Playne alias Playden of Thurrock; Richard Price of Thurrock; Daniel Carter of Low Layton; Mary Tye of Blackmore. Hertfordshire: George Marshall of Totteridge; William Harrison of St. Peter, Hertford; Marjory Roberts of Hitchin; Thomas Johnson of Stondon. Kent: Jonathan Davies of Leyborne; Henry Thompson of Leybourne; John Baker of Pluckley; Charles Hill of Leybourne; Isaac Banford alias Bradford; Robert Welsh alias Shipmarsh of Hadlow (still in prison in July 1691). Surrey: Thomas Field of Lambeth; John Powell of St. Saviour, Southwark; Francis Lowe of Bermondsey; William Jones of Camberwell; Ann Spencer alias Mary Browne of St. Saviour, Southwark; Robert Sedgewick of Croydon (still in prison in February 1690); Henry Pottinger of Kingston on Thames (still in prison in February 1690). Sussex: John Miles of Horsted Keynes; Charles Bisrow of Slinfold; William Castleden of Fant. (PRO: C66/3305/8).

19 July. Northern Circuit prisoners reprieved to be transported to Barbados. Northumberland: John Leighton of Newcastle upon Tync. Yorkshire: Richard Morton of Foulby; John Bradshawe Jr. of Calsett, clothmaker. (PRO: C66/3305/9).

24-26 July. Shipper by the *Lusitania*, Mr. John Browne, bound from London for Maryland: Thomas Ellis. (PRO: E190/145/1).

30 July-5 September. Shippers by the *James*, Mr. Nicholas Dumaresque, bound from London for New York: Peter Wallis, Joseph Welch, Edward Fox, Daniell Brulon, Lewis Gorvaire, Symon Duport. (PRO: E190/145/1).

July. Administration of John Arrowsmith of Virginia, bachelor, who died overseas. (AW).

July. Administration of John Johnson of Virginia, bachelor. (AW).

July. Administration of Edward King of Virginia, bachelor. (AW).

July. Administration with will of Anthony Roby of parts overseas who died in Carolina. (AW).

July. Administration with will of John Read of Bristol, who died in Virginia. (AW).

July. Probate of will of Henry Woodhouse of Linhaven, Norfolk County, Virginia. (AW).

2-31 August. Shippers by the *Sarah*, Mr. Francis Parsons, bound from London for Virginia: Edward Parsons, Richard Park, John Singler, Richard Moseley, Thomas Palmer. (PRO: E190/145/1).

3-10 August. Shippers by the *Averilla*, Mr. Abraham Wild, bound from London for Maryland: John Pettit, Samuell Sanford, John Cary, Robert Baldwin, Jeremy Sap, Samuell Billing, Thomas Chamberlaine. (PRO: E190/145/1).

3-17 August. Shippers by the *Success*, Mr. Edward Tatnall, bound from London for Virginia: Benjamin Whiston, Thomas Jennings, Thomas Marshall, John Shelton. (PRO: E190/145/1).

3-18 August. Shippers by the *Anne & Elizabeth*, Mr. William Orton, bound from London for Virginia: William Gibbs, Blaze Clarke, Arthur Selake. (PRO: E190/145/1).

4-11 August. Shippers by the *Samuell*, Mr. Daniell Bradley and Mr. John Atkins, bound from London for Virginia: Thomas Stark, Arthur North, Micajah Perry. (PRO: E190/145/1).

8 August. Deposition by Roger Atlee, citizen and merchant tailor of London, aged 40, and his servant, Richard Blundell, aged 20, that they consigned goods to Richard Banks in New England in 1685 and 1686 by the *Adventure*, Mr. John Bolston. (LMCD).

8-11 August. Shippers by the *Benedict Leonard*, Mr. Nicholas Spurn, bound from London for Maryland: James Wagstaffe, Joseph Pile, Anthony Lacon. (PRO: E190/145/1).

8-18 August. Shippers by the *Return*, Mr. Michael Shute, bound from London for New England: John Beighton, John Hill. (PRO: E190/145/1).

8 August-11 September. Shippers by the *Providence*, Mr. Joseph Bryer, bound from London for Pennsylvania: James Kelk, Richard Whitpan, Richard Dymond, James Denew, Roger Leavery, John Vans, Roger Levins. (PRO: E190/145/1).

8 August-13 October. Shippers by the *Abigall & Sarah*, Mr. John Selleck, bound from London for New York: William Stonehewer, Paul Minivell, John

Gardner, Mark Manbert, Thomas Whitehill, Hercules Beaufoy, Nathan Wilmer, Joseph Bladenbird, Thomas Pipping. (PRO: E190/145/1).

11 August. Shipper by the *Adventure*, Mr. Francis Fisher, bound from London for Virginia: Micajah Perry. (PRO: E190/145/1).

11-13 August. Shippers by the *Bird*, Mr. Benjamin Hall, bound from London for Virginia: Micajah Perry, Jonathan Mathews. (PRO: E190/145/1).

14 August-22 September. Shippers by the *Bristol Merchant* bound from Bristol for Virginia and Pennsylvania: James Ransom, John Stratton, John Roberts, Thomas Withers, Henry Lodge, Giles Persons, William Stocker, Margaret Smith, John Lovell, William Smith. (PRO: E190/1149/1).

15-25 August. Shippers by the *Mary*, Mr. John Gardner, bound from London for New England: John Raven, Jeremy Chivers, James Jackson, Edward Goodwin. (PRO: E190/145/1).

17 August. Shipper by the *Charles*, Mr. Timothy Armitage, bound from London for New England: Arthur Shallett. (PRO: E190/145/1).

17 August-19 October. Shippers by the *Jeffreys*, Mr. Thomas Arnold, bound from London for Virginia: John Hind, Daniell Sheriffe, George Richards, Thomas Potter. (PRO: E190/145/1).

20 August. Shipper by the *Stark*, Mr. John Ransom, bound from London for Maryland: Thomas Stark. (PRO: E190/145/1).

20-22 August. Shippers by the *Spencer*, Mr. Nicholas Goodridge, bound from London for Virginia: Thomas Stark, Gilbert Metcalf, Nicholas Hayward. (PRO: E190/145/1).

20-27 August. Shippers by the *Adventure*, Mr. John Nore, bound from London for Virginia: Samuell Groome, Thomas Ellis. (PRO: E190/145/1).

21 August-18 September. Shipper by the *Jacob*, Mr. Edward Audley, bound from London for Maryland: Benjamin Williams. (PRO: E190/145/1).

25 August. Shipper by the *James*, Mr. Symon Emberley, bound from London for Virginia: William Paggen. (PRO: E190/145/1).

25 August. Shipper by the *Martin* of Belfast bound from Bristol for Virginia: Charles Jones. (PRO: E190/1149/1).

25 August. Shippers by the *James* of Bristol bound from Bristol for Virginia: William French, Richard Day. (PRO: E190/1149/1).

25-30 August. Shippers by the *Elizabeth & Katherine*, Mr. John Hide, bound from London for Virginia: William Paggen, Thomas Stark. (PRO: E190/145/1).

25 August-1 September. Shippers by the *Booth*, Mr. Timothy Keysar, bound from London for Virginia: William Paggen, John Taylor. (PRO: E190/145/1).

25 August-3 September. Shippers by the *Sarah & Elizabeth* of Bristol, Mr. John Miller, bound from Bristol for Virginia: John Duddleston, John Millerd, Edward Field. (PRO: E190/1149/1).

25 August-10 September. Shippers by the *Abraham & Francis*, Mr. Edward Burford, bound from London for Virginia: William Paggen, Edward Round. (PRO: E190/145/1).

28-30 August. Shippers by the *Anne*, Mr. Richard Howard, bound from London for Virginia: John Jefferies, James Cary, Thomas Wych. (PRO: E190/145/1).

29 August. Anthony Eales, aged 18, apprenticed from Christ's Hospital to Benjamin King, commander of the *Constant Richard* bound for Barbados. (CH).

29 August-4 September. Shippers by the *Concord* of Bristol, Mr. Samuell Hartnell, bound from Bristol for Virginia: William Danes & Co., John Peirson. (PRO: E190/1149/1).

29 August-5 September. Shippers by the *Isaac & Sarah*, Mr. Samuell Isaac, bound from London for Virginia: Robert Bristow, Jeremy Bearman, Micajah Perry. (PRO: E190/145/1).

30 August-1 September. Shippers by the *Owners Adventure*, Mr. Wharton, bound from London for Maryland: John Robinson, Robert Cullant. (PRO: E190/145/1).

30 August-2 October. Shippers by the *Potomack Merchant* bound from Bristol for Barbados and Virginia: Richard Gotly, William Fry, Richard Crumpe. (PRO: E190/1149/1).

31 August-4 September. Shippers by the *Maryland Merchant*, Mr. John Dorman, bound from London for Virginia: Samson Dorrell, William Peel, James Dryden. (PRO: E190/145/1).

31 August-19 November. Shippers by the *Richard*, Mr. William Harris, bound from London for New England: Richard Watts, Wigfall & Gell, Timothy Armitage, James Rawliston, John Lambert, Joseph Cane, David Clarkson, John Pym, David Kelly, Sir Humphrey Edwin, Rowland Platt, John Cranmer, Samuell Wood. (PRO: E190/145/1).

August. Administration of John Addams of St. Botolph Aldgate, London, who died in Virginia, bachelor. (AW).

August. Administration with will of Simon Keech of Stepney, Middlesex, who died in Virginia, bachelor. (AW).

August. Administration of Matthew Rowlson of the ship *Susan* of London, who died in Virginia, bachelor. (AW).

1 September. Shipper by the *Diligence* of London, Mr. Robert Bishop, bound from Bristol for Virginia: Benjamin Dolinge. (PRO: E190/1149/1).

4-20 September. Shippers by the *Stephen & Edward*, Mr. Sebastian Ginge, bound from London for Virginia: John Hobbs, Micajah Perry. (PRO: E190/145/1).

6-15 September. Shippers by the *Bailey*, Mr. William Norrington, bound from London for Virginia: Arthur Baily, James Wagstaffe, Samuell Spicer, Thomas Brittle. (PRO: E190/145/1).

7 September. Shipper by the [blank] *Merchants Adventure?*, Mr. [Richard] Langley, bound from London for Virginia: Thomas Potter. (PRO: E190/145/1).

7-11 September. Shippers by the *Perry & Lane*, Mr. Morgan, bound from London for Virginia: William King, Robert Gimbleton, Micajah Perry. (PRO: E190/145/1).

7 September-2 October. Shippers by the *Swan*, Mr. Andrew Belcher, bound from London for New England: Timothy Fowler, Thomas Gwin, Mary Bradly, James Aynsworth, John Newark, Abraham Austin, Henry Hatfield, Roger Pitkin, John Gilbert, Sir William Phipps, Jeffrey Pollard. (PRO: E190/145/1).

10 September. Deposition by William Baker of London, gent aged 38, that Thomas Cook, formerly of London but late of Maryland, merchant, signed a deed of 20 October 1681 whereby he conveyed his lands in Maryland to Edmund White and Thomas Hunt of London, merchants. (LMCD).

11 September. Shippers by the *John & William* of Bristol for Virginia and Jamaica: John Boussac, Peter Mougleworth. (PRO: E190/1149/1).

12 September. Shipper by the *Laurell*, Mr. Gill Lindsey, bound from London for Virginia: said Gill Lindsey. (PRO: E190/145/1).

12-18 September. Shippers by the *Benjamin*, Mr. Frederick Johnson, bound from London for Virginia: Francis Wheeler, Samuell Curle, Benjamin Braine, Jacob Bell. (PRO: E190/145/1).

13-15 September. Shippers by the *Hound*, Mr. Phineas Hide, bound from London for Virginia: Edward Leman, Anthony Stratton. (PRO: E190/145/1).

14-17 September. Shippers by the *Three Brothers*, Mr. James Braine, bound from London for Virginia: John Pryor, William Irwin. (PRO: E190/145/1).

14-20 September. Shippers by the *Judith*, Mr. Mathew Trim, bound from London for Virginia: Edmond Littlepage, John Handford. (PRO: E190/145/1).

14 September-19 October. Shippers by the *Augustine*, Mr. Zachary Taylor, bound from London for Virginia: Richard Nicholson, Anthony Stratton, Francis Southworth, Thomas Dolphin, Richard Atkinson, John Viner, Thomas Mynne. (PRO: E190/145/1).

17 September. Shipper by the [blank], Mr. Rowland, bound from Carolina: Anthony Sebastia. (PRO: E190/145/1).

17-29 September. Shippers by the *Mary* of Bristol, Mr. Thomas Opie, bound from Bristol for Virginia: John Bubb, Thomas Cole, John Howlett. (PRO: E190/1149/1).

18-24 September. Shippers by the *Eastland Merchant*, Mr. Michael Holmes, bound from London for Maryland: Edward Carlton, Thomas Wilkin. (PRO: E190/145/1).

18 September-22 October. Shippers by the *Katherine*, Mr. Samuell Dodson, bound from London for Carolina: John Ryon, Peter Albertus, William Grace, Moses Lamouch, Thomas Amy, Christopher Willing, Humphrey Cock, John Garrett. (PRO: E190/145/1).

19 September-17 December. Shippers by the *Lemon*, Mr. Thomas Hasted, bound from London for Virginia: Francis Lee, Thomas Wych, John Gore. (PRO: E190/145/1).

20 September-10 October. Shippers by the *Hopewell*, Mr. John Rudds, bound from London for Virginia: John Phelps, Daniell Claphamson, John Brodnax, William Lovell. (PRO: E190/145/1).

20 September-17 October. Shipper by the *Concord*, Mr. William Jefferies, bound from London for Virginia: Micajah Perry. (PRO: E190/145/1).

22 September-4 October. Shippers by the *John*, Mr. Robert Roberts, bound from London for Carolina: Thomas Browne, John Cockram. (PRO: E190/145/1).

25 September-29 November. Shippers by the *Globe*, Mr. [Bartholomew] Watts, bound from London for Virginia and Maryland: Ann Lambert, William Oyles, William Rousby. (PRO: E190/145/1).

27 September. Shipper by the *Lyon* of Plymouth, Mr. Charles Blight, bound from Plymouth for Virginia: James Blight. (PRO: E190/1052/21).

27 September-2 October. Shippers by the *Diligence* of Bristol, Mr. John Evans, bound from Bristol for Virginia: Jacob Beale & Co., Michaell Wharton. (PRO: E190/1149/1).

28 September. Shipper by the *Seaflower* of Bristol, Mr. John Shewell, bound from Bristol for Virginia: Richard Paine. (PRO: E190/1149/1).

September. Administration of Joseph Oliver of Virginia, bachelor. (AW).

September. Probate of will of Michael Griggs of Lancaster County, Virginia, but late of St. Botolph Aldgate, London, who died in St. Matthew, Friday Street, London. (AW).

3 October. Newgate prisoners reprieved to be transported to Barbados or Jamaica. London: John Barnes alias Anderson; Anne Yates alias Mills alias Clarke, spinster; Mary Bathurst, spinster; John Avery; ; William alias John Stafford of St. Giles in the Fields; Henry Sprosely of the same; John Sutton of the same; Tabitha Porter of the same; Samuel Smith of the same; Solomon

Spring of Hornsey; John Wyatt of St. Clement Danes; William Goodman of the same; Elizabeth Parsons of St. Mary Savoy, spinster; John Jackson of Whitechapel; James Nicholls of the same; William Goddard of Edmonton; Thomas Percivall of Hendon; John Browne of the same; James Pidgley of Fulham; John Collett of St. Andrew Holborn; Valentine Cogswell of the same; Robert Lambourn of St. Margaret Westminster; George Emmett of the same. (PRO: C66/3309/1).

5 October. Shipper by the *Richard & James* of Bristol bound from Bristol for Virginia: Sarath Porter. (PRO: E190/1149/1).

5-8 October. Shippers by the *Mary* of Plymouth, Mr. John Jory, bound from Plymouth for Virginia: John Rogers, John Edgcombe. (PRO: E190/1052/21).

21 October-9 November. Shippers by the *Unicorn*, Mr. John Brumskill, bound from London for Virginia: James Smith, Ambrose Talbott. (PRO: E190/145/1).

24 October-12 November. Shippers by the *[St.] Thomas*, Mr. Henry Sutton, bound from London for Virginia: Richard Fifoot, Francis Camfield, Thomas Coman. (PRO: E190/145/1).

30 October. Shipper by the *Barbados Merchant*, Mr. Cuthbert Sharpless, bound from Weymouth for Virginia: David Arbuthnot & Co. (PRO: E190/888/9).

31 October. Shipper by the *Hopewell* of Bristol bound from Bristol for Virginia: Joseph Whitchurch. (PRO: E190/1149/1).

October. Administration of Francis Epes the elder, of Virginia. (AW).

19-22 November. Shipper by the *Mary*, Mr. John Harris, bound from London for Maryland: James Braine. (PRO: E190/145/1).

21 November. Shipper by the *Endeavour* of Plymouth, Mr. Robert Gooding, bound from Plymouth for Virginia: William Martyn. (PRO: E190/1052/21).

24 November. Deposition by John Crofts Barker of London, aged 24, that Joseph Harris of Pennsylvania, merchant, deceased, became indebted by bond of 8 June 1687 to John Leapidge of London, skinner, for goods shipped on the *Brothers Adventure*, Mr. Henry Tregany. Harris also became indebted by bond of 20 May 1687 to Thomas Seaborne, barber surgeon of London, deceased, to whom the deponent was then servant. John Leapidge, aged 28, deposes that Joseph Harris also became indebted to Thomas Zachary of London, merchant, on 4 June 1687 for goods shipped by the *Brothers Adventure*. Daniel Le Febvre deposes that Harris also became indebted to his master, William Doldern, citizen and skinner of London, on 6 June 1687 for goods shipped by the same vessel. Thomas Zachary, aged 33, affirms that he has not received satisfaction. (LMCD).

29 November-7 December. Shippers by the *Virginia Factor*, Mr. William Hill, bound from London for Maryland: Michael Yoakley, Roger Leavens, Robert Hamilton. (PRO: E190/145/1).

30 November. Deposition by John Science of London, stationer aged 26, that Thomas Wynn of Philadelphia, physician, became indebted to Michael Jones of London, merchant, by bond of 23 July 1686. Zachary Whitpen and Charles Sanders of Pennsylvania, merchants, have been appointed as attorneys. (LMCD).

November. Administration of John Rose of Deptford, Kent, who died in Virginia, bachelor. (AW).

November. Administration of Thomas Arnold of St. Sepulchre, London, who died in Carolina. (AW).

November. Administration of Bartholomew Wills of New England, bachelor. (AW).

1 December. Shipper by the *Crown*, Mr. Bartholomew Watts, bound from London for Maryland: Joseph Foscey(?). (PRO: E190/145/1).

4 December. Shipper by the *Loyal Effingham*, Mr. John Purvis, bound from London for Virginia: said John Purvis. (PRO: E190/145/1).

5 December. Shipper by the *Olive Branch* of Plymouth, Mr. William Sellwood, bound from Plymouth for Virginia: Marke Batt. (PRO: E190/1052/21).

18-24 December. Shipper by the *London Merchant*, Mr. John Prentis, bound from London for New England: Samuell Cudworth. (PRO: E190/145/1).

19 December. Shipper by the *Daniell & Elizabeth* of Plymouth, Mr. William Ginnis, bound from Plymouth for Virginia: William Martyn. (PRO: E190/1052/21).

20 December. Shipper by the *Young Prince*, Mr. Robert Lurting, bound from London for Virginia: William Paggen. (PRO: E190/145/1).

December. Probate of will of Thomas Blagrave of Westminster, Middlesex, whose kinswoman, Anne Williams, was in Virginia. (AW).

1689

9 January. Ezekiel Muller, aged 18, apprenticed from Christ's Hospital to Robert Lurting, commander of the *Young Prince* bound for Virginia. (CH).

26 January. Paul Payne, aged 17, apprenticed from Christ's Hospital to Thomas Burrell, commander of the *Turkey Merchant* bound for the West Indies. (CH).

January. Probate of will of Sir John Bawdon of All Hallows the Great, London, who had lands in New England. (AW).

February. Administration of Thomas Burton of New England, who died on the ship *Quaker Ketch*. (AW).

February. Administration of John Smith of Pennsylvania. (AW).

28 March-3 April. Shipper by the *Katherine* of Lancaster, Mr. William Reynolds, bound from Lancaster for Virginia: John Hodgson (PRO: E190/1350/6).

1 April-30 May. On the petition of Alderman Edward Thompson he is to be granted the right to register servants for the plantations for a period of 21 years, the patent formerly granted to Colonel John Legg, Christopher Guise and John Robins having been vacated. The fees payable are to be five shillings for indentures and six pence for the registration of each name. (APC & CSPC).

27 April. Thomas Rogers, aged 14, apprenticed from Christ's Hospital to John Brome, commander of the *Ruth* bound for Barbados. (CH).

April. Probate of will of Henry Whearley of Barbados, whose brother, Francis Whearley, was in Pennsylvania. (AW).

April. Probate of will of Alexander Parker of St. Edmund Lombard Street, London, who had lands in Pennsylvania. (AW).

April. Probate of will of George Reeves of Virginia, widower. (AW).

3 May. Petition by John Clapp, Joseph Pitts and John Gould of Colyton, Devon, and Daniel Cleveland and Nathaniel Smith of Honiton, Devon, that the following persons, men of industrious and sober lives, who were sentenced to be sold as slaves to America, be allowed to return home to their families. All were taken into custody after the defeat of the Duke of Monmouth, some having take up arms against the King, others having supplied provisions to the rebels but many not having assisted at all: Judge Jefferies required all of them to plead guilty or face immediate execution and they were therefore terrified into making false confessions and accepting banishment for ten years.

John Smith, Thomas Franklyn, Abraham Thomas, John Baker, James Fowick, Christopher Irwell, Richard Pyne, John White, Samuell Pinson, Richard Parker, Francis Smith, Emanuel Marchant, Thomas Meade, Nicholas Salter,

Benjamin Whicker, John Heathfield, Nicholas Braddon, Francis Puckett, John Gey, William Harvey, Thomas Quick, Thomas Pester, John Conant, William Clarke, Edmund Bovett, Thomas Bovett, Peter Kent, John Clode, Argenton Roost, Gideon Dare, Humphrey Slade, John Skiffe, John Bagwell, Henry Tizard, John Alston, George Macey, Richard Greene, John Edwards, Robert Spurway, Edward Vildue, William Browne. (PRO: SP32/43, 44/236).

13 May. The following apprenticed in London: David Tristid to Richard Whitpaine, citizen and butcher of London, 4 years Pennsylvania. (LMWB 13).

14 May. The following apprenticed in London: Elizabeth Whittle to William Smith, mariner, 4 years Pennsylvania. (LMWB 13).

May. Administration of Richard Farmer of Virginia, who died on the ship *Quaker Ketch* at sea, bachelor. (AW).

27 July. The following apprenticed from Christ's Hospital: Samuell Edwards, aged 17, to Stephen Carket, commander of the *Charity* bound for the West Indies; John Sadler, aged 19, to John Williams, commander of the *Richard & Michael* bound for Barbados. (CH).

July. Administration of John Smith of Boston, New England, who died on the ship *Nonsuch*. (AW).

July. Administration of Edward Nowell of Virginia, bachelor. (AW).

July. Administration with will of William Burges of South River, Anne Arundell County, Maryland. (AW).

July. Administration with will of Charles Stepkin the elder of London who died in Virginia. (AW).

July. Administration of James Muire of Virginia. (AW).

21 August. The following apprenticed from Christ's Hospital: John Hooke, aged 15, to Michael Staples, commander of the *Edward & Mary* bound for the West Indies; John Sherrington, aged 16, to James Smith, commander of the *Sedgwick* bound for Barbados and Jamaica. (CH).

27 September-2 October. Shipper by the *Grape* of Liverpool, Mr. Thomas Preeson, bound from Liverpool for Virginia: William Preeson. (PRO: E190/1350/1).

September. Administration with will of Nowell Hilton of Charles Town, Middlesex County, New England, mariner. (AW).

15-17 October. Shipper by the *Morning Star* of Lancaster, Mr. Henry Baggott, bound from Lancaster for Virginia: Thomas Medcalfe. (PRO: E190/1350/6).

17 October-19 December. Shipper by the *Barbados Merchant* of Liverpool, Mr. Cuthbert Sharples, bound from Liverpool for Virginia: David Arbuthnot. (PRO: E190/1350/1).

October. Administration of Stephen Meeres of Boston, New England, who died on H.M. ship *Warspite*, bachelor. (AW).

4 November-10 December. Shippers by the *Reserve* of Liverpool, Mr. Christopher Moore, bound from Liverpool for Maryland: Clement Sayle, Thomas Johnson, David Arbuthnot. (PRO: E190/1350/1).

November. Edmond Gethings, aged 14, apprenticed from Christ's Hospital to Robert Morton, barber surgeon living in Wapping, bound to Jamaica as surgeon of one of H.M. ships. (CH).

November. Probate of will of Dame Alicia Lisle of Moyles Court, Hampshire, whose daughter, Bridget, was in New England. (AW).

November. Administration of Elizabeth Griffin of Virginia, widow. (AW).

4 December. Robert Edwards of Periton, Somerset, husbandman, bound to John Bull of Lyme Regis, mariner, to serve 7 years in Virginia or Maryland; Nathaniell Smith of Doressetton (*sic*), Devon; Thomas Midford of Langport, Somerset, husbandman; Katherine Midford of Langport, spinster, Joane Gyle of Trull [*Trysull*?], Somerset, spinster; Ann Pearce of Taunton, Somerset, spinster; Susanna Williams of the same place, spinster; and Elizabeth Stevens of Exeter, Devon, spinster, bound to the same to serve 4 years in Virginia or Maryland. (DRO B7/M9).

10 December. Newgate prisoners reprieved to be transported to Barbados or Jamaica. London: Mary Davis, spinster; Anne Harris, spinster; Jane Field, spinster, alias wife of Joseph Field; Katherine White alias Whitwood, spinster; John Moore; Thomas Harrison; Barbara Woolfe, spinster; Laurence Welch; Job Meddison; Elizabeth Browne alias Latham, spinster. Middlesex: Richard Davis of Fulham; John Bargier of St. Katherine's and his wife Abigail Bargier alias Mettham; Thomas Hillman of St. Martin in the Fields; Ann Robertson alias Robinson of the same; Elizabeth Locker alias Dye of the same, widow; Elizabeth Boyle, wife of William Boyle of St. Paul Covent Garden; Thomas Kelsey of the same; Jane Read of St. Andrew Holborn, spinster; Bold Billingsley of St. Giles in the Fields; Edward Thompson alias Blake of the same; Robert Evans of Stoke Newington; Thomas Lee of Norton Folgate; Mary Crosse, wife of Thomas Crosse of St. Giles Cripplegate; Mary Amor of Chiswick, spinster; Isaac Ford of St. Pancras; William Battin of St. James Westminster, yeoman; Ann Holding of Whitechapel; Thomas Barlow of St. Clement Danes; Sarah Burroughs alias Welstead of St. Mary Savoy, widow; Anne Dye alias Thomas alias Whitwood of the same, spinster. (PRO: C66/3332/5).

10-24 December. Shipper by the *Recovery* of Liverpool, Mr. John Banks, bound from Liverpool for Virginia: David Arbuthnott. (PRO: E190/1350/1).

19 December. George Quintine, aged 13, sent from Christ's Hospital to his uncle Henry Quintine and to Micajah Perry and Thomas Lane of St. Katherine Creechurch, merchants, to serve William Cole Esq. in Virginia. (CH).

20 December. Shipper by the *Lyon* of Liverpool, Mr. John Crompton, bound from Liverpool for Virginia: John Molynex. (PRO: E190/1350/1).

20 December. Shipper by the *Adventure* of Lancaster, Mr. Ebenezer Featherston, bound from Lancaster for Virginia: Augustus Greenwood. (PRO: E190/1350/6).

28 December. Edward Athy, aged 14, apprenticed from Christ's Hospital to Col. Philip Ludwell of Virginia by the consent of his brother John Athy, cooper. (CH).

December. Probate of will of Robert Clarke of St. Giles Cripplegate, London, but late of Maryland. (AW).

December. Administration of Thomas Langhorne of Pennsylvania. (AW).

1690

2 January. William Wright, aged 16, from Christ's Hospital to his cousin William Skelton to serve Daniel Park of York River, Virginia, merchant. (CH).

9 January. By order of the King the provision of 1686 whereby those convicted of complicity in Monmouth's rebellion were to serve ten years in the plantations is now revoked. Pardons may be given to those who desire them. (CSPC).

9-28 January. Shippers by the *Resolution* of Hull, Mr. Mathew Hexon, bound from Hull for Maryland: Gilbert Metcalfe, William St. Quintin. (PRO: E190/331/15).

10 January-15 February. Shippers by the *Recovery* bound from Exeter for New England: John Ellery, Francis Lidstone, Walter Lyle. (PRO: E190/966/8).

16 January-1 February. Shippers by the *Jefferys*, Mr. Thomas Arnold, bound from London for Virginia: William Anderson, William Bates, George Richards, William Hiccock, John Jefferyes. (PRO: E190/148/6).

22 January-2 March. Shippers by the *Elizabeth*, Mr. John Wylde, bound from London for New England: Nathaniel Loe, Froud Emberly, Francis Fox, Joseph Whetham, Joseph Bowles, John Wase, David Jefferys, Francis Barksteed, William Barre, John Mason, Gilbert Heathcott, Joseph Whesham, Owen Phillips. (PRO: E190/148/6).

26 January-4 February. Shippers by the *Unicorn*, Mr. William Norrington, bound from London for Virginia: Thomas Potter, Phillip Ford, Jonathan Woodley, John Jackson, Robert Walkeman. (PRO: E190/148/6).

26 January-8 March. Shippers by the *Thomas & Ann*, Mr. Andrew Elton, bound from London for New York: William Sanders, David Conyard, Anthony Tomkins, Samuell Wickens, Thomas Hanson, William Short, Thomas Gibbs, Phillip Woodward, Thomas Rawlinson, John Lonero, Nathaniel Rokeby, John Hackshaw, Robert Hackshaw, John Longuet, Jacob Jesson, Paul Manvill, Charles & Samuel Mitchell, Robert Spicer. (PRO: E190/148/6).

January. Probate of will of John Baynton of Bristol (bound for Virginia). (AW).

January. Probate of will of John Bulkeley of St. Katherine by the Tower, London, whose brother, Thomas Bulkeley, was in New England. (AW).

4 February & 5 March. Oxford Circuit prisoners reprieved to be transported to America. Berkshire: William Wright of Reading; John Connell of the same; William Guilman of the same; Bartholomew Brasier of the same; William Ditch of the same; Huckvill Wright of the same; Edward Money of the same. Gloucestershire: Richard Barnesfield of Gloucester. Herefordshire: William Weaver of Hereford. Oxfordshire: John Hall of Spelsbury; Thomas Bue of

Oxford; William Ashley of Woodstock. Worcestershire: John Davis of Worcester; John Biddle of Norton Regis; Robert Wakelin of Chaddesley Corbett; William Ashfield alias Ashwell alias Attaway of Northfield. (PRO: C66/3335/17 & 3339/3).

5 February-6 April. Shippers by the *Thomas*, Mr. Thomas Colebrooke, bound from London for New York: John Teshmaker, Thomas Bonney, William Fortune, Joseph Billop, Daniell Wherley. (PRO: E190/148/6).

12 February. The following apprenticed from Christ's Hospital: John French, aged 18, to Peregrine Browne, commander of the *Anne* bound for Virginia; Francis Booth, aged 17, to William Covell, commander of the *William & Mary* bound for the West Indies. (CH).

12 February. Shipper by the *Hopewell*, Mr. John Pennywall, bound from London for New England: said John Pennywall. (PRO: E190/148/6).

12 February. Shipper by the English-built *New York* of Dartmouth, Mr. Gilbert Bond, bound from Dartmouth for Virginia: Henry Lane. (PRO: E190/966/11).

12-16 February. Shippers by the *Blessing*, Mr. Ralph Potts, bound from London for Carolina: Nathaniell Johnson, Anthony Laxon, Thomas Pitts, John Covoore(?), Charles Fancheraw, William Thornburgh, John Rose, Walter Ryan, Paul Bruneall. (PRO: E190/148/6).

15 February. Shipper by the *John* of Exeter, Mr. Isaac Stone, bound from Exeter for Virginia: William Ekin. (PRO: E190/966/8).

16 February-27 April. Shippers by the *Amity*, Mr. Richard Dymond, bound from London for Pennsylvania: Joseph Richards, Thomas Merritt, Joseph Sedgwick, George Barr, Peter Keckwith, Thomas Cooper, Thomas Nicholl, William Gould, James Blackman, Richard Thacker, Daniell Wherley, John Willis, Phillip Ford, Edward Hartwell, Richard Willard, William Cockram, Richard Greenway, William Crouch, Abraham Chitty, Richard Edmondson. (PRO: E190/148/6).

22 February-21 March. Shippers by the *Happy Return* of New York, Mr. John Crouch, bound from Exeter for New York: Jacob Leisler, Charles Francom. (PRO: E190/966/8).

27 February. Western Circuit prisoners reprieved to be transported to Barbados. Devon: Roger Tucker of Alfington; Morgan Jenkin of Cullompton; Thomas Maunders of Halberton; John Jarvis of Alphington; Katherine Mitchell of Abbotskerswell; John Somers of St. Thomas Apostle, Exeter, worsted comber. Dorset: Robert Dare of Stockland. Somerset: Walter Peppen of Stogumber, blacksmith; William Quant of Pitminster; Richard Latham of Stratton Wedmore. (PRO: C66/3334/21).

28 February. Home Circuit prisoners reprieved to be transported to Barbados or Jamaica. Essex: John Lackrow of Harwich; Thomas Spencer of Witham;

William Suffold of Danbury. Hertfordshire: William Bew of Great Amwell. Kent: Richard Cole of Greenwich; William Bayley of Halling; William Peate of Halling; Richard Pritchard of Layborne; Alexander Woodward of Gravesend; Henry Shorter of Sevenoaks. Surrey: William Cumber of Bermondsey; Lydia Stocker of Knighton (pardoned absolutely in 1691); Robert Cliffe of Bermondsey; Mary Edmunds of Newington; Elizabeth Clarke, wife of John of St. George, Southwark; Matthew Eldridge of Holy Trinity, Guildford; Ann Heyton of St. Saviour, Southwark. (PRO: C66/3337/16).

1-24 March. Shippers by the *William*, Mr. William Deering, bound from London for New York: Daniel Ingall, Henry Maynard, William Cornelius, John Osmond, Thomas Crundall, Paul Freeman, Peter Hacker, John Hopkin, Thomas Cuddon. (PRO: E190/148/6).

3-27 March. Shippers by the *Dolphin*, Mr. John Foy, bound from London for New England: Charles Feltham, Edward Chotenham, Benjamin Bullivant, Robert Hodson, John Balstone, John Shelton, Rebecca Shrimpton, John Ware, Thomas Brindley, Thomas Phipps. Benjamin Bull, Joseph Whethorne, John Waser, John Shipton, William Scowen, Nicholas Burnett, Joseph Alford, Richard Edmondson. (PRO: E190/148/6).

3 March-22 April. Shippers by the *Society*, Mr. Peter Clarke & Mr. Thomas Fairweather, bound from London for New England: Godfrey Matthews, John Lynch, Walter Monk, Michael Watts, Thomas Powell, Christopher Booth, John Sindry, James (or Jonas) Blackman, Samuell Gerrard, Richard Gooding, Edward Hull, William Stretton, John Beighton, John Bletsoe, Samuell Ball, Richard Parrott, Mathew Carlton, John Fisher, James Galwith, Samuell Procter, Jeffrey Stanes, John Colton, Noah Lawrence, John Crow, Richard Humphries, James Jesson, Thomas Dodge, Nathaniel Holson, Elias Russell, Thomas Brattle, John Coltman, Thomas Cuddon. (PRO: E190/148/6).

11 March. Shipper by the *Elizabeth* of Boston, Mr. John Peck, bound from Hull for New England: said John Peck. (PRO: E190/331/15).

19 March-2 May. Depositions in London re the sale of the *William & Thomas* (then renamed the *Averilla*), Mr. Abraham Wilde, which was captured by the French while on a voyage from Virginia to London in 1689. (EA).

29 March-20 April. Shippers by the *Charles*, Mr. Edmond Copping, bound from London for Carolina: William Trist, Anthony Hatch, Stephen Peters, Benjamin Bradly, Eldred Lancelott, John Ashbey, William Thornburgh, John Rayner, John Singleton, Thomas Coman, William & John Scowen. (PRO: E190/148/6).

March. Administration of Rowland Stringer of Plymouth, Devon, who died on the ship *Daniel and Elizabeth* in Virginia, bachelor. (AW).

March. Cheshire prisoner reprieved to be transported to America: Margaret Phillips of Congleton, spinster. (EB).

17 April. Newgate prisoners reprieved to be transported to Barbados or Jamaica. London: Martin Seward; Mary Eades, spinster; Joseph Taylor; Daniel Grove. Middlesex: Benjamin Hall of Norton Folgate; Ruth Knight of St. Giles in the Fields, spinster; Thomas Mountague of the same; John Culliford of St. Martin in the Fields; Margaret Jones of St. Margaret Westminster; James Smith of Stepney. (PRO: C66/3335/9).

22 April-4 May. Shippers by the *Tryal*, Mr. William Dry, bound from London for New England: John Hackshaw, Oliver Andrew, Daniell Foye. (PRO: E190/148/6).

April. Administration of Samuel Dobson of New England, who died in Holborn, Middlesex, bachelor. (AW).

April. Probate of will of Richard Wharton of Boston, New England, merchant. (AW).

4 May-4 June. Shippers by the *Elizabeth*, Mr. John —ston, bound from London for New England: Henry Palmer, Daniell Atkins, Ezekiel Hutchinson, Rebecca Garrard, Edward Mann, Richard Seale, Thomas Major, John Smallwood, John Teshmaker, Edward Ellis, John Cabell, Thomas Ruck, Thomas Godfrey, Roger Allet, Jeremiah Bradfield, James Oldfield, Joseph Webb, Thomas Cuddon. (PRO: E190/148/6).

10 May. Thomas Tranter, aged 17, apprenticed from Christ's Hospital to Samuell Isaac, commander of the *Virginia Factor* bound for Virginia. (CH).

31 May. The following apprenticed from Christ's Hospital: Joseph Wallis, aged 17, to John Soane, commander of the *Jeffrey* bound for Guinea and the West Indies; Edmond Edon, aged 18, to Richard Whiffing, commander of the *Port Royal Merchant* bound for Jamaica. (CH).

May. Administration of John Halford of St. Katherine Creechurch, London, who died in Virginia, bachelor. (AW).

May. Administration of Thomas Bullen of Virginia, bachelor. (AW).

May. Probate of will of Joshua Holland of Shadwell, Middlesex, whose daughter, Elizabeth, was in Pennsylvania. (AW).

5-17 June. Shippers by the *Susanna*, Mr. Thomas Meeke, bound from London for New York: Paul Freeman, Samuell Burlingham, Isaac Demonds. (PRO: E190/148/6).

17 June-12 July. Depositions in London re the voyage of the *Constant*, Mr. William Burnham, from London to Virginia in 1689 with seven passengers including a servant, Elizabeth Garstell, and a child, and her capture by the French on her homeward voyage. (EA).

18 June-15 July. Shippers by the *Betty*, Mr. Edmond Hendfield, bound from London for New England: Thomas Glover, Timothy Jowles, Stephen Alexander. (PRO: E190/148/6).

19 June-27 July. Shippers by the *Ann & Elizabeth*, Mr. William Orton, bound from London for Virginia: Micajah Perry, Robert Christopher, Gabriel Glover, Robert Spicer. (PRO: E190/148/6).

27 June -15 June 1691. Depositions in London re the voyage of the *Partis*, Mr. Charles Partis, from Shoreham, Sussex, to Virginia in 1688 and her seizure by the French on her homeward voyage. The deponents include David White, merchant aged 30, of Houndsditch, London, who was born in Boston, New England. (EA).

1-7 July. Shippers by the *Success*, Mr. Edward Tatnall, bound from London for Virginia: Richard Buller, Blewet ———, Thomas Parker. [names mostly illegible]. (PRO: E190/148/6).

1-19 July. Shipper by the *John & Sarah*, Mr. John Francis, bound from London for Virginia: Micajah Perry. (PRO: E190/148/6).

2-28 July. Shippers by the *Elizabeth*, Mr. Elisha Bennett, bound from London for New England: Thomas Hunt, Joseph Martin, Aristophane(?) Churchill, William Coleman. (PRO: E190/148/6).

10-15 July. Shippers by the *Dove*, Mr. John Walker, bound from London for New England: Edward Manning, Nicholas Brattle. (PRO: E190/148/6).

12-19 July. Shipper by the *William & Mary*, Mr. Benjamin Hall, bound from London for Virginia: Micajah Perry. (PRO: E190/148/6).

15-21 July. Shippers by the *Samuel*, Mr. Daniel Bradley, bound from London for Virginia: Nowell Bassano, Micajah Perry. (PRO: E190/148/6).

15-21 July. Shippers by the *Rose*, Mr. William Tucker, bound from London for New England: Abraham Jellard, Francis Eggaree. (PRO: E190/148/6).

18-30 July. Shippers by the *Booth*, Mr. Simon Emberley, bound from London for Virginia: Henry Dennis, William Paggen, Thomas Cudden. (PRO: E190/148/6).

24 July. Shipper by the *Antelope*, Mr. Edward Cooke, bound from London for Virginia: James Arbuckle. (PRO: E190/148/6).

27 July. Shippers by the *Owners Adventure*, Mr. Peter Browne, bound from London for Maryland: Anthony Bayley, Arthur Bayley, Thomas Parker. (PRO: E190/148/6).

30 July. Northern Circuit prisoners reprieved to be transported to Barbados. Durham: William Moore of Durham City. Northumberland: Thomas Fairley of Morpeth. Yorkshire: John Cobb of Birdsall; William Bateman of

Dunkswick; Joseph Newhouse of York; William Pott of Fewston; John Hanley of South Kirby; John Goodyeare of Walton. (PRO: C66/3337/1).

July. Shippers by the *Hopewell*, Mr. ———, bound from London for Virginia: [names illegible]. (PRO: E190/148/6).

July. Shippers by the *Three Brothers*, Mr. James Brames, bound from London for Maryland: Henry Phillips, William Adams. (PRO: E190/148/6).

July. Shippers by the *Francis & Jane*, Mr. Edmond Polson, bound from London for Virginia: [names illegible]. (PRO: E190/148/6).

7-13 August. Shippers by the *John*, Mr. Daniel Pensax, bound from London for Virginia: Thomas Starke, Thomas Cuddon. (PRO: E190/148/6).

10 August. Shippers by the *Crown Mallago*, Mr. Michael Staples, bound from London for Virginia: —— Martin [other names illegible]. (PRO: E190/148/6).

12-16 August. Shipper by the *Abraham & Francis*, Mr. Edmond Burford, bound from London for Virginia: William Paggen. (PRO: E190/148/6).

12-18 August. Shippers by the *Elizabeth & Katherine*, Mr. Timothy Keyser, bound from London for Virginia: William Paggen, Edmond Harrison, Samuel Thayer. (PRO: E190/148/6).

16 August. Shippers by the *Thomas & Rebecca*, Mr. Thomas Wynn, bound from London for Carolina: Charles Fossett, Samuell Burdett. (PRO: E190/148/6).

17-26 August. Shippers by the *Hopewell*, Mr. Tompson Stodard, bound from London for New England: Walter Mico, John Shorter. (PRO: E190/148/6).

21 August. Shipper by the *Thomas*, Mr. Robert Limbrey, bound from London for New England: Paul Bristow. (PRO: E190/148/6).

31 August. Shippers by the *Averilla*, Mr. Abraham Wild, bound from London for Maryland: [names illegible]. (PRO: E190/148/6).

August. Shippers by the *Jacob*, Mr. Charles Reeve, bound from London for Maryland: [names illegible]. (PRO: E190/148/6).

August. Shippers by the *Adventure*, Mr. Thomas Sweeting, bound from London for Maryland: [names illegible]. (PRO: E190/148/6).

August. Shippers by the *Benedict Leonard*, Mr. Francis Partis, bound from London for Maryland: [names illegible]. (PRO: E190/148/6).

August. Shippers by the *Elizabeth*, Mr. Peter ———, bound from London for New England: Charles Seabright, Richard Merriweather, William Mead. (PRO: E190/148/6).

August. Shippers by the ——*Adventure*, Mr. Ralph Cooper, bound from London for Virginia: [names illegible]. (PRO: E190/148/6).

10-30 September. Shippers by the *Jefferys*, Mr. Thomas Arnold, bound from London for Virginia: William Woodbee, Thomas Hill, Thomas Lawrence, John Hanford, Richard Haines, Edward Round, Samuell Newson, Hugh Lamb, Richard Whitpain, Arthur North, Oliver Williams, Edward Hartwell, Ambrose Crawley, Nicholas Daw, Jonathan Smith, Thomas Beene, Walter Benthall, Daniell Wherley. (PRO: E190/148/6).

20 September. Shipper by the *Standerberg* of Barnstaple, Mr. Robert Fishley, bound from Barnstaple for Maryland: John Christmas. (PRO: E190/966/10).

24 September-4 December. Shippers by the *Exeter Merchant*, Mr. John Lyle, bound from Exeter for Virginia: Roger Prowse, Edward Pynder, Richard Shuckburg, James Radcliffe, George Bass. (PRO: E190/966/8).

September. Shippers by the *Thomas & Susan*, Mr. Robert Lewis, bound from London for New England: [names illegible]. (PRO: E190/148/6).

September. Probate of will of William Dyre of Sussex County, Pennsylvania. (AW).

8 October. Shipper by the *Friendship* of Barnstaple, Mr. Henry Wickey, bound from Barnstaple for Maryland: Richard Parminter. (PRO: E190/966/10).

11 October. The following apprenticed from Christ's Hospital: William Vaile, aged 16, to Thomas Willey, commander of the *Laurel* bound for the West Indies; Edward Wilton, aged 17, to Matthew Ryder, commander of the *Caecilia* bound for Virginia. (CH).

13 October. Pass issued in London for Mr. Heathcote and three others to embark at Portsmouth, Hampshire, for New York, witnessed by Mr. Byfield of Walbrook, London. (LMWB 15/18).

17 October. Newgate prisoners reprieved to be transported to Barbados or Jamaica. London: Philip Williams; Christopher Jones; Mary Jones, spinster; William Banister; Thomas Allen. Middlesex: Philip Magner of Twickenham; George Craford of the same; Andrew Browne of St. Pancras; William Rolph of the same; William Bristue of the same; John Wilson of Kensington; William Wright of St. Clement Danes; James Gawen alias Gardiner of St. Andrew Holborn; William Tripett of St. Martin in the Fields; William Gould of St. Margaret Westminster; Sarah Taylor of the same; Thomas Effoll of Hampstead; Isaac Woollens of the same; Jonathan Hawkes of the same; Thomas Fisher of Stepney; Richard Bourne of the same; Thomas Dodd of the same; John Lowe of the same; James Ardin of the same; Thomas Read of Hornsey; John Carter of the same; William Wilson of Edmonton; Anne Hereford alias Roberts of St. Giles in the Fields, widow; Susan Terrill of the same, spinster. (PRO: C66/3338/12).

18 October. Pass issued in London for Elias Heath to go to the place of his abode in Boston, New England, embarking at Portsmouth, Hampshire. (LMWB 15/18).

29 October. Nathan Gase, aged 17, apprenticed from Christ's Hospital to Elihu Robinson, commander of the *Francis & Samuell* bound for Virginia. (CH).

29 October. Shipper by the *Hopewell*, Mr. John Venard, bound from Exeter for Virginia: said John Venard. (PRO: E190/966/8).

30 October-10 December. Shipper by the *Success*, Mr. Phillip Ware, bound from Exeter for Virginia: John Bastard. (PRO: E190/966/8).

6 November. John Whittorne, aged 11, sent from Christ's Hospital to his mother Ruth Whittorne and Mr. Thomas Lane of St. Katherine Creechurch, merchant, to serve Col. James Powell in Virginia. (CH).

7 November. Newgate prisoners reprieved to be transported to Barbados or Jamaica. London: John Loveridge alias Spencer; Jane Eaton; John Stevens. Middlesex: Thomas Chawke of Hillingdon. (PRO: C66/3338/4).

7 November. Shipper by the English-built *Tiger* of Dartmouth, Mr. Robert Gooding, bound from Dartmouth for Virginia: Silvanus [Evans]. (PRO: E190/966/11).

8 November. Shipper by the foreign-built *Phoenix* of Dartmouth, Mr. Jeremy Sicks, bound from Dartmouth for Virginia: William Hayne. (PRO: E190/966/11).

8 November. Shipper by the English-built *Providence* of Dartmouth, Mr. Robert Streete, bound from Dartmouth for Virginia: Anthony Streete. (PRO: E190/966/11).

8 November. Shippers by the English-built *Merrimack* of New England, Mr. William Lord, bound from Dartmouth for Barbados and New England: Joseph Bully for Benjamin Masters, George Dottin. (PRO: E190/966/11).

8 November. Deposition in London by Samuel Johnson, sailor aged 23 of Boston, New England, where he was born, re the voyage of the *Providence*, Mr. Robert Lewis, from Boston to New York in April 1690. (EA).

10 November. Passes issued in London for the following to go to Barbados: Robert Blacklock and John Martin at the instance of Mr. Kirke, saddler; Mr. Goddard at the instance of William Longland of Cornhill, London, spectacle maker; Abraham Decasseris, his wife, son and daughter; Mary Gray, widow, witnessed by Henry Osman of Southwark, Surrey, chandler; William Charnly (also to go to Antigua), witnessed by Joseph Cheer of Cannon Street, London, silkman. Pass to Pennsylvania for John Busby and William Davis at the instance of Mr. Fair— of Scotch Yard. Pass to Jamaica for Isaac Decasseris, witnessed by Mr. Samuel Decasseris; David Machere; Isaac Meers; Stephen Elliot, witnessed by William Longland of Cornhill, London, spectacle maker; John Godfrey, his wife, his brother-in-law, Jonathan Stiffe, and a kinswoman, witnessed by Nathaniel Carpenter of St. Clement's Lane, London, upholder; John Wake, witnessed by Mr. Bray of Abchurch Lane, London, glazier; John

Wayte, son of John Wayte, with the same witness; William Rose, clerk, witnessed by Thomas Maccloch, merchant. (LMWB 15/19).

11 November. Passes issued in London for the following to go to Jamaica: Richard Chitty with his wife, son and maidservant, witnessed by William Atwell of St. Antholin, carpenter and Samuel Fowler; John Gale to go to his father in Port Royal, same witnesses; James Glasse, witnessed by John Barnard of King Street, London, upholder; John Slaughter, surgeon, witnessed by the same; John Meux, witnessed by Lawrence Hatsell of Birching Lane, London, scrivener. Pass for Justinian Sherborne to go to New England, witnessed by Mr. Linch of Leadenhall Street, London, surgeon. Pass to Barbados for Sarah Moore to go to her husband, Richard M., distiller, witnessed by Elizabeth Randall of the Royal Exchange, London. (LMWB 15/20).

12 November. William Parsons, aged 15, sent from Christ's Hospital to Mr. John Blaxtone, apothecary in Newgate Market, and Richard Bell, citizen and haberdasher, on Ludgate Hill, to serve Capt. William Matthews, merchant at Port Royal, Jamaica. (CH).

12 November. Pass issued in London for the following to go to Barbados: Mary Fenton, witnessed by Benjamin Harrison of Bridewell, London, weaver; Anne Wayte, witnessed by Robert Swinfield of Bread Street, London, milliner. Pass for William Godfrey to go to St. Christopher's, witnessed by Mr. Mabley of Skinners' Hall, London, coffee man. Pass to Jamaica for Richard Voysey with servants Thomas Butcher and Michael Higgins, witnessed by Mrs. Ann Pilkington. (LMWB 15/20).

13 November. Passes issued in London for the following to go to New England: Jane Edwards; Lott Gurney; Thomas Field, witnessed by Henry Chamberlain of the Royal Exchange, surgeon. Pass to Barbados for William Harris with servants Robert Cunyngham, Katherine Pegson, Mary Pegson and a negro boy, witnessed by Mr. Hurst of Wood Street, London, tailor. Pass to Jamaica for Anne Simonds and Elizabeth Williams. Pass to Antigua for Richard Street, witnessed by Joseph Carpenter of Aldermanbury, London, haberdasher. (LMWB 15/21,22).

14 November. Passes issued in London for the following to go to Jamaica: Edward Pattison the elder, his wife Elizabeth P., Edward Pattison the younger and Sarah Pattison, witnessed by Mr. Wasse of St. Clement's Lane, London, surgeon; Sarah Swetman; Ralph Greatorex; Katherine Greatorex. Pass to Boston, New England, for Peter Chabot and Andrew Faneuil, French Protestants, witnessed by Daniel Bruton of Cornhill, London, tobacconist. Pass to Barbados for Samuel Aungier. (LMWB 15/20,22)

15 November. Passes issued in London for the following to go to Jamaica: Peter Beckford with servants Edward Broughton, Anthony Major, Richard Inge, Charles Faller, Mary Farrer, Thomas Allen, John Meales and Dorcas King.

Passes for the following to go to New England: George Nicholson and Addington Davenport, witnessed by Mr. Marthwaite of Dowgate, London, wire drawer; John Bell and Epaphras Shrimpton of New England, witnessed by John Richards of Friday Street, London, linen draper. Pass for the following to go to Barbados: Ursula Gould, witnessed by Mr. Wynn of Leadenhall Street, London; Mary Jane; Richard Beale, witnessed by Mr. Levett of Lombard Street, London, silkman; Thomas Edmonds. witnessed by John Wright of Cheapside, London, joiner. (LMWB 15/22,23).

22 November. Following a petition for the release of those transported after Monmouth's rebellion, the Governors of West Indian colonies are ordered to repeal their servitude but to impose such restrictions as to prevent their leaving the islands without royal permission. (CSPC).

November. Administration of Robert Granger of Maryland. (AW).

November. Administration of John Hacker of Bermondsey, Surrey, who died in Virginia. (AW).

November. Probate of will of Elizabeth Matthewes of St. Mary Woolnoth, London, who died in New England. (AW).

November. Administration of Thomas Viggory of New England, who died in Deptford, Kent, bachelor. (AW).

November. Administration with will of Thomas Barnes of H.M. ship *Rose*, who died near New England. (AW).

19 December. Report on the petition of Philip Ludwell, who married the executrix of Sir William Berkeley deceased, Governor of Virginia, and who was sued by John Toton. (APC).

December. Probate of will of Elizabeth Bretland of Barbados, widow, whose brother, Adam Coulson, was of New England. (AW).

December. Administration of William Owen of Carolina. (AW).

1691

January. Probate of will of David Jeffries of Taunton, Somerset, whose son, David Jeffries, was in New England. (AW).

January. Probate of will of Martha Hunlocke of Clapham, Surrey, widow, whose son, Edward Hunlocke, was in New England. (AW).

January. Administration with will of John Enton of Virginia. (AW).

6 February. Passes issued in London for the following to go to Barbados: Thomas Walker and Mr. Robert Hall, merchant, witnessed by John Pitt of Watling Street, London, merchant. (LMWB 15/28).

February. Administration of John Burrowes of Bristol, who died in Virginia. (AW).

February. Administration of Evans Carter of the ship *Rose*, who died in Boston, New England, bachelor. (AW).

February. Administration of Philipp Sage of Stepney, Middlesex, who died in Virginia. (AW).

5 March. Midland Circuit prisoners reprieved to be transported to America. Derbyshire: William Bocking; John Shropshire. Leicestershire: Matthew Hutchinson; Thomas Deacon. Lincolnshire: Jane Jackson; Deborah Greene; Robert Grimes. Northamptonshire: Mary Hollowell. Nottinghamshire: Gervase Scratchard; Ralph Leadbeter. Warwickshire: Mary Bowyer; Joseph Higginson of Coventry; Elizabeth Barry. (PRO: C66/3340/6).

5 March. Western Circuit prisoners reprieved to be transported to Barbados. Devon: Richard Luxton of Cheriton Fitzpaine; Henry Chaire of Tiverton; John Heard of Holcombe Burnell. Dorset: Anne Golton of Dorchester. Wiltshire: Thomas Clargoe of Swindon. Isaac Jackson of Clerkenwell (Middlesex). (PRO: C66/3340/7).

6 March. Pass issued in London for William Elliot and Thomas Buckley to go to Maryland and New Jersey, witnessed by Mr. Wasse of St. Clement's Lane, surgeon. (LMWB 15/31).

April. Probate of will of Francis Willis of East Greenwich, Kent, and Ware River, Virginia. (AW).

April. Administration of Ralph Wythers of Bishops Canning, Wiltshire, who died in Pennsylvania. (AW).

April. Administration of Anne Clymer alias Ennis of Maryland. (AW).

April. Administration with will of Andrew Clarke of St. Sepulchre, London, who died in Maryland. (AW).

April. Probate of will of Francis Macaire who died in Charles Town, South Carolina. (AW).

7 May. Jeffrey Atkinson, aged 17, apprenticed from Christ's Hospital to Christopher Prissie, commander of the *Bridgetown* bound for Barbados. (CH).

11 May. Robert Jenkins, 15, sent from Christ's Hospital to his brother Jeremiah Jenkins to be bound to Francis Bond Esq. of Barbados, merchant. (CH).

27 May. Newgate prisoners reprieved to be transported to Barbados or Jamaica. Katherine Jones, spinster; Elizabeth MacDonnell, spinster, for coin clipping; Margaret Jones, spinster; Anne Yates, spinster, for burning Newgate Gaol; Jane Carr, spinster, alias wife of Robert Carr; Eleanor Edgerton; Mary Smith, spinster; Elizabeth Busby alias Noble, spinster, alias wife of John Busby; Elizabeth Wilson; Anne Harris, spinster, alias wife of William Harris; Ruth Staines, spinster; Elizabeth Fairbank, widow; John Anderson; John Leech Jr.; John Thompson; Elizabeth Walton, spinster, for manslaughter. Middlesex: Peter Volard of St. Marylebone; Thomas Rogers and his wife Anne Rogers of Ealing for coin clipping; Benjamin Harvey of Fulham; John Payson of St. Sepulchre; Margaret Roberts of the same, spinster; Francis Freeman of the same; Samuel Chaplin of St. Giles in the Fields; William Arrowsmith of the same; Margaret Batchelor of St. Martin in the Fields, spinster; Peter Desiong of the same for highway robbery; Sarah Steele of St. Anne Westminster, spinster; William Cole of St. James Westminster; Thomas Williams of the same; William Yorke of St. Margaret Westminster; John Rands of St. Andrew Holborn; Nicholas Upton of the same; Thomas Barlow of St. Clement Danes; Henry Chawke of Hillingdon; John Kirby alias William Trapp of Acton; George Read of Heston. (PRO: C66/3345/2).

22 June. Passes issued in London for the following to go to Jamaica: Pheasant Crispe and his servant; Sarah Love; Lucy Mayo with her servant. (LMWB 15/39).

24 June. Passes issued in London for the following to go to Maryland: John Stephens and his wife; Edward Killingworth; John Hanson; Elizabeth Johnson; Edward Phillips. Pass for Joanna Markham to go to the Governor of Pennsylvania, witnessed by John Foster of Gracechurch Street, London, ironmonger. (LMWB 15/40).

June. Probate of will of Joshua Pordage of St. Botolph Bishopsgate, London, whose son, George Pordage, was in Boston, New England. (AW).

June. Administration with will of Elias Provoast of New York, who died on H.M. ship *Samuel and Henry* in Virginia. (AW).

June. Administration of Thomas Ayres of Carolina, bachelor. (AW).

14 July. Oxford Circuit prisoners reprieved to be transported to America. Berkshire: Rebecca Shorter of Hurst. Gloucestershire: John Clarke of Gloucester. Shropshire: Hugh Roberts of Hodnet. Worcestershire: Robert

Launder of Dudley; William Marrowe of Stourbridge; William Bird of Whiteladies Aston; Francis Bathoe of Whiteladies Aston; John Miller of Bromsgrove; Thomas Saunders of Bromsgrove; Thomas Russen of Dudley; John Elt of Whiteladies Aston. (PRO: C66/3345/5).

14 July. Home Circuit prisoners reprieved to be transported to Barbados or Jamaica. Kent: Robert Welsh alias Shipmarsh of Hadlow. Sussex: Edward Hawton of Worth; John Mulzar of Feering (still in prison in June 1692). (PRO: C66/3345/4).

17 July. Yorkshire prisoner reprieved to be transported to Barbados: George Butler alias Buttles of York. (PRO: C66/3345/3).

22 July. Norfolk prisoners reprieved to be transported to America: Thomas Snelling alias Marison of Barton Turf; Richard Brett of Drayton; Thomas Breese of Drayton. (PRO: C66/3345/6).

July. Probate of will of Hesther Pritchard of Holborn, Middlesex, widow, whose granddaughter, Elizabeth, daughter of Robert Pritchard, was in Virginia. (AW).

28 August-27 November. Depositions in London re the voyage of the *Young Prince* from London to Virginia in 1690 with eight servants and her capture by the French on her return voyage. (EA).

August. Administration of Nathaniel Souther of the ship *Samuel and Henry*, bachelor, granted to the brother, Samuel Souther, attorney for the father, Joseph Souther, in Boston, New England. (AW).

September. Administration with will of Hugh Arrowsmith of the ship *Edgar* and of New York, who died at sea. (AW).

September. Administration of Arthur Herring of Maryland. (AW).

10 October. Thomas Nash, aged 15, sent from Christ's Hospital to his mother Rebecca Creed to serve Richard Bate of Fauston, Derbys, Esq. and to go with him to Barbados. (CH).

12 October. Petition of Elizabeth, widow of Thomas Jarvis deceased, and of their son, Thomas Jarvis, for the grant to them of the estate of Nathaniel Bacon which was forfeited by his rebellion. (APC).

14 October. The following apprenticed from Christ's Hospital: Edward Jones, aged 17, to Robert Bell, commander of the *Chesterfield* bound for Jamaica; Benjamin Wallington, aged 17, to Joseph Old, commander of the *Good Success* bound for the West Indies; Thomas Panck, aged 16, to John Smith, commander of the *Diamond* bound for Jamaica. (CH).

14 October. Pass issued in London for Abraham Fernandes to go to Jamaica, witnessed by Mr. France of Leadenhall Street, London, merchant. (LMWB 15/53).

October. Probate of will of Thomas Wyborne of New England, surgeon, who died at sea, bachelor. (AW).

October. Administration of Thomas Swan of Southwark, Surrey, who died in Virginia. (AW).

October. Administration of James Willington of St. Giles Cripplegate, London, who died on the ship *Burdis Factor* in Virginia. (AW).

October. Administration with will of William Coward of Boston, New England, who died in the King's service on the ship *Neptune*. (AW).

October. Probate of will of Lawrence Deledicq of the ship *Bever*, bound for New York, who died overseas. (AW).

10 November. The following apprenticed from Christ's Hospital: Samuell Smith, aged 14, sent to his sister Sarah Underhill and Micajah Perry, merchant, to serve William Edwards, Clerk of the Council in Virginia; John Chidley, aged 14, sent to his father John Chidley and Micajah Perry of London, merchant, to serve William Bird Esq. of James River, merchant. (CH).

19 November. Petition of Nicholas Sewall. He went from his plantation in Maryland to Virginia where he was seized from his vessel in Patuxent River by Mr. John Payne. During an exchange of fire, Payne was killed and the petitioner and his crew were tried for murder. John Woodcock was executed but the execution of two others was deferred. He prays for a pardon. (APC).

20 November. Thompson Hayne, aged 14, sent from Christ's Hospital to his father Thomas H. and Micajah Perry, merchant, to serve Capt. John Lane of York River, Virginia, merchant. (CH).

27 November. Isaac Browne, aged 12, sent from Christ's Hospital to his grandmother Joane Underhill to serve George Polegreen of York River, Virginia. (CH).

November. Administration of Richard Bray of Rappahannock River, Virginia. (AW).

November. Limited administration of Henry Fortee of Lambeth, Surrey, who died on the East India ship *Josiah* in Virginia. (AW).

November. Probate of will of John West formerly of New York but late of Boston, New England, who died in St. Martin Ludgate, London. (AW).

November. Probate of will of John Wayte of Worcester, who had lands in Pennsylvania. (AW).

2 December. James Walters, aged 14, sent from Christ's Hospital to his mother Ellinor Walters and Micajah Perry, merchant, to serve Major Arthur Allen of James River, Virginia, surveyor. (CH).

2 December-25 April 1692. Depositions in London re the voyage of the *Success*, Mr. Edward Tatnall, from London to Virginia in 1690 with four passengers and her capture by the French on her homeward voyage. Deponents include Micajah Perry, merchant aged 51 of St. Katherine Creechurch, London, but born in New England and engaged in the Virginia trade for 26 years. (EA).

December. Limited administration of John Bowman of Stepney, Middlesex, who died in Virginia. (AW).

December. Administration of Robert Archer of St. Dunstan in the West, London, who died in Carolina. (AW).

1692

15 January. Newgate prisoners reprieved to be transported to Barbados or Jamaica. London: Robert Bennison, Margaret Beard, spinster; Jane Williams, wife of Henry Williams; John Killpatrick; Mary Horsepoole, spinster; Francis Exall. Middlesex: Matthew Thomas of St. James Westminster; Martha Walters alias Wilson, spinster, alias wife of John Wilson of St. Anne Westminster; Daniel Wilcocks of St. Martin in the Fields; Elizabeth Hancock of St. Martin in the Fields; William Gray of Whitechapel; Elizabeth Jones of the same; Richard Jackson of the same; John Strutton of the same; Matthew Earsell of Enfield; Robert Chatfield of the same; Francis Bluck of St. Pancras; Charles Trevitt of Islington; John Friend of the same; Daniel Bramsbury of St. Sepulchre; Thomas Mercy of Heston. (PRO: C66/3348/11).

January. Probate of will of John Follett of Cape Henry, Virginia, who died on H.M. ship *Deptford*. (AW).

January. Probate of will of Francis Benskin of St. Martin in the Fields, Middlesex, whose son, Henry Benskin, was in Virginia. (AW).

January. Administration of John Stanesby of Maryland, widower. (AW).

January. Administration of William Burrell of Stepney, Middlesex, who died in Virginia on the ship *Mary*. (AW).

January. Administration of Richard Merritt of Stepney, Middlesex, who died in Virginia. (AW).

January. Administration of Thomas Baytop the elder of Virginia, widower. (AW).

13 February. Benjamin Langley, aged 16, from Christ's Hospital to his friend Mr. Edmond Lightfoot and Micajah Perry, merchant, to serve Col. James Powell of James River, Virginia, merchant. (CH).

19 February-4 July. Depositions in London by John Edwards, resident of Salem, New England, for 20 years but born at Christ Church, Southampton, England; Jacob Mauritz, mariner aged 47, resident of New York for 33 years but born in Harlem, Holland; Jacob Teller, mariner aged 37, born and resident in New York; and Isaac Derimer, mariner aged 26, born and resident in New York, re the voyage of the *Anne & Katherine*, Mr. John Couchee, from New York to Maryland where she was seized by the Royal Navy and taken to London in 1690. (EA).

22 February. Midland Circuit prisoners reprieved to be transported to America. Derbyshire: James Roberts; Laurence Nixon; Joseph Ford; Thomas Tomkinson; Grace Browne. Leicestershire: Thomas Verbracken; William Hickling. Lincolnshire: George Chappell; John Fowler; William Wisdom alias

Cambell. Northamptonshire: John Goodwyn; John Fetherston, yeoman; Edward Waddingham; Samuel Challenge. Nottinghamshire: Edward Ricketts; Thomas Osborne. Rutland: John Dickens. Warwickshire: John Pack. (PRO: C66/3349/15).

29 February. Western Circuit prisoners reprieved to be transported to Barbados. Cornwall: Joan Herdon alias Heyton. Hampshire: Richard Coles of Godshill, Isle of Wight. Somerset: John Hore of Stoke St. Gregory; William Curry of Charlinch. Wiltshire: Robert May of Sennington; Michael Longford of Kempton Langley, sergeweaver. Samuel Lee of London. (PRO: C66/3349/12).

February. Probate of will of William Bolton of Harrow on the Hill, Middlesex, clerk, whose brother, Henry Bolton, was in Virginia. (AW).

10 March. Deposition in London by John Barton, sailor aged 46, of Wapping, Middlesex, formerly resident for 26 years in Virginia, but born at St. Sepulchre's, London, re the voyage of the *Lucas*, Mr. Richard Tolliver, from Providence to Virginia and London. (EA).

30 March. Depositions by Gilbert Bant, mariner aged 30, of Boston, New England, but born in Cornwall, and John Bant, mariner aged 21, of Boston but born in the Isles of Scilly, re the voyage of the *Mehitabel*, commanded by the said Gilbert Bant, from Montserrat bound for London in 1691 and her capture by the French. (EA).

March. Probate of will of Elianor Trye of St. Lawrence Jewry, London, spinster, whose nephew, Thomas Buckley, was in New England. (AW).

April. Probate of will of John Stolpys alias Stolpee of Virginia who died on the ship *Mary*. (AW).

April. Probate of will of Nathaniel Snell of Hillingdon, Middlesex, who made a bequest to David Maybanke in Carolina. (AW).

April. Administration of William Joddrell of H.M. ship *Dunbarton*, who died in Virginia, bachelor. (AW).

April. Probate of will of John Aungier of Drome Derrick, Cavan County, Ireland, clerk, who died in St. Clement Danes, Middlesex, or in Virginia. (AW).

4 May. The following apprenticed from Christ's Hospital: Thomas Pickering, aged 18, to John Corbett, commander of the *Beaver* bound for New York; John Swetnam, aged 18, to William Jeffreys, commander of the *Sarah* bound for Virginia. (CH).

May. Administration of Stephen Crego of New York, who died on H.M. ship *Archangel*. (AW).

May. Administration of Richard Nicholls of St. Olave, Southwark, Surrey, who died on the ship *Susanna* in Virginia. (AW).

May. Limited administration with will of John Scott of Southampton, York County, Long Island, New England, who died in St. Thomas, Southwark, Surrey. (AW).

24 June. Oxford Circuit prisoners reprieved to be transported to America. Berkshire: Thomas Hall of Newbury; Richard Williams of Newbury. Gloucestershire: Thomas Smith of Bishops Norton. Staffordshire: Humphrey Pott of Lichfield; Richard Dutton of Sutton; William Browne of Wolverhampton; Anthony Rider of Stafford. Worcestershire: Richard Ballard of Pershore; Thomas Oreton of Worcester. (PRO: C66/3353/16).

28 June. Yorkshire prisoners reprieved to be transported to Barbados: George Whittaker of York; John Lee of Saulby; Henry Walker of Whitchurch; Benjamin Lee of Saulby; John Wilson of York. (PRO: C66/3353/13).

30 June. Home Circuit prisoners reprieved to be transported to Barbados or Jamaica. Essex: Benjamin Morrell of Hallingbury; James Sowgate of Great Holland; John Kendall of Beaumont; Caleb Clarke of Great Braxted. Hertfordshire: Thomas Nuttin of Hitchin. Kent: Charles Fincher of Ightham; Thomas Usborne of Ightham. Surrey: Mary Robinson of St. Saviour, Southwark, spinster; John Wright of Egham; Jane Williams of St. Saviour, Southwark, spinster. (PRO: C66/3353/12).

June. Administration with nuncupative will of John Lee of Charles Town, New England, who died at sea on the ship *Swallow*. (AW).

June. Probate of will of John Carter of Whitechapel, Middlesex, whose brother, Robert Skelton, was in New York. (AW).

July. Administration of George Nicholson of Boston, New England, who died in Virginia. (AW).

18 August. Probate of will of Elizabeth Whitburne of St. Botolph Aldgate, London, widow, whose granddaughter, Elizabeth, was wife of William Erby of Virginia. (NGSQ 76/3).

19 September. Depositions in Bristol to establish the validity of the will of Thomas Foulkes of Princess Anne County, Virginia, planter. (NGSQ 66/3).

September. Administration with will of John Grave of Virginia. (AW).

September. Probate of will of William Read of New England and of the ship *Granada*, who died in Jamaica. (AW).

September. Probate of will of Thomas Foulks of Princess Ann County, Virginia. (AW).

September. Probate of will of Walter Upington of Bristol, who died in Maryland. (AW).

September. Administration of Stephen Sargent of H.M. ship *Swan* bachelor, granted to the sister, Elizabeth, wife of John Davis, attorney for the father, Stephen Sargent, in Boston, New England. (AW).

5 October. The following apprenticed from Christ's Hospital: James Mires, aged 17, to Edmond Drake, commander of the *Amity* bound for Barbados; William Rowland, aged 18, to Robert Curtis, commander of the *Seven Brothers* bound for Barbados. (CH).

October. Probate of will of Henry Benskin formerly of St. Martin in the Fields, Middlesex, but late of Virginia. (AW).

October. Administration of Edward Howell of St. Mary Woolnoth, London, who died in Carolina. (AW).

October. Probate of will of John Seaman of St. Dunstan in the East London, who died in Maryland. (AW).

October. Probate of will of Joseph Wade of Boston, New England, who died on the ship *Mary*. (AW).

October. Probate of will of John Gibson of the ship *Assurance*, who died at James River, Virginia. (AW).

November. Probate of will of John Archbell of the ship *Ephraim*, who died in Virginia. (AW).

November. Probate of will of William Weedon of St. Botolph Bishopsgate, London, whose nephew and niece, William and Ann Weedon, were in Maryland. (AW).

29 December. Petition of Martha Dolby, wife of William Dolby, late boatswain of the *Assurance* in the West Indies. She prays a pardon for her husband who is detained in Virginia under sentence of death as an accessory to the murder of Mr. William Marshall, an inhabitant of Virginia. (APC).

1693

13 January. Newgate prisoners reprieved to be transported to Barbados or Jamaica. London: Robert Smith; William Dixey; Richard Smith; Edward Kelloway; William Carter; Margaret Pleadwell, spinster; Christopher Abell; John Demy. Middlesex: Robert Scofield of Stepney; John Overton alias Tucker of the same; Elizabeth Lee, spinster, alias wife of John Lee of the same; Abraham Welch of the same; Joseph Mead of Whitechapel; John Child of the same; Richard Harris of Islington; Joseph Jones alias Maurice Moore of Clerkenwell; Thomas Wheeler alias Richard Tovey of the same; Richard Page of St. Andrew Holborn, gent; Sarah Chandler of St. Paul Covent Garden; James Duncombe alias Dunckin of St. Clement Danes; William Warrington of St. Giles in the Fields. (PRO: C66/3356/11)

28 January-14 March. Depositions in London re the voyage of the *Samuel & Henry*, Mr. John Mead, from London to Maryland and her capture by the French on her return voyage. Deponents include John Dorman, sailor aged 45, of Stepney, Middlesex, who was born in Northampton County, Virginia. (EA).

31 January. Samuell Hinton, aged 15, sent from Christ's Hospital to his mother Mary Hinton and Mr. George Richards, citizen and weaver, to serve John Lane of York River, Virginia. (CH).

January. Administration of Richard Randall of St. Olave, Southwark, Surrey, who died in Virginia. (AW).

January. Administration of John Scrimgeour, Rector of Nominie, Westmoreland County, Virginia, bachelor. (AW).

January. Administration with will of Caleb Philipps of New England, who died on H.M. ship *Expedition*. (AW).

February. Probate of will of Samuel Jackson of New England, who died on H.M. ship *Windsor Castle*. (AW).

1 March. Gloucestershire prisoners reprieved to be transported to Barbados: Walter Taylor of Cirencester; Jane Greene of Cirencester, spinster. (PRO: C66/3359/11).

March. Administration with will of Henry Gerrard of St. Martin Brandon, Charles City County, Virginia. (AW).

March. Administration of Peter Lucas of Chipping Norton, Oxfordshire, who died in Virginia, bachelor. (AW).

March. Administration of Edward Blagge of Plymouth, Devon, who died in Virginia. (AW).

7 April. Benjamin Bridges, aged 15, apprenticed from Christ's Hospital to John Morris, mariner, to serve him in New York with the consent of his friends. (CH).

April. Administration of Peter Perdrian of Carolina, bachelor. (AW).

10 May. Buckinghamshire prisoners reprieved to be transported to America: Henry Cole of Bletchley; John Williamson of Bletchley; Richard Busby of Bletchley. (PRO: C66/3359/5).

May. Probate of will of John Symonds of Great Yeldham, Essex, whose cousin, William Symonds, was in New England. (AW).

May. Probate of will of William Shaw of St. Dunstan in the East, London, whose brother, John Shaw, was in New England. (AW).

May. Probate of will of Samuel Topping of Stepney, Middlesex, who had lands in Virginia. (AW).

May. Probate of will of Samuel Jones of the ship *James* who died on the ship *York* bound for Virginia. (AW).

June. Probate of will of John Harris of Hillmarton, Wiltshire, who had lands in Pennsylvania. (AW).

19 July. Western Circuit prisoners reprieved to be transported to Barbados. Cornwall: Matthew Hoare of Pillaton; Petronella Daw of Tywordreth, spinster; Grace Goodman of Tywordreth, spinster. Devon: Robert Ellworthy of Chulmleigh, weaver. Dorset: William Guy of Bere Regis; William Parker of Corscombe. Hampshire: Mary Prince of Newport, Isle of Wight; Mary Jolliffe of Romsey, spinster; Jane Goldring of Portsmouth, spinster. Somerset: Richard Westlake of Kings Brimpton; Benjamin Windmill of Compton Dando; Damaras Day of Compton Dando, spinster; John Jones of Crewkerne; Richard Beadon of Taunton, woolcomber. Wiltshire: Hanna Batten of East Coulston, singlewoman; Anne Belbin of New Sarum, singlewoman. (PRO: C66/3365/7).

22 July. Midland Circuit prisoners reprieved to be transported to America. Derbyshire: Joseph Bishopp; David Middleton; John Sikes. Leicestershire: John Bone. Northamptonshire: John Lovell. Nottinghamshire: John Roberts; John Caldwell. Rutland: William Dorman. Warwickshire: William Johnson; Jane Milward; John Bedding. (PRO: C66/3365/8).

22 July. Oxford Circuit prisoners reprieved to be transported to America. Gloucestershire: John Purcell of Bitton; Benjamin Searle of Bitton; John Pringell of Bitton; Thomas Kilford of Westbury; Thomas Brighty of Prestbury; Samuel Wintle of Westbury; Joseph Walker of Bitton. Oxfordshire: Henry Thomas of Adderbury. Shropshire: Benjamin Davis of Dorrington, blacksmith; Thomas Brookes of Pontesbury; William Hughes of Stokesay. Staffordshire: Richard Fogg of Bromley; William Berrisford of Alstonfield;

Zachary Benson of Rowley Regis, nailer; John Benson of Rowley Regis, nailer. Worcestershire: Thomas Mathews of Kidderminster; Evans Jones of Worcester; Simon Croley of Dudley, nailer; Thomas Williams of Kidderminster. (PRO: C66/3365/5).

22 July. Buckinghamshire prisoner reprieved to be transported to America. Francis Murrey of Marsh Gibbon. (PRO: C66/3365/6).

July. Probate of will of John Noore of Stepney, Middlesex, bound for Virginia. (AW).

July. Probate of will of John Abbott of St. Saviour, Southwark, Surrey, whose son, Josiah Abbott, was in New England.

July. Administration of Elizabeth Cawood of Boston, New England, widow. (AW).

August. Probate of will of Peter Johnson of the ship *Anne*, who died in Virginia, bachelor. (AW).

August. Probate of will of John Nicholson of Maryland, who died on the ship *Anne*. (AW).

September. Probate of will of Francis Petty of the ship *Hope*, bound for New England.(AW).

September-November. Depositions taken in Gloucester County, Virginia, re accounts between Thomas Starke of London, merchant, and William Seager, master of the *Concord*. Deponents include: James Ransone, aged 48; Thomas Merricke, aged 36; Thomas Edmundson; Lewis Burwell, aged 41; Thomas Merriden, aged 36; John Smith, aged 34; William Buckner, aged 36. (NGSQ 70/1).

October. Probate of will of John Cole of Exeter, Devon, who died in Pennsylvania. (AW).

6 November. The following apprenticed from Christ's Hospital: John Frognall, aged 12, sent to his grandmother Margaret Birt to serve John Breholt, commander of the *New Exchange* bound for Barbados; John Cheese, aged 13, to the same. (CH).

7 November. Peter Jenks, aged 17, apprenticed from Christ's Hospital to Michael Staples, commander of the *Edward & Mary* bound for the West Indies. (CH).

November. Probate of will of William Campbell of Wapping, Middlesex, who died on the ship *Anne* in Virginia. (AW).

November. Probate of will of Thomas Browne of the fireship *Hart* who died in New England, bachelor. (AW).

6 December. Newgate prisoners reprieved to be transported to Barbados or Jamaica. London: Elizabeth Harris, spinster; Elizabeth Wanne, spinster; John

Symonds; Walter Stephens; Mary Williams, spinster; Elizabeth Birkin, spinster; Thomas Granger; Anne Harris; Hester King; Isabel Clerke; Tobias Craddock; Charles Gale; Matthew Jones; Thomas Hudson alias Peirce; John Williams; Mary Gingen, spinster; Joseph Stephens; George Winder; Anne Smith, spinster; Edward Tear. Middlesex: Elizabeth Morgan alias Jones of St. Paul Covent Garden, widow; John Barker of the same; Eleanor Jones of St. Pancras, spinster; Isaac Blunt of Hackney; Joseph Mansfield of Acton; Ruth Harris of St. Martin in the Fields, spinster; Elizabeth Smith of the same; John Pitford of the same; Elizabeth Ridgeway alias Granger of the same, widow; Thomas Percivall of the same for coin clipping; William Smith alias Francklyn alias Bavington of Whitechapel; John Hoe of the same; Susan Lucas, spinster, alias wife of John Lucas of the same; Susan Martin of the same; Mary Child, spinster, alias wife of John Child of the same; Ralph Smith of Stoke Newington; John Jennings of Shoreditch; Thomas Taverner of Stepney; James Carey of Holy Trinity Minories; James Robins of St. Giles in the Fields; Cornelius Slayman of Hackney; Phillip MacDonnell of the same; John Chitwood of Willesden; John Algood of St. James Westminster; Elizabeth Gardner of St. Anne, Westminster; Mary Browne, spinster, alias wife of John Browne of Clerkenwell; Robert Wootton alias Parkway alias Watton; William Foreman of Isle of Ely, Cambridgeshire; John Platt of Harding, St. Albans, Hertfordshire. (PRO: C66/3360/15)

18 December. Chancery suit of Basilia Durban of St. Clement Danes, Middlesex, relict and executrix of Anthony Durban, v. Nathan Knight Esq. and others re the Manor of Tilehurst, Berkshire. Depositions were taken in London in 1695 to establish whether Francis Williamson, who had claim to part of the Manor, was still living. Deponents include: Jervis Gunthorpe, formerly resident in Antigua, Barbados and New York, surgeon aged 30, says that he saw Williamson in Flushing, New York, in June 1694 where he kept a school; Winifred Barnett of St. Clement Danes, widow aged 72, who says that Williamson went to New York before 1686; Obadiah Haig, merchant of New York, aged 20, that he had met Williamson several times in New York. (NGSQ 71/2).

December. Administration with will of George Deane of New England, who died on the ship *Princess Anne* in Barbados, bachelor. (AW).

December. Administration of Peter Holding of the ship *Resolution*, who died in New England, widower. (AW).

December. Administration of George Hollister of Boston, New England, who died on H.M. fireship *Hawk*, bachelor. (AW).

1694

9 January. Shipper by the *Submission* bound from Liverpool [*no destination shown*]: William Porter. (PRO: E190/1352/14).

12 January. Shipper by the *Oak* of Liverpool, Mr. Edward Tarlton, bound from Liverpool for Virginia: Thomas Johnson for Jonas Kenyon. (PRO: E190/1352/14).

20 January-10 November. Depositions in London re an expedition from New York into Canada in 1690 against the French by the ships *Blessed William*, Mr. William Mason, and the *John & Catherine*, Mr. Francis Gooderis. Deponents include: Jacob Teller, mariner aged 37, of Gracechurch Street, London, born and resident in New York; Robert Sinclair, mariner aged 34, resident of New York but born in the Orkneys, Scotland; Jacob Leisler, merchant aged 27, born and resident in New York; Edward Anketill, merchant aged 34, born and resident in Richmond, Surrey, but for six years previously resident in New York; Joseph Dudley Esq., aged 46, born and resident in Roxbury, New England; George Farwell Esq., aged 30, of Enfield, Middlesex, and formerly of New York, but born in the parish of St. Matthew, Friday Street, London; and Thomas Wenham, merchant aged 30, of St. Mildred, Bread Street, London, formerly resident for eight years in New York, but born in Hailsham, Sussex. (EA).

22 January. Humphrey Baldwin, aged 15, apprenticed from Christ's Hospital to Peter Dickary living in Bermondsey, Master of the *Hopewell* bound for Barbados. (CH).

January. Probate of will of John Green of Petsoe, Gloucester County, Virginia. (AW).

1-16 February. Shippers by the *Charity* of Liverpool, Mr. John Rimer, bound from Liverpool for Virginia: Richard Norris, Benjamin Weston. (PRO: E190/1352/14).

23 February. Shipper by the *Lamb* of Bideford, Mr. Phillip Prance, bound from Bideford for Maryland: John Davie. (PRO: E190/968/10).

23-26 February. Shippers by the *Expedition* of Bideford, Mr. Richard Martin, bound from Bideford for Maryland: John Davie, John Hockaday. (PRO: E190/968/10).

28 February-27 September. Depositions in London re the voyage of the *Mary* from London to Virginia in 1692 with four passengers and her capture by the French on her homeward voyage. (EA).

February. Administration with will of David Waugh of Stafford County, Virginia, who died on the ship *Elizabeth*. (AW).

February. Probate of will of Jone Cole of Exeter, Devon, spinster (*sic*), whose husband, John Cole, was intended for Philadelphia. (AW).

February. Administration of Samuel Marshall of Great Waltham, Essex, who died in New England. (AW).

3 March. Western Circuit prisoners reprieved to be transported to Barbados. Cornwall: Peter Hobbs of Menheniot. Devon: Richard Dodd of Manaton; Roger Prowse of Exeter; Margery Smith of Exeter; Mary Smith of Exeter; Richard Pittwood of Exeter. Hampshire: Daniel Cleverley of Waltham; Nathaniel Wentworth alias Winckworth of Husborne Tarrant. Somerset: Thomas Shaw of Taunton; John Burbage alias Chapple alias Stephen Hutchins of Almsea. Wiltshire: Thomas Bradfield of Yatesbury. (PRO: C66/3369/21).

9 March. Home Circuit prisoners reprieved to be transported to Barbados or Jamaica. Essex: William Brooman of Hatfield Broadoak; Thomas Layton of Hornchurch; Jonas Willmott of Danbury; John Byfill of Hornchurch. Hertfordshire: Edward Gardner of Bishops Stortford; John Ducke of Thorley; Sarah Abraham alias Browne of Hunsdon (still in prison in February 1696); Mary Brand, spinster of Felsted (still in prison in February 1696). Kent: David King of Tonbridge. Surrey: Benjamin Meecham of St. Olave, Southwark; John Hyatt of Lambeth. Sussex: Sarah Heath of Beeding or Seale (?Surrey). (PRO: C66/3369/20).

12 March-18 June. Depositions in London re the voyage in 1692 of the *Joseph*, Mr. Thomas Fairweather, from New England to Barbados where she was commandeered by the Royal Navy. Deponents include David Waterhouse, merchant aged 35, of St. Mary at Hill, London, formerly for seven years resident in Boston, New England, but born at Ash Bockinghall, Suffolk; and James Whitehead, sailor aged 41, resident of Spights Bay, Barbados, for 20 years, but born in Plymouth, Devon. (EA).

17 March. Chester Circuit prisoners reprieved to be transported to Barbados or Jamaica. Cheshire: John Stewart of Northwich; John Oldham of Chester; Enock Bartington of Somerford Booths. Lancashire: Robert Walker of Denton. Yorkshire: Dickey Smith of Pontefract, slater. Staffordshire: Robert Johnson of Stoke, yeoman. (PRO: C66/3369/19).

March. Probate of will of Henrick Harrison of the ship *Barnardiston*, who died in Virginia. (AW).

March. Administration of Nicholas Daniell of Stepney, Middlesex, Captain of the ship *Hampshire*, who died in Virginia. (AW).

4 April. Shipper by the *Truelove* of Bideford, Mr. Isaac Cleere, bound from Bideford for Maryland: said Isaac Cleere. (PRO: E190/968/10).

April. Administration of Andrew Charter of Wapping, Middlesex, who died on the ship *Edward and Francis* in Virginia, bachelor. (AW).

April. Limited administration with will of Abraham Cully of Stafford County, Virginia, bachelor. (AW).

April. Probate of will of Sir Peter Colleton of St. James, Westminster, Middlesex, who had lands in Carolina. (AW).

April. Probate of will of John Booth of Stepney, Middlesex, who died on the ship *Industry* in Virginia. (AW).

April. Administration of Charles Jeffs of the ship *St. John*, who died in Virginia, bachelor. (AW).

April. Administration of James White who died on the ship *Archangel* in Virginia, bachelor. (AW).

April. Administration of Edward Stevens of Bristol, who died in Virginia. (AW).

April. Probate of will of Richard Charlett of Calvert County, Maryland, who died at sea or abroad. (AW).

May. Administration of William Howes of Virginia. (AW).

May. Administration of Edward Westlake of Maryland. (AW).

27 June. Northern Circuit prisoners reprieved to be transported to Barbados. Cumberland: John Watson of Bewcastle, blacksmith. Northumberland: John Tough of Newcastle upon Tyne. Yorkshire: William May of Casingwould; George Mills of Skelton. (PRO: C66/3370/12).

June. Probate of will of Samuel Thomson of Shadwell, Middlesex, who died in Virginia. (AW).

June. Administration of Thomas Bowman of Stepney, Middlesex, who died on the ship *Henry* in Virginia. (AW).

June. Probate of will of Thomas Austin of H.M. ship *Richmond*, who died in New York. (AW).

June. Probate of will of John Larabee of New England. (AW).

June. Probate of will of John Osgood of Leytonstone, Essex, who had lands in New Jersey. (AW).

16 July. Midland Circuit prisoners reprieved to be transported to America. Derbyshire: Richard Gray. Leicestershire: Mary Ruddiford; John Shrouder; Charles Wrexham; John Getley. Lincolnshire: Robert Lacy; Joseph Bothomly; John Cade; John Burton; William Foulham; John Toms; Tirwhite Turpin; Edward Wilson; John Storey. Northamptonshire: Thomas Colson; William Tomkins; Thomas Bryan; John Smithergill; Thomas Tecton; Thomas Hawkes; James Satchwell; Thomas Burrough; William Bryan; Nicholas Rowell; John Browne; William Diccons. Warwickshire: John Wiatt; John Sherwood; Robert Shreve. (PRO: C66/3371/10).

July. Administration with will of John Abington of St. Faith the Virgin, London, who had lands in Maryland. (AW).

July. Limited administration of John Ware of Boston, New England, who died at sea on the ship *Friendship*. (AW).

28 August. Deposition by Thomas Raven of North Shields, Northumberland, mariner aged 40, that in 1690 Francis Gatonby Jr. was apprenticed to Frederick Fletcher of Newcastle upon Tyne, mariner, before being turned over to John Spring of Shadwell, Middlesex, who shipped him to Virginia in January 1693 as a mariner on board the *Baltimore*, Mr. Samuel Phillips. Henry Hickman of St. Giles Cripplegate, London, deposes similarly. (LMCD).

August. Probate of will of William Davis of New York, who died on the ketch *Aldborough*. (AW).

August. Administration of Alexander Fullerton of Maryland, who died on the ship *Elizabeth*, bachelor. (AW).

August. Administration of Andrew Dolbery of New England, who died in France, widower. (AW).

17 September. Shipper by the *Elizabeth & Ann*, Mr. Andrew Malpas, bound from Liverpool for Virginia: William Clayton. (PRO: E190/1352/14).

September. Probate of will of Thomas Hayward of Beverley, New York, who died on H.M. ship *Royal William*. (AW).

September. Administration with nuncupative will of Samuel Crabb of New England, who died in Stepney, Middlesex, bachelor. (AW).

1-8 October. Shipper by the *Thomas* of London, Mr. Christopher Buskin, bound from Newcastle for Virginia: Francis Partis. (PRO: E190/204/5).

5-11 October. Shippers by the *Torrington Merchant* of Bideford, Mr. William Giddy, bound from Bideford for Maryland: James Busuargus, John Joce. (PRO: E190/968/10).

10 October. Newgate prisoners reprieved to be transported to Barbados or Jamaica. London: John Webb; Abraham Turner; John Shorter; William Randall; Robert Beck; Mary Smith, spinster; William Gillett; Thomas Kerton; Richard Lorriman; John Edwards; Diana Lawrence, spinster; William Browne; Martha Shorter; John Cooke; Erasmus Townsend; Richard Clements; William Brewer; Thomas Allen; Isaac Syms; Isabel Harris alias Clerke, spinster. Middlesex: Nicholas Chappell alias Chaplin of Whitechapel; William Carter of the same; Thomas Cooper of the same; Francis Piper of the same; James Bends of St. Andrew Holborn; Samuel Hughes of the same; Henry Huper of the same; Charles Norman alias Pennington of the same; Joane Browne of St. Giles in the Fields, spinster; William Daintry of the same; Thomas Breed alias Richard Buckingham of the same; Elizabeth Bird of the same, spinster; Sarah Newell, spinster, alias wife of John Newell of the same;

Complete Book of Emigrants 1661-1699

Elias Stevens of Hees (*sic*); John Steward of St. Margaret Westminster; John Norris of St. Giles Cripplegate; John Nunn of St. Botolph Aldgate; Grace Cutler of the same, spinster; Anne Bowcher alias Davis alias Smith of St. Botolph Aldersgate, spinster; William Evans of Tottenham High Cross; Samuel Smith of St. James Westminster; Thomas Mitchell of the same; William Stafford of St. Paul Covent Garden; Samuel Eades of the same; Edward Tobin of St. Mary Savoy; Sarah Willmore, spinster, alias wife of John Willmore of Clerkenwell; Phillip Constable of Edmonton; Frances Wroth of St. Martin in the Fields, spinster; Susan Martin, spinster, of St. Martin in the Fields, alias wife of Thomas Martin of Whitechapel; Anne Goddard alias Wilson of Hackney, widow. (PRO: C66/3375/12).

16 October. London prisoners reprieved to be transported to Barbados or Jamaica: Charles Goddin; Mary Morrell alias Cambridge Moll, spinster; Lewis Lerosse; Humphrey Burton; John Thompson; William Whiteway; Eleanor Pelsome, widow; Elizabeth Storey, spinster; Elizabeth Edwards; Mary Sheppard, widow. (PRO: C66/3375/11).

20 October. Shipper by the *Expedition* of Bideford, Mr. John Banbury, bound from Bideford for Maryland: John Davie. (PRO: E190/968/10).

22-24 October. Shippers by the *Ann & Sarah*, Mr. Robert Middleton, bound from Liverpool for Virginia: Thomas Johnson, Thomas Preeson. (PRO: E190/1352/14).

22 October. Shipper by the *Loyalty* of Liverpool, Mr. Henry Browne, bound from Liverpool for Virginia: Richard Houghton. (PRO: E190/1352/14).

30 October. Shipper by the *Morning Star* bound from Liverpool [*destination not stated*]: Thomas Seacome. (PRO: E190/1352/14).

31 October. Samuell Chaddock, aged 16, apprenticed from Christ's Hospital to Humphry Ayler, commander of the *Jeffrey* bound for Jamaica. (CH).

October. Administration of Susanna Johnson alias Duncombe of Virginia. (AW).

October. Administration of Elizabeth Lloyd alias Carter of Richmond County, Virginia. (AW).

October. Probate of will of Joseph Newton of the ship *Dreadnaught*, bound for Virginia. (AW).

October. Limited administration of John Mead of Wapping, Whitechapel, Middlesex, who had goods in Maryland. (AW).

October. Probate of will of Edward Severy of the ship *America*, who died in Barbados, and whose brother, Andrew Severy, was in New England. (AW).

9-27 November. Depositions in London re the voyage of the *Mayflower*, Mr. Samuel Saunders, from Dartmouth, Devon, to Virginia in 1693 which carried a woman passenger. (EA).

10 November. Christopher Smith, aged 15, sent from Christ's Hospital to his friend Hugh Squire Esq. and Ralph Marshall of St. Paul Covent Garden Esq. to serve Sir Edmond Andrews, Governor of Virginia. (CH).

15-21 November. Shippers by the *Society* of Liverpool, Mr. Jonathan Livesley, bound from Liverpool for Virginia: John Pemberton, Robert Taylor, John Custis, William Watters, John Cockshutt, Richard Woodward, Samuel Sandford. (PRO: E190/1352/14).

19-20 November. Shipper by the *Amity* of Liverpool, Mr. Lewis Jenkins, bound from Liverpool for Virginia: John Molyneux. (PRO: E190/1352/14).

22 November. Oxford Circuit prisoners reprieved to be transported to America. Berkshire: Richard Miller of Waltham St. Lawrence; Andrew Peterson of White Waltham; John Parr of Reading; Edward Howse of Abingdon. Gloucestershire: Stephen Beard of Randwicke; William Parker of Yeave; Margaret Martin of Tuffley; William Jones of Welford; John Floyd alias Lloyd of Gloucester; Stephen Parker of Yeave. Herefordshire: Thomas Smith of Hentland; Thomas Horley of Hentland. Oxfordshire: Elizabeth Norton of Deddington; John Jeffreys of Nettlebed; Henry James of Bampton; James Plott of Tetsworth; Robert Smyth. Shropshire: Richard Carden of Dorrington. Staffordshire: John Hill of Stafford; Samuel Lakin of Stone; John Greenfield of Patshull. Worcestershire: Richard Bankes of Salwarpe; John Meredith of Tardebigg; Thomas Orton of Salwarpe; William Russell of Tardebigge. (PRO: C66/3375/2).

November. Administration of Elisha Lancaster of Bristol, who died in Virginia. (AW).

November. Probate of will of Thomas Arnall of Whitechapel, who died at sea on a voyage to Virginia. (AW).

November. Administration of Stephen Butler of New England, who died on the ship *John* of London in Sierra Leone, Gambia. (AW).

November. Administration of Mary Townsend of Newton or Higham Ferrers, Northamptonshire, who died in Virginia, widow. (AW).

November. Administration of Ralph Shurley of Whitechapel, Middlesex, who died in Virginia. (AW).

3-8 December. Shipper by the *Happy Return* of Bideford, Mr. John Hartnoll, bound from Bideford for Maryland: John Buck. (PRO: E190/968/10).

7 December. Shipper by the *Vine*, Mr. William Fletcher, bound from Liverpool for Virginia: Walter Brice. (PRO: E190/1352/14).

7 December. Shippers by the *Lyon*, Mr. John Crompton, bound from Liverpool for Virginia: Isaac Foxcroft, William Clayton. (PRO: E190/1352/14).

29 December. Shippers by the *Society*, Mr. Thomas Ely, bound from Bristol for Virginia: Samuell Parker, Mordecai Greene. (PRO: E190/1151/1).

December. Administration of John Foissin of Virginia, bachelor. (AW).

December. Probate of will of Edward Cresfield the younger who died at sea, merchant, and whose daughter-in-law, Lucy, was wife of Thomas Reed of Gloucester, Virginia. (AW).

December. Administration of James Laurence of Kingston, Warwickshire, who died in Virginia, bachelor. (AW).

December. Probate of will of Robert Thomson of Stoke Newington, Middlesex, who had lands in New England. (AW).

1695

7 January. Shippers by the *Margaret*, Mr. John Walker, bound from Bristol for Virginia: Mathew Yeamans, John Pope, John Bowman, Abraham Elton, Edward Fry. (PRO: E190/1151/1).

22 January. Shipper by the *Maryland*, Mr. Richard Townsend, bound from Bristol for Virginia: Roger Bird. (PRO: E190/1151/1).

28 January. Shipper by the *Swan*, Mr. David Robinson, bound from Portsmouth Roads for New England: Thomas Barton. (PRO: E190/837/6).

31 January. Shipper by the *Swan*, Mr. David Robertson, bound from Southampton for Boston, New England: Charles Newland. (PRO: E190/837/4).

January. Administration of David Carwithen of Boston, New England, who died on H.M. ship *Coronation*. (AW).

25 February. Home Circuit prisoners reprieved to be transported to Barbados. Essex: Mary Brand of Felstead; Lucas Page of Romford; William Baker of Messing; Richard Jackson of Little Wakering; Zachary Vails of Witham; John Ford of Takeley; John Turmidge of Steeple cum Stansgate; John Farrowe of Bulphan; Thomas Manning alias Cowell of Tolleshunt. Hertfordshire: Sarah Abraham alias Browne, spinster, alias wife of John Browne of Hunsdon. Kent: Margaret Johnson alias Mason alias Edwards of East Greenwich, spinster; William Jefferson of Chalk. Surrey: Joan Appleby, wife of William Appleby of St. George, Southwark; John Topham of St. Saviour, Southwark; William Stevens of Egham; John Blaxton of Camberwell. Sussex: William Pickerell of Sandhurst (*sic*). (PRO: C66/3380/15).

26 February. Norfolk Circuit prisoners reprieved to be transported to America. Buckinghamshire: John Edmonds of Amersham; William Jones of Beaconsfield. Cambridgeshire: William Papworth of Reach; Thomas Hall of Barnwell. Norfolk: Humphrey Jex of Barton Bendish; Henry Emerson of Garbich Thorne (*sic*); Thomas Ellinor of Wilby; Christopher Brice of Walpole St. Andrew; Richard Wright of Northwold. Suffolk: George Lagden of Stanningfield; Joseph Dye of Felsham; William Claydon of Hawstead. (PRO: C66/3380/13).

February. Administration of John Cornish of Ottery St. Mary, Devon, who died in New England, bachelor. (AW).

February. Administration of William Wright of Boston, New England, who died on H.M. ship *Mermaid*, bachelor. (AW).

1 March. Shipper by the *Bristol Factor* bound from Bristol for Virginia: Abraham Perkins. (PRO: E190/1151/1).

4 March. Western Circuit prisoners reprieved to be transported to Barbados. Cornwall: John Parsons of St. Agnes, tinner. Devon: William Kennick alias Thomas Lamprey of Crediton. Somerset: John Hillard of North Cadbury. (PRO: C66/3380/9).

6-10 March. Shippers by the *Elizabeth*, Mr. John Hooper, bound from Bristol for New England: William Clarke, Thomas Jackson, Michaell Pope, Paul Bowcher, Mordecai Greene. (PRO: E190/1151/1).

12-20 March. Shippers by the *Mary Ann*, Mr. Phillip Bass, bound from London for New England: Stephen Wesendonck, Samuel Nelham, John Ludlow, Samuel Ball, Thomas Ruch. (PRO: E190/150/1).

30 March-6 May. Shippers by the *Jago*, Mr. Robert Pincarton, bound from London for New England: George Brazier, Sampson Coleclough, Richard Clarke, George Anderson, Michael Plumsted. (PRO: E190/150/1).

March. Administration of Grace Gray of Symondsbury, Dorset, widow. (AW).

March. Probate of will of William Pawlett of Bicton, Hampshire, who died in Maryland. (AW).

March. Probate of will of John Endicott of Salem, New England. (AW).

5 April-11 May. Shippers by the *Adventure*, Mr. Thomas Parker, bound from London for New England: Francis Ambrass, John Glover, Thomas Washington, Joseph Crouch, Henry Gray, Matthew Eyles, Martin Goddard. (PRO: E190/150/1).

24 April-24 May. Shippers by the *Robert*, Mr. John Mullaney, bound from London for New York: William Cornelison, John Richardson, John Lucas, John Blackall, Robert Hackshaw, Francis Terene, John White, Joseph Trebell, John Barroby, Benjamin De Jaine. (PRO: E190/150/1).

April. Administration of Thomas Indian of Bristol Township, New England, who died at Barbados on H.M. ship *Dolphin*, bachelor. (AW).

April. Administration of Eleanor Hey of East Greenwich, Kent, granted to John Grant of East Greenwich, glover, attorney for the husband, James Hey, now in New England. (AW).

April. Administration of Charles Banford of Boston, New England, who died on H.M. ship *Nonsuch*. (AW).

April. Administration with will of Osmond Crabbe of Brislington, Somerset, whose brother, John Crabbe, was in Virginia. (AW).

April. Probate of will of George Richards of St. Botolph Aldgate London, who had goods in Virginia. (AW).

7 May-6 July. Shippers by the *Johnson*, Mr. Samuell White, bound from London for New England: John Stillman, Robert Meyer, Elizabeth Saunders, Phillip

Fell, Sir William Gore, John Shelton, Samuell Thare, Charles Middleton, Charles Haller, William Cony. (PRO: E190/150/1).

May. Probate of will of Mary Janson, relict of Bryan Janson, whose son, George Janson, was in Virginia. (AW).

May. Probate of will of Thomas Deane of Freefolk, Hampshire, but formerly of Boston, New England. (AW).

26 June. Shipper by the *Dolphin's Prize*, Mr. John Atkins, bound from Portsmouth for New England: William Bedford. (PRO: E190/837/6).

27 June-6 July. Shippers by the *Fir Tree*, Mr. John West, bound from London for New England: John Taylor, John Hill, William Stonehouse, Humphrey Spurway, Lewis Jones, Thomas Wilson. (PRO: E190/150/1).

30 June-12 August. Shippers by the *Bristol Factor* bound from Bristol for Virginia: Edward Harford, Henry Watts, Abraham Elton, Edward Hackett, Peter Saunders, John Clarke, Nicholas Chancey, —— Wilcox, Henry Lloyd, Sh. Pelloquin, Richard Nicholls, Jonathan Hornblow. (PRO: E190/1151/1).

June. Administration with will of Thomas Broome of H.M. ship *Dunkirk* bound from the Leeward Islands to Boston, bachelor. (AW).

11 July. Shipper by the *Endeavour*, Mr. Samuel Paine, bound from London for New England: Samuel Wickins. (PRO: E190/150/1).

17 July. Shipper by the *Granada*, Mr. William Holman Jr., bound from Portsmouth for New England: said William Holman. (PRO: E190/837/6).

17-18 July. Shippers by the *Supply*, Mr. John Long, bound from Portsmouth for New England: John Hopkins, William Troward. (PRO: E190/837/6).

19 July. Western Circuit prisoners reprieved to be transported to Barbados. Devon: Elizabeth Downe of Chittlehampton, spinster; John Traverse of Plymouth; Isaac Moore of Modbury; William Spikeman of Modbury; Philip Washington of Honiton; Edward Bragg of Dolton; John Merryman of Heavitree. Somerset: Elizabeth Roche of Stogumber, spinster. William Rose of London, yeoman; John Miller of Chelsea (Middlesex). (PRO: C66/3378/13).

24 July-29 November. Shippers by the *London Merchant*, Mr. James Thomas, bound from London for New York: Robert Hackshaw, William Grayham, Richard Clarke, Thomas Rascoe, Edward Hampton, George Norcott, Goddard Guy, Benjamin Knight, Paul Merlin, Abraham Barvetier. (PRO: E190/150/1).

26 July. Shipper by the *Johnson* frigate, Mr. Samuel White, bound from Portsmouth Roads for Boston, New England: Benjamin Quelch. (PRO: E190/837/6).

29 July-5 August. Shippers by the *St. Mallo*, Mr. Christopher Pollard, bound from Barnstaple for Newfoundland and Virginia: Anthony Juliott, Richard Parminter. (PRO: E190/969/7).

July. Probate of will of William Carpenter of St. George, Southwark, Surrey, who died in New York on H.M. ship *Richmond*. (AW).

July. Probate of will of John Colvill of Cranbrook, Kent, whose nephew, John Colvill, was in New England. (AW).

July. Administration of Samuel Teare of the ship *Anne*, who died in Virginia. (AW).

10 August. Shipper by the *James & Elizabeth*, Mr. Deane Cock, bound from London for New York: Samuell Clarke. (PRO: E190/150/1).

10 August. Shipper by the *America* of Bideford, Mr. Robert Northcott, bound from Bideford for Maryland: John Smith. (PRO: E190/969/7).

August. Administration of Richard Heywood of Stepney, Middlesex, who died in Virginia. (AW).

August. Probate of will of William Marsh of Charles Town, New England, who died on the ship *Mary* in Stepney, Middlesex. (AW).

August. Probate of will of Samuel Hill of Virginia, bachelor. (AW).

2 September. Shipper by the *Orange Tree* of Piscataway, Mr. John Hatch, bound from Plymouth for Boston, New England: Philip Pentire. (PRO: E190/1055/3).

5-26 September. Shippers by the *Carolina* sloop bound from Bristol for Carolina: Thomas Bower, Charles Nicholls, Mathew Worgan, Thomas Melton, John Dyer. (PRO: E190/1151/1).

16 September-6 November. Shippers by the *Bengall*, Mr. Christopher Scandrett, bound from Bristol for Virginia: Richard Franklin, Peter Wadding, Sir William Davies, Charles Harford, Thomas Hodges, Roger Kirk, Thomas Tyler, William Scott, Thomas Longman, Thomas Harbert. (PRO: E190/1151/1).

24 September. Chancery suit brought by John Herbert, merchant of London, against Rebecca Buller, relict and administratrix of Richard Buller of London, merchant. The plaintiff was appointed by Richard Buller as his factor in Virginia in place of Essex Bevell. In 1691, when he was nearly 70, Buller married his chambermaid, Rebecca Finney, and died in 1695. The suit relates to accounts between them and depositions were taken in London in December 1695 from: Henry Batt of Virginia, aged 53; John Harrison, mariner aged 31, who was a master of ships trading to Virginia; Roger Jones of Great Tower Hill, London, aged 54, who lived in Virginia in 1680-1691. (NGSQ 70/2).

26 September-23 October. Shippers by the *Antigua*, Mr. William Kidd, bound from London for New York: John Richardson, William Shepherd, John Rowett, Joseph Trebell, Robert Leving, Richard Parke. (PRO: E190/150/1).

September. Administration of John Bennett of Boston, New England, who died on H.M. ship *New Norwich*. (AW).

4-15 October. Depositions in London re the signatures of Benjamin Fletcher, Commander in Chief of New York, and Abraham de Peyster, Mayor of New York. Deponents include Giles Shelley, mariner aged 31, of New York, who was raised in the parish of St. Olave, Southwark, Surrey, and William Kidd, mariner aged 41, of New York, who was raised in Dundee, Scotland. (EA).

8 October-15 November. Shippers by the *Phillip*, Mr. Benjamin Norwood, bound from Bristol for New York: Edward Hackett, Peter Ketelcar(?), James Doning. (PRO: E190/1151/1).

8 October-14 January. Shippers by the *Nassau*, Mr. Giles Shelley, bound from London for New York: John Jackson, Joseph Lawson, Thomas Armstrong, Nune Fernandes, Henry Stodderley, William Teshmaker, Lewis Gullean, John Longuett, Simon Leblane, Gilbert Heathcott, Samson Gideon. (PRO: E190/150/1, 155/5).

9-10 October. Shippers by the *Henrietta*, Mr. Scipio Row, bound from Barnstaple and Bideford for Maryland: John Davie, Phillip Greenslade. (PRO: E190/969/7).

10 October. Shipper by the *America* bound from Exeter for Virginia: John Addams. (PRO: E190/969/6).

11-14 October. Shippers by the *Phoenix* of Bideford, Mr. Walter Power, bound from Bideford for Maryland: John Smith, John Joce. (PRO: E190/969/7).

11-19 October. Shipper by the *Happy Return* of Bideford, Mr. Henry Rock, bound from Bideford for Maryland: George Buck. (PRO: E190/969/7).

15 October. Shipper by the *Olive Branch* of Plymouth, Mr. Peter Werden, bound from Plymouth for Virginia: Mark Batte. (PRO: E190/1055/3).

30 October-27 November. Shippers by the *Bristol Merchant*, Mr. John Chapline and Mr. John Stevens, bound from Bristol for Virginia: Charles Jones, Thomas Machen, Samuell Packer, Thomas Longman, William Jordan, Thomas Tyler, Israell Hobbs, John Gilbert, John Putten. (PRO: E190/1151/1).

October. Probate of will of Maximilian Robinson of Rotherhithe, Surrey, who died on the ship *Aurelia* at sea, mariner, and who had lands in Virginia. (AW).

October. Probate of will of Robert Smithett formerly of Bermondsey, Surrey, but late of H.M. ships *Humber* and *Newport*, who died in Boston, New England. (AW).

2-7 November. Shippers by the *Sea Flower*, Mr. Robert Hodge, bound from London for Virginia: John March, Abraham Wild. (PRO: E190/150/1).

2-13 November. Shippers by the *Lilly*, Mr. Robert Redhead, bound from London for Pennsylvania: Thomas Couls, John Forbess. (PRO: E190/150/1).

2-23 November. Shippers by the *Lyon*, Mr. Roger Bayly, bound from Bristol for Virginia: Charles Jones, Sir William Davies, John Stroude, William Burrow, Abraham Elton, James Long. (PRO: E190/1151/1).

7-12 November. Shippers by the *Unity*, Mr. Joseph Gaich, bound from Lyme for Virginia: John Burridge & Co., Daniell Gundry, Simon Bayly. (PRO: E190/890/5).

8 November. Shipper by the *George* of Plymouth, Mr. Richard Dowling, bound from Plymouth for Virginia: George Lapthorne. (PRO: E190/1055/3).

8-12 November. Shippers by the *Adventure*, Mr. John Opie, bound from Bristol for Virginia: Peter Wadding, Thomas Opie, Thomas Hort, Alexander Piney. (PRO: E190/1151/1).

8-27 November. Shippers by the *Benjamin & Hester*, Mr. Richard Chesshire, bound from Bristol for Virginia: John Dudlestone, John Millard, Arthur Jackson. (PRO: E190/1151/1).

9 November. Shipper by the *Richard & Sarah*, Mr. Freegrace Bendall, bound from London for Maryland: Edward Warner. (PRO: E190/150/1).

9 November. Shipper by the *Bonetta* of Plymouth, Mr. Daniell Williams, bound from Plymouth for Virginia: Henry Ceane. (PRO: E190/1055/3).

9 November-18 December. Shippers by the *Sarah*, Mr. Benjamin Guillam, bound from London for New England: Lewis Grolleau, John Het, Richard Whittingham, John Pemble, William Moor, Oliver Corr, Joseph Butler, Matthew Plumsted, Phillip Sanderson, John Wightman, George Brazier, Benjamin Degane, Francis Tyrence. (PRO: E190/150/1).

11 November-11 December. Shippers by the *Fortune* of Plymouth, Mr. Peter Baker, bound from Plymouth for Virginia: Thomas Warne, James Busvergus, Isaac Pickes, John Alsop. (PRO: E190/1055/3).

12 November. Shipper by the *William & Brian*, Mr. Jeffrey Bayly, bound from Bristol for Virginia: Sir John Dudlestone. (PRO: E190/1151/1).

12-28 November. Shippers by the *Mountjoy*, Mr. James Scott, bound from Bristol for Virginia: Thomas Longman, Thomas Rogerson. (PRO: E190/1151/1).

13 November-12 December. Shippers by the *Virginia Merchant* of Plymouth, Mr. Phineas Harwood, bound from Plymouth for Virginia: John Rogers, Thomas Aishweek. (PRO: E190/1055/3).

13 November-13 January. Shippers by the *Speaker* of London, Mr. Humphrey Pellen, bound from Plymouth for Maryland: Phillip Pentire, Anthony Stratton, Samuell Ayre, James Burdett. (PRO: E190/1055/3, 1056/14).

14 November. Shipper by the *Margaret*, Mr. John Walker, bound from Bristol for Virginia: Whitchurch Phippen. (PRO: E190/1151/1).

14 November. Shipper by the *Content* of Plymouth, Mr. Mathew Hutchings, bound from Plymouth for Virginia: Joseph Palmer. (PRO: E190/1055/3).

14 November-2 December. Shippers by the *George* of Plymouth, Mr. Thomas Blake, bound from Plymouth for Virginia: Richard Burlace, George Lapthorne. (PRO: E190/1055/3).

14 November-9 December. Shipper by the *Mercy* of Plymouth, Mr. John Luke, bound from Plymouth for Virginia: George Lapthorne. (PRO: E190/1055/3).

14 November-14 December. Shippers by the *Maryan* of Plymouth, Mr. Charles Blighe, bound from Plymouth for Virginia: Nathaniell Dowrish, John Westlake, James Cocke. (PRO: E190/1055/3, 1056/14).

19 November. Shipper by the *Integrity* of Bideford, Mr. Matthew Dyer, bound from Bideford for Maryland: Peter Wellington. (PRO: E190/969/7).

19-26 November. Shippers by the *Friendship* bound from Bristol for Virginia: Sir John Dudlestone, Lott Wickins, John Morgan, Thomas Terry, John Millard. (PRO: E190/1151/1).

21 November-5 December. Shippers by the *Hampshire*, Mr. Francis Fisher, bound from London for Virginia: Edward Hastnoll, John Marsh. (PRO: E190/150/1).

22 November. Shipper by the *Abraham & Francis*, Mr. Bartholomew Whitehorne, bound from London for Virginia: Peter Paggen. (PRO: E190/150/1).

22-27 November. Shippers by the *Richard & John*, Mr. John Jones, bound from Bristol for Virginia: Thomas Machen, Jasper Tyler, John Kinnestone. (PRO: E190/1151/1).

22 November-14 December. Shippers by the *Joseph*, Mr. Daniel Bradley, bound from London for Virginia: Thomas Rascoe, Richard Chancey. (PRO: E190/150/1).

22 November-4 January. Shippers by the *James*, Mr. Robert Lurting, bound from London for Virginia: Peter Paggen, Peregrine Browne. (PRO: E190/150/1, 156/5).

25 November. Shipper by the *John*, Mr. William Phippard, bound from London for Maryland: John Charles. (PRO: E190/150/1).

25 November-31 December. Shippers by the *Lyon*, Mr. Robert Ransom, bound from London for Virginia: Robert Bristow, Peter Mercer, Andrew Percivall, Peter Albert, John Reynolds. (PRO: E190/150/1, 156/5).

26 November. Shipper by the *John & Betty*, Mr. Joshua Whiteing, bound from Bristol for Virginia: Sir John Dudlestone. (PRO: E190/1151/1).

27 November. Shipper by the *Rebecca*, Mr. Henry Martin, bound from London for Virginia: Peter Renew. (PRO: E190/150/1).

27-28 November. Shippers by the *James & Elizabeth* of Weymouth, Mr. John Wall, bound from Poole and Weymouth for Virginia: David Arbuthnott & Co., Robert Bennett, Thomas Young (PRO: E190/890/7, 890/12).

27 November-2 January. Shippers by the *Baltimore*, Mr. William Robins & Mr. Samuell Phillips, bound from London for Virginia: Nicholas Jones, Walter Honton, John Taylor. (PRO: E190/150/1, 156/5).

29 November. Shipper by the *Rayner*, Mr. John Munden, bound from Weymouth for Virginia: David Arbuthnott & Co. (PRO: E190/890/7).

29 November-14 December. Shippers by the *London Merchant*, Mr. Nicholas Smith, bound from London for Virginia: Anthony Palmer, Ambrose Bray, Thomas Quiney, Thomas Ruscoe, Peter Bimton. (PRO: E190/150/1).

November. Probate of will of Isaac Reed of Boston, New England, who died on H.M. ship *Tyger*'s prize. (AW).

November. Probate of will of Joseph Facy of Maryland, who died on the ship *James* in Virginia. (AW).

November. Administration of Catherine Thorpe of Middle Plantation, York County, [Virginia], widow. (AW).

2-23 December. Shippers by the *America*, Mr. Thomas Graves, bound from London for Virginia: Arthur Baily, Hopfar Bendall, Arthur Nash, Thomas Ellis. (PRO: E190/150/1).

3-30 December. Shippers by the *Adventure*, Mr. Thomas Martin, bound from London for Virginia: Edward Leman, Samuel Wickins, Thomas Starke. (PRO: E190/150/1, 156/5).

4 December. Shipper by the *John*, Mr. John Tanner, bound from London for Maryland: Cornelius Mason. (PRO: E190/150/1).

4-12 December. Shippers by the *Canterbury*, Mr. Henry Treganny, bound from London for Virginia: Benjamin Braine, Micajah Perry. (PRO: E190/150/1).

4-23 December. Shippers by the *Robert & Samuell*, Mr. Matthew Trim & Mr. Samuell Dodson, bound from London for Virginia: Thomas Rascoe, Phillip Lassell, Giles Shuter, Nehemiah Russell, Benjamin Hatley, Abraham Spranger, Robert Bloone, Peregrine Browne. (PRO: E190/150/1).

4-24 December. Shippers by the *Hopewell*, Mr. Nicholas Smith, Mr. Thomas Yoakly & Mr. Henry Munday, bound from London for Virginia: Benjamin Hatley, David Dennis, John Munday, Edward Burford, Phillip Lloyd, Thomas Hudson, Anthony Stratton, John Pettit, Matthew Jones, Henry Dennis. (PRO: E190/150/1).

4 December-11 January. Shippers by the *Sarah*, Mr. William Jefferys, bound from London for Virginia: Zachary Taylor, Edward Colthrop, Joseph Cresset, William Willis, Sarah Dobins. (PRO: E190/150/1, 155/5).

5-18 December. Shippers by the *Burton*, Mr. William Ingledon, bound from London for Virginia: John Handford, John Purvis, William Leader. (PRO: E190/150/1).

6-23 December. Shippers by the *Employment*, Mr. Edward Barecock & Mr. John Soare, bound from London for Virginia: Timothy Keyser, Jona Mathews, Samuell Sandford, John Goodwin, Phillip Fincher. (PRO: E190/150/1).

7 December. Shipper by the *Richard & James*, Mr. James Greenwell, bound from London for Virginia: Edward Warner. (PRO: E190/150/1).

7-20 December. Shippers by the *Diligence*, Mr. Isaac Wild & Mr. Jonas Motts, bound from London for Virginia: Abraham Wild, Francis Lee, Thomas Wickins. (PRO: E190/150/1).

7-16 December. Shippers by the *Henry*, Mr. Daniel Watts, bound from London for Virginia: Samuell Groome, John Blackhall. (PRO: E190/150/1).

7-23 December. Shippers by the *Josiah*, Mr. Splendor Ramm, bound from London for Virginia: Samuell Grove, Corne Mason. (PRO: E190/150/1).

9 December. Shipper by the *Richard & Margaret*, Mr. Andrew Senhouse, bound from London for Maryland: John Hide. (PRO: E190/150/1).

9-31 December. Shippers by the *Owners Adventure*, Mr. Benjamin Lotherington, bound from London for Virginia: John Purvis, Cornelius Mason, Edward Mason. (PRO: E190/150/1, 156/5).

10 December. Shipper by the *Providence*, Mr. Thomas Pitts, bound from London for Virginia: William Morgan. (PRO: E190/150/1).

10 December-10 January. Shippers by the *Ann & Mary*, Mr. Richard Tibbott, bound from London for Virginia: Roger Jones, Micajah Perry, Thomas Clark. (PRO: E190/150/1, 155/5).

10-18 December. Shippers by the *Adventure*, Mr. John Buckshire, bound from London for Virginia: Samuell Hoyle, Benjamin Travers, Arthur North. (PRO: E190/150/1).

10-20 December. Shippers by the *Ann & Mary*, Mr. John Gandy, bound from London for Virginia: Robert Meyers, John Hyde, Thomas Wharton, Reynold Smith, Joseph Lambert. (PRO: E190/150/1, 156/5).

10 December-10 January. Shippers by the *Friendship*, Mr. Benjamin Emes, bound from London for Virginia: Thomas Kirkpatrick, Stephen Wesendunck, Joseph Pace, Thomas King, Thomas Washington, John Norton, Thomas Waterer, Gabriel Smith, Sarah Callender, Samuell Theyer, Nicholas Oursell. (PRO: E190/150/1, 155/5, 156/5).

10 December-7 January. Shippers by the *Perry & Lane*, Mr. James Morgan, bound from London for Virginia: Thomas Stannard, Micajah Perry, Anthony Cornwell, Thomas Macullock, Christopher Morgan. (PRO: E190/150/1, 156/5).

12 December. Shipper by the *London Arms*, Mr. John Gatton, bound from London for Virginia: Edward Hastwell. (PRO: E190/150/1).

12 December. Shipper by the *Benjamin*, Mr. Thomas Bagwell, bound from London for Virginia: Benjamin Braine. (PRO: E190/150/1).

12 December. Shipper by the *Adventure*, Mr. Michael Cole, bound from London for Virginia: Richard Haynes. (PRO: E190/150/1).

12-24 December. Shippers by the *Mary*, Mr. Frederick Johnson, bound from London for Virginia: Peter Banton, James Braine. (PRO: E190/150/1).

13-14 December. Shippers by the *Endeavour*, Mr. James Mitchell & Mr. Nathaniel Davis, bound from London for Maryland & Virginia: Robert Plumsted, John Munday. (PRO: E190/150/1).

13-18 December. Shippers by the *John*, Mr. William Cann, bound from London for Virginia: John Hide, Thomas Wharton. (PRO: E190/150/1).

13-20 December. Shippers by the *Samuell*, Mr. John Harrison, bound from London for Virginia: Benjamin Bradley, Humphrey Pye, Richard Parle. (PRO: E190/150/1).

14-24 December. Shippers by the *Hope*, Mr. John Cotterell, bound from London for Virginia: Edward Warner, Anthony Stratton. (PRO: E190/150/1).

16 December. Shipper by the *Habitation*, Mr. John Salmon, bound from London for Virginia: John Hayes. (PRO: E190/150/1).

16 December. Shipper by the *Ann* pink bound from Exeter for Virginia: Daniel Joie. (PRO: E190/969/6).

17 December. Shipper by the *Abraham*, Mr. Joseph Cooke, bound from London for Virginia: Richard Parke. (PRO: E190/150/1).

17-18 December. Shippers by the *Consent*, Mr. John Garfoot, bound from London for Virginia: Jonathan Mathews, Thomas Ellis. (PRO: E190/150/1).

17-24 December. Shippers by the *Abraham*, Mr. Nicholas Purdue, bound from London for Maryland: Richard Parke, Joseph Cooke, Samuell Deane. (PRO: E190/150/1).

17 December-15 January. Shippers by the *Adventure*, Mr. Francis Harbin, bound from London for Virginia: Robert Levinstone, James Wagstaffe, John Reynolds. (PRO: E190/150/1, 155/5, 156/5).

17 December-2 January. Shippers by the *Leare* frigate, Mr. William Norrington, bound from London for Virginia: John Hall, Edward & Dudley Carleton, John Morris, Roger Jones, Edmund Hilldyard. (PRO: E190/150/1, 156/5).

18 December. Shipper by the *Mary & Johanna*, Mr. William Harvey, bound from London for Virginia: said William Harvey. (PRO: E190/150/1).

19 December. Shipper by the *John & Margaret*, Mr. Thomas Salmon, bound from London for Virginia: John Taylor. (PRO: E190/150/1).

19 December. Shipper by the *William & John*, Mr. Jonathan Scarfe, bound from London for Maryland: John Mathew. (PRO: E190/150/1).

19-20 December. Shippers by the *Mary*, Mr. Thomas Whittington, bound from London for Virginia: John Marsh & Co., Edward Haistwell. (PRO: E190/150/1).

19 December-9 January. Shippers by the *York Merchant*, Mr. John Hollard, bound from London for Virginia: John Marsh & Co. (PRO: E190/150/1, 156/5).

20 December. Shipper by the *Providence*, Mr. William Cant, bound from London for Virginia: John Wright. (PRO: E190/150/1).

20 December. Shipper by the *Deptford*, Mr. Joseph Munday, bound from London for Virginia: Micajah Perry. (PRO: E190/150/1).

20 December. Shipper by the *Thorowgood*, Mr. John Nall, bound from London for Virginia: Joseph Jackson. (PRO: E190/150/1).

20 December-15 January. Shippers by the *Edward & Francis*, Mr. Thomas Mann, bound from London for Carolina: John Flavell, Ralph Izard, Joseph Gillmore. (PRO: E190/150/1, 155/5).

20 December. Shippers by the *Johanna & Ann*, Mr. Jeremiah Deble, bound from London for Virginia: Edward Haistwell, Benjamin Dolbin. (PRO: E190/150/1).

20-24 December. Shippers by the *Industry*, Mr. William Mobbs, bound from London for Virginia: Michael Jones, Alexander Caine. (PRO: E190/150/1).

22 December. James Newman, aged 15, sent from Christ's Hospital to his mother Ellinor Newman to serve Edward Mitchell of London, merchant, in Jamaica. (CH).

23 December. Shipper by the *John*, Mr. Richard Biswick, bound from London for Virginia: Benjamin Brame, Richard Swinfield. (PRO: E190/150/1).

23 December. Shipper by the *John & Thomas*, Mr. Joseph Scotting, bound from London for Virginia: John Hitchcock. (PRO: E190/150/1).

23 December. Shipper by the *Eagle*, Mr. Jonathan Clifton, bound from London for Maryland: Peregrine Browne. (PRO: E190/150/1).

23-24 December. Shippers by the *Swan*, Mr. Samuell Scurry, bound from London for Virginia: Edward Leman, Samuell Wickins. (PRO: E190/150/1).

23-30 December. Shippers by the *Preservation*, Mr. Benjamin Emms, bound from London for Maryland: Joseph Jackson, Thomas Washington, John Morton. (PRO: E190/150/1).

24 December. Shippers by the *Jonathan*, Mr. Rand, bound from London for Maryland: Robert & John Askew. (PRO: E190/150/1).

24 December-3 January. Shippers by the *James*, Mr. Benjamin Braine, bound from London for Maryland: Augustine Mumford, John Barbott, James Braine. (PRO: E190/150/1).

26 December. Newgate prisoners reprieved to be transported to Barbados or Jamaica. London: John Marshall; George Deracke; Mary Bennett, spinster; Mary Newman alias Colthropp, spinster; Samuel Herd; John Thompson; Humphrey Burton; John Jenkins alias Browne; William Ingram; Elizabeth Lott, spinster; Jane Pretious alias Browne, spinster; Jane Blewett, spinster; John Ayre; James Waite; Thomas Whipp; Christopher Atkinson; William Nordish; John Blithman; James Smith, yeoman; Aubrey Price, yeoman. Middlesex: John Weaver of Whitechapel; Susan Davis of the same, spinster; Christian Carter of Stepney, spinster; Susan Clayton of the same, spinster; Richard Scott of St. Clement Danes; Johanna Bates alias Clerke alias Elizabeth Lambeth of the same; Thomas Johnson of Islington; Peter Lawman of the same; Francis Buckley of the same; John Davis alias Davy of St. Pancras; Elizabeth Harris of the same, spinster; John Shaw of St. Martin in the Fields; John Terry of the same; William Wake alias Demogy of St. Dunstan in the West; Thomas Mitchell of St. James Westminster; Elizabeth Mitchell of the same, spinster; Jane Pritchard alias Lyall alias Larke of the same; John Jones alias Hodge of St. Giles in the Fields; Thomas Butcher of Kensington; William Morgan of the same; Elizabeth Titherington of Shoreditch, spinster; Mary Middleton of Clerkenwell, spinster. (PRO: C66/3381/14).

29 December. Shipper by the *Fidelity* of Jersey, Mr. Amias Danvers, bound from Southampton for Virginia: Elias De Grut. (PRO: E190/837/4).

31 December. Shipper by the *Success*, Mr. Taylor, bound from London for Carolina: Daniell Lodge. (PRO: E190/150/1, 156/5).

31 December-14 January. Shipper by the *James & Elizabeth*, Mr. Dean Cock, bound from London for Virginia and Maryland: John Shelton, John Norton, Samuell Clark. (PRO: E190/155/5, 156/5).

31 December-3 April. Shippers by the *New York Merchant* of London, Mr. Thomas Jefferys, bound from Portsmouth for New York: Benjamin Dejeime, Tierens & Cruger. (PRO: E190/838/5).

December. John Draycott, aged 14, sent from Christ's Hospital to his mother Mary D. to serve John Tills, Mr. of the *Mary* of Colchester bound for Barbados. (CH).

December. Administration with will of Thomas Cornwell of London, who died in Maryland, bachelor. (AW).

December. Probate of will of Francis Atkinson of H.M. ship *Deptford* who died in Virginia. (AW).

1695. Chancery suit brought by Thomas Starke of London, merchant, against Katherine Arnall, relict and executrix of Thomas Arnall, master of the *Merchants Adventure*, deceased, re accounts between Starke and William Bates, mariner. Depositions were taken in King and Queen County, Virginia, (in 1700) from: William Leigh, aged 50; Mr. John Walker, aged 45; James Edwards, aged 50; Mr. William Seamore, aged 45. (NGSQ 70/1).

1696

3 January. Shipper by the [blank] *Three Brothers*?, Mr. James Braine, bound from London for Virginia: John Barbot. (PRO: E190/156/5).

3-7 January. Shippers by the *Providence*, Mr. George Keble, bound from London for Maryland: Edward & Dudley Carleton, William Penn. (PRO: E190/150/1, 156/5).

10-20 January. Shippers by the *Lion*, Mr. Saxon, bound from London for New England: Thomas Dodge, Peter Lynch, Thomas Draper, Samuell White, Joshua Solard. (PRO: E190/150/1, 155/5).

13-23 January. Shippers by the *Maynerd*, Mr. John Hill, bound from London for Virginia: Sir John Parsons, Peter Wallis. (PRO: E190/150/1, 155/5).

14 January. Shipper by the *John*, Mr. Richard Bilwick, bound from London for Virginia: said Richard Bilwick. (PRO: E190/155/5).

14 January-3 February. Shippers by the *James & Thomas* of Plymouth, Mr. William Broaded, bound from Plymouth for Virginia: James Blighe, Abraham Beele, Henry Ceane. (PRO: E190/1056/14).

15 January. Shipper by the *Hope*, Mr. George Purvis, bound from London for Virginia: John Woolfe. (PRO: E190/155/5).

30 January. Newgate prisoners reprieved to be transported to Barbados or Jamaica. [*See list of 26 December 1695 which this pardon virtually duplicates*]. (PRO: C66/3381/2).

January. Probate of will of William Raydon of Philadelphia. (AW).

January. Probate of will of Joseph Swett of Boston, New England, who died on H.M. ship *Defiant*. (AW).

January. Probate of will of Samuel Huckstep of King and Queen County, Virginia, and Ewhurst, Sussex. (AW).

January. Probate of will of William Nall of Boston, New England, who died on the ship *Greenwich*, bachelor. (AW).

January. Administration of Peter Hearne of Carolina, who died on H.M. ship *Monmouth*. (AW).

15 February-28 May. Shippers by the *Recovery* of Exeter, Mr. Benjamin Parsons, bound from Plymouth for Virginia: John Addis, William Drake, Tristram Whitter. (PRO: E190/1056/14).

21 February. Chancery case of George Janson, citizen and apothecary of London, v. John Edwards of Ness, Shropshire. The plaintiff married Mary, daughter of the defendant John Edwards, in 1688 but was obliged to give up his trade and go to Virginia in 1693. He returned to London but again went to Virginia in 1696 with his wife. Deponents in this case include Edmund Berkeley, aged 26, who was born in Virginia. (NGSQ 67/4).

22 February. Shipper by the *America* of Plymouth bound from Plymouth for Virginia: Josias Daniell. (PRO: E190/1056/14).

13 March. Shipper by the *Recovery* bound from Exeter for Virginia: Richard Smith. (PRO: E190/970/1).

March. Administration of William Parsons of Newcastle-upon-Tyne, Northumberland, bachelor, granted to Samuel Sheafe, attorney for the brothers, Humphrey and Joseph Parsons, in Boston, New England. (AW).

2 April-11 May. Shippers by the *Fir Tree*, Mr. Richard Newman, bound from London for New England: Ambrose Crawley, George Long, Samuell Checkley, Richard Eyles, John Coltman. (PRO: E190/155/5).

22 April. The following apprenticed from Christ's Hospital: Thomas Case, aged 16, to Robert Lurting, commander of the *James* bound for Virginia; Edward Audley to Thomas Graves, commander of the *America* bound for Virginia; William Foster, aged 13, to John Brooke, commander of the *Joseph* bound for Jamaica. (CH).

April. Probate of will of Edward Gadsby of Stepney, Middlesex, and of the ship *Redbridge*, bound for Virginia. (AW).

April. Probate of will of Daniel Johnson of Lynn, New England, seaman of H.M. ship *Advice*, who died in St. Thomas's Hospital, Southwark, Surrey. (AW).

April. Probate of will of James Lloyd of Boston, New England. (AW).

2-8 May. Shippers by the *Friendly Society*, Mr. Habbakuk Wild, bound from London for Virginia: Edward Leman, Thomas Stark. (PRO: E190/155/5).

2-13 May. Shippers by the *William & Richard*, Mr. Nicholas Follett, bound from London for New England: Joseph Paice, Thomas Truss, Thomas Bletsoe, Joseph Roswell, Christopher Merriweather, John Ballentine, Thomas Cook. (PRO: E190/155/5).

2-16 May. Shippers by the *New Hampshire*, Mr. Mark Hunking and Mr. John Sherburn, bound from London for New England: Joseph Paice, Richard Pittman, David Garrie, Reginald Heber, John Lambert, William Ellingham, Samuell Theyer, John Brogees, Humphrey Strode, Henry Caswell, Nicholas Oursell, Nune Fernandes, Samson Parrie, Jaziell Crowch, Richard Soames, Sutton Sharpe, Elizabeth Chadwell, Edward Hooker. (PRO: E190/155/5).

2 May-12 June. Shippers by the *Johns Adventure*, Mr. Thomas Parker, bound from London for New England: Edward Smith, Thomas Zachary, Martha Wale, Nicholas Liddiard, John Lordell, Samuell Rider, Henry Ventris, John Beal, George Barr, John Roberrie, William Manton, Isaac Bonneire, Thomas Buckly, Zachary Tuttle, Phillip Sanderson, Thomas Blythe, Peter Richards. (PRO: E190/155/5).

2 May-16 June. Shippers by the *Blossom*, Mr. David Collins, bound from London for New York: John White, George Hammond, William Snelling, Gilbert Heathcott, George Brazier, Thomas Mead, Henry Penn, David Sarrazin, John Morton, Henry Pennell, Richard Stermer, Ebenezer Webb, John Hanwood, John Grove. (PRO: E190/155/5).

4 May. Shipper by the *Prudent Sarah* of London, Mr. Benjamin Guillam, bound from Portsmouth for New England: Thomas Barton. (PRO: E190/838/5).

8 May. Shipper by the *Prudent Sarah*, Mr. Benjamin Gillum, bound from London for New England: John Hill. (PRO: E190/155/5).

8 May. Richard Smith, aged 15, sent from Christ's Hospital to his uncle Abraham Jordan at College Hill to be bound to his uncle Nicholas Smith, commander of a ship bound for Virginia. (CH).

14 May. Shipper by the *Hope*, Mr. Aaron Emerson, bound from London for New England: Samuell White. (PRO: E190/155/5).

14 May. Shipper by the *Lyon* of London, Mr. William Saxon, bound from Portsmouth for New England: Thomas Barton. (PRO: E190/838/5).

18 May. Shipper by the *Diligence* of Plymouth, Mr. Elias King, bound from Plymouth for Virginia: James Cocke. (PRO: E190/1056/14).

18-19 May. Shippers by the *London Merchant* of London, Mr. James Thomas, bound from Plymouth for New York: Richard Burlace, Peter Parpoint. (PRO: E190/1056/14).

19 May. Shipper by the *Nassau*, Mr. George Shelly, bound from Cowes for New York: John Righton. (PRO: E190/838/4).

19 May. Shipper by the *George* of Plymouth bound from Plymouth for Virginia: Thomas Burgis. (PRO: E190/1056/14).

25 May. Shipper by the *Betty*, Mr. Edward Ireland, bound from London for Virginia: Thomas Clark. (PRO: E190/155/5).

26 May. Shipper by the *Eagle*, Mr. Josiah Clifton, bound from Portsmouth for Maryland: John Colvar. (PRO: E190/838/5).

27 May. Shipper by the *Hope* of London, Mr. Arthur Everdon, bound from Portsmouth for New England: said Arthur Everdon. (PRO: E190/838/5).

27 May. Shipper by the *Golden Lyon* of London, Mr. Robert Rounsam, bound from Portsmouth for Virginia: James Clarke. (PRO: E190/838/5).

28 May. Shipper by the *Betty* of London, Mr. George —ster, bound from Portsmouth for Virginia: Thomas Barton. (PRO: E190/838/5).

28 May. Shipper by the *Eagle*, Mr. John Clifton, bound from London for Virginia: John C—lier. (PRO: E190/155/5).

May. Administration of Sarah Hales of New England. (AW).

May. Administration of Stephen Paul of New England, who died on the ship *New Castle Merchant*. (AW).

17 June-9 July. Shippers by the *[St.] Joseph*, Mr. Michael Shute, bound from London for New England: Edward Hocker, Christopher Truss, Henry Spurham, John Tiler, Richard Pitman, Nicholas Cursell, John Markham, Anthony Walker. (PRO: E190/155/5).

20 June. Shipper by the *Friendship*, Mr. J[ohn] Searle, bound from London for Virginia: Phebe(?) Fairman. (PRO: E190/155/5).

23 June-5 August. Shippers by the *Albemarle*, Mr. Thomas Lucas, bound from London for New York: King & Pratt, William Nicholls. (PRO: E190/155/5).

25 June. Shipper by the *Thomas & Francis* ketch, Mr. Stephen Salman, bound from Plymouth for Virginia: Thomas Bryan & Co. (PRO: E190/1056/14).

30 June-11 November. Shippers by the *Antelope*, Mr. John Dunne, bound from Bristol for Virginia: Renedy Insley, John Stephens, Abraham Hooke, Thomas Meachin, Thomas Warren, Joseph Jeffries, Thomas Whittop, George Lason, Elisha James, Edward Groome. (PRO: E190/1152/3).

2 July. Shipper by the *Agnes* of Bristol, Mr. John Richardson, bound from Plymouth for Virginia: said John Richardson. (PRO: E190/1056/14).

7 July. Western Circuit prisoners reprieved to be transported to America. Berkshire: William Davis of Newbury, glover. Bristol: John Brewer, blacksmith. Cornwall: William Thompson of Falmouth. Devon: William Trehane of Walkhampton, husbandman; William Hopkins of Fremington; John Browne of Sydwells, Exeter, alehouse keeper; Andrew Gaskyn of Exeter; David Hamilton of the same; Richard Martin of Great Torrington, husbandman; William Lemon of Dartmouth, blacksmith; Richard Drew of Okehampton, blacksmith; William Bright of Pimm(?); Cornelius Bartlett of Ugborough, husbandman; Christopher Latwood of Rockbeare, husbandman. Dorset: Benjamin Varin of Blandford Forum; William Genge of West Stafford. Hampshire: John Ayres of Hartley Wintney; William Taylor of the same; George Martin of Elverton. Somerset: John Markes alias Hollard alias Peyce of Bishops Lydeard, husbandman; Thomas Hunt of London; Robert Fest of Wincanton. Wiltshire: Joseph Merris alias Merrick of Calne; John West of Lyneham; John Elmes of Lacock, tucker;

Henry Pitt of Laverstock; Edward Skuse of Tinhead, Westbury, husbandman; Thomas Croome of Longbridge Deverill, broad weaver; Richard Deere of Castle Combe, husbandman. (PRO: C66/3384/11).

7-10 July. Shippers by the *Submission*, Mr. Thomas Lurting, bound from London for Pennsylvania: Cornelius Mason, William Eburne. (PRO: E190/155/5).

9 July. Shippers by the *Friendship*, Mr. Daniell Coverdale, bound from London for Virginia: Edward Haistwell, Richard Marsh. (PRO: E190/155/5).

9 July-27 September. Shippers by the *Primrose*, Mr. William Sankey, bound from Bristol for Virginia: Phillip Freake, Thomas Freeke, John Jelfe, Sir William Deanes, Anthony Swymmer, Robert Bagly. (PRO: E190/1152/3).

11 July. Shipper by the *New Hampshire*, Mr. Mark Hunking, bound from Portsmouth for New England: James Barton. (PRO: E190/838/5).

14 July. Shipper by the English-built *Blossom* of London, Mr. David Collings, bound from Portsmouth for New England: Hugh Watts. (PRO: E190/838/5).

15 July. Home Circuit prisoners reprieved to be transported to Barbados or Jamaica. Essex: Thomas Steale of Wanstead; David Dye of Chigwell; James Bennett alias Benne of Ilford. Hertfordshire: William Jarvis of Cheshunt; John Stratford of Hemel Hempstead; Joseph Bunn of North Hall; Joseph Munn of Hatfield. Kent: Thomas Thackston of Bromley; Emanuel Bishopp of Otford; John Ford of Bethersden; William Taylor of Swanscombe; Elizabeth Tanner of Newington by Sittingbourne; John Jackson of Offham. Surrey: Mary Gay alias Johnson of Bermondsey, spinster; Elizabeth Hart of the same, spinster; Mary Meachum alias Grimes of the same, spinster; William Cockerill of St. George, Southwark; Sarah Thomas, wife of John Thomas of St. Saviour, Southwark; William Combe of East Molesey; Thomas Grainger of Addington; William Cockerill of the same; Mary Christian of St. Olave, Southwark, spinster; Thomas Arthur of Horsell. Sussex: Philip Pritchard of Worth; Jonas Pritchard of the same; Henry Shove of Worth; John Stacey of the same; John Hatcher of the same; Nicholas Hatcher of the same; Henry Shove of the same. Unidentified: John Ryan, John Gold, John Samster, Constant Dougherty, Richard Cheevers. (PRO: C66/3384/7).

16 July. Oxford Circuit prisoners reprieved to be transported to America. Gloucestershire: Richard Bansom of Hawkesbury; Robert Hughes of St. Philip & Jacob; Isaac Baston alias Bastings of Bitton; John Elsmore of Longhope; Thomas Wilcox of St. Philip & Jacob; Thomas Stephens of Cirencester; Abraham Sandford of Uley; Roger Gastrell of Uley. Herefordshire: Edward Preece alias Mathew Parry of Almeley; John Nott of Hereford; John Bishopp of Leominster. Shropshire: David Lloyd of Bridgenorth. Staffordshire: Charles Smart of Edial; John Davis of Cannock; Anthony Biddulph of Ediall. Worcestershire: Richard Jenkins of Worcester. (PRO: C66/3384/6).

23 July-16 September. Shippers by the *Friendship*, Mr. Benjamin Allen, bound from Bristol for New England: Peter Wadding, John Perrot, William Clerke, Joseph Way, James Long, Charles Chancy, Giles Merrick, Paul Boucher, Thomas Scroope. (PRO: E190/1152/3).

July. Probate of will of Edward Lloyd, formerly of Maryland but late of Whitechapel, Middlesex. (AW).

6-12 August. Shippers by the *European*, Mr. John Foy, bound from London for New England: Richard Diamond, Samuell Drinkwater, John Gerald. (PRO: E190/155/5).

7 August. Shipper by the *Bonnivir*, Mr. William Brittaine, bound from Bristol for Virginia: Abraham Hooke. (PRO: E190/1152/3).

8-31 August. Shippers by the *William & Mary*, Mr. Joseph Leach, bound from Bristol for Boston: Richard Gibbons, Samuell Weekes, Erasmus Dole. (PRO: E190/1152/3).

12 August. Shipper by the *Virginia*, Mr. Edward Whittaker, bound from London for Virginia: Edmond Littlepage. (PRO: E190/155/5).

12-19 August. Shipper by the *Hope*, Mr. Charles Hartford, bound from Bristol for Virginia: Samuell Jacob. (PRO: E190/1152/3).

13 August. Shipper by the *Globe*, Mr. John Harris, bound from London for Maryland: Benjamin Braine. (PRO: E190/155/5).

17-20 August. Shippers by the *New Hampshire* of Piscataway, Mr. John Sherburne, bound from Plymouth for Boston, New England: George Lillington, Thomas Turner & Co., Abraham Goswell, John Ellery. (PRO: E190/1056/14).

22 August-5 September. Shippers by the *Susanna & Sarah* of Boston, Mr. John Tucker, bound from Newcastle for Boston, New England: John Wilkinson, Thomas Stellhaven, Thomas Steele. (PRO: E190/205/1).

30 August-9 September. Shippers by the *Swift*, Mr. Nicholas Mitchell, bound from Bristol for New York: Abraham Elton, Samuell Packer, Henry Hobbs, James Stephens. (PRO: E190/1152/3).

August. Administration of Adam Gembell of St. Martin in the Fields, Middlesex, who died in Carolina, bachelor. (AW).

15 September-9 October. Shippers by the *Phillip*, Mr. Joseph Smith, bound from Bristol for New York: Edward Hacket, Stephen Peloquin, Benjamin Norwood. (PRO: E190/1152/3).

24 September. Petition of Jeffrey Jones of East New Jersey against the judgment awarded by a court in Perth Amboy to James Fullerton. (APC).

September. Administration with will of Benjamin Whitmore of Middletown, New England, who died on H.M. ship *Royal Katherine*. (AW).

5 October. Depositions taken in London to establish the circumstances of the death of William Pawlett Esq. of Bicton, Devon, who went to Maryland and died there in August 1694 leaving a will. Deponents include: Edward Randolph Esq., aged 57, Surveyor-General of Customs in Maryland; Miles Burroughs, aged 33, innholder of Maryland. (NGSQ 67/4).

7 October-19 November. Shippers by the *Rebecca*, Mr. Wybron Lestoner, bound from Bristol for New York: Henry Lloyd, Stephen Peloquin, John Hobbs, John Dunning, John Smart. (PRO: E190/1152/3).

16 October. Shipper by the *Richmond* pink of London, Mr. William C——, bound from Portsmouth Roads for Virginia: John Hydall. (PRO: E190/838/5).

23-30 October. Shippers by the *Submission* from Liverpool [*no destination given*]: Daniel Danvers, John Withington. (PRO: E190/1355/1).

13-23 November. Shippers by the *Gloucester*, Mr. William Reed, bound from Bristol for Cork and Virginia: Charles Nicholas, Mark Goddard, Abraham Elton. (PRO: E190/1152/3).

17 November-8 December. Shippers by the *Providence*, Mr. John Read, bound from Bristol for Virginia: Michael Pope, John Junior. (PRO: E190/1152/3).

21 November-5 December. Shippers by the *Concord* of Liverpool, Mr. William Chantrell, bound from Liverpool for Virginia: John Pemberton, William Fletcher, Nicholas Reynolds. (PRO: E190/1355/1).

25 November-5 December. Shippers by the *Little John*, Mr. William Webb, bound from Bristol for Virginia: John Jones & Co., John Miler, Peter Wadding, John Hurlestone, John Loveday. (PRO: E190/1152/3).

27 November-7 December. Shippers by the *Carolina*, Mr. John Parker, bound from Bristol for Carolina: Charles Nicholas, John Chancey, William Barron, Edward Hutton, Abraham Eve, Thomas Spread. (PRO: E190/1152/3).

November. Administration of Thomas Dudley of New England, bachelor. (AW).

7-19 December. Shippers by the *Susanna* brigantine of Plymouth, Mr. Symon Pascoe, bound from Plymouth for Virginia: Henry Ceane & Co. (PRO: E190/1056/14).

7-27 December. Shippers by the *Mountjoy*, Mr. James Scott, bound from Bristol for Virginia: Thomas Longman, William French, Joseph James, George Mason, John Taylor, John Batchelor, Richard Franklin, Arthur Jackson, John Olliver. (PRO: E190/1152/3).

8-22 December. Shippers by the *James & Mary*, Mr. George Hitchings and Mr. Jeremy Perce, bound from Bristol for Virginia: Richard Gibbons & Co., James Thomas. (PRO: E190/1152/3).

14-22 December. Shippers by the *Dispatch*, Mr. John Thomas, bound from Bristol for Virginia: Sir John Duddlestone & Co., Thomas Tyler, Edward Lloyd & Co., Robert Tunbridge, Samuell Packer. (PRO: E190/1152/3).

18-23 December. Shippers by the *Mulberry* of Liverpool, Mr. Bryan Blundell, bound from Liverpool for Virginia: Walter Bryce, Robert Bell, Isaac Foxcroft, William Watts, Charles Scarborough, Robert Moore, Thomas Chapman. (PRO: E190/1355/1).

23 December. Shipper by the *Morning Star*, Mr. Shadrack Roal, bound from Bristol for New England: Joseph Whitchurch. (PRO: E190/1152/3).

29 December-29 January. Shippers by the *John & Ann*, Mr. John Hobby, bound from London for New England: James Cheecly, Anthony Merry, George Ford. (PRO: E190/159/1).

30 December. Shipper by the *Jeremiah* of Bideford bound from Plymouth for Virginia: Henry Rock. (PRO: E190/1057/1).

December. Administration with will of Job Tookey of H.M. ship *Newport*, bachelor, granted to Henry Fitzhugh, brother and attorney of the executor, Robert Fitzhugh, in Boston, New England. (AW).

December. Administration of Peter Simondson of the ship *Merchants Adventure* granted to Susan, wife and attorney of the next heir, Michael Deane, in Virginia. (AW).

December. Probate of will of Simon Wotton of Calvert County, Maryland, who died in Jamaica. (AW).

December. Administration of Samuel Newman of Boston, New England, who died in Barbados. (AW).

December. Administration of James Amsed of Virginia. (AW).

December. Probate of will of John Geary of Dunsley, Hertfordshire, who had lands in Pennsylvania. (AW).

1697

4-9 January. Shippers by the *Oak* of Liverpool, Mr. Edward Tarleton, bound from Liverpool for Virginia: Thomas Johnson, Gilbert Livesley. (PRO: E190/1357/5).

13 January-4 February. Shippers by the *Jefferies*, Mr. William Cooper, bound from London for Maryland: John Cornish, Anthony Stratton, Thomas Browne. (PRO: E190/159/1).

14-22 January. Shipper by the *Planter* of Liverpool, Mr. John Rimer, bound from Liverpool for Virginia: John Molyneux. (PRO: E190/1357/5).

19 January. Shipper by the *Peter & Anthony*, Mr. John Thomas, bound from London for New England: Robert Hackshaw. (PRO: E190/159/1).

19 January-12 February. Shippers by the *Barbados Merchant*, Mr. Robert Middleton, bound from Liverpool for Virginia: Cuthbert Sharples, Thomas Sweeting, Richard Scarborough, John Custis, Samuell Young. (PRO: E190/1357/5).

22 January-4 February. Shippers by the *Johanna*, Mr. Robert Griffin, bound from London for New York: Thomas Couts, David Sarazin, Robert Hackshaw, John Kimis. (PRO: E190/159/1).

26 January. Shipper by the *Margaret*, Mr. Robert Kells(?), bound from London for New York: Robert Hackshaw. (PRO: E190/159/1).

26 January. Shipper by the *Supply* of New York, Mr. Richard Newman, bound from Portsmouth for New England: James Barton. (PRO: E190/839/5).

26 January. Shipper by the *Peter & Anthony*, Mr. James Thomas, bound from Portsmouth for Boston, New England: James Barton. (PRO: E190/839/5).

27-29 January. Shippers by the *Pennsylvania Merchant*, Mr. Samuell Harrison, bound from London for Pennsylvania: Richard Haynes, Mathew Plumstead. (PRO: E190/159/1).

27-29 January. Shippers by the *Mehitabel*, Mr. Gregory Sugar, bound from London for New England: George Hyam, George Ford. (PRO: E190/159/1).

28 January. Shipper by the *Elizabeth & Ann*, Mr. Andrew Malpas, bound from Liverpool for Virginia: William Clayton. (PRO: E190/1357/5).

28 January-26 February. Shippers by the *Lamb*, Mr. John Thomas, bound from Liverpool for Virginia: John Mathewson, Richard Willis, Andrew Moore, John Stockley. (PRO: E190/1357/5).

29 January-5 February. Shippers by the *Elizabeth & Judith*, Mr. James Wingfield, bound from Liverpool for Virginia: Hugh Markland, Silvanus Richmond. (PRO: E190/1357/5).

January. Probate of will of Sir William Phipps, Governor of New England, who died in London. (AW).

January. Administration of John Walter of New England, bachelor. (AW).

January. Administration of Thomas Nicholson of Marblehead, New England. (AW).

1 February. The Council of Trade and Plantations report that the only colony now prepared to received pardoned convicts is Barbados where any who are fit for laborious service will be received but not women, children or the infirm. (CSPC).

3-9 February. Shippers by the *Charity*, Mr. Ralph Williamson, bound from Liverpool for Virginia: Richard Norres, Thomas Chapman. (PRO: E190/1357/5).

6 February. Shipper by the *European*, Mr. John Foy, bound from London for New England: Samuell White. (PRO: E190/159/1).

15 February. Yorkshire prisoners reprieved to be transported to Barbados: Edward Gleaves alias Cleaves of York City; Hannah Hurd of York, spinster; John Clarke of Caleshall. (PRO: C66/3393/20).

16 February. Shipper by the *America* of Bideford, Mr. John Dalling, bound from Bideford for Maryland: John Jeffery. (PRO: E190/971/6).

18 February-11 March. Shippers by the *William & Sarah*, Mr. Samuell Wood, bound from London for Pennsylvania: Mathew Plumstead, Joseph Ormstone, Thomas Emmerson. (PRO: E190/159/1).

22 February. Western Circuit prisoners reprieved to be transported to Barbados. Devon: Benjamin Crocker of Crediton; Richard Rice alias John Jones of Tiverton, brickmaker. Bristol: Thomas Allen, John Barker, George Helsteed. (PRO: C66/3393/19).

February. Administration with will of Seth Southell of Virginia. (AW).

February. Probate of will of Benjamin Willdy of Carolina. (AW).

February. Administration of James Larkins of New York. (AW).

1 March. Oxford Circuit prisoners reprieved to be transported to America. Berkshire: Martha Stroud of Reading, spinster; Elianor Salmon of Stratfield Mortimer; Thomas Cooke of Cumnor; Nathaniel Johnson of Cumnor. Shropshire: Abigael Doughty of Milsom; John Cruckson of Worthen. Thomas Sacheverill of Marlborough (Wiltshire). (PRO: C66/3393/16).

3 March. Midland Circuit prisoners reprieved to be transported to America. Derbyshire: Thomas Palfreman, John Tayler alias Richardson. Leicestershire: Elizabeth Williams, Theophilus Gumley, Gabriel Hall. Lincolnshire: Ann Cawger, spinster. Northamptonshire: Richard Heybourne. Nottinghamshire: Thomas Cooke. Rutland: William Barlow, Zachary Fessand. (PRO: C66/3393/14).

6 March. Norfolk Circuit prisoners reprieved to be transported to Barbados or Jamaica. Buckinghamshire: Richard Munday of West Wycombe; Thomas Burgis of Fenny Stratford; John Browne alias Beazely of West Wycombe; Thomas Eaton of West Wycombe; George Lee alias Laye of Amersham. Huntingdonshire: William Berry of Great Catworth; John Bulmer of Whittlesey. Norfolk: John Watts of Besthorpe; William Craske of Besthorpe; Nicholas Scott of Aslacton; John Garland of Besthorpe; George Harrison of Swaildale. Suffolk: John Manning of Honington; Thomas Statham of Badwell Ash; Anthony Hutton of Newmarket; George Hunt alias Leech of Bury St. Edmunds; George Lagdell alias John Britten of Great Cornard. (PRO: C66/3393/13).

8-18 March. Shippers by the *Love's Increase*, Mr. John Lancaster, bound from Liverpool for Virginia: Thomas Hind, Edward Roberts. (PRO: E190/1357/5).

11 March. Shipper by the *Leeds* galley, Mr. William Humble, bound from London for Carolina: Samuell Wickins. (PRO: E190/159/1).

16 March. Shipper by the *Betty* sloop of Bristol, Mr. James Barry, bound from Bristol for Virginia: Abraham Elton. (PRO: E190/1154/2).

17-26 March. Shippers by the *Star*, Mr. Thomas Leckonby, bound from Liverpool for Virginia: John Hughes, Christopher Anderton, Capt. Thomas Pound. (PRO: E190/1357/5).

23 March. Shipper by the *Cole* galley, Mr. Robert Blake, bound from London for New England: Samuell Wickins. (PRO: E190/159/1).

30 March. Shipper by the English-built *Mary & Elizabeth*, Mr. Thomas Brittijohn, bound from Dartmouth for Virginia: Nathaniell Gallpine. (PRO: E190/971/7).

31 March-1 June. Shippers by the *Prudent Sarah*, Mr. Benjamin Guillam, bound from London for New England: John Tydcombe, James Rawles, John Chickering, George Shored, Nicholas Batchelor, William Pymble, Daniell Saunders, Stephen Wesenduncke. (PRO: E190/159/1).

26 March-25 June. Shippers by the *Success*, Mr. Samuell Terrell, bound from London for New England: Joseph Paice, John Love, David Garricke, William Fisher, Stephen Mason, Thomas Basley, Sampson Gidcomb, James & Richard Eyton, Thomas Rich, Samuell Penhallow, Isaac Bouven. (PRO: E190/159/1).

March. Administration with will of Winifred Mallett alias Wolseley of Maryland, widow. (AW).

8 April. Norfolk Circuit prisoners reprieved to be transported to America. Bedfordshire: John Budwell of Ampthill; William Capell of Woburn; Edward McDonnell of Biggleswade. Cambridgeshire: Thomas Fordham of Chesterton. Huntingdonshire: James Shackley of Spaldwick; John Newham of Dekesdon. Norfolk: Peter Millard of Gillingham; Nathaniel Copps of Hunstanton. Suffolk: John Phillips of Bury St. Edmunds; Robert Money of Fornham; Simon Whibby of Fornham; Robert King of Fornham; John Lilley of Bury St. Edmunds; William Smith of Fornham. (PRO: C66/3391/3).

April. Probate of will of Richard Foote of St. Dunstan in the East, London, who had lands in Virginia. (AW).

April. Probate of will of John Mundell of Newcastle, Pennsylvania, who died in Boston, merchant. (AW).

4-6 May. Shippers by the *Assistance* of Bristol, Mr. William Cole, bound from Bristol for New England: Erasmus Dole, Richard Nicholls, William French, Abraham Elton. (PRO: E190/1154/2).

23 May-8 September. Shippers by the *Antelope* of Bristol, Mr. John Donne, bound from Bristol for Virginia: William Clark, John Stevens, George Lason, Edward Green, Abraham Stooke, Renedes Imbres, Thomas Machen, John Day, William Skinner, John Fisher, Elisha James, Joseph Jefferies, Thomas Warren, William Rishton, Thomas Hungerford. (PRO: E190/1154/2).

28 May. Newgate prisoners reprieved to be transported to Barbados or Jamaica. London: Mary Newman alias Colthropp, spinster; Elizabeth Lott, spinster; Jane Pretious, spinster; Jane Blewitt, spinster; Jane Jenkins alias Browne, spinster; Richard Talent; Jane Gillett, spinster; Sarah Mohoone alias Moone alias Murry, spinster; John Cumberland; William Painter; Daniel Phillips; Jane Mayfield, spinster; Martha Clements, spinster; Robert Royston; Edward Troope; Zipora Ireland, spinster; Elizabeth Scarre alias Osborne, spinster; Elizabeth Perry, spinster; Anne Povey, spinster; Elizabeth Hutton, spinster; Mary Mitchell, spinster; Mary Booker alias Fagg alias Robinson, spinster; Dorothy Cozin alias Bourne, spinster; Sarah Burroughs alias Pritchard alias Hill, spinster; Anne Raymond, spinster, alias wife of James Raymond; Anne Jones, spinster, alias wife of Edward Jones; William Smith alias John Carroll. Middlesex: Christian Carter of Stepney, spinster; Susan Clayton of the same, widow; John Brewer of the same; Susan Davis of Whitechapel, spinster; Anne Greene, wife of John Greene of the same; Mary Wood of the same, widow; Joan Bates alias Clarke alias Elizabeth Lambeth of St. Clement Danes, spinster; Sarah Wittall, spinster, alias wife of John Wittall of the same; Gabriel Tuckey of the same; James Pritchard of the same; Anne Hampton, spinster, alias wife of John Hampton of the same; Elizabeth Harris of St. Pancras, spinster; Elizabeth Titherington of Shoreditch, spinster; Mary Middleton of

Clerkenwell, spinster; Marmaduke Cooke of the same; Anne Walters of St. Martin in the Fields, spinster; Susan Powell alias Holden, spinster, alias wife of Timothy Holden of the same; Henry Atkinson of the same; Thomas Blunderfield of the same; William Denny of the same; Thomas Shaw of St. Paul Covent Garden; James Arnoe of Heston; Thomas Boone alias Booth of St. Giles in the Fields; Elizabeth Bryan of the same, spinster; John Jones of the same; Dorothy Abbis, wife of Edward Abbis of the same; Mary Chambers of the same, widow; Peter Paul of St. James Westminster; John Marshall of the same; Eleanor Jefferys, spinster, alias wife of Giles Jefferys of the same; John Allen of St. Margaret Westminster; Jane Sherry of St. Anne Westminster, widow; Mary Waters alias Pines alias Gibbins, spinster, alias wife of Thomas Waters of the same; Urianus Pulford of Hackney; Elizabeth Wright of the same, widow; John Bresbone of Tottenham; William Moulton of Paddington; Joseph Inkenbottom of the same; Richard Yates of the same; Mary Williams alias Glasse, spinster, alias wife of William Glasse; Sarah Densdale of St. Mary Savoy, widow; Thomas Pasmore and his wife Rosamond Pasmore of St. Andrew Holborn; Jane Juxon, spinster, alias wife of Daniel Juxon of the same. (PRO: C66/3390/13).

May. Administration of Robert Prewitt of New England, who died on H.M. ship *Devonshire*. (AW).

6 June-16 September. Shippers by the *Friendship* of New England, Mr. Benjamin Allen, bound from Bristol for New England: William Burgis, John Perrott, Joseph Way, James Webb, Thomas Gooding, James Long, Paul Boucher, Thomas Scroope, Samuel Boussac. (PRO: E190/1154/2).

21 June-8 September. Shippers by the *Jeremy*, Mr. Gilbert Bant, bound from London for New England: Samuell Keeling, Samuell White, John Bridge, Hugh Watts, Edward Dowdwell, Richard Bothwell, Sir Henry Ashurst, John Thorne, Richard Jenkison, Robert Maxwell, Henry Gray, Joseph Martin. (PRO: E190/159/1).

June. Administration of Thomas Cox of Nansemum, Virginia, bachelor. (AW).

June. Administration of Joseph Hobbs of Crewkerne, Somerset, who died in New England, bachelor. (AW).

1 July. The Council of Trade and Plantations are to report what places will receive women convicts. There are some 50 such women in Newgate awaiting transportation which will now have to be provided at the King's expense and the Treasury have agreed to pay for their removal to the West Indies. (CSPC).

6-21 July. Replies by Agents for the colonies to a request for information about the disposal of pardoned convicts. Virginia and Maryland have found the entertainment of convicts prejudicial and have passed laws against their importation. It will be no advantage to Barbados to have 50 Newgate women for no English women in the colony work in the fields and the people will not receive them into their homes - so they will be useless. These women would be of no use in Jamaica but rather a burden which would contribute nothing to the defence of the colony; they would be received only if 150 male convicts went with them. Carolina might accept women convicts where they may find a better reception than elsewhere. The Leeward Islands will accept the women convicts. (CSPC).

8-27 July. Depositions in London re the voyage in 1695 of the *Joan* from Boston, New England, to Barbados and London and her capture by the French. Deponents include Benjamin Smith, sailor aged 26, of Hartford, New England. (EA).

9-27 July. Shippers by the *Speedwell* of Boston bound for from Liverpool for New England: Thomas Barrington, Daniel Danvers, David Ferguson. (PRO: E190/1357/5).

9 July-24 September. Shippers by the *Primrose* of Bristol, Mr. John Jelfe, bound from Bristol for Virginia: Phillip Freake, Sir William Daines, Stephen Watts, William Rishton, William Swymmer, Anthony Swymmer. (PRO: E190/1154/2).

13 July. Shipper by the [blank], Mr. James Berry, bound from London for New England: Stephen Mason. (PRO: E190/159/1).

21 July. Shippers by the *Halem*, Mr. Samuell Bradford, bound from London for New York: Richard Wise, John Blackhall. (PRO: E190/159/1).

21 July. Shippers by an English ship, Mr. John Gureen, bound from Southampton for New England: Col. Joseph Dudley for wearing apparel. (PRO: E190/839/1).

21 July. Marmaduke How, aged 17, apprenticed from Christ's Hospital to Samuell Phillips, commander of the *Baltimore* bound for Virginia. (CH).

22 July. Shipper by the *Loyalty* of Belfast, Mr. William Pringle, bound from Liverpool for Virginia: Robert Andrews. (PRO: E190/1357/5).

July. Administration of John Holton of H.M. ship *Greenwich*, who died in Maryland, bachelor. (AW)

July. Administration of William Norrington master of the frigate ?*Leart*, who died in Virginia. (AW).

July. Probate of will of John Sinckler of the ship *Owners Adventure*, who died in Virginia, widower. (AW).

July. Probate of will of Thomas Griffin of the ship *Hope*, who died in Virginia, widower. (AW).

July. Administration with will of Gabriel Predix of Virginia. (AW).

July. Probate of will of Lewis Perdrian of Carolina who died in Barbados. (AW).

7-14 August. Shipper by the *Bonavir Merchant*, Mr. William Brittaine, bound from Bristol for Virginia: Abraham Hooke. (PRO: E190/1154/2).

13 August. Shipper by the *Hope* brigantine, Mr. Charles Harford, bound from Bristol for Virginia: said Charles Harford. (PRO: E190/1154/2).

17 August. Shipper by the *Seven Sons*, Mr. James Perry, bound from London for Virginia: John Denew. (PRO: E190/159/1).

18-25 August. Shipper by the *Ann & Mary*, Mr. William Watts, bound from Liverpool for Virginia: Thomas Johnson. (PRO: E190/1357/5).

18 August-23 September. Shippers by the *Charles*, Mr. Lewis Middleton and Mr. Benjamin Stow, bound from London for Carolina: Robert Myre, Peter Mercer, John Charon, Joseph Puddephat, Joseph Boone, Daniell Puckle. (PRO: E190/159/1).

28 August-7 September. Shippers by the *Esther*, Mr. John Jewell, bound from London for New York: John Whichcombe, Walter Yerbury, Lewis Davids, Paroculus Pearmiter. (PRO: E190/159/1).

31 August-1 September. Shippers by the *Supply*, Mr. James Barry, bound from Portsmouth for Boston, New England: Stephen Worledge, James Barron. (PRO: E190/839/5).

31 August-30 September. Shippers by the *Recovery* of Topsham, Mr. Benjamin Parsons, bound from Portsmouth for Boston, New England: James Barton, John Tousey. (PRO: E190/839/5).

August. Administration of Philip Watson of New England, widower. (AW).

August. Probate of will of Joel Horwood of Boston, New England, seaman of H.M. ship *Sheerness*. (AW).

August. Probate of will of William Robinson of Maryland. (AW).

August. Administration of Henry Sturges of the ship *John and Margaret*, who died in Maryland. (AW).

1-5 September. Shippers by the *Unity* of Lyme, Mr. Joseph Gaich, bound from Lyme for Virginia: John Burridge, Daniell Gundry, Thomas Bowdidge. (PRO: E190/891/19).

1 September-6 November. Shippers by the *Phillip* brigantine, Mr. Joseph Smith, bound from Bristol for New York: Edward Hackett, Stephen Peloquin, Benjamin Norwood. (PRO: E190/1154/2).

10 September. Shippers by the *Hester*, Mr. Joshua Hubbert, bound from London for New York: John Lofting, Pad. Paring. (PRO: E190/159/1).

10 September-11 October. Shippers by the *Jeremiah*, Mr. Gilbert Bant, bound from Portsmouth for New England: Stephen Wesendunk, John Winthrop, James Arnold. (PRO: E190/839/5).

15-24 September. Shippers by the *Nassau*, Mr. Giles Shelley, bound from London for New York: John Stacy, Samuell Monk, John Piteanne, Robert Hackshaw, Gilbert Heath, William Cornelison. (PRO: E190/159/1).

16 September. Shipper by the *Loyal Factor*, Mr. Timothy Auchambold, bound from London for New York: John Strienson. (PRO: E190/159/1).

22-29 September. Shippers by the *Annapolis* of Bideford, Mr. John Hartnoll, bound from Bideford for Maryland: George Buck, Thomas Marshall. (PRO: E190/971/6).

24 September. Shipper by the *Speaker*, Mr. Nicholas Lidston, bound from London for Virginia: Anthony Stratton. (PRO: E190/159/1).

27 September. Shipper by the *Dorothy*, Mr. Anthony Knack, bound from London for New England: Anthony Burren. (PRO: E190/159/1).

30 September. Shipper by the *Prudent Sarah*, Mr. William Guillam, bound from Portsmouth for New England: William Wallis. (PRO: E190/839/5).

September. Administration of Nathaniel Rhodes of Virginia, bachelor. (AW).

September. Administration of Thomas Hubbard of Virginia, bachelor. (AW).

September. Probate of will of William White of H.M. ship *St. Albans'* prize, who was drowned in Virginia. (AW).

September. Administration with will of Gawen Lawrie, Governor of East Jersey. (AW).

September. Probate of will of James Gault alias Gallt of Stepney, Middlesex, who died on a prize of H.M. ship *Dove* in Virginia. (AW).

September. Administration of Henrietta Maria Lloyd of Talbot County, Maryland, widow. (AW).

12 October. Shipper by the *Hallam* frigate, Mr. Samuel Bradford, bound from Portsmouth for New York: Charles Woolley. (PRO: E190/839/5).

12 October. Shipper by the *Marygold* of Bideford bound from Bideford for Maryland: Joseph Poardon. (PRO: E190/971/6).

12 October. Shipper by the *Crown* of Bideford, Mr. Thomas Phillips, bound from Bideford for Maryland: John Smith. (PRO: E190/971/6).

15 October-2 November. Shippers by the *Mulberry*, Mr. Bryan Blundell, bound from Liverpool for Virginia: Richard Scarborough, Thomas Edgar, William Green, Robert Moon, Walter Bryce, John Cockshutt, Thomas Preeson, Thomas Benn. (PRO: E190/1357/5).

16 October. Shipper by the *Pearl* of Bideford, Mr. Samuell Ellis, bound from Bideford for Maryland: Thomas Smith. (PRO: E190/971/6).

19 October-18 November. Depositions in London re the voyage of the *St. Peter*, Mr. Robert Delbridge, from Topsham to Virginia in 1696 and her return. Deponents include William Matthew of Westminster, Middlesex, aged 16, who was born in Virginia. (EA).

21 October. Shipper by the *Jeremiah* of New England, Mr. Gilbert Banks, bound from Cowes for New England: Richard Warder. (PRO: E190/839/1).

27 October. The following apprenticed in Liverpool: Martin Heyes to Thomas Johnson Jr., 4 years Virginia or Maryland. (LTB).

28 October. The following apprenticed in Liverpool: Robert Hilton to Bryan Blundell, 11 years Virginia or Maryland. (LTB).

29 October. The following apprenticed in Liverpool: William Mosson to Lewis Jenkins, 5 years Virginia or Maryland. (LTB).

October. Administration with will of William Barton of H.M. ship *Play's* prize, who had children in Pennsylvania. (AW).

October. Probate of will of John Primus of H.M. ship *St. Albans'* prize, who died in Virginia, bachelor. (AW).

2-10 November. Shippers by the *Lyon* of Liverpool, Mr. John Crompton, bound from Liverpool for Virginia: Andrew Leach, Henry Preston, Henry Chads, Peter Fauves. (PRO: E190/1357/5).

2-19 November. Shippers by the *Rebecca* brigantine, Mr. Waybert Lazenby, bound from Bristol for New York: Edward Hackett, Abraham Thomas, John Smart, Henry Lloyd, John Hobbs, James Donning. (PRO: E190/1154/2).

6 November. Shipper by the *Hopewell*, Mr. Thomas Yoakley, bound from London for Maryland: Henry Dennis. (PRO: E190/159/1).

6-9 November. Shippers by the *Providence*, Mr. John Kinkade, bound from London for Virginia: Daniell Puckle, John Cary. (PRO: E190/159/1).

8-15 November. Shipper by the *Josiah*, Mr. Thomas Lurting, bound from London for Maryland and Virginia: Samuell Groome. (PRO: E190/159/1).

8-20 November. Shipper by the *Henry*, Mr. Daniell Watts, bound from London for Maryland and Virginia: Samuell Groome. (PRO: E190/159/1).

8-24 November. Shippers by the *John & Margaret*, Mr. Thomas Salmon, bound from London for Maryland and Virginia: Peregrine Browne, John Tayler, James Ayres. (PRO: E190/159/1).

8-27 November. Shippers by the *Bachelor's Endeavour* of Stockton, Mr. Richard Danby, bound from Newcastle for Maryland: Francis Partis, Robert Grason. (PRO: E190/206/8).

11 November. The following apprenticed in Liverpool to Henry Farrar to serve in Virginia or Maryland: Margery Blundell, 4 years; Lewis Gillgrist, 7 years; Thomas Silvester, 7 years. (LTB).

12 November. Shipper by the *Joseph*, Mr. Anthony Matthews, bound from London for Carolina: Gibson Clap. (PRO: E190/159/1).

12 November. Shipper by the *Jane & Sarah*, Mr. Thomas Witchington, bound from London for Virginia: Matthias Jones. (PRO: E190/159/1).

13 November. Shipper by the *William & Mary* of Poole, Mr. Thomas Gentle, bound from Poole for Virginia: William Phippard. (PRO: E190/891/16).

15 November. Shipper by the *Vine*, Mr. William Smith, bound from London for Virginia: Thomas Harrington. (PRO: E190/159/1).

15-18 November. Depositions in London re the capture by the French of the New England ship *Joseph & Mary*, Mr. George Beard, in 1696. Deponents include William Phillips, mariner aged 30, of Boston, New England, where he was born. (EA).

15 November-7 December. Shipper by the *Deptford*, Mr. John [or Joseph] Munday, bound from London for Virginia: Benjamin Hatley, Francis Willis. (PRO: E190/159/1).

15 November-23 December. Shippers by the *Hopewell*, Mr. Nicholas Smith, bound from London for Maryland and Virginia: Thomas Rascoe, Richard Diamond, Abraham Wilde, Bennett & Dennis, Silvanus Grove, John Knight, Richard Chambers, Stephen Noguier. (PRO: E190/159/1).

16-25 November. Shippers by the *Gloucester*, Mr. William Read, bound from Bristol for Cork and Virginia: Mark Goddard, John Stevens, Thomas Cockaine, Samuell Combes, Charles Nicholls, William Galbraith. (PRO: E190/1154/2).

18 November. Shipper by the *Merchants Adventure*, Mr. Michaell White, bound from London for Carolina: John Constantine. (PRO: E190/159/1).

18 November. Shipper by the *Adventure* of Bideford, Mr. Thomas Leach, bound from Bideford for Maryland: said Thomas Leach. (PRO: E190/971/6).

18 November-8 December. Shippers by the *Providence* of Bristol, Mr. John Read, bound from Bristol for Virginia: Michaell Pope, John Bubb, John Jones. (PRO: E190/1154/2).

19 November-14 December. Shippers by the *Friends Endeavour*, Mr. John Bond, bound from London for New York: Thomas Powell, Thomas Noell, John Robery, Thomas Bond, John Desene, Paul Palliott. (PRO: E190/159/1).

20 November. Shipper by the *Friends Goodwill*, Mr. Thomas Moyse, bound from London for Maryland: John Tayler. (PRO: E190/159/1).

22 November. Shipper by the *John*, Mr. Henry Munday, bound from London for Maryland: John Pettet. (PRO: E190/159/1).

22-24 November. Shippers by the *Dover Merchant*, Mr. Henry Coleman, bound from London for Carolina: Ambrose Garrett, James Brayne. (PRO: E190/159/1).

22-26 November. Shippers by the *Friends Adventure*, Mr. Michaell Cole, bound from London for Carolina: Richard Haynes, Peter De Marland, Burtwell & Walker, Patrick Miles. (PRO: E190/159/1).

23 November. The following apprenticed in Liverpool: Isabell Conley to Lewis Jenkins, 7 years Virginia or Maryland. (LTB).

23 November-1 December. Shippers by the *Richmond*, Mr. Richard Hill, bound from London for Maryland: Matthew Plumstead, Thomas Wharton. (PRO: E190/159/1).

23 November-7 December. Shippers by the *Scarborough*, Mr. Robert Allison, bound from London for Virginia: Samuell Shefford, John Bullen. (PRO: E190/159/1).

24 November. Shipper by the [blank], Mr. Samuell Pacey, bound from London for Maryland: John Searle(?). (PRO: E190/159/1).

24 November. Shippers by the *Providence*, Mr. George Keeble, bound from London for Maryland: Edward & Dudley Carleton. (PRO: E190/159/1).

24 November. Shipper by the *Hopewell*, Mr. Henry Munday, bound from London for Maryland: John Munday. (PRO: E190/159/1).

24 November-1 December. Shippers by the *Richard & Mary*, Mr. Andrew Senhouse, bound from London for Maryland: John Munday, John Hyde, Thomas Wharton. (PRO: E190/159/1).

25 November. The Council of Trade and Plantations to consider and report how and where convicts pardoned for transportation may be sent and what punishment might be more proper in the place of transportation. (CSPC).

25 November. Shipper by the *Integrity* of Bideford, Mr. Aaron Whitton, bound from Bideford for Maryland: said Aaron Whitton. (PRO: E190/971/6).

25 November-4 December. Shippers by the *Jeffery*, Mr. Daniell Watts, bound from London for Maryland: Thomas Walsh, Robert Bundy. (PRO: E190/159/1).

25 November-7 December. Shippers by the *John*, Mr. John Tanner, bound from London for Maryland: Samuell Harwood, Thomas Starke, Cornelius Mason. (PRO: E190/159/1).

1697

25 November-11 December. Shippers by the *Hope*, Mr. John Cottrell, bound from London for Maryland: Edward Warner, Anthony Strutton. (PRO: E190/159/1).

26 November-12 December. Shippers by the *[St.] George*, Mr. George Purvis, bound from London for Virginia: Thomas Ellis, Edward & Thomas Haistwell, Thomas Corbin, Sir John Woolfe. (PRO: E190/159/1).

27 November-16 December. Shippers by the *York Merchant*, Mr. Wyall and Mr. Attwood, bound from London for Virginia: John Weith, Ambrose Smith. (PRO: E190/159/1).

30 November. Shipper by the *Henrietta* bound from Bideford for Maryland: John Davie. (PRO: E190/971/6).

November. Administration with will of Ambrose Cleare of Great Stratton, New Kent County, Virginia. (AW).

November. Probate of will of William Penn of Patuxent River, Maryland. (AW).

November. Probate of will of John Nevill of St. Margaret, Westminster, Middlesex, who died in Virginia, Vice-Admiral. (AW).

November. Probate of will of Richard Baker of Stonedeane, Chalfont, Buckinghamshire, who had lands in Pennsylvania. (AW).

November. Probate of will of Thomas Jones of H.M. ship *Pembroke*, who died in Virginia. (AW).

1 December. The following apprenticed in Liverpool to serve in Virginia or Maryland: John Leek to Lewis Jenkins, 5 years; William Ludloe of Bradford, Yorkshire, to William Chantrell, 5 years; William Gibson to Randle Galloway, 4 years; John Webster to the same, 8 years; Paul Leighmans to the same, 9 years; John Moores to the same, 9 years;—— Green and —— Haddam to William Chantrell, 4 years. (LTB).

1-3 December. Shippers by the *Little John*, Mr. William Webb, bound from Bristol for Virginia: John Jones, John Miller, Thomas Hollister, John Bubb, Thomas Blayden. (PRO: E190/1154/2).

1-3 December. Shippers by the *Amity*, Mr. Lewis Jenkins, bound from Liverpool for Virginia: John Molineux, William Addison. (PRO: E190/1357/5).

1-5 December. Shippers by the *Carolina* sloop, Mr. John Parker, bound from Bristol for Carolina: Charles Chauncey, William Barron, Abraham Eve, Thomas Spread, Arthur Jackson, William Bath, John Baker, Edward Hutton. (PRO: E190/1154/2).

1-14 December. Shipper by the *Ann*, Mr. Benjamin Dolling, bound from London for Maryland: Robert Dunklin. (PRO: E190/159/1).

681

1-22 December. Shippers by the *Benjamin*, Mr. Gerrish, bound from London for New England: Joseph Paice, Anthony Merry. (PRO: E190/159/1).

1-23 December. Shippers by the *Dispatch* of Bristol, Mr. John Thomas, bound from Bristol for Virginia: John Scandrett, Richard Franklin, Abraham Lewis, Robert Tunbridge, Thomas Tyler, Edward Lloyd, Sir John Duddlestone. (PRO: E190/1154/2).

3 December. Shipper by the *Employment*, Mr. Edward Barecock, bound from London for Maryland: Timothy Keysar. (PRO: E190/159/1).

3 December. Shipper by the *Amity* of Bideford, Mr. John Rock, bound from Bideford for Maryland: George Buck. (PRO: E190/971/6).

3-7 December. Shipper by the *America*, Mr. Thomas Graves, bound from London for Virginia: Arthur Bailey. (PRO: E190/159/1).

3-16 December. Shipper by the *Mary*, Mr. John Gundy, bound from London for Virginia: John Marsh. (PRO: E190/159/1).

4-15 December. Shippers by the *Friendship*, Mr. Robert Dickson, bound from London for Pennsylvania: Edward Hampson, Benjamin Olive, Mathew Day. (PRO: E190/159/1).

4 December-2 February. Shippers by the *Mountjoy*, Mr. James Scott, bound from Bristol for Virginia: Ezekiel(?) Wallis, John Bachelor, Thomas Longman, William French, Samuell Weekes, Joseph Temple, George Mason, Richard Franklin, Joseph James, John Oliver, Joseph Brittain, William Stafford, Thomas Mountjoy, William Burges, Sir Richard Crumpe. (PRO: E190/1154/2).

6 December. Shipper by the *Jeffery*, Mr. Cole, bound from London for Carolina: John Beaufield. (PRO: E190/159/1).

6-16 December. Shippers by the *Mary & Johanna*, Mr. William Harris, bound from London for Virginia: Robert Bristow, John Owen. (PRO: E190/159/1).

6-20 December. Shippers by the *Baltimore*, Mr. Samuell Phillips, bound from London for Maryland: Peter Paggen, John Tayler. (PRO: E190/159/1).

6-20 December. Shippers by the *John & Thomas*, Mr. Thomas Scotting, bound from London for Maryland: Edward & Thomas Haistwell. (PRO: E190/159/1).

7 December. Shipper by the *Recovery*, Mr. William Mabb, bound from London for Maryland: Michaell Jones. (PRO: E190/159/1).

7-10 December. Shippers by the *Providence*, Mr. William Cant, bound from London for Virginia: John Wright, James Ayres. (PRO: E190/159/1).

7-14 December. Shippers by the *Virginia*, Mr. Edward Whittaker, bound from London for Virginia: Thomas Kelsey, Samuell Manyne. (PRO: E190/159/1).

8 December. William King, aged 15, apprenticed from Christ's Hospital to Samuell Phillips, commander of the *Catherine* bound for Jamaica. (CH).

8-22 December. Shippers by the *James & Mary*, Mr. Jeremy Pearce, bound from Bristol for Virginia: Richard Gibbons, Abraham Gibbons, John Taylor. (PRO: E190/1154/2).

9-19 December. Shippers by the *Concord*, Mr. William Chantrill, bound from Liverpool for Virginia: John Pemberton, John Cockshutt. (PRO: E190/1357/5).

10 December. Shipper by the *Hope*, Mr. John Castle, bound from London for Virginia: Edward Warner. (PRO: E190/159/1).

11 December. Shipper by the *Postillion*, Mr. Richard Potts, bound from London for Virginia: John Purvis. (PRO: E190/159/1).

11-16 December. Shippers by the *Harrison*, Mr. John Harrison, bound from London for Virginia: Humphrey Pye, Richard Cooke, Arthur North. (PRO: E190/159/1).

13 December. Shippers by the *Levett*, Mr. Edward Rhodes, bound from London for Virginia: Arthur Bailey, Robert Broslow. (PRO: E190/159/1).

13-15 December. Shipper by the *Hartwell* of London, Nicholas Humphrey, bound from Southampton for Virginia: John Norton. (PRO: E190/839/1).

14 December. Shipper by the *Elizabeth & Mary*, Mr. John Bradford, bound from London for Virginia: Samuell Sandford. (PRO: E190/159/1).

15 December. Shipper by the *Gloucester*, Mr. Edward Ellis, bound from London for Virginia: Edmond Littlepage. (PRO: E190/159/1).

15 December. Shipper by the *Jacob*, Mr. Edward Rhodes, bound from London for Virginia: John Mumford. (PRO: E190/159/1).

15 December. Shipper by the *Mary Anne* of Weymouth, Mr. William Cleeves, bound from Poole for Virginia: David Arbuthnott. (PRO: E190/891/16).

16 December. Shipper by the [blank], Mr. Nathaniell Mason, bound from London for Maryland: Thomas Rascoe. (PRO: E190/159/1).

16 December. Shipper by the *Golden Lyon*, Mr. Robert Ranton, bound from London for Virginia: William Madgwick. (PRO: E190/159/1).

16 December. Shipper by the *Preservation*, Mr. Thomas Ellis, bound from London for Maryland: Joseph Jackson. (PRO: E190/159/1).

16 December. Shipper by the *Recovery*, Mr. Peter Reeves, bound from London for Virginia: Thomas Nisbett. (PRO: E190/159/1).

16 December. Shipper by the *Richard & James*, Mr. James Greenwell, bound from London for Virginia: Peter Paggen. (PRO: E190/159/1).

16-22 December. Shippers by the *Robert & Samuell*, Mr. Mathew Trym, bound from London for Virginia: Thomas Hart, John Cooper, John Tiplady, Samuell Maynes. (PRO: E190/159/1).

16-22 December. Shippers by the [blank], Mr. John Buckshire, bound from London for Virginia: Robert Farish, Samuell Hoyle. (PRO: E190/159/1).

17 December. Shipper by the *William & Elizabeth* of Poole, Mr. Richard Tregian, bound from Poole for Virginia: William Phippard. (PRO: E190/891/16).

20 December. Shipper by the *John*, Mr. Richard Biswick, bound from London for Virginia: Thomas Corbin. (PRO: E190/159/1).

20 December. Shipper by the *James*, Mr. Edward Burford, bound from London for Maryland: Isaac Milner. (PRO: E190/159/1).

20 December. Shipper by the *Gerrard*, Mr. William Dennis, bound from London for Virginia: Edward Leman. (PRO: E190/159/1).

22 December. Shipper by the [blank], Mr. Benjamin Dowting, bound from London for Virginia: Benjamin Hatley. (PRO: E190/159/1).

22 December. Shipper by the *Abraham*, Mr. Joseph Cooke, bound from London for Virginia: Thomas Starke. (PRO: E190/159/1).

23 December. Shipper by the *Thorogood*, Mr. John Noll, bound from London for Virginia: John Purvis. (PRO: E190/159/1).

24 December. Shipper by the [blank], Mr. Francis Fisher, bound from London for Virginia: Matthias Jones. (PRO: E190/159/1).

29 December-24 June 1698. Depositions in London re the capture by the French of the New England ship *Joseph*, Mr. Richard Anthony, in 1696. Deponents include John Smith, mariner aged 43, resident for 20 years in Boston, New England, but born in Selby, Yorkshire. (EA).

30 December-18 January. Shippers by the *Ann & Sarah* of Liverpool, Mr. John Brazhall, bound from Liverpool for Virginia: Alexander Reed, George Heaper, Gilbert Jackson, John Baynes, Thomas Sweeting. (PRO: E190/1359/11).

December. Probate of will of Peter Hodges of East West Jersey who died in Bermondsey, Surrey. (AW).

December. Probate of will of James Mountgomery of James River, Virginia, who died in St. Katherine Creechurch, London. (AW).

December. Administration with will of Solomon Stedman of Boston, New England. (AW).

1698

3 January. The following apprenticed in Liverpool: George Worrs of Lancashire to Randle Galloway, 8 years Virginia or Maryland. (LTB).

5 January. The following apprenticed in Liverpool to William Webster to serve in Virginia or Maryland: Maudlin Davis of Ruthin, Wales, 5 years; Katherine Perry of Ruthin, 5 years; Joan Rowland of Bangor, Wales, 5 years; Richard Jones of Denbighshire, 5 years; Edward Jones of Willison [?Willington], Cheshire, 5 years; Thomas Cook of Frodsham, [Cheshire], 5 years; William Smith of Dover, [Kent], 4 years. (LTB).

7 January. Shipper by the *Four Sisters* of Liverpool, Mr. Randolph Galloway, bound from Liverpool for Virginia: William Clayton by Mathias Gibson. (PRO: E190/1359/11).

7 January. Shipper by the *Mary & Isabella*, Mr. Henry Rogers, bound from Exeter for Virginia: John Pole. (PRO: E190/972/9).

8 January. The following apprenticed in Liverpool: John White of Cirencester, Gloucestershire, [to] John Tonnard, 4 years Barbados; Hugh Gryffeth of Denbigh [*prob.* Denbigh, Wales], to Randle Galloway, 4 years [Virginia or Maryland]; William Gryffeth to the same for the same term. (LTB).

8 January. Shipper by the *Katherine* of Poole, Mr. Hugh Rockett, bound from Poole for Virginia: William Phippard. (PRO: E190/892/7).

10 January. The following apprenticed in Liverpool: Hugh Partington to Randle Galloway, 4 years [Virginia or Maryland]; John Thomas of St. Asaph, [Wales], to the same for the same term. (LTB).

10-11 January. Shippers by the *Maryland Merchant* of Plymouth, Mr. Walter Lugger, bound from Plymouth for Virginia: John Rogers, John Arnold. (PRO: E190/1058/2).

18 January. The following apprenticed in Liverpool to serve William Webster [in Virginia or Maryland]: Thomas Humphrey, 9 years; Edward Jones of Merioneth, 4 years; Elizabeth Gryffeth, 5 years. (LTB).

19-26 January. Shippers by the *Society* of Liverpool, Mr. Jonathan Livesley, bound from Liverpool for Virginia: John Pemberton, John Hughes. (PRO: E190/1359/11).

20 January. The following apprenticed in Liverpool: Hugh Roberts of Anglesey, Wales, to Jonathan Livesey, 4 years [Virginia or Maryland]; John Gryffin of Caernarvon to the same for the same term; Ann Jones of Anglesey to the same for 6 years. (LTB).

21 January. The following apprenticed in Liverpool to serve William Webster [in Virginia or Maryland]: Robert Hughes of St. Asaph, [Flint]; William Ellis of Clantastelh [?Llanstadwell], Wales, 7 years; John Alvin of Shaftesbury, Dorset; John Hughes, 7 years; William Davis of Caires (*sic*), Wales, 7 years. (LTB).

21 January. The following apprenticed from Christ's Hospital: Stephen Clarke, aged 16, sent to his friend James Kirby and Micajah Perry, merchant in Leadenhall Street, to serve Mr. Robert Beverley of James City, Virginia; Thomas Knight, aged 16, to Micajah Perry to serve Hon. William Bird of James River, Virginia. (CH).

28 January. The following apprenticed in Liverpool to William Webster to serve in Virginia or Maryland: Jane Evans of Denbighshire, 5 years; Henry Evans of Denbighshire, 4 years; Mary Gryffith of Merioneth, 4 years; Ame Watkins of Denbighshire, 4 years; Robert Matthew of Denbigh, 9 years; Robert Jones of Denbighshire, 4 years; Richard Jones of Caernarvon, 4 years; Ann Watkins, 4 years; Finch Morris of Denbigh, 9 years; Mary Norman of Egremont, [Cumberland], 5 years; Isabel Troughton of Catton [?Yorkshire], 5 years; William Moor of Antrim, Ireland, 4 years; Mary Williams of Flintshire, 5 years. (LTB).

?January. The following apprenticed in Liverpool to serve John Marshall, master of the *Ann & Sarah*, for 4 years [in Virginia or Maryland]: Henry Ripley of York; Daniel Showland of Cork, [Ireland], John Wilson of Nycrofe(?), Leicestershire; James Eccles of Loughlavin, Ireland; John Steward of London. (LTB).

January. Probate of will of Michael Musgrave of Virginia, who died in St. Sepulchre, London. (AW).

January. Administration with will of Thomas Yale of London merchant, whose uncle, Thomas Yale, was in New England. (AW).

1 February-2 March. Shippers by the *Plymouth* of Plymouth, Mr. Thomas Willington, bound from Plymouth for Virginia: Phillip Pontyn, Allen Witherson, John Addis & Co., Charles Huddy. (PRO: E190/1058/2).

2 February-13 April. Depositions in London re the capture by the French in 1695 of the New England ship the *Dove*, Mr. Andrew Way. Deponents include Petre Machee, mariner aged 27, for six years resident in New York but born in France. (EA).

3 February. The following apprenticed in Liverpool to serve Jonathan Livesey [in Virginia or Maryland]: Jacob Boulton Sr. of Ashton Keynes, Wiltshire, 3 years; William Darter of the same parish, 3 years; William Prior of Flintshire, 4 years. (LTB).

7 February. Shipper by the *Nicholas & John* of Dartmouth, Mr. John Torier, bound from Dartmouth for Virginia: James Silby. (PRO: E190/972/12).

10 February. Shipper by the *Susanna & Sarah* of Boston, Mr. John Tucker, bound from Newcastle for Boston, New England: William Skinner. (PRO: E190/206/1).

14 February. Warrant for Cecilia Labree, imprisoned in Newgate for counterfeiting coins, to be pardoned on condition of transportation. (SP Dom).

16 February. The following apprenticed in Liverpool to William Webster [to serve in Virginia or Maryland]: Henry Brobbin of Warrington, [Lancashire], 5 years; John Brobbin, 5 years; Elizabeth Brobbin, 5 years; Mary Cloud, 5 years; Mary Steel of Harperthe (*sic*), Cheshire, 5 years; Katherine Williams. (LTB).

17-18 February. The following apprenticed in Liverpool: William Ertome of London to William Webster, 4 years Virginia or Maryland; Robert Clark to the same, 4 years. (LTB).

22 February. Shipper by the *Two Sisters* of Guernsey, Mr. John Bassett, bound from Plymouth for Virginia: Elias Brett & Co. (PRO: E190/1058/2).

23 February. Western Circuit prisoners reprieved to be transported to Barbados. Cornwall: Robert Richards alias Bartley of Truro; William Humphrey of Probus. Devon: Nicholas Dunstone of Exeter; Thomas Strang alias Strong of Bickington; John Creebar of Meavy, blacksmith; Thomas Downham of Clyst Honiton, cordwainer; Nicholas Marshall of Dunkeswell. Hampshire: John Willson of Elvetham. Somerset: Richard Hawkins alias Wood of Stogumber; George Thompson of Binegar, barber surgeon; George Mead of Ilminster, weaver. Wiltshire: George Dickenson of Purton (who will not be reformed except by transportation); Thomas Bradfield of Maston, Potterne. Nicholas Northover of St. Ann's, London. (PRO: C66/3403/15).

24 February. The following apprenticed in Liverpool to William Webster to serve in Virginia or Maryland: Elizabeth Jones of near Ruthin, [Wales], 5 years; Ann Jones of Wrexham, [Wales], 7 years; Robert Williams of near Ruthin, 7 years; Thomas Davies of Wrexham, [Wales], 7 years; Mary Tue of Houghtonton (*sic*), Cheshire, 5 years; Thomas Babington of Appleton, Cheshire, 9 years; Joan Williams of Ruthin, 5 years; Ellen Hughes of Ruthin, 5 years; Thomas Owen of Denbigh, 7 years; Katherine Hughes of Ruthin, 5 years. (LTB).

28 February. The following apprenticed in Liverpool [to William Webster to serve in Virginia or Maryland]: Richard Edward of Denbigh, 4 years; John Thomas of Denbigh, 9 years; William Hughes of Denbigh, 9 years; Thomas Roberts of Denbigh, 9 years; John Owens of Caernarvon, 6 years; Owen Jones of Anglesey, 4 years; Christian Ireland of Chester, 4 years; John Jones of Anglesey, 4 years; Henry Perry of Montgomery, 4 years; (LTB).

February. Administration of Hugh Merriken of Maryland. (AW).

February. Probate of will of Robert Fargusion of Kenton, Northumberland, and of the ship *Falkland*, who died in New England. (AW).

2 March. The following apprenticed in Liverpool [to William Webster to serve in Virginia or Maryland]: William Bennet of Ashbourne, Derbyshire. (LTB).

5-18 March. Shippers by the *Liverpool Merchant*, Mr. William Webster, bound from Liverpool for Virginia: William Clayton, Richard Houghton. (PRO: E190/1359/11).

10-12 March. The following apprenticed in Liverpool [to William Webster to serve in Virginia or Maryland]: Thomas Steward of Wybunbury, Cheshire, 7 years; Thomas Whitaker of Eastquein [?Eastham], Cheshire, 8 years; John Wright of Uxbridge, Middlesex, 4 years; John Davis of Wapping, Middlesex, 4 years; George Baddoe of Clee, Shropshire, 4 years; Edward Buckley of Buglawton, Cheshire, 4 years; William Dickinson of Farn[don], Cheshire, 4 years; Joseph Jinkins of Warton, Cheshire, 4 years. (LTB).

10-26 March. Shippers by the *Planter* of Liverpool, Mr. John Rimer, bound from Liverpool for Virginia: John Molyneux, John Dunbar, William Dent. (PRO: E190/1359/11).

12 March. Home Circuit prisoners reprieved to be transported to Barbados or Jamaica. Essex: John Leach of Witham; Philip Tims; John Skill; Leonard Fryer of Epping; Thomas Rogers of Chadwell; Nicholas Olliver of Burnham. Hertfordshire: William Hixson of Brickenden; Mary wife of Thomas Dennis, "an old convict" of All Saints, Hertford; William Woodward of Brickenden. Kent. Robert Garlett of Chatham; William Hunt of Chislet; James Smith of Iwade; Simon Hulstone of Chislet; Dorothy Kidwell of Great Chart; William Carter of Chislet; John Ganfield of Chatham; John Richardson alias Moore of Eltham; James Smith alias Hubbart of Ightham; Mary Martin alias Meechin of Lewisham, spinster; John Duboyce of Beckenham. Surrey: Stephen Bird of St. Saviour, Southwark; John Hunt of Camberwell; Mary Bevill of St. Saviour, Southwark; Mary wife of Robert Compton of St. Olave, Southwark; Elizabeth Wilson of St. Saviour, Southwark; Peter Eaton of Camberwell; Edward Brommedge of Christ Church; Ambrose Mead of Wandsworth; Joan Martin of Croydon; George Cridon of Leatherhead; Robert Allen of Camberwell. Sussex: Stephen Owen of Hellingly; William Bowler of Sillington. (PRO: C66/3403/11).

16 March. The following apprenticed in Liverpool [to William Webster to serve in Virginia or Maryland]: Samuel Low of Knutsford, Cheshire, 4 years; Thomas Farrel of Dublin, [Ireland], 4 years. (LTB).

18 March. Buckinghamshire prisoners reprieved to be transported to America: Thomas Wilkinson of Chesham; Henry Quarrington of Ivinghoe. (PRO: C66/3403/9).

18 March. Cheshire prisoners reprieved to be transported to America: John Port of Sutton, watchmaker; William Smith of Sandbach, nailer. (PRO: C66/3403/8).

21-24 March. The following apprenticed in Liverpool [to William Webster to serve in Virginia or Maryland]: John Baggeley, 4 years; Joseph Brosier of London, 5 years; John Stol of Sunhen (*sic*), 9 years; Margery Hunt of Knutsford, Cheshire, 5 years; Henry Prescott of Wigan, [Lancashire], 4 years; Ann Coulburne of Preston, [Lancashire], 8 years; Peter Fothner of Tattenhall, Cheshire, 4 years; Hugh Jones of Wrexham, [Wales], 9 years; John Lloyd of Denbighshire, 8 years; Charles Webster of Denbigh, 8 years; William Hughes of Denbighshire, 8 years; Edward Hughes of Flint, 9 years; Edward Howell of St. Asaph, Flint, 9 years; John Morgan of Denbighshire, 8 years; Edward Roberts of Denbighshire, 6 years; Gabriel Roberts of Flint, 4 years; Thomas Hughes of Ruthin, 5 years; Robert Hughes of Denbighshire, 4 years; Thomas Roberts of Denbighshire, 5 years; Thomas Perrey of Denbigh, 4 years; Owen Hughes of Ruthin, 8 years. (LTB).

March. Administration of Anne Wotton of Calvert County, Maryland, spinster. (AW).

March. Probate of nuncupative will of John Fly of Piscataway, New England, who died on H.M. ship *Catherine*, widower. (AW).

1-13 April. The following apprenticed in Liverpool [to William Webster to serve in Virginia or Maryland]: Elizabeth Roberts of Denbighshire, 7 years; Margaret Williams of Anglesey, 5 years; Dorathy Edwards of Denbighshire, 7 years; James Yates of Blackburn, [Lancashire], 4 years; Charles Shehy of Dublin, [Ireland], 4 years; Thomas Moor of Dublin, 4 years; John Edmunds of Merioneth, 4 years; Robert Warner of Gloucestershire, 4 years; Thomas Morris of Shropshire, 4 years; Richard Worden of Essex, 4 years. (LTB).

7 April. Shipper by the *Rose* of Plymouth, Mr. William Willshman, bound from Plymouth for Virginia: James Keating. (PRO: E190/1058/2).

19 April. The following apprenticed in Liverpool: Thomas Evans of Denbighshire, carpenter, to Richard Adams and William Lewis, 4 years Pennsylvania. (LTB).

April. Administration of Thomas Groome of the ship *Falkland* in H.M. service, who died in New England. (AW).

April. Administration of Edward Guy of Appleby, Westmorland, who died in Philadelphia. (AW).

5 May. The following apprenticed in Liverpool to James Gordon to serve 4 years [in Virginia or Maryland]: Joseph Stile of Talkell Hill [?Tatenhill], Staffordshire; William English of Farr, Scotland; Samuel Wallington of Prestbury, [Gloucestershire]; Roger Sharples of Lealand [?Leyland, Lancashire]; Richard Hughes of Mould, [Flint]. (LTB).

11 May. The following apprenticed in Liverpool to serve James Gordon [in Virginia or Maryland]: Thomas Prichard of Beaumaris, [Anglesey], 7 years; Peter Jones of Flintshire, 4 years. (LTB).

16 May. The following apprenticed in Liverpool to serve James Gordon [in Virginia or Maryland]: John Prior of Pisor(?), Flint. (LTB).

28 May. The following apprenticed from Christ's Hospital: Thomas Costine, aged 16, to Francis Rogers, commander of the *Castle* frigate bound for Jamaica; John White, aged 16, to Michaell Staples, commander of the *Hopewell* bound for the West Indies. (CH).

May. Administration with will of Charles Lidget, formerly of Boston, New England, who died in St. Bride, London. (AW).

May. Probate of will of John Bennett of St. Gabriel, Fenchurch Street, London, who had lands in Maryland. (AW).

May. Probate of will of Michael Dickenson of Altrincham, Cheshire, whose nephew, James Talier, was in Virginia. (AW).

May. Probate of will of John Warnsley of St. Olave Southwark, Surrey, bound for Virginia. (AW).

4 June. Shipper by the *Greyhound* of Boston, Mr. James Pitt, bound from Dartmouth for New England: Joseph Bully. (PRO: E190/972/12).

4 June. Shipper by the *William* of Jersey, Mr. John Ballaine, bound from Dartmouth for New England: Daniell Janwrin. (PRO: E190/972/12).

7 June. The following apprenticed in Liverpool: William Russell of Kinsale [Ireland], to James Gordon, 4 years [Virginia or Maryland]. (LTB).

21 June. The following apprenticed in Liverpool: Jane Horton of Windle, [Cheshire], to Edward Tarleton, 4 years [Virginia or Maryland]; Richard Cowland of Thornton, Leicestershire, to [James] Gordon, 7 years [Virginia or Maryland]; William Wilson of Laughton, Leicestershire, to the same, 7 years. (LTB).

23 June. Shipper by the *Manley* of Southampton, Mr. Phillip Denevile, bound from Southampton for Virginia: said Philip Denevile. (PRO: E190/840/3).

27 June. The following apprenticed in Liverpool to serve James Gordon for four years [in Virginia or Maryland]: Jonathan Davis; Augustine Carr; Richard Werton. (LTB).

27 June-1 July. Shipper by the *Friendship* of Whitby, Mr. William Dowell, bound from Southampton for Pennsylvania: Richard Warder. (PRO: E190/840/3).

June. Administration of John Gribb of Stepney, Middlesex, who died in Virginia. (AW).

June. Administration of Thomas Bossinger of New England, who died on the ship *Elizabeth*. (AW).

2 July. The following apprenticed in Liverpool to serve John Thomas for seven years in Virginia or Maryland: John Mason, son of John M. of London, mariner, deceased; William Mason. (LTB).

5 July. Shipper by the *Rogers* of Plymouth, Mr. John Saunders, bound from Plymouth for Virginia: Sir John Rogers. (PRO: E190/1058/2).

7 July. The following apprenticed in Liverpool to Edward Tarleton to serve four years in Virginia or Maryland: William Holt of Preston on the Hill, Cheshire; George Oldham. (LTB).

8 July. The following apprenticed to James Gordon to serve in Barbados: Humphry Roberts of Caernarvonshire, 7 years; William Gryffith of Cardinganshire, 4 years; Peter Prior of Denbighshire, 7 years; John Browne of Lincolnshire, stationer, 4 years; Maurice Roberts of Denbighshire, 7 years; Richard Merton of Denbighshire, 7 years; John Hughes of Merionethshire, sawyer, 4 years; Peter Matthew of Denbighshire. And the following to serve Peter Atherton [in Virginia or Maryland]: John Roberts, son of Edward R. of Queekleys(?), Flint, 4 years; John Lloyd, son of John L. of Abergele, Denbighshire, 9 years. (LTB).

12 July. Shipper by the *Fisher* of Bideford, Mr. Thomas Lashbrook, bound from Bideford for Maryland: Peter Luxon. (PRO: E190/972/8).

16 July. Western Circuit prisoners reprieved to be transported to Barbados. Cornwall: Mathew Nicholls alias Nicholas of Gwermop, tinner. Devon: Richard Lane alias James Francis of Ilsington, tinner; Richard alias John Bright of Bow or Nuntracy; John Thomas alias Bonady alias Inon of Bideford. Hampshire: John Barker of Southampton. Somerset: Richard Comer of Huntspill; George Yeo of Orchard; Ann Cowdall wife of Saul of Frome Selwood; Henry Brimble of South Petherton; John Yeo of Orchard Portman; William Foweracres of Wellington; Jonathan Palfrey alias Parfrey of Huntspill. Wiltshire: Roger Wheeler Jr.; Charles Harris of Rowde; Benjamin Wyatt of Fisherton Anger. Thomas Smith of Grantham (Lincolnshire); Richard Gass of Acton (Middlesex), mariner. (PRO: C66/3405/8).

16 July. Northern Circuit prisoners reprieved to be transported to Barbados. Durham: Gerard Meaburne of Hett; Ralph Emmerson of Barnard Castle. (PRO: C66/3405/7).

16 July. Appeal by Daniel Pierce and other tenants of William Brown and Benjamin Brown of New England against a verdict given at Newport, Rhode Island, in favour of Edmond Willie and Margaret his wife and Richard Hancock and Judith his wife for a moiety of Prudence Island, New England. (APC).

19 July. The following apprenticed in Liverpool to serve [in Virginia or Maryland]: Laurence Downes of Macclesfield, [Cheshire], to James Gordon, 4 years; Ann Green of Bretherton, [Lancashire], to [Edward] Tarleton, 4 years; Mary Smith of Grosli(?), Flint, to the same, 4 years. (LTB).

20 July. Oxford Circuit prisoners reprieved to be transported to America. Berkshire: Richard Harris alias Castle of Botley; Richard North of Speen; Anthony Care of Wantage. Gloucestershire: John Mead alias Lawrence of St. Peter & James, Gloucester; Jeremiah Buck alias Churches of Frocester; Susan Holloway of Tewkesbury. Monmouthshire: Charles William Monmouth of Panteg. Oxfordshire: William Baker of Glympton; John Scayle of Aston Rowant; Samuel Westbrooke of Kirtlington. Shropshire: Edward Jones of Whitchurch; Owen Jones of Llanymynech. Staffordshire: Joseph Hutchins alias Hutchinson of Weston under Lizard; Edward Ratcliffe alias Butterworth of Park Yate, Ipstones; John Fenton of Shelton. Worcestershire: Thomas Gibson of Worcester; Thomas Wagg alias Wagstaffe of Doverdale; John Truelove of Worcester; Edward Daunce of Underhill; Matthew Cooper of Worcester; John Ladd of Bishopstraw (Wiltshire). (PRO: C66/3405/3).

22 July. The following apprenticed in Liverpool to [James] Gordon [to serve in Virginia or Maryland]: Richard Evans of Caernarvon, 4 years; Elkana Telson, 7 years; William Roberts of Denbighshire, 4 years. (LTB).

27 July. Shipper by the *George*, Mr. George Phippard, bound from Poole for Virginia: William Phippard. (PRO: E190/892/7).

27 July. Shipper by the *Phoenix* of London, Mr. John Jane, bound from Plymouth for Virginia: said John Jane. (PRO: E190/1058/2).

27 July. The following apprenticed in Liverpool to serve John Thomas [in Virginia or Maryland]: Thomas Lloyd of Cardiganshire, 4 years; Watkin Prior of Cardigan, 4 years; John Harrison of Babbington, [Nottinghamshire], 8 years; William Chancellor of Harbro(?), Yorkshire, 7 years; Rowland Jones of Ruthin, [Wales], 5 years; Ellin Cook of London, spinster, 5 years; Margaret Blake, daughter of John B. of London, 4 years; John Bird of Preston, Oxfordshire (*sic*), 4 years. (LTB).

29 July. The following apprenticed in Liverpool [to serve in Virginia or Maryland]: Gaynold Thomas of Caernarvon to [Edward] Tarleton, 4 years; Thomas Row of Flintshire, tailor, to [James] Gordon, 4 years. (LTB).

30 July. The following apprenticed in Liverpool: Mary Jones, daughter of John J. of Wrexham, Denbighshire, to John Thomas, 4 years [Virginia or Maryland]. (LTB).

July. Probate of will of Rigoult Bew of Virginia, who died in St. Giles Cripplegate, London, bachelor. (AW).

July. Probate of will of David Edwards of Boston, New England. (AW).

July. Administration of William Steward of Deptford, Kent, who died on H.M. ship *Deptford* in Boston, New England. (AW).

July. Limited administration of Samuel Pond of Virginia. (AW).

2 August. Shipper by the *Salem* Galley, Mr. Thomas Walters, bound from Dartmouth for New England: George Dottin. (PRO: E190/972/12).

2 August. Shipper by the *Charles* of Guernsey, Mr. John Vincent, bound from Dartmouth for New England: George Dottin. (PRO: E190/972/12).

4-9 August. The following apprenticed in Liverpool to John Thomas [to serve in Virginia or Maryland]: Robert Jones of Denbighshire, 4 years; Edward Jones of Wrexham, [Wales], 7 years; Thomas Dukes of Tarvin, Cheshire, 7 years; Mary Cowly, 4 years; Robert Faux of Denbighshire, 4 years. (LTB).

5 August. Shipper by the *Hopewell* of Plymouth, Mr. Robert Hobbs, bound from Plymouth for Virginia: James Bligh & Co. (PRO: E190/1058/2).

13 August. The following apprenticed in Liverpool to Henry Brown to serve 4 years in Virginia or Maryland: Joseph Troughweare of Crosby, Cumberland, tailor; William Kitchin of Erton(?), Cumberland, tailor. (LTB).

16 August. The following apprenticed in Liverpool: Elizabeth Jones of Denbighshire to John Thomas, 5 years [Virginia or Maryland]. (LTB).

16 August. Shipper by the *Pearl* of Bideford, Mr. Samuell Ellis, bound from Bideford for Virginia: Thomas Smith. (PRO: E190/972/8).

17 August. The following apprenticed in Liverpool: John Stedman of Padiham, Lancashire, to Edward Tarleton, 4 years Virginia; Rowland Thomas of Anglesey, tailor, to John Thomas, 5 years [Virginia or Maryland]; Robert Hughes of Conway, [Wales], to the same, 4 years; Richard Woods of Adlington [?Aldingham], Lancashire, to the same, 7 years; William Lawson of Lievsay (*sic*), Lancashire, to the same, 7 years. (LTB).

20 August. Governor Nicholson of Maryland to the Council of Trade and Plantations. When I was in Virginia I heard it was the common practice to take up 50 acres for every person imported and rights were bought from the Clerk of the Secretary. Sometimes the Clerk purchased rights from those who were really imported, sometimes he would write down names of his own invention, and sometimes those who brought names to be registered would do so too. Several cheats passed undiscovered and the names of those who were really imported were used several times. (CSPC).

21 August. Shipper by the *John* of Topsham, Mr. George Colsworthy, bound from Exeter for Virginia: Richard Lowbridge. (PRO: E190/972/9).

23 August. The following apprenticed in Liverpool to John Thomas to serve four years [in Virginia or Maryland]: John Prescott. (LTB).

24 August. The following apprenticed in Liverpool to John Thomas to serve [in Virginia or Maryland]: John Pritchett of Wrexham, [Wales], 4 years; Thomas Powell of Wrexham, 7 years; Hugh Jones of Wrexham, 7 years; Hugh Lealand of Westhoughton, [Lancashire], 7 years; Ann Blyth of York, spinster, 4 years. (LTB).

27 August. The following apprenticed in Liverpool: Joseph Reyburne of Waser [?Walsall], Staffordshire, shoemaker, to Mr. Bryan Blundell, 5 years Virginia. (LTB).

28 August. Shipper by the *Loyalty* of Belfast, Mr. William Pringle, bound from Liverpool for Virginia: Henry Chades. (PRO: E190/1359/11).

29 August. The following apprenticed in Liverpool: Thomas Dunbalin, son of William D., to [Edward] Tarleton, 6 years [Virginia or Maryland]; John Foster of [?Durham] Bishopric to the same, 4 years; John Kirk to the same, 4 years; John Jones of Wrexham, [Wales], Hannah his wife and a child, 4 years. (LTB).

30 August. The following apprenticed in Liverpool: Gryffith Thomas, labourer, to Edward Tarleton, 4 years [Virginia or Maryland]; Elizabeth Markley of Latham (*sic*) to the same, 5 years. (LTB).

30 August-20 September. Shippers by the English-built *Elizabeth*, Mr. William Harris, bound from Exeter for Virginia: John Hornebrook, William Drake, Dorothy Carpenter, Thomas Whitehaire. (PRO: E190/972/9).

31 August. The following apprenticed in Liverpool to John Thomas [to serve in Virginia or Maryland]: Jonas Davis of Cork, [Ireland], 4 years; Richard Owen of Flintshire, 4 years; Henry Bond, son of James B. of Garstang, [Lancashire], 7 years (LTB).

?August. The following apprenticed in Liverpool to Mr. Lewis Jenkins [?for Virginia or Maryland]: Richard Alcock of Bolton, [Lancashire], tailor, 5 years; John Houseman of Bolton, tailor, 5 years; Robert Chalis of Castleton, Derbyshire, 4 years; John Bramwale of Preston, [Lancashire], 4 years; William Rycroft of Preston, 4 years. (LTB).

August. Administration of George Stanton of Virginia. (AW).

August. Probate of will of Adam Kennedy of Antigua, intending for New York. (AW).

August. Probate of will of Thomas Baker of the ship *Elizabeth*, who died in Virginia. (AW).

August. Probate of will of Edward Greene of Bristol, who died in Virginia. (AW).

1-20 September. Shippers by the *Ann*, Mr. John Venard, bound from Exeter for Virginia: John Hornbroke, Dorothy Carpenter. (PRO: E190/972/9).

2 September. The following apprenticed in Liverpool to John Thomas [to serve in Virginia or Maryland]: Thomas Ellis of Daliraven(?), Wales, 7 years; Thomas Ellis of Dalmen (*sic*), Wales, 4 years. (LTB).

3-16 September. Shippers by the *Lamb* of Liverpool, Mr. John Thomas, bound from Liverpool for Virginia: Peter Atherton, James King, Richard Bridge, John Cleveland, John Pemberton. (PRO: E190/1359/11).

5 September. The following apprenticed in Liverpool to Mr. Porter [to serve in Virginia or Maryland]: Elizabeth King, daughter of Abraham K. of Dublin, [Ireland], 4 years; Charity Barlor of Kilkenny, [Ireland], 5 years. (LTB).

5 September-9 December. The following apprenticed in Liverpool to go to Virginia by the *Eleanor* of Liverpool, Mr. Nicholas Reynolds: Charles Barber of Kilkenny, [Ireland], 5 years; Elizabeth King of Dublin, [Ireland], 4 years; Martha Jackson, 4 years (but remained); John Pennant of Flintshire, 7 years; Mary Terpin of Lytham in Fyle, [Lancashire], 5 years; John Posthous of Harding, Wales, 5 years; Ralph Thomas of Bolton, Lancashire, (falsified his name as Ralph Haliwale), 4 years; Diana Johnson of Prestbury, Cheshire, 4 years; Margaret Bantum of Coppul, Lancashire, 4 years; Mary Smallwood of Barthomley, Cheshire, 4 years; Peter Shellom of Prestbury, Cheshire, 7 years; Thomas Upton of Prestbury, 4 years; John Upton of Prestbury, 5 years; Elizabeth Upton of Prestbury, 4 years; Martha Jackson of Prestbury, 5 years; Susanna Pound of Devon, widow, 4 years; John Haggarty of Ireland, 4 years; William Beck of Underbarrow, Westmorland, 4 years; Robert Lawson of Burnley, Lancashire, 4 years; Richard Holmes of Preston, Lancashire, 4 years; Peter Jones of Anglesey, 4 years; Hugh Owen of Anglesey, 4 years; William Owen of Anglesey, 4 years; James Morden of Bristol, 7 years; Elizabeth Wilson of Carleton, Lancashire, 4 years; John Hartopp of Coventry, [Warwickshire], 4 years; John Porter of Wimbersley, Cheshire, 4 years; James Barbour, apprentice of John Tyrer, 7 years; Katherine Ritchley of Ayr, Scotland; William Blundell of Cheadle Hulme, Cheshire, 5 years; Ralph Relshaw of Lendy [?Lund], Yorkshire, 7 years. (LTB).

6 September. Shipper by the *Samuell* of Bideford, Mr. Thomas Cantrell, bound from Bideford for Virginia: Thomas Smith. (PRO: E190/972/8).

7 September. The following bound in Liverpool to serve Henry Browne for four years [in Virginia or Maryland]: John Threlfell of Preston, [Lancashire], gardener; John Dobson of Bolton, Lancashire; Ralph Kettle of Warmingham, Cheshire; Henry Bell of Carlisle, [Cumberland]; James Boudler of Oswestry, Shropshire. (LTB).

7-22 September. Shippers by the *Andrew & Samuel* of Boston, Mr. William Rouse, bound from Dartmouth for New England: George Dottin. (PRO: E190/972/12).

9 September. Shipper by the *James & Elizabeth* of Weymouth, Mr. John Swetnam, bound from Weymouth for Scotland and Virginia: David Arbuthnot. (PRO: E190/892/2).

10 September. The following apprenticed in Liverpool to serve John Thomas for four years [in Virginia or Maryland]: John Owen; Edward Jones. (LTB).

10 September. Shipper by the *Henrietta* of Bideford, Mr. William Browne, bound from Bideford for Maryland: John Davie. (PRO: E190/972/8).

10 September. Shipper by the *John* of Guernsey, Mr. John Stephens, bound from Dartmouth for New England: Thomas Plumtree. (PRO: E190/972/12).

13 September. The following apprenticed in Liverpool to serve Henry Browne for four years [in Virginia or Maryland]: Robert Tongue. (LTB).

14 September. The following apprenticed in Liverpool [to serve in Virginia or Maryland]: Elizabeth Wilson of Kirkham, [Lancashire], to Edward Tarleton, 4 years; Edward Steele of Westtirlie [?Westerleigh, Gloucestershire], 4 years; John Ducker of Tarvin, [Cheshire], tailor, to the same, 4 years; Richard Darrell of Chester to the same, 4 years; Elizabeth Barlow of Knutsford, [Cheshire], to the same, 4 years; Hannah Vaughan of Chester to the same, 4 years. (LTB).

15 September. The following apprenticed in Liverpool to Richard Bridge: Robert Rallester of Leeds, [Yorkshire], 4 years [Virginia]. (LTB).

15 September. Shipper by the *George* of Plymouth, Mr. Richard Dowling, bound from Plymouth for Virginia: George Lapthorne. (PRO: E190/1058/2).

15-20 September. The following apprenticed in Liverpool to serve Henry Browne in Virginia: Charles Ellis of Macclesfield, [Cheshire], 5 years; Edward Thornicroft of Sutton, Cheshire, 5 years; John Davies of Denbighshire, grocer, 4 years; Humphrey Howell of Merioneth, 4 years; John Wynn of Denbighshire, 5 years; Thomas Marland of Ashton under Lyne, 7 years; John Carneagee of Aberdeen, Scotland, 4 years; John Walker of Ashton under Lyne, [Lancashire], 5 years; Thomas Walker of the same, 7 years; John Beecham of Chester, 4 years. And the following apprenticed to Edward Tarleton to serve in Virginia: James Jameson of Newcastle [?Northumberland], 4 years; Robert Pollet, son of Robert P. of Bolton, [Lancashire], deceased, 9 years; John Nichols, 4 years; Samuell Hemming, 4 years. (LTB).

15-20 September. Shippers by the *Oak* of Liverpool, Mr. Edward Tarleton, bound from Liverpool for Virginia: Thomas Johnson, Robert Carter. (PRO: E190/1359/11).

15-30 September. Shippers by the *Content* of Plymouth, Mr. Daniell Williams, bound from Plymouth for Virginia: James Bligh & Co., Elizabeth Banks. (PRO: E190/1058/2).

15 September-22 November. Shippers by the *Success*, Mr. Robert Lyle, bound from Exeter for Virginia: John Hornbroke, Roger Prowse. (PRO: E190/972/9).

16-30 September. Shipper by the *Seaflower* of New England, Mr. John Jenkins, bound from Newcastle for New England: William Johnson. (PRO: E190/206/1).

17-20 September. The following apprenticed in Liverpool to serve John Neild of Pennsylvania for five years: Edward Hardman; Richard Newell. (LTB).

18 September-14 January 1699. Depositions in London re the New York ship *Frederick*, Mr. Humphrey Parking, captured by the Dutch in 1698 and taken to Hamburg. Deponents include: Humphrey Parking, mariner aged 30, resident in New York for eight years but born at Empicombe, Devon; Richard S. Sampson, fisherman aged 23, resident of Piscataway, New England, for 16 years but born at Stonehouse, Devon; John Lawrence, sailor aged 23, born and resident in Long Island, New York; Philip French, merchant aged 31, resident in New York for 12 years but born at the Hermitage, Wapping, Middlesex; and John Narramore, shipwright aged 21, born and resident in Boston, New England. (EA).

20-27 September. The following apprenticed in Liverpool to John Thomas [to serve in Virginia or Maryland]: John Price of Merioneth, surgeon, 4 years; Richard Owen of Caernarvonshire, 4 years. (LTB).

22 September. The following apprenticed in Liverpool: Thomas Wilding of Liverpool [*but see below where he is described as of Lichfield*] to William Bushell, 5 years Virginia. (LTB).

24 September. Shipper by the *Integrity* of Bideford, Mr. Aaron Whitton, bound from Bideford for Maryland: Peter Wellington. (PRO: E190/972/8).

24 September-13 October. Shippers by the *Mulberry* bound from Liverpool for Virginia: Walter Bryce, James Clarke, John Needle, Richard Scarborough. (PRO: E190/1359/11).

26 September-4 October. Shippers by the *Blessing* of Boston, Mr. John Phillips, bound from Plymouth for Boston, New England: John Rogers, Andrew Stuckey. (PRO: E190/1058/2).

27-28 September. The following apprenticed in Liverpool: John Lamb of Liverpool to Ezekiell Parr, 4 years [Virginia]; Mary Floyd of Shrewsbury, Shropshire, to the same, 5 years; John Ricketts of Lavanshie [?Llavaches], Wales, to same, 4 years; Jonathan Clarke of Little Messin [?Little Marsden], Lancashire, to Henry Browne, 7 years [Virginia]; Mary Terpin of Lytham, [Lancashire], to William Porter, 5 years [Virginia]; Jane Hide of Manchester, [Lancashire], spinster, to Nicholas Smith, 5 years [Virginia]. (LTB).

27 September-13 October. Shippers by the *Virginia Merchant* of Plymouth, Mr. William Ginnis, bound from Plymouth for Virginia: John Rogers, George Boyce. (PRO: E190/1058/2).

27 September-5 December. Shippers by the *Mary & Isabella*, Mr. Henry Rogers, bound from Exeter for Virginia: John Hornbroke, Richard Veale(?), Anthony Vicary, John Southcome, John Pike. (PRO: E190/972/9).

30 September. The following apprenticed in Liverpool: Matthew Moreton of Prestbury, Cheshire, to Henry Browne, 4 years [Virginia]. (LTB).

September. Probate of will of John Eades of New England. (AW).

September. Probate of will of Thomas Plowden of Lasham, Hampshire, who had lands in Virginia. (AW).

September. Probate of will of Benjamin Williams of Stoke by Guildford, Surrey, whose cousins, Samuel, Thomas and Benjamin Williams, and Elizabeth Bird, were in New England. (AW).

September. Administration of Thomas Barker of Stepney, Middlesex, who died in Maryland. (AW).

3 October. Shipper by the *Factor* of Bideford, Mr. John Yeo, bound from Bideford for Maryland: John Smith. (PRO: E190/972/8).

3-10 October. Shippers by the *Unity* of Lyme, Mr. Robert Colbard, bound from Lyme for Virginia: John Burridge, Robert Fowler, Samuell Courtnay, Simon Bayly. (PRO: E190/892/5).

4-11 October. Shippers by the *Employment* of Lancaster, Mr. James Mires, bound from Lancaster for Virginia: Joseph Lawson, Robert Lawson. (PRO: E190/1359/16).

5 October. The following apprenticed in Liverpool: Robert Vaughan, son of Thomas V. [?of Shropshire] to Andrew Leed, 5 years [?Virginia]. (LTB).

7 October-23 November. The following apprenticed in Liverpool to Mr. John Hughes to go to Virginia by the *Submission* of Liverpool, Mr. Thomas Seacome: William Relict of Gatlemellit (*sic*), Flint, 4 years; John Young of Wandsworth, Surrey, 4 years; William Bradshaw of Lond Green, Cheshire, 4 years; John Adams of Shotton, Flint, 4 years; John Thompson of Coleraine, Ireland, 4 years; Henry Woods of Chester, 4 years; Mary Standish of Stafford, spinster, 4 years; Mary Faulkner of Manchester, [Lancashire], spinster, 4 years; Martha Newton of Macclesfield, [Cheshire], 4 years; Joan Witter of Taporley, Cheshire, 4 years; Philip Finn of Harding, Wales, 4 years; John Finn of Harding, 6 years; Richard Finn of Harding, 4 years; Robert Middleton of Oaks, Derbyshire, 4 years; Ellin Barlow of Macclesfield, Cheshire, 4 years; Thomas Williams of Caernarvon, Wales, 5 years; Francis Glanford of Buckinghamshire, 4 years; Andrew Hamilton of Edinburgh, [Scotland], 4 years; William Pilkington of Brindle, [Lancashire], 5 years. And the following servants of Mr. John Marsden, merchant: Paul Riglie of Hey, Lancashire, 7 years; Jeremiah Jones of Bury, [Lancashire], 7 years; David Bevis of Burslem, Staffordshire, 7 years; John Newton of Bolton, [Lancashire], 7 years; William

Fartley of Orrell near Wigan, [Lancashire], husbandman, 4 years; John Winstanley of Orrell, husbandman, 4 years; Isaac Firth of Bradford, Yorkshire, 5 years; Joseph Parr of Little Hulton, Lancashire, 5 years. (LTB).

11-13 October. Shippers by the *Loyalty*, Mr. Henry Brown, bound from Liverpool for Virginia: Richard Houghton, Silvanus Richmond. (PRO: E190/1359/11).

12-19 October. Shippers by the *Amity*, Mr. Lewis Jenkins, bound from Liverpool for Virginia: John Molyneux, William Bassnett. (PRO: E190/1359/11).

13 October. The following apprenticed in Liverpool to serve Nicholas Smith for five years in Virginia or Maryland: William Hudson; Miles Grimshaw; Mary Boardman. (LTB).

13 October. Shipper by the *William & Mary*, Mr. Thomas Gentle, bound from Poole for Virginia: William Phippard. (PRO: E190/892/7).

14 October. Shipper by the *Adventure* of Bideford, Mr. Thomas Bleek, bound from Bideford for Maryland: John Atkin. (PRO: E190/972/8).

14 October. Shipper by the *Exchange* of Bideford, Mr. Roger More, bound from Bideford for Maryland: Thomas Power. (PRO: E190/972/8).

14 October. Shipper by the *Tryall* of Northam, Mr. Thomas Gribble, bound from Bideford for Maryland: said Thomas Gribble. (PRO: E190/972/8).

15-17 October. Shippers by the *James* of Plymouth bound from Plymouth for Virginia: Robert Edgcombe, James Bligh & Co., James Cock. (PRO: E190/1058/2).

17 October. The following apprenticed in Liverpool: Thomas Higham of Warrington, [Lancashire], to Mr. Scarborough, 4 years [?Virginia]. (LTB).

17 October. Shipper by the *Content* of Lyme, Mr. Isaac Davy, bound from Lyme for Virginia: Nathan Gundry. (PRO: E190/892/5).

19 October. The following apprenticed in Liverpool to go to Virginia by the *Loyalty*, Mr. Henry Browne: Ralph Kettle of Warmingham, Cheshire, 4 years; Robert Tongue of Farnworth near Manchester, [Lancashire], 4 years; John Threlfell of Preston, gardener, 4 years; Charles Ellis of Macclesfield, 5 years; Alexander Sinkler of Glasgow, [Scotland], 4 years; John Wright of Middlesex, 4 years; William Taylor of Scarbrick [Scarborough], [Yorkshire], 8 years; James Streete, 10 years; Thomas Walker of Ashton under Lyne, 7 years; John Walker of the same, 5 years; David Taylor of Mottram, Cheshire, 8 years; Charles Taylor of Mottram, 7 years; John Beecham of Cheshire, 4 years; George Low of Gawsworth, Cheshire, 10 years; George Brasfield, 11 years; John Carneagee of Aberdeen, Scotland, 4 years; John Harrison of Ashton under Lyne, 7 years; Robert Bower of Macclesfield, Cheshire, 7 years; James Bouldler of Augettree [?Oswestry], Shropshire, 4 years; John Dobson of Bolton, Lancashire, 4 years; Edward Thornicroft of Sutton, Cheshire, 5 years;

Thomas Marland of Ashton under Lyne, 7 years; Humphrey Howell of Merioneth, 4 years; John Davies of Denbighshire, grocer, 4 years; Edward Perry of Denbighshire, 4 years; Thomas Upton of Prestbury, Cheshire, 10 years; John Wynn of Ruthin, Denbighshire, 5 years; Jonathan Clark of Little Messin, Lancashire, 7 years; Nathaniel Taylor of Mottram, Cheshire, 9 years; Thomas Taylor of Mottram, 11 years; Mathew Moreton of Prestbury, Cheshire, 4 years; Joseph Troughweare of Crosby, Cumberland, 4 years; William Kitchen of Erton, Cumberland, tailor, 4 years; Joyce Cooper of Caernarvonshire, 4 years; Henry Bell of Carlisle, 4 years; Thomas Wilding of Lichfield, [Staffordshire], (apprentice of William Bushell, mate of the *Loyalty*), 5 years; James Barton, apprentice of James Hawkshaw, to serve in Montserrat for four years. (LTB).

21-24 October. Shipper by the *Concord*, Mr. John Walls, bound from Liverpool for Virginia: Henry Parr. (PRO: E190/1359/11).

22 October. Shipper by the *Annapolis* of Bideford, Mr. Thomas Marshall, bound from Bideford for Maryland: George Buck. (PRO: E190/972/8).

22-29 October. Shippers by the *Mary Rose* of Bideford, Mr. Scipio Row, bound from Bideford for Virginia: John Davie, Benjamin Hussie, Thomas Jeffery. (PRO: E190/972/8).

23 October-13 December. The following apprenticed in Liverpool to go to Virginia by the *Society* of Liverpool, Mr. Jonathan Livesley: Andrew Martin of Huttale [?Huttock], Lancashire, 5 years; John Ramsbottem of Lancashire, 5 years; John Brown of Cheadle, Cheshire, 5 years; Isaac Taylor of Newton, Lancashire, 5 years; Elizabeth Williams of Clutton, Cheshire, 8 years; George Wisson of Inglewhite, Lancashire, 5 years; Mary Clowd of Brereton, Cheshire, 6 years; Jane Banks of Chorley, Lancashire, 6 years; John Taylor of Coulden [?Colton], Lancashire, 5 years; Robert Noblett of Aston Bank, Lancashire [?Aston Blank, Gloucestershire], 6 years; Ayley Blackwell of Brereton, Cheshire, 6 years; John Briggs of Waddington, Yorkshire [?Lancashire], 5 years. (LTB).

24 October. Shippers by the *Lyon*, Mr. John Crompton, bound from Liverpool for Virginia: William Clayton, John Yeoman. (PRO: E190/1359/11).

24 October-31 December. The following apprenticed in Liverpool to go to Virginia by the *St. John the Baptist*, Mr. Nicholas French: John Thompson of Cumberland, 7 years; John Rudd of Liverpool, webster, 4 years; Peter Winstanley of Orrell, [Lancashire], 4 years; Abraham Rudd of Rochdale, [Lancashire], clothier, 4 years; John Gilburt of Holtbridge [?Heybridge], Essex, 4 years; John Morgan of Apsom [?Epsom, Surrey], 4 years; John Fisher of Holmes Chapel, [Cheshire], 4 years; Samuell Williams of Wrexham, [Denbighshire], 10 years; Thomas Williams of Wrexham, 10 years; William Collins of Bristol, 4 years; Robert Lewis of Denbighshire, 4 years; John Redding of Canterbury, [Kent], 4 years; Daniell Child of Whitechapel,

[Lancashire], 4 years; Richard Lewis of Branford [?Bramford, Suffolk, or Bransford, Worcestershire], 4 years; Robert Finch of Wrexham, 10 years; Elizabeth Holding of Lancashire, spinster, 4 years; Caelia Woods of Bury, Lancashire, 6 years; Elizabeth Hunt of Wrexham, 4 years; Ruth Davies of Wrexham, spinster, 4 years; Henry Woods of Derry, [Ireland], 4 years; Alexander Challenor of Macclesfield, [Cheshire], 4 years; Ann Evans of Wrexham, 4 years; Edward Clark of Uttoxeter, Staffordshire, 4 years; Edward Williams of Wrexham, 4 years; John Taylor of Wellington, Shropshire, 4 years; John Cheetum of Oldham, Lancashire, 4 years; James Pye of Lydgate, Lancashire, 4 years; Margaret Rendle of Pilling, [Lancashire], apprentice of John Fox, mate of the ship, 7 years; Newman Steward of Norfolk, 4 years; William Hodgkins, apprentice of Mr. Conly of Blockley, Worcestershire, 4 years. (LTB).

25 October 1689. The following apprentices of Ezechiel Parr of Liverpool to go to Virginia by the *Concord*, Mr. John Walls: Jane Johnson of Wigan, [Lancashire], spinster, 4 years; Isaac Carpenter, 4 years; John Prescot of Wigan, tailor, 4 years; Roger Taylor of Abram, Lancashire, husbandman, 4 years; John Leyland of Abram, weaver, 4 years; Oliver Whalley alias Wood, 7 years; Francis Catterall of Wigan, 4 years; Alice Catterall of Wigan, 4 years; Elizabeth Ashton of Wigan, spinster, 4 years; Sarah Heyes, 4 years; William Scott of Wigan, 7 years; John Gasway, 4 years; William Fox, 4 years; James Exx, 4 years; James Butterworth, weaver, 4 years; Mary Moss, 4 years; Joshua Spencer of Upholland, [Lancashire], 7 years; Mary Gibbs of Wigan, 4 years; John Wood, 4 years; Alice Heaton, 4 years; Richard Heaton, 4 years; Edward Heaton, 4 years; Elizabeth Heaton, 4 years; Margaret Kearfoote of Wigan, spinster, 4 years. All the above bound at Wigan. Also the following: Charles Wilkinson of Burnley, Lancashire, 7 years; Elizabeth Rollins of Raby, Cheshire, 4 years; Edward Wilson of Tarleton, Lancashire, 5 years; Joseph Stanthrop of Yorkshire, tanner, 4 years; Ann Eccles of Preston, [Lancashire], 4 years; Charles Coop of Bolton, [Lancashire], tailor, 4 years; James Gambell on Nantwich, [Cheshire], 4 years; Thomas Clayton of Preston, 7 years; Martha Lloyd of Shrewsbury, Shropshire, 5 years; James Boardman of Bolton, butcher, 4 years; Thomas Turner of Warrington, [Lancashire], 4 years; Hester Ford of Wigan, spinster, 4 years; Daniel Lyon of Rainford, [Lancashire], blacksmith, 4 years; Thursden Mather of Hindley, Lancashire, 4 years; James Dangerfield of Rappahannock River, Virginia, 4 years; Ellen Peatiason of Fylde, Lancashire, 4 years; John Lamb of Liverpool, 4 years; John Ricketts, joiner, 4 years; Elizabeth Crompton of Bury, Lancashire, 5 years; William Thomas of Caernarvonshire, 4 years; John Johnson of Ipstones, Staffordshire, shoemaker, 4 years; Edward Houghton of Macclesfield, [Cheshire], 4 years. (LTB).

26 October. Shipper by the *George* of Plymouth, Mr. Thomas Blake, bound from Plymouth for Virginia: Richard Burlace. (PRO: E190/1058/2).

27 October. Richard Crompton, aged 15, sent from Christ's Hospital to his mother Anne Crompton and Benjamin Woolley, merchant in Mincing Lane, to serve Major Beverley of Gloucester Co., Virginia. (CH).

27-29 October. Shipper by the *John* of Bideford, Mr. Thomas Leach, bound from Bideford for Maryland: John Smith. (PRO: E190/972/8).

29 October. Shipper by the *Fidelity* of Jersey, Mr. John Legent, bound from Dartmouth for Virginia: George Dottin. (PRO: E190/972/9).

29 October-9 November. Shippers by the *John & Sarah*, Mr. John Dumersq, bound from Dartmouth for Virginia: George Dottin, George Bennett. (PRO: E190/972/9).

October. Administration of James Scott of Bristol, who died in Virginia. (AW).

October. Probate of will of Dr. Thomas Hobbs of St. Clement Danes, Middlesex, whose sister, Elizabeth, was wife of Francis Weekes in Middlesex County, Virginia. (AW).

October. Administration of Thomas Hayward of Rappahannock River, Virginia, who died at sea on the ship *William and Mary*. (AW).

October. Administration of George Butler of Maryland. (AW).

October. Limited probate of will of Owen Jones of H.M. ship *Richmond*, who died in New York. (AW).

October. Administration of John Ive of Boston, New England. (AW).

October. Administration of John Hayward of Rappahannock River, Virginia, bachelor. (AW).

4 November-23 December. The following apprenticed in Liverpool to go to Virginia by the *Ann & Sarah*, Mr. John Marshall: John Bruin of Chester, 4 years; Michael Godwin of Winchester, [Hampshire], 4 years; John Shaw, son of John S. of Congleton, Cheshire, 7 years; Thomas Jennison, son of Thomas J. of Lunt(?), Lancashire, deceased, 7 years; John Williams, son of John W. of Wybunbury, Cheshire, 5 years; Walter Crampton, son of William C. of Whittington, Shropshire, 7 years; Herbert Patterson, son of Thomas P. of Chester, chapman, deceased, 7 years; Thomas Hawkshaw, son of George H. of Dunham, Cheshire, 5 years; John Hoague of Cloud, Cheshire, 9 years; Wharton Fallowfield of Penrith, Cumberland, 4 years; William Wood of Tarvin, Cheshire, 5 years; John Lloyd of Weppen [?Wepre], Flint, 8 years; John Lyon of Huntspill, Somerset, 4 years; John Baker of Astbury, Cheshire, 5 years; John Shaw of Millhouse, Lancashire [?Cheshire], 4 years; William Heaton of Heaton, Lancashire, 4 years; Job Howard of Salford, Lancashire, 5 years; Ann Dumbile of Middlewich, Cheshire, 4 years; Sarah Pinkston of Middlewich, 4 years; John Rothell of Tottington, Lancashire, 5 years; Samuell McCreky of Carlisle, Cumberland, 5 years; Elizabeth Valentine of Liverpool, 6 years; Daniell Walker of Poulton-le-Sands, Lancashire, 4 years; Joseph Brosents of Burnley, Lancashire, 4 years; Adam Mottershed of Macclesfield, Cheshire, 4 years; John Milner of Holbrook, Yorkshire, 5 years. (LTB).

7-24 November. Shippers by the *Ellenor*, Mr. Nicholas Reynolds, bound from Liverpool for Virginia: William Porter, James McCleire, Thomas Tench. (PRO: E190/1359/11).

8 November. Shipper by the *Adventure*, Mr. William Middleton, bound from Liverpool for Virginia: William Clayton. (PRO: E190/1359/11).

10-25 November. Shippers by the *Submission*, Mr. Thomas Seacome, bound from Liverpool for Virginia: John Marsden, Thomas Tyrer for Gilbert Eden. (PRO: E190/1359/11).

12-16 November. Shippers by the *Society*, Mr. Jonathan Livesley, bound from Liverpool for Virginia: John Pemberton, John Brown, John Stanton, Richard Houghton. (PRO: E190/1359/11).

14 November. Shipper by the *John* of Topsham, Mr. George Colsworthy, bound from Exeter for Virginia: John Hornbroke. (PRO: E190/972/9).

14 November. Bartholomew Tatham, aged 14, sent from Christ's Hospital to his aunt Mary Tatham to serve Philip French of New York City, merchant. (CH).

15-17 November. The following apprenticed in Liverpool to go to Virginia by the *Lamb* of Dublin, Mr. William Burnsides: Judith Butterworth of Middleston, Lancashire, 5 years; Sarah Celliam of Manchester, [Lancashire], 5 years; Ann Sickley of Cheadle, Cheshire, 5 years; Martha Peak of Brogden, Lancashire, 7 years; Ann King of Clitheroe, [Lancashire], 5 years; Matthew Newall of Minshull, Cheshire, 7 years; William Sheapheard of Manchester, 7 years; Jonathan Preestley of Snelland, Yorkshire [?Lincolnshire], 7 years; William Guy of Dukinfield, Cheshire [?Lancashire], 5 years; John Penberry of Manchester, 7 years; Robert Leafield of Lancaster, 5 years; Abigail Burnett of Manchester, 5 years. (LTB).

17 November-9 December. Shippers by the *John Baptist*, Mr. Nicholas French, bound from Liverpool for Virginia: Thomas Hind, John McCollough, Silvanus Richmond by Thomas Coore, Isaac Martin. (PRO: E190/1359/11).

21-25 November. Shipper by the *Barbados Merchant*, Mr. William Fletcher, bound from Liverpool for Virginia: Cuthbert Sharples. (PRO: E190/1359/11).

23 November-12 December. The following apprenticed in Liverpool to go to Virginia by the *Barbados Merchant*, Mr. Cuthbert Sharples: Josiah Mayers of Macclesfield, Cheshire, 4 years; Jane Swindle of Maxfield [*prob.* Macclesfield, Cheshire], apprentice of Alderman Houghton, 5 years; Thomas Yates of Whiston, [Lancashire], 5 years; Aaron Summers of St. Helen's, Lancashire, 5 years; William Davies of Mostyn, Flintshire, 5 years; John France of Huddersfield, Yorkshire, 4 years; Elizabeth Dickin of Denbigh, 4 years; Mary Holme of Bolton, [Lancashire], 4 years; Mary Case of Bolton, 4 years; Joyce Cooper of Caernarvonshire, 4 years; Sarah Gibbons of Macclesfield, [Cheshire], 4 years; Benjamin Royal of Macclesfield, 7 years; Samuel Dagnell of St. Helen's, Lancashire, 5 years; William Cragge of

Denton, Yorkshire, 5 years; Robert Ward of Bolton, Lancashire, 6 years. (LTB).

24 November. Shipper by the *Lamb* of Dublin, Mr. William Bornside, bound from Liverpool for Virginia: Andrew Moore. (PRO: E190/1359/11).

November. Administration of Catherine Everigin of Virginia, spinster. (AW).

November. Administration of Robert Barrett of Christ Church, Surrey, who died in Virginia. (AW).

November. Limited probate of will of George Robotham of Talbot County, Maryland. (AW).

1-31 December. Shippers by the *Augustin* of Liverpool, Mr. Thomas Preeson, bound from Liverpool for Virginia: William Preeson, William Oliver, Robert Middleton, John Curtis. (PRO: E190/1359/11, 1360/17).

2-15 December. The following apprenticed in Liverpool to go to Virginia by the *Globe*, Mr. Simpson: John Strachine of Scotland, 4 years; Alexander Marsh of Aughton, Lancashire, 8 years; Homer Rodan of Scotland, apprentice of Mr. Neilson, 4 years; James Douglas of Scotland, apprentice of Mr. Neilson, 4 years; Peter Holland of Middlewich, [Cheshire], 6 years; James Corry of Scotland, 4 years. (LTB).

8 December. The following apprenticed in Liverpool: Nathaniel Fogg to Mr. Abraham Dyson, 4 years [Virginia]. (LTB).

8-31 December. Shippers by the *Globe* of Liverpool, Mr. George Simpson, bound from Liverpool for Virginia: Abraham Dyson, William Neilson, Thomas Hind. (PRO: E190/1359/11, 1360/17).

10 December. Newgate prisoners reprieved to be transported to Barbados or Jamaica. London: Charles Harding; David Owen; Thomas Davice; William Ingram; Thomas Niccolls; William Riggs; John Shackford; John Arnold; William Howell; Emanuel Hambleton; Samuel Apps; Robert Ingram; Jane Browne; John Davenport; Lawrence Ford; John Clarke; Caleb Millett; William Thompson. Middlesex: Thomas Pherley alias Blyth of St. Giles in the Fields; Edward Wike alias Deacombe of St. Margaret Westminster; William Hitchcock alias Bristol Jack of the same; Thomas Doddy alias Dodd of St. Anne Westminster; William Stone of the same; William Richardson of St. James Westminster; William Hayes of the same; John Penny of St. Margaret Westminster; John Norcott of St. Andrew Holborn; Elizabeth Barraclough alias Grant alias Reeves of the same, spinster; Phillip Carew of Twickenham; Thomas Payne of the same; William Skillington of Edgware; Isaac Bridges of Shadwell; James Niblett of the same; Elizabeth Hawkins of the same, widow; William Dodson of Stepney; Thomas Wells of the same; Charles Gibson of the same; Thomas Smith of St. Pancras; John Williams of the same; William Beasley of St. Martin in the Fields; Francis Exon alias Eames of the same; Richard Humphreys of the same; Edward Short the same; Elizabeth Lowe, wife of Francis Lowe of the same; John Adsitt alias Davenport of the same; Daniel Crookes of the same; David Martinshrider of the same; Simon Hollis of the same; John Ketling of the same; John Thomas of St. Clement Danes; William Jackson of the same; John Murrey of the same; William Harris of the same; John Waters of Isleworth; Edward Boddily of Clerkenwell; Oliver Brent of Staines; Christian Callow of St. Mary Savoy, spinster; Mary Taylor of Willesden, spinster; Anne Richardson of the same, spinster; Elizabeth Hall; William Bishopp of St. Katherine's; Thomas Sherborne of Enfield; Alexander Pepperell of Acton; John Sparrow of Edmonton; Thomas Read; John Douglas of Paddington. (PRO: C66/3398/12).

12 December-5 January. Shippers by the *Ann & Sarah*, Mr. John Marshall, bound from Liverpool for Virginia: John Cleveland, William Bixter, Thomas Johnson. (PRO: E190/1359/11, 1360/17).

14 December. The following apprenticed from Christ's Hospital: George Hale, aged 16, to Bartholomew Whitehorne, commander of the [blank] bound for Virginia; John Watson, aged 15, to Micajah Perry, merchant in Leadenhall Street, to serve him in Virginia with the consent of his father-in-law Peter Griffith; Thomas King, aged 16, to Thomas Leman, commander of the *Isabella, Anne & Katherine* bound for Barbados. (CH).

22 December. Shipper by the *Mary & Ann* of Weymouth, Mr. William Cleeves, bound from Weymouth for Virginia: David Arbuthnott. (PRO: E190/892/2).

December. Probate of will of Sarah Eckley of Philadelphia. (AW).

December. Administration of John Butler the elder of Connecticut, New England. (AW).

1699

7-10 January. Shippers by the *Hester*, Mr. Elisha James, bound from Bristol for Virginia: John Gwinnie, Richard Sandford, William Galbraith, John Butcher. (PRO: E190/1156/1).

12 January. Shipper by the *Adventure* bound from Exeter for New England: Samuel Eveleigh. (PRO: E190/973/1).

13 January. Shipper by the *Welcome* bound from Exeter for New England: Roger Prowse. (PRO: E190/973/1).

25 January. Shipper by the *John & Samuell* of Poole, Mr. William Pike, bound from Poole for Virginia: William Pike Sr. (PRO: E190/892/13).

26 January. Shipper by the *Josiah & Betty* of Plymouth, Mr. Jonas Nowell, bound from Plymouth for Pennsylvania: Henry Ceane & Co. (PRO: E190/1059/4).

28 January-1 March. Shippers by the *Hopewell*, Mr. Thomas Braster, bound from Exeter for New England: Bernard Sampson, John Turner, Sir Edward Seaward, James Tuthill, Richard Ponsford. (PRO: E190/973/1).

January. Administration of Joas Blackler of the Tower of London, who died in Virginia, bachelor. (AW).

January. Administration of John Ireland of Boston, New England, who died at sea. (AW).

January. Administration of Joseph Dauncey, chaplain of the ship *Falcon*, granted to Samuel Wallin, father of the relict, Anne Myles alias Dauncey, in New England. (AW).

24 January-10 March. Shippers by the *Adventure* of Lancaster, Mr. Thomas Marshall, bound from Lancaster for New England: John Hodgson, Charles Rigby. (PRO: E190/1360/6).

3-17 February. Shippers by the *Pennsylvania Merchant*, Mr. John Hitchings, bound from Bristol for Pennsylvania: Samuell Packer, Jeoffrey Pinnell, Edward Bayly, Edward Martindale. (PRO: E190/1156/1).

18 February. Western Circuit prisoners reprieved to be transported to Barbados. Cornwall: Griffith Thomas of Probus; Richard Miller of Halberton; David Colwall alias Colwell of Morchard Bishop, shoemaker. Dorset: Thomas Cumbershall of Forcehill, West Chaldon. Hampshire: John Tewksbury of Gosport; John Callaway of Berriton. Somerset: Thomas Newman alias Harding of Cucklington, linenweaver; John Turner of Cudworth, butcher; William Fort of Ilminster, sergeweaver; Henry Harding of Bruton, butcher; John Gully of Withypool. Wiltshire: Sarah Hamblyn of Shalbourne, widow;

John Lawrence of Graton, Great Bedwin; Edward Lawrence of Graton, Great Bedwin; Henry Purton of Shalbourne. Nehemiah Peed of Wotton under Edge (Gloucestershire); Michael Norris of London; Robert Smith of London; John Hazlewood of London; George Holmes of London, shoemaker; Elizabeth wife of John Hazelwood. (PRO: C66/3412/16).

21-27 February. The following apprenticed in Liverpool to William Middleton for four years to go to Newfoundland by the *Irish Lawrell*, said William Middleton master: Henry Powell of Wells, Somerset, aged 21; James Tucker of Wells, aged 20; Thomas Jones of Caernarvon, aged 20; Thomas Jackson of Blackley, Lancashire, aged 19 (ran away); William Williams of Narberth, Pembrokeshire, aged 21. (LTB).

23 February. Midland Circuit prisoners reprieved to be transported to America. Derbyshire: Robert Naylor of Derby; John Soulter of the same. Leicestershire: Elizabeth Grimes, wife of Charles Grimes of Leicester; Thomas Heath of the same; William Carrawin of the same; Thomas Welch of the same; John Crane of the same; Daniel Clayton of the same; John Dilks of the same. Lincolnshire: Francis Clifton of Lincoln. Northamptonshire: Thomas White of Northampton; John Hopkins of the same; John Butler of the same; Thomas Gent of the same; William Allifull of the same. Nottinghamshire: Penitent Saywood of Nottingham, spinster; Thomas Cooke of the same; Thomas Hall of the same. Rutland: John Mason of Oakham. Warwickshire: Edward Joyner of Warwick. (PRO: C66/3412/13).

23 February. Oxford Circuit prisoners reprieved to be transported to America. Gloucestershire: Charles Ashley of Stow in the Wold, joiner; John Roberts of Winchcombe, cordwainer. Herefordshire: Isaac Jones alias Devan of Leominster. Oxfordshire: John Spruce of Waterstock. Shropshire: James Crumpe of Rushbury. Staffordshire: Francis Bather alias Batho of Leek, baker; Edward Smith of Leigh, yeoman. Worcestershire: Robert Russell of Redston Ferry; Richard Davis of St. Chad's, Worcester. (PRO: C66/3412/14).

25 February-10 May. Shippers by the *Earl* galley, Mr. Edward Bird, bound from Bristol for New England and Pennsylvania: Joseph Earle, James Clemson & Co., John Corsley, Bourchier Goldstone, Joshua Cart, Matthew Worgan, Edward Tippett, Nathaniel Kill, John Taunton, John Lucas, David Kill, Cornelius Serjeante, William Fry, Samuell Greenaway, James Peter, John Phillips, Charles Grevile, John Kienton, James Bullman, Athel Tyndale, William Fursden, Hugh Wilson, James Wills, Thomas Goldney, Edward Bullock, Thomas Whitehead. (PRO: E190/1156/1).

27-28 February. The following apprenticed in Liverpool to Edward Tarleton to go to Newfoundland by the *Yorkshire Lawrell*, said Edward Tarleton master: Evan Owen of Oswestry, Shropshire, aged 20, 4 years; Thomas Williams of Caernarvon, aged 12, 9 years; Hugh Reddish of Kearsley, Lancashire, aged 19, 4 years; John Stock of Rochdale, Lancashire, aged 23, 4 years; John Barnes of Haslingden, Lancashire, aged 15, 7 years; John Wood of Haslingden, aged 13, 8 years; John Bretherton of Nantwich, Cheshire, aged 20, 4 years. (LTB).

27 February-3 March. Shippers by the *Violet* sloop, Mr. John Davies, bound from Bristol for New England: Francis Rogers, John Donning. (PRO: E190/1156/1).

28 February-19 April. Shippers by the *Expectation*, Mr. William Curtis, bound from Bristol for New England: Walter Oborne, Samuell Hunt, Thomas Hord, John Webb, John Day, Ann Lambert, William Turton, Anselm Jenner(?), George Winter, John Bodenham, Moses Deane, Edward Tippett, Thomas Careless, Thomas Fry, Phillip Stone, Richard Sullock, John Corsley, Thomas Whitehead, Robert White. (PRO: E190/1156/1).

February. Administration of Thomas Hasted of Stepney, Middlesex, who died on the ship *Bristow* in Virginia, widower. (AW).

February. Probate of will of John Langley of St. Saviour, Southwark, Surrey, doctor of medicine, whose daughter, Margaret Day, was in Maryland. (AW).

February. Administration with will of John Eckley of Philadelphia. (AW).

3-6 March. The following apprenticed in Liverpool to go to New England by the *Virginia Merchant*, Mr. Edmund Ball: Jane Radcliff of Rochdale, Lancashire, spinster aged 20, 7 years; Mary Gleddale of Hepworth, Yorkshire, aged 20, 7 years; Daniell Clows of Alston Field, Staffordshire, aged 23, 6 years; John Holgrave of Haslingden, Lancashire, aged 28, 7 years; James Nuttes of Blackburn, Lancashire, aged 18, 7 years; Paul Widdop of Halifax, Yorkshire, aged 26, 7 years; John Walker of Titherington, Cheshire, aged 19, 7 years; Christopher Patrick of Great Musgrave, Westmorland, aged 20, 7 years; Mathew Mooreton of Prestbury, Cheshire, aged 20, 7 years; John Jones of Clanderry [?Llandyrnog], Denbighshire, aged 17, 7 years; James Thompson of Scotland, aged 19, 7 years; Josiah Maires of Macclesfield, Cheshire, aged 19, 7 years; Mary Dawson of Leeds, Yorkshire, aged 22, 7 years; Margaret Jones of Ruthin, Denbighshire, aged 32, 7 years; James Chaddock of Rochdale, Lancashire, aged 22, 7 years; Jane Swindle of Macclesfield, Cheshire, aged 23, 7 years; Edward Cook of Hope, Derbyshire, aged 19, 7 years; Richard Thomas of Dublin, Ireland, aged 18, 7 years; Nicholas Hurd of Ponsonby, Cumberland, aged 19, 7 years; Thomas Stringer of Buckton [?Burton], Yorkshire, aged 22, 7 years; John Beaver of Hepworth, Yorkshire, aged 22, 7 years; Jonathan Hartly of Marton, Yorkshire, aged 18, 7 years; Edward Glover of Manchester, Lancashire, aged 20, 7 years; Peter Hughes of Anglesey, aged 19, 7 years; Peter Bole of Poynton, Cheshire, aged 20, 7 years; Margaret Todd of Ingleton, Yorkshire, aged 19, 7 years; Mary Taylor of Rochdale, Lancashire, aged 22, 7 years; James Clarke of Newton Heath, Cheshire [?Lancashire], aged 17, 7 years; Edward Faux of Flint, aged 19, 7 years; Mathew Williams of Blew Morrice [?Beaumaris], Wales, aged 26, 7 years; Humphrey Salsbury of Glandiray(?), Denbighshire, aged 19, 7 years;

Margaret Bishop of Loughborough, Leicestershire, aged 25, 7 years; Peirce Tickle of Lymm, Cheshire, aged 17, 10 years; John Smith of Craven, Yorkshire, aged 17, 7 years; John Williams of Woolwich, Kent, aged 29, 7 years (turned off); John Roadly of Norwich, aged 17, 7 years; Daniell Clew of Manchester, Lancashire, aged 21, 7 years; John Rochett of Blackburn, Lancashire, aged 19, 7 years; Maudlin Lewis of Carmarthen Town, Wales, aged 15, 7 years; John Mills of Oldham, Lancashire, aged 12, 10 years (turned off); Joseph Bell of Newcastle upon Tyne, [Northumberland], aged 23, 7 years (ran away); Lawrence Scotland of Scotland, aged 21, 7 years (ran away); Ann Singleton of Firwood(?), Lancashire, apprentice of John Moody, aged 23, 7 years. (LTB).

3-28 March. Shippers by the *Adventure*, Mr. Abraham Winter, bound from Exeter for New England: Sir Edward Seaward, Peter Park, William Drake, James Gould, Richard Reynolds, Richard Simmons, Richard Ponsford, Jacob Rowe, John Upcott, Edward Marden, George Poe, William Heathfield, Philip Hooper, Edward Mann, Robert Tristram, John Dewes, Joseph Mawry, John Avery, Eyles Pierce. (PRO: E190/973/1).

14 March. Cheshire prisoner reprieved to be transported to America: Samuel Knipe for coining. (PRO: C66/3412/7).

14 March-8 April. Shippers by the *William & Mary*, Mr. Nicholas Downe, bound from Exeter for New England: Edward Marden, Richard Parminter, Thomas Turner, George & James Gould, John Evans, John York, Peter Parr, Richard Reynolds, Edward Gatchell, John Gandy, Daniell Joie, Thomas Tripe, Benjamin Bake, Alice Bamfield, John Turner, John Poole, Roger Prowse. (PRO: E190/973/1).

20 March-8 April. Shippers by the *Sarah & Elizabeth*, Mr. William Coggan, bound from Exeter for New England: Thomas Hayne, Benjamin Bake, Richard Halfe, John Munckley, Thomas Turner, Jonathan Came. (PRO: E190/973/1).

28 March-4 April. The following apprenticed in Liverpool to John Dann to go to the West Indies by the *Ann & Mary*, said John Dann master: Thomas Roper of Wrightingham [?Whittington], Lancashire, aged 19, 4 years; Henry Halewood of Ormskirk, Lancashire, aged 25, 4 years. (LTB).

28 March-13 April. Shippers by the *Virginia Merchant* bound from Liverpool [*destination not stated*]: Edmund Ball, Richard Houghton, John Moody, Andrew Swan(?). (PRO: E190/1360/17).

29 March. Shipper by the *Mary & Ann* of Weymouth, Mr. William Cleeves, bound from Weymouth for Virginia: David Arbuthnott. (PRO: E190/892/9).

March. Probate of will of Jonas Dixon of the ship *Preservation*, who died in Virginia. (AW).

1 April. Shippers by the *Frederick* of New York, Mr. Humphrey Parking, bound from Southampton for New York: Adolphus Phillips, Augustine Jay, John Cosaert. (PRO: E190/841/1).

4 April. Chancery proceedings initiated in Weeks v. Hobbs to establish inheritance under the will of Dr. Thomas Hobbs of Lincolns Inn Fields, London. Dr. Hobbs' sister, Elizabeth, married Francis Weeks of Middlesex County, Virginia. (NGSQ 61/4).

15 April-5 May. Shippers by the *Britannia*, Mr. Richard Nicholls, bound from Liverpool for Virginia: Richard Scarborough, Thomas Musgrewe, George Godsalve, Joseph Stretch, Robert Heaton, Christopher Atkinson, Robert Haydock, John Brookes, James Brookes, Hugh Croxton, Jonathan Higginson. (PRO: E190/1360/17).

26-29 April. Shippers by the *Three Sisters*, Mr. David Fortune, bound from Bristol for New England: Peter Wadding, James Hollidge, Francis Brome. (PRO: E190/1156/1).

26 April-28 September. Shippers by the *James & Elizabeth*, Mr. John Mather, bound from Exeter for New England: John Munckley, Roger Prowse, John Turner, Arthur Jeffery, Jacob Rowe, Peter Parr, Abraham Goswill, John Poole, James Sparke, Samuell Cooke. (PRO: E190/973/1).

28 April. Shippers by the *Hopewell* of Guernsey, Mr. Thomas Le Measurier, bound from Dartmouth for New England: Thomas Plumleigh, John Dobree. (PRO: E190/968/1).

April. Probate of will of John Thompson of Virginia. (AW).

April. Probate of will of James Trent of the ship *Charles* in the King's service who died in Pennsylvania. (AW).

April. Administration of Thomas Pendergrass of Stepney, Middlesex, who died in Virginia. (AW).

2 May. Shipper by the *Experience & Susannah* of London, Mr. John Sharp, bound from Southampton for New England: said John Sharp. (PRO: E190/841/1).

2-12 May. Shippers by the *Hopewell* of New York, Mr. William Fryer, bound from Southampton for New York: Adolphus Phillips, Ann Van Scaick, Derrick Banker, John Cosaert, Nicholas Garret. (PRO: E190/841/1).

10-15 May. Shippers by the *George*, Mr. Richard Arding, bound from Bristol for New England: George Lewis, Phillip Freeke, William Challoner, Abraham Hooke, Abell Kelly, Humphrey Corsley, Moses Deane, Benjamin Turner. (PRO: E190/1156/1).

12 May. Shippers by the *Mary* of Guernsey, Mr. Peter Le Measurier, bound from Dartmouth for New England: Thomas Plumleigh, Thomas Le Measurier. (PRO: E190/968/1).

17 May. Shipper by the *Margaret*, Mr. Charles Hayden, bound from Bristol for Virginia: Sir John Duddlestone. (PRO: E190/1156/1).

18-23 May. Shippers by the *Jane* of Jersey, Mr. John Dovergne, bound from Dartmouth for New England: George Dottin, Ellis Nicholls, Lawrence Raymond, Samuell Pewse. (PRO: E190/968/1).

25 May. Shippers by the *Owners Adventure* of Guernsey, Mr. Peter Turner, bound from Dartmouth for New England: Thomas Plumleigh, John Gruchy. (PRO: E190/968/1).

26 May. Shipper by the *Owners Adventure* of London, Mr. James Mitchell, bound from Southampton for Pennsylvania: Joseph Todd. (PRO: E190/841/1).

31 May-9 June. Shipperrs by the *Helena* of New York, Mr. Johannes Van Allen, bound from Southampton for New York: Henry Van Bael, Mydert Schuyler, Garret Banker, Henry Dally. (PRO: E190/841/1).

May. Probate of will of John Morton who died in Carolina. (AW).

May. Probate of will of Robert Throckmorton of Paxton Parva, Huntingdonshire, who had lands in Virginia. (AW).

20 June-15 August. The following apprenticed in Liverpool to John Hughes to go to Pennsylvania, Virginia or Maryland by the *Experiment* of Liverpool, Mr. Cavaleiro Christian: Mary Lee of Peak, Derbyshire, spinster aged 19, 6 years; Richard Worrall of St. Bridget, Chester, tailor aged 21, 5 years; Stephen Fletcher of London, tailor aged 21, 6 years; William Windsor of Potters Marston, Leicestershire, blacksmith aged 18, 6 years; James Johnson of Salford, Lancashire, weaver aged 23, 5 years; Ellin Acres of Sefton, Lancashire, spinster aged 22, 6 years; Ellin Rushton of Whalley, Lancashire, aged 18, 6 years; George Griffith of Colwyn, Flint, aged 23, 6 years; Margaret Plaise of Stainburn, Yorkshire, aged 20, 6 years; John Rhodes of Halifax, Yorkshire, weaver aged 21, 5 years; Margaret Ellis of Merionethshire, Wales, aged 28, 5 years; William Ellis of the same place, aged 26, 5 years; Elizabeth Wharton of Frodsham, Cheshire, aged 22, 6 years; Jane Lackey of Carrickfergus, Ireland, aged 18, 5 years; John Jones of Northop, Flint, aged 28, 5 years; John Richard of Llanarmon, Denbighshire, aged 16, 7 years. (LTB).

28 June. Benjamin Mills, aged 16, apprenticed from Christ's Hospital to James Smith, commander of the *Sedgwick* bound for Jamaica. (CH).

29 June. Western Circuit prisoners reprieved to be transported to Barbados. Bristol: Martha West; Sarah Williams. Cornwall: John Barnicott alias Arney of Bodmin, miller. Devon: John Cross of Lustleigh, tanner. Dorset: Roger Fudge of Stallbridge Weston. Hampshire: John Harde alias Harden of Gosport; Mary Foster of Benmead, Hambleton, spinster. Somerset: William Woodcock of Wells; William Martin of Weare; Richard Cross of Marke, tinker. Wiltshire: William Olive of Devizes. Henry Peirce of London; William Reynolds of London. (PRO: C66/3413/17).

30 June. Home Circuit prisoners reprieved to be transported to Barbados or Jamaica. Essex: Francis Hambleton of South Hanningfield; George Naylor of Barking; Thomas Moore of Hornchurch; James Bycham alias Belcham of High Ongar; John Owell alias Overhill of Rayleigh; John Mason of Rayne; Richard Mortar of Inworth. Hertfordshire: William Beere of Braughin; John Phipps of Braughin; Florence Vaughan of Braughing; Daniel McDugdale of Little Hormead; John Greene of Harpenden. Kent: William Leicester of Cobham; Thomas Rich of Selling; George Howard of Cobham; Robert Jennings of Gravesend; Augustine Parker of Cuxton; Richard Hyder of Cobham; John Sanderson of Lewisham. Surrey: Nicholas Oliver of Camberwell; Mary Day of Lambeth; John Gingin alias Kingan of St. Olave, Southwark; Mary Bignall alias Ward of Bermondsey; Thomas Johns of Walton on Thames; Susan Wood of Lambeth; Elizabeth Snaxton of Croydon. Sussex: Richard Stitchborne of Frant. (PRO: C66/3413/16).

30 June-31 August. Shippers by the *Blossom* pink, Mr. Robert Darkin, bound from Bristol for New York: Robert Lurting, Henry Langley, Jeremy Pearce, John Droilehett (*sic*), John Morin, Stephen Delancey, Edward Hackett, John Mayson. (PRO: E190/1156/1).

June. Administration of Robert Wilson of Wapping, Middlesex, who died on the ship *James and Elizabeth* in Virginia. (AW).

June. Probate of will of Charles Hall, citizen and fishmonger of London, who died in Virginia, bachelor. (AW).

7 July. Oxford Circuit prisoners reprieved to be transported to America. Berkshire: William Mobson of Didcot. Gloucestershire: Stephen Bull of Bisley; Joseph Elton of Newent, blacksmith; Joane Ellis of Newland. Herefordshire: John Parker of Harewood. Oxfordshire: John Baldwyn of Toersey. Shropshire: Richard Downes of Hadnall. Staffordshire: Daniel Heron of Newcastle under Lyme; Thomas Scragg of Cheddleton. Worcestershire: Robert Dyson of Bradley. Mary Smith of Nottingham, spinster. (PRO: C66/3413/13).

7 July. Northern Circuit prisoners reprieved to be transported to Barbados. Cumberland: John Lowther of Rose Causeway, Dalston, gent. Durham: Thomas Harrison Jr. of Sheraton; Robert Hutchinson of Fine; Ralph Hall of Murton. Lancashire: Edward Gooden of Lancaster; Jonathan Shaw of the same; Bonaventure Mills of the same; George Fryer of the same; Mary Barwell of the same; Sarah Breasly of the same; Elizabeth Wrenshaw of the same; Richard Baxforth of the same; John Dixon of the same. Yorkshire: William Hind of Sutton; William Harper of York; Joseph Nordon of South Milford; John Hinchcliffe of Leeds; John Mabell of Scarborough; John Stainton of Wrenthorpe, Wakefield, yeoman; John Wheldrake of Pocklington; Christopher Robinson of York; Edward Cunningham of the same. (PRO: C66/3413/14).

15 July. Shipper by the *Friendship* of Boston, Mr. Zachary Alden, bound from Newcastle for New England: John Wilkinson. (PRO: E190/207/6).

15-22 July. Shippers by the *Pearl*, Mr. Samuell Ellis, bound from Barnstaple for Virginia: RIchard Parminter, Thomas Smith. (PRO: E190/973/5, 973/11).

21 July-7 September. Shippers by the *Adventure*, Mr. Abraham Winter, bound from Exeter for New England: John Upcott, Joseph Mawry. (PRO: E190/973/1).

28 July. Shippers by the *Essex* Galley of New England, Mr. Eliazer Linsley, bound from Dartmouth for New England: George Dottin, Phillip Hooper, Silvanus Evans, Joseph Bully, James Pitt. (PRO: E190/968/1).

July. Probate of will of John West of St. Sepulchre, London, whose grandson, John East, and daughter, Hannah Streete, were in Pennsylvania. (AW).

July. Administration of John Weedon of Boston, New England, who died on H.M. ship *Mary*. (AW).

July. Administration of Charles Gough of Maryland, widower. (AW).

1 August-1 September. Shippers by the *Sarah*, Mr. John Miller, bound from Bristol for Virginia and Pennsylvania: Jacob Beale, John Baker, William Penn Esq., George Birkbeck, Charles Watkins, John Atkins, William Dowdney, Benjamin Gwyn, William Gibbons, George Milborne, Christopher White. (PRO: E190/1156/1).

3 August. Cheshire prisoners reprieved to be transported to America: Samuel Jellicoe of Kingsley; John Hooley of Wynrith; Samuel Knype of Broughton (Lancashire). (PRO: C66/3413/8).

8-11 August. Shippers by the *Antigua Merchant* of Boston, Mr. Anthony Ayroust, bound from Plymouth for Boston, New England: Sir John Rogers, Andrew Stuckey. (PRO: E190/1059/4).

10-29 August. Shippers by the *Richard & John*, Mr. John Jones, bound from Bristol for Virginia: Sir Richard Crumpe & Co., Edward Foye, William Whitehead, Edmund Mountjoy, William Williams, Hugh Hayward, Joseph Rudge, Cornelius Read, John Collier, Barnaby Shuttleworth. (PRO: E190/1156/1).

12-16 August. Shippers by the *Tryal*, Mr. Abraham Lewis, bound from Bristol for Virginia: Samuell Packer, William Smith. (PRO: E190/1156/1).

14 August. Shipper by the *Happy Union* of London, Mr. John Browne, bound from Southampton for Virginia: John Harley. (PRO: E190/841/1).

16 August-28 September. Shippers by the *Charles & Sarah*, Mr. Edward Wilmott, bound from Bristol for New England: William Beale, John Webb, Samuell Greenaway, Joseph Burges, Marmaduke Bowdler, Robert Lawes,

James Oborne, Robert Devonshire, John Lloyd, Simon Facey, William Temple. (PRO: E190/1156/1).

19 August. Shippers by the *Canterbury* of London, Mr. Henry Tregany, bound from Southampton for Pennsylvania: Solomon Warder, Thomas Applin. (PRO: E190/841/1).

21-28 August. Shippers by the *Canterbury* of London, Mr. Henry Tregany, bound from Portsmouth Roads for Pennsylvania: James Sweeter, William Barr. (PRO: E190/841/8).

22 August. William Hoome of Manchester, dyer, whose apprentice, Richard Berlow, ran away to be asked whether he consents to his going to sea. (LTB).

22 August-21 October. Shippers by the *Resolution*, Mr. William Courtney, bound from Bristol for Virginia: George Mason, Hugh Hayward, Thomas Hodges, William Salwood. (PRO: E190/1156/1).

23 August. Shipper by the *Samuell* of Bideford, Mr. Thomas Cantrell, bound from Bideford for Virginia: Thomas Smith. (PRO: E190/973/11).

29 August. Shipper by the *Michael*, Mr. James Wheeler, bound from Bristol for Virginia: said James Wheeler. (PRO: E190/1156/1).

29-30 August. Shippers by the *Lamb* of Dublin, Mr. Richard Murphey, bound from Liverpool for Virginia: Andrew Moore, John Preston. (PRO: E190/1360/17).

29 August-27 September. Shippers by the *Welcome* bound from Exeter for New England: Roger Prowse, Edward Mann, Thomas Turner, Peter Parr, William Lewis, William Sanford, William Heathfield, Thomas Winter, Philip Hooper, Humphrey Limbry. (PRO: E190/973/1).

30 August. Shipper by the *Francis* of Bideford, Mr. John Yeo, bound from Bideford for Maryland: John Smith. (PRO: E190/973/11).

August. Probate of will of John Payton of Portbury, Somerset, who had assets in Virginia and Maryland. (AW).

August. Administration of Stephen Harris of Norham, Devon County, Virginia or Maryland. (AW).

August. Probate of will of Thomas Hunt of Chalfont St. Giles, Buckinghamshire, who died in Carolina. (AW).

August. Probate of will of Augustine Lyndon of Boston, New England, shipwright, who died in Shadwell, Middlesex. (AW).

August. Probate of will of Henry Hartwell of Stepney, Middlesex, who died in Virginia. (AW).

August. Probate of will of Jacob Tompson of Bristol, who died on the ship *Sarah* of Bristol in Virginia. (AW).

1-6 September. Shippers by the *Lamb* of Liverpool, Mr. William Benson, bound from Liverpool for Virginia: Peter Atherton, William Bassnett, John Pemberton, Richard Geldart, Henry Parr. (PRO: E190/1360/17).

1-26 September. Shippers by the *Beginning*, Mr. Stephen Nicholas, bound from Bristol for Carolina: John Yeamans, William Birte, John Baker, Isaac Shepard, Joshua Cart, Ellis Ashby, George Newland, Nicholas Seaborne, Edward Bittle, Thomas Yeamans, Humphrey Hancock. (PRO: E190/1156/1).

1-27 September. Shippers by the *James & Mary*, Mr. John Walter, bound from Bristol for Virginia: Jeremy Pearce, James Wallis, Lewis Burrill, John Freman, James Lloyd, Michael White, Thomas Hort. (PRO: E190/1156/1).

2 September-17 October. Shippers by the *Primrose* pink, Mr. Lott Nickins, bound from Bristol for Carolina: Richard Cheshire, Phillip Freeke. (PRO: E190/1156/1).

4-6 September. The following apprenticed in Liverpool to Richard Murphy to go to Virginia by the *Lamb* of Dublin, said Richard Murphy master: Phebe Leed of Oldham, Lancashire, aged 19, 5 years; Robert Owen of Sale, Cheshire, tailor aged 18, 5 years; Mary Speakman of Clifton, Lancashire, aged 20, 5 years; Thomas Lindsay of Pendleton, Lancashire, aged 16, 9 years; Ellen Holt of Rochdale, Lancashire, aged 27, 5 years; John Andrew of Oldham, Lancashire, aged 22, 4 years. (LTB).

4-25 September. Shippers by the *John & Susanna*, Mr. Thomas Cooper, bound from Bristol for Virginia: Daniel Hickman, Thomas Tyler, Christopher Shuttleworth, Joseph Triggs, Thomas Mercer, John Swift, Constant Overton. (PRO: E190/1156/1).

7-14 September. Shippers by the *Hope* of Virginia bound from Plymouth for Virginia: Henry Ceane, George Boyce, James Cock & Co., Abraham Carter, Benjamin Harrison. (PRO: E190/1059/4).

8 September. Shipper by the *Annapolis* of Bideford, Mr. Thomas Marshall, bound from Bideford for Maryland: George Buck. (PRO: E190/973/5).

9-10 September. Shippers by the *Andrew & Samuel* of Boston, Mr. Thomas Pearson, bound from Dartmouth for New England: William Carter, Silvanus Evans. (PRO: E190/968/1).

11 September. Shipper by the *Rogers* of Plymouth, Mr. John Saunders, bound from Plymouth for Virginia: Sir John Rogers. (PRO: E190/1059/4).

11-28 September. Shippers by the *George* of Plymouth, Mr. John Carne, bound from Plymouth for Virginia: George Lapthorne, William Williams, John Harvey. (PRO: E190/1059/4).

12 September. Shipper by the *Samuell* dogger of London, Mr. Thomas Tyler, bound from Liverpool for Boston, New England: said Thomas Tyler. (PRO: E190/1360/17).

12 September. The following apprenticed in Liverpool: John Nicholson of Lancaster, aged 20, to Thomas Tyler, 7 years New England. (LTB).

13-30 September. Shippers by the *Rachel*, Mr. Richard Nicholls, bound from Bristol for New England: Thomas Cole, Abraham Hooke, Eleazar Derby, Thomas Coysgarne, Anthony Swymmer, John Harper. (PRO: E190/1156/1).

14 September. The following apprenticed in Liverpool to Capt. Clayton: John Thomas of Clandethlow [?Llandilo], Carmarthenshire, aged 18, 7 years West Indies. (LTB).

14 September. Shippers by the *Unity* of Lyme, Mr. Robert Colbard, bound from Lyme for Virginia: Daniell Gundry, Simon Bayly, John Stone. (PRO: E190/892/8).

14-16 September. Shippers by the *Faithful Prize*, Mr. Thomas Cox, bound from Bristol for Barbados and Virginia: Aaron Williams, Henry Watts, Joseph Harris, Thomas Tyler. (PRO: E190/1156/1).

15-27 September. Shippers by the *Expectation*, Mr. Christopher Scandrett, bound from Bristol for Virginia: Samuell Packer, Abraham Lloyd, Samuell Boussac. (PRO: E190/1156/1).

18-27 September. Shippers by the *Bristol* pink, Mr. John Thomas, bound from Bristol for Virginia: Charles Harford, Robert Day, Amy Ryland, William Jordan, Thomas Ford. (PRO: E190/1156/1).

19 September. The following apprenticed in Liverpool: Mary Atkinson of Knottingley, Yorkshire, aged 21, to Mr. Henry Smith of Liverpool, merchant, 5 years [Virginia]. (LTB).

20 September-2 October. Shippers by the *William & Orian*, Mr. Jeffrey Bayly, bound from Bristol for Virginia: Henry Lynthorne, Sir John Duddlestone, John Watkins. (PRO: E190/1156/1).

25 September-4 October. Shippers by the *Lyon*, Mr. Robert Bayly, bound from Bristol for Virginia: Sir William Daines, John Day, Jacob Hollister, William Perrott, Charles Nicholls, John Cornish, Edward Croft, Stephen Hollister. (PRO: E190/1156/1).

25 September-6 November. Shippers by the *Elizabeth*, Mr. William Harris, bound from Exeter for Virginia: William Drake, William Pennick. (PRO: E190/973/1).

27-30 September. Shippers by the *Virginia Merchant*, Mr. Walter Bayly, bound from Bristol for Virginia: John Day, Thomas Tyler, Edward Lloyd, Nicholas Lott, Samuell Whitchurch. (PRO: E190/1156/1).

30 September. Shippers by the *Seaverne* galley, Mr. Hugh Rainstrip, bound from Bristol for Virginia: James Hollidge, James Vaughan, Edward Hackett. (PRO: E190/1156/1).

September. Administration of Thomas Luscombe of Boston, New England. (AW).

September. Probate of will of Peter Noyes of Sudbury, New England. (AW).

September. Probate of will of Thomas Scottow of Boston, New England, surgeon, who died on the ship *Gerard* of London. (AW).

3 October. Shipper by the *Orange Branch*, Mr. John Wright, bound from Southampton for Carolina: George Barron. (PRO: E190/841/1).

5 October. Shipper by the *Factor* of Bideford, Mr. John Banbury, bound from Bideford for Maryland: John Smith. (PRO: E190/973/5).

5-10 October. Shippers by the *John*, Mr. John Mylam, bound from Bristol for Virginia: John Jenkins, Daniel Hickman, Stephen Baker, Sir Richard Crumpe, Robert Bodenham, Francis Pinnell. (PRO: E190/1156/1).

6 October. Shippers by the *Laurel* of New York, Mr. John Many, bound from Southampton for New York: John Cosaerts, Lucinius Van Scaick, John Many & Co., William Duncanson, Peter Thouvett(?). (PRO: E190/841/1).

7 October. The following apprenticed in Liverpool to Mr. Robert Fleetwood: John Nutting of Burnley, Lancashire, aged 12, 10 years [Virginia]. (LTB).

7 October. Shippers by the *Anne* of Newcastle, Mr. Robert Allen, bound from Newcastle for Virginia: Francis Partis, Thomas Allen. (PRO: E190/207/6).

11-17 October. Shippers by the *Elizabeth*, Mr. Gilbert Livesley, bound from Liverpool for Virginia: Thomas Johnson, William Hurst, Joseph Atkins, Thomas Chapman, Thomas Bowling, Thomas Edgar. (PRO: E190/1360/17).

11-19 October. Shippers by the *Blossom* of Plymouth, Mr. Henry Munyon, bound from Plymouth for Virginia: John Anderson, John Christmas. (PRO: E190/1059/4).

12-18 October. Shippers by the *James*, Mr. William Browning, bound from Barnstaple and Bideford for Virginia: John Crabb, John Smith, John Davie. (PRO: E190/973/5, 973/11).

14 October. The following apprenticed in Liverpool to Thomas Bowling of Euxton, Lancashire, husbandman, and to go by the *Elizabeth*, Mr. Gilbert Livesey, to Virginia or Maryland: James Hall of Euxton, aged 11, 12 years; Joshua Holden of Charnock Heath, Lancashire, aged 16, 8 years; Thomas Colson of Chorley, [Lancashire], aged 18, 8 years; William Dickinson of Flockton, Yorkshire, aged 14, 8 years; William Conly of Walton, Lancashire, aged 9, 13 years. (LTB).

16 October. Shipper by the *James* of Plymouth, Mr. Daniell Williams, bound from Plymouth for Virginia: James Bligh. (PRO: E190/1059/4).

17-20 October. Shippers by the *George* of Plymouth, Mr. Thomas Black, bound from Plymouth for Virginia: Richard Burlace, John Scott. (PRO: E190/1059/4).

21 October-22 November. Shippers by the *Richard & Mary*, Mr. Philip Franklin, bound from Bristol for Virginia: Ambrose Dudley, John Cades, Robert Peyton, Edmond Mountjoy, William Lisle, James Addis, Richard Franklin, Henry Whitehead, John Knight, Thomas Whittup, William Bath, Richard Burgis, William House, Humphrey Clarke. (PRO: E190/1156/1).

23 October-3 November. Shippers by the *Mulberry*, Mr. Bryan Blundell, bound from Liverpool for Virginia: William Waters, John Browne, Richard Roe. (PRO: E190/1360/17).

24 October. The following apprenticed in Liverpool to Mr. Bryan Blundell, master of the *Mulberry*, to serve 11 years [in Virginia]: Isaac Scofield of Chadderton, Lancashire, aged 13; James Scofield his brother, aged 11; Edward Lunt of Meols, Lancashire, aged 13. And the following apprenticed to Henry Brown to go to Virginia or Maryland by the *Loyalty*, said Henry Brown master: Francis Boardman of Gorton, [Lancashire], aged 21, 4 years; Ann Williams of Denbighshire, aged 22, 7 years; James Kershaw of Blackley, Lancashire, aged 18, 7 years; William Kinder of Disley, Cheshire, aged 16, 7 years; Mathew Stabbs Sr. of Rushton, Staffordshire, aged 44, 6 years; Mathew Stabbs Jr. of the same, aged 15, 9 years; Edward Stabbs of the same, aged 16, 8 years; Ewen Lommas of Bury, Lancashire, aged 21, 5 years. (LTB).

24-27 October. Shippers by the *Amity*, Mr. Lewis Jenkins, bound from Liverpool for Virginia: John Pemberton, Love Houston, Adam Oldfield. (PRO: E190/1360/17).

26 October. The following apprenticed in Liverpool: William Scott of Portsmouth, [Hampshire], aged 14, to Mr. John Parker, 7 years [Virginia]. (LTB).

October. Probate of will of Richard Tull of Maryland, bachelor. (AW).

October. Probate of will of Jacob Gradwell who died on the ship *Preston* on Cooper River, South Carolina. (AW).

3-8 November. Shippers by the *Loyalty*, Mr. Henry Browne, bound from Liverpool for Virginia: Richard Houghton, John Booth. (PRO: E190/1360/17).

7-17 November. Shippers by the *Robert & Elizabeth*, Mr. Ralph Williamson, bound from Liverpool for Virginia: Thomas Johnson, William Fitzhugh, Cornelius Brenan, Jonas Kenyon, Randall Platt, Thomas Clifton. (PRO: E190/1360/17).

9 November. The following from Denbighshire apprenticed in Liverpool to Mr. Lewis Jenkins [to serve in Virginia?]: Richard Edwards, aged 14, 7 years; John

Edward, aged 18, 5 years; Robert Powell, aged 20, 6 years; Robert Davies, aged 21, 6 years.

And the following apprenticed to Richard Singleton: Jacob Rylance of Morley, Cheshire, aged 24, 5 years [Virginia]. (LTB).

14-21 November. Shippers by the *Society*, Mr. Jonathan Livesley, bound from Liverpool for Virginia: William Bassnett, John Curtis, Robert Middleton. (PRO: E190/1360/17).

16 November. Shipper by the *Industry* of Boston, Mr. William Watts, bound from Dartmouth for New England: said William Watts. (PRO: E190/968/1).

16-23 November. Shippers by the *Samuell & James* of London, Mr. Richard Foster, bound from Plymouth for Boston, New England: Sir John Rogers, Henry Ceane, Josiah Austin. (PRO: E190/1059/4).

17 November. Shipper by the *Endeavour* of London, Mr. John Bond, bound from Plymouth for New York: Henry Ceane & Co. (PRO: E190/1059/4).

17 November. Shipper by the *Supply* of London, Mr. Peter Blackstone, bound from Plymouth for Virginia: Thomas Darracott. (PRO: E190/1059/4).

20 November. The following apprenticed in Liverpool: Joseph Elwood of Garston, [Lancashire], tailor aged 19, to Henry Smith, 4 years [Virginia]. (LTB).

21 November. Chancery suit brought by Sarah Bowditch, relict of William Bowditch Jr. of Thornecombe, Devon, deceased, v. William Bowditch Sr., in which the defendant declares that his son, William Bowditch Jr., married Sarah Beare in 1663 and went to New England shortly afterwards to be followed by his wife five years later after she had had a child named Giles. (NGSQ 69/4).

21-27 November. Shipper by the *Concord*, Mr. John Walls, bound from Liverpool for Virginia: John Pemberton. (PRO: E190/1360/17).

28 November. Shipper by the *Speedwell* of Hull, Mr. Jeremy Bentley, bound from Hull for Maryland: William Crowle & Co. (PRO: E190/334/21).

4-13 December. Shippers by the *Virginia Merchant* of Plymouth, Mr. Robert Edgcombe, bound from Plymouth for Virginia: Sir John Rogers, John Arnold. (PRO: E190/1059/4).

5 December. Newgate prisoners reprieved to be transported to Barbados or Jamaica. London: John Goodwin alias Plumpe; William Dickate alias Coffee; William Smith alias Williams; John Westcutt; Thomas Grover; John Serjeant alias Field; Dedereux Peasant; Peter Anderson alias Davis; John Wheeler; Samuel Stubbs; John Smith; Richard Larkin; Barnaby Brabazon; Richard Howlin alias Browne. Middlesex: Mary Price of St. Giles in the Fields, spinster; William Guy of St. Clement Danes; Robert Taylor of Tottenham; Metthew Walton of the same; John Gayling alias Gamling of Wapping; Mary

Day of Hillingdon; Richard Apsley of the same; Herbert Herring of Stepney; Thomas Badge of the same; John Covey of the same; Thomas Wood of the same; James Hewett of the same; Joseph Fisher of the same; Thomas Elderton of the same; Frances Fox of the same, spinster; Charles Congill alias Concklin of Whitechapel; Anne Lambert of the same, spinster; Charles Gale alias Silvester of the same; Daniel Johnson alias Bogg of St. James Westminster; David Williams of the same; Nicholas Stanzell of St. Margaret Westminster; John Holmes of St. Anne Westminster; Daniel Staines of Edmonton; Francis Waller of Hayes; John Ingram of Clerkenwell; John Holliday of St. Martin in the Fields; John Thompson of the same; Peter Wise of the same; John Fryer of Shoreditch; John Linvill of St. Katherine's; Thomas Smith of St. Andrew Holborn; John Lee of Heston; Francis Lee of St. Paul Covent Garden; William Browne of Hayes; Sarah Day of Kensington, spinster; Mary Robinson of the same, spinster; Henry Chapman of Marylebone; John Bramsey of Kingsbury. (PRO: C66/3411/16).

13 December. Thomas Graven, aged 17, apprenticed from Christ's Hospital to James England, commander of the *Tryon* bound for Barbados. (CH).

1699. Chancery proceedings of Brayley v. Stocker establishing that Ephraim Stocker went from Bristol to Virginia before 1694 but he and his ship were never heard of again. (NGSQ 67/3).

Index of Persons

Entries are arranged as nearly as possible in accordance with modern spellings, the principal alternatives being shown in square brackets. The inclusion of an asterisk after a page number indicates that the name occurs more than once on that page.

Arlington, Lydia 399,
400
Armitage, Henry 330
Richard 80
Timothy 504,609,610
Armory, Robert 144
Armstrong, Alexander
589
Ann 334
Elizabeth 513
James 513
John 424,475
Jonas 313
Mary 551
Thomas 551,653
Arnall [Arnell],
Anthony 101
Benjamin 514
John 101
Katherine 661
Mary 101
Thomas 540,647,661
Arnaux, Jane 507
Arnes, Thomas 573
Arney [Arnee], John
256,711
Arnoe, James 674
Arnold, Alice 98
Anthony 282
Benedict 335
Edward 191
Elizabeth 230
James 676
Jeremiah 463,476
John 77,280,526,685,
704,719
Sibyl 87
Stephen 335
Thomas 198,289,299,
341,345,352,362,379,
397,398,419,463,
474*,476,478,536,
564,583,609,614,
619,625
William 116,335
Arnoll, Robert 229*
William 24
Arnsley, Richard 97
Arren, Richard 71
Arrendon, Thomas 99
Arres, Thomas 375
Arriall, George 114

Arrowsmith, Hugh 631
John 607
Richard 154,438
Thomas 85
William 630
Arsdel, John 412
Arthur, Archibald 487
Edward 410
Henry 570
John 30,63,268
Katherine 334
Miriam 446
Robert 76,85,92
Thomas 666
Arundell, Charity 418,
596
Daniel 435
Israel 378
Ascue. *See Askew.*
Ash, Isaac 407,518
James 174,266
John 26
Jonathan 78
Margaret 484
Richard 344
Ashall, Richard 224
Ashby, Champion 282,
294,326
Ellis 303,715
George 3,41,42,43,44
Hester 46
John 86,334,361,386,
393,401,416,456,588,
596,621
William 224
Ashcombe, Mary 606
Nathaniel 334
Ashenden, Robert 408
Ashenhurst, John 145
Ashfield, Thomas 598
William 620
Ashford, Ambrose 548
Andrew 60
James 442
John 499
Ashley, Lord 149,150,
160
Andrew 433
Charles 707
Christopher 455
Elizabeth 511
Gilbert 432

Ashley, *(contd.)*
Hester 6
Jeremiah 509
John 433
Rebecca 509
Richard 511
William 236,620
Ashlock, John 442
Ashman, George 24
Ashmore, John 248
Ashton, Elizabeth 701
Henry 487
James 597
Jonathan 532
Joseph 299,382
Thomas 442
William 178,277
Ashurst, Edward 281
Henry 61,77,123,126,
187*,189*,190,213,
237,247,265,284,335
Sir Henry 674
Robert 441
William 329,382,400,
421,584,593
Ashwell, William 620
Asken, John 325
Askew [Ascue], John
290,329,660
Mary 129
Robert 660
Samuel 9
Thomas 345,368
Askin, Michael 431
Aspinall, Katherine 245
Asplyn, Samuel 567
Aspray, Henry 100
Asson, Cornelius 87
Samuel 54
Ast, John 447
Aston(e), Robert 31
Rowland 65
Atchley, Christopher 69
John 102,105
Athay, Richard 480
Atherton, Peter 117,487,
547,584,691,695,
715
William 333
Atherwood, Peter 137
Athowe, Thomas 234
Athurst, William 518

Ayres, *(contd.)*
  Robert 452
  Samuel 569
  Thomas 544,630
Ayroust, Anthony 713
Ayson, Thomas 23

Babb, John 392*
Babbett, Joan 86
Babbidge, George 236
Bab(b)ington, Randall
  524,552,565
  Thomas 352,687
Babell, Hugh 330
Baber, John 354,386,430
  Robert 342
Baby, Anthony 20
Bach(e), Bartholomew
  348
  Elizabeth 318
  John 128
  Peter 352
  Samuel 25
  Thomas 226
Bachelor. *See* **Batchelor.**
Backer, James 91
Backham, Richard 524
Backrell, Henry 14
Backwell, Hannah 27
  Henry 44,119
  James 447
Backworth, William 230
Bacon, Daniel 91
  Edward 181
  John 161,172
  Josiah 302,559
  Nathaniel 282,301,303,
    304*,306,422,492,
    542,560,585,631
  Richard 600
  Thomas 304
  William 102
Badcock, Thomas 199
Baddam, James 45
  Thomas 45
Baddason, John 382
Baddily, John 253
Baddoe, George 688
Baden, John 303
Badenham, John 595

Badge, Jane 197
  Thomas 720
Badger, Jeffery 468
  William 175
Badman, Edward 320
  John 97
Badmington, Mary 88
Baesh, John 328
Bagg, John 556
  Matthew 517
  Roger 279,501
  Thomas 606
  William 148,304
Bag(g)ott, Henry 616
  William 454
Baggs, Thomas 528
Bag(ge)ley, John 689
  Mary 513
  Ralph 513
  Robert 666
  Roger 304
  Thomas 513
Bagnall, George 317
  John 132,332,562
Bagnell, Robert 118,133
Bagwell, Francis 524
  George 23
  Jane 114
  John 523,616
  Peter 523,549
  Thomas 658
Bail, Samuel 429
Bailey [Bayly] [Bayley],
  Alice 60,149
  Ananias 530,533
  Anne 28,158
  Ansell 17
  Anthony 623,188,221
  Arthur 67,200,205*,215,
    237,266,290,292,294,
    295,301,343,344,345,
    381,396,421,470*,
    533,579*,582,597,
    611,623,656,682,683
  Benjamin 592
  Charles 211
  Dorothy 202
  Edward 285,706
  Elizabeth 12,59,81,91,
    533
  Francis 3
  George 198,256,351

Bailey, *(contd.)*
  Hannah 189
  Henry 60*,65,266
  James 45,204,247,288,
    291,300,345,437
  Jane 148,438
  Jeffery 654,716
  John 11,14,61,116,168,
    347,376,413,458
  Joseph 148
  Lancelot 458
  Margaret 51
  Nathan 232
  Richard 2,122,378,462,
    482
  Robert 308,318,354,
    368,483,716
  Roger 654
  Sarah 225
  Simon 654,698,716
  Thomas 11,123,168*,
    188,228,294,561*
  Walter 280,311,716
  William 201,207,259,
    266,523,621
Baillergeau, Jacob 406
Baine(s). *See* **Bayne(s).**
Bainham, Richard 271
Baisnett, William 451
Baison. *See* **Bason.**
Baiton, John 511
Bake, Benjamin 709*
Bakehouse, Joan 12
Baker, Andrew 171
  Anne 133,177,225
  Bartholomew 481
  Charles 7,221,440,524
  Daniel 55
  Edward 212
  Eleanor 288
  Fortunate 288
  Francis 51,62,181,237,
    468
  George 124,193,215,
    270,290,427,483,549
  Giles 535
  Henry 37,67,229,230,
    235,243,253,257,
    274,281,330,361,
    388,392,452,457
  James 524*,526,555,
    568

Bateman, *(contd.)*
Rebecca 180
Sir Thomas 308
William 623
Ba(i)tes, Anne 45
Edward 558
Joan 673
Johanna 660
John 265,558
Jonathan 236
Robert 145,146
Roger 145,146
Thomas 213,375
William 10,385,619,661
Bath, John 245
Mary 28
William 681,718
Bather, Francis 707
Batho, Francis 631,707
Bathum, Thomas 45
Bathurst, John 441
Mary 612
Batt, Edward 237
Henry 652
Israel 165,521
Mark 351,371,401,478,
591,614,653
Richard 229,308,415*,
416,425,468,483
Robert 526,549
Batten, Benjamin 54
Hannah 639
Battersby, George 329
Batterton, Thomas 488
Battey, Thomas 414
Battin, John 577
Thomas 19
William 617
Batting, Thomas 281,
283*,293
Battison, Julian 349
Battle, William 169
Batton, Ishmael 342
Batts, Richard 414,435,
438*,446,448,450,
453,456
Battsly, Richard 132
Baudinell, Elias 588
Bauds, Thomas 595
Baugh, Edward 208
John 223
Joseph 418,461

Bauldry, Elizabeth 533
Jean 533
Bavington, William 641
Bawdon [Bawden,
Humphrey 582
Sir John 615
John 192,213,294,337,
341,355,365,374,
376,378,385,406,
435,438,517*,568
Bawman, Thomas 472
Bawton, John 243
Bax, John 1
Baxforth, Richard 712
Baxter [Backster],
David 485
Edward 149,375
George 1,122,578
John 440,485,542
Richard 463
Robert 119
Sarah 11
Thomas 46,331
William 243,463
Bay, John 116*
Sarah 269
Bayliffe, John 256
Baylis, William 278
Baymer, Thomas 326
Baynam, John 230
Pleasant 571
Richard 571
Solomon 571
Ba(y)ne [Bain], John
561
William 101,136
Baynes [Bains], John
684
Thomas 575
Baynham [Bainham],
Mary 551
Robert 551
Thomas 551
Baynton, John 619
Bays, John 551
Bayton, George 34
Baytop, Thomas 634
Bazen, James 502
William 502
Beach. *See* **Beech.**
Beacham [Beecham]
[Bicham], James 511

Beacham, *(contd.)*
John 696,699
Robert 269
Thomas 355
Beacher, Richard 592
Be(a)con, Edward 217
John 168,171,172,183,
185
Mary 226
Bead, Francis 63
Beadle [Beedle],
Lawrence 189,191
William 258
Beadon, Richard 639
Beake, Benjamin 231
Elias 291
Joseph 247
Samuell 424
Beaker, George 259
Beakes, William 403
Beale [Beele], Abraham
252,351,429,662
Henry 134,150
Jacob 386,507,544,612,
713
John 199,293,338,664
Leonard 567
Richard 628
Robert 525
Samuel 159
Thomas 240
William 713
Bealey, John 162
Beaman, Henry 589
Beames, Robert 604
Roger 14
Beamhouse, Edward 78
Beane, Peter 67
Beanes, Mary 441
Bearcroft [Barecroft],
Humphrey 32
Stephen 301,354,381,
426,539,586
Beard, Elizabeth 83
Francis 284
George 322,679
Godfrey 408
Margaret 634
Robert 72
Stephen 647
Thomas 87,88
William 162,555

Beardmore, John 451
Beardsly, Alexander 415
Beare, Elizabeth 191
 George 450
 Humphrey 16
 John 28,56,70,116,117,
 229
 Peter 604
 Sarah 719
Bearman, Robert 610
Bearnes, Thomas 1
Bearsly, Peter 283
Beart, John 255
Beasley, Elizabeth 467
 William 704
Beate, Richard 69
Be(a)ton, Jerman 143
 John 170,311,598
 Nathaniel 526,549
 Richard 22
 Robert 525
 Timothy 596
Beatson, Susanna 430
Beauchamp, Abel 324
 John 134
 Richard 196
Beaufield, John 682
Beaufoy, Hercules 609
Beaumont [Bemont],
 Abraham 213
 Blewett 246,577
 James 586
 Jane 351
 Richard 437,554
 William 351
Be(a)ver, Elizabeth 463
 John 708
Beazely, John 672
Beazer, Edward 415
 John 384
Becher, Richard 584,603
Beck, Robert 645
 Roger 469
 Sarah 439
 William 1,695
Becker, John 427
Beckett, Humphrey 249
 John 477
 Philip 503
 Thomas 477
Beckford, Edward 15
 Peter 627

Beckford, *(contd.)*
 Richard 296
Beckin, Edward 289
Beckmore, Conyers 120
Becknall, James 302
Becon. *See* Beacon.
Bedding, John 639
 Joseph 516
Beddoe, John 447
Bedell, John 605
Bedford, Edward 451
 Francis 424
 Margaret 3
 Robert 603
 Thomas 122*,163,164*,
 208,216*
 William 651
Bedingfield, Thomas 39
Bedingham, John 342
Beech [Beach], George
 247
 James 446
 John 127
Beecham. *See* Beacham.
Beechley, Grace 76
Beeders, George 37
Beeding, William 453,
 454
Beedle. *See* Beadle.
Beeker, Richard 591
Beele. *See* Beale.
Beels, William 313
Beene, Thomas 625
Beer(e), Edward 196
 John 491,598,607
 Thomas 583
 William 712
Beetle, Frances 60
Beex, John 1
Beford, Thomas 62
Begham, Robert 267
Beighton, John 572,584,
 588,608,621
Beind, John 21
Belbin, Anne 639
Belcham, James 712
Belche(i)r, Andrew 425,
 473,543,595,611
 Frances 161
 James 172*
 John 251,317,399,400
 Thomas 66,140,512

Belche(i)r, *(contd.)*
 William 87,117
Belcherre, Anne 113
Belfore, William 278
Belfour, James 346
Belgood, George 494
 John 494
Bell, Alison 160
 Anne 8
 Henry 695,700
 Jacob 349,601,611
 James 497
 Jane 497
 John 188,197,304,574,
 628
 Joseph 709
 Mary 574
 Nicholas 584
 Richard 627
 Robert 631,669
 Sarah 522
 Susan 212
 Thomas 59,61,191,418,
 502,574
 William 41,443
Bellamy, Edward 524, 553
 Henry 386
 John 249
 Robert 386
 William 596
Bellchamber, Richard 35
Bellew, William 71
Bellgrave, Thomas 379
Bellico, Pasco 100
Belling, John 437
Bellingham, Richard 157
Bellow, William 100
Bellrenger, Margaret 584
Belman, Peter 178
Belshire, Henry 261
 James 4
Belt, Elias 176
 Jonathan 341
Beman, Elizabeth 456
Bemister, Enoch 540
Benan, Charles 35
Benborne, John 307
Benbow, Francis 59,76
 Thomas 210
Bence, Elizabeth 107
Bendall, Freegrace 654
 Hopfar 656

Bendall, *(contd.)*
James 245
Bendon, John 447
Bendry, William 284,286
Bends, James 645
Benerley, John 407
Benfield, Henry 220
Maurice 215
Benford, Alice 186
Walter 178
Benham, William 165,290
Benioge, Richard 186
Benjon, Richard 186
Benn, James 666
Thomas 677
Bennell, William 131
Bennett, Charles 103,
523,552
David 366
Edward 536
Elisha 284,379,392,481,
574,577,623
Evan 26
Francis 197
George 379,702
Henry 574
Hester 57
Isaac 291,292
Isaiah 198
Jacob 63,65
James 433,666
Joan 191
John 33,44,85,91,129,
178,190,364,428,433,
436,467,524,525,
552,596,653,690
Jonas 115
Joseph 570
Margaret 45
Mary 478,660
Nicholas 569
Onisopherus 12
Peter 199,378,436
Philip 45*,49,50*,61
Richard 78,101,142,
270,300,322,536
Robert 25,66,327,368,
382,402,437,544*,656
Samuel 412
Sarah 321
Thomas 103,122,290,
475,548,561

Bennett, *(contd.)*
Timothy 30
William 11,164,165,
252,257,258,297,
548,561,688
Bennett & Dennis 679
Benning, James 246
Bennison, Robert 634
Benny, Alexander 160
Benon, Daniel 10
Benskin, Francis 634
Henry 634,637
Benson, Anne 578
Edward 201
George 345,348
Henry 62
John 126,357,569,640
Mary 165,167,349
Nathaniel 175
Richard 121,191,194,
321*,372,385*,404,
419,430,489,554,
590,601
Robert 98
Rowland 442
William 715
Zachary 640
Bent, John 73
Peter 242
Richard 427,495
Bent(h)all, Walter 503,
583,589,598,605,625
William 597
Bentler, Stephen 219
Bentley, —— 284
Cornelius 61
Jeremy 719
John 135,262,288
Katherine 61
Martin 353
Roger 156,157
Thomas 136,247*,250
William 184*
Benton, George 151
Nathaniel 526
Benum, Temperance 29
Benwell, Joseph 483
Benyon, Daniel 67
Beresford, Henry 252
Berife, Miles 286
Berkeley, Lady 550
Edmund 663

Berkeley, *(contd.)*
Robert 276
Sir William 291,294,
301,303,304,305*,
628
Berkhead. *See*
Birkhead.
Berkin. *See* **Birkin.**
Berkle, Edward 36
Berlow, Richard 714
Berman, Gabriel 603
Bernard [Burnard],
Anne 418
Daniel 406
James 38
John 121,432,455
William 524
Bernford, Henry 252
Berrington, Samuel 604
Berrisford, Thomas 480
William 639
Berrow, Anthony 81,157
Christopher 80,81,328
Elizabeth 72
George 35
John 31,71
Joseph 167
Matthew 10
Nathaniel 32
Philip 544
William 36
Berry, Christopher 230,
250
Edward 35
George 297
Grace 151
James 675
John 20,80,424,601
Richard 51
Robert 112
Samuel 283,482
Thomas 120,122,147,
275,325,553
Walter 175
William 55,529,672
Berryman, John 252
Berton. *See* **Burton.**
Besor, Anne 535
Besouth, James 52
Joan 52
Bessant, Thomas 205
Best, Cuthbert 344

Blanchard, Anthony 270
Blanchflower, Benjamin 519
Bland, Anne 399
 Giles 264
 James 508
 John 16,264,331,362
 Matthew 232
 Michael 299
 Nathaniel 419
 Nicholas 290
 Sarah 264,362
Blan(d)ford, Giles 378
 John 491
Blane, Anne 400
Blaney, John 39,234
Blank(e), Hezekiah 297
 John 165
Blannyer, Henry 396
Blase, Robert 149
Blatchley, John 235
Blathen, Joan 107
Blathern, William 44
Blathwaite, Mabel 418
Blaton, John 547
Blatt, James 131
Blavor, John 343
Blaxton, John 649,627
Blayden, Thomas 681
Blayfield, Giles 402
Blaymor, Henry 280
Blayton, Thomas 98,118
Bleakman, Thomas 505
Blease, Joseph 424
Bleathen, Joan 179
Bleek, Edward 385
 Thomas 699
Blendall. *See* Blindall.
Blenton, John 240
Bless, Thomas 569
Blessly, Elizabeth 149
Blest, Joseph 200
Bletsoe, John 621
 Thomas 569,663
Blew, Walter 523
Blewett [Blewitt], Jane 594,660,673
 Johanna 129
 John 242,538
 Samuel 357,329,395, 416
 William 169

Bligh [Bly], Charles 655
 James 662,693,696,699, 717
 John 65
Blight, Charles 612
 James 545,599,612
Blindall [Blendall], John 74,79
Blindman, Benjamin 7, 8,9,12,30,31,50
Blinkhorn, John 61
Blinnar, Thomas 27
Bliss(e), John 2,9,110
 Thomas 115
 William 508
Blither, Robert 68
Bloome, John 179
 Robert 656
Blount, John 56
Blount, Margaret 12
Blower, James 173
 Richard 534
Blowers, Pyam 412
Bluck, Francis 634
 Thomas 212
Blundell, Bryan 669,677, 678,694,718*
 Daniel 424
 Margery 679
 Mary 424
 Richard 608
 William 695
Blunderfield, Thomas 674
Blunston, John 389,395
Blunt, Benjamin 200,202
 Charles 124
 Christopher 186
 George 347
 Isaac 641
 James 220
 Joan 154
Bly. *See* Bligh.
Blyth, Ann 694
 Thomas 664,704
Blythman, John 427,660
Boake, John 238
Board, Jacob 98
Boardman, Francis 718
 James 701
 Mary 699
Boarken, James 362

Bobby, Thomas 282
Bobett, Anne 342
Bocking, William 629
Boddard, Henry 434
Boddily, Edward 705
Bodenar, Henry 93
Bodenham, John 7,27, 28,30,67*,69,97, 165,182,214,216, 230,231*,232,708
 Robert 20,717
 Thomas 231
Bodesey, John 77
Bodewin, Rene 578
Bodkin, Martin 312,340
 Nicholas 340
Bo(u)dley, Jane 242
 John 188,212
 Thomas 92,126,187,189, 213*,247,248,309
 William 188*
Bodman, Edward 494
 John 181
 Mary 194
 Thomas 49,61,160*
Bod(d)y, John 202,276, 299,385,417
 Thomas 526,551
Bogg, Daniel 720
Bois, Elkanah 336
Bolcher, James 36
Bo(u)ld, William 551
Boldero, Arthur 255
 John 255
Boldero, Mary 255
Bole, Peter 708
Boles, James 47
Bollard, Charles 352
Bollen, John 98,99,100
 Sarah 116
Boll(e)s, Andrew 346
 John 92
 Joseph 92
Bolster, Isaac 525
Bo(u)lt, Andrew 286, 293*,294,296,299, 340,345*,398
 John 423
 Joseph 532
 Joshua 470
Bo(u)lter, Robert 284, 376,388

Bo(u)lton, Edward 566
　Elizabeth 231
　Enoch 32
　Henry 635
　Jacob 686
　James 183
　Job 306
　John 64,177,595
　Mary 38
　Philip 213
　Robert 38
　Thomas 258,375,388*,
　　574
　Timothy 410
　William 406,454,529,
　　635
Bomer, Andrew 301
Bonady, John 691
Bond, Abraham 254
　Elizabeth 113
　Francis 606,630
　Gilbert 620
　Giles 433
　Henry 694
　James 251,253,361,694
　John 378,472,485,679,
　　719
　Judith 328
　Nicholas 1,39
　Rebecca 562
　Samuel 523,553
　Thomas 335,679
　Timothy 340
　Walter 137
　William 562
Bone, Ann 286
　John 639
Boniface, Silvester 522
　William 517
Boniton, John 605
Bonneire, Isaac 664
Bonnell, Jeremy 15
Bonner, Gabriel 564*
　Henry 73
　John 338
　Richard 142,143
　Thomas 66
　William 84,97,248
Bonnet, Phillip 22
Bonney, Thomas 620
Bonns, Jonathan 502
Bonome, Humphrey 69

Boobier, Robert 20
Boodle, Robert 565
Boodly, Robert 597
Booker, Edward 346,404,
　　493,580
　Hannah 456
　Mary 673
Bookey, John 527
Boole, Edward 269
　Jane 269
Boone, Andrew 268,293,
　　297,325,333,359,391
　Gresham 391,413,504,
　　591
　James 178*
　John 581
　Joseph 676
　Richard 331
　Samuel 524,555
　Thomas 250,330,674
　William 62
Boore, John 214
Boote, Charles 436
　Henry 62
　Samuel 436
Booteflower, John 48
Booth, Andrew 133
　Charles 515
　Christopher 383,504,
　　569,621
　Edward 142
　Elizabeth 409,565
　Francis 620
　John 644,718
　Joseph 603
　Richard 69,202,203,215,
　　247,250,253,261,272,
　　292,293,296,301,331,
　　344,346,366,379*,
　　430,535,586
　Thomas 565,674
　Sir William 565
　William 262
Booty, Richard 200
Border, William 207
Bordridge, George 6
Boreham, Thomas 129
Boreman, Joseph 465
　Thomas 327
Boren, John 61
Borer, William 594
Borges, Samuell 420

Borne. *See* Bourne.
Borrodon, Robert 408
Borse, George 74
Borsley, Anne 117
Borton, Edmund 86
Bosiar, James 247
Bosley, Jacob 474
Boss(e), Isaac 55
　Peter 201,328,352,503
　Richard 201
Bossinger, Thomas 329,
　　691
Boston, Nathaniell 572
Boswell, Arthur 343
　Elizabeth 539
　John 138,393,415
　Richard 187,364
Boswick, Venetia 11
Bosworth, Joseph 606
Botfield, Elizabeth 375
Bothomley, Joseph 644
Bothwell, Richard 674
Botley, Samuell 239
Bott, Edward 76
　Elinor 122
Bottle, Jane 164
　John 445
Botton, William 297
Boucher. *See* Bowcher.
Boudenell, Alice 583
Bough, William 349
Boughey, Thomas 369
Boules, Thomas 230
Boullay, Augustine 545,
　　546
　John 543
Boulston, Edward 291
Boult. *See* Bolt.
Boulton. *See* Bolton.
Bound, Robert 96,145
　Thomas 516
Bounsford, Richard 273
Bo(u)rne, Dorothy 673
　Edward 75
　Francis 19,20,21*,42,
　　43*,44,78,87,172
　Henry 436,449
　Jane 507
　John 119,180,196
　Nehemiah 78,214,243,
　　374,591
　Ralph 417

Bo(u)rne, *(contd.)*
Richard 625
Samuel 428
William 62,138
Bourton. *See* **Burton.**
Boussac, John 611
Samuel 674,716
Bouven, Isaac 672
Bovett, Edmond 523,
549,616
Edward 523
John 523,549
Thomas 548,616
Bovey, John 28
Bow, Simon 406
Bowater, William 567
Bowcher [Boucher],
Anne 646
Francis 172
George 47*,48,49
John 584
Paul 650,667,674
Richard 587
Bowdell, Thomas 195
Bowden [Bowdon],
Dorothy 61
Elizabeth 175
John 15
Martha 2
Richard 328
Roger 389
Thomas 229
Bowdenett, Elias 592
Bowdey, Richard 176
Bowdidge, Thomas 676
Bowditch, Giles 719
Sarah 719
Thomas 476
William 719
Bowdler, Andrew 327
Henry 246
James 695,699
Marmaduke 320,353,
368,713
Bowdley, Elizabeth 191
Bowdry, George 338
Bowell, Diana 515
Dorothy 7
Robert 515
Bowels, Arthur 64
Bowen [Bowin]
[Bowne], Arthur 17,340

Bowen, *(contd.)*
Bridget 90
David 184
Edward 83
Griffith 108
Honor 176
Isaac 24
Jane 69
Jenkin 57
John 14,46,165,261,
280
Joyce 14
Judith 128
Lewis 177
Mark 12
Matthew 259
Philotheus 55
Richard 33,133,236
Roger 55
Sarah 280,410
Thomas 226,238,244*,
245,328
William 108,180,223
Bower, Edward 531
James 478
Robert 699
Thomas 5,598,652
William 113
Bowerman, John 241
Thomas 192
Bowers, John 318
Bowes, Arthur 467
Joshua 410
Bowker, Simon 37
Bowkin, Thomas 113
Bowler, Deborah 161
John 161,199
Sarah 199
William 688
Bowles, John 183,254,431
Joseph 280,284,287*,
293,326,332,376,
384,388,393,396,
411,566,619
Thomas 4
Bowley, John 362
Robert 75
Bowling, Thomas 717*
Bowman, James 470,479
John 206,240,399,413,
414*,484,584,633,
649

Bowman, *(contd.)*
Robert 527
Thomas 305,325,389,
396,415,416*,463,
464,527,580,597,
606,644
William 148
Bowry, Benjamin 34
Francis 472
John 110,388,407
Joseph 332
Richard 88
Bowser, Thomas 494
Bowsie, John 282
Bowston, Mary 560
Bowtell, Joseph 491
Thomas 280
Bowyer, Mary 629
William 82
Box, Anne 334
Ralph 187,212,247,278,
283,284,325,326,
383,480
Boxer, William 604
Boxwell, John 55
Boyce [Boys], Andrew
523
George 697,715
Jacob 520
John 112,211,360
Robert 101,440
Rowland 472
Sarah 472
Thomas 270
Boyd, John 68
Mary 181
Boydon, James 389
Boyer, James 413
Nathaniel 236
Robert 420
Boykin, Thomas 97,135,
175,177,178,179,214
Boyle, Elizabeth 617
John 575
Thomas 112,430
William 617
Boylen, Edward 97
Boylston, Anne 471
Richard 77
Boynton, Deborah 541
Boys. *See* **Boyce.**
Boysom, William 116

Boyston, Edward 54
Thomas 268
Boyter, John 465
Braban, Sarah 28
Brabazon, Barnaby 719
Brace, George 447
Giles 224
James 350
Bracebridge, Shem 575
Bracegirdle, John 218
Bracket, Anthony 80
Bradburne, Thomas 88
Bradbury, Thomas 3
Braddon, Nicholas 616
Bradenham, John 283,
294,337
Bradfield, Jeremy 428,
494,559,568,587,622
Thomas 643,687
Bradford, Ambrose 476
Edward 38
Isaac 607
John 408,603,683
Margaret 75
Robert 21
Samuel 675,677
Thomas 21,75,185,391
William 483,549
Brading, John 316
Bradley, Benjamin 238,
411,422,486,572,
621,658
Daniel 131,155,369,381,
398,422,470,528,578,
596,598,608,623,655
George 479
Henry 12
John 295,491
Margaret 515
Mary 611
Michael 290
Simon 491
Thomas 396
William 279,303,351,
443,493
Bradnock, Elinor 16
Bradshaw, Adam 15
Chedley 196
James 508
John 268,312,486,607
Ralph 75
Thomas 264,473

Bradshaw, *(contd.)*
William 565*,698
Bradway, Samuel 517,518
Bradwell, Mary 546
Bradwill, Edward 283
Brady, Andrew 220
Henry 179
Bradyll, Benjamin 592
Bragg(e), Andrew 123
Edward 651
Jenkin 17,40,56,69*,
81,85,100,154
John 524
Brailsford, John 575
Thomas 329
Braine [Brayne],
Benjamin 584,591,611,
656,658,659,660,667
Darby 122
Edward 582
Henry 133,149
James 290,295,371,580,
611,613,658,660,662,
680,624
John 103,136
Martha 10,12,16,29
Matthew 55
Robert 143
Susanna 268
Thomas 13
William 254
Braines, James 199,409,
464,522,539
Bra(i)thwaite, Ezechiel
117
James 82,101,174
Simon 409
Thomas 409
Brakes, John 449
Braking, Joseph 429
Bramble, John 526
Brames, James 239,251,
302
John 239
Bramley, Joshua 503
Thomas 408
Bramsbury, Daniel 634
Bramsey, John 720
Bramsgrove, Benjamin 83
Bramwale, John 694
Branch, Cecilia 109
Nicholas 88

Brand, Charles 50
John 147,267,375
Mary 643,649
Brandby, Elizabeth 348
Brankenwell, Justinian
98
Brannidge, Elizabeth 55
Branscombe, Andrew
146
Branson, Francis 407
Brant, Samuel 197
Thomas 14
Brasey [Brasie], Richard
26
Thomas 392
Brasfield, George 699
Brasier, Bartholomew
619
William 446
Braster, Thomas 706
Bratch, Nicholas 291,
329
Brathwaite. *See*
Braithwaite.
Brattle, John 80
Nicholas 283,286,329,
331,341,347,408,623
Thomas 568,621
Bratton, William 379
Brawne, John 418
Bray, Ambrose 656
Charles 512
Elizabeth 512,576
Henry 286,479,488,519,
526,549
James 551
John 524
Katherine 128
Rachel 512
Richard 67,479,573,
632
Robert 181,233
Thomas 132,134,523
William 512
Brayley, Henry 365
Brayne. *See* **Braine.**
Brayner, John 461
Braywood, Sarah 411
Brazhall, John 684
Brazier, George 650,654,
664
Breach, John 20,153,203

Brown(e), *(contd.)*
John 46,50,54,64,76,
137,145,148,174,185,
193,204,220,273,297,
342,348,350,367,380,
391,395,440,446,448,
449,456*,457,459,
463*,464,468,483,
508,524*,528,530,
541,548,558,566,575,
580,597,607,613,641,
644,649,660,665,672,
691,700,703,713,718
Jonas 524,553
Joseph 228,424,519*,
521,528
Joshua 453
Katherine 531
Leonard 575
Margaret 50
Martha 79,350
Mary 182,227,607,641
Michael 54
Moses 61,358,390,412,
606
Nicholas 112,448
Patrick 29
Peregrine 367,461,464,
533,579,598,620,
655,656,660,678
Peter 623
Philip 82,214
Rachel 328
Ralph 566
Randall 97
Rebecca 279
Richard 146,232,332,
409,531,578,719
Robert 146,231,262,
418,419,604
Roger 67,154,579
Samuel 179,310
Sarah 410,511,606,643,
649
Simon 47,132
Thomas 4,31,52,65,68,
87,178,221,225,331,
374,415,520,522,524,
534,541,612,640,670
William 16,40,44,45,47,
200,225,250,282,285,
312,335,370,389,395,

Brown(e), *(contd.)*
William *(contd.)*
415,529,548,557,616,
636,645,691,696,720,
96,99,119,127,131,
145,154
Brownest, Thomas 77
Browning, Ann 165
Charles 595
Christopher 100
John 165
Richard 12,486*,492
Thomas 350
William 717
Brownsford, James 382,
483
Broxup, Nathaniel 293
Brucy, Thomas 91
Bruett. *See* **Brewett.**
Bruin, John 702
William 463
Brulan [Brulon], Daniel
592,593,596,607
Brumidge, Anne 56
John 183
Brumpsted, Rose 94
Brumskill, John 613
Brune, Rachel 32
Bruneall, Paul 620
Bruton, Daniel 627
Elizabeth 544
George 544
John 192
William 399,476
Bryan [Brian], Andrew
546
Benjamin 506
Elizabeth 439,506,674
George 600
Hugh 606
John 537,140,153
Joseph 277
Lewis 161,162,166
Margaret 63
Margery 31
Mary 546
Nicholas 442
Robert 81,403
Tarlough 144
Thomas 52,244,644,
665
William 152,492,644

Bryant [Briant],
Bernard 548
George 452
Hugh 595
James 296
John 44
Mary 435
Richard 150
Robert 205
Roger 523,549
William 50
Bryar [Briar] [Bryer],
Henry 123
John 523
Joseph 346,608
Nathaniel 571
Bryce. *See* **Brice.**
Brytell, Matthew 404
Bubb, Giles 11*,12
John 304,316*,317,
321*,358,488,612,
679,681
Richard 276
Buck, Gabriel 496
George 653,677,682,
700,715
Hartwell 100,365*,598
Henrietta 453
Hester 127
James 453
Jane 437
Jeremiah 692
Joan 40
John 12,39,588,647
Matthew 59
Obadiah 453
Owen 357
Peter 226
Richard 582
Roger 467
Thomas 279,526
William 90
Bucker, Robert 417
Buckey, John 296
Buckham, Richard 364
Thomas 283
Buckingham, Richard 645
Bucklan, John 467
Buckle, Robert 243
Buckler, Charles 507
William 280,281*,283*,
294,326

Buckley, Ambrose 347
  Edward 688
  Francis 660
  Peter 347
  Richard 283,576,599
  Robert 278
  Rowland 510,511*
  Samuell 393
  Sarah 599
  Thomas 629,635,664
  William 319
Buckmaster, John 66
Bucknell [Bucknall],
  Elizabeth 452
  Ferdinando 452
  Humphrey 375
Buckner, William 640
Buckridge, Edmond
  280,283,325
  Edward 73
Buckshire, John 657,684
Budd, Elizabeth 50
  James 150
  Thomas 150,472,486,
  534,547
Budden [Budding], Joan
  243
  Mary 149
  Susanna 149
  Thomas 594
Budds, Richard 286,287
Budge, John 524,555,591
  Jonathan 299
  Josias 299
Budley. *See* **Bodley**.
Budstarte, John 125
Budwell, John 673
Bue. *See* **Bew**.
Buffield, Isaac 603
Bugby, Samuel 129
Bugden, Jane 378
Buggin, Ann 234
  Benjamin 349
Buglar, Thomas 524,552
Bugle, Daniel 259
Bugnall, Richard 161
  Robert 161
Bulk(e)ley, John 310,619
  Thomas 619
  William 63,342
Bull, Benjamin 621
  James 452

Bull, *(contd.)*
  John 122,164,349,382,
  426,462,478,482,582,
  584,598*,617
  Joseph 328
  Josias 588
  Katherine 435
  Mary 230
  Richard 487
  Stephen 148,712
  Thomas 91,231
  William 32,179*,196,
  254,275,523
Bullard, Richard 577
Bullay, James 406
Bullen, John 221
  John 680
  Thomas 622
Buller, Rebecca 652
  Richard 290*,292,295,
  348,354,365,371,380,
  398,470,528,591,
  597,623,652
Bullery, Humphrey 24
Bullet, John 192
Bullgam, John 83
Bullivant, Benjamin
  336,410,569,621
Bullman, James 707
Bullock, Edmund 408
  Edward 707
  Giles 251,271,395,402,
  403,417,468
  Hugh 148,162
  John 77,86,153,462,511
  Joseph 364,391
  Katherine 38
  Mary 160,511
  Robert 148,162
  Thomas 15,38,160
  William 24,33,80,148,
  192,206
Bullowes, Alice 594
Bully, Joseph 626,690,
  713
Bulmer, John 672
Bulte, John 101
Bummer, Thomas 461
Bum(p)stead, John 128*
  Stephen 455
Buncarr, Humphrey 495
Bunce, John 573

Bunchcombe, William
  289
Bundy, Robert 680
Bunford, John 555
  Mary 555
Bungy, William 31
Bunn, Joseph 666
  William 111
Bunney, Ursula 68
Bunting, John 416
Burbage, John 643
Burbridge, Elizabeth 600
  William 254
Burch. *See* **Birch**.
Burchen, Christopher
  257*
Burcocks [Burkox],
  Eleanor 520
  Thomas 520
Burd. *See* **Bird**.
Burdack, William 69
Burden [Burdon],
  Richard 279,292
  Samuell 294
  William 59
Burdett, Henry 292
  James 655
  Robert 202
  Samuel 581,624
Bure, John 105
Burfoot, Ralph 336
Burford, Edmond 624
  Edward 379,395,420,
  463,470,472,581,
  610,657,684
  George 235
  John 538
  Margaret 27,148
  Matthew 5
  Richard 9,29
Burgan, Elizabeth 437
Burge, John 66
  Samuel 556
Burges(s) [Burgis],
  Abraham 333
  Anne 50
  Anthony 349
  Elizabeth 54,600
  George 354
  John 164,276,357,391,
  476,479,524,556
  Joseph 207,713

Checkley *(contd.)*
John 159
Samuell 663
Thomas 484
Checky, Joan 162
Chedbun, Richard 142
Chedd, James 194,256
Chedsey, William 232
Chedzoy, Edward 526
Cheeke, Philip 524,553
Cheer, Joseph 626
Cheese, Elizabeth 440
John 640
Robert 62
Thomas 437
Chees(e)man, John 18,
34,78
Margaret 364
Robert 475,566
Thomas 382,383
William 326
Cheetum, John 701
Cheevers, Richard 666
Chegley, Jane 168
Chelcutt, Anne 226
Chelderey, Margaret 545
Chelsham, John 436
Cheltenham, Edward 421
Peter 515
Cheltman, Edward 400
Cheltnam, Jacob 73
Chemix, Robert 307
Cherrey, Francis 512
John 421
William 408
Cheshire, Richard 417,
654,715
Chesley, Philip 243
Chesson, Anthony 262
Chester, Granad 363
John 313
Thomas 510
Chetwell, John 448
Chetwin, Thomas 508
Chetwood, Isaac 213,247
Chew, Robert 73
Cheyney [Chayny],
Anne 114
John 46
Chibbett, George 146
Chicheley, Dame Agatha
276

Chicheley, *(contd.)*
Sir Henry 149,276
Sir Thomas 240,241
Chichester, Edward 223
Chick, George 499
Thomas 221
Chickering, John 672
Chicking, Lawrence 411
Chidley, Elizabeth 460
John 632
Katherine 562
Chilcott, John 61,524,
556
Thomas 46,90
William 526
Child, Abraham 2
Alice 31
Ann 603
Daniel 700
Edward 1
Elizabeth 464
James 279
Jeremy 451
John 187,193,212,213,
214,237,241,247*,
263,280,283,381,395,
454,501,513,638,641
Sir Josiah 510
Margaret 561
Mary 641
Matthias 561
Richard 464
Thomas 120,122
Ursula 465
Childersley, Joan 236
Thomas 236
Childerton, Benjamin 15
Ch(e)ilds, George 248
William 324
Chilkin, Tristram 504
Chilton, Alice 295,311
Chilver, John 51
Chiner, Richard 210
Chiners, Humphrey 50
Chiney, John 350
Chinnery, Thomas 333,
459,519
Chipp, Robert 29
Chippett, George 76
Chisman, Thomas 587
Chissers, Abraham 343
Chiston, James 136

Chiswell, Mary 428
Richard 400
Chitty, Abraham 389,620
Matthew 294,547
Richard 627
Chitwood, John 641
Chivers, Jeremy 609
Robert 172
Walter 13
William 93
Chivet, Richard 390
Chock, Alice 95
Cholmley, Job 485
Cholwell [Cholwill],
John 310,359,377,390,
409,450,509*,568,
576
Chooke, Samuel 593
Chope, Joseph 111,204
Chotenham, Edward 621
Chresseham, Daniel 46
Christason, Winlock 166
Christer, Thomas 63
Christian, Abraham 330
Cavaleiro 711
Christian 507
John 544,598,607
Mary 666
Christmas, John 625,717
Richard 129,133
Christofs, Grisby 174
Christon, Daniel 324
Christopher, Katherine 43
Robert 456,494,562,
579,581,623
Thomas 236
William 86*,87,135,
139,204
Winslow 163
Christy, William 84
Chubb, Jacob 320
Chudley, William 108
Chudworth, John 237
Chumley, John 290
Chune, Elizabeth 65
Church, Charles 483
Daniel 453
Elizabeth 600
Henry 68
James 453
John 80
William 16,443

Cooke, Aaron 243
  Abraham 351
  Anne 17
  Arthur 279
  Benjamin 275
  Christopher 578
  Edward 232,243,268,
    409,623,708
  Elizabeth 30,441,543
  Ellen 692
  George 56,442
  Gilbert 336
  Henry 525,543,589
  James 570
  Joan 25
  John 4,53,54,55,57,63,
    78,90,96,106,107,
    128,138,163,176,
    194*,247,282,325,
    361,377,380,389,
    407,450,517,526*,
    531,543,549*,645
  Joseph 38,658*,684
  Lucy 575
  Marmaduke 674
  Martha 376
  Mary 51,575
  Matthew 524,553
  Miles 585
  Nicholas 447
  Philip 233,234,312,
    314,315,543,545,
    546*,550
  Ralph 572,585
  Richard 212,474,683
  Robert 14,440
  Roger 208
  Samuel 150,531,588,
    710
  Sarah 14,300
  Stephen 282,472
  Thomas 15,201,219,243,
    252,357,369,370,575,
    611,663,671,672,685,
    707
  William 62,64,164,231,
    443,492,493,497,
    578
Cooker, Thomas 433
Cookham, James 151
Cookney, William 38
Cooksey, Daniel 251

Cooksley, Mary 569
Cookson, Edward 157,
  158*
Co(o)mbe, Hanna 11
  John 11,238,470
  Simon 426
  William 524,556,666
Co(o)mbes, Adam 458
  Edward 509
  Henry 6,451
  James 523
  John 155,190,225,451
  Richard 560
  Robert 235
  Samuel 367,679
Coop, Charles 701
  Thomas 517
Cooper [Cowper], Ann
  575
  Benjamin 206,252,273,
    301,427
  Christopher 220*,
    523,549
  David 10
  Elizabeth 124,275
  George 94
  Henry 124,444
  James 290
  Jane 94
  John 87,145,193*,208,
    240,273,289,346,424,
    427,442,486,532,544,
    596,603,684
  Joyce 700,703
  Judith 117
  Margaretta M. 531
  Mary 332
  Matthew 375,692
  Peter 55
  Ralph 94,364,379,396,
    419,464*,583,596,
    606,624
  Richard 417
  Robert 126,430
  Samuel 70,126,307,
    522
  Sarah 175
  Thomas 164,223,267,
    268,280,313,330,331,
    351,353,359,372,375,
    381,484,503,532,600,
    620,645,715

Cooper *(contd.)*
  Timothy 87
  William 61,99,427,
    442,670
Coopes, Edward 565
Coopy, Henry 117
Coore, Thomas 703
Coote, Jacob 83
Cooton, John 113
Cope, Hugh 359
  Thomas 455
Copeland, John 79
Copeman, George 59
Copley [Copplee], Jane
  561
  Lionel 1
  Samuel 561
  Thomas 78
Coppacle, Bartholomew
  392
Copping, Edmond 572,
  603,621
  George 234
  William 62
Coppinger, Matthew 236
Copps, Nathaniel 673
Corbett, Abraham 80125
  Edward 313,471,583
  Francis 221
  Gawin 67
  John 236,635
  Richard 161
  William 354
Corbin, Gawen 102,200,
    203,206,213,239,249,
    250,252,286,292*,
    295,301,306,338,
    342,344,345
  George 538
  Henry 95
  Thomas 681,684
Cordelion, Peter 526,549
Corder, John 389
Corderoy, William 114
Cordin(g), Anne 14,21
  John 4
Cordwell, Henry 349
Cordwint, Roger 38
Core, Elizabeth 522
Corens, Charles 112
Corey. *See* Cory.
Corfield, Jane 469

Cripps, *(contd.)*
John 505
Robert 279
Crisp(e), Edward 296,
605
Elizabeth 442
John 301
Joseph 314
Pheasant 630
Richard 138,516,572
Robert 292
Thomas 342,398
Crispin, Thomas 421,
539,581
Crock, John 87,98
Crocker, Benjamin 671
George 47
Joan 203
John 3
Richard 407
William 142,231
Crockett, Richard 414
Crockford, Nathaniel
605
Rebecca 605
Richard 403
Crode, Abel 452
Crofford, Thomas 258
Croft, Edward 716
Elizabeth 211
James 391
John 408
Thomas 447
William 523
Crofts, John 465,486,544,
578
Sarah 359
Crome, Thomas 593
Crompton [Crumpton],
Anne 701
Elizabeth 56,701
Fitzallan 190
Hugh 31
John 391,416,487,550,
618,647,678,700
Margaret 122
Richard 701
Thomas 201
William 56
Cromwell, John 320,343,
345
Crone, George 305

Crooke, Ann 493
Benjamin 522
Phillip 417
Robert 79
Thomas 378
Crookes, Daniel 596,705
Edward 596
Henry 69
Crookshanks
[Cruickshanks], John
336,559
Croom, John 524
Thomas 666
Cropley, Luke 293
Croppin, William 558
Crosby, Henry 22
Croscombe, Eric 69
Ezekiel 134,250
Crosdell, Roger 424
Croson, George 471
Cross(e), Edward 531
Jane 545
Jasper 5,23,33,51*,
52,73*,83*,98
John 4,524,545,553,711
Jonas 524,555
Joshua 489
Leonard 545
Mary 160,617
Peter 211
Richard 711
Robert 471
Samuel 108,160
Thomas 12,246,523,617
William 412,524,552
Crossing, William 332
Crossley, Michael 46
Nehemiah 593
Crossman, Ezechiel 193,
201
Robert 370,420*,550
William 420
Croston, Edmond 550,585
Robert 392
Crothwine, Joseph 63
Crouch [Crowch],
Gilbert 560
Jaziell 663
John 366,620
Joseph 650
William 199,238,247,
277,278,279,280*,

Crouch, *(contd.)*
William *(contd.)*
282,283,284,286,
287*,290,291*,293,
294*,297,302,325,
326,331,332,335,336,
341,343,346,347,400,
410,447,578,620
Croucher, William 134
Crouchley, John 176
Crow, Ang. 540
Ann 275
Benjamin 548
John 279,280,283,326,
329,331,343,345,346,
357*,368,376,383,
388,390,407,505,568,
569,591,601,621
Ralph 25,597
Richard 68
Robert 44
Sarah 147
Thomas 339,446
Walter 80
Crowder, Archibald 1
John 404
John 577
Crowle, William 719
Cro(w)ley, Alice 15
Simon 640
Crown, John 1,327
William 327
Crowther, John 543
Croxton, Hugh 710
James 286
Cruckson, John 671
Cruden, Joan 38
Crump(e), Alice 112
Edward 27,31,33,37
James 707
John 16,202
Joseph 259
Sir Richard 604,682,
713,717
Richard 118,196,304,
323,373,387*,599,610
Thomas 68
Crumpton. *See*
Crompton.
Crundall, Thomas 206,
248,275,293,301,354,
358,375,388,391,

Dagg, Edward 111
Daggett, Richard 321
Dagnell, Samuel 703
Daile. *See* Dale.
Daine, John 137,494
    Joseph 424
Daines, Sir William
    675,716
    William 157,384,
    557,599,610
Dainton, Eleanor 211
Daintry, William 645
    Eleanor 537
Dainty, Katherine 537
    William 537
Dakeyn, Gregory 417
Dakins, Richard 603
Dalby, Isachar 494
    John 131,467
    Thomas 467
Dalcott, John 30
Da(i)le, Edward 202
    John 39*,567
    Jon. 173
    Moses 137
    Peter 397
    Robert 30,294
    Samuel 30
    Thomas 83,222
    William 38,69,98,118,
    165,440
Dallen, Jane 70
Dalling, John 671
Dallison, Martin 199
Dally, Henry 711
    Richard 492
Dalton, James 169
    Joseph 148
    Peter 236
    Thomas 157,344,487
Damarin, Henry 335,401
Dammes, John 201
Damster, Sarah 495
    William 495
Danby, Edward 481
    John 481
    Richard 678
Da(u)nce, Edward 692
    Nicholas 105
Dancer, Robert 83
    Thomas 176
Dand, John 1,15

Dands, Thomas 250
Dandy, Henry 292,295,
    329,347,400,423,540
    James 9
    John 54,118
Dang, Margaret 328
Dangerfield, Edward 81
    James 701
    John 544
    Wartus 19
Daniell, Ann 602
    Christopher 475,478
    Darby 12,602
    Elizabeth 41
    Griffith 143
    Henry 28,38,84,140,
    159,160,188,196,
    224,316,320,321,
    322,353,384,421
    John 299,328,331,333,
    342,338,374,449,
    495,595,605
    Josias 663
    Judith 23
    Nicholas 643
    Richard 339,523,549
    Robert 133,332
    Teague 20
    Thomas 180,181,197,
    250,253,267,309,
    322,525
    Wilbert 239,330,348
    William 101,150
Dann, John 709
    Thomas 438,499
    William 516
Dansy, Anthony 299
Danvers, Amias 660
    Daniel 668,675
    Samuell 358
Dapwell, Robert 6,8,43,
    76*,195,196,261,320
Darber, William 686
Darby [Derby], Bernard
    604
    Charles 56
    Eleazar 716
    Elizabeth 109
    Grace 100
    John 69
    Martin 512*,514
    Miles 132

Darby, *(contd.)*
    Paul 126,187,190,192
    Thomas 14,97,606
    William 411
Darbyshire, Charles 441
Dare, Gideon 616
    Michael 317
    Robert 620
Dark(e), Abigail 343
    James 416
    Thomas 520
Darkenwell, Nathaniel
    148
    Sampson 148
Darkin, Richard 573
    Robert 338,712
Darling, John 469
Darnell, Henry 396
    Thomas 466
Darracott, Ethelred 272
    John 96,100,401,479
    Richard 290
    Thomas 719
Darrant, Frances 473
Darrell, Richard 696
Darricott, John 599
Darson, Edmond 567
    James 567
Darte, Mark 166
Darton, Mary 186
Darvall, Cornelius 374
    Richard 374
    Thomas 377
    William 291,324,377,410
Dashashire, Mary 359
Dashwood, Francis 131
    Samuell 284
Dassey, Thomas 357
Dately, Francis 520
Daughton, Thomas 536
Dauncey, Anne 706
    Joseph 706
Dave, James 100
    Thomas 76
    Welthian 91
Davenport, Addington
    628
    Edward 421
    John 704,705
    Lawrence 546
Daveson, Grace 474
    Henry 474

Dawden, John 370
Dawes, Nicholas 583
  Samuel 472,502,539
  William 469
Dawkes, Davis 112
Dawkins, George 32
  Mary 389
  Richard 326,332
  Simon 246
Dawson [Dorson],
  Abraham 135
  Anne 560
  Barbara 38
  Bartholomew 313
  Christopher 51,59
  John 568
  Mark 38
  Mary 560,708
  Matthew 539
  Maurice 359
  Rebecca 424
  Robert 291
  Samuel 436
  Sarah 254
  Tremmit 341
Dawtrey, William 410
Dax, Thomas 220
Day, Agnes 559
  Anne 215
  Damaris 639
  Edmond 234
  Edward 295
  Eleanor 389
  Elizabeth 151,499*
  George 331
  John 121,135,190,215,
    393,484,673,708,716*
  Joseph 1,3,4,18,22,26,
    47,90,133,147,168
  Leonard 557
  Margaret 708
  Mary 712,720
  Matthew 32,682
  Merrian 557
  Michael 79
  Nathaniel 200,271,298,
    536
  Nicholas 471,533
  Richard 49,51,53,161*,
    482,609
  Robert 5,268,322,367,
    716

Day, *(contd.)*
  Sarah 720
  Thomas 30,33,37,368,
    403,440,467
  William 6,244,325
Daybrinke, Elizabeth
  318
Dayman, John 92
Deacombe, Edward 704
Deacon, Thomas 629
Deakins, Alice 488
  Robert 488
Deale, James 592
  Robert 462
  Thomas 595
  William 523,549
Dealtry, Margaret 236
Deame, William 289
Deane, Abel 417
  Anne 27
  Christopher 431
  Emanuel 128
  Francis 423
  Gabriel 32,34,36,128,
    133*,197,202
  George 176,641
  Jeremiah 79
  John 109,123,156,169,
    175,185,282
  Martha 320
  Michael 289,669
  Moses 708,710
  Richard 217*,461,518
  Samuel 397,588,658
  Sarah 592
  Silvester 345,368,383
  Susan 669
  Thomas 122,187,190,
    191,261,329,343,
    388,390,454,651
  William 341
  Zachariah 203
Deanes, James 540
  Sir William 666
Deare. *See* **Deere.**
Dearing. *See* Deering.
Dearsley, Thomas 272
Death, Andrew 248
Deble, Jeremiah 659
Debnam, Thomas 523
Deboard, James 558
De Camps, Isaac 442

Decasseris, Abraham 626
  Isaac 626
  Samuel 626
Decent, John 30
Dedbridge, William 340
Dedicott, James 31
Dedman, Anne 540
Dee, Margery 84
Deere [Deare], John 519
  Richard 666
  Thomas 176
Deering [Dearing],
  Samuel 166
  William 411,568,621
Defell, Sarah 24
Deffield, John 35,37
  William 37
Defrane, Benjamin 358
De Gelder, Cornelius 330
Degrave, John 411,479,
  532
De Grut, Elias 660
De Hague, Godfrey 128
Deighton, Henry 201
Dejeane [Degane]
  [Dejane], Benjamin
    291,294,370,375,
    390,479,594,650,
    654,660
De Jorden, Olandia 10
Delahay, William 140
Delamott, Margaret 574
Delancey, Stephen 712
Delaplace, Henry 406
De la Prairie, Robert 223
Delarmer, Thomas 171
Delavall, John 325,358
Delbridge, Robert 678
Deledicq, Lawrence 632
Delillers, Isaac 446
Dell, John 132,193,554
  Joseph 244
  Thomas 468,607
Deloge, Michael 54
Delytree, Isaac 422
De Marland, Peter 680
Demarry, Thomas 375
Dembry, John 139
Demerick, Sarah 326
Demerry, Philip 376
Demetrius, John 50
Demogy, William 660

Dickenson *(contd.)*
John 564
Joseph 294
Michael 690
Robert 520
Thomas 546
William 145,688,717
Dicker, William 152
Dickeson. *See* **Dixon.**
Dickfield, John 133
Dicks. *See* **Dix.**
Dickson. *See* Dixon.
Diddall, William 102
Digby, Charles 222
John 15
Sarah 37
Diggery, Joan 411
Diggs, William 424
Dight, Mary 40
Dighton, William 140
Dike. *See* **Dyke**
Dilks, John 707
Dill, Thomas 596
Dilling, Penelope 113
Dilloway, John 567
Dilworth, James 393
Dimmock [Dymocke],
Alice 45
John 18,54
Robert 21,59,65,78*
Dimpsey, Philip 188
Dimsdall, Joshua 336
Dinant, George 296
Dingley, William 238,
241,250*,287,326,
331,341,382,384,
399
Dinnett, John 526
Dinsdall, Joshua 279
Diptale, Ann 481
John 481
Dirrick, Gertrude 410
Disher, William 357,368,
383,416,454
Disney, Robert 51
Ditch, William 619,
Ditcher, Anne 376,400
John 192,376,400
Ditty, Edmund 90,156*,
170,278
Richard 32,36
Richard 543

Dix [Dicks], Alice 277
James 146
John 146,382,447,448,
464,469,492
Milbrow 24
Thomas 22
Dixey [Dicksey],
William 306,638
Dixon [Dick(e)eson],
Andrew 381
Charles 247
Elizabeth 124
Humphrey 433
John 146,310,359,513,
712
Jonas 709
Mary 513
Robert 682
Roger 152
Samuel 562
Sarah 6
Thomas 92
William 131,515,588
Dobbins, George 214
Henry 202
Sarah 657
Dobree, John 710
Dobson, John 695,699
Samuel 509,622
Dockwra, William 423,
427,439,486,508,583
Docton, Nicholas 426
Dodd, John 158
Richard 643
Robert 212
Simon 505
Thomas 506,591,625,
704
Dodderidge, George 163
John 164
Dodds, Archiman 154
John 526,549
Doddy, Thomas 704
Do(i)dge, Amos 537
John 224
Thomas 254,568,569,
572,621,662
Dodimet, Walter 261
Dodson, Katherine 376
Lancelot 386
Samuel 551,589,612,656
Thomas 410

Dodson, *(contd.)*
William 25,299,366,
399,704
Dodsworth, Anthony 444
Christopher 386,390,
392,466,527
John 393,461
Doe, James 542
Richard 568
Doggett, Ann 471
John 335,357
Dolbeare, Samuel 523,
549
Dolberry, Andrew 310,
330,416,645
William 433
Dolbin, Benjamin 659
Dolby, Martha 637
William 237,275,281,
344,420,637
Doldern, William 613
Dole, Erasmus 122,310,
323,330,333,355,
358,377,380,480,
591,667,673
Grace 33
John 109
Tobias 467
Dollery, Anthony 148
Dolling, Benjamin 610,
681
John 3
Thomas 5*,22*,23*,24*,
25,523,549
Dol(e)man, Alexander
369,418
John 105,245,287
Mary 316
Thomas 526
Dolphin, Thomas 611
Dominee, Ann 495
Matthias 495
Donalson, James 247,289
Done, John 550
Donfellow, William 244
Doniphan, Alexander
282
Donne, John 673
Robert 403
Donning, James 678
John 708
Thomas 116

Drew, *(contd.)*
  Anthony 293,370
  Garrett 54
  James 15
  Joan 118
  John 205
  Jonathan 525
  Richard 665
  Roger 314,339,343,
    348*,366,369,395,
    418,546
  Thomas 50,567
  William 223,524,555
Drewett [Druett], John
  164
  William 258
  Morgan 281
Drignion, Rene 454
Dring, Matthias 178
  Stephen 121,240*
Drinkwater, John 38
  Richard 238
  Samuel 667
  William 68
Driscoll, Florence 152
Drive, John 84
Driver, Edmond 11,259,
  386
  Edward 259,377
  Elizabeth 497
  Henry 461,488,491
  John 17
  William 377
Droilehett, John 712
Drope, William 288,380,
  395,402
Drower, Robert 525,526
Druen, Richard 358
Druett. *See* **Drewett.**
Drummer, Francis 462
  Michael 447,462
Drummond, Sarah 301,
  302,368
  William 158,301,302
Drumont, James 104
Drunckourt, Anthony 545
  James 545
  Susanna 545
Drury, Elizabeth 343
  Thomas 528
Dry, George 61
  William 622

Drydall, Joshua 283
Dryden, Henry 439
  James 340,419,527,581,
    582,585,610
  Thomas 440
Dryer, Samuel 98
  Tobias 523
Dubbs, Richard 130
Duboys [Duboyce], John
  335,688
Ducane, Peter 358
Duchais, Daniel 414
Duck, Arthur 230
  John 643
  Mary 359
Duckenfield, Thomas 495
  William 495
Ducker, John 696
Duckett, Alice 451
Duddleston(e), Sir John
  654,655,656,669,
  682,711,716
  John 122,129,202,203,
    353,546,654,610
  Jone 317
  Thomas 102,110,191,
    358,364*,380,412,
    599
Dudlett, William 55
Dudley, Ambrose 718
  Charles 189,190
  Elizabeth 282,305
  James 282
  Joseph 642,675
  Thomas 282,668
  William 282,305
Dudson, Edward 132
  Thomas 283
Duffield, Edward 61,332,
  348,352
  Isabel 567
Dufoy, David 588
Dugar, Anthony 578
Dugard, John 56
Dugden, Margaret 322
Dugmore, Christopher
  289
  Dorcas 375
Duke, Charles 396,416,
  423,446,505,554,
  576,584
  John 55

Duke, *(contd.)*
  William 24,253
Dukes, Ann 410
  Thomas 9,693
  William 333
Dukesell, Margaret 124
Dull, Richard 340
Dumaresque, John 702
  Nicholas 607
Dumbile, Ann 702
Dumbleton, Abraham 292
Dummutt, Richard 181
Dunbalin, Thomas 694
  William 694
Dunbar, John 462,688
Duncan, James 594
Duncanson, William 717
Dunch, Barnaby 241,271,
  286,288,299*,302,
  334,345,349,350,
  363,374
  Daniel 299
  Elizabeth 379,381
  John 70,182,200,203,
    270,292,307
  Mary 271
  Walter 250,271,273,
    299,474
Duncombe, James 638
  John 333
  Richard 27
  Susanna 646
Dundas, William 341
Dune, Daniel 178
Dunfield, Thomas 240
Dunkerton, William 272
Dunkin, James 638
  John 592
Dunkley, Abraham 495
  Elizabeth 540
  Joseph 435
  Moses 117*
  Thomas 443,475,495
Dunklin, Robert 681
Dunlop, John 409
Dunn(e), George 11
  John 325,485,586,665
  Richard 165
  Sibilla 535
  Thomas 435*
  Tobias 203
Dunning, Francis 525

764

Edwards, *(contd.)*
　Walter 8
　William 17,27,33,232,
　　318,321,461,523,632
Edwin, Elizabeth 488*,489
　Francis 486,488*,489
　Sir Humphrey 610
　Humphrey 357,591,603
　William 443
Edwins, William 106
Eeff, Nathan 536
Effoll, Thomas 625
Efford, Peter 87
Eggaree, Francis 623
Eggleston, Philip 254,319
Eglin, Thomas 526
Eilsey, Robert 26
Eke, George 251
　Joan 251
Ekin, William 620
Elbiston, Peter 134
Elbridge, Aldworth 125,
　201
　John 29
　Thomas 26,30,33,60,62
Elbur, Mary 121
Elbury, Mordecai 12
Elcock, Edward 77
　Thomas 323
Elcombe, Eleazar 219
Elder, William 15
Elderkin, John 457
　William 539
Eldershire, John 418
Elderton, Thomas 720
Eldridge, Joseph 554
　Matthew 621
　Robert 564*
Eleate, William 21
Elemond, Robert 36
Elered, John 592
Eley. *See* **Ely.**
Elford, James 525*
Elger, Elizabeth 25
Elkin, George 542
　Nathaniel 340
　Thomas 126,237,243*,
　　244,247*,282,283,
　　286,286,294,374
Elkins, Richard 424
Ellers, John 357
　Thomas 366

Ellery, John 619,667
Ellett, Frances 225
　Josias 426
　Mary 52
　Peter 543
　Robert 122
　Thomas 543
Elletts, Richard 467
　Robert 467
Ellgood, Richard 501
Ellice. *See* **Ellis.**
Ellicott, Vines 335
Ellingham, William 663
Ellingworth, John 578
Ellinor, Thomas 649
Ellinsworth, William 346
Elliott, Anne 212
　Anthony 498
　Charles 519
　Cornelius 525
　George 80,530
　Henry 346
　James 68,431
　John 212,467,496
　Lionell 578
　Matthew 13,523
　Robert 122
　Roger 582
　Samuel 82,598
　Stephen 626
　Thomas 56,205,253,540
　William 484,586,629
Ellis [Ellice], Charles
　696,699
　Edward 257,271,282,
　　287,347,379,390,396,
　　404,408,411,451,505,
　　566,578,582,622,683
　Humphry 395
　James 95,96
　Jeffrey 532
　Joan 712
　John 55,116,294,298,
　　326,336,423,433,484
　Margaret 711
　Mary 539
　Percival 552
　Richard 163,325,331
　Robert 220,383,584
　Samuel 221,392,677,
　　693,713
　Simon 420

Ellis, *(contd.)*
　Thomas 42,63,83,84,85,
　　225,294*,347,418,
　　437,480,487,528,540,
　　543,580,588,607,609,
　　656,658,681,683,695*
　William 35,140,225,
　　528,686,711
Ellis & Cheesley 593
Ellison, George 457
　John 4
　Thomas 232
　William 457
Elliston, George 333
Ellmore, Thomas 178
Ellor, Enoch 135
Ellott, John 245
Ellwill, John 359
Elmes, John 665
　Mary 64,103
　William 87
Elowes, John 204
Elsam, Dorothy 445
Elsden, Aaron 184
Elsey, Thomas 507
Elsing, Thomas 591
Elsley, Matthew 295
Elsmore, John 666
　Mary 211
　Robert 211
Elson, James 247,265,
　293
　Thomas 326
　William 330
Elston(e, Robert 418,596
　William 426,548
Elsworthy, John 591,604
Elt, John 631
　Thomas 184
Elton, Abraham 391,412,
　　484,546,601,649,651,
　　654,667,668,672,673
　Andrew 503,565,619
　Anthony 397
　Jacob 99
　Joseph 712
　Thomas 103
　William 440
Eltworth, John 192
Elver, James 114
Elverd, James 10
Elvins, Hannah 315

Elwand, Alan 213
Elwes [Elwys], George
544,559
Jeremy 473,487
Thomas 250,270,296,
299,350,369,370,
Thomas 381,385,397,
419,423,429,432,469,
522,527,559
Elwick, John 487
El(l)wood, Cipper 518
Joseph 719
William 179
El(l(worthy, Robert 639
Samuel 525
El(e)y, Gabriel 456
George 456
John 267,296
Richard 355
Thomas 329,648
William 378,578,603
Emannuel, Mary 131
Emberley, Froud 566,
619
John 413
Simon 466,528,579,598,
609,623
William 498
Emberry, Edward 35
William 507
Emberton, Francis 381
Emblin, Elizabeth 85
Embling, Christopher
204
Emerson, Aaron 664
Henry 649
James 432,442
Ralph 691
Thomas 671
Emerton, Anne 446
Emery, John 341
Margaret 191
Richard 442
Simon 268
Emes. *See* **Eames**.
Emley, Mary 390
Emmes, William 50
Emmett, George 613
John 14
Josias 58
Emmont, Edward 140
Empson, Cornel 470

Enbree, John 292
End, William 255
Endecott, John 1,3,4,650
Enderby, Oliver 330
England, Allen 523,549
Anne 10
Barenthia 413
Dorothy 204
Francis 417
James 720
Jane 180
John 153,165,183,236,
261,321,344,355,
364,524,534,552
Philip 249,413,525
Richard 123
Robert 180
Samuel 86
Susan 180
Thomas 523
William 172*,184
Engleton, Jane 42
English, Giles 279
John 37,105,400
Joseph 391
Peter 395
Philip 395
Robert 518
Walter 482
William 279,689
Ennis, Anne 629
Ennott, William 318
Enos, Richard 507
Ensdale, Anthony 493
Enton, John 629
Epes, Francis 613
Erbury, Edward 168
Thomas 28
Erby, Elizabeth 409,636
William 636
Erdeswick, John 64
Eridge, John 130
Ernell, Anne 82
Erpe, Elizabeth 148
Mary 148
Sarah 148
Errington, Gerrard 35
Erskin, Archibald 391,461
Ertome, William 687
Ervin, Andrew 474
John 525
Escott, Thomas 360

Esden, Richard 77
Eshall, George 559
Espin, George 313
John 313
Essex, William 116
Essington, John 3,109,
290,293,328,375,
405,413,494
Estob, Ralph 552
Eston, John 597
Estop, John 29
Estwick, Phessent 193
Etherington, Thomas 47
Ethewe, Rachel 430
Eton. *See* **Eaton**.
Evan, Jenkin 100
Mary 153
Reece 163,226
William 135
Evans [Evance] [Evins],
Abraham 249,251,268,
602
Alice 2
Anne 378,453,701
Charles 410,546
Cicely 208
David 35,228,273
Edward 27,105,113,142,
227,337,372,438,469
Elinor 181,275
Elizabeth 3,83,101,280,
311,561
Ellis 508
Emanuel 161
Evan 433,577
Gainer 25
Griffin 255,258
Helen 557
Henry 46,221,503,686
Hugh 181
James 132
Jane 122,686
Joan 58,327
John 10,27,32,55,69,
101,127,147,174,262,
478,510,530,539,557,
589,594,606,612,709
Lewis 2,82,332,464,477
Margaret 544
Mark 93
Mary 37,142,208,220,
258,351,475,536

Fanster, Clement 293
Fantin, William 198
Farclue. *See* Fairclue.
Farding, Ann 7
 John 7
Far(e)well, Elizabeth 550
 George 605,642
 John 91
 Margaret 605
 William 37,359
Fargusion, Robert 688
Farish, Robert 684
Farle, Elizabeth 40
Farley, Elizabeth 225
 John 420
 Margaret 26
Farlow, William 64
Farmer, Alice 40
 Anthony 539
 Helen 211
 Henry 34
 James 362
 John 254,524,556
 Margaret 229
 Richard 267,616
 Robert 49
 Samuel 525*
 Thomas 129
 William 471,482,535,
 540
Farnell, William 390
Farnfield, John 150
Farr, Edmund 280
 Johanna 50
 Richard 490
Farrell, Daniel 5
 Hubert 217
 Hugh 351
 Roger 354
 Thomas 688
Farrer [Farrar], Henry
 679
 Mary 627
 Robert 226,293*,344
Farrier, Richard 321
Farrin, John 174
Farrington, John 92
 Michael 24
 Thomas 326
Farrow, Edmond 445
 Francis 431
 John 649

Farrow, *(contd.)*
 Susanna 347
Farthing, John 73
Fartley, William 699
Fa(i)rvacks, Daniel 152,
 153,161
 David 138
 John 152,161
Farworth, Joseph 269
Fassaker, Richard 267
Fassett, James 64
Fathers, John 526
Faulkner [Falconer],
 Deborah 470
 Edward 48
 Frances 297
 Francis 48
 John 101
 Mary 698
 Peter 588
 Robert 470
 Sarah 405,470
 Thomas 384,410
 William 125,126,227,
 338*,360
Fauntleroy, James 335
Fauves, Peter 678
Faux, Edward 708
 Robert 693
Fawcett, James 501
 Richard 131,423,479,
 542
 Walter 470
 William 532
Fawconer. *See* Faulkner.
Fawne, Elizabeth 91
 George 544
 John 91
 Luke 91
 Robert 523
Fawthropp, Christopher
 196
Fay, Peter 349
Feaghery, Thomas 334
Feakes, Joyce 409
Feakley, Charles 177
Fear, Francis 349
Fearclue. *See* Fairclue.
Feare, Cicely 154
 John 151
 William 525
Fearne. *See* Ferne.

Feast, Henry 79
Featherston(e),
 Ebenezer 618
 John 245,635
 Richard 589
Feaver, Henry 388
Feaveryear, Edmond
 393*,397
Febber, Peter 547
Fechom, Robert 386
Felgate, Samuel 530
Felix [Phelix], Henry 448
Fell, Elinor 266
 John 124
 Lydia 336
 Phillip 651
Fellowes, William 391
Felt(h)am, Andrew 99
 Charles 569,621
Felton, Alice 40
 Edward 152
 Richard 40
 William 210
Fenace, Charles 605
Fendall, James 374
 Joseph 134
Fenn, Anthony 303,307
 Benjamin 238
 Henry 324
 Humphrey 329
 Thomas 121,502
Fennell, Richard 472,491
Fennick, Lionel 522
Fenott, Nicholas 11
Fenshaw, Edward 551
Fenton, Edward 280,358
 John 692
 Mary 627
 Pres 362
 Robert 394
 William 544
Fentzell, John 540
Fenwick, Edward 325
 Lionel 567
 Robert 469,601
 William 469
Ferguson, David 675
 William 151
Fermin, Thomas 278
Fernandes, Abraham 631
 Nune 653,663
Fernauld, Samuel 80

Fletcher, Anne 225
  Benjamin 653
  Elizabeth 406,505,506
  Frederick 645
  James 416
  John 172,335,505,506
  Mary 148
  Richard 138
  Robert 228
  Samuel 134
  Stephen 711
  William 10,27,50,66,
    135,455,647,668,
    703
Fleuriott, Daniel 533
  Jean 533
  Louise 533
Flew, Simon 420,440
Flexny, Robert 353
Fley, William 207
Flicknoll, Henry 562
  Rebecca 562
Flint, Henry 604
Flixon, John 565
Flood, William 492,545,
  547
Flooke, John 193
Flory, John 110
Flower, Daniel 160,163,
  551,578
  Elizabeth 176
  Enock 415
  Frances 435
  John 146,162,176,
    280,525
  Mary 551
  Phillip 8
  Richard 175
  William 33,34,36,49,
    50,51*,52,53,54
Flowerdew, John 276
Flownes, Samuel 189
Floyd, Edward 62,237,
  296*,299
  Henry 151
  John 144,163,245,414,
    421,477,503,565,
    647
  Margaret 460
  Margery 22
  Mary 236,697
  Nicholas 213*

Floyd, *(contd.)*
  Noah 61,70,76,90,120,
    121,123,125,126,132,
    173,187*,189*,190,
    192,193,195,206,212,
    237*,268
  Reece 94
  Richard 193,213,266
  Roger 170
  Thomas 53
  William 98,579
Fluellin. *See* **Llewellin.**
Fly, John 689
  Richard 474
Flyd, Hugh 64
  John 39
  Thomas 43
  William 42
Flyfoote, John 208
Foach, Henry 192
Foane, Robert 523
Foe, Daniel 449,566,583,
  589,594,604
Fogg, David 334,338
  Ezechiel 140,210
  Nathaniel 704
  Richard 595,639
Foissin, John 648
Foley, Thomas 1
Foller, Thomas 458
Follett, Henry 116
  John 523,549,634
  Nicholas 663
Follington, Richard 315
Follint, Richard 334
Folliott, Elinor 108
Follitt, John 325
Fonken, Henry 496
Fontenew, Peter 42
Foode, William 548
Foote, Henry 366
  John 108,526,549
  Richard 287,298,328,
    673
  Thomas 350
Forbes(s), Arthur 398,
  440
  John 654
  Robert 512,570,573
Forbush, James 328
Forby, Felix 3
  John 412

Forcey, Thomas 523,549
Ford, Abraham 250
  Amos 360,378
  Anne 98,206
  Arthur 525*
  Charles 512
  Edward 73,525
  Elinor 274
  Elizabeth 73
  Francis 338
  George 210,669,670
  Giles 98
  Hannah 269,275
  Hester 701
  Isaac 617
  Joan 3,225
  John 6,72,171,185,191,
    233,288,306,371,381,
    452,478,591,649,666
  Joseph 540,634
  Lawrence 704
  Lettice 218
  Philip 383,388,389,
    394*,420,581,619,
    620
  Richard 455
  Sarah 324
  Thomas 252,256,319,
    716
  William 129,166,191*,
    192,194*,199,215,
    219,229,438,452
Fordham, John 397
  Thomas 673
Fordick, William 49
Foredom, William 433
Foreman. *See* **Forman.**
Foresight, George 193
Forest, Francis 286
Forger, Ann 529
Forley, Elizabeth 234
For(e)man, Henry 198,
  216,241,250,289,290,
  292*,296,297,298,
  326*,331*,392,395,
  418
  Jacob 206
  Jeremiah 192,216,268,
    337
  William 641
Forrester, Dorothy 571
Forset, John 33

Garfoot, John 658
  Sarah 419,482,540
  William 239,288,289,
    334,338,379,395,398
Garland, Elizabeth 265
  John 672
  Randolph 544
  William 124
Garlett, Robert 688
Garlick, Hannibal 112
Garlington, Lydia 399,
  400
Garman, John 44
Garmant, George 151
Garner, Thomas 12,43
Garnesay, Edward 84
  James 14
Garnet(t), Elizabeth 151
  James 532
  John 532
  Sarah 546
  Thomas 419
Garnish, Thomas 115
Garolls, James 181
Garrard, Rebecca 622
Garraway, Edward 113
  Richard 128
Garrett [Garratt],
  Ambrose 680
  Elizabeth 27
  George 224,228
  Henry 409
  Joan 224
  John 224,228,283,578
  Joseph 519
  Judith 224
  Nicholas 710
  Thomas 603
  Walter 183
Garricke, David 672
Garrie, David 663
Garrington, Lydia 399,
  400
Garrold, George 524
Garroway, Walter 172
Garstell, Elizabeth 622
Garth, Avery 560
  Richard 560
Garvis, Humphrey 93
Garway, John 146,147
  William 441
Gase, Nathaniel 626

Gaskin, Andrew 665
Gass, Richard 691
Gasson, Thomas 152,312
Gastrell, Anthony 246
  Roger 666
Gasway, John 701
Gatchell, Edward 709
  John 457
Gate, John 88
Gatehouse, Elizabeth
  437
Gater, Mary 176
Gates, Capt. 79
Gathering, Thomas 49
Gatlock, Joan 23
Gatly, John 23
Gatonby, Francis 645
Gatton, John 658
  Thomas 279,357,438
Gaudrum, Matthew 247
Ga(u)lt, James 677
Gauslin, William 603
Gausset, William 45
Gawden, Isabel 375
Gawen, James 625
Gawes, Sarah 513
Gawler, Katherine 582
Gawthorne, Richard 283,
  294,326,347,377
Gay, Anthony 194,196
  George 61,272,283*,294,
    295
  Mary 228,666
  Matthew 151
  Richard 102,519
  Thomas 160,519
  William 17,90,140
Gayling, John 719
Gayner [Gainer],
  Samuel 268
  Thomas 12,28,29,30,31,
    86,95,99
Geale, Joseph 525
Geange, Henry 157
Geare, Christopher 214
  John 224
  William 578
Geary, John 669
  Thomas 205
Geaston, Andrew 4
Geay, Peter 479
Gee [Jee], George 211

Gee, *(contd.)*
  John 291
  Rebecca 246
  Thomas 198
Gefford, John 203
Gelbenon, James 445
Geldart, Richard 715
Gellisoe, Elizabeth 103
Gembell, Adam 667
Generall, James 578
Genge, William 665
Genings. *See* **Jennings.**
Genn, John 229
Gennett, Margaret 409
  William 409
Gent, Richard 414
  Samuel 448
  Thomas 707
Gentle, Thomas 679,699
Gentleman, Evers 531
  Thomas 531
  William 463
George, Benjamin 117
  John 7,94,119,212,282,
    290,445,482,601
  Joseph 445
  Lambert 165*,177*,178*,
    179*,180*
  Mary 196
  Richard 463
  Ryer 105
  Sarah 34
  Shadrach 177
  Thomas 57,116,117
  Walter 3
  William 147,167,448,
    522
Gerald, John 667
German, James 525
  John 482
  Thomas 35
  William 277
Gerrard, Anthony 193
  Benjamin 279,331,400,
    423
  Edward 143
  Francis 408
  Henry 638
  John 585
  Samuel 267,326,621
  Susan 568
  Thomas 241

Gerring, Robert 60
Gerrish, ——— 682
  Benjamin 331
Gerry, Luke 10
Gervaire, Lewis 578
Gester, Ambrose 540
  Anthony 300,342,381,
    398,423,547,554,597
  Arthur 482
Gethin, Simon 269
Gething, Anthony 24
  Elizabeth 14,16
  John 25
Gethings, Edmond 617
Getley, John 644
  Richard 138
Gettings, Richard 16,27
Geuether, Nathaniel 358
Gey, John 616
Gibb, Robert 248
Gibbins, James 126
  Mary 674
Gibbitus, William 573
Gibble, Robert 454
  William 454
Gibbon, Elizabeth 399
  John 389
  Matthew 331
  Ralph 237
  Thomas 22
Gibbons, Abraham 683
  Agnis 396
  Henry 488,524,555
  John 70,145,415,488,
    504
  Jonathan 361
  Mary 603
  Richard 321,388,407,
    455,592,602,667,668,
    683
  Samuel 503
  Sarah 703
  Thomas 128,347,348,
    349,354
  William 713
Gibbs, Abraham 33
  Amy 576
  Anne 108
  Edward 4,5,21,34,217,
    228
  Elizabeth 457
  Francis 488

Gibbs, *(contd.)*
  George 2
  Henry 100,331,349,368,
    377,392,591,604
  Isaac 399,450,556
  John 62,85,116,117,409*,
    410,502,523*,530,553
  Mary 471,701
  Matthew 31
  Nicholas 576
  Philip 230
  Ralph 440
  Rebecca 139
  Richard 149,166*,432
  Robert 303
  Samuel 369
  Sarah 576
  Susan 180
  Thomas 95,138,139,177,
    461,471,569,584,
    592,619
  William 447,473,608
Gibson, Anne 191
  Charles 704
  Elizabeth 295
  John 637
  Matthias 685
  Richard 76,78,172,173,
    174,282
  Susan 311
  Thomas 692
  William 503,681
Gidcomb, Sampson 672
Giddy, William 645
Gideon, Samson 653
Gidney, George 124
  John 157
Gifford [Giffard], John
  1*,39,140,274
  Nicholas 310,469,532
Gilbert, Edward 526
  James 266,285,312
  Jane 65
  John 189,191,611,653,
    700
  Katherine 95
  Mary 410,471,530
  Thomas 250,285,312,
    441
  William 108
Gilborne, Christian 64
  John 64

Gilby, Jacob 96
Gilchrist [Gillgrist],
  John 408
  Lewis 679
Gild, Thomas 166
Gildar, Benjamin 274
Gilder, John 189,191
Giles [Gyles],
  Athanasius 99
  Cornelius 277
  John 146,176,293,501,
    512,526,540
  Mark 62
  Mary 501
  Roger 491
  Thomas 21,280
  William 246,433,501,
    523,549
Gilford, Robert 407
Gilham, Emanuel 79
  Josiah 526
  Samuel 421
  Susanna 15
Gill, Edward 19
  Elizabeth 420
  George 35
  Hugh 523
  James 8
  John 15,57,83,93,149,
    178,195,214,232,
    233*,234,253,339,
  John 526,549,575
  Nicholas 526
  Peter 232,363
  Ralph 420
  Richard 229
  Robert 307
  William 128
Gillam, Benjamin 363,
    385
  Margaret 547
  Zachary 296
Gillard, Richard 441
Gillars, Anthony 62
Gillart, Samuel 253
Gillett, Jane 673
  William 245,645
Gillhampton, Francis 129
Gilling, Robert 169
Gillis, Adam 588
Gillum. *See* **Guillam.**
Gil(l)man, Elizabeth 409

Gil(l)man, *(contd.)*
Thomas 366
Walter 409
Gilmore, John 431
Joseph 659
Samuel 59,76
Gilpin, Robert 410
Gilson, Edward 165
John 123
Gimbleton, Robert 611
Ginge, George 216
Sebastian 300,380,395,
422,472,538,583,611
William 202
Gingell, Isaac 177
Thomas 233,289
Gingen, Mary 641
Ginger, William 215
Gingin, John 712
Ginnings, Henry 379
Ginnis [Ginnes],
Nicholas 479
William 426,484,545,
585,600,614,697
Ginny, William 352,353
Ginsey, Nathaniel 479
Girton, Arthur 15
Gist, Nathaniel 409
Walter 370
William 93
Githins, John 309
Gittes, Henry 332
Gittin(g)s, Adam 166
Thomas 11
Givan, John 517
Glace, Margery 21
Gladdin, Thomas 352
Gladwin, Edward 120
Glam, William 282
Glamen, Thomas 97
Glamster, Thomas 567
Glanford, Francis 698
Glanvell, William 134
Glanvill, James 523
Glascock, George 145
Richard 60
Glasier, Abraham 52
George 521
Glassbrook, Roger 538
Glasse, James 627
Mary 674
Robert 3,25,26*,28,35

Glasse, *(contd.)*
Samuell 559
William 674
Glassingham, Ann 558
Glavin, Bartholomew
314
James 314
Thomas 314
Gleaves, Edward 671
Francis 11
Gleddale, Mary 708
Gleed, Henry 153
Glegg, Robert 70
Glenn, Samuel 27
Glenton, Thomas 32
Glosty, Richard 268
Gloucester, Mark 159
Robert 159
Glover, Anne 188
Bennett 13
Blanch 530
Charles 318
Edward 708
Gabriel 623
Hugh 124
John 395,527,528,650
Joseph 488,552
Mary 13,427
Richard 181,241,250,
252,253,270,278,289,
292,307,329,335,338,
345,383,483
Thomas 61,125,187,200,
202,213,242,247*,
279,282*,283,285,
313,468,623
William 434,487,584
Glue, William 259
Goad, Samuel 5
Gobell, Thomas 433
Godbold, Thomas 439
Goddard, Anne 646
Bernard 480,547
Edmund 387
Edward 190,225
Elizabeth 498
Henry 571
Isaac 486,545
Mark 668,679
Martin 650
Mary 443
Stephen 498

Goddard, *(contd.)*
Thomas 388,397,399,
470,532,534,554,600
Vincent 344,382,427,
441,483,545,551,
591
William 399,613
Goddart, Anthony 30
Godden, Thomas 192
Goddin, Charles 646
James 534
Godfrey, Edward 1,4,68
Gilbert 342
Hugh 50
James 69,200,240,268,
273,296,301,347
Jane 13
John 113,514,547,626
Mary 332
Michael 188,595
Richard 83
Samuel 300
Sarah 113
Thomas 572,591,622
William 627
Godlington, Thomas 90
Godman, Thomas 13,74
Godsalve, George 710
Godsell [Godsall], John
40,524,553
Thomas 365
Godson, Jane 167
Robert 380
Godward, Giles 348
Joseph 114
Godwin, Anne 85
John 165
Joseph 398
Mary 116,172
Michael 251,702
Richard 82
Sarah 398
William 245
Goedean, Andrew 282
Goffe, Anthony 559
George 409
John 71,98,118,538
Mary 438
Nehemiah 525
Roger 538
William 1,189
Gold. *See* **Gould.**

Griffin, *(contd.)*
James 228
Joanna 6
John 98,159*,228,685
Katherine 313,316
Margaret 85,162
Phillip 14
Rice 236
Richard 262,468
Robert 206,239,250,670
Samuel 356,398
Sarah 83
Simon 264
Thomas 223,321,386,
480,485,538,675
Walter 86
William 14,369
Griffith, Capt. 244
Bridget 300
David 19,240
Edward 283*,331
Elizabeth 685
Francis 211
George 711
Henry
Hugh 685
James 455
John 56,207,218,339,
340
Joyce 162
Lewis 167
Margaret 143,144*
Mary 211,686
Peter 531,705
Richard 242,422
Roger 371
Thomas 201,248,281,
282,284,307*,322,
596
Walter 498
William 59,533,596,
685,691
Griffiths [Griffis],
Andrew 147,148
Bridget 349
Elizabeth 137,297
Griffith 203,298
John 361
Margaret 138
Mary 43
Richard 248
Robert 121

Griffiths, *(contd.)*
Walter 165
William 363
Grigg, Alice 332
Henry 290
Mary 207
Robert 332
Thomas 75,98
Griggs, John 462
Mary 553
Michael 612
Thomas 308,553
Timothy 462
Grigson, Thomas 2
Grimditch, Thomas 451
Grime, Ann 502
Robert 418
Grimes, Charles 707
Elizabeth 707
John 25
Mary 666
Philip 607
Robert 492,629
William 51
Grimsby, Jasper 8
Grimshaw, Miles 699
Grindall, Richard 132
William 90
Grindley, Charles 147
Grindon, Thomas 239,
240,252,272,290,
297*,345
William 14
Grindy, Philip 475
Thomas 475
Grinfield, John 38
Grining, Jane 106
Grinson, Elizabeth 439
Grissell, John 595
Grizell, Jane 46
Roger 43
Groce. *See* **Grosse.**
Grocer, John 131
Grolleau, Lewis 654
Gronen, Frederick 365
Groombright, George 416
Groome, Edward 665
Samuel 132,157,253,293,
294,302,355,371,385,
394,397,416,464,527,
535,581,596,606,609,
657,678*

Groome, *(contd.)*
Thomas 415,689
Zacharias 313
Grosilia, Ezekiel 593
Grosse [Groce], Daniel
91
Henry 12,69
Jasper 11
Grosvenor, Philip 246
Grove, Daniel 622
Elinor 3
Elizabeth 110
George 325
Grace 566
John 3,664
Margaret 248
Rayner 411
Richard 166
Robert 602
Samuel 657
Silvanus 679
Thomas 248
Grover, Thomas 719
William 295
Groves, James 346
John 17*
Roger 204
Thomas 288,348,371,385
William 225
Growden, Joseph 392
Groyn, Christopher 491
Grubb, Penelope 234
Philip 339
Thomas 476
Gruchy, John 711
Grundy, James 378
Grunwin, Gabriel 476,
536,581
James 296
Gualter, Thomas 515
G(u)ard, William 287,
330,338
Gubden, Matthew 95
Gubry, Frances 51
Gudden, Thomas 595
Gueff, Auffris 151
Guerard, Jacob 335,351
Guerin, Gasper 108*,
109*,110
Gueshard, Samuel 406
Guest, Anthony 221,552
Daniel 506

Hardman, Edward 697
  George 542
  Mathew 299
  Robert 420
Hardon, John 604
Hardwick, James 385,
  482,487
  John 112
  Joseph 12,16
  Thomas 12,201,223*,
  224,237
  William 8,15,26,27,
  28,29,522
Hardwith, Grace 482
Hardy, Andrew 406
  James 247
  Jane 178
  Joseph 194,248,327,332,
  543
  Mary 496,532
  Samuel 321
  Thomas 397,511
  William 9,27,28*
Hare, Henry 124
  John 232,301,442
  Mary 38
  Thomas 283,297
Har(t)ford, Charles 196,
  318,351,354,529,544,
  652,667,676,716
  Edward 418,651
  Guy 148
  John 451,543
  Mary 246
  William 67,72
Hargesse, John 100
Hargoose, Stephen 430
Hargrave, Edward 417
Harke, John 33
  Thomas 346
Harker, John 347
Harkwood, Samuel 49
Harle, Henry 208
  John 72
  Mary 208
  Randall 208
  Symon 320
  William 103
Harlewood, John 67
Harley, John 713
  Thomas 287
Harlock, William 7

Harlow, John 236
Harman, Anne 376,386,
  400
  Edmond 239
  Henry 381
  James 525
  John 527
  Matthias 527
  Robert 594
  Thomas 463,580,581
  William 527
Harmant, Clement 109
Harmer, Ephraim 408
  George 438
  Ignatius 204
  Richard 118
  Timothy 251
  William 546
Harnaman, Edward 606
Harne, Robert 597
Harper, Christopher 2*,6
  Edmond 292
  Edward 286,292,300,
  344,371
  George 132
  Jane 131
  John 34,482,595,716
  Richard 248
  Robert 394
  Thomas 65,280
  William 712
Harpfield, Michael 251
Harpum, George 73
Harrad, John 244
Harrard, William 37
Harrell, Christopher 320
  Henry 320
Harrendon, Tristian 384
  William 442
Harridge, Abraham 213
  Mary 550
Harrington, Charles 134
  Edward 374,429
  John 76,224,301
  Thomas 679
Harris, Anne 68,248,617,
  630,641
  Anthony 36
  Charles 207,215,227,
  245,691
  Christopher 293
  Daniel 593

Harris, *(contd.)*
  David 288
  Edward 30,55,77,525
  Elizabeth 25,68,80,225,
  455,640,660,673
  Erasmus 56
  Francis 21,111,156,255
  Frederick 484
  George 26,89,172,227,
  272
  Henry 31*,253,353,361,
  362,380,410,453
  Huddy 153
  Humphrey 21
  Isabel 645
  James 15,57,178,184,
  202,205,207*,221*,
  395,397,402,404,
  423,443,468,480,
  483,484*,486,496,
  536,550
  Jane 18,24,280,311,535
  Jeremy 142,288
  Joan 152,238
  Johanna 362
  John 1,9,25,17*,31,37*,
  35,36,38*,45,46,56,
  59,151,173,181,202,
  206,221,255,256*,
  261*,262*,264,295,
  296,304,307*,336,
  352,353*,360,371,
  384,399,403,413,424,
  426,446,458,481,484,
  524,531,535,539,555,
  577,578,586,613,639,
  667
  Jonas 17
  Joseph 594,613,716
  Joshua 390
  Katherine 182
  Margaret 276,346,531
  Mary 38,399,400*,428,
  438,473
  Michael 68
  Morrice 31
  Nathaniel 59*
  Nicholas 479
  Phillip 21,22,23*,25*,36
  Richard 5*,9,317,406,
  534,638,692
  Robert 8,439

Heaton, Alice 701
  Edward 701
  Elizabeth 701
  Richard 701
  Robert 710
  Thomas 409,565
  William 702
Hebb, Andrew 287
Heber, Reginald 449,663
Hedge, Thomas 200,204
Hedges, Anthony 235
  Grace 10
  Joseph 112
  Robert 16
  Sarah 54
  William 94,232,233
Hedon, Richard 505
Heiman, Abraham 96,
  111,204,368
  John 343
Helcott, Matthew 407
Hele, Tobias 23
Helford, Christopher 7
Helland, Samuel 447
Hellerd, Thomas 202
Helleway, Richard 493
Hellier [Helliar], ——
  169
  Henry 227*
  Isaac 29
  John 135,163,317
  Mary 92
  Peter 177
  Rebecca 162
  Richard 529
  Robert 494,548
  Thomas 494,548
  William 536
Helligan, Katherine 188
Helman, James 524
Helmes, John 335
Helps, John 526
Helsteed, George 671
Hemens, Thomas 72
Hemming, John 96,312
  Samuel 696
  Thomas 368
Hemmings, Joseph 110
  Thomas 289
Henbitch, William 52
Henbury, John 111
Henchman, Thomas 529

Henderson, Archibald 1*
  Henry 232
Hendfield, Edmond 623
Hendray, Robert 19
Hendry, Thomas 151
Hendy, Thomas 523
Hene, Thomas 425
Henfield, Edward 576
Henley, Joan 436
  Reynold 219
Hennagin, John 433
Hennen, Abraham 52
Henning, William 30
Hennis, Miles 531
  William 148
Henrick, Joachim 562
Henry, John 230,430
  William 458
Hensley, John 523
  Joseph 592
Hensman, Richard 60
Henson, John 525
Henton, Christopher 104
Hepart, Richard 410
Hepper, John 16,38
Herbert, Edward 224,240
  Elizabeth 164,349
  John 652
Hercy, Edward 132
Herd. *See* **Hurd.**
Herder, Lawrence 254,
  269
Herdon, Joan 635
Hereford, Anne 625
Heritage, Thomas 108,
  595
He(a)rne, George 475
  Henry 16
  James 249
  Jeremiah 74,79
  Joseph 326,357
  Sir Nathaniel 344
  Nathaniel 199
  Peter 662
  Robert 606
  Samuel 296
  Thomas 176,484
  William 43
Heron, Daniel 712
  Philip 78,130
  Thomas 430
Herren, Edward 104

Herrick, Isaac 330
  Thomas 453
  William 453
Herring, Andrew 499
  Arthur 631
  Herbert 720
  James 235,525
  Raphael 3
  Simon 51
Herriott, Ambrose 133
Hersent, Samuel 295
Herve, Thomas 533
Hescock, Easter 530
Hesketh, Ann 588
Heskins, Robert 21
Het, John 654
Hetherley, John 25
Hetty, Christopher 426
Heunan, George 159
Heverdine, William 124
Hewell, Anne 217
Hewes. *See* **Hughes.**
Hewins, John 278
Hewitt [Hewett] [Huet],
  Elizabeth 265,295
  Henry 497
  James 286,720
  Mary 350,474,567
  Thomas 386,567
  William 124
Hewlett [Hulett], Joan 13
  John 254
Hewling [Huling],
  Benjamin 61,64,70,
    193,239,242,252,262,
    263,268,281,283*,
    291,293,325,331,388,
    411
  James 103,128
  Margaret 112,139
  Nicholas 502
Hewlingson, James 113
Hewman, Alice 58
Hewson, David 176
Hexon, Matthew 619
Hext, Hugh 598
Hey. *See* **Hay.**
Heybourne, Richard 672
Heydock. *See* **Haydock.**
Heyes. *See* **Hayes.**
Heyhurste, Cuthberd 393
Heynes. *See* **Haynes.**

Hillier, Christopher 131
Hil(l)man, James 524,
  555
  Joan 103
  Margaret 176
  Richard 14
  Robert 57*,78
  Thomas 88,285,328,
   358,521,617
Hills, John 602
  Margaret 490
  Robert 43
  Thomas 490
  William 262
Hilsey, Philip 351
Hilson, George 195,289,
  291,336
  John 215
  Jonathan 298
Hilton, John 227,461
  Margaret 542
  Nowell 616
  Robert 678
  Samuel 161
  Sarah 463
  Thomas 510
Hilzy, Robert 22
Himby, Samuel 268
Himons, Joseph 391
Hinchcliffe, John 712
Hinchman, Samuel 62
Hind, Edward 328
  James 303
  John 156,202,372,393,
  609
  Richard 428
  Robert 335,357,374,
  456
  Thomas 672,703,704
  William 212,712
Hindmarsh, Jeremy 575
  Joseph 575
Hindmore, William 368
Hinds, Simon 221
Hine [Hyne], Isaac 255
  John 592
  Robert 400,410,484
  William 153
Hingston, John 244
Hinks, Samuel 254,584
Hinsell, Susan 311
Hinsley, Thomas 302

Hinson, Thomas 290
Hinton, Mary 638
  Samuel 638
Hipkin, Edward 418
Hipkins, Mary 343
Hippesley [Hipsly],
  William 257
Hippy, William 456
Hire, James 324
Hiscox, Joseph 194,196,
  297
  William 24
Hisley, John 69
Hissing, David 108
Hitchbourne, David 142
  Katherine 142
Hitchcock, Edward 192
  John 549,659
  William 704
Hitchcott, John 523
Hitchin(g)s [Hitchens],
  Anne 86
  Daniel 356
  George 668
  John 706
  Joseph 356
  Margaret 120,147
  Samuel 192,356
  Thomas 38,117
Hitchman, Thomas 306
Hitchold, Francis 55
Hoague, John 702
Ho(a)re, Christopher 151
  Elizabeth 84
  George 218
  Henry 303
  John 523,635
  Leonard 187
  Matthew 639
  Philip 86
  Richard 523,526,549
  Thomas 548
  William 282
Hoasden, John 409
Hobbart, James 567
Hobbs, Elizabeth 702,710
  Henry 241,339,667
  Israell 653
  John 15,176,250,540,
  611,668,678
  Joseph 674
  Joshua 44

Hobbs, *(contd.)*
  Oliver 523,549
  Peter 643
  Richard 158
  Robert 693
  Roger 548
  Thomas 546,702,710
Hobby, John 669
Hoblyn, Christopher 524,
  553
Hobson, Benjamin 239*,
  289,324
  Cuthbert 211
  Elizabeth 29
  Francis 146
  John 81,136,165,196
  Mary 218,498
  Miles 133
  Paul 77
  Richard 401
  Stephen 59
  Thomas 220,236,255,
  257
Hockaday, John 642
Hockenhull, George 247
Hocker, Edward 665
Hockle, John 484
Hockley, Michael 181,183
Hocknell, Daniel 236
Hocroft, Thomas 478
Hoddy, James 263
  John 263
Hodge, Edward 151
  Humphrey 525
  John 8*,9,11,88,95,137,
  253,340,345,424,660
  Peter 400
  Philip 571
  Robert 49,269,654
  Thomas 152,254
  William 208
Hodgen, Gawen 165
Hodges, Charles 41
  Elizabeth 497
  Hercules 244*
  Humphrey 64
  Jane 263
  John 7*,98,177,181,200,
  550
  Lawrence 182
  Peter 684
  Samuel 550

Ho(l)mes, Daniel 287
Edward 76,132
Elizabeth 57
George 366,707
Henry 513
John 238,265,420,507,
525,570,720
Michael 612
Richard 469,530,695
Thomas 160,388,389,
416
William 457
Holroyd, Isaac 541,554,
579
Holsey, Richard 334
Holson, Nathaniel 621
Holster, William 402
Holston, Henry 438
Holt, Charles 142
Edward 465
Ellen 715
Joseph 287,351
Richard 277,283,358,
450
Robert 127,325,337,
345,376,413
Thomas 595
William 691
Holtham, John 507
Thomas 471
Holton, Isaac 544
John 675
Mary 544
Richard 544
Holway [Holwey], Anne
101
Dorothy 120
Isaac 8
Jeremy 122,202
John 97
Jonas 229
Holwood, Hugh 20
Homan, Anthony 54
Homby, Johanna 124
William 124
Homead, Richard 13
Homer, Matthew 112
Homersham, Charles
578
Homes. *See* **Holmes.**
Homittslett, George 109
Hone, Edmund 9

Hon(e)ywell, Joseph 477
Thomas 435,513
William 435,477
Honnott, John 571
Mary 571
Honour, John 437
Honton, Walter 656
Hood, John 146,206
Julian 5
Richard 220
Hooke(e), Abraham 488,
544*,665,667,676,
710,716
Elizabeth 105
Francis 125
Grace 105
John 79,616
Robert 280
Thomas 181
William 337
Hooker, Edward 663
John 187
Mary 403
Michael 319
Ralph 78
Robert 242,243,247,
248,284,447
Thomas 217,218
Hookes, Ellis 7
Hoolby, John 583
Hoole, George 527
John 333
Hooley, Anthony 60
John 713
Hoome, William 714
Hooper [Huper], Daniel
335
Edward 171
Henry 523,645
James 17,408
John 8,100,139,263,
523,526*,549,650
Margaret 86
Philip 709,713,714
Richard 268,271,526
Robert 86,394
Roger 523
Simon 31
Thomas 51,525,594
Walter 453
William 38,105,171*,
172,185,188*,209,

Hooper, *(contd.)*
William *(contd.)*
324,329*,330,362,
506,509
Hooton, Thomas 392
Hoover, Christopher 4
Hopcroft, John 338
Hope, Anthony 450
Walter 550
William 450
Hopkin, Edward 13
George 78
John 621
Hopkins, Andrew 272,
401
Anne 128
Charles 232,234
Edward 74
Elizabeth 138
George 186
Isaac 299
Joan 92
John 53,55*,57,67,71,
72,73*,80,81,84,85,
94*,95,175,455,651,
707
Jonas 195
Matthew 27
Millisent 415
Richard 210,220
Samuel 159
Susan 7
Thomas 217,554,595
Walter 42
William 39,216,236,284,
300,446,665
Hopley, George 7*
Hoppells, Matthew 204
Hopper, John 310,443
Sarah 509
William 327,578
Hopps, Barbara 515
Hopson, Richard 312
Thomas 339
Hopton, Charles 596
Elizabeth 545
George 350
Joseph 325
Hopwood, Matthew 69
Sarah 45
Hord, Thomas 708
Horden, John 198

Hutchinson, Abraham
  594
  Ann 417
  Benjamin 249
  Dorothy 446
  Elizabeth 213,253
  Ezechiel 192,193,212,
    213,239,247,279,293,
    348,376,408,472,572,
    593,622
  George 486,547
  Joseph 692
  Matthew 629
  Richard 39,159,241,
    270
  Robert 712
  Thomas 340
Hutson, Emanuel 414
  William 124
Hutt, Daniel 182
  John 182
Hutton, Ann 473
  Anthony 672
  Carnan 251
  David 591
  Edward 668,681
  Elizabeth 673
  George 10
  John 202
  Leonard 447
  Mary 574
  Richard 378,521
  Susan 473
  Thomas 391,467
Huxley, Leversedge 235
Hyam, George 670
Hyatt. *See* **Hyett**.
Hydall, John 668
Hyde [Hide], Andrew
  458
  Francis 105
  Jane 697
  John 357,609,657*,
    658,680
  Joseph 383,200,357,591
  Philip 458
  Phineas 217*,231,398,
    421,469,479,526,583,
    611
  Stephen 519
  Thomas 97,398,600
  Walter 86,121,154,166

Hyde, *(contd.)*
  William 171,394
  William A. 592
Hyder, Richard 712
Hye, Henry 414
Hyett [Hyatt], Abraham
  60
  Elizabeth 102,103
  Jane 103
  John 259,643
  Thomas 83,102,111,168
Hyfield. *See* **Highfield**.
Hyland, James 481
Hynch, John 393
Hyne. *See* **Hine**.

Ian, Nathaniel 539
Ibbetson, Joshua 380
Ibrooke, Henry 128
Iden, John 68
Idens, Elizabeth 76
Idle, William 166,205,
  222,434
Ifield [Ifell], James 558
  Susanna 192*,200
Igne, John 470
Igorne, John 69
Ilea, Edward 16
I(s)les, Charles 171
  Christopher 100
  Edward 20,509
  Elizabeth 177
  James 502
  Joan 348
  Lewis 460
  Rebecca 460
  Timothy 22
Iliffe, Robert 43
Ilsco, John 342
Imay, John 243
Imbres, Renedes 673
Impey, John 284
Ince, Anne 202
  Thomas 9
Ind, John 278
Indian, Thomas 650
Inds, John 341
  Thomas 341
Infield, John 568
Inge, Richard 627

Ingersole, John 416
Ingleby, John 289,328,
  335
  Nicholas 337
Ingledon, James 256
  William 657
Ingles, John 429
  Jonathan 541
  Penelope 541
Ingleson, George 2*
Ingleton, Jane 30
Ingold, Mary 189,190
Ingoldsby, Mary 590
Ingoll [Ingle], Daniel
  189,279,293,325,
  413,568,591,621
  William 513
Ingram, Clement 241
  Edward 211
  Henry 465
  John 178,720
  Ralph 173,240,283,284,
    293,294,302,332,341,
    345,374,476,522,
    527,535,536,554
  Richard 308
  Robert 704
  Thomas 421
  Walter 477
  William 660,704
Ingrave, Ralph 505
Inion, John 79,138
Inkenbottom, Joseph
  674
Inkoe, Andrew 567
Inman, Henry 138
  Margaret 236
  Robert 236
Innis, William 137
Inon, Daniel 371
  Griffith 3
  John 375,691
  William 14,361
Insley, Renedy 665
Ipey, Robert 463
Ireland, Anne 257
  Christian 687
  Edward 664
  John 375,706
  Mary 224
  Richard 598
  William 211

Jameson, James 696
  William 383
Jancey [Jauncy], James
  240
  John 18
Ja(y)ne, Anne 509
  Eleanor 288
  Elizabeth 3,4*
  John 692
  Mary 628
  Thomas 514
  William 93,147
Janie, Rosser 138
  William 20
Janney, James 205
Jannins, James 442
Janson, Bryan 651
  George 651,663
  Mary 651,663
Janurin, Daniel 586,690
Ja(c)ques, Thomas 270,
  293,383,423,424,
  467
Jare, William 199
Jarratt, Mark 296
  William 457
Jarrow, Bridget 50
  John 50
Jarvis [Jervis], Edward
  113
  Elizabeth 631
  Francis 563,584
  Henry 64
  Humphrey 76,93,289,
  292
  Jane 113
  Joan 223
  John 331,620
  Mark 75
  Paul 412
  Richard 228
  Robert 185
  Thomas 99,115,130,131,
  133,454,506,596,631
  Walter 350
  William 350,666
Jary, William 179
Jasper, Joan 188
Jaspers, Nicholas 61
Jauncy. *See* **Jancey.**
Jay, Augustine 710
  Richard 179

Jay, *(contd.)*
  Stephen 4
  Thomas 132
  William 153
Jayne. *See* **Jane.**
Jeale, Overington 153
Jeane, William 499
Jeanes, Ezekiel 511
  John 523
  Thomas 295
Jeapson, William 147
Jeddrell, Elizabeth 191
  John 191
Jedds, William 438
Jee. *See* **Gee**
Jefcole, John 467
Jeffard, Bartholomew
  175
  Joan 176
Jefferies [Jeffreys],
  Judge 615
  Charles 502
  Daniel 391
  David 572,619,629
  Deborah 237
  Edward 114
  Eleanor 674
  George 190,491
  Giles 674
  Henry 404,487
  Herbert 336
  Jennet 104
  Jerome 167
  John 67,69,70,149,
  202,216,237,239,247,
  276,289,291,295,296,
  301,311,323,328,343,
  345,346,390,434,466,
  478,497,527,537,571,
  610,619,647
  Joseph 557,665,673
  Josias 505
  Mary 48,169
  Nathaniel 152,232*
  Peter 334*
  Philip 411,460,590
  Reece 460
  Rice 328,601
  Richard 405
  Stephen 524,552
  Thomas 41,46,75,152,
  254,338,660

Jefferies, *(contd.)*
  William 87,257,303*,
  353,385,414,417*,
  483,549,588,612,
  635,657
Jefferson, Christopher
  435,454,566,567*
  Samuel 357,488
  William 649
Jeffery [Jeffrey], Arthur
  710
  Digery 126
  Edward 252,271
  John 207,306,307,490,
  671
  Thomas 237,490,700
  William 187
Jefford, Bartholomew
  240
  David 213
Jeffs, Charles 644
  John 204
Jeffson, Jacob 235
Jelfe, John 666,675
  Margaret 125
  William 10,53,67,84,
  164,215,226,229,
  258,259*,260
Jelford, Francis 90
Jelks, Richard 101
Jellard, Abraham 623
Jellicoe, Samuel 713
Jelly, Richard 421
Jelson, Edward 166
Jenkin, Edward 250
  Margaret 43
  Morgan 340,620
  Thomas 270
  William 137,174
Jenkins [Jinkins], Anne
  67,160
  Austin 210
  Charles 63
  David 224,560
  Edward 63,226
  Eleanor 287
  Elizabeth 107
  Evan 23
  Francis 344
  George 122,232
  Henry 76,138,259,282
  James 11,70,307

Karkeese, William 42
Kates, Jane 248
 John 248
Katherine, Dorothy 169
Kaurhell, Samuel 236
Kay, Silvester 179
Kayes, John 133
Keable. *See* Keeble.
Keale. *See* Keele.
Kearfoote, Margaret 701
Keate, John 177
Keating, James 689
Kecke, Lawrence 565
Keckerbecke, Anna 554
 Ernesto 425,529,531*,
 532*,535*
Kedger, Elizabeth 61
Kedgwin, John 112,146,
 147
Ke(e)ble [Kible],
 Benjamin 524
 Christopher 411,575*
 George 662,680
 Hannah 462
 Henry 262
 John 462
Kee(t)ch, James 68
 Richard 548
 Simon 610
 Stephen 23
 William 110*,111
Keege, John 115
Keele [Keale], George
 524,555
 John 556
 Malachi 370
 Robert 595
Keeling, Josiah 347
 Katherine 225
 Samuell 674
Keen(e), Christopher
 382,559
 Ralph 601
 William 16,49
Keepe, Samuel 573
Keeping, Philip 525
Keightley, William 15
Keir, Allian 497
 Caleb 497
 James 210
Keisin, Alexander 3
Keith, Henry 341

Kekwich, Peter 569,620
Kelford, Nicholas 525
Kelk, James 427,591,
 603,608
 Nicholas 591
Kellam, William 105
Kelland, Walter 404
Kellett, Samuel 437
Kellock, James 14
Kellond, John 340
 Thomas 340
Kelloway, Edward 638
Kellowhill, Francis 102
Kells, Robert 670
Kellsar, Samuel 74
Kellway, Robert 300
 Thomas 142
Kelly, Abell 710
 Charles 16,131,147,
 148
 David 388,610
 Edward 12,88
 John 140
 Martin 100
 Mary 248
 Peter 129
 Thomas 130,147
 William 527
Kelsey, Richard 121
 Thomas 617,682
Kelson, Thomas 433
Kelwin, Alexander 155
Kembe, Margaret 88
 Thomas 88
Kemble, John 204,297
Kemp, Barbara 442
 Edward 404,526,592
 Francis 326
 Joseph 64
 Mary 83
 Roger 494,557
 Thomas 314
 William 408
Kemplin, John 523,549
Kempster, John 61,213,
 264,594
Kempton, John 39
Kemys [Kimis], John
 670
Kenall, John 547
Kendall [Kendell],
 Freegrace 123

Kendall, *(contd.)*
 James 231,285,292,471,
 548
 John 56,477,636
 William 402,422,440
Ken(d)rick, Andrew 293,
 294,325,328,348,
 430,542,568
 Stephen 425
Kennedy, Adam 694
 Elizabeth 572
 George 401
 Michael 572
Kenner, Anne 256
 John 37
Kennery, James 392
Kennick, William 650
Kenniston, William 335
Kenny, Roger 124
Kensey, John 283
Kent, Abraham 499
 Anne 300
 Edward 523*,553
 Elizabeth 362
 George 211
 Henry 269,383
 Joan 160
 Joel 553
 John 29,215,233,237,
 239,247,252,253,261,
 265,292*,295,344
 Peter 549,616
 William 139
Kenten, Banks 407
Kenton, Ann 38
Kenyon, Jonas 642,718
Kerby. *See* Kirby.
Kerie, John 17
Kerk, Gilbert 593
Kerle. *See* Kirle.
Kerne, Barnaby 330
Kerr, Andrew 566
Kerrington, Robert 283
Kershaw, James 718
Kerslake, John 493
Kerswell, Joan 492
 Richard 161
 Walter 193
Kerton, Thomas 606,645
Kesterman, Peter 291,358
Kestin, Francis 104
 Thomas 104

Macarty, Honor 152
Maccadie, James 151
MacCleire, James 703
Maccloth, Thomas 627
—MacCollough, John 703
MacCreky, Samuel 702
MacDaniell, Patrick 342
MacDonnell, Edward 673
Elizabeth 630
James 510
Philip 641
MacDugdale, Daniel 712
MacEnree, John 338
MacKee, Patrick 164
Mace, Edward 151
Mac(e)y, George 548,616
Joseph 534
Katherine 221
MacGregor, Margaret 543
Macguider, John 491
Machee, Petre 686
Machell, John 133
Machen, John 122,133, 141,161,203,389
Oliver 137
Thomas 653,655,673
Machere, David 626
Mackall, James 53
Mackalla, George 151
Mackcloth, Sarah 436
Mackelow, Ambrose 35
Mackenchin, John 418
Mackenna, Daniel 441
Mackerith [Macrith], William 571,572
Mackerness, Edward 478
Mackfarly, John 131
Macklyn, John 410
Mackrell, John 224
Mackrow, Daniel 522
Macks, George 136
Mackworth, John 13
MacQuin, Daniel 448
Macullock, Alexander 367
Thomas 658
Madberry, Thomas 62
Madden, John 153
Patrick 346
Madder, William 549

Madders, John 548
Maddin, James 545
Mary 545
Maddock, Cornelius 433, 550
Henry 416,420,581
Maddox [Maddocks], Ann 306
Edward 157
Gilbert 443
Joan 330
Richard 148
Robert 292,293
Thomas 254
William 54,288
Madford, William 548
Madgwick, Jonathan 160
William 683
Madler, Gertude 80
Magdalene, Miriam 446
Mager, Peter 88
Mag(g)ott, Richard 300
Sarah 437
Maggs, Alexander 227
George 242
Maglockly, Scalam 28
Magner, Philip 625
Mahew, John 286
Mahone, James 341
Mahony, Daniel 333
Maiden, James 112
Richard 522
Maine. *See* Mayne.
Maires, Josiah 708
Major, Anthony 627
Jerman 19
Mary 295
Peter 191,333
Thomas 279,572,622
Thomas 62
William 332
Makepeace, George 51
Makins, Edward 204
Richard 139
Thomas 191
Malacha, Peter 583
Malcone, Robert 123
Maldon [Malden], Francis 370,419,480
Ma(y)le, Anthony 287, 423
John 498

Malin [Malyn], John 428
Thomas 197,249,326,352
Mallett, John 88,143
Winifred 673
Mallins, Thomas 295,304
Mallion, William 221
Mallory, Phillip 13
Malpas, Andrew 645,670
Malpus, Ann 147
Malraven, Mathew 550
Manarty, Samuel 455
Manbert, Mark 605,609
Manby, James 377,416
Manckly, John 582
Mancroft, John 579
Mander. *See* Maunder.
Mandle, John 161
Mandler, Mary 13
Manfield, George 162
Manford, Elizabeth 115
Manie, Abraham 281
Manistry, Clement 287
Manley, Elizabeth 101
Mann, Deborah 113
Edward 193,214,237, 238,242,262,277,283, 287,290,291,293*, 294,299,328,332,343, 393,429,517,622,709, 714
John 295,346,366,381, 404,420
Katherine 149
Samuel 462
Thomas 211,659
William 12,148
Mannerick, Nathaniel 353
Mannering, Ralph 423
Manners, Joseph 375
Mannian, David 120
Manning, Abigail 475
Anne 98
Daniel 565
Edward 623
John 81,548,672
Mary 94,264
Nicholas 337
Philip 192,242,282,382
Robert 512
Thomas 649
William 25

Martin, *(contd.)*
  Elinor 4
  Elizabeth 59,79,343
  George 163,289,665
  Gilbert 459
  Henry 24,48,550,587,
    656
  Humphrey 448
  Isaac 393,703
  James 131,410
  Jane 235
  Joan 174,688
  John 59,124,198,221,
    261,268,382,414,462,
    493*,495,506,514,
    519,391,402,403,567,
    626
  Jonathan 495,569
  Joseph 109,400,446,447,
    449,454,484,623,674
  Judith 183
  Margaret 15,647
  Martha 506
  Mary 248,688
  Michael 354
  Nicholas 81
  Philip 514
  Richard 3,24*,36,93,122,
    127,145,165,171,195,
    213,280*,283,316,
    376*,413,447,468,529,
    575,642,665
  Robert 95,136
  Susan 641,646
  Thomas 69,98,112,174,
    183,235,261,438,459,
    464,479,491,522,546,
    551,580,606,646,656
  Walter 383
  William 60,68,99,105,
    129,137,151,160,175,
    179,198,242,243*,
    248,255,260,265,269*,
    277,351,371,402,443,
    484,498*,499*,506,
    585,600*,613,614,711
Martindale, Edward 138,
    196*,202,317,321,
    323*,372,386,430,706
Martinshrider, David
    705
Marty, Joseph 472

Marvin, Mary 104
Marwood, Arthur 454
  John 524,552
Maryon, Walter 413
Mascall, John 63
  William 6
Mash, John 171
  Thomas 173
Maslin, William 550
Mason, Capt. 355
  Anne 15,154
  Anthony 368
  Charles 526
  Cornelius 656,657*,666,
    680
  Edward 657
  Elizabeth 420
  George 229,277,349,447,
    600,668,682,714
  Humphrey 235,327,328
  John 173*,177*,178,
    179,187,197,217,218,
    248,249*,252,253,254,
    255,274,275*,276,302,
    303,322,339,393,418,
    448,619,691,707,712
  Lemuel 364
  Luke 558
  Margaret 649
  Mason 543
  Nathaniel 273,319,683
  Phillip 52
  Richard 163
  Robert 322,411,559
  Sarah 359
  Stephen 602,672,675
  Sylam 335
  Thomas 173,235,286,
    447
  William 246,303,420,
    642,691
Massey, Edward 29
  John 103
  Joseph 413
  Sigismund 542
  Thomas 120
Masson, George 384,
    387,484,592
  Henry 436
Master, Herriat 593
Masters, Alice 248
  Anne 217

Masters, *(contd.)*
  Benjamin 272,626
  Christopher 525
  George 520
  Henry 328
  Hugh 44
  John 22,23,25*,248,
    580
  Richard 523
  Robert 322
  Simon 204,206,239
  Thomas 264*,300,424,
    453,504*,561
Maston, John 251
Mastys, Margaret 425
Masy, Henry 175
Matchett, John 236
  Thomas 190
Mathen, Elizabeth 100
Mather, David 28
  Gilbert 128
  John 460,710
  Thomas 211,593
  Thursden 701
Mathewson, John 670
Mathias, John 244
Mathyson, John 164
Matkins, Elizabeth 293
Matthew, James 459
  John 371,659
  Jonathan 597
  Mary 105
  Peter 691
  Robert 686
  Thomas 105,208,307,
    570
  William 22,678
Matthew(e)s, Abraham
    194
  Anne 314
  Anthony 679
  Christopher 424
  Dorothy 375
  Edward 68
  Elizabeth 148,339,628
  George 227,268
  Godfrey 621
  Henry 574
  James 211,280,375
  Jane 111
  John 9,184,237,304,
    364

Meecham. *See*
Meacham.
Meechin. *See* **Meachin.**
Meeke [Meake], Francis
302
George 15
John 130
Margaret 603
Thomas 576,622
William 229
Meekes, John 164*
Meeres [Meares],
Elizabeth 513
Isaac 626
John 545
Stephen 617
Meese [Mease], Edward
313
Henry 198,200,205,216,
227,237,239,249,252,
286,289,290,294,295,
296,301,307,311,326,
337,341,342,345,346,
381,392
Richard 423
Meivy, Thomas 135
Melborne, Thomas 540
Mell, James 605
Mellard, Elizabeth 603
Meller, Charles 120
Mellichap, Richard 546
Mellin, Richard 487
Melloly, James 349
Mellowes, John 335
Melony, Timothy 330
Melton, Joseph 295
Philip 313
Thomas 652
Membry, John 203
Mendam, Thomas 71
Mennick, Susanna 67
Mens, Robert 207
Mercer, Elizabeth 480
John 246
Peter 656,676
Richard 572
Robert 453
Samuell 568
Thomas 715
Merchant [Marchant],
Edmond 329
Elizabeth 24

Merchant, *(contd.)*
Emanuel 523,553,615
George 225
John 595
Joseph 320
Thomas 371,503
William 523,552
Mercy [Marcy], Anne
439
Margaret 439
Thomas 634
Meredith, Charles 274
Elizabeth 23
Howell 23
John 39,113,647
Robert 292
Roger 320
Mer(r)iton, John 326
Joshua 230
Matthew 215
Merlin, Paul 651
Merrell, John 312
Merrett, William 12
Merriatt, John 2
Merrick [Meyrick],
Elizabeth 72
Giles 21,24,43,55,56,70,
195,453,458,667
John 229
Joseph 665
Robert 114
Thomas 375,640
William 29,39,121,175,
176,220,525
Merriday, John 400
Merriden, John 399
Thomas 640
Merrifield, Thomas 218
William 28
Merriken, Hugh 687
Merrill, John 188
Merriman
[Merryman], John
651
Nicholas 339
Richard 19
William 23,50
Merrin, Richard 277
Merring, Elizabeth 451
John 248,269
Merriott, Robert 309
Merris, Joseph 665

Merritt, Francis 416
Isaac 202,207,215,216*,
240,252,253*,268,289*,
295,299,345*,353
Richard 634
Thomas 393,620
William 281
Merriweather,
Christopher 540,663
Edward 61,187,188,193,
213,237,247,254,278,
282,283,284*,285,
291*,293
Jane 13,102
John 2,50,146
Joseph 251
Richard 284,291,332,
336,396,407,568,624
Merry, Anthony 669,682
Edward 190
Henry 358,398
Humphrey 409
Robert 22
Thomas 11,534
Merryman. *See*
Merriman.
Merton, Richard 691
Merveillean, Peter 399,
400
Messe, Thomas 79
Mesurer, John 96
Metcalfe [Medcalfe],
Abraham 535
Elizabeth 535
Gilbert 113,286,294,341,
379,429,609,619
Jane 423,483,540
Richard 166,340,364,
380,384,429,434
Thomas 616
Mettham, Abigail 617
Margaret 136
Metyard, John 523
Meunix, Giles 330
Peter 330
Meux, John 627
Mew, Ellis 175
Samuel 175
Sarah 175
Mewington, Samuel 204
Meyer, Henry 524
Robert 650

818

Meyers, Robert 657
Meynell, Christopher 313
Meyrick. *See* **Merrick.**
Mibber, William 24
Micail, John 26
Michael, Abraham 543
  Jane 180
Michalls, Olla 234
Michelborne, Richard
  120,125,126
Micher, Stephen 308
Mico, Walter 277,279,
  325,336,347,390,
  624
Middlecott, Francis 377
  Richard 122
  William 310,312,376
Middlecutt, Richard 81,
  85
Middlelow, Mary 300
Middlemore, Thomas
  109
Middleton, Andrew 113
  Arthur 342
  Charles 522,583,651
  David 639
  Diana 383
  Edmund 25
  Edward 136,358
  Elizabeth 113,148
  George 100
  Gerrard 455
  James 98
  Jane 326
  John 307,325,370
  Joseph 433
  Lewis 676
  Mary 437,512,660,673
  Ralph 525
  Robert 34,646,670,698,
  704,719
  Thomas 10,15,148,209,
  443,524,555
  William 279,286,360,
  595,703,707
Midford, Katherine 617
  Thomas 617
Midgley, Elizabeth 531
  Henry 494
  John 494
Milbank, Mark 229
Milberry, John 182

Milborne [Milburne],
  George 713
  Jacob 449,577
  James 497
  Nicholas 498,551
  Paul 508
  Ralph 416
Milden, William 84,85
Miles, Anne 706
  Arthur 298
  Christopher 138
  David 546
  Elizabeth 53
  Hannah 433
  John 571*,607
  Mary 437
  Patrick 680
  Robert 62
  Roger 84
  Samuel 440
  Susanna 571
  William 57
Milford, James 100
  John 436
Millard [Millerd], Anne
  133
  Archibald 139
  Daniel 278
  Edward 302
  George 273,365
  James 196,206,316,353,
  373,384,396,399,480,
  600
  John 95,418,596,610,
  654,655
  Peter 673
  Philip 13,65,183
  Richard 116,371
  Robert 174,525
  William 31,68,155,157,
  225,371
Miller, Ann 221
  Edward 282
  Francis 341
  John 524,553,610,631,
  651,668,681,713
  Jonathan 451
  Mary 251,460
  Nicholas 300
  Otwell 113
  Richard 50,526,647,706
  Robert 146,319

Miller, *(contd.)*
  Thomas 311,440
Millett, Caleb 704
  John 159
  William 194
Millicheap, Samuel 518
Millier, Elizabeth 113
Milliner, Thomas 84
Millis, John 324
Mills, Alice 148
  Andrew 428
  Anne 612
  Benjamin 711
  Bonaventure 712
  Charles 428
  Edward 229
  Elizabeth 116
  George 644
  Gideon 79
  Henry 133,498,525
  Hugh 91
  Humphrey 302
  John 48,102,217,255,
  442,473,554,583,
  592,709
  Margaret 239
  Mary 265
  Richard 148
  Roger 421,552
  Sarah 498
  Thomas 1,17,33,234,
  235,389,481,525
  William 13,195,247,285,
  315,319,320,509
Milner, Anne 134,135
  Elizabeth 113
  Isaac 684
  James 416
  John 494,702
  Percival 506
  Thomas 69,84
Milsham, Richard 273
Mil(l)som [Milsum],
  Edward 97
  Elizabeth 86
  John 255
  Mary 99
  Richard 274,297,322*,
  559
  William 24
Milson, Charles 193
  Thomas 222

Milstead, Edward 221
Milton, Alice 30
  Robert 520
  William 40
Milward, Jane 639
  Richard 526
Minard, Edward 19
  Samuel 152
Mince, Anne 100
Minchall, Samuell 581
Minchard, Henry 599
Minchin, Hannah 551
Mines, Charles 261
Mingham, Francis 436,
  559
  William 457,522
Mingian, Mr. 456
Mingo, Francis 493
Minifie, John 548
Minivell, Paul 601,608
Minns, Elizabeth 265
  John 175,265
  Pasche 576
Minny, Thomas 174
Minor, John 97,347
  Samuel 320
  William 221,352,364
Minord, Edward 234
Minsher, Robert 311
Minson, Joan 110
Minthen, John 217
Minton, Rowland 183
Mire [Myre], Henry 555
  Humphrey 140
  Robert 676
Mires, James 637,698
Mishew, William 193
Miskell, Margaret 192
Mitchell, Abram 601
  Benjamin 285
  Bernard 202,252,275
  Charles 92,252,578,
    619
  Edward 151,525,596,
    659
  Eleanor 522
  Elizabeth 215,439,660
  George 5,524,555
  James 658,711
  Joan 18
  John 333,427,524,548,
    556

Mitchell, *(contd.)*
  Katherine 620
  Mary 465,673
  Nicholas 667
  Peter 599
  Richard 76,333,534
  Robert 28,524,555
  Samuel 92,619
  Stephen 562
  Thomas 3,25,101,160,
    200,525,646,660
  William 129,225,306
Mitford, Robert 290
Mittins, George 494
  Richard 412
Mitton, Edward 301
Moate, Elizabeth 144
Mobbs, William 659
Mobson, William 712
Mocker, Joseph 372
Mockeridge, Joan 14
Mockesby, John 177
Mockley, Jonas 147
Modyford, Sir James 74
Moggeridge, John 524,
  549,553
Moggs, Jacob 487,601
  Martha 110
  Thomas 177
Mohoone, Sarah 673
Mohun, John 126,307
  Paul 241
Moir, Archibald 438
  Elizabeth 490
Molbourn, Richard 466
Moles, George 186
Molineux [Mullinex],
  John 467,581,618,647,
    670,681,688,699
  Richard 467
  Robert 530
  Thomas 439
Mollone, Charles 513
Molque, Abraham 545
Molyn, Abraham 483
Mompesson, John 158
  Richard 158
Moncks, John 36
  Thomas 22
Monell, John 580
Money, Edward 619
  Robert 673

Money, *(contd.)*
  Roger 68
Monk(e), George 111,374
  James 81
  John 114,409,437
  Richard 409
  Roger 185
  Samuell 677
  Walter 242,299,569,
    587,621
Monkhouse, George 210
Monkles, James 589
Monlylockes, Jacob 125
Monmouth, Charles W.
  692
Monnseir, Mary 440
Monsly, Valentine 14
Mo(u)ntague, Francis 80
  Stephen 301,363*,373
  Thomas 400,441,513,
    622
Monteage, Deane 517
  Stephen 382,397
Montforth, Edward 242
Montgomery, Anne 466
  James 684
  Robert 466
Monyon, John 251,254
Moody, Edward 29
  George 82
  James 185,525
  John 383,457,709*
  Sarah 341
  Thomas 28,157
  William 254
Moone, Dennis 330,332
  George 317,372
  John 5,357,403,424
  Patrick 356
  Robert 677
  Sarah 673
Mo(o)re, Abraham 542
  Andrew 670,704,714
  Barbara 183
  Benjamin 214,242*
  Christopher 390,435,
    542,587,617
  Dorothy 211,280
  Edmund 300
  Edward 159
  George 329,359,570,596
  Henry 7,9*,398

Mullins, *(contd.)*
  William 39
Mullocke, Charles 529
Mulzar, John 631
Mumford [Munford],
  Augustine 660
  Benjamin 279
  Edward 237,283
  Henry 192,279
  John 204,215,247,298,
    380,562*,564,683
  William 299,305,319
Munbedd, Thomas 172
Munckley, John 709,710
Mund(a)y, Anne 2
  Arthur 440
  Bridget 479
  Daniel 156
  Elizabeth 49
  Henry 657,680*
  John 657,658,679,680*
  Joseph 659,679
  Nicholas 501
  Richard 2,672
  Robert 492,501
  Samuel 152
  Thomas 37
  William 220
Mundell, John 673
Munden, John 656
  Robert 132
Mundin, Thomas 486
Munding, George 12
Munfie, John 447
Munfield, John 587
Munford, Augustine 90
  Robert 526
Munksley, Elinor 42
Munn, Joseph 666
Munt, Henry 192
Munyon, Henry 717
Murdoch, David 600
Murgett, Edward 375
Murphy, Richard 420,
  714,715
  Thomas 177
  William 342,352
Murray [Murrey],
  Anthony 176
  Francis 640
  John 48,705
  Roger 177

Murray, *(contd.)*
  Sarah 673
  Thomas 506
Murrell, Jonathan 597
Murton, John 515
Muscot, Joseph 212
Musgrave, Michael 686
  Nathaniel 523
Musgrewe, Thomas 710
Musgrove, John 145
  Robert 536
Muskett, Sarah 292
  William 348
Muspott, Joseph 214
Muspratt, John 162,560
  Thomas 224,560
Mussaven, William 274
Mutchmore, Walter 66
Muttit, Elizabeth 124
  Stephen 124
Muttlebury, Anne 227
  John 525
Mylam, John 717
Mynn, Thomas 584,611
Myre. *See* **Mire.**

Nabrick, Andrew 523
Naden, Richard 312
  Thomas 312,447
Nagis, Ann 296
Nall, John 659
  William 662
Nantford, Francis 189,
  190
Napp, Edith 538
  Margaret 538
Napper, John 461,521*,
    522,527*,528*,529,
    530*,531*,532,533*,
    534*
  Robert 72
  Thomas 257
  William 444,455
Narramore, John 697
Nasey, Richard 64
Nash, Arthur 656
  Giles 271
  Joseph 484,531
  Mary 157,217
  Rebecca 631

Nash, (contd.)
  Richard 526,549
  Samuel 408
  Sarah 252
  Thomas 15,631
  William 547
Nashion, Thomas 526
Nasir, Jane 305
Nason, John 427
  Joshua 193
  Thomas 425
Nasy, Daniel 347
Nathan, John 280
Nauty, William 217
Naylor, Charles 380
  George 712
  John 295,585
  Robert 707
  Thomas 475,585
  William 75
Neads. *See* **Needes.**
Neagle, Martin 341
Neagles, Andrew 545
Neale [Neel] [Neil],
  Alexander 460
  Andrew 234
  Elizabeth 410
  Hannah 151
  John 145,401,448
  Peter 361
  Sarah 234,460
  Thomas 253
  William 154,231,280,
    493
Neame, William 188
Nean, Thomas 37
Neason, John 278
  Philip 269,292,315,317
Nedham. *See* **Needham.**
Needes [Neads], John 14,
    489,490,524,552,170,
    171,210,216,257,259,
    278
  William 269,285*,286,
    287*,289,314,315
Ne(e)dham, Benjamin 126
  James 279
  John 187,188,388
  Mary 437
Needle, John 697
Needler, James 452
  John 338

Nicholas, *(contd.)*
Samuel 44*,45*,46
Stephen 715
Thomas 132,166
William 166,167,199,
201,202,273,322*,
385,482,487,552
Nicholl, Andrew 487
John 120,217
Thomas 620
Nicholls [Niccolls],
Allen 190*
Anne 160
Charles 437,652,679,
716
Daniel 125
David 107,345,349
Dorothy 494
Elia 399
Elizabeth 537
Ellis 711
Francis 436
Grace 21
Henry 473
Humphrey 331
James 566,613
Jane 552
Joan 323,455
John 22,78,85,447,569,
696
Joseph 552
Marian 45
Matthew 132,691
Nicholson 334
Paul 76
Richard 635,651,673,
710,716
Robert 21,165
Samuel 22,23,24,43
Solomon 543
Stephen 290
Thomas 168,416,550,
552,564,570,571,
572,573*,704
William 85,203,263,282,
288,290,341,665
Nicholson, Governor 693
George 628,636
Sir Humphrey 388
Humphrey 189,190,215,
283*,293,325
James 325

Nicholson, *(contd.)*
John 640,716
Richard 344,363,368,
383,486,611
Thomas 671
Nickins, Lott 715
Robert 277
Nickles, George 96
Nickson. *See* **Nixon.**
Nightingale, Edward
196,340,364,372,384
Nilie, Thomas 231
Nilston, Mary 163
Ninnis, Thomas 28*
Nisbett, Thomas 369,
470,683
Nixon [Nickson],
Dorothy 590
John 416
Lawrence 634
Thomas 50,570,591
No(a)kes, Anthony 80*
Diana 275
Rebecca 558
Thomas 603
William 558
Noble, Allen 404
Ann 602
Edward 96*,106,164
Elizabeth 630
Francis 588
John 602
Ralph 103
Robert 55,70,97,203,
204
Simon 289
William 467
Noblett, Robert 700
Nock, Elizabeth 85
William 85
Noell. *See* **Nowell.**
Noguier, Stephen 679
Nolbrough, Henry 35
Nolder, Mary 446
Noll, John 684
Nollard, Woolfrey 7
Nonson, John 440
Noone, Fortune 246
Henry 526
Norcombe [Nurcombe],
Francis 188
William 109

Norcott [Norcutt], Ann
464
George 651
Henry 464
John 704
Richard 464
Susanna 294
William 230
Nordish, William 660
Nordon, Joseph 712
Nore, John 204,297,609,
640
Norgate, Sarah 221
William 88
Norman, Charles 645
Dorman 355
Edward 137
Elizabeth 68,211,542
Henry 11
John 132,137,140,165,
180,348
Joseph 436
Mary 157,686
Robert 410
Samuel 433
Thomas 22,61,63,116*,
123,126,162,173,175,
187,189,190,192,193,
213,214,244,247*,
282,283,284,295,332,
532
William 273,343,523
Normand, William 492
Norover, Thomas 122
Norres. *See* **Norris.**
Norrington, —— 363
Alice 85
John 431*
William 381,402,430,
564,591,611,619,
659,675
**Norris [Norres]
[Norrice],** Abel 196
Alexander 587
Daniel 299
Eleanor 550
Elizabeth 539,540
George 168,540
Henry 102
Joan 581
John 437,550,448,646
Mary 26

Norris, *(contd.)*
Michael 707
Richard 642,671
Samuel
Thomas 573
Norrish, John 178
Norroway, Phillip 566
North, Arthur 289,296,
344,368,381,395,399,
404,417,528,528,578,
608,625,657,683
Daniel 98
John 236
Joseph 498
Mary 359
Richard 692
Thomas 133,303
William 76
Northcott, George 262
Katherine 541
Robert 652
William 151
Northerne, Ellis 225
Sarah 216
Thomas 24,127
Northerow, Samuel 426
Northover, Nicholas 687
Norton, Anthony 166
Christopher 270
Edward 47
Elizabeth 546,647
Francis 72
George 44
Jeremiah 142
John 1,75,77,360,388,
658,660,683
Robert 525
Thomas 77,407,492,
526
William 77
Norvill [Norvell], James
526
Thomas 30,33,201
Norwich, Erasmus 472,
539
Eros 347
Arthur 111
Benjamin 653,667,676
Edward 360
Matthew 300
Thomas 354
Nosman, Thomas 370

Nossiter, Thomas 281
Notey, Alexander 583
Notley, John 352
Matthew 152
Thomas 270
Nott, John 666
Margaret 140
Nottell, William 423
Notts, Alexander 597
Novis, George 601
No(w)ell, Edward 616
George 524,555
John 152
Jonas 706
Jonathan 58
Michael 460
Richard 212
Samuel 49
Thomas 127,679
Nowes, Percival 553,523
Noyes [Noyce], Peter
456,717
Sarah 606
William 146
Nucke, Richard 603
Nugent [Newgent],
Edward 592
Nunn, John 646
Nurse, Luke 342,358,
366,382
Nutchall, John 15
Nutt, Job 200
John 40,139,227,252,
258,262
Thomas 121
William 206,297,346
Nuttall, Richard 38
Thomas 38
Nuttes, James 708
Nuttier, James 93
Nuttin(g), John 717
Thomas 34,536,636

O(a)ker, Abraham 109
Oakes, Elizabeth 542
William 66
O(a)key, Ann 297
Henry 347
John 414
Thomas 529

O(a)key, *(contd.)*
William 246
Oakford, Elizabeth 165
Katherine 165
Oakley, Francis 138
George 13
John 497
Peter 55
Oates, Bartholomew 476
Obie, John 424
Obonny, John 183
Oborne, James 714
Walter 708
Obridge, John 276
Obryan, Sarah 342
Oburne, John 46
Ockford, Samuel 327
Odams, William 111,354
Odell, John 248
Odeon, William 271
Odingsells, Gabriel 413
Odwin, Samuel 151
Offer, Elizabeth 266
Offerton, William 62
Ofield, John 32
Thomas 11,14,26,122
Ogden, Abraham 466
Samuel 466
Thomas 289,389
Oghen, Hugh 113
Ogilvie, Alexander 462
David 462
Ogle, John 353
Katherine 236
Thomas 236
Ogleby, George 603
O'Holtenhan, Edward
569
Oilbear, John 490
Oker. *See* **Oaker.**
Old, Joseph 631
Oldbury, Elizabeth 156
John 4,21,154,156
Olden, William 236
Oldfield, Adam 718
James 622
John 479
Thomas 145*,146*,163
Oldham, George 691
John 643
Oldis, William 296
Oldridge, Abel 352

Owen, *(contd.)*
Morgan 38
Richard 113,139,306,
307,415,475,694,697
Robert 715
Sarah 184
Stephen 688
Thomas 2,35,66,79,422,
687
William 21,628,695
Owens, James 312,447
John 687
Thomas 425
William 148
Owing, Elizabeth 42
Oxe, Robert 189,279,355
Oxenbourd, John 528
Oxenbridge, —— 590
Oxford, Thomas 17
Oyles, William 612

Pace. *See* **Paice.**
Pacey [Pacie], Edward
313
Elizabeth 488
Samuel 680
Pack, James 364
John 187,635
Michael 205,284,331,
360,389,451,507
Packenden, Robert 47
Packer, Charles 418
Daniel 592
George 252
Henry 256
Jonathan 321
Samuel 372,403,418,424,
461,557,598,653,667,
669,706,713,716
Thomas 18,338
William 268
Paddinghall, Richard 68
Paddock, William 132
Paddon, Anthony 108
Padley, Edward 452
Pafford, Henry 576
Thomas 603
Pagan. *See* **Paggen.**
Pa(i)ge, Ann 44
Edmond 92

Pa(i)ge, *(contd.)*
Edward 189,191
Elizabeth 166
Gregory 284
Henry 38,439
Joan 215
John 323,295,388,600,
605
Lucas 649
Margaret 44
Matthew 102,240,243,
289,296,383,580
Richard 50,302,638
Robert 290
Samuel 248
Thomas 234
William 440,523
Pagett, Edmond 398
John 283,331,337,469
Paggen [Pagan],
Edward 193
Peter 292,365,395,416,
420,457,458,655*,
682,683
William 193,234,237,
250,266*,292,296,
395*,402,404,420*,
472,528,533,551,579,
580,581,585,598*,
609*,610,614,623,
624*
Pagrowne, Joseph 453
Pa(i)ce, Jacob 448
Joseph 454,658,663*,
672,682
Paige. *See* **Page.**
Paine. *See* **Payne.**
Paines, Henry 65
William 512
Painter [Paynter],
Nicholas 440,479,481,
482,483,556
Roger 19
Samuel 256
Stephen 463
Thomas 173
William 673
Painton, George 14
Paisley, William 117
Palfreman, Thomas 672
Palfrey, Jonathan 691
Pall, Nathaniel 137

Pall, *(contd.)*
Richard 113
Thomas 212
Palleday, Richard 188
Palliott, Paul 679
Palmer, Ambrose 53
Andrew 525
Anthony 342,381,423,
656
Benjamin 93
Cadwallader 224,311
Edward 35
Elizabeth 438
Elizahias 475
Henry 622
Humphrey 412
James 32,190
Joan 190
John 279,288,357,385,
525*,594,604
Joseph 436,655
Mary 40
Matthew 562
Nathaniel 475
Nicholas 548
Oliver 476
Paul 293
Peter 262
Samuell 283
Sarah 507
Thomas 106,256,279,
282,293,439*,608
Ursula 81
William 93,117,225,368,
426,481,514
Pamle, Nicholas 481
Paniwell, William 50
Pank, Thomas 631
Panton, John 198
Papillon, Thomas 247,
345,376
Papworth, William 649
Paradice, John 30
Timothy 90
Pard, Robert 128
Pardie, Philip 85
Pardon, Henry 85
William 223
Parfrey, Jonathan 691
Pargiter, John 603
Sarah 13
Paring, Pad. 676

Parsons, *(contd.)*
  Reynald 443
  Richard 566
  Robert 300
  Susanna 143*
  Thomas 275,548
  William 627,663
Partington, Hugh 685
  John 80
Partis, Charles 369,396,
  419,420,466,467,
  527,582,623
  Francis 225,247,298,347,
  380,396,421*,439,
  462,469,522,537,581,
  624,645,678,717
Parton, Joseph 283
Partridge, Arthur 538
  Edward 600
  Elizabeth 405,538
  Isabel 462
  James 75
  John 80,526
  Robert 572
  Samuel 345,580
  Sarah 345
  Susan 138
  William 570
Parvey, Charles 151
Pascall, George 132
  James 132
  Robert 5
  Thomas 391
Pascoe, Sarah 601
  Simon 668
Pasfield, Nicholas 597
Pashellor, Anne 574
  William 574
Passell, Jonathan 490
  Sarah 490
Passmore, John 454
  Robert 266
  Rosamond 674
  Thomas 674
Paston, Robert 326
Patch, Philip 318,451,
  537
Pate, Edward 204,344,
  423,429,596
  Hannah 273
  John 105,212
  Thomas 198,596

Pate, *(contd.)*
  William 214,254,294,
  374,540
Patience, Alexander 4
Patrick, Christopher 708
  Henry 486,547
  Jonathan 439
  Nicholas 583
Patrone, Jean Louis 406
Patten [Patton],
  Gabriell 325
  James 524,552
  Robert 325*,336,363,
  429
  Thomas 122,153
  William 161
Pattent, Thomas 127
Patterson, Herbert 702
  Thomas 702
Pattfield, Thomas 304
Pattin, Anne 50
  John 50
  Thomas 449
Pattison, Edward 406,627
  Elizabeth 627
  Richard 496*,499
  Sarah 627
Pattman, Edmund 451
  Thomas 444,515
Paty, Elizabeth 325
Paul, Henry 95
  Joseph 546,548
  Margaret 455
  Peter 674
  Richard 102,111,548
  Robert 524,555
  Samuel 523,577
  Stephen 665
Pauson, Mary 578
Pavier, John 323
Paviott, John 143
Pavy, Richard 496
Pawlett, William 650,668
Pawling, Elizabeth 538
Paxton, Roger 193,197
Payne [Paine], Alice 572
  Anne 286,310
  Anthony 518
  Edmond 294,381,450,
  451,452,454,585
  Edward 156,342,365,
  476

Payne, *(contd.)*
  Elizabeth 64
  Francis 251,434
  George 350
  Harbett 565
  Henry 34
  Hester 565
  James 200,525
  Jane 253
  Joan 92
  John 61,74,110,174,204,
  345,409,501,535,547,
  549,550,632
  Joseph 74,429,559
  Margaret 136
  Matthew 135,206,251,
  269,306,369,403,588
  Nathaniel 238
  Paul 615
  Peter 266
  Richard 501,612
  Robert 384
  Samuel 651
  Sarah 140
  Silvanus 341
  Thomas 99,433,704
  Timothy 196
  William 105,113,164,
  283,520
Payson, John 630
Payton, John 488,714
  Joshua 488
  Phillip 82
Peabody, John 435
Peach, John 116
Peachey [Peachie], John
  407
  Thomas 363
Peacock, Daniel 91
  Edward 213
  Francis 284
  John 398
  Richard 465
  Robert 151
  William 15
Pead. *See* **Peed.**
Peak(e) [Peeke],
  Benjamin 189,192*,
  193,212,233,242,272
  Elizabeth 140
  George 313
  Sir John 281,293,311

Phillips, *(contd.)*
Silas 525
Susan 44
Thomas 16,60,76,135,
143,154,211,253,254,
264,353,378,463,532,
598,677
Walter 523
William 125,126,161,
163,250,253,263,342,
430,450,503,513,679
Phillis, Alexander 82
Philpott, John 357
Mary 10,13
Thomas 32,532
William 24
Philpotts, Elizabeth 546
Phinnimore, John 523
Phippard, George 692
William 375,392,655,
679,684,685,692,699
Phippen, Whitchurch
655
William 524,556
Phipps, Henry 216
James 223
John 216,712
Robert 195
Samuel 489
Thomas 366,532,621
Sir William 611,671
William 24*,43,359
Phippy, John 15
Pible, William 672
Pickard, Edmond 82
Pickerell, Richard 2
William 649
Pickering, Ann 148
Charles 393
John 80,85,227
Thomas 635
Pickes, Isaac 654
Josiah 91
Josias 219
Pickett, Anthony 123
John 79
Pickford, Bennett 538
Jedediah 218
Mary 148
Robert 342,345
William 538
Pickman, Richard 334

Pickmore, Simon 353,
483
Picknall, Mascall 132
Pidden, James 17
Piddesley, Matthew 211
Piddock, Elizabeth 458
Pidgeon, Richard 240,241
Pidgley, James 613
Pierpoint, Peter 664
Piggott, Richard 190
Spencer 58,187,189,190,
192,212,238,247*,
248,254,278,279,
280*,282,283,291,
293,296,325,326,329,
331,336,341,346
William 164
Piggs, Mark 262
Richard 396
Pike, John 16,293,548,
698
Lydia 464
Oliver 47
Samuel 164
Timothy 386
William 16,320,355,374,
706
Pilborow, John 522
Pilcher, Stephen 476
Pilchert, William 220
Pile [Pyle], George 558
John 471,555
Joseph 200,252,381,404,
423,440,467,560,606,
608
William 330
Pilgram, Anne 14
Pilkington, Ann 627
John 530
Margaret 465
William 460,698
Pille, Francis 125
Pill(e)s, Francis 490
Joseph 130
Pilson, Edward 347
John 67
Pilsworth, Samuel 229,
304,306
Pilt, John 562
Pinchback, William 344
Pinchon [Pinchen], John
42,61,345

Pinchon, *(contd.)*
Joseph 283
Margaret 42
Thomas 325
William 42,93
Pinckney, Richard 38
Pincus, Thomas 26*
Pinder [Pindar],
Edward 625
Mary 88
Matthew 246
Tobias 87,88
William 400
Pine. *See* **Pyne.**
Pines, Mary 674
Pinfield, William 197
Pinfold, Elizabeth 31
George 389
Ping, Jonathan 120
Pingrey, Francis 604
Pinhorne, William 263
Pink(e), John 334
Mary 565
Pinkard, Richard 602
William 466
Pinkerton [Pincarton],
Robert 650
Pinkston, Sarah 702
Pinnall, Thomas 87
Pinnell [Pinnill], Francis
717
Jeffery 706
Miles 173
William 52
Pinner, John 151
William 38
Pinney, Alexander 537,654
Azarias 523,549
Pinnick, Edward 478
John 478
Pinson, Roger 77
Samuel 523,549,615
Thomas 81
Pipe, William 329
Piper, Francis 645
Henry 257
Joan 249
John 249
Joseph 93
Pippard, William 403
Pippin(g), John 535
Joseph 591

Pont, Anne 54
Margaret 64
Pontin, Philip 686
Pook(e), Joseph 294
Simon 424
Poole, Anthony 293,322,
376
Arthur 20
Benjamin 265
Cicely 13
Daniel 60
David 114,323,376,404,
434,493,527,552,568,
579
Edward 336
Ellis 230
Emanuel 12
Francis 453
Hester 13
Jeremy 523,553
Joan 541
John 9,59,151,318,524,
709,710
Lydia 376
Matthew 453
Phillip 242
Ralph 258
Richard 15,41,117
Silvester 524,553
Simon 524,556
Theophilus 541
Timothy 93
William 24,222
Pooler, John 504
Pooley, William 34
Poore, Anne 17,61
Edward 81,112,128,
140
Gregory 248
John 233
Mary 342
Miles 340
Robert 193
Thomas 515
William 81
Pope, Charles 451,537
Dorothy 463
Elizabeth 295
Humphrey 524,555
James 150,178,196,318,
368,380,384,385,463
Jane 472,487,537

Pope, *(contd.)*
John 34,98,114,192,309,
523,525,649
Matthew 184
Michael 100,144,201,
316,318,320,321,353,
354,364,371,372,377,
380,544,552,650,668,
679
Nicholas 314
Philip 534
Richard 31,40,86,133,
148,157,202,210,318,
363,364
Robert 189,190
Sarah 280
Thomas 12,64,66,84,86,
87,102,108,137,139,
143,162,163,183*,
217,218,219,220,221*,
226,229*,230*,294,
306*,321,322,350,
353,365,367*,371,
482,556
William 403
Popejoy, William 365
Popham, Henry 82
Popkin, John 110
Roger 347
Popley, Edward 89
William 255
Poppin, George 57
Popple, Charles 525
Magnus 349
Popplestone, John 137
Popton, John 189
Porch, Elizabeth 41
George 604
Henry 18,35
Porcher, Matthew 312
Richard 197
Pordage, George 630
Joseph 374
Joshua 363,364,407,412,
423,630
Port, John 69,307,689
Porten, Robert 303,508
Sarah 113
William 113
Porter, Anthony 547
Benjamin 452
George 457

Porter, *(contd.)*
James 61,76,261*,262,
374,490,493,496,497*,
498,499,501
John 77,99,182,306,318,
327,380,396,420,457,
470,472,478,695
Luke 524,553
Lyson 197
Mary 547
Matthew 312,548
Peter 49
Robert 268,282
Samuel 381,421,429
Sarah 613
Stephen 99,153
Tabitha 612
Thomas 414,441,564,
592
William 176,642,697,
703
Porteus, Edward 247
Portman, Christopher
349
Henry 357
Robert 32
Portnell, John 525
Portry, Lyson 163,343
Pory, Katherine 499
Posterne, Elizabeth 490
William 490
Posthous, John 695
Postons, Thomas 490
Poticary, Elizabeth 314
Pott, George 119
Humphrey 636
William 385,566,624
Potter, Cuthbert 240
David 279
Edward 79
Elizabeth 378
John 153,202,241
Joseph 331
Richard 418
Thomas 357,361,380,
406,411,421,434,482,
533,536,589,600,609,
611,619
William 279
Potteridge, John 38
Pottinger, Henry 607
John 487

Pottle, Matthew 523
Potto, Abraham 508
  Jacob 508
Potts, George 308*
  Henry 578
  John 345
  Ralph 566,620
  Richard 683
  Theophilus 314
  Thomas 410,435,439,
    566
Pouley, Thomas 239
  William 154
Pouls, Paul 456
Po(u)lson, Edmond 624
  Edward 496,559,579
  John 251
  Paul 456
Poulter, Richard 65*
Pound, James 494
  John 59,76
  Susanna 695
  Thomas 672
Pounsey, Alice 529
  William 529
Pounty, Edward 75
Povey, Anne 673
  Charles 548
Pow, Katherine 92
Powell [Powle], Aaron 83
  Alice 248,476
  Andrew 17
  Ann 235
  Benjamin 221
  Charles 6,238
  David 45,47
  Edward 446
  Elizabeth 71,474,546,
    547
  Francis 140
  George 100,392
  Henry 26,288,460,707
  Hugh 2
  Isaac 492
  Jacob 524,552
  James 38,128,139,153,
    212,282,326,626,634
  Jane 82
  John 14,19,33,57,112,
    132,134,174,203,205,
    212,242,284,10,327,
    607

Powell, *(contd.)*
  Joseph 179,392,546,581
  Judith 20
  Katherine 505
  Lettice 84
  Margaret 9
  Martha 148
  Mary 56,150,303,320,
    495,555
  Matthew 57*
  Michael 524,556
  Nathaniel 408
  Oliver 492
  Peter 9
  Rice 29
  Richard 13,46,47,146,
    181,269
  Robert 23,281,719
  Samuel 249,299,345
  Susan 386,674
  Thomas 11,43,65,167,
    176,213,250,251,270,
    279,280,285,312,322,
    339,382,502,550,569,
    585,599,621,679,694
  William 16,20,65,148,
    176,243,255,259,262,
    458,526
Power, Anthony 136
  Herbert 271
  John 26
  Thomas 271,580,699
  Walter 529,653
Powlin, Edward 65
Pownell [Pownall],
  Christopher 604
  George 392
  Samuel 362
Powter, Henry 276
  Jane 274
  John 481
Powys, Thomas 489
Poyner, Ann 175
  Peter 122
  Thomas 529
Poynter, Samuell 588
  William 312
Poynting, Mary 35
Poynton, William 592
Poyntz, Joseph 258
  Thomas 299,324,367
Poyson, Peter 369

Pragg, John 502
Pralse, Roger 131
Prance, Aaron 220,247
  John 180
  Philip 642
Pranch, John 8
  Morgan 137
Prater, Henry 93
  Israel 116
Pratt, Dorcas 437
  Edward 572
  Lawrence 257
  Robert 58*,60,74
  Samuel 499,557
Prattin, Charles 242
Praul, John 342
Precept, William 445
Predix, Gabriel 675
Preece, Edward 666
  Richard 258
  Thomas 232
  Walter 85
Preed, William 8
Preeson, Thomas 541,
    581,616,646,677,704
  William 323,370,384,
    402,422,457,541,581,
    616,704
Prenstes, John 599
Prentis [Prentice], John
    614
  William 453
Prescott, Charles 358
  Elizabeth 438
  Henry 689
  James 403,419,486,542
  John 693,701
  William 234,380
Prest, Susan 145
Preston, Christopher 101
  Edward 326
  Elizabeth 430
  George 452
  Henry 678
  Jacob 329,348
  John 240,249,714
  Ralph 265
  Richard 113,164
  Thomas 115,252
  William 19,55
Pretious, Jane 660,673
Pretty, Anne 512

Prosly, Thomas 65
Prosser, Francis 39
  John 327,501
  Matthias 111
  William 24,455
Protheroe, Elizabeth 72
Prou, Cyprian 479
  Margaret 479
Proudman, William 498
Prough, Stephen 39
Prout, Timothy 146,337
  William 279,316
Provender, John 60
Provin, Edward 181
Provise, Capt. 89
Provist, John 498
Provo, George 290
  Nathaniel 316
Provost, Elias 630
Prowse, John 251
  Richard 714
  Roger 625,643,696,706,
    709,710
  William 447,525,526
Prudrow, Elizabeth 228
Prust, Peter 393,598
Pruther, Robert 49
Prynn [Prinn], John 401
  Nicholas 220,266,296,
    301,304,346,366,424,
    429,456
Pryor [Prior], Anthony
    52,316,417,535
  Francis 74,79
  Henry 559
  Isaac 525
  John 124,342,365,384,
    399,421,548,611,
    690
  Jonathan 92
  Matthew 410,526
  Peter 691
  Samuel 471
  Watkin 692
  William 418,686
Prytherch, Rowland 341
Puberly, Edward 232
Publin, James 226
Puckett, Francis 523,616
Puckle, Daniel 676,678
  Thomas 461,518
  William 316

Puddefatt, Joseph 334,
    361,676
Puddeford, Daniel 48
Pudding, Joan 127,133,
    134
Puddington, George 207
  John 126
Pugh [Pew], Christian 141
  Francis 409
  Hugh 169
  James 281
  Richard 81
  Samuel 143
  William 46
Pugsley, James 32,33
  Richard 23
  William 393
Pulford, Richard 388
  Urianus 674
  William 62
Pulham, Robert 592
Pullborne, Moses 529
Pullen, Abraham 84
  William 76
Puller, Elizabeth 13
  Isaac 345
Pullin(g), Richard 5*
  Thomas 414
Pullison, Roger 225
Pul(l)man, Elizabeth 573
  James 242,386
  Robert 573
  William 386,447
Pullridge, William 445
Pumfry, Elizabeth 131
Pumphret, Robert 178
Punford, Edmund 167
Punnet, Daniel 26*
Punny, Prudence 162
Punt, Augustine 249
Purcell [Percell], John
    248,639
  William 68,96
Purchase [Purchise],
    Daniel 494
  John 494
  Richard 88
Purdey, John 39
Purdue, Nicholas 658
  Simon 201
Purefoy, Michael 345,
    381,410

Purkis, George 391
Purnell, John 11,358,560
  Thomas 562
  William 562
Purnis, John 345
Purryer, William 470,
    532
Purse, Anne 60,68
  John 68
Purton, Henry 707
  Jane 432
  John 432
Purvis [Purvice],
  George 238,270,276,
    301,346,370,381,398,
    422,484,537,551,557,
    586,662,681
  Isabel 439
  John 204,239,271,295,
    345,367,382,402,429,
    431,432,492,556,614,
    657*,683,684
  Katherine 236
Pury, Thomas 1
Pussell, Elinor 27
Pustone, George 130
Putford, John 344
Putman, Amy 564
  Edmund 431
  Edward 432
  James 525
  William 526
Putt, Grace 606
  Samuell 239
Putteford, John 250,383,
    399
Putten, John 653
Puttley, Mary 366
Puxton, Thomas 382
Pybus, Richard 59
Pye, Edward 365
  Elizabeth 154
  George 407,501
  Humphrey 658,683
  James 701
  John 192,543
  Nicholas 113
  Philip 147
  Richard 2
  Walter 33,491
Pyland, Jane 324
  Robert 324

Redhead, Robert 654
Redman, Henry 212
Joan 49
John 112,366
Nathaniel 572
William 120
Redmond, Mary 13
Robert 18
Redwick, Sampson 17
Redwood, Philip 422
Ree [Rea], Nicholas 290
Thomas 263
William 213
Reece [Rees], Ann 45
David 17
Francis 176
Henry 229
Howell 132,530
Hugh 363
Jane 149,230
Jenkin 162
John 34,37,289
Margaret 163
Morgan 171
Richard 125,241,251
Roger 179,603
Thomas 5,43,216
Walter 519
William 37,74,147,226,
323
Reed(e). *See* **Reade.**
Reeker, Robert 493
Reekes, Henry 232
Reene, John 360
Reepe, William 36
Rees. *See* **Reece.**
Reeve [Reave], Charles
624
Diana 568
Edward 477
John 112,477
Judith 168
Walter 391
Reeves, Charles 581,597
Edward 13
Elizabeth 704
Francis 588
George 615
John 107,275,526,549
Katherine 215
Peter 683
Richard 262

Reeves, *(contd.)*
Robert 525
Thomas 141
William 15
Reid. *See* **Reade.**
Relict, William 698
Relk, James 576,582
Nicholas 576,582
Relshaw, Ralph 695
Remington, Robert 313
Thomas 151
Remmon, Lawrence 411
Renald, Hugh 357,373
William 496
Rench, Simon 33
Rendall, Giles 183
Thomas 168
Rendle, Margaret 701
Renell, Randolph 205
Renew, Peter 656
Renn, Richard 85
Rennalls, Anthony 103
Francis 86
Rennington, Richard 297
Rescons, Abraham 503
Resler, Jeremiah 541
Reston, William 35
Revell, Katherine 168
Randall 197
William 514
Revis, Thomas 244
Rey, Roger 208
Reyburne, Joseph 694
Reyden, William 360
Reyland, Gregory 215
Reynault, Elizabeth 533
Francois 533
Henry 533
Marie 533
Reyney, William 37
Reynold [Reignold],
John 297
Samuel 190
William 119
Reynolds [Raynolls]
[Rennols], Ann 16,486
Anthony 300,363
Daniel 442
Edward 128
Elizabeth 514
Gabriel 15
Henry 10,99

Reynolds, *(contd.)*
James 28,592
John 6,13,64,161,279*,
280*,284,286,294,
325,326,332,341,347,
376,388,398,514,525,
569,578,656,659
Katherine 215
Nathaniel 348,349
Nicholas 668,695,703
Richard 450,709*
Robert 407
Sarah 227
Thomas 13,16,128,351,
486,603
William 124,539,615,711
Reyse, John 360
Rhodes [Roads],
Edward 587,683*,380,
397,423,483,540,545,
286,337,363
Elizabeth 30
Francis 603
John 14,711
Nathaniel 677
Robert 515,595
Ribton, George 579
Rice, Arthur 507
David 445
Edmund 431
Evan 20,21,153
Hugh 177
James 340,341,347
Jenkin 173,174
John 178,241,321,340,
445,502
Katherine 28
Mary 145,515
Richard 671
Simon 258
Thomas 22,350,360,515
William 55,152
Rich, George 187
Henry 80,81,83,86,115,
116*,117,203
Humphrey 576
Jeremy 350,369,395
Joseph 56
Peter 358
Richard 47,247
Robert 342
Thomas 3,672,712

Richard, David 178
  Evan 135
  Griffin 390
  Henry 24,157,205
  James 338
  John 280,711
  Margaret 177
  Robert 174,606
Richards, Abraham 166
  Alexander 257
  Charles 278,569,570*,
   571*,572,573*
  Christopher 525
  Edward 8,251,334
  Elizabeth 571
  Francis 45
  George 193,198,202,237,
   272,289*,290,293,296,
   301,311,338,344,345,
   355,363,385,386,399,
   402,420,429,432,492,
   600,609,619,638,650
  Henry 15,22,129
  Hugh 27
  Humphrey 390
  James 230,246
  John 24,31,53,84,102,
   126,139,174,180,282,
   293,297,303,326,442,
   491,492,493,495,496,
   501,502,573*,574*,
   587,628
  Joseph 389,569,620
  Lot 81,115,162,196,
   317,384
  Margaret 4
  Mary 22
  Matthew 27
  Oliver 61
  Owen 59
  Paul 115
  Peter 664
  Robert 524,553,687
  Roger 97
  Samuel 120,381,384,
   399,402
  Thomas 140,206,246,
   252,275,291
  William 32,81,312,338,
   389,546,571
Richardson, Anne
  150,705

Richardson, *(contd.)*
  Edward 359
  Elizabeth 359
  Francis 337,358,375,
   409*,411,437,503
  George 324
  John 99,103,196,214,
   232,280,283,285,288,
   290*,292,293,296,
   310,312*,316,322,
   323,325,328,330,
   333*,337,340,346,
   353,358*,364,376,
   389,394,418,511,530,
   573,578*,585,591,
   592,650,653,665,672,
   688
  Joseph 135
  Martha 488
  Nicholas 282,490
  Richard 232
  Robert 62,169
  Samuel 217,420
  Sarah 10
  Thomas 110,437,451
  Walter 147
  William 132,134,240,
   259,488,704
Richbell, John 97,337
  Robert 199,315,335
  Roger 172
Richerson, Mary 483
Riches, John 326
Richeson, Charles 393
Ri(t)chley, Jane 11
  Katherine 695
Richman, Elinor 149
Richmond, Margaret 503
  Richard 503
  Silvanus 541,550,671,
   699,703
  Silvester 587
Richson, Samuel 205,
Rickard, Samuel 332
Rickards, Nathaniell 391
Rickens, Thomas 37
Rickett, Edward 308
Ricketts, Benjamin 295
  Edward 635
  George 1,443
  James 105
  Joan 342

Ricketts, *(contd.)*
  John 30,697,701
  Richard 165
  William 227,565
Ricky, Abraham 445
  Isaac 445
Riddell, Thomas 603
Ridder, Katherine 542
  Thomas 542
Riddle, Thomas 14,148
Rideon, Joseph 575
Rider. *See* **Ryder.**
Ridewood, Richard 59
Ridge, Jane 602
Ridgell, William 493
Ridgley, William 121
Ridgway, Edward 61
  Elizabeth 641
  Nicholas 61
  William 211
Riding, Thomas 182
Ridley, Daniel 333
  George 332
  John 171
  Thomas 176,308
Ridon. *See* **Rydon.**
Ridout, Nicholas 487,491
Riffin, William 284
Rigault, Christopher 190,
  425
Rigby, Charles 706
  Elinor 211
  Thomas 63
Rigglestone, Richard 3
Riggs, James 473
  John 15,225
  Robert 443
  Thomas 223
  William 435,704
Righton, John 664
  Mary 239
Rigley, Paul 698
Rignold, John 280
Riley, John 375
  William 440
Rime, Mary 445
Rimer, John 587,642,
  670,688
Rines, John 50
Ring, Ann 230
  John 366
  Richard 85

Ringwood, Anthony 189,
204,238,247,292,295
Ripley, Henry 686
Lionel 350
Richard 333
Rippin, Thomas 18
Risdon, Colon 520
Riser, Elizabeth 72
Riseton, Jarvis 137
Rishton, William 673,
675
Rishworth, Edward 125
Rither, James 559
Rivers, John 49,105,148
Joseph 21,25
Rives. *See* **Ryves.**
Rivington, Francis 578
Rivis, Edward 236
Roach. *See* **Roche.**
Roades. *See* **Rhodes.**
Roadly, John 709
Roal, Shadrach 669
Ro(a)ne, Charles 265
Robert 265
William 441
Robbs, John 76*
Robe, Stephen 464
Robert, Edward 169
John 243
Roberts, Anne 229,625
Charles 6,435
Christopher 147,161
David 246
Edmond 295,584
Edward 460,567,672,
689,691
Eliab 284
Elie 285
Elinor 92
Elizabeth 503,689
Evan 67,106
Fortune 22
Francis 514
Gabriel 689
Gayner 419
George 244
Gerrard 213,237
Griffith 265
Hugh 419,630,685
Humphrey 691
James 634
Joan 30

Roberts, *(contd.)*
John 7,42,72,91,137,
165,223,252,268,322,
344,419,482,538,609,
639,691,707
Joseph 11,275
Katherine 419
Lewis 72,518
Lydia 102
Margaret 101,149,630
Margery 607
Matthew 143
Maurice 691
Nicholas 76,187,192,
200,202,205,212,213,
239,243,247*,250,
252,503
Phillip 8,13,48
Richard 8,153,243,256,
288,368,606
Richard William 159
Robert 612
Samuel 263,439,471,
545,546
Thomas 238,239,291,
306,34,57,59,76,99,
102,105,136,443,
603,687,689
William 11,51,69,144,
161,196,223,268,
402,471,487,514,692
Robertson, Ann 617
Barnabas 248,249,315
David 593,649
George 523
Gerrard 238
Robins, Arthur 28
Henry 346,368
Humphrey 26
James 641
Jane 24
Jasper 281
Jeremy 184
John 22,59,345,524,
552,615
Joseph 525
Lewin 540
Mary 86
Nathaniel 112,144
Rachel 197
Rebecca 82,184
Richard 249

Robins, *(contd.)*
Samuel 7
Thomas 28,147,248,320
William 237,340,656
Robinson, Alexander
330,460,525
Andrew 244,247
Ann 617
Bartholomew 370
Christopher 478,479,
587,712
Daniel 573
David 649
Deborah 573
Edward 37,139,226,
270,293,313,367,401
Elihu 626
Elizabeth 438,541
Francis 37
Henige 422
Henry 236,541
Humphrey 52
Jane 153,389
John 15,225,410,465,
574*,580,606,610
Joseph 460
Mary 343,604,636,673,
720
Matthew 384,581,594
Maximilian 480,653
Rebecca 574
Richard 604
Robert 579
Samuel 64,508
Susan 52
Thomas 61,65,70,595
William 226,248,337,
604,676
Robotham, George 530,
547,573,704
John 297,298
William 345
Robson, John 482
William 59
Roby, Anthony 608
Samuel 80
William 357,503
Roche [Roach],
Elizabeth 651
George 192*,237,279,
282,325,329,343,357,
376,388

Rumney, Phoebe 440
Rumsey, Thomas 410
  William 18
Ruscoe, Thomas 656
Rusdon, Moses 293
Ruse, Thomas 17
Rusher, Robert 17
Rushton, Edward 54
  Ellen 711
Russ, James 269,498
  John 498
Russell, Edward 132,335
  Elias 621
  Elizabeth 96
  Frances 265
  Francis 386,400,416
  George 53,525
  Henry 57,153,326*
  Sir James 222,223*
  James 186
  Joan 494
  John 65,149,145,173,
    192,262
  Lawrence 543
  Mary 78
  Michael 529,583
  Nehemiah 656
  Nicholas 423
  Richard 71,347
  Robert 434,707
  Sarah 404
  Thomas 33,54,64,510
  Tobias 316
  Walter 567
Russell, William 80,112,
  455,647,690
Russells, Thomas 323
Russen, Thomas 631
Russy, Hugh 45
Rust, Argentine 525
  Daniel 469
  Finch 475
  John 247,495
  Moses 475
  Thomas 495
Ruth, Elizabeth 557
Ruther, Ann 39
Ruthra, Arthur 111
Rutland, John 253,267
Rutter, Daniel 523,553
  William 281
Rutty, Thomas 454

Ryan, John 612,666
  Philip 424
  Walter 392,393,438,578,
    596,620
Rycroft, Elizabeth 386,
  578
  John 116
  William 694
Ryde, Job 50
Ryder [Rider], Anne 202
  Anthony 636
  John 379,605
  Matthew 247,272,299,
    345,368,383,402,425,
    429,431*,551,584,625
  Richard 147
  Samuell 664
  Simon 329
  William 126
Rydon [Ridon], George
  510
Ryfield, James 179
Rylance, Jacob 719
Ryland, Amy 716
Ryves [Rives], Charles
  248,250
  Mary 507

Sabin, John 279,290,296,
  297,302,304,325,334
  Joseph 204
Saby, John 437
Sacheverell, Thomas 671
Sack, Sidrach 76
Sadbury, Christopher
  110,112
Sadd, Thomas 542
Sadler, Jane 295,326
  John 205,295,343,616
  Richard 81
  Samuel 410
  Thomas 21,25,29,211,
    236
  William 236,391
Saffin, John 40
  Michael 21
  Thomas 603
Safford, Thomas 219
Sage, Henry 124
  Philip 629

Sage, *(contd.)*
  William 183
Sailes, Richard 332
Sainbry, Rebecca 327
Sainsbury, John 204
Saint, James 467
St. Alban, Jonathan 180
Saintbury, Rebecca 327
Sainthill, Nicholas 370,
  382,424
St. John, Thomas 14
St. Quintin, William 619
Sair, Alice 30
Saker, David 361
Sa(y)le, Clement 580,617
  Martin 32
  Samuell 297
Salisbury, Ann 202
  David 13
  Gilbert 296,344
  Humphrey 708
  Richard 472
  Robert 14
  Thomas 525
  William 130,368
Sall, Lawrence 24
Sallett, Margaret 227
Salley, John 280
Sallock, Edward 442
Salloway [Sallaway],
  John 54
  Robert 359
  William 424
Salmon [Salman],
  Eleanor 671
  James 290
  John 504,658
  Richard 51
  Stephen 665
  Thomas 659,678
  William 89,244
Salt, Benjamin 96,99,
  103,134,137
Salter, Anne 83,220
  George 154,352
  Henry 205,238,281,286
  James 548
  John 11,13,266,286
  Joseph 53
  Nicholas 549,615
  Richard 61,335,516
  Theophilus 1

Salter, *(contd.)*
  Thomas 301,339,355,
    369,550
Salthouse, Mark 135
Saltmarsh, Thomas 522
Saltonstall, Richard 61,
  92
  Thomas 243
Salwey, Anthony 51,197
Salwood, William 714
Saly, George 457
  Mary 457
Samborne, Barnaby 164
  Mawdley 164
Same, Thomas 470
Samm, Daniel 29,31,95,
  99,120*,145
  John 20,150,523,549
  Thomas 187
Samms, Edith 14
  William 50
Sample, Robert 372
Sampson, Capt. 374
  Bernard 706
  Elizabeth 275
  Francis 562
  Gerrard 35
  Henry 104
  John 46,284
  Peter 160
  Richard S. 697
  Robert 14
  Samuel 570
Samster, John 666
Samuell, Richard 185
  Roger 435
Sanby, William 364
Sand, John 202
Sandell, Richard 231
Sanders. *See* **Saunders.**
Sa(u)nderson, Elizabeth
  226
  John 604,712
  Margaret 604
  Phillip 654,664
  William 226,436
San(d)ford, Abraham
  666
  Anne 109
  Edmond 472,476,538
  Giles 255
  Henry 332

San(d)ford, *(contd.)*
  John 304,316,320,323,
    349,384,396,558,606
  Mary 407
  Richard 143,706,415
  Samuel 296
  Samuel 202,608,647,
    657,683
  Thomas 123,434,547,
    583,584
  William 55,390,714
Sandon, Christopher 532
Sandy, John 28
  Mary 28
  Robert 549
  William 28
Sand(y)s, Henry 282,410
  Robert 523
  Thomas 25,239,266,266,
    286,290,296,299,307,
    311,338,349,374,393,
    430,464,483,522
Sankes, William 128
Sankey, William 164,
  176,177,256,257,
  365*,666
Sankin, William 228
Sankley, Richard 253
Sanny, William 421
Sansom(e), Francis 461
  George 76
Sapp, Edward 69
  Jeremy 608
Sare, William 237,303,
  387,484
Sargent. *See* **Serjeant.**
Sarrazin, David 664,670
Sarsfield, Patrick 451
Sartaine, James 167
Sarys, Charles 253
Sa(t)chwell, George 125,
  190,195,376
  James 644
Sauchy, William 322
Saudon, Joseph 358
Saught, James 250
Saul, Thomas 39
  Thomasine 100
Saunder, John 143
  Philip 278
Sa(u)nders, Abraham
  390,304,354

Sa(u)nders, *(contd.)*
  Alice 68,71
  Anne 371
  Anthony 600
  Benjamin 330
  Charles 614
  Daniel 672
  David 451,596
  Edward 290
  Elizabeth 225,589,650
  Francis 35
  George 272,371
  Henry 185*,589
  Humphrey 523
  James 171
  John 26,67,68,121,196,
    198,221,229,230*,
    329,333,413,447,466,
    525,534,589,691,715
  Joseph 217,365,380,396,
    402,413,466,510,532,
    533,537,539,582
  Joshua 535
  Nathaniel 257,277
  Peter 593,651
  Phillip 34,67
  Richard 147,200,589
  Robert 140
  Samuel 646
  Sarah 85
  Silvester 259
  Thomas 29,35,61,121,
    122,300,310,312,330,
    332,333,358,361,376,
    441,453,526,631
  William 29,83,101*,138,
    147,163,179,200,205,
    221,224*,354,469,
    503,523,548,553,557,
    565,619
Saunderson. *See*
  Sanderson.
Sauty, William 322
Savage, Abraham 489
  Charles 572
  Edward 59
  Francis 494,525
  Henry 80
  John 68,293,295,378,
    489
  Rowland 43
  Thomas 158,452,489

850

Sol(l)ey, *(contd.)*
Richard 532
Thomas 450
Solloway, Richard 191,
253
Solomon, Elizabeth 247,
292
Somer, John 158
Somerford, Geoffrey 28
Somerley, Thomas 256
Somers. *See* **Summers.**
Somerset, John 467
Richard 302
William 467
Somner, Jonas 105,113
Sondes, Thomas 263
Sonier, Jonas 105
Sontley, Thomas 213,
238,283,284,390,
454,587
Soper, Elizabeth 442
James 523
Sopper, Robert 133
Sorrell, Thomas 459
Sotheby, James 237,280
William 237
Soulter, John 707
South, Francis 131
Henry 388
Humphrey 499
James 250
John 280,283
Southake, Cyprian 378
Southby, Thomas 357
Southcome, John 698
Southcott, Leonard 286
Richard 426
So(u)thell, Seth 292,671
Thomas 170
William 169
Souther, Joseph 631
Nathaniel 631
Samuel 158,631
Southerly, William 144
Southe(r)n, George 18,
218,392
Isaac 39
Leonard 52
William 285
Southin, Thomas 151
Southley, Thomas 285,
286

Southwell, Robert 150
Southworth, Francis
334,338,409,611
Soutley, Thomas 335,336
Soux, Augustine 406
Sowdell, William 280
Sowell, Jeremy 211
John 105
Sowgate, James 636
Sowlard, Lewis 578
Spales, Leonard 553
Sparke, Benjamin 523
James 710
Richard 95
Thomas 19
William 112
Sparkes, Elizabeth 375
Francis 153
Henry 94
John 9,60
Joseph 448
Peter 165
Robert 165
Samuel 335
Thomas 21,22,45,78,
264,443
William 57
Sparrow, Elizabeth 175
John 705
Joseph 135,204,206,
241,249,297,298
Sparry, Ann 595
Speake, Henry 192
Speakman, Frances 471
George 471
Mary 715
Spear, Stephen 556
Speed(e), Hester 545
John 23,133,140,195,
196,203
Phillip 588
Richard 203,251,257,
278*,279,305
Thomas 38,74,112,130,
156*,196,203,206,
215,223,245,252*,
268,271,316,317,322,
352,354,364,371*,
526,600
Speering, John 548
Spence, James 548
Mary 461

Spence, *(contd.)*
Patrick 227,230
Richard 554
Thomas 593
Spencer, Ann 607
Arthur 146
Dorothy 214
George 429,434
Henry 313
John 40,167,214,236,
318,436,626
Joshua 701
Margery 33
Nicholas 577
Robert 112*,113,115
Thomas 40,167,239,
620
William 213,577
Spender, Joan 14
Spendler, John 293
Spendlove, Charles 129
Sperin, Rebecca 504
Sperring, John 235
Sperry, Elizabeth 142
Henry 142
William 164
Spicer, Elizabeth 438
John 263
Robert 619,623
Samuel 576,603,611
Spickett, William 158
Spigurnell, George 124
Spikeman, William 651
Spiller, John 95
Oliver 14
Richard 526
Spilman, George 482,
576
Mary 29
Thomas 29
Spinke, Thomas 256
Spinnedge, Joseph 512
Spinner, John 112
Spire, Andrew 343
John 534
Spittle, John 326,400
Richard 378
Robert 354
Spooner, Edward 516
Henry 252
Sprackland, James 596
John 98,294

Starkey [Starkie], John
  153
  Richard 581
  Thomas 440
  William 59
Starling, George 265
  William 532
Starnell, William 310
Starr, Joan 47
  Stephen 54
Start(e)e, Arthur 100
  George 29
  John 426
  Thomas 56
Statham, Thomas 672
Stathorne, William 534
Staty, John 253
Staunton. *See* Stanton.
Staverton, Edward 291
Stayne, John 318
Stead, Elizabeth 10
Steane. *See* Steene.
Steart, Arthur 19
  George 34,36,38
Stebbins, John 248
Stechley, Thomas 589
Stedman, Hugh 384
  John 457,693
  Solomon 684
  William 64
Steed, William 54
Steele [Steale], Alice 312
  Edward 606,696
  Giles 254
  Isaac 431*,434,436,
    566
  John 398
  Mary 687
  Robert 431
  Samuel 359
  Sarah 630
  Thomas 666,667
Steene [Steane], Abel
  408
  Anne 134
Steere, Elizabeth 339
Steeres, John 579
  Mary 394
Stegge, Thomas 175
Stellhaven, Thomas 667
Stennett, John 466
Stenning, William 68

Stent, Henry 79
  William 361
Stenton, Samuel 243
Stephens [Stevens],
  Abigail 540
  Alice 135,477
  Angell 48
  Anne 84,125
  Benjamin 417,540
  Charles 203,298
  Christopher 30
  David 499
  Edward 139,219,409,
    644
  Elias 548,646
  Elizabeth 287,617
  Frances 159
  George 317
  Godfrey 355
  Hannah 409
  Henry 157,460
  James 103,124,667
  Jane 295,326
  Joan 13,65
  John 12,76,85,92,110,
    210,254,267,317,
    318*,350,360,361,
    389,439,467,471,477,
    480,490,529,598,626,
    630,653,665,673,679,
    696
  Jones 24
  Joseph 10,12,28,277,
    641
  Lewis 68
  Lodowick 107,109,110
  Mary 29,156,265,343
  Matthew 5,36,45*,56,63,
    64,106,109,116,222,
    323
  Nathaniel 264*,333,337
  Rebecca 269,460
  Richard 51,85,105,248,
    524,527,529,535,555
  Robert 10,15,72,177,
    508
  Samuel 159
  Silvester 335
  Simon 31,228,229*,353
  Thomas 26,27,159,274*,
    318,322,341*,431,
    666

Stephens, *(contd.)*
  Walter 36,99,312,320,
    372,392,415,418,480,
    593,641
  William 37,40,88,90,
    144*,156,296,470,
    490,606,649
Stephenson [Stevenson],
  Edward 62
  Elizabeth 431
  Humphrey 295
  Jane 164
  John 298,431,496
  Mary 581
  Robert 193
  Thomas 507
  Valentine 259
Stephson, Thomas 70
Stepkin, Charles 572,616
  Thomas 203
Stepkins, Charles 231,
    233,289,291,293,299,
    340,433
Stepmon, Andrew 45
Stepney, Robert 409,478,
    536
  Samuel 115
Stermer, Richard 664
Sterne, William 159
Sterry, James 74*
  William 557
Stert. *See* Sturt.
Steven, Martha 273
Stevens. *See* Stephens.
Stevenson. *See*
  Stephenson.
Steventon, John 269,301,
    347
Steward, Anne 311
  Charles 132
  George 436
  James 368
  Jane 389
  Joan 309
  John 184,308,309,416,
    577,646,686
  Newman 701
  Peter 254
  Thomas 688
  William 416,420*,693
Stewart, James 507
  John 643

859

Symms, *(contd.)*
John 381,436
Mary 138,306
Richard 15
Robert 157,436
Samuel 27
William 301,435
Symon(d) [Simon],
Daniel 275
John 525
Sarah 81
Symon(d)s [Simmons]
[Simmonds], Andrew
116
Anne 378,627
Elizabeth 567*
Florence 42
Francis 579
Henry 300
Humphrey 130
Jacob 408
James 193,229
Jane 248
John 27,28,59,76,144,
236,639,641
Jonathan 467
Katherine 60,511
Margery 141,156*
Ralph 103
Richard 40,297,567,
709,524,553
Robert 129,240
Samuel 189,327
Sarah 81,83
Thomas 5,22,24*,30,42,
43,44,52,153*,154,
155,157*,158*,159,
187*,188*,189,222*,
248,257*,261,262,
286,326,439,511
William 407,435,521,
546,639
Synschall, John 215

Taberfield, Edward 116
Tabor, William 280
Tackley, John 295
William 295
Tacy, Thomas 352
Walter 172

Taffe, Mary 280,326
Taffey, Benjamin 398
Tagwell, John 462
William 462
Tailby, William 560*
Tainton, Benjamin 336
John 11
Talbot(t), Ambrose 613
Christopher 334
Edward 464,465
George 505
Jane 68
Matthew 346
Richard 123
William 374
Talent, Richard 673
Talier, James 690
Tallis, Clement 175
Tally, Elizabeth 604
John 261
Thomazine 604
William 196
Tamar, Jane 148
Tammas, Grace 319
Tandy, Bryan 167,229,
249,254,256,322,352,
371,423,487
James 10,11,12,13,28
Margery 87
Sarah 129
Thomas 226*,227*,274,
275,276,320,351
Tankard, Dillington 357,
376,388
Tankyn, John 439
Tanner, Anthony 472
Arthur 85,280,398,445,
504,605
Elizabeth 666
Henry 319
Jane 59,447
John 70,80,87,343,484,
535,540,583,656,
680
Lawrence 330
Martha 309
Mary 166
Robert 165,166
Thomas 320,345,449
William 309,359
Tansly, Thomas 432
Tanton. *See* **Taunton.**

Taplady, Charles 54
George 53
Tapley, Edward 52
Giles 376,601
William 539
Tapling, John 514
Tapp, Thomas 172
Tapper, Richard 526
Tappin, Johanna 189
William 189
Tapping, John 124
Tapscott, William 523
Tapsfield, John 78
Tarbert, Richard 45
Tarbutt, Elizabeth 445
Richard 275
Tarleton, Edward 325,
329,336,347,374,381,
396,416,554,581,587,
596,642,670,690,691,
692*,693,694*,696*,
707
Stephen 282
Tarnell, Mary 338
Tarrs, William 359
Tasker, John 292
Robert 455
Thomas 129,439
William 578
Taster, Anne 359
Taswell, William 460
Tate, Mary 529
Tatem, John 605
Tatham, Bartholomew
703
Mary 703
Tatlock, Henry 182
Tatnall [Tattnell],
Edward 73,577,597,
608,623,633
Thomas 478
William 357
Tatten [Tatton], William
17,389
Tattle, Margaret 138
Tattnam, James 374
Tatum, Samuell 238
Ta(u)nton, Benjamin 283
Giles 46
John 707
Robert 552
Samuel 50

Terrick, Samuel 157
Terrold, George 464
    Joseph 464
Terry, John 423,660
    Joseph 290
    Richard 145,225
    Thomas 655
Tervin, Thomas 357
Teshmaker, John 565,
    572,587,620,622
    William 653
Testard, Isaac 455
Tether, John 84
Tetlow, Jonathan 399
Teverton. *See* Tiverton.
Tew [Tue], Henry 243
    Mary 687
    Richard 222,213
Teward, John 446
Tewksbury, John 706
Tewsey, Thomas 337
Thacker, Elizabeth 567
    John 579
    Richard 569,620
Thackham, Thomas 383,
    390,402
Thackster, Thomas 515
Thackston, Thomas 666
Tha(i)re, John 152
    Robert 161
Thatcher, Francis 3
    Peter 281
    Samuel 3
    Thomas 492
Thatchwell, John 343
Thayer [Theyer],
    Nathaniel 338
    Samuel 580,624,651,
    658,663
Theckstone, Jeffery 587
Thedam, John 318,319
Theed, Thomas 481
Thelball, Elizabeth 364
Th(i)ery, James 162,260,
    354
Thieron, Anthony 320
Thiew [Thewe], William
    175,308
Thomas, Abraham 523,
    549,615,678
    Alexander 246
    Alice 136,137*,139

Thomas, *(contd.)*
    Ambrose 28
    Anne 12,112,218,221,
    339,439,487,617
    Baldwin 222
    Bartholomew 21,22*,
    218
    Benjamin 136,277
    Blanch 375
    Cornelius 27
    Daniel 134,439
    David 14,32,108,526,
    567
    Dorothy 343,359
    Edmund 25,75
    Edward 3,4,19,36,44,45,
    97,108,144,153,154,
    226,232,567
    Elinor 109
    Elizabeth 7,63,131,255,
    485
    Evan 3,58,116,136,150,
    248,249,351
    Francis 31,216,302,341,
    489,557
    Gaynold 692
    George 14,64,130,187,
    210,335,442
    Griffith 694,706
    Gwilliam 260
    Henry 38,51,68,224,639
    Howell 48,232,242,243
    Hugh 128,165,258,268
    Humphrey 94
    Isaac 25
    Jacob 164
    James 8,86,199,322,357,
    372,403,510,515,543,
    602,651,664,668
    Jane 57
    Jenkin 9,42,152,270
    Jenner, 542
    John 5,16,17*,22,27,29,
    30,38,49,53,58,76,82,
    86,87,95,104,137,144,
    162*,196,220,255,269,
    315,325,368,376,443,
    457,493,552,592,666,
    669,670*,682,685,687,
    691*,692*,693*,694*,
    695*,696,697,705,
    716*

Thomas, *(contd.)*
    Joseph 257,597
    Joyce 37
    Judith 15
    Katherine 26,546
    Lambert 561
    Lambrook 560
    Lewis 18,174
    Llewellin 24
    Margaret 12,176,583
    Mary 9,11,81,255,299,
    567
    Matthew 634
    Morgan 81,83,168,179,
    187
    Morris 2
    Philip 60,81,135,137
    Ralph 42,695
    Rebecca 26,87
    Reece 115,184,205
    Rice 25,540
    Richard 1,79,227,419,
    510,581,708
    Robert 1,19,99,136,176,
    180,268,543
    Rosser 28
    Rowland 693
    Sarah 158,516,666
    Saye 73
    Silvanus 422
    Stephen 27
    Thomas 24,443
    Ursula 255
    Walter 60,250,363
    Watkin 133
    Welthian 116
    William 18,33,37,60,70,
    119,123,159,171,
    174*,185,193*,216,
    218,235,244,252,254,
    255,268,278,426,460,
    507,701
    Zacharias 183
Thomasman, Markham
    436
T(h)ompson, Alexander
    131*,257,314,357,
    372,403
    Bryant 136
    Christopher 599
    Daniel 120
    David 337

Truman, Thomas 288
Trump, Humphrey 524, 556
Trunkett, Jane 480
Truren, John 548
Truss, Christopher 665
  Thomas 663
Trusty, Gabriel 84
Try(e), Eleanor 635
  Mellisant 238
Tryon, Rowland 569
  Thomas 278,279,326, 357,376,540
Tryon & Perkins 588
Tryton, James 364
Tubb, James 311
  John 408
Tubley, John 369
Tuck, John 17*,35,67,69
  Reginald 206
  Richard 304
  Stephen 323
  Susan 134,137
  Thomas 82,286,341
Tucker, David 83*,84,104
  Edmond 546
  Edward 145,385
  Elizabeth 37,99,262, 288
  Francis 416
  George 11
  Grace 211
  Henry 548
  James 382,582,707
  John 29,105,112,137, 198,255*,638,667, 687
  Joseph 30,31,32,55,80, 263
  Maurice 493
  Nathaniel 111
  Pugh 223*
  Reginald 127,283,297
  Richard 99,189,199, 211,213
  Roger 620
  Samuel 10,53,72,96,132, 166
  Thomas 156,303
  Walter 10,51,72,81,82,87, 96*,136,164,180,181, 198,200,201

Tucker, *(contd.)*
  William 359,548,578, 579,623
Tuckey, Gabriel 673
  Richard 106
  Thomas 83,526
Tuckfield, James 123
  Joseph 390
Tuckwell, Thomas 396
Tudway, Clement 443,564
Tue. *See* Tew.
Tuften, Frances 149
Tuftin, Richard 24
Tuick, Jane 150
Tull, Richard 718
Tullidge, Richard 21
Tullis, Thomas 478
Tulloch, Margaret 543
Tully, John 13,67,71,238
  Ralph 288
Tunbridge, Robert 669, 682
Tupe. *See* Toope.
Turdall, John 342
Turdin, Philip 315
Turford, Edward 60
  Theophilus 298
Turk, Richard 224
Turley, George 230
  Jane 437
Turmidge, John 649
Turner, Abraham 645
  Alice 113,582
  Anne 300
  Benjamin 710
  Charles 300
  Elizabeth 223
  Ephraim 173
  Grace 201
  Henry 489*,528,550
  Hester 502
  James 327*,492,577
  Jane 339
  John 6,23,113,165,173, 322,333,340,551,607, 706*,709,710
  Margaret 81
  Martha 551
  Mary 101
  Matthew 248
  Peter 711
  Richard 50,152,189,526

Turner, *(contd.)*
  Robert 14
  Samuel 489
  Susan 502
  Theophilus 420
  Thomas 47,76,223,244, 252,318,321,339,351, 383,391,423,482,502, 570,594,667,701,709*, 714
  William 68,150,414
Turney, Anthony 326
Turpin [Terpin], Henry 331
  James 311
  John 454
  Mary 695,697
  Oliver 312
  Robert 208,249,313,316
  Tirwhite 644
Turrell, Alice 60
Turton, Francis 455
  Thomas 178
  William 708
Turvey, Edward 589
Tushingham, George 113,114*
Tustey, Thomas 59
Tustin, Thomas 555
Tuston, Ann 264
Tutfold, William 339
Tuthill, George 92,98, 389,480,542
  James 706
  John 482
Tutt, Alexander 249
  Anthony 441
  John 468,581
  Susan 249
Tuttle, Zachary 664
Tuxon, William 307
Twiggs, Allan 511
Twisden, Elizabeth 192
  John 126
Twisleton, Ezechiell 247
Twist, Ann 211
  Charles 568
  Joan 300
  Mary 104
  William 199
Twitt, Fortune 30,31*, 135,183

White, *(contd.)*
  Robert 134,238,269,445,
    523,544,708
  Samuel 428,438,650,651,
    662,664,671,674
  Thomas 29,82*,222,310,
    331,707
  Walter 247,495
  William 10,13,64,131,
    223,276,277,279,280,
    284,286,290,291,293,
    294,298,314,325,326,
    335,342,343,385,398,
    425,470,510,593,607,
    677
Whiteacre. *See*
  Whittaker.
Whiteborough, John 554
Whitecake, Thomas 73
Whitecraft, John 32
Whitefield. *See* **Whitfield**.
Whitefoot, Amos 332
Whit(e)haire, Robert
    199,224
  Thomas 382,386*,424,
    694
Whitehall, Edward 326,
    588
  Stephen 446
Whitehand, William 176
Whitehart, Richard 186
Whit(e)head, Benjamin
    414
  Elizabeth 280
  George 187,329
  Henry 209,718
  James 643
  John 457
  Jonathan 545
  Joseph 260,352
  Margaret 182
  Mary 336,546
  Ninian 545
  Richard 336
  Rose 138
  Samuel 522*
  Thomas 251,457,707,
    708
  William 410,522,713
Whitehill, Thomas 609
Whitehorne,
  Bartholomew 655,705

Whitehorne, *(contd.)*
  Elizabeth 280
  Robert 200,202
  Stephen 446
Whit(e)house, Elizabeth
    131
  John 305
  Lawrence 14
Whiteman, Abel 502
Whitenit, William 313
Whitethorne, Bridget
    343
Whiteway, William 646
Whitewood. *See*
  Whitwood.
Whit(e)field, Barbara 535
  Daniel 61
  Jane 451
  John 184,257,273*,
    274*,360,361,466,
    472,474,478,565
  Matthew 69,334
  Nathaniel 63,449
  Richard 414
  Roger 165,347,581
  Thomas 78
  William 179
Whitford, Hannah 176
Whitgreave, Dorothy
    214
  Frances 214
  Thomas 214
Whit(e)ing, George 90
  John 295,517,521
  Joshua 656
  Mary 131
  Thomas 79,183,460
  William 7,115,279,335,
    398,450,460,605
Whitley, Gabriel 280*,
    282,283,294,325,
    336
  Roger 307,405
Whitlock, —— 344
  Anthony 362
  Godfrey 49
  John 362*
  Thomas 362,364
Whitman, Edward 177
Whitmore, Benjamin
    668
  Thomas 313

Whitpa(i)n, Richard
    455*,486,547,583,
    608,616,625
  Zachary 614
Whitson, Mary 13
  Samuel 53
Whitstone, William 111
Whittaker [Whiteacre],
  Edward 667,682
  George 636
  Hester 530
  Richard 342
  Thomas 688
  William 279
Whittamore, John 406
Whitten, John 70
Whittenbury, Mary 79
Whitter, Tristram 662
Whittingham, Richard
    654
  Sarah 298
  Thomas 493
  William 190
Whittington, Elizabeth
    14
  Thomas 659
Whittle [Whittell],
  Elizabeth 457,490,616
  Giles 525
  James 490
  John 192,415
  Joseph 506
  Thomas 281,347
Whittoes, Isaac 13
Whitton. *See* **Witton**.
Whittop [Whitetopp],
  Thomas 31,50,128,168,
    223,396,420,531,544,
    665,718
Whittorne, John 626
  Ruth 626
Whitturd, Richard 179
W(h)itty, John 98,106,
    136
  Margaret 98
  Mary 330
  Sarah 98,106
  Thomas 10*,55,288,
    523
Whitwell, Edward 296
  John 236
  Thurston 346

Whit(e)wood, Abigail
  328
  Anne 14,617
  Katherine 617
  Mary 358,482
  Michael 257
  Thomas 257
Whoms, John 516
Whore, Allen 194
  William 282
Whusden, John 88
Wibberd, Gabriel 3
Wiburne. *See* **Wyborne.**
Wibury, William 84
Wick, Samuell 336
Wickers, John 176
Wickey, Henry 625
Wickham, Alice 37
  Benjamin 335
  Elizabeth 344
  Joseph 524,555
  Thomas 230,338,346,496
Wickins [Wickens],
  Edward 282
  John 190,212
  Lott 655
  Samuel 214,267,268*,
    278,279,286,294,325,
    326,341,400,619,651,
    656,660,672*
  Thomas 293,657
Wickmans, Thomas 290
Wicks [Wix], Anne 27
  Elizabeth 550,556,557*
  Francis 550,557*
  Jane 561
  Joseph 32,33*
  Paul 588
  Richard 29,603
  Susanna 496
  Thomas 561
  Tobias 123
Widdop, Paul 708
Widdowes [Widdus],
  Cassandra 567
  Robert 23
  Richard 276
  William 207
Widdowson, Richard 419
Widger, Samuel 94
Widlake, Godfrey 16
Wigfall & Bell 603,610

Wigg, Richard 217
Wiggin, Samuell 336
Wiggington, William
    146,147,204*,205,
    206,223*,266
Wiggins, Richard 313
Wigglesworth, Ambrose
  468
Wiggleworth, Thomas
  393
Wigham, William 394
Wight, Thomas 392
Wightman, John 654
Wigley, John 133
Wigmore, Nathaniel 116
Wilbow, Eustace 529
  Jacob 529
Wilcock, Richard 252
Wilcox [Wilcocks],
  Alexander 294
  Barnaby 424
  Daniel 634
  George 502
  John 101,256
  Josias 117
  Philip 428,472,554
  Richard 196,270,526
  Thomas 666
  William 98
Wildblood, Thomas 595
Wildbore, Edmond 592
Wild(e), Abraham 3,183,
    191,320,321,322,323,
    363*,365,366*,396,
    422,478*,479,480,
    538,550,582,608,621,
    624,654,657,679
  Alice 547
  Andrew 369
  Daniel 274
  Elizabeth 151
  Habbacuck 663
  Isaac 657
  Jane 64
  John 64,278,358,376,
    390,411,447,566,602,
    619
  Joseph 296
  Richard 151
  Susan 172
Wilder, John 399
Wildes, Mary 128

Wildgoose, Richard 68
Wilding, Richard 27
  Thomas 697,700
Wildman, Henry 298
Wiles [Wyles], Martha
  130
  William 359
Wiley, Isaac 174
Wilk(e)s, Benjamin 358
  Henry 189
  John 137,413
  Richard 61
  William 230,543
Wilkey, Henry 101
  John 463
Wilkin, Maudlin 3
  Thomas 120,326*,602,
    612
Wilkins, Giles 84
  Henry 359
  James 195,397
  John 22,71,333,594
  Mary 50
  Michael 135,379
  Richard 134,594
  Robert 526
  Samuel 283,290,388,
    389,390
  Thomas 87,195,277,
    284,331
  William 19,229,445
Wilkinson, Benjamin 389
  Charles 701
  Daniel 333
  Elizabeth 375,446
  Gabriel 522
  George 8,322,485,490,
    492
  Henry 365
  Isabel 582
  John 119,416,573,667,
    713
  Martin 574
  Matthew 201,206,219,
    260,319
  Nathaniel 201,285,290
  Philip 380
  Richard 452
  Robert 443
  Thomas 443,594,688
  William 27,66,378,390
Willard, Richard 569,620

Wood, *(contd.)*
Joan 221
John 145,151,226,253,
344,345,358,381,388,
396,425,439,461,472,
474,532,701,708
Jonathan 178,211
Margaret 59
Mary 89,473,673
Nathaniell 591
Oliver 701
Richard 30,55,97,467,
687
Robert 15,32,124
Roger 390
Samuel 610,671
Sarah 502
Susan 712
Thomas 359,480,593,720
William 137,243,307,
419,475,539,702
Woodall, Joseph 398
Woodard, Richard 131
Woodbee, William 397,
419,455,486,534,547,
583,625
Woodburne, Adine 537*
Mary 537
Thomas 537
Woodbury, John 210
Samuel 582
Woodcock, John 518,
568,632
Nicholas 418
Richard 286
Thomas 310
William 85,524,553,711
Woodden, Edward 326,
355
Mary 326,355
Woodfield, Samuel 528
Thomas 167
Woodford, Mary 68
Thomas 242
Woodgate, Daniel 36
Edward 268
Woodham, William 562
Woodherd, John 258
Woodhouse, Elizabeth
521
Henry 608
Jonathan 281,283

Woodhouse, *(contd.)*
Robert 291
Woodiard, George 420
Woodland, Henry 97
Joseph 597
Matthew 526
Woodley, Elizabeth 249*
John 121
Jonathan 564,619
Thomas 232
William 247
Woodman, John 243
Woodmanson, Richard
190
Woodner, Anne 31
Woodrow, Anthony 525
John 525
Woodruffe, Edmund
112,114
Woods, Celia 701
Henry 43,698,701
Jane 268
John 233,484,508,545,
586,600
Margery 12
Mary 140
Richard 693
Virtue 442
William 568
Woodward, Alexander
621
Alice 27
Anne 99
Christopher 577
George 337
John 19,80,316,353,
371,523
Martha 438
Phillip 619
Richard 30*,32,57,647
Samuel 39
Thomas 19,68,80,234,
511
William 38,197,688
Woolcott, Henry 139
Woolem, John 161
Wooles, Thomas 18
Woollams, Joan 78
Woollaston, Thomas 259
Woollball, James 199
Woollens, Isaac 625
Wooler, George 16

Woolley, Benjamin 701
Charles 677
Ezechiell 403
John 88,241
Martin 405
Richard 400
Robert 119,120,121,123,
125,126,187,188,189,
190,192,193,195,196,
212,213*,238,243,
248*,249*,250,252,
253,254,262,263*,
268,279,280,282,283*,
284,285,289,291,293*,
294,298,325*,331
Woolman, Gilbert 420
Woolnough, John 509
Thomas 509
Woolridge, Richard 331
William 524,556
Woolsey, Robert 286
Woolton, John 163
Woolvin, John 205,216,
219,255,275,276,303
Woory, John 13,69,91,
117,125,126,127,129,
171
Woosley, John 426
Richard 473
Wootlane, Julian 13
Wootters, John 204*
Wo(o)tton [Wootten],
Anne 689
Edward 112,529,603
John 163,165,529
Mary 603
Richard 280
Robert 641
Silvester 536
Simon 669
Thomas 165,434
William 539
Worden, Richard 689
Worgan, John 32
Mathias 194,403,480
Matthew 198,320,652,
707
Richard 306,346,361
Robert 315,316,320,344
William 226,228*,324*,
327,328,498,555
Worger, John 605

Workman [Warkman],
  Anthony 139
  Mark 159,307
  Robert 159,288,484
  Samuel 373
  Thomas 2,10,19
Worledge, Richard 329
  Samuel 312
  Stephen 676
  Thomas 248,289
Worley, Anne 23
Worlock, Thomas 85
Wormall, Israell 591
Worme, Anthony 402
Wormer, William 460
Wormlayton, Robert 124
  Thomas 124
Wornall, Philip 97
Worne, Elizabeth 484
Wornell, George 339
  John 14
Worrall [Worrell],
  Charles 38
  John 526
  Richard 456,711
  Sarah 568
  William 191,272,521
Worrs, George 685
Worsam, Richard 327
Worsencroft, Elizabeth
  442
Worsley, Richard 54
Worster, John 408
Worth, James 290
Worthington, John 64,
  366,483,485*
Wosey, Joseph 478
Wotner, William 113
Wotton. *See* **Wootton.**
Wovenden, Ralph 246
Wrangham, George 446
Wraxall [Wraxell],
  John 544
  Peter 183,258,269,
  320,350
  William 352
Wray, Leonard 82
  Rebecca 82
  Susanna 200
Wrayford, William 435,
  540,604
Wrenn, Elizabeth 443

Wrenn, *(contd.)*
  Francis 18
  John 334
  Susan 61
Wrenshaw, Elizabeth 712
Wrentmore, Henry 523
  John 332
  Nicholas 22
  Thomas 203
Wrexham, Charles 644
Wright, Alice 338
  Andrew 253
  Daniel 486,547
  Elizabeth 55,128,236,674
  Frances 265
  Henry 156
  Huckvill 619
  Isaac 30
  James 165
  Joan 50
  John 62,64,108*,113,
  122,158,163,196,274,
  325,375*,437,462*,
  468,595,628,636,659,
  682,688,699,717
  Jonas 61
  Joseph 340,343,571
  Katherine 61
  Margaret 34
  Mary 148,330
  Peter 338
  Richard 331,649
  Robert 70,330,409,464
  Savill 334
  Stephen 462
  Thomas 24,111,179,232
  Tobias 151
  Walter 475
  William 80,124,176,
  286,359,394,462,475,
  619*,625,649
Wrighton, William 360
Wrinch, Mary 424
Wroth, Frances 646
  Richard 131
Wyatt [Wyett], Anne 53
  Benjamin 691
  Davy 519
  Henry 568
  John 438,448,613,644
  Katherine 188
  Mary 287

Wyatt, *(contd.)*
  Nicholas 98*
  Richard 121
  Thomas 448,603
  William 123,437
  W. 282
Wybo(u)rne [Wiburne],
  Jane 551
  John 94
  Thomas 632
Wych(e), Elizabeth 174
  James 174
  Thomas
  368,369,381,386,
  395,396,400,409,414,
  428,588,589,610,612
Wyell, Francis 587
Wyerdale, Nathaniel 478
Wyke [Wike], Edward
  704
  Joan 171
Wyles. *See* **Wiles.**
Wynn(e), Anne 326
  James 64
  John 258,384,404,406,
  428,486,488,489,544,
  696,700
  Jonathan 364
  Mary 326
  Priscilla 375
  Ralph 63
  Richard 249,422
  Symon 357
  Robert 242,256,257*,
  258,280,281,286,287,
  293,317
  Thomas 326,397,399,
  581*,614,624
Wyre [Wyer], John 592,
  602
Wyron, Grace 605
  John 605
Wyth(e) [With], James
  143
  John 681
  Thomas 300

Yalden, Robert 449
Yale, Thomas 686
Yalland, Robert 121
Yallop, Richard 289

Index of Ships

Falkland 688,689
Fellowship 99,122,164,
 306,323,328,562,564
Fidelity 361,660,702
Fir Tree 651,663
Fisher 691
Flanell 384
Flower 225,248
Flowerpot 129
Fly 393
Fortune 56,204,234,237,
 263,271,272,277,354,
 538,654
Four Anns 240
Four Sisters 685
Francis 98,131,169,217,
 233,272,277,302,303,
 315,334*,378,714
Francis & Dorothy 448,
 593
Francis & Jane 624
Francis & Mary 138,
 165*,180*,181*,183*,
 273*,274*,275*,276*,
 297*,298,299,301,
 302*,320,322*,323,
 352*,354,371,385,
 402,426,476,482*,
 487,488,552
Francis & Samuel 626
Francis & Stephen 335
Fraternity 290
Frederick 385,697,710
Freeman 374,392,579
Friendly Society 663
Friends' Adventure 333,
 374,392,449,473,474,
 480,508,587,606,680
Friends' Endeavour 679
Friends' Goodwill 679
Friends' Increase 268,
 289,298,336,384
Friendship 13,16,34,128,
 172,173,206,239,243,
 271,327,342,347,348,
 368,392,396,401,413,
 420*,421,425,427,453,
 544,550,587,595,596,
 605*,625,645,655,
 658,665,666,667,674,
 682,690,713
Fyall Merchant 52

Gabriel 119,167,168*,
 169*,170,171*,172*,
 184,185*,186,261*,
 262*,279*,280,306*,
 327,374
Gally 568
Genoa Merchant 384,
 404,406,428,486,544
George 52,136,137,164,
 199,215,229,269,274*,
 275*,276*,288,299*,
 302*,303,318,321*,
 322*,353,374,448,
 450,497,502*,602,
 654,655,664,692,696,
 701,710,715,718
Gerrard 384,684,717
Gift 117,238
Globe 302,355,371,385,
 397,400,421,471,535*,
 559,588,612,667,704,
 704
Gloucester 668,679,683
Golden Falcon 237
Golden Fleece 414
Golden Fortune 15,55,
 70,86,303,353,387
Golden Hart 324,327,
 329,330,506
Golden Hind 393
Golden Lion 70,169,
 171*,215,277*,278,
 304,350,467,470,579,
 597,604,665,683
Golden Phoenix 241
Golden Wheatsheaf 13,
 69
Good Hope 172,239,262,
 293,301
Good Success 631
Goodwill 36
Grace 404,557
Granada 636,651
Grane 239
Grape 616
Great Society. *See*
 Society.
Greenwich 662,675
Greyhound 283,399,472,
 534,690
Griffin 206,239,250
Guillielmo 447

Habitation 658
Hallam 675,677
Hambro 411
Hampshire 643,655
Handmaid 95
Hannah 261,300,303,
 342,369,381,398,423,
 425,471,482,540,595
Hannah & Elizabeth
 318,352*
Hannah & Katherine 93
Hannah & Sarah 585
Happy Entrance 132
Happy Return 193,239,
 423,548,620,647,653
Happy Union 713
Harrison 683
Hart 371,381,429,640
Hartwell 683
Hawk 641
Helena 711
Henrietta 396,422,598,
 653,681,696
Henry 341,606,644,657,
 678
Henry & Ann 299,345,
 362,379
Henry & Francis 71,521
Hercules 179
Herne 296,326,357,376,
 388
Heron 267,298,377,378
Hester 676,706
Hester & Hannah 388
Hind 526
Honor 11,69
Honor & Dorothy 252,
 300
Honor's Desire 32
Hope 105,130,145,166,
 171,181,182,196,198,
 207,237,243,250,297,
 300,334,347,374,428,
 434,479,496,531,552,
 586,640,658,662,664*,
 667,675,676,681,683,
 715
Hopeful Katherine 175*
Hoper 53
Hopewell 123,163,195,
 205,239,244,255,265,
 267,272,284*,285,292,

891

Unity 33,54,78,96,127,
173,285,309,332,354,
362,369,382,428,478,
582,598*,654,676,
698,716
Vealz Merchant 575*
Victory 315*,316*,317*,
318*,320*,321,348,
350*,353,372,385
Vine 323,360,370,384,
402,413,422,457,541,
581,647,679
Vinetree 96
Vineyard 329
Violet 708
Virgin 349,391
Virginia 667,682
Virginia Factor 251,268,
296,350,370,385,432*,
490,491,584,614,622
Virginia Merchant 96,
111,121,130,140,194,
204,253,269,343,552,
596,654,697,708,709,
716,719
Virgin Queen 69
Walsingham 21
Warspite 216,617
Waterhouse 10
Welcome 263,360,378,
394,421,551,706,714
Weymouth Merchant 96

Wheatsheaf 12,120,241
White Dove 19
White Fox 398,422,484,
537,586
William 63,99,178,197,
198,255,269,320,335,
366,388,407,421,433,
452,593,621,690
William & Anne 164,
165*,166*,182,197,
200,257*,258*,269,
273*,274*,275*,276*,
306*,323,328,411,417,
458,568
William & Bryan 654
William & Daniel 594
William & Edward 16
William & Elizabeth
375,392,583,588,684
William & Ellen 139
William & Henry 291,
331
William & Jane 198
William & John 190,
201,269,282,329,333,
335,336,659
William & Joseph 322
William & Mary 19,92,
132,157,205,239,360*,
361*,456,468,527,
579,586,620,623,667,
679,699,702,709

William & Nicholas 63
William & Orian 716
William & Ralph 187
William & Richard 663
William & Robert 433
William & Sarah 671
William & Susan 330
William & Thomas 26,
177,380,396,427*,
486,545,561,587,
621
Willing Mind 96,202,
215,216,286,337,
346,384
Windmill 381,399,430,
482,534,582,593
Windsor Bridge 388
Windsor Castle 638
Wren 411
York 602,639
York Merchant 91,305,
324,659,681
Yorkshire Laurel 707
Young Prince 250,266,
290,292,299,304,430,
585,614,615,631
Young William 340
Zant 411
Zebulon 242,252,263*,
294,347,367,400,401,
423,483,485,540,560